University Casebook Series

May, 1985

ACCOUNTING AND THE LAW, Fourth Edition (1978), with Problems Pamphlet (Successor to Dohr, Phillips, Thompson & Warren)

George C. Thompson, Professor, Columbia University Graduate School of Business.
Robert Whitman, Professor of Law, University of Connecticut.
Ellis L. Phillips, Jr., Member of the New York Bar.
William C. Warren, Professor of Law Emeritus, Columbia University.

ACCOUNTING FOR LAWYERS, MATERIALS ON (1980)

David R. Herwitz, Professor of Law, Harvard University.

ADMINISTRATIVE LAW, Seventh Edition (1979), with 1983 Problems Supplement (Supplement edited in association with Paul R. Verkuil, Dean and Professor of Law, Tulane University)

Walter Gellhorn, University Professor Emeritus, Columbia University.
Clark Byse, Professor of Law, Harvard University.
Peter L. Strauss, Professor of Law, Columbia University.

ADMIRALTY, Second Edition (1978), with Statute and Rule Supplement

Jo Desha Lucas, Professor of Law, University of Chicago.

ADVOCACY, see also Lawyering Process

AGENCY, see also Enterprise Organization

AGENCY—PARTNERSHIPS, Third Edition (1982)

Abridgement from Conard, Knauss & Siegel's Enterprise Organization, Third Edition.

ANTITRUST: FREE ENTERPRISE AND ECONOMIC ORGANIZATION, Sixth Edition (1983), with Problems in Antitrust Supplement

Louis B. Schwartz, Professor of Law, University of Pennsylvania.
John J. Flynn, Professor of Law, University of Utah.
Harry First, Professor of Law, New York University.

BANKRUPTCY (1985)

Robert L. Jordan, Professor of Law, University of California, Los Angeles.
William D. Warren, Professor of Law, University of California, Los Angeles.

BUSINESS ORGANIZATION, see also Enterprise Organization

BUSINESS PLANNING, Temporary Second Edition (1984)

David R. Herwitz, Professor of Law, Harvard University.

BUSINESS TORTS (1972)

Milton Handler, Professor of Law Emeritus, Columbia University.

CHILDREN IN THE LEGAL SYSTEM (1983)

Walter Wadlington, Professor of Law, University of Virginia.
Charles H. Whitebread, Professor of Law, University of Southern California.
Samuel Davis, Professor of Law, University of Georgia.

CIVIL PROCEDURE, see Procedure

CLINIC, see also Lawyering Process

COMMERCIAL LAW (1983)

Robert L. Jordan, Professor of Law, University of California, Los Angeles.
William D. Warren, Professor of Law, University of California, Los Angeles.

COMMERCIAL LAW, CASES & MATERIALS ON, Fourth Edition (1985)

E. Allan Farnsworth, Professor of Law, Columbia University.
John Honnold, Professor of Law, University of Pennsylvania.

COMMERCIAL PAPER, Third Edition (1984)

E. Allan Farnsworth, Professor of Law, Columbia University.

COMMERCIAL PAPER (1983) (Reprinted from COMMERCIAL LAW)

Robert L. Jordan, Professor of Law, University of California, Los Angeles.
William D. Warren, Professor of Law, University of California, Los Angeles.

COMMERCIAL PAPER AND BANK DEPOSITS AND COLLECTIONS (1967), with Statutory Supplement

William D. Hawkland, Professor of Law, University of Illinois.

COMMERCIAL TRANSACTIONS—Principles and Policies (1982)

Alan Schwartz, Professor of Law, University of Southern California.
Robert E. Scott, Professor of Law, University of Virginia.

COMPARATIVE LAW, Fourth Edition (1980)

Rudolf B. Schlesinger, Professor of Law, Hastings College of the Law.

COMPETITIVE PROCESS, LEGAL REGULATION OF THE, Second Edition (1979), with 1984 Statutory Supplement and 1984 Case Supplement

Edmund W. Kitch, Professor of Law, University of Chicago.
Harvey S. Perlman, Professor of Law, University of Virginia.

CONFLICT OF LAWS, Eighth Edition (1984)

Willis L. M. Reese, Professor of Law, Columbia University.
Maurice Rosenberg, Professor of Law, Columbia University.

CONSTITUTIONAL LAW, Seventh Edition (1985), with 1985 Supplement

Edward L. Barrett, Jr., Professor of Law, University of California, Davis.
William Cohen, Professor of Law, Stanford University.

CONSTITUTIONAL LAW: THE STRUCTURE OF GOVERNMENT (Reprinted from CONSTITUTIONAL LAW, Sixth Edition), with 1985 Supplement

Edward L. Barrett, Jr., Professor of Law, University of California, Davis.
William Cohen, Professor of Law, Stanford University.

CONSTITUTIONAL LAW, CIVIL LIBERTY AND INDIVIDUAL RIGHTS, Second Edition (1982), with 1985 Supplement

William Cohen, Professor of Law, Stanford University.
John Kaplan, Professor of Law, Stanford University.

CONSTITUTIONAL LAW, Eleventh Edition (1985), with 1985 Supplement (Supplement edited in association with Frederick F. Schauer, Professor of Law, University of Michigan)

Gerald Gunther, Professor of Law, Stanford University.

CONSTITUTIONAL LAW, INDIVIDUAL RIGHTS IN, Third Edition (1981), (Reprinted from CONSTITUTIONAL LAW, Tenth Edition), with 1984 Supplement (Supplement edited in association with Frederick F. Schauer, Professor of Law, University of Michigan)

Gerald Gunther, Professor of Law, Stanford University.

CONSUMER TRANSACTIONS (1983), with Selected Statutes and Regulations Supplement

Michael M. Greenfield, Professor of Law, Washington University.

CONTRACT LAW AND ITS APPLICATION, Third Edition (1983)

The late Addison Mueller, Professor of Law, University of California, Los Angeles.
Arthur I. Rosett, Professor of Law, University of California, Los Angeles.
Gerald P. Lopez, Professor of Law, University of California, Los Angeles.

CONTRACT LAW, STUDIES IN, Third Edition (1984)

Edward J. Murphy, Professor of Law, University of Notre Dame.
Richard E. Speidel, Professor of Law, Northwestern University.

CONTRACTS, Fourth Edition (1982)

John P. Dawson, Professor of Law Emeritus, Harvard University.
William Burnett Harvey, Professor of Law and Political Science, Boston University.
Stanley D. Henderson, Professor of Law, University of Virginia.

CONTRACTS, Third Edition (1980), with Statutory Supplement

E. Allan Farnsworth, Professor of Law, Columbia University.
William F. Young, Professor of Law, Columbia University.

CONTRACTS, Second Edition (1978), with Statutory and Administrative Law Supplement (1978)

Ian R. Macneil, Professor of Law, Cornell University.

COPYRIGHT, PATENTS AND TRADEMARKS, see also Competitive Process

COPYRIGHT, PATENT, TRADEMARK AND RELATED STATE DOCTRINES, Second Edition (1981), with 1985 Case Supplement and 1985 Statute Supplement

Paul Goldstein, Professor of Law, Stanford University.

COPYRIGHT, Unfair Competition, and Other Topics Bearing on the Protection of Literary, Musical, and Artistic Works, Fourth Edition (1985), with 1985 Statutory Supplement

Ralph S. Brown, Jr., Professor of Law, Yale University.
Robert C. Denicola, Professor of Law, University of Nebraska.

CORPORATE FINANCE, Second Edition (1979), with 1984 Supplement

Victor Brudney, Professor of Law, Harvard University.
Marvin A. Chirelstein, Professor of Law, Columbia University.

CORPORATE READJUSTMENTS AND REORGANIZATIONS (1976)

Walter J. Blum, Professor of Law, University of Chicago.
Stanley A. Kaplan, Professor of Law, University of Chicago.

CORPORATION LAW, BASIC, Second Edition (1979), with 1983 Case and Documentary Supplement

Detlev F. Vagts, Professor of Law, Harvard University.

CORPORATIONS, see also Enterprise Organization

CORPORATIONS, Fifth Edition—Unabridged (1980), with 1984 Supplement

The late William L. Cary, Professor of Law, Columbia University.
Melvin Aron Eisenberg, Professor of Law, University of California, Berkeley.

CORPORATIONS, Fifth Edition—Abridged (1980), with 1984 Supplement

The late William L. Cary, Professor of Law, Columbia University.
Melvin Aron Eisenberg, Professor of Law, University of California, Berkeley.

CORPORATIONS, Second Edition (1982), with 1982 Corporation and Partnership Statutes, Rules and Forms

Alfred F. Conard, Professor of Law, University of Michigan.
Robert N. Knauss, Dean of the Law School, University of Houston.
Stanley Siegel, Professor of Law, University of California, Los Angeles.

CORPORATIONS COURSE GAME PLAN (1975)

David R. Herwitz, Professor of Law, Harvard University.

CORRECTIONS, SEE SENTENCING

CREDITORS' RIGHTS, see also Debtor-Creditor Law

CRIMINAL JUSTICE ADMINISTRATION, Second Edition (1982), with 1985 Supplement

Frank W. Miller, Professor of Law, Washington University.
Robert O. Dawson, Professor of Law, University of Texas.
George E. Dix, Professor of Law, University of Texas.
Raymond I. Parnas, Professor of Law, University of California, Davis.

CRIMINAL LAW, Third Edition (1983)

Fred E. Inbau, Professor of Law Emeritus, Northwestern University.
James R. Thompson, Professor of Law Emeritus, Northwestern University.
Andre A. Moenssens, Professor of Law, University of Richmond.

CRIMINAL LAW (1982), with 1983 Supplement

Peter W. Low, Professor of Law, University of Virginia.
John C. Jeffries, Jr., Professor of Law, University of Virginia.
Richard C. Bonnie, Professor of Law, University of Virginia.

CRIMINAL LAW, Third Edition (1980)

Lloyd L. Weinreb, Professor of Law, Harvard University.

CRIMINAL LAW AND PROCEDURE, Sixth Edition (1985)

Rollin M. Perkins, Professor of Law Emeritus, University of California, Hastings College of the Law.
Ronald N. Boyce, Professor of Law, University of Utah.

CRIMINAL PROCEDURE, Second Edition (1980), with 1985 Supplement

Fred E. Inbau, Professor of Law Emeritus, Northwestern University.
James R. Thompson, Professor of Law Emeritus, Northwestern University.
James B. Haddad, Professor of Law, Northwestern University.
James B. Zagel, Chief, Criminal Justice Division, Office of Attorney General of Illinois.
Gary L. Starkman, Assistant U. S. Attorney, Northern District of Illinois.

UNIVERSITY CASEBOOK SERIES—Continued

CRIMINAL PROCESS, Third Edition (1978), with 1985 Supplement

Lloyd L. Weinreb, Professor of Law, Harvard University.

DAMAGES, Second Edition (1952)

Charles T. McCormick, late Professor of Law, University of Texas.
William F. Fritz, late Professor of Law, University of Texas.

DEBTOR–CREDITOR LAW (1984)

Theodore Eisenberg, Professor of Law, Cornell University.

DEBTOR–CREDITOR LAW, Second Edition (1981), with Statutory Supplement

William D. Warren, Dean of the School of Law, University of California, Los Angeles.
William E. Hogan, Professor of Law, New York University.

DECEDENTS' ESTATES (1971)

Max Rheinstein, late Professor of Law Emeritus, University of Chicago.
Mary Ann Glendon, Professor of Law, Boston College.

DECEDENTS' ESTATES AND TRUSTS, Sixth Edition (1982)

John Ritchie, Emeritus Dean and Wigmore Professor of Law, Northwestern University.
Neill H. Alford, Jr., Professor of Law, University of Virginia.
Richard W. Effland, Professor of Law, Arizona State University.

DOMESTIC RELATIONS, see also Family Law

DOMESTIC RELATIONS, Successor Edition (1984) with 1985 Supplement

Walter Wadlington, Professor of Law, University of Virginia.

ELECTRONIC MASS MEDIA, Second Edition (1979)

William K. Jones, Professor of Law, Columbia University.

EMPLOYMENT DISCRIMINATION (1983)

Joel W. Friedman, Professor of Law, Tulane University.
George M. Strickler, Professor of Law, Tulane University.

ENERGY LAW (1983)

Donald N. Zillman, Professor of Law, University of Utah.
Laurence Lattman, Dean of Mines and Engineering, University of Utah.

ENTERPRISE ORGANIZATION, Third Edition (1982), with 1982 Corporation and Partnership Statutes, Rules and Forms Supplement

Alfred F. Conard, Professor of Law, University of Michigan.
Robert L. Knauss, Dean of the Law School, University of Houston.
Stanley Siegel, Professor of Law, University of California, Los Angeles.

ENVIRONMENTAL POLICY LAW 1985 Edition, with 1985 Problems Supplement (Supplement in association with Ronald H. Rosenberg, Professor of Law, College of William and Mary)

Thomas J. Schoenbaum, Professor of Law, University of Georgia.

EQUITY, see also Remedies

EQUITY, RESTITUTION AND DAMAGES, Second Edition (1974)

Robert Childres, late Professor of Law, Northwestern University.
William F. Johnson, Jr., Professor of Law, New York University.

ESTATE PLANNING, Second Edition (1982), with 1985 Case, Text and Documentary Supplement

David Westfall, Professor of Law, Harvard University.

ETHICS, see Legal Profession, and Professional Responsibility

ETHICS AND PROFESSIONAL RESPONSIBILITY (1981) (Reprinted from THE LAWYERING PROCESS)

Gary Bellow, Professor of Law, Harvard University.
Bea Moulton, Legal Services Corporation.

EVIDENCE, Fifth Edition (1984)

John Kaplan, Professor of Law, Stanford University.
Jon R. Waltz, Professor of Law, Northwestern University.

EVIDENCE, Seventh Edition (1983) with Rules and Statute Supplement (1984)

Jack B. Weinstein, Chief Judge, United States District Court.
John H. Mansfield, Professor of Law, Harvard University.
Norman Abrams, Professor of Law, University of California, Los Angeles.
Margaret Berger, Professor of Law, Brooklyn Law School.

FAMILY LAW, see also Domestic Relations

FAMILY LAW Second Edition (1985)

Judith C. Areen, Professor of Law, Georgetown University.

FAMILY LAW AND CHILDREN IN THE LEGAL SYSTEM, STATUTORY MATERIALS (1981)

Walter Wadlington, Professor of Law, University of Virginia.

FEDERAL COURTS, Seventh Edition (1982), with 1985 Supplement

Charles T. McCormick, late Professor of Law, University of Texas.
James H. Chadbourn, late Professor of Law, Harvard University.
Charles Alan Wright, Professor of Law, University of Texas.

FEDERAL COURTS AND THE FEDERAL SYSTEM, Hart and Wechsler's Second Edition (1973), with 1981 Supplement

Paul M. Bator, Professor of Law, Harvard University.
Paul J. Mishkin, Professor of Law, University of California, Berkeley.
David L. Shapiro, Professor of Law, Harvard University.
Herbert Wechsler, Professor of Law, Columbia University.

FEDERAL PUBLIC LAND AND RESOURCES LAW (1981), with 1983 Case Supplement and 1984 Statutory Supplement

George C. Coggins, Professor of Law, University of Kansas.
Charles F. Wilkinson, Professor of Law, University of Oregon.

FEDERAL RULES OF CIVIL PROCEDURE, 1984 Edition

FEDERAL TAXATION, see Taxation

FOOD AND DRUG LAW (1980), with Statutory Supplement

Richard A. Merrill, Dean of the School of Law, University of Virginia.
Peter Barton Hutt, Esq.

FUTURE INTERESTS (1958)

Philip Mechem, late Professor of Law Emeritus, University of Pennsylvania.

FUTURE INTERESTS (1970)

Howard R. Williams, Professor of Law, Stanford University.

FUTURE INTERESTS AND ESTATE PLANNING (1961), with 1962 Supplement

W. Barton Leach, late Professor of Law, Harvard University.
James K. Logan, formerly Dean of the Law School, University of Kansas.

GOVERNMENT CONTRACTS, FEDERAL, Successor Edition (1985)

John W. Whelan, Professor of Law, Hastings College of the Law.

**GOVERNMENT REGULATION: FREE ENTERPRISE AND ECONOMIC ORGANI-
ZATION, Sixth Edition (1985)**

Louis B. Schwartz, Professor of Law, University of Pennsylvania.
John J. Flynn, Professor of Law, University of Utah.
Harry First, Professor of Law, New York University.

INJUNCTIONS, Second Edition (1984)

Owen M. Fiss, Professor of Law, Yale University.
Doug Rendleman, Professor of Law, College of William and Mary.

INSTITUTIONAL INVESTORS, 1978

David L. Ratner, Professor of Law, Cornell University.

INSURANCE, Second Edition (1985)

William F. Young, Professor of Law, Columbia University.
Eric M. Holmes, Professor of Law, University of Georgia.

**INTERNATIONAL LAW, see also Transnational Legal Problems and United
Nations Law**

**INTERNATIONAL LAW IN CONTEMPORARY PERSPECTIVE (1981), with Essay
Supplement**

Myres S. McDougal, Professor of Law, Yale University.
W. Michael Reisman, Professor of Law, Yale University.

**INTERNATIONAL LEGAL SYSTEM, Second Edition (1981), with Documentary
Supplement**

Joseph Modeste Sweeney, Professor of Law, Tulane University.
Covey T. Oliver, Professor of Law, University of Pennsylvania.
Noyes E. Leech, Professor of Law, University of Pennsylvania.

**INTRODUCTION TO LAW, see also Legal Method, On Law in Courts, and
Dynamics of American Law**

INTRODUCTION TO THE STUDY OF LAW (1970)

E. Wayne Thode, late Professor of Law, University of Utah.
Leon Lebowitz, Professor of Law, University of Texas.
Lester J. Mazor, Professor of Law, University of Utah.

**JUDICIAL CODE and Rules of Procedure in the Federal Courts with Excerpts
from the Criminal Code, 1984 Edition**

Henry M. Hart, Jr., late Professor of Law, Harvard University.
Herbert Wechsler, Professor of Law, Columbia University.

JURISPRUDENCE (Temporary Edition Hardbound) (1949)

Lon L. Fuller, Professor of Law Emeritus, Harvard University.

JUVENILE, see also Children

JUVENILE JUSTICE PROCESS, Third Edition (1985)

Frank W. Miller, Professor of Law, Washington University.
Robert O. Dawson, Professor of Law, University of Texas.
George E. Dix, Professor of Law, University of Texas.
Raymond I. Parnas, Professor of Law, University of California, Davis.

LABOR LAW, Ninth Edition (1981), with 1983 Case Supplement and 1977 Statutory Supplement

Archibald Cox, Professor of Law, Harvard University.
Derek C. Bok, President, Harvard University.
Robert A. Gorman, Professor of Law, University of Pennsylvania.

LABOR LAW, Second Edition (1982), with Statutory Supplement

Clyde W. Summers, Professor of Law, University of Pennsylvania.
Harry H. Wellington, Dean of the Law School, Yale University.
Alan Hyde, Professor of Law, Rutgers University.

LAND FINANCING, Third Edition (1985)

The late Norman Penney, Professor of Law, Cornell University.
Richard F. Broude, Member of the California Bar.
Roger Cunningham, Professor of Law, University of Michigan.

LAW AND MEDICINE (1980)

Walter Wadlington, Professor of Law and Professor of Legal Medicine, University of Virginia.
Jon R. Waltz, Professor of Law, Northwestern University.
Roger B. Dworkin, Professor of Law, Indiana University, and Professor of Biomedical History, University of Washington.

LAW, LANGUAGE AND ETHICS (1972)

William R. Bishin, Professor of Law, University of Southern California.
Christopher D. Stone, Professor of Law, University of Southern California.

LAW, SCIENCE AND MEDICINE (1984)

Judith C. Areen, Professor of Law, Georgetown University.
Patricia A. King, Professor of Law, Georgetown University.
Steven P. Goldberg, Professor of Law, Georgetown University.
Alexander M. Capron, Professor of Law, Georgetown University.

LAWYERING PROCESS (1978), with Civil Problem Supplement and Criminal Problem Supplement

Gary Bellow, Professor of Law, Harvard University.
Bea Moulton, Professor of Law, Arizona State University.

LEGAL METHOD (1980)

Harry W. Jones, Professor of Law Emeritus, Columbia University.
John M. Kernochan, Professor of Law, Columbia University.
Arthur W. Murphy, Professor of Law, Columbia University.

LEGAL METHODS (1969)

Robert N. Covington, Professor of Law, Vanderbilt University.
E. Blythe Stason, late Professor of Law, Vanderbilt University.
John W. Wade, Professor of Law, Vanderbilt University.
Elliott E. Cheatham, late Professor of Law, Vanderbilt University.
Theodore A. Smedley, Professor of Law, Vanderbilt University.

LEGAL PROFESSION (1970)

Samuel D. Thurman, Dean of the College of Law, University of Utah.
Ellis L. Phillips, Jr., Professor of Law, Columbia University.
Elliott E. Cheatham, late Professor of Law, Vanderbilt University.

LEGAL PROFESSION, THE, Responsibility and Regulation (1985)

Geoffrey C. Hazard, Jr., Professor of Law, Yale University.
Deborah L. Rhode, Professor of Law, Stanford University.

LEGISLATION, Fourth Edition (1982) (by Fordham)

Horace E. Read, late Vice President, Dalhousie University.
John W. MacDonald, Professor of Law Emeritus, Cornell Law School.
Jefferson B. Fordham, Professor of Law, University of Utah.
William J. Pierce, Professor of Law, University of Michigan.

LEGISLATIVE AND ADMINISTRATIVE PROCESSES, Second Edition (1981)

Hans A. Linde, Judge, Supreme Court of Oregon.
George Bunn, Professor of Law, University of Wisconsin.
Fredericka Paff, Professor of Law, University of Wisconsin.
W. Lawrence Church, Professor of Law, University of Wisconsin.

LOCAL GOVERNMENT LAW, Revised Edition (1975)

Jefferson B. Fordham, Professor of Law, University of Utah.

MASS MEDIA LAW, Second Edition (1982), with 1985 Supplement

Marc A. Franklin, Professor of Law, Stanford University.

MENTAL HEALTH PROCESS, Second Edition (1976), with 1981 Supplement

Frank W. Miller, Professor of Law, Washington University.
Robert O. Dawson, Professor of Law, University of Texas.
George E. Dix, Professor of Law, University of Texas.
Raymond I. Parnas, Professor of Law, University of California, Davis.

MUNICIPAL CORPORATIONS, see Local Government Law

NEGOTIABLE INSTRUMENTS, see Commercial Paper

NEGOTIATION (1981) (Reprinted from THE LAWYERING PROCESS)

Gary Bellow, Professor of Law, Harvard Law School.
Bea Moulton, Legal Services Corporation.

NEW YORK PRACTICE, Fourth Edition (1978)

Herbert Peterfreund, Professor of Law, New York University.
Joseph M. McLaughlin, Dean of the Law School, Fordham University.

OIL AND GAS, Fourth Edition (1979)

Howard R. Williams, Professor of Law, Stanford University.
Richard C. Maxwell, Professor of Law, University of California, Los Angeles.
Charles J. Meyers, Dean of the Law School, Stanford University.

ON LAW IN COURTS (1965)

Paul J. Mishkin, Professor of Law, University of California, Berkeley.
Clarence Morris, Professor of Law Emeritus, University of Pennsylvania.

PATENTS AND ANTITRUST (Pamphlet) (1983)

Milton Handler, Professor of Law Emeritus, Columbia University.
Harlan M. Blake, Professor of Law, Columbia University.
Robert Pitofsky, Professor of Law, Georgetown University.
Harvey J. Goldschmid, Professor of Law, Columbia University.

UNIVERSITY CASEBOOK SERIES—Continued

PERSPECTIVES ON THE LAWYER AS PLANNER (Reprint of Chapters One through Five of Planning by Lawyers) (1978)

Louis M. Brown, Professor of Law, University of Southern California.
Edward A. Dauer, Professor of Law, Yale University.

PLANNING BY LAWYERS, MATERIALS ON A NONADVERSARIAL LEGAL PROCESS (1978)

Louis M. Brown, Professor of Law, University of Southern California.
Edward A. Dauer, Professor of Law, Yale University.

PLEADING AND PROCEDURE, see Procedure, Civil

POLICE FUNCTION, Third Edition (1982), with 1985 Supplement

Reprint of Chapters 1–10 of Miller, Dawson, Dix and Parnas's CRIMINAL JUSTICE ADMINISTRATION, Second Edition.

PREPARING AND PRESENTING THE CASE (1981) (Reprinted from THE LAWYERING PROCESS)

Gary Bellow, Professor of Law, Harvard Law School.
Bea Moulton, Legal Services Corporation.

PREVENTIVE LAW, see also Planning by Lawyers

PROCEDURE—CIVIL PROCEDURE, Second Edition (1974), with 1979 Supplement

The late James H. Chadbourn, Professor of Law, Harvard University.
A. Leo Levin, Professor of Law, University of Pennsylvania.
Philip Shuchman, Professor of Law, Cornell University.

PROCEDURE—CIVIL PROCEDURE, Fifth Edition (1984)

Richard H. Field, late Professor of Law, Harvard University.
Benjamin Kaplan, Professor of Law Emeritus, Harvard University.
Kevin M. Clermont, Professor of Law, Cornell University.

PROCEDURE—CIVIL PROCEDURE, Fourth Edition (1985)

Maurice Rosenberg, Professor of Law, Columbia University.
Hans Smit, Professor of Law, Columbia University.
Harold L. Korn, Professor of Law, Columbia University.

PROCEDURE—PLEADING AND PROCEDURE: State and Federal, Fifth Edition (1983), with 1985 Supplement

David W. Louisell, late Professor of Law, University of California, Berkeley.
Geoffrey C. Hazard, Jr., Professor of Law, Yale University.
Colin C. Tait, Professor of Law, University of Connecticut.

PROCEDURE—FEDERAL RULES OF CIVIL PROCEDURE, 1984 Edition

PRODUCTS LIABILITY (1980)

Marshall S. Shapo, Professor of Law, Northwestern University.

PRODUCTS LIABILITY AND SAFETY (1980), with 1985 Case and Documentary Supplement

W. Page Keeton, Professor of Law, University of Texas.
David G. Owen, Professor of Law, University of South Carolina.
John E. Montgomery, Professor of Law, University of South Carolina.

PROFESSIONAL RESPONSIBILITY, Third Edition (1984), with 1985 Selected National Standards Supplement

Thomas D. Morgan, Dean of the Law School, Emory University.
Ronald D. Rotunda, Professor of Law, University of Illinois.

PROPERTY, Fifth Edition (1984)

John E. Cribbet, Dean of the Law School, University of Illinois.
Corwin W. Johnson, Professor of Law, University of Texas.

PROPERTY—PERSONAL (1953)

S. Kenneth Skolfield, late Professor of Law Emeritus, Boston University.

PROPERTY—PERSONAL, Third Edition (1954)

Everett Fraser, late Dean of the Law School Emeritus, University of Minnesota.
Third Edition by Charles W. Taintor, late Professor of Law, University of Pittsburgh.

PROPERTY—INTRODUCTION, TO REAL PROPERTY, Third Edition (1954)

Everett Fraser, late Dean of the Law School Emeritus, University of Minnesota.

PROPERTY—REAL AND PERSONAL, Combined Edition (1954)

Everett Fraser, late Dean of the Law School Emeritus, University of Minnesota.
Third Edition of Personal Property by Charles W. Taintor, late Professor of Law, University of Pittsburgh.

PROPERTY—FUNDAMENTALS OF MODERN REAL PROPERTY, Second Edition (1982), with 1985 Supplement

Edward H. Rabin, Professor of Law, University of California, Davis.

PROPERTY—PROBLEMS IN REAL PROPERTY (Pamphlet) (1969)

Edward H. Rabin, Professor of Law, University of California, Davis.

PROPERTY, REAL (1984)

Paul Goldstein, Professor of Law, Stanford University.

PROSECUTION AND ADJUDICATION, Second Edition (1982), with 1985 Supplement

Reprint of Chapters 11–26 of Miller, Dawson, Dix and Parnas's CRIMINAL JUSTICE ADMINISTRATION, Second Edition.

PUBLIC REGULATION OF DANGEROUS PRODUCTS (paperback) (1980)

Marshall S. Shapo, Professor of Law, Northwestern University.

PUBLIC UTILITY LAW, see Free Enterprise, also Regulated Industries

REAL ESTATE PLANNING (1980), with 1980 Problems, Statutes and New Materials Supplement

Norton L. Steuben, Professor of Law, University of Colorado.

REAL ESTATE TRANSACTIONS, Second Edition (1985), with 1985 Statute, Form and Problem Supplement

Paul Goldstein, Professor of Law, Stanford University.

RECEIVERSHIP AND CORPORATE REORGANIZATION, see Creditors' Rights

REGULATED INDUSTRIES, Second Edition, 1976

William K. Jones, Professor of Law, Columbia University.

TAXATION, FEDERAL INCOME, Fifth Edition (1985)

James J. Freeland, Professor of Law, University of Florida.
Stephen A. Lind, Professor of Law, University of Florida.
Richard B. Stephens, Professor of Law Emeritus, University of Florida.

TAXATION, FEDERAL INCOME, Volume I, Personal Income Taxation (1972), with 1985 Case Supplement; Volume II, Taxation of Partnerships and Corporations, Second Edition (1980), with 1985 Legislative Supplement

Stanley S. Surrey, late Professor of Law, Harvard University.
William C. Warren, Professor of Law Emeritus, Columbia University.
Paul R. McDaniel, Professor of Law, Boston College Law School.
Hugh J. Ault, Professor of Law, Boston College Law School.

TAXATION, FEDERAL WEALTH TRANSFER, Second Edition (1982) with 1985 Legislative Supplement

Stanley S. Surrey, late Professor of Law, Harvard University.
William C. Warren, Professor of Law Emeritus, Columbia University.
Paul R. McDaniel, Professor of Law, Boston College Law School.
Harry L. Gutman, Instructor, Harvard Law School and Boston College Law School.

TAXATION, FUNDAMENTALS OF CORPORATE, Cases and Materials (1985)

Stephen A. Lind, Professor of Law, University of Florida.
Stephen Schwarz, Professor of Law, University of California, Hastings.
Daniel J. Lathrope, Professor of Law, University of California, Hastings.
Joshua Rosenberg, Professor of Law, University of San Francisco.

TAXATION, PROBLEMS IN THE FUNDAMENTALS OF FEDERAL INCOME, Second Edition (1985)

Norton L. Steuben, Professor of Law, University of Colorado.
William J. Turnier, Professor of Law, University of North Carolina.

TAXES AND FINANCE—STATE AND LOCAL (1974)

Oliver Oldman, Professor of Law, Harvard University.
Ferdinand P. Schoettle, Professor of Law, University of Minnesota.

TORT LAW AND ALTERNATIVES, Third Edition (1983)

Marc A. Franklin, Professor of Law, Stanford University.
Robert L. Rabin, Professor of Law, Stanford University.

TORTS, Seventh Edition (1982)

William L. Prosser, late Professor of Law, University of California, Hastings College.
John W. Wade, Professor of Law, Vanderbilt University.
Victor E. Schwartz, Professor of Law, American University.

TORTS, Third Edition (1976)

Harry Shulman, late Dean of the Law School, Yale University.
Fleming James, Jr., Professor of Law Emeritus, Yale University.
Oscar S. Gray, Professor of Law, University of Maryland.

TRADE REGULATION, Second Edition (1983), with 1985 Supplement

Milton Handler, Professor of Law Emeritus, Columbia University.
Harlan M. Blake, Professor of Law, Columbia University.
Robert Pitofsky, Professor of Law, Georgetown University.
Harvey J. Goldschmid, Professor of Law, Columbia University.

TRADE REGULATION, see Antitrust

UNIVERSITY CASEBOOK SERIES—Continued

TRANSNATIONAL LEGAL PROBLEMS, Second Edition (1976) with 1982 Case and Documentary Supplement

Henry J. Steiner, Professor of Law, Harvard University.
Detlev F. Vagts, Professor of Law, Harvard University.

TRIAL, see also Evidence, Making the Record, Lawyering Process and Preparing and Presenting the Case

TRIAL ADVOCACY (1968)

A. Leo Levin, Professor of Law, University of Pennsylvania.
Harold Cramer, of the Pennsylvania Bar.
Maurice Rosenberg, Professor of Law, Columbia University, Consultant.

TRUSTS, Fifth Edition (1978)

George G. Bogert, late Professor of Law Emeritus, University of Chicago.
Dallin H. Oaks, President, Brigham Young University.

TRUSTS AND SUCCESSION (Palmer's), Fourth Edition (1983)

Richard V. Wellman, Professor of Law, University of Georgia.
Lawrence W. Waggoner, Professor of Law, University of Michigan.
Olin L. Browder, Jr., Professor of Law, University of Michigan.

UNFAIR COMPETITION, see Competitive Process and Business Torts

UNITED NATIONS LAW, Second Edition (1967), with Documentary Supplement (1968)

Louis B. Sohn, Professor of Law, Harvard University.

WATER RESOURCE MANAGEMENT, Second Edition (1980), with 1983 Supplement

Charles J. Meyers, Dean of the Law School, Stanford University.
A. Dan Tarlock, Professor of Law, Indiana University.

WILLS AND ADMINISTRATION, Fifth Edition (1961)

Philip Mechem, late Professor of Law, University of Pennsylvania.
Thomas E. Atkinson, late Professor of Law, New York University.

WORLD LAW, see United Nations Law

THE
JUVENILE JUSTICE
PROCESS

By

FRANK W. MILLER

James Carr Professor of Criminal Jurisprudence,
Washington University

ROBERT O. DAWSON

Judge Benjamin Harrison Powell Professor of Law,
University of Texas

GEORGE E. DIX

Vinson and Elkins Professor of Law, University of Texas

RAYMOND I. PARNAS

Professor of Law, University of California, Davis

THIRD EDITION

Mineola, New York
THE FOUNDATION PRESS, INC.
1985

COPYRIGHT © 1971, 1976 THE FOUNDATION PRESS, INC.
COPYRIGHT © 1985 By THE FOUNDATION PRESS, INC.
All rights reserved
Printed in the United States of America

Library of Congress Cataloging in Publication Data

Main entry under title:

The Juvenile justice process.

  (University casebook series)
  Includes bibliographies and index.
   1. Juvenile courts—United States—Cases.
2. Juvenile justice, Administration of—United
States—Cases. I. Miller, Frank William, 1921–.
II. Series.
KF9793.J88 1985   345.73'08   85–10268
ISBN 0–88277–243–0 347.3058

PREFACE TO THIRD EDITION

Since 1979, when we finished selecting material for the 1980 Supplement to the second edition of The Juvenile Justice Process, courts, legislatures and commentators have contributed an exceptional amount of new law and theory to and about the field of juvenile justice. Indeed, it is fair to say that between the time of the first edition and this one, juvenile law changed from a subject about which definitive legal answers to legitimate inquiries could only occasionally be discovered to as fast a growing field as can be found. This is not to say that uniform answers are now common—either about the acceptability of underlying sociological theories or about the appropriateness of legal responses. It is to say that massive efforts have been undertaken, that the general trend has shifted, and that in a given jurisdiction the answers to more questions can be found than was true at an earlier time.

Once in 1984 and already in 1985, the Supreme Court of the United States has added two more major decisions to the field. In 1984 in *Schall v. Martin*, the Court upheld the constitutionality of statutes providing for preventive detention of juveniles, and in the 1985 case of *New Jersey v. T.L.O.*, the court established a "reasonableness" standard for searches of students by school officials.

As the field of juvenile law becomes increasingly complex, we felt the need to provide a more carefully structured method of presenting it to the students. In earlier editions, we thought it useful to group together all Supreme Court decisions so that students would have a sense of the extent of Supreme Court examination of the numerous problems as well as an awareness of what had been firmly established as constitutional limitations on the juvenile process. In this edition, we have sought to accomplish those goals less directly: we have placed the Supreme Court cases in their appropriate subject-matter categories.

Because legislative activity has been so great, we felt required thoroughly to update the statutory authorities cited and reproduced in the second edition and its supplement. Specifically, we expanded our treatment of determinate dispositions by including updated versions of the relevant State of Washington statutes, as well as the Official Juvenile Disposition Sentencing Standards used by Washington to implement its statutory scheme. We added more IJA–ABA Juvenile Justice Standards where pertinent. The Standards we reprint represent the final drafts approved by the IJA and ABA in 1980. A list of the standards reprinted is attached to this preface. We wish to thank Ballinger Publishing Company for its gracious permission to reprint standards, and we recommend to students perusal of the excellent commentary to those standards found in the Ballinger publication. We have also included standards issued in 1980 by the National Advisory Committee for Juvenile Justice and Delinquency Prevention for additional views about the appropriateness of future legislation.

* * *

Standards Relating to Adjudication §§ 3.1 to 3.7; Alternate §§ 3.3 and 3.4.

Standards Relating to Dispositional Procedures §§ 6.3; 7.1.

Standards Relating to Dispositions §§ 3.2; 5.1 to 5.4.

Standards Relating to Interim Status §§ 6.6; 7.7.

Standards Relating to Juvenile Delinquency and Sanctions §§ 3.1; 3.2; 3.5; 5.2; 6.2 to 6.4.

Standards Relating to Juvenile Probation Function §§ 2.2 to 2.5; 2.12 to 2.16.

Standards Relating to Juvenile Records and Information Services §§ 5.6; 5.7; 17.1 to 17.3; 17.7; 18.4; 19.6; 20.1 to 20.3.

Standards Relating to Police Handling of Juvenile Problems §§ 2.4; 2.5; 3.2.

Standards Relating to Pretrial Court Proceedings §§ 6.1 to 6.4.

Standards Relating to Transfer Between Courts §§ 1.1; 2.2.

* * *

Finally, the editors wish to express their appreciation for the exceptional research help provided by Pamela Schmidt Greer and Jo Anne Levy, and to Mrs. Herbert A. Bettlach, who has once again managed to keep the material organized as the revision proceeded and to display her usual patience when asked to re-do some material that she had just finished when the editors had one of their numerous changes of mind about the best way to do things some thirty minutes after a contrary decision has been reached.

F. W. M.
R. O. D.
G. E. D.
R. I. P

June, 1985

SUMMARY OF CONTENTS

TABLE OF CONTENTS

xxvii

Miller et.al. Juv.Just.Proc. 3rd Ed. UCB—2

TABLE OF CONTENTS

TABLE OF CONTENTS

TABLE OF CASES

The principal cases are in italic type. Cases cited or discussed are in roman. References are to Pages.

THE
JUVENILE JUSTICE
PROCESS

INTRODUCTION *

Many myths surround the area of juvenile crime: that juvenile crime is increasing, that juvenile crime is becoming more violent, that juvenile crime is directed at persons more often than at property, that juveniles prey on the elderly and on females, and that juveniles more often attack strangers than acquaintances. To gain a clear understanding of the juvenile justice system, one must attempt to separate facts from fiction about the extent and nature of juvenile crime. This introduction does not purport to give answers. Instead, it attempts to articulate the difficulties involved in pinpointing an accurate picture of juvenile crime.

I. What are the sources of information on juvenile crime?

There are three basic national sources of information on juvenile crime. The first is the National Crime Survey (NCS) conducted by the U.S. Bureau of the Census and the Law Enforcement Assistance Association. A random survey of households and businesses, the NCS requests information regarding the type and amount of crime to which the surveyed persons have been subjected. When personal victimization offenses are reported, the surveyed persons are also requested to estimate the age of the offender and to describe the severity of the offense. These data are used by researchers to correlate the age of offenders with the seriousness of their offenses.

One problem with the NCS, however, is that the accuracy of the victims' estimates of age remains untested.[a] For example, the victims' observational skills may be impaired during the commission of a crime. Victims' memories may be faulty if surveyed significantly after the crime's occurrence. In addition, small age differences may be extremely difficult for victims to judge. The latter would be of particular significance if the victims' estimates of the offenders' age determined whether the offense was categorized as a juvenile or an adult offense.

Another problem is that the NCS reports only the number of violent juvenile crimes rather than the number of juvenile offenders. In doing so, the NCS not only fails to report accurately the number of juveniles committing violent crimes, but also ignores the fact (belief) that much violent juvenile crime is committed by juveniles acting in groups.[b]

---

* A slightly revised version appears in 1985 Southern Illinois Law Journal ___.

[a] Snyder, Howard N., and John L. Hutzler, "The Serious Juvenile Offender: The Scope of the Problem and the Response of Juvenile Courts" (Pittsburgh: National Center for Juvenile Justice, 1981), p. 1 [hereinafter cited as Snyder and Hutzler].

[b] McDermott, M. Joan, and Michael J. Hindelang, "Analysis of National Crime Victimization Survey Data to Study Serious Delinquent Behavior, Monograph 1" (Albany: U.S. Dept. of Justice, National Institute for Juvenile Justice and Delinquency Prevention, 1981), p. 10 [hereinafter cited as McDermott and Hindelang].

The second source of information on juvenile crime are the Uniform Crime Reports (UCR) compiled by the FBI. The UCR record the number of reported crimes and of arrests made in police departments across the country. Snyder and Hutzler point out that the UCR may be deceptive. They argue that because the percentage of unreported crimes is high[c], the UCR do not give a true measure of the total number of crimes committed,[d] making any determination of the percentage of actual crimes committed by juveniles inherently faulty. Since the number of unreported juvenile crimes cannot be determined, at best figures can show only the percentage of total reported crimes for which juveniles are responsible.

The number of reported crimes changes from year to year. The reason for those changes cannot be accurately determined using the UCR. If the UCR show an increase, for example, the increase can be due either to an increase in the number of reports of crime or to an actual increase in crime. This ultimately makes determination of the percentage and trends of crimes committed by juveniles very difficult.

In addition, measuring the number of arrests rather than the number of offenses may exaggerate the amount of juvenile crime. Since juveniles are (perhaps) more likely than adults to commit group crimes, a single offense may more often result in multiple arrests.[e] If one compared the number of juvenile arrests to the number of adult arrests in an attempt to compare the proportion of crime attributable to juveniles, and if the assumption is made that group criminality is more common among juveniles than among adults, the result would, of course, be distorted.

The third source of information is the National Juvenile Court Archive established and maintained by the National Center for Juvenile Justice and the National Institute for Juvenile Justice and Delinquency Prevention. The Archive collects information on courts' responses to juvenile offenders through analysis of juvenile case records. But, as a measure of juvenile crime, the Archive fails in two ways: (1) it offers no information on unsolved crimes and (2) it excludes juveniles who are tried in adult courts. Since many juveniles charged with serious crimes are certified to adult court for trial, the Archive's figures on serious juvenile crime may tend to be underestimates since they rely only on juvenile case records.[f]

II. How significant is the problem of juvenile crime?

Generally, the amount of juvenile crime has been perceived as rapidly increasing. In 1978, Strasburg reported that juvenile arrests

---

[c] The NCS estimates that over half of all violent crimes are unreported. Snyder, Howard N., "Violent Juvenile Crime: The Problem in Perspective," Today's Delinquent (Pittsburgh: National Center for Juvenile Justice, 1982), p. 10 [hereinafter cited as Snyder].

[d] Snyder and Hutzler, supra note a, at 1.

[e] For example, if a juvenile theft results in four juvenile arrests while an adult theft results in only one adult arrest, the UCR's arrest data will show that juvenile thefts are occurring at a four times greater rate than adult thefts. Id. at 1.

[f] Snyder and Hutzler, supra note a, at 2.

for violent crimes increased 293% between 1960 and 1975.[g] In 1976, the National Advisory Committee on Criminal Justice Standards and Goals reported that "* * * for many years the growth rate of juvenile delinquency has been outstripping that of adult crimes by wide * * * margins."[h] The Committee refers to this increase as "frightening and relatively steady."[i] The National Advisory Committee relied in part on a 1967 report by the President's Commission on Law Enforcement and Administration of Justice. The President's Commission reported that "in recent years the number of delinquency arrests has increased sharply * * * [T]he Commission is of the opinion that juvenile delinquency has increased significantly in recent years."[j] *(1967)*

Recent studies, however, suggest that juvenile crime is *not* increasing. Doleschal and Newton recently concluded that the "perceived increase in youthful violence in the U.S. today appears to stem from the interest by the mass media in the problem of crime rather than to reflect any real increases."[k] In a speech at the 1979 National Council of Juvenile and Family Court Judges meeting, Judge William Sylvester White also noted the media-induced perception of increasing juvenile crime. He referred to a 1977 Time magazine article that stated, "Since 1960, juvenile crime has risen twice as fast as that of adults." In 1978, Judge White continued, Senator Edward M. Kennedy (Mass.) spoke of a "plague" of violent juvenile crime. Also in 1978, Judge White noted, Senator John Culver (Iowa) announced a doubling since 1968 in the commission of violent crime by juveniles.[l]

Apparently, the public has believed media announcements about increasing violent juvenile crime.[m] With respect to crime in general, James Garofalo wrote in 1977 that opinion polls showed the public felt that not only was crime increasing, but also violent crime was a

[g] Strasburg, Paul A., "Violent Delinquents: A Report to the Ford Foundation from the Vera Institute of Justice" (New York: Monarch, 1978), p. 13 [hereinafter cited as Strasburg]. As Armstrong and Altschuler point out, Strasburg's figure must be qualified by the corresponding 52% increase in juvenile population during the 1960's. Armstrong, Troy L., and David M. Altschuler, "Community Based Program Interventions for Serious Juvenile Offenders: Targeting, Strategies, and Issues" (Chicago: National Center for the Assessment of Alternatives to Juvenile Justice Processing, 1982), p. 18.

[h] "Juvenile Justice and Delinquency Prevention: Report of the Task Force on Juvenile Justice and Delinquency Prevention" (Washington, D.C.: National Advisory Committee on Criminal Justice Standards and Goals, 1976), p. 1.

[i] Id. at 5.

[j] "The Challenge of Crime in a Free Society" (Washington, D.C.: The President's Commission on Law Enforcement and Administration of Justice, 1967), p. 56.

[k] Doleschal, Eugene, and Anne Newton, "The Violent Juvenile: A Review," Criminal Justice Abstracts 10, no. 4 (1978): 539–573.

[l] White, William Sylvester, "Debunking Three Myths About America's Children and the Courts that Serve Them," Juvenile and Family Court Journal (Reno: National Council of Juvenile and Family Court Judges, Aug. 1979), p. 3–4.

[m] McDermott, M. Joan, "Facts About Violent Juvenile Crime" (Washington, D.C.: U.S. Dept. of Justice, National Council on Crime and Delinquency, July 1982), p. 1 [hereinafter cited as McDermott].

major factor in that increase.[n] It seems unlikely that the public perception of an increasing quantity of violent crime in general would not also include a public belief that violence by juveniles was also on the increase.

Federal agencies and state legislatures shared the public's perception.

Some of the actions taken in recent years have focused on dealing with the role of juvenile offenders in committing violent crimes. The OJJDP at the federal level has suggested that 30% of formula grant funds be earmarked for efforts directed at the serious and violent juvenile offender. Many states have passed so-called "get tough" legislation to allow or mandate more severe penalties to deal with violent juvenile offenders. A recent report states that half of the state legislatures in the past five years have changed their states' juvenile codes to make it easier to refer juveniles to criminal courts to be tried as adults.[o]

It should be noted that there have been some media announcements that did not endorse the belief in increasing juvenile crime. In January, 1983, USA Today printed an article by Judge Seymour Gelber noting that, "Juvenile crime is not pervasive, not violent, not increasing, and not destined to destroy our society." Gelber also noted that between 1970 and 1980, the five to fourteen-year-old population declined by 6,000,000. Gelber felt that the population decrease "foreshadows a continued decrease in juvenile crime during the 1980's." [p]

Schuster's study of Ohio juvenile offenders supported this view: "The findings of this study do not support the media-generated belief in widespread, serious juvenile violence * * *" [q] McDermott and Hindelang also concluded that "to the extent that recent legislative changes are premised on the assumption of generally increasing involvement of juveniles in violent personal offenses or on the assumption that juveniles constitute an increasing proportion of those committing violent personal offenses, the data presented to this point simply do not support such changes." [r] McDermott and Hindelang

[n] Garofalo, James, "Public Opinion about Crime: The Attitudes of Victims and Nonvictims in Selected Cities" (Washington, D.C.: U.S. Dept. of Justice, National Criminal Justice Information and Statistics Service, 1977), p. 15–17.

[o] "Juveniles and Violent Crime in Missouri" (Jefferson City: Missouri Juvenile Justice Review Committee, 1983), p. 1 [hereinafter cited as Missouri Juvenile Justice Review Committee].

[p] Gelber, Seymour, "Treating Juvenile Crime," USA Today (New York: Society for the Advancement of Education, January 1983), p. 26.

[q] Schuster studied juveniles in one Ohio county who were born between 1956–58 and who had at least one contact with police for a violent offense. He measured the extent of violent juvenile behavior that was handled by Ohio's juvenile justice system. Schuster noted a media distortion of the extent of juvenile crime. He summarized by warning that across-the-board juvenile justice reforms would be too drastic. Instead, he concluded, reforms should be made to deal specifically with the minority of hardened juvenile offenders. Schuster, Richard L., "Violent Juveniles and Proposed Changes in Juvenile Justice: A Case of Overkill?," Juvenile and Family Court Journal (Reno: National Council of Juvenile and Family Court Judges, Nov. 1982), p. 41.

[r] McDermott and Hindelang, supra note b, p. 16.

found that the raw number of personal crimes committed by juveniles decreased from 1976 (1,311,000) to 1977 (1,179,000). They also found that juvenile rates of offending (i.e., the raw number of personal crimes committed by juveniles divided by the juvenile population) per 100,000 persons decreased 8.7% from 1976 (5,317) to 1977 (4,852).[s]

In a separate study, McDermott found that of the two million juvenile arrests in 1980, only 4% were for serious violent crimes, a decrease of 1.8% from 1976.[t]

III. Why are accurate reports of current trends in juvenile crime so elusive?

The discrepancies in the figures on juvenile crime can be partly explained by the inherent problems in the three types of available information, described above. In addition, the definition of violent juvenile offender varies from one jurisdiction to another. Altschuler and Armstrong noted "considerable variation across jurisdictional boundaries * * * [T]here is no common definition of the serious juvenile offender." [u]

Definitions of violent juvenile offenders that are based on the offenses labeled as violent by the FBI (i.e., murder/voluntary manslaughter, forcible rape, robbery, and aggravated assault) are fairly common. Similarly, typical definitions of juvenile property offenders are based on FBI Index Crimes (i.e., burglary, larceny, and motor vehicle theft).

Occasionally, the juvenile offender is termed violent because the offense he committed is usually committed in a violent way. The amount of violence that actually occurred may or may not be considered. For example, a juvenile who committed a robbery might be termed a serious offender even though no violence—as most of us would understand the term—was threatened or used. In other jurisdictions, the juvenile's offense history is used to determine whether he is to be classified as a violent offender.[v]

McDermott and Joppich observed that definitional differences centered around two questions: (1) What is the violent juvenile offense? and (2) Who is the violent juvenile offender? [w] Jurisdictions that concentrate on the former question focus on the type of offense the juvenile committed. Jurisdictions that concentrate on the latter question focus on the juvenile's offense history.

[s] Id. at 16.

[t] McDermott, supra note m, p. 2. The Missouri study, see supra note o at 5, states that of 35,000 referrals to juvenile courts in that state in 1981, 0.5% were adjudicated delinquent or certified to adult courts for violent offenses.

[u] Altschuler, David M., and Troy L. Armstrong, "Community Based Programs for Serious Juvenile Offenders," Change: A Juvenile Justice Quarterly 5, No. 1 (1981), p. 5 [hereinafter cited as Altschuler and Armstrong].

[v] McDermott, M. Joan, and Gisela Joppich, "The Serious Juvenile Offender" (Hackensack: National Council on Crime and Delinquency, 1980), p. 2.

[w] Id. at 2.

IV. How violent are offenses committed by juveniles as compared to the same offenses committed by adults?

According to Snyder, juveniles were consistently less likely than
adults to possess some type of weapon even during a violent crime.
Snyder found that from 1973 to 1977, adults possessed weapons in
about 79% of their violent crimes while juveniles possessed weapons
in 63% of their violent crimes.[x] Strasburg found that weapons were
present in less than 17% of the violent juvenile crimes committed in
three New York/New Jersey counties.[y] McDermott and Hindelang
found that from 1973 to 1977, juveniles used a weapon in 27% of their
personal incidents (and a gun in less than 5%) while adults used a
weapon in about 38% of their personal incidents.[z]

Specifically, Snyder found that juveniles were approximately
four times less likely than adults to possess a gun during a violent
crime.[aa] McDermott and Hindelang attribute at least part of this
difference to the greater availability of guns to adults than to
juveniles.[bb]

Snyder and Hutzler also found that "the likelihood of serious
injury to the victim is significantly higher when the offender is an
adult than when he is a child."[cc] This is not surprising because
juveniles less frequently use either weapons or physical force. On
the other hand, McDermott and Hindelang found no substantial
difference in the seriousness or type of injury sustained by victims of
juvenile crime and victims of adult crime.[dd]

Researchers have also found that economic losses resulting from
juvenile crimes were less than those resulting from adult crimes.
Snyder and Hutzler found that cash losses of ten dollars or more
occurred in 10% of juvenile robberies and in 34% of adult robberies.
He found that cash losses of ten dollars or more occurred in 28% of
juvenile personal larcenies and in 59% of adult personal larcenies.[ee]
McDermott and Hindelang reached similar results, concluding that
"financial losses were consistently greater in crimes committed by
adult offenders than they were in crimes committed by juveniles
* * *."[ff]

V. Are there types of crimes that juveniles are more likely to
commit?

Apparently, juveniles are more likely to commit serious property
offenses than personal offenses. In 1979, juvenile arrests resulted in
only 12% of cleared violent offenses (i.e., those so labeled by the FBI)
and in 30% of cleared serious property offenses (i.e., those so labeled

[x] Snyder, supra note c, p. 19.

[y] Strasburg, supra note g, p. 73.

[z] McDermott and Hindelang, supra
note b, p. 21.

[aa] Snyder, supra note c, p. 19.

[bb] McDermott and Hindelang, supra
note b, p. 23.

[cc] Snyder and Hutzler, supra note a, p.
2.

[dd] McDermott and Hindelang, supra
note b, p. 36–37.

[ee] Snyder and Hutzler, supra note a, p.
2.

[ff] McDermott and Hindelang, supra
note b, p. 61.

by the FBI).gg The prevalence of property offenses in juvenile crimes appears appropriate in light of the findings that juveniles generally use fewer weapons and less physical force than adults in the commission of a crime.

Altschuler and Armstrong found that in contrast to violent crimes against persons, "serious property crimes are committed in greatest numbers by juvenile offenders." hh McDermott also found that of the 1.3 million cases "processed" ii by juvenile courts in 1979, "4.6% involved serious violent crimes, 37.8% were serious property offenses, 37.8% were less serious offenses * * * and 19.8% involved noncriminal behavior such as truancy * * *" jj Other researchers found that the proportion of serious property arrests to violent crime arrests of juveniles was approximately 9:1. Strasburg observed that 90% of the juveniles arrested in 1975 were arrested for property offenses.kk Smith et al. noted a rapid increase in juvenile violent crime arrests in the 1960's, but then observed a stabilization in the 1970's at a 9:1 ratio of serious property to personal offenses.ll

VI. Who is likely to be a violent juvenile offender?

Snyder and Hutzler found that 1.3 million cases were processed by juvenile courts in 1979.mm Of those cases, 78% of the juveniles were male and 22% female. In the serious offenses cases (4.6% of the total cases), 82% of the juveniles were male and 18% female.nn In property crime and non-index cases, males also outnumbered females. In the status offense category, there was an approximately equal percentage of males and females until age 15 years when males again outnumbered females.oo

Snyder and Hutzler found that the 1.3 million cases involved 69% white and 31% non-white juveniles. In dividing the cases into offense categories, Snyder and Hutzler found that non-whites comprised 60% of violent crime cases, 33% of property crime cases, 30% of non-index cases, and 19% of status offense cases.pp

Walter and Ostrander conducted a study of the demographic characteristics of 627 juveniles who appeared in official and unofficial juvenile court hearings. The hearings took place over a ten-week period in a large, north central city. Walter and Ostrander found that 54% of the juveniles were white and 46% were non-white. Males comprised 73% of the juveniles and were more likely to appear on

gg Snyder and Hutzler, supra note a, p. 3.

hh Altschuler and Armstrong, supra note u, p. 21.

ii See note mm, infra.

jj McDermott, supra note m, p. 2.

kk Strasburg, supra note g, p. 13.

ll Smith, Charles P. et al., "A National Assessment of Serious Juvenile Crime and the Juvenile Justice System: The Need for a Rational Response," Vol. II (Sacramento: National Juvenile Justice System Assessment Center, 1979), p. 91.

mm As used by Snyder and Hutzler, "processed" does not mean only "adjudicated." Their 1.3 million figure includes all juveniles who enter the juvenile justice system (e.g., those who are certified to adult court, those unofficially disposed, and those adjudicated in some fashion). Snyder and Hutzler, supra note a, p. 3.

nn Id. at 3.

oo Id. at 3.

pp Id. at 4.

delinquency charges. The remaining 27% were female and were more likely to appear on unruly behavior charges. Of the juveniles whose age was mentioned by the court, 27% were 17–18 years old, 43% were 15–16 years old, 25% were 13–14 years old, and 5% were 12 years old and younger. Of the juveniles with known residences, 68% resided in urban areas and 32% in suburban areas.[qq] Walter and Ostrander also found that 50% of the juveniles had "generally poor" school records with only 12% having "generally good" school records. Fifteen percent of the juveniles had "average" school records and 8% were not attending school. Walter and Ostrander did not find any significant difference between white and non-white juveniles' school records.[rr]

In a Missouri study of all juveniles adjudicated delinquent or certified to adult courts for a violent offense in 1981, 88.6% of the juveniles were male and 11.4% female. In Missouri's general population, there are 51.1% males and 48.9% females.[ss] The Missouri study also found that 42.4% of the offenders were white, 57.0% black, and 0.6% other. In Missouri's general population, there are 85.3% whites, 13.4% blacks, and 0.8% others.[tt]

VII. Who is likely to be a victim of a violent juvenile offender?

The Missouri study found that 90% of violent juvenile crime victims were under 60 years old. Fifty-one percent of those victims were 16 years old or younger. Sixty-two percent of the victims were male.[uu] It is unclear whether the Missouri Committee took the populations of the age groups of victims into account. In other words, the fact that 90% of juvenile crime victims were under 60 years old must be viewed in terms of the percentage of Missouri's general population under 60 years old.

The same study also found that 51% of the violent crime victims were at least acquaintances of the offender.[vv] The Missouri Committee observed that the chance of the victim and offender being strangers depended on the type of offense. For instance, the victim and the offender were strangers in 77% of robberies while they were strangers in only 13% of the sex offenses.[ww]

McDermott also found that young males were the most likely victims of violent juvenile crimes.[xx]

[qq] Walter, James D., and Susan A. Ostrander, "An Observational Study of a Juvenile Court," Juvenile and Family Court Journal (Reno: National Council of Juvenile and Family Court Judges, Aug. 1982), p. 57.

[rr] Id. at 64.

[ss] Missouri Juvenile Justice Review Committee, supra note o, p. 7.

[tt] Id. at 7. For further statistics, see Snyder, supra note c, p. 21–23.

[uu] Missouri Juvenile Justice Review Committee, supra note o, p. 9.

[vv] Id. at 10.

[ww] Id. at 10.

[xx] McDermott, supra note m, p. 4–5.

Chapter 1

LEGAL AND PHILOSOPHICAL BASES FOR A SEPARATE JUVENILE JUSTICE PROCESS

A. DESCRIPTION OF THE JUVENILE JUSTICE SYSTEM

DAWSON, LEGAL NORMS AND THE JUVENILE CORREC-
TIONAL PROCESS, IN F. COHEN, THE LEGAL CHAL-
LENGE TO CORRECTIONS 88–90 (1969)

Juvenile justice is a system separate from, though parallel to, the criminal justice system. Separation is established by statutes which give juvenile courts exclusive jurisdiction over persons under specified age who are alleged to have committed criminal offenses. Statutes substitute adjudication of delinquency for conviction of crime and provide that an adjudication does not create the civil disabilities that result from a criminal conviction. Upon adjudication, the juvenile court's statutory powers of disposition include commitment to a juvenile correctional institution until the juvenile becomes 21 years of age, without regard to the seriousness or pettiness of the offense as measured by the sentence authorized upon conviction in criminal court.

Even more important than the differences created by legal structure are those that occur in the actual operation of the system. Police investigation may be conducted by a special juvenile bureau of the police department rather than detective bureaus organized on the basis of offense categories, and the juvenile bureau may operate programs for the adjustment of cases without referral to juvenile court. Juveniles taken into police custody in some places are not photographed or fingerprinted. Juvenile police records may be kept separate from adult records with special restrictions on public access to them; furthermore, juvenile records in some places are not sent to state or national criminal identification centers.

Offenders referred to juvenile court may be detained before trial in a juvenile detention center rather than in a city or county jail. Although the juvenile offender may be denied an opportunity for release on bail, he may have greater opportunity than the adult offender for release without security. A preliminary determination as to whether the juvenile engaged in delinquent conduct may be made by a social worker in the juvenile court's intake department. Even when it is concluded that delinquency can be proved, the case may be informally adjusted without a juvenile court hearing.

In the criminal system, the prosecuting attorney's office may make a preliminary determination as to whether there is sufficient evidence of guilt to justify prosecution, and this decision may be

9

reviewed in a brief judicial proceeding (preliminary examination or hearing) or by a grand jury, or both. Even if the prosecutor's office determines there is sufficient evidence of guilt to justify prosecution, it may conclude prosecution is not in the public interest and dismiss the case, conditionally or unconditionally.

* * * [T]he adjudication of criminal cases is accomplished most frequently by a plea of guilty entered by the defendant as a result of negotiations between his attorney and a prosecuting attorney. The comparatively small number of "not guilty" pleas leads to contested trials. In the juvenile system, bargaining for guilty pleas is much less likely to occur, although the percentage of cases that are not contested by the defendant may be even greater than in criminal court. Despite full implementation of the *Gault* requirements, the juvenile court hearing is likely to be more informal than the criminal trial, and a jury is far less likely to be present.

If the defendant is convicted in criminal court, he is sentenced (normally by the judge, but in some jurisdictions by the jury); sentencing may be postponed to permit a presentence investigation into the offense and the defendant's background. After adjudication of delinquency in juvenile court, the judge normally consults a social history report in making his disposition. Unlike the presentence report in adult cases, the juvenile social history investigation may have been conducted before the juvenile court hearing and adjudication of delinquency. A juvenile is more likely to receive probation than an adult.

An adult sentenced to a correctional institution often must serve a specified length of time or percentage of his sentence before he becomes eligible for release on parole; a juvenile committed to a training school normally does not have statutory durational requirements to satisfy to become eligible for release. Furthermore, he is likely to be released earlier than his counterpart sentenced for a criminal offense.

A juvenile is likely to be confined in a minimum-security institution in which the daily routine consists of a mixture of academic education, vocational training, and maintenance of the institution. An adult offender is likely to be confined in a maximum- or medium-security institution with a daily routine of prison maintenance, prison industry work, and vocational training.

NOTE

Older state statutes defining juvenile delinquency typically included status offenses, i.e., non-criminal conduct that is illegal only if committed by children, such as truancy and curfew violations. Furthermore, children who did not fall within the above category might have come within the juvenile court's delinquency jurisdiction for "being incorrigible" or for leading "immoral lives." The Alabama statute printed below is an example of the older-style statute. It has since been repealed. Currently, most, if not all, state statutes exclude status offenses and conduct embodying judgments about "immorality" from definitions of juvenile delinquency. Delinquency is now usually defined as those acts which if committed by an adult would be criminal. Status offenses are now usually included in either a relatively new juvenile category, children in need of supervision (CHINS) (sometimes PINS, MINS, YINS), or a category sometimes labelled "unruly children" or "wayward children." Jurisdiction based on findings of immorality survives in the modern statutes in two principal contexts: (1) to the extent that the concept is subsumed within the CHINS (or "wayward" or "unruly children") jurisdiction under the more common heading of habitual disobedience or incorrigibility; and (2) when the explicit morality language is transferred to the dependency or neglect jurisdiction or placed in the "wayward" or "unruly children" category. The second (current) Alabama statute places the "disobedient" and "beyond control" language in its CHINS definition and refers explicitly to endangerment of morals in its dependency definition. The Rhode Island statute which follows places both the "immorality" and the "disobedience" language in its definition of a "wayward child."

ALABAMA CODE TITLE 13, CHAPTER 7 (repealed)

§ 350. * * * **Definitions.**—(1) For the purposes of this chapter the words "dependent child" shall mean any child, who, while under sixteen years of age, for any reason, is destitute, homeless, or is dependent on the public for support; or who is without a parent or guardian able to provide for his support, training and education; or whose custody is the subject of controversy. (2) The words "neglected child" shall mean any child, who, while under sixteen years of age is abandoned by both parents, or if one parent is dead, by the survivor, or by his guardian, or custodian; or who has no proper parental care or guardianship or whose home, by reason of neglect, cruelty, or depravity, on the part of his parent or parents, guardian or other person in whose care he may be, is an unfit or improper place for such child; or who is found begging, receiving or gathering alms, or who is found in any street, road or public place for the purpose of so doing, whether actually begging or doing so under the pretext of selling or offering for sale any article or articles, or of singing or playing on any musical instrument, or of giving any public entertainment or accompanying or being used in aid of any person so doing; or for whom his parent, parents, guardian or custodian, neglect or refuse, when able to do so, or when such service is offered without charge, to provide, or allow, medical, surgical, or other care necessary for his health, or well-being; or whose parent, parents, guardian or custodian permits such child to engage in an occupation or calling contrary to the provisions of the child labor law of this state; or whose parent, parents, guardian or custodian fail, refuse or neglect to send such child to school in accordance with the terms of the compulsory attendance law of this state; or who is in such condition or surroundings, or is under such improper or insufficient guardianship or control as to endanger the morals, health or general welfare of such child; or who is not being reared or cared for in accordance with the provisions of any law, regulation or ordinance for the education, care and protection of children; or who for any other cause is in need of the care and protection of the state. (3) The words "delinquent child" shall mean any child who while under sixteen years of age violates any penal law of the United States or of this state, or any regulation, ordinance or law of any city, town or municipality, or who commits any offense or act for which an adult could be prosecuted in a method partaking of the nature of a criminal action or proceeding; or who is beyond the control of his parent, parents, guardian, or custodian, or who is otherwise incorrigible, or who is guilty of immoral conduct; or who is leading an idle, dissolute, lewd or immoral life; or who engages in any calling, occupation or exhibition punishable by law or is found in any place for permitting which an adult may be punished by law. (4) All such children, hereinabove described dependent, neglected or delinquent, shall be subject to the guardianship of the state and entitled to its care and protection. The state shall exercise its right of guardianship and control over such children in the manner and form hereinafter provided. * * *

ALABAMA CODE OF 1975 (1983 Supplement) TITLE 12,
CHAPTER 15, ARTICLE 1

§ 12-15-1. Definitions

* * *

(3) CHILD.

a. Such term, before January 1, 1978, means an individual under the age of 17 or under 19 years of age who committed the act of delinquency with which he is charged before reaching the age of 17 years.

b. Such term, after December 31, 1977, means an individual under the age of 18 or under 19 years of age and who committed the act of delinquency with which he is charged before reaching the age of 18 years.

(4) CHILD IN NEED OF SUPERVISION. A child who:

a. Being subject to compulsory school attendance, is habitually truant from school; or

b. Disobeys the reasonable and lawful demands of his parents, guardian or other custodian and is beyond their control; or

c. Has committed an offense established by law but not classified as criminal or one applicable only to children; and

d. In any of the foregoing, is in need of care or rehabilitation.

* * *

(8) DELINQUENT ACT. An act designated a crime under the law of this state or of another state if the act occurred in another state or under federal law or a violation of a municipal ordinance; provided, however, that traffic offenses committed by one 16 years of age or older shall be excepted unless transferred to the juvenile court by the court having jurisdiction.

(9) DELINQUENT CHILD. A child who has committed a delinquent act and is in need of care or rehabilitation.

(10) DEPENDENT CHILD. A child:

    a. Who, for any reason is destitute, homeless or dependent on the public for support; or

    b. Who is without a parent or guardian able to provide for his support, training or education; or

    c. Whose custody is the subject of controversy; or

    d. Whose home, by reason of neglect, cruelty or depravity on the part of his parent, parents, guardian or other person in whose care he may be, is an unfit and improper place for him; or

    e. Whose parent, parents, guardian or other custodian neglects or refuses, when able to do so or when such service is offered without charge, to provide or allow medical, surgical or other care necessary for such child's health or well-being; or

    f. Who is in such condition or surroundings or is under such improper or insufficient guardianship or control as to endanger his morals, health or general welfare; or

    g. Who has no proper parental care or guardianship; or

    h. Whose parent, parents, guardian or custodian fail, refuse or neglect to send such child to school in accordance with the terms of the compulsory school attendance laws of this state; or

    i. Who has been abandoned by his parents, guardian or other custodian; or

    j. Who is physically, mentally or emotionally abused by his parents, guardian or other custodian or who is without proper parental care and control necessary for his well-being because of the faults or habits of his parents, guardian or other custodian or their neglect or refusal, when able to do so, to provide them; or

    k. Whose parents, guardian or other custodian are unable to discharge their responsibilities to and for the child; or

    l. Who has been placed for care or adoption in violation of the law; or

    m. Who for any other cause is in need of the care and protection of the state; and

    n. In any of the foregoing, is in need of care or supervision.

GENERAL LAWS OF RHODE ISLAND (1981) TITLE 14,
CHAPTER I

14-1-3. Definitions.—The following words and phrases when used in this chapter shall, unless the context otherwise requires, be construed as follows:

*   *   *

C. The term "child" shall mean a person under eighteen (18) years of age.

D. The term "adult" shall mean a person eighteen (18) years of age or older.

* * *

F. The term "delinquent" when applied to a child shall mean and include any child—

Who has committed any offense which, if committed by an adult, would constitute a felony, or who has on more than one (1) occasion violated any of the other laws of the state or of the United States or any of the ordinances of cities and towns, other than ordinances relating to the operation of motor vehicles.

G. The term "wayward" when applied to a child shall mean and include any child—

1. Who has deserted his home without good or sufficient cause; or

2. Who habitually associates with dissolute, vicious or immoral persons; or

3. Who is leading an immoral or vicious life; or

4. Who is habitually disobedient to the reasonable and lawful commands of his parent or parents, guardian or other lawful custodian; or

5. Who, being required by chapter 19 of title 16 to attend school, wilfully and habitually absents himself therefrom, or habitually violates rules and regulations of the school when he attends; or

6. Who has on any occasion violated any of the laws of the state or of the United States or any of the ordinances of cities and towns, other than ordinances relating to the operation of motor vehicles.

H. The terms "dependent" and/or "neglected" when applied to a child shall mean and include any child—

Who is homeless or destitute or abandoned or dependent upon the public for support, or who has not the parental care or guardianship or who habitually begs or receives alms, or whose home, by reason of neglect, cruelty, drunkenness or depravity on the part of the parent or parents having custody or control of such child is an unfit place for such child, or any child under eight (8) years of age found peddling in the streets or any child found engaging in an occupation or being in a situation dangerous to life, or limb or injurious to the health or well-being of such child, or who has had physical injury or injuries which may adversely affect his health and welfare inflicted upon him other than by accidental means.

* * *

ORLANDO AND BLACK, CLASSIFICATION IN JUVENILE
COURT: THE DELINQUENT CHILD AND THE
CHILD IN NEED OF SUPERVISION, 25 JUVE-
NILE JUSTICE, No. 1, 13–14, 16–23 (1974) *

Antisocial behavior and juvenile delinquent behavior encompasses conduct ranging from acts of murder and armed robbery to curfew
violations and running away from home, to conduct not resulting in
court action but resulting in a label of pre-delinquent. This latter
activity often includes conduct such as fighting in school which would
be subsumed under the umbrella of the juvenile court, but which
agencies do not feel warrants court action at this time. Studies
reveal that 90 per cent of all youth have engaged in activities which
could have led to involvement with the juvenile court.

The focus of this paper is on an examination of the classifications
employed by the juvenile court and their impact upon the lives of
children, especially the reality of that impact when contrasted with
the theory of the juvenile justice system. Although there exists a
need for inquiry into the economic, social, and ethnic composition of
those children before the court, this paper excludes that consideration. The focus here is on the extremely wide range of conduct
included within the juvenile court jurisdiction and the consequences to
children coming within its mandate. However, it would be misleading to suggest that all antisocial acts are simply examples of youths
acting out or "boys being boys," for youths are responsible for a
substantial portion of serious criminal activity. In 1965, 30 per cent
of all persons arrested were under 21 years of age and 20 per cent
under 18. One-half of the arrests for serious property crimes were
of youths aged 11 through 17.

The classification of juveniles for antisocial conduct is an embodiment of the concept that juveniles, like adults, are accountable at law
for violations of the law. The problem is to reconcile the interests of
society in being safe and secure in life and property with the interest
of the society and the child in having that child become a productive
citizen. Juvenile courts have traditionally been thought of as vehicles to accommodate these interests and as a means of securing aid
and rehabilitation for deviant children.

To comprehend more fully the task with which society has
saddled the court, one needs to recognize the multiplicity and complexity of the causes of youth crime and then to assess the ability of
the state to effectively modify the behavior of antisocial children.

Crime and delinquency are multi-causal phenomena with roots in
the political, social, and economic inequalities which exist in a large,
heterogeneous society. An individual's norms, values, and code of
conduct are shaped by his life experiences which in great measure,
are dictated by the physical and moral environment of his youth.

Among the forces, conditions, and circumstances most often singled out as "breeders" of crime and delinquency are:

(a) The undesirable and pervasive condition associated with poverty;

(b) The weakening of the traditional institutions (family, school, religions) as agents of socialization and social control;

(c) The failure of the educational system to meet the academic and vocational needs of today's youth;

(d) The prolongation of childhood as a period of nonresponsibility;

(e) The failure of society to provide meaningful work opportunities and vocational training for those lacking the ability or desire for higher (academic) education;

(f) The lack of youth and community involvement in policy-making and decision-making in matters which directly affect them;

(g) The failure of society to provide adequate and relevant services (medical, dental, social, psychological, psychiatric) to large segments of the population;

(h) The inability of our judicial and correctional systems to provide adequate and effective rehabilitation programs for those already enmeshed in the delinquent, deviant, and criminal subcultures.

While recent studies are calling into question the stereotype juvenile delinquent, it is clear that those children who are caught in the system demand more than a man with a gavel, they need a fairy godmother with a magic wand.

* * *

CLASSIFICATION SYSTEM

Juvenile courts are involved with children who commit acts which violate criminal laws, children who commit acts which violate laws applicable to children alone (running away from home), children who are habitually ungovernable by their natural guardian and children who are neglected or abused by their guardian. Juvenile court legislation forms the basis for the distinctions between the delinquent, the child in need of supervision, and the neglected and dependent child. The classifications "delinquent and child in need of supervision" involve proceedings initiated as a result of some act by the child himself. On the other hand, neglect and dependency proceedings are essentially actions against the parents or guardians, and are initiated because of some act of misfeasance, malfeasance or nonfeasance on the part of the parent with respect to the welfare of the child. Since the category of neglected and dependent children does not involve children who commit antisocial acts it will not be covered by this paper.

The classifications "juvenile delinquent" and "child in need of supervision" are nonscientific classifications representing legislative attempts to delimit the boundaries between conduct which warrants state intervention and conduct which does not. Consistent with the original formulation of the juvenile court the concept "delinquency" included conduct which was injurious to the community such as property crimes, and conduct which was basically injurious to the child himself, such as running away from home. Sussman listed the acts subsumed under delinquency definitions as: violations of any law or ordinance; habitual truancy, knowingly associating with thieves, vicious, or immoral persons; incorrigibility, being beyond control of parent or guardian; growing up in idleness or crime; deporting self so as to injure self or others; absenting self without just cause, without consent; immoral or indecent conduct; habitual use of vile, obscene or vulgar language in a public place; jumping trains or entering cars or engine without authority; patronizing public poolroom or bucket shop; immoral conduct around school; engaging in illegal occupation; engaging in occupation or situation dangerous or injurious to self or others; smoking cigarettes or using tobacco in any form; frequenting place whose existence violates the law; being found in a place for permitting which an adult may be punished; being addicted to drugs; being disorderly; begging; using intoxicating liquor; making an indecent proposal; loitering; sleeping in alleys; vagrancy; running away from state or charity institution; attempting to marry without consent in violation of law; being given to sexual irregularities. The state, acting as *parens patriae*, was basically unlimited in the type of conduct proscribed and was relatively free in intervening in the child's life. Natural parents would be expected to be concerned with the whole gambit of undesirable behavior—from criminal activity to smoking cigarettes—and the statutes were drawn to permit state intervention in these instances as well.

In many jurisdictions the classification "juvenile delinquency" has been refined to include only conduct which if committed by an adult would be a violation of the criminal law. Those persons, who are habitually truant, who persistently refuse to obey the reasonable commands of their guardians, who commit violations of the law applicable only to children, are classified as "children in need of supervision," "persons in need of supervision," "incorrigibles" or "unruly children." Two main reasons exist for the development of these new categories. First, the *Gault* decision required procedural safeguards for children and necessitated more precise notice of charges that (sic) the loose language of many of the juvenile court act definitions of delinquency. Secondly, legislatures became concerned with the stigma attached to the label "delinquent" and sought to limit that label to violations of the criminal law. Furthermore, the legislatures prohibited placement of children classified CINS in the same institutions as delinquents. At present, 22 states have created a separate legal status for children charged as runaway, truant, incorrigible, or wayward.

In order to find a child delinquent or in need of supervision, two essential elements must be present. First, if the child is to be found delinquent he must have committed an act which constitutes a crime if committed by an adult; if he is to be found in need of supervision, he must have engaged in a pattern of conduct which makes him unruly. The second essential element is that the child must also be found to be in need of treatment or rehabilitation. Thus, to determine that a child committed an act without determining a need for treatment should be insufficient to support a finding of delinquency and lead to no action by the court.

* * *

ASSESSMENT OF THE SYSTEM

The juvenile court, to be sure, has a number of beneficial aspects which make it preferable to its adult counterpart, the criminal court. Judges in juvenile court normally view their role differently from that of the criminal court judge. The emphasis in juvenile court is primarily on helping the child. Although these are frequently inadequate, the courts do rely on diagnostic and rehabilitation services. The end result of a finding of delinquency is significantly different from that of a criminal proceeding. A finding of delinquency does not result in civil disabilities such as loss of the right to vote, the right to hold public office, or the right to be employed under the civil service system. The system allows for wide discretion in the intake procedure, and there is certainly more flexibility at the dispositional phase of the proceedings.

The juvenile court system, however, has major shortcomings as well as strengths. There are serious flaws in the classification scheme employed by the court. Difficulties are encountered when the interests of society and of the child do not coincide. The labels *delinquent* and *child in need of supervision* often have unintended consequences in stigmatizing the children so labeled. Also, constitutional problems arise from many statutes concerning children in need of supervision which attempt to reach children guilty of no specific anti-social conduct.

CONFLICTS

As was indicated earlier, juvenile courts are required to make two findings: (1) that the child committed the alleged antisocial act; and (2) that he is in need of treatment. This is consistent with the original philosophy of the juvenile court movement and with the requirements of *Gault*. The first finding involves the procedural safeguards of *Gault*. The second finding centers on helping children rather than punishing them. It is based upon the premise that the best interests of the child and the community are identical and that if a child does not need help, the interests of the community are fully served when he is released. Many judges appear to have difficulty in adjudging a child not delinquent where the child committed the act but has no need for treatment. This is especially true where the child committed a substantial anti-social act such as malicious destruction of property. Undoubtedly part of the difficulty lies with the fact that the community feels a very real need to be protected, to make an example out of this wrongdoer, and to punish him for his indiscretion. Even in cases where treatment is needed, often the court is called upon to correct conditions which are beyond its capabilities, with the result that the inadequate "treatment" prescribed is more like punishment.

The failure to assess accurately the role that the court plays in protecting the community has several unintended consequences which are detrimental to the child. Society has allowed laxness and unfairness in the classification process because of the assumption that it is simply looking out for the welfare of the child, when it is clear that what the court is being called upon to do is to protect the community. Furthermore, the emphasis upon the therapeutic efforts of the court creates the danger of unrealistic expectations with the result that the court is called upon to right situations which can be better handled by other agencies in the community. Finally, this unrealistic picture of the role of the court has led society to escape critical evaluation of the system and to overburden the system to such an extent that it is unlikely to be effective even in those areas where it could operate successfully.

STIGMA

There has been considerable discussion recently on the consequences of juvenile court adjudications. In analyzing these materials, it must be recognized from the outset that the official label of *delinquency*, delinquent behavior, and the public's concept of delinquency are not interchangeably synonymous. The public fails to make distinctions between the delinquent child who commits a criminal act and the CINS who commits an act of truancy or curfew violation. Rather it considers any juvenile to be "delinquent" if he has been subjected to juvenile court intervention. Stigma thus attaches when the public conceives the child to be delinquent. Stigma operates as an additional means of sanction for the child other than the specific statutory consequences of a finding of delinquency.

The ensuing discussion will examine the legal awareness of the problem of stigma, the sociological and psychological effects of the delinquency stigma and the economic consequences to the child.

The traditional stance of the courts was that adjudication of delinquency was not criminal in nature and that no adverse consequences attached to the adjudication. This was consistent with the goals set out in the statutes. However, it ignored reality. The Supreme Court expressly rejected that approach in *Gault* where it maintained that classification as a delinquent involved "only slightly less stigma than the term 'criminal.'" The Court has since reaffirmed that position in *In re Winship*.

As early as 1946, the Virginia Supreme Court noted that,

> The judgment against a youth that he is delinquent is a serious reflection upon his character and habits. The stain against him is not removed merely because the statute says no judgment in this particular proceeding shall be deemed a conviction for crime or so considered. The stigma of conviction will reflect upon him for life. It hurts his self respect. It may, at some inopportune, unfortunate moment, rear its ugly head to destroy his opportunity for advancement, and blast his ambition to build up a character and reputation entitling him to esteem and respect of his fellow man.

Similar awareness was made known by other courts in the following years. Judge Orman Ketcham of the District of Columbia listed as one of the unfulfilled promises of the juvenile court the fact that the findings resulted in a stigma much akin to a criminal court connotation. There has also been judicial recognition of the inherent dangers involved in the exposition of juvenile records.

Recent socio-psychological research suggests that official response to delinquent behavior may often act to push the juvenile further into deviant conduct. This theory has generally been called the "labeling hypothesis." The thrust of the concept is that being identified as a juvenile results in a "spoiled" public identity. The label results in a degree of public liability through exclusion from participation in groups and events which would not occur without the prior attachment of the label. The social liability has the further effect of reinforcing the deviance.

> The assumption is that the public responds to a person informally and in an unorganized way unless that person has been defined as falling into a clear category. The official labeling of a misbehaving youth as 'delinquent' has the effect of placing him in such a category. This official stamp may help to organize responses different from those that would have arisen without the official action. The result is that the label has an important effect upon how the individual is regarded by others. If official processing results in an individual's being segregated with others so labeled, an additional push toward deviant behavior may result. * * * (T)he individual begins to think of himself as delinquent, and he organizes his behavior accordingly.

Under this theory, the societal reaction is initially critical. Society, of course, first determines what behavior is to be considered as deviant. Stigma results when the deviant behavior and the offender are exposed. At this point, the delinquent's self-concept becomes crucial. The social rejections caused by the stigma can reinforce a negative self-image and persuade the juvenile that he cannot make it in normal society. The result is continued delinquency. This is what Robert Merton has termed the "self-fulfilling prophecy." If a person is treated like a criminal, he is likely to become one. "Under the impact of negative social reactions the individual may, then, be propelled from isolated acts of criminality into more complete involvement in criminal ways of life (heightened 'commitment' to criminal roles) and he may come increasingly to view himself as an enemy of society (since society seems so determined to consider him one)."

Several writers have seen delinquency as cyclical in nature. One recent study has advanced the hypothesis that when juveniles are confronted with poor institutional relationships—family, school, social contacts, employment situations—strain and tension result. Often the more intense the resulting strain becomes, the worse the institutional ties become. Peer pressures may add to the tension. Finally, the strain results in a deviant act. However, the tension is not necessarily broken, as society's reaction to the delinquency often heightens the strain. The societal reaction is expressed through stigma. As the strain worsens again so do the institutional ties, and when delinquency reoccurs, it is most likely of a more serious nature, with the resulting stigma more severe and the pattern starting anew. Thus the cycle has two "feedback loops"; strain worsening institutional ties, and stigma intensifying strain.

According to the noted criminologist Shoham, stigma is used as a "generic tool of social control," demanding conformity to established norms while threatening individualism. It often leaves the offender facing almost total "apartness" from regular society, the only alternative being association with others having the same handicap, delinquency. Thus, stigma can have the effect of creating deviant subcultures.

Empirical research attempts to support the labeling hypothesis have been inconclusive. However, significant work has been done by Martin Gold and Jay Williams at the University of Michigan. In one of their studies, the researchers assembled thirty-five matched pairs, in which one member of the match had escaped apprehension for essentially the same delinquent act which resulted in apprehension for his "twin." (Variables were matched as evenly as possible between the members of each pair). The subsequent records of the two youths were then compared. The survey concluded that "apprehension itself encourages rather than discourages delinquency." The rate of recidivism was higher when there was any type of official intervention, from apprehension to incarceration, than if nothing at all had been done. These same conclusions were also reached by Gold in an independent research project using similar methods.

In response to the above findings, Juvenile Court Judge John Steketee maintained that the study certainly lent credence to the theory that there is a self-fulfilling prophecy at work.

The effects of court adjudication on a juvenile's school performance have also received empirical study. A 1966 study concluded that "the school itself inadvertently contributes to alienation, rejection, misbehavior, and delinquency in its very attempt to do the opposite." An alienating cycle was detected, and the labeling process was held responsible.

On the other side of the coin, there are recent studies which conclude that an adverse reaction does not necessarily arise as a serious obstacle to school achievement for those labeled deviant. The data demonstrated that there is a negative association between public status as a delinquent and school performance, but that the association existed before the identification of the juvenile as deviant, as well as after. The label may, however, exacerbate the already ongoing process.

Recent studies also have raised questions concerning the validity of the labeling hypothesis. One study found that variations between those classified delinquent and those not so classified but who committed delinquent acts to be of such low magnitude as to result in the conclusion that "actually having a delinquent record does not appear to be particularly stigmatic by itself."

The second study focused upon the extent to which delinquent boys perceived themselves as having incurred any social liability as a consequence of public intervention. The project took cases in an urban community from both the police department and the juvenile court, and interviewed all the chosen subjects within a week to ten days after disposition of their cases. Recognizing that stigma may result in subtle and diffuse ways, the researchers are planning follow-up studies, but their early research supports the following conclusions:

(1) only a relatively small proportion of youths perceive any significant change in interpersonal relationships with friends or family;

(2) only a relatively small proportion anticipate any difficulties in completing school as a direct consequence of the public intervention;

(3) slightly more than one-half of the youths expect increased police surveillance as a consequence of public intervention;

(4) slightly less than one-half of the youths perceive that they may have endangered their chances of obtaining desired employment.

From the results of this study the authors felt that the extent of the perceived stigmatization at the time of intervention was overestimated.

The economic problems of the classification of delinquency arise despite statutes in every state requiring the confidentiality of juvenile court records. The statutes fail for a number of reasons. First they apply only to court records, thus leaving police departments free to form their own policies concerning their records of juvenile arrests. The loopholes in the statutes are significant, and information is regularly supplied to the FBI, the military, government agencies, and even private employers. In addition, employers can obtain the information simply by asking for it on the application forms or in interviews.

The classical study on the economic problems was performed in 1962 by Schwartz and Skolnick. They sent identical employment information of 100 employees in application for the same type of unskilled labor vacancy. The only variable was that 25 of the dossiers admitted an arrest and conviction for assault, 25 showed an arrest but no conviction, 25 included a letter from the judge affirming the applicant's innocence of the charges, while the remaining 25 made no mention of any arrest. Nine employers gave positive responses to the "no-record" folder, six accepted the applicant with the letter from the judge, only three offered employment to the arrestee without the letter, and only one would accept the convicted applicant. Subsequent studies demonstrate that a juvenile record can be almost as damaging as an adult record.

Employment opportunities are affected in more subtle ways. Obtaining bonds required for many jobs is made extremely difficult, and there may be substantial obstacles in procuring automobile liability coverage, thus making impossible any employment which would require driving a vehicle. "The delinquency label may preclude membership in labor unions, or participation in apprenticeship training." Occupational licensing practices may also prevent those with a record of juvenile delinquency from engaging in certain careers.

When an individual's avenues for financial stability are closed off, he has little choice but to resort to crime for needed funds and status. Some courts have recognized that a juvenile record "may stigmatize and impede its victim throughout his lifetime," and have accordingly ordered expungement of his records in certain circumstances. However, expungement is not the total answer since employers can still demand the information from the individual.

The child in need of supervision. As a response both to the growing awareness of the stigma attaching to the classification of *delinquent* and to *Gault,* legislatures developed that category called "child in need of supervision." The experience gained in the attempts to separate criminal from noncriminal behavior is not extensive, but recent indications indicate that the attempt is a failure. The President's Commission on Law Enforcement and Administration of Justice recommended that noncriminal conduct be removed from juvenile court jurisdiction as early as 1967. It reached this position after concluding "that even the most earnest efforts to narrow broad jurisdictional bases in language or practice will not remove the possibility of over-extension." Although many states attempt to treat the child in need of supervision differently from the delinquent, the attempts have not proven successful.

The children called children in need of supervision are "guilty" of committing what can only be called status offenses. That is, their antisocial act is one of being truant or of being a runaway. The statutes have omnibus clauses which are broad, all-encompassing, and incapable of precise definition. The omnibus clauses represent attempts by the legislature to reach children who are likely to become delinquent because they are presently leading lives of idleness or are in danger of becoming "morally depraved." The Department of Health, Education and Welfare has estimated that 40% of the cases disposed of by juvenile courts involve this type of behavior.

The net result of these status offenses is that children are being swept up into the juvenile court system unnecessarily and are being stigmatized by the court process just as are the delinquent children. In addition, children in need of supervision are faced with allegations of conduct which deprive them of their constitutional right to due process because the statutes are so imprecisely drawn as to afford them no notice of the prescribed conduct. Two recent federal courts have found these statutes to be unconstitutionally vague.

The answer to the problem does not appear to be more precise definition of status offenses. The clear alternative is to adopt the recommendations of the President's Commission of Law Enforcement and Administration of Justice and to eliminate status offenses from the court's jurisdiction. The benefits derived from the classification child in need of supervision would appear to be nonexistent for the child and society. The cycle of recidivism would be grounds alone to eliminate the category.

The child in need of supervision is one experiencing problems in his home, school, or community. He can be dealt with much more effectively outside the court setting. Family counseling, improved living conditions, educational opportunities and in general an improved existence for the child would seem much more positive than the present classification of status offenses. In the case of *Gesicki* the court referred to a statement of Milton Luger, Commissioner of the New York Division of Youth, in which Mr. Luger observed:

> With the exception of a relatively few youths, it would probably be better for all concerned if young delinquents were not detected, apprehended or institutionalized. Too many of them get worse in our care.

FJELD, NEWSOM AND FJELD, DELINQUENTS AND
STATUS OFFENDERS: THE SIMILARITY OF DIF-
FERENCES, 32 JUVENILE AND FAMILY COURT
JOURNAL, No. 2, 3–10 (1981) *

In recent years, juvenile court systems have become increasingly involved when offenses are committed by adolescents, as such offenses are less frequently handled informally in the community. There has been a particularly sharp rise in the number of offenses classified as delinquent—that is, offenses involving law violations which would incur legal penalties, regardless of whether the offender were a juvenile or an adult. Many other individuals who appear within the jurisdiction of a juvenile court are charged with status offenses—that is, offenses which would not result in a court appear-

* Copyright by The National Council of
Juvenile and Family Court Judges.

ance if the individual were an adult. The separate classification of juvenile offenders as delinquents or status offenders became widespread in the 1970s because many juvenile experts felt that status offenders were inappropriately handled by the court system. In their view, status offenders are different from delinquents, and status offenses are not ordinarily expected to be precursors of later delinquent offenses.

The proposal to separate delinquent and status offenders and remove the latter from the jurisdiction of the juvenile court has aroused considerable controversy. The three most important reasons given for removing the status offenders from the courts include avoiding the stigma of going to a juvenile court, avoiding the possible harmful effects of containing some of these children with delinquent offenders in juvenile facilities and releasing more of the court's time to handle the increasing number of delinquent offenses.[1] These objections to court handling of status offenders seem reasonable if it is true that status offenders are in fact different from delinquents— that is, if status offenders do not ordinarily have subsequent offenses which are classified as delinquent.

Is Separating Programs Practical?

Judge Robert L. Drake [2] points out that the distinction between delinquents and status offenders is of little practical value when one looks at the services which are required as, for example, in the evaluation and screening of adolescent offenders. The seriousness of an adolescent's problems cannot be determined solely on the basis of classifying his or her offense as status or delinquent. Separate classification cannot simplify the problem of identifying and meeting the needs of youthful offenders. Indeed, separating programs may only further complicate the rendering of services. Furthermore, Judge Lindsay G. Arthur points out that needed services may not be obtained unless the authority of the court is used to mandate protection and controls in cases where voluntary measures fail:

> Probably about 50% of the cases that come before the court can be diverted to the parents after a conference, to community social service agencies, to a private psychiatrist, to a private social work practitioner, or to a clergyman. This can be done *only* when the family and child are *ready, willing* and *able* to accept that help voluntarily.

> But if the child or the family cannot or will not accept needed treatment * * * then the court should be there to impose the needed treatment.[3]

[1] President's Commission on Law Enforcement and the Administration of Justice *Task Force Report: Juvenile Delinquency and Youth Crime* (Washington, D.C., 1977).

[2] Robert L. Drake, "Elimination of Status Offenses: The Myth, Fallacies and More Juvenile Crime," *Juvenile and Family Court Journal* (29, 1978) pp. 33–40.

[3] Lindsay G. Arthur, "Status Offenders Need Help, Too," *Juvenile Justice* (26, 1975) pp. 3–8.

Regardless of one's predilections for or against the arguments to remove status offenders completely from juvenile court jurisdiction, what is frequently proposed is a new agency to correct the shortcomings of an old agency. As anyone familiar with the history of bureaucracy knows, this type of cure is only temporary. The new agency is soon guilty of as many, albeit different, sins as was the old. However, if the status offenders are truly dissimilar to delinquents and tend not to engage in subsequent delinquent acts, then removal of these offenders from court jurisdiction to a different agency would have empirical justification. The picture would be further complicated, of course, if a substantial number of delinquents were found to also commit status offenses as part of their adjustment histories. Any shifting of the type of offense would involve the problem of overlapping agency jurisdiction, the shuffling of the juvenile and his family between agencies and would undoubtedly lead to duplication of services in intake procedures, psychological services and counseling.

THE NEED FOR DATA

There have been very few studies of the stability of juvenile offenses when they are separated into delinquent and status categories. The inadvisability of making radical changes in the juvenile justice system without first obtaining sufficient data to support such a change is the subject of a paper by Christopher Martin. The following excerpts summarize his arguments:

> For the most part, there is an absolute scarcity of empirical research justifying movement in these directions. As a matter of fact * * * the concept that the juvenile justice system encourages deviance through an ongoing labeling process, appears to be soundly repudiated by the studies dealing with it. Also, relative to every argument supporting either deinstitutionalization or decriminalization, there seems to be a logical counterargument * * *

> * * * [t]he Law Enforcement Assistance Administration, in its program announcement relative to the impending deinstitutionalization of status offenders indicated that very little research has been completed, either supportive or non-supportive, relative to the status offenders situation. It appears to be a noteworthy shortcoming of the entire criminal justice system that allows significant changes (and perhaps changes that will have far-reaching repercussions) to occur without a substantial data base to validate them. Many people have contended that the present system for handling status offenders has failed, yet there is no empirical data to validate that hypothesis. The rhetorical question relative to that issue keeps arising: Failed? Relative to what?[4]

4 Christopher Martin, "Offenders in the Juvenile Justice System: Where Do They Belong?", *Juvenile Justice* (28, 1977) pp. 438–55.

One study which has been done involved more than 2,000 juveniles and found substantial shifts between offenses when subsequent court appearances were involved.[5] Thomas, who directed this study, found that almost 60% of those originally classified as status offenders were later charged as delinquents when they reappeared before the court. If a figure of this magnitude is supported by further research, the arguments for removing status offenders from any jurisdiction by the juvenile court would seem to be considerably weakened.

Since the determination of stability of type of offense would seem to have an important bearing on the question of appropriate agency jurisdiction, the authors of the present study analyzed the behavior of a group of juveniles over a period of more than three years. As a part of this study, some of the personality characteristics of status offenders and delinquents were analyzed. Several questions seemed pertinent: Do individuals initially charged with status offenses tend to have subsequent delinquent charges? Or do those that are status offenders tend to remain status offenders? Do those that are delinquent tend to remain delinquent? Are subsequent court appearances as frequent for those charged with status offenses as for those charged with delinquency?

DESCRIPTION OF STUDY SAMPLE

In this study of the behavior of status offenders and delinquents, the psychological services of the Hamilton County Juvenile Court studied in detail 92 consecutive psychological referrals over a period of approximately 14 months in 1975–1976 who met the following conditions: IQ greater than 80, reading skills at least sixth grade level, 13 years of age or older and residence in the court's service area for at least six months. There were 106 other referrals to the psychological services during the time of this study who did not meet all of the above criteria. During this time, the court adjudicated about 470 delinquents, 270 dependent and neglected cases and formally processed about 260 status offenders. Males accounted for 62% of these 1,000 cases and for 80% of the 470 delinquents. Approximately 28% of those coming before the court were black.

Of the 92 cases who met the study criteria, 51 were classified as status offenders, 32 as delinquents and nine as dependent and neglected. The dependent and neglected cases are underrepresented in terms of referral to the psychological services. These nine cases undoubtedly represent referrals made because evidence of personal problems was quite clear but which the Department of Human Services had not yet referred to mental health clinics. The status offenders studied are overrepresented in the sample. This is partly because of the fact that during the period of the study, the psycho-

---

[5] Charles W. Thomas, "Are Status Offenders Really So Different?", *Crime and Delinquency* (22, 1976) pp. 438–55.

logical services were heavily involved in planning, treatment and follow-up of status offenders. Some of these offenders were unofficial (petitions not filed) and do not appear as formally processed in the statistical summaries of the court. Juveniles charged with delinquent offenses and referred for evaluation presumably represented individuals about whom the judges or probation workers had questions related to intellectual or personality functioning.

Of the study group (N=92), about half were male (N=47) and half were female. The mean age was 15.4 years, and the modal age was 16.0 years. The mean IQ of the sample was 98.0. Only five of the sample were *not* white. In terms of parental status, 36 lived with both natural parents, 26 came from one-parent families, 15 came from families with one natural and one stepparent and 15 came from adoptive homes, foster placements, families of relatives, etc. Most were attending school or, at least, had not officially dropped out. Of those 22 juveniles who had dropped out of school, none were working at the time they appeared before the court.

Almost two-thirds of the 106 referrals who did not meet the study criteria were rejected because of low intelligence or reading test scores. The remaining third were rejected for a variety of reasons: some were under age, some failed to complete testing, several had incomplete histories, a few were non-residents, etc. This rejected group was slightly more than half male (N=60) and about one-third black (N=32). These figures were fairly representative of cases brought to the court. (It is noted that the ratio of blacks meeting study criteria was substantially lower than their representation in the total population of court cases.) There were 26 individuals with IQ scores of 80 or higher, but who were rejected from the study because their reading skills were below sixth grade level. The average reading score for those individuals was a grade equivalent of 3.5, approximately five years below their expected average grade level. More than half of those cases rejected were status offenders (N=58), about one-third were delinquents and approximately one-tenth (N=12) were dependent and neglected cases. These ratios are quite comparable with the distribution of offenses in the study sample.

In the study group, there were some differences between delinquents, status offenders and dependent and neglected cases on variables such as sex, age, intelligence and personality characteristics. For example, only eight of the 45 females in the study were classified as delinquents. Court appearances of the females in the study were classified as delinquents. Court appearances of the females tended to be on dependent and neglected petitions or status offenses. In regard to age variables, it should not be surprising that dependent and neglected children and first-time status offenders were found to be somewhat younger. Delinquents charged with multiple offenses tended to be the oldest. In regard to intellectual differences, status offenders tended to score somewhat higher on IQ tests than delinquents (99.7 vs. 95.3, p=.05).

With respect to personality variables, the dependent and neglected subjects in the present study were more apt to have elevated MMPI profiles. They had the highest average scores on F and on eight of the nine clinical scales. This finding suggests that dependent and neglected adolescents tend to exhibit greater emotional disturbance, which is consistent with the observation that the home situations of these individuals typically appeared to be the most severely disruptive in terms of psychological development. A comparison of status offenders and delinquents on personality variables indicated that status offenders tended to score higher on most MMPI scales, although the size of the differences on most of the scales was typically not large. Only on scale 4 (a scale concerned with hostility toward authority figures, acting out tendencies, etc.) were the scores of status offenders significantly higher (71.3 vs. 65.8, p=.05). It is interesting that the feelings of hostility toward authority seemed to be somewhat stronger in status offenders than in delinquents. There was also a definite tendency for status offenders to score higher on scale eight (61.8 vs. 55.8, p=.07), suggesting that status offenders may have more personality problems and more difficulty in getting along socially than do delinquents.

FREQUENCY OF COURT APPEARANCES

In terms of the frequency of offenses, almost one-third of the juveniles (N=29) in our sample had no previous court record and committed no subsequent offenses during a two-year period following the study. Almost half of the subjects in the present study (N=41) had only one additional appearance before the court. However, one-fourth (N=22) had two or more additional appearances over this three-year period. Sixteen had only two additional appearances before the court, but six appeared before the court in all of the years covered by this study (i.e. prior to, during the study and in each of the two years following).

There were nine adolescents in this study classified as dependent and neglected. Of these, two had no additional court appearances, five had one additional appearance and two had two additional appearances.

TABLE 1
Appearances of Study Sample Before the Court
(N=83)

	Number of Court Appearances				
	N	1	2	3	4
Status Offenders	51	23	24	3	1
Delinquents	32	4	12	11	5

TABLE 1—Continued
When Court Appearances Occurred

	N	Study Only	Prior to Study	Subsequent to Study	
				1st Year	2nd Year
Status Offenders	51	23	22	13	3
Delinquents	32	4	17	16	11

**Number of Juveniles Shifting From One Type
of Offense to Another**

	Prior to Study	Subsequent to Study	
		1st Year	2nd Year
Status Offenses to Delinquent	6	6	1
Delinquent to Status Offenses	7	2	1

The nine cases classified as dependent and neglected will not be included in the analysis which follows, because their unusually poor home situations created difficulties and necessitated court appearances which were unrelated to the behavior of the juveniles themselves.

An analysis of the frequency of appearances before the court based on subjects classification as status offenders or delinquents at the time of the study is reported in Table 1. Almost half of those classified as status offenders have no previous or subsequent charges. On the other hand, 28 of 32 delinquents had additional charges on record. A comparatively large number of the status offenders and delinquents who had charges prior to the study had no additional charges in the first or second year following. Of the 13 status offenders who had additional charges in the first year after the study, nine had only one additional court appearance. This contrasts rather sharply with the finding that of the 16 delinquents who had additional charges in the first year, nine had *only* one additional court appearance. More than one-third of these 16 delinquents had two subsequent appearances; another third had both a prior and a subsequent court appearance; and still another third had both a prior court appearance and two subsequent appearances.

SHIFTS IN TYPE OF OFFENCE

The above data suggest a tendency for delinquents to continue as delinquents and to have more charges than status offenders. A detailed analysis of prior versus subsequent charges also support this conclusion. Of the 18 individuals who had prior status offenses, only three had subsequent offenses in the first year. On the other hand, of 21 individuals with prior delinquent offenses, nine had additional delinquent charges brought against them in the first year following the study. In the second year, six of the 21 delinquents with prior offenses were brought before the court on additional delinquent charges. None of the individuals with delinquent charges prior to the present study shifted to the status offender category during the first or second year of follow-up study.

In this study, delinquents were more apt than status offenders to have multiple court appearances. Almost three of every four delinquents in the sample had prior charges, while only one of every three status offenders had previously been before the court. During the first year following the initial study, one of every two delinquents reappeared before the court while only one of every five status offenders re-appeared. In the second year following the study, only three of the 51 status offenders appeared before the court, compared with 11 of the 32 delinquents.

Some shifting in classification was observed in regard to juveniles with multiple court appearances. When charges made prior to this study were examined, it was noted that seven delinquents had previously been charged with status offenses and six status offenders had previously been charged with delinquency. In the first year following the study, six status offenders shifted to delinquent offenses, compared to only two delinquents who shifted to status offenses. During the second year following the study, only one delinquent and one status offender shifted categories. Overall, the data suggest that fairly frequent shifts between status offenses and delinquency occur. In general, more shifts occur when the offenders are younger. Also, status offenders appear more likely to shift to delinquent offenses than delinquents appear likely to shift to status charges.

COMPARISON TO PREVIOUS STUDIES

In several respects, the results of this study are not strikingly different from those of Thomas' study despite the fact that our sample represents a more intelligent group of offenders followed over a shorter time. In Thomas' sample, 72% of the individuals had only one court appearance, approximately 14% had three official court appearances and approximately 7% had four contacts. In the present study, approximately 65% (54 of 83) had no subsequent appearance before the court, and only approximately 7.5% of offenders appeared before the court in every year of the study. As Thomas noted, the rate of recidivism among juvenile offenders is quite low, "thus any suggestion that formal court appearances are so stigmatizing that they encourage recidivism is difficult to substantiate with the data available on those in this sample." The relatively low rate of recidivism noted in the present study supports Thomas' conclusion.

Thomas' data suggest considerable instability of status offenders with respect to subsequent offenses. He states, " * * * any contention that those initially charged with a status offense will remain status offenders finds no support in this analysis: 59.15 percent (N=223) of the re-appearances charged against those initially appearing for status offense involve either misdemeanors or felonies." In the present study, 43% of 28 status offenders with multiple court appearances also had delinquent charges on prior or later court appearances. Although this percentage of status offenders shifting to delinquent offenses is somewhat lower than in Thomas' study, it should be noted that 10 of 28 delinquents had also shifted offenses either prior to the study or in the two years following. Overall, 23 multiple offenders shifted their classification in the period of this study. On the basis of the data, there would seem little doubt that adolescent offenders are not highly stable.

Conclusions

In summary, the data in this study suggest the following conclusions regarding differences between status offenders and delinquents:

1. Delinquents are more apt to repeat offenses than status offenders and, when they repeat, are more apt to repeat delinquent offenses.

2. Status offenders are much less apt to repeat offenses. When they do repeat, they tend to be more variable in the type of offense.

3. The younger offender is more likely to shift offense.

4. The older the delinquent, the less likely he is to shift to status offenses.

The clear tendency of the status offenders to have fewer court appearances than the delinquents may be due to several factors. In the present study, a difference in intervention may be reflected by the data. For example, the status offenders referred to psychological services during the initial period of the study tended to get placement in a brief family treatment program much more frequently than did delinquents. One would certainly hope that intervention did have some effect on the juvenile's future behavior, i.e. reducing recidivism. Another explanation which must be considered is that status offenses in general may be more symptomatic of problems in interaction between the individual and those emotionally closest to him—namely the family and the school. On the other hand, delinquent acts are more a product of the activities of the individual interacting with relative strangers. Consequently, therapeutic intervention with delinquents is necessarily less effective because the problem environment is not accessible to treatment.

Yet another hypothesis is that status offenses may simply be more directly reflective of adolescent turmoil in general than are delinquent offenses. This may partially account for the tendency of status offenders not to repeat as frequently as the delinquents. As the status offender grows a little more mature and works through some of his problems, he has less need to act out.

Those who would remove status offenders from the jurisdiction of the juvenile court argue that it is the stigma of being under the jurisdiction of the court that results in the status offender repeating his behavior. As Thomas concluded earlier, those who make this argument do not have data to support this conclusion. The data in this study suggests that the rate of recidivism, especially for status offenders, is quite low. Approximately 65% of the total sample did not re-appear before the court during the two years following the study. Only 50% of those classified as delinquents in our study had additional court appearances during these two years. It is noted that only 7.5% had four or more court appearances (i.e. in every year of the study and follow-up). Since only one of the 51 status offenders had court appearances in every year covered by the present study, it appears clear that handling status offenders in the juvenile court system does *not* increase recidivism rates. The harmful effects of court appearances would appear to be minimal considering the complexity of factors which underlie delinquency and status offenders, e.g. poor family situations, reading difficulties, disturbed personalities, etc.

Those who would separate the status offenders entirely from court jurisdiction also argue that status offenders are so different from delinquents that the court and its supporting services are inappropriate. Again, the data do not support this argument. In our study, 43% (12 of 28) of those charged as status offenders also had a delinquency charge. Thomas' data even more strikingly refutes this argument and almost 60% of his status offenders also had delinquency charges. Furthermore, almost 40% (10 of 28) of those juveniles charged as delinquents in the present study had status offense charges. In short, adolescent offenders in both classification groups tend to be quite unpredictable with respect to type of future offenses. As Thomas noted in his study summary "* * * knowledge of the type of behavior which brought about an initial court appearance is an exceedingly poor predictor of whether a juvenile would reappear and, if so, the type of misconduct that would prompt the reappearance."

The results of our study suggest that because status offenders and delinquents share a substantial amount of unpredictability in their behavior, the two groups cannot be clearly separated. This conclusion regarding the unpredictable nature of juvenile offenders should not be surprising in view of what we know about adolescent psychology in general. Adolescents are typically viewed as being unsure of themselves and unsure of the roles they are to play. As a consequence, adolescent behavior is viewed as more erratic and unpredictable than the behavior of adults. Clinically, adolescents are found to have more evidence of mental disturbance on personality tests, and adolescent test norms have been established for evaluating responses. These adolescent test norms support the theory that adolescent behavior is expected to be somewhat more erratic than that of adults.

As the law now stands, parents and schools are charged with the responsibility for the welfare and the behavior of the child. Statutes allow adolescents to be deemed status offenders on the basis of behaviors which would be regarded as unconstitutionally vague for adults. Where the responsibility for adolescent behavior lies, and whether the statutes regarding status offenders are desirable, are questions which this study does not and cannot attempt to answer. The results of this and other studies do suggest, however, that status offenders are *not* substantially different enough from delinquents that separate handling of these types of offenders is necessary or even desirable. It appears unlikely that any program, regardless of where situated, would do substantially better than the juvenile court system. Indeed, in view of the overlap of the behavior of these types of offenders, it is reasonable to conclude that separate programs would frequently result in an individual offender being shuffled from one agency to another as his behavior fluctuated.

The real need is to treat the juvenile, regardless of offense, in as effective a manner as possible. This would seem especially important with younger offenders who are less apt to have established a fixed behavioral pattern. Our data suggest that juvenile offenders, whatever their charge, are quite variable. Intervention deemed desirable for the status offender might also be the most desirable intervention for the early delinquent offender. Determination of the most valuable forms of intervention would appear to be a more profitable pursuit than debating *in vacuo* the desirability of removing the status offender from the jurisdiction of the juvenile courts. There is no reason to suppose that the type of treatment intervention could not be varied substantially within a single agency. For example, most if not all courts now handle the typical status offender quite differently from the typical delinquent, particularly with regard to formal court processing. In conclusion, the available evidence would appear to support the argument that a single agency is the most appropriate method of handling individuals whose behaviors are, in many respects, so closely similar.

IN RE GAULT
Supreme Court of the United States, 1967.
387 U.S. 1, 87 S.Ct. 1428, 18 L.Ed.2d 527.

[The statement of facts and most of the opinion in this case appear at p. 489 et seq., infra.]

MR. JUSTICE FORTAS delivered the opinion of the Court.

* * *

From the inception of the juvenile court system, wide differences have been tolerated—indeed insisted upon—between the procedural rights accorded to adults and those of juveniles. In practically all jurisdictions, there are rights granted to adults which are withheld from juveniles. In addition to the specific problems involved in the present case, for example, it has been held that the juvenile is not entitled to bail, to indictment by grand jury, to a public trial or to trial by jury. It is frequent practice that rules governing the arrest and interrogation of adults by the police are not observed in the case of juveniles.

The history and theory underlying this development are well-known, but a recapitulation is necessary for purposes of this opinion. The Juvenile Court movement began in this country at the end of the last century. From the juvenile court statute adopted in Illinois in 1899, the system has spread to every State in the Union, the District of Columbia, and Puerto Rico.[6] The constitutionality of juvenile court laws has been sustained in over 40 jurisdictions against a variety of attacks.

The early reformers were appalled by adult procedures and penalties, and by the fact that children could be given long prison sentences and mixed in jails with hardened criminals. They were profoundly convinced that society's duty to the child could not be confined by the concept of justice alone. They believed that society's role was not to ascertain whether the child was "guilty" or "innocent," but "What is he, how has he become what he is, and what had best be done in his interest and in the interest of the state to save him from a downward career."[7] The child—essentially good, as they saw it—was to be made "to feel that he is the object of [the state's] care and solicitude," not that he was under arrest or on trial. The rules of criminal procedure were therefore altogether inapplicable. The apparent rigidities, technicalities, and harshness which they observed in both substantive and procedural criminal law were therefore to be discarded. The idea of crime and punishment was to be abandoned. The child was to be "treated" and "rehabilitated" and the procedures, from apprehension through institutionalization, were to be "clinical" rather than punitive.

These results were to be achieved, without coming to conceptual and constitutional grief, by insisting that the proceedings were not adversary, but that the state was proceeding as *parens patriae*. The Latin phrase proved to be a great help to those who sought to rationalize the exclusion of juveniles from the constitutional scheme; but its meaning is murky and its historic credentials are of dubious relevance. The phrase was taken from chancery practice, where, however, it was used to describe the power of the state to act *in loco*

[6] See National Council of Juvenile Court Judges, Directory and Manual (1964), p. 1. The number of Juvenile Judges as of 1964 is listed as 2,987, of whom 213 are full-time Juvenile Court Judges. Id., at 305. The Nat'l Crime Comm'n Report indicates that half of these judges have no undergraduate degree, a fifth have no college education at all, a fifth are not members of the bar, and three-quarters devote less than one-quarter of their time to juvenile matters. See also McCune, Profile of the Nation's Juvenile Court Judges (monograph, George Washington University, Center for the Behavioral Sciences, 1965), which is a detailed statistical study of Juvenile Court Judges, and indicates additionally that about a quarter of these judges have no law school training at all. About one-third of all judges have no probation and social work staff available to them; between eighty and ninety percent have no available psychologist or psychiatrist. Ibid. It has been observed that while "good will, compassion, and similar virtues are * * * admirably prevalent throughout the system * * * expertise, the keystone of the whole venture, is lacking." Harvard Law Review Note, p. 809. In 1965, over 697,000 delinquency cases (excluding traffic) were disposed of in these courts, involving some 601,000 children, or 2% of all children between 10 and 17. Juvenile Court Statistics—1965, Children's Bureau Statistical Series No. 85 (1966), p. 2.

[7] Julian Mack, The Juvenile Court, 23 Harv.L.Rev. 104, 119–120 (1909).

parentis for the purpose of protecting the property interests and the person of the child. But there is no trace of the doctrine in the history of criminal jurisprudence. At common law, children under seven were considered incapable of possessing criminal intent. Beyond that age, they were subjected to arrest, trial, and in theory to punishment like adult offenders. In these old days, the state was not deemed to have authority to accord them fewer procedural rights than adults.

The right of the state, as *parens patriae*, to deny to the child procedural rights available to his elders was elaborated by the assertion that a child, unlike an adult, has a right "not to liberty but to custody." He can be made to attorn to his parents, to go to school, etc. If his parents default in effectively performing their custodial functions—that is, if the child is "delinquent"—the state may intervene. In doing so, it does not deprive the child of any rights, because he has none. It merely provides the "custody" to which the child is entitled.[8] On this basis, proceedings involving juveniles were described as "civil" not "criminal" and therefore not subject to the requirements which restrict the state when it seeks to deprive a person of his liberty.[9]

Accordingly, the highest motives and most enlightened impulses led to a peculiar system for juveniles, unknown to our law in any comparable context. The constitutional and theoretical basis for this peculiar system is—to say the least—debatable. And in practice, as we remarked in the *Kent* case, supra, the results have not been entirely satisfactory.[10] Juvenile Court history has again demonstrated that unbridled discretion, however benevolently motivated, is frequently a poor substitute for principle and procedure. In 1937, Dean Pound wrote: "The powers of the Star Chamber were a trifle in comparison with those of our juvenile courts * * *."[11] The ab-

[8] See, e.g., Shears, Legal Problems Peculiar to Children's Courts, 48 A.B.A.J. 719, 720 (1962) ("The basic right of a juvenile is not to liberty but to custody. He has the right to have someone take care of him, and if his parents do not afford him this custodial privilege, the law must do so."); Ex parte Crouse, 4 Whart. 9, 11 (Sup.Ct.Pa.1839); Petition of Ferrier, 103 Ill. 367, 371–373 (1882).

[9] The Appendix to the opinion of Judge Prettyman in Pee v. United States, 107 U.S.App.D.C. 47, 274 F.2d 556 (1959), lists authority in 51 jurisdictions to this effect. Even rules required by due process in civil proceedings, however, have not generally been deemed compulsory as to proceedings affecting juveniles. For example, constitutional requirements as to notice of issues, which would commonly apply in civil cases, are commonly disregarded in juvenile proceedings, as this case illustrates.

[10] "There is evidence * * * that there may be grounds for concern that

the child receives the worst of both worlds: that he gets neither the protections accorded to adults nor the solicitous care and regenerative treatment postulated for children." 383 U.S., at 556, 86 S.Ct., at 1054.

On the other hand, while this opinion and much recent writing concentrate upon the failures of the Juvenile Court system to live up to the expectations of its founders, the observation of the Nat'l Crime Comm'n Report should be kept in mind:

"Although its shortcomings are many and its results too often disappointing, the juvenile justice system in many cities is operated by people who are better educated and more highly skilled, can call on more and better facilities and services, and has more ancillary agencies to which to refer its clientele than its adult counterpart." Id., at 78.

[11] Foreword to Young, Social Treatment in Probation and Delinquency

sence of substantive standards has not necessarily meant that children receive careful, compassionate, individualized treatment. The absence of procedural rules based upon constitutional principle has not always produced fair, efficient, and effective procedures. Departures from established principles of due process have frequently resulted not in enlightened procedure, but in arbitrariness. The Chairman of the Pennsylvania Council of Juvenile Court Judges has recently observed: "Unfortunately, loose procedures, high-handed methods and crowded court calendars, either singly or in combination, all too often, have resulted in depriving some juveniles of fundamental rights that have resulted in a denial of due process." [12]

Failure to observe the fundamental requirements of due process has resulted in instances, which might have been avoided, of unfairness to individuals and inadequate or inaccurate findings of fact and unfortunate prescriptions of remedy. Due process of law is the primary and indispensable foundation of individual freedom. It is the basic and essential term in the social compact which defines the rights of the individual and delimits the powers which the state may exercise.[13] As Mr. Justice Frankfurter has said: "The history of

(1937), p. xxvii. The 1965 Report of the United States Commission on Civil Rights, "Law Enforcement—A Report on Equal Protection in the South," pp. 80–83, documents numerous instances in which "local authorities used the broad discretion afforded them by the absence of safeguards [in the juvenile process]" to punish, intimidate, and obstruct youthful participants in civil rights demonstrations.

[12] Lehman, A Juvenile's Right to Counsel in a Delinquency Hearing, 17 Juvenile Court Judges Journal 53, 54 (1966).

Compare the observation of the late Arthur T. Vanderbilt, Chief Justice of the Supreme Court of New Jersey, in a foreword to Virtue, Basic Structure for Children's Services in Michigan (1953), p. x; "In their zeal to care for children neither juvenile judges nor welfare workers can be permitted to violate the Constitution, especially the constitutional provisions as to due process that are involved in moving a child from its home. The indispensable elements of due process are: first, a tribunal with jurisdiction; second, notice of a hearing to the proper parties; and finally, a fair hearing. All three must be present if we are to treat the child as an individual human being and not to revert in spite of good intentions, to the more primitive days when he was treated as a chattel."

We are warned that the system must not "degenerate into a star chamber proceeding with the judge imposing his own particular brand of culture and morals on indigent people * * *." Judge Marion

G. Woodward, letter reproduced in 18 Social Service Review 366, 368 (1944). Doctor Bovet, the Swiss psychiatrist, in his monograph for the World Health Organization, Psychiatric Aspects of Juvenile Delinquency (1951), p. 79, stated that: "One of the most definite conclusions of this investigation is that few fields exist in which more serious coercive measures are applied, on such flimsy objective evidence, than in that of juvenile delinquency." We are told that "The Judge as amateur psychologist, experimenting upon the unfortunate children who must appear before him, is neither an attractive nor a convincing figure." Harvard Law Review Note, at 808.

[13] The impact of denying fundamental procedural due process to juveniles involved in "delinquency" charges is dramatized by the following considerations: (1) In 1965, persons under 18 accounted for about one-fifth of all arrests for serious crimes (Nat'l Crime Comm'n, Report, p. 55) and over half of all arrests for serious property offenses (id., at 56), and in the same year some 601,000 children under 18, or 2% of all children between 10 and 17, came before juvenile courts (Juvenile Court Statistics—1965, Children's Bureau Statistical Series No. 85 (1966) p. 2). About one out of nine youths will be referred to juvenile court in connection with a delinquent act (excluding traffic offenses) before he is 18 (Nat'l Crime Comm'n Report, p. 55). * * * Furthermore, most juvenile crime apparently goes undetected or not formally punished. Wheeler & Cottrell,

American freedom is, in no small measure, the history of procedure." But, in addition, the procedural rules which have been fashioned from the generality of due process are our best instruments for the distillation and evaluation of essential facts from the conflicting welter of data that life and our adversary methods present. It is these instruments of due process which enhance the possibility that truth will emerge from the confrontation of opposing versions and conflicting data. "Procedure is to law what 'scientific method' is to science."

It is claimed that juveniles obtain benefits from the special procedures applicable to them which more than offset the disadvantages of denial of the substance of normal due process. As we shall discuss, the observance of due process standards, intelligently and not ruthlessly administered, will not compel the States to abandon or displace any of the substantive benefits of the juvenile process. But it is important, we think, that the claimed benefits of the juvenile process should be candidly appraised. Neither sentiment nor folklore should cause us to shut our eyes, for example, to such startling findings as that reported in an exceptionally reliable study of repeaters or recidivism conducted by the Stanford Research Institute for the President's Commission on Crime in the District of Columbia. This Commission's Report states:

> "In fiscal 1966 approximately 66 percent of the 16- and 17-year-old juveniles referred to the court by the Youth Aid Division had been before the court previously. In 1965, 56 percent of those in the Receiving Home were repeaters. The SRI study revealed that 61 percent of the sample Juvenile Court referrals in 1965 had been previously referred at least once and that 42 percent had been referred at least twice before." Id., at 773.

Certainly, these figures and the high crime rates among juveniles to which we have referred could not lead us to conclude that the absence of constitutional protections reduces crime, or that the juve-

supra, observe that "[A]lmost all youngsters have committed at least one of the petty forms of theft and vandalism in the course of their adolescence." Id., at 28–29. See also Nat'l Crime Comm'n Report, p. 55, where it is stated that "self-report studies reveal that perhaps 90 percent of all young people have committed at least one act for which they could have been brought to juvenile court." It seems that the rate of juvenile delinquency is also steadily rising. See Nat'l Crime Comm'n Report, p. 56; Juvenile Court Statistics, supra, pp. 2–3. (2) In New York, where most juveniles are represented by counsel * * * and substantial procedural rights are afforded * * * out of a fiscal year 1965–1966 total of 10,755 juvenile proceedings involving boys, 2,242 were dismissed for failure of proof at the fact-finding hearing; for girls, the figures were 306 out of a total of 1,051. New York Judicial Conference, Twelfth Annual Report, pp. 314, 316 (1967). (3) In about one-half of the States, a juvenile may be transferred to an adult penal institution after a juvenile court has found him "delinquent" (Delinquent Children in Penal Institutions, Children's Bureau Pub. No. 415–1964, p. 1). (4) In some jurisdictions a juvenile may be subjected to criminal prosecution for the same offense for which he has served under a juvenile court commitment. However, the Texas procedure to this effect has recently been held unconstitutional by a federal district court judge, in a habeas corpus action. Sawyer v. Hauck, 245 F.Supp. 55 (D.C. W.D.Tex.1965). (5) In most of the States the juvenile may end in criminal court through waiver (Harvard Law Review Note, p. 793).

nile system, functioning free of constitutional inhibitions as it has largely done, is effective to reduce crime or rehabilitate offenders. We do not mean by this to denigrate the juvenile court process or to suggest that there are not aspects of the juvenile system relating to offenders which are valuable.   But the features of the juvenile system which its proponents have asserted are of unique benefit will not be impaired by constitutional domestication.   For example, the commendable principles relating to the processing and treatment of juveniles separately from adults are in no way involved or affected by the procedural issues under discussion.[14] Further, we are told that one of the important benefits of the special juvenile court procedures is that they avoid classifying the juvenile as a "criminal." The juvenile offender is now classed as a "delinquent."   There is, of course, no reason why this should not continue.   It is disconcerting, however, that this term has come to involve only slightly less stigma than the term "criminal" applied to adults.[15]   It is also emphasized that in practically all jurisdictions, statutes provide that an adjudication of the child as a delinquent shall not operate as a civil disability or disqualify him for civil service appointment.   There is no reason why the application of due process requirements should interfere with such provisions.

Beyond this, it is frequently said that juveniles are protected by the process from disclosure of their deviational behavior.   As the Supreme Court of Arizona phrased it in the present case, the summary procedures of Juvenile Courts are sometimes defended by a statement that it is the law's policy "to hide youthful errors from the full gaze of the public and bury them in the graveyard of the forgotten past."   This claim of secrecy, however, is more rhetoric than reality.   Disclosure of court records is discretionary with the judge in most jurisdictions.   Statutory restrictions almost invariably apply only to the court records, and even as to those the evidence is that many courts routinely furnish information to the FBI and the military, and on request to government agencies and even to private employers.   Of more importance are police records.   In most States the police keep a complete file of juvenile "police contacts" and have complete discretion as to disclosure of juvenile records.   Police de-

---

[14] Here again, however, there is substantial question as to whether fact and pretension, with respect to the separate handling and treatment of children, coincide.

While we are concerned only with procedure before the juvenile court in this case, it should be noted that to the extent that the special procedures for juveniles are thought to be justified by the special consideration and treatment afforded them, there is reason to doubt that juveniles always receive the benefits of such a *quid pro quo.*

In fact, some courts have recently indicated that appropriate treatment is essential to the validity of juvenile custody,

and therefore that a juvenile may challenge the validity of his custody on the ground that he is not in fact receiving any special treatment.   See Creek v. Stone, 379 F.2d 106 (D.C.Cir.1967); Kautter v. Reid, 183 F.Supp. 352 (D.C.D.C. 1960).

[15] "[T]he word 'delinquent' has today developed such invidious connotations that the terminology is in the process of being altered; the new descriptive phrase is 'persons in need of supervision,' usually shorted to 'pins.' "   Harvard Law Review Note, p. 799, n. 140.   The N.Y. Family Court Act § 712 distinguishes between "delinquents" and "persons in need of supervision."

partments receive requests for information from the FBI and other law-enforcement agencies, the Armed Forces, and social service agencies, and most of them generally comply. Private employers word their application forms to produce information concerning juvenile arrests and court proceedings, and in some jurisdictions information concerning juvenile police contacts is furnished private employers as well as government agencies.

In any event, there is no reason why, consistently with due process, a State cannot continue if it deems it appropriate, to provide and to improve provision for the confidentiality of records of police contacts and court action relating to juveniles. It is interesting to note, however, that the Arizona Supreme Court used the confidentiality argument as a justification for the type of notice which is here attacked as inadequate for due process purposes. The parents were given merely general notice that their child was charged with "delinquency." No facts were specified. The Arizona court held, however, as we shall discuss, that in addition to this general "notice," the child and his parents must be advised "of the facts involved in the case" no later than the initial hearing by the judge. Obviously, this does not "bury" the word about the child's transgressions. It merely defers the time of disclosure to a point when it is of limited use to the child or his parents in preparing his defense or explanation.

Further, it is urged that the juvenile benefits from informal proceedings in the court. The early conception of the Juvenile Court proceeding was one in which a fatherly judge touched the heart and conscience of the erring youth by talking over his problems, by paternal advice and admonition, and in which, in extreme situations, benevolent and wise institutions of the State provided guidance and help "to save him from a downward career." Then, as now, goodwill and compassion were admirably prevalent. But recent studies have, with surprising unanimity, entered sharp dissent as to the validity of this gentle conception. They suggest that the appearance as well as the actuality of fairness, impartiality and orderliness—in short, the essentials of due process—may be a more impressive and more therapeutic attitude so far as the juvenile is concerned. For example, in a recent study, the sociologists Wheeler and Cottrell observe that when the procedural laxness of the *"parens patriae"* attitude is followed by stern disciplining, the contrast may have an adverse effect upon the child, who feels that he has been deceived or enticed. They conclude as follows: "Unless appropriate due process of law is followed, even the juvenile who has violated the law may not feel that he is being fairly treated and may therefore resist the rehabilitative efforts of court personnel." Of course, it is not suggested that juvenile court judges should fail appropriately to take account, in their demeanor and conduct, of the emotional and psychological attitude of the juveniles with whom they are confronted. While due process requirements will, in some instances, introduce a degree of order and regularity to Juvenile Court proceedings to determine delinquency, and in contested cases will introduce some elements of the adversary system, nothing will require that the conception of the kindly juvenile judge be replaced by its opposite, nor do we here rule upon the question whether ordinary due process requirements must be observed with respect to hearings to determine the disposition of the delinquent child.

Ultimately, however, we confront the reality of that portion of the Juvenile Court process with which we deal in this case. A boy is charged with misconduct. The boy is committed to an institution where he may be restrained of liberty for years. It is of no constitutional consequence—and of limited practical meaning—that the institution to which he is committed is called an Industrial School. The fact of the matter is that, however euphemistic the title, a "receiving home" or an "industrial school" for juveniles is an institution of confinement in which the child is incarcerated for a greater or lesser time. His world becomes "a building with whitewashed walls, regimented routine and institutional hours * * *." Instead of mother and father and sisters and brothers and friends and class-mates, his world is peopled by guards, custodians, state employees, and "delinquents" confined with him for anything from waywardness to rape and homicide.

* * *

NOTE

A question of current academic interest is the extent to which earlier studies and descriptions of the history of the juvenile court movement—particularly of its immediate forerunners—are fact or fiction. The very title of Anthony Platt's well-known little book "The Child Savers: The Invention of Delinquency," (1969) carries the suggestion of past fiction. The theme is developed in Fox, Juvenile Justice Reform: An Historical Perspective, 22 Stanford Law Review 1187 (1970). The breadth of the conclusions is challenged in Schultz, The Cycle of Juvenile Court History, 19 Crime and Delinquency 457 (1973). For a careful history of the treatment of delinquents during the last three quarters of the nineteenth century and the first forty years of the twentieth, see Mennel, Thorns and Thistles (1973).

B. CONSTITUTIONAL CONSIDERATIONS

SMITH v. STATE

Court of Civil Appeals of Texas, 1969.
444 S.W.2d 941.

CADENA, JUSTICE. Appellant, a child adjudged delinquent and facing confinement in the State training school for boys for a period not extending beyond his twenty-first birthday—a period of almost five years—complains of the action of the district court denying his application for a writ of habeas corpus and ordering his return to the school. He argues that he faces confinement for a period of almost five years for carrying a switch-blade knife; that an adult who engaged in the same conduct could not be confined for a period in excess of one year and might escape with no more than the payment of a fine,[16] and that this difference in the authorized period of confinement solely because of his tender years denies him the equal protection of the laws and deprives him of his liberty without due process of law in violation of the Fourteenth Amendment to the Constitution of the United States.

In Texas, as in perhaps all other states, where confinement is deemed necessary in the case of a delinquent child, the child is committed to an institution for an indeterminate period not extending beyond his twenty-first birthday. Stated simply, the authorized period of confinement depends solely on the age of the child—the younger the child, the longer the permitted period of detention. Such factors as the child's background, his previous history of anti-social conduct, his response to rehabilitative programs, if any, not involving confinement,[17] and the seriousness of the conduct, criminal or otherwise,[18] upon which the finding of delinquency is based, are irrelevant in determining the length of the period during which he may be held. Conceivably, a child of ten may be kept in an institution for eleven years for conduct which would subject an adult to no more than a fine or confinement for a few days or months.[19]

No citation of authority is required in support of the statement that a State may classify its citizens for various purposes, for to deny to government the power to classify is to divest it of the power to legislate intelligently. Since classification is a necessity, and since discrimination is the fortuitous result of classification in legislation, it is clear that a statute cannot be branded constitutionally offensive

[16] Vernon's Ann.P.C. Art. 483 prescribes a punishment for adult violators of a fine not exceeding $500.00, or imprisonment for not more than one year, or both such fine and imprisonment.

[17] The alternatives to commitment to the Youth Council are placement of the child on probation or under supervision in his own home or in the custody of a relative or other fit person, upon such terms as the court shall determine; or commit the child to a suitable private institution or agency authorized to care for children; or place the child in a suitable family home; or make such other disposition as the court may deem to be for the best interest of the child. Art. 2338–1, § 13(c). The Youth Council, upon receiving a delinquent child, is under the duty to examine the child and make an investigation of "all pertinent circumstances of his life and behavior." The Council may permit the child his liberty under supervision and upon such conditions as are believed conducive to acceptable behavior; or order his confinement under such conditions as are believed best designed for the child's welfare and the interests of the public; or order reconfinement or renewed releases as

often as conditions indicate to be desirable; or discharge him from control when it is believed that such discharge will best serve the child's welfare and the protection of the public. Any order of the Council affecting a child, other than an order of final discharge, may be revoked or modified as often as conditions indicate to be desirable. Article 5143d, §§ 16, 17.

[18] A finding of delinquency is authorized where the child "habitually so deports himself as to injure or endanger [his] morals or health." Art. 2338–1, § 3(f).

[19] In re Gault, 387 U.S. 1, 87 S.Ct. 1428, 18 L.Ed.2d 527 (1967), is a good example of the potential inequality. There the child was ordered confined for a maximum period of six years for an offense which, if committed by an adult, carries with it a maximum punishment of a fine of not less than $25.00 and not more than $50.00, or imprisonment for not more than two months. In Texas, a finding of delinquency could be based on the fact that the child habitually associates with prostitutes, Art. 2338–1, § 3(g). An adult committing the same offense would face only a fine not exceeding $200.00. Tex.Ann.P.C. Arts. 607, 608.

merely because it singles out a class of persons for disparate treatment which is more oppressive than non-members of the class must tolerate. As sometimes said, the Equal Protection Clause does not require that things different in fact be treated in law as though they were the same. It does not require equal treatment for all persons without recognition of differences in relevant circumstances.

Where a class is selected for differential treatment, the pertinent inquiry concerns the existence of some reasonable nexus between the classification adopted and a valid governmental objective. A classification is invulnerable to an "equal protection" attack if it is reasonable, and a classification is reasonable if it includes all persons who are similarly situated with respect to the law.

In dealing with equal protection problems raised by legislative classifications, the Supreme Court of the United States has used at least two different approaches. In some cases, such as those involving taxation or regulation of economic activity, a classification will be upheld unless it is palpably arbitrary, irrational or capricious. According to this test, which may be designated as "permissive review," a statute will be upheld if any state of facts may reasonably be conceived which would sustain the rationality of the classification. This standard assigns to the Legislature the primary responsibility for evaluating the relevant facts and results in a judicial tolerance of a rather loose relationship between the classifying trait and the legislative purpose, without inquiring whether the social benefits resulting from the statute are important enough to justify the burdens imposed upon the affected class. Perhaps the most important practical effect of this method of inquiring into the reasonableness of a classification is that it places upon the person attacking the statute the burden of demonstrating that the classification is utterly lacking in rational justification.

If, in considering appellant's contentions, we adopt this restrained or permissive mode of review, we must conclude that appellant's contentions are without merit. The purpose of our statutes relating to the handling of youthful offenders is, as in other states having juvenile court systems, the education, treatment and rehabilitation of the child, rather than retributive punishment.[20] The emphasis on training and rehabilitation, rather than punishment, is under-

---

[20] "The purpose of this Act is to secure for each child * * * such care, guidance and control, preferably in his own home, as will serve the child's welfare and the best interest of the state; and when such child is removed from his own family, to secure for him custody, care and discipline as nearly as possible equivalent to that which should have been given him by his parents." Art. 2338–1, § 1. "The purpose of this Act is * * * to provide a program of constructive training aimed at rehabilitation and reestablishment in society of children adjudged delinquent by the courts of this state and committed to the Texas Youth Council, and to provide active parole supervision for such delinquent children until officially discharged from custody of the Texas Youth Council." Art. 5143d, § 1. The purpose of the training schools, "and of all education, work, training, discipline, recreation, and other activities carried on in the schools and other facilities shall be to restore and build up the self-respect and self-reliance of the children and youth lodged therein to qualify them for good citizenship and honorable employment." Id., § 21.

scored by the declaration that juvenile proceedings are civil, rather than criminal, in nature. Instead of a complaint or indictment we have a "petition." The hearing never results in a conviction, but may lead to an "adjudication of delinquency." Where confinement of the delinquent child is indicated as the proper treatment, the child is not sentenced to prison but, instead, is "committed" to a "training school." The adjudication of delinquency does not carry with it any of the civil disabilities ordinarily resulting from conviction of crime, nor is the child considered to be a criminal because of such adjudication.

Since the purpose of the legislation is to salvage youthful offenders, it requires no straining of the judicial imagination to find the existence of a reasonable relationship between the legislative purpose and the use of age as the classifying trait. It is indisputably the province of the Legislature to determine the manner in which various offenders will be treated, and if the difference in treatment is founded upon an arguably rational basis, the legislative decision is determinative. The Legislature could reasonably have concluded that children, as a class, should be subject to indefinite periods of confinement, not to extend beyond their twenty-first birthday, in order to insure sufficient time to accord the child sufficient treatment of the type required for his effective rehabilitation. This conclusion might be based on physiological and psychological differences between children and adults, the types of crimes committed by children, their relation to the criminal world, their unique susceptibility to rehabilitation, and their reaction, as a class, to confinement and discipline, as well as reformative treatment. It is true that some or all of these conclusions are based on sociological, psychological and penological theories which are not universally agreed on among so-called social scientists, but the fact that eminent scholars believe such theories to be valid prevents us from branding them as palpably irrational.

Since appellant has produced no data refuting the legislative conclusion that children who engage in deviant conduct require a different type and manner of confinement than do adult criminals, the presumption of validity with which the permissive method of review shields the statute remains unpierced.

However, in some cases, the Supreme Court of the United States has applied a stricter standard, demanding more than a conceivable rational relationship between the classification and the statutory purpose. In these cases, the statute is subjected to "the most rigid scrutiny," and the ordinary presumption of constitutionality seems to melt away, so that the burden is on the person defending the statute to show a substantial, empirically grounded justification to support the differentiation.

Statutory classifications have been subjected to this rigid scrutiny, at least ostensibly, in cases where the classification is based on one of certain "suspect" traits and the statutory class is subjected to disparate treatment which impinges seriously on personal rights considered as "fundamental."

Strict or "active" review results from the interaction of these two factors—suspect classification and serious impingement of fundamental personal liberties. Thus, if the classification is of the type considered highly suspect, such as a classification based on race, the statute will be subjected to close scrutiny even though the interest affected is not regarded as meriting a high position in the hierarchy of protected personal interests. On the other hand, the fact that the classification is relatively free from suspicion will not result in the application of a restrained or permissive standard of review if the operation of the statute seriously affects interests high on the list of the so-called "fundamental liberties."

Classifications based on age are no strangers to our law. Especially familiar are laws designed for the protection of children, such as those prohibiting the sale of intoxicants to minors. Although classifications based on age have sometimes been struck down, our attention has been called to no case indicating that age is a suspect basis for classification.

If, then, a strict standard of review is to be applied in this case, the reason must be that the legislation in question seriously impinges on an important fundamental right. It might persuasively be argued that a statute which permits longer confinement of children does impinge on fundamental personal liberties, although, in the area of criminal law, courts have traditionally allowed legislatures considerable leeway in classifying offenses and offenders for sentencing purposes. Apparently, it has not been thought that the possibility of a longer period of confinement, standing alone, calls for a strict standard of review.[21]

If the purpose of permitting longer periods of detention for children was to punish youthful offenders more severely than adult criminals, the application of a strict standard of review would seem justified. But where the legislative purpose is to benefit the affected class, a less strict standard would seem proper. We are familiar with the literature reflecting disillusionment concerning the practical administration of the rehabilitative ideal, and the burgeoning literature of criticism of the juvenile system in this country. But, as the Texas Supreme Court pointed out only a few days ago, "while we must accept as true much of the dismal picture painted in *Gault* as to the abuses of the juvenile system, we cannot condemn out of hand the Texas Youth Council, the juvenile judges, and other trained people working in this field. The policy of the juvenile laws has been fixed by the Texas Legislature; and we conceive it to be our duty to uphold the spirit of that law * * *."

[21] An exception is Commonwealth v. Daniel, 430 Pa. 642, 243 A.2d 400 (1968), holding that a statute imposing longer sentences on women than on men convicted of the same offense was a denial of equal protection. Prior to the Daniel decision the courts were consistent in upholding the imposition of longer periods of confinement, via the indeterminate sentence or commitment route, on women and youthful offenders. Rubin, Disparity and Equality of Sentencing, 40 F.R.D. 55, 76 (1966); Note, 82 Harv.L.Rev. 921, 924 (1969).

The purpose of our juvenile laws is benign, rather than invidious. Whether the law is actually beneficial to the affected class is a question which is not susceptible of easy judicial determination. The determination of the beneficial effects of our system depends, at least in part, on complicated factual judgments of whether our juvenile program helps or impedes the salvation of child offenders. It is not necessary, in this case, to hold that the required judgment is of the sort that should be left to the political processes. But we do hold that, in the absence of at least some data indicating that the legislative promise of treatment rather than punishment is not, in fact, being kept, we should not attempt, by a reasoning process alone, to determine whether the promised benefits are, in fact, being accorded to juvenile offenders.

If, in fact, in Texas the term "training school" is but a euphemism for prison; if the promised "treatment" consists of nothing more than confinement and disciplinary measures not substantially different from those characteristic of our adult penitentiaries; if, in fact, what is called rehabilitative treatment is indistinguishable from ordinary penal confinement in caged and demoralizing idleness, then, perhaps, a court would not be unwilling to cut through the verbal camouflage and condemn the system because of the exposed realities. But the record before us is bare of any indication that the promise of treatment and rehabilitation has been broken, and that the legislative declaration of purpose is no more than cant and hypocrisy used to justify what is essentially a system that does no more than provide longer terms of imprisonment for children.

The judgment of the trial court is affirmed.

IN RE ERIC J.

Supreme Court of California, 1980.
25 Cal.3d 522, 159 Cal.Rptr. 317, 601 P.2d 549.

CLARK, JUSTICE.

Eric J., a minor, appeals from an order continuing his juvenile court wardship and committing him to the Youth Authority (Welf. & Inst.Code, §§ 602, 731) after findings he committed burglary (Pen. Code, § 459) and was in contempt of court for violating conditions of an earlier order granting probation (Pen.Code, § 166, subd. 4). The maximum term for which he might be confined was determined to be three and one-half years—three years for the burglary and six months for the misdemeanor contempt. The commitment order must be modified to recite that appellant's maximum term is three years, two months, and that he is to receive forty-six days credit for time in custody prior to commitment. As modified, the judgment will be affirmed.

* * *

Equal Protection

Relying on People v. Olivas (1976) 17 Cal.3d 236, 131 Cal.Rptr. 55, 551 P.2d 375, appellant contends Welfare and Institutions Code section 726 denies him equal protection of the laws by providing that the maximum term of confinement for a juvenile is the longest term imposable upon an adult for the same offense, without the necessity of finding circumstances in aggravation of the crime justifying imposition of the upper term as is required in adult criminal procedure by Penal Code section 1170, subdivision (b).

Section 726, subdivision (c), of the Welfare and Institutions Code provides in relevant part: "In any case in which the minor is removed from the physical custody of his parent or guardian as the result of an order of wardship made pursuant to Section 602, the order shall specify that the minor may not be held in physical confinement for a period in excess of the maximum term of imprisonment which could be imposed upon an adult convicted of the offense or offenses which brought or continued the minor under the jurisdiction of the juvenile court. [¶] As used in this section and in Section 731, 'maximum term of imprisonment' means the longest of the three time periods set forth in paragraph (2) of subdivision (a) of Section 1170 of the Penal Code, but without the need to follow the provisions of subdivision (b) of Section 1170 of the Penal Code or to consider time for good behavior or participation pursuant to Sections 2930, 2931, and 2932 of the Penal Code, plus enhancements which must be proven if pled."

Section 1170, subdivision (b), of the Penal Code provides: "When a judgment of imprisonment is to be imposed and the statute specifies three possible terms, the court shall order imposition of the middle term, unless there are circumstances in aggravation or mitigation of the crime. At least four days prior to the time set for imposition of judgment either party may submit a statement in aggravation or mitigation to dispute facts in the record or the probation officer's report, or to present additional facts. In determining whether there are circumstances that justify imposition of the upper or lower term, the court may consider the record in the case, the probation officer's report, other reports including reports received pursuant to Section 1203.03 and statements in aggravation or mitigation submitted by the prosecution or the defendant, and any further evidence introduced at the sentencing hearing. The court shall set forth on the record the facts and reasons for imposing the upper or lower term * * *."

Appellant was found to have committed burglary. (Pen.Code, § 459.) Because the court failed to find the degree of the offense, it is deemed to be of the second degree. (Pen.Code, § 1157.) Second degree burglary is punishable "by imprisonment in the county jail not exceeding one year or in the state prison." (Pen.Code, § 461, subd. 2.) Where it is not otherwise specified, the term for an offense punishable by imprisonment in a state prison is "16 months, or two or three years." (Pen.Code, § 18.) Pursuant to Welfare and Institutions Code section 726, subdivision (c), the maximum term for which appellant might be confined for the burglary was determined to be three years. He contends that, in the absence of any finding of aggravation, it is a denial of equal protection of the law not to set the maximum at two years.

In People v. Olivas (1976) 17 Cal.3d 236, 131 Cal.Rptr. 55, 551 P.2d 375, this court held that section 1770 of the Welfare and Institutions Code violated the equal protection clauses of the California and United States Constitutions insofar as it permitted misdemeanants between the ages of 16 and 21 to be committed to the Youth Authority (Welf. & Inst.Code, § 1731.5) for a term potentially longer than the maximum jail term which might have been imposed for the same offense if committed by a person over the age of 21 years. We emphasized that youthful misdemeanants committed pursuant to section 1731.5 "have been prosecuted as *adults*, adjudged by the same standards which apply to *any competent adult*, and convicted as adults *in adult courts.*" (17 Cal.3d at pp. 242–243, 131 Cal. Rptr. at p. 59, 551 P.2d at p. 379, original italics.) "We are not confronted," we stressed, "by a situation in which a juvenile adjudged *under the Juvenile Court Law as a juvenile* contends that his term of involuntary confinement may exceed that which might have been imposed on an adult or juvenile who committed the identical unlawful act and was thereafter convicted *in the criminal courts.* Since that situation is not before us, we reserve consideration of the issue should it arise in some future case and we express no opinion on the merits of such a contention." (Id. at p. 243, fn. 11, 131 Cal.Rptr. at p. 59, fn. 11, 551 P.2d at p. 379, fn. 11, original italics.)

The situation not before us in *Olivas* is presented here. Appellant was adjudged under Juvenile Court Law as a juvenile. Pursuant to Welfare and Institutions Code section 726, subdivision (c), the maximum term for which he might be confined for the burglary was automatically set at three years. An adult or juvenile convicted in the criminal courts of committing the identical unlawful act could not, without a finding of aggravating circumstances, be imprisoned more than two years.

Despite this disparity, appellant has not been denied equal protection of the laws. The first prerequisite to a meritorious claim under the equal protection clause is a showing that the state has adopted a classification that affects two or more *similarly situated* groups in an unequal manner. Adults convicted in the criminal courts and sentenced to prison and youths adjudged wards of the juvenile courts and committed to the Youth Authority are not "similarly situated."

For purposes of this discussion, the most significant difference between minors and adults is that "[t]he liberty interest of a minor is qualitatively different than that of an adult, being subject both to reasonable regulation by the state to an extent not permissible with adults, and to an even greater extent to the control of the minor's parents unless 'it appears that the parental decisions will jeopardize the health or safety of the child or have a potential for significant social burdens.' " When the minor must be removed from the custody of his parents for his own welfare or for the safety and protection of the public (Welf. & Inst.Code, § 202), the state assuming the parents' role, the state also assumes the parents' authority to limit the minor's freedom of action.

" 'The concept of the equal protection of the laws compels recognition of the proposition that persons similarly situated with respect to the legitimate purpose of the law receive like treatment.' " (In re Gary W. (1971) 5 Cal.3d 296, 303, 96 Cal.Rptr. 1, 7, 486 P.2d 1201, 1207, quoting Purdy & Fitzpatrick v. State of California (1969) 71 Cal.2d 566, 578, 79 Cal.Rptr. 77, 85.) The state does not have the same purpose in sentencing adults to prison that it has in committing minors to the Youth Authority. Adults convicted in the criminal courts are sentenced to prison as punishment (Pen.Code, § 1170, subd. (a)(1)) while minors adjudged wards of the juvenile courts are committed to the Youth Authority for the purposes of treatment and rehabilitation.

This distinction has been significantly sharpened recently. Under the Indeterminate Sentence Law, which was the system under review in *Olivas*, the purposes of imprisonment were deterrence, isolation and rehabilitation. Not the least of these was rehabilitation. "It is generally recognized by the courts and by modern penologists that the purpose of the indeterminate sentence law, like other modern laws in relation to the administration of the criminal law, is to mitigate the punishment which would otherwise be imposed upon the offender. These laws place emphasis upon the reformation of the offender. They seek to make the punishment fit the criminal rather than the crime." (In re Lee (1918) 177 Cal. 690, 692, 171 P. 958, 959; see In re Foss (1974) 10 Cal.3d 910, 923, 112 Cal.Rptr. 649, 519 P.2d 1073.)

The enactment of the Uniform Determinate Sentencing Act marked a significant change in the penal philosophy of this state regarding adult offenders. "The Legislature finds and declares that the purpose of imprisonment for crime is punishment. This purpose is best served by terms proportionate to the seriousness of the offense with provision for uniformity in the sentences of offenders committing the same offense under similar circumstances. The Legislature further finds and declares that the elimination of disparity and the provision of uniformity of sentences can best be achieved by determinate sentences fixed by statute in proportion to the seriousness of the offense as determined by the Legislature to be imposed by the court with specified discretion." (Pen.Code, § 1170, subd. (a) (1).)

There has been no like revolution in society's attitude toward juvenile offenders. It is still true that "[j]uvenile commitment proceedings are designed for the purposes of rehabilitation and treatment, not punishment." (In re Aline D., supra, 14 Cal.3d 557, 567, 121 Cal.Rptr. 816, 822, 536 P.2d 65, 70.) Therefore, Juvenile Court Law continues to provide for indeterminate terms, with provision for parole as soon as appropriate. (Welf. & Inst.Code, § 1176.)

In *Olivas* this court objected that "[t]here has been no showing made that youthful offenders *necessarily* require longer periods of confinement for rehabilitative purposes than older adults." (17 Cal. 3d at p. 256, 131 Cal.Rptr. at p. 68, 551 P.2d at p. 388.) No such objection is appropriate here since under the Determinate Sentencing Act rehabilitation is no longer the standard for term fixing.

It is significant, however, that in *Olivas* we approved of a federal law having essentially the same features challenged here. "In the context of juveniles adjudged as delinquents and committed under the Federal Youth Corrections Act the United States Congress has recently revised custody limitations so that they are now within constitutional bounds. (18 U.S.C. § 5037(b).) The new provisions now accord juveniles confined as delinquents (as opposed to misdemeanants) the constitutional protection we find required in the instant case." (17 Cal.3d at pp. 255–256, 131 Cal.Rptr. at p. 68, 551 P.2d at p. 388, fn. omitted.)

The statute mentioned provides in pertinent part: "Probation, commitment * * * shall not extend beyond the juvenile's twenty-first birthday or the maximum term which could have been imposed on an adult convicted of the same offense, whichever is sooner." (18 U.S.C. § 5037(b).) In the federal system, the trial judge is informed of the maximum sentence for each crime from the federal code. The judge, in his sound discretion, sets the determinate sentence at any point up to the maximum. (Fed.Rules Crim.Proc., rule 32(a); United States v. Buck (9th Cir.1977) 548 F.2d 871, 877.) Thus, the judge in each criminal case carries on what is essentially a mitigation/aggravation hearing. No such discretion exists in a youth commitment made pursuant to 18 United States Code section 5037. The juvenile is simply sent to the rehabilitative authority to be treated as the authority in its professional judgment deems best. In *Olivas* our court was aware of this facet of the federal juvenile system. The court nonetheless found the system to have avoided the defects of the old California juvenile sentencing scheme. *Olivas* has thus sanctioned the system now defined in California by Welfare and Institutions Code sections 726 and 731, including provision for commitment up to the maximum adult term without review by the trial court.

In conclusion, because minors and adults are not "similarly situated" with respect to their interest in liberty, and because minors adjudged wards of the juvenile courts and committed to the Youth Authority and adults convicted in the criminal courts and sentenced to prison are not confined for the same purposes, Welfare and Institutions Code section 726 does not deny minors equal protection of the laws.

* * *

Computing the Maximum Term

Under section 726, if the juvenile court chooses to "sentence" consecutively on multiple counts or multiple petitions, the maximum term must be specified in accordance with the formula set forth in subdivision (a) of Penal Code section 1170.1, i.e., the sum of the "principal term" (the longest term imposed for any of the offenses) and "subordinate terms" (one-third of the middle term imposed for each other offense).[22]

Appellant contends the maximum term specified here was erroneously computed. As stated, the maximum term was determined to be three and one-half years—three years for the burglary and six months for the misdemeanor contempt. In other words, the "aggregate maximum term" was computed here by adding the maximum terms prescribed by law for both the burglary (the principal term) and the misdemeanor contempt (the subordinate term). Appellant contends the court should have imposed only one-third of the maximum of the subordinate offense, i.e., two months. The People respond that Penal Code section 1170.1, subdivision (a), by its terms applies only to consecutive terms imposed for *felony* offenses and that the juvenile court should therefore aggregate any subordinate misdemeanor term by imposing the maximum term prescribed by law, as it did here.

"[W]here the language of a statutory provision is susceptible of two constructions, one of which, in application, will render it reasonable, fair and harmonious with its manifest purpose, and another which would be productive of absurd consequences, the former construction will be adopted." (Clements v. T.R. Bechtel Co. (1954) 43 Cal.2d 227, 233, 273 P.2d 5, 9.)

The interpretation of section 726 urged by the People would lead to the following result: A minor committed for the period of the maximum term for a principal felony offense, and to one-third of the middle term of a 'sixteen months, two years, three years' subordinate felony offense, could be confined for an aggregate maximum period four months shorter than a minor committed for the same principal

---

[22] Welfare and Institutions Code section 726, subdivision (c), provides in relevant part: "If the court elects to aggregate the period of physical confinement on multiple counts, or multiple petitions, including previously sustained petitions adjudging the minor a ward within Section 602, the 'maximum term of imprisonment' shall be specified in accordance with subdivision (a) of Section 1170.1 of the Penal Code."

Penal Code section 1170.1, subdivision (a), provides: "Except as provided in subdivision (b) and subject to Section 654, when any person is convicted of two or more felonies, whether in the same proceeding or court or in different proceedings or courts, and whether by judgment rendered by the same judge or by a different court, and a consecutive term of imprisonment is imposed under Sections 669 and 1170, the aggregate term of imprisonment for all such convictions shall be the sum of the principal term, the

subordinate term and any additional term imposed pursuant to Section 667.5. The principal term shall consist of the greatest term of imprisonment imposed by the court for any of the crimes, including any enhancements imposed pursuant to Sections 12022, 12022.5, 12022.6, and 12022.7. The subordinate term for each consecutive offense shall consist of one-third of the middle term of imprisonment prescribed for each other felony conviction for which a consecutive term of imprisonment is imposed, and shall exclude any enhancements when the consecutive offense is not listed in subdivision (c) of Section 667.5, but shall include one-third of any enhancement imposed pursuant to Section 12022, 12022.5 or 12022.7 when the consecutive offense is listed in subdivision (c) of Section 667.5. In no case shall the total of subordinate terms for consecutive offenses not listed in subdivision (c) of Section 667.5 exceed five years."

offense but with a subordinate misdemeanor offense having a one-year maximum term. This anomaly does not appear to have been within the contemplation of the Legislature.

Although the Legislature clearly indicated its intent that the aggregation provisions of Penal Code section 1170.1, which limit consecutive terms to one-third of the middle determinate term, apply only in imposing sentence for felonies, we are not persuaded that the Legislature intended that this distinction apply in determining the maximum period of confinement for minors committed by the juvenile court. The limitation of section 1170.1 reflects a legislative recognition that misdemeanor terms, unless imposed concurrently with a felony term, are served in local detention facilities and are not part of a continuous period of imprisonment under the supervision of the same correctional officials. The judge who orders that a misdemeanor term be served consecutively to a previously imposed felony term thus retains discretion as to the length of the misdemeanor term and the power to maintain supervision over the defendant through probation by suspension of execution of the term for an appropriate period. The latter option would in many cases be foreclosed were the term limited to one-third of the maximum term since no realistic sanction for violation of probation would be available.

It is apparent that the considerations leading to the limitation on physical confinement of minors differ markedly from those involved in adult sentencing. The physical confinement to which Welfare and Institutions Code section 726 refers is typically a commitment for a single continuous period of custody under the supervision of a single agency with a unitary rehabilitation plan. By directing in section 726 that the juvenile court measure the maximum period of confinement for 'multiple counts' in accordance with subdivision (a) of Penal Code section 1170.1, without restricting the application of the consecutive term provisions of that subdivision to felony counts, the Legislature recognized the different circumstances of juvenile and adult commitments, and indicated its intent that the aggregation provisions of section 1170.1 be applied whether the offenses committed by the minor are felonies or misdemeanors.

The commitment order is modified to recite that appellant's maximum term is three years, two months, and that he is to receive forty-six days credit for time in custody prior to commitment. As modified, the judgment is affirmed.

TOBRINER, MOSK, RICHARDSON and MANUEL, JJ., concur.

NEWMAN, JUSTICE, dissenting:

I dissent because I agree with views that Justice Wiener articulated as follows when he wrote the opinion for the court of appeal in this case (except that I would rely solely on the California Constitution):

"The Attorney General argues the differential in the period of confinement imposed on youthful offenders is not so disproportionate to the term imposed on adult offenders to involve the application of

Olivas. When this argument is examined in light of the fundamental interest involved, we conclude the difference in time, modest as it may appear to those whose liberty is not restricted, cannot be constitutionally condoned.

"There are those who will undoubtedly say the juvenile has the best of both worlds. He obtains the benefits of the Indeterminate Sentencing Law within the juvenile system with the opportunity of being released earlier than the outer limits of his commitment and the benefits of the limitation of a maximum term determined in accordance with the adult penal system. We do not view this as a dramatic result. It is only consistent with the purpose of the juvenile justice system which will still permit the juvenile to be released at any time before the service of the maximum term if deemed rehabilitated or retained for the maximum term if efforts at rehabilitation are unsuccessful. (Welf. & Inst.Code, § 1176.) As a practical matter, we suspect our decision will have little or no impact on the operation of the Youth Authority. There should be a direct correlation between the length of term imposed and successful rehabilitation of youthful offenders, i.e., those who are more likely to be rehabilitated will be given lesser terms; those less likely, longer terms. We anticipate the same class of offenders upon whom are imposed the upper term because of circumstances in aggravation will be identical to the class that would have otherwise remained incarcerated for the upper term.

"We recognize our decision creates an additional facet to the dispositional hearing (Welf. & Inst.Code, § 706) causing additional work for the presently overburdened personnel within the juvenile court system. We cannot allow this administrative consideration, important as it is, to outweigh the guarantees afforded to minors.

"Because of equal protection of the laws (U.S.Const., 14th Amend.; Cal.Const. art. I, § 7, subd. (a)), we conclude the provision within Welfare and Institutions Code section 726 relating to the automatic imposition of the upper term of confinement is unconstitutional. Juvenile courts shall be required to apply the substantive rule of Penal Code section 1170 [, subd.] (b) providing for the sentencing of the middle term unless aggravating or mitigating circumstances have been established in determining a minor's potential term of incarceration."

BIRD, C.J., concurs.

NOTES

1. Is the answer to the Equal Protection argument affected by an explicit legislative recognition of punishment and of societal protection as additional purposes of juvenile justice statutes? The Supreme Judicial Court of Maine says "no." In State v. Gleason, 404 A.2d 573 (Me.1979), the court found that the rehabilitative purpose of the Juvenile Code retained sufficient significance to overcome the argument that equal protection requirements demanded that juveniles were now entitled to the full panoply of rights given to adults charged with crime.

In analyzing the scope of the procedural due process to be accorded a juvenile, we must ascertain at the threshold whether the State retains a rehabilitative purpose in the establishment of a specialized system of juvenile justice.

The Legislature expressly set forth its purposes in enacting the Maine Juvenile Code:

The purposes of this Part are:

A. To secure for each juvenile subject to these provisions such care and guidance, preferably in his own home, as will best serve his welfare and the interests of society;

B. To preserve and strengthen family ties whenever possible, including improvement of home environment;

C. To remove a juvenile from the custody of his parents only when his welfare and safety or the protection of the public would otherwise be endangered or where necessary to punish a child adjudicated, pursuant to chapter 507, as having committed a juvenile crime;

D. To secure for any juvenile removed from the custody of his parents the necessary treatment, care, guidance and discipline to assist him in becoming a responsible and productive member of society;

E. To provide procedures through which the provisions of the law are executed and enforced and which will assure the parties fair hearings at which their rights as citizens are recognized and protected. 15 M.R.S.A. § 3002(1) (Supp.1978).

These purposes continue the goals of rehabilitation and treatment which have historically characterized the juvenile justice system in Maine. Preservation of home and family ties is a goal of the new Juvenile Code. It further seeks to secure for any juvenile treatment, care, guidance and discipline to assist him in becoming a responsible and productive member of society. These goals and purposes are substantially the same as those underpinning the prior treatment of juveniles.

Under the Maine Juvenile Code, an adjudication of the commission of a juvenile crime is not deemed a conviction of a crime, and it does not lead to the civil disabilities which conviction of an adult crime may entail. 15 M.R.S.A. § 3310(6).

Proceedings under the new Code retain as much informality as is permitted by the state and federal constitutions. The flexibility of the dispositional alternatives and the criteria for selection of the proper disposition demonstrate the compassion which the Legislature still has in large measure for the welfare of the juvenile. These are the substantive benefits justifying separate treatment of these offenders.

404 A.2d at 581.

* * *

There is, admittedly, an element of deterrence through restraint in the approach of the Maine Juvenile Code, but this is found to some degree in all juvenile systems. So long as rehabilitation remains the primary goal, and so long as it is not destructive to the fact-finding process, certain informality in the juvenile procedures is appropriate and simplified procedures in juvenile matters are a legitimate objective for such a Code as this.[23]

> In summary, it cannot be said that under the Maine Juvenile Code the young offender is treated in an essentially punitive manner for the violation of a criminal statute. The benevolent purposes of our prior juvenile laws remain uppermost. Our Code creates a separate and distinctive juvenile justice system designed primarily for the rehabilitation, not the punishment, of the young offender.

Id. at 582.

2. Would the result (or rationale) be different if there were a "more determinate" disposition (sentencing) scheme for juveniles than for adults? Under the recent Washington juvenile code, the juvenile judge may vary the length of the disposition (longer or shorter) from the disposition derived from the point scale authorized for juveniles by the Washington legislature. Sentencing of adults in Washington, on the other hand, is largely within the discretion of the trial judge subject to broad legislatively-set limits. There is no point scale required for adult sentencing, and thus no "departure" from "it" could exist. In State v. Rice, 98 Wn.2d 384, 655 P.2d 1145 (1982), the court found no violation of equal protection. The majority emphasized the need for longer juvenile dispositions in the face of the Juvenile Code's substantial rehabilitative purpose.

> If we were to apply the adult maximum to the disposition provisions of the JJA, we would leave the juvenile courts without a means of responding to the obvious needs of juveniles like the defendants. It would be, in effect, telling the juvenile court to ignore the needs of the juvenile until he is convicted of committing an even more serious offense. Such an approach is necessary under the adult system in which punishment is the paramount purpose and where the punishment must fit the crime. But it is inimical to the rehabilitative purpose of the juvenile justice system. It would destroy the flexibility the legislature built into the system to allow the court, in appropriate cases, to fit the disposition to the offender, rather than to the offense.

Id. at 397, 655 P.2d at 1152. The dissent takes a different view. Relying on the language of *In re Gault*, the dissent argues that the loss of liberty suffered by juveniles and adults alike demands the same maximum lengths of disposition (sentences).

> Even assuming that the state provides substantial "treatment" benefits to juveniles, the Washington court has rejected the proposition that these benefits sufficiently compensate a juvenile for the loss of liberty to dispense with the need for strict scrutiny. A juvenile still shares with an adult offender the one feature that

---

[23] The Legislature has taken a stricter approach in its treatment of juveniles at the adjudicatory stage. See 15 M.R.S.A. §§ 3307, 3314(1)(D). However, when we balance the interest of the state in an effective juvenile justice system against the interest of the juvenile in the safeguards of due process, we conclude that the Maine Juvenile Code retains the substantive benefits crucial to maintenance of this separate system of juvenile justice.

For a discussion of recent radical surgery to New York's juvenile law which now in large measure treats serious juvenile crime very much as in the adult criminal system (in sharp contrast with Maine's approach), see Carey, A Positive Perspective, 15 Trial 31 (January, 1979); and Thorpe, Juvenile Justice Reform, 15 Trial 26 (January, 1979).

overwhelms the differences between their circumstances—they are both incarcerated against their will. While conceding the rehabilitation purposes of the Washington juvenile system even in 1976, the Supreme Court said:

> However, where a restraint of liberty is involved, the fact of the beneficent, civil nature of the juvenile code loses its significance. Although the proceedings may be deemed "civil," "rehabilitative," or "remedial," they are subject to the same strict constitutional scrutiny they would be if they were deemed "criminal" proceedings.

Johnson v. Morris, 87 Wash.2d 922, 929, 557 P.2d 1299 (1976). The United States Supreme Court made the same point. "It is incarceration against one's will, whether it is called 'criminal' or 'civil'." In re Gault, 387 U.S. 1, 50, 87 S.Ct. 1428, 1455, 18 L.Ed.2d 527 (1967). * * * The State's allegation of available treatment benefits should not divert the court's attention from this primary feature of incarceration, whether juvenile or adult.

Id. at 408, 655 P.2d at 1158–59.

3. Suppose that juveniles who attack the elderly are subject to lengthier dispositions than juveniles who attack younger persons, and that no comparable distinction is found in the Penal Code governing adults. Does either characteristic—or both in combination—amount to a denial of equal protection?

The New York Court of Appeals, though reversing on other grounds in Matter of Quinton A., 49 N.Y.2d 328, 402 N.E.2d 126 (1980), found no violation of equal protection. The court applied the rational relation rather than strict scrutiny standard.

4. In R.R. v. State, 448 S.W.2d 187 (1969), writ refused n.r.e., appeal dismissed, Rios v. Texas, 400 U.S. 808, 91 S.Ct. 35, 27 L.Ed.2d 37 (1970), the appellant, age sixteen, was adjudicated delinquent and committed to the state training school for an indefinite term not extending beyond his minority for conduct that would have subjected an adult to a maximum of one year's incarceration. The Texas Court of Civil Appeals upheld the juvenile statute against contentions that, as applied in this case, it inflicted cruel and unusual punishment:

> For the purposes of this opinion, we assume that, as appellant contends, a penalty may run afoul of the constitutional prohibition if it is excessive and that, implicit in this principle is the notion that the prohibition against cruel and unusual punishment requires that punishment should be proportioned to the crime.

> But even if we accept appellant's basic contentions as true, they would be relevant only in cases involving punishment for crime.
> * * *

> The record before us contains no evidence concerning the conditions at the state training schools or the facilities available at such institutions for the rehabilitation of youthful offenders. In the absence of evidence that the dismal picture painted in Gault reflects the conditions in the institutions of this State, and giving due consideration to the legislative declaration of policy and purpose, "we are not prepared to condemn out of hand the Texas Youth Council, the juvenile judges, and other trained people working in the field."

Id. at 188–90.

5.   Should the equal protection argument be handled differently when both juveniles and adults are committed to the same correctional institution? The Supreme Court of Pennsylvania was faced with that problem in In re Wilson, 438 Pa. 425, 264 A.2d 614 (1970):

> Wilson's delinquency petition was based on two charges of simple assault and battery. Having been found delinquent as a result of that conduct he was committed to Camp Hill for an indefinite period of time not to extend beyond his twenty-first birthday. Since he was sixteen at the time the maximum possible commitment was five years. Had Wilson been tried as an adult and been convicted of simple assault and battery his punishment would again probably have been commitment to Camp Hill, but since the maximum sentence for one count of simple assault and battery is two years, he could have been given a maximum sentence of only four years.
>
> Under the Equal Protection Clause of the Fourteenth Amendment to the United States Constitution a state may make distinctions only upon the basis of reasonable classifications. If the Commonwealth wishes to make individuals guilty of similar conduct eligible for maximum sentences of varying lengths it must demonstrate that the distinctions which it makes are based on some relevant and reasonable classification. * * *
>
> It is our view that there can be no constitutionally valid distinction between a juvenile and an adult offender which justifies making one of them subject to a longer maximum commitment in the same institution for the same conduct.
>
> There can be circumstances under which a longer maximum commitment may be permissible, but only if three factors are present: (1) The juvenile must have notice at the outset of the proceedings of any and all factors upon which the state proposes to base the adjudication of delinquency; (2) the ultimate conclusions upon which the finding of delinquency is based, and the facts supporting each of them, must be clearly found and set forth in the adjudication; and (3) it must be clear that the longer commitment will result in the juvenile's receiving appropriate rehabilitative care and not just in his being deprived of his liberty for a longer time. If all three of these conditions are present, a juvenile may be deprived of his liberty for a period in excess of the maximum sentence which he could have received if treated as an adult.

264 A.2d at 617–18.

In a number of states, juveniles committed to a training school can later be transferred administratively to an adult correctional institution. Should the principles of In re Wilson apply to juveniles who are later transferred to a prison or reformatory? To all juveniles committed to a training school in a state in which transfer to an adult institution is a lawful and realistic possibility?

6.   If the equal protection argument is accepted and juveniles are not permitted to be incarcerated for a longer period of time than an adult could be confined for the same conduct, does an adult subject to a longer period of confinement than would be permissible for a juvenile who engaged in the same conduct have an equal protection claim? If so, how is his confinement to be limited, since the length of confinement for a juvenile depends upon his age at the time of commitment?

7. The Federal Juvenile Delinquency Act provides in 18 U.S.C.A. § 5037:

(b) The court may suspend the adjudication of delinquency or the disposition of the delinquent on such conditions as it deems proper, place him on probation, or commit him to the custody of the Attorney General. Probation, commitment, or commitment in accordance with subsection (c) shall not extend beyond the juvenile's twenty-first birthday or the maximum term which could have been imposed on an adult convicted of the same offense, whichever is sooner, unless the juvenile has attained his nineteenth birthday at the time of disposition, in which case probation, commitment, or commitment in accordance with subsection (c) shall not exceed the lesser of two years or the maximum term which could have been imposed on an adult convicted of the same offense.

(c) If the court desires more detailed information concerning an alleged or adjudicated delinquent, it may commit him, after notice and hearing at which the juvenile is represented by counsel, to the custody of the Attorney General for observation and study by an appropriate agency. Such observation and study shall be conducted on an outpatient basis, unless the court determines that inpatient observation and study are necessary to obtain the desired information. In the case of an alleged juvenile delinquent, inpatient study may be ordered only with the consent of the juvenile and his attorney. The agency shall make a complete study of the alleged or adjudicated delinquent to ascertain his personal traits, his capabilities, his background, any previous delinquency or criminal experience, any mental or physical defect, and any other relevant factors. The Attorney General shall submit to the court and the attorneys for the juvenile and the Government the results of the study within thirty days after the commitment of the juvenile, unless the court grants additional time.

Does this provision solve the equal protection problem? How important is this limitation in light of (1) the fact that most minor criminal violations and noncriminal acts of delinquency are disposed of by the juvenile system before adjudication or by a term of probation and (2) the availability of consecutive sentences and extended terms for habitual offenders in the criminal system? If such a provision were engrafted onto a state juvenile justice system, what effect would it have upon charging and adjudication practices in juvenile court, the incidence of plea bargaining in juvenile court and the system's response to noncriminal violations of the juvenile statute?

8. Some juvenile statutes depart from the traditional notion that any training school commitment must be for an indefinite term not exceeding the minority of the offender. For example, an initial juvenile court commitment to a New York training school may not exceed 18 months in the case of a felony and 12 months in the case of a misdemeanor. N.Y.—McKinney's Family Court Act § 353.3.

9. Suppose for the same conduct an adult is subject only to a fine, i.e., cannot even be placed on probation, while a juvenile can be placed on probation. Is there a denial of equal protection? The California Court of Appeal found no constitutional violation, in the Matter of Wayne J., 97 Cal. App.3d 776, 159 Cal.Rptr. 106 (1979).

Chapter 2

THE SUBSTANTIVE LAW GOVERNING
JUVENILE CONDUCT

The substantive law governing juvenile conduct is, in its most important aspects, divided into three parts: conduct that were it committed by any adult would constitute a crime (or a violation); conduct that is illegal for all children including those beyond the age over which the juvenile court has jurisdiction; and conduct which is forbidden only to children young enough to fall within the jurisdiction of the juvenile court. Within the last category falls what are commonly referred to as "status offenses." (The student should consider carefully, as we proceed through the chapter, in what sense that label is accurate.)

In addition, the typical juvenile or family court has jurisdiction over "dependent" or "neglected" children. As indicated in the Preface, no emphasis is placed on these categories. Occasionally problems arise in one of two ways: (1) There may be a jurisdictional question whether the "law" creates an overlap of categories; or (2) officials, in exercising discretion, choose to use the less restricting jurisdiction for conduct technically falling under other jurisdictional heads.

A. CRIMINAL VIOLATIONS

1. INFANCY DEFENSE

IN RE R.

Supreme Court of California, 1970.
83 Cal.Rptr. 671, 464 P.2d 127, 1 Cal.3d 855.

* * *

2. *A child under the age of 14 must appreciate the wrongfulness of her conduct in order to become a ward of the juvenile court under section 602.*

As we have stated, section 602 provides that any minor who violates "any law of this State," that defines crime, comes under the jurisdiction of the juvenile court. We shall point out that in order to become a ward of the court under that section, clear proof must show that a child under the age of 14 years at the time of committing the act appreciated its wrongfulness. This conclusion follows from the statutory postulate that the jurisdiction of the court must rest upon a violation of a law that defines crime and from the further statutory requirement of Penal Code section 26, subdivision One,[1] that, by

---

[1] "All persons are capable of committing crimes except those belonging to the following classes: One—Children under the age of fourteen, in the absence of clear proof that at the time of committing the act charged against them, they knew its wrongfulness." (Pen.Code § 26, subd. One.) References hereinaf-

definition, a child under the age of 14 years does not commit a crime in the absence of clear proof that he "knew its wrongfulness."

A ruling that a child could be committed to the juvenile court under section 602, in the absence of such clear proof, would compel the disregard of section 26 or the assumption of its repeal. Indeed, the Welfare and Institutions Code provides that the juvenile courts exercise exclusive jurisdiction over all minors under the age of 16; these children cannot otherwise be tried as criminal offenders.

Hence, if section 26 pertains at all to a definition of criminal conduct it must apply to proceedings under section 602 which, in turn, covers "[a]ny person under the age of 21 years who violates any law of this State * * *."

We cannot presume the repeal of section 26 by implication; the decisions clearly establish the contrary presumption. We have said that "To overcome the presumption the two acts must be irreconcilable, clearly repugnant, and so inconsistent that the two cannot have concurrent operation. The courts are bound, if possible, to maintain the integrity of both statutes if the two may stand together."

In enacting section 602 of the Welfare and Institutions Code, the Legislature must have considered the pre-existing section 26; that section constituted practically the only special provision for children in the entire legal system. Section 26 did not lie at the periphery of the statutory scheme, bearing only tangentially upon juvenile offenders. Necessarily confronted with the section, the Legislature must have intended in its later enactment of section 602 a definition of crime consistent with the older section. If the Legislature had intended to repeal section 26 or to sever it from section 602, it could have done so expressly. Yet the legislative history of the present California Juvenile Court Law, of which section 602 forms a part, indicates no such intent. In fact, the commission that drafted the present law refers to the necessity of "respectable proof of the jurisdictional facts" for the institution of proceedings under section 602 for the violation of "*serious* crimes against persons and property."

Section 26 accords with the historical treatment of juveniles, deriving from the early common law that children under the age of seven could not be held responsible for criminal conduct. Between the ages of seven and fourteen the common law rebuttably presumed children incapable of criminal acts, unless the particular child possessed the requisite age and experience to understand the wrongfulness of his act.

California likewise rebuttably presumes all minors under the age of 14 incapable of committing a crime, but does not totally exclude any child from criminal responsibility. Section 26 embodies a venerable truth, which is no less true for its extreme age, that a young child cannot be held to the same standard of criminal responsibility as

ter to section 26, without mention of any
code, are to the quoted section.

his more experienced elders. A juvenile court must therefore consider a child's age, experience, and understanding in determining whether he would be capable of committing conduct proscribed by section 602.

As we observed in People v. Lara (1967) 67 Cal.2d 365, 380, 62 Cal.Rptr. 586, 432 P.2d 202, section 26 plays a very definite role in the overall system of protections afforded to minors under the criminal law and under our special juvenile court system. We know of no change that has occurred since the rendition of this decision that prompts its abandonment. To the contrary, one Court of Appeal has apparently considered Penal Code section 26 applicable to section 602 proceedings.

Furthermore, section 26 provides the kind of fundamental protection to children charged under section 602 which this court should not lightly discard. Section 602 is clearly distinguishable from sections 600 and 601 with respect to the consequences of their operation upon the child: upon the application of section 602, commitment of the youth to the custody of the California Youth Authority becomes far more likely. Section 600 concerns dependent children who need care because of home conditions or medical deficiencies.[2] Section 601 covers delinquent children whose acts fall short of criminal conduct.[3] Section 602 pertains to minors who have violated a court order or a criminal law.

If a juvenile court finds a lack of clear proof that a child under 14 years at the time of committing the act possessed knowledge of its wrongfulness under sections 602 and 26, the court might well declare the child a ward under section 600 or 601. These latter provisions carry far less severe consequences for the liberty and life of the child. After all, it is the purpose of the Welfare and Institutions Code to "insure that the rights or physical, mental or moral welfare of children are not violated or threatened by their present circumstances or environment."

[2] Section 600. "Any person under the age of 21 years who comes within any of the following descriptions is within the jurisdiction of the juvenile court which may adjudge such person to be a dependent child of the court: (a) Who is in need of proper and effective parental care or control and has no parent or guardian, or has no parent or guardian willing to exercise or capable of exercising such care or control, or has no parent or guardian actually exercising such care or control. (b) Who is destitute, or who is not provided with the necessities of life, or who is not provided with a home or suitable place of abode, or whose home is an unfit place for him by reason of neglect, cruelty, or depravity of either of his parents, or of his guardian or other person in whose custody or care he is. (c) Who is physically dangerous to the public because of a mental or physical deficiency, disorder or abnormality." (Welf. & Inst. Code, § 600.)

[3] Section 601. "Any person under the age of 21 years who persistently or habitually refuses to obey the reasonable and proper orders or directions of his parents, guardian, custodian or school authorities, or who is beyond the control of such person, or any person who is a habitual truant from school within the meaning of any law of this State, or who from any cause is in danger of leading an idle, dissolute, lewd, or immoral life, is within the jurisdiction of the juvenile court which may adjudge such person to be a ward of the court." (Welf. & Inst. Code, § 601.)

Strong policy reasons cast doubt upon the placement of a child who is unable to appreciate the wrongfulness of his conduct with an institution where he will come into contact with many youths who are well versed in criminality. To argue that we should trust entirely to the discretion of the juvenile court in this matter does not justify a ruling that section 26 is inapplicable to the definition of crime within section 602. We cannot condone a decision which would both misinterpret the statute and expose the child to consequences possibly disastrous to himself and society as a whole.

Other sections may possibly be invoked to provide for a wardship for this child with no injurious potentials. Section 601 provides that a child who disobeys the lawful orders of his parents or school authorities, who is beyond the control of such persons, or who is in danger of leading an immoral life may be adjudged a ward of the court. Section 601 might clearly cover younger children who lacked the age or experience to understand the wrongfulness of their conduct. If the juvenile court considers section 601 inappropriate for the particular child, he may be covered by the even broader provisions of section 600.

Section 602 should apply only to those who are over 14 and may be presumed to understand the wrongfulness of their acts and to those under the age of 14 who clearly appreciate the wrongfulness of their conduct. In the instant case we are confronted with a 12-year-old girl of the social and mental age of a 7-year-old. Section 26 stands to protect her and other young people like her from the harsh strictures of section 602. Only if the age, experience, knowledge, and conduct of the child demonstrate by clear proof that he has violated a criminal law should he be declared a ward of the court under section 602.

*   *   *

In reaching our second ruling we have recognized that over the past centuries our society has attained a stage of relative sophistication in which it recognizes that antisocial conduct in most cases stems from psychological motivation in the individual that cannot be segregated into the easy categories of "criminal" or "noncriminal." It would be particularly undesirable for a juvenile court, arbitrarily, without analysis of the child's appreciation of the "wrongfulness" of her conduct, to hold this emotionally disturbed child of 12 years guilty of criminal conduct. To reach that result we would, in our judgment, be compelled to misread the pertinent statutes, to disregard even our presently inadequate knowledge of psychology, and to retreat to an approach which pre-dates the early common law.

The judgment is reversed and the case is remanded to the Santa Clara County Superior Court, sitting as a juvenile court, for further proceedings consistent with this opinion.

TRAYNOR, C.J., and PETERS, MOSK and SULLIVAN, JJ., concur.

BURKE, JUSTICE (concurring and dissenting.)

I concur with the majority opinion except the portion which holds that in order for a minor under 14 to be within the jurisdiction of the juvenile court under Welfare and Institutions Code section 602 there must be "clear proof" that the minor at the time of committing the crime knew of its wrongfulness (Pen.Code, § 26, subd. One). With respect to that portion I dissent.

Proceedings in the juvenile court are conducted for the protection and benefit of minors and not to prosecute them as law violators. It is unreasonable to believe that the Legislature intended Penal Code section 26, subdivision One, to apply in a proceeding instituted for the minor's benefit and which seeks to determine whether the minor comes within the terms of section 602.[4] Application of that subdivision in such juvenile court proceedings could result in excluding some minors who are in dire need of the care and guidance afforded by the Juvenile Court Law from receiving those benefits. It appears likely that the very minors so excluded would be those in greater need of receiving such care than others more sophisticated who plainly knew that their acts were wrongful.

The majority state, "If a juvenile court finds a lack of clear proof that a child under 14 years at the time of committing the act possessed knowledge of its wrongfulness under sections 602 and 26, the court might well declare the child a ward under [Welfare and Institutions Code] sections 600 or 601. The quoted statement, however, fails to give adequate consideration to the fact that many children who violate a law defining a crime may not be found to come within either section 600 or 601. Under the majority position such children will be deprived of the attention they need in order to become law-abiding citizens. For example, a 12-year-old boy on one occasion exhibits a loaded gun in a threatening manner in the presence of another (Pen.Code, § 417), and the evidence does not show his conduct was the result of "a mental or physical deficiency, disorder, or abnormality," (see Welf. & Inst.Code, § 600, subd. (c)). A 13-year-old girl has possession of marijuana (Health & Saf.Code, § 1530). A 13-year-old boy on one occasion commits statutory rape (Pen.Code, § 261, subd. 1), with a willing 13-year-old girl in a private place, or goes joyriding (Pen.Code, § 499b) or commits petty theft (Pen.Code, § 488). In none of the foregoing instances is there "clear proof" that the minor at the time of committing the crime had knowledge of its wrongfulness. In the foregoing instances some juvenile courts might conclude that the minor did not come within either section 600 or 601,

---

[4] Section 502 reads: "The purpose of this chapter [the Arnold Kennick Juvenile Court Law] is to secure for each minor under the jurisdiction of the juvenile court such care and guidance, preferably in his own home, as will serve the spiritual, emotional, mental, and physical welfare of the minor and the best interests of the State; to preserve and strengthen the minor's family ties whenever possible, removing him from the custody of his parents only when his welfare or safety and protection of the public cannot be adequately safeguarded without removal; and, when the minor is removed from his own family, to secure for him custody, care, and discipline as nearly as possible equivalent to that which should have been given by his parents. This chapter shall be liberally construed to carry out these purposes."

and additional proof to bring the minor within section 600 or 601 might not be available.

It is implicit in the above quoted statement of the majority that knowledge of the wrongfulness of the act is not required for an adjudication that a minor under 14 is a person described by section 601. A minor may be adjudicated to come within section 601 where he has persistently refused to obey the reasonable and proper orders of school authorities. It would have been anomalous had the Legislature required knowledge of the wrongfulness of his act by a minor under 14 who committed a serious crime in order for the court to have jurisdiction under one section and not to have required it for a relatively lesser transgression under another. The welfare of the child and the best interests of society manifestly would make jurisdiction of the former child more imperative than jurisdiction over the latter child. Although one difference exists with respect to the disposition that may be made of a minor found to come within section 601 and a minor found to come within section 602,[5] otherwise the same dispositions are authorized for both such minors and both may be ordered confined, for example, in a juvenile home.

The common law rebuttable presumption of lack of criminal capacity of a child between 7 and 14 has been regarded as inapplicable in juvenile court proceedings. (Borders v. United States (1958) 256 F.2d 458, 459; see Juvenile Court v. State (1918) 139 Tenn. 549, 201 S.W. 771, 773; 31 Am.Jur. (1958 ed.) Juvenile Courts, etc., § 39, p. 317; Rubin, Crime and Juvenile Delinquency (1961) p. 56.) The cited cases reasoned that juvenile court proceedings are not criminal in nature and are not instituted to punish the child for any offense but rather have the purpose of providing for the child's welfare. In this state the Legislature has specifically provided that a juvenile court proceeding shall not be deemed a criminal proceeding. (Welf. & Inst.Code, § 503.) In the light of In re Gault (1967) 387 U.S. 1, 87 S.Ct. 1428, 18 L.Ed.2d 527 which held that certain procedural protections required by due process are applicable in juvenile court proceedings, such proceedings may not be regarded in all cases for every purpose as civil rather than criminal. However, as we pointed out in In re Dennis M., supra, 70 A.C. 460, 472, 75 Cal.Rptr. 1, 8, 450 P.2d 296, 303, "even after *Gault * * ** juvenile proceedings retain a *sui generis* character: although certain basic rules of due process must be observed, the proceedings are nevertheless conducted for the protection and benefit of the youth in question. * * *" Thus the conclusion reached in *Borders* and *Juvenile Court* remains valid.

In support of its position that subdivision One of section 26 applies in a juvenile court proceeding under section 602, the majority state that "the juvenile courts exercise exclusive jurisdiction over all minors under the age of 16" and that "we cannot presume the repeal of [subdivision One of] section 26 by implication; the decisions clearly

---

[5] The circumstances under which a section 601 ward and a section 602 ward may be committed to the Youth Authority are not identical. (See Welf. & Inst. Code, §§ 602, 730, 731, 733, and 734.)

establish the contrary presumption." Even if it be assumed that the former quoted statement is correct, it does not follow that subdivision One of section 26 is repealed by implication by a determination of the inapplicability of that subdivision in a juvenile court proceeding under section 602. As the majority recognize, that subdivision is applicable where an adult defendant charged with a sex crime against a child contends that the latter is an accomplice whose testimony requires corroboration (Pen.Code, § 1111).

The majority also note that "section 602 is clearly distinguishable from sections 600 and 601 with respect to the consequences of their operation upon the child: upon the application of section 602, commitment of the youth to the custody of the California Youth Authority becomes far more likely." However, the Welfare and Institutions Code places restrictions on such a commitment (§§ 733 and 734),[6] and where such a commitment is authorized it is only one of several possible alternatives.[7] Under the circumstances the fact that Youth Authority commitment may be an alternative available for a minor found to be a person described by section 602 should not preclude holding subdivision One of section 26 is inapplicable in a juvenile court proceeding under section 602.

*   *   *

Subdivision *Three* of Penal Code section 26 (insanity) has been held applicable in a juvenile court proceeding to determine whether a minor is a person described by section 602 (In re M.G.S., 267 Cal.App. 2d 329, 337, 72 Cal.Rptr. 808), but it does not follow that subdivision *One* of section 26 is likewise applicable in such a proceeding. Permitting the defense of insanity in such a proceeding does not deprive the minor of needed care (see, e.g., Welf. & Inst.Code, § 705), whereas holding subdivision One of section 26 applicable in such a proceeding can, as we have seen, deprive minors of needed care.

For the reasons above stated I would uphold the position of the Attorney General that subdivision One of section 26 is inapplicable in

---

[6] Section 733 prohibits commitment to the Youth Authority of specified persons including, among others, a ward under 8 years of age, and section 734 prohibits such a commitment "unless the judge * * * is fully satisfied that the mental and physical condition and qualifications of the ward are such as to render it probable that he will be benefited by the reformatory educational discipline or other treatment provided by the Youth Authority."

[7] Where the court has found the minor to be a person described by section 602, it may, without adjudging the minor a ward of the court, place the minor on probation under the supervision of the probation officer, or the court may adjudge the minor to be a ward of the court. (Welf. & Inst.Code, § 725.) "* * * no ward * * * shall be taken from the physical custody of a parent * * * unless upon the hearing the court finds" one of several enumerated facts (e.g. the minor has been tried on probation and has failed to reform). (Welf. & Inst.Code, § 726.) Where the court has found such a fact exists, it may order for a section 602 ward any of the types treatment authorized for a section 600 or 601 ward (e.g. commit minor to care of probation officer to be placed in suitable family home or suitable private institution, commit minor to juvenile home) or may commit the minor to the Youth Authority (Welf. & Inst.Code, § 731), subject to the restrictions heretofore mentioned.

a juvenile court proceeding to determine whether a minor comes within section 602.

McComb, J., concurs.

NOTES

1. Consider the following from In the Matter of Andrew M., 91 Misc.2d 813, 398 N.Y.S.2d 824 (Fam.Ct.1977):

> The crucial determinant of criminal behavior in the classic Common Law sense was the so-called "evil intent" or *mens rea* without which an act could not be deemed criminal in nature. *Mens rea* has been defined in terms of knowledge of the anti-social consequences of one's acts. In a perceptive analysis in the Cambridge Law Journal, Sanford H. Kadish points out the existence of two separate categories of *mens rea.* First, there is *mens rea* in its special sense in which it "—refers only to the mental state which is required by the definition of the offense to accompany the act which produces or threatens the harm" * * *. Without this intent, there can be no criminal liability for any act in question.

> The second category of *mens rea* addresses the question of legal responsibility for one's acts and classically includes the defenses of infancy and insanity * * * requiring a determination of the capacity of the perpetrator to understand the nature and wrongfulness of his act.

Id. at 825–26.

2. Even if the common law defense of infancy is not recognized in juvenile proceedings, are there circumstances in which *mens rea* cannot be proved because of the age or immaturity of the respondent? In *In the Matter of Robert M.,* 110 Misc.2d 113, 441 N.Y.S.2d 860 (Fam.Ct.1981), a different judge of the court which decided *In the Matter of Andrew M.,* supra note 1, after holding that the common law rebuttable presumption of incapacity of children 7–14 was not applicable in delinquency proceedings, went on to discuss the issue of "specific intent."

> The issue of specific intent appears to be more troublesome. The legislative scheme is based on an assumption that a child over seven is capable of forming a specific criminal intent, for surely the legislature did not intend to create a system of strict liability for children. However, there may well be cases in which a child between seven and sixteen who is developmentally slow does in fact lack the capacity to form the requisite specific intent. Appellate Courts in at least two jurisdictions have, in the face of such cases, held that the common law presumption of incapacity by reason of infancy is applicable in all delinquency trials.[8] The first of these cases, and the record of "unanimous rejection of the infancy defense in delinquency proceedings by every court that * * * faced the issue * * * [before] 1970", are reviewed in Fox, Responsibility in the Juvenile Court, 11 William and Mary L.Rev. 659, 664–74 (1970) with the conclusion that the policy of protecting a "grossly immature" or "developmentally abnormal" child from delinquency adjudication makes good sense.[9] It does not, however, seem sensible to

---

[8] Commonwealth v. Durham, 255 Pa. Super. 539, 389 A.2d 108 (1978) (involving an act by a nine year old girl who suffered from borderline retardation, id. at 109, 110); In re Gladys R., 83 Cal.Rptr. 671, 464 P.2d 127 (1970) (involving an "emotionally disturbed child of 12 years", id. at 138).

[9] Id. at 672.

give the petitioner in every delinquency case involving a child under
fourteen the burden of overcoming a presumption that the respondent could not have had the requisite specific intent, Commonwealth
v. Durham, supra, 255 Pa.Super. 545, 389 A.2d at 110–111 (dissenting opinion of Price, J.) [10]

The petitioner in a delinquency matter does, however, have the
burden of proving, beyond reasonable doubt, every element of the
crime charged, including the element of intent. In this case it is
asserted that Respondent intended to play rather than to rob. An
adult charged with robbery is entitled to acquittal if the prosecution
fails to overcome, beyond reasonable doubt, evidence that he intended to play a practical joke rather than to rob, People v. Stetz, 206
App.Div. 223, 201 N.Y.S. 79 (2d Dept. 1923). Respondent is entitled
to the same protection. Moreover, if the Respondent offers evidence that any combination of factors, including immaturity, nega-
tives the requisite specific intent, he will be exonerated unless his
evidence is overcome beyond reasonable doubt.[11]

The application of these principles protects against imposition
of undeserved punishment upon those who are "developmentally
abnormal" or "grossly immature" without imposing a common law
presumption which is inappropriate in the usual case and inconsistent with the legislative scheme for the adjudication of juvenile
offenses.

The court finds beyond reasonable doubt that Respondent intentionally committed acts which would have been criminal had he been
sixteen or older.

3. Should different principles apply to *mens rea* requirements in juvenile cases than in criminal cases? Consider the following from IJA–ABA
Juvenile Justice Standards Project, Standards Relating to Juvenile Delinquency and Sanctions (1980):

3.1 * Mens rea—lack of mens rea an affirmative defense

Where an applicable criminal statute or ordinance does not require
proof of some culpable mental state, it should be an affirmative defense
to delinquency liability that the juvenile:

[10] "* * * the law is that a child under the age of seven is conclusively presumed to lack the capacity to commit a
crime, that a child between ages seven
and fourteen is entitled to a rebuttable
presumption of incapacity and when the
age of fourteen is reached any special
immunity or presumption of incapacity
ceases. But these presumptions * * *
have been applied where the child under
discussion is being measured against
adult standards. * * * That application I can accept. However, to make the
application in juvenile proceedings is, to
me, contrary to the whole concept of the
creation of juvenile courts, which were
created throughout the country in an attempt to depart from the traditional
treatment of children as ordinary criminal defendants. Indeed, the use of presumptions concerning a child's capacity
to commit crime was earlier born of the
same effort. The majority would give
* * * [a respondent] the benefit of
both these efforts. I would not."

[11] We do not reach the question whether in the case of a respondent near the
age of six the circumstances of the crime
and the age of the accused could, without
more, raise a reasonable doubt as to intent, see In re Andrew M., 91 Misc.2d
813, 398 N.Y.S.2d 824 (Family Ct. Kings
Co. 1977). For discussion of an analogous situation involving the insanity defense, see People v. Woodworth, 47
A.D.2d 991, 366 N.Y.S.2d 707 (4th Dept.
1975).

* Reprinted with permission from
STANDARDS RELATING TO JUVE-
NILE DELINQUENCY AND SANC-
TIONS, Copyright 1980, Ballinger Pub-
lishing Company.

A. was neither negligent nor reckless with respect to any material element of an offense penalizing the unintended consequence of risk-creating conduct; or

B. acted without knowledge or intention with respect to any material element of an offense penalizing conduct or the circumstances or consequences of such conduct.

3.2 * Mens rea—reasonableness defense

Where an applicable criminal statute or ordinance penalizes risk-creating conduct, it should be a defense to juvenile delinquency liability that the juvenile's conduct conformed to the standard of care that a reasonable person of the juvenile's age, maturity, and mental capacity would observe in the juvenile's situation.

2. INSANITY DEFENSE

STATE IN THE INTEREST OF CAUSEY

Supreme Court of Louisiana, 1978.
363 So.2d 472.

TATE, JUSTICE.

At the instance of a juvenile made defendant in juvenile proceedings, we granted certiorari to determine whether a juvenile has a right to plead not guilty by reason of insanity and a right to a hearing to determine his mental capacity to assist in his defense. La., 357 So.2d 1159.

Facts

Pate Causey, age 16, was petitioned into the Orleans Parish juvenile court, charged with armed robbery. His attorney filed a motion, the substance of which was that defendant be allowed to plead not guilty and not guilty by reason of insanity, and that the judge appoint a panel of psychiatrists to perform comprehensive tests to determine whether defendant was legally insane at the time the act was committed, and also whether defendant was legally competent to aid in his own defense.

Several psychological tests had been performed upon the defendant, and the report of the testing psychologists had recommended psychiatric evaluation. A psychiatrist had interviewed the defendant, without access to the psychological test results. Defense counsel wished to subpoena the psychiatrist, whose report he had been given by the judge at the time of the hearing on the motion. After indicating his inclination to deny the motion, the judge asked the defense attorney if he would "submit it [the question whether defendant was competent to assist in his defense] on that [the psychiatrist's report]." Defense counsel responded, "I submit on the report," and the court denied the motion.

* Reprinted with permission from STANDARDS RELATING TO JUVENILE DELINQUENCY AND SANC-TIONS, Copyright 1980, Ballinger Publishing Company.

The Right of a Juvenile to Plead Insanity

There is no statutory right to plead not guilty by reason of insanity in a Louisiana juvenile proceeding, since such proceedings are conducted as civil proceedings, with certain enumerated differences. La.R.S. 13:1579 (1977).[12] We hold, however, that the due process guaranties of the Fourteenth Amendment to the United States Constitution, and of Article I, Section 2 of the Louisiana Constitution, require that a juvenile be granted this right.

The only courts ever squarely confronted with the issue have held that, at least in adult proceedings, the denial of the right to plead insanity, with no alternative means of exculpation or special treatment for an insane person unable to understand the nature of his act, violates the concept of fundamental fairness implicit in the due process guaranties. Some recent federal cases have also spoken of the insanity plea in terms indicating that the right to assert it has constitutional dimensions of a due process (fundamental fairness) nature.

The insanity defense, and the underlying notion that an accused must understand the nature of his acts in order to be criminally responsible (the *mens rea* concept), are deeply rooted in our legal tradition and philosophy, as the cited decisions note. We deem it clear, as held by the Mississippi and Washington supreme courts, that the due process-fundamental fairness concepts of our state and federal constitutions would be violated, at least in adult prosecutions for crimes requiring intent, if an accused were denied the right to plead the insanity defense. Cf. also Robinson v. California, 370 U.S. 660, 82 S.Ct. 1417, 8 L.Ed.2d 758 (1962).

However, not every constitutional right guaranteed to adults by the concept of fundamental fairness is automatically guaranteed to juveniles.

The United States Supreme Court has undertaken a case-by-case analysis of juvenile proceedings, making not only the historical inquiry into whether the rights asserted were part of fundamental fairness, but also a functional analysis of whether giving the particular right in question to the juvenile defendant would interfere with any of the beneficial aspects of a juvenile proceeding. Only those rights that are both "fundamental" and "essential," in that they perform a function too important to sacrifice in favor of the benefits theoretically afforded by a civil-style juvenile proceeding, have been held to be required in such proceedings. McKeiver v. Pennsylvania, 403 U.S. 528, 91 S.Ct. 1976, 29 L.Ed.2d 647 (1970); In re Winship, 397 U.S. 358, 90 S.Ct. 1068, 25 L.Ed.2d 368 (1970); In re Gault, 387 U.S. 1, 87 S.Ct. 1428, 18 L.Ed.2d 527 (1967).

The same approach was adopted by a majority of this court in determining which due process rights are guaranteed to juveniles by the Louisiana Constitution, in State in Interest of Dino, 359 So.2d 586

---

[12] Act 172 of 1978 enacted a Code of Juvenile Procedure (C.J.P.) which replaces much prior statutory regulation. La.C.J.P. art. 24 provides similarly to former La.R.S. 13:1579 (1977).

(La.1978). (Since we ultimately find this defendant's right to plead insanity to be guaranteed by the state and federal due process clauses, we need not reach the additional equal protection argument advanced, by which juveniles would be denied the equal protection of the laws if they were not permitted as are adults to be exculpated by insanity from criminal responsibility.)

McKeiver, Winship, and *Gault* imposed on juvenile proceedings a host of traditional criminal trial safeguards—the right to appropriate notice, to counsel, to confrontation and cross-examination, and the privilege against self-incrimination—and declined to impose only one safeguard, the right to a jury trial.

While the due process right to a jury trial has been held to be an element of "fundamental fairness," at least in non-petty adult proceedings, Duncan v. Louisiana, 391 U.S. 145, 88 S.Ct. 1444, 20 L.Ed.2d 491 (1968), the court's emphasis in *McKeiver* was not on the degree of "fundamentality," but on the *function* served by the jury trial. The plurality saw the jury as a component in the factfinding process, and as such, *not* "a necessary component of accurate factfinding." 403 U.S. at 543, 91 S.Ct. at 1985. Only after finding that the jury trial—although "fundamental" for adults—was not really "essential" to a fair trial proceeding, i.e., did not perform a function that could not be adequately performed by some other procedure, did the court examine the impact of a jury trial upon the beneficial effects of the juvenile system, and conclude that it would "bring with it into that system the traditional delay, the formality, and the clamor of the adversary system and, possibly, the public trial." Id. at 550, 91 S.Ct. at 1988.

In *Winship,* the court held that a juvenile could not be adjudged to have violated a criminal statute by a mere preponderance of the evidence. The standard of proof "beyond a reasonable doubt" was held to play "a vital role in the American scheme of criminal procedure. It is a prime instrument for reducing the risk of convictions resting on factual error. * * * '[A] person accused of a crime * * * would be at a severe disadvantage * * * if he could be adjudged guilty and imprisoned for years on the strength of the same evidence as would suffice in a civil case.'" 397 U.S. at 363, 90 S.Ct. at 1072.

Underlying the functional analysis of the two procedures examined in *McKeiver* and *Winship,* was not only the consideration of whether equally effective safeguards existed to the rights sought to be imported into juvenile proceedings, but also a consideration of the realistic role played by these two rights in safeguarding juvenile rights at actual trials: the "beyond a reasonable doubt standard" actually kept the juvenile in *Winship* out of jail, whereas there was no evidence that a jury trial in *McKeiver* would have done so.

The availability of some procedure for differentiating between those who are culpably responsible for their act and those who are merely ill is, as we have seen, a part of "fundamental fairness." Moreover, it is hard to see that any important aim of the juvenile system is thwarted by affording such a distinction to the mentally ill juvenile.

The function of the insanity plea is much more akin to that of the burden of proof imposed on juvenile proceedings in *Winship*, than of the jury trial involved in *McKeiver* and *Dino*. An insanity defense, like a high burden of proof, will generically spell the difference between conviction and acquittal. That there is perhaps a lesser stigma associated with an adjudication of juvenile delinquency than with an adult criminal conviction, and that juvenile incarceration is theoretically calculated to rehabilitate rather than to punish, were deemed constitutionally insignificant in *Winship*.

In the present case, further, the state expressly does not contest the issue whether this juvenile should be allowed to plead not guilty and not guilty by reason of insanity when charged with a serious crime.

*   *   *

Conclusion

The right to plead insanity, absent some other effective means of distinguishing mental illness from moral culpability, is also fundamental. There is no compelling reason to deny either of these constitutional rights to juveniles charged with conduct that would be serious crimes if committed by adults.

Here, there were facts in the record to put the trial court on notice that the defendant might be mentally retarded or insane. A defendant in a juvenile proceeding has the right to plead not guilty and not guilty by reason of insanity. Under the showing made, this defendant also had the right to a more thorough mental (psychiatric) examination, followed by a contradictory hearing.

Decree

For the foregoing reasons, the ruling of the trial judge denying applicant's motion is reversed, and the case is remanded to the district court for further proceedings consistent with the views expressed by this opinion.

Reversed and remanded.

SANDERS, C.J., dissents and assigns reasons.

SUMMERS, J., dissents.

MARCUS, J., dissents for reasons assigned by SANDERS, C.J.

SANDERS, CHIEF JUSTICE (dissenting).

This proceeding was instituted by petition in the Juvenile Court for the Parish of Orleans, alleging that Pate Causey, age 16, had committed armed robbery upon Margarette Williams. After a preliminary hearing, the judge ruled that there was probable cause to hold the youth for hearing on the petition.

Later, defense counsel filed two motions, a motion to suspend proceedings and a motion to enter a plea of "not guilty and not guilty by reason of insanity." Both motions were founded upon the following allegations:

"(1) Defendant's inability to assist his attorney in the preparation of his defense;

"(2) Certain psychiatric tests that have been administered at the Youth Study Center in New Orleans, seemingly substantiate the fact that this defendant is mentally incompetent and should not be allowed to stand trial in this condition."

At the hearing on the motions, defense counsel submitted the motions on the psychiatric evaluation of Dr. Patrick Dowling of the court's Youth Study Center.

Based upon the submission, the court ruled that the youth was competent to assist counsel and indicated that the case would later be assigned for hearing. The court made no ruling on his psychiatric condition at the time of the offense.

In this Court, the defense submits one assignment of error, reciting two arguments: * * * (2) that the defense should be allowed to plead "not guilty and not guilty by reason of insanity."

The majority * * * also holds that due process guarantees require that a juvenile be accorded the right to plead not guilty by reason of insanity. * * *

The holding that a plea of not guilty by reason of insanity is constitutionally required in Louisiana juvenile law is based upon the premise that the present statute is constitutionally deficient in not providing procedures for exploring insanity at the time of the offense.

In my opinion, the basic premise is untenable. The Juvenile Court Law contains ample procedures to deal with the issue. LSA–R.S. 13:1570 provides in pertinent part:

"Except as otherwise provided herein, the court shall have exclusive original jurisdiction in proceedings:

" * * *

"E. For the commitment of a mentally defective or mentally disordered child in accordance with the provisions of law for commitment of such persons. If it shall appear that any child concerning whom a petition has been filed is mentally defective or mentally disordered, the court, before committing him to an institution, may cause such child to be examined by a qualified psychiatrist, physician, or psychologist. On the written statement of such psychiatrist or physician that such child is mentally disordered, or on the written statement of such psychologist that such child is mentally defective, or at the discretion of the court, the court may, by observing the procedure prescribed by existing laws commit such child to an appropriate institution authorized by law to receive and care for such children. The parent, tutor or person having the care of such child shall be given due notice of any proceedings hereunder."

LSA–R.S. 13:1583 authorizes the psychiatric examination and commitment of a child to a hospital in any case.

LSA–R.S. 13:1579 authorizes consideration of "social, psychological and psychiatric studies" at the hearing on a delinquency petition.

LSA–R.S. 13:1580 provides in pertinent part:

"A.　If the court finds that a child is within the purview of R.S. 13:1561 through 13:1592, it may adjudge the child to be a neglected child or delinquent child, as defined in R.S. 13:1569, or a child in need of supervision.　The court, in its judgment, after giving consideration to the gravity of the alleged offense, the police record of the juvenile, and when available the social, psychological, and psychiatric studies conducted on the juvenile, may:

"＊　＊　＊

"(3) Make such other disposition of the child as the court deems to be for the best interests of the child, including commitment to a public mental hospital or institution for the mentally defective.　However, nothing herein shall be construed as authorizing the removal of the child from the custody of his parents unless his welfare or the safety and protection of the public cannot, in the opinion of the court, be adequately safeguarded without such removal.

"＊　＊　＊

"B.　No adjudication by the court upon the status of any child shall operate to impose any of the civil disabilities ordinarily resulting from conviction, nor shall any child be deemed a criminal by reason of such adjudication, and such adjudication shall not be deemed a conviction.　The disposition of a child or any evidence given in the court shall not operate to disqualify the child in any future civil service application or appointment."

The 1978 Code of Juvenile Procedure contains similar procedures. See Articles 61, 70, 81, 83A(7), 86D.

Thus, there is built into the juvenile court law procedures for pre-hearing mental and psychiatric examinations.　Further examinations may be made in connection with the hearing.　In the event a mental defect or insanity is found, the court is authorized to commit the child to a mental institution at any stage of the proceeding.

Juvenile proceedings are non-criminal.　LSA–R.S. 13:1580B. Hence, there is no provision for formal criminal-court pleas.　The essential inquiry is whether the child admits or denies the factual allegations of the petition.　See Art. 55, Code of Juvenile Procedure (1978).[13]　Whether he admits or denies the allegations, however, his competence to assist counsel and his sanity are always pertinent issues under juvenile procedures.　There is no room in these proce-

---

[13] Because of the criminal law experience of counsel, the response to the petition is frequently voiced as "not guilty." This expression, though technically inap-propriate since juvenile proceedings are non-criminal, is received as a denial of the allegations of the petition.

dures for a plea of not guilty by reason of insanity, because the competence and sanity of the child are before the court at all stages.

The majority holding imports into the juvenile law formal criminal-court pleading and procedure by means of constitutional analysis based upon what I believe to be an erroneous premise. I greatly fear that the constitutional holding will disrupt juvenile procedures, so recently codified in the Code of Juvenile Procedure of 1978.

For the reasons assigned, I respectfully dissent.

NOTES

1. Similarly to the *Causey* dissent, the majority in In the Matter of C.W.M., 407 A.2d 617 (D.C.App.1979), held that because the mental illness of the juvenile must be taken into account by the authority making the disposition, there is no need, under either due process or equal protection standards, to consider the insanity defense—qua insanity defense—at the adjudication stage of a delinquency proceeding.

2. The court in State v. Ferrell, 209 S.W.2d 642 (Tex.Civ.App.1948) resolved the question whether insanity can be a defense in delinquency cases with this comment: "Art. 2338–1 provides that one is a delinquent child who violates any penal law of this state of the grade of felony. It is our opinion that Mary Katheryn Ferrell was not guilty of a felony if she was insane at the time of the killing." Id. at 643.

3. IJA–ABA Juvenile Justice Standards Project, Standards Relating to Juvenile Delinquency and Sanctions (1980) proposes the following standard concerning the insanity defense:

3.5 * Responsibility

Juvenile delinquency liability should not be imposed if, at the time of the conduct charged to constitute the offense, as a result of mental disease or defect, the juvenile lacked substantial capacity to appreciate the criminality of his or her conduct or to conform his or her conduct to the requirements of the law.

4. There is a split of authority concerning the availability of the insanity defense in juvenile delinquency determinations. In some states, case law has determined whether the defense is available. In other states, the legislature has made this decision. For example, N.J.S.A. 2A:4A–40 provides in pertinent part: "All defenses available to an adult charged with a crime, offense or violation shall be available to a juvenile charged with committing an act of delinquency." In State in the Interest of R.G.W., 135 N.J.Super. 125, 342 A.2d 869 (1975), *affirmed*, 70 N.J. 185, 358 A.2d 473 (1976), the Superior Court of New Jersey held that "all defenses" included the insanity defense, thereby overriding the holding of State in the Interest of H.C., 106 N.J.Super. 583, 256 A.2d 322 (1969), an earlier case in which the same court held that the insanity defense was not available to juveniles in delinquency determinations.

3. WHO IS AN "ADULT?"

All juvenile codes provide an upper age limit on the jurisdiction of the juvenile court. The variations are considerable, but most of the problems are resolved simply by resolution of factual inquiries. (How old was Jenny when she stabbed Billy?) There is an occasional problem concerning whether age at the time of the act or age at the time of the petition is controlling, statutes and cases on the point are not in agreement.

In some instances conduct is subject to penal sanctions for persons who are somewhat beyond the upper age of juvenile court jurisdiction, but not for still older persons. The following sequence of cases from New Mexico illustrates the problem.

IN RE DOE

New Mexico Court of Appeals, 1975.
87 N.M. 466, 535 P.2d 1092.

HENDLEY, JUDGE. A petition, pursuant to the Children's Code, § 13–14–1 through § 13–14–45, N.M.S.A.1953 (Repl.Vol. 3, 1969, Supp.1973), was filed alleging that the child, age sixteen, was a delinquent and in need of care or rehabilitation, in that he did violate the Village of Carrizozo curfew ordinance and that he did possess alcoholic beverages "* * * contrary to the provisions of Sections 45–10–12 and 46–10–19 N.M.S.A. (1953)." The child and his parents were pro se at the hearing on the petition. The child admitted he committed the two offenses. On the basis of the admissions the Children's Court entered a Judgment and Order and the child was "* * * committed to the custody of the New Mexico Department of [C]orrections for no more than sixty (60) days for comprehensive social and psychological evaluation. * * *" The child appeals alleging the petition was defective and therefore the Children's Court was without jurisdiction to enter its Judgment and Order. We agree.

Section 13–14–3(O), supra, defines a *delinquent child* as a child who has committed a delinquent act and is in need of care or rehabilitation. Section 13–14–3(N), supra, defines delinquent act as an act committed by a child, *which would be designated as a crime under the law if committed by an adult,* except for offenses under municipal traffic codes or the Motor Vehicle Code.

The restricted hours section of the Village of Carrizozo curfew ordinance states:

"* * * It shall be unlawful for any juvenile, male or female, under the age of eighteen (18) years to be upon any of the streets of the Town at any time between the hours of nine thirty o'clock (9:30) P.M. and five o'clock (5:00) A.M., unless accompanied by a parent or guardian. * * *"

This section does not come within the purview of § 13–14–3(N), supra, defining a delinquent act. The ordinance relates to any juvenile under the age of eighteen years.

As to the second charge, § 45–10–12, N.M.S.A.1953 (Repl.Vol. 7, 1966), relates to the conduct of election for the creation of a weed control district. Section 46–10–19, N.M.S.A.1953 (Repl.Vol. 7, 1966) is the penalty section of the Alcoholic Beverage Act. Neither of these sections constitutes a delinquent act as defined by § 13–14–3(N), supra.

Further, the fact that the child did possess alcoholic beverages does not constitute a delinquent act as defined in § 13–14–3(N), supra. The possession of alcoholic beverages would not be a crime under the law if committed by an adult.

Accordingly, neither of the charges constituted a delinquent act. The Children's Court was without jurisdiction to enter the Judgment and Order. See In Re Doe, 87 N.M. 170, 531 P.2d 218 (Ct.App.1975).

By the foregoing, we are not saying that a valid petition pursuant to § 13–14–3(M), supra, and § 13–14–9(A)(2), supra,[a] asserting the aforementioned two counts, would be jurisdictionally defective. The cause is reversed and remanded with instructions to dismiss the petition with prejudice.

It is so ordered.

WOOD, C.J., and SUTIN, J., concur.

STATE v. DOE

Supreme Court of New Mexico, 1975.
88 N.M. 137, 537 P.2d 1399.

OPINION

MONTOYA, JUSTICE.

On February 27, 1975, an amended petition was filed in the Children's Court Division of the District Court of Lincoln County, allegedly pursuant to the Children's Code, §§ 13–14–1 to 45, N.M.S.A. 1953 (Repl.Vol. 3, 1973 Supp.). The petition alleged that John Doe, age sixteen, was a "delinquent child, and in need of care or rehabilitation" in that he had violated the Village of Carrizozo curfew ordinance § 6–9–1 (actually § 6–8–1) and possessed alcoholic beverages

[a] Children's Code, New Mexico Statutes Annotated, section 13–14–3(M) reads:

" 'child in need of supervision' means a child who:

(1) being subject to compulsory school attendance, is habitually truant from school; or

(2) habitually disobeys the reasonable and lawful demands of his parents, guardian or custodian and is ungovernable and beyond their control; or

(3) has committed an offense not classified as criminal or one applicable only to children; and

(4) in any of the foregoing situations is in need of care or rehabilitation;"

Section 13–14–9(A) reads:

"The court has exclusive original jurisdiction of all proceedings under the Children's Code [13–14–1 to 13–14–45] in which a child is alleged to be:

(1) a delinquent child; or

(2) for the adoption of a minor; or

(3) a neglected child."

It seems obvious that (2) is a misprint. A check of the source, Laws of New Mexico, 1972, chapter 97, section 9, shows that (2) should read: "(2) a child in need of supervision; or"

contrary to § 45–10–12 (actually §§ 46–10–12 and 46–10–19, N.M. S.A., 1953 (Repl.Vol. 7, 1973 Supp.)).

At the lower court hearing the child and his parents appeared pro se, and the child admitted that he had committed the two violations. Based on these admissions, the court entered a judgment and order stating that "the Child is a Delinquent Child and in need of care and rehabilitation." In addition, the child was ordered committed to the New Mexico Department of Corrections "for no more than sixty (60) days for comprehensive social and psychological evaluation."

On March 20, 1975, the child filed a notice of appeal. The Court *P/S* of Appeals ruled that the petition filed in Children's Court was jurisdictionally defective on the grounds that neither charge constituted a "delinquent act" as the term is defined in § 13–14–3(N), supra. The cause was reversed and remanded with instructions to dismiss the petition with prejudice. A petition for writ of certiorari was then filed by the State on May 20, 1975, and granted by this court on May 26, 1975.

The sole issue which this court must decide is whether the Children's Court had jurisdiction over this cause; more specifically, whether count II, possession of alcoholic beverages, can be characterized as a "delinquent act." Petitioner has previously conceded that count I, the curfew violation, does not constitute a delinquent act.

The Court of Appeals stated in its opinion that:

> "Further, the fact that the child did possess alcoholic beverages does not constitute a delinquent act as defined in § 13–14–3(N), supra. The possession of alcoholic beverages would not be a crime under the law if committed by an adult."

This statement is incorrect, as an examination of the relevant statutes reveals.

Generally, the Children's Court has exclusive original jurisdiction of all proceedings under the Children's Code, supra, in which a child is alleged to be (1) a delinquent child; (2) a child in need of supervision; or (3) a neglected child. See § 13–14–9, supra. In this particular case, the child was charged with being a "delinquent child" which is defined in § 13–14–3(O), supra, as:

> "* * * a child who has committed a delinquent act and is in need of care or rehabilitation[.]"

In turn, a "delinquent act" is defined in § 13–14–3(N), supra, as:

> "* * * an act committed by a child, which would be designated as a crime under the law if committed by an adult, * * *."

And, according to § 13–14–3(B):

> "'adult' means an individual who is eighteen [18] years of age or older[.]"

Referring to § 46–10–12, supra, the statutory section which concerns possession of alcoholic beverages, subsection "(B)" states:

"It is a violation of the Liquor Control Act for any minor to buy, receive, possess or permit himself to be served with any alcoholic liquor except when accompanied by his parent, * * *."

Subsections "(E) and (F)" of the same statute read as follows:

"E. As used in the Liquor Control Act 'minor' means any person under twenty-one [21] years of age.

"F. Violation of this section by a minor with respect to possession is a petty misdemeanor."

When all of these statutory sections are considered together, it appears that an adult, as defined by § 13–14–3(B), supra, between the ages of eighteen and twenty-one, even though a minor, as defined by § 46–10–12(E), supra, may under certain circumstances be guilty of a crime under § 46–10–12(B), supra, when in possession of alcoholic beverages. It certainly cannot apply to any minor under the age of eighteen since, under the Children's Code, the Children's Court has exclusive jurisdiction and any illegal act committed by a child under the age of eighteen is not considered a crime, unless there is a specific exception made in the Code itself. See § 13–14–45, supra. In addition, § 13–14–30, supra, provides in pertinent part as follows:

"* * *. A judgment in proceedings on a petition under the Children's Code [13–14–1 to 13–14–45] shall not be deemed a conviction of crime nor shall it impose any civil disabilities ordinarily resulting from conviction of a crime, nor shall it operate to disqualify the child in any civil service application or appointment. * * *"

Thus, it logically follows that the act of possession of alcoholic beverages with which the child was charged may be characterized as a "delinquent act," and the allegation of "delinquent child" was proper. No other conclusion can be reached if the statutes with which we are concerned, and referred to above, are to be harmonized and given a reasonable interpretation. We are unable to discern how the Court of Appeals could hold otherwise.

Also in relation to count II, the Court of Appeals ruled that the mistaken reference to § 45–10–12, supra, constituted a jurisdictional defect. Since that statute concerned the conduct of elections for the creation of a weed control district and § 46–10–19, supra, was only a penalty section, the Court of Appeals felt that violation of neither of these statutes would constitute a "delinquent act" as defined by § 13–14–3(N), supra. We are unable to agree with this treatment of the problem.

In our opinion, the Court of Appeals was overly concerned with technicalities, exalting form over substance. First of all, it would appear that citation of § 45–10–12, supra, was a mere typographical error. By no stretch of the imagination did this child's conduct involve violation of election laws for the creation of weed control districts. And no one has seriously contended that it did. Secondly, count II did state that the specific charge was possession of alcoholic beverages, and the correct penalty provision was cited. Also, during the Children's Court hearing, the judge asked the child:

> "Next, they tell me that on the same date and place you did possess alcoholic beverages contrary to law. Do you admit or deny it?"

The child admitted this charge.

The record reveals that the child and his parents had adequate notice and knowledge of the charge, and there has been no showing of prejudice. We are aware, of course, of § 13–14–17, supra, which states that the petition must present charges with "specificity" and cite the appropriate law when violation of a statute is charged. However, we do not believe that the facts of this case amount to a violation of that statute or amount to jurisdictional defect. Certainly, the Children's Court had jurisdiction over the child, and as far as the second charge is concerned, we conclude that the court was acting within the bounds of its subject matter jurisdiction. See Grace v. Oil Conservation Commission of New Mexico, 87 N.M. 205, 531 P.2d 939 (1975).

In view of the foregoing, the cause is remanded to the Court of Appeals for further proceedings in accordance with the views expressed by this court.

It is so ordered.

McMANUS, C.J., and OMAN, and STEPHENSON, JJ., concur.

4. "EXCLUDED" OFFENSES

In many states, murder (and sometimes other very serious offenses) are excluded by statute from the jurisdiction of the juvenile court. Those legislative decisions result in little litigation. The student should keep this in mind when considering statutes which permit prosecutors to determine whether to proceed against the perpetrators of certain serious acts as criminals rather than as juvenile delinquents. The matter is considered in detail in Chapter 6 infra.

At the other end of the scale, most statutes exclude traffic offenses from the jurisdiction of the juvenile court. Why? Occasionally a problem arises determining whether particular conduct constitutes a "traffic offense." For example, in Gressel v. State, 429 N.E.2d 8 (Ind.App.1981), the court held that reckless driving was a traffic offense and therefore was excluded from juvenile court jurisdiction.

B. NON–CRIMINAL MISCONDUCT

GESICKI v. OSWALD

United States District Court, Southern District of New York, 1971.
336 F.Supp. 371, affirmed without opinion sub. nom. Oswald v. Gesicki, 406
U.S. 913, 92 S.Ct. 1773, 32 L.Ed.2d 113 (1972).

OPINION

IRVING R. KAUFMAN, CIRCUIT JUDGE:

This class action presents an issue of fundamental importance concerning the power of a state to enforce against juveniles a purportedly non-criminal statute which permits commitment of defendants to adult criminal correctional programs and facilities, but is impermissibly vague if judged by the standards applicable to penal laws. We hold that the particular provisions at issue, on their face, violate due process of law.

The procedural and factual background is well presented in Judge Lasker's opinion requesting that this three-judge court be convened. D.C., 336 F.Supp. 365. We need reiterate only the essential details necessary to frame the questions we now resolve.

Each of the three named plaintiffs was "deemed" by a County Court of New York State to be a "wayward minor" between the ages of 16 and 21, under N.Y.Code Crim.Proc. § 913–a(5) or (6), each having been found "morally depraved" or "in danger of becoming morally depraved." [14] As a result, each was subsequently sentenced to terms in the Albion and Bedford Hills Correctional Facilities, penal institutions for adult criminals.[15] All three have since been paroled from Bedford Hills, and each currently remains on parole status.

Plaintiffs rely on three arguments in requesting that we set aside their convictions, declare §§ 913–a(5) and (6) unconstitutional, and enjoin the further enforcement of those provisions. They urge that the provisions are unconstitutionally vague, that they permit

---

[14] "Any person between the ages of sixteen and twenty-one who either * * * (5) is wilfully disobedient to the reasonable and lawful commands of parent, guardian or other custodian and is morally depraved or is in danger of becoming morally depraved, or (6) who without just cause and without the consent of parents, guardians or other custodians, deserts his or her home or place of abode, and is morally depraved or is in danger of becoming morally depraved * * * may be deemed a wayward minor." Each of these provisions states two elements in the disjunctive which together constitute "waywardness." Because we find that the repeated phrase, "morally depraved or is in danger of becoming morally depraved," is impermissibly vague, we express no opinion as to plaintiffs' assertion that the other elements of these provisions are also unconstitutional on their face.

Section 913–a was allowed by the state legislature to expire August 31, 1971, but, as Judge Lasker noted, persons found to have violated the statute before that date "remain subject to its provisions until the expiration of their term in custody, parole, or probation."

[15] Plaintiffs Esther Gesicki and Dominica Morelli were both initially placed on probation. Each was subsequently found to have violated a condition of probation and sentenced to Bedford Hills. Plaintiff Marion Johnson was transferred to Bedford Hills after she had violated a condition of her parole following release from another state correctional institution.

punishment of a status or condition rather than a criminal act, and that their enforcement violates the equal protection of the laws by discriminating against 16-to-21-year olds in relation both to adults and to younger children who are not subject to the Wayward Minor statute. Since we agree with plaintiffs that the provisions under which they were convicted are unconstitutionally vague and impermissibly punish a status, we do not reach the equal protection claim.

* * *

1. *Vagueness* [16]

It is clear to us that the terms "morally depraved" and "in danger of becoming morally depraved" fall far beyond the bounds of permissible ambiguity in a standard defining a criminal act. Indeed, a penal statute purporting to outlaw "evil," as these criteria essentially do, is a paradigm of a statute "so vague that men of common intelligence must necessarily guess at its meaning and differ as to its application." Connally v. General Construction Co., 269 U.S. 385, 391, 46 S.Ct. 126, 127, 70 L.Ed. 322 (1926). The concept of morality has occupied men of extraordinary intelligence for centuries, without notable progress (among even philosophers and theologians) toward a common understanding.

By contrast with the language in question, criteria previously found too vague to pass constitutional scrutiny are models of precision. See Coates v. Cincinnati, 402 U.S. 611, 91 S.Ct. 1686, 29 L.Ed.2d 214 (1971) ("conduct * * * annoying to persons passing by"); Palmer v. City of Euclid, 402 U.S. 544, 91 S.Ct. 1563, 29 L.Ed.2d 98 (1971) ("suspicious person"); Lanzetta v. New Jersey, 306 U.S. 451, 59 S.Ct. 618, 83 L.Ed. 888 (1939) ("known to be a member of any gang"); Connally v. General Construction Co., 269 U.S. 385, 46 S.Ct. 126, 70 L.Ed. 322 (1926) ("not less than the current rate per diem wages in the locality where the work is performed").

To require more definite standards of criminal behavior than those at issue is hardly to require the "impossible." The cases the State relies on to buttress its argument that a penal statute is not unconstitutional merely because there are doubtful hypothetical cases at the margins of a basically clear standard, to the contrary, amply illustrate the intangible, diffuse, and chameleonic nature of the concept of "moral depravity." See United States v. Petrillo, 332 U.S. 1, 67 S.Ct. 1538, 91 L.Ed. 1877 (1947) ("unlawfully" and "by the use of * * * force" or threat of force "to coerce, compel or constrain");

[16] The New York Court of Appeals rejected, without setting forth its reasons, the argument that Section 913-a(5) and (6) are unconstitutionally vague in People v. Salisbury, 18 N.Y.2d 899, 276 N.Y.S.2d 634, 223 N.E.2d 43 (1966). In recent cases postdating In re Gault, 387 U.S. 1, 87 S.Ct. 1428, 18 L.Ed.2d 527 (1967), the court has refused to reconsider *Salisbury*, holding simply that determinations of waywardness were not sustained by the record. See People v. Gregory E. (anon.), 26 N.Y.2d 622, 307 N.Y.S.2d 465, 255 N.E.2d 721 (1970); People v. Martinez, 23 N.Y.2d 780, 297 N.Y.S.2d 144, 244 N.E.2d 711 (1968). Since these decisions illustrate only a scant number of instances, in which the Court of Appeals believed the facts established the juveniles were not included in the universe of "morally depraved" children, they do not appreciably diminish the vagueness of the class of remaining cases that *are* included.

United States v. Irwin, 354 F.2d 192 (2d Cir.), cert. denied 383 U.S. 967, 86 S.Ct. 1272, 16 L.Ed.2d 308 (1965) (statute prohibited giving "anything of value to any public official").

An excellent object lesson in the lack of meaning of the challenged standards is provided by the specific allegations that were the apparent basis for the adjudications of the named plaintiffs here. The state urges that those charges—involving pregnancy out of wedlock, sexual promiscuity, *suspected* drug use and truancy—are clear instances of "moral depravity," so clear, that even if the standards are otherwise vague, when applied to these plaintiffs they are clear and certain.[17] We cannot agree.

Justice Jackson, in Musser v. Utah, 333 U.S. 95, 97, 68 S.Ct. 397, 398, 92 L.Ed. 562 (1948), described the similar phrase "injurious to public morals:"

> Standing by itself it would seem to be warrant for conviction for agreement to do almost any act which a judge and jury might find at the moment contrary to his or its notions of what was good for health, morals, trade, commerce, justice or order. In some States the phrase "injurious to public morals" would be likely to punish acts which it would not punish in others because of the varying policies on such matters as use of cigarettes or liquor and the permissibility of gambling. This led to the inquiry as to whether the statute attempts to cover so much that it effectively covers nothing. Statutes defining crimes may fail of their purpose if they do not provide some reasonable standards of guilt. See, for example, United States v. [L.] Cohen Grocery Co., 255 U.S. 81, 41 S.Ct. 298, 65 L.Ed. 516, 14 A.L.R. 1045. Legislation may run afoul of the Due Process Clause because it fails to give adequate guidance to those who would be law-abiding, to advise defendants of the nature of the offense with which they are charged, or to guide courts in trying those who are accused.

[17] Esther Gesicki, who was living alone because her mother had been committed to a state mental hospital, was expelled from school because the school principal charged her with "sexual promiscuity" and later adjudicated a wayward minor. She was placed in a foster home. When her social worker refused to allow her to return home after her mother was released, Esther ran away. She then was sent to Albion and later to Bedford Hills for violating probation.

Marion Johnson lived in foster homes from the time she was 5. At 17, she had an out-of-wedlock child. When her social worker pressured her to give up the child for adoption and she refused, Marion was adjudicated a wayward minor (she previously had run away from her foster home when she was not allowed to see the father of the child). Her social work-

er allegedly told her: "If you had signed the adoption papers, you wouldn't be going to Albion."

Dominica Morelli, the first of eight children, grew up in a broken home. Her mother remarried four times, and one of her stepfathers sexually assaulted her. After her mother, an alcoholic, was found to be unfit, all the children were placed in foster homes. When Dominica ran away, her mother secured a warrant for her arrest. Dominica was allowed to remain at home, but was placed under a curfew. She has no recollection of being placed on probation. After she journeyed to Williamsport, Pennsylvania, with a friend and without her mother's permission (she was suspected of having attended a drug party), she was charged with violating probation.

2. *"Status" or "condition"*

In a sense, the question whether the statute is sufficiently precise to guide the actions of men of ordinary intelligence and understanding hearts misses the core of the issue raised by the language in question. By its terms, "morally depraved" does not refer to conduct at all, but to a condition or status of immorality. Thus, a second objection to subsections (5) and (6) is that they permit the unconstitutional punishment of a minor's condition, rather than of any specific actions,[18] as did the statute penalizing narcotics addiction condemned in *Robinson v. California*, 370 U.S. 660, 82 S.Ct. 1417, 8 L.Ed.2d 758 (1962). In *Robinson*, the Court held "that a state law which imprisons a person [afflicted with narcotics addiction] * * * as a criminal * * * inflicts a cruel and unusual punishment in violation of the Fourteenth Amendment * * *. Even one day in prison would be cruel and unusual punishment for the 'crime' of having a common cold." Id. at 667, 82 S.Ct. at 1421. Plaintiffs similarly argue that any kind of punishment for the misfortune of being a "morally depraved" minor is cruel and unusual in the constitutional sense.

3. *Parens Patriae rationale*

The state's reply to this line of argument, and implicitly to the vagueness attack as well, is that the Wayward Minor statute is not a penal statute at all, that it does not provide for criminal punishment, and hence that it is irrelevant whether as a criminal provision the standard "moral depravity" would be condemned on either asserted ground. In short, the state asserts the power of the government to act as *parens patriae* for the benefit of children and adolescents who would otherwise graduate from their youthful "wayward" tendencies to a criminal or at least unhealthy adult life. This has been the reasoning relied upon by innumerable courts in the past to sustain the constitutionality of statutes regulating or "protecting" juveniles by standards equally as vague and all-embracing as that before us. See, e.g., State v. L.N., 109 N.J.Super. 278, 263 A.2d 150 (1970); People v. Deibert, 117 Cal.App.2d 410, 256 P.2d 355 (1953). It is a rationale which has its roots deep in the history of this country's praiseworthy efforts to treat *troublesome* juveniles differently than adult criminals. See Ex parte Crouse, 4 Whart. 9 (Pa.1838) (commitment to house of detention for "incorrigible conduct"). See generally Fox, Juvenile Justice Reform: An Historical Perspective, 22 Stan.L. Rev. 1187, 1198ff. (1970).

More to the point, the state's position is that the provisions of subsection (5) and (6) are constitutional for two reasons. (First) it is

---

[18] A finding that the juvenile has been "wilfully disobedient to the reasonable and lawful commands of parent * * *" or "without just cause and without the consent of parents * * * [deserted] his or her home" is a *sine qua non* of an adjudication of "waywardness." Since these acts, as opposed to a status, are not criminal and the State singles out for punishment only those juveniles who commit the act and in addition are "morally depraved or in danger of becoming morally depraved," the State effectively hinges punishment on the status. N.Y. Code Crim.Proc. §§ 913-a(5), (6).

asserted that the statute applies only to minors, as to whom the state has not only a special authority, but a positive duty, to act when parental responsibility proves insufficient. Second, we are urged to recognize that adolescents found to be "wayward minors" are treated on the basis of their individual needs, not punished (unless punishment is a prescribed "treatment"). In connection with the latter point, we are invited to take evidence that would demonstrate that the named plaintiffs, like other members of their class, receive such ameliorative treatment as remedial schooling and vocational training following their commitment to adult penal institutions.

For the reasons developed below, we reject these arguments and find that the statute in question is, on its face, an unconstitutionally vague penal law, regardless of the nature of the treatment actually accorded these or any other defendants adjudicated "wayward." Another way of stating our conclusion is that the statute provides wholly inadequate safeguards against arbitrary application, and insufficient guarantees that minors sentenced as "wayward" will be treated non-punitively.[19]

4. *The Penal Character of the "Wayward Minor" Statute*

In attempting to show that the statute is not criminal or penal, the state relies on N.Y.Code Crim.Proc. § 913–dd, which provides that an adjudication under § 913–a may not disqualify the minor from public employment or deprive him or her of any right or privilege. Nor is a wayward minor "denominated a criminal * * * nor shall such determination be deemed a conviction."

Of the two points, the second is at the same time the least tenable and the most pernicious, because it suggests that constitutional protections can be circumvented by "soft" language. Professor Lon Fuller has aptly captured in a sentence the potential for eroding due process guarantees were labels unquestionably accepted as describing reality: "When an attempt is made to hide the harsh realities of criminal justice behind euphemistic descriptions, a corrupting irony may be introduced into ordinary speech that is fully as frightening as Orwell's 'Newspeak.'" Anatomy of the Law 57 (Mentor ed., 1968). As Justice Fortas observed in a similar context, speaking (for the Court) of the discrepancy between procedures in adult and juvenile courts, "So wide a gulf between the State's treatment of the adult and of the child requires a bridge sturdier than mere verbiage. * * *"[20] In re Gault, 387 U.S. 1, 29–30, 87 S.Ct. 1428, 1445, 18 L.Ed.2d 527 (1957).

[19] We emphasize that we are not concerned here with state procedures which lead to special supervision of juveniles, and not incarceration with adult criminals. We fully recognize the justification and wisdom of identifying and affording bona fide treatment to juveniles who exhibit behavioral deviations requiring treatment and intervention without which they might, in time, become adult criminals.

[20] In Giaccio v. Pennsylvania, 382 U.S. 399, 86 S.Ct. 518, 15 L.Ed.2d 447 (1966), the Court curtly dismissed an assertion that an assessment of costs permitted to be made by a jury against a defendant following his acquittal of criminal charges, guided by no standards whatever, was merely a "civil" sanction and hence not subject to the vagueness test applicable to criminal statutes:

The penal character of the Wayward Minor statute is clearly indicated by several factors. It is important to distinguish the now-expired Wayward Minor statute at issue in this litigation from New York's statutory scheme for treating juvenile offenders. Except where jurisdiction in cases of unusually serious crimes is transferred to the adult courts, all offenses committed by minors under the age of 16 in New York are heard by the Family Courts. These juvenile offenders may not be incarcerated in an adult prison, and the provisions conferring jurisdiction on the Family Courts in these juvenile cases is contained in the Family Court Act, not in the Criminal Code. See N.Y.—McKinney's Family Court Act, art. 7.

By contrast, the Wayward Minor statute permits the incarceration of those adjudicated under it in any of the correctional institutions maintained by the State of New York for the incarceration of adult criminals, the statute itself is contained in the Criminal Code, and trials are conducted in courts of general criminal jurisdiction. Confinement in an adult prison may continue for as long as three years. The New York Court of Appeals has recently drawn attention to the gulf between New York's methods of dealing with juvenile delinquents and with wayward minors:

> "The public safety factors involved in [the release of "wayward minors, youthful offenders, and other young criminals"] are deemed much more important than those connected with juvenile delinquents. Rehabilitation is, of course, a factor, a hopefully desired goal, in the treatment of every type of criminal, and there are special reformative and rehabilitative measures applied and adopted to young criminals * * *. Moreover, the punitive and custodial aspects of their incarceration are much more rigorous than those prescribed for juveniles and, for the State's own protection, much more closely resemble those mandated for adult criminals." (footnote omitted) Matter of Jesmer, 29 N.Y.2d 5, 10, 323 N.Y.S.2d 417, 421, 271 N.E.2d 905, 907 (1971).

5. *Absence of Limits to Discretion*

As the quotation from *Jesmer* suggests, it is not an acceptable answer to say that some minors found "wayward" are in fact treated appropriately for medical, psychological, or social disorders. Such instances of effective treatment, if they exist, would fail to distinguish the Wayward Minor statute from criminal legislation generally. It is safe to say that few if any prison administrators today would describe the function of the institutions they direct as entirely punitive, and most would undoubtedly cite "rehabilitation" or the equivalent as their most important goal. Surely the vagueness doctrine would not become obsolete if all criminal statutes were denominated "correctional statutes" and civil penalties for criminal convictions were abolished, but that is the implication of the state's argument.

"Both liberty and property are specifically protected by the Fourteenth Amendment against any state deprivation which does not meet the standards of due process, and this protection is not to be avoided by the simple label a State chooses to fasten upon its conduct or its statute." Id. at 402, 86 S.Ct. at 520.

It is instructive to recall in this connection that the first state institution for troublesome juveniles the New York House of Refuge, was designed in part to "treat" youngsters through such methods as "solitary confinement, strict discipline, and a coarse diet." Fox, supra, at 1198.

Moreover, we cannot blind ourselves to the deplorable state of prisons in this country. Prison focus on confinement rather than therapy and education certainly cannot be the answer to preventing juveniles from growing into adult criminals. The papers submitted to this court disclose that New York wayward minors suffer the misfortune of forced association with those who already have adopted crime as a way of life. It must be a painful experience when the Director of the State's Division for Youth, Milton Luger, is driven to state: "With the exception of a relatively few youths, it would probably be better for all concerned if young delinquents were not detected, apprehended or institutionalized. Too many of them get worse in our care." Samuels, When Children Collide with the Law, New York Times, Magazine Section 44, 146 (Dec. 5, 1971).

The central fallacy in the assertion that the statute might be viewed as the equivalent of a provision for the compulsory treatment of narcotics addiction, for example, see Robinson v. California, 370 U.S. 660, 665, 82 S.Ct. 1417, 1419, 8 L.Ed.2d 758 (1962),[21] is that the statute fails to require any course of treatment at all. Specifically, *there is no assurance that wayward minors will be given special treatment substantially distinguishable from that accorded to criminals and reasonably related to the condition upon which the adjudication of waywardness is based.*[22] Absent such a minimal guarantee against arbitrary application of the statute, the juvenile must rely on the good intentions and skills of courts and administrators. But "unbridled discretion, however benevolently motivated, is frequently a poor substitute for principle and procedure." In re Gault, supra, 387 U.S. at 18, 87 S.Ct. at 1439. Like the statute at issue in *Robinson*, the wayward minors statute "is not a law which even purports to provide or require medical treatment." 370 U.S. at 666, 82 S.Ct. at 1420.

That these plaintiffs are juveniles does not render the failure to guard against arbitrariness any less intolerable. In McKeiver v. Pennsylvania, 403 U.S. 528, 91 S.Ct. 1976, 29 L.Ed.2d 647 (1971), the Supreme Court held that juveniles do not have a constitutional right to a jury trial in delinquency proceedings, thus finding that not all the safeguards afforded adults in criminal trials apply to juvenile proceedings. But, as we have observed, the wayward minor statute does

---

21 "[I]n the interest of the general health or welfare of its inhabitants, a State might establish a program of compulsory treatment for those addicted to narcotics."

22 * * * We do not intend to intimate that a statute which does provide sufficient guarantees against arbitrariness on its face would be immune from attack as failing to provide treatment in practice. See, e.g., Rouse v. Cameron, 125 U.S. App.D.C. 366, 373 F.2d 451 (1966); Lake v. Cameron, 124 U.S.App.D.C. 264, 254 F.2d 657 (1966). See generally, Note, The Nascent Right to Treatment, 53 Va. L.Rev. 1134 (1967).

not establish a juvenile delinquency proceeding. It is substantially equivalent to a criminal statute. Moreover, in *McKeiver*, Justice Blackmun speaking for the court reaffirmed that "the applicable due process standard in juvenile proceedings * * * is fundamental fairness." 403 U.S. at 543, 91 S.Ct. at 1985. We are told, however, that lack of specificity in a penal statute "violates the first essential of due process of law," Connally v. General Construction, 269 U.S. 385, 391, 46 S.Ct. 126, 127, 70 L.Ed. 322 (1926). "One cannot measure our just treatment with a yardstick made of rubber." L. Fuller, supra, at 56. A statute indistinguishable in any substantial respect from a criminal provision, which fails to define the conduct that will bring a juvenile within its reach with sufficient specificity to protect against arbitrary application and to alert the malefactor to the conduct proscribed, does not comport with fundamental fairness.[23]

6. *Conclusion*

For the reasons stated, we set aside the convictions of the named plaintiffs and all members of the class they represent, declare former N.Y.Code Crim.Proc. §§ 913–a(5) and (6) unconstitutional, and enjoin defendants, their employees, agents, successors and all persons in active concert and participation with them, from enforcing these provisions.

JOHNSON v. OPELOUSAS

United States Court of Appeals, Fifth Circuit, 1981.
658 F.2d 1065.

Before INGRAHAM, POLITZ and WILLIAMS, CIRCUIT JUDGES.

JERRE S. WILLIAMS, CIRCUIT JUDGE:

This case involves an action by a mother and her son to challenge the constitutionality of the nocturnal juvenile curfew ordinance of the City of Opelousas, Louisiana. The district court upheld, with a minor exception, the constitutionality of the ordinance. See Johnson v. City of Opelousas, 488 F.Supp. 433 (W.D.La.1980). We reverse.

I. Facts

On August 16, 1978, appellant Madeline Johnson's son, James Johnson, then fourteen years old, was arrested at 2:05 a.m. by a police officer of the City of Opelousas under Opelousas Code § 18–8.1

---

[23] See People v. Munoz, 9 N.Y.2d 51, 211 N.Y.S.2d 146, 172 N.E.2d 535 (1961), holding unconstitutional for vagueness a New York City Administrative Code provision permitting criminal prosecution of minors under 21 years of age who carried "any knife or sharp pointed or edged instrument * * *." "Juvenile delinquents," the court observed, "can be highly dangerous, especially in large cities. They cannot be legislated out of existence, however, *nor be held guilty of offenses on the sole basis of status*, or except insofar as they may be found guilty from their conduct of violating criminal or quasi-criminal statutes that are sufficiently definite so that one may know in advance what is prohibited * * *." Id. at 60, 211 N.Y.S.2d at 153, 172 N.E.2d at 540 (emphasis added). The court concluded that "The purpose could only be to enable prosecution of those whom the police believe to be bad boys and girls." Id. at 58, 211 N.Y.S.2d at 151, 172 N.E.2d at 539.

(1972),[24] the nocturnal juvenile curfew ordinance of Opelousas. James Johnson subsequently was found to be in violation of the ordinance as a result of this incident. He was first placed on probation, then was placed in a private juvenile residential facility, and eventually was released and allowed to live at home with his mother in Opelousas. No appeal was taken from this adjudication.

Appellants, Madeline Johnson, on the behalf of herself, her then minor son, James Johnson, and all other minors similarly situated, and James Johnson, suing by his mother as his next friend, then brought this action in the United States District Court for the Western District of Louisiana pursuant to 42 U.S.C. § 1983 challenging the constitutionality of Opelousas' juvenile curfew ordinance on several grounds. The defendants are the City of Opelousas, Thomas Edwards, Mayor of Opelousas, and Howard Zerangue, Police Chief of Opelousas.

Appellants sought to maintain the suit as a class action under Rule 23(b)(2) of the Federal Rules of Civil Procedure, the class being "all persons who have been or in the future will be arrested or detained under § 18–8.1." Although it expressly found that all of the requirements of Rule 23(a) and (b)(2), Fed.R.Civ.P., had been satisfied, the district court nevertheless denied class status to appellants. The court reasoned that a class action was "unnecessary" because "any declaratory or injunctive relief to the named plaintiffs would inure to the benefit of other similarly situated minors." 488 F.Supp. at 435–36.

On April 16, 1980, the district court upheld the constitutionality of the curfew ordinance, with one minor exception.[25] The court entered a final judgment dismissing the action on the merits.

Appellants now appeal from this judgment. They initially claim that the district court abused its discretion in denying class certification. As to the merits of their suit, they assert, as they did below, a

---

[24] Opelousas Code § 18–8.1 provides as follows:

(a) It shall be unlawful for any unemancipated minor under the age of seventeen (17) years to travel, loiter, wander, stroll, or play in or upon or traverse any public streets, highways, roads, alleys, parks, places of amusements and entertainment, places and buildings, vacant lots or other unsupervised places in the City of Opelousas, Louisiana, between the hours of 11:00 p.m. on any Sunday, Monday, Tuesday, Wednesday or Thursday night and 4:00 a.m. of the following day, or 1:00 a.m. on any Friday or Saturday night and 4:00 a.m. of the following day, all official time of the City of Opelousas, Louisiana, unless the said minor is accompanied by his parents, tutor or other responsible adult or unless the said minor is upon an emergency errand.

(b) Any minor violating any of the provisions of this section shall be deemed a neglected child, as such term is defined in Louisiana Revised Statutes, Title 13, Sections 1569 and 1570, as now enacted or hereafter amended or reenacted and such minor and his parents, tutor or other adult having the care and custody of such minor shall be dealt with under proper procedure in any juvenile court having jurisdiction of such child. (Ord. No. 3, §§ 1, 2, 6–14–72)

[25] The district court held that the portion in subsection (b) of the ordinance which provides that a violator would be deemed a "neglected child" is unconstitutionally vague and must be deleted in the application of that subsection. 488 F.Supp. at 441–44.

broad challenge to the constitutionality of the curfew ordinance under the United States Constitution specifically urging that the ordinance: (1) is unconstitutionally vague and overbroad on its face, in violation of the due process clause of the Fourteenth Amendment; (2) violates the minor appellant's rights of freedom of speech, freedom of association, freedom of assembly, and freedom of religion under the First and Fourteenth Amendments; (3) violates the minor's substantive due process rights under the Fourteenth Amendment to move freely and to use the public streets in a way that does not interfere with the personal liberties of others; (4) violates the constitutional rights of parents under the Fourteenth Amendment to direct the upbringing of their children and the constitutional guarantee of family autonomy; (5) violates the minor appellant's constitutional rights of interstate and intrastate travel guaranteed by the commerce clause of Article 1, Section 8 and the privileges and immunities clauses of the Fourteenth Amendment and Article 4, Section 2; and (5) violates the equal protection clause of the Fourteenth Amendment.

* * *

Having reversed the class certification denial, certified the class, and found appellants to be proper class representatives, we need not return the case to the district court before we address the merits of appellants' constitutional claim. Although the district court did not consider the case as a class action, its refusal to certify the class for "lack of need" implicitly recognized that the questions presented for judicial determination would remain the same whether the case proceeded as a personal or as a class action. James Johnson made a facial attack on the constitutionality of the ordinance, raising no factual dispute concerning the particular circumstances of his arrest and conviction. He and his mother could and did raise all pertinent issues, and further factual development in the court is not necessary to avoid prejudice to the class. In sum, this is a purely legal dispute arising from stipulated facts, 434 F.Supp. at 434, and we proceed to the merits of the Johnsons' challenge.

IV. Overbreadth

We turn to appellants' contention that the Opelousas juvenile curfew ordinance is unconstitutionally overbroad. The ordinance prohibits unemancipated minors under seventeen years of age from being on the public streets or in a public place between 11:00 p.m. and 4:00 a.m., Sunday through Thursday, and 1:00 a.m. and 4:00 a.m., Friday and Saturday. The only exceptions to this prohibition arise when the minor is accompanied by a parent or "responsible adult," or is upon an "emergency errand."

Although juvenile curfew ordinances are fairly common, only three federal cases to our knowledge have considered the constitutionality of such ordinances. None of the ordinances involved in these cases, however, encompassed nearly the breadth of the Opelousas ordinances. A review of the Opelousas juvenile curfew ordinance and pertinent legal authority convinces us that this curfew ordinance is constitutionally infirm in its breadth.

Rule

"A law is void on its face for overbreadth if it 'does not aim specifically at evils within the allowable area of [government] control but, * * * sweeps within its ambit other activities that in ordinary circumstances constitute an exercise' of protected expressive or associational rights." Aladdin's Castle, Inc. v. City of Mesquite, 630 F.2d 1029, 1038 n. 13 (5th Cir.1980), prob. juris. noted, 451 U.S. 981, 101 S.Ct. 2312, 68 L.Ed.2d 838 (1981) (quoting Thornhill v. Alabama, 310 U.S. 88, 97, 60 S.Ct. 736, 741, 84 L.Ed. 1093 (1940); see also Keyishian v. Board of Regents, 385 U.S. 589, 87 S.Ct. 675, 17 L.Ed.2d 629 (1967).[26] Even though the government has a legitimate and substantial purpose behind the legislation, that purpose cannot be sought by means that "broadly stifle fundamental personal liberties" when "less drastic means for achieving the same basic purpose" are available. A state statute should not be found to be overbroad, however, unless "it is not readily subject to a narrowing construction by the state courts," Erznoznik v. City of Jacksonville, 422 U.S. 205, 216, 95 S.Ct. 2268, 2276, 45 L.Ed.2d 125 (1975) and its deterrent effect on legitimate first amendment activity is both real and substantial. Id.

The Opelousas curfew ordinance is directed at nighttime activities of minors rather than adults. Minors are "persons" under the United States Constitution, and have fundamental rights which the state must respect. Tinker v. Des Moines Independent Com. Sch. Dist., 393 U.S. 503, 511, 89 S.Ct. 733, 739, 21 L.Ed.2d 731 (1969). Although the totality of the relationship between the juvenile and the state is undefined, it is clear that minors as well as adults are protected by the Bill of Rights and the Fourteenth Amendment. In re Gault, 387 U.S. 1, 13, 87 S.Ct. 1428, 1436, 18 L.Ed.2d 527 (1967); accord, Planned Parenthood v. Danforth, 428 U.S. 52, 74, 96 S.Ct. 2831, 2843, 49 L.Ed.2d 788 (1976). Minors "are entitled to a significant measure of First Amendment protection * * *," Erznoznik v. City of Jacksonville, 422 U.S. at 212–13, 95 S.Ct. at 2274 (citing Tinker v. Des Moines Independent Community School District, supra), even though their First Amendment rights are not coextensive with those of adults. Id. 422 U.S. at 214 n. 11, 95 S.Ct. at 2275. The First Amendment rights of minors include freedom of speech, Tinker v. Des Moines Independent Community School District, supra, and freedom of religion. West Virginia State Board of Education v. Barnette, 319 U.S. 624, 63 S.Ct. 1178, 87 L.Ed. 1628 (1943). To some degree,

---

[26] In *Aladdin's Castle*, this court struck down as overbroad a municipal ordinance that barred operators of "pinball" parlors from allowing minors under seventeen to play the machines unless accompanied by a parent or guardian. We found this restriction on the fundamental associational rights of minors constitutionally infirm since it neither promoted "a sufficiently important interest [nor] employ[ed] means closely drawn to avoid unnecessary abridgement of associational freedoms." 630 F.2d at 1041 (quoting Buckley v. Valeo, 424 U.S. 1, 25, 96 S.Ct. 612, 637, 46 L.Ed.2d 659 (1976)). The ordinance at issue here targets the same age group, but casts a much broader net over the associational rights of minors by seeking to keep them off the streets altogether during certain hours.

these rights undoubtedly also entail the right to associate freely, which, like the right of adults, see Sawyer v. Sandstrom, 615 F.2d 311, 316 (5th Cir.1980), is not limited to political associations but includes associations for social, legal, or economic purposes.

Moreover, the right of "all citizens" to be free to travel within and between the states uninhibited by statutes or regulations which unreasonably burden this movement, Shapiro v. Thompson, 394 U.S. 618, 629, 89 S.Ct. 1322, 1328, 22 L.Ed.2d 600 (1969); United States v. Guest, 383 U.S. 745, 757–59, 86 S.Ct. 1170, 1177–78, 16 L.Ed.2d 239 (1966), certainly extends in some measure to juveniles, as citizens of the United States.

It is clear that these rights of minors in Opelousas currently are being burdened by that city's juvenile curfew ordinance. The curfew ordinance prohibits unemancipated minors generally from being on public streets between certain hours without their parents, with exception for minors on "emergency errands." We express no opinion on validity of curfew ordinances narrowly drawn to accomplish proper social objectives. See, e.g., Bykofsky v. Borough of Middletown, 401 F.Supp. 1242 (M.D.Penn.1975), aff'd mem., 535 F.2d 1235 (3d Cir.), cert. denied, 429 U.S. 964, 97 S.Ct. 394, 50 L.Ed.2d 333 (1976). But, under this curfew ordinance minors are prohibited from attending associational activities such as religious or school meetings, organized dances, and theater and sporting events, when reasonable and direct travel to or from these activities has to be made during the curfew period. The same inhibition prohibits parents from urging and consenting to such protected associational activity by their minor children. The curfew ordinance also prohibits a minor during the curfew period from, for example, being on the sidewalk in front of his house, engaging in legitimate employment, or traveling through Opelousas even on an interstate trip. These implicit prohibitions of the curfew ordinance overtly and manifestly infringe upon the constitutional rights of minors in Opelousas.

We are aware, of course, that in some situations the state may have the power to place regulations upon the conduct of minors that would be unconstitutional if placed upon the conduct of adults. "[T]he power of the state to control the conduct of children reaches beyond the scope of its authority over adults. * * *" Prince v. Commonwealth of Massachusetts, 321 U.S. 158, 170, 64 S.Ct. 438, 444, 88 L.Ed. 645 (1944). Restrictions on minors that would be constitutionally invalid if applied to adults may be justified only if the restrictions serve a "significant state interest * * * that is not present in the case of an adult.'" Carey v. Population Services International, 431 U.S. 678, 693, 97 S.Ct. 2010, 2020, 52 L.Ed.2d 675 (1977) (quoting Planned Parenthood v. Danforth, 428 U.S. 52, 75, 96 S.Ct. 2831, 2844, 49 L.Ed.2d 788 (1976)); see also Ginsberg v. New York, 390 U.S. 629, 638–41, 88 S.Ct. 1274, 1279–81, 20 L.Ed.2d 195 (1968).

In Bellotti v. Baird, 443 U.S. 622, 633–39, 99 S.Ct. 3035, 3043–46, 61 L.Ed.2d 797 (1979), four of the eight Justices joining in the majority holding set out three reasons explaining why some situations justify the placement of restraints on minors which would be unconstitutional if placed on adults: "the peculiar vulnerability of children; their inability to make critical decisions in an informed, mature manner; and the importance of the parental role in childrearing." Id. at 634, 99 S.Ct. at 3043. In Aladdin's Castle, Inc. v. City of Mesquite, 630 F.2d at 1043, this Court said that "[t]hese reasons may be viewed as threshold criteria." If the statute, regulation, or ordinance under question is based on any of these factors, "we would be required to determine the strength of the support provided, its relation to the [enactment] as a whole, and the extent, if any, to which it might serve to justify any special restraints on the * * * rights of minors." Id. Noting that "[n]either the Supreme Court nor this circuit has set forth the appropriate standards under which such an inquiry would be conducted," id., we found it unnecessary in *Aladdin's Castle* to engage in such analysis, due to the inapplicability of any of the factors in that case. Id.

We need not conduct such an inquiry in this case either, since none of the three factors, while possibly relevant to a general curfew mandate,[27] apply to the overly broad restrictions with which we are concerned. First, there is no issue of *peculiar* vulnerability of children with respect to their attending or traveling to or from a religious, school, commercial, or other bona fide organized activity during nighttime. Similarly, no issue of peculiar vulnerability of children is presented by a minor's being on the sidewalk in front of his house at night, engaging in legitimate nighttime employment, or traveling through Opelousas at night. These activities do not involve a minor's special vulnerability to the extent which justifies differing juvenile criminal proceedings, see e.g., In re Gault; McKeiver v. Pennsylvania, 403 U.S. 528, 91 S.Ct. 1976, 29 L.Ed.2d 647 (1978), or special control of obscene materials, see Ginsberg v. New York, both of which have been held to warrant distinguishing the rights of minors from those of adults. Instead, the activities we describe are, in terms of juvenile vulnerability, more like a minor's patronizing a coin-operated amusement center, an activity which we found in *Aladdin's Castle* to present no substantial issue regarding the special vulnerability of children. 630 F.2d at 1043.

Second, the associational, employment, and travel activities with which we are concerned and which are prohibited by the Opelousas curfew ordinance do not involve any "critical decisions" on the part of minors. It would be anomalous to permit minors to express their views on divisive public issues, Tinker v. Des Moines Independent Community School District, and to obtain abortions without parental consent, Bellotti v. Baird; Planned Parenthood v. Danforth, but to deny them the right to decide, within the bounds of parental judgment, whether or not to engage in the above activities which at present are proscribed by the curfew ordinance.

---

[27] Opelousas' asserted purposes underlying the curfew ordinance are to protect youths from nighttime dangers, reduce nocturnal juvenile crime, and enforce parental control and responsibility for their children.

Finally, to the extent that it prohibits minors from engaging in these activities, the curfew ordinance inhibits rather than promotes the parental role in child-rearing, the third listed justification for greater restrictions on the rights of minors. While Opelousas may have legitimate concern over minors being on the streets at night in general, a point on which we express no opinion here, its interest in whether juveniles engage in these specific nighttime activities is not sufficient to justify the removal of the decision as to these activities from the childrens' parents. "[T]he custody, care and nurture of the child reside first in the parents, whose primary function and freedom include preparation for obligations the state can neither supply nor hinder." Prince v. Commonwealth of Massachusetts, 321 U.S. at 166, 64 S.Ct. at 442; see also Aladdin's Castle, Inc. v. City of Mesquite, 630 F.2d at 1043.

Hence, Opelousas has no "significant * * * interest * * * that is not present in the case of an adult," Carey v. Population Services International, 431 U.S. at 693, 97 S.Ct. at 2020, which would justify the prohibition its curfew ordinance places on the specific activities of minors we have described. Therefore, this curfew ordinance, however valid might be a narrowly drawn curfew to protect society's valid interests, sweeps within its ambit a number of innocent activities which are constitutionally protected. The stifling effect upon these legitimate activities is overt and is both real and substantial. Regardless of the legitimacy of Opelousas' stated purposes of protecting youths, reducing nocturnal juvenile crime, and promoting parental control over their children, less drastic means are available for achieving these goals. Since the absence of exceptions in the curfew ordinance precludes a narrowing construction, we are compelled to rule that the ordinance is constitutionally overbroad. We accordingly reverse the district court's holding to the contrary.

Our holding is expressly limited to the unconstitutional overbreadth of the ordinance. Because we reverse on this ground, and since at oral argument appellants waived their general challenge to the constitutional authority of Opelousas to enact a properly drafted nocturnal juvenile curfew ordinance, it is unnecessary for us to address the merits of appellants' other attacks on the ordinance.

Reversed.

NOTES

1. Juvenile curfew ordinances have given rise to numerous constitutional challenges with the courts differing in their treatment of these challenges. In the first federal case to confront the issue of a juvenile curfew ordinance's constitutionality, Bykofsky v. Borough of Middletown, 401 F.Supp. 1242, affirmed mem., 535 F.2d 1245 (3d Cir.1976), cert. denied, 429 U.S. 964, 97 S.Ct. 394, 50 L.Ed.2d 333 (1976), the District Court sustained a narrowly-drawn curfew ordinance against charges of violations of due process, equal protection, first amendment rights, parental rights to control over children, and freedom of movement rights. The court noted that the state's authority to restrict juveniles' activities is greater than its authority to restrict adults' activities. The court then used the reasonable relation test

to determine whether the curfew was a reasonable means of fulfilling the state's expressed purposes of protecting juveniles, enforcing parental control, protecting the public, and reducing juvenile crime. The court found that the interests of juveniles were outweighed by these governmental purposes. For a detailed analysis and criticism of the court's holding in *Bykofsky*, see 54 Tex.L.Rev. 812 (1976) in which the author argued that the court "failed to address" increased judicial recognition of juvenile rights. In *Naprstek v. Norwich*, 545 F.2d 815 (2d Cir.1976), an ordinance without a termination time was held void for vagueness.

A clear discussion of the general constitutional issues that surround juvenile curfew ordinances is presented in 76 Mich.L.Rev. 109 (1977). The author concluded that only carefully and narrowly-drawn curfew ordinances would be upheld by the courts. An appendix to the Note contains a "Model Curfew Ordinance," id. at 152. The author of 97 Harv.L.Rev. 1163 (1984) presented an overview of recent juvenile curfew cases, concluding that because juvenile rights affected by curfews are fundamental, strict scrutiny is the appropriate test for courts to apply in deciding the constitutionality of juvenile curfew ordinances. See also 52 Notre Dame Law. 858 (1977).

2. In *In re People*, 32 Colo.App. 79, 506 P.2d 409 (1973), the court answered a contention that because a curfew ordinance can be violated only by a child, and because the statute authorized a warrantless arrest only on reasonable grounds to believe the individual "* * * committed an act which would be a * * * [crime] * * * if committed by an adult * * *" there could be no valid warrantless arrest for a curfew violation.

* * *. We disagree.

The statute must be read and construed as part of the entire Children's Code, 1967 Perm.Supp., C.R.S.1963, 22–1–1 et seq. One of the underlying purposes of the Code is to create a distinction between adults and children who violate the law. A child who violates the law may be adjudicated a delinquent child and thus become subject to correction by the state; however, he is not subject to the specific penalties imposed upon adult offenders. So that a child might not be labeled a criminal, it is necessary to define the offenses for which he might be adjudicated delinquent in terms other than as crimes.

Careful study of the Children's Code demonstrates that the use of phraseology, such as "acts which if committed by an adult," was intended to define, by analogy, a general type of conduct for which a child might be taken into custody and for which he might be adjudicated a delinquent. Viewed from this perspective, the phrase relied upon by respondent does not create a limitation on the power of the state, but merely establishes a general category of behavior for which children may be adjudicated delinquent. This intent is further evidenced by the fact that children may be taken into custody for conduct which is not expressly prohibited by statute but which requires the state's intervention in the interest of the child or society. See 1967 Perm.Supp., C.R.S.1963, 22–2–1(1)(d) and (e), supra. Thus, a child may be taken into temporary custody pursuant to 1969 Perm.Supp., C.R.S.1963, 22–2–1(1)(c), if he violates a statute or ordinance which makes specific behavior by children unlawful, even though such behavior if committed by an adult is not unlawful.

We hold that the exercise of temporary custody over B.M.C. and his subsequent release to his parents was lawful and proper.

Id. at 410–11.

IN THE INTEREST OF E.B.

Supreme Court of North Dakota, 1980.
287 N.W.2d 462.

PEDERSON, JUSTICE.

E.B., a juvenile, appeals from a decision of the juvenile court entered May 16, 1979, finding him to be an unruly child in that he was "habitually and without justification truant from school" in violation of § 27–20–02(4)(a), NDCC. We find that § 27–20–02(4)(a) is not unconstitutionally vague, and affirm the holding that E.B. is an unruly child.

* * *

E.B. is fifteen years old and lives with his mother. He was involved in an informal adjustment before a juvenile supervisor in May of 1978, at which time he admitted committing the unruly act of truancy during the 1977–78 school year, and was placed on probation.

The problem reoccurred the following year and on January 30, 1979, a petition was filed alleging that E.B. was an unruly child in that he was habitually truant from school. He missed a total of eighteen days of school, six and one-half of which were unexcused, between September 5, 1978, and January 30, 1979.

E.B.'s attorney moved to dismiss the petition on the ground that § 27–20–02(4)(a) was unconstitutionally vague. The juvenile supervisor denied the motion and found that E.B. was an unruly child. The district court confirmed the supervisor's finding.

As grounds for reversal, E.B. contends that the terms "habitually" and "without justification" are too vague for the fair administration of justice; secondly, that the State must prove that the child's absences from school were willful and that there was no justification for them; and, lastly, that six and one-half days of unexcused absences do not constitute habitual truancy.

Section 27–20–02(4) provides as follows:

"4. 'Unruly child' means a child who:

a. Is habitually and without justification truant from school;

b. * * *

c. * * *

d. In any of the foregoing is in need of treatment or rehabilitation."

E.B. asserts that the terms "habitually" and "without justification" do not provide adequate standards for the juvenile court in applying the statute so that § 27–20–02(4)(a) violates the due process clause of the Fourteenth Amendment to the United States Constitution and Section 13 of the North Dakota Constitution. It is admitted that this is a minority position and that a number of courts have ruled that those words are not unconstitutionally vague.

In United States v. Harriss, 347 U.S. 612, 74 S.Ct. 808, 98 L.Ed. 989 (1954), the Supreme Court set forth applicable principles for determining whether a statute is void for vagueness:

> "The underlying principle is that no man shall be held criminally responsible for conduct which he could not reasonably understand to be proscribed. [Footnote omitted.]" Id. at 617, 74 S.Ct. at 812.

This guarantee of due process is applicable to civil statutes as well as criminal. Alsager v. District Court of Polk Cty., Iowa, 406 F.Supp. 10 (S.D.Iowa 1975). In In re J.Z., 190 N.W.2d 27 (N.D.1971), this court considered a vagueness challenge to a portion of the Uniform Juvenile Court Act and stated:

> "A statute which either forbids or requires the doing of an act in terms so vague that men of common intelligence must necessarily guess at its meaning and differ as to its application violates the first essential of due process of law. On the other hand, where the words assailed, taken in connection with the context, are commonly understood, their use does not render a statute invalid. * * * (footnotes omitted.)" Id. at 35.

This directive to look to see if the words assailed are commonly understood is also found in § 1–02–02, NDCC, on rules of interpretation of statutes.[28]

We find the argument less than persuasive that the words "habitually" and "without justification" are too vague to provide adequate standards.

* * *

It appears that the phrase "habitually truant" has been used in numerous statutes and courts have uniformly upheld them. Although the phrase may lack mathematical precision, it has a common-sense meaning which provides adequate standards for the guidance of the court. Attempting to delineate precisely how many times a child can "skip" school for the sake of exact guidelines would be a futile gesture and may invite students to test its limits. * * * [W]e decline to interfere with the reasonable discretion to be exercised by school authorities in defining exactly where the thin ice ends.

We also decline to hold that the words "without justification" are unconstitutionally vague. These words are not ambiguous and have a meaning well understood in common language. These are also terms which have withstood previous vagueness challenges. See Ex parte Strong, 95 Tex.Cr.R. 250, 252 S.W. 767 (Texas 1923); State v. Gardner, 51 N.J. 444, 242 A.2d 1 (1968); State v. Norflett, 67 N.J. 268, 337 A.2d 609 (1975), "without lawful justification."

---

28 1–02–02. "Words used in any statute are to be understood in their ordinary sense, unless a contrary intention plainly appears, but any words explained in this code are to be understood as thus explained."

E.B. asserts that the State must prove that the child's absences were at least "voluntary" and perhaps "willful," and he asserts that oversleeping is not the kind of conduct the statute meant to proscribe. Our state requires each child to attend school every day. Chapter 15–34.1, NDCC. If the child does not attend, and his or her parent did not give permission for the absence—the child's absence is marked unexcused. This is the exact conduct meant to be proscribed, whether the reason for the absence was oversleeping or something else. We are hard-pressed to see how oversleeping is not volitional conduct, unless the fatigue producing the oversleeping is due to illness or other conditions beyond the juvenile's control.

E.B. also maintains that the culpability requirement of "willfulness" must be implied as a part of the offense by analogizing the Uniform Juvenile Court Act to criminal law. The purpose of the Uniform Juvenile Court Act is to improve the child's condition and to remove the taint of criminality. Section 27–20–01, NDCC. It should not be construed as a punitive statute.

The State does not have to prove there was no justification for the absences. The Compulsory School Attendance chapter, 15–34.1, provides several exceptions to compulsory attendance and places the burden of proving them on the parent. See § 15–34.1–03, NDCC. We see no reason why a child charged with habitual truancy should not have the same burden. See Simmons v. State, supra.

Lastly, E.B. contends that six and one-half days of unexcused absences do not constitute habitual truancy.

We are to consider this matter using a broad review of the files, records, and transcript of the juvenile court. Section 27–20–56, NDCC.

The findings of the juvenile referee and the record below indicate that E.B. admitted committing the act of truancy for the previous school year (1977–78). There is a separate finding of fact that E.B.'s mother had difficulty controlling the child and that he did not submit to her reasonable wishes. The transcript indicates that she had not given E.B. permission to miss school on the days he was marked unexcused. E.B. was absent from school a total of 18 times during the five months in question, not just the six and one-half days marked unexcused. Viewing the total picture, school authorities were able to detect a developing, consistent pattern of truancy in E.B. for the 1978–79 school year. With this conclusion we agree.

The Uniform Juvenile Court Act has separate provisions for the "unruly child" to remove any taint of criminality and to provide for treatment or rehabilitation. School officials should be encouraged to act upon developing patterns of truancy so that the child can be helped and the problem cured.

Having reviewed the evidence anew, we find that § 27–20–02(4) (a) is not unconstitutionally vague and affirm the district court's holding that E.B. was an unruly child in that he was habitually and without justification truant from school.

ERICKSTAD, C.J., and PAULSON, SAND and VANDE WALLE, JJ., concur.

IN THE INTEREST OF GRAS

Louisiana Court of Appeals, 1976.
337 So.2d 641.

Before REDMANN, BOUTALL and MORIAL, JJ.

MORIAL, JUDGE.

This matter previously was before this court (La.App., 320 So.2d 578) and remanded to us by the Supreme Court (La., 323 So.2d 473).

The sole issue for our determination on remand is whether LSA–R.S. 13:1569, subd. 15(b), (c), and (d) [29] and LSA–R.S. 13:1570, subd. A(3) [30] are constitutional.

Appellant attacks the statutes on three grounds:

1. LSA–R.S. 13:1569, subd. 15(b), (c), and (d) on their face violate the due process clause of the 14th Amendment to the United States Constitution because they are vague and overbroad.

2. The provisions of LSA–R.S. 13:1569, subd. 15(b), (c), and (d) punish a status rather than specific acts in violation of the 8th Amendment to the United States Constitution.

3. Adjudication pursuant to LSA–R.S. 13:1569, subd. 15(b), (c), and (d) and LSA–R.S. 13:1570, subd. A(3) constitutes a restraint of the child's liberty for non-criminal behavior without a legitimate state purpose.

The language of LSA–R.S. 13:1569, subd. 15(b), (c), and (d), is not vague on its face as to deny a "child in need of supervision" (CINS) due process of law. A reading of the statute clearly indicates the intent of the legislature is to provide for judicial supervision of a certain class of children who are engaging in conduct which is detrimental to their development and well-being in lieu of affixing the

---

[29] LSA–R.S. 13:1569 in pertinent part provides:

* * *

"15. 'Child in need of supervision' means a child who:

* * *

"b. habitually disobeys the reasonable and lawful demands of his parents, tutor, or other custodian, and is ungovernable and beyond their control; or

"c. has committed an offense not classified as criminal or one applicable only to children; and

"d. in any of the foregoing, is in need of care or rehabilitation."

[30] LSA–R.S. 13:1570 in pertinent part provides:

"Except as otherwise provided herein, the court shall have exclusive original jurisdiction in proceedings:

"A. Concerning any child whose domicile is within the parish or who is found within the parish:

* * *

"(3) Who absents himself from home or usual place of abode without the consent of his parent or other custodian or who is habitually disobedient or beyond the control of his parent or other custodian."

stigma of delinquence on such children upon adjudication. Where there is an allegation of a violation of section (b) or (c), the court must also consider section (d) which contains a mandatory prerequisite second element for a CINS adjudication. Inherent in LSA–R.S. 13:1569, subd. 15(b), (c), and (d) is the requirement for an adjudicatory hearing to determine judicially if the elements of either (a) or (b) are present and that the child is "in need of care or rehabilitation." [31] Appellant's fear that a child who engages in normal adolescent misbehavior or trivial juvenile conduct will be adjudicated a CINS arbitrarily is without merit. That danger is eliminated by the requirement of LSA–R.S. 13:1569, subd. 15(d).   *   *   *

A detailed listing of every type of behavior falling within the purview of "child in need of supervision" is unrealistic. A cursory attempt to define all types of behavior injurious to a child with mathematical precision makes the reason for granting Broad and general jurisdiction obvious. The state's interests in protecting the physical, moral or mental well-being of children under seventeen years of age is at the heart of the juvenile act. See La. Const. 1921, Art. 7, § 52; La. Const. 1974, Art. 14, § 16(A); LSA–R.S. 13:1580.

We are of the opinion that an adolescent child is capable of discerning conduct on his part which is contrary to the reasonable demands of his parent or guardian. Further, at the statutorily mandated inquiry the child becomes aware of his conduct which will result in further court action, i.e., an informal adjustment or the filing of a petition. See LSA–R.S. 13:1574.

The contention of appellant that the statute prevents a child from adequately preparing a defense is without merit. LSA–R.S. 13:1574 requires a specific pleading of the facts which bring the child within the purview of the provisions of Chapter 6 of the Revised Statutes. Additional procedural due process safeguards are provided by LSA–R.S. 13:1574 and 1575.

Appellant relies heavily on Gesicki v. Oswald, 336 F.Supp. 371, aff'd, 406 U.S. 913, 92 S.Ct. 1773, 32 L.Ed.2d 113 (1972), in which a portion of the New York Wayward Minor Act (N.Y.Code of Crim.Pro. § 913(a)–(dd)) was held unconstitutional on the ground of vagueness. However, in Gesicki the court clearly distinguished between the penal nature of the Wayward Minor Act and the state's statutory scheme for treatment of juvenile offenders. The Wayward Minor Act, which was contained in the New York Code of Criminal Procedure, provided for trials of juveniles in the courts of general criminal jurisdiction, and permitted placement of minors in *adult* correctional facilities. The court was concerned with the probability that these children would not be treated substantially different from adult criminals. *Gesicki* is not persuasive in the interpretation of our statutory scheme for the treatment of juveniles.

[31] LSA–R.S. 13:1569(18) states: " 'Adjudicatory hearing' means a hearing to determine whether the allegations of a petition under this chapter are supported by the standard of proof applicable to that case or class of case."

Appellant's argument that a "child in need of supervision" may be punished for constitutionally protected behavior is less than persuasive and unrealistic. A CINS child is not being adjudicated a criminal and placed in a facility as a punitive measure. See In re Parker, 118 La. 471, 43 So. 54 (1907). The object of the CINS statute is to provide rehabilitation and treatment for juveniles who engage in the sort of conduct therein proscribed. Although marginal cases could be placed where doubts might arise that is no basis to strike down the statute for vagueness. See United States v. Harriss, 347 U.S. 612, 618, 74 S.Ct. 808, 98 L.Ed. 989.

We do not find that LSA–R.S. 13:1569, subd. 15(b), (c), and (d) punish a status which does not involve any specific acts on the part of the child. The statute requires a finding by the court that the child in question is engaging in the type of conduct proscribed by the statute.

Tina Marie Gras ran away six times and violated the provisions of her probation agreement. On the basis of those actions, the court found it necessary to classify Tina as a "child in need of supervision" and to place her in a closed setting.

This court is cognizant of the difficulties experienced in the adolescent years. However, we agree with the judge of the juvenile court that Tina Marie needed some form of control and discipline in her life. A child who is having a particularly difficult time in adjusting during the difficult adolescent period is more than likely to benefit from a state program when his parents or guardians can no longer provide him with the necessary guidance and supervision.

We find that the placement by the juvenile court of CINS children in approved facilities with qualified staffs is a valid exercise of *parens patriae* and serves a legitimate state purpose. Under the theory of *parens patriae*, the state is responsible for the welfare of its children. In the case of CINS the state is attempting to provide these children with the treatment, guidance, and care which under normal circumstances is provided in the home. The proceedings in the instant case illustrate the concerted effort of the juvenile court and its probation office to act in the best interest of the child by providing her with an environment best suited to meet her adolescent behavior problems.

We agree that a child adjudicated a CINS should not be placed in custody with children who have been adjudicated delinquents. Nevertheless, such placement, which is alleged to be a constitutional violation, is not a defect in the statute; it is a potential defect in the state's performance of its custodial function following a dispositional order. The placement does not invalidate the statutory provision which authorized the CINS adjudication preceding placement. See Vann v. Scott, 7 Cir., 467 F.2d 1235. Furthermore, appellant was not committed to the Department of Corrections following her CINS adjudication. She was committed to the Department of Corrections at a dispositional hearing following her adjudication as a delinquent. See LSA–R.S. 13:1580(2). This adjudication was based upon her admission to the charges in a petition alleging her to be a delinquent by virtue of the extreme violation of the terms of her probation placement.

For the foregoing reasons the judgment of the Juvenile Court for the Parish of Jefferson is affirmed.

Affirmed.

NOTES

1. In *In re Napier*, 532 P.2d 423 (Okl.1975), children ran away from home, were verbally abusive to their grandparents and refused to attend school. Among other attacks on the validity of the CINS statute, the appellants contended that:

"* * * the statute chills the exercise of constitutionally protected rights and may involve the state in actual interference with these rights.

"In this respect appellants contend the statute chills the exercise of constitutional rights because a child who seeks to exercise his religion or express his political views against the wishes of his parents might be found to be a child 'beyond the control of his parents.'

"They further contend judicial proceedings upon a petition alleging such acts would constitute state interference with the child's exercise of his constitutional rights.

"We note no contention is made appellants herein were exercising constitutionally protected rights when they engaged in the acts alleged in the petition.

"In A. v. City of New York, supra, the court considered a similar contention and stated:

'The danger that Family Court judges may make an unduly restrictive application of the statute in marginal cases seems unrealistic. As the Supreme Court declared in Harriss * * * a "statute will not be struck down as vague even though marginal cases could be put where doubts might arise." '

"Likewise in *In re Jackson*, supra, the court stated:

'Any claim of unconstitutionality based upon the possible overbreadth of RCW 13.04.010(7), if applied to unreasonable parental demands, is unavailable to Jennifer. Her conduct was of a kind properly within the control of a parent. In the absence of compelling countervailing considerations in the public interest, which do not appear here, unconstitutionality of a statute may not be urged by resort to hypothetical applications. State v. Cashaw, 4 Wash. App. 243, 480 P.2d 528 (1971).' "

Id. at 426.

2. Suppose a child runs away from home once. Is that sufficient to authorize a finding that the child is "incorrigible, ungovernable, or habitually disobedient and beyond the control of a parent or other lawful authority?" Even if the child ran away several times, may a court infer that the child so behaved "without just cause?" Is it necessary that there be evidence, by way of inference or otherwise, that the behavior was "without just cause?" If so, who has the burden of proof? See Matter of Kathie L., 418 N.Y.S.2d 859 (Fam. Ct. 1979).

C. DEPENDENCY AND NEGLECT AS AN ALTERNATIVE BASIS

TASK FORCE REPORT: JUVENILE DELINQUENCY AND YOUTH CRIME. THE PRESIDENT'S COMMISSION ON LAW ENFORCEMENT AND ADMINISTRATION OF JUSTICE pp. 27–8 (1967)

NEGLECT AND DEPENDENCY

Besides delinquency, the other major branch of juvenile court jurisdiction deals with cases of neglect (usually including dependency). Neglect cases generally concern children whose parents have abandoned them or are neglecting or refusing to provide proper care (including medical care) or education or a fit environment. A protective function in such situations is conferred by statute on almost all juvenile courts (although legislative language and criteria vary) and is widely exercised (157,000 dependency and neglect cases in 1965.) It is estimated that more than half of all neglect proceedings involve children under 6, 90 percent children under 12 years old.

The juvenile court's neglect jurisdiction should not be used to impose a judge's childrearing preferences any more than its delinquency jurisdiction should be exercised against an adolescent's nonconformity. It is undeniable, however, that numbers of parents are either unfit or dangerously erratic to a degree that actually endangers the physical or emotional well-being of their children, and that in many such instances the State is the only available intervening party. The neglect jurisdiction of the juvenile court should therefore be retained, as an appropriate embodiment of the State's concern and responsibility for the welfare of children.

Although the effort in a case of parental neglect is always to improve the home and leave the child in it, there are instances in which his own interest requires that he be removed. Since in such an order the State is contravening the basic custodial rights of parenthood, the order should be issued by a court as the outcome of judicial proceedings conducted with all the safeguards commonly observed when conflicting custodial rights are adjudicated.

Dependency, where it is defined separately from neglect, usually means either complete absence of a legal custodian or lack of proper care not as a result of willful failure to provide but because of physical, mental, or financial inability. Thus the new Illinois act provides that a neglected minor is anyone under 18 years of age:

(a) Who is neglected as to proper or necessary support, education as required by law, or as to medical or other remedial care recognized under State law or other care necessary for his well-being, or who is abandoned by his parents, guardian, or custodian; * * *.

While a dependent minor is one under 18:

    (*a*) Who is without a parent, guardian, or legal custodian; or

    (*b*) Who is without proper care because of the physical or mental disability of his parent, guardian, or custodian * * *.

Accepting that common distinction, based on willfulness, between neglect and dependency, dependency should be eliminated from the jurisdiction of the juvenile court. The Children's Bureau Standards do not use the term dependent child on the ground that:

    No child should be subject to the jurisdiction of the court for economic reasons alone. The term dependent child generally implies a child in need of economic assistance. Such assistance should be provided by a social agency. Unless there is an element of neglect involved, the court's jurisdiction should not be exercised in situations of dependency.

The New York Family Court Act likewise restricts the court's jurisdiction to neglect: Cases in which those responsible for the child, though having or being offered financial means, fail to provide adequate "food, clothing, shelter, education, or medical or surgical care" or "moral supervision" or abandon or desert him. Problems caused by financial inability are to be "dealt with administratively under the Social Welfare law rather than judicially under the Family Court Act." The Illinois act appears to reach the same result by specifying, as set out above, the sorts of parental incapacity on which a finding of dependency may be based and by excluding in section 5–7 (Placement; Legal Custody or Guardianship), wards of the court whose guardians fail to provide properly for them for "financial circumstances alone."

The Standards point out in a note that "there are situations where the parent, however willing, is unable to provide the child with proper care because of parental incapacity—mental, physical, or otherwise," and that in such cases protection of the child may require court action even in the absence of neglect. The note states, however, that the drafters believe such action to be provided for by the jurisdiction already given the court, especially in connection with other proceedings such as adoption, termination of the legal relationship between parent and child, and appointment of a guardian. Similarly, the New York Family Court Act appears to deal with dependency cases involving absence of a custodian under provisions for permanent termination of parental rights, adoption, guardianship, and custody.

Where the child's dependency stems from his guardian's good-faith failure to cope, what is needed is not the force of law but the assistance of a social agency. Courts, even ones as informal and socially oriented as the juvenile court, traditionally deal with willful or at least negligent harmful conduct. Maximum use of social services and facilities to treat the causes of illegal conduct is a most desirable juvenile court goal. Acting as a mere conduit for the referral of well-meaning people overwhelmed by life to a source of assistance for their economic and social ills is a burdensome task for any court, and one there is no need to handle judicially. Especially in view of the inevitably stigmatizing effects of going to court, whatever the court and outcome are called, dependency alone should not be a subject for court consideration. As demonstrated by the Children's Bureau Standards and the New York Family Court Act, the cases in which adjudication of rights and coercion are required raise problems in addition to dependency and can be comprehended by other jurisdictional bases.

IN RE GARNER

Superior Court of Pennsylvania, 1974.
230 Pa.Super. 476, 326 A.2d 581.

PRICE, JUDGE. A petition was filed in the Montgomery County Juvenile Court on February 21, 1974, by William Schlachter, Director of the Child Welfare Services of Montgomery County, in the interest of Donna Garner. Donna is fourteen years old, and resides with her mother. The petition alleged that Donna repeatedly exhibited extremely incorrigible behavior, including constant truancy from school, which recurred despite Donna's repeated promises that she would go back to school and attend classes.

The petition also alleged the following circumstances:

On October 22, 1973, with the consent of Donna's parents, the lower court awarded temporary custody of Donna to the Child Welfare Service which placed Donna in the Good Shepherd Diagnostic Center in Philadelphia. On October 23, 1973, with her parents' consent, Donna entered the Good Shepherd Diagnostic Center. On October 28, 1973, Donna left the grounds with her mother and was later reported to have run away. On October 29, 1973, Donna went to her mother's home, where she was found on October 30, 1973.

Donna requested that she not be returned to the Philadelphia Center, and promised to attend school regularly if she were permitted to stay at home. She was re-registered in school, but was truant after a few days. As a result of this truancy, an application was made for Donna at the Topton Lutheran Home, where she was admitted on January 29, 1974. On that same day, Donna told her caseworker that she had spent the previous Saturday night driving a friend's car, and that she had stayed out all night.

On February 4, 1974, Donna ran away from the Topton Lutheran Home. No one knew her whereabouts until February 13, 1974, when she returned to her mother's home. Although she had agreed to return to Topton in a telephone conversation with her caseworker, when the caseworker arrived, Donna refused to move or to speak, despite the efforts of her mother and the caseworker.

The petition concluded that, while Donna had been provided with several opportunities to avoid legal action, she had failed to use any to her advantage, because she continually refused to listen to anyone—whether her mother or father, her caseworker or personnel of a school or placement facility. On the basis of Donna's "incorrigible behavior", the petitioner requested that Donna be adjudicated a delinquent and placed in a security setting.

At her adjudicatory hearing on March 6, 1974, Donna admitted running away from her mother's home and the institutions in which she had been placed, and also her truancies from school. Donna's counsel also admitted these facts, but denied that they were sufficient to prove Donna ungovernable or delinquent. Judge Scirica adjudicated Donna both a delinquent and deprived child under the Pennsylvania Juvenile Act, Act of Dec. 6, 1972, P.L. —, No. 333, 11 P.S. § 50–101.

At the disposition hearing on March 21, 1974, Donna was released from Montgomery Hall on probation, in the custody of her mother, upon the condition that she attend school regularly and receive counselling through services provided by the probation department.

This appeal challenges the adjudication, alleging that the trial judge improperly overruled a demurrer to the evidence related to the allegation that Donna is an ungovernable child, and seeking a determination of whether persistent truancy is an act of delinquency or deprivation under the Juvenile Act. The appeal alleges that the finding of delinquency should be reversed, and that Donna should again be placed in the custody and under the supervision of the Child Welfare Service.

* * *

The question we must resolve is whether Donna's actions constituted sufficient evidence of incorrigibility to uphold an adjudication of delinquency. The adjudication of deprivation is not contested.

Section 50–102(2) of the Juvenile Act defines a "delinquent act" as follows:

> "(2) 'Delinquent Act' means: (i) an act designated a crime under the law of this State, or of another state if the act occurred in that state, or under Federal law, or under local ordinances; or (ii) *a specific act or acts or habitual disobedience of the reasonable and lawful commands of his parent, guardian, or other custodian committed by a child who is ungovernable.* 'Delinquent act' shall not include the crime of murder nor shall it include summary offenses unless the child fails to pay a fine levied thereunder, in which event notice of such fact shall be certified to the court." [Emphasis added.]

A "delinquent child" is one whom the court has found to have committed a delinquent act, and who is in need of treatment, rehabilitation, or supervision.

Section 50–102(4) of the Juvenile Act defines a "deprived child" as follows:

"(4) 'Deprived child' means a child who: (i) is without proper parental care or control, subsistence, education as required by law, or other care or control necessary for his physical, mental, or emotional health, or morals; or (ii) has been placed for care or adoption in violation of law; or (iii) has been abandoned by his parents, guardian, or other custodian; or (iv) is without a parent, guardian, or legal custodian; or (v) *while subject to compulsory school attendance is habitually and without justification truant from schools.*" [Emphasis added.]

The testimony reveals that Donna was taken to the Good Shepherd Diagnostic Center with her parents' consent, after her mother and father had determined that they could not control Donna's truancy. Donna's mother testified that Donna would not obey when told to go to school. Donna would sometimes leave the house for school, but not stay at school during the day. On most occasions, Donna did not go to school at all, despite directions from her mother that she go.

The record also establishes that Donna did not stay at the Good Shepherd Diagnostic Center, despite the requests of her mother that she do so. Donna ran away from the Center after spending only five days there. This behavior was in defiance not only of the Center's rules, but also of her parents' wishes.

Donna was permitted to remain at home, rather than be returned to the Center, after promising to attend school regularly. However, she did not keep her promise, and, in fact, did not attend classes at all during the months of November and December of 1973, and January of 1974, despite her mother's requests that she do so. During this time, Donna's mother had to pay three fines, due to Donna's truancy. Such behavior supports the lower court's conclusion that Donna is an ungovernable child who needs supervision by the probation department.

In addition to this evidence, there was undisputed testimony from Paul Ernst, Director of the Topton Home Children's Services, which revealed that Donna's disobedience to the rules and regulations of Topton Home began the first night she was there. She refused to move from a chair, to take a shower, or to go to bed, demanding to be taken home to her mother. After several hours of persuasion, Donna did go to bed, but the next morning, refused to arise until the house father personally insisted that she do so. She consistently demanded to see her mother or to be taken home, and upon a refusal, would not move from wherever she was sitting at the time. When she realized, after several such incidents, that Topton Home administrators could not comply with her requests, she ran away from the Home and refused to return. Instead, she ran to a house near Topton Home, in an effort to avoid going back. When she was finally caught, Donna shouted obscenities at the administrators, but did submit.

All was well until the following weekend, when Donna again ran away from the Home with two boys, and began hitch-hiking out of Topton.

Donna ran to a friend's home and from there, was driven to her mother's home.

Mr. Ernst testified that while she was at Topton, Donna cut classes on one occasion and spent the time in the company of two boys. Testimony from Mr. Ernst also established that Donna would engage in temper tantrums and crying spells when confronted with a rule which she was obliged to, yet did not want to, obey. If those antics were not fruitful, she would get angry and refuse to move until she had her way. Mr. Ernst stated that Donna's disobedience "was manipulative" but that he did not see Donna "as a completely delinquent child in terms of a criminal-type child, but so manipulating [sic] that she is headed for a very difficult life." (NT 14) In his opinion, Donna is an ungovernable child who refuses to cooperate.

Another witness, Gwendolyn Morgan, testified to other specific actions of Donna's disobedience during her brief stay at Topton.

When Donna took the stand, she admitted all these facts, and further admitted the facts alleged in the petition which began this proceeding.

In reviewing this record, it is clear that the trial judge acted properly in overruling the demurrer and in adjudicating delinquency. The evidence was more than adequate to prove Donna a delinquent beyond a reasonable doubt. The Juvenile Act does not require that an adjudicated delinquent be a criminally-involved child. Delinquency can be shown, as it has been here, by habitual disobedience to a parent, guardian, or custodian who makes reasonable and lawful requests of the child. In this case, Donna chose to enroll in Topton Home, and knew the rules and regulations she would live by before she was admitted. (NT 38) She promised to abide by these rules, but failed to keep that promise as of her first night there. Her behavior was incorrigible, and established that Donna is an ungovernable child, in need of supervision.

This appeal also alleges that an adjudication of delinquency is not proper under the Juvenile Act, when the basis for that determination is persistent truancy. We agree that the Juvenile Act establishes that a child who is habitually truant without justification is a deprived child under § 50–102(4)(v), and not a delinquent child. However, such an allegation is of no moment in the instant case. Donna has been adjudicated both delinquent *and* deprived. Both determinations are supported by the evidence—the adjudication of delinquency by Donna's habitual disobedience and that of deprivation by her habitual truancy.

Judgment affirmed.

IN THE MATTER OF RICHARD C. (ANONYMOUS)

Appellate Division, Supreme Court of New York, 1974.
43 App.Div.2d 862, 352 N.Y.S.2d 15.

Before GULOTTA, P.J., and SHAPIRO, CHRIST, BRENNAN and BENJAMIN, JJ.

MEMORANDUM BY THE COURT

Appeal from an order of Family Court, Queens County, dated August 17, 1973, which adjudicated appellant as being a juvenile delinquent, after a hearing, and directed that he be placed in the State Training School for a period not to exceed 18 months.

Order reversed, on the law and in the exercise of discretion, without costs, and proceeding remanded to the Family Court for further proceedings consistent herewith.

Appellant, presently confined in the Warwick State Training School, is now 15 years old. In September of 1972, he began to take automobiles for "joy-riding". Since that time he has been arrested four times for taking cars, at least two of which incidents resulted in automobile chases and wrecks. His taking of a car on July 31, 1973 resulted in the filing of the petition in the instant proceeding.

At a fact-finding hearing held August 8, 1973 appellant admitted taking the automobile, which taking, if committed by an adult, would constitute a crime. His mother failed to attend the hearing, as she had failed to attend two previously scheduled hearings. In order to obtain her presence at the dispositional hearing, the Family Court issued a warrant requiring her presence. Despite the warrant, and despite several attempts to call the mother to secure her presence at the hearing, she failed to appear at the dispositional hearing on August 17, 1973.

Appellant's law guardian, who was present, moved the court to adjourn the proceeding until the mother would be present, but the court denied the motion, stating that appellant's interests could be adequately protected by the law guardian. The court asserted that it was not surprised that the mother was absent since she had apparently given up hope on appellant and wanted nothing further to do with him. The court found that the mother's failure to appear "may constitute neglect."

The probation officer then presented evidence of appellant's history, including psychiatric reports which recommended "individual supportive therapy". The probation officer recommended confinement of appellant at the State Training School although he was uncertain that the recommended therapy was available there.

After hearing further objections of the law guardian on the basis of the absence of the mother, the court stated its decision to place appellant in the State Training School with the qualification that he was to be given the required therapy there. The court made this disposition despite the fact that it was not sure facilities for the required treatment were available.

We are impressed by two of appellant's arguments on this appeal. First, it is asserted that the Family Court abused its discretion in failing to substitute a neglect petition for the juvenile delinquency one, in view of the court's own comment that failure of appellant's mother to appear "may constitute neglect." The procedure to which appellant refers is provided in section 716 of the Family Court Act, which states that such a substitution may be made on the court's own motion. The provision recognizes that some children are juvenile delinquents because they are neglected and that they can be better treated as neglected children (Joint Legislative Committee Comments in McKinney's Cons.Laws of N.Y., Book 29A, p. 301).

We agree with appellant. To fail to substitute a neglect petition in this case was an abuse of the court's discretion since the court, on the record, stated that appellant may be a neglected child. The instant case is precisely the kind of case to which this provision was intended to apply.

* * *

Since we hold that the Family Court did abuse its discretion, both in failing to substitute a petition of neglect under the circumstances and in imposing a term in the State Training School without proper inquiry to determine if the appropriate facilities were available, we reverse and remand the proceeding to the Family Court for further disposition in accordance with this opinion.

IN RE PAUL H.

Appellate Division, Supreme Court of New York, 1975.
47 A.D.2d 853, 365 N.Y.S.2d 900.

Before MARTUSCELLO, ACTING P.J., and LATHAM, COHALAN, BRENNAN and MUNDER, JJ.

MEMORANDUM BY THE COURT

In a proceeding pursuant to article 7 of the Family Court Act, the appeal is from an order of the Family Court, Dutchess County, dated April 2, 1974, which, upon a prior determination that appellant was a person in need of supervision (PINS), placed him in the custody of a New York State Division For Youth facility.

Order reversed, on the law and in the interest of justice, without costs, and proceeding remanded to the Family Court for further proceedings not inconsistent herewith.

Appellant, Paul H., at about 14 years of age, was brought before the Family Court pursuant to two PINS petitions. The first, filed by his father, alleged in substance that Paul was a truant and generally disobedient and beyond the father's control. The second, filed by the attendance officer of the Arlington Central School District, also alleged that Paul was a truant. On February 21, 1974, a fact-finding hearing was held on both petitions. Paul appeared with his father, but was not represented by an attorney. He was advised of the contents of the two petitions, that he could be placed in an institution for up to 18 months and that he was entitled to a hearing in which his father would testify. Additionally, he was informed of his right to remain silent and his right to an attorney. When asked by the court what he wished to do, he stated, "I don't really care, to tell you the truth". He later admitted that the allegations in the first petition were true and similarly admitted the truthfulness of the allegations in the second petition after again being perfunctorily informed of his right to an attorney. At no time in the proceeding was he informed of the desirability of being represented by counsel.

Following his admissions, Paul was adjudicated a PINS. Prior to the dispositional hearing the Probation Department completed an investigation of Paul and his background. The probation report indicates that his home environment was less than ideal. The probation officer found that the home was "filthy with food, clothing and debris scattered about." The father, because of his ill health, is unemployed and cannot meet his everyday expenses. He accepted most of the blame for Paul's truancy and explained that because of his ill health he could not "adequately supervise" his son. The probation report recommended that Paul be immediately removed from his father's home.

Following a dispositional hearing held on March 12, 1974, Paul was placed in the custody of the Department of Social Services for placement at the McQuade Foundation for 18 months. Approximately two weeks later the department filed a petition to terminate placement. A second dispositional hearing was held on April 2, 1974. At the conclusion of the hearing the court stated, "The boy isn't going to get the guidance he needs at home. The home isn't suitable at the present time * * *. [Appellant's] home environment is bad * * *. I would suggest that you seek counseling, Mr. [the father]. Make some effort to understand this boy." The court thereupon directed Paul's placement in a State Training School for 18 months.

Appellant argues that the PINS adjudication should be vacated on two grounds: first, that the court abused its discretion in not substituting a neglect petition in place of the PINS petitions; and second, that the fact-finding hearing was defective, since appellant was denied his right to counsel. We agree on both grounds. Section 716 (subd. [b]) of the Family Court Act allows the court "on its own motion and at any time in the proceedings [to] substitute a neglect petition * * * for a petition to determine * * * whether a person is in need of supervision." This provision reflects a recognition by the Legislature that some children who are "in need of supervision" often are "neglected" and are better treated that way (see Comments of the Joint Legislative Committee on Court Reorganization on Family Ct. Act, § 716, in McKinney's Cons.Laws of N.Y., Book 29A, Part 1, p. 301). The results of the investigation conducted by the Probation Department irresistably lead to the conclusion that Paul is a neglected child within the meaning of section 1012 (subd. [f]) of the Family Court Act. Moreover, the court's statements at the conclusion of the second dispositional hearing are tantamount to a finding of neglect (see Matter of Richard C., 43 A.D.2d 862, 352 N.Y.S.2d 15; cf. Matter of Lloyd, 33 A.D.2d 385, 308 N.Y.S.2d 419).

* * *

D. "IN NEED OF TREATMENT" AS AN ADDITIONAL PRE-REQUISITE TO A DETERMINATION OF DELINQUENCY OR INCORRIGIBILITY

GEORGIA JUVENILE COURT CODE OF 1981

§ 24A–401   Definitions

As used in this chapter, the term:

(1) "Adult" means any individual who is not a child under the definition in paragraph (2) of this Code section.

(2) "Child" means any individual who is:

(A) Under the age of 17 years;

(B) Under the age of 21 years, who committed an act of delinquency before reaching the age of 17 years, and who has been placed under the supervision of the court or on probation to the court; or

(C) Under the age of 18 years, if alleged to be a "deprived child" as defined by this chapter.

* * *

(6) "Delinquent act" means:

(A) An act designated a crime by the laws of this state, or by the laws of another state if the act occurred in that state, under federal laws, or by local ordinance, where the crime does not fall under subparagraph (12)(C) of this Code section and is not a juvenile traffic offense as defined in Code Section 15–11–49;

(B) The act of disobeying the terms of supervision contained in a court order which has been directed to a child who has been adjudged to have committed a delinquent act; or

(C) Failing to appear as required by a citation issued with regard to a violation of Code Section 3–3–23.

(7) "Delinquent child" means a child who has committed a delinquent act and is in need of treatment or rehabilitation.

(8) "Deprived child" means a child who:

(A) Is without proper parental care or control, subsistence, education as required by law, or other care or control necessary for his physical, mental, or emotional health or morals;

(B) Has been placed for care or adoption in violation of law;

(C) Has been abandoned by his parents or other legal custodian; or

(D) Is without a parent, guardian, or custodian.

No child who in good faith is being treated solely by spiritual means through prayer in accordance with the tenets and practices of a recognized church or religious denomination by a duly accredited practitioner thereof shall, for that reason alone, be considered to be a "deprived child."

*   *   *

(11) "Status offender" means a juvenile who is charged with or adjudicated of an offense which would not be a crime if it were committed by an adult, in other words, an act which is only an offense because of the perpetrator's status as a juvenile. Such offenses shall include, but are not limited to, truancy, running away from home, incorrigibility, and unruly behavior.

(12) "Unruly child" means a child who:

(A) While subject to compulsory school attendance is habitually and without justification truant from school;

(B) Is habitually disobedient of the reasonable and lawful commands of his parent, guardian, or other custodian and is ungovernable;

(C) Has committed an offense applicable only to a child;

(D) Without just cause and without the consent of his parent or legal custodian deserts his home or place of abode;

(E) Wanders or loiters about the streets of any city, or in or about any highway or any public place, between the hours of 12:00 Midnight and 5:00 A.M.;

(F) Disobeys the terms of supervision contained in a court order which has been directed to such child, who has been adjudicated unruly; or

(G) Patronizes any bar where alcoholic beverages are being sold, unaccompanied by such child's parents, guardian, or custodian, or possesses alcoholic beverages; and

(H) In any of the foregoing, is in need of supervision, treatment, or rehabilitation; or

(I) Has committed a delinquent act is in need of supervision, but not of treatment or rehabilitation.

YOUNG v. STATE

Georgia Court of Appeals, 1969.
120 Ga.App. 605, 171 S.E.2d 756.

SYLLABUS OPINION BY THE COURT

JORDAN, PRESIDING JUDGE. This is an appeal from an order of indefinite commitment of a juvenile, born on February 27, 1954, to the Division for Children and Youth, Department of Family and Children Services, as provided in § 13 of the Children and Youth Act, Ga.L.1963, pp. 81, 105; Code Ann. § 99–213. The order is dated December 28, 1968. The juvenile was released on February 21, 1969,

on bail, pursuant to the provisions of a federal court order. Young v.
Proctor, Civil Action No. 12,475, United States District Court, Northern District of Georgia. The Supreme Court transferred the appeal
from the juvenile court order to this court. Young v. State, 225 Ga.
221, 167 S.E.2d 591. Held:

The evidence adduced at the juvenile court hearing, stripped of
hearsay and in relation to the only alleged misconduct of the child,
that she used vile, obscene, and profane language on more than one
occasion, shows that she used the term, "kiss my ass" on one
occasion in a classroom of boys and girls about her same age, the
evidence being in conflict as to whether similarly offensive language
was directed to her, and that on a previous occasion on a school bus
she called another student a "cross-eyed bastard" perhaps in response to a reference to her as a "nigger," and that on still another
occasion on a school bus she called another student a "bitch," also
perhaps preceded by provoking remarks. Nothing appears to rebut
the uncontradicted evidence disclosing the disapproval of the parents
of the use of such offensive language, or otherwise indicating that
they are not capable of supervising the correction and training of the
child. We do not regard this evidence as sufficient to authorize a
determination of a juvenile court that the child is one, even if
delinquent, who is "in need of correction, treatment, care and rehabilitation" as set forth in the order, warranting commitment to a State
welfare agency, having authority, absent further action, to keep her
in confinement until she reaches age 21. See Ga.L.1963, pp. 81, 107,
109; Code Ann. § 99–213(d)(2), (j). Such action necessarily deprives
her parents of their prima facie prerogative of training and supervision, and implies that the juvenile is, within the terms of the juvenile
law, one who is in need of supervision beyond the control of her
parents and in need of correction and training which the parents
cannot provide. See Ga.L.1968, pp. 1013, 1016, 1019; Code Ann.
§§ 24–2401, 24–2408. The State concedes it was not the purpose of
the petition to accuse the juvenile of the commission of a punishable
offense, and the recent decision of Wilson v. Gooding, 303 F.Supp.
952, United States District Court, Northern District of Georgia, July
7, 1969, held unconstitutional Georgia Code § 26–6303 dealing with
the use of opprobrious words or abusive language in the presence of
another.

While in no way condoning the use of such alleged language by
school students, this court merely observes that such conduct as
proved here is usually the subject of disciplinary action by school
officials without the necessity of invoking the aid of the courts.
Indeed, the record shows that white students who used similar
language were appropriately punished at the school level. To bring
all students accused of this or similar deeds of misconduct before the
courts would be taking advantage of the real purpose of and necessity for the Juvenile Court Act and would place burdens on the courts
which rightfully belong to parents and school officials. It is only
when such corrective measures are totally without avail that the

courts should be asked to invoke the sometimes awesome consequences of the law.

Judgment reversed.

HALL, P.J., concurs.

WHITMAN, J., concurs in the judgment.

NOTES

1. Georgia statutes contained no jurisdictional requirement of "need
for treatment" in 1969. The Georgia statute containing such a requirement—in one form for delinquent children, in another form for unruly
children—was not passed until 1971. In 1974 the Georgia Court of Appeals
referred to the *Young* case, citing it at least with approval, perhaps as
controlling:

SYLLABUS OPINION BY THE COURT

HALL, PRESIDING JUDGE. M.S.K., an eleven year old black boy,
came before the Effingham County Juvenile Court judge on charges of
having touched two eleven year old white girls, who were dressed in
pants, in the genital area. He did not contest the statements of the two
girls, one of whom said it had happened other times before; but neither
of the girls said he had kicked or otherwise hurt them, whereas M.S.K.
and his two witnesses seemed to testify to some kicking. The record of
the hearing indicates that M.S.K. had not been generally thought to be a
behavior problem; that his teacher administered a spanking following
this offense; and that the girls' parents had not particularly wanted the
matter to go as far as juvenile court. The complaint was filed by the
local sheriff.

The judge ordered M.S.K. placed on probation and allowed him to
remain in his home, but ordered "that you don't go to school anymore. I
want to get you out of that school * * * You just haven't got any
business in school."

1. The motion to dismiss the appeal is denied. See Rule 14 (124
Ga.App. 873).

2. This case should not have been brought before the juvenile
court. "While in no way condoning the * * * [act done by this eleven
year old child] this court merely observes that such conduct as proved
here is usually the subject of disciplinary action by school officials
without the necessity of invoking the aid of the courts. * * * To
bring all students accused of this or similar deeds of misconduct before
the courts would be taking advantage of the real purpose of and
necessity for the Juvenile Court Act and would place burdens on the
courts which rightfully belong to parents and school officials. It is only
when such corrective measures are totally without avail that the courts
should be asked to invoke the sometimes awesome consequences of the
law." Young v. State, 120 Ga.App. 605, 606, 171 S.E.2d 756.

It should be noted that this youth is below the age of criminal
accountability as set by the General Assembly of Georgia. Code Ann.
§ 26–701. See Code Ann. § 24A–401 for the definition of a "delinquent
child" and an "unruly child."

As to his right to an education, the laws of Georgia require children
to attend a public or private school between their seventh and sixteenth

birthdays. Code Ann. § 32–2104. The American Bar Association Standards relating to probation of adult criminals recommend that a condition for probation is the pursuit of educational training. See pp. 44–45.

Judgment reversed.

DEEN and STOLZ, JJ., concur.

M.S.K. v. State, 131 Ga.App. 1, 205 S.E.2d 59 (1974).

2. "On remand, the court counselor conducted a study of the child and his home. The report of the counselor, dated 5 August 1974, was submitted to the court. This report reveals that the child appeared to be a well-mannered, intelligent boy, who was active in the Boy Scouts, attended 4–H Camp, was president of the Beta Club at his school, and maintained an almost perfect A average at school. His school principal reported that he had not experienced any behavior or attendance problems with the child, and the child's parents made a similar report. The counselor concluded that the child was a fine student and was involved in many worthwhile activities, and that his parents were concerned and 'very capable of providing adequate supervision for him.' Accordingly, the counselor recommended 'that supervision by the court be withheld at this time.'

"On 30 August 1974 the judge signed what are denominated in the record as 'Exceptions and Appeal Entries.' These contain the following:

'1. Upon hearing oral evidence from the petitioner and witnesses for the petitioner the Court finds the following facts and beyond a reasonable doubt: that on or about September 25, 1973, in the daytime this child did break and enter the home of Stamey Pierce of Rt. 3, High Point, North Carolina; that entry was apparently gained by opening a basement window; that no damage was done to the home; the child admitted this to Deputy R.C. Ward and later to Mrs. Pierce, the wife of the owner of the home.

'2. That the child is delinquent as alleged in the petition.

'3. That it would be to the best interest of this child that prayer for judgment be continued.'

To the foregoing, the respondent juvenile excepted and appealed.

* * *

[In the omitted part of the opinion the court decided that other grounds existed for requiring a new hearing.]

"Since there must be a new hearing, we direct attention to the following provision in G.S. § 7A–285 relating to juvenile hearings:

'If the court finds that the conditions alleged do not exist, *or that the child is not in need of the care, protection or discipline of the State, the petition shall be dismissed.*' (Emphasis added.)

In view of the information contained in the court counselor's report, the court may wish to give consideration to that provision of the statute in any further proceedings in this matter.

The order adjudicating appellant a delinquent is reversed and this proceeding is remanded to the district court.

Reversed and remanded."

In re Meyers, 25 N.C.App. 555, 214 S.E.2d 268, 269–70 (1975).

Chapter 3

ARREST AND INVESTIGATION OF
THE JUVENILE

IJA–ABA JUVENILE JUSTICE STANDARDS PROJECT,
STANDARDS RELATING TO POLICE HANDLING
OF JUVENILE PROBLEMS (1980)

3.2 * Police investigation into criminal matters should be similar whether the suspect is an adult or a juvenile. Juveniles, therefore, should receive at least the same safeguards available to adults in the criminal justice system. This should apply to:

    A. preliminary investigations (e.g., stop and frisk);

    B. the arrest process;

    C. search and seizure;

    D. questioning;

    E. pretrial identification; and

    F. prehearing detention and release.

For some investigative procedures, greater constitutional safeguards are needed because of the vulnerability of juveniles. Juveniles should not be permitted to waive constitutional rights on their own. In certain investigative areas not governed by constitutional guidelines, guidance to police officers should be provided either legislatively or administratively by court rules or through police agency policies.

A. SEARCH AND SEIZURE PROBLEMS

Until the decision in New Jersey v. T.L.O., infra, the Supreme Court had never directly addressed the question of whether Fourth Amendment protections against unreasonable searches and seizures are applicable to juveniles. The question remains whether the extent of the protections are, or should be, identical in adult cases and (all) (some) juvenile delinquency cases. For example, the Court in *T.L.O.* expressly declined to rule whether the exclusionary rule applicable under *Mapp* in criminal cases is also applicable in juvenile delinquency cases. The uncertainty is even greater when the juvenile is taken into custody with the intention of invoking a different juvenile court jurisdiction such as PINS, dependency or neglect. In particular the scope of private party search rules may be different in some, but perhaps not all, juvenile search cases. Similarly the consent search doctrines, both primary and third party, may not be the same in adult and juvenile cases.

Uncertainty also arises when the question is the validity of an arrest, and the subsequent application of an exclusionary rule to the fruits, physical or verbal, of that arrest. E.g., is an arrest warrant for juveniles required under precisely the same conditions which would invalidate an arrest of an adult without a warrant?

The section begins with some representative statutes, some in force as legislative enactments, others proposed as models. While the student is considering the cases and other materials in this section, the statutes set out at the beginning should be examined to determine (1) whether the cases would have turned out differently under all or any of them; and (2) whether any of them create (or solve) problems of federal constitutional dimension.

————

UNIFORM JUVENILE COURT ACT

SECTION 13. [*Taking into Custody.*]

(a) A child may be taken into custody:

(1) pursuant to an order of the court under this Act;

(2) pursuant to the laws of arrest;

(3) by a law enforcement officer [or duly authorized officer of the court] if there are reasonable grounds to believe that the child is suffering from illness or injury or is in immediate danger from his surroundings, and that his removal is necessary; or

(4) by a law enforcement officer [or duly authorized officer of the court] if there are reasonable grounds to believe that the child has run away from his parents, guardian, or other custodian.

(b) The taking of a child into custody is not an arrest, except for the purpose of determining its validity under the constitution of this State or of the United States.

————

NEW YORK FAMILY COURT ACT

29A McKinney's Consolidated Laws of New York (1983)

§ 305.2 Custody by a peace officer or a police officer without a warrant

1. For purposes of this section, the word "officer" means a peace officer or a police officer.

2. An officer may take a child under the age of sixteen into custody without a warrant in cases in which he may arrest a person for a crime under article one hundred forty of the criminal procedure law.

PENNSYLVANIA JUVENILE COURT ACT

Purdon's Pennsylvania Statutes Annotated (1982)

§ 6324. Taking into custody

A child may be taken into custody:

(1) Pursuant to an order of the court under this chapter.

(2) Pursuant to the laws of arrest.

(3) By a law enforcement officer or duly authorized officer of the court if there are reasonable grounds to believe that the child is suffering from illness or injury or is in imminent danger from his surroundings, and that his removal is necessary.

(4) By a law enforcement officer or duly authorized officer of the court if there are reasonable grounds to believe that the child has run away from his parents, guardian, or other custodian.

(5) By a law enforcement officer or duly authorized officer of the court if there are reasonable grounds to believe that the child has violated conditions of his probation.

WISCONSIN CHILDREN'S CODE

Wisconsin Statutes Annotated (1979 & Supp.1983–4)

HOLDING A CHILD IN CUSTODY

48.19 Taking a child into custody

(1) A child may be taken into custody under:

(a) A warrant;

(b) A capias issued by a judge of the court assigned to exercise jurisdiction under this chapter in accordance with s. 48.28;

(c) An order of the judge if made upon a showing satisfactory to the judge that the welfare of the child demands that the child be immediately removed from his or her present custody. The order shall specify that the child be held in custody under s. 48.207; or

(d) Circumstances in which a law enforcement officer believes on reasonable grounds that:

1. A capias or a warrant for the child's apprehension has been issued in this state, or that the child is a fugitive from justice;

2. A capias or a warrant for the child's apprehension has been issued in another state;

3. The child is committing or has committed an act which if committed by an adult is a violation of a state or federal criminal law;

4. The child has run away from his or her parents, guardian or legal or physical custodian;

    5.   The child is suffering from illness or injury or is in immediate danger from his or her surroundings and removal from those surroundings is necessary;

    6.   The child has violated the terms of court-ordered supervision or aftercare supervision administered by the department;

    7.   The child has violated the conditions of an order under s. 48.21(4) [a] or the conditions of an order for temporary physical custody by an intake worker; or

    8.   The child has violated a civil law or a local ordinance punishable by a forfeiture, provided that in any such case the child shall be released as soon as reasonably possible under s. 48.20(2).

* * *

    (3) Taking into custody is not an arrest except for the purpose of determining whether the taking into custody or the obtaining of any evidence is lawful.

1. ARREST

IN RE APPEAL IN PIMA COUNTY ANONYMOUS, JUVENILE ACTION NO. J 24818–2

Arizona Supreme Court, 1973.
110 Ariz. 98, 515 P.2d 600, appeal dismissed, cert. denied Michaels v. Arizona, 417 U.S. 939, 94 S.Ct. 3063, 41 L.Ed.2d 661 (1974).

HAYS, CHIEF JUSTICE.   This appeal arises from the April 13, 1971, order of the Juvenile Division of the Superior Court of Pima County, Juvenile Court No. 24818–2, declaring appellant to be a delinquent; and from the denial on June 17, 1971, of appellant's motion for a new trial, and in the alternative to alter or amend judgment. Thereafter, on request of the Court of Appeals, Division Two, this court took this case as a direct appeal.

    Between March 4 and March 7, 1971, a series of daylight attempted robberies and robberies took place in the vicinity of Nash Elementary School. The victims ranged between the ages of eight and twelve years old. The items involved included cash not exceeding $2.00, a bike lock and some keys. None of the victims could provide a detailed description of their assailant but a few common facts were given by all of the victims. The assailant was a white male, junior high school age, riding a red bicycle, wearing a red T-shirt, and using a switchblade knife.

    Due to these incidents, the police established a mobile stake-out surveillance of the area. Involved in this stake-out were two officers, one of whom was a school resource officer for Amphitheater Junior High School and Nash Elementary School.

    On March 8, 1971, one of the detectives observed the juvenile, appellant herein, on two occasions. The first observation placed the

---

[a] Section 48.21(4) referred to above authorizes a judge or commissioner on a finding of a need for continued custody to make certain placement orders including certain restrictions on travel and association and requiring reporting, among other things.

juvenile by a building under construction. The second occasion occurred just five minutes later and placed the juvenile as heading towards an area of a hotel in the immediate vicinity of the first sighting. The detective then left his unmarked car and ran towards the juvenile and caught up with him in the coke machine area.

At this point, the juvenile was ordered off his bicycle and was searched by the detective. The juvenile was asked where the knife was, to which he responded that he did not have a knife, nor did the search produce one. The juvenile was also questioned as to where he was going and why he was absent from school. The juvenile responded that he was going to a nearby gas station to have his bicycle fixed. The detective then asked the juvenile to accompany him to his car so that they could proceed to Nash Elementary School. From testimony at the hearing, it is clear that the detective took the juvenile into custody as a possible suspect in the robberies.

Upon arrival at Nash School, the juvenile was placed in the reception room outside the principal's office. The detective then requested that the robbery victims be called into the office. In substance, each victim was asked to walk into the room and inform the detective if there was anyone there that they knew. Each of the victims complied with this request and each identified the juvenile in question as the assailant.

The juvenile was subsequently charged with five counts of armed robbery, one count of assault with a deadly weapon and one count of theft. The theft count was dismissed in the trial court's minute entry of April 12, 1971, and order of April 13, 1971, and the assault charge was reduced to simple assault. At the adjudicatory hearing of April 8–9, 1971, counsel for the juvenile made a continuing objection to the use of the testimony of those witnesses who participated in the identification at Nash School. The county attorney attempted to validate the in-court identification by propounding a series of hypothetical questions that required the witnesses to block out from their memories the identification at the school. In defense, the juvenile offered the testimony of a relative as to his whereabouts on one of the days involved.

On April 12, 1971, by a minute entry and by an order filed April 13, 1971, the juvenile was declared a delinquent. Counsel for the juvenile moved for a new trial or in the alternative to alter or amend judgment. This motion was denied by the court by a minute entry on June 17, 1971. The dispositional hearing was held on July 9, 1971, and the juvenile was placed on probation by an order filed July 12, 1971.

* * *

Appellant's second contention concerns the taking of the juvenile into custody on March 8, 1971. Appellant argues that this was an arrest wanting in probable cause. The trial court concluded that the juvenile was taken into custody pursuant to the Juvenile Code, but did not couch its conclusion in terms of an arrest.

A.R.S. § 13–1401(A) reads:

> "An arrest is made by actual restraint of the person to be arrested, or by his submission to the custody of the person making the arrest."

When the detective took appellant from the coke machine area to his car and did not inform appellant that he was free to go, an arrest had been consummated. This conclusion is corroborated by two factors. First, the detective testified at the hearing that he took the appellant into custody as a possible suspect in the armed robberies. The second factor is the conclusion of the trial court that the Juvenile Code gave the detective authority to seize the appellant. A.R.S. § 8–223(A)(1–4) as amended provides four grounds for taking custody of a juvenile. Subsection 1 allows for custody pursuant to an order of the juvenile court. Subsection 3 allows for custody if there are reasonable grounds to believe that the juvenile is ill or injured or in immediate danger of his surroundings and removal is necessary. Subsection 4 allows for custody where there are reasonable grounds to believe that the child is a runaway.

In the instant case, it is clear that subsections 1, 3 and 4 of A.R.S. § 8–223(A) are inapplicable to support the seizure of appellant's person. It is subsection 2 that provided the basis for the detective's action. Subsection 2 allows a juvenile to be taken into custody.

> "Pursuant to the laws of arrest, without a warrant, when there are reasonable grounds to believe that he has committed a delinquent act or is incorrigible." A.R.S. § 8–223(A)(2).

Before determining whether the arrest of March 8, 1971, was lacking in probable cause, it is necessary to clarify the phrase "reasonable grounds" as used in A.R.S. § 8–223(A)(2). The trial court expressed some concern that this phrase might support an arrest on less than probable cause. We think that is not the case, as A.R.S. § 8–223(A)(2) should be read in light of A.R.S. § 13–1403(1–4) as amended. Section 13–1403 sets forth four situations in which a peace officer may, without a warrant, arrest an individual. Sections 1 through 4 use the language "probable cause." A.R.S. § 8–223(A)(2) begins with "[p]ursuant to the laws of arrest, without a warrant * * *." To the extent that these sections conflict, it is a conflict of semantics and not substance. The terms "probable cause" and "reasonable grounds" are often used interchangeably. It would do violence to the concept of equal protection of the law to allow a juvenile to be taken into custody pursuant to A.R.S. § 8–223(A)(2) without the standard being probable cause.

Having determined that an arrest took place on March 8, 1971, we consider now the second prong of appellant's argument—that the arrest was made without probable cause. "Arrest with or without warrant must stand upon firmer ground than mere suspicion * * *." State v. Dessureault, supra. The totality of facts in the instant case persuades us that the arrest was predicated on mere suspicion.

Appellant's behavior consisted of being by a building under construction and riding his bike into the coke machine area of a hotel. Neither of the two acts could arouse a reasonable belief that appellant had committed a crime. Nor did appellant's appearance at the time provide any more of a basis. Appellant was not wearing any of the clothes described by the victims and he was riding a gold bicycle, while a red bicycle was the one used by the unknown assailant. There is a conflict in the testimony as to appellant's alleged attempt to run from the detective. Standing alone, this fact would not provide the basis for an arrest. Indeed, the only characteristic that appellant possessed in common with the alleged assailant was being a white male of junior high school age. Nor does the case at bar present any exigent circumstances, such as a possibility of appellant's fleeing the jurisdiction. There was sufficient time to make application pursuant to A.R.S. § 13–1424 as amended to detain appellant for identification purposes.

The effect of this illegal arrest is to taint the evidence of the show-ups at Nash Elementary School and that evidence should have been excluded at the hearing. Wong Sun v. United States, 371 U.S. 471, 83 S.Ct. 407, 9 L.Ed.2d 441 (1963). However, that is not to say that subsequent identifications are also excluded. The procedure in State v. Dessureault, supra, should have been followed and the court should have made a finding as to whether or not the subsequent identifications were tainted by the original show-ups.

The trial judge further expressed some doubts as to the show-ups because of their suggestive nature. We need not meet this because of the foregoing position as to the arrest.

The adjudication of delinquency was based on a number of charges, all but one of which were subject to the tainted identification problem. It is appellant's contention that all the charges had a cumulative effect in the adjudication of delinquency and that this court must find beyond a reasonable doubt that the tainted identifications did not lead to the trial court's decision. We find to the contrary. Each charge in and of itself is a sufficient basis for the determination of delinquency. Striking the charges which may have rested on tainted identifications, one count of attempted robbery still remains. Finding no clear error on this charge, we affirm that adjudication and the disposition order entered by the juvenile court.

CAMERON, V.C.J., LOCKWOOD, J., and STEVENS and HAIRE, Judges of the Court of Appeals, Division One, concur.

NOTES

1. In In re _____, 194 N.E.2d 797 (Juv.Ct. Cuyahoga City, Ohio 1963) the court held that a police officer was authorized to take into custody any child who he had reasonable grounds to believe was delinquent, neglected or dependent even though the child had committed no misdemeanor in his presence nor with respect to whom the officer had reasonable grounds to

believe he had committed a felony. The court said that the law of arrest was not applicable to the taking into custody of minors. The student should compare that reasoning with Section 13 of the Uniform Juvenile Court Act, printed supra this section.

2. In Baldwin v. Lewis, 300 F.Supp. 1220 (E.D.Wis.1969), *reversed on jurisdictional grounds* 442 F.2d 29 (7th Cir.1971), the court, in the course of an opinion granting habeas corpus to a juvenile held in detention without a probable cause hearing, discussed the relationship between the Fourth and Fourteenth Amendment restrictions on arrests on adults and the arrest powers over juveniles:

" * * *

"MUST PROBABLE CAUSE EXIST BEFORE A JUVENILE MAY BE TAKEN INTO CUSTODY ON SUSPICION OF HAVING COMMITTED A VIOLATION OF LAW WHICH WOULD CONSTITUTE A CRIME IF COMMITTED BY AN ADULT?[1]

"The Fourth Amendment of the United States Constitution provides:

'The right of the people to be secure in their persons, houses, papers, and effects, against unreasonable searches and seizures, shall not be violated, and no Warrants shall issue, but upon probable cause, supported by Oath or affirmation, and particularly describing the place to be searched, and the persons or things to be seized.'

"As the United States Supreme Court has interpreted this amendment, it requires that a person may be validly arrested only if there is probable cause to believe that a crime has been committed and that the person to be arrested has committed such crime. * * * While the Fourth Amendment is a limitation upon the powers of the Federal Government only, it is well settled that the prohibition of the Fourth Amendment against unreasonable arrest is enforceable against the states through the due process clause of the Fourteenth Amendment; hence, a state has no power to sanction arrests prohibited by the Fourth Amendment.

* * *

"The State contends, however, that the Fourth Amendment requirement that an arrest be based upon 'probable cause' does not apply to a juvenile taken into custody and held in detention pursuant to § 48.28 of the Wisconsin Children's Code. It is the State's contention that such a juvenile has technically never been placed under arrest. Subsection (2) of § 48.28 of the Children's Code specifically states that 'Taking into custody under this section shall not be considered an arrest.'

"It is my opinion, however, that when the petitioner was taken into custody by the Milwaukee Police Department, he was clearly subjected to a 'seizure' or arrest within the meaning of the Fourth Amendment. Perhaps the most concise statement of what constitutes such a seizure was made by the Ninth Circuit Court of Appeals in Gilbert v. United States, 366 F.2d 923, 928 (1966), in which the court made it clear that 'any official exertion of custody over the person is a "seizure" within the

---

[1] This opinion is directed only to the issue of the circumstances under which the police may take into custody a juvenile who is suspected of having committed an act which would have been a crime had such act been committed by an adult. I am in no way expressing any opinion on the power of the police to take juveniles into custody under other circumstances, such as when a juvenile of tender years is taken into custody for his own safety.

meaning of the Fourth Amendment, and may be sustained only if not "unreasonable" under the circumstances.'

"According to the record, the petitioner is before the Children's Court because he is suspected of having committed an act which would be considered a crime if committed by an adult. Pursuant to such allegation, he was taken into custody and deprived of his liberty under authority of law.

"It is the view of this court that when Richard Baldwin was taken into custody by the Milwaukee Police Department, placed in the Milwaukee County Detention Center, and not allowed to leave the Detention Center on order of persons acting under authority of State statute, his liberty was clearly restrained by the State regardless of the name the State chooses to apply to his seizure and subsequent detention. Consequently, in my opinion, the probable cause requirement of the Fourth Amendment does apply to the present case.

"MUST THE DETERMINATION OF PROBABLE CAUSE BE MADE BY A JUDICIAL OFFICER PRIOR TO ARREST?

"The Fourth Amendment requirement of probable cause for arrest does not necessarily require that an arrest warrant be obtained. An arrest can be validly effected without an arrest warrant or any prior judicial determination of probable cause if the officer making the arrest, at the time of the arrest, had knowledge of facts sufficient to establish probable cause. * * *

"DID THE OFFICERS AT THE TIME OF THE ARREST HAVE KNOWLEDGE OF FACTS SUFFICIENT TO ESTABLISH PROBABLE CAUSE?

"It therefore becomes the duty of this court to determine whether the facts available to the officers at the moment of arrest would 'warrant a man of reasonable caution in the belief' that an offense had been committed and that the petitioner had committed the offense. Carroll v. United States, supra, 267 U.S. at 162, 45 S.Ct. at 288.

"The juvenile report of the Milwaukee Police Department (one of the voluminous records deposited with this court) indicates that the Fire Department's 6th Batallion Chief, Clarence Rydlewicz, found that the fire at the North Division High School 'was set by unknown means of arson.' The report indicates that as a result of this finding and on the basis of statements received from two eyewitnesses and an alleged accomplice, the petitioner was taken into custody. The report further indicates that the two eyewitnesses are teachers at the North Division High School who observed the petitioner and another youth on the high school stage in the area where the fire broke out. They then observed the petitioner and the other youth run from the stage as the fire developed. The other youth, who is referred to as an 'associate or accomplice' in the report, indicated to the police officers that the petitioner had started the fire.

"While the credibility of the 'associate or accomplice's' testimony may be questioned, it appears to me that the information which the officers received from the teachers is sufficiently reliable and definite to constitute probable cause for taking the petitioner into custody. I find that this information, coupled with the finding of the Fire Department investigation as to the cause of the fire, amounted to facts available to the officers at the moment of the arrest which would warrant a man of reasonable caution in the belief that an offense had been committed and that the petitioner had committed the offense. I therefore am of the opinion that the petitioner's arrest was validly effected and was not accomplished in violation of his Fourth Amendment rights.

"The petitioner contends, however, that aside from the issue of whether the officers had probable cause to take him into custody, his arrest is invalid because approximately twenty-five days had elapsed between the fire and his arrest, and that under such circumstances the Fourth Amendment requires that the arresting officers first obtain an arrest warrant.

"The record indicates that the fire at the North Division High School occurred on March 27, 1969, and that the petitioner was taken into custody on April 22, 1969. The record does not indicate, however, the point in time at which the police first obtained evidence sufficient to warrant taking the defendant into custody. If this evidence was obtained shortly after the fire, it would appear to me that the police should have obtained a warrant prior to the petitioner's arrest. If, on the other hand, the police did not obtain information constituting probable cause to arrest the petitioner until shortly before he was taken into custody, the police were justified in promptly taking him into custody if they thought such action was necessary to protect the interests of the school. But in light of the fact that there is no evidence as to when the officers did obtain probable cause to pick up the defendant, and in as much as they did in fact have such probable cause, I am not prepared to hold that under these circumstances the failure of the police to obtain a warrant requires that the petitioner's arrest be held invalid. * * * "

Id. at 1229–1231.

3. In Payton v. New York, 445 U.S. 573, 100 S.Ct. 1371, 63 L.Ed.2d 639 (1980), the Supreme Court held that

"the Fourth Amendment to the United States Constitution, made applicable to the States by the Fourteenth Amendment, prohibits the police from making a warrantless and nonconsensual entry into a suspect's home in order to make a routine felony arrest."

445 U.S. at 576, 100 S.Ct. at 1374.

Even prior to the *Payton* decision, in In the Matter of R.A.J., No. J–4709–78 (Dec. 11, 1978), the Superior Court of the District of Columbia, relying on *Gault*, and the negative inference from United States v. Watson, 423 U.S. 411, 96 S.Ct. 820, 46 L.Ed.2d 598 (1976) and United States v. Santana, 427 U.S. 38, 96 S.Ct. 2406, 49 L.Ed.2d 300 (1976), which had upheld warrantless arrests without exigent circumstances or consent in public, held that such arrests in a private home would require a warrant.

Subsequently, the Maryland Court of Special Appeals stated in dicta that

Payton should serve as a poignant signal to law enforcement officers that the issue we have discussed could easily be avoided by obtaining an arrest warrant in order to make a routine felony arrest of a suspect.

In re Anthony F., 49 Md.App. 294, 297–98, 431 A.2d 1361, 1363 (1981).

4. The common law rules for misdemeanor arrests by police officers are more restrictive than those applicable to felony arrests. In particular, in most jurisdictions arrests without a warrant may be made only if the misdemeanor was committed in the officer's presence. Should a similar limitation be imposed in the case of juveniles?

While New Jersey statutes guarantee juveniles "the right to be secure from unreasonable searches and seizures," N.J.S.A. 2A:4–60, section 54(a)(2) delegates authority to the New Jersey Supreme Court to establish standards relating to warrantless arrests of juveniles. That court, in turn, promulgated Rule 5:8–2:

> A law enforcement officer may take into custody without process any juvenile who he has probable cause to believe is delinquent or in need of supervision.

In State in the Interest of J.B., Jr., 131 N.J.Super. 6, 328 A.2d 46 (1974), the juvenile was taken into custody prior to the effective date of the rule. The court—as was not unusual in adult cases of that period—found the arrest valid on the theory that the juvenile was "idly roaming the streets at night" in the presence of the officer. The court, in dicta, described its new rule as abolishing the in-presence requirement. In doing so, they found no denial of due process in establishing one rule for adults and another for juveniles. Id. at 20, 328 A.2d at 53–54.

5. The sanctions for an illegal arrest of an adult are numerous. Absent a privilege, or an immunity, a police officer may be sued in tort or even prosecuted for a crime. The sanction which is most controversial, of course, is the rule which requires exclusion of evidence searched for or seized as a result of an arrest which violates the Fourth or Fourteenth Amendment. The evidence excluded includes "fruits" of the illegality, physical or intangible. The cases above suggest, or assume, that the rule is applicable in juvenile cases, although the Supreme Court has never addressed the question. But suppose a state imposes requirements for a valid arrest or search beyond those demanded by the Federal Constitution. States are clearly free to impose the exclusionary rule sanction in such cases as well. See Dawson, "State-Created Exclusionary Rules in Search and Seizure: A Study of the Texas Experience," 59 Tex.L.Rev. 191 (1981) for a discussion of the Texas situation.

In the juvenile context, the issue is most likely to arise under one of two typical statutes: (1) a statute requiring prompt notification of parents when a juvenile is taken into custody; and (2) a statute requiring that the juvenile be turned over immediately to juvenile authorities. The latter situation is considered infra section (B)(1). For light on the former situation, the student should consult the full report of In re Anthony F., supra Note 3, and Davidson v. Commonwealth, 613 S.W.2d 431 (Ky.App.1981).

2. SEARCHES

IN RE PEOPLE IN THE INTEREST OF B.M.C.

Colorado Court of Appeals, 1973.
32 Colo.App. 79, 506 P.2d 409.

SMITH, JUDGE.

B.M.C. seeks reversal of a judgment, entered after an adjudicatory hearing, which declared him to be a delinquent child.

On Saturday, November 21, 1970, at approximately 12:15 A.M., police officers observed three young men walking along a downtown Denver street. The officers stopped the men and asked for identification. Two of them, one being the minor-appellant, had no identification and were under the age of eighteen years. The officers took appellant and the other minor into custody for violation of the Denver curfew ordinance, Denver Revised Municipal Code 813.1, which reads in pertinent part as follows:

> "It shall be unlawful for any child under the age of eighteen (18) years to be or remain upon any street, alley or to remain or be in any establishment open to the public generally after the hour of 10:30 p.m. or prior to the hour of 5:00 a.m., * * * provided, that on Friday and Saturday nights, the curfew hour for children under eighteen (18) years shall be extended to the hour of 11:30 p.m."

Appellant was then taken to the Delinquency Control Division of the Denver Police Department at 13th and Champa Streets. There the officers conducted a search of his clothing and found a small quantity of hashish, a refined form of marijuana. The officers contacted appellant's parents, to whom he was released upon their arrival at the police station. No charges were filed at that time.

More than three months later, on March 3, 1971, a delinquency petition was filed. The petition made no mention of the curfew violation but alleged that appellant had violated C.R.S.1963, 48–5–2, by having in his possession a derivative of *cannabis sativa L* (hashish). Such violation, it was urged, required that B.M.C. should be adjudicated a delinquent. Defendant subsequently filed a motion to suppress the drugs seized claiming that the search of his clothing at the police station was unlawful. After a hearing, the court denied appellant's motion. The matter came on for trial to the court on June 11, 1971. The court found that B.M.C. had violated C.R.S.1963, 48–5–2, sustained the petition, and adjudicated him a delinquent child. B.M.C. appeals from this adjudication asserting that the court erred in not granting his motion to suppress.

* * *

II.

Appellant next argues that 1967 Perm.Supp., C.R.S.1963, 22–2–2(3)(a) prohibits the search of juveniles taken into temporary custody under the Children's Code. We do not agree. That section reads as follows:

> "A child shall not be detained by law enforcement officials any longer than is reasonably necessary to obtain his name, age, residence, and other necessary information and to contact his parents, guardian, or legal custodian."

B.M.C. would have us hold that because this section does not expressly authorize the search of a child, any search would be violative of the child's Fourth Amendment rights. We disagree. The purposes of the entire article of which this section is a part, are to insure initially, that children taken into temporary custody are promptly brought before the court or released to their parents and, secondly, that they are not stigmatized as criminals.

A search properly conducted in accordance with the safeguards arising out of the Fourth Amendment to the Constitution of the

United States is not, however, inconsistent with these provisions of the Children's Code. The same tests apply to the search of a child as of an adult, with the exception that certain searches of children require additional safeguards. For example, "a search by consent" of a child requires that a parent, guardian or legal custodian must freely and intelligently consent to the search. People v. Reyes, Colo., 483 P.2d 1342. A child who is the subject of a petition for adjudication as a delinquent is entitled to the constitutional protections afforded an adult defendant in a criminal case. People in Interest of P.L.V., Colo., 490 P.2d 685. B.M.C.'s protection from an unauthorized search does not arise from the silence of the statute, as B.M.C. argues, but from the constitutional guarantee against unreasonable searches and seizures. Therefore, the right of the police to conduct a search does not depend on express legislative authorization.

III.

B.M.C. contends that the search conducted at police headquarters, although incident to a lawful "arrest," was unreasonable because of its general exploratory nature. We agree. Even though the taking of B.M.C. into temporary custody was not an arrest, 1967 Perm.Supp., C.R.S.1963, 22–2–1(3), it was a detention for an unlawful act. Since B.M.C. has the same constitutional protections as his adult counterpart, the validity of the search must be measured by the same standards.

The people argue that the warrantless search was justified as an inventory search or alternatively as a search incident to the lawful taking of B.M.C. into temporary custody. The District Attorney relies on Baca v. People, 160 Colo. 477, 418 P.2d 182, which approved inventory searches. However, in that case the search was authorized and reasonable, not because of the arrest, but rather as a necessary protective procedure prior to the incarceration of the defendant. The holding in *Baca*, supra, is not applicable to the present facts where B.M.C. was detained only until he could be released to his parents. In the instant case, there was never any intention that B.M.C. be incarcerated. The search conducted was not therefore an inventory search, but an exploratory search conducted for the purpose of discovering whether appellant had violated any law in addition to the curfew ordinance.

In determining whether the search may be justified as incident to the lawful taking of B.M.C. into temporary custody, we refer to the standards for such searches as enunciated by our Supreme Court:

> "The decisions have not been altogether harmonious, but throughout all the cases and all the learned treatises on the subject runs the dominant theme that the search, whether under a valid search warrant or whether as incident to a lawful arrest, must be one in which the officers are looking for specific articles and must be conducted in a manner reasonably calculated to uncover such articles. Any search more extensive than this constitutes a general exploratory search and is squarely within

the interdiction of the constitutional guarantee against unreasonable search and seizure. * * * It was against just such
exploratory searches that the Fourth Amendment was specifically directed. On the other hand, it appears from the authorities
that if an officer is conducting a search, either under a valid
search warrant or incident to a valid arrest where the search is
such as is reasonably designed to uncover the articles for which
he is looking and in the course of such search discovers contraband or articles the possession of which is a crime, other than
those for which he was originally searching, he is not required to
shut his eyes and refrain from seizing that material under the
penalty that if he does seize it it cannot be admitted in evidence."
Hernandez v. People, 153 Colo. 316, 385 P.2d 996.

In the present case, the record discloses that the search in question
was not one conducted at the time and place of arrest for the purpose
of insuring that B.M.C. was not armed with a weapon by which he
could injure the officers or effect an escape. See People v. Navran,
Colo., 483 P.2d 228, applying Terry v. Ohio, 392 U.S. 1, 88 S.Ct. 1868,
20 L.Ed.2d 889; and Chimel v. California, 395 U.S. 752, 89 S.Ct. 2034,
23 L.Ed.2d 685. Since we have held that it was not an inventory
search pursuant to *Baca,* supra, it must be concluded that the sole
purpose of the search at issue was to obtain evidence.

However, the only evidence necessary to support a finding that
B.M.C. had violated the curfew ordinance would be that which would
establish his age and his presence on the street after a certain hour.
Proof of the offense by these elements did not require evidence which
could have been obtained from a personal search of B.M.C.

The scope of a warrantless evidentiary search incident to an
arrest is limited to evidence related to the offense for which the
arrest was made. See Cowdin v. People, Colo., 491 P.2d 569. The
search of B.M.C. was beyond the scope of the curfew offense for
which he was taken into custody and cannot be justified as properly
conducted incident to the taking of B.M.C. into temporary custody.
The search was a general exploratory search in violation of B.M.C.'s
constitutional rights. Hernandez v. People, supra.

IV.

The remaining question is whether the evidence obtained as a
result of a violation of B.M.C.'s constitutional rights should have
been suppressed at the adjudicatory hearing. Since a child subject to
delinquency adjudication is entitled to the same constitutional safeguards as an adult accused of a crime, the evidence obtained as the
result of the unlawful search should have been suppressed. Mapp v.
Ohio, 367 U.S. 643, 81 S.Ct. 1684, 6 L.Ed.2d 1081. Gonzalez v.
People, 156 Colo. 252, 398 P.2d 236. The failure to exclude such
evidence was reversible error.

Judgment reversed and order adjudicating B.M.C. a delinquent set aside.

COYTE and DWYER, JJ., concur.

NOTES

1. *B.M.C.* was decided shortly before the Supreme Court decided two cases which cast considerable doubt on *B.M.C.*'s continued vitality. In United States v. Robinson, 414 U.S. 218, 94 S.Ct. 467, 38 L.Ed.2d 427 and Gustafson v. Florida, 414 U.S. 260, 94 S.Ct. 488, 38 L.Ed.2d 456, both decided in 1973, the Court permitted full custodial searches of persons validly arrested for crimes without fruits (driving after revocation of license—*Robinson*; and driving without valid license in possession—*Gustafson*) even when there were no circumstances suggesting particular danger to the arresting officers or others. Of course, the state courts are free to impose stricter *state* standards than the Federal Constitution requires. Do you believe a state legislature—or court—should impose stricter search standards when the police take a juvenile into custody than when they arrest an adult?

2. In D.L.C. v. State, 298 So.2d 480 (Fla.App.1974), the court held that a full custodial search of a juvenile at the time and place of his lawful arrest for a curfew violation was justified as incident to that arrest and that marijuana seized from him at that time was therefore admissible evidence. In its discussion, the court did not address any issue regarding the constitutionality of the curfew ordinance (see Chapter 2, Section B, infra).

3. Does the "stop and frisk" doctrine, announced in Terry v. Ohio, 392 U.S. 1, 88 S.Ct. 1868, 20 L.Ed.2d 889 (1968) and developed in later cases, apply to "stops" and "frisks" of juveniles? In simplest terms, *Terry* permits a limited search—variously called a "frisk" or "patdown"—of an individual believed to be armed and dangerous and whom the officer reasonably suspects, based on articulable facts, to have committed or be in the process of committing a crime.

In In re Harvey, 222 Pa.Super. 222, 295 A.2d 93 (1972), the court ruled that the quantum of evidence needed to reach the level of "reasonable suspicion" was lacking, that absent that amount of evidence the "frisk" which turned up a revolver was illegal, but strongly implied that if the reasonable suspicion standard had been met, the search for and seizure of the revolver would have passed constitutional muster.

IN THE MATTER OF J.M.A. v. STATE

Supreme Court of Alaska, 1975.
542 P.2d 170.

BOOCHEVER, JUSTICE.

On this appeal, we are presented with the novel question of whether foster parents are to be considered agents of the state for purposes of the constitutional proscription against unreasonable searches and seizures. Appellant J.M.A. also raises issues concerning the constitutional guarantee against self-incrimination involved in a failure to give a *Miranda* warning before interrogation, and the constitutional guarantee of due process of law, as applied to the judge's review of J.M.A.'s juvenile record prior to the adjudication of his case.

In May 1974, appellant J.M.A. was placed in the home of Mr. and Mrs. Blankenship as a foster child. The Blankenships were licensed by the State of Alaska to operate a foster home for as many as five children. For their efforts in this regard, they received a monthly allowance from the state of $233.00 for each child so housed.

In early August 1974, Mrs. Blankenship became concerned with the fact that children who were strangers to her were coming into her home, staying briefly and departing. She suspected that these visits were related to trafficking in drugs. As a result of these suspicions, Mrs. Blankenship began periodically searching J.M.A.'s room during the first week of August. On August 8, 1974, Mrs. Blankenship listened on another extension to one of J.M.A.'s telephone calls without his knowledge or permission. During the course of this conversation, she heard J.M.A. tell the other party he had only a little pot left and needed to pick up some more plus some pills. Mrs. Blankenship again searched J.M.A.'s room and discovered no drugs, although earlier that day she had found and confiscated a pipe. During the evening of August 8, Mrs. Blankenship returned to J.M.A.'s room and searched a jacket she saw lying on the bed. Discovering a plastic bag of marijuana in one of the pockets, she removed the bag and placed it in her purse. No mention of the discovery was made to J.M.A. that day.

The next day Mrs. Blankenship called Jerry Shriner, the social worker assigned to J.M.A., seeking advice on how to deal with the problem. Mr. Shriner advised Mrs. Blankenship to place the marijuana in an envelope for safekeeping and assured her that he would visit her home in the afternoon. Mr. Shriner then called the Alaska State Troopers, and later on the same day, Mr. Shriner and a plainclothesman went to the Blankenship residence. J.M.A., who had been asked to stay home, was called into the living room where he was confronted by Mr. Shriner, Officer Fullerton and Mrs. Blankenship. Mrs. Blankenship then handed the marijuana to Officer Fullerton, who identified it as such and began questioning J.M.A. about it. The officer asked J.M.A. whether the jacket in which the marijuana was found was his jacket. J.M.A. admitted that the jacket was his but denied any knowledge of the marijuana. During the course of the meeting, J.M.A. was never advised of his rights.

J.M.A. was removed from the Blankenship home by Mr. Shriner and Officer Fullerton immediately after this meeting and placed in detention pending consideration of his case by the juvenile court. Counsel for J.M.A. filed a motion to suppress all evidence obtained as a result of the overheard telephone conversation and the searches of J.M.A.'s room. On October 8, 1974, a hearing on the motion to suppress was held, and on October 29, 1974, Judge Occhipinti issued his decision denying J.M.A.'s motion to suppress the evidence gathered against him. The adjudication hearing was held on October 31, 1974, resulting in a finding of delinquency. The superior court ordered that J.M.A. be committed to the Department of Health and Social Services for an indeterminate period not to extend beyond his nineteenth birthday, and that he be placed in a correctional or detention facility.

J.M.A. now appeals both from the ruling on the motion to suppress and from the adjudication of delinquency. J.M.A. alleges that the trial court erred in failing to suppress evidence obtained by the foster mother's eavesdropping on J.M.A.'s phone call; in failing to suppress evidence obtained through her searches of J.M.A.'s room; in failing to suppress statements made by J.M.A. in response to police questioning conducted without being prefaced by the *Miranda* warnings; and in considering J.M.A.'s entire juvenile record during the adjudication phase of the delinquency proceedings.

With regard to J.M.A.'s allegation that the lower court erred in failing to suppress the evidence obtained by Mrs. Blankenship through her eavesdropping on J.M.A.'s telephone conversation and her searches of his room, we must determine whether the state and federal constitutional prohibitions against unreasonable searches and seizures apply to a foster parent, licensed and paid by the state, and if so, whether the exclusionary rule, whereby evidence obtained in violation of the constitution is held inadmissible, should apply. Our analysis must initially focus on the question of whether the foster parent stands in such a relationship to the state as to be subject to the constitutional prohibitions against unreasonable searches and seizures. J.M.A. contends that the evidence gathered by Mrs. Blankenship should be suppressed since these warrantless searches were executed while Mrs. Blankenship was acting as an agent of the state, and thus did not comport with constitutional requirements concerning such actions. The state, to the contrary, argues that Mrs. Blankenship, as a foster parent, is not an agent of the state for purposes of the fourth amendment.

Although the constitutional prohibitions against unreasonable searches and seizures have not been specifically limited to state action, there is little doubt but that that was the original intent. We stated in Bell v. State:

> A search by a private citizen not acting in conjunction with or at the direction of the police does not violate the constitutional prohibitions against unreasonable search and seizure.

There is a further limitation on the scope of the fourth amendment in that it does not apply to searches engaged in by governmental officials when such officials act for a private purpose or outside the scope of duties related to law enforcement. Such a limitation involves a question of the capacity in which the state agent acts during the course of the search. In *Bell,* this court held an airport security officer to be subject to the same fourth amendment standards as a law enforcement officer, reasoning:

> The controlling principle does not depend so much upon which department of state government employs the officer, but instead upon the nature of the duties performed and the part the officer may have played in the course of events leading to appellant's

arrest and the seizure which followed. His duties were to provide crash and rescue services and to assure physical security in the airport and parking areas. He carried a sidearm.

Considering the question of when official involvement may be said to exist for purposes of the fourth amendment, the Oregon Court of Appeals in State v. Pearson, 15 Or.App. 1, 514 P.2d 884, 886 (1973), stated:

> * * * [O]fficial involvement is not measured by the primary occupation of the actor, but by the *capacity* in which he acts at the time in question.

Similarly, in People v. Wolder, 4 Cal.App.3d 984, 84 Cal.Rptr. 788 (1970), the action of an off-duty police officer in searching his daughter's apartment was found not subject to the fourth amendment, since, at the time, the police officer was acting in a private capacity as a concerned parent.

Applying these principles to the instant case, it is apparent that, in some respects, Mrs. Blankenship is an agent of the state. Her home is licensed and regulated by the state, and she is paid by the state for caring for foster children. But she also acts in a private capacity in managing the home for her family and herself. In all likelihood, her search of J.M.A.'s room and her listening to his telephone conversation involved both her state duties and her private functions. In both capacities, she had a need to supervise the young people placed under her control, and, solely as a private person, she had a legitimate concern about the illegal activities taking place in her home.

The mere fact that Mrs. Blankenship may have been acting in part as an agent of the state, however, does not necessarily mean that fourth amendment prohibitions apply. As we indicated in *Bell*, the real question is whether the nature of one's duties is related to law enforcement. In that regard, the activities of even a private citizen, acting on behalf of the police, would be subject to the prohibitions of the fourth amendment.

A foster parent is required both to assume temporarily the role of a natural parent to the child committed to his custody and to aid in the discharge of the government's obligation to care for and supervise those juveniles who have become the responsibility of the state. In substituting for a natural parent, the foster parent is no more an agent of the police than would be any natural parent. The actions of Mrs. Blankenship were in no manner instigated by the police. She testified that she did not want her children to get into trouble with the police and that she sought to work out such problems without police involvement. In fact, even after discovering the marijuana, she contacted J.M.A.'s social worker rather than the police. There is no reason for regarding Mrs. Blankenship's actions undertaken while fulfilling this parental role, which did not involve collaboration with the police, as being any different from the actions of a private parent, and, therefore, not subject to fourth amendment constitutional restraints.

The second function undertaken by foster parents, that of caring for and supervising foster children on behalf of the state, quite obviously involves the foster parent in a relationship with the state which may be characterized as an agency relationship. At least insofar as the supervision of J.M.A. is concerned, even as an agent of the state, we suggest without deciding that Mrs. Blankenship had the right to search J.M.A.'s room. He had previously been declared a delinquent and was placed in the Blankenship home as an alternative to placement in a correctional institution. Had he been placed in a correctional institution, his room would have been legally subject to searches. "In prison, official surveillance has traditionally been the order of the day."

Thus, if Mrs. Blankenship's relationship with J.M.A. is analogized to that of parent and child, the search did not violate the fourth amendment, and if the relationship were to be construed as similar to that involved had J.M.A. been placed in a correctional institution, again there would be no violation. In this instance, the operator of a foster home is in the extremely difficult position of endeavoring to fulfill the role of parent, and, at the same time, perform the task of supervising the activities of a minor found to be a delinquent. Under the circumstances of such a relationship, a search of the room can hardly be regarded as the type of unreasonable activity constitutionally prohibited. Nevertheless, we believe that the privacy of both natural and foster children should be respected to the fullest extent consistent with parental responsibilities.

Quite obviously, the duties of foster parents do not encompass responsibilities of a law enforcement officer similar to those discussed in *Bell*. Foster parents are not charged with the enforcement of penal statutes or regulations, nor are they entrusted with ensuring the physical security of the public. They are no more responsible for the detection of criminal activity or the apprehension of those participating in such activity than would be any other private citizen. They merely supervise on behalf of the state those children committed to their care. Such responsibilities are not of the same nature as those discussed in *Bell*, and accordingly, we hold that foster parents are not agents of the state for purposes of the fourth amendment.

Our conclusion that the trial court did not err in denying the motion to suppress is bolstered by application of the policies underlying the exclusionary rule to the facts of this case. The rule was first enunciated by the United States Supreme Court in *Weeks* v. United States, 232 U.S. 383, 34 S.Ct. 341, 58 L.Ed. 652 (1914), which held that evidence acquired by federal officers in violation of the fourth amendment must be excluded. Eventually, the rule was applied to criminal actions in state courts by Mapp v. Ohio, 367 U.S. 643, 81 S.Ct. 1684, 6 L.Ed.2d 1081 (1961). The United States Supreme Court has described the rule as one calculated to prevent, not to repair. Its purpose is to deter—to compel respect for the constitutional guaranty in the only effectively available way—by removing the incentive to disregard it.

As explained by the California Supreme Court in Dyas v. Superior Court, 114 Cal.Rptr. at 117, 522 P.2d at 677:

The two-fold purpose of the exclusionary rule is to deter law enforcement officers from engaging in unconstitutional searches and seizures by removing their incentive to do so, and to relieve the courts from being compelled to participate in such illegal conduct.

Thus,

[W]hether the exclusionary rule should be invoked depends instead on whether to do so would deter the particular governmental employee, and others similarly situated, from engaging in illegal searches of private citizens.

Thus the purpose of the rule is not to give shelter to those who have violated criminal laws but to insure that the constitutional rights of all citizens will be maintained. Police, knowing that illegally-obtained evidence cannot be used, are encouraged to comply with constitutional provisions. In the instant case, a principal motivating factor of Mrs. Blankenship's actions must have been a desire to aid her foster child as well as to have her home free of illegal drugs and criminal activity. Excluding the evidence seized herein would do nothing to deter similar future conduct by the Blankenships and other foster parents as that interest is entirely separate from a desire to have a person convicted of a crime or adjudged a delinquent. Put another way, the incentive to make a search under the circumstances here involved would not be lessened because of the likelihood that the evidence would be suppressed. In short, the primary purpose to be served by the exclusionary rule would not be served by its application in this case or ones similar to it.

Appellant J.M.A. suggests in passing that AS 11.60.280(b) which prohibits unauthorized eavesdropping on telephone conversations might also provide an alternative basis for barring the admission of Mrs. Blankenship's testimony concerning J.M.A.'s telephone call. In Roberts v. State, 453 P.2d 898 (Alaska 1969), cert. denied, 396 U.S. 1022, 90 S.Ct. 594, 24 L.Ed.2d 515 (1970), reh. denied, 397 U.S. 1059, 90 S.Ct. 1368, 25 L.Ed.2d 681 (1970), we noted that no provision excluding testimony obtained by eavesdropping had been enacted in conjunction with AS 11.60.280(b). In determining whether Mrs. Robert's conduct should come under a court fashioned exclusionary rule, we emphasized that her interception of a telephone conversation was not in any manner initiated or solicited by the police. Mrs. Roberts was acting as a private citizen in good faith and on her own initiative. Similarly, in this case, Mrs. Blankenship acted independently of the police as a private citizen, and no purpose would be served by ruling her testimony of the conversation to be inadmissable under the circumstances here involved.

In summary, in view of our holding that foster parents are not agents of the state for purposes of the fourth amendment, we conclude that the evidence secured by Mrs. Blankenship's efforts, both the testimony regarding the telephone conversation and the marijuana, was properly admitted.

* * *

Affirmed.

BURKE, J., not participating.

NOTES

1.   Whether a suspect consented to a search (and thereby waived his fourth amendment rights) presents perplexing problems for law enforcement and the judiciary. The problems are magnified when the suspect is a child. In In re Williams, 49 Misc.2d 154, 267 N.Y.S.2d 91 (1966) the Family Court judge concluded that the defendant's consent had not been given freely:

> The reasonableness of the search of the respondent's bungalow depends entirely upon the reality of his consent. * * * [T]he consent of this 15 year old boy given at 2 o'clock in the morning while in police custody under a charge of 3rd degree burglary and after he had been questioned for several hours without the presence of his parents or any other adult friend cannot be held to be a consent that was given freely and intelligently without any duress or coercion, express or implied. Unless we are prepared to say that because this boy is charged with juvenile delinquency and not a crime he has no right to be secure in his person, papers, house and effects against unreasonable searches and seizure the jewelry discovered in his bungalow is inadmissible against him and must be suppressed. * * * I think that due process of law and fair treatment require that even juveniles be held to be secure against unreasonable search and seizure.

Id. at 169–170, 267 N.Y.S.2d at 110.

2.   In In re Robert H., 78 Cal.App.3d 894, 144 Cal.Rptr. 565 (1978) the California Court of Appeals held that a minor suspected of a crime could give valid consent to a search of the dwelling house in which both he and his parents lived. The evidence seized was used in a delinquency proceeding involving the minor over his objection that he was not authorized to consent to a search of his parents' residence.

3.   In adult cases, under some circumstances the consent of a person other than the defendant may validate a discovery and seizure of things belonging to or otherwise incriminating the defendant. In juvenile cases the relationship of parent and child may enlarge the circumstances under which a valid third party consent can be given. In In re Scott, 24 Cal.3d 395, 155 Cal.Rptr. 671, 595 P.2d 105, cert. denied, Fare v. K., 444 U.S. 973, 100 S.Ct. 468, 62 L.Ed.2d 388 (1979), the court recognized that the rights of juveniles and adults were not co-extensive but, nevertheless, invalidated a father's consent to a search by a police officer of his son's locked tool box located in the juvenile's bedroom. And in State v. Flowers, 23 Mich.App. 523, 179 N.W. 2d 56 (1970), the court went considerably further—possibly beyond what most courts would do in adult third party consent cases—to invalidate a father's consent to a search of the room of his 17-year-old son living at home, attending school and being supported by his parents.

On the other hand, the court in Commonwealth v. Hardy, 423 Pa. 208, 223 A.2d 719 (1966), had little difficulty in sustaining a father's consent to a search of his son's room.

> Under the circumstances presented here the voluntary consent of Hardy's father to search *his own* premises is binding on Hardy and precludes his claim of violation of constitutional rights * * *.

423 Pa. at 216, 223 A.2d at 723.

STATE IN THE INTEREST OF R.H.

New Jersey Juvenile and Domestic Relations Court, 1979.
170 N.J.Super. 518, 406 A.2d 1350.

FERRANTE, P.J.J.D.R.C.

At issue in this case is the extent of a probationer's 4th Amendment rights. This matter raises the following issue of first impression in New Jersey: does the 4th Amendment to the United States Constitution prohibit the admission in a criminal juvenile delinquency complaint of evidence seized from a probationer by her probation officer without a search warrant or probable cause justifying a warrantless search. The prosecutor contends that R.H. lost her 4th Amendment right against illegal searches and seizures as a probationer.

There has been no evidentiary hearing, the parties have stipulated to the pertinent facts.

The facts as stipulated are as follows. On June 30, 1978 R.H.'s probation officer received an anonymous telephone call that R.H. was coming to the Passaic County Probation Department with a dangerous weapon. On arrival, and at her officer's request, R.H. emptied her purse, causing a knife to fall into view. The probation officer then caused a criminal juvenile delinquency complaint to be sworn out against R.H. for illegal possession of a dangerous weapon. To date no charge of violation of probation has been brought against R.H. pursuant to this incident.

The State argues the validity of the search. It contends that when defendant signed a statement acknowledging the rules and conditions of probation, she thereby waived certain constitutional rights possessed by one charged with a crime. The state specifically relies on four probation conditions as constituting such waiver: No. 1, refrain from crimes; No. 6, avoid injurious habits; No. 9, answer all reasonable inquiries, and No. 10, cooperate with the probation department in its efforts to help the probationer maintain a satisfactory standard of conduct. Nowhere does the State cite a condition which is a specific waiver of constitutional rights. The State also contends that defendant consented to the search.

Defendant argues that standard New Jersey conditions of probation do not clearly and positively inform a probationer that he waives his constitutional right against illegal searches and seizures. Defendant also contends that the State has not proven unequivocal, intelligent and voluntary consent to the search.

Moreover, defendant contends that the receipt of an anonymous telephone call, without more, does not give rise to probable cause sufficient to justify a warrantless search.

I agree with defendant's position.

The court disagrees that mere acknowledgment of the standard conditions of probation implies a waiver of constitutional rights.

A basic tenet of constitutional law is that a waiver of constitutional rights is not easily upheld.   *   *   *

A waiver must be clearly understood by the defendant; as stated in Karr v. Blay, 413 F.Supp. 579, 583 (N.D.Ohio 1976), "a defendant cannot be deprived of his liberty by an unknowing and silent waiver of his rights."

Simply put, the standard conditions of probation in New Jersey do not sufficiently apprise a probationer that he is waiving any of his 4th Amendment rights. It is a fundamental principle that a waiver must be known and intentional, not presumed or inferred. Clearly, there was no valid waiver by R.H. of her constitutional rights when she signed the acknowledgment of probation form and the standard conditions therein. None of the conditions quoted by the prosecutor includes a clear waiver of constitutional rights.

If the terms of probation governing R.H. had been more specific, a different result might have occurred.[2]

This court holds that a probationer does not waive his 4th Amendment rights in a new criminal action merely by his status as a probationer.[3]

People v. Jackson, 46 N.Y.2d 171, 385 N.E.2d 621, 412 N.Y.S.2d 884 (Ct.App.1978), is instructive; the facts are similar. In that case there was also no probable cause to believe defendant-probationer was committing a crime; there was only an anonymous accusation given by telephone to his probation officer. On the basis of this call the probation officer searched the probationer's work locker, finding a small hand gun. A probation revocation hearing was held and a new criminal complaint sworn out. The Court of Appeals admitted the gun to the revocation hearing but suppressed it in the new criminal action. The court stated:

To uphold the search in this case would hardly be consistent with the recognition of a probationer's constitutional right to be

---

2. The law of the nation, and recently of New Jersey, upholds warrantless searches of probationers when only pursuant to specific probation terms that clearly waive constitutional rights. State v. Bollinger, 169 N.J.Super. 553, 405 A.2d 432 (Law Div. 1979), addressed the constitutionality of special probation terms. The *Bollinger* court upheld the otherwise illegal search of a probationer's home and car on the basis of special probation drug rules. Special rule No. 6 permitted at any time a search by a probation officer of any place or thing under a proba-

tioner's immediate control. The court held that by agreeing to the drug dependency rules, the defendant waived his 4th Amendment rights in regard to illegal searches.

3. Though not a specific issue in this matter, it is clear that the knife in question would be admissible in a revocation of probation hearing. Although a probation revocation may result in a defendant's loss of liberty, it is not a stage of a criminal prosecution.

free of unreasonable searches and seizures. If that right means anything it must at least mean that a probationer who has not previously violated the conditions of his sentence should not be subjected to a complete search of his person and property whenever his probation officer receives an anonymous phone call. [385 N.E.2d at 624, 412 N.Y.S.2d at 887]

* * *

Therefore, absent probable cause, the warrantless search of defendant cannot be justified by her status as a probationer.

The prosecutor contends that R.H. consented to the search, thereby validating it. The defendant claims it was involuntary and coerced. In regard to the issue of consent the court is governed by Schneckloth v. Bustamonte, 412 U.S. 218, 93 S.Ct. 2041, 36 L.Ed.2d 854 (1973), wherein the minimum constitutional requirements are outlined. This court is also bound by State v. Johnson, 68 N.J. 349, 346 A.2d 66 (1975), wherein our Supreme Court (at 354, 346 A.2d at 68) imposed the additional requirement of the State having to show "that the person involved knew that he had a right to refuse to accede to such a request."

This court is satisfied that the consent was valid under *Bustamonte*, supra; based upon the totality of all the circumstances it was voluntary and not the product of duress or coercion.

However, as a threshold matter, the court is satisfied from the facts of this case that the State has failed to meet the additional requirement imposed by *Johnson*, supra—specifically, that the State has not demonstrated knowledge on the part of R.H. that she had a choice as to the probation officer's demand to empty her pocketbook. The probation officer made no effort to inform R.H. of her rights; instead she quickly demanded that the purse be emptied. R.H. is a confused juvenile with psychiatric problems. She is almost naive in her knowledge of society; to expect her to have had a knowledge of her right to withhold consent is erroneous. The court holds, accordingly, that R.H.'s consent was not unequivocally, intelligently and voluntarily given, as required in State v. King, 44 N.J. 346, 209 A.2d 110 (1965), and State v. Rice, 115 N.J.Super. 128, 278 A.2d 498 (App. Div.1971).

In determining the existence of probable cause the court finds it permissible to rely on a less stringent standard when defendant is a probationer. * * * Obviously, a defendant's status as a probationer is a relevant element in deciding whether probable cause existed * * * "probationary status may be taken into account in determining whether a particular search was in fact reasonable." The *Jackson* ((supra) court also stated at 385 N.E.2d at 623, 412 N.Y.S.2d 886), "Of course the defendant's status as a parolee or probationer is relevant in determining the reasonableness of the search."

R.H.'s probation status is a factor that would normally weigh in favor of finding probable cause. The facts of the case, however, negate this presumptive inclination. R.H. was on probation for a JINS (juvenile in need of supervision) offense, not for a juvenile delinquency criminal offense. She has never, in fact, been guilty of any criminal act. Her probation officer was aware of her noncriminal history. When the background of R.H.'s probation is revealed, little support for probable cause is evidenced.

The probation officer based her search solely on an anonymous telephone call. These facts do not constitute probable cause justifying the warrantless search.

For all the foregoing reasons the court suppresses the knife as admissible evidence in the criminal action for illegal possession of a dangerous weapon.

NEW JERSEY v. T.L.O.*

Supreme Court of the United States, 1985.
___ U.S. ___, 105 S.Ct. 733, 83 L.Ed.2d 720.

JUSTICE WHITE delivered the opinion of the Court.**

We granted certiorari in this case to examine the appropriateness of the exclusionary rule as a remedy for searches carried out in violation of the Fourth Amendment by public school authorities. Our consideration of the proper application of the Fourth Amendment to the public schools, however, has led us to conclude that the search that gave rise to the case now before us did not violate the Fourth Amendment. Accordingly, we here address only the questions of the proper standard for assessing the legality of searches conducted by public school officials and the application of that standard to the facts of this case.

I

On March 7, 1980, a teacher at Piscataway High School in Middlesex County, N.J., discovered two girls smoking in a lavatory. One of the two girls was the respondent T.L.O., who at that time was a 14-year-old high school freshman. Because smoking in the lavatory was a violation of a school rule, the teacher took the two girls to the Principal's office, where they met with Assistant Vice Principal Theodore Choplick. In response to questioning by Mr. Choplick, T.L.O.'s companion admitted that she had violated the rule. T.L.O., however, denied that she had been smoking in the lavatory and claimed that she did not smoke at all.

---

* Because this case was decided after completion of the manuscript, we have decided to depart from our usual practice and leave the footnote numbers as they appear in the original official reports.

** WHITE, J., delivered the opinion of the Court, in which BURGER, C.J., and POWELL, REHNQUIST, and O'CONNOR, JJ., joined and in Part II of which BRENNAN, MARSHALL, and STEVENS, JJ., joined.

POWELL, J., filed a concurring opinion, in which O'CONNOR, J., joined. BLACKMUN, J., filed an opinion concurring in the judgment. BRENNAN, J., filed an opinion concurring in part and dissenting in part, in which MARSHALL, J., joined. STEVENS, J., filed an opinion concurring in part and dissenting in part, in which MARSHALL, J., joined and in Part I of which BRENNAN, J., joined.

Mr. Choplick asked T.L.O. to come into his private office and demanded to see her purse. Opening the purse, he found a pack of cigarettes, which he removed from the purse and held before T.L.O. as he accused her of having lied to him. As he reached into the purse for the cigarettes, Mr. Choplick also noticed a package of cigarette rolling papers. In his experience, possession of rolling papers by high school students was closely associated with the use of marihuana. Suspecting that a closer examination of the purse might yield further evidence of drug use, Mr. Choplick proceeded to search the purse thoroughly. The search revealed a small amount of marihuana, a pipe, a number of empty plastic bags, a substantial quantity of money in one-dollar bills, an index card that appeared to be a list of students who owed T.L.O. money, and two letters that implicated T.L.O. in marihuana dealing.

Mr. Choplick notified T.L.O.'s mother and the police, and turned the evidence of drug dealing over to the police. At the request of the police, T.L.O.'s mother took her daughter to police headquarters, where T.L.O. confessed that she had been selling marihuana at the high school. On the basis of the confession and the evidence seized by Mr. Choplick, the State brought delinquency charges against T.L.O. in the Juvenile and Domestic Relations Court of Middlesex County.[1] Contending that Mr. Choplick's search of her purse violated the Fourth Amendment, T.L.O. moved to suppress the evidence found in her purse as well her confession, which, she argued, was tainted by the allegedly unlawful search. The Juvenile Court denied the motion to suppress. State ex rel. T.L.O., 178 N.J.Super. 329, 428 A.2d 1327 (1980). Although the court concluded that the Fourth Amendment did apply to searches carried out by school officials, it held that

> "a school official may properly conduct a search of a student's person if the official has a reasonable suspicion that a crime has been or is in the process of being committed, *or* reasonable cause to believe that the search is necessary to maintain school discipline or enforce school policies." Id., 178 N.J.Super., at 341, 428 A.2d, at 1333 (emphasis in original).

Applying this standard, the court concluded that the search conducted by Mr. Choplick was a reasonable one. The initial decision to open the purse was justified by Mr. Choplick's well-founded suspicion that T.L.O. had violated the rule forbidding smoking in the lavatory. Once the purse was open, evidence of marihuana violations was in plain view, and Mr. Choplick was entitled to conduct a thorough search to determine the nature and extent of T.L.O.'s drug-related activities. Id., 178 N.J.Super., at 343, 428 A.2d, at 1334. Having denied the motion to suppress, the court on March 23, 1981

---

[1] T.L.O. also received a 3-day suspension from school for smoking cigarettes in a nonsmoking area and a 7-day suspension for possession of marihuana. On T.L.O.'s motion, the Superior Court of New Jersey, Chancery Division, set aside the 7-day suspension on the ground that it was based on evidence seized in violation of the Fourth Amendment. (T.L.O.) v. Piscataway Bd. of Ed., No. C.2865–79 (Super.Ct.N.J., Ch.Div., Mar. 31, 1980). The Board of Education apparently did not appeal the decision of the Chancery Division.

found T.L.O. to be a delinquent and on January 8, 1982, sentenced her to a year's probation.

On appeal from the final judgment of the Juvenile Court, a divided Appellate Division affirmed the trial court's finding that there had been no Fourth Amendment violation, but vacated the adjudication of delinquency and remanded for a determination whether T.L.O. had knowingly and voluntarily waived her Fifth Amendment rights before confessing. State ex rel. T.L.O., 185 N.J.Super. 279, 448 A.2d 493 (1982). T.L.O. appealed the Fourth Amendment ruling, and the Supreme Court of New Jersey reversed the judgment of the Appellate Division and ordered the suppression of the evidence found in T.L.O.'s purse. State ex rel. T.L.O., 94 N.J. 331, 463 A.2d 934 (1983).

The New Jersey Supreme Court agreed with the lower courts that the Fourth Amendment applies to searches conducted by school officials. The court also rejected the State of New Jersey's argument that the exclusionary rule should not be employed to prevent the use in juvenile proceedings of evidence unlawfully seized by school officials. Declining to consider whether applying the rule to the fruits of searches by school officials would have any deterrent value, the court held simply that the precedents of this Court establish that "if an official search violates constitutional rights, the evidence is not admissible in criminal proceedings." Id., 94 N.J., at 341, 463 A.2d, at 939 (footnote omitted).

With respect to the question of the legality of the search before it, the court agreed with the Juvenile Court that a warrantless search by a school official does not violate the Fourth Amendment so long as the official "has reasonable grounds to believe that a student possesses evidence of illegal activity or activity that would interfere with school discipline and order." Id., 94 N.J., at 346, 463 A.2d, at 941–942. However, the court, with two justices dissenting, sharply disagreed with the Juvenile Court's conclusion that the search of the purse was reasonable. According to the majority, the contents of T.L.O.'s purse had no bearing on the accusation against T.L.O., for possession of cigarettes (as opposed to smoking them in the lavatory) did not violate school rules, and a mere desire for evidence that would impeach T.L.O.'s claim that she did not smoke cigarettes could not justify the search. Moreover, even if a reasonable suspicion that T.L.O. had cigarettes in her purse would justify a search, Mr. Choplick had no such suspicion, as no one had furnished him with any specific information that there were cigarettes in the purse. Finally, leaving aside the question whether Mr. Choplick was justified in opening the purse, the court held that the evidence of drug use that he saw inside did not justify the extensive "rummaging" through T.L.O.'s papers and effects that followed. Id., 94 N.J., at 347, 463 A.2d, at 942–943.

We granted the State of New Jersey's petition for certiorari. 464 U.S. ___, 104 S.Ct. 480, 78 L.Ed.2d 678 (1983). Although the State had argued in the Supreme Court of New Jersey that the search of T.L.O.'s purse did not violate the Fourth Amendment, the petition for certiorari raised only the question whether the exclusionary rule should operate to bar consideration in juvenile delinquency proceedings of evidence unlawfully seized by a school official without the involvement of law enforcement officers. When this case was first argued last Term, the State conceded for the purpose of argument that the standard devised by the New Jersey Supreme Court for determining the legality of school searches was appropriate and that the court had correctly applied that standard; the State contended only that the remedial purposes of the exclusionary rule were not well served by applying it to searches conducted by public authorities not primarily engaged in law enforcement.

Although we originally granted certiorari to decide the issue of the appropriate remedy in juvenile court proceedings for unlawful school searches, our doubts regarding the wisdom of deciding that question in isolation from the broader question of what limits, if any, the Fourth Amendment places on the activities of school authorities prompted us to order reargument on that question.[2] Having heard

[2] State and federal courts considering these questions have struggled to accommodate the interests protected by the Fourth Amendment and the interest of the States in providing a safe environment conducive to education in the public schools. Some courts have resolved the tension between these interests by giving full force to one or the other side of the balance. Thus, in a number of cases courts have held that school officials conducting in-school searches of students are private parties acting *in loco parentis* and are therefore not subject to the constraints of the Fourth Amendment. See, e.g., D.R.C. v. State, 646 P.2d 252 (Alaska App.1982); In re G., 11 Cal.App. 3d 1193, 90 Cal.Rptr. 361 (1970); In re Donaldson, 269 Cal.App.2d 509, 75 Cal. Rptr. 220 (1969); R.C.M. v. State, 660 S.W.2d 552 (Tex.App.1983); Mercer v. State, 450 S.W.2d 715 (Tex.Civ.App.1970). At least one court has held, on the other hand, that the Fourth Amendment applies in full to in-school searches by school officials and that a search conducted without probable cause is unreasonable, see State v. Mora, 307 So.2d 317 (La.), vacated, 423 U.S. 809, 96 S.Ct. 20, 46 L.Ed.2d 29 (1975), on remand, 330 So. 2d 900 (La.1976); others have held or suggested that the probable-cause standard is applicable at least where the police are involved in a search, see M. v. Board of Ed. Ball-Chatham Community Unit School Dist. No. 5, 429 F.Supp. 288, 292 (SD Ill.1977); Picha v. Wielgos, 410 F.Supp. 1214, 1219–1221 (ND Ill.1976); State v. Young, 234 Ga. 488, 498, 216 S.E.2d 586, 594 (1975); or where the search is highly intrusive, see M.M. v. Anker, 607 F.2d 588, 589 (CA2 1979).

The majority of courts that have addressed the issue of the Fourth Amendment in the schools have, like the Supreme Court of New Jersey in this case, reached a middle position: the Fourth Amendment applies to searches conducted by school authorities, but the special needs of the school environment require assessment of the legality of such searches against a standard less exacting than that of probable cause. These courts have, by and large, upheld warrantless searches by school authorities provided that they are supported by a reasonable suspicion that the search will uncover evidence of an infraction of school disciplinary rules or a violation of the law. See, e.g., Tarter v. Raybuck, 742 F.2d 977 (CA6 1984); Bilbrey v. Brown, 738 F.2d 1462 (CA9 1984); Horton v. Goose Creek Independent School Dist., 690 F.2d 470 (CA5 1982); Bellnier v. Lund, 438 F.Supp. 47 (NDNY 1977); M. v. Board of Ed. Ball-Chatham Community Unit School Dist. No. 5, supra; In re W., 29 Cal.App.3d 777, 105 Cal.Rptr. 775 (1973); State v. Baccino 282 A.2d 869 (Del.Super.1971); State v. D.T.W., 425 So.2d 1383 (Fla.Dist.Ct.App.1983); State v. Young, supra; In re J.A., 85 Ill.App.3d 567, 40 Ill.Dec. 755, 406 N.E.2d 958 (1980); People v. Ward, 62 Mich.App. 46, 233 N.W.2d 180 (1975); Doe v. State, 88 N.M. 347, 540 P.2d 827 (App.1975); People v. D., 34 N.Y.2d 483, 358 N.Y.S.2d 403, 315 N.E.2d 466 (1974); State v. McKinnon, 88 Wash.2d 75, 558 P.2d 781 (1977); In re L.L., 90 Wis.2d 585, 280 N.W.2d 343 (App.1979).

Although few have considered the matter, courts have also split over whether the exclusionary rule is an appropriate

argument on the legality of the search of T.L.O.'s purse, we are satisfied that the search did not violate the Fourth Amendment.[3]

II

In determining whether the search at issue in this case violated the Fourth Amendment, we are faced initially with the question whether that Amendment's prohibition on unreasonable searches and seizures applies to searches conducted by public school officials. We hold that it does.

It is now beyond dispute that "the Federal Constitution, by virtue of the Fourteenth Amendment, prohibits unreasonable searches and seizures by state officers." Elkins v. United States, 364 U.S. 206, 213, 80 S.Ct. 1437, 1442, 4 L.Ed.2d 1669 (1960); accord, Mapp v. Ohio, 367 U.S. 643, 81 S.Ct. 1684, 6 L.Ed.2d 1081 (1961); Wolf v. Colorado, 338 U.S. 25, 69 S.Ct. 1359, 93 L.Ed. 1782 (1949). Equally indisputable is the proposition that the Fourteenth Amendment protects the rights of students against encroachment by public school officials:

> "The Fourteenth Amendment, as now applied to the States, protects the citizen against the State itself and all of its creatures—Boards of Education not excepted. These have, of course, delicate, and highly discretionary functions, but none that they may not perform within the limits of the Bill of Rights. That they are educating the young for citizenship is reason for scrupulous protection of Constitutional freedoms of the individual, if we are not to strangle the free mind at its source and teach youth to discount important principles of our government as mere platitudes." West Virginia State Bd. of Ed. v. Barnette, 319 U.S. 624, 637, 63 S.Ct. 1178, 1185, 87 L.Ed. 1628 (1943).

These two propositions—that the Fourth Amendment applies to the States through the Fourteenth Amendment, and that the actions of public school officials are subject to the limits placed on state action by the Fourteenth Amendment—might appear sufficient to answer the suggestion that the Fourth Amendment does not proscribe unreasonable searches by school officials. On reargument, however, the State of New Jersey has argued that the history of the

remedy for Fourth Amendment violations committed by school authorities. The Georgia courts have held that although the Fourth Amendment applies to the schools, the exclusionary rule does not. See, e.g., State v. Young, supra; State v. Lamb, 137 Ga.App. 437, 224 S.E.2d 51 (1976). Other jurisdictions have applied the rule to exclude the fruits of unlawful school searches from criminal trials and delinquency proceedings. See State v. Mora, supra; People v. D., supra.

[3] In holding that the search of T.L.O.'s purse did not violate the Fourth Amendment, we do not implicitly determine that the exclusionary rule applies to the fruits of unlawful searches conducted by school authorities. The question whether evidence should be excluded from a criminal proceeding involves two discrete inquiries: whether the evidence was seized in violation of the Fourth Amendment, and whether the exclusionary rule is the appropriate remedy for the violation. Neither question is logically antecedent to the other, for a negative answer to either question is sufficient to dispose of the case. Thus, our determination that the search at issue in this case did not violate the Fourth Amendment implies no particular resolution of the question of the applicability of the exclusionary rule.

Fourth Amendment indicates that the Amendment was intended to regulate only searches and seizures carried out by law enforcement officers; accordingly, although public school officials are concededly state agents for purposes of the Fourteenth Amendment, the Fourth Amendment creates no rights enforceable against them.[4]

It may well be true that the evil toward which the Fourth Amendment was primarily directed was the resurrection of the pre-Revolutionary practice of using general warrants or "writs of assistance" to authorize searches for contraband by officers of the Crown. See United States v. Chadwick, 433 U.S. 1, 7–8, 97 S.Ct. 2476, 2481, 53 L.Ed.2d 538 (1977); Boyd v. United States, 116 U.S. 616, 624–629, 6 S.Ct. 524, 528–531, 29 L.Ed. 746 (1886). But this Court has never limited the Amendment's prohibition on unreasonable searches and seizures to operations conducted by the police. Rather, the Court has long spoken of the Fourth Amendment's strictures as restraints imposed upon "governmental action"—that is, "upon the activities of sovereign authority." Burdeau v. McDowell, 256 U.S. 465, 475, 41 S.Ct. 574, 576, 65 L.Ed. 1048 (1921). Accordingly, we have held the Fourth Amendment applicable to the activities of civil as well as criminal authorities: building inspectors, see Camara v. Municipal Court, 387 U.S. 523, 528, 87 S.Ct. 1727, 1730, 18 L.Ed.2d 930 (1967), OSHA inspectors, see Marshall v. Barlow's Inc., 436 U.S. 307, 312–313, 98 S.Ct. 1816, 1820, 56 L.Ed.2d 305 (1978), and even firemen entering privately owned premises to battle a fire, see Michigan v. Tyler, 436 U.S. 499, 506, 98 S.Ct. 1942, 1948, 56 L.Ed.2d 486 (1978), are all subject to the restraints imposed by the Fourth Amendment. As we observed in Camara v. Municipal Court, supra, "[t]he basic purpose of this Amendment, as recognized in countless decisions of this Court, is to safeguard the privacy and security of individuals against arbitrary invasions by governmental officials." 387 U.S., at 528, 87 S.Ct., at 1730. Because the individual's interest in privacy and personal security "suffers whether the government's motivation is to investigate violations of criminal laws or breaches of other statutory or regulatory standards," Marshall v. Barlow's, Inc., supra, 436 U.S., at 312–313, 98 S.Ct., at 1820, it would be "anomalous to say that the individual and his private property are fully protected by the Fourth Amendment only when the individual is suspected of criminal behavior." Camara v. Municipal Court, 387 U.S., at 530, 87 S.Ct., at 1732.

Notwithstanding the general applicability of the Fourth Amendment to the activities of civil authorities, a few courts have concluded that school officials are exempt from the dictates of the Fourth Amendment by virtue of the special nature of their authority over schoolchildren. See, e.g., R.C.M. v. State, 660 S.W.2d 552 (Tex.App. 1983). Teachers and school administrators, it is said, act *in loco parentis* in their dealings with students; their authority is that of the

[4] Cf. Ingraham v. Wright, 430 U.S. 651, 97 S.Ct. 1401, 51 L.Ed.2d 711 (1977) (holding that the Eighth Amendment's prohibition of cruel and unusual punishment applies only to punishments imposed after criminal convictions and hence does not apply to the punishment of schoolchildren by public school officials).

parent, not the State, and is therefore not subject to the limits of the Fourth Amendment. Ibid.

Such reasoning is in tension with contemporary reality and the teachings of this Court. We have held school officials subject to the commands of the First Amendment, see Tinker v. Des Moines Independent Community School District, 393 U.S. 503, 89 S.Ct. 733, 21 L.Ed.2d 731 (1969), and the Due Process Clause of the Fourteenth Amendment, see Goss v. Lopez, 419 U.S. 565, 95 S.Ct. 729, 42 L.Ed.2d 725 (1975). If school authorities are state actors for purposes of the constitutional guarantees of freedom of expression and due process, it is difficult to understand why they should be deemed to be exercising parental rather than public authority when conducting searches of their students. More generally, the Court has recognized that "the concept of parental delegation" as a source of school authority is not entirely "consonant with compulsory education laws." Ingraham v. Wright, 430 U.S. 651, 662, 97 S.Ct. 1401, 1407, 51 L.Ed.2d 711 (1977). Today's public school officials do not merely exercise authority voluntarily conferred on them by individual parents; rather, they act in furtherance of publicly mandated educational and disciplinary policies. See, e.g., the opinion in State ex rel. T.L.O., 94 N.J., at 343, 463 A.2d, at 934, 940, describing the New Jersey statutes regulating school disciplinary policies and establishing the authority of school officials over their students. In carrying out searches and other disciplinary functions pursuant to such policies, school officials act as representatives of the State, not merely as surrogates for the parents, and they cannot claim the parents' immunity from the strictures of the Fourth Amendment.

III

To hold that the Fourth Amendment applies to searches conducted by school authorities is only to begin the inquiry into the standards governing such searches. Although the underlying command of the Fourth Amendment is always that searches and seizures be reasonable, what is reasonable depends on the context within which a search takes place. The determination of the standard of reasonableness governing any specific class of searches requires "balancing the need to search against the invasion which the search entails." Camara v. Municipal Court, supra, 387 U.S., at 536–537, 87 S.Ct., at 1735. On one side of the balance are arrayed the individual's legitimate expectations of privacy and personal security; on the other, the government's need for effective methods to deal with breaches of public order.

We have recognized that even a limited search of the person is a substantial invasion of privacy. Terry v. Ohio, 392 U.S. 1, 24–25, 88 S.Ct. 1868, 1881–1882, 20 L.Ed.2d 889 (1967). We have also recognized that searches of closed items of personal luggage are intrusions on protected privacy interests, for "the Fourth Amendment provides protection to the owner of every container that conceals its contents from plain view." United States v. Ross, 456 U.S. 798, 822–823, 102

S.Ct. 2157, 2171, 72 L.Ed.2d 572 (1982). A search of a child's person or of a closed purse or other bag carried on her person,[5] no less than a similar search carried out on an adult, is undoubtedly a severe violation of subjective expectations of privacy.

Of course, the Fourth Amendment does not protect subjective expectations of privacy that are unreasonable or otherwise "illegitimate." See, e.g., Hudson v. Palmer, 468 U.S. ___, 104 S.Ct. 3194, 82 L.Ed.2d 393 (1984); Rawlings v. Kentucky, 448 U.S. 98, 100 S.Ct. 2556, 65 L.Ed.2d 633 (1980). To receive the protection of the Fourth Amendment, an expectation of privacy must be one that society is "prepared to recognize as legitimate." Hudson v. Palmer, supra, 468 U.S., at ___, 104 S.Ct., at 3200. The State of New Jersey has argued that because of the pervasive supervision to which children in the schools are necessarily subject, a child has virtually no legitimate expectation of privacy in articles of personal property "unnecessarily" carried into a school. This argument has two factual premises: (1) the fundamental incompatibility of expectations of privacy with the maintenance of a sound educational environment; and (2) the minimal interest of the child in bringing any items of personal property into the school. Both premises are severely flawed.

Although this Court may take notice of the difficulty of maintaining discipline in the public schools today, the situation is not so dire that students in the schools may claim no legitimate expectations of privacy. We have recently recognized that the need to maintain order in a prison is such that prisoners retain no legitimate expectations of privacy in their cells, but it goes almost without saying that "[t]he prisoner and the schoolchild stand in wholly different circumstances, separated by the harsh facts of criminal conviction and incarceration." Ingraham v. Wright, 430 U.S., at 669, 97 S.Ct., at 1411. We are not yet ready to hold that the schools and the prisons need be equated for purposes of the Fourth Amendment.

Nor does the State's suggestion that children have no legitimate need to bring personal property into the schools seem well anchored in reality. Students at a minimum must bring to school not only the supplies needed for their studies, but also keys, money, and the necessaries of personal hygiene and grooming. In addition, students may carry on their persons or in purses or wallets such nondisruptive

[5] We do not address the question, not presented by this case, whether a schoolchild has a legitimate expectation of privacy in lockers, desks, or other school property provided for the storage of school supplies. Nor do we express any opinion on the standards (if any) governing searches of such areas by school officials or by other public authorities acting at the request of school officials. Compare Zamora v. Pomeroy, 639 F.2d 662, 670 (CA10 1981) ("Inasmuch as the school had assumed joint control of the locker it cannot be successfully maintained that the school did not have a right to inspect it."), and People v. Overton, 24 N.Y.2d 522, 249 N.E.2d 366, 301 N.Y.S.2d 479 (1969) (school administrators have power to consent to search of a student's locker), with State v. Engerud, 94 N.J. 331, 348, 463 A.2d 934, 943 (1983) ("We are satisfied that in the context of this case the student had an expectation of privacy in the contents of his locker * * *. For the four years of high school, the school locker is a home away from home. In it the student stores the kind of personal 'effects' protected by the Fourth Amendment").

yet highly personal items as photographs, letters, and diaries. Finally, students may have perfectly legitimate reasons to carry with them articles of property needed in connection with extracurricular or recreational activities. In short, schoolchildren may find it necessary to carry with them a variety of legitimate, noncontraband items, and there is no reason to conclude that they have necessarily waived all rights to privacy in such items merely by bringing them onto school grounds.

Against the child's interest in privacy must be set the substantial interest of teachers and administrators in maintaining discipline in the classroom and on school grounds. Maintaining order in the classroom has never been easy, but in recent years, school disorder has often taken particularly ugly forms: drug use and violent crime in the schools have become major social problems. See generally 1 NIE, U.S. Dept. of Health, Education and Welfare, Violent Schools— Safe Schools: The Safe School Study Report to the Congress (1978). Even in schools that have been spared the most severe disciplinary problems, the preservation of order and a proper educational environment requires close supervision of schoolchildren, as well as the enforcement of rules against conduct that would be perfectly permissible if undertaken by an adult. "Events calling for discipline are frequent occurrences and sometimes require immediate, effective action." Gross v. Lopez, 419 U.S., at 580, 95 S.Ct., at 739. Accordingly, we have recognized that maintaining security and order in the schools requires a certain degree of flexibility in school disciplinary procedures, and we have respected the value of preserving the informality of the student-teacher relationship. See id., at 582–583, 95 S.Ct., at 740; Ingraham v. Wright, 430 U.S., at 680–682, 97 S.Ct., at 1417–1418.

How, then, should we strike the balance between the schoolchild's legitimate expectations of privacy and the school's equally legitimate need to maintain an environment in which learning can take place? It is evident that the school setting requires some easing of the restrictions to which searches by public authorities are ordinarily subject. The warrant requirement, in particular, is unsuited to the school environment: requiring a teacher to obtain a warrant before searching a child suspected of an infraction of school rules (or of the criminal law) would unduly interfere with the maintenance of the swift and informal disciplinary procedures needed in the schools. Just as we have in other cases dispensed with the warrant requirement when "the burden of obtaining a warrant is likely to frustrate the governmental purpose behind the search," Camara v. Municipal Court, 387 U.S., at 532–533, 87 S.Ct., at 1733, we hold today that school officials need not obtain a warrant before searching a student who is under their authority.

The school setting also requires some modification of the level of suspicion of illicit activity needed to justify a search. Ordinarily, a search—even one that may permissibly be carried out without a warrant—must be based upon "probable cause" to believe that a violation of the law has occurred. See, e.g., Almeida-Sanchez v. United States, 413 U.S. 266, 273, 93 S.Ct. 2535, 2540, 37 L.Ed.2d 596 (1973); Sibron v. New York, 392 U.S. 40, 62–66, 88 S.Ct. 1889, 1902–1904, 20 L.Ed.2d 917 (1968). However, "probable cause" is not an irreducible requirement of a valid search. The fundamental command of the Fourth Amendment is that searches and seizures be reasonable, and although "both the concept of probable cause and the requirement of a warrant bear on the reasonableness of a search, * * * in certain limited circumstances neither is required." Almeida-Sanchez v. United States, supra, 413 U.S., at 277, 93 S.Ct., at 2541 (POWELL, J., concurring). Thus, we have in a number of cases recognized the legality of searches and seizures based on suspicions that, although "reasonable," do not rise to the level of probable cause. See, e.g., Terry v. Ohio, 392 U.S. 1, 88 S.Ct. 1868, 20 L.Ed.2d 889 (1968); United States v. Brignoni-Ponce, 422 U.S. 873, 881, 95 S.Ct. 2574, 2580, 45 L.Ed.2d 607 (1975); Delaware v. Prouse, 440 U.S. 648, 654–655, 99 S.Ct. 1391, 1396, 59 L.Ed.2d 660 (1979); United States v. Martinez-Fuerte, 428 U.S. 543, 96 S.Ct. 3074, 49 L.Ed.2d 1116 (1976); cf. Camara v. Municipal Court, 387 U.S., at 534–539, 87 S.Ct., at 1733–1736. Where a careful balancing of governmental and private interests suggests that the public interest is best served by a Fourth Amendment standard of reasonableness that stops short of probable cause, we have not hesitated to adopt such a standard.

We join the majority of courts that have examined this issue [6] in concluding that the accommodation of the privacy interests of schoolchildren with the substantial need of teachers and administrators for freedom to maintain order in the schools does not require strict adherence to the requirement that searches be based on probable cause to believe that the subject of the search has violated or is violating the law. Rather, the legality of a search of a student should depend simply on the reasonableness, under all the circumstances, of the search. Determining the reasonableness of any search involves a twofold inquiry: first, one must consider "whether the * * * action was justified at its inception," Terry v. Ohio, 392 U.S., at 20, 88 S.Ct., at 1879; second, one must determine whether the search as actually conducted "was reasonably related in scope to the circumstances which justified the interference in the first place," ibid. Under ordinary circumstances, a search of a student by a teacher or other school official [7] will be "justified at its inception" when there are reasonable grounds for suspecting that the search will turn up evidence that the student has violated or is violating either the law or the rules of the school.[8] Such a search will be permissible in its scope

[6] See cases cited in n. 2, supra.

[7] We here consider only searches carried out by school authorities acting alone and on their own authority. This case does not present the question of the appropriate standard for assessing the legality of searches conducted by school officials in conjunction with or at the behest of law enforcement agencies, and

we express no opinion on that question. Cf. Picha v. Wielgos, 410 F.Supp. 1214, 1219–1221 (ND Ill.1976) (holding probable cause standard applicable to searches involving the police).

[8] We do not decide whether individualized suspicion is an essential element of the reasonableness standard we adopt for searches by school authorities. In

when the measures adopted are reasonably related to the objectives of the search and not excessively intrusive in light of the age and sex of the student and the nature of the infraction.[9]

This standard will, we trust, neither unduly burden the efforts of school authorities to maintain order in their schools nor authorize unrestrained intrusions upon the privacy of schoolchildren. By focusing attention on the question of reasonableness, the standard will spare teachers and school administrators the necessity of schooling themselves in the niceties of probable cause and permit them to regulate their conduct according to the dictates of reason and common sense. At the same time, the reasonableness standard should ensure that the interests of students will be invaded no more than is necessary to achieve the legitimate end of preserving order in the schools.

IV

There remains the question of the legality of the search in this case. We recognize that the "reasonable grounds" standard applied by the New Jersey Supreme Court in its consideration of this question is not substantially different from the standard that we have adopted today. Nonetheless, we believe that the New Jersey court's application of that standard to strike down the search of T.L.O.'s

other contexts, however, we have held that although "some quantum of individualized suspicion is usually a prerequisite to a constitutional search or seizure[,] * * * the Fourth Amendment imposes no irreducible requirement of such suspicion." United States v. Martinez-Fuerte, 428 U.S. 543, 560–561, 96 S.Ct. 3074, 3084, 49 L.Ed.2d 1116 (1976). See also Camara v. Municipal Court, 387 U.S. 523, 87 S.Ct. 1727, 18 L.Ed.2d 930 (1967). Exceptions to the requirement of individualized suspicion are generally appropriate only where the privacy interests implicated by a search are minimal and where "other safeguards" are available "to assure that the individual's reasonable expectation of privacy is not 'subject to the discretion of the official in the field.'" Delaware v. Prouse, 440 U.S. 648, 654–655, 99 S.Ct. 1391, 1396–1397, 59 L.Ed.2d 660 (1979) (citation omitted). Because the search of T.L.O.'s purse was based upon an individualized suspicion that she had violated school rules, see infra, at 745–746, we need not consider the circumstances that might justify school authorities in conducting searches unsupported by individualized suspicion.

[9] Our reference to the nature of the infraction is not intended as an endorsement of Justice Stevens' suggestion that some rules regarding student conduct are by nature too "trivial" to justify a search based upon reasonable suspicion.

See post, at 763–765. We are unwilling to adopt a standard under which the legality of a search is dependent upon a judge's evaluation of the relative importance of various school rules. The maintenance of discipline in the schools requires not only that students be restrained from assaulting one another, abusing drugs and alcohol, and committing other crimes, but also that students conform themselves to the standards of conduct prescribed by school authorities. We have "repeatedly emphasized the need for affirming the comprehensive authority of the States and of school officials, consistent with fundamental constitutional safeguards, to prescribe and control conduct in the schools." Tinker v. Des Moines Independent Community School Dist., 393 U.S. 503, 507, 89 S.Ct. 733, 737, 21 L.Ed.2d 731 (1969). The promulgation of a rule forbidding specified conduct presumably reflects a judgment on the part of school officials that such conduct is destructive of school order or of a proper educational environment. Absent any suggestion that the rule violates some substantive constitutional guarantee, the courts should, as a general matter, defer to that judgment and refrain from attempting to distinguish between rules that are important to the preservation of order in the schools and rules that are not.

purse reflects a somewhat crabbed notion of reasonableness. Our review of the facts surrounding the search leads us to conclude that the search was in no sense unreasonable for Fourth Amendment purposes.[10]

The incident that gave rise to this case actually involved two separate searches, with the first—the search for cigarettes—providing the suspicion that gave rise to the second—the search for marihuana. Although it is the fruits of the second search that are at issue here, the validity of the search for marihuana must depend on the reasonableness of the initial search for cigarettes, as there would have been no reason to suspect that T.L.O. possessed marihuana had the first search not taken place. Accordingly, it is to the search for cigarettes that we first turn our attention.

The New Jersey Supreme Court pointed to two grounds for its holding that the search for cigarettes was unreasonable. First, the court observed that possession of cigarettes was not in itself illegal or a violation of school rules. Because the contents of T.L.O.'s purse would therefore have "no direct bearing on the infraction" of which she was accused (smoking in a lavatory where smoking was prohibited), there was no reason to search her purse.[11] Second, even assuming that a search of T.L.O.'s purse might under some circumstances be reasonable in light of the accusation made against T.L.O., the New Jersey court concluded that Mr. Choplick in this particular case had no reasonable grounds to suspect that T.L.O. had cigarettes in her purse. At best, according to the court, Mr. Choplick had "a good hunch." 94 N.J., at 347, 463 A.2d at 942.

Both these conclusions are implausible. T.L.O. had been accused of smoking, and had denied the accusation in the strongest possible terms when she stated that she did not smoke at all. Surely it cannot be said that under these circumstances, T.L.O.'s possession of cigarettes would be irrelevant to the charges against her or to her response to those charges. T.L.O.'s possession of cigarettes, once it was discovered, would both corroborate the report that she had been smoking and undermine the credibility of her defense to the charge

[10] Of course, New Jersey may insist on a more demanding standard under its own Constitution or statutes. In that case, its courts would not purport to be applying the Fourth Amendment when they invalidate a search.

[11] Justice Stevens interprets these statements as a holding that enforcement of the school's smoking regulations was not sufficiently related to the goal of maintaining discipline or order in the school to justify a search under the standard adopted by the New Jersey court. See post, at 765. We do not agree that this is an accurate characterization of the New Jersey Supreme Court's opinion. The New Jersey court did not hold that the school's smoking rules were unrelated to the goal of maintaining discipline or order, nor did it suggest that a search that would produce evidence bearing directly on an accusation that a student had violated the smoking rules would be impermissible under the court's reasonable suspicion standard; rather, the court concluded that any evidence a search of T.L.O.'s purse was likely to produce would not have a sufficiently direct bearing on the infraction to justify a search— a conclusion with which we cannot agree for the reasons set forth infra, at 745–746. Justice Stevens' suggestion that the New Jersey Supreme Court's decision rested on the perceived triviality of the smoking infraction appears to be a reflection of his own views rather than those of the New Jersey court.

of smoking. To be sure, the discovery of the cigarettes would not prove that T.L.O. had been smoking in the lavatory; nor would it, strictly speaking, necessarily be inconsistent with her claim that she did not smoke at all. But it is universally recognized that evidence, to be relevant to an inquiry, need not conclusively prove the ultimate fact in issue, but only have "any tendency to make the existence of any fact that is of consequence to the determination of the action more probable or less probable than it would be without the evidence." Fed.Rule Evid. 401. The relevance of T.L.O.'s possession of cigarettes to the question whether she had been smoking and to the credibility of her denial that she smoked supplied the necessary "nexus" between the item searched for and the infraction under investigation. See Warden v. Hayden, 387 U.S. 294, 306–307, 87 S.Ct. 1642, 1649–1650, 18 L.Ed.2d 782 (1967). Thus, if Mr. Choplick in fact had a reasonable suspicion that T.L.O. had cigarettes in her purse, the search was justified despite the fact that the cigarettes, if found, would constitute "mere evidence" of a violation. Ibid.

Of course, the New Jersey Supreme Court also held that Mr. Choplick had no reasonable suspicion that the purse would contain cigarettes. This conclusion is puzzling. A teacher had reported that T.L.O. was smoking in the lavatory. Certainly this report gave Mr. Choplick reason to suspect that T.L.O. was carrying cigarettes with her; and if she did have cigarettes, her purse was the obvious place in which to find them. Mr. Choplick's suspicion that there were cigarettes in the purse was not an "inchoate and unparticularized suspicion or 'hunch,' " Terry v. Ohio, 392 U.S., at 27, 88 S.Ct., at 1883; rather, it was the sort of "common-sense conclusio[n] about human behavior" upon which "practical people"—including government officials—are entitled to rely. United States v. Cortez, 449 U.S. 411, 418, 101 S.Ct. 690, 695, 66 L.Ed.2d 621 (1981). Of course, even if the teacher's report were true, T.L.O. *might* not have had a pack of cigarettes with her; she might have borrowed a cigarette from someone else or have been sharing a cigarette with another student. But the requirement of reasonable suspicion is not a requirement of absolute certainty: "sufficient probability, not certainty, is the touchstone of reasonableness under the Fourth Amendment * * *." Hill v. California, 401 U.S. 797, 804, 91 S.Ct. 1106, 1111, 28 L.Ed.2d 484 (1971). Because the hypothesis that T.L.O. was carrying cigarettes in her purse was itself not unreasonable, it is irrelevant that other hypotheses were also consistent with the teacher's accusation. Accordingly, it cannot be said that Mr. Choplick acted unreasonably when he examined T.L.O.'s purse to see if it contained cigarettes.[12]

---

[12] T.L.O. contends that even if it was reasonable for Mr. Choplick to open her purse to look for cigarettes, it was not reasonable for him to reach in and take the cigarettes out of her purse once he found them. Had he not removed the cigarettes from the purse, she asserts, he would not have observed the rolling papers that suggested the presence of marihuana, and the search for marihuana could not have taken place. T.L.O.'s argument is based on the fact that the cigarettes were not "contraband," as no school rule forbade her to have them. Thus, according to T.L.O., the cigarettes were not subject to seizure or confiscation by school authorities, and Mr. Choplick was not entitled to take them out of T.L.O.'s purse regardless of whether he was entitled to peer into the

Our conclusion that Mr. Choplick's decision to open T.L.O.'s purse was reasonable brings us to the question of the further search for marihuana once the pack of cigarettes was located. The suspicion upon which the search for marihuana was founded was provided when Mr. Choplick observed a package of rolling papers in the purse as he removed the pack of cigarettes. Although T.L.O. does not dispute the reasonableness of Mr. Choplick's belief that the rolling papers indicated the presence of marihuana, she does contend that the scope of the search Mr. Choplick conducted exceeded permissible bounds when he seized and read certain letters that implicated T.L.O. in drug dealing. This argument, too, is unpersuasive. The discovery of the rolling papers concededly gave rise to a reasonable suspicion that T.L.O. was carrying marihuana as well as cigarettes in her purse. This suspicion justified further exploration of T.L.O.'s purse, which turned up more evidence of drug-related activities: a pipe, a number of plastic bags of the type commonly used to store marihuana, a small quantity of marihuana, and a fairly substantial amount of money. Under these circumstances, it was not unreasonable to extend the search to a separate zippered compartment of the purse; and when a search of that compartment revealed an index card containing a list of "people who owe me money" as well as two letters, the inference that T.L.O. was involved in marihuana trafficking was substantial enough to justify Mr. Choplick in examining the letters to determine whether they contained any further evidence. In short, we cannot conclude that the search for marihuana was unreasonable in any respect.

Because the search resulting in the discovery of the evidence of marihuana dealing by T.L.O. was reasonable, the New Jersey Supreme Court's decision to exclude that evidence from T.L.O.'s juvenile delinquency proceedings on Fourth Amendment grounds was erroneous. Accordingly, the judgment of the Supreme Court of New Jersey is

Reversed.

JUSTICE STEVENS, with whom JUSTICE MARSHALL joins, and with whom JUSTICE BRENNAN joins as to Part I, concurring in part and dissenting in part.

*   *   *

II

The search of a young woman's purse by a school administrator is a serious invasion of her legitimate expectations of privacy. A purse "is a common repository for one's personal effects and therefore is inevitably associated with the expectation of privacy." Arkan-

purse to see if they were there. Such hairsplitting argumentation has no place in an inquiry addressed to the issue of reasonableness. If Mr. Choplick could permissibly search T.L.O.'s purse for cigarettes, it hardly seems reasonable to suggest that his natural reaction to finding them—picking them up—could be a constitutional violation. We find that neither in opening the purse nor in reaching into it to remove the cigarettes did Mr. Choplick violate the Fourth Amendment.

sas v. Sanders, 442 U.S. 753, 762, 99 S.Ct. 2586, 2592, 61 L.Ed.2d 235 (1979). Although such expectations must sometimes yield to the legitimate requirements of government, in assessing the constitutionality of a warrantless search, our decision must be guided by the language of the Fourth Amendment: "The right of the people to be secure in their persons, houses, papers and effects, against *unreasonable* searches and seizures, shall not be violated * * *." In order to evaluate the reasonableness of such searches, "it is necessary 'first to focus upon the governmental interest which allegedly justifies official intrusion upon the constitutionally protected interests of the private citizen,' for there is 'no ready test for determining reasonableness other than by balancing the need to search [or seize] against the invasion which the search [or seizure] entails.' " Terry v. Ohio, 392 U.S. 1, 20–21, 88 S.Ct. 1868, 1879–1880, 20 L.Ed.2d 889 (1968) (quoting Camara v. Municipal Court, 387 U.S. 523, 528, 534–537, 87 S.Ct. 1727, 1730, 1733–1735, 18 L.Ed.2d 930 (1967)).[14]

The "limited search for weapons" in *Terry* was justified by the "immediate interest of the police officer in taking steps to assure himself that the person with whom he is dealing is not armed with a weapon that could unexpectedly and fatally be used against him." 392 U.S., at 23, 25, 88 S.Ct., at 1881, 1882. When viewed from the institutional perspective, "the substantial need of teachers and administrators for freedom to maintain order in the schools," ante, at 743 (majority opinion), is no less acute. Violent, unlawful, or seriously disruptive conduct is fundamentally inconsistent with the principal function of teaching institutions which is to educate young people and prepare them for citizenship.[15] When such conduct occurs amidst a sizable group of impressionable young people, it creates an explosive atmosphere that requires a prompt and effective response.

Thus, warrantless searches of students by school administrators are reasonable when undertaken for those purposes. But the majority's statement of the standard for evaluating the reasonableness of such searches is not suitably adapted to that end. The majority holds that "a search of a student by a teacher or other school official will be 'justified at its inception' when there are reasonable grounds for suspecting that the search will turn up evidence *that the student has violated or is violating either the law or the rules of the school.*" Ante, at 743–744. This standard will permit teachers and school administrators to search students when they suspect that the search will reveal evidence of even the most trivial school regulation or precatory guideline for student behavior. The Court's standard for

---

[14] See also United States v. Brigoni-Ponce, 422 U.S. 873, 881–882, 95 S.Ct. 2574, 2580–2581, 45 L.Ed.2d 607 (1975); United States v. Martinez-Fuerte, 428 U.S. 543, 567, 96 S.Ct. 3074, 3087, 49 L.Ed.2d 1116 (1976).

[15] Cf. ante, at 750 (BLACKMUN, J., concurring in judgment) ("The special need for an immediate response to behavior that threatens either the safety of school children and teachers or the educational process itself justifies the Court in excepting school searches from the warrant and probable cause requirement"); ante, at 748 (POWELL, J., concurring, joined by O'CONNOR, J.) ("Without first establishing discipline and maintaining order, teachers cannot begin to educate their students").

deciding whether a search is justified "at its inception" treats all violations of the rules of the school as though they were fungible. For the Court, a search for curlers and sunglasses in order to enforce the school dress code [16] is apparently just as important as a search for evidence of heroin addiction or violent gang activity.

The majority, however, does not contend that school administrators have a compelling need to search students in order to achieve optimum enforcement of minor school regulations.[17] To the contrary, when minor violations are involved, there is every indication that the informal school disciplinary process, with only minimum requirements of due process,[18] can function effectively without the power to search for enough evidence to prove a criminal case. In arguing that teachers and school administrators need the power to search students based on a lessened standard, the United States as *amicus curiae* relies heavily on empirical evidence of a contemporary crisis of violence and unlawful behavior that is seriously undermining the process of education in American schools.[19] A standard better attuned to this concern would permit teachers and school administrators to search a student when they have reason to believe that the search will uncover *evidence that the student is violating the law or engaging in conduct that is seriously disruptive of school order, or the educational process.*

[16] Parent-Student Handbook of Piscataway [N.J.] H.S. (1979), Record Doc. S–1, p. 7. A brief survey of school rule books reveals that, under the majority's approach, teachers and school administrators may also search students to enforce school rules regulating:

(i) secret societies;

(ii) students driving to school;

(iii) parking and use of parking lots during school hours;

(iv) smoking on campus;

(v) the direction of traffic in the hallways;

(vi) student presence in the hallways during class hours without a pass;

(vii) profanity;

(viii) school attendance of interscholastic athletes on the day of a game, meet or match;

(ix) cafeteria use and cleanup;

(x) eating lunch off-campus; and

(xi) unauthorized absence.

See id., 7–18; Student Handbook of South Windsor [Conn.] H.S. (1984); Fairfax County [Va.] Public Schools, Student Responsibilities and Rights (1980); Student Handbook of Chantilly [Va.] H.S. (1984).

[17] Cf. Camara v. Municipal Court, 387 U.S. 523, 535, 87 S.Ct. 1727, 1734, 18 L.Ed.2d 930 (1967) ("There is unanimous agreement among those most familiar with this field that the only effective way to seek universal compliance with the minimum standards required by municipal codes is through routine periodic inspections of all structures * * *. [I]f the probable cause standard * * * is adopted, * * * the reasonable goals of code enforcement will be dealt a crushing blow").

[18] See Goss v. Lopez, 419 U.S. 565, 583–584, 95 S.Ct. 729, 740–741, 42 L.Ed. 2d 725 (1975).

[19] "The sad truth is that many classrooms across the country are not temples of learning teaching the lessons of good will, civility, and wisdom that are central to the fabric of American life. To the contrary, many schools are in such a state of disorder that not only is the educational atmosphere polluted, but the very safety of students and teachers is imperiled." Brief for United States as *Amicus Curiae* 23.

See also Brief for National Education Association as *Amicus Curiae* 21 ("If a suspected violation of a rule threatens to disrupt the school or threatens to harm students, school officials should be free to search for evidence of it").

This standard is properly directed at "[t]he sole justification for the [warrantless] search." [20] In addition, a standard that varies the extent of the permissible intrusion with the gravity of the suspected offense is also more consistent with common-law experience and this Court's precedent. Criminal law has traditionally recognized a distinction between essentially regulatory offenses and serious violations of the peace, and graduated the response of the criminal justice system depending on the character of the violation. [21] The application of a similar distinction in evaluating the reasonableness of warrantless searches and seizures "is not a novel idea." Welsh v. Wisconsin, 466 U.S. ___, ___, 104 S.Ct. 2091, 80 L.Ed.2d 732 (1984). [22]

In *Welsh*, police officers arrived at the scene of a traffic accident and obtained information indicating that the driver of the automobile involved was guilty of a first offense of driving while intoxicated—a civil violation with a maximum fine of $200. The driver had left the scene of the accident, and the officers followed the suspect to his home where they arrested him without a warrant. Absent exigent circumstances, the warrantless invasion of the home was a clear violation of Payton v. New York, 445 U.S. 573, 100 S.Ct. 1371, 63 L.Ed.2d 639 (1980). In holding that the warrantless arrest for the "noncriminal, traffic offense" in *Welsh* was unconstitutional, the Court noted that "application of the exigent-circumstances exception in the context of a home entry should rarely be sanctioned when there is probable cause to believe that only a minor offense * * * has been committed." 466 U.S., at ___, 104 S.Ct., at 2099.

The logic of distinguishing between minor and serious offenses in evaluating the reasonableness of school searches is almost too clear for argument. In order to justify the serious intrusion on the persons and privacy of young people that New Jersey asks this Court to approve, the State must identify "some real immediate and serious

[20] Terry v. Ohio, 392 U.S. 1, 29, 88 S.Ct. 1868, 1884, 20 L.Ed.2d 889 (1968); United States v. Brigoni-Ponce, 422 U.S., at 881–882, 95 S.Ct., at 2580–2581.

[21] Throughout the criminal law this dichotomy has been expressed by classifying crimes as misdemeanors or felonies, *malum prohibitum* or *malum in se*, crimes that do not involve moral turpitude or those that do, and major or petty offenses. See generally W. LaFave, Handbook on Criminal Law § 6 (1972).

Some codes of student behavior also provide a system of graduated response by distinguishing between violent, unlawful, or seriously disruptive conduct, and conduct that will only warrant serious sanctions when the student engages in repetitive offenses. See, e.g., Parent-Student Handbook of Piscataway [N.J.] H.S. (1979), Record Doc. S–1, pp. 15–16; Student Handbook of South Windsor [Conn.] H.S. ¶ E (1984); Rules of the Board of Education of the District of Columbia, Chap. IV, §§ 431.1–.10 (1982).

Indeed, at Piscataway High School a violation of smoking regulations that is "[a] student's first offense will result in assignment of up to three (3) days of after school classes concerning hazards of smoking." Record Doc. S–1, p. 15.

[22] In Goss v. Lopez, 419 U.S., at 582–583, 95 S.Ct., at 740–741 (emphasis added), the Court noted that similar considerations require some variance in the requirements of due process in the school disciplinary context:

"[A]s a general rule notice and hearing should precede removal of the student from school. We agree * * *, however, that there are recurring situations in which prior notice and hearing cannot be insisted upon. *Students whose presence poses a continuing danger to persons or property or an ongoing threat of disrupting the academic process may be immediately removed from school.* In such cases the necessary notice and rudimentary hearing should follow as soon as practicable * * *."

consequences." McDonald v. United States, 335 U.S. 451, 460, 69 S.Ct. 191, 195, 93 L.Ed. 153 (1948) (Jackson, J., concurring, joined by Frankfurter, J.).[23] While school administrators have entirely legitimate reasons for adopting school regulations and guidelines for student behavior, the authorization of searches to enforce them "displays a shocking lack of all sense of proportion." Id., 459, 69 S.Ct., at 195.[24]

The majority offers weak deference to these principles of balance and decency by announcing that school searches will only be reasonable in scope "when the measures adopted are reasonably related to the objectives of the search and not excessively intrusive in light of the age and sex of the student, *and the nature of the infraction.*" Ante, at 743 (emphasis added). The majority offers no explanation why a two-part standard is necessary to evaluate the reasonableness of the ordinary school search. Significantly, in the balance of its opinion the Court pretermits any discussion of the nature of T.L.O.'s infraction of the "no smoking" rule.

The "rider" to the Court's standard for evaluating the reasonableness of the initial intrusion apparently is the Court's perception that its standard is overly generous and does not, by itself, achieve a fair balance between the administrator's right to search and the student's reasonable expectations of privacy. The Court's standard for evaluating the "scope" of reasonable school searches is obviously designed to prohibit physically intrusive searches of students by persons of the opposite sex for relatively minor offenses. The Court's effort to establish a standard that is, at once, clear enough to allow searches to be upheld in nearly every case, and flexible enough to prohibit obviously unreasonable intrusions of young adults' privacy only creates uncertainty in the extent of its resolve to prohibit the latter. Moreover, the majority's application of its standard in this case—to permit a male administrator to rummage through the purse

---

[23] In *McDonald* police officers made a warrantless search of the office of an illegal "numbers" operation. Justice Jackson rejected the view that the search could be supported by exigent circumstances:

"Even if one were to conclude that urgent circumstances might justify a forced entry without a warrant, no such emergency was present in this case * * *. *Whether there is reasonable necessity for a search without waiting to obtain a warrant certainly depends somewhat upon the gravity of the offense thought to be in progress* as well as the hazards of the method of attempting to reach it * * *. [The defendant's] criminal operation, while a shabby swindle that the police are quite right in suppressing, was not one which endangered life or limb or the peace and good order of the community * * *." 335 U.S., at 459–460, 69 S.Ct., at 195.

[24] While a policeman who sees a person smoking in an elevator in violation of a city ordinance may conduct a full-blown search for evidence of the smoking violation in the unlikely event of a custodial arrest, United States v. Robinson, 414 U.S. 218, 236, 94 S.Ct. 467, 477, 38 L.Ed. 2d 427 (1973); Gustafson v. Florida, 414 U.S. 260, 265–266, 94 S.Ct. 488, 491–492, 38 L.Ed.2d 456 (1973), it is more doubtful whether a search of this kind would be reasonable if the officer only planned to issue a citation to the offender and depart, see Robinson, 414 U.S., at 236, n. 6, 94 S.Ct., at 477, n. 6. In any case, the majority offers no rationale supporting its conclusion that a student detained by school officials for questioning, on reasonable suspicion that she has violated a school rule, is entitled to no more protection under the Fourth Amendment than a criminal suspect under custodial arrest.

of a female high school student in order to obtain evidence that she was smoking in a bathroom—raises grave doubts in my mind whether its effort will be effective.[25] Unlike the Court, I believe the nature of the suspected infraction is a matter of first importance in deciding whether *any* invasion of privacy is permissible.

Privacy!

III

The Court embraces the standard applied by the New Jersey Supreme Court as equivalent to its own, and then deprecates the state court's application of the standard as reflecting "a somewhat crabbed notion of reasonableness." Ante, at 745. There is no mystery, however, in the state court's finding that the search in this case was unconstitutional; the decision below was not based on a manipulation of reasonable suspicion, but on the trivial character of the activity that promoted the official search. The New Jersey Supreme Court wrote:

> "We are satisfied that when a school official has reasonable grounds to believe that a student possesses evidence of *illegal activity or activity that would interfere with school discipline and order,* the school official has the right to conduct a reasonable search for such evidence.

> "In determining whether the school official has reasonable grounds, courts should consider 'the child's age, history, and school record, *the prevalence and seriousness of the problem in the school to which the search was directed,* the exigency to make the search without delay, and the probative value and reliability of the information used as a justification for the search.' "[26]

The emphasized language in the state court's opinion focuses on the character of the rule infraction that is to be the object of the search.

In the view of the state court, there is a quite obvious, and material difference between a search for evidence relating to violent or disruptive activity, and a search for evidence of a smoking rule violation. This distinction does not imply that a no smoking rule is a matter of minor importance. Rather, like a rule that prohibits a student from being tardy, its occasional violation in a context that poses no threat of disrupting school order and discipline offers no reason to believe that an immediate search is necessary to avoid

[25] One thing is clear under any standard—the shocking strip searches that are described in some cases have no place in the school house. See Doe v. Renfrow, 631 F.2d 91, 92–93 (CA7 1980) ("It does not require a constitutional scholar to conclude that a nude search of a 13-year-old child is an invasion of constitutional rights of some magnitude"), cert. denied, 451 U.S. 1022, 101 S.Ct. 3015, 69 L.Ed.2d 395 (1981); Bellnier v. Lund, 438 F.Supp. 47 (NDNY 1977); People v. D., 34 N.Y.2d 483, 358 N.Y.S.2d 403, 315 N.E.2d 466, (1974); J. v. State, 399 So.2d 996 (Fla.App.1981). To the extent that deeply intrusive searches are ever reasonable outside the custodial context, it surely must only be to prevent imminent, and serious harm.

[26] 94 N.J., at 346, 463 A.2d, at 941–942 (quoting State v. McKinnon, 88 Wash.2d 75, 81, 558 P.2d 781, 784 (1977)) (emphasis added).

unlawful conduct, violence, or a serious impairment of the educational process.

A correct understanding of the New Jersey court's standard explains why that court concluded in T.L.O.'s case that "the assistant principal did not have reasonable grounds to believe that the student was concealing in her purse evidence of criminal activity or evidence of activity that *would seriously interfere with school discipline or order*." [27] The importance of the nature of the rule infraction to the New Jersey Supreme Court's holding is evident from its brief explanation of the principal basis for its decision:

> "A student has an expectation of privacy in the contents of her purse. Mere possession of cigarettes did not violate school rule or policy, since the school allowed smoking in designated areas. The contents of the handbag had no direct bearing on the infraction.

> "The assistant principal's desire, legal in itself, to gather evidence to impeach the student's credibility at a hearing on the disciplinary infraction does not validate the search." [28]

Like the New Jersey Supreme Court, I would view this case differently if the Assistant Principal had reason to believe T.L.O.'s purse contained evidence of criminal activity, or of an activity that would seriously disrupt school discipline. There was, however, absolutely no basis for any such assumption—not even a "hunch."

In this case, Mr. Choplick overreacted to what appeared to be nothing more than a minor infraction—a rule prohibiting smoking in the bathroom of the freshmen's and sophomores' building.[29] It is, of course, true that he actually found evidence of serious wrongdoing by T.L.O., but no one claims that the prior search may be justified by his unexpected discovery. As far as the smoking infraction is concerned, the search for cigarettes merely tended to corroborate a teacher's eyewitness account of T.L.O.'s violation of a minor regulation designed to channel student smoking behavior into designated locations. Because this conduct was neither unlawful nor significantly disruptive of school order or the educational process, the invasion of privacy associated with the forcible opening of the T.L.O.'s purse was entirely unjustified at its inception.

A review of the sampling of school search cases relied on by the Court demonstrates how different this case is from those in which

---

[27] 94 N.J., at 347, 463 A.2d, at 942 (emphasis added).

[28] Ibid. The court added:

"Moreover, there were not reasonable grounds to believe that the purse contained cigarettes, if they were the object of the search. No one had furnished information to that effect to the school official. He had, at best, a good hunch. No doubt good hunches would unearth much more evidence of crime on the persons of students and citizens as a whole.

But more is required to sustain a search." Id., at 347, 463 A.2d, at 942–943.

It is this portion of the New Jersey Supreme Court's reasoning—a portion that was not necessary to its holding—to which this Court makes its principal response. See ante, at 745.

[29] See Parent-Student Handbook of Piscataway [N.J.] H.S. 15, 18 (1979), Record Doc. S–1. See also Tr. of Mar. 31, 1980, Hearing 13–14.

there was indeed a valid justification for intruding on a student's privacy. In most of them the student was suspected of a criminal violation; [30] in the remainder either violence or substantial disruption of school order or the integrity of the academic process was at stake.[31] Few involved matters as trivial as the no smoking rule violated by T.L.O.[32] The rule the Court adopts today is so open-ended that it may make the Fourth Amendment virtually meaningless in the school context. Although I agree that school administrators must have broad latitude to maintain order and discipline in our classrooms, that authority is not unlimited.

IV

The schoolroom is the first opportunity most citizens have to experience the power of government. Through it passes every citizen and public official, from schoolteachers to policemen and prison guards. The values they learn there, they take with them in life. One of our most cherished ideals is the one contained in the Fourth Amendment: that the Government may not intrude on the personal privacy of its citizens without a warrant or compelling circumstance. The Court's decision today is a curious moral for the Nation's youth. Although the search of T.L.O.'s purse does not trouble today's majority, I submit that we are not dealing with "matters relatively trivial to the welfare of the Nation. There are village tyrants as well as village Hampdens, but none who acts under color of law is beyond the reach of the Constitution." West Virginia State Board of Education v. Barnette, 319 U.S. 624, 638, 63 S.Ct. 1178, 1185, 87 L.Ed. 1628 (1943).

I respectfully dissent.

NOTES

1. An interesting, if novel, view was taken by the Georgia Supreme Court in State v. Young, 234 Ga. 488, 216 S.E.2d 586, cert. denied, 423 U.S. 1039, 96 S.Ct. 576, 46 L.Ed.2d 413 (1975).

[30] See, e.g., Tarter v. Raybuck, 742 F.2d 977 (CA6 1984) (search for marihuana); M. v. Board of Education Ball-Chatham Community Unit School Dist. No. 5, 429 F.Supp. 288 (SD Ill.1977) (drugs and large amount of money); D.R.C. v. State, 646 P.2d 252 (Alaska App.1982) (stolen money); In re W., 29 Cal.App.3d 777, 105 Cal.Rptr. 775 (1973) (marihuana); In re G., 11 Cal.App.3d 1193, 90 Cal.Rptr. 361 (1970) (amphetamine pills); In re Donaldson, 269 Cal.App.2d 509, 75 Cal.Rptr. 220 (1969) (methedrine pills); State v. Baccino, 282 A.2d 869 (Del.Super.1971) (drugs); State v. D.T.W., 425 So.2d 1383 (Fla.App.1983) (drugs); In re J.A., 85 Ill. App.3d 567, 40 Ill.Dec. 755, 406 N.E.2d 958 (1980) (marihuana); People v. Ward, 62 Mich.App. 46, 233 N.W.2d 180 (1975) (drug pills); Mercer v. State, 450 S.W.2d 715 (Tex.Civ.App.1970) (marihuana);

State v. McKinnon, 88 Wash.2d 75, 558 P.2d 781 (1977) ("speed").

[31] See, e.g., In re L.L., 90 Wis.2d 585, 280 N.W.2d 343 (App.1979) (search for knife or razor blade); R.C.M. v. State, 660 S.W.2d 552 (Tex.App.1983) (student with bloodshot eyes wandering halls in violation of school rule requiring students to remain in examination room or at home during midterm examinations).

[32] See, e.g., State v. Young, 234 Ga. 488, 216 S.E.2d 586 (three students searched when they made furtive gestures and displayed obvious consciousness of guilt), cert. denied, 423 U.S. 1039, 96 S.Ct. 576, 46 L.Ed.2d 413 (1975); Doe v. State, 88 N.M. 347, 540 P.2d 827 (1975) (student searched for pipe when a teacher saw him using it to violate smoking regulations).

"We find that these cases in the main have failed to separate the issues with sufficient sensitivity to delineate comprehensively the rights we are considering. They have tended to divide those making searches, for purposes of the Fourth Amendment, into two groups: private persons, and government agents. We conclude that there are really three groups: private persons; governmental agents whose conduct is state action invoking the Fourth Amendment; and governmental *law enforcement* agents for whose violations of the Fourth Amendment the exclusionary rule will be applied.

"With reference to searches by private persons, there is no Fourth Amendment prohibition and therefore no occasion for applying the exclusionary rule. Burdeau v. McDowell, supra. The third group, law-enforcement officers, of course, are bound by the full panoply of Fourth Amendment rights and are subject to the application of the exclusionary rule. But the intermediate group, including public school officials, plainly are state officers whose action is state action bringing the Fourth Amendment into play; but they are not state law enforcement officials, with respect to whom the exclusionary rule is applied.

"In explanation of our conclusion that these three categories exist separately, we think it too plain to be controverted that public school officials are state officers acting under color of law, whose action is therefore state action which must comport with the Fourth Amendment standards applicable to the given situation. "If an individual is possessed of state authority and purports to act under that authority, his action is state action." Griffin v. Maryland, 378 U.S. 130, 135, 84 S.Ct. 1770, 1773, 12 L.Ed.2d 754 (1964). However, the mere fact that action is taken by state officials is not adequate to invoke the exclusionary rule even if that action violates the Fourth Amendment. As we noted above, the exclusionary rule does not reach so far as does the Fourth Amendment and the rule has not been applied save to action taken by law enforcement personnel. The tide is turning, we think properly, away from the exclusionary rule; and we decline to extend it to apply to searches by non-law enforcement persons. There can be no serious contention that public school officials are law enforcement personnel. Therefore, it follows that although school officials are governmental officers subject to some Fourth Amendment limitations in searching their students, should they violate those limitations the exclusionary rule would not be available to the students to exclude from evidence items illegally seized. Instead, for the violation of their constitutional rights the students would be relegated to such other remedies as the law affords them, whether by actions based upon a claimed violation of their civil rights by state officers, or by some tort claim seeking damages."

Id. at 493–94, 216 S.E.2d at 591.

2. Suppose a high school teacher's aide, hired to patrol hallways and parking lots to ensure compliance with the school code, while routinely checking the parking lot, looked into a student's car and saw a partially covered object that he could identify as a "bong." (For a definition of a "bong" teachers and older students are referred to Footnote 1 of the court's opinion). Is the "bong" admissible in evidence? See State v. D.T.W., 425 So. 2d 1383 (Fla.App.1983).

3. Is the "sniffing" of students, by dogs trained to detect drugs a search? Of students' lockers? Of students' cars? See Horton v. Goose Creek Independent School District, 690 F.2d 470, rehearing en banc denied, 693 F.2d 524 (5th Cir.1982).

B. POLICE INTERROGATION

Despite the assertion by the Supreme Court in Fare v. Michael C., infra, p. 174, that it

> * * * has not yet held that *Miranda* applies with full force to exclude evidence obtained in violation of its prescriptions from consideration in juvenile proceedings * * *,

nearly all cases which have addressed the problem have assumed or decided that *Miranda,* in some form or another, is applicable in delinquency proceedings. Indeed, there is some indication that there is an even greater obligation to make certain that the juvenile understands the import of the warnings.

Because the issue arises most often, as in the adult cases, in the context of waiver, some legislatures and courts have imposed stricter waiver requirements for juveniles than the Supreme Court apparently requires for adults.

1. THE CUSTODY REQUIREMENT

One of the necessary conditions to the requirement that *Miranda* warnings be given is that the suspect be "in custody." In the adult cases the issue frequently is whether the individual being questioned is "free to leave," or, alternatively, whether he perceives he is—or is not—free to leave. The latter may depend on his subjective perception or the test may be an objective one.

The problem is most likely to arise in a fashion peculiar to juveniles when the child is questioned in the office of a school administrator. In In the Matter of Gage, 49 Or.App. 599, 624 P.2d 1076 (1980) the court concluded that a public school principal was a "public official" for Fourth-Fourteenth Amendment purposes. On the assumption that he was also a public official for Fifth-Fourteenth Amendment purposes and that *Miranda* was applicable in juvenile delinquency cases, the court held that on the following stipulated facts, the child was in an "investigative stage" rather than a "custodial situation."

The relevant portion of the stipulation reads:

> 'On November 27, 1979, he [the school principal] discovered one thousand school lunch tickets missing from their appropriate location in the student store. That he investigated and found that tickets with numbers indicating that they were among those stolen were being used by students at the school. That based on conversations with the students he questioned James Wade Gage in the principal's office on November 28, 1979. * * *'

Id. at 601, 624 P.2d at 1077.

IN THE MATTER OF KILLITZ

Oregon Court of Appeals, 1982.
59 Or.App. 720, 651 P.2d 1382.

ROSSMAN, JUDGE.

This case involves the admissibility of incriminating statements made by a junior high school student while being questioned in the principal's office by a police officer. A resolution of the case turns on whether defendant was in "custody" for *Miranda* purposes when the statements were made. If he was in custody, the statements are not admissible, because he was not advised of his rights before the interrogation began. If he was not in custody, the statements are admissible.

Defendant was charged with having committed an act that, if done by an adult, would be a violation of ORS 164.215, Burglary in the Second Degree. The court found that he committed the act and thus found him to be within the jurisdiction of the Juvenile Court. ORS 419.476(1)(a). Defendant assigns as error the denial of his motion to suppress the evidence on which the finding of jurisdiction was based. We conclude that the motion to suppress should have been granted, and we reverse.

FACTS

Defendant was summoned to the principal's office, as he had been on previous occasions. Students are obliged to respond to these directives; if they do not appear, they are sought out. When defendant arrived at the office, he was instructed to wait outside. At the time, another student was in the office being questioned. That student implicated defendant in the burglary.

After defendant was ushered into the office, the police officer questioned him about the burglary. The officer was in uniform and armed. The principal was present. Neither the officer nor the principal told defendant he was free to leave. During the interrogation, defendant made incriminating statements about the burglary. He was then sent back to class. The following day, defendant was again questioned by the same police officer and made further incriminating statements, under substantially the same circumstances as the day before. This proceeding followed.

DECISION AND DISCUSSION

Because the statements at issue were elicited in response to police questioning, "interrogation" did take place. The issue is whether the interrogation was "custodial" within the meaning of *Miranda*, so that defendant should have been advised of his rights before the questioning occurred. In State v. Paz, 31 Or.App. 851, 572 P.2d 1036 (1977), this court set forth criteria for determining when an interrogation is custodial: (1) whether defendant could have left the scene of the interrogation voluntarily; (2) whether defendant was being questioned as a suspect or merely as a witness; [13] and (3) whether defendant freely and voluntarily accompanied the officer to the place of questioning.

Here, the *Paz* indicia of custodial interrogation are all present. *First,* defendant was not free to leave during the interrogation. He was in school during regular hours, where his movements were controlled to a great extent by school personnel. Defendant was interrogated by an armed, uniformed police officer in the principal's office with the principal present. Neither the police officer nor the principal said or did anything to dispel the clear impression communicated to defendant that he was not free to leave.[14] *Second,* the fact that another student had implicated defendant in the burglary indicates that he was being questioned as a suspect rather than as a witness. *Third,* defendant cannot be said to have come voluntarily to the place of questioning. He would likely have been subject to the usual school disciplinary procedures had he not complied with the principal's request that he come to the office. In addition, defendant did not know that a police officer awaited him at the principal's office. He can hardly be said to have come voluntarily to the place of police questioning when he had no idea a police officer would be present.

For these reasons, we hold that defendant was so deprived of his freedom of action as to render his interrogation custodial.

The state argues that State ex rel. Juv. Dept. v. Gage, 49 Or. App. 599, 624 P.2d 1076 (1980), is controlling and requires a different result. In *Gage,* defendant was questioned by school authorities regarding the theft of school lunch tickets from within the school. There was no official police involvement. The court held that *Miranda* warnings were not required, apparently because the questioning occurred without police participation and for a school-related purpose, and was, therefore, not a criminal investigation. In contrast, where a police officer conducts an inquiry regarding criminal activity that took place outside school, the criminal nature of the investigation is manifest. *Gage* does not control under the circumstances presented here.

The factual basis for jurisdiction is derived entirely from the statements defendant made in the two interrogations. Because his

---

[13] In State v. Roberti, 293 Or. 59, 644 P.2d 1104, 293 Or. 236, 646 P.2d 1341 (1982), the Supreme Court held that, at least where the interrogating officer has made the determination to arrest the defendant, *Miranda* warnings must be given, regardless whether defendant is aware of the officer's decision. Nothing in *Roberti* casts doubt on the applicability of the *Paz* factors, where evidence of the police officer's state of mind does not aid the custody determination. Here, although another student had implicated defendant in a burglary, the record does not indicate that the officer had decided before interrogating defendant to take him into formal custody.

[14] Cf. State v. Fields, 291 Or. 872, 635 P.2d 376 (1981) (holding that interview held in probation office and conducted by police officer after probationer was told he was not under arrest or obligation to answer questions did not constitute custodial interrogation).

motion to suppress those statements should have been granted, the order of jurisdiction is reversed.

Reversed.

2. THE INTERROGATION REQUIREMENT

Miranda is also not applicable unless "interrogation" by a "public official"—almost always a police officer—occurs. The test for interrogation was established in Rhode Island v. Innis, 446 U.S. 291, 100 S.Ct. 1682, 64 L.Ed.2d 297 (1980).

> We conclude that the *Miranda* safeguards come into play whenever a person in custody is subjected to either express questioning or its functional equivalent. That is to say, the term "interrogation" under *Miranda* refers not only to express questioning, but also to any words or actions on the part of the police (other than those normally attendant to arrest and custody) that the police should know are reasonably likely to elicit an incriminating response from the suspect. The latter portion of this definition focuses primarily upon the perceptions of the suspect, rather than the intent of the police. This focus reflects the fact that the *Miranda* safeguards were designed to vest a suspect in custody with an added measure of protection against coercive police practices, without regard to objective proof of the underlying intent of the police. A practice that the police should know is reasonably likely to evoke an incriminating response from a suspect thus amounts to interrogation.[15] But, since the police surely cannot be held accountable for the unforeseeable results of their words or actions, the definition of interrogation can extend only to words or actions on the part of police officers that they *should have known* were reasonably likely to elicit an incriminating response.[16]

Id. at 300–02, 100 S.Ct. at 1689–90, 64 L.Ed.2d at 307–08.

Of course, the aspect of the interrogation issue highlighted in *Innis* could as easily arise in a juvenile delinquency context. Presumably, though not certainly, the test would be the same, doubtless with special weight attached to the youth of the suspect.

Another aspect of the "interrogation" problem, of course, is the requirement that the interrogating person be a government official. Although adults might be persuaded by friends or family to "do the

[15] This is not to say that the intent of the police is irrelevant, for it may well have a bearing on whether the police should have known that their words or actions were reasonably likely to evoke an incriminating response. In particular, where a police practice is designed to elicit an incriminating response from the accused, it is unlikely that the practice will not also be one which the police should have known was reasonably likely to have that effect.

[16] Any knowledge the police may have had concerning the unusual susceptibility of a defendant to a particular form of persuasion might be an important factor in determining whether the police should have known that their words or actions were reasonably likely to elicit an incriminating response from the suspect.

right thing" and confess, the situation is much more likely to arise when a juvenile is urged by his parents to "admit what he has done."

In In the Matter of C.P., 411 A.2d 643, cert. granted and remanded for further consideration in light of Rhode Island v. Innis, 449 U.S. 945, 101 S.Ct. 345, 66 L.Ed.2d 210 (1980), while the juvenile remained in police custody after refusing to answer questions and requesting an attorney, his mother, in the presence of the police but not the result of a trick on their part to induce the juvenile to give up his rights, successfully persuaded him to confess. The court held his statement made to his mother in the police presence was admissible in a juvenile delinquency case. After the Supreme Court granted certiorari and remanded for reconsideration in the light of its recently decided *Innis* case, the Court of Appeals of the District of Columbia remanded the case to the trial court for additional findings in the light of Edwards v. Arizona, 451 U.S. 477, 101 S.Ct. 1880, 68 L.Ed.2d 378 (1981), but with a recommendation that the case be dismissed. 439 A.2d 460 (D.C.App.1981). (In *Edwards,* the Supreme Court held that, absent "initiation" of conversations by the suspect, one who has invoked his right not to be interrogated without counsel does not lose that right simply because he responds to police-initiated interrogation.)

Suppose a statement to the police made by a juvenile would be inadmissible under *Miranda*, but that a similar statement was made later to the child's father outside the presence of the police. Would the inculpatory statement made to the father be admissible? See In the Matter of McCluskey, 59 Or.App. 575, 652 P.2d 812 (1982), rejecting the juvenile's contention that his father was an "agent of the police."

3. NEED FOR ADDITIONAL WARNINGS

a. TRANSFER POSSIBILITY

In a number of cases the question has arisen whether statements or confessions made in compliance with *Miranda* are admissible in criminal prosecutions instituted after a transfer hearing. Piersma, Ganousis, Bolenik, Swanger and Connell, Law and Tactics in Juvenile Cases (3d ed. 1977) suggest that four positions have been taken by various courts on the issue:

1. Any statement made while in police custody is inadmissible in a criminal prosecution following a transfer hearing. This is the position taken in Harling v. United States, 295 F.2d 161 (D.C.Cir.1961);

2. Such a statement is inadmissible unless the juvenile and his parents are advised that criminal proceedings are a possibility (citing State v. Maloney, 102 Ariz. 495, 433 P.2d 625 [1967]);

3. Such a statement is admissible so long as it was made "in an adversarial atmosphere" (citing, among others, State v. Gullings, 244 Or. 173, 416 P.2d 311 [1966]);

3a. [The Illinois Supreme Court in People v. Prude, 66 Ill.2d 470, 6 Ill.Dec. 689, 363 N.E.2d 371 (1977), subsequently read *Gullings* as requiring the "atmosphere" to be "sufficiently adversary" to warrant charging the juvenile with knowledge that he could be prosecuted criminally, which may represent a fifth position];

4. Any statement by a juvenile in compliance with *Miranda* is admissible in a subsequent criminal proceeding. See Mitchell v. State, 3 Tenn.Cr.App. 494, 464 S.W.2d 307 (1971).

In United States v. Cheyenne, 420 F.Supp. 960 (D.S.D.1976) the court interpreted Title 18, § 5032 of the U.S. Code

"Statements made by a juvenile prior to or during a transfer hearing under this section shall not be admissible at subsequent criminal prosecutions"

as prohibiting the use of statements made "prior to but in connection with proceedings for transfer * * *," id. at 962, in either subsequent criminal proceedings *or in subsequent juvenile delinquency adjudication hearings* even if *Miranda* is complied with. On the other hand, statements *without an adequate nexus with a transfer proceeding* are admissible in either juvenile delinquency adjudication hearings or in post-transfer criminal proceedings "* * * if found to be voluntary according to legally established criteria * * *." Id. at 964.

b. "THE FIFTH MIRANDA WARNING"

Professor Thomas Grisso, a psychologist, reports that empirical studies show

"* * * that younger juveniles as a class do not understand the nature and significance of their *Miranda* rights * * *."

Grisso, Juveniles' Capacities to Waive Miranda Rights: An Empirical Analysis, 68 Cal.L.Rev. 1134, 1166 (1980). Putting aside for the moment whether the report bears more directly on waiver standards, it might suggest that at least younger juveniles might be given more extensive warnings or that the need to explain them carefully should be emphasized. In some adult cases courts have either urged the giving of a "fifth" *Miranda* warning ["you have the right to stop answering questions at any time"], see Commonwealth v. Lewis, 374 Mass. 203, 371 N.E.2d 775 (1978), or have held as a matter of federal constitutional law that "* * * the officer should have advised the accused that the accused could decide at anytime to exercise these rights and not answer any questions or make any statements * * *." Micale v. State, 76 Wis.2d 370 at 374, 251 N.W.2d 458, 460 (1977).

In State v. Nicholas S., 444 A.2d 373 (Me.1982), the court discussed the effect of a failure to give the "fifth warning" to a juvenile:

There may be no express requirement that the police, prior to the commencement of interrogation, give the "fifth"

Miranda warning, that is, inform the accused of his right to terminate questioning at any time. * * * The failure to give this warning, however, will generally raise a serious question as to the adequacy of a juvenile's understanding of his rights and, in this case, specifically raises serious doubt as to the claimed elaboration of the *Miranda* rights. Cf. United States v. DiGiacoma, 579 F.2d 1211, 1214–15 (10th Cir.1978). Law enforcement officials would be well advised to fully explain the rights enunciated in the *Miranda* warning when dealing with juvenile offenders in order to assure adequate comprehension of these important safeguards.

Id. at 378.

c. WARNINGS TO PARENTS

Although usually discussed in terms of whether there was an effective waiver, the question whether parents, as well as the juvenile, must be informed of the juvenile's *Miranda* rights might logically be conceived as a question of whether additional warnings are required in juvenile custodial interrogation cases. The Supreme Judicial Court of Maine found such a practice preferable. State v. Michael L., 441 A.2d 684 (Me.1982). And in Commonwealth v. Christmas, 502 Pa. 218, 465 A.2d 989 (1983) the Pennsylvania Supreme Court said:

> It is clear that the presumption of inadmissibility of appellee's confession, arising because the record fails to establish that appellee's father was advised of an accused's constitutional rights prior to consulting with appellee, is rebutted by the existence of circumstances which clearly demonstrate that the appellee was fully competent to understand, and in fact understand his rights, and knowingly, intelligently, and voluntarily waived them. At the time of his arrest, appellee was just four months under the age of eighteen years. Appellee had extensive experience with the criminal justice system, having been arrested on seventeen previous occasions and adjudicated delinquent on three different occasions, and having been committed to two separate youth detention facilities as well as serving "intensive" probation. Indeed, appellee was a veteran arrestee and a seasoned delinquent, not a naive and inexperienced youth needing the advice of an interested and informed adult to deal with a legal situation with which he was unfamiliar, or which he did not understand. Appellee did, nevertheless, confer with his father, an experienced police officer. In the presence of his father, appellee was then informed of his constitutional rights, waived them, and gave an inculpatory statement. The evidence also shows that appellee's physical condition was normal and that appellee was not subjected to physical or psychological abuse, and that no threats or promises were utilized to induce his confession. Further,

appellee's reasonable requests, such as the use of restroom facilities, were granted. Given these circumstances, the record clearly demonstrates that appellee's confession was knowingly, intelligently, and voluntarily made.[17]

Id. at 224–25, 465 A.2d at 992–93.

4. PROMPT RELEASE TO CUSTODY OF JUVENILE AUTHORITIES

IN THE INTEREST OF SCHIRNER

Superior Court of Pennsylvania, 1979.
264 Pa.Super. 185, 399 A.2d 728.

Before CERCONE, HESTER and HOFFMAN, JJ.

HOFFMAN, JUDGE:

Appellant, a juvenile adjudicated delinquent below, contends that the court below erred in failing to suppress inculpatory extrajudicial statements obtained from him during his unlawful detention at the Bristol Township police station. We agree, and accordingly reverse the adjudication of delinquency and remand for a new hearing.

The facts are as follows. On April 2, 1978, at 10:30 a.m., William Melbourne and appellant Richard Schirner were arrested while in flight from the scene of an attempted burglary. They were taken to the Bristol Township police station at 11:00 a.m., and were each placed in detention cells. The police notified their parents, who arrived at the station at noon.

After questioning Melbourne, Detective Edward Ward, the Juvenile Officer of the Bristol Township police, began to question Schirner at 1:30 p.m. in the presence of his mother, after warning him of his *Miranda* rights. Schirner admitted that he was at the scene of one prior unsolved burglary but maintained that he was simply an innocent bystander. Schirner was returned to his cell at 3:00 p.m. At that point, Ward resumed questioning of Melbourne. Melbourne then admitted to numerous burglaries on which the police had open files, and implicated Schirner along with two other juveniles named Michael White * * * and John Jones.

At 5:30 p.m., an officer telephoned Michael White at his home, and spoke to his father, who agreed to bring his son to the station for questioning. The Whites arrived at 5:30 p.m., and Detective Ward gave Michael his *Miranda* rights and questioned him in the presence of his father. Michael White orally admitted to his participation in numerous burglaries with Schirner, Melbourne, and Jones. Ward finished questioning Michael White at 7:00 p.m. and placed him in his own detention cell. No one questioned White further that day.

Officer John Schwab arrived at the station at 7:30 p.m. in response to a call from Detective Ward for help in interviewing the

---

[17] Ironically, appellee's father is a police officer with many years of experience, required by the nature of his employment to be always prepared to inform arrestees of their constitutional rights.

juveniles in custody. At 8:00 p.m., he brought Schirner out of his cell and questioned him until 10:00 p.m., during which time (with his mother no longer present) Schirner admitted to his participation in many burglaries with the others. At 10:00 p.m., all three juveniles were informed that they would stay overnight in their cells. The next morning, the juveniles' confessions were transcribed into written statements and signed. The juveniles were then given lunch and taken to the Bucks County Youth Center early in the afternoon.

The Juvenile Act, 11 P.S. § 50–101 et seq., provides a specific procedure to be followed when a juvenile is taken into custody. First, the officer must with all reasonable speed notify the parents of the child's apprehension and whereabouts, and then must do one of two things: (1) release the juvenile to his parents, or (2) if his detention is required to protect the person or property of others, detain the child at an appropriate place which is licensed or approved by the court or the Department of Public Welfare for the detention of delinquents. 11 P.S. §§ 50–309 to 311. For the purpose of determining which of these options to follow, the Act permits the "temporary detention or questioning" of the juvenile. 11 P.S. § 50–310(a)(3). Any extrajudicial statements taken from the juvenile during the course of a violation of these procedures may not be used against him. 11 P.S. § 50–318(b).

In In Interest of Anderson, 227 Pa.Super. 439, 313 A.2d 260 (1973), the juvenile was taken into custody at 9:00 p.m. and questioned about his participation in a gang shooting of a passerby. After he confessed to his participation in the shooting, he was taken to a juvenile detention center around 11:30 p.m. We held that Section 310(a)(3) does not forbid custodial interrogations of juveniles and found that a 2½ hour delay prior to detention in a juvenile center was permissible under the "all reasonable speed" standard of the Juvenile Act. On the other hand, in Commonwealth v. Bey, 249 Pa.Super. 185, 375 A.2d 1304 (1977), the juvenile was arrested at 10:00 p.m. and taken to the local police station. The police did not question him but they did place him in a lineup four hours later at 2:00 a.m., at which time the complainant positively identified him. The juvenile was then transferred to another police station and, in the morning, was taken to the Youth Study Center in Philadelphia. We held that this delay was in violation of the Juvenile Act:

"The [juvenile] * * * upon his arrest * * * was 'in custody' within the meaning of the Juvenile Act. Consequently, before he was taken elsewhere, allowing for a period in which the authorities could administratively process the juvenile suspect, he should have either been released in the custody of his parents * * * or delivered to a detention * * * center * * *. In view of the serious charges [rape] for which [the juvenile] was arrested it would have been quite impractical for the police to have released [him]. However, this does not alter the fact that his lengthy detention at the * * * police districts was not * * * in conformity with the mandatory provisions of [the Juvenile Act, 11 P.S. § 50–310]." Commonwealth v. Bey, supra at 198, 375 A.2d at 1313. We also held that a police station is *not* an appropriate detention center for juveniles under the requirements of 11 P.S. § 50–311(a). Id. at 199, 375 A.2d 1312. Therefore, we held that the admission of this pre-trial identification was erroneous.[18]

Here, applying the Juvenile Act as construed by *Anderson* and *Bey*, we conclude that it was error to admit Schirner's statements. Schirner did not begin to make his inculpatory statements until he had been in custody for 9½ hours after his arrest. When Schirner was brought into custody, he was not immediately questioned to determine whether he should be released to his parents or detained. Rather, Schirner was placed in a detention cell for 2½ hours, questioned for 1½ hours, during which time he denied any criminal conduct, and then returned to his cell where he stayed for the next five hours. This delay prior to his confession is even greater than the four hours delay in *Bey* between the arrest and the lineup, which was there held to be a violation of the Juvenile Act. Only after this delay did Schirner begin to make the inculpatory statements that were later used against him, and this when his mother was no longer present.[19] We conclude that keeping Schirner in custody for 9½ hours prior to his confession, when he should have been taken to a juvenile detention center "with all reasonable speed," was a violation of the Juvenile Act. As the confession was obtained during the course of a violation of the Act, his statement should have been suppressed.

The adjudication of delinquency is reversed and the case is remanded for a new hearing.

HESTER, J. dissents.

NOTES

1. In Commonwealth v. Wallace, 346 Mass. 9, 190 N.E.2d 224 (1963) the Supreme Judicial Court of Massachusetts held that a confession obtained in violation of a statute requiring the police immediately to notify the probation

---

[18] The Juvenile Act, 11 P.S. § 50–318, provides that "extrajudicial statements * * * shall not be used against [a juvenile]." However, this Section does not specifically address the suppression of pretrial identifications taken during the course of an unlawful delay. Accordingly, in *Bey* we held that since the procedures mandated by the Juvenile Act were not followed, the Commonwealth would be required to adhere to the Rule of Criminal Procedure, specifically Rule 130, which provides that persons subjected to warrantless arrests must be taken to arraignment without unnecessary delay. Thus we stated in *Bey* that a *Futch* analysis would apply. Commonwealth v. Futch, 447 Pa. 389, 290 A.2d 417 (1972), but refused to order a rehearing because the reliability of the victim's in-court identification rendered harmless any er-

ror in the admission of the pre-trial line-up identification. Commonwealth v. Bey, 249 Pa.Super. 185, 202, 375 A.2d 1304, 1314 (1977). Here, we have no need to resort to a *Futch* analysis, since the Juvenile Act explicitly requires the suppression of statements in these circumstances. Our analysis must be under the Juvenile Act's standard of "with all reasonable speed." Still, the "unnecessary delay" standard of *Futch* and Commonwealth v. Williams, 455 Pa. 569, 319 A.2d 419 (1974) remains relevant by analogy. *See In Interest of Anderson*, 227 Pa. Super. 439, 441, 313 A.2d 260, 261 (1973).

[19] Appellant does not challenge the legality of the resumption of questioning without the continued presence of his mother, and thus we do not discuss that issue. * * *

officer and a parent when a child is taken into custody is not for that reason inadmissible:

> A violation of this statute, however, accompanied by lengthy questioning by the police would be an important factor to be considered in determining whether a detained juvenile had been overreached or coerced by the police in the obtaining of a statement constituting a confession or an admission. We hold only that a violation of the statute in and of itself does not render a statement inadmissible, if otherwise competent.

Id. at 229.

2. "The defendant was arrested at approximately 12:51 a.m. on April 5, 1981. He was questioned at approximately 5:00 a.m., was advised of his *Miranda* rights, and shortly thereafter gave a confession to the police. He was taken before a juvenile judge at 7:00 a.m., and his aunt was notified of his arrest at approximately 9:30 a.m. The defendant was ten (10) days short of his eighteenth birthday when arrested. The defendant contends that the questioning and detention of him prior to being released to his guardian or being taken before a juvenile judge violated the provisions of T.C.A. § 37–215 and, citing T.C.A. § 37–227(b), says that this violation precluded the use of his confession at the juvenile court transfer hearing and at the circuit court acceptance hearing.

"The defendant relies on two (2) Tennessee Supreme Court cases, State v. Strickland, 532 S.W.2d 912 (Tenn.1975) and Colyer v. State, 577 S.W.2d 460 (Tenn.1979) which held that in the absence of police compliance with the requirements of T.C.A. § 37–215, questioning of juvenile defendants was barred. This reliance is misplaced since both *Strickland* and *Colyer* were construing T.C.A. § 37–215 as originally drafted, and this statute was significantly amended in 1976. The former version of T.C.A. § 37–215 required that the child be brought before the court or released to his parents or guardian, "directly with all reasonable speed," and further required that "any temporary detention or questioning of the child necessary to comply with this subsection shall conform to the procedures and conditions prescribed in this chapter and rules of court." As noted in *Colyer*, supra, the legislature amended this section by the Public Acts of 1976, ch. 745 § 1 (effective March 22, 1976), deleting entirely the sentence pertaining to the detention and questioning of juveniles, and changing the words "directly with all reasonable speed" to "within a reasonable time." *Colyer*, supra, at 462. Both this Court, and the Court of Appeals have held that by virtue of this amendment, T.C.A. § 37–215(a) no longer specifies requirements for custodial interrogation of juveniles. Randall Wade Proctor v. State, Nos. 997–998 (Tenn.Cr.App., Nashville, July 18, 1977); State v. Johnny Manus, Cannon Law (Tenn.App., February 1, 1982).

"Thus, since there is no longer any statutory prohibition against the questioning of a juvenile defendant after his arrest, there only remains the statutory issue of whether the "reasonable time" requirements of T.C.A. § 37–215(a) have been met, and the constitutional issue of whether under the totality of the circumstances the defendant's confession was the result of a knowing and intelligent waiver of his constitutional rights. Both the juvenile

court judge and the circuit court judge answered these questions in
the affirmative and we agree."

State v. Gordon, 642 S.W.2d 742, 743–44 (Tenn.Cr.App.1982).

3. Suppose the following statute is in force.

"A law enforcement officer who takes a minor into custody with or
without a warrant under Section 3–1 shall immediately make a reasonable attempt to notify the parent or other person legally responsible for
the minor's care or the person with whom the minor resides that the
minor has been taken into custody and where he is being held; and the
officer shall without unnecessary delay take the minor to the nearest
juvenile police officer designated for such purposes in the county of
venue or shall surrender the minor to a juvenile police officer in the city
or village where the offense is alleged to have been committed."

Would the statute be violated—and a statement given by a juvenile while
still in police custody be inadmissible—if the police officer in a medium-sized
city tried on Sunday to locate the appropriate juvenile official but was
unsuccessful because that official was not on duty?   Should the juvenile's
rights depend on whether the city sufficiently staffs its departments to
permit full compliance with state statutes?   In People v. Baxtrom, 81 Ill.
App.3d 653, 37 Ill.Dec. 437, 402 N.E.2d 327 (1980), the court concluded that a
reasonable effort was sufficient to satisfy the statute, but that even if it
were not "* * * the law is clear that such violation would not render the
statement inadmissible * * *."   Id. at 661, 37 Ill.Dec. at 442, 402 N.E.2d at
332.

C. WAIVER

FARE v. MICHAEL C.

Supreme Court of the United States, 1979.
442 U.S. 707, 99 S.Ct. 2560, 61 L.Ed.2d 197.

MR. JUSTICE BLACKMUN delivered the opinion of the Court.

In Miranda v. Arizona, 384 U.S. 436, 86 S.Ct. 1602, 16 L.Ed.2d
694 (1966), this Court established certain procedural safeguards designed to protect the rights of an accused, under the Fifth and
Fourteenth Amendments, to be free from compelled self-incrimination
during custodial interrogation.   The Court specified, among other
things, that if the accused indicates in any manner that he wishes to
remain silent or to consult an attorney, interrogation must cease, and
any statement obtained from him during interrogation thereafter
may not be admitted against him at his trial.   Id., at 444–445, 473–
474, 86 S.Ct., at 1612–1613, 1627–1628.

In this case, the State of California, in the person of its acting
chief probation officer, attacks the conclusion of the Supreme Court
of California that a juvenile's request, made while undergoing custodial interrogation, to see his *probation officer* is *per se* an invocation
of the juvenile's Fifth Amendment rights as pronounced in *Miranda*.

I

Respondent Michael C. was implicated in the murder of Robert
Yeager.   The murder occurred during a robbery of the victim's home

on January 19, 1976. A small truck registered in the name of respondent's mother was identified as having been near the Yeager home at the time of the killing, and a young man answering respondent's description was seen by witnesses near the truck and near the home shortly before Yeager was murdered.

On the basis of this information, Van Nuys, Cal., police took respondent into custody at approximately 6:30 p.m. on February 4. Respondent then was 16½ years old and on probation to the juvenile court. He had been on probation since the age of 12. Approximately one year earlier he had served a term in a youth corrections camp under the supervision of the juvenile court. He had a record of several previous offenses, including burglary of guns and purse snatching, stretching back over several years.

Upon respondent's arrival at the Van Nuys station house two police officers began to interrogate him. The officers and respondent were the only persons in the room during the interrogation. The conversation was tape recorded. One of the officers initiated the interview by informing respondent that he had been brought in for questioning in relation to a murder. The officer fully advised respondent of his *Miranda* rights. The following exchange then occurred, as set out in the opinion of the California Supreme Court, In re Michael C., 21 Cal.3d 471, 473–474, 146 Cal.Rptr. 358, 359–360, 579 P.2d 7, 8 (1978) (emphasis added by that court):

"Q. * * * Do you understand all of these rights as I have explained them to you?

"A. Yeah.

"Q. Okay, do you wish to give up your right to remain silent and talk to us about this murder?

"A. What murder? I don't know about no murder.

"Q. I'll explain to you which one it is if you want to talk to us about it.

"A. Yeah, I might talk to you.

"Q. Do you want to give up your right to have an attorney present here while we talk about it?

"A. *Can I have my probation officer here?*

"Q. Well I can't get a hold of your probation officer right now. You have the right to an attorney.

"A. How I know you guys won't pull no police officer in and tell me he's an attorney?

"Q. Huh?

"A. [How I know you guys won't pull no police officer in and tell me he's an attorney?]

"Q. Your probation officer is Mr. Christiansen.

"A. Yeah.

"Q. Well I'm not going to call Mr. Christiansen tonight. There's a good chance we can talk to him later, but I'm not going to call him right now. If you want to talk to us without an attorney present, you can. If you don't want to, you don't have to. But if you want to say something, you can, and if you don't want to say something you don't have to. That's your right. You understand that right?

"A. Yeah.

"Q. Okay, will you talk to us without an attorney present?

"A. Yeah I want to talk to you."

Respondent thereupon proceeded to answer questions put to him by the officers. He made statements and drew sketches that incriminated him in the Yeager murder.

Largely on the basis of respondent's incriminating statements, probation authorities filed a petition in juvenile court alleging that respondent had murdered Robert Yeager, in violation of Cal.Penal Code Ann. § 187 (West) (Supp.1979), and that respondent therefore should be adjudged a ward of the juvenile court, pursuant to Cal. Welf. & Inst. Code Ann. § 602 (West) (Supp.1979). App. 4–5. Respondent thereupon moved to suppress the statements and sketches he gave the police during the interrogation. He alleged that the statements had been obtained in violation of *Miranda* in that his request to see his probation officer at the outset of the questioning constituted an invocation of his Fifth Amendment right to remain silent, just as if he had requested the assistance of an attorney. Accordingly, respondent argued that since the interrogation did not cease until he had a chance to confer with his probation officer, the statements and sketches could not be admitted against him in the juvenile court proceedings. In so arguing, respondent relied by analogy on the decision in *People v. Burton*, 6 Cal.3d 375, 99 Cal.Rptr. 1, 491 P.2d 793 (1971), where the Supreme Court of California had held that a minor's request, made during custodial interrogation, to see his parents constituted an invocation of the minor's Fifth Amendment rights.

In support of his suppression motion, respondent called his probation officer, Charles P. Christiansen, as a witness. Christiansen testified that he had instructed respondent that if at any time he had "a concern with his family," or ever had "a police contact," App. 27, he should get in touch with his probation officer immediately. The witness stated that, on a previous occasion, when respondent had had a police contact and had failed to communicate with Christiansen, the probation officer had reprimanded him. Id., at 28. This testimony, respondent argued, indicated that when he asked for his probation officer, he was in fact asserting his right to remain silent in the face of further questioning.

In a ruling from the bench, the court denied the motion to suppress. Id., at 41–42. It held that the question whether respondent had waived his right to remain silent was one of fact to be determined on a case-by-case basis, and that the facts of this case showed a "clear waiver" by respondent of that right. Id., at 42. The court observed that the transcript of the interrogation revealed that respondent specifically had told the officers that he would talk with them, and that this waiver had come at the outset of the interrogation and not after prolonged questioning. The court noted that respondent was a "16 and a half year old minor who has been through the court system before, has been to [probation] camp, has a probation officer, [and is not] a young, naive minor with no experience with the courts." Ibid. Accordingly, it found that on the facts of the case respondent had waived his Fifth Amendment rights, notwithstanding the request to see his probation officer.

On appeal, the Supreme Court of California took the case by transfer from the California Court of Appeal and, by a divided vote, reversed. In re Michael C., 21 Cal.3d 471, 146 Cal.Rptr. 358, 579 P.2d 7 (1978). The court held that respondent's "request to see his probation officer at the commencement of interrogation negated any possible willingness on his part to discuss his case with the police [and] thereby invoked his Fifth Amendment privilege." Id., at 474, 146 Cal.Rptr., at 360, 579 P.2d, at 8. The court based this conclusion on its view that, because of the juvenile court system's emphasis on the relationship between a probation officer and the probationer, the officer was "a trusted guardian figure who exercises the authority of the state as *parens patriae* and whose duty it is to implement the protective and rehabilitative powers of the juvenile court." Id., at 476, 146 Cal.Rptr., at 361, 579 P.2d, at 10. As a consequence, the court found that a minor's request for his probation officer was the same as a request to see his parents during interrogation, and thus under the rule of *Burton* constituted an invocation of the minor's Fifth Amendment rights.

The fact that the probation officer also served as a peace officer, and, whenever a proceeding against a juvenile was contemplated, was charged with a duty to file a petition alleging that the minor had committed an offense, did not alter, in the court's view, the fact that the officer in the eyes of the juvenile was a trusted guardian figure to whom the minor normally would turn for help when in trouble with the police. 21 Cal.3d, at 476, 146 Cal.Rptr., at 361, 579 P.2d, at 10. Relying on *Burton*, the court ruled that it would unduly restrict *Miranda* to limit its reach in a case involving a minor to a request by the minor for an attorney, since it would be " 'fatuous to assume that a minor in custody will be in a position to call an attorney for assistance and it is unrealistic to attribute no significance to his call for help from the only person to whom he normally looks—a parent or guardian.' " 21 Cal.3d, at 475–476, 146 Cal.Rptr., at 360, 579 P.2d, at 9, quoting People v. Burton, 6 Cal.3d, at 382, 99 Cal.Rptr., at 6, 491 P.2d, at 797–798. The court dismissed the concern expressed by the State that a request for a probation officer could not be distinguished from a request for one's football coach, music teacher, or clergyman on the ground that the probation officer, unlike those other figures in the juvenile's life, was charged by statute to represent the interests of the juvenile.   21 Cal.3d, at 477, 146 Cal.Rptr., at 361, 579 P.2d, at 10.

The court accordingly held that the probation officer would act to protect the minor's Fifth Amendment rights in precisely the way an attorney would act if called for by the accused.   In so holding, the court found the request for a probation officer to be a *per se* invocation of Fifth Amendment rights in the same way the request for an attorney was found in *Miranda* to be, regardless of what the interrogation otherwise might reveal.   In rejecting a totality of the circumstances inquiry, the court stated:

> "Here, however, we face conduct which, regardless of considerations of capacity, coercion or voluntariness, per se invokes the privilege against self-incrimination.   Thus our question turns not on whether the [respondent] had the ability, capacity or willingness to give a knowledgeable waiver, and hence whether he acted voluntarily, but whether, when he called for his probation officer, he exercised his Fifth Amendment privilege.   We hold that in doing so he no less invoked the protection against self-incrimination than if he asked for the presence of an attorney."   Ibid., 146 Cal.Rptr., at 362, 579 P.2d, at 10–11.

See also id., at 478 n. 4, 146 Cal.Rptr., at 362 n. 4, 579 P.2d, at 11 n. 4.   The court went on to conclude that since the State had not met its "burden of proving that a minor who requests to see his probation officer does not intend to assert his Fifth Amendment privilege," id., at 478, 146 Cal.Rptr., at 362, 579 P.2d, at 11, the trial court should not have admitted the confessions obtained after respondent had requested his probation officer.

The State of California petitioned this Court for a writ of certiorari.   Mr. Justice Rehnquist, as Circuit Justice, stayed the execution of the mandate of the Supreme Court of California.   439 U.S. 1310 99 S.Ct. 3, 58 L.Ed.2d 19 (1978).   Because the California judgment extending the *per se* aspects of *Miranda* presents an important question about the reach of that case, we thereafter issued the writ.   439 U.S. 925, 99 S.Ct. 308, 58 L.Ed.2d 318 (1978).

II

We note at the outset that it is clear that the judgment of the California Supreme Court rests firmly on that court's interpretation of federal law.   This Court, however, has not heretofore extended the *per se* aspects of the *Miranda* safeguards beyond the scope of the holding in the *Miranda* case itself.[20]   We therefore must examine the California court's decision to determine whether that court's conclu-

[20] Indeed, this Court has not yet held that *Miranda* applies with full force to exclude evidence obtained in violation of its prescriptions from consideration in juvenile proceedings, which for certain purposes have been distinguished from formal criminal prosecutions.   See McKeiver v. Pennsylvania, 403 U.S. 528, 540–541, 91 S.Ct. 1976, 1983–1984, 29 L.Ed.2d 647 (1971) (plurality opinion). We do not decide that issue today.   In view of our disposition of this case, we assume without deciding that the *Miranda* principles were fully applicable to the present proceedings.

sion so to extend *Miranda* is in harmony with *Miranda's* underlying principles. For it is clear that "a State may not impose * * * greater restrictions as a matter of *federal constitutional law* when this Court specifically refrains from imposing them." Oregon v. Hass, 420 U.S. 714, 719, 95 S.Ct. 1215, 1219, 43 L.Ed.2d 570 (1975) (emphasis in original). See North Carolina v. Butler, 441 U.S. 369, 99 S.Ct. 1755, 60 L.Ed.2d 286 (1979).

The rule the Court established in *Miranda* is clear. In order to be able to use statements obtained during custodial interrogation of the accused, the State must warn the accused prior to such questioning of his right to remain silent and of his right to have counsel, retained or appointed, present during interrogation. 384 U.S., at 473, 86 S.Ct., at 1627. "Once [such] warnings have been given, the subsequent procedure is clear." Ibid.

> "If the individual indicates in any manner, at any time prior to or during questioning, that he wishes to remain silent, the interrogation must cease. At this point he has shown that he intends to exercise his Fifth Amendment privilege; any statement taken after the person invokes his privilege cannot be other than the product of compulsion, subtle or otherwise. * * * If the individual states that he wants an attorney, the interrogation must cease until an attorney is present. At that time, the individual must have an opportunity to confer with the attorney and to have him present during any subsequent questioning. If the individual cannot obtain an attorney and he indicates that he wants one before speaking to police, they must respect his decision to remain silent." Id., at 473–474, 86 S.Ct., at 1627, 1628 (footnote omitted).

Any statements obtained during custodial interrogation conducted in violation of these rules may not be admitted against the accused, at least during the State's case-in-chief. Id., at 479, 86 S.Ct., at 1630. Cf. Harris v. New York, 401 U.S. 222, 224, 91 S.Ct. 643, 645, 28 L.Ed. 2d 1 (1971).

Whatever the defects, if any, of this relatively rigid requirement that interrogation must cease upon the accused's request for an attorney, *Miranda's* holding has the virtue of informing police and prosecutors with specificity as to what they may do in conducting custodial interrogation, and of informing courts under what circumstances statements obtained during such interrogation are not admissible. This gain in specificity, which benefits the accused and the State alike, has been thought to outweigh the burdens that the decision in *Miranda* imposes on law-enforcement agencies and the courts by requiring the suppression of trustworthy and highly probative evidence even though the confession might be voluntary under traditional Fifth Amendment analysis. See Michigan v. Tucker, 417 U.S. 433, 443–446, 94 S.Ct. 2357, 2363–2365, 41 L.Ed.2d 182 (1974).

The California court in this case, however, significantly has extended this rule by providing that a request by a juvenile for his probation officer has the same effect as a request for an attorney.

Based on the court's belief that the probation officer occupies a position as a trusted guardian figure in the minor's life that would make it normal for the minor to turn to the officer when apprehended by the police, and based as well on the state-law requirement that the officer represent the interest of the juvenile, the California decision found that consultation with a probation officer fulfilled the role for the juvenile that consultation with an attorney does in general, acting as a " 'protective [device] * * * to dispel the compulsion inherent in custodial surroundings.' " 21 Cal.3d, at 477, 146 Cal.Rptr., at 361, 579 P.2d, at 10, quoting Miranda v. Arizona, 384 U.S., at 458, 86 S.Ct., at 1619.

The rule in *Miranda,* however, was based on this Court's perception that the lawyer occupies a critical position in our legal system because of his unique ability to protect the Fifth Amendment rights of a client undergoing custodial interrogation. Because of this special ability of the lawyer to help the client preserve his Fifth Amendment rights once the client becomes enmeshed in the adversarial process, the Court found that "the right to have counsel present at the interrogation is indispensable to the protection of the Fifth Amendment privilege under the system" established by the Court. Id., at 469, 86 S.Ct., at 1625. Moreover, the lawyer's presence helps guard against overreaching by the police and ensures that any statements actually obtained are accurately transcribed for presentation into evidence. Id., at 470, 86 S.Ct., at 1625.

The *per se* aspect of *Miranda* was thus based on the unique role the lawyer plays in the adversarial system of criminal justice in this country. Whether it is a minor or an adult who stands accused, the lawyer is the one person to whom society as a whole looks as the protector of the legal rights of that person in his dealings with the police and the courts. For this reason the Court fashioned in *Miranda* the rigid rule that an accused's request for an attorney is *per se* an invocation of his Fifth Amendment rights, requiring that all interrogation cease.

A probation officer is not in the same posture with regard to either the accused or the system of justice as a whole. Often he is not trained in the law, and so is not in a position to advise the accused as to his legal rights. Neither is he a trained advocate, skilled in the representation of the interests of his client before both police and courts. He does not assume the power to act on behalf of his client by virtue of his status as advisor, nor are the communications of the accused to the probation officer shielded by the lawyer-client privilege.

Moreover, the probation officer is the employee of the State which seeks to prosecute the alleged offender. He is a peace officer, and as such is allied, to a greater or lesser extent, with his fellow peace officers. He owes an obligation to the State, notwithstanding the obligation he may also owe the juvenile under his supervision. In most cases the probation officer is duty bound to report wrongdoing by the juvenile when it comes to his attention, even if by communication from the juvenile himself. Indeed, when this case arose, the probation officer had the responsibility for filing the petition alleging wrongdoing by the juvenile and seeking to have him taken into the custody of the juvenile court. It was respondent's probation officer who filed the petition against him, and it is the acting chief of probation for the State of California, a probation officer, who is petitioner in this Court today.

In these circumstances, it cannot be said that the probation officer is able to offer the type of independent advice that an accused would expect from a lawyer retained or assigned to assist him during questioning. Indeed, the probation officer's duty to his employer in many, if not most, cases, would conflict sharply with the interests of the juvenile. For where an attorney might well advise his client to remain silent in the face of interrogation by the police, and in doing so would be "exercising [his] good professional judgment * * * to protect to the extent of his ability the rights of his client." Miranda v. Arizona, 384 U.S., at 480–481, 86 S.Ct., at 1631, a probation officer would be bound to advise his charge to cooperate with the police. The justices who concurred in the opinion of the California Supreme Court in this case aptly noted: "Where a conflict between the minor and the law arises, the probation officer can be neither neutral nor in the minor's corner." 21 Cal.3d, at 479, 146 Cal.Rptr., at 363, 579 P.2d, at 12. It thus is doubtful that a general rule can be established that a juvenile, in every case, looks to his probation officer as a "trusted guardian figure" rather than as an officer of the court system that imposes punishment.

By the same token, a lawyer is able to protect his client's rights by learning the extent, if any, of the client's involvement in the crime under investigation, and advising his client accordingly. To facilitate this, the law rightly protects the communications between client and attorney from discovery. We doubt, however, that similar protection will be afforded the communications between the probation officer and the minor. Indeed, we doubt that a probation officer, consistent with his responsibilities to the public and his profession, could withhold from the police or the courts facts made known to him by the juvenile implicating the juvenile in the crime under investigation.

We thus believe it clear that the probation officer is not in a position to offer the type of legal assistance necessary to protect the Fifth Amendment rights of an accused undergoing custodial interrogation that a lawyer can offer. The Court in *Miranda* recognized that "the attorney plays a vital role in the administration of criminal justice under our Constitution." 384 U.S., at 481, 86 S.Ct., at 1631. It is this pivotal role of legal counsel that justifies the *per se* rule established in *Miranda*, and that distinguishes the request for counsel from the request for a probation officer, a clergyman, or a close friend. A probation officer simply is not necessary, in the way an attorney is, for the protection of the legal rights of the accused, juvenile or adult. He is significantly handicapped by the position he occupies in the juvenile system from serving as an effective protector of the rights of a juvenile suspected of a crime.

The California Supreme Court, however, found that the close relationship between juveniles and their probation officers compelled the conclusion that a probation officer, for purposes of *Miranda*, was sufficiently like a lawyer to justify extension of the *per se* rule. 21 Cal.3d, at 476, 146 Cal.Rptr., at 361, 579 P.2d, at 10. The fact that a relationship of trust and cooperation between a probation officer and a juvenile might exist, however, does not indicate that the probation officer is capable of rendering effective legal advice sufficient to protect the juvenile's rights during interrogation by the police, or of providing the other services rendered by a lawyer. To find otherwise would be "an extension of the *Miranda* requirements [that] would cut this Court's holding in that case completely loose from its own explicitly stated rationale." Beckwith v. United States, 425 U.S. 341, 345, 96 S.Ct. 1612, 1615, 48 L.Ed.2d (1976). Such an extension would impose the burdens associated with the rule of *Miranda* on the juvenile justice system and the police without serving the interests that rule was designed simultaneously to protect. If it were otherwise, a juvenile's request for almost anyone he considered trustworthy enough to give him reliable advice would trigger the rigid rule of *Miranda*.

Similarly, the fact that the State has created a statutory duty on the part of the probation officer to protect the interests of the juvenile does not render the probation officer any more capable of rendering legal assistance to the juvenile or of protecting his legal rights, especially in light of the fact that the State has also legislated a duty on the part of the officer to report wrongdoing by the juvenile and serve the ends of the juvenile court system. The State cannot transmute the relationship between probation officer and juvenile offender into the type of relationship between attorney and client that was essential to the holding of *Miranda* simply by legislating an amorphous "duty to advise and care for the juvenile defendant." 21 Cal.3d, at 477, 146 Cal.Rptr., at 361, 579 P.2d, at 10. Though such a statutory duty might serve to distinguish to some degree the probation officer from the coach and the clergyman, it does not justify the extension of *Miranda* to requests to see probation officers. If it did, the State could expand the class of persons covered by the *Miranda* *per se* rule simply by creating a duty to care for the juvenile on the part of other persons, regardless of whether the logic of *Miranda* would justify that extension.

Nor do we believe that a request by a juvenile to speak with his probation officer constitutes a *per se* request to remain silent. As indicated, since a probation officer does not fulfill the important role in protecting the rights of the accused juvenile that an attorney plays, we decline to find that the request for the probation officer is tantamount to the request for an attorney. And there is nothing inherent in the request for a probation officer that requires us to find that a juvenile's request to see one necessarily constitutes an expression of the juvenile's right to remain silent. As discussed below, courts may take into account such a request in evaluating whether a juvenile in fact had waived his Fifth Amendment rights before confessing. But in other circumstances such a request might well be consistent with a desire to speak with the police. In the absence of further evidence that the minor intended in the circumstances to invoke his Fifth Amendment rights by such a request, we decline to attach such overwhelming significance to this request.

We hold, therefore, that it was error to find that the request by respondent to speak with his probation officer *per se* constituted an invocation of respondent's Fifth Amendment right to be free from compelled self-incrimination. It therefore was also error to hold that because the police did not then cease interrogating respondent the statements he made during interrogation should have been suppressed.

III

Miranda further recognized that after the required warnings are given the accused, "[i]f the interrogation continues without the presence of an attorney and a statement is taken, a heavy burden rests on the government to demonstrate that the defendant knowingly and intelligently waived his privilege against self-incrimination and his right to retained or appointed counsel." 384 U.S., at 475, 86 S.Ct., at 1628. We noted in North Carolina v. Butler, 441 U.S., at 373, 99 S.Ct. at 1757, that the question whether the accused waived his rights "is not one of form, but rather whether the defendant in fact knowingly and voluntarily waived the rights delineated in the *Miranda* case." Thus, the determination whether statements obtained during custodial interrogation are admissible against the accused is to be made upon an inquiry into the totality of the circumstances surrounding the interrogation, to ascertain whether the accused in fact knowingly and voluntarily decided to forgo his rights to remain silent and to have the assistance of counsel. Miranda v. Arizona, 384 U.S., at 475–477, 86 S.Ct., at 1628–1629.

This totality of the circumstances approach is adequate to determine whether there has been a waiver even where interrogation of juveniles is involved. We discern no persuasive reasons why any other approach is required where the question is whether a juvenile has waived his rights, as opposed to whether an adult has done so. The totality approach permits—indeed, it mandates—inquiry into all the circumstances surrounding the interrogation. This includes evaluation of the juvenile's age, experience, education, background, and intelligence, and into whether he has the capacity to understand the warnings given him, the nature of his Fifth Amendment rights, and the consequences of waiving those rights. See North Carolina v. Butler, supra.

Courts repeatedly must deal with these issues of waiver with regard to a broad variety of constitutional rights. There is no reason to assume that such courts—especially juvenile courts, with their special expertise in this area—will be unable to apply the totality of the circumstances analysis so as to take into account those special concerns that are present when young persons, often with limited experience and education and with immature judgment, are involved. Where the age and experience of a juvenile indicate that his request for his probation officer or his parents is, in fact, an invocation of his right to remain silent, the totality approach will allow the court the necessary flexibility to take this into account in making a waiver determination. At the same time, that approach refrains from imposing rigid restraints on police and courts in dealing with an experienced older juvenile with an extensive prior record who knowingly and intelligently waives his Fifth Amendment rights and voluntarily consents to interrogation.

In this case, we conclude that the California Supreme Court should have determined the issue of waiver on the basis of all the circumstances surrounding the interrogation of respondent. The juvenile court found that under this approach, respondent in fact had waived his Fifth Amendment rights and consented to interrogation by the police after his request to see his probation officer was denied. Given its view of the case, of course, the California Supreme Court did not consider this issue, though it did hold that the State had failed to prove that, notwithstanding respondent's request to see his probation officer, respondent had not intended to invoke his Fifth Amendment rights.

We feel that the conclusion of the juvenile court was correct. The transcript of the interrogation reveals that the police officers conducting the interrogation took care to ensure that respondent understood his rights. They fully explained to respondent that he was being questioned in connection with a murder. They then informed him of all the rights delineated in *Miranda,* and ascertained that respondent understood those rights. There is no indication in the record that respondent failed to understand what the officers told him. Moreover, after his request to see his probation officer had been denied, and after the police officer once more had explained his rights to him, respondent clearly expressed his willingness to waive his rights and continue the interrogation.

Further, no special factors indicate that respondent was unable to understand the nature of his actions. He was a 16½-year-old juvenile with considerable experience with the police. He had a record of several arrests. He had served time in a youth camp, and he had been on probation for several years. He was under the full-time supervision of probation authorities. There is no indication that he was of insufficient intelligence to understand the rights he was waiving, or what the consequences of that waiver would be. He was not worn down by improper interrogation tactics or lengthy questioning or by trickery or deceit.

On these facts, we think it clear that respondent voluntarily and knowingly waived his Fifth Amendment rights. Respondent argues, however, that any statements he made during interrogation were coerced. Specifically, respondent alleges that the police made threats and promises during the interrogation to pressure him into cooperating in the hope of obtaining leniency for his cooperative attitude. He notes also that he repeatedly told the officers during his interrogation that he wished to stop answering their questions, but that the officers ignored his pleas. He argues further that the record reveals that he was afraid that the police would coerce him, and that this fear caused him to cooperate. He points out that at one point the transcript revealed that he wept during the interrogation.

Review of the entire transcript reveals that respondent's claims of coercion are without merit. As noted, the police took care to inform respondent of his rights and to ensure that he understood them. The officers did not intimidate or threaten respondent in any way. Their questioning was restrained and free from the abuses that so concerned the Court in *Miranda*. See 384 U.S., at 445–455, 86 S.Ct., at 1612–1618. The police did indeed indicate that a cooperative attitude would be to respondent's benefit, but their remarks in this regard were far from threatening or coercive. And respondent's allegation that he repeatedly asked that the interrogation cease goes too far: at some points he did state that he did not know the answer to a question put to him or that he could not, or would not, answer the question, but these statements were not assertions of his right to remain silent.

IV

We hold, in short, that the California Supreme Court erred in finding that a juvenile's request for his probation officer was a *per se* invocation of that juvenile's Fifth Amendment rights under *Miranda*. We conclude, rather, that whether the statements obtained during subsequent interrogation of a juvenile who has asked to see his probation officer, but who has not asked to consult an attorney or expressly asserted his right to remain silent, are admissible on the basis of waiver remains a question to be resolved on the totality of the circumstances surrounding the interrogation. On the basis of the record in this case, we hold that the juvenile court's findings that respondent voluntarily and knowingly waived his rights and consented to continued interrogation, and that the statements obtained from him were voluntary, were proper, and that the admission of those statements in the proceeding against respondent in juvenile court was correct.

The judgment of the Supreme Court of California is reversed and the case is remanded for further proceedings not inconsistent with this opinion.

It is so ordered.

MR. JUSTICE MARSHALL, with whom MR. JUSTICE BRENNAN and MR. JUSTICE STEVENS join, dissenting.

In Miranda v. Arizona, 384 U.S. 436, 86 S.Ct. 1602, 16 L.Ed.2d 694 (1966), this Court sought to ensure that the inherently coercive pressures of custodial interrogation would not vitiate a suspect's privilege against self-incrimination. Noting that these pressures "can operate very quickly to overbear the will of one merely made aware of his privilege," the Court held:

> "If [a suspect in custody] indicates in any manner, at any time prior to or during questioning, that he wishes to remain silent, the interrogation must cease. At this point he has shown that he intends to exercise his Fifth Amendment privilege; any statement taken after the person invokes his privilege cannot be other than the product of compulsion, subtle or otherwise. * * * If the individual states that he wants an attorney, the interrogation must cease until an attorney is present." Id., at 473–474, 86 S.Ct., at 1627–1628 (footnote omitted).

See also id., at 444–445.

As this Court has consistently recognized, the coerciveness of the custodial setting is of heightened concern where, as here, a juvenile is under investigation. In Haley v. Ohio, 332 U.S. 596, 68 S.Ct. 302, 92 L.Ed. 224 (1948), the plurality reasoned that because a 15½-year-old minor was particularly susceptible to overbearing interrogation tactics, the voluntariness of his confession could not "be judged by the more exacting standards of maturity." Id., at 599, 68 S.Ct., at 304. The Court reiterated this point in Gallegos v. Colorado, 370 U.S. 49, 54, 82 S.Ct. 1209, 1213, 8 L.Ed.2d 325 (1962), observing that a 14-year-old suspect could not "be compared with an adult in full possession of his senses and knowledgeable of the consequences of his admissions." The juvenile defendant, in the Court's view, required

> "the aid of more mature judgment as to the steps he should take in the predicament in which he found himself. A lawyer or an adult relative or friend could have given the petitioner the protection which his own immaturity could not." Ibid.

And, in In re Gault, 387 U.S. 1, 55, 87 S.Ct. 1428, 1458, 18 L.Ed.2d 527 (1967), the Court admonished that "the greatest care must be taken to assure that [a minor's] admission was voluntary."

It is therefore critical in the present context that we construe *Miranda's* prophylactic requirements broadly to accomplish their intended purpose—"dispel[ling] the compulsion inherent in custodial surroundings." 384 U.S., at 458, 86 S.Ct., at 1619. To effectuate this purpose, the Court must ensure that the "protective device" of legal counsel, id., at 465–466, 469, 86 S.Ct., at 1623–1624, 1625, be readily available, and that any intimation of a desire to preclude questioning be scrupulously honored. Thus, I believe *Miranda* requires that interrogation cease whenever a juvenile requests an adult who is obligated to represent his interests. Such a request, in my judgment, constitutes both an attempt to obtain advice and a general invocation of the right to silence. For, as the California Supreme Court recognized, " 'it is fatuous to assume that a minor in custody will be in a position to call an attorney for assistance,' " 21 Cal.3d, at 475–476, 146 Cal.Rptr. 358, 360, 579 P.2d 7, 9 quoting People v. Burton, 6 Cal.

3d, at 382, 99 Cal.Rptr. 1, 6, 491 P.2d 793, 797 (1971), or that he will trust the police to obtain a lawyer for him. A juvenile in these circumstances will likely turn to his parents, or another adult responsible for his welfare, as the only means of securing legal counsel. Moreover, a request for such adult assistance is surely inconsistent with a present desire to speak freely. Requiring a strict verbal formula to invoke the protections of *Miranda* would "protect the knowledgeable accused from stationhouse coercion while abandoning the young person who knows no more than to ask for the * * * person he trusts." Chaney v. Wainwright, 561 F.2d 1129, 1134 (CA5 1977) (Goldberg, J., dissenting).

On my reading of *Miranda*, a California juvenile's request for his probation officer should be treated as a *per se* assertion of Fifth Amendment rights. The California Supreme Court determined that probation officers have a statutory duty to represent minors' interests and indeed, are "trusted guardian figure[s]" to whom a juvenile would likely turn for assistance. 21 Cal.3d, at 476, 146 Cal.Rptr., at 361, 579 P.2d, at 10. In addition, the court found, probation officers are particularly well-suited to assist a juvenile "on such matters as whether or not he should obtain an attorney" and "how to conduct himself with police." Id., at 476, 477, 146 Cal.Rptr., at 361, 579 P.2d, at 10. Hence, a juvenile's request for a probation officer may frequently be an attempt to secure protection from the coercive aspects of custodial questioning.

This Court concludes, however, that because a probation officer has law-enforcement duties, juveniles generally would not call upon him to represent their interests, and if they did, would not be well-served. * * * But that conclusion ignores the California Supreme Court's express determination that the officer's responsibility to initiate juvenile proceedings did not negate his function as personal advisor to his wards. I decline to second-guess that court's assessment of state law. See Murdock v. City of Memphis, 20 Wall. 590, 626, 22 L.Ed. 429 (1875); General Trading Co. v. State Tax Comm'n, 322 U.S. 335, 337, 64 S.Ct. 1028, 1029, 88 L.Ed. 1309 (1944); Scripto v. Carson, 362 U.S. 207, 210, 80 S.Ct. 619, 621, 4 L.Ed.2d 660 (1960). Further, although the majority here speculates that probation officers have a duty to advise cooperation with the police, * * *—a proposition suggested only in the concurring opinion of two justices below, 21 Cal.3d, at 479, 146 Cal.Rptr., at 363, 579 P.2d, at 11–12 (Mosk, J., concurring)—respondent's probation officer instructed all his charges "not to go and admit openly to an offense, [but rather] to get some type of advice from * * * parents or a lawyer." App. 30. Absent an explicit statutory provision or judicial holding, the officer's assessment of the obligations imposed by state law is entitled to deference by this Court.

Thus, given the role of probation officers under California law, a juvenile's request to see his officer may reflect a desire for precisely the kind of assistance *Miranda* guarantees an accused before he waives his Fifth Amendment rights. At the very least, such a request signals a desire to remain silent until contact with the officer is made. Because the Court's contrary determination withdraws the safeguards of *Miranda* from those most in need of protection, I respectfully dissent.

MR. JUSTICE POWELL, dissenting.

Although I agree with the Court that the Supreme Court of California misconstrued Miranda v. Arizona, 384 U.S. 436, 86 S.Ct. 1602, 16 L.Ed.2d 694 (1966), I would not reverse the California court's judgment. This Court repeatedly has recognized that "the greatest care" must be taken to assure that an alleged confession of a juvenile was voluntary. See, e.g., In re Gault, 387 U.S. 1, 55, 87 S.Ct. 1428, 1458, 18 L.Ed.2d 527 (1967); Gallegos v. Colorado, 370 U.S. 49, 54, 82 S.Ct. 1209, 1212, 8 L.Ed.2d 325 (1962); Haley v. Ohio, 332 U.S. 596, 559–600, 68 S.Ct. 302, 303–304, 92 L.Ed. 224 (1948) (plurality). Respondent was a young person, 16 years old at the time of his arrest and the subsequent prolonged interrogation at the stationhouse. Although respondent had had prior brushes with the law, and was under supervision by a probation officer, the taped transcript of his interrogation—as well as his testimony at the suppression hearing—demonstrates that he was immature, emotional, and uneducated, and therefore was likely to be vulnerable to the skillful, two-on-one, repetitive style of interrogation to which he was subjected. App., at 54–82.

When given *Miranda* warnings and asked whether he desired an attorney, respondent requested permission to "have my probation officer here," a request that was refused. App., at 55. That officer testified later that he had communicated frequently with respondent, that respondent had serious and "extensive" family problems, and that the officer had instructed respondent to call him immediately "at any time he has a police contact, even if they stop him and talk to him on the street." App. 26–31. The reasons given by the probation officer for having so instructed his charge were substantially the same reasons that prompt this Court to examine with special care the circumstances under which a minor's alleged confession was obtained. After stating that respondent had been "going through problems," the officer observed that "many times kids don't understand what is going on, and what they are supposed to do relative to police * * *." App. 29. This view of the limited understanding of the average 16-year-old was borne out by respondent's question when, during interrogation, he was advised of his right to an attorney: "How I know you guys won't pull no police officer in and tell me he is an attorney?" App. 55. It was during this part of the interrogation that the police had denied respondent's request to "have my probation officer here." App. 55.

The police then proceeded, despite respondent's repeated denial of any connection to the murders under investigation, see App. 56–60, persistently to press interrogation until they extracted a confession. In In re Gault, in addressing police interrogation of detained juveniles, the Court stated:

"If counsel was not present for some permissible reason when an admission was obtained [from a child], the greatest care must be taken to assure that the admission was voluntary, in the sense not only that it was not coerced or suggested, but also that it was not the product of ignorance of rights or of adolescent fantasy, fright or despair." Supra, at 55.

It is clear that the interrogating police did not exercise "the greatest care" to assure that respondent's "admission was voluntary." [21] In the absence of counsel, and having refused to call the probation officer, they nevertheless engaged in protracted interrogation.

Although I view the case as close, I am not satisfied that this particular 16-year-old boy, in this particular situation, was subjected to a fair interrogation free from inherently coercive circumstances. For these reasons, I would affirm the judgment of the Supreme Court of California.

STATE IN THE INTEREST OF DINO

Supreme Court of Louisiana, 1978.
359 So.2d 586, cert. denied, 439 U.S. 1047, 99 S.Ct. 722, 58 L.Ed.2d 706.

DENNIS, JUSTICE.

On August 3, 1977 a petition was filed in the Caddo Parish Juvenile court seeking to have thirteen year old Andrew Leonard Dino, relator, adjudicated a delinquent based on the allegation that he committed the first degree murder of Cynthia Tew on June 26, 1977 in violation of La.R.S. 14:30. Relator denied the allegations contained in the petition.

Prior to the adjudicatory hearing relator filed a motion to suppress an inculpatory statement given to the Shreveport police on the ground that it was obtained in violation of his constitutional rights. Following a five day hearing the juvenile court denied the motion to suppress. The juvenile court also denied relator's motion for a trial by jury and his motion for a public trial.

We granted writs to review the pre-trial rulings of the juvenile court. State of Louisiana in the Interest of Dino, 353 So.2d 1334 (La. 1978).

Waiver of Rights by a Juvenile

During the late afternoon of June 26, 1977 the parents of nine year old Cynthia Tew discovered that she was missing from home. Several residents in the neighborhood, including relator Andrew

[21] Minors who become embroiled with the law range from the very young up to those on the brink of majority. Some of the older minors become fully "street-wise," hardened criminals, deserving no greater consideration than that properly accorded all persons suspected of crime. Other minors are more of a child than an adult. As the Court indicated in In re Gault, 387 U.S. 1, 87 S.Ct. 1428, 18 L.Ed. 2d 527 (1967), the facts relevant to the care to be exercised in a particular case vary widely. They include the minor's age, actual maturity, family environment, education, emotional and mental stability, and, of course, any prior record he might have.

Dino, commenced a search for her. Early that evening the relator reported that he had found Cynthia, critically injured, in a wooded area behind the Tew and Dino houses. Cynthia was taken to the hospital and died shortly thereafter from severe head wounds without regaining consciousness.

The police began an investigation which extended over a period of about six weeks. Because relator was the one who discovered Cynthia the police were in frequent contact with him and his parents during the investigation. However, during the initial stages of the investigation the relator was regarded merely as a potential witness, rather than as a suspect, by the police.

On July 8, 1977, the relator at the request of the investigating officers went to the police station with his parents and gave the police a "witness informational" statement. On this occasion he did not implicate himself in the crime. His parents were not present in the room during the taking of the statement, which was recorded. Because of discrepancies between Andrew's statement and information from other sources, it was agreed that Andrew should take a polygraph test to clarify his earlier statement and to eliminate him as a potential suspect.[22] One test was cancelled by Andrew's father because of the youth's nervousness. Another test was scheduled but never performed when the polygraph examiner went on vacation.

On August 1, 1977 Andrew's father gave a witness statement to the police. Mr. Dino's account of Andrew's activities on the afternoon in question differed from that of his son. One of the officers testified that Andrew definitely became a suspect at this time.

On the afternoon of August 2, 1977, Andrew awoke from a nap and a bad dream. He told his mother he remembered being in the woods with Cynthia, that something "blue" had come toward them, and that he ran away leaving Cynthia alone. Mrs. Dino called one of the officers with whom she had become acquainted during the investigation and told him what Andrew had said. She asked the officer to come talk with Andrew after her husband came home from work. However, at the insistence of the officer Mrs. Dino agreed to bring Andrew to police headquarters. The officer agreed to leave word at her husband's office for him to join his wife and son at the stationhouse. Mrs. Dino attempted to call the family attorney to ask for advice before leaving her house, but he was not in.

Upon arrival at the station Andrew was taken into an office by the chief of police and one of the investigating officers. Mrs. Dino was left to wait in a separate room and was not asked if she wished to be present while they talked to Andrew. She was not told that the investigation had focused on Andrew as a suspect. She was not informed of her son's constitutional rights or given an opportunity to confer with him about whether he should give a statement without consulting a lawyer. Because they had not previously met the chief

[22] At this point several residents in the neighborhood were considered by the police as "potential suspects."

of police, Mrs. Dino and Andrew were asked if they objected to his presence during the interrogation. No objection was made, and no other conversation occurred before the interrogation began.

Apparently, the youth was not told either that he was free to leave or required to remain during questioning. According to the record Andrew was in the office with the chief of police and the other officer for approximately four to eight minutes. During this short period of time, the officers testified, Andrew read and listened to explanations of his constitutional rights, he waived his rights both orally and in writing, and he gave them an oral inculpatory statement. The officers' testimony was not detailed as to the oral explanation or the means by which it was determined that the warnings were fully understood by the thirteen year old youth. Contrary to the testimony of the officers, Andrew testified that they gave no explanation of his rights and that he did not understand what was on the paper signed by him. At the motion to suppress hearing a psychiatrist and a clinical psychologist testified that Andrew was incapable of understanding the language contained on the standard waiver form, but that he could have comprehended a statement of constitutional rights phrased in simpler terms. From our review of the officers' testimony it appears that the warnings given the youth were either quoted or paraphrased from a standard waiver form.

After the statement was given, the police informed Mrs. Dino that Andrew had confessed to the murder and asked her to sign the waiver card. She signed it without reading the warnings. Mr. Dino arrived at the station shortly after these events transpired. The youth was not allowed to leave the stationhouse with his parents but was placed in confinement in the juvenile detention center.

The constitutional privilege against self-incrimination and the rights to counsel and to confront and cross-examine witnesses are applicable in the case of juveniles as they are with respect to adult accuseds. Article I, § 13 of the 1974 Louisiana Constitution requires that any person arrested or detained in connection with the investigation or commission of any offense must be advised fully of the reason for his arrest or detention, his right to remain silent, his right against self-incrimination, his right to the assistance of counsel and, if indigent, his right to court appointed counsel. By the adoption of this provision Louisiana enhanced and incorporated the prophylactic rules of Miranda v. Arizona, which in essence require that the state, before it may use a confession at trial, establish that a defendant was informed of his right against self-incrimination and to have an attorney present at the interrogation; that he fully understood the consequences of waiving those rights; and that he did in fact waive those rights voluntarily and without physical or mental coercion. This protection must have been given "when the individual [was] first subjected to police interrogation while in custody at the station or otherwise deprived of his freedom of action in any significant way."

The State raises a threshold issue by contending that the warnings required by *Miranda* and Article 1, § 13 of our constitution do not come into play in the instant case because the youth was brought to the police station and placed in an office with his interrogators through the voluntary action of his own mother. Perhaps in recognition that the circumstances surrounding young Dino rather plainly qualified him as a person who had been taken into custody or otherwise deprived of his freedom of action in a significant way, the State relies primarily upon the Supreme Court's decision in Oregon v. Mathiason,[23] which may to some extent modify *Miranda.*

The State's arguments must be rejected for several reasons. First, the precedent relied upon is distinguishable on its facts from the circumstances involved in Dino's interrogation. In *Mathiason* the Court held that police were not obliged to administer warnings to an adult parolee who came to the stationhouse at the request of a policeman to answer questions about his possible involvement in a recent burglary under investigation. Heavily emphasizing that Mathiason voluntarily came to the stationhouse as a possible suspect and was allowed to leave without hindrance when the questioning was over, the Court held that this was not the sort of coercive environment to which *Miranda* applies. The ingredients of the instant case are significantly different. The relator became the primary suspect in the murder investigation when the police learned of his admission to being in the woods with the victim before she was attacked. It cannot be said that young Dino, who was only thirteen years old and subject to the legal custody of his parents, acted voluntarily when he was brought to the stationhouse by his mother. Nor could one conclude realistically that he was not deprived of his freedom of action in a significant way when he was closeted with two adult policemen in the interrogation room, without counsel, parents, or friends. Insofar as the record reflects, young Dino was not "streetwise" and did not have any previous experience as a juvenile accused. The youth was never told that he was free to leave the police station, and he was placed in confinement immediately after his confession was taken. Second, if *Mathiason* represents a constriction of the *Miranda* definition of significant deprivation of freedom of action, its holding clearly does not govern our interpretation of Article I, § 13 of the 1974 Louisiana Constitution whose framers intended to adopt the *Miranda* edicts full-blown and unfettered.[24] Finally, it appears that, in fact, there was an intention by the convention to go beyond *Miranda* and to require more of the State regarding the precise issue now under discussion. In Article I, § 13 the cautions are triggered and must be given "when any person has been arrested or detained in connection with the investigation or commission of any offense." The use of "detained" in addition to

[23] 429 U.S. 492, 97 S.Ct. 711, 50 L.Ed. 2d 714 (1977).

[24] State of Louisiana Constitutional Convention of 1973 Verbatim Transcripts, September 1–7, 1973, Vol. XIII, pp. 68–112, Vol. XIV, pp. 1–51; Hargrave, The Declaration of Rights of the Louisiana Constitution of 1974, 35 La.L. Rev. 1, 40–48 (1974). See, State v. Welch, 337 So.2d 1114 (La.1976).

"arrested" was intended to prevent a narrow construction of the latter term.[25]

It is well settled under *Miranda* and our state constitution that if a statement is taken without the presence of an attorney, under circumstances in which the warnings are required, a heavy burden rests on the State to demonstrate that the accused knowingly and intelligently waived his privilege against self-incrimination and his right to retained or appointed counsel. Since the warnings were required before a statement could be taken in the instant case, the State must discharge a heavy burden in order to prove a valid waiver of his constitutional rights by young Dino.

This Court has not expressly stated under what circumstances a juvenile may be deemed to have knowingly and intelligently waived his privilege against self-incrimination and his right to retained or appointed counsel. One Louisiana court of appeal has taken the position that the age of a person under interrogation does not necessarily require additional protections and has employed a "totality of circumstances" test similar to that articulated in *West v. United States*.[26] That test consists of an illustrative list of factors to be considered in determining whether a juvenile has knowingly and intelligently waived his privilege against self-incrimination and his right to retained or appointed counsel:

> "* * * 1) age of the accused; 2) education of the accused; 3) knowledge of the accused as to both the substance of the charge, if any has been filed, and the nature of his rights to consult with an attorney and remain silent; 4) whether the accused is held incommunicado or allowed to consult with relatives, friends or an attorney; 5) whether the accused was interrogated before or after formal charges had been filed; 6) methods used in interrogation; 7) length of interrogations; 8) whether vel non the accused refused to voluntarily give statements on prior occasions; and 9) whether the accused has repudiated an extra judicial statement at a later date." 399 F.2d 467, 469.

The totality of circumstances in the instant case shows, inter alia, that Andrew's knowledge and education pertaining to his constitutional liberties were no greater than that of an average thirteen year old Louisiana youth; that he was not allowed to consult with relatives, friends or an attorney during the interrogation; that he was interrogated before formal charges had been filed and without being told that the investigation had focused on him as the primary suspect; that he was interrogated in an office at the police station by the chief of police and another officer; that the interrogation itself lasted no longer than eight minutes, but it occurred after an intensive six-week investigation involving many previous contacts between relator and the police, and it followed closely his awakening from a frightening dream related to the murder incident; that the youth had not refused

[25] Id. See, State v. Segers, 355 So.2d 238 (La.1978).

[26] 399 F.2d 467 (5th Cir.1968) cert. den. 393 U.S. 1102, 89 S.Ct. 903, 21 L.Ed.2d 795 (1969).

to give statements on prior occasions, but his father had cancelled a lie detector test because of his emotional condition; and that Andrew had repudiated the waiver of his rights. Thus the factors of the present case raise grave doubts as to whether there was real understanding and intelligent exercise of the constitutional liberties. Accordingly, were we to rely solely upon the totality of circumstances test in this case, we would conclude that the State has not carried its heavy burden in proving that young Dino was aware not only of his rights, but also of the consequences of foregoing them, that he knew he was faced with a phase of the adversary system, and that he was aware that he was not in the presence of persons acting solely in his interest.

However, exclusive use of the totality of circumstances test in relation to waivers by juveniles tends to mire the courts in a morass of speculation similar to that from which *Miranda* was designed to extricate them in adult cases. Although the *Miranda* court did not express itself specifically on the special needs of juveniles confronted with police interrogation, the reasons given for making the warnings an absolute prerequisite to interrogation point up the need for an absolute requirement that juveniles not be permitted to waive constitutional rights on their own. The Court stated:

> "The Fifth Amendment privilege is so fundamental to our system of constitutional rule and the expedient of giving an adequate warning as to the availability of the privilege so simple, we will not pause to inquire in individual cases whether the defendant was aware of his rights without a warning being given. Assessments of the knowledge the defendant possessed, based on information as to his age, education, intelligence, or prior contact with authorities, can never be more than speculation; a warning is a clearcut fact. More important, whatever the background of the person interrogated, a warning at the time of the interrogation is indispensable to overcome its pressures and to insure that the individual knows he is free to exercise the privilege at that point in time." 384 U.S. 436, 468–9, 86 S.Ct. 1602, 1625, 16 L.Ed.2d 694, 720.

> "   *   *   *

> "No amount of circumstantial evidence that the person may have been aware of this right will suffice to stand in its stead. Only through such a warning is there ascertainable assurance that the accused was aware of this right." 384 U.S. 436, 471–2, 86 S.Ct. 1602, 1626, 16 L.Ed.2d 694, 722.

Similarly, the rights which a juvenile may waive before interrogation are so fundamental to our system of constitutional rule and the expedient of requiring the advice of a parent, counsel or adviser so relatively simple and well established as a safeguard against a juvenile's improvident judicial acts, that we should not pause to inquire in individual cases whether the juvenile could, on his own, understand and effectively exercise his rights. Assessments of how the "totality of the circumstances" affected a juvenile in a particular case can never be more than speculation. Furthermore, whatever the background of the juvenile interrogated, assistance of an adult acting in his interest is indispensable to overcome the pressures of the interrogation and to insure that the juvenile knows he is free to exercise his rights at that point in time.

The presence of a parent, counsel, or other adult acting in the juvenile's interest at the interrogation may serve several significant subsidiary functions as well. If the juvenile decides to talk to his interrogators, the assistance of an adult can mitigate the dangers of untrustworthiness. With an adult acting in his interest present the likelihood that the police will practice coercion is reduced, and if coercion is nevertheless exercised the adult can testify to it in court. The presence of such an adult can also help to guarantee that the accused gives a fully accurate statement and that the statement is rightly reported by the prosecution at trial.

Moreover, such a rule will relieve the police from having to make a subjective judgment in each case. As noted by the Indiana Supreme Court in Lewis v. State, 259 Ind. 431, 288 N.E.2d 138, 141 (1972):

> "The authorities seeking to question a juvenile enter into an area of doubt and confusion when the child appears to waive his rights to counsel and against self-incrimination. They are faced with the possibility of taking a statement from him only to have a court later find that his age and the surrounding circumstances precluded the child from making a valid waiver. There are no concrete guidelines for the authorities to follow in order to insure that the waiver will be upheld. The police are forced to speculate as to whether the law will judge this accused juvenile on the same plane as an adult in regard to the waiver of his constitutional rights, or whether the court will take cognizance of the age of the child and apply different standards.
>
> "   *   *   *
>
> " *   *   * It is harmful to the system of criminal justice to require law enforcement authorities to second guess the courts in the area of constitutional rights. Clearly defined procedures should be established in areas which lend themselves to such standards in order to assure both efficient police procedure and protection of the important constitutional rights of the accused. Age is one area which lends itself to clearly defined standards."

One study indicates that many law enforcement officers in Louisiana are presently following this procedure.[27]

[27] See, Comment, Louisiana's Youth Law: Rules and Practice, 35 La.L.Rev. 851, 856 (1975):

"The practice of many of the Louisiana police departments interviewed was to advise a youth who was suspected of committing a serious offense that he could remain silent and that he could consult with and have counsel present during interrogation. Police often delay interrogation until the parents of the youth are present and orally consent to the questioning. Some departments go even further and obtain a written waiver from the juvenile and his parents before seeking an admission. A few authorities interviewed, however, were lax in consistently enforcing such procedures. Fail-

Although a majority of jurisdictions allow a juvenile to waive his privilege against incrimination and his right to counsel without mature guidance,[28] a growing number of courts and scholars recognize that a more ascertainable assurance of a knowing and intelligent waiver of constitutional rights should precede juvenile interrogation.[29]

The courts of Pennsylvania, Indiana and Georgia, for example, have recently concluded that the administering of *Miranda* warnings to a juvenile, without providing an opportunity to consult with a mature, informed individual concerned primarily with the interest of the juvenile, is inadequate to offset the disadvantage occasioned by youth.[30] Moreover, the Pennsylvania Supreme Court has held that the impediment of immaturity can only be overcome where the record establishes that the youth had access to the advice of an attorney, parent or other interested adult, and that the consulted adult was informed as to the constitutional rights available to the minor and aware of the consequences that might follow the election to be made.[31]

ure to employ these and other safeguards may not only deny fundamental due process, but may also weaken the state's case against a delinquent youth by threatening the validity of the confession thereby obtained."

See also, Tentative Draft, ABA Standards Relating to Police Handling of Juvenile Problems, § 3.2 and comments (1977).

[28] E.g., State v. Gullings, 244 Or. 173, 416 P.2d 311, 315 (1966); See, S. Davis, Right of Juveniles: The Juvenile System, §§ 3.11 et seq. (1974); IJA–ABA Juvenile Justice Standards Project, Standards Relating to Police Handling of Juvenile Problems (1977), § 3.2, p. 70.

[29] See, e.g., Commonwealth v. Jamison, 474 Pa. 541, 379 A.2d 87 (1977); Commonwealth v. Smith, 472 Pa. 492, 372 A.2d 797 (1977); Commonwealth v. McCutchen, 463 Pa. 90, 343 A.2d 669 (1975); Lewis v. State, 259 Ind. 431, 288 N.E.2d 138 (1972); Freeman v. Wilcox, 119 Ga. App. 325, 167 S.E.2d 163 (1969).

See, Comment, Interrogation of Juveniles: The Right to a Parent's Presence, 22 Dick.L.Rev. 543 (1972–73); Comment, Recent Developments—Criminal Law, 1972 Univ. of Ill.L. Forum 625; Note, 34 U. of Pitt.L.Rev. 321 (1972); Note, 3 Seton Hall L.Rev. 482 (1972); Note, 23 Baylor L.Rev. 467 (1971); Note, 68 Col.L.Rev. 1149 (1968).

In § 3.2 of the IJA–ABA Juvenile Justice Standards Project, Standards Relating to Police Handling of Juvenile Problems (1977), it is stated:

" * * * For some investigative procedures, greater constitutional safeguards are needed because of the vulnerability of juveniles. Juveniles should not be permitted to waive constitutional rights on their own. * * *"

See, also, the Commentary commencing on p. 69.

Rule 25 of the Model Rules for Juvenile Courts prepared by the Council of Judges of the National Council on Crime and Delinquency (1969) recommends, in part:

"No extrajudicial statement by the child to a peace officer or court officer shall be admitted into evidence unless it was made in the presence of the child's parent or guardian or counsel. No such statement shall be admitted into evidence unless the person offering the statement demonstrates to the satisfaction of the court that, before making the statement, the child and his parents were informed and intelligently comprehended that he need not make a statement, that any statement made might be used in a court proceeding, and that he had a right to consult with counsel before or during the making of a statement."

[30] See, e.g., Commonwealth v. Jamison, 474 Pa. 541, 379 A.2d 87 (1977); Commonwealth v. Smith, 472 Pa. 492, 372 A.2d 797 (1977); Commonwealth v. McCutchen, 463 Pa. 90, 343 A.2d 669 (1975); Lewis v. State, 259 Ind. 431, 288 N.E.2d 138 (1972); Freeman v. Wilcox, 119 Ga. App. 325, 167 S.E.2d 163 (1969).

[31] See, e.g., Commonwealth v. Smith, 472 Pa. 492, 372 A.2d 797 (1977).

Some "sophisticated" juveniles, without the benefit of adult advice, may understand the serious consequences flowing from a waiver of constitutional rights. However, one empirical study indicates that a large percentage of juveniles are incapable of knowingly and intelligently waiving constitutional rights.[32] In any event, it is the general policy of our law to protect all minors from the possible consequences of immaturity.

Because most juveniles are not mature enough to understand their rights and are not competent to exercise them,[33] the concepts of fundamental fairness embodied in the Declaration of Rights of our constitution[34] require that juveniles not be permitted to waive constitutional rights on their own. For these reasons we hold that in order for the State to meet its heavy burden of demonstrating that a waiver is made knowingly and intelligently, it must affirmatively show that the juvenile engaged in a meaningful consultation with an attorney or an informed parent, guardian, or other adult interested in his welfare before he waived his right to counsel and privilege against self-incrimination.

Accordingly, the purported waiver by a juvenile must be adjudged ineffective upon the failure by the State to establish any of three prerequisites to waiver, viz.: that the juvenile actually consulted with an attorney or an adult before waiver, that the attorney or adult consulted was interested in the welfare of the juvenile, or that, if an adult other than an attorney was consulted, the adult was fully advised of the rights of the juvenile. In the instant case the record establishes that Andrew Dino's mother, who was interested in his welfare, was present at the police station during the interrogation. However, the State did not show that Mrs. Dino was fully advised of her juvenile son's rights or that Andrew actually consulted with her in waiving his rights. We are therefore constrained to conclude that the statement should have been suppressed.

* * *

NOTES

1. Who is an interested adult? There are three fundamental cases: (1) If the juvenile wishes to talk to a particular person and is refused the right to do so, what must be the characteristics of that person before a denial will violate the Constitution? This is, in essence, the problem in *Fare v. Michael C.* (2)(a) If there is an "interested adult" rule in the jurisdiction, what must

[32] A. Ferguson and A. Douglas, A Study of Juvenile Waiver, 7 San Diego L.Rev. 39 (1970).

[33] IJA–ABA Juvenile Justice Standards Project, Standards Relating to Police Handling of Juvenile Problems, § 3.2 at p. 70; Ferster and Countless, The Beginning of Juvenile Justice, Police Practices and the Juvenile Offender, 22 Vand.L. Rev. 567, 569–97 (1969); see the concurring opinion of Fedoroff, J., State in the Interest of Holifield, supra: " * * * I cannot fathom how a minor, who lacks [see La.C.C. art. 1785 and La.C.C.P. art. 4501] the capacity to sell, mortgage, donate or release (who could not even contract with the lawyer whose services he waives) can be said to possess the capacity to waive constitutional privileges and lose his freedom as a consequence." 319 So.2d at 475.

[34] La.Const.1974, Art. I, §§ 2 (Due Process of Law), 3 (Right to Individual Dignity [equality]), 13 (Rights of the Accused), 16 (Right to a Fair Trial [right against self-incrimination]).

be the generic characteristics of the person to whom the juvenile *has been permitted* to talk? (2)(b) If there is a person to whom the juvenile wishes to speak and is refused permission to do so, what must be that person's generic characteristics in order to find a violation of the rule, though not of the Federal Constitution?

Example (2)(a) is represented by Borum v. State, ___ Ind.App. ___, 434 N.E.2d 581 (1982) (caseworker who filed the petition not an "interested adult") and by Commonwealth v. Thomas, 486 Pa. 568, 406 A.2d 1037 (1979) (prison counselor not an "interested adult.") and by Spradley v. State, 161 Ga.App. 180, 288 S.E.2d 133 (1982) (brother-in-law with whom juvenile lived is an "interested adult.")

Example (2)(b) is represented by In re Patrick W., 104 Cal.App.3d 615, 163 Cal.Rptr. 848 (1980), cert. denied, 449 U.S. 1096, 101 S.Ct. 893, 66 L.Ed. 2d 824 (1981) (grandparents of youth who killed father and refused to talk to his mother were denied permission to talk to youth who did not know of their presence, but who asserts that he would have liked to talk to them, were "interested adults" in sense that youth should have been offered opportunity to talk to them).

Of course, the ultimate issue in all of these cases is the admissibility of statements made by the juvenile when the rule was not complied with.

2. May a juvenile waive rights without the advice of an attorney? In 1974 the Texas Court of Civil Appeals held that under the Texas Family Code (prior to its 1975 revision) no federal or state constitutional right could be waived by a juvenile unless he is joined in that waiver by his attorney and has been informed of both his rights and the consequences of waiving them. In the Matter of S.E.B., 514 S.W.2d 948 (Tex.Civ.App.1974).

Subsequently the statute was expanded to provide an alternative:

VERNON'S TEXAS CODE ANN., FAMILY CODE § 51.09

§ 51.09 Waiver of Rights

(a) Unless a contrary intent clearly appears elsewhere in this title, any right granted to a child by this title or by the constitution or laws of this state or the United States may be waived in proceedings under this title if:

(1) the waiver is made by the child and the attorney for the child;

(2) the child and the attorney waiving the right are informed of and understand the right and the possible consequences of waiving it;

(3) the waiver is voluntary; and

(4) the waiver is made in writing or in court proceedings that are recorded.

(b) Notwithstanding any of the provisions of Subsection (a) of this section, the statement of a child is admissible in evidence in any future proceeding concerning the matter about which the statement was given if:

(1) when the child is in a detention facility or other place of confinement or in the custody of an officer, the statement is made in writing and the statement shows that the child has at some time prior to the making thereof received from a magistrate a warning that:

(A) he may remain silent and not make any statement at all and that any statement he makes may be used in evidence against him;

(B) he has the right to have an attorney present to advise him either prior to any questioning or during the questioning;

(C) if he is unable to employ an attorney, he has the right to have an attorney to counsel with him prior to or during any interviews with peace officers or attorneys representing the state;

(D) he has the right to terminate the interview at any time;

(E) if he is 15 years of age or older at the time of the violation of a penal law of the grade of felony the juvenile court may waive its jurisdiction and he may be tried as an adult; and

(F) the statement must be signed in the presence of a magistrate by the child with no law enforcement officer or prosecuting attorney present. The magistrate must be fully convinced that the child understands the nature and contents of the statement and that the child is signing the same voluntarily. If such a statement is taken, the magistrate shall sign a written statement verifying the foregoing requisites have been met.

The child must knowingly, intelligently, and voluntarily waive these rights prior to and during the making of the statement and sign the statement in the presence of a magistrate who must certify that he has examined the child independent of any law enforcement officer or prosecuting attorney and determined that the child understands the nature and contents of the statement and has knowingly, intelligently, and voluntarily waived these rights.

(2) it be made orally and the child makes a statement of facts or circumstances that are found to be true, which conduct tends to establish his guilt, such as the finding of secreted or stolen property, or the instrument with which he states the offense was committed.

(3) the statement was res gestae of the delinquent conduct or the conduct indicating a need for supervision or of the arrest.

3.   Does the following provision of the Colorado statutes seem to be a more or less satisfactory resolution than that of Texas?

Colorado Revised Statutes, Children's Code, § 19–2–102

* * *

(3)(c)(I) No statements or admissions of a child made as a result of interrogation of the child by a law enforcement official concerning acts alleged to have been committed by the child which would constitute a crime if committed by an adult shall be admissible in evidence against that child unless a parent, guardian, or legal or physical custodian of the child was present at such interrogation and the child and his parent, guardian, or legal or physical custodian were advised of the child's right to remain silent, that any statements made may be used against him in a court of law, the right of the presence of an attorney during such interrogation, and the right to have counsel appointed if so requested at the time of the interrogation; except that, if a public defender or counsel representing the child is present at such interrogation, such statements or admissions may be admissible in evidence even though the child's parent, guardian, or legal or physical custodian was not present.

4.   In Forest v. State, 76 Wn.2d 84, 455 P.2d 368 (1969) the Supreme Court of Washington held that a confession given by a juvenile was inadmissible because the officer had omitted one of the *Miranda* warnings. However, it refused to reverse the adjudication of delinquency:

* * * We are not here concerned with the prejudice to a defendant of the introduction into evidence of an invalid confession before a jury in a criminal trial. * * * The informal instant proceedings were conducted before a juvenile judge only. We recognize that there is a difference between the effect of error committed before a jury and that committed before a judge. * * * It is also recognized in this state that a hearing to determine delinquency is not a criminal proceeding, * * * and an order adjudicating a child delinquent is not deemed a criminal conviction. * * * Because juvenile proceedings are civil, rather than criminal, we have held that a finding of delinquency must be supported by a preponderance of the evidence only; the normal evidentiary standard used in civil cases. * * * It must be pointed out that, while this was the rule at the time of the instant proceedings and so governs them, it is no longer the rule. Pursuant to Juvenile Court Rule 4.4(b), RCW vol. 0, effective January 10, 1969, the degree of proof required in a fact finding hearing on a petition alleging delinquency is "beyond a reasonable doubt."

The language in In re Gault * * * indicates that the invalidation of a juvenile's admissions which have been considered by the juvenile court may not require automatic reversal. In *Gault* the petitioner made certain admissions before the juvenile court sitting without a jury. The United States Supreme Court found the use of these admissions to violate petitioner's privilege against self-incrimination for he was not advised of his right to remain silent or his right to counsel. In reversing the finding of delinquency the court said at 56–57 of 387 U.S., at 1458–1459 of 87 S.Ct.:

> The "confession" of Gerald Gault was first obtained by Officer Flagg, out of the presence of Gerald's parents, without counsel and without advising him of his right to silence, as far as appears. The judgment of the Juvenile Court was stated by the judge to be based on Gerald's admissions in court. Neither "admission" was reduced to writing, and, to say the least, the process by which the "admissions" were obtained and received must be characterized as lacking the certainty and order which are required of proceedings of such formidable consequences. Apart from the "admissions," there was nothing upon which a judgment or finding might be based. There was no sworn testimony. Mrs. Cook, the complainant, was not present. * * *
>
> * * *
>
> * * * We now hold, that, absent *a valid confession,* a determination of delinquency and an order of commitment to a state institution cannot be sustained in the absence of sworn testimony subjected to the opportunity for cross-examination in accordance with our law and constitutional requirements.

(Italics ours.) * * * If the invalidation of petitioner's admissions in In re Gault, supra, had required automatic reversal of the finding of delinquency, there would have been no need to review the additional facts surrounding the hearing. Furthermore, the ultimate holding of the case would not have been framed in terms of necessary requirements of fair treatment in a juvenile proceeding in which a juvenile's admissions were found to be invalid.

Unlike the situation in *Gault,* in the instant case the juvenile judge did not state that his finding was based upon petitioner's admissions; there was sworn testimony subject to cross-examination with regard to every act of delinquency petitioner was found to have committed; the complaining witnesses were present and testified; and there was evidence, *independent* of petitioner's admissions, sufficient to support a finding of delinquency with regard to two of the counts. As to one act of malicious destruction of property, one of petitioner's neighbors testified that she witnessed petitioner and another boy break a number of windows in her house. In addition, when police officers went to petitioner's home to question him about a number of burglaries, one of which was the burglary of Louisa Boren Junior High School, they discovered three caged rats taken from that school with the name "Louisa Borden Junior High" attached to the cages. This evidence was discovered prior to petitioner's arrest and admissions and was testified to by the investigating officers. There was no issue raised with regard to the legality of the search and seizure to obtain this evidence.

It must be remembered that all that was necessary to a finding of delinquency at the time of the instant proceedings, although no longer the rule, was that it be shown by a preponderance of the evidence that the child violated any law of this state, or any ordinance of any town, city or county. See RCW 13.04.010. While the juvenile court must have considered petitioner's admissions, we cannot say petitioner was necessarily prejudiced thereby. Even absent petitioner's admissions, there was sufficient evidence derived from sworn testimony by witnesses available for cross-examination to support the finding of delinquency in the instant juvenile proceedings.

Id. at 370–71.

D. PROCEDURE FOR DETERMINING ADMISSIBILITY

In Jackson v. Denno, 378 U.S. 368, 84 S.Ct. 1774, 12 L.Ed.2d 908 (1964), the Supreme Court held that a trial judge in a criminal case must make an independent determination whether a confession challenged on the ground that it was "involuntary" was indeed "involuntary." If he finds that it was, he must exclude the confession. He cannot allow the jury to make that determination, although he may, if he finds the confession to be "voluntary," permit the jury to find it to be "involuntary."

IN RE SIMMONS

North Carolina Court of Appeals, 1974.
24 N.C.App. 28, 210 S.E.2d 84.

PARKER, JUDGE.

* * *

Respondent also contends the District Court erred in failing to conduct a voir dire examination and in failing to make express findings as to voluntariness before admitting testimony as to the statements. In a criminal case tried before judge and jury when objection is made to introduction of evidence as to an accused's extrajudicial confession, it is the duty of the judge to conduct a hearing in the absence of the jury at which the State has the burden of demonstrating that the confession was voluntarily and understandingly made. State v. Vickers, 274 N.C. 311, 163 S.E.2d 481 (1968). If conflicting evidence is presented at the voir dire hearing and the judge overrules the objection, he must make findings of fact which support his ruling. State v. Barnes, 264 N.C. 517, 142 S.E.2d 344 (1965). If no conflicting testimony is presented, no findings of fact need be made, State v. Keith, 266 N.C. 263, 145 S.E.2d 841 (1966), although "it is always the better practice for the court to find the facts upon which it concludes any confession is admissible." State v. Lynch, 279 N.C. 1, 15, 181 S.E.2d 561, 570 (1971).

Certainly an involuntary confession made by a child is no more admissible than would be an involuntary confession of an adult accused of the same criminal offense. In re Ingram, 8 N.C.App. 266, 174 S.E.2d 89 (1970), and basic requirements of due process apply to juvenile proceedings. In re Burrus, 275 N.C. 517, 169 S.E.2d 879 (1969). Nevertheless, there are significant differences between a juvenile proceeding and a criminal trial in the superior court. The absence of a jury and the fact that the District Judge rules on admissibility as well as on credibility and weight of evidence, makes largely artificial and meaningless any clear-cut distinction between that portion of the juvenile hearing during which the District Judge is hearing testimony bearing upon the admissibility of evidence and portions of the hearing when he receives and considers the evidence as it bears upon the ultimate factual issues presented for his determination. In the present case, we find no conflict in the evidence as it bears upon the circumstances under which respondent's confessions to Mr. and Mrs. Robinson were made. While it would have been the better practice for the District Judge to make express findings of fact as to those circumstances, since there was no conflict in the evidence it was not essential that he do so, and the Judge's overruling of respondent's objections amounted to an implied finding that respondent's confessions had been voluntarily made. Respondent's assignments of error directed to the court's admission of his confessions are overruled.

The judgment appealed from is

Affirmed.

BROCK, C.J., and BALEY, J., concur.

E. CUSTODIAL IDENTIFICATION PROCEDURES

The Supreme Court of the United States has formulated a series of rules to govern the conduct of some pre-trial identification procedures—line-ups, show-ups, photographic displays. Central issues are whether counsel is needed because the particular kind of confrontation, or the particular kind only when it occurs at a particular time, can somehow be thought of as a critical stage in a criminal proceeding; whether in those that do not require the presence of counsel to satisfy the constitution, the method of conducting the particular procedure is "unduly suggestive" to the witness; and finally, because most often the challenge is to in-court-identification testimony which has been preceded by one or more kinds of pre-trial confrontations, whether despite problems with the pre-trial procedures, the in-court-identification has an "independent basis."

The problem arises in some delinquency proceedings, perhaps more often when the juvenile has been transferred to adult court after he has been identified in some suspect fashion before the waiver occurred. The student should know that not all of the cases involving criminal trials of adults were decided by the Supreme Court on the same day, and so the juvenile identification cases must be assessed with some knowledge of which of the Supreme Court cases had been decided at that particular time.

IN RE McKELVIN
District of Columbia Court of Appeals, 1969.
258 A.2d 452.

Before HOOD, CHIEF JUDGE, KERN and GALLAGHER, ASSOCIATE JUDGES.

GALLAGHER, ASSOCIATE JUDGE:

This is an appeal from a judgment finding appellant within the jurisdiction of the Juvenile Court, based upon a jury verdict of guilt in the unauthorized use of a motor vehicle. Appellant was placed on probation for an indeterminate period.

On the evening of September 11, 1967, an 11-year-old boy observed one of three youths, known to him as "Earl", break into a parked car, admit two others and drive away in it. A fourth boy in the group refused to enter the car and "ran home." The boy knew the woman who owned the vehicle and told her what he had seen the next morning. He also told her he knew the youths when he saw them and that one was named "Earl."

Three days later appellant and three youths were riding in another car which was stopped by an officer for excessive smoking. On observing that the inspection sticker was improperly attached to the windshield with tape, the officer asked the youths to accompany him to the police station. A check of the sticker number revealed that it belonged to the car stolen on September 11th. The owner of that car was called, told the police there was an eyewitness, and was asked to bring him to the station to make an identification. After walking through the room in which the youths were seated, the 11-year-old identified three of the four, including appellant, as those involved in the theft. Appellant was without counsel at the time.

Prior to trial appellant filed a written motion to suppress any in court identification by the boy on the ground that his identification of appellant at the police precinct absent counsel violated the constitutional precepts of Gilbert v. California, 388 U.S. 263, 87 S.Ct. 1951, 18 L.Ed.2d 1178 (1967), and United States v. Wade, 388 U.S. 218, 87 S.Ct. 1926, 18 L.Ed.2d 1149 (1967), or that the identification was so tainted by suggestion as to constitute a violation of due process under Stovall v. Denno, 388 U.S. 293, 87 S.Ct. 1967, 18 L.Ed.2d 1199 (1967).

At the same time appellant moved orally for a hearing, out of the presence of the jury, to determine whether an in-court identification of appellant could properly be made by the boy due to the allegedly suggestive circumstances of the identification at the precinct. The motions were denied without prejudice to their reconsideration during trial.

The government's first witness at trial was the young eyewitness. After he related what he observed during the car theft, the government attempted to elicit from him whether he recognized anyone in the courtroom as having been involved in the incident that evening. Appellant interposed an objection on the basis of his pretrial motions, which was overruled. The witness then identified appellant and testified that he had seen him on Gay Street "a whole lot of times" before; that he knew the house in which appellant lived; and that, when reporting the theft to the car owner, he told her that he knew the boys involved in the theft when he saw them. The remainder of his testimony related to photographic and in-person identification at the police station. There was additional testimony for the government by police officers about the arrest of the four suspects and the identification process employed.

At the close of the government's case appellant renewed his motion to suppress or strike the in-court identification and offered a motion for a judgment of acquittal. Both motions were denied by the trial judge, who reasoned that it was unnecessary to reach the issues of suggestiveness and absence of counsel at the police station since the witness based his in-court identification on his recognition of appellant at the time of the incident. Thereupon appellant took the stand in his own behalf and denied his involvement in the incident. After the same motions were made by appellant and again denied, the case was submitted to the jury which returned a verdict of "guilty."

Appellant contends *Gilbert, Wade* and *Stovall,* supra, should apply to juvenile as well as adult proceedings, and therefore the trial court erred in admitting the in-court identification because of suggestive circumstances at the station house "walk-through" and the absence of counsel at that time. One could hardly dispute that a juvenile suspect is as much entitled as an adult to fundamentally fair identification procedures. If it appeared here that the in-court identification had no independent basis and might have been polluted by suggestive precinct identification procedures without counsel present we would have the serious question of whether the holdings of the Supreme Court in *Wade* and *Gilbert,* as illuminated by its prior holdings in In re Gault, 387 U.S. 1, 87 S.Ct. 1428, 18 L.Ed.2d 527 (1967), should not logically be just as binding in a juvenile court proceeding as in a criminal trial. We agree with the court below, however, that the in-court identification was based on the witness' recognition at the time of the theft that he knew appellant[35] and,

---

[35] While the boy's testimony may at times be read as conflicting, this may well be attributable to his age and inexperience. On the record as a whole the trial court's conclusion that the in-court identification had this independent basis had sufficient evidentiary support.

consequently, we do not have here a factual situation requiring a decision on that question. Moreover, since the witness knew appellant, and had so informed the owner of the vehicle who in turn informed the police before the station house identification, there was no danger that the identification procedures might be "so unnecessarily suggestive and conducive to irreparable mistaken identification" as to amount to a denial of due process of law. Stovall v. Denno, 388 U.S. 293, 302, 87 S.Ct. 1967, 1972, 18 L.Ed.2d 1199 (1967).

Under the circumstances, appellant's further contention that it was prejudicial error to deny his motion for a hearing out of the presence of the jury to determine whether an independent basis existed for the in-court identification is without merit. A substantial portion of the government's case was occupied with establishing the reliability of the 11-year-old witness' identification. In this particular case, we see no prejudice to appellant because this took place before the jury. It was clear that the station house identification merely verified for the police that a person with whom the witness was familiar prior to the incident was in their custody and had been involved in the theft. The identification might have been made by asking the boy to show the police appellant's house and to point him out in the neighborhood. That an identification occurred at the station house does not make it legally suspect on these facts.

We find no substantial error in the proceedings.

Affirmed.

NOTE

In Jackson v. State, 17 Md.App. 167, 300 A.2d 430 (1973), the Maryland Court of Special Appeals showed some frustration at the sequence of decisions in the Supreme Court of the United States. In a pre-*Kirby* decision, the same Maryland court had held that whether the line-up was pre- or post-indictment was not material on the counsel issue in a case involving adults. In *Jackson*, a juvenile had been picked out of a police line-up when he was not represented by counsel. *Subsequently*, a juvenile petition charging delinquency was filed. He was then transferred for trial as an adult on a criminal charge. After overruling their previous decision, the Court applied its new rule in the instant case.

"On the day of trial, but prior to its start, Jackson filed a motion 'to suppress and exclude in-court identification of him by the prosecuting witness.' The motion was heard as a preliminary matter and denied. The sole contention on appeal is that the court below erred in denying the motion to suppress and in not excluding the judicial identification of him by Ritter upon objection at the guilt stage of the trial. As argued, the contention is bottomed only upon the absence of counsel at the lineup, Jackson urging that a waiver, executed by him, of his right to the presence of counsel at the lineup, was ineffective. He makes no claim that there was a deprivation of due process in the particularized circumstances of this case.

"It is patent that the lineup here was conducted before the initiation of an adversary judicial criminal proceeding. The record before us does not indicate that Jackson had been formally charged [36] or that a preliminary hearing had been held prior to the lineup. It shows that, at the time of the lineup, he had not been presented, he had not been arraigned, and neither an indictment nor an information had been filed against him. Even if the proceedings in the Juvenile Court be deemed "an adversary judicial criminal proceeding" within the contemplation of *Kirby*, which we expressly do not now decide,[37] such proceedings postdated the lineup. Therefore, Jackson had no constitutional right to the assistance of counsel at the lineup, and, as he was not entitled to counsel as of right, the absence of counsel did not violate the Sixth and Fourteenth Amendments.

"We hold that the court below did not err in denying the pretrial motion to suppress the in-court identification evidence or in overruling the objection at trial to such evidence."

Id. at 173–75, 300 A.2d at 435.

PEOPLE IN INTEREST OF M.B.
Colorado Court of Appeals, 1973.
513 P.2d 230.

COYTE, JUDGE. The appellant, a minor child, appeals from the trial court's adjudication of her as a delinquent child entered after a jury verdict finding that she committed acts which if committed by an adult would have constituted the crime of theft.

The complaining witness testified that he had been bar-hopping and met appellant on the evening of August 12, 1971. After dining at a restaurant, they went to his hotel room. The complaining witness said he placed his wallet under the mattress and left the room for a few moments. When he returned the wallet was lying empty on the floor, and, despite his protests, appellant left immediately. He reported the incident to the police. The following day the complaining witness was shown four photographs and selected the picture of appellant as the person who stole his money.

Prior to trial a hearing was held on a motion to suppress any identification of appellant by the complaining witness. The judge

---

[36] We note that we do not deem an "offense report" submitted by a police officer to be a "formal charge" within the contemplation of *Kirby*. And we observe that it is patent in *Kirby* that an "adversary judicial criminal proceeding" is not attained merely by the focusing of an investigation on an accused. In Miranda v. Arizona, * * * the Court said that when it spoke of "an investigation which had focused on an accused" in Escobedo v. Illinois, supra, it meant "questioning initiated by law enforcement officers after a person has been taken into custody or otherwise deprived of his freedom of action in any significant way." This was the meaning of "custodial interrogation" as spelled out in *Miranda*. The focusing of an investigation on an accused invokes the right to

counsel with respect to self-incrimination but not with respect to pretrial confrontations.

[37] We point out, however, that the Juvenile Court had exclusive original jurisdiction over Jackson. Code, Art. 26, § 70–2; Code, Art. 27, § 12 and § 488. See Ch. 514, Acts 1972, effective 1 July 1972, codified as Art. 26, § 70–2(d)(3). Juvenile proceedings are not criminal proceedings. Matter of Nawrocki, 15 Md.App. 252, 289 A.2d 846. No criminal proceedings against Jackson could in any event be commenced until the Juvenile Court had waived its jurisdiction over him. He was not subject to criminal prosecution before the case was transferred to the criminal court as authorized by Code, Art. 26, § 70–16.

ruled that the photographic identification was inadmissible, but allowed an in-court identification by the complaining witness. The ruling was based largely upon the complaining witness's testimony that he could identify the thief independently of the photographs. At trial, appellant was also identified in court by a waitress as the person who dined with the complaining witness on the night the theft occurred.

Although proceedings under the Colorado Children's Code are civil in nature, a respondent child in such proceedings is entitled to the same constitutional protections as are afforded an adult defendant in a criminal case.

*   *   *

II.

Appellant next contends that the trial court erred by allowing the complaining witness to identify appellant in court because the identification was "tainted" by a prior improper photographic identification. We disagree. She makes a two-pronged attack on the propriety of the photographic identification. First, she argues that the photographic identification was improper because no attorney representing appellant was present. However, it is clear that no adversary judicial criminal proceeding had been initiated at that time, and, thus, the right to counsel had not yet arisen. Kirby v. Illinois, 406 U.S. 682, 92 S.Ct. 1877, 32 L.Ed.2d 411; United States v. Von Roeder, 10 Cir., 435 F.2d 1004. Secondly, appellant contends the photographic identification was "impermissibly suggestive." The witness was presented with four photographs and only one other besides appellant's was of a girl of Hispanic ancestry. However, the officer who conducted the photographic identification testified that he used that mixture of photographs because they were the only ones he had in the appellant's age bracket. Moreover, all the subjects were about the same height and one of the Anglo girls appeared to be of Hispanic ancestry. There was no showing that any suggestive comments were made at the time the photographic identification was made. We note that the complaining witness had been in appellant's company for a considerable period of time on the evening the theft occurred. There was no "improper identification" made of appellant. See Simmons v. United States, 390 U.S. 377, 88 S.Ct. 967, 19 L.Ed.2d 1247.

*   *   *

UNITED STATES v. SECHRIST
United States Court of Appeals, Seventh Circuit, 1981.
640 F.2d 81.

SWYGERT, CIRCUIT JUDGE.

Defendant William Luther Sechrist, a Menominee Indian youth, appeals from an adjudication of delinquency. He contends that this adjudication was barred by the speedy trial provisions of the Federal

Juvenile Delinquency Act, as amended,[38] and that certain fingerprint evidence was illegally obtained and should have been suppressed. We affirm the district court's rulings on both grounds.

* * *

Sechrist also contends that the district court improperly rejected his motion to suppress his fingerprint exemplars which were taken pursuant to an *ex parte* order issued by a federal magistrate, in accordance with 18 U.S.C. § 5038(d)(1) (1976). He argues that there was no probable cause to issue that order and that it therefore violated his Fourth Amendment rights. The Government concedes that there was not sufficient evidence before the magistrate to constitute probable cause. Recent Supreme Court opinions have made clear, however, that no probable cause was necessary to take the fingerprint impressions in this case, when the juvenile was already in lawful custody. We therefore hold that no Fourth Amendment violation occurred.

The analysis of any Fourth Amendment claim involves a potential violation at two different levels: "the 'seizure' of the 'person' necessary to bring him into contact with government agents * * * and the subsequent search for and seizure of the evidence." United States v. Dionisio, 410 U.S. 1, 8, 93 S.Ct. 764, 768, 35 L.Ed.2d 67 (1973). When the FBI agent took Sechrist's fingerprints in December 1979, Sechrist was incarcerated in the Shawano County Jail, as he was awaiting trial before the Menominee Tribal Court on an unrelated matter. Because he was in lawful custody at the time, there could be no Fourth Amendment violation with respect to the first level of analysis: the "seizure" of the person.[39]

We therefore turn to consider whether the actual taking of the fingerprint exemplars without probable cause infringed Sechrist's Fourth Amendment rights. The Fourth Amendment tests a search or seizure under a standard of reasonableness, in which the need to search or seize is balanced against the invasion into one's privacy that the search or seizure entails. Although the Government in this case could not establish probable cause, it did have grounds to suspect that Sechrist was the thief. Latent fingerprints had been found on several items left thrown in the clerk's office, and the clerk suspected Sechrist because the youth had recently learned the location of the cash box. In fact, Sechrist was working in the clerk's office to make restitution for a previous theft.

The degree of invasion of one's privacy is measured by a person's "reasonable expectation of privacy" and the process of the search or seizure. "What the Constitution forbids is not all searches and seizures, but unreasonable searches and seizures." Elkins v. United States, 364 U.S. 206, 222, 80 S.Ct. 1437, 1446, 4 L.Ed.2d 1669 (1960). The taking of a person's fingerprints simply does not entail a

[38] 18 U.S.C. §§ 5031–5042 (1976).

[39] United States v. Rogers, 475 F.2d 821 (7th Cir.1973); United States v. Sanders, 477 F.2d 112, 113 (5th Cir.1973) (taking palm print while "legally under arrest * * * removes the first level of a potential Fourth Amendment infringement.").

significant invasion of one's privacy. The Supreme Court noted in Davis v. Mississippi, 394 U.S. 721, 727, 89 S.Ct. 1394, 1397, 22 L.Ed.2d 676 (1969), that "fingerprinting involves none of the probing into an individual's private life and thoughts that marks an interrogation or search."[40] The procedure involves only passive participation by the individual and very little inconvenience, particularly in this case where Sechrist was already in legal custody. Fingerprinting is such an unobtrusive process that it is even used in many noncriminal contexts. The Supreme Court in *Davis* found the fingerprinting process to involve such a minimal intrusion into one's privacy that it was arguable that "the requirements of the Fourth Amendment could be met by narrowly circumscribed procedures for obtaining, during the course of a criminal investigation, the fingerprints of individuals for whom there is no probable cause to arrest." 394 U.S. at 728, 89 S.Ct. at 1398. In United States v. Dionisio, supra, the Court confirmed that this statement was not mere dictum when it was cited in holding that the taking of voice exemplars without probable cause did not infringe upon any interest protected by the Fourth Amendment. The Court held "there was no justification for requiring * * * even the minimal requirement of 'reasonableness' imposed by the Court of Appeals." 410 U.S. at 15, 93 S.Ct. at 772. The minimal burden imposed on Sechrist in requiring him to submit to fingerprinting did not therefore infringe his Fourth Amendment rights.[41]

Sechrist argues that section 5038(d)(1) of the Federal Juvenile Delinquency Act, as amended, which requires that the photograph or fingerprints of a juvenile be taken only with the written consent of a judge,[42] invests greater rights in a juvenile than in an adult and that a juvenile like Sechrist therefore is entitled to a *Miranda*-type warning that he may contest the order. He is correct that the statute grants a juvenile greater protection, for it requires that a judge (or magistrate) consider the order, while an adult could be required to give his fingerprints without any such consideration by a neutral third party. The statute nowhere mandates—nor does its legislative history anywhere indicate—that the judge or magistrate is bound by a probable cause standard. The Congressional purpose was to protect the privacy of a juvenile by granting discretion in an impartial official who could weigh the interests of the juvenile against the interests of the investigating authorities and their reasonable belief that there were grounds for taking the fingerprints. Adults have no such protection. By enacting section 5038(d)(1) in the midst of a section requiring the confidentiality of juvenile records, Congress created a mechanism to ensure that a juvenile's fingerprints or photograph would not be taken unnecessarily and that once

---

[40] In that case, the Court held that the particular procedures involved—including an illegal detention—rendered the fingerprints unconstitutional. Because Sechrist was already in legal custody, no such problems arise in this case.

[41] See also Schmerber v. California, 384 U.S. 757, 86 S.Ct. 1826, 16 L.Ed.2d 908

(1966) (taking of blood sample during lawful arrest was reasonable in light of circumstances), and Terry v. Ohio, supra ("patdown" of clothing for weapons did not violate Fourth Amendment).

[42] 18 U.S.C. § 5038(d)(1) (1976).

taken, they would remain secret.[43] Although a juvenile could under some circumstances contest an order requiring fingerprinting, the statute neither implicitly nor explicitly requires that the juvenile be told in advance he might have that right.[44] The procedure followed in this case gave Sechrist the protections to which he was entitled under the Act.[45]

IV

The trial court properly denied Sechrist's motions to dismiss the information and to suppress the fingerprint evidence. We affirm the adjudication of delinquency.

Affirmed.

NOTES

1. In common with statutory provisions in many states, a Washington statute restricts the right of the police to fingerprint or photograph juveniles taken into custody:

> Neither the fingerprints nor a photograph shall be taken of any child under the age of eighteen years taken into custody for any purpose without the consent of juvenile court.

Under such a statute, would a general order of a juvenile court giving police authority to fingerprint in all cases be valid? See Vovos v. Grant, 87 Wash. 2d 697, 555 P.2d 1343 (1976) (holding that consent of the juvenile court on a case-by-case basis is required).

Subsequently, the statute was amended.

West's Revised Code of Washington Annotated,
Title 13

13.04.130. Fingerprinting or Photographing Juvenile

(1) Neither the fingerprints nor a photograph of any juvenile may be taken without the consent of juvenile court, except as provided in subsections (2) and (3) of this section and RCW 10.64.110.

(2) A law enforcement agency may fingerprint and photograph a juvenile arrested for a felony offense. If the court finds a juvenile's arrest for a felony offense unlawful, the court shall order the fingerprints and photographs of the juvenile taken pursuant to that arrest expunged, unless the court, after a hearing, orders otherwise.

* * *

2. Vernon's Texas Code Annotated, Family Code § 51.15

§ 51.15. Fingerprints and Photographs

(a) No child may be fingerprinted without the consent of the juvenile court except as provided in Subsection (f) of this section. However, if a child

---

[43] 93rd Cong., 2d Sess., S.Rep. No. 93–1011, as reprinted in 1974 U.S.Code Cong. & Admin. News 5283, 5312.

[44] We note, for example, that when a search warrant is executed—pursuant to an *ex parte* order similar to that required by section 5038(d)(1)—the party whose property is to be searched has no right to a *Miranda*-type warning that he could contest it.

[45] Sechrist also argues that the Government could have protected his rights by taking him before a grand jury to consider whether his fingerprints should be taken. We find it unnecessary to decide whether a juvenile may be called before a grand jury, since we have held that no probable cause was necessary to compel his fingerprints and that the statute, which makes no mention of grand juries, grants him all the protections to which he was entitled.

15 years of age or older is referred to the juvenile court for a felony, his fingerprints may be taken and filed by a law-enforcement officer investigating the case.

(b) Except as provided in Subsection (h) of this section, no child taken into custody may be photographed without the consent of the juvenile court unless the child is transferred to criminal court for prosecution under Section 54.02 of this code.

(c) Fingerpint and photograph files or records of children shall be kept separate from those of adults, and fingerprints or photographs known to be those of a child shall be maintained on a local basis only and not sent to a central state or federal depository.

(d) Fingerprint and photograph files or records of children are subject to inspection as provided in Subsections (a) and (d) of Section 51.14 of this code.

(e) Fingerprints and photographs of a child shall be removed from files or records and destroyed if:

(1) a petition alleging that the child engaged in delinquent conduct or conduct indicating a need for supervision is not filed, or the proceedings are dismissed after a petition is filed, or the child is found not to have engaged in the alleged conduct; or

(2) the person reaches 18 years of age and there is no record that he committed a criminal offense after reaching 17 years of age.

(f) If latent fingerprints are found during the investigation of an offense, and a law-enforcement officer has reasonable cause to believe that they are those of a particular child, if otherwise authorized by law, he may fingerprint the child regardless of the age or offense for purpose of immediate comparison with the latent fingerprints. If the comparison is negative, the fingerprint card and other copies of the fingerprints taken shall be destroyed immediately. If the comparison is positive, and the child is referred to the juvenile court, the fingerprint card and other copies of the fingerprints taken shall be delivered to the court for disposition. If the child is not referred to the court, the fingerprint card and other copies of the fingerprints taken shall be destroyed immediately.

(g) When destruction of fingerprints or photographs is required by Subsection (e), (f), or (h) of this section, the agency with custody of the fingerprints or photographs shall proceed with destruction without judicial order. However, if the fingerprints or photographs are not destroyed, the juvenile court, on its own motion or on application by the person fingerprinted or photographed, shall order the destruction as required by this section.

(h) If, during the investigation of a criminal offense, a law enforcement officer has reason to believe that a photograph of a child taken into custody or detained as permitted under this title will assist in the identification of the offender and if not otherwise prohibited by law, the officer may photograph the face of the child. If the child is not identified as an offender, the photograph and its negative shall be destroyed immediately. If the child is identified through the photograph and the child is referred to the juvenile court for the offense investigated, the photograph and its negative shall be delivered to the juvenile court for disposition. If the child is not referred to the juvenile court for the offense investigated, the photograph and its negative shall be destroyed immediately.

Chapter 4

INFORMAL PROCESSES IN EARLY STAGES

A. THE POLICE DECISION WHETHER TO REFER A CHILD TO JUVENILE COURT

NOTE, JUVENILE DELINQUENTS: THE POLICE, STATE COURTS, AND INDIVIDUALIZED JUSTICE *

79 Harv.L.Rev. 775, 776–85 (1966).

I. THE SCREENING PROCESS

In most cases, a juvenile who is taken into custody will never see a judge. He will be released after a nonappealable screening process administered by individuals without legal training; he will not be represented by counsel, nor are the screening officials likely to acknowledge a right of silence. The result of the screening may be the creation of an official record of contact with the police or court or both, and, possibly, a substantial interference with the juvenile's liberty. This basic process is in use, in one variant or another, in virtually all cities. It is broken down into two stages, the first administered by the police and the second by "intake" departments attached to the courts.

A. Police Screening

1. *Introduction.*—The importance of the police screening power is apparent: the vast majority of juveniles who appear in court are police referrals and half of all police contacts are settled without referral.[1] The role of the police in the handling of juveniles has thus

[1] In Chicago in 1964, 98.4% of juvenile court cases were referred by law enforcement agencies. Citizens Committee on the Family Court, Bulletin No. 4, April 1965. The Youth Division in Chicago recorded 40,352 juvenile offenses in 1964, of which 26,978 were adjusted at the station level and 13,374 referred to court. Chicago Police Department, Youth Division, Annual Report 1964.

In Kansas City, of 3,360 officially recorded delinquency contacts in 1964, 1,379 were settled by the juvenile bureau and 1,981 referred to court. Kansas City Police Department, Annual Statistical Report 1964, p. 46.

In Wisconsin Rapids, Wis., it was estimated that there were 343 police contacts with juveniles in 1964: 110 juveniles were referred to court; 33 were officially warned and released; and "about 200" were talked to informally and released.

* * *

The FBI national estimates are that 47.2% of the cases in which a juvenile is taken into custody are handled within the police department, 1.6% are referred to a welfare agency, 2.7% are referred to another police agency, 46.8% are referred to juvenile court, and 1.8% are referred to criminal or adult courts. Uniform Crime Reports—1964, at 102.

It is, of course, impossible to know how many police contacts were not recorded, but the number is undoubtedly large. Thus, the effect of police screening is probably significantly greater than these statistics indicate. Cf. Carr, Delinquency Control 226 (rev.ed.1950).

expanded considerably beyond the discretion in the decision to arrest that has long been recognized. In part this expansion reflects police acceptance of the idea that juvenile offenders have a great potential for reformation and the conclusion that there is a need for rehabilitative treatment at the police level. Juvenile court acts may have indirectly aided this trend by the language they employ: juveniles are "taken into custody," not arrested, and "referred to court," not arraigned or booked. Of course, the acts have also added to the role of the police in the definitions of prohibited conduct: juveniles are often subject to condemnation as "delinquents" for acts that would not be criminal if committed by adults. Moreover, police departments in virtually all major cities indicate that in the postwar decades there has been a significant increase in complaints arising out of incidents that would have been settled privately in earlier years. These factors, combined with the continuing rise in the number of detected violations committed by juveniles,[2] have led most of the larger police departments to establish separate divisions or to designate special officers to coordinate the handling of juvenile cases, in order to create and enforce a uniform policy.[3] At the same time, the lack of sufficient court personnel has led many judges to increase the power of the police indirectly, by condoning or encouraging the settlement of complaints without referral to courts.

2. Invocation of Police Authority.—Initial police contact may result either from a complaint received or from apprehension at the time of an alleged offense. If the offender is identified in a complaint as a juvenile the matter will either be handled initially by an officer of the police juvenile bureau or given to the appropriate unit (for example, burglary or homicide) for investigation and later turned over to the juvenile bureau for disposition. More often, initial contact is made by the patrolman on the beat, who will usually have a range of alternatives, often including all of the following: (1) release the juvenile, with or without a warning, but without making an official record or taking further action; (2) release the juvenile, but write up a brief "field report" for the juvenile bureau describing the contact, or file a more formal report referring the matter to the juvenile bureau for possible action; (3) turn the youth over to the juvenile bureau immediately; or (4) refer the case directly to the juvenile court.

In a few cities, if the patrolman does not choose the first alternative, the child is automatically turned over to a member of the juvenile bureau, who makes all decisions in the matter. If the child is

---

[2] "A review of total arrests of persons under the age of 18 reveals a continued upswing in their involvement with police. The nationwide increase in all arrests, again excluding traffic, for persons under 18 was 17 percent." Uniform Crime Reports—1964, at 24. See also id. at 110–11.

[3] A survey undertaken by the International Association of Chiefs of Police revealed that even in cities in the 10,000–24,000 population range, 72% had some sort of specialization; in the 25,000–49,000 range the percentage was 92.5%; and all cities of 250,000 or more have a specialized program. O'Connor & Watson, Juvenile Delinquency and Youth Crime: The Police Role 85 (1964) [hereinafter cited as IACP Survey.]

to be referred to court, a further decision in which the police are involved is whether the juvenile should be released or detained. Juvenile court acts often require that once a juvenile has been taken into custody, he may be released only to his parent or guardian; where such is the law, a decision to detain will automatically follow if it is not possible to locate a parent or guardian. In other situations, the detention decision may be the tail that wags the dog: a detained juvenile must be referred to the court and his case cannot be settled by the police.

Standards to guide the patrolman's decision are absorbed from the informal learning process involved in contacts between patrolman and youth bureau officers, and formally imparted in written instructions from police and court authorities. These standards take account of both the nature of the offense and the background of the juvenile. Mandatory referral to the juvenile bureau, or even directly to court, may be required for all crimes of violence, felonies, and "serious" misdemeanors.[4] Similarly, referral to court may be required if it is determined that the juvenile is currently on parole or probation, or if he has had previous contacts with police. Since such information is normally available only from a central records center, the patrolman's decision is more difficult in areas that do not man such a center on a twenty-four hour basis, for his failure to report even a very minor offense may result in the nonrecognition of a parole or probation violation.[5]

The patrolmen interviewed generally acknowledged that they do not write up offenses of a minor nature but rather terminate the conduct and perhaps admonish the offenders. In the larger metropolitan areas, this policy reflects both a condonation of a certain amount of "horseplay" and a recognition of the fact that the juvenile bureau has limited resources; in smaller towns, where patrolmen are likely to know the juveniles involved or their families, similar allowances are made. But such a permissive attitude in regard to very minor offenses may be modified where the juvenile bureau strongly believes that treatment and rehabilitation will be made more effective through

[4] The Salt Lake City guide for police officers, for instance, states that "minor *first* offenders [curfew violators, petty shoplifters] are to be referred to our Youth Division," and then lists the cases requiring direct referral to the juvenile court: felonies, car thefts, fireworks violations, sex offenses, offenses involving large amounts of restitution, escapes from the state industrial school, runaway cases, traffic violations, drinking and glue sniffing, and second violations "even when offenses are minor." Juvenile Arrest Procedure, pp. 1–2.

The juvenile officer in Wisconsin Rapids, Wis., has formulated his own standards; he refers to court all theft offenses, for example, since he feels that these violators need aid that he is unable to supply. * * *

[5] The policeman's task is further complicated by the fact that it may be difficult to determine from appearance alone whether a suspect is a "juvenile." A youth's motives for lying about his age are generally practical in nature; for example, Chicago youth officers indicated that juveniles taken into custody for minor offenses such as disorderly conduct often claim to be over the age limit, reasoning that if they are treated as adults they will simply be forced to spend a night in jail and to hear a lecture by the judge in the morning, but that if they are identified as juveniles the interference with their liberty may well be more substantial. * * *

early discovery and handling of delinquent traits; this belief may lead to a policy of encouraging patrolmen to bring even minor offenses to the attention of the bureau.[6]

An obvious further qualification to permissive police attitudes is the reaction of the juvenile: a polite, cooperative, or obsequious attitude on his part may result in a simple warning, whereas insolence will influence the patrolman to "write up" the incident or even to take the juvenile into custody. Police officials, youth bureau officers, and patrolmen, while admitting that the youth's attitude is often determinative, claimed that simple emotional reaction is not the reason for considering such a factor; rather, they maintained that the explanation is in part a belief in the importance of fostering a positive and cooperative attitude toward police authority and in part the notion that a negative attitude is indicative of delinquent tendencies. Discriminatory enforcement on the basis of factors such as race or economic status, however, was emphatically denied by all those who were interviewed.

When the offender is referred to the juvenile bureau, the court referral decision will be made by the juvenile officer, and an inappropriate invocation of the legal process can be corrected at this stage. The patrolman is thus insulated from the pressure of direct judicial review of his decision, and the importance of learning proper standards is diminished. Moreover, the release of an offender by the juvenile bureau, normally accompanied by a sharp reprimand to the youth, does not imply an incorrect decision on the part of the patrolman, as release by the court might. Consequently, one would expect patrolmen to decide doubtful cases in favor of referral. This tendency was confirmed by the head of the juvenile division in Chicago, who further indicated a belief that contact with the police is usually beneficial and that the overall effect of the trend is therefore constructive.

3. The Police Hearing.—In some cities, the offender is immediately brought before a juvenile officer, who decides whether to refer the case to court or to "adjust" or "settle" (terminate) it at the police stage. In most cities, the process of making this decision has assumed the form of a police hearing whenever the nature of the offense or the juvenile's status (as parolee or runaway) do not call for an automatic court referral. The alleged purpose of these proceedings is not to adjudicate guilt, but to determine (according to a standard that concentrates on the likelihood of recidivism) which cases require the attention of the court. In fact, an equally important function of the hearing is to provide an authoritarian setting in which the police can, with a severe lecture, impress upon the juvenile the error of his ways and "counsel" him so that he will avoid future difficulties.

[6] There is a widespread belief that "the early discovery of the pre-delinquent or potential delinquent is the key to the preventive program." Winters, The Youth Aid Division, Metropolitan Police Department, Washington, D.C., 1964, p. 11.

(a) Procedure.—After the juvenile bureau has investigated a complaint, or after the receipt of a report from a patrolman or investigating unit, a time is set for the hearing. A notice of the time and place of the proceeding is then either mailed to the juvenile's parents or delivered to them by a patrolman. The juvenile and his parents appear before a "hearing officer" or "counselor," and the juvenile is questioned about his participation in the offense under investigation. Only rarely is the youth accompanied by counsel or advised of a right to remain silent. In none of the notice forms that were examined is there any mention of a right to counsel. Indeed, to the police the "right" to counsel or to remain silent is simply not in accord with the nature of the process, because both the hearing and the decision are matters completely within their discretion.

The police have no authority to compel the juvenile or his parents to attend the hearing,[7] much less to accept any eventual restrictions on the juvenile's freedom. But in fact, the police have the necessary leverage: the possibilities of court referral and of the creation of a permanent police or court record are made clear in order to obtain the cooperation of both the parents and the child. An obvious additional influence on the juvenile's response is the quasi-judicial appearance of the hearing—service of "notice," preset time and place, location at the seat of authority (police headquarters), and a "hearing officer" in uniform, usually seated behind a desk. These quasi-judicial forms are adopted in order to magnify the apparent authority of the hearing officer, and thereby both to solemnify the inevitable lecture to the juvenile and to increase the chances that he will confess. The rationale usually offered by hearing officers for the emphasis on confessions was that police rehabilitation of the youth cannot be undertaken unless by confession he recognizes his guilt in a moral sense; if the juvenile remains impenitent there is no insurance against further illegal acts. A persistent denial of guilt is taken to indicate that the juvenile is not amenable to the "noncompulsory" approaches of his parents, local agencies, or the police, and requires referral to court. A more practical motive for requiring confession may be fear that a practice of "adjusting" denied offenses might antagonize the juvenile court judges and thus jeopardize the extra-statutory police authority to act in such matters.

[7] The phrasing of the notices sent to parents raises many problems. Although the police have no power to compel attendance at a "hearing," an appearance of authority may in practice be an adequate substitution. The Washington, D.C., form reads:

You are hereby requested to be present in the Office of the Juvenile Bureau * * * on (xxx) and to bring with you (xxx) at which time an inquiry will be made into a complaint placed against (xxx).

In Salt Lake City, the notice, which bears the printed signature of the Chief of Police, reads:

Dear (xxx), On (xxx) your (xxx) was referred to this office instead of the Juvenile Court on a charge of (xxx). We would like you and your child to come in and see our counselor, Sgt. Yospe, at the Police Department * * * on (xxx). Please make every effort to keep this appointment as we are making it at the request of the Juvenile Court. If further information is necessary, contact the Youth Bureau, phone number (xxx).

In Kansas City, the child is released to the custody of the parent only after the parent signs a "summons notice" requiring a later appearance at the juvenile bureau. * * *

Since police hearings are based on confessions, they obviously would not work if juveniles refused to speak. To most of the police departments interviewed, it follows logically that there is no role for a lawyer at the police hearing stage: there was a nearly uniform belief that an attorney would instruct his client to remain silent and thus obstruct the hearing process. In at least one city there was admitted hostility to the introduction of lawyers at "adjustment" decisions: a juvenile's request to contact his parents is honored, but "if he asks for an attorney, we don't let that interfere with our investigation." Most departments noted that there had been a greater demand for lawyers in recent years, especially by the older and more "sophisticated" juveniles, though the request is still unusual. The increase was blamed on the influence of increased publicity (especially through popular television shows) of the ability of a "mouthpiece" to "beat the rap."

(b) Factors Affecting the Dispositional Decision.—If the juvenile maintains his innocence, the hearing is terminated. The juvenile officer must then decide whether the case is to be referred to court. The police generally refer to court all cases in which the juvenile does not confess, in order to prevent the referral threat from losing its potency. However, they will not refer a case when the evidence available is insufficient or the offense is trivial, because the court is likely to dismiss the proceeding; but even in this situation the juvenile is unlikely to be released without a lecture, and will probably be led to believe that his release is due to a decision to give him another chance, rather than to a recognition of the likelihood of release by the court. The police are rarely faced with this problem, however, since only a tiny percentage of juveniles who are given police hearings deny their guilt.

If the juvenile confesses, most hearing officers (or if there is no hearing procedure in the jurisdiction, the juvenile officer making the adjudication decision) have three courses open to them: release the child to his parents with a reprimand or warning; direct the child (and perhaps his parents) to a community social service agency; or refer the case to court. Some hearing officers have the additional alternative of imposing direct sanctions on the juvenile. Both the hearing and disposition are generally viewed by the police as fulfilling a crime prevention function. They therefore claim that their decision-making process—like that of the juvenile court—centers on the child rather than on the offense. The decision as to disposition is supposedly based upon a calculation of the risk of future illegal activity on the part of the juvenile. If it seems probable that the parents will be able to control the child's behavior, either on their own or with the aid of counseling by a private or public agency, there will be no referral to court. When at a later stage a juvenile court judge is faced with an analogous decision, he is usually provided with a comprehensive family history and social profile, including a recommended disposition prepared by a probation officer with training in social work. The police have come to recognize the importance of such background information to their own dispositional decision,[8] and in an increasing number of departments a serious attempt is made to secure some of the relevant material.[9]

Certain facts—the juvenile's previous record, the seriousness of the offense charged, and the degree of criminal sophistication in the mode of commission of the crime—are validly related to the referral decision but are obviously of no aid in the broad range of cases involving juveniles who have no significant record and whose offense is not of a serious nature. In such cases the probability of recidivism is allegedly tested almost exclusively by considerations such as the extent of parental control, factors that require an investigation more extensive than police resources allow and analytic techniques for which the police are not trained. The not unpredictable result is reliance upon factors that are visible and easily ascertainable but arguably irrelevant. For example, many of the hearing officers questioned indicated that they would refer to court all cases in which the parents were uncooperative and attempted to "shield" the child from the authorities. Whether this police attitude stems from a judgment about emotional relationships within the family is questionable; rather, it may well represent a simple attempt to bolster the position of the police. The few empirical studies made have examined on-the-spot decisions by juvenile officers rather than hearings, but confirm in that setting the tendency to rely on improper criteria. One study concluded that the determinative factors are the juvenile's demeanor, his appearance, and his race;[10] another confirms the reliance on race and notes wryly that "athletes and altar boys will rarely be referred to court for their offenses."[11]

A further factor influencing referral decisions—and one of the most important causes of the great difference among jurisdictions in the percentage of cases referred to court—is the wide variation among departments in their attitude towards court appearance. In Wisconsin Rapids, Wisconsin, for instance, the juvenile officer refers all youths involved in serious crimes and thefts and most repeaters of minor offenses, while in a neighboring community the juvenile officer reportedly refrains from referring in a large proportion of cases and

---

[8] In the large number of cases that are disposed of at the police level, at least a minimum of information relating to the family situation, economic status, and personality development of the juvenile is needed in order to make an intelligent decision. Since these cases are handled entirely by the police, it is they who must obtain the necessary background data. IACP Survey 72.

[9] The "Case Investigation Report" employed in New York City, for example, provides rating scales for the neighborhood, the physical facilities of the home, the supervision, affection, and discipline of the parents, the family atmosphere, and various physical, mental, and social characteristics of the juvenile.

[10] Piliavin & Briar, Police Encounters With Juveniles, 70 American J. Sociology 206 (1964).

[11] Goldman, The Differential Selection of Juvenile Offenders for Court Appearance 131 (1963). In this study the police admitted that race was a factor but denied that this indicated prejudice; rather, they contended that statistics and their experience had demonstrated that there is a significantly higher crime rate among Negroes.

attempts to work with the juveniles, even when there have been a significant number of past violations. This difference in policy may stem from varying judgments as to the success of crime prevention at the police level or from varying degrees of dissatisfaction with juvenile court operations. Of course, the hearing officer's decision whether or not to retain cases depends largely on the range of alternatives available between release after the hearing, with whatever "counseling" that entails, and referral to court.

In a few cities, the police must refer all offenders who require outside aid to court: in Tucson, for instance, the only alternative to referral is immediate reprimand and release.[12] But in the majority of departments, one possibility is referral to a "community agency." The Chicago Youth Division, for example, has compiled an extensive manual of available community resources and maintains direct contact with all such organizations. Many departments request that parents utilize the services of the agencies, but they differ on the extent to which they check to ensure compliance. Some tell the parents frankly that any action on their part is purely voluntary; others attempt to enforce the agency referral, commonly by conditioning police settlement on continued adherence to the program for reform outlined at the hearing. The ability of the police to enforce such threats of future court referral depends, however, upon the willingness of the court to accept referrals a considerable time after apprehension of the offender, and several courts will not. However, it is the opinion of many of those interviewed that, when a juvenile who requires agency aid does not receive it, he will commit another offense within a relatively short period of time; the inability of the police to require him to seek the assistance of an agency will therefore simply result in a short-term delay in the initiation of "treatment," for presumably he will be referred to court after his next offense.

In some cities, the judges apparently allow the police, with the consent of the parents, to place restrictions of varying degrees of severity on the juvenile's freedom. In Kansas City, for example, the police administer a stringent though informal discipline program called "grounding." A typical "grounded" youth must attend school unless a doctor's explanation is obtained for his absence. At all other times he may leave the house only if accompanied by a parent, and then not for any activity that is primarily engaged in for pleasure. He must dress conventionally and have his hair cut in a reasonable manner; and he must study at home for a minimum prescribed period each day. After this schedule is enforced for a month, lesser

---

[12] The situation in Tucson results from an express agreement between the court and the police that all probation work and "counseling" will be done by the probation department. * * * But in nearby Phoenix, the police involvement is reportedly much more extensive. * * * The extent of police activity may differ even within the same small area: the Sheriff's Office of Pima County, in which Tucson is located, does "counsel" although the Tucson police do not. * * * Thus, the treatment a juvenile receives may depend upon which law enforcement agency apprehends him.

conditions will be imposed for the duration of the school year. A high degree of success in preventing future offenses is claimed to result from this program.[13]

(c) Records.—It has been recognized since the inception of separate treatment for juveniles that a "criminal record" severely limits the juvenile offender's career opportunities and often hinders rehabilitation. The solution offered by the juvenile court acts has been to classify *court* records as confidential, giving the juvenile court judge discretionary power to disclose them when necessary; recently, a few states have established procedures for expunging court records. However, despite the attention paid to the matter of court records, little has been done about the analogous problems caused by separate police records; this is particularly ironic since the rationale often advanced for the expansion of police screening authority is that it will avoid the creation of possibly harmful court records.[14] In many jurisdictions the police attempt to maintain complete records of every contact with a juvenile. In some, a duplicate record, available to other enforcement agencies, is kept in a central index. When the offense involved is serious, fingerprints and other identification material may be forwarded to the FBI, although this is not the general practice.[15] However, unless the police contact results in court referral, the court is rarely notified of the contact at all.

The typical police record is a card containing, in addition to identification items, the date of apprehension, the alleged offense, and the disposition. Cards are maintained in an "active file," separate from the adult records, until the individual passes the juvenile age limit. The cards are then generally transferred to a separate "overage" file, for use as a reference source by the police; or, in the case of an "adjusted" juvenile who has committed only one offense, they may be destroyed in accordance with the promise made at the police hearing.

Most departments maintain that complete files of police contacts are essential to successful law enforcement, since adult criminals almost inevitably have a juvenile record and since intelligent use of record information greatly increases the efficiency of police work.

---

[13] * * * Lt. Hollenbeck estimated that 40 to 50% of juvenile contacts were settled without court referral, and that in this group there was a repeat rate of 18%. He indicated that informal settlement methods are most suitable for those whose economic standing permits utilization of private resources such as private psychiatric counseling or military boarding schools; but he thinks that better economic situations are no guarantee of the necessary stable family relationship. Almost all of the police officials who were interviewed agreed. See also IACP Survey 134.

[14] The delegation of screening authority to police "has the definite purpose of avoiding the creation of an official record for a child * * *" Washington, D.C., Metropolitan Police Department Youth Aid Division, Annual Report, Fiscal Year 1965, p. 23. Similarly, the Salt Lake City Police Department Youth Bureau finds that "by handling the minor offender in the Youth Bureau * * * the individual being handled for the first time can avoid receiving * * * [an] official court record that he would receive if he were referred to the Juvenile Court." "Youth Bureau Counseling," p. I (1964).

[15] Uniform Crime Reports—1964, at 26–27. It is usually said that information is sent to the FBI only in "rare" cases, usually crimes of violence. * * *

But even if this argument is persuasive, it does not reach the central problem—control of access to the information. All police departments routinely receive requests from other law enforcement agencies, the armed forces, the FBI, social service agencies, and private employers. Disclosure practices vary widely: some departments will release information to private employers, reasoning that the employers have a right to know of the past delinquent conduct of prospective employees, while others will reply only to other law enforcement agencies. But except in a few states where statutes place control of the records in the hands of the juvenile court judge, the police have complete discretion to release information and destroy records as they see fit.

ROCHE, POLICE DISPOSITION OF JUVENILE CASES IN
SOUTH DAKOTA *

24 South Dakota Law Review 61 (1979).

* * *

Agency Disposition of Juvenile Offenders

A. *Definitions*

After a law enforcement officer has made contact with a youth and the youth has been taken to the station house, the law enforcement agency is confronted with a number of possible solutions. A good framework for examining agency dispositions is provided by dividing the possible dispositions into two broad categories—the referral and the informal disposition.

A referral is the result of a law enforcement agency's decision to use the formal juvenile court system and to turn the youth's case over to the juvenile court. The court referral consists of the law enforcement agency turning the juvenile, or the name of the youth (if he has been released pending adjudication) over to court personnel along with a report detailing the facts of the case. The court then determines how to handle the child.

The law enforcement agency can also choose to divert the youth from the formal juvenile justice system by not referring the youth to court personnel. This second category of disposition is designated informal disposition and primarily includes the following options:

(1) the juvenile is warned and released without notifying the parents or guardian;

(2) the juvenile is warned and released to a parent or guardian;

(3) the juvenile is released to a parent or guardian following monetary restitution to the victim of the offense;

(4) the juvenile, although released to a parent, must complete a work restitution program; or

---

(5) the juvenile is released to a parent on the condition that the youth receive counseling from an agency approved source.

B. Disposition Policies

Of the twenty-four police departments supplying 1975 juvenile offense data, twenty reported using a combination of factors in determining whether a contact should be referred to juvenile court. The remaining four stated it was their policy to refer almost all juvenile offenders to court intake personnel. Over one-half of the sheriff's departments declared using several criteria in the dispositional decision, while the remainder indicated a general policy of automatic court referral. The criteria reportedly used in determining whether to refer a youth to court appear in Table 1.

One-third of the police and sheriff's departments with a policy of automatic court referral stated that the court directed them to refer all juvenile contacts to their court service workers. The other departments which automatically referred all or most juvenile contacts to court reported that they did so voluntarily.

TABLE 1

Criteria Used By Law Enforcement Agencies in Determining Disposition in Juvenile Cases

Criterion	Police Departments (N=20)	Sheriff's Departments (N=8)	Total (N=28)
Past Offenses	19	8	27
Seriousness of offense	16	8	24
Age	10	3	13
Parents' cooperation	6	6	12
Attitude	1	2	3
Seriousness of past offense	2	1	3
Acquainted w/family	0	1	1
Degree of involvement	1	0	1
Time since previous offense	1	0	1

The most frequently related criteria were the juvenile's past offenses and the seriousness of the present offense. The juvenile's age and the cooperativeness of the parents were also frequently mentioned. Although the departments probably used the full range of criteria listed in Table 1 in their disposition decisions, the general practice was that if the offense was not serious, if the juvenile had no past offenses, if the parents cooperated, and especially if the juvenile was young, the case was handled informally; otherwise it was referred to court. Almost every department, however, varied from this general policy to some extent.

C. Disposition Data Reported by Law Enforcement Agencies

The sample law enforcement agencies referred fifty-six percent of the 5322 reported contacts to court; thus forty-four percent were handled informally by the agencies surveyed. The percentage of contacts referred to court varied widely, with all juvenile contacts for murder-manslaughter, rape, robbery, and driving while intoxicated resulting in referral, while only nine percent of the truancy cases produced court referrals. For all offenses except truancy, at least thirty-five percent of the contacts were referred to court.

TABLE 2

Disposition of Juvenile Offenders According to Offense by All Agencies Surveyed

	Offense Total		
	Informal	Referral	% Referred
Murder or manslaughter	0	2	100
Forcible rape	0	2	100
Robbery	0	19	100
Aggravated assault	1	15	94
Burglary	73	353	83
Larceny-theft	523	653	56
Auto theft	11	168	94
Other assaults	21	48	70
Arson	3	2	40
Forgery	8	28	78
Fraud or embezzlement	6	18	75
Stolen property	12	24	67
Vandalism	324	255	44
Weapons	13	7	35
Sex offense	5	12	71
Drug violation	80	156	66
DWI	0	54	100
Liquor laws	636	475	43
Disorderly conduct	51	103	67
Curfew	165	92	36
Runaway	219	245	53
Truancy	21	2	9
All other non-traffic offenses	185	232	56
Total	2357	2965	56

Generally, status offenders were less likely to be referred to court than delinquent offenders, forty-six percent of status offenses as compared to fifty-seven percent of delinquent offenses were referred to court. There was substantial disparity, however, in court referral rates for the various status offenses. As stated above, only nine percent of truancy cases were referred to court. Curfew violations were referred to juvenile court in thirty-six percent of the reported cases. The percentage of runaways referred to court was much higher at fifty-three percent, nearly equal to the referral rate for delinquent offenses.

The survey disclosed that police departments were more likely to refer juveniles to court than their counterparts at the county level. Providing statistical information without analysis, however, can be deceiving. Liquor law violations accounted for almost one-half of the contacts handled by sheriff's departments, and only eighteen percent of these violations resulted in court referral as opposed to sixty percent of liquor law violations referred by police departments. Thus, it can be shown that if liquor law violations were excluded, sheriff's departments were more apt to transfer juveniles to court than the police.

Examination of the relationship between the population of the jurisdiction and the court referral rates revealed that generally, for both police and sheriff's departments, as the population decreased so did the percentage of juvenile contacts referred to court (Figure 1). For police departments this is evidenced by the declivity of referral rates from sixty percent, to sixty-two percent, to forty percent, and then to thirty-one percent—each rate corresponding to a progressively declining population category. Similarly, for sheriff's departments, the percent of juveniles referred to court drops from seventy-nine percent, to fifty-three percent, and then to thirty-seven percent for the three departments above five thousand population. The referral rate increases to forty-nine percent for the one thousand to five thousand population category.

This correlation can be attributed to three factors. First, departments in less populous areas handled smaller percentages of the "serious offenses," which generally mandate automatic court referral. These serious offenses accounted for twenty-five percent, eleven percent, six percent, and eight percent of all offenses reported by police departments in the four city population categories in declining order of population. For sheriff's departments, as population decreased, these offenses accounted for thirty percent, twenty-one percent, fifteen percent, and sixteen percent of all offenses. Second, law enforcement personnel in less populous areas are more likely to know the offender's family, thus increasing the agency's perceptions of its ability to handle juvenile cases informally. Third, department personnel in smaller towns and counties expressed a more negative opinion about the ability of the court to deal effectively with juvenile offenders. This feeling was even stronger in departments that were isolated from the court service worker for their area. The combined effect probably accounts for the unwillingness of law enforcement agencies in less populated, more isolated areas to refer youths to court.[16]

[16] A similar correlation between population and court referral is reported by Goldman for four Pennsylvania communities. He attributes high referral rates in certain cities to "an objective, impersonal relation between police and the public * * *," while informal handling is more indicative of "a personal face-to-face relation between the police and public * * *." Goldman, The Differential Selection of Juvenile Offenders for Court Appearance, printed in Crime and the Legal Process 264, 286 (W. Chambliss ed. 1969).

Figure 1

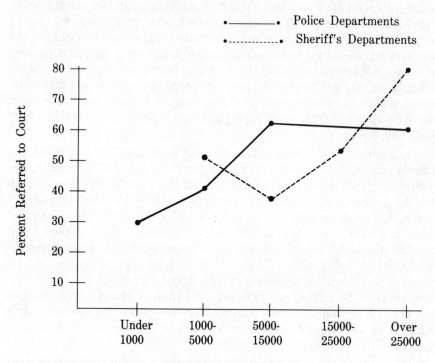

PERCENT OF JUVENILE OFFENDERS REFERRED TO COURT BY
POLICE AND SHERIFF'S DEPARTMENTS ACCORDING TO
POPULATION OF JURISDICTION

[D2484]

There was extensive disparity in the rates of court referrals among individual agencies in the survey sample. This can be ascribed, in part, to the widely different disposition policies, which are represented at all population levels and geographic areas of the state. Thus, although it is possible to generalize about court referral rates on the basis of the type of agency and the population of the jurisdiction, it is impossible to predict referral rates for individual agencies without additional information on disposition policy and offense rates.

JUVENILE LAW ENFORCEMENT IN SOUTH DAKOTA

Practices Utilized By the Sample Agencies in Handling Juveniles

In interviewing the forty sample agencies, an attempt was made to obtain a general picture of the practices employed by South Dakota law enforcement personnel in handling juveniles, beyond those relating to the decision to refer the youth to court. The South Dakota Juvenile Code [17] would be the logical base for any discussion of the procedures governing police handling of juveniles. The most

---

[17] S.D.C.L. chs. 26–7 through 13 (1976).

salient feature of the Code, however, is the absence of specific procedural guidelines to be followed by police in their on-the-street dealings with youths. For example, although South Dakota Code section 26–8–19.1 provides that an officer "may" take a child into custody under certain specified circumstances, thus at least tacitly recognizing the officer's discretionary power, there is nothing to give the officer guidance.

Law enforcement agencies have responded to this inadequate statutory direction by developing their own juvenile procedures. Since many of these procedures vary from agency to agency, the ultimate result is considerable disparity in juvenile procedures across the state. The survey exposed the dearth of written juvenile procedures—a full ninety percent of the agencies surveyed did not specify any juvenile procedures in the department procedure manual. The ten percent with written procedures for juveniles were all in the state's larger cities.[18]

While few agencies had written juvenile procedures, most claimed to follow relatively standard, unwritten procedures. Commonly, this involved transporting the youth to the department after apprehension. Most departments reported they called the youth's parents immediately and did not question the youth without a parent present. With a minor offense, which could be best handled outside of court, the agency would handle the matter informally only if the parents agreed on an out-of-court settlement and cooperated with the informal disposition. Several agencies, upon conclusive proof of the juvenile's guilt,[19] insisted upon an admission of guilt from the juvenile before informal handling.

[18] For example, the Brookings Police Department Procedures Manual contains the following section:

It shall be the policy of this department that when juveniles are handled that have violated the law the officer should contact the parents as soon as possible. The parents should be given as much information about the violation as the officer has * * *. If a juvenile is talked to about a minor offense, the officer should make contact with the juvenile's parents explaining why the youth was talked to. Juveniles committing more serious crimes that result in being in jail are entitled to the same rights as an adult; however, the juvenile could be released in most cases to a reliable parent or other adult of the family. In the absence of all adults of the family, the juvenile can be released to the minister or a neighbor who is a good friend. There should be no bonds posted on juveniles unless required by the Judge. The states attorney or judge should be contacted when a juvenile is to be held in jail for any length of time. The above policy will not cover all juvenile cases handled so the Chief will expect compliance with the laws and a common sense measure.

[19] There is no real statutory authority for any type of informal handling of juveniles by police, with possible exception of the word "may" in S.D.C.L. § 26–8–19.1. See also S.D.C.L. § 26–8–1.1 which gives the state's attorney the power to "[r]efer the case to a court service worker who may make whatever informal adjustment under the supervisions of the court that is practicable * * *." This suggests that the legislature intended that the state's attorney have exclusive authority in this area. Informal police diversion is subject to criticism. Lemert, Instead of Court: Diversion in Juvenile Justice printed in Back on the Street: The Diversion of Juvenile Offenders 123, 142 (R. Carter & M. Klein, eds. 1976) and Kobetz, Police Discretion: The Need for Guidelines printed in Back on the Street 207, 209.

In departments with a juvenile officer or division, after the initial contact, the youth was transferred to the custody of a juvenile officer to be processed. While some departments without juvenile officers had one or two officers who handled all the juvenile cases, most required that the officer making the initial contact process the juvenile.

While all the law enforcement agencies surveyed approximated the general practices outlined above, most agencies departed from them in some respect. For example, although station house detention during disposition was the general practice, nearly one-half of the sample agencies reported that officers would sometimes immediately release a juvenile with only a warning. This, however, was not standard procedure for informal dispositions and was used for only very minor offenses. Two police departments stated they generally did not inform parents of their child's contact with the law unless the child was to be referred to court. They reasoned that, for informal dispositions, if they avoided "getting him in trouble" with his parents he would return the favor by avoiding future entanglements with the law.[20]

Several departments admitted that parents were not always present during questioning and one agency stated that it would sometimes intentionally delay calling parents if it felt more information could be obtained without their presence.[21] Contrast this with another agency's policy of insisting on having parents sign a form stating that they had been completely apprised of all facts known to the department,[22] in addition to having a parent present during all questioning.

Finally, several agencies can be distinguished by their unique methods of informal disposition. Generally, the agency would emphasize the serious consequences of the act and release the youth to his parents with the parents making monetary restitution for any property damage done. Several departments, however, had release programs resembling more formalized "diversion" programs. "Diversion," as defined by the International Association of Chiefs of Police (IACP) is "an exercise of discretionary authority to substitute an informal disposition prior to a formal hearing on an alleged

---

[20] This procedure does not comply with S.D.C.L. § 26-8-19.2 (1976), which does not exempt non-court referrals from the requirement of notifying the parents, if the child is taken into temporary custody.

[21] This practice clearly violates S.D. C.L. § 26-8-19.2 (1976). It requires that "the officer shall notify the parents, guardian, or custodian *without unnecessary delay*" (emphasis added) after he has taken the child into custody. Additionally, any lengthy interrogation appears to violate S.D.C.L. § 26-8-19.3 (1976), which prescribes the term of detention by law enforcement officials as no longer than necessary to obtain the youth's name, age, residence, and other necessary information.

[22] Hopefully, this information would include proper constitutional warnings. None of the departments interviewed, however, volunteered any information concerning the giving of Miranda rights to juveniles or their parents. Since the repeal of S.D.C.L. § 23-44-2 by 1973 S.D.Sess.Laws, ch. 155, South Dakota has not statutorily mandated the giving of Miranda rights by police before questioning of adults or juveniles.

violation," where the youth is released and/or referred to some non-judicial agency.

Several police departments stated they would occasionally release the youth to his parent's custody on the condition that the youth receive professional counseling. This occurred in cases where the police felt the youth's misbehavior could be symptomatic of psychological problems.[23]

Another variation in informal dispositions involved work restitution programs. Three police departments reported offering such programs as an alternative to court referral for some juveniles. Under one program first offenses for shoplifting, vandalism, and some other minor offenses were handled by referral to the work restitution program. The juveniles were required to sign a work agreement and satisfactorily complete its terms or be referred to court. In another program, again primarily for shoplifting and vandalism, the juvenile debt was assessed on the basis of the cost of the item stolen or amount of damage done by the juvenile and was worked off at an hourly rate. Work was done for the victim or a public agency. The third program was used for all youthful violators except serious or chronic offenders. The juvenile was required to work for the victim or the city for a specified length of time, again under threat of court referral. The agencies said that the programs were operated with the full approval of the court.[24]

The instant section emphasizes the tremendous discretion exercised by law enforcement agencies in devising specific procedures for handling juveniles. This results in not only inconsistent law enforcement practices between departments, but also dissonance between the "standard, unwritten procedures" (and the inevitable variation allowed therefrom) and the admittedly brief and superficial state law governing the handling of juveniles.

Two factors contribute to this high degree of diversity in juvenile procedure and lack of adherence to the juvenile code. First, nearly all agencies felt that their primary goal was deterring juveniles from further crime, not strict law enforcement. Furthermore, most departments believed they were more effective in providing deterrence than the juvenile court. Second, the problem of disparity in handling juveniles can be attributed to the lack of training in juvenile law and procedure as evidenced below. Both factors demonstrate the need for adequate statutory and administrative guidelines for structuring discretion, as well as the importance of specific juvenile training and an educational background in juvenile justice philosophy.

[23] Such an assessment, without specific guidelines or psychological training, appears to exceed the capabilities of most agencies. See Ferster & Courtless, Legislation: The Beginning of Juvenile Justice, Police Practices, and the Juvenile Offender, 22 Vand.L.Rev. 567, 581–82 (1969). have no real statutory basis and are subject to the same objections raised earlier. See note 19 supra. Some definite due process problems also arise in the instituting of what can be considered punishment without a hearing or adjudication of guilt.

[24] The court-approved work restitution programs, laudable as they might be,

* * *

LEGAL IMPLICATIONS

* * *

Police Diversion of Juvenile Cases

The role of the police as the primary agents of referral or diversion in the juvenile justice system is clearly recognized. The authors of the IJA/ABA Standards contend that the police have always performed such a function but without public recognition or scrutiny. The problematical aspect of this practice is not that police dispose of most juvenile cases in one manner or another before they become court issues, "it is that most police actions are taken on an *ad hoc* basis by individual officers and are not guided either by departmental policies or joint policies with other juvenile justice agencies." [25]

The IJA/ABA Standards offer data from a recent FBI Uniform Crime Reports to reveal only a fraction of the total extent of police diversion of juveniles:

According to the over 8500 reporting police agencies, 1,709,564 juveniles were taken into custody during 1974. This figure reflects not only Crime Index offenses, but covers all offenses except traffic and neglect cases. Of this total police agencies report that 44.4 percent of the juveniles were handled within their respective police departments and were released; 47 percent were referred to juvenile court jurisdiction; 2.5 percent were referred to welfare agencies; 2.4 percent were referred to other police agencies; and 3.7 percent were referred to criminal courts * * *. These figures reveal only the percentage of referrals made *after* a child is taken into custody. An even higher percentage of all problems with juveniles are dealt with on the street without any formal action being taken. [26]

The extensiveness of on-the-street informal dispositions is reflected in a study which found that only forty percent of arrested youths reached the court intake process and only twenty percent actually reached the court. In light of this data and the opinions of police officers questioned throughout the study, the authors approximate that every one hundred youths the police arrest represents five hundred "probable cause" arrest situations.

In South Dakota, our data reveals that forty-four percent (2357) of the 5322 juvenile contacts reported by the law enforcement agencies surveyed were handled informally. Since the agencies reported it was general practice for an officer to bring a juvenile to the department for disposition and that only occasionally did an officer make an informal disposition in the field, it can be assumed that most

[25] Institute of Judicial Administration, American Bar Association, Standards Relating to Police Handling of Juvenile Problems, § 4.1A (Tentative Draft 1977).

[26] Id., at 32–33.

contacts in South Dakota involved custody and therefore, our data clearly conforms to that reported by the FBI in a recent Uniform Crime Reports.

The preceding paragraph documents the extent of informal handling of juveniles but does little to reveal the effects of police diversion. A number of writers have commented on the consequences of the extensive authority of law enforcement officers. These findings can be summarized as follows:

> The significance of the police in this process has been suggested by Lemert when he writes that through arrests and court referrals the police have the "strategic power to determine what proportions and what kinds of youth problems become official and which ones are absorbed back into the community." Beside this gate-keeping function for the justice system and its potential labeling effect on the juvenile, the police may also have their own labeling effect on the juvenile. For instance, Wattenberg and Bufe concluded from their study of initial police juvenile contacts that "the relatively brief contact between a boy or his family and a police officer may be highly influential on a future 'career' in delinquency." Also, Gold attributed apprehension by police as the factor which explained recidivism among a matched group of juveniles.[27]

As we have previously observed, law enforcement authorities in South Dakota are not governed by sufficient statutory or administrative directives in the exercise of their tremendous discretion in dealing with juveniles. South Dakota, however, is certainly not alone in this regard. Nationally, statutes rarely recognize the exercise of police discretion and police officers must necessarily resort to their own judgment to decide whether to make an arrest and whether detention is appropriate. In terms of administrative guidelines, many larger police departments across the country publish police-juvenile procedural manuals which are designed to assist the individual officer in making the correct disposition of the case.

The National Council on Crime and Delinquency suggests that police consider the following criteria in determining whether to refer a juvenile to court:

    (1) the seriousness of the offense;

    (2) totality of the circumstances, even if the particular offense is minor;

    (3) repeated offenses;

    (4) lack of cooperation by the child or parents in seeking voluntary help;

    (5) failure of previous casework on a voluntary basis;

    (6) the services needed are best obtained through the court and court related agencies;

---

[27] Sundeen, Police Professionalization and Community Attachments and Diversion of Juveniles from the Justice System, printed in Back on the Street, supra note 19, at 314.

(7) the child denies the charge and sufficient evidence apparently exists to prove his involvement; and

(8) any case in which the child has been placed in detention or should be.

Very few agencies have adopted such stringent and explicit guidelines, or any guidelines whatsoever, and it is clear that police behavior seldom conforms to such recommendations. "To understand the process of police diversion of juveniles, which takes place with little outside scrutiny and largely in the absence of formal criteria, it is essential to know how the police actually make their decisions." [28] Over the past decade and a half, a variety of significant studies have been conducted which have attempted to isolate criteria employed by police in determining juvenile dispositions. Some interesting comparisons can be made between those previous efforts and the data produced in the present study.

In one of the most influential excursions into this realm, it was concluded that the seriousness of the offense committed by the juvenile was the single most important factor influencing police dispositional decisions. Police were much more inclined to refer serious cases than less serious cases to court. A number of subsequent studies have confirmed this finding and in our investigation the seriousness of the offense, along with the juvenile's past offenses, were the two most frequently mentioned criteria by the police and sheriff's departments surveyed. Other studies also agree with the notion that the prior record of the offender is also a significant determinant of juvenile dispositions.

Age also appeared from our data to be an important consideration in the dispositional decision. Other studies show that police tend to avoid arresting younger adolescents unless the nature of their offense or the amount of harm and damage they have caused is relatively severe. One commentator has observed:

> There appears to be an under-representation in court of arrests below the age of twelve, and an over-representation of arrests in the sixteen- and seventeen-year groups. It is possible, if not probable, that the nature of the offenses of children under age twelve is much less serious than that of the older boys and girls. For a variety of other reasons, however, police are loathe to refer younger children to court. Some, referring back to their own early childhood escapades, find justification for the informal rather than official treatment of such children. Other police, referring to court and institution experiences as leading to habituation in the ways of delinquency, use court referral only as a last resort. Some, in terms of their self-conceptions as professional antagonists of the criminal, are embarrassed at having to assume a police role with respect to a young child. They prefer, then, to overlook juvenile offenses.[29]

---

[28] D. Besharov, Juvenile Justice Advocacy: Practice in a Unique Court 107–8 at 109 (1974).

[29] Goldman, supra note 16, at 274.

Another criterion which researchers have considered to be an important factor is the demeanor of the juvenile who comes into contact with the police. It has been observed as follows:

The cues used by police to assess demeanor were fairly simple. Juveniles who were contrite about their infractions, respectful to officers, and fearful of the sanctions that might be employed against them tended to be viewed by patrolmen as basically law-abiding or at least "salvageable." For these youths it was usually assumed that informal or formal reprimand would suffice to guarantee their future conformity. In contrast, youthful offenders who were fractious, obdurate, or who appeared nonchalant in their encounters with patrolmen were likely to be viewed as "would-be tough guys" or "punks" who fully deserve the most severe sanction: arrest.[30]

Similarly, another study found police ranked the juvenile's attitude as the second most significant dispositional criterion. In contrast, only three of the twenty-eight South Dakota law enforcement agencies identified attitude as a significant factor affecting dispositional decisions. Perhaps this can be explained by the reticence of South Dakota authorities to openly recognize a determinant which has been identified as an entirely inappropriate foundation upon which to base a dispositional decision.

Other factors, such as race and sex, may also affect police decisions. A South Dakota Statistical Analysis Center report noted:

Non-white juveniles were far more likely to be referred to court than white juveniles * * *. Of the 575 non-white juvenile contacts, 77 percent (443) were referred to court, compared to only 58 percent (1971) of the 3370 white juvenile contacts. Again, however, much of this difference is probably due to the fact that 59 percent of non-whites and only 37 percent of whites were being charged more often [i.e., were recidivists]. Also, whereas non-whites accounted for 12 percent of all offenses, they accounted for 15 percent of those offenses resulting in a high rate of court referrals. Thus, all other things being equal, there is no indication that non-whites were more likely than whites to be referred to court.[31]

Even though some studies have concluded that blacks receive harsher police dispositions than whites, other research efforts have been equally insistent that race is not a factor at this stage in the process.

Clearly, consensus is lacking in this area. One leading study evaluates the issue in the following manner:

Consequently, despite the widely held belief that police openly discriminate against minority group members, particularly Blacks, our evaluation of these and other research reports leads us to infer that the nature of this linkage is far from simplistic.

---

[30] Piliavin & Briar, Police Encounters with Juveniles, 70 Am.J.Soc. 206 at 210 (1964).

[31] Statistical Analysis Center, The Juvenile Offender in South Dakota at 75–76 (December 1976).

Instead, the association between ethnic origin and type of police reaction appears to diminish considerably when other relevant factors are taken into consideration, factors that tend to be correlated with both ethnicity and police decisions. Thus, it would appear that simply being Black does not appreciably influence police decisions to arrest. On the other hand, because being Black in this society implies that one is more likely to fall into a variety of other categories that are associated with this ethnic membership, the odds that Blacks will be arrested are higher than for those who are not Black.[32]

Another variable might be the sex of the juvenile. Virtually no evidence exists, however, that the sex of the child is a factor in the disposition of juvenile cases in South Dakota. This finding corresponds with the analysis of other researchers. "[T]he apparent relationship between sex and decisions to arrest may more appropriately be viewed as a function of other variables." [33] Another study seems to have isolated one of these variables by noting a relationship between sex and offense type in police decision-making. Their data revealed that petitions were more likely to be requested by police for boys than girls for the more serious adult offenses and less likely to be sought for boys in status offense situations. Our data does not indicate such a clean distinction between status and non-status offenses; only in the status offense category of runaway, however, did the number of females contacted exceed the number of males.

Before concluding this discussion of police disposition of juveniles, we would be remiss if we did not mention two factors which are not dispositional criteria but most certainly affect the employment of such criteria. One of these factors is the organizational structure of the department. Sundeen adroitly describes Wilson's landmark work in this area:

> Wilson attributed the difference in diversion rates between a Western and an Eastern police department to whether or not the department had a "fraternal" or a "professional" ethos. The professional department officers had more formal education and police training, more complex attitudes toward delinquency, tended to enforce the law more impartially and impersonally, were more likely to come in contact with juveniles, and, once in contact, to arrest or cite (as opposed to reprimand) than their counterparts in the fraternal department. On the other hand, the fraternal department officers were allowed a wide range of discretion in dealing with juveniles. With regard to community attachments, the fraternal force officers tended to be locals from lower-class backgrounds, while the officers from the professional force came from areas outside the city and had not been exposed as youth to lower-class culture.[34]

---

[32] Thomas & Fitch, The Exercise of Discretionary Decision-Making by the Police, 54 N.D.L.Rev. 61 at 75 (1977).

[33] Id. at 77.

[34] Sundeen, supra note 27, at 315.

Since the instant study does not undertake a categorization of South Dakota law enforcement agencies into professional or fraternal, and the individual characteristics of the agencies surveyed are not easily secured, any observations concerning organizational structure would be tentative.

The second factor deserving specific mention is the impressions law enforcement personnel maintain regarding the juvenile court and the correctional agencies which will handle formally adjudicated children. The potential impact of such perceptions has been described as follows:

> Where police view the efforts of such agencies as unsuccessful or inappropriate, they may be tempted to exercise dispositional alternatives within their departments * * *. Thus, where there is no compelling reason, such as severity of the delinquent or criminal act, for referral to the court, the police frequently dispose of the case themselves rather than expose the child to what they consider to be ineffective agencies utilized by the juvenile court system.[35]

This type of reaction is confirmed by our data to the extent that law enforcement personnel in the less populous areas of South Dakota were found to possess relatively negative opinions regarding the ability of the juvenile court (and assumedly its related agencies) to deal effectively with juvenile offenders. This disenchantment is apparently reflected in a smaller rate of court referrals in less populous areas than in the larger jurisdictions.

This comparative analysis of police decision-making emphasizes the extent and effects of informal handling of youths and the criteria used in varying degrees by law enforcement agencies throughout South Dakota and the rest of the country. It also demonstrates the astounding amount of discretion resting in the hands of the police. This point is stressed and the attendant dangers recognized by the President's Commission on Law Enforcement and the Administration of Justice:

> There are grave disadvantages and perils, however, in that vast continent of sublegal dispositions. It exists outside of and hence beyond the guidance and control of articulated policies and legal restraints. It is largely invisible—unknown in its detailed operations—and hence beyond sustained scrutiny and criticism. Discretion too often is exercised haphazardly and episodically, without the salutary obligation to account and without a foundation in full and comprehensive information about the offender and about the availability and likelihood of alternative dispositions. Opportunities occur for illegal and even discriminatory results, for abuse of authority by the ill-intentioned, the prejudiced, the overzealous. Irrelevant, improper considerations—race, nonconformity, punitiveness, sentimentality, understaffing, overburdening loads—may govern officials in their largely personal exercise

---

[35] Ferster & Courtless, supra note 23, at 580–81.

of discretion. The consequence may be not only injustice to the juvenile but diversion out of the formal channels of those whom the best interests of the community require to be dealt with through the formal adjudicatory and dispositional processes.[36]

The real issue is not whether we are going to retain or eliminate this discretion; law enforcement personnel should and will continue to exercise discretion in their decision to refer youths to court. The issue and the struggle is how to structure the discretion in police operations to prevent the abuses documented above and preserve the benefits of informal handling of juveniles.

* * *

TEXAS FAMILY CODE, TITLE III, VERNON'S TEXAS CODES ANNOTATED (1983)

Sec. 52.03   Disposition Without Referral to Court

(a) A law-enforcement officer authorized by this subtitle to take a child into custody may dispose of the case of a child taken into custody without referral to juvenile court, if:

(1) guidelines for such disposition have been issued by the law-enforcement agency in which the officer works;

(2) the guidelines have been approved by the juvenile court of the county in which the disposition is made;

(3) the disposition is authorized by the guidelines; and

(4) the officer makes a written report of his disposition to the law-enforcement agency, identifying the child and specifying the grounds for believing that the taking into custody was authorized.

(b) No disposition authorized by this section may involve:

(1) keeping the child in law-enforcement custody; or

(2) requiring periodic reporting of the child to a law-enforcement officer, law-enforcement agency, or other agency.

(c) A disposition authorized by this section may involve:

(1) referral of the child to an agency other than the juvenile court; or

(2) a brief conference with the child and his parent, * * * guardian, or custodian.

(d) Statistics indicating the number and kind of dispositions made by a law-enforcement agency under the authority of this section shall be reported at least annually to the office or official designated by the juvenile court, as ordered by the court.

---

[36] President's Commission on Law Enforcement and Administration of Justice,   The Challenge of Crime in a Free Society 82 (1967).

REPORT OF THE NATIONAL ADVISORY COMMITTEE FOR JUVENILE JUSTICE AND DELINQUENCY PREVENTION, STANDARDS FOR THE ADMINISTRATION OF JUVENILE JUSTICE (1980)

Section 2.241   Procedures Following A Decision Not to Refer to Intake

Individuals who are not referred to intake by a law enforcement officer should be released without condition or ongoing supervision. Although those individuals and their families may be referred or taken to community resources offering services on a voluntary basis.

QUESTIONS

1. What position should the legal system take on the issue of the desirability of broad police discretion in the handling of juveniles believed to be offenders? How important are the following considerations? (1) Police referral of all juveniles believed to be offenders would greatly increase, probably double, the number of children referred to the juvenile court. (2) Juvenile police officers are often untrained to make the "correctional" decisions they are now making. (3) Many of the cases not now referred to juvenile court are of such minor importance that they would receive only cursory treatment if referred to court personnel. (4) The legal system may be impotent to change the current practice.

2. Does the lawyer have any contribution to make to the way police handle juveniles believed to be offenders, either in representing a client or changing the system?

3. IJA–ABA Juvenile Justice Standards Project, Standards Relating to Police Handling of Juvenile Problems (1980) takes the following position with regard to informal disposition of juveniles by policing agencies:

2.4 * For juvenile matters involving nuisance, mischievous behavior, minor criminal conduct (e.g., being intoxicated, engaging in minor thefts), or parental misconduct (such as neglect) not involving apparent criminal behavior, police should select the least restrictive alternative from the following courses of action, depending upon the circumstances:

A. nonintervention;

B. temporary assistance to those seeking or obviously needing such assistance (including situations in which the potential of serious physical harm is apparent);

C. short-term mediation and crisis intervention (e.g., resolution of family conflicts);

D. voluntary referral to appropriate community agencies; or

E. mandatory temporary referral to mental or public health agencies under statutory authorization to make such referrals (e.g., to detoxification program).

In dealing with juvenile problems, police agencies should not attempt to initiate their own deterrence or treatment programs (such as

* Reprinted with permission from STANDARDS RELATING TO POLICE HANDLING OF JUVENILE PROB-   LEMS, Copyright 1980, Ballinger Publishing Company.

informal probation), but rather should limit their services to short-term intervention and referral.

2.5 * In order to stimulate police handling of juvenile problems (both criminal and noncriminal) in ways that are consistent with previous and subsequent standards, the following steps should be taken:

A. Juvenile codes should narrowly limit police authority to utilize the formal juvenile justice process.

B. Juvenile codes should clarify the authority and immunity from civil liability of police to intervene in problems involving juveniles in ways other than through use of their arrest power in dealing with matters in which the juvenile or criminal courts are to be involved. This means authority and emphasis should be given to the use of summons in lieu of arrest. For matters in which police must act to assist a juvenile in need against his or her will, authority to take a juvenile into protective custody or to make a mandatory temporary referral should be specified and should be properly limited. It should also be specified that a juvenile cannot be detained, even temporarily, in adult detention facilities.

C. Police agencies should formulate administrative policies structuring the discretion of and providing guidance to individual officers in the handling of juvenile problems, particularly those that do not involve serious criminal matters. Such policies should stress:

1. avoiding the formal juvenile justice process unless clearly indicated and unless alternatives do not exist;

2. using the least restrictive alternative in attempting to resolve juvenile problems; and

3. dealing with all classes and races of juveniles in an even-handed manner.

D. Police training programs should give high priority, in both recruit and inservice training, to available and desirable alternatives for handling juvenile problems.

E. Police administrators should work collaboratively with both public and private agencies in ensuring that adequate services are available in various neighborhoods and districts so that referrals can be made to such services, and ensuring that joint policies and common understandings are reached whenever necessary. In addition, police administrators, because of their knowledge of deficiencies in this area, should focus attention on gaps in public and private resources that must be filled in order to meet the needs of juveniles and their families, and on the unwillingness or inability of existing agencies and institutions to respond to the needs.

B. THE DECISION WHETHER TO FILE A PETITION: THE INTAKE PROCESS

In felony prosecutions, the law usually requires that a determination be made prior to trial that there is probable cause to believe an offense was committed and that the defendant committed it. In some jurisdictions, this determination is made by a grand jury, while in

* Reprinted with permission from STANDARDS RELATING TO POLICE HANDLING OF JUVENILE PROB- LEMS, Copyright 1980, Ballinger Publishing Company.

other jurisdictions the probable cause determination is made by a magistrate in a preliminary examination. Some jurisdictions use both devices.

Juvenile court statutes usually require a determination that a case referred to the court has merit before a petition for court hearing is filed. This determination is made administratively, usually by a juvenile probation officer. In larger juvenile probation departments, this function and related ones are handled by probation officers whose sole responsibility is handling cases at the "intake" level.

IJA–ABA JUVENILE JUSTICE STANDARDS, STANDARDS RELATING TO THE JUVENILE PROBATION FUNCTION: INTAKE AND PREDISPOSITION INVESTIGATIVE SERVICES (1980)

Section II: Dispositional Alternatives at Intake

2.2 * Judicial disposition of a complaint.

"Judicial disposition of a complaint" is the initiation of formal judicial proceedings against the juvenile who is the subject of a complaint through the filing of a petition. After intake screening, judicial disposition of a complaint may be made.

2.3 * Unconditional dismissal of a complaint.

The "unconditional dismissal of a complaint" is the termination of all proceedings against a juvenile. Unconditional dismissal of a complaint is a permissible intake dispositional alternative.

2.4 * Nonjudicial disposition of a complaint.

A. "Nonjudicial disposition of a complaint" is the taking of some action on a complaint without the initiation of formal judicial proceedings through the filing of a petition or the issuance of a court order.

B. The existing types of nonjudicial dispositions are as follows:

1. "Nonjudicial probation" is a nonjudicial disposition involving the supervision by juvenile intake or probation personnel of a juvenile who is the subject of a complaint, for a period of time during which the juvenile may be required to comply with certain restrictive conditions with respect to his or her conduct and activities.

2. The "provision of intake services" is the direct provision of services by juvenile intake and probation personnel on a continuing basis to a juvenile who is the subject of a complaint.

3. A "conditional dismissal of a complaint" is the termination of all proceedings against a juvenile subject to certain *nonjudicial* conditions not involving the acceptance of nonjudicial supervision or intake services. It includes a "community agency referral," which is the referral of a juvenile who is the subject of a complaint to a community agency or agencies for services.

This is the only permissible non-judicial disposition

C. A "community agency referral" is the only permissible nonjudicial disposition, subject to the conditions set forth in Standard 2.4 E. Intake personnel should refer juveniles in need of services whenever possible to youth service bureaus and other public and private community agencies. Juvenile probation agencies and other agencies responsible for the administration and provision of intake services and intake personnel should actively promote and encourage the establishment and the development of a wide range of community-based services and programs for delinquent and nondelinquent juveniles.

D. Nonjudicial probation, provision of intake services, and conditional dismissal other than community agency referral are not permissible intake dispositions.

E. A nonjudicial disposition should be utilized only under the following conditions:

Subject to these

1. A nonjudicial disposition should take the form of an agreement of a contractual nature under which the intake officer promises not to file a petition in exchange for certain commitments by the juvenile and his or her parents or legal guardian or both with respect to their future conduct and activities.

2. The juvenile and his or her parents or legal guardian should voluntarily and intelligently enter into the agreement.

3. The intake officer should advise the juvenile and his or her parents or legal guardian that they have the right to refuse to enter into an agreement for a nonjudicial disposition and to request a formal adjudication.

4. A nonjudicial disposition agreement should be limited in duration.

5. The juvenile and his or her parents or legal guardian should be able to terminate the agreement at any time and to request formal adjudication.

6. The terms of the nonjudicial agreement should be clearly stated in writing. This written agreement should contain a statement of the requirements set forth in subsections 2.–5. It should be signed by all the parties to the agreement and a copy should be given to the juvenile and his or her parents or legal guardian.

7.   Once a nonjudicial disposition of a complaint has been made, the subsequent filing of a petition based upon the events out of which the original complaint arose should be permitted for a period of [three (3)] months from the date the nonjudicial disposition agreement was entered into. If no petition is filed within that period its subsequent filing should be prohibited. The juvenile's compliance with all proper and reasonable terms of the agreement should be an affirmative defense to a petition filed within the [three-month] period.

2.5   * Consent decree.

A.   A consent decree is a court order authorizing supervision of a juvenile for a specified period of time during which the juvenile may be required to fulfill certain conditions or some other disposition of the complaint without the filing of a petition and a formal adjudicatory proceeding.

A consent decree should be permissible under the following conditions:

1.   The juvenile and his or her parents or legal guardian should voluntarily and intelligently consent to the decree.

2.   The intake officer and the judge should advise the juvenile and his or her parents or legal guardian that they have the right to refuse to consent to the decree and to request a formal adjudication.

3.   The juvenile should have an unwaivable right to the assistance of counsel in connection with an application for a consent decree. The intake officer should advise the juvenile of this right.

4.   The terms of the decree should be clearly stated in the decree and a copy should be given to all the parties to the decree.

5.   The decree should not remain in force for a period in excess of six (6) months. Upon application of any of the parties to the decree, made before expiration of the decree, the decree, after notice and hearing, may be extended for not more than an additional three (3) months by the court.

6.   The juvenile and his or her parents or legal guardian should be able to terminate the agreement at any time and to request the filing of a petition and formal adjudication.

7.   Once a consent decree has been entered, the subsequent filing of a petition based upon the events out of which the original complaint arose should be permitted for a period of [three (3)] months from the date the decree was entered. If no petition is filed within that period its subsequent filing should be prohibited. The juvenile's compliance with all proper and reason-

* Reprinted with permission from Standards Relating to the Juvenile Probation Function: Intake and Predisposition Investigative Services, Copyright 1980, Ballinger Publishing Company.

able terms of the decree should be an affirmative defense to a petition filed within the [three-month] period.

* * *

2.14 * Intake interviews and dispositional conferences.

A. If the intake officer deems it advisable, the officer may request and arrange an interview with the juvenile and his or her parents or legal guardian.

B. Participation in an intake interview by the juvenile and his or her parents or legal guardian should be voluntary. They should have the right to refuse to participate in an interview, and the officer should have no authority to compel their attendance.

C. At the time the request to attend the interview is made, the intake officer should inform the juvenile and his or her parents or legal guardian either in writing or orally that attendance is voluntary and that the juvenile has the right to be represented by counsel.

D. At the commencement of the interview, the intake officer should:

1. explain to the juvenile and his or her parents or legal guardian that a complaint has been made and explain the allegations of the complaint;

2. explain the function of the intake process, the dispositional powers of the intake officer, and intake procedures;

3. explain that participation in the intake interview is voluntary and that they may refuse to participate; and

4. notify them of the right of the juvenile to remain silent and the right to counsel as heretofore defined in Standard 2.13.

E. Subsequent to the intake interview, the intake officer may schedule one or more dispositional conferences with the juvenile and his or her parents or legal guardian in order to effect a nonjudicial disposition.

F. Participation in a dispositional conference by a juvenile and his or her parents or legal guardian should be voluntary. They should have the right to refuse to participate, and the intake officer should have no authority to compel their attendance.

G. The intake officer may conduct dispositional conferences in accordance with the procedures for intake interviews set forth in subsections D. and E.

2.15 * Length of intake process.

A decision at the intake level as to the disposition of a complaint should be made as expeditiously as possible. The period within which the decision is made should not exceed thirty (30) days from the date the complaint is filed in cases in which the juvenile who is the subject of a complaint has not been placed in detention or shelter care facilities.

FERSTER AND COURTLESS, THE INTAKE PROCESS AND THE AFFLUENT COUNTY JUVENILE COURT *

22 Hastings Law Journal 1127 (1971).

A judicial hearing is not held on every delinquent complaint made to the juvenile court. Rather, statistics indicate that in 1967, 53 percent, or 428,000 of all cases referred to juvenile courts were not formally adjudicated. In some large cities and counties the percentage of cases handled in an unofficial manner is even larger. Affluent County,[37] however, has a considerably lower rate of informal disposition than the national average. In 1967, 39 percent of the cases referred to the court were handled informally. The Affluent County rate of informal cases increased in the next 2 years—to 45 percent in 1968 and to 50 percent in 1969.

Although approximately half of all juvenile cases referred to courts in the United States are processed informally, the percentage variation from community to community, as shown below, is very large.

TABLE 1

Percentage of Delinquency Cases (Excluding Traffic Cases) Handled Informally in 1967

City	Percent	County	Percent
St. Louis	80.0	Trumbull, Ohio	80.7
Milwaukee	70.2	Westchester, New York	73.8
Houston	59.5	Yakima, Washington	72.7
Detroit	50.4	Polk, Iowa	68.5
District of Columbia	49.4	San Joaquin, California	65.0
Atlanta	47.2	Orange, Florida	63.3
Los Angeles	43.0	Mecklenburg, N. Carolina	59.4
New York	40.3	Delaware, Pennsylvania	39.0
Cleveland	38.5	Macomb, Michigan	38.7
Philadelphia	27.0	Spartanburg, S. Carolina	29.0

Manifestly, these communities use different criteria to determine which cases shall be subject to informal disposition because no other explanation will support a range of percentages from 27.0 percent to 80.7 percent. The purpose of this article is to discover the criteria

* Copyright 1971, Hastings College of the Law, reprinted from Volume 22, No. 5 Hastings Law Journal page 1127 with permission.

[37] Affluent County is located in the Middle-Atlantic region. Its estimated 1969 population was 500,000. The name "Affluent" was chosen because the county has the highest median income of any county in the United States. Dep't of Community Development, Affluent County, Population and Social Characteristics 2 (CRP Rep. No. 6, 1968).

and procedures which are used to make intake decisions and to evaluate them in light of the purposes of intake.

The Purposes of Intake

It is generally agreed that the chief function of intake is to determine which complaints should be referred for a judicial hearing, although differences of opinion do exist concerning the criteria and procedures which are to be used in making this determination. Intake is supposed to eliminate three basic situations. First, intake should eliminate complaints involving acts over which the juvenile court has no jurisdiction. For example, the juvenile court may be requested to adjudicate a child to be incorrigible merely because he failed to do his homework or cut his hair. Second, intake should dismiss complaints which, although they allege sufficient grounds for juvenile court jurisdiction, are not supported by sufficient evidence. Third, intake should eliminate those cases which may invoke court jurisdiction and are supported by sufficient evidence but involve only minor offenses, such as breaking a street light or possessing liquor.

Thus, in performing this screening function, the intake staff should affirmatively answer the following questions before referring a complaint for judicial hearing: Is the complaint one over which the juvenile court has jurisdiction? Is there sufficient evidence to support the allegations of the petition? Will filing of a petition be in the best interest of the child and the public?

It is also generally agreed that intake should decide whether the juvenile is to be released to his family or detained until the court hearing. There is much less agreement, however, concerning the propriety of a third function which is performed by the intake staff of many courts: supervision and treatment of juveniles against whom a delinquency complaint has been made but who are not referred to the judge for a hearing. Before examining these functions, however, it will be helpful to discuss intake personnel, the procedures which they follow, and the criteria which they employ to implement the screening process.

A. Intake Personnel

The number and quality of personnel performing the screening function vary from jurisdiction to jurisdiction and from court to court. The wide variety of procedures and personnel used to screen cases in juvenile courts often reflect pragmatic factors, such as workload of the court, size of the staff and degree of prescreening performed by the police. Juvenile courts located in larger cities often have complete and separate intake sections composed of trained probation officers. In contrast, some courts located in less populated jurisdictions have no intake personnel and the intake functions are performed entirely outside the court. In one such court, the judge had delegated authority for most screening and agency referral to the police.

Statutes in most jurisdictions require that the decision to adjudicate a complaint formally be preceded by, and be based on, a "preliminary inquiry" or investigation, but many of these same statutes do not indicate who shall make the investigation. Some statutes simply designate "the court," while others require that the probation officer make the initial inquiry. In contrast, organizations which propose model standards recommend that the intake function be performed by probation officers who would constitute a separate intake unit.

This latter procedure is followed in Affluent County. At the time of this study the intake unit consisted of three workers and one supervisor who performed all the screening for the 2,283 cases which were referred to the court during 1968.

The authority delegated to intake also varies from state to state. Although based on a preliminary investigation, the intake worker's decision about the necessity of a judicial hearing is not always final. In some jurisdictions, for example, complainants can insist on filing a petition for formal adjudication, thereby overruling the probation officer's decision. In a few other jurisdictions complainants, although they cannot compel a judicial hearing, can demand that the probation officer's determination be reviewed by a prosecution official.

There is no statutory authority for review of the probation officer's decision by a prosecutor in Affluent County; neither is there authority for overruling the probation officer's decision.[38] However, at least some intake workers believe that the complainant has the right to insist on formal court action. Several of the intake reports in sample cases contained comments by the intake worker that many cases not requiring formal court action were referred at the insistence of the complainant.

Statutes which limit intake authority have been criticized by some experts because they restrict the power of officials to prevent petty disputes from burdening the courts. Proponents of such statutes, on the other hand, contend that if intake officials have exclusive authority to determine whether a complaint should be referred to a judge, the rights of the public and the juvenile may not be protected. The validity of this contention cannot be determined until current intake procedures and practices have been examined.

B. Intake Procedures

As explained above, the first question that an intake worker must decide is whether the complaint is within the jurisdiction of the juvenile court. For example, if the juvenile court is only authorized to handle delinquency complaints involving children 15 years of age

[38] The pertinent provisions of the Affluent County Code are as follows: § 81 provides that "the probation officers * * * shall perform such duties * * * as may be prescribed by the judge, including the duty of investigating complaints made to the court * * *."

§ 86(a) states that "whenever any person informs the court that a child is within the purview of this subtitle, the court shall make a preliminary inquiry to determine whether the interests of the public or * * * the child require that further action be taken. Thereupon the court may make such informal adjustment as is practicable with a petition, or may authorize a petition to be filed by any person."

and under and the complaint involves a charge of automobile theft by a boy who was 16 at the time of the alleged act, the juvenile court would have no jurisdiction. Ordinarily, the intake worker is able to determine whether the court has jurisdiction, but he may need to consult legal counsel if he encounters difficult jurisdictional questions. Affluent County intake personnel indicated their need for either legal training or assistance to handle these legal questions.

After determining that the juvenile court has jurisdiction over the complaint, the intake worker must decide whether the evidence is sufficient to support the allegations of delinquent conduct. The extent of the investigation the intake worker makes to determine the sufficiency of the evidence varies from jurisdiction to jurisdiction. The intake worker's function in some jurisdictions is to gather evidence; in others, like Affluent County, he is simply to review the evidence presented.

Statistics on the number of cases closed by the intake determination that the court has no jurisdiction would of course be helpful to determine how many cases are unnecessarily referred to the juvenile court. Data on the number of cases closed because of lack of evidence would be useful for the same reason. Unfortunately, juvenile courts usually do not keep such records.

To compensate for this lack of information, data concerning intake dispositions were obtained in Affluent County by an examination of 162 of the intake case records, including the intake worker's comments. Eighty-nine, or 65 percent, of these cases were closed at intake, but in only five of these cases were lack of jurisdiction or lack of evidence given as the reason for the decision not to refer the case to juvenile court. In six instances the record gave no reason for closing the case. Even if these last six cases were added to those known to be closed because intake found that the juvenile was not involved in the offense, the percentage of cases closed for this reason would be less than 10 percent. Since no comparable data were available from other jurisdictions, however, it is impossible to generalize accurately whether intake departments of other juvenile courts also dismiss only a small number of complaints for lack of jurisdiction or lack of evidence.

C. Intake Criteria

Determination of the juvenile court's jurisdiction and the sufficiency of the evidence to support the complaint is relatively simple in comparison to the most important function performed by the intake officer: deciding whether referral of the case for judicial hearing is in the best interests of the public or the child. The statutes offer little guidance. The typical statute provides that petitions should be filed when formal adjudication is in the interests of the public or the child, but it fails to specify the criteria which are to be used in making this decision. Juvenile courts also normally fail to provide written guidelines. Even organizations which propose model standards refer only to the "best interests" of the public and the child. This informal and vague approach has not gone unnoticed, however, and has been criticized by the President's Crime Commission on Law Enforcement and Administration of Justice:

> Written guides and standards should be formulated and imparted in the course of inservice training. Reliance on word of mouth creates the risk of misunderstanding and conveys the impression that pre-judicial dispositions are neither desirable nor common. Explicit written criteria would also facilitate achieving greater consistency in decision making.[39]

The lack of definite intake criteria is presently being challenged in Conover v. Montemuro,[40] on the grounds that

> the failure to provide standards reasonably related to probable cause or the purposes of the Juvenile Court Act results in an overbroad scope of the worker's discretion and in arbitrary and irrational choice of cases in which to file petitions.[41]

Intake units do base their decision on some criteria, which, however, are frequently neither stated explicitly nor applied consistently. Factors apparently considered most important by courts and commentators when evaluating the desirability of referring the complaint to the judge for a judicial hearing include: the seriousness of the act, prior court and police contacts and the attitude of the child and his parents. Some commentators suggest that the intake worker should also consider the age of the child,[42] the time of day of the offense[43] and the type of neighborhood in which the juveniles live.[44]

Most authorities agree that "serious" cases unquestionably should be routed to the juvenile court. It is not clear, however, what offenses are to be considered serious. One authority suggests that in the absence of unusual circumstances, complaints of homicide, forcible rape, robbery, purse snatching, aggravated assault, auto theft and burglary should be referred to court. The District of Columbia Crime Commission, however, cautions against automatic

[39] President's Comm'n on Law Enforcement and Administration of Justice, Task Force Report: Juvenile Delinquency and Youth Crime 17 at 21 (1967).

[40] 304 F.Supp. 259 (E.D.Pa.1969). This class action to enjoin the Philadelphia pretrial procedure for juveniles has withstood a motion to dismiss and awaits a hearing on the plaintiff's request for declaratory judgment. Id. at 263.

[41] Id.

[42] Sheridan considers the age of the juvenile important since the act of a young child may "be only the immature impulse of a child." However, he warns against excusing the conduct of a young child, since it may expose the community to more danger and negate opportunities for early detection and treatment of delinquent children. Sheridan, Juvenile Court Intake, 2 J. Family L. 139 at 150 (1962). A 1964 study of the St. Louis County Juvenile Court found age has little influence unless the child is very young when the most effective handling is informal or private. Note, Informal Disposition of Juvenile Cases, 1965 Wash.U.L.Q. 256, 269.

[43] Sheridan points out that the time of day the offense took place is a clue to the home supervision. The more unusual the hour and the younger the child, the greater the significance. Sheridan, Juvenile Court Intake, supra note 42, at 150.

[44] The impact of the child's neighborhood is disputed. Sheridan considers a high delinquency rate area as creating "environmental pressures." Id. at 150–51. The President's Commission warns that neighborhoods "may bear an indirect association with the avowedly irrelevant factor of race." Juvenile Delinquency, supra note 39, at 17.

referral to court on the basis of the classification of the act as a felony. That an act would be classified as a felony, if committed by an adult, is not considered a sufficient definition of "serious" by the Crime Commission. For example, joyriding in an automobile around the block is technically a felony, as is grabbing a playmate's pocketbook with a quarter in it. The commission pointed out that children who commit these offenses may not always demand full-scale court treatment.

An analysis of the data from the Affluent County field study conducted by the authors demonstrates the problems involved in trying to determine intake criteria and in evaluating whether an intake unit is making decisions which protect the public. Affluent County has no written intake criteria. Although neither Affluent County Juvenile Court judge suggested that written criteria are necessary, they both believed that present criteria need to be sharpened. Both judges agreed that the court and the intake staff should cooperate in formulating intake criteria; they differed somewhat on the disposition of a case when intake and the court were not in agreement. Judge A was of the opinion that the court must have the final word, while Judge B seemed more inclined to defer to intake.

Only one criterion has been imposed by the court in Affluent County on the intake staff: Whenever two or more juveniles are charged with a single offense, if intake refers one of these children to court, they must refer all. The judges think that the court can evaluate those differences in the children which would cause intake to treat them differently. While it is true that differences can be handled at disposition, the practice of automatically referring accomplices undermines intake's role of screening out children who do not need court services.

Except for this one rule, intake in fact establishes the criteria for court referral in Affluent County. As the description below indicates, however, these criteria are unclear. Intake personnel said that the basic premise of the intake unit is that court referral should be avoided if possible. However, there is a somewhat inconsistent second premise that children who commit "serious" offenses are automatically referred to court. For these cases intake does not employ its normal procedure of conferences with juveniles and parents. The cases are merely given a hearing date. Furthermore, intake personnel were unable to specify the offenses which are serious enough to justify automatic court referral. Therefore an attempt was made by an analysis of intake records to determine empirically which offenses intake regards as "serious."

The authors examined the records of the 162 cases in the informal sample, and those of the 49 juveniles in the formal sample for whom there had been no prior court petitions. The records show that there is no single offense for which court referral is automatic, despite intake's statements that seriousness of offense controls the intake decision. The table below lists the offense for which the juveniles in our samples were charged and indicates the frequency with which each offense was handled formally and informally.

TABLE 2

Crimes Which Were Handled Formally and Informally in 1968

	Formal	Informal *
Aggravated Assault	3	2
Assault	7	4
Auto Theft	0	0
Burglary, Breaking and Entering	7	16
Disorderly Conduct	1	5
Drugs (Narcotics)	0	1
Drunkenness	0	2
Larceny	5	13
Robbery	3	3
Sex Offenses	0	4
Shoplifting	4	18
Vandalism	6	4
All Others	13	12
Total	49	84

* The total of this column is less than 162 because it includes only crimes. No "status" offenses such as running away from home or truancy are included in this comparison.

The other, nonautomatic criteria which intake uses are age and prior police and court contacts. A comparison of 49 cases which were handled formally in 1968 with the 1968 informal sample disclosed that the average ages were 15.6 and 14.5 years respectively. This difference of about 1 year is not significant. As far as prior encounters with the juvenile justice system are concerned, the informal group had considerably more contact with the police than did the juveniles who were processed formally for the first time in 1968. While prior intake contact was the same for both groups (about 6 percent for each), 39 percent of the informals and only 22 percent of the formals had prior police contacts. Nor were there any significant differences discovered between the two groups when they were compared on various combinations of age, prior intake and prior police contact variables.

Clearly, intake decisions are not made on the basis of the criteria enunciated by the intake staff. This situation is not confined to Affluent County. There are apparently no studies or reports which provide any information concerning the standards to be used in making intake decisions. The absence of written criteria, the belief of some judges that intake workers should use common sense and a certain amount of intuition in making their assessment and the failure of some intake workers to record reasons for their decisions probably all help to explain the lack of precise and consistently applied criteria. Since intake's reported criteria are not those which are employed, a detailed analysis of the 162 informal cases and the 49 formal cases was undertaken to determine the actual criteria used. As the table below indicates, the reasons for handling juveniles on an informal basis were found in the intake records for only 83 (51.2 percent) of the cases.

TABLE 3

Reasons for Handling Cases Informally

Reason:	Number	Percent of All Cases
Juvenile found not involved	5	
Referral offense was minor	9	
Family found able to cope with problem	28	
Juvenile receiving service from another agency in the community	9	
Restitution made	5	
Juvenile was a non-resident	11	
No further difficulties noted since referral [45]	16	
Total Cases with Reasons	83	51.2%
Total Cases where Reasons Unknown	79	48.8%

Reasons for the intake decisions were given in an even smaller percentage of the formal cases. Fourteen (29.8 percent) of these cases have intake reports, with the stated reasons for formal disposition given in the following table.

TABLE 4

Reasons for Formal Disposition

	Number
Request of victim	5
Seriousness of offense	1
Request of parent for away-from-home placement	3
Unknown—record lost, partial data available	1
Endorsed summons of court	1
Probation to another court	1
Additional offenses	1
Denial of offense	1

[45] The reason of "no further difficulties" for closing cases at intake is undoubtedly confusing to the reader. It was used because that was the reason stated by intake in its closing note for these 16 cases. Normally, an intake conference takes place within a few days after a juvenile is referred to court. In most of these 16 cases, however, conferences were not held for several weeks.

Affluent County authorities have attributed lack of intake data in the records of so many children to two factors. The principal reason is automatic court action. Presumably, if the child meets the criteria for automatic referral to court, intake does not interview the child or his parents. Since no such criteria were found, this explanation does not account for the scarcity of data. Nor, of course, would this reason explain the lack of data of the cases which did not go to court. The second reason, and the most plausible explanation, is the intake worker has very little time to write reports. However, it does not justify the absence of such data if they are necessary for the effective operation of the court. It is impossible for the court or the community to determine whether the screening function is being performed properly if the basis for the decision is unknown.

Even the cases analyzed as part of this study are unsatisfactory for evaluating intake screening because it cannot be determined whether these cases are representative of all intake cases. The appropriateness of the decision in the cases for which data was found is speculative at best.

The decisions in the informal cases for which data were available seem to be consistent with the basic premise of this intake department: to keep children out of court whenever possible. The decisions about children whose cases went to court also seem to be consistent with that premise because in 10 of the 13 cases where information was available intake was of the opinion that a court hearing was required. For example, the records showed that intake workers thought a complainant has a right to insist on judicial action.

Another way of evaluating intake decisions is to follow the child's progress after the intake decision. For this purpose the children in the sample were followed for at least 18 months. Intake re-referred forty-seven (29 percent) of the children in the informal sample to court during that period. The cases against four were dismissed, and another eight had their cases held open without finding. Only one case was formally adjudicated. These findings suggest that many intake decisions are inappropriate. Since the criteria used to make these decisions cannot be determined, it is impossible to discover which specific factors were weighted improperly. The task of deciding which cases should be referred for a judicial hearing need not be difficult if the sole function of the intake department is to screen out inappropriate cases. Establishment of precise definitions of such terms as "serious offense" and "prior contacts" by the legislature or juvenile court would enable intake workers to make decisions consistently if their function is solely to eliminate cases in which the court lacks jurisdiction, the evidence of involvement is insufficient, or the act is clearly an isolated incident.

It is doubtful, however, that the elimination of inappropriate cases is the sole function of either the typical intake unit, or the one in Affluent County. They attempt to perform three additional functions: saving judicial time by reducing the number of formal hearings; preventing delinquency by giving service to children who are likely to get into trouble again; and avoiding the stigma of adjudicating a child "delinquent." The belief that many intake decisions are made in furtherance of these three functions is supported by the large number of nonreferred cases which are put on informal probation.

Informal Probation

The use of informal probation as a method of disposition of juvenile complaints has been the subject of some controversy. Those who advocate its use claim that it has several distinct advantages. The principle benefit is that it avoids the evils incident to formal adjudication, such as curtailment of employment opportunities, stigma of quasi-criminal records, harm to personal reputation and reinforcement of antisocial tendencies. A second major advantage of informal probation is that it saves judicial time and is therefore economical. Those who criticize informal probation allege that existing practices are too informal and do not adequately protect the juvenile's rights. For example, any child on informal probation faces the risk for a considerable period of time that formal court action on the original charge will be prosecuted if he violates his probation conditions. Some commentators believe that the result of filing a petition on the original complaint after an informal adjustment has begun "is practical and perhaps legal double jeopardy."

Children in Affluent County are subject to this double jeopardy for a 3-month period. Although a new state law prohibits formal court action if the case has been processed informally,[46] Affluent County is not subject to this law and thus far has allowed formal action within the 3-month period.

Most intake units permit informal probation only for those children who have admitted their offenses and automatically refer every case for formal adjudication if the juvenile denies the facts. But other courts allow factually disputed cases to be informally adjusted. According to a 1966 study, intake workers in Philadelphia claimed the power to adjust cases of contested involvement. In Affluent County the intake section may informally adjust some cases where the child has denied his involvement. This power includes the granting of informal probation.

Seventy (44 percent) of the children retained by intake were put on informal probation. Presumably, intake believed that these children needed some guidance but that a court order was not required.

[46] Although Affluent County does not come under the state statute, its Chief Probation Officer felt that the county would shortly conform to the new provision. Interviews with two Affluent County Juvenile Court Judges, August 5th and 21st, 1970. But this view is not shared by Judge A, who said he found the Affluent County practice satisfactory.

The children did not differ from those whose cases were closed at intake in age, seriousness of offense or prior contacts with the juvenile justice system. This absence of any noticeable difference between these children is consistent with the finding that all of the juveniles handled formally were similar to those who were referred to court for the first time.

No reason was given for placing a child on informal probation in an overwhelming majority of cases. In the few cases where reasons were given, they tended to be vague or contradictory. For example, one statement read, "It is felt that a period of informal probation for R—is very much in order at this point," but the file contained no other information about the girl. The cases of two teenage boys illustrate how conflicting reasons are sometimes given to justify the need for supervision. One boy was granted probation because his offense of drinking was considered mild and he had not previously been referred, while the other boy was placed on probation because he had a prior referral.

A probation officer is assigned in most cases, but the records usually showed no contact between the probation officer and the child or his family. Although the overwhelming majority of records was bare except for a closing summary, a few of the records showed several contacts, while others indicated that the family did not respond to a letter from the probation office, or refused the court's services.

Some children seem to have been placed on informal supervision because of emotional problems. A few records indicate that the parents agreed to take the child to a mental health clinic or a private psychiatrist. Most of these children were not put on probation. The records do not indicate if the child began treatment or even if he was taken for an examination. They do suggest, however, that neither intake nor probation seems to follow the progress of these mental health referrals. Interviews with probation officers substantiated the impression that little service is provided juveniles with informal status. They believe that if the case was not serious enough to justify judicial treatment, it is not sufficiently important to require their services.

Since little is known about most of these children besides the nature of their offense, it is difficult to evaluate the effect of informal supervision on their problems. The reasons given in the court records for closing informal supervision cases shed little light on the success of informal probation. As the table below shows, the most frequently given reason for closure was that the probation officer found the child encountered "no further difficulties" during the period of supervision. However, almost as many cases were closed for the opposite reason—continuing difficulties. When the child committed a new offense or the parents reported continuing home difficulties, a petition was filed on the original offense.

TABLE 5

Reasons for Closing Informal Supervision Cases

	Number	Percent
No Further Difficulties	28	41.2
Converted to Formal Status	25	36.8
Other Agency or Service Satisfactory	4	5.9
Moved Out of Affluent County	5	7.4
Reached 18th Birthday	1	1.4
Parents or Juvenile Uncooperative	4	5.9
No Reason Noted	1	1.4
Totals	68	100.0

If the effectiveness of informal supervision is merely defined as the absence of subsequent court referrals, the experience can be called successful for 37, or 53 percent, of the informal probation cases because no court record was found for these children within 18 months of their placement on informal probation. However, it should be noted that there is no way to determine whether the children continued to live in Affluent County during this period. Nor would the Affluent County records show a referral to a juvenile court in a neighboring community.

It is also worth noting that a much larger percentage of children whose cases were closed at intake could be called successful because 87 percent of this group had no subsequent court record, while of the children referred for formal hearings for the first time 97 percent had no further court referral. (It should be remembered that the 3 percent figure reflects only recidivism rate for those who appear in court formally for the first time. The rate of recidivism for the total formal sample is in excess of 50 percent).

The absence of criteria for informal supervision makes it almost impossible to assess accurately the propriety of the decisions and usefulness of informal probation. From the data that were available, the intake criteria used seem to vary from worker to worker. Thus, while some children are unnecessarily referred to court, others who do not seem to meet the generally offered criteria for nonjudicial supervision are kept at the intake stage. Furthermore, intake workers and some probation officers apparently disagree about the use of informal probation because several interviewees said they gave little or no time to cases which were not serious enough to be referred to a judge.

Informal supervision in Affluent County seems to be a waiting period to see if the child encounters further difficulties; it certainly cannot be characterized as an active treatment or supervision program. This approach seems inconsistent not only with the term "informal probation," but also with the prevalent assumption that certain children who have problems can be helped without court-ordered treatment. The records give several examples of this passive approach. First, large numbers of children on informal supervision are apparently not seen during the supervisory period. Second, intake does attempt to discover whether services are provided to referrals to community services. Third, the closing summaries say no more than that the child has not been in further difficulty. No mention is made of the progress of the child and his family in resolving the problem which occasioned the supervision. In some cases it was clear that the worker thought the problems were not resolved because the closing summary specified that the parents did not respond to, or actively rejected, the court's services.

* * *

1. CONTROL OF THE DECISION TO FILE A PETITION

IN THE MATTER OF THE APPEAL IN MARICOPA COUNTY, JUVENILE ACTION NO. J–81405–S

Supreme Court of Arizona, 1979.
122 Ariz. 252, 594 P.2d 506.

HOLOHAN, JUSTICE.

The presiding judge of the juvenile division of the Maricopa County Superior Court found the juvenile in this cause to have violated the terms of his probation. The court continued the juvenile on probation. An appeal was then taken from the judgment of the court. The Court of Appeals set aside the judgment of the juvenile court. Matter of the Appeal in Maricopa County, Juvenile Action, 122 Ariz. 279, 594 P.2d 533 (App.1978). We granted the petition of the state for review. The opinion of the Court of Appeals is vacated. The judgment of the juvenile division of the superior court is affirmed.

The facts surrounding this case arose out of an incident in which the subject juvenile was taken into custody after disturbing the peace and releasing a large German Shepherd to attack the police.

A formal complaint was filed with the juvenile court describing the conduct of the juvenile. For reasons unexplained in the record, the juvenile probation officer to whom the case was referred decided to hold the complaint for possible adjustment. See 17A A.R.S. Juv. Ct.Rules of Proc., rules 1 & 2.

Subsequently the county attorney's office received a report from the police describing the incident, and a deputy county attorney filed a formal petition in juvenile court alleging that the juvenile, who was on probation at the time, had violated his probation by disturbing the peace.

Counsel for the juvenile moved to dismiss the petition, but the juvenile court judge denied the motion. The case was thereafter heard by the court on the merits with the result above described.

On appeal there is no challenge to the facts upon which the juvenile court based its judgment. The issues presented may be stated as:

1. Does the juvenile probation officer, by choosing to "adjust" a juvenile matter pursuant to the Rules of Procedure for the Juvenile Court, preclude the county attorney from filing a juvenile petition?

2. Does the procedure established for filing juvenile petitions violate equal protection by failing to provide for a determination of probable cause similar to the procedure required by adult prosecutions?

Counsel for the juvenile argues that the juvenile probation officer has the discretion to charge or not charge the juvenile with an act of delinquency or violation of probation. As authority he refers to the Rules of Procedure for the Juvenile Court. He points out that Rule 1 defines the word "adjusted" as meaning "the handling of a juvenile referral or complaint in a manner which obviates the necessity of filing a petition." Counsel also points out that Rule 2 provides in part:

* * *

"(b) The juvenile probation officer shall make a record of the complaint and investigate the matter to determine whether the facts, if true, are sufficient to bring the child within the court's jurisdiction, and whether they appear serious enough on their face to warrant some form of court action. If the facts are insufficient to meet the foregoing conditions, the complaint may be *adjusted*.

"(c) If a child has acknowledged his responsibility for the delinquent act and the juvenile probation officer has found from his investigation of the child's total circumstances that court action is not necessary, the child may be referred to other agencies or to the parents, guardian or custodian for corrective action, and the complaint adjusted."

Finally, he points out that A.R.S. § 8–221 provides that the commencement of proceedings in juvenile court is accomplished by the filing of a petition in accordance with the Rules of Procedure for the Juvenile Court.

From the foregoing authorities counsel concludes that the decision to initiate a juvenile court proceeding is within the exclusive domain of the juvenile probation office. We find this position fallacious as based on an incomplete reading and understanding of the rules and statutes applicable to juvenile courts.

To determine the first issue in this case it is necessary to keep in mind that the rules for juvenile court were adopted prior to the revision of the juvenile code. Under the 1956 code the juvenile probation officer had the authority that counsel describes. The probation officer made investigations and filed petitions; he represented children and their interests in court; he was to be notified when a child was arrested and he would decide the disposition to be made of the child. See A.R.S. §§ 8–204 and 8–221 prior to the 1970 revision.

In 1967, modifications in Arizona's juvenile justice system were mandated by the United States Supreme Court in Application of Gault, 387 U.S. 1, 87 S.Ct. 1428, 18 L.Ed.2d 527 (1967). The Supreme Court stated:

> "Probation officers, in the Arizona scheme, are also arresting officers. They initiate proceedings and file petitions which they verify, as here, alleging the delinquency of the child; and they testify, as here, against the child. * * * The probation officer cannot act as counsel for the child." 387 U.S. at 35–36, 87 S.Ct. at 1448, 18 L.Ed.2d at 551.

Gault held that juveniles charged with delinquent acts were entitled to the assistance of counsel. The case also held that juveniles were entitled to a number of other constitutional rights including the privilege against self-incrimination, and the rights of confrontation and cross-examination. Application of *Gault*, 387 U.S. at 55–57, 87 S.Ct. at 1458–59, 18 L.Ed.2d at 561–63.

This court promulgated the juvenile rules recognizing that due process required substantial changes in Arizona's procedure in juvenile court, but the legislature had not changed the juvenile code at the time the rules became effective. Subsequently the legislature made a comprehensive revision of the juvenile code.

Under the revised juvenile code the powers of the juvenile probation officer were significantly changed. These changes were necessary to make the role of the probation officer comport with due process. The code changed his role to that of an officer of the court charged with the responsibility of gathering and evaluating information for the court and supervising those children assigned to him by the juvenile court after an adjudication of delinquency or incorrigibility.

The new code provided that the probation officer would:

> "Receive and examine complaints involving an alleged delinquent or incorrigible child for the purpose of considering the commencement of proceedings under this chapter." A.R.S. § 8–205(1)

The new code did not, however, specifically authorize the probation officer to file petitions. It should be noted that there is a distinction between "complaints" and "petitions" in juvenile law. The complaint or referral is the written statement by an individual or agency setting forth facts describing the acts of a juvenile which may constitute delinquent conduct. The petition is the formal initiation of court action by a written instrument under oath filed with the juvenile court alleging an act of juvenile delinquency or incorrigibility. A complaint in juvenile law is somewhat similar to a complaint in criminal law, and the petition may, in a sense, be compared to an information or indictment.

The new juvenile code recognized that the adversary system had been introduced to juvenile law by *Gault*. Provision was made for the appointment of counsel for juveniles under A.R.S. § 8–225, and the role of the prosecutor was defined under A.R.S. § 8–233 which provided:

"A. The county attorney shall:

"1. Direct such investigation he deems necessary of acts of alleged delinquent behavior;

"2. Cause petitions alleging delinquent behavior to be drafted and filed with the juvenile court as he deems necessary in the public interest; and

"3. Attend the juvenile court within his county and conduct on behalf of the state all contested hearings involving allegations of delinquent acts or incorrigibility.

"B. In a juvenile court hearing where the child who is the subject of the petition not alleging a delinquent act or incorrigibility is represented by counsel in a contested matter, the county attorney shall, when requested by the juvenile court judge, appear and participate in the hearing to assist in the ascertaining and presenting of evidence."

The authority to file petitions alleging delinquent behavior was granted to the county attorney. No restriction was placed on that authority. The code left the matter to the county attorney to file petitions as he deemed necessary in the public interest. In McBeth v. Rose, 111 Ariz. 399, 531 P.2d 156 (1975), we recognized the change which the juvenile code had made in the method of prosecuting juvenile cases, and we noted that the decision to file a delinquency petition in juvenile court was a matter exclusively for the prosecutor.

The position of counsel for the juvenile on the authority of the probation officer is a reversion to the pre-Gault era where the probation officer occupied too many roles. We do not propose to reinvest the probation officer with the role of prosecutor. At the complaint or referral stage in a juvenile case the probation officer may, as the statute provides, examine complaints "for the purpose of considering the commencement of proceedings * * *." The probation officer could decide that the matter should not be referred to the county attorney for the filing of a petition; that it be adjusted. The juvenile code, however, no longer leaves the decision solely to the probation officer. The decision to file a petition is now a function of the prosecutor. In his discretion the county attorney may, notwithstanding the opinion of the probation officer, deem it necessary in the public interest to file a petition alleging delinquent behavior. We believe this construction of the juvenile code and our rules is in harmony with due process and the changes in the juvenile system of justice.

Counsel for the juvenile argues that the prosecutorial freedom to file a petition without establishment of probable cause violates the juvenile's right to equal protection of the laws. U.S. Const. amend. XIV; A.R.S.Const. art. 2 § 13.

In In re Maricopa County, Juvenile Action, 18 Ariz.App. 560, 504 P.2d 501 (1972), a juvenile appellant attacked the validity of the juvenile appellate procedures, claiming that the shorter time limits for juvenile appeals violated equal protection. The Court of Appeals stated:

> "Appellant's equal protection argument breaks down under analysis, for the Equal Protection Clause of the 14th Amendment to the U.S. Constitution does not require that all persons be treated alike, only that individuals within a certain class be treated equally and that there exist reasonable grounds for the classification. [Citations omitted.] In this regard, appellant admits there exists a reasonable ground for treating juvenile offenders in a different classification than adults." 18 Ariz.App. at 565, 504 P.2d at 506.

We believe that the same principle applies to this issue. The separate and comprehensive statutory and procedural system applicable to persons under the age of eighteen is a classification based upon the obvious difference between the maturity of adults and children. Under the juvenile system the often severe consequences following conviction of crime have been avoided by substituting civil penalties of limited duration and consequence. See A.R.S. §§ 8–207 and 8–246. We believe the classification to be reasonable and furnishes the basis for the different treatment of the class.

Gault did not require that a juvenile receive all the requirements of a criminal trial. See Application of Gault, 387 U.S. at 30, 87 S.Ct. at 1445, 18 L.Ed.2d at 548. The matter of the petition in juvenile court was considered in *Gault*, and the court held that the petition must give notice of the charges which would be deemed constitutionally adequate in a civil or criminal proceedings. Id., 387 U.S. at 33, 87 S.Ct. at 1446, 18 L.Ed.2d at 549. No requirement for establishment of probable cause prior to filing was mentioned.

The United States Supreme Court in McKeiver v. Pennsylvania, 403 U.S. 528, 91 S.Ct. 1976, 29 L.Ed.2d 647 (1971) cautioned that all rights constitutionally assured for adults accused of crime are not imposed upon a state juvenile proceeding. The court then held that there was no constitutional right to a jury trial in juvenile court.

We do not believe that either "due process" or "equal protection" requires the establishment of probable cause before filing a petition in juvenile court. We note in passing that the juvenile rules have recently been amended to provide additional protection to a juvenile who may be subject to detention pending action by the juvenile court. 17A A.R.S. Juv.Ct.Rules of Proc., rule 3 as amended, 1978. The amended rule now requires that a determination of probable cause be made that the juvenile committed the acts alleged before the juvenile can be detained.

Finding the judgment and rulings of the juvenile court legally correct, we affirm the judgment.

CAMERON, C.J., STRUCKMEYER, V.C.J., and HAYS and GORDON, JJ., concur.

IJA–ABA JUVENILE JUSTICE STANDARDS, STANDARDS
RELATING TO THE JUVENILE PROBATION FUNC-
TION: INTAKE AND PREDISPOSITION INVESTI-
GATIVE SERVICES (1980)

Section V: Scope of Intake Officer's Dispositional Powers

**2.16   * Role of intake officer and prosecutor in filing of petition:
right of complainant to file a petition.**

A. If the intake officer determines that a petition should be
filed, the officer should submit a written report to the appropriate
prosecuting official requesting that a petition should be filed. The
officer should also submit a written statement of his or her decision
and of the reasons for the decision to the juvenile and his or her
parents or legal guardian. All petitions should be countersigned and
filed by the appropriate prosecuting official. The prosecutor may
refuse the request of the intake officer to file a petition. Any
determination by the prosecutor that a petition should not be filed
should be final.

B. If the intake officer determines that a petition should not be
filed, the officer should notify the complainant of his or her decision
and of the reasons for the decision and should advise the complainant
that he or she may submit the complaint to the appropriate prosecuting official for review. Upon receiving a request for review, the
prosecutor should consider the facts presented by the complainant,
consult with the intake officer who made the initial decision, and then
make the final determination as to whether a petition should be filed.

C. In the absence of a complainant's request for a review of the
intake officer's determination that a petition should not be filed, the
intake officer should notify the appropriate prosecuting official of the
officer's decision not to request the filing of a petition in those cases
in which the conduct charged would constitute a crime if committed
by an adult. The prosecutor should have the right in all such cases,
after consultation with the intake officer, to file a petition.

REPORT OF THE NATIONAL ADVISORY COMMITTEE
FOR JUVENILE JUSTICE AND DELINQUENCY PRE-
VENTION, STANDARDS FOR THE ADMINISTRA-
TION OF JUVENILE JUSTICE (U.S. Depart-
ment of Justice, 1980).

3.143   Criteria for Intake Decisions—Delinquency

State and local agencies responsible for intake services should
develop and publish written guidelines and rules regarding intake
decisions for complaints based on the delinquency jurisdiction of the
family court.

* Reprinted with permission from Standards Relating to the Juvenile Probation
Function: Intake and Predisposition Investigative Services, Copyright 1980, Ballinger Publishing Company.

In determining what disposition of a sufficient delinquency complaint best serves the interests of the community and of the juvenile, the following factors should be considered:

a.   The seriousness of the alleged offense;

b.   The role of the juvenile in that offense;

c.   The nature and number of contacts with the intake unit and family court that the juvenile has had and the results of those contacts;

d.   The juvenile's age and maturity; and

e.   The availability of appropriate services outside the juvenile justice system.

Referral for services or dismissal should not be precluded for the sole reason that the complainant objects or that the juvenile denies the allegations.

Sources:

See generally Institute of Judicial Administration/American Bar Association Joint Commission on Juvenile Justice Standards, Standards Relating to the Juvenile Probation Function: Intake and Predisposition Investigative Services, Standards 1.6 and 1.8 (tentative draft, 1977) [hereinafter cited as IJA/ABA, Probation Function].

Commentary

This standard outlines the basis on which intake officers should make the intake decisions described in Standard 3.142. Although the standard sets forth the general criteria to be used, detailed rules and guidelines should be developed to operationalize these criteria and other procedures and to promote consistency in intake decisions. See, e.g., Florida Department of Health and Rehabilitative Services, Manual: Intake for Delinquency and Dependency Juvenile Programs, Section 5.6.1(b)(i-xiii) (1976). The family court and the state and local agencies, departments, and programs affected by intake decisions should participate in the development of these guidelines, but final responsibility for their promulgation should rest with the agency directly responsible for the provision of intake services. *The National Advisory Committee recommends the development of rules and guidelines governing intake decisions as an action that states can take immediately, without a major reallocation of resources, to improve the administration of juvenile justice.*

The standard outlines five criteria on which intake decisions in delinquency cases should be based. These five factors should be considered in concert with each other in reaching the intake decision.

The first criterion listed is the seriousness of the delinquent conduct, i.e., the nature and extent of harm to others resulting from the alleged offense. The provision approved by the IJA/ABA Joint Commission on which this standard is based lists as specific criteria: "whether the conduct caused death or personal injury, severity of personal injury, extent of property damage, value of property damaged or taken, whether property taken is recovered and whether victim was threatened or intimidated by display of weapons, physical force or verbally." IJA/ABA, Probation Function, supra at 1.8(b)(1). See also Florida, Manual, supra at 5.6.1(b); California Proposed Juvenile Court Rules, Rule 1307 (tentatively adopted, May 1976). Others have suggested that a serious offense be defined in terms of the felony-misdemeanor distinction or in terms of a list of specified offenses. See, e.g., Ferster, Courtless, and Snethen, "Separating Official and Unofficial Delinquents: Juvenile Court Intake," 55 Iowa L.Rev. 874 (1970); California Juvenile Court Deskbook, Section 4.7 (1972). However, juveniles who commit some acts that are technically felonies or one of the enumerated offenses, may not constitute such a threat to society as to warrant judicial handling of the matter on that basis. The President's Commission on Crime in the District of Columbia, Report, 661 (1966); R. Kobetz and B. Bosarge, Juvenile Justice Administration, 247–248 (International Association of Chiefs of Police, 1973).

The second criterion is the role that the juvenile allegedly played in the offense. The provision adopted by the IJA/ABA Joint Commission proposes that when a group of juveniles are alleged to have committed a delinquent act together, equity requires that they be treated alike. Hence, in a leader/follower situation, if the intake officer determines on the basis of the seriousness of the prior record and other factors that a petition should be filed against the leader of the group, a petition should ordinarily be filed against all. Although not intending to denigrate the importance of equal treatment, the National Advisory Committee goes no further than recommending role as an appropriate point to consider.

The third criterion is the nature, number, and result of prior contacts with intake services and the family court. See Standards 1.531–1.534. Information regarding past referrals and the juvenile's response to them seems essential if diversion for services is to be retained and encouraged as an alternative, and there is little doubt that prior adjudications are relevant to intake decisions. Use of such records does imply that the threshold decision on whether a delinquency case should or should not proceed may be based, in part, on unproven allegations. This use appears little different than the commonly accepted practice of using arrest records in determining dispositions and sentences in delinquency and criminal proceedings. To assure that incomplete or inaccurate information is not used and that unwarranted assumptions are not made from records of prior contacts, the standard requires that the results of any prior contact— not only the nature and number of those contacts—be considered and that the right to counsel be extended to intake proceedings. See Standards. 1.54–1.56, 3.132, and 3.133. The IJA/ABA Joint Commission and a number of commentators and standards-setting groups have endorsed consideration of a juvenile's prior contacts with intake and the family court. See, e.g., IJA/ABA, Probation Function, supra; Kobetz and Bosarge, supra at 248; President's Commission on Law

(handwritten margin note) But some felonies don't pose juvenile as a threat to society!

Enforcement and the Administration of Justice, Task Force Report on Juvenile Justice and Youth Crime, 17 (1967); Ferster, Courtless, and Snethen, supra at 1151; see also Florida, Manual, supra at 5.6.1(b); California Proposed Juvenile Court Rules, supra. Standards 1.51–1.56 govern the retention and dissemination of such records.

The fourth consideration is the juvenile's age and maturity. The fact that a particular juvenile is ten or seventeen years of age should not in and of itself be determinative whether or not to recommend the filing of a petition. It must be weighed together with all of the other factors. See IJA/ABA, Probation Function, supra; Florida, Manual, supra.

The final criterion is the availability of services outside the juvenile justice system that are suited to the juvenile's needs. The unavailability of services should not necessarily imply that a petition should be filed when other criteria suggest that dismissal of the complaint is the proper disposition.

Absent from this list are factors such as school attendance and behavior and the juvenile's relationship with his/her family. See, e.g., Kobetz and Bosarge, supra, at 248; Florida, Manual, supra; California Proposed Juvenile Court Rules, supra. Serious questions can be raised regarding the equity in differentiating between two youths accused of burglary or armed robbery on the basis of their school attendance or ability to communicate with their parents. However, if the listed criteria point to dismissal, these social factors may be considered in determining which if any available services may be appropriate.

Also absent is consideration of the accused youth's "attitude." See IJA/ABA, Probation Function, supra at Standard 1.8; Kobetz and Bosarge, supra at 248; Florida, Manual, supra; California Proposed Juvenile Court Rules, supra. As noted in President's Commission on Law Enforcement and Administration of Justice, Task Force Report: Juvenile Justice and Youth Crime, 17 (1967):

> Even more troubling is the question of the significance of a juvenile's demeanor. Is his attitude, remorseful or defiant, a sound measure of his suitability for pre-judicial handling? Can the police, or anyone else for that matter, accurately detect the difference between feigned and genuine resolve to mend one's ways, or between genuine indifference to the law's commands and fear engendered defiance?

Finally, the standard urges that a recommendation to file a petition should not be made merely because the subject of a complaint is unwilling to acknowledge responsibility or the complainant objects to a dismissal of the complaint. However, as is noted in the Commentary to Standard 3.142, if a juvenile, after consultation with counsel, requests a judicial determination of the allegations, that request should be honored.

3.144   Criteria for Intake Decisions—Noncriminal Misbehavior

State and local agencies responsible for intake services should develop and publish written guidelines and rules regarding intake decisions for complaints based on the jurisdiction of the family court over noncriminal misbehavior.

In determining what disposition of a sufficient noncriminal misbehavior complaint best serves the interests of the juvenile, the family, and the community, the following factors should be considered:

a. The seriousness of the alleged conduct and the circumstances in which it occurred;

b. The age and maturity of the juvenile with regard to whom the complaint was filed;

c. The nature and number of contacts with the intake unit and the family court that the subject of the complaint and his/her family has had;

d. The outcome of those contacts, including the services to which the juvenile and/or family have been referred and the results of those referrals; and

e. The availability of appropriate services outside the juvenile justice system.

Referral for services or dismissal should not be precluded for the sole reason that the complainant objects or that the person named in the complaint denies the allegations.

Sources:

Standard 3.144 is based on the jurisdiction of the family court over noncriminal misbehavior defined in Standard 3.112 and draws on criteria set forth in Institute of Judicial Administration/American Bar Association Joint Commission on Juvenile Justice Standards, Standards Relating to the Juvenile Probation Function: Intake Predisposition Investigative Services, Standards 1.6 and 1.8 (tentative draft, 1977).

Commentary

This standard outlines the issues to be considered in making the intake decision on complaints filed under the noncriminal misbehavior jurisdiction of the family court. Although similar to the criteria specified for intake in delinquency cases, the criteria in this standard focus on the family rather than the juvenile alone and are designed to fulfill the requirement in Standard 3.112 that "the family court should not exercise its jurisdiction over noncriminal misbehavior unless all available and appropriate noncoercive alternatives to assist the juvenile and his/her family have been exhausted. Also in keeping with the provisions of Standard 3.112, the term "seriousness" in paragraph (a) is intended to refer to such factors as the length of the juvenile's absences from home, the number of days missed from school, and the nature of the parental demand disregarded or misused, rather than to the extent of harm caused to others.

As in Standard 3.143 the *National Advisory Committee recommends the development of rules and guidelines governing the intake process in noncriminal misbehavior cases as an action that each state can take immediately, without a major reallocation of resources, to improve the administration of juvenile justice.* The development of such guidelines is especially critical for noncriminal misbehavior cases because of the abuses to which this type of jurisdiction has been subject, see Commentary to Standard 3.112, and the emphasis in these standards on the use of voluntary services. Although the rules and guidelines should be issued by the agency responsible for intake, see e.g., Florida Department of Health and Rehabilitative Services, Manual: Intake for Delinquency and Dependency Juvenile Programs (1976), the family court and the state and local agencies, departments, and programs affected by intake decisions should participate in their development.

2. JUVENILES' RIGHTS DURING INTAKE

a. THE "RIGHT" TO DIVERSION

In the adult criminal justice system, more or less formal diversion programs have been established in many jurisdictions. Basically a diversion program is one in which the individual is subjected to less than the full course of criminal proceedings provided he participates in some rehabilitation program. In the juvenile justice system the functions regularly performed by an intake staff have been partly formalized by statutory establishment of juvenile diversion programs. In a sense, the juvenile diversion program is a modern label—in terms of function—for the older terms "informal handling"—"consent decrees"—"informal probation"—"informal adjustment"—"unofficial handling." They ordinarily, however, have in common one characteristic that is—at least formally—lacking in the older and, indeed current, systems: there is recognition in formal law of authority to retain control over the juvenile on diversion and, under some circumstances and with appropriate safeguards, to terminate diversion and return the individual to the formal adjudicative process. This trend raises the question whether the intake process requires the same or similar constitutional domestication that the Supreme Court ultimately imposed on the adjudicative process in *Gault* and *Winship*.

The student should also keep the problem of the cost of diversion in mind. Extensive diversionary programs demand funding and trained personnel. It has been recommended that the juvenile justice system be restructured so that money intended for expansion of juvenile police, court, and correctional facilities be instead used for increased diversionary purposes. Note, "Funding Juvenile Justice," 60 Iowa L.Rev. 1149 at 1300 (1975). In this way, it is argued, the available money is being used more effectively since diversion may have greater potential for successful rehabilitation than traditional corrections. Id. at 1300.

Once it is determined that funding should be allocated to diversionary programs, the question arises as to the source of the funding. In In the Matter of 1978 Passaic County Budget Relating to Juvenile and Domestic Relations Court, 165 N.J.Super. 598, 398 A.2d 1295 (1979), the New Jersey Superior Court held that "since the intake service program is an integral part of the juvenile and domestic relations justice system, for the administration of which the Supreme Court has exclusive authority, the judiciary has the inherent power to order it financed by [the counties]." 398 A.2d at 1297.

WEST'S REVISED CODE OF WASHINGTON ANNOTATED
(1983 PP. Supp.) Chapter 13.40, Juvenile Justice
Act of 1977

13.40.070. Complaints alleging offenses—Screening of, scope—Filing information, when—Diversion of case, when—Motion to modify community supervision—Notification of parent or guardian—Probation counselor may act for prosecutor, when

(1) Complaints referred to the juvenile court alleging the commission of an offense shall be referred directly to the prosecutor. The prosecutor, upon receipt of a complaint, shall screen the complaint to determine whether:

(a) The alleged facts bring the case within the jurisdiction of the court; and

(b) On a basis of available evidence there is probable cause to believe that the juvenile did commit the offense.

(2) If the identical alleged acts constitute an offense under both the law of this state and an ordinance of any city or county of this state, state law shall govern the prosecutor's screening and charging decision for both filed and diverted cases.

(3) If the requirements of subsections (1)(a) and (b) of this section are met, the prosecutor shall either file an information in juvenile court or divert the case, as set forth in subsections (5), (6), and (7) of this section. If the prosecutor neither files nor diverts the case, he shall maintain a record, for one year, of such decision and the reasons therefor. In lieu of filing an information or diverting an offense a prosecutor may file a motion to modify community supervision where such offense constitutes a violation of community supervision.

(4) An information shall be a plain, concise, and definite written statement of the essential facts constituting the offense charged. It shall be signed by the prosecuting attorney and conform to chapter 10.37 RCW.

(5) Where a case is legally sufficient, the prosecutor shall file an information with the juvenile court if:

(a) An alleged offender is accused of a class A felony, a class B felony, an attempt to commit a class B felony, assault in the third degree, rape in the third degree, or any other offense listed in RCW 13.40.020(1)(b) or (c); or

(b) An alleged offender is accused of a felony and has a criminal history of at least one class A or class B felony, or two class C felonies, or at least two gross misdemeanors, or at least two misdemeanors and one additional misdemeanor or gross misdemeanor, or at least one class C felony and one misdemeanor or gross misdemeanor; or

(c) An alleged offender has been referred by a diversion unit for prosecution or desires prosecution instead of diversion.

(6) Where a case is legally sufficient the prosecutor shall divert the case if the alleged offense is a misdemeanor or gross misdemeanor or violation and the alleged offense(s) in combination with the alleged offender's criminal history do not exceed three offenses or violations and do not include any felonies: *Provided,* That if the alleged offender is charged with a related offense that must or may be filed under subsections (5) and (7) of this section, a case under this subsection may also be filed.

(7) Where a case is legally sufficient and falls into neither subsection (5) nor (6) of this section, it may be filed or diverted. In deciding whether to file or divert an offense under this section the prosecutor shall be guided only by the length, seriousness, and recency of the alleged offender's criminal history and the circumstances surrounding the commission of the alleged offense.

(8) Whenever a juvenile is placed in custody or, where not placed in custody, referred to a diversionary interview, the parent or legal guardian of the juvenile shall be notified as soon as possible concerning the allegation made against the juvenile and the current status of the juvenile.

(9) The responsibilities of the prosecutor under subsections (1) through (8) of this section may be performed by a juvenile court probation counselor for any complaint referred to the court alleging the commission of an offense which would not be a felony if committed by an adult, if the prosecutor has given sufficient written notice to the juvenile court that the prosecutor will not review such complaints.

13.40.080. Diversion agreement—Defined—Scope—Modification— Limitations on—Divertee's rights—Diversionary unit's powers and duties—Use of fines—Termination of authority to impose or collect fines

(1) A diversion agreement shall be a contract between a juvenile accused of an offense and a diversionary unit whereby the juvenile agrees to fulfill certain conditions in lieu of prosecution. Such agreements may be entered into only after the prosecutor, or probation counselor pursuant to this chapter, has determined that probable

cause exists to believe that a crime has been committed and that the juvenile committed it.

(2) A diversion agreement shall be limited to:

(a) Community service not to exceed one hundred fifty hours, not to be performed during school hours if the juvenile is attending school;

(b) Restitution limited to the amount of actual loss incurred by the victim, and to an amount the juvenile has the means or potential means to pay;

(c) Attendance at up to two hours of counseling and/or up to ten hours of educational or informational sessions at a community agency: *Provided,* That the state shall not be liable for costs resulting from the diversionary unit exercising the option to permit diversion agreements to mandate attendance at up to two hours of counseling and/or up to ten hours of educational or informational sessions; and

(d) A fine, not to exceed one hundred dollars. In determining the amount of the fine, the diversion unit shall consider only the juvenile's financial resources and whether the juvenile has the means to pay the fine. The diversion unit shall not consider the financial resources of the juvenile's parents, guardian, or custodian in determining the fine to be imposed.

(3) In assessing periods of community service to be performed and restitution to be paid by a juvenile who has entered into a diversion agreement, the court officer to whom this task is assigned shall to the extent possible involve members of the community. Such members of the community shall meet with the juvenile and advise the court officer as to the terms of the diversion agreement and shall supervise the juvenile in carrying out its terms.

(4) A diversion agreement may not exceed a period of six months for a misdemeanor or gross misdemeanor or one year for a felony and may include a period extending beyond the eighteenth birthday of the divertee. Any restitution assessed during its term may not exceed an amount which the juvenile could be reasonably expected to pay during this period. If additional time is necessary for the juvenile to complete restitution to the victim, the time period limitations of this subsection may be extended by an additional six months.

(5) The juvenile shall retain the right to be referred to the court at any time prior to the signing of the diversion agreement.

(6) Divertees and potential divertees shall be afforded due process in all contacts with a diversionary unit regardless of whether the juveniles are accepted for diversion or whether the diversion program is successfully completed. Such due process shall include, but not be limited to, the following:

(a) A written diversion agreement shall be executed stating all conditions in clearly understandable language;

(b) Violation of the terms of the agreement shall be the only grounds for termination;

(c) No divertee may be terminated from a diversion program without being given a court hearing, which hearing shall be preceded by:

(i) Written notice of alleged violations of the conditions of the diversion program; and

(ii) Disclosure of all evidence to be offered against the divertee;

(d) The hearing shall be conducted by the juvenile court and shall include:

(i) Opportunity to be heard in person and to present evidence;

(ii) The right to confront and cross-examine all adverse witnesses;

(iii) A written statement by the court as to the evidence relied on and the reasons for termination, should that be the decision; and

(iv) Demonstration by evidence that the divertee has substantially violated the terms of his or her diversion agreement.

(e) The prosecutor may file an information on the offense for which the divertee was diverted:

(i) In juvenile court if the divertee is under eighteen years of age; or

(ii) In superior court or the appropriate court of limited jurisdiction if the divertee is eighteen years of age or older.

(7) The diversion unit shall be responsible for advising a divertee of his or her rights as provided in this chapter.

(8) The right to counsel shall inure prior to the initial interview for purposes of advising the juvenile as to whether he or she desires to participate in the diversion process or to appear in the juvenile court. The juvenile may be represented by counsel at any critical stage of the diversion process, including intake interviews and termination hearings. The juvenile shall be fully advised at the intake of his or her right to an attorney and of the relevant services an attorney can provide. For the purpose of this section, intake interviews mean all interviews regarding the diversion agreement process.

The juvenile shall be advised that a diversion agreement shall constitute a part of the juvenile's criminal history as defined by RCW 13.40.020(6) as now or hereafter amended. A signed acknowledgment of such advisement shall be obtained from the juvenile, and the document shall be maintained by the diversionary unit together with the diversion agreement, and a copy of both documents shall be delivered to the prosecutor if requested by the prosecutor. The supreme court shall promulgate rules setting forth the content of such advisement in simple language.

(9) When a juvenile enters into a diversion agreement, the juvenile court may receive only the following information for dispositional purposes:

(a) The fact that a charge or charges were made;

(b) The fact that a diversion agreement was entered into;

(c) The juvenile's obligations under such agreement;

(d) Whether the alleged offender performed his or her obligations under such agreement; and

(e) The facts of the alleged offense.

(10) A diversionary unit may refuse to enter into a diversion agreement with a juvenile. It shall immediately refer such juvenile to the court for action and shall forward to the court the criminal complaint and a detailed statement of its reasons for refusing to enter into a diversion agreement. The diversionary unit shall also immediately refer the case to the prosecuting attorney for action if such juvenile violates the terms of the diversion agreement.

(11) A diversionary unit may, in instances where it determines that the act or omission of an act for which a juvenile has been referred to it involved no victim, or where it determines that the juvenile referred to it has no prior criminal history and is alleged to have committed an illegal act involving no threat of or instance of actual physical harm and involving not more than fifty dollars in property loss or damage and that there is no loss outstanding to the person or firm suffering such damage or loss, counsel and release or release such a juvenile without entering into a diversion agreement: *Provided,* That any juvenile so handled shall be advised that the act or omission of any act for which he or she had been referred shall constitute a part of the juvenile's criminal history as defined by RCW 13.40.020(6) as now or hereafter amended. A signed acknowledgment of such advisement shall be obtained from the juvenile, and the document shall be maintained by the unit, and a copy of the document shall be delivered to the prosecutor if requested by the prosecutor. The supreme court shall promulgate rules setting forth the content of such advisement in simple language: *Provided further,* That a juvenile determined to be eligible by a diversionary unit for such release shall retain the same right to counsel and right to have his or her case referred to the court for formal action as any other juvenile referred to the unit.

(12) A diversion unit may supervise the fulfillment of a diversion agreement entered into before the juvenile's eighteenth birthday and which includes a period extending beyond the divertee's eighteenth birthday.

(13) If a fine required by a diversion agreement cannot reasonably be paid due to a change of circumstance, the diversion agreement may be modified at the request of the divertee and with the concurrence of the diversion unit to convert an unpaid fine into community service. The modification of the diversion agreement shall be in writing and signed by the divertee and the diversion unit. The

number of hours of community service in lieu of a monetary penalty shall be converted at the rate of the prevailing state minimum wage per hour.

(14) Fines imposed under this section shall be collected and paid into the county general fund in accordance with procedures established by the juvenile court administrator under RCW 13.04.040 and may be used only for juvenile services. In the expenditure of funds for juvenile services, there shall be a maintenance of effort whereby counties exhaust existing resources before using amounts collected under this section.

(15) The authority to impose and collect fines under this section shall terminate on June 30, 1985.

STATE v. CHATHAM
Court of Appeals of Washington, 1981.
28 Wash.App. 580, 624 P.2d 1180.

ANDERSEN, JUDGE.

FACTS OF CASE

Charles C. Chatham, a juvenile at the time of the events herein, appeals his juvenile court conviction of simple assault. RCW 9A.36.040.

The charge arose from an altercation between a group of juveniles (including Chatham) and several adult golfers at the Fairwood Golf Club near Kent, Washington. During the altercation, one of the golfers sustained a serious and permanent eye injury caused, as the juvenile court later determined, by blows struck by the juvenile Chatham. At least one of the juveniles involved in the melee was armed with a club.

This appeal involves the juvenile's right to "diversion", as that term is used in this State's Juvenile Justice Act of 1977, RCW 13.40.[47] That act established a comprehensive system for the disposition of complaints lodged against juveniles. One such disposition is a juvenile diversion program in which eligible juvenile offenders perform community services as an alternative to prosecution. RCW 13.40.080. The diversion unit is a community-based correctional unit where local citizens enter into contracts (diversion agreements) with eligible juveniles to pay restitution and perform community service in lieu of prosecution. See Comment, Diversion Agreements Under Washington's Juvenile Justice Act of 1977, 14 Gonz.L.Rev. 423 (1978–1979).

In diverting this juvenile's case, a member of the prosecuting attorney's staff phoned the chairperson of the local diversion unit, the Kent Conference Committee, and related the facts of the case as they appeared from the police reports. The chairperson thereupon declined to accept diversion of the juvenile's case because the serious

---

[47] It should be noted that many procedural aspects of juvenile cases are governed by Juvenile Court Rules (JuCR) promulgated by the State Supreme Court, and in King County, by Local Juvenile Court Rules (LJuCR).

nature of this case did not fall within the committee's eligibility standards for diversion.

The case then went before the juvenile court for an adjudicatory hearing and the defendant was found guilty of assault as charged. One ultimate issue is presented by this appeal.

ISSUE

Was reversible error committed in the manner in which the juvenile's diversion was handled and rejected?

DECISION

CONCLUSION. Although the juvenile did have a right to have his case referred to a diversionary unit, that unit also had the right to refuse to enter into a diversionary agreement with him. The procedures employed herein did not, under the circumstances presented, violate the juvenile's due process or other legal rights.

A juvenile's eligibility for diversion is determined by statute. RCW 13.40.070–.080. See JuCR 6.1.

Since the juvenile in this case was a first offender not charged with a felony, he had a right to have his case referred to a diversionary unit, RCW 13.40.070(5); and the prosecuting attorney's office, in turn, had the duty to so refer it, RCW 13.40.070(6).

The juvenile contends that the procedures used resulted in his being denied his right to be handled by a diversion unit, did not comply with the provisions of the juvenile code and denied him due process of law by forcing him to proceed with an adjudicatory hearing which he was entitled to avoid. RCW 13.40.080(6). We do not agree.

The juvenile's statutory right to have his or her case referred to a diversion unit does not guarantee that the unit will enter into a diversion agreement with the juvenile. Diversion is not always an appropriate disposition, even in first-offender juvenile cases.

As one of the sponsors of the legislation which resulted in the new juvenile code has written concerning the purpose of diversion:

> Diversion represents the intent to preserve a species of informal adjustment for those youngsters whose offenses have been so few and so minor that involvement with a court would be counter-productive. The intent is to foster community accountability boards, a means for straightening out youthful offenders that has proved both popular and effective in the past.

(Footnote omitted.) M. Becker, Washington State's New Juvenile Code: An Introduction, 14 Gonz.L.Rev. 289, 308 (1978–1979).

The juvenile code grants a diversion unit the authority to exercise sound discretion and to reject a case referred to it for diversion:

> A diversionary unit may refuse to enter into a diversion agreement with a juvenile. It shall immediately refer such juvenile to the court for action and shall forward to the court the

criminal complaint and a detailed statement of its reasons for refusing to enter into a diversion agreement.

RCW 13.40.080(10) (part). By providing that the reasons for refusing to enter a diversion agreement be in writing, the statute assures fair and reasoned decisions for rejecting diversion and insures juvenile court control over the fairness of the procedure. The informal phone conversation by which this juvenile was referred and rejected prompted the juvenile court to conduct a special hearing into the reasons for rejecting this juvenile's diversion referral.

The chairperson of the Kent Conference Committee testified at that hearing that in order to accommodate 300 to 350 diversions a year, the committee delegates to her the task of conducting a prescreening of diversion referrals to see that each one meets the committee's minimum standards of acceptance. These minimum standards excluded those cases involving serious injury or weapons from further consideration for diversion.

This prescreening by the chairperson of the diversionary unit is done, according to her uncontroverted testimony, prior to the juvenile being notified and appearing and prior to the invocation of the detailed diversionary procedures provided by the juvenile code. See RCW 13.40.080; JuCR 6.1–6.6.

Of some 300 cases handled, the chairperson testified that this was the only case she could recall in which the prescreening procedure was not carried out in writing. Thus the usual prescreening by the diversion unit is handled in accordance with the course outlined by statute, RCW 13.40.080(10), set out above.

Satisfied that the committee standards used in refusing this juvenile's diversion provided a reasonable and fair basis for rejecting the diversion referral, the juvenile court determined any errors in the procedural handling of the matter were merely formalistic and not prejudicial.

Although the informal procedures followed in this case are not exemplary, the juvenile's case was referred to a diversionary unit, was considered by that unit through its authorized representative and was rejected for reasons that were neither arbitrary nor capricious. The juvenile court was satisfied that this juvenile's diversion was unacceptable to the diversion unit and that, therefore, no purpose would be served by sending the case back to perform some ritualistic paper work. We agree.

The prescreening procedure of the diversionary unit in this case is not prohibited by statute, and is contemplated by RCW 13.40.080(10), set out above. Because the rejection of this juvenile's referral was based on standardized safeguards properly adopted and reasonably applied to determine candidates with whom the committee would be likely to enter diversion agreements, it is not violative of due process. On these facts, exercise of some degree of informality in these preliminary proceedings did not deprive the defendant of a fair and reasoned decision or deny him his right to due process. See In re Noble, 15 Wash.App. 51, 57, 547 P.2d 880 (1976).

Affirmed.

SWANSON and WILLIAMS, JJ., concur.

NOTE

There are striking differences of view about whether all juvenile offenders should be eligible for consideration for diversion or whether only "minor offenders" should merit consideration, or even whether only repeat misdemeanor offenders and first time felony offenders should be eligible. Another difference in the statutory schemes is the extent to which the legislature should provide specific procedures or guidelines for diversion. For example, the Kansas Judicial Council drafted and recommended for adoption a detailed and specific diversion procedure—see Reynolds, Survey of Kansas Law: Juvenile Law, 32 Kans.L.Rev. 371 at 387 (1984)—but the legislature produced the result printed immediately below.

KANSAS STATUTES ANNOTATED (1983 Cum.Supp.)

38–1635. Diversion. Each court may adopt a policy and establish guidelines for a diversion program by which a respondent who has not been previously adjudged to be a juvenile offender may avoid such an adjudication.

COLORADO REVISED STATUTES (1983 Cum.Supp.)

19–2.5–101. Juvenile diversion program—authorization. (1) In order to more fully implement the stated objectives of this title, the general assembly declares its intent to establish a juvenile diversion program to provide community-based alternatives to the formal court system that will reduce juvenile crime and recidivism, change juvenile offenders' behavior and attitudes, and reduce the costs within the juvenile justice system.

(2) The division of youth services in the department of institutions is authorized to establish and administer a juvenile diversion program. In order to effectuate the program, the division may contract with governmental units and nongovernmental agencies to provide services for eligible youth, as defined in section 19–2.5–103, through community-based projects providing an alternative to a petition filed pursuant to section 19–3–101, an adjudicatory hearing pursuant to section 19–3–106, or dispositions of a delinquent pursuant to section 19–3–113.

19–2.5–102. Definitions. As used in this article, unless the context otherwise requires:

(1) "Director" means the executive director of the department of institutions.

(2) "Governmental unit" means any county, city and county, city, town, judicial district attorney office, or school district.

(3) "Nongovernmental agency" means any person, private nonprofit agency, corporation, association, or other nongovernmental agency.

(4) "Services" may include, but is not limited to, provision of diagnostic needs assessment, general counseling and counseling during a crisis situation, specialized tutoring, job training and placement, restitution programs, constructive recreational activities, and follow-up activities.

19–2.5–103. Eligible youth. Juveniles eligible for services under this article are those who have been taken into temporary custody more than once for crimes which would have constituted a misdemeanor if committed by an adult or once for a crime which would have constituted a felony if committed by an adult.

19–2.5–104. Criteria for program eligibility. (1) Projects soliciting service contracts pursuant to section 19–2.5–101(2) must demonstrate that they meet the following eligibility requirements:

(a) Meet a demonstrated community need as shown by a survey of the type of community, its special circumstances, and the type and number of youth who will be served by the project;

(b) Provide services that do not duplicate services already provided in the community;

(c) Show community support of the project through receipt of nonstate funds or in-kind supplies or services to meet at least twenty-five percent of the total cost of the project.

19–2.5–105. Application by project. When applying for a contract with the division of youth services to provide services to youths under the juvenile diversion program, a community project shall submit for review by the division a list of the project's objectives, a report of the progress made during the previous year if applicable toward implementing the stated objectives, an annual budget, and such other documentation as may be required by the director.

19–2.5–106. Evaluation. (1) Each project providing services under this article shall develop objectives and report progress toward such objectives as required by rules and regulations promulgated by the director.

(2) The director shall regularly monitor these diversion projects to insure that progress is being made to accomplish the objectives of this article.

FLORIDA STATUTES ANNOTATED (1983 PP.Supp.)

39.331. Community arbitration program

(1) Any county may establish a community arbitration program designed to complement the juvenile intake process provided in this chapter. The program shall provide one or more community juvenile arbitrators or community juvenile arbitration panels to hear cases informally involving alleged commissions of certain offenses by children.

(2) Cases which may be heard by a community juvenile arbitrator or arbitration panel shall be limited to those involving misdemeanors and violations of local ordinances which have been agreed upon, in writing, as being subject to community arbitration by the state attorney, senior circuit court judge assigned to juvenile cases in the circuit, and the Department of Health and Rehabilitative Services.

39.332. Community juvenile arbitrators

(1) Each community juvenile arbitrator or member of a community arbitration panel shall be selected by the chief judge of the circuit, the senior circuit court judge assigned to juvenile cases in the circuit, and the state attorney.

(2) A community juvenile arbitrator or member of a community arbitration panel may be a person specially trained or experienced in juvenile causes and the problems of persons likely to appear before him, but shall be:

(a) Either a graduate of an accredited law school or of an accredited school with a degree in behavioral social work or trained in conflict resolution techniques; and

(b) A person of the temperament necessary to deal properly with the cases and persons likely to appear before him.

39.333. Procedure for initiating cases for arbitration

(1) Any law enforcement officer or other person authorized under the program may issue a complaint, along with a recommendation for arbitration against any child whom such officer or person has reason to believe has committed any offense that is eligible for arbitration. The complaint shall specify the offense and the reasons why the law enforcement officer or authorized person feels that the offense should be handled by arbitration. A copy of the complaint shall be forwarded to the appropriate intake officer and the parent or legal guardian of the child. In addition to the complaint, the child's parent or legal guardian shall be informed of the objectives of the arbitration process, the conditions and procedures under which it will be conducted, and the fact that it is not obligatory. The intake officer shall contact the child's parent or legal guardian within 3 days after the date on which the complaint was forwarded. At this time, the child's parent or legal guardian shall inform the intake officer of the decision to approve or reject the handling of the complaint through arbitration.

(2) If the child's parent or legal guardian rejects the handling of the complaint through arbitration, the intake officer shall consult with the state attorney or assistant state attorney for the possible filing of formal juvenile proceedings.

(3) If the child's parent or legal guardian accepts the handling of the complaint through arbitration, the intake officer shall provide copies of the complaint to the arbitrator or panel within 24 hours.

(4) The arbitrator or panel shall, upon receipt of the complaint, set a time and date for a hearing within 7 days and shall inform the child's parent or legal guardian, the complaining witness, and any victims of the time, date, and place of the hearing.

39.334. Arbitration hearings

(1) The law enforcement officer or authorized person who issued the complaint need not appear at the scheduled hearing. However, prior to the hearing, he shall file with the community arbitrator or the community arbitration panel a comprehensive report setting forth the facts and circumstances surrounding the allegation.

(2) Records and reports submitted by interested agencies and parties, including, but not limited to, complaining witnesses and victims, may be received in evidence before the community arbitrator or the community arbitration panel without the necessity of formal proof.

(3) The testimony of the complaining witness and any alleged victim may be received when available, and these individuals may be present during the entire course of the proceedings.

(4) Any statement or admission made by the child appearing before the community arbitrator or the community arbitration panel relating to the

offense for which he was cited is privileged and may not be used as evidence against him either in a subsequent juvenile proceeding or in any subsequent civil or criminal action.

(5) If a child fails to appear on the original hearing date, the matter shall be referred back to the intake officer who shall consult with the state attorney or an assistant state attorney regarding possible filing of formal juvenile proceedings.

39.335. Disposition of cases

(1) Subsequent to any hearing held as provided in s. 39.334, the community arbitrator or community arbitration panel may:

(a) Dismiss the case.

(b) Dismiss the case with a warning to the child.

(c) Refer the child for placement in a community-based program.

(d) Refer the child to community counseling.

(e) Refer the child to a safety and education program related to juvenile offenders.

(f) Refer the child to a work program related to juvenile offenders.

(g) Refer the child to a nonprofit organization for volunteer work in the community.

(h) Order restitution in case of property damage.

(i) Continue the case for further investigation.

(j) Impose any other restrictions or sanctions that are designed to encourage noncriminal behavior and are agreed upon by the participants of the arbitration proceedings.

(2) Any person or agency to whom a child is referred pursuant to this section shall periodically report the progress of the child to the referring arbitrator or panel in the manner prescribed by such arbitrator or panel.

(3) If a child consents to an informal adjustment and, with his parent or legal guardian and the community arbitrator or community arbitration panel, agrees to comply with any disposition suggested or ordered by the arbitrator or panel and subsequently fails to abide by the terms of such agreement, the arbitrator or panel may, after a careful review of the circumstances, forward the case back to the intake officer who shall consult with the state attorney or the assistant state attorney regarding the possible filing of formal juvenile proceedings.

39.336. Review

Any interested agency or party, including, but not limited to, the complaining witness and victim, who is dissatisfied with the disposition provided by the community arbitrator or the community arbitration panel may request a review of the disposition to the appropriate intake officer within 15 days of the community arbitration hearing. Upon receipt of the request for review, the intake officer shall consult with the state attorney or assistant state attorney who shall consider the request for review and may file formal juvenile proceedings or take such other action as may be warranted.

39.337. Funding

Funding for the provisions of this act shall be provided through federal grant or through any appropriations as authorized by the county participating in the community arbitration program.

b. THE RIGHT TO COUNSEL

IN RE H.

New York City Family Court, 1972.
71 Misc.2d 1042, 337 N.Y.S.2d 118.

DECISION AND ORDER

RALPH E. CORY, JUDGE: The petition alleges that the respondent "while acting in concert with one other, also apprehended, was in a 1971 Pontiac Le Mans—no registration—the property of Robbins Reef Buick Corporation, 44 Hannah Street, Staten Island, New York. The respondent had no permission to use the above vehicle ∗ ∗ ∗".

The respondent, on his first appearance before the court, was assigned counsel pursuant to article 18-B of the County Law. When the assigned attorney appeared in this proceeding, he made a motion to vacate the petition and send the case back to intake for consideration de novo on the ground that the respondent had been denied his constitutional right to counsel at the intake stage of the Family Court proceeding. The court directed that the respondent's attorney file a memorandum of law in his behalf. The fact-finding hearing has not commenced pending decision on the motion by the court.

The sole question for determination is whether the initial intake conference is a critical stage in the proceedings within the meaning of the constitutional guarantee of the right to counsel thereby depriving the respondent of this right. This initial intake conference occurs before a petition is ordered drawn and prior to the holding of a Family Court hearing.

The intake procedure of the Family Court insofar as it applies to juvenile delinquency cases is provided for in Section 734 of the Family Court Act and section 2506.3 of the Uniform Family Court Rules (22 NYCRR 2506.3). Section 2506.3 provides in part:

> "The probation service is authorized to confer with any person seeking to originate a juvenile delinquency or person in need of supervision proceeding under Article 7 of the Family Court Act, with the potential respondent and other interested persons concerning the advisability of filing a petition under said Article and to attempt to adjust suitable cases before a petition is filed ∗ ∗ ∗."

The intake officer can adjust a case at intake where the accused youth denies his guilt of any offense. Intake process in juvenile courts is a specialized proceeding in the constellation of court services and procedures. There are more social than legal issues involved. Adjustment is not mandatory and the Rules specifically provide that the probation service may not prevent any person or complainant from having access to the court if he insists that a petition be filed.

It permits informal adjustments to be made at intake but includes provisions designed to protect the rights of the parties in this process. No person can be compelled to appear at any conference, produce any papers or visit any place.

Under Section 734(c) of the Family Court Act, "Efforts at adjustment pursuant to rules of court * * * may not extend for a period of more than two months without leave of a judge of the court, who may extend the period for an additional sixty days."

Intake is not a legal term and with the exception of juvenile and family courts, is foreign to the court field. Its use in juvenile and family courts has no doubt been adopted from the field of social welfare. In the welfare field, the client has complete freedom of choice. He comes to the agency and he may or may not decide to accept the service if offered. At the same time, the agency also has freedom of choice. It may or may not accept the client for service, particularly in the private welfare field.

The same is not true with court intake. The "client" defined as the person complained about or alleged to be in a situation necessitating action, has no freedom of choice. Here the request for action is initiated by someone other than the client. Whatever freedom of choice exists as to whether action will be taken rests in the court, not in the client. Unlike the private welfare agency, the court's authority to deny the right to file a petition is controlled by the nature of the case. Certainly giving the court this power can be justified and is fairly well established, at least by custom in delinquency cases. 2 Journal of Family Law 139, University of Louisville, Juvenile Court Intake by William H. Sheridan, (1962).

Delinquency cases involve offenses which if committed by an adult would be a crime. Here the State is usually a party to the action. The decisions made at intake level, affect individual and community rights—the right of the child and family to personal freedom and privacy and at the same time the right of the child and family to receive the services of the State for care, protection and treatment. 2 Journal of Family Law, supra, p. 141.

The New York Family Court Act provides for due process of law in Section 711, stating: "The purpose of this article is to provide a due process of law (a) for considering a claim that a person is a juvenile delinquent or a person in need of supervision and (b) for devising an appropriate order of disposition for any person adjudged a juvenile delinquent or in need of supervision." The landmark case in the area of due process for juveniles is In re Gault, 387 U.S. 1, 87 S.Ct. 1428, 18 L.Ed.2d 527. In this case, the New York Family Court Act was quoted with approval on several occasions. In determining whether the *Gault* decision and the New York Family Court Act should be expanded to provide a right of counsel at intake proceedings it is first necessary to examine the relevant provisions of the Family Court Act and the specific holdings of *Gault*.

Section 241 of the Family Court Act provides: "that minors who are the subject of family court proceedings should be represented by counsel of their own choosing or by law guardians. This declaration is based on a finding that counsel is often indispensable to a practical realization of due process of law and may be helpful in making reasoned determinations of fact and proper orders of disposition."

This act preceded *Gault* by some five years and obviously the right to counsel in juvenile proceedings already existed in New York at the time of that case. *Gault* is limited to adjudicatory hearings resulting in incarceration. The question then becomes whether right to counsel also exists at intake proceedings. No specific answers to whether the intake stage of a juvenile delinquency proceeding is a critical stage of the proceedings wherein the right to counsel attaches is supplied by Section 241 or the entire Family Court Act. Nor does *Gault* provide any answers to this specific question.

The answer does however lie in Section 735 of the Family Court Act indicating strong legislative intent that no counsel is necessary at the intake stage of proceedings. This section provides that: "No statement made during a preliminary conference may be admitted into evidence at a fact-finding hearing or, if the proceeding is transferred to a criminal court, at any time prior to a conviction."

See also Rules of the Family Court, Section 2506.3(d) (22 NYCRR 2506.3[d]). This section makes inadmissible at a fact-finding hearing any statement made during a preliminary conference carried on under probation service connected with the Family Court and does not refer to questioning by police and statements made to police which are not within the proscription of this section. Matter of Williams, 49 Misc.2d 154, 267 N.Y.S.2d 91; Matter of Addison, 20 A.D.2d 90, 245 N.Y.S.2d 243.

This preserves the spirit of cooperation which it is to be hoped prevails, at a preliminary conference such as intake and guards against self-incrimination, a prohibition in *Gault*. Furthermore, Section 734(b) provides that: "The probation service may not prevent any person who wishes to file a petition under this article from having access to the court for that purpose." See also 22 NYCRR 2506.3(a). This is further protection to the respondent because this is still the pre-fact-finding hearing level where the presiding judge, rather than the intake officer, will make the determination as to whether or not a petition will issue.

Counsel for respondent elaborates at length in his memorandum of law on holdings in adult criminal cases which find preliminary conferences to be a critical stage of the proceedings requiring Constitutional safeguards. However, these all refer to police custodial interrogations. Intake officers do not make arrests or charge anyone with acts which if committed by adults would be crimes. This is all done before the respondent arrives at the intake door.

In other words, Section 735 accomplishes in effect what *Miranda* (Miranda v. Arizona, 384 U.S. 436, 86 S.Ct. 1602, 16 L.Ed.2d 694) accomplishes: If the juvenile is to be encouraged to make admissions, despite the privilege against self-incrimination, he should be protected against the use of such admissions at ensuing proceedings. 1 Family Law Quarterly, No. 4, "Gault and the Future of Juvenile Law," by Dorsen and Rezneck, December, 1967. Furthermore, there can be no unnecessary detention of the juvenile in the Family Court. If the probation service for any reason should not release the child before the filing of a petition, he must be brought before a judge of the Family Court and "the judge shall hold a hearing for the purpose of making a preliminary determination of whether the court appears to have jurisdiction over the child. At the commencement of the hearing, the judge shall advise the child of his right to remain silent, his right to be represented by counsel of his own choosing, and of his right to have a law guardian assigned * * *. He (the Judge) must also allow the child a reasonable time to send for his parents or other person legally responsible for his care, and for counsel, and adjourn the hearing for that purpose." Family Court Act Section 728(a); See also: Family Court Act Sections 727(d) and 741(a).

Thus both *Gault* and the New York Family Court Act provide for counsel at adjudication at the very least. The question is how far *Gault* can be expanded. In fact, *Gault* stated " * * * we are not here concerned with the procedures or constitutional rights applicable to the pre-judicial stages of the juvenile process * * *." In re Gault, supra, at p. 13, 87 S.Ct. at p. 1436.

The threat of self-incrimination is mitigated by the exclusion provision of Section 735. Counsel for the respondent argues that the mere presence of counsel for the respondent at the intake level will prevent the issuance of a petition. This is not necessarily true and is a legal non sequitur. The fact that a petition may issue and a record created for the juvenile depends on what develops at the subsequent fact-finding hearing. The petition may be dismissed for lack of credible or legal evidence. The standard of proof is now "beyond a reasonable doubt" rather than mere preponderance. Is intake level to be designated a critical stage for the juvenile because it determines whether an official record of delinquency adjudication will become part of the child's dossier? Intake referral for petition per se would not create an institutional commitment. It may well be that the desired openness of the intake interview can be maintained with counsel present as well as absent at least where under Section 735 of the Family Court Act admissions made by the juvenile may not be used at the hearing. 8 Journal of Family Law 243, Counsel in Juvenile Court Proceedings; A Total Criminal Justice Prospective by Daniel L. Skoler (1968).

To require counsel at intake would be an intolerable burden on an already overburdened court. The lack of manpower is both frightful and appalling. This is a valid argument entitled to great weight and has great relevancy. If there was no Section 735 of the Family Court Act with its exclusionary rule, the argument would have no merit over the greater right to be represented at a critical stage of the proceeding, for it would then become truly a critical stage of the proceedings where counsel would be required.

In addition, it should be carefully noted that under Section 735 of the Family Court Act there is an *absolute prohibition* of the use of any statements or confession made at the intake interview, even though voluntarily made and without coercion or undue influence or even where a waiver of that right was knowingly and intelligently made. Contrast this with admission statements and confessions voluntarily made after *Miranda* warning or waiver of such rights, intelligently and knowingly made, in adult criminal proceedings where such statements or confessions, voluntarily made can be used against the respondent or defendant.

What greater right then does the juvenile need at intake proceedings than the tremendous protection afforded him under the exclusionary rule of Section 735 of the Family Court Act or the equally great right of having the court or judge determine whether or not any petition will issue against him if a petitioner does not wish an adjustment at intake level and insists upon a petition being drawn.

If intake proceedings are to be classified as critical stages of proceedings despite all the legal protections for the juveniles above enumerated as already in existing law, rules and procedures, then there would be no need for intake proceedings for accused juveniles in furtherance of Family Court policy of *rehabilitation and not punishment for crime* and petitions should be drawn automatically in all cases and set down for fact-finding hearings.

There is accordingly, no basis based on all of the foregoing for interpreting a logical extension of *Gault* to provide counsel at the intake level. There are no abuses in the pre-hearing stage as to impose the procedural requirement of counsel for the respondent at the intake interview. There is no present violation of due process clause of the 14th Amendment by not providing such counsel at the informal intake conference.

Motion to vacate the petition and send the case back to intake for consideration de novo on the ground that the respondent had been denied his constitutional right to counsel at the intake stage of the present Family Court proceeding is denied.

The fact-finding hearing is ordered to commence October 2, 1972.

NOTES

1. The same conclusion was reached in In re S, 73 Misc.2d 187, 341 N.Y.S.2d 11 (Fam.Ct.1973).

2. Would the result be different if the following statute were in force?

"At his first appearance before the court, the child and his parents, guardian, or other legal custodian shall be fully advised by the court of their constitutional and legal rights, including * * * the right to be represented by counsel at every stage of the proceedings * * *."

Colo.Rev.Stat. § 19–1–106(1)(a) (1978).

3. In Conover v. Montemuro, 477 F.2d 1073 (3d Cir.1973), the court remanded for appropriate findings of fact a class action suit brought under 42 U.S.C. § 1983 in which the following contentions were made:

"a. that juvenile defendants were denied equal protection on the ground that Pennsylvania law provides for discharge of adults at a preliminary hearing against whom a prima facie case is not established, but does not provide for the discharge of juveniles at the intake interview against whom a prima facie case of delinquency is not established.

"b. that juvenile defendants were denied due process because of the overbroad discretion allowed to the intake interviewer and the vagueness of the standards for his decision whether to file a delinquency petition.

"c. that juvenile defendants were denied due process by the arbitrary and irrational choice of cases in which to file delinquency petitions.

"d. that juvenile defendants were denied due process because the intake standards were not reasonably related either to probable cause or to the purposes of the Juvenile Court Law."

Id. at 1077.

4. Ferster and Courtless, The Intake Process in the Affluent County Juvenile Court, supra p. 243 at 1145 suggest that whether counsel is needed at intake depends on the functions intake workers are permitted to perform, the "informal sanctions" they impose, and, in particular, the extent to which they have unsupervised discretion in all these matters. The authors also point out that, even in jurisdictions whose statutes provide for counsel as soon as the child is taken into custody, counsel is ordinarily appointed only after the intake process. Indeed, even retained counsel do not often appear at intake conferences.

5. IJA–ABA JUVENILE JUSTICE STANDARDS, STANDARDS RELATING TO THE JUVENILE PROBATION FUNCTION: INTAKE AND PREDISPOSITION INVESTIGATIVE SERVICES (1980).

2.13   * Juvenile's right to assistance of counsel at intake.

A juvenile should have an unwaivable right to the assistance of counsel at intake:

A. in connection with any questioning by intake personnel at an intake interview involving questioning in accordance with Standard 2.14 or other questioning by intake personnel; and

B. in connection with any discussions or negotiations regarding a nonjudicial disposition, including discussions and negotiations in the course of a dispositional conference in accordance with Standard 2.14.

c. The Right to an Impartial Trial

Because the Intake Workers are part of the juvenile court, it has been argued that the juvenile judge's involvement with that process combined with his role as a judge violates the equal protection and due process clauses. The issue has been raised a number of times, with the usual result being that reached in Arizona. In In the Matter

* Reprinted with permission from Standards Relating to the Juvenile Probation Function: Intake and Predisposition Investigative Services, Copyright 1980, Ballinger Publishing Company.

of the Appeal in Pima County Anonymous, Juvenile Action No. J 24818–2, 110 Ariz. 98, 515 P.2d 600 (1973), appeal dismissed cert. denied Michaels v. Arizona, 417 U.S. 939, 94 S.Ct. 3063, 41 L.Ed.2d 661 (1974), the court said:

"Appellant's attack on the involvement of the juvenile court in the accusatory process rests upon the Equal Protection and Due Process Clause of the Fourteenth Amendment of the United States Constitution and Article II, Section 4, and Article VI, Section 26 of the Arizona Constitution. The effect of these provisions is to guarantee to all who are brought before the bar of justice, a fair and impartial trial by a fair and impartial judge. With that premise we cannot disagree for such a right ' *   *   * is a valuable substantive right originating in the common law and recognized by statute in both criminal and civil cases.' Marsin v. Udall, 78 Ariz. 309, 312, 279 P.2d 721, 723 (1955). Appellant concludes that the supervisory relationship between the juvenile court judge and the court staff violate the premise that an impartial trier of fact is indispensable to the integrity of the adjudicatory process. With that conclusion we cannot agree.

"The juvenile court system was originally conceived as an attempt to perform a rehabilitative function. By not treating the juvenile as a criminal, there was the possibility of preventing a future life of crime. Accordingly, rules of procedure were relaxed in order to achieve this rehabilitative goal. Over a period of years, the question arose as to whether the juvenile was receiving the worst of both worlds. Neither adequate facilities and staff nor time available for rehabilitation, nor rules of procedure could be equated with the fundamentals of due process of law. In re Gault, 387 U.S. 1, 87 S.Ct. 1428, 18 L.Ed.2d 527 (1967), seemingly answered that question. Thus, Gault, supra, mandated certain changes in procedure in order to comply with due process requirements. Yet, there is nothing in Gault to foreclose the possibility that the rehabilitative function and due process could function together. The juvenile code of this state, we believe, has made the two compatible and functional.

"We have read many of the cases cited to us by appellant. Certain categories arise in which the right to an impartial finder of fact has been violated. First, those cases in which the judge has become so personally involved as to be rendered unfit. In Mayberry v. Pennsylvania, 400 U.S. 455, 91 S.Ct. 499, 27 L.Ed.2d 532 (1971), the defendant repeatedly insulted the trial judge and interrupted the trial. The court held that in a criminal contempt charge a defendant should be given a public trial by a judge not vilified by the contemnor. [See also Pickering v. Board of Education, 391 U.S. 563, 88 S.Ct. 1731, 20 L.Ed.2d 811 (1968), where the trier of fact was both the victim of appellant's statement and the prosecutor that brought charges seeking dismissal]. This category is not applicable for describing the juvenile justice system in this state. Furthermore, when a party feels that the juvenile judge is or may be biased against him, an affidavit of bias and prejudice may be filed pursuant to

A.R.S. § 12–409. Such an affidavit can be used to disqualify the juvenile judge. Anonymous v. Superior Court in and for Pima County, 14 Ariz.App. 502, 484 P.2d 655 (1971).

"A second line of cases deals with the situation where the prosecutorial and adjudicatory functions become intertwined. In Figueroa Ruiz v. Delgado, 359 F.2d 718 (1 Cir., 1966), the Commonwealth of Puerto Rico provided no prosecutors in the District Court, and the judge introduced the government's evidence and conducted cross-examination for the government. See also Wong Yang Sun v. McGrath, 339 U.S. 33, 70 S.Ct. 445, 94 L.Ed. 616 (1950). Again, the Juvenile Code of this state does not allow the duties of the judge to merge with the duties of the prosecutor. A.R.S. § 8–233.

"A third category of cases concerns situations in which the trier of fact has participated in a preliminary finding of fact. In In re Murchison, 349 U.S. 133, 75 S.Ct. 623, 99 L.Ed. 942 (1955), the United States Supreme Court found that a single judge grand jury was such a part of the accusatory process that the judge '* * * cannot be, in the very nature of things, wholly disinterested in the conviction or acquittal of those accused.' 349 U.S. at 137, 75 S.Ct. at 626. This line of cases strikes at prejudgment of the trier of fact prior to a particular case's being adjudicated. American Cyanamid v. F.T.C., 363 F.2d 757 (6 Cir., 1966), also raised the issue of prejudgment. There, the F.T.C. brought charges against certain drug companies. These charges were based, to some extent, on a report issued by a Senate subcommittee. One of the F.T.C. members had been chief counsel to the subcommittee and had helped in preparing and drafting the report. The plaintiff sought disqualification of that F.T.C. commissioner and the court agreed. The Court of Appeals for the Third Circuit, in Falcone v. Dantinne, 420 F.2d 1157 (1969), found nothing inherently improper in having a union officer attend and participate in the informal hearing and then act as a trier of fact '* * * provided there is no element of bias or prejudgment, as we find to be the case here.' 420 F.2d at 1160–61.

"The fourth category of cases involves a situation in which the trier of fact has an interest in finding against the accused. Tumey v. Ohio, 273 U.S. 510, 47 S.Ct. 437, 71 L.Ed. 749 (1927). None of the categories described above are applicable in describing the relationship between the juvenile judge and the juvenile court of this state. Nor are we persuaded by the recent decision of In re Reis, 7 BNA Cr. L. 2151 (1970), which struck down the Rhode Island juvenile justice system because of the juvenile court's participation in the accusatory process. We are persuaded by appellee's contention that the juvenile court merely supervises the operation of the court employees. The juvenile court does not pass on investigation reports and therefore does not have any involvement in a case prior to the adjudicatory hearing.

"Therefore, we hold that the Juvenile Code of Arizona does not contravene juveniles' rights to the Equal Protection and Due Process of Law as guaranteed by the federal and state constitutions."
Id. at pp. 100–102, 515 P.2d at 602–04.

The same result was reached in In re Leon, 122 R.I. 548, 410 A.2d 121 (1980).

"In any event, counsel for respondent conceded at oral argument that the justice who heard this particular case had in no way participated in any preliminary investigation or accepted any report that related thereto. Thus we need not reach the question of whether contact by a justice with an intake investigation or materials developed therefrom could in a different context operate to deny a juvenile respondent's right to a fair and impartial tribunal."

Id. at 124.

d. INTAKE AND SELF-INCRIMINATION

IN RE WAYNE H.

Supreme Court of California, 1979.
24 Cal.3d 595, 156 Cal.Rptr. 344, 596 P.2d 1.

RICHARDSON, JUSTICE.

The defendant appeals from judgment declaring him a ward of the juvenile court and committing him to the Youth Authority. (Welf. & Inst. Code, § 602; all statutory references are to that code unless otherwise indicated.) The wardship adjudication is based on a finding that he committed armed robbery. (Pen.Code, § 211.) We will uphold the defendant's contention that his incriminating statement to a probation officer was improperly admitted as substantive evidence of guilt.

Near 9 p.m. on November 23, 1976, a black male brandishing a pistol robbed a Lerner gas station in Gardena, and escaped with $54 in denominations of $20, $5 and $1 bills. The station attendant described the robber as wearing a "yellowish-goldish-brown" jacket and a dark knit cap. Shortly before the robbery an attendant at another Lerner station in the vicinity had noticed the suspicious movements of a gray Chevrolet containing two persons, one of whom was wearing a dark knit cap. She telephoned the police.

Responding to the robbery call, Police Officer Williams observed a gray Chevrolet Nova with driver and passenger travelling away from the crime scene at a high speed. After the Chevrolet "ran" a stop sign, Officer Williams pursued the vehicle. When the passenger threw a pistol out the automobile's window, the officer stopped the vehicle and arrested the occupants. Defendant, a 16-year-old black male, was identified as the passenger. He was wearing a yellow jacket. A beanie cap, a dark knit cap, and $54 in $20, $5 and $1 bills were found on the floorboard of the passenger side of the Chevrolet.

The arrests occurred around 9:10 p.m. Both suspects were taken to the Gardena police station, booked, and held overnight. The next morning, November 24, defendant was questioned by Detective Lynn. Defendant denied any involvement in the robbery and offered an alibi.

At 8:10 p.m. on the 24th, defendant was taken to the Los Padrinos Juvenile Hall where he was interviewed by Probation Officer Wright. Officer Wright gave defendant *Miranda* warnings and explained that the results of the interview would bear on the determination of whether or not defendant would be detained and whether juvenile fitness proceedings would be recommended. Defendant agreed to discuss the case and again denied involvement. When, at the end of the interview, Officer Wright announced that he intended to recommend detention and a fitness hearing, defendant replied, "I did this one."

Defendant was detained in custody and a petition under section 650 was filed charging him with armed robbery (Pen.Code, § 211) (par. I) and possession of stolen property, i.e., the pistol (id., § 496, subd. 1) (par. II). At a subsequent fitness hearing, defendant was found amenable to treatment as a juvenile. In the ensuing jurisdictional hearing, defendant's statement to the probation officer was admitted over objection as evidence of his guilt. The charges contained in paragraph II were dismissed, the allegations of paragraph I were found to be true, and, as noted, defendant appeals from the subsequent wardship adjudication.

Defendant contends that statements by a juvenile to a probation officer are inadmissible in any subsequent proceeding as confessions or admissions of guilt, or for purposes of impeachment. We agree that the statement in question should have been excluded.

Section 626 affords several options to a peace officer who takes a minor into custody: he may release the minor outright (subd. (a)) or upon a written promise to appear (subd. (b)), or "without unnecessary delay" he may deliver custody of the minor to the probation officer (subd. (c)). If the minor is brought to a probation officer, the latter must investigate the need for further detention, and must release the minor unless specific circumstances are found. (§ 628.) At the time here relevant the probation officer was also charged with filing a wardship petition on any minor he detained (former § 630); the probation department has further responsibility to recommend a hearing on the issue of transfer to adult court. (§ 707.)

Courts have recognized a number of situations in which the use of statements by adult defendants to a probation officer as admissions in a trial on the issue of guilt would be unfair. Thus, we have held that statements made to a probation officer in the hope that candor will induce a favorable sentencing report are inadmissible against the defendant in any retrial (People v. Harrington (1970) 2 Cal.3d 991, 999, 88 Cal.Rptr. 161, 471 P.2d 961) unless "volunteered" by the defendant under the guiding hand of counsel (id., at p. 1000, 88 Cal.Rptr. 161, 471 P.2d 961; People v. Alesi (1967) 67 Cal.2d 856, 861–862, 64 Cal.Rptr. 104, 434 P.2d 360). Postconviction admissions to the adult criminal court made on a probation officer's advice in hope of lenient treatment are also excluded from use at any subsequent trial. (People v. Hicks (1971) 4 Cal.3d 757, 762, 94 Cal.Rptr. 393, 484 P.2d 65.)

Similar results have been reached under the Juvenile Court Law. Admissions by a juvenile to a probation officer for use in the preparation of the social study, and to the juvenile court itself in the course of a section 602 jurisdictional hearing, have both been excluded from subsequent adult criminal proceedings. (Bryan v. Superior Court (1972) 7 Cal.3d 575, 587–588, 102 Cal.Rptr. 831, 498 P.2d 1079.) Similarly, it has been held that, where a probation officer obtains damaging statements from a juvenile in the course of preparing the social study, without prior advice to the minor's counsel when the attorney's identity is known, the statements must be excluded from any subsequent juvenile adjudication proceeding. (In re Paul T. (1971) 15 Cal.App.3d 886, 893–894, 93 Cal.Rptr. 510.)

The cases have stressed the law's interest in encouraging complete candor between a defendant and his probation officer in the probation interview. The purpose of such an interview is not the marshalling of evidence on the issue of guilt, but rather the assembling of all available information relevant to an informed disposition of the case if guilt is established (§§ 280, 702; Pen.Code, § 1203), or to assist in the evaluation of the minor's fitness for treatment as a juvenile (§ 707). Such decisions, courts have uniformly concluded, should be based on the most complete knowledge of the defendant's background that is possible. His description and explanation of the circumstances of the alleged offense, and his acknowledgment of guilt and demonstration of remorse, may significantly affect decisions about punishment or transfer for adult proceedings. (Bryan v. Superior Court, supra, 7 Cal.3d 575, 587, 102 Cal.Rptr. 831, 498 P.2d 1079.)

Thus, "[a]s stated in People v. Garcia (1966) 240 Cal.App.2d 9, 13, 49 Cal.Rptr. 146, 148, * * * quoted approvingly in Hicks [supra, 4 Cal.3d 757, 94 Cal.Rptr. 393, 484 P.2d 65], 'in order [for the probation officer] to get full cooperation from a defendant he should be advised that any statement he makes will be used only for the information of the court in a probationary hearing. We do not doubt that defendants have that belief and that if they knew their damaging admissions could be used against them in another trial they would not talk freely and the purpose of the interview would be frustrated.' [¶] * * * The minor who is subject to the possibility of a transfer order should not be put to the unfair choice of being considered uncooperative by the juvenile probation officer and juvenile court because of his refusal to discuss his case with the probation officer, or of having his statements to that officer used against him in subsequent criminal proceedings. (Cf. In re Paul T. [supra] * * * 15 Cal.App.3d 886, 894, 93 Cal.Rptr. 510 * * *.)" (Bryan, supra, 7 Cal.3d at pp. 587–588, 102 Cal.Rptr. at pp. 839–840, 498 P.2d at pp. 1087–1088.) Such a result would frustrate the rehabilitative purposes of the Juvenile Court Law.

The People suggest that the rule excluding statements to juvenile probation officers applies only to subsequent *adult criminal proceedings*, and, in the case of minors, only *after an adjudication of guilt,* when the proper treatment of the minor is being considered. In contrast, it is urged, the section 628 interview which precedes guilt adjudication is primarily accusatorial, and the "dilemma" faced by a minor in this situation is common to any criminal suspect who must decide whether to cooperate with the police. The cases, and the Juvenile Court Law itself, however, compel a contrary conclusion.

Both *Bryan* and *Paul T.*, supra, involved statements by juveniles made *before* determination of criminal culpability, and the *Paul T.* court held that the statements there at issue were inadmissible in a subsequent *juvenile adjudication proceeding.* (See also In re R. (1970) 1 Cal.3d 855, 859–861, 83 Cal.Rptr. 671, 464 P.2d 127 [juvenile judge may not, *prior to jurisdictional hearing,* read social study prepared by probation officer].) *Bryan* stressed the importance of the relationship between the minor and probation officer in the juvenile court setting (7 Cal.3d at p. 587, 102 Cal.Rptr. 831, 498 P.2d 1079).

The interview required by a juvenile probation officer under section 628 is conducted in a nonaccusatorial setting. Contrary to the People's contention, the consultation is not analogous to police interrogation of an adult suspect. In fact, the section 628 interview has no counterpart in adult criminal proceedings in which the defendant confers with his probation officer only after conviction. (Pen.Code, § 1203, subd. (a).) The primary purpose of the section 628 interview, as the statutes make clear, is not to elicit evidence of guilt—the function of police questioning—but to assist the probation officer in deciding at the outset of the case whether the minor need be further detained pending a court hearing. (§§ 626, 628, 630.) This approach thereby serves a paramount concern of the Juvenile Court Law—that a minor be treated in the least restrictive means feasible under the circumstances (§ 626, subd. (c); see § 202, subd. (a)).

While the purposes of such an interview are relatively restricted, however, the latitude given the probation officer in reaching a detention decision, and the effect of that decision on the minor, are substantial. The probation officer is required to investigate "the circumstances of the minor *and the facts surrounding his being taken into custody*" in order to determine whether such detention is appropriate. (§ 628, subd. (a), italics added.) Among the factors justifying detention are the risk of the defendant's flight and the possibility that his freedom will present a danger to person or property. (Id., subds. (a)(4), (a)(5).) The probation officer's decision may cause the minor to be detained for a period not exceeding 72 hours after arrest before he receives a court hearing on the detention issue. (See §§ 631, 632.)

Under these circumstances, the minor's frank discussion of the offense may indicate that his involvement was innocent or secondary, or, more to the point, that he is cooperative and remorseful, and is therefore a good candidate for release pending further proceedings. Candor will assist the probation officer in discharging his statutory duty to determine the least restrictive feasible treatment of the minor. (See § 626, subd. (c).) A free interchange between minor and officer should therefore be encouraged.

In considering the nature of the section 628 interview we are not unmindful of section 627.5, which requires the probation officer to advise the minor and his parents that anything the minor says may be used against him, and of his rights to silence, appointment of counsel, and presence of counsel "during *any* interrogation." (Italics added.) The statute further provides that if the minor requests counsel, the probation officer shall so advise the juvenile court and counsel "shall" be appointed under section 634.

While the legislative origins of section 627.5 are unclear, its adoption within the year after the United States Supreme Court's *Miranda* and *Gault* decisions suggest strongly that the statute's purpose was simply to assure that the minor would be advised as early as possible of his rights in "any" interrogation, and to make the probation officer responsible for seeing that a request for counsel is honored. Nothing in section 627.5 overcomes the clearly nonaccusatorial import of the interview required by section 628.

We conclude that the subsequent use of statements made by a juvenile to a probation officer in a section 628 interview would frustrate important purposes of that statute, and of the Juvenile Court Law generally. We therefore hold that such statements are not admissible as substantive evidence, or for impeachment, in any subsequent proceeding to determine criminal guilt, whether juvenile or adult. Such statements may, of course, be admitted and considered in hearings on the issues of detention and fitness for juvenile treatment.

It follows from the foregoing that the defendant's incriminating statement to Officer Wright should not have been admitted at the jurisdictional hearing. We need not determine whether defendant's declaration "I did this one" constituted a *confession* which requires a per se reversal. (People v. McClary (1977) 20 Cal.3d 218, 230, 142 Cal.Rptr. 163, 571 P.2d 620; People v. Fioritto (1968) 68 Cal.2d 714, 720, 68 Cal.Rptr. 817, 441 P.2d 625.) Even if these words are deemed a mere *admission*, their improper introduction invalidates the judgment of wardship unless the error was harmless beyond a reasonable doubt. (Chapman v. California (1967) 386 U.S. 18, 23–24, 87 S.Ct. 824, 17 L.Ed.2d 705; McClary, supra, 20 Cal.3d at p. 230, 142 Cal.Rptr. 163, 571 P.2d 620.) Did the admission of the damaging statement influence the judgment?

There was, to be sure, strong circumstantial evidence against defendant. His description matched that of the robber. His jacket, and the gun he discarded during the pursuit by Officer Williams, were identified in court as similar to the gun displayed and the jacket worn by the thief. Defendant was a passenger in a car moving quickly away from the crime location minutes after the robbery was committed. Currency, in amounts and denominations identical to that taken in the holdup, and a cap, like that worn by the robber, were found in the vehicle on the side on which defendant had been riding. The alibi he gave to Detective Lynn proved false.

On the other hand, no witness was able to identify defendant positively. The presence of another black male of similar description in the gray Chevrolet raises a reasonable doubt about who had dominion and control of the currency and the dark cap found in the automobile. The trial judge referred to the incriminating statement in his oral review of the evidence against defendant suggesting that the court may have relied on it. We cannot say that, in the absence of admission of the incriminating statement, the charges against defendant would have been sustained. We must therefore reverse the judgment.

Our disposition of this case makes it unnecessary to reach defendant's additional contentions.

The judgment is reversed.

BIRD, C.J., and TOBRINER, MOSK, MANUEL and NEWMAN, JJ., concur.

CLARK, JUSTICE, dissenting.

The majority have, in effect, made a policy decision. They have decided that the interest in encouraging the juvenile to be candid and confiding in the section 626 interview outweighs the interest in protecting the juvenile and society by resolving guilt on the basis of admissions and confessions obtained in such an interview. This is an arguable position. But the Legislature appears to have taken the opposite position when it enacted section 627.5 requiring the probation officer to advise the minor at the section 626 interview that anything he says may be used against him. Therefore, the judgment should be affirmed.

[handwritten margin note: took care of problem by saying stop if want a lawyer!]

NOTES

1. In In the Matter of Luis R., 92 Misc.2d 55, 399 N.Y.S.2d 847 (1977), the argument was made that Sec. 735 of the Family Court Act, "No statement made during a preliminary conference may be admitted into evidence at a fact-finding hearing * * *," required not only that declarations made at the intake conference and evidence which was the fruit of those declarations must be excluded, but also that the further sanction of outright dismissal should follow. The court, consistent with both the criminal cases and other juvenile cases, rejected the contention.

> It is settled law that outright dismissal of charges is mandated only when there exists such basic prosecutorial misconduct which makes the very pendency of the charges themselves immoral (People v. Collier, 85 Misc.2d 529, 376 N.Y.S.2d 954). We do not have such conduct before us.

Id. at 850.

2. IJA–ABA JUVENILE JUSTICE STANDARDS, STANDARDS RELATING TO THE JUVENILE PROBATION FUNCTION: INTAKE AND PREDISPOSITION INVESTIGATIVE SERVICES (1980).

2.12 * Juvenile's privilege against self-incrimination at intake.

A. A juvenile should have a privilege against self-incrimination in connection with questioning by intake personnel during the intake process.

B. Any statement made by a juvenile to an intake officer or other information derived directly or indirectly from such a statement is inadmissible in evidence in any judicial proceeding prior to a formal finding of delinquency unless the statement was made after consultation with and in the presence of counsel.

* Reprinted with permission from Standards Relating to the Juvenile Probation Function: Intake and Predisposition Investigative Services, Copyright 1980, Ballinger Publishing Company.

Chapter 5

PRE-TRIAL DETENTION

CHILDREN IN NEED: OBSERVATIONS OF PRACTICES OF THE DENVER JUVENILE COURT.*

C. *Probation Department Decision to Detain Pending Detention Hearing:*

I try to look at the child and look at the parents, and I see if there is a possibility that the parents can supervise that child at home * * * I have to feel that the child can be relatively safe staying at home * * * because I think that is where he should be if at all possible.

Intake Probation Counselor [1]

Almost hourly, a patrol car will turn into the alley behind juvenile hall with a child or two for the admissions office. The door is locked, and a buzzer must be pushed to notify the counselor that another child is awaiting admission. The child will pass through the door into a poorly lit office area. Behind a large counter, a juvenile hall employee waits to get basic information from the child and to relieve him or her of all valuables. If an intake screening counselor is not readily available,[2] the child will be placed in a small locked room across from the admissions office until an interview can be arranged which will aid in determining whether or not the child will be detained pending a detention hearing before the court.

Frequently, no explanation of the procedures which are being followed or what can be expected is given to the child; generally he has a fairly clear idea why he is where he is, but little insight into what is coming next. Therefore, when the screening probation counselor arrives, he may appear to the child as a friend. The child has just been impersonally treated by police officers or overwrought parents and a juvenile hall employee, and anyone who will talk to him is an improvement. The screening probation counselor already has

* Permission to reprint the following article written by Hufnagel and Davidson has been obtained from the Denver Law Journal, University of Denver, (Colorado Seminary), College of Law. This article appeared in Volume 51 of the Denver Law Journal at pages 355 through 370. Copyright 1974 by the Denver Law Journal, University of Denver, (Colorado Seminary), College of Law.

[1] During fiscal year 1971-72, 4,739 children were admitted to Denver Juvenile Hall. The projected figures for the following year suggest that 5,876 will be admitted. On an average day in 1971-72, 83 youngsters were detained at the hall—some serving time on the school program, some waiting for court hearings, some waiting for placement in group homes, and some waiting for their parents to want them home again.

[2] Beginning in early 1972, unit III of the intake division of the probation department located at juvenile hall, initiated a work schedule which required one counselor from the unit to be responsible for the screening of children brought to the hall. There is a "screening counselor" on duty from 7:00 a.m. to 11:00 p.m. daily, including weekends. A child brought to the hall after 11:00 p.m. would be transferred to a unit upstairs to spend the night, and would be interviewed the following morning.

obtained some information on the child from the police summary sheet accompanying him. If the child is currently on probation or awaiting other court action, the screening counselor will defer to the counselor already involved. If the child is new to the court, the screening counselor will make the detention decision himself.

If the screening counselor determines that the child can be released, the child will usually wait in the admissions area for his parent or probation counselor to take him home. He and his parents may be asked to promise to return for further interviews at a later date. Some children who are not potential runaways are released to shelter care because of parental refusal to respond or because of the child's fear of returning home.[3] If it is determined that the child must be held pending a detention hearing, he will be taken to one of the units upstairs, relieved of his own clothing, given juvenile hall clothing, and introduced to his "home" and "roommates" for at least the next 48-hour period.

Although it is not part of the administrative guidelines for hold or release from juvenile hall, an informal procedure was noted by a screening counselor:

> Now, if they are 16 or over [and on parole], they'll just be taken to city jail and you won't have to make that decision. You do have to make the decision to have them go to city jail * * * but that's kind of a policy, if they are 16 or over and on parole, then they go to city jail.

The screening unit is a relatively new administrative innovation in the court.[4] Before its inception, children brought to the hall were interviewed by a juvenile hall employee and transferred immediately to units upstairs. The probation counselors had the authority to release a child prior to his detention hearing, but because there was

---

[3] According to one intake probation counselor who serves as a screening counselor at least 1 day a week, well over half of the children who are brought to juvenile hall are released prior to their detention hearings—that is, within 48 hours.

[4] The efficient operation of the juvenile hall screening unit has probably been the most notable reform effected in Denver Juvenile Court during the period of time covered by this study. Its purpose and structure were described by the acting assistant director of court services as follows:

[T]he unit at the hall was set up so there would be a professional approach— dialogue—between the child first coming into detention and professional decisions being made at that point.

The way it's structured is that when a child is picked up anywhere in the city, the child will go through the Delinquency Control Division and they have a receiving officer on duty 24 hours a day, 7 days a week. This receiving officer makes the initial decision whether the child should be released or detained.

* * *

Once that decision is made, if the decision is made for detention, the child comes to juvenile hall. Immediately upon the child's arrival, he is interviewed— screened—by an intake probation officer. This officer has the final say as to whether the child is to be detained or not, and there are certainly cases where we don't go along with the police department's recommendation. They might have recommended detention but we might release the child. So it has to be clear—it is clear—to the police department and the probation department that the final decision is made by that particular officer. * * * If the police are saying "hold" and the probation officer is saying "release", the supervisor is contacted and has to agree with the probation officer before the child is released. * * *

no efficient mechanism for contacting the counselor and because a full unit of intake counselors was not housed in the hall, release was much less frequent. This resulted in detention hearing dockets of 10 to 20 children daily and massive overuse of detention facilities.

The Code does not provide for the establishment of special screening units, nor does it delineate, except in the most general language, the criteria to be considered in deciding to detain a child. It defines detention and shelter care as follows:

> (12) "Detention" means the temporary care of a child who requires secure custody in physically restricting facilities pending court disposition or an execution of a court order for placement or commitment.

> (13) "Shelter" means the temporary care of a child in physically unrestricting facilities pending court disposition or execution of a court order for placement.

The authority of the intake division of the probation department to act on detention prior to a detention hearing is apparently derived, as a delegated responsibility, from the following Code section:

> (4) The court may at any time order the release of any child, except children being held pursuant to paragraphs (b) and (c) of subsection (3) of this section, from detention or shelter care without holding a hearing, either without restriction or upon written promise of the parent, guardian, or legal custodian to bring the child to the court at a time set or to be set by the court.

The Code requires the use of shelter care rather than detention where appropriate, but it does not require that a hearing be held to determine its necessity. Presumably, the authority to release a child to shelter care has also been delegated to probation counselors by the court, although shelter is not mentioned in the court's administrative guidelines reprinted below.[5]

The only other official guidelines on detention standards are found in the Colorado Rules of Juvenile Procedure. Rule 58(a) uses as a standard the child's "immediate welfare or the protection of the community," while the comparable language of Rule 59(a) is "the child's best interest or that of the community."

The court has interpreted these broad statutory guidelines and has formulated a court policy on hold or release from juvenile hall. Its policy statement was written by the director of field services and the acting director of intake with the help of their staff supervisors, and reads as follows:

---

[5] One reason for this omission may be the crucial lack of shelter facilities available to the Denver Juvenile Court and the presumption, probably legitimate, that the agency charged with the responsibility of establishing and making available to the court adequate shelter care would respond more quickly to an order for shelter placement by the court than a request for it by a screening counselor.

I. *Discretion To Release:*

A. When any child is brought to Juvenile Hall to be detained, the proper probation officer, Intake or Field, will make the final determination on the Hold or Release of the juvenile.

II. *Reasons For Holding a Child:*

A. Unless otherwise committed to a probation program, or ordered by the Court, no child should be detained in Juvenile Hall, unless the child is a danger to himself or to the community.

B. A child is not to be held in Juvenile Hall merely as a disciplinary measure.

C. A child is not to be held in Juvenile Hall merely for investigation. If investigation of unsolved complaints becomes a factor in danger to self or community, the probation officer should take this into careful consideration.

* * *

E. A child should be held if there is strong evidence he is a danger to himself or the community even though that danger is not at the moment completely established.

1. Danger to self or community must be established by taking into consideration all involved factors—probable cause, seriousness of alleged offense, pending court action, past behavior pattern, social and psychological history, and knowledge of home and community environments.

The discretion allowed a probation officer in deciding to release a child varies depending on the DCD's request to hold or release. If the DCD wishes the child to be held, the proper supervisor or director must approve the child's release, unless the police hold was requested because the child is alleged to have committed a delinquent act which would constitute a felony if committed by an adult, in which case the child must be held for a detention hearing. Before a release is permitted, a conference between the probation counselor and the child must take place. If a decision cannot be reached, the child is held pending a final decision by the director. If the DCD indicates that the child may be released, the probation counselor has full discretion over the detention decision.

After the above guidelines had been promulgated, structured interviews were conducted with probation counselors to determine their own practices. The counselors were asked what criteria were used in the decision to hold or release and were asked whether the decision was theirs alone to make. Most of those interviewed were familiar with the guidelines but had embellished and interpreted them substantially to reflect their own philosophies and experiences. Many of these embellishments are consistent with the statutory requirement of detention where the child's "immediate welfare or the protection of the community" can be served. Certainly repeated runaways, users of hard drugs, and juveniles whose conduct suggests the probability that they will commit further similar offenses might reasonably be detained under this standard. However, detaining a child for the purpose of forcing parental involvement in a treatment plan or of gathering investigative information, as one intake screening counselor suggested, would seem to be only indirectly related to the best interests of the child. Surely, a recommendation of detention because shelter care or other alternative holding facilities are unavailable is not acceptable.

All of the line-staff probation counselors questioned indicated that in most cases, they would not ask that a child be detained unless a formal petition on the alleged offense was going to be filed. The acting assistant director of court services, however, did not feel this was an absolute requirement. In spite of the guidelines promulgated by the court administrators, the counselors felt the detention decision was theirs alone to make in the first instance. One suggested conferring with the supervisor only for the sake of communication, another, with DCD for informational purposes.

The decision to release a child is obviously not reviewed by the court since the child will not appear for a detention hearing. Nor can it be assumed that the decision is reviewed by a supervising probation counselor. On the other hand, if the decision is made to detain the youngster, that decision will be reviewed by the court within 48 hours.

D.　*Detention Hearing*

Effective Monday, December 13, 1971, members of the Court Intake Staff will advise all children detained at Juvenile Hall of their right to an attorney and a list will be compiled daily of the children on the Detention Docket who desire attorneys. This list will be available to the Public Defenders and Legal Aid Attorneys at the Admitting Office. The children will be brought from the units to be interviewed by the attorneys in the interviewing rooms across from the Admitting Office.[6]

The referee who sits at juvenile hall in Division III of the Denver Juvenile Court averages eight to nine detention hearings an afternoon, Monday through Friday. Until the establishment of the intake screening unit at the hall, hearings were often held for as many as 20 youngsters in a single day. Most children are now represented by counsel, and a representative of the district attorney's office attends all hearings, arguing vigorously for detention in many of the more serious delinquency allegation cases and taking no role whatsoever in most CHINS cases.

The child who is detained as a result of his interview with a probation counselor often waits in an upstairs living unit at juvenile hall for at least one full day following the interview. On the day of

---

[6] Memorandum to Public Defenders and Legal Aid Attorneys from the Presiding Judge of Denver Juvenile Court, Dec. 9, 1971. The memorandum is court policy only and is not drawn from the Children's Code which requires only that children and parents be advised of the child's right to counsel "at his first appearance before the court." Colo.Rev. Stat.Ann. § 22–1–6(1)(a) (Supp.1967).

his scheduled detention hearing, he will be brought to the lobby area of the visiting or interviewing rooms across from the admitting office. The child may or may not have been advised as to the purpose of this removal. Generally, promptly at 1 p.m., a representative of the public defender's office and a student attorney from the University of Denver's Clinical Legal Education Program will arrive, detention docket in hand.

The child may be impressed by the youth and the rather "hip" appearance of his attorney. Most are in their twenties, many are women, and all have a casual attitude with regard to their own and the court's status as authority figures. The attorneys, on the whole, show concern for helping the child to understand what is going to happen in the detention hearing, and most of the children readily choose to be represented. Those who are unsure or unconcerned about being represented are generally represented anyway.

When the attorney tells the child that the purpose of the detention hearing is to determine whether he is going to remain at juvenile hall, return home, or go to a welfare shelter placement, the child, when asked, will almost always respond that he wants to go home. In the rare case where the child may fear abuse at home, he will select the protective closed environment of juvenile hall. Even though the majority of the children interviewed had been represented by counsel before, most seemed genuinely surprised that anyone cared about their feelings.

The typical attorney-child interview lasts for 5 to 15 minutes, although often the attorney is able to speak with the child immediately before the hearing to tell him whether his parents are present and whether the child's assessment of their willingness to take him home is correct. After all of the children have been interviewed, they are escorted upstairs through many corridors and locked doors. The children are then moved downstairs in the other wing of the building where they sit in a cramped stairwell to await being called by the sheriff, who attends all detention hearings.[7]

When each child's name is called, the locked door to the stairwell opens, and the child is led by the sheriff across a hall to the courtroom. The child's attorney either is sitting at defense counsel table or meets him in the hall. The parents of the child, who have been waiting near the courtroom in a lobby area, are now called and join the child and his attorney at counsel table. This is often the first time that the child and his parents have seen each other in 2 days.

After questioning counsel about his or her willingness to proceed before a referee and to waive formal advisement of the child's rights, the referee will ask the probation counselor to proceed. In almost all cases, the probation counselor is the same person who made the

[7] The sheriff has become a permanent fixture at detention hearings because of the large number of children who have escaped by running down the carpeted hall about 20 feet to an open door used by the general public as the entrance to the courtroom area. In fiscal year 1971–72, 76 children were "AWOL" from juvenile hall, a decrease of 22 from the previous year.

initial decision to detain the child. He will relate why the child is before the court, often stating as fact the alleged offense. The counselor's information is derived from the police summary sheet, past court records of the child, and interviews with the child and his parent. On the basis of this information, the probation counselor makes a recommendation as to detention or release. After this presentation, the child's attorney is permitted to question the counselor about the statements made or about omissions in the presentation. In addition, the referee and opposing counsel may question the probation counselor about his recommendation. Experienced probation counselors are careful to recite the alternative litanies that the child is "a danger to himself or the community" or that his detention or release is "in his best interest or in the best interest of the community." With newer counselors, however, the referee may have to consciously lead the presentation so that the counselor ends by articulating these statutory standards for detention.

The evidentiary rules applicable to detention hearings are informal. Witnesses are rarely sworn, opinion testimony and hearsay are widespread, and probation counselors often urge as the basis for detention the commission of offenses by a child which have not been admitted or proved. Repeated objections by attorneys are frowned upon by the court.

After the counselor's presentation is completed, the attorney for the child will present the child's case. Usually this consists of either relating or having the child relate what he wants to do, arguing that the child's situation does not fall within the parameters of the standards for detention, and possibly enlisting the support of the parent for the child's viewpoint. If the parent's view is contrary to the child's wishes, the attorney will at least make the parent's view clear to the court and then attack it. The attorney for the child will also suggest the alternative shelter replacement if it is appropriate and desired by the child. The referee may question the child or the attorney following this presentation. In addition, the court will usually ask the parents how they feel about the situation.

If serious allegations of delinquency are at issue, the representative of the district attorney's office may then present the case for the "prosecution." If the counselor is recommending release, some elements of a contested hearing may ensue, and the representative may choose to cross-examine any of the persons who testified. It must be remembered that the district attorney's representative generally has available for review only that information which has been developed in the hearing and additional reports from the files of the police department or district attorney. Rarely has this representative interviewed either the child or the child's parents.

After listening to these arguments, the referee will make findings and will recommend further detention, shelter placement, or release to the parents. The recommendation may be followed by emotional appeals from the parents or child or by an oral request on the record from counsel for the child for a rehearing before a judge.

If the child is released to his parents, they may leave the hall within approximately one-half hour, possibly with orders to return to speak further with a probation counselor about contemplated court action. If a shelter placement is ordered for the child, the probation counselor is charged with the duty of contacting the Denver Department of Welfare to request that a child welfare worker transport the child from juvenile hall to the shelter facility.[8] This will occur 2 hours to 2 days following the court's recommendation, during which time, of course, the child remains in detention. Probation counselors are not authorized by the welfare department to place the child in a shelter facility.

If further detention is recommended for the child, he will be returned to his detention unit. This recommendation may be reviewed by a judge and can be re-evaluated at any of the later critical junctures. During detention, psychological and medical evaluations of the child may be performed, and the probation counselor will probably visit with him again. However, the child will receive no counseling or treatment, except for the limited amount provided by the unit counselors. A detained child may understandably become depressed following the detention hearing since the average length of stay in Denver's Juvenile Hall in 1971 was 28.7 days.

The provisions of the Code and the Colorado Rules of Juvenile Procedure which deal specifically with the detention hearing are sparse. As a result, an administrative overlay has been developed. But because the detention hearing is the child's first appearance before the court, it may be instructive to examine the provisions of the Code dealing with court hearings generally.

The Code provides that upon a first appearance before the court, the child and his legal custodian are to be fully advised of their constitutional and legal rights, including the right to a jury trial and the right to be represented by counsel.[9] It would seem that the rights accorded juveniles as a result of United States Supreme Court decisions should therefore be explained to the child at his first appearance before the court. Those rights include timely written notice to parents and child of the specific charge and factual allegations to be considered at any adjudicatory hearing, retained or appointed counsel for the child in that hearing, the privilege against self-incrimination, confrontation and cross-examination of witnesses

---

[8] Presently there is one shelter facility for girls available to the court and one for boys, so this argument for shelter placement may in many cases be futile. The standard for detention is so vague that almost any behavior can be said to fulfill it, and often does, when there are no placements available in shelter care. In recent months the court has shown decreasing reticence in ordering the placement despite the absence of shelter placements. Only upon occasion will it force the Denver Department of Welfare, to whom the court has delegated the responsibility for the establishment of shelter facilities, to bear the burden of finding *some* nonrestrictive placement or risk being held in contempt of court.

[9] Colo.Rev.Stat.Ann. § 22–1–6(1)(a) (Supp.1967). Subsection (b) provides for court-appointed counsel if the family "requests an attorney and is found to be without sufficient financial means." Id. §§ 22–1–6(4)(i), (ii) provide for a "trial by a jury of not more than six."

against the child, and the right to have the allegations in the adjudicatory hearing proved beyond a reasonable doubt.

These constitutional rights, as well as the right under the Code to a jury trial, apply only to an adjudicatory hearing. Consequently, referees rarely advise the child and his parents of them at the detention hearing. In practice, this is of little significance since in most cases a petition, even if contemplated, has not as yet been filed, and under *Gault*, the court has the responsibility of again advising the child prior to both the plea and the adjudicatory hearings.

Inasmuch as detention hearings are generally held before a referee, the child and his parents should also be advised of the child's right to a hearing before a judge in the first instance, of the effect of the recommendation of the referee, and, following the findings and recommendations of the referee, of the right of the parties to a rehearing before a judge if requested within 5 days.

If a formal advisement is given by the court at the detention hearing, it generally includes discussion only of the child's right to a hearing before a judge in the first instance, of the right to counsel at every stage of the proceedings, and of the privilege against self-incrimination in the detention hearing. Rarely is the child or parent advised of the child's right to a rehearing before a judge if they dispute the recommendations of the referee.

Other provisions of the Code also apply specifically to detention hearings. "[T]emporary care in a shelter facility designated by the court or the county department of public welfare" is required for those children who must be taken from home but do not require physical restriction. Such children should not be placed in detention.[10] However, all children taken into custody by the police and not released to their parents are in fact placed in Denver's Juvenile Hall at least temporarily, since the police officers are not permitted by the Denver Department of Welfare to take such children directly to a shelter facility.

Some provisions of the Code are applicable to all hearings in Juvenile Court. The Colorado Rules of Juvenile Procedure govern, hearings "may be conducted in an informal manner," the general public is not excluded unless the court determines such exclusion is in the best interest of the child, a verbatim record is required in all hearings unless waived, and publicity including names or pictures of the parties is forbidden unless specifically ordered by the court.

Generally these provisions, as well as those referring specifically to detention hearings, are well followed by the court. Yet in some instances, the administrative overlay of court structure and procedure has the effect of abridging or nullifying many of the rights included in the formal law. For example, all detention hearing

[10] Ch. 110, § 13, [1973] Colo.Sess. Laws 389, amending Colo.Rev.Stat.Ann. § 22-2-3(3) (Supp.1967), Colo.R.Juv.P. 59 is more explicit in its guidelines for detention, stating that "[i]f the court finds release will not be contrary to the child's best interest or that of the community it shall release the child to the custody of its parents or other responsible adult."

proceedings are recorded by tape recorder, as mandated, and the tapes retained in the court clerk's office. However, even if counsel immediately files a request for a rehearing of the referee's detention decision, it is often at least 5 days before the judge receives the request, locates and listens to the tape, and is prepared for the rehearing. If the child has been detained, the judge's subsequent decision to release the child benefits him only after 5 to 10 days of detention, and the child's right to a redetermination of the referee's detention decision thus becomes less meaningful.

Similarly, although hearings "may be conducted in an informal manner," the detention hearing is the only type of hearing conducted in the court in which informality is peculiarly pronounced. Although the injustice which may result to the child is only further detention, and neither commitment nor branding as a delinquent, the following section of the *Gault* decision is apropos:

> [T]here is increasing evidence that the informal procedures, contrary to the original expectation may themselves constitute a further obstacle to effective treatment of the delinquent to the extent that they engender in the child a sense of injustice provoked by seemingly all-powerful and challengeless exercise of authority by judges and probation officers.

The brief description of a typical detention hearing contained in the first part of this section gives some indication of the confused and confusing nature of the hearings in division III of the court. Because the child is usually represented by an attorney, the allegations and authority of the probation counselor and the court may not go totally unchallenged. However, because the informality of the hearing is so extreme, and because those involved generally have only limited information to work with, it may often seem to the child that the recommendations of the probation counselor are always followed by the referee, and the objections of counsel regarding gross hearsay and opinion evidence always ignored. As presently conducted, a detention hearing is an ill-defined hybrid governed only minimally by the formal law. It is too formal in some respects, devastatingly informal in others; sometimes evidentiary, other times oblivious of the rules of evidence; adversary as to participants involved, nonadversary as to the conduct of the hearings; governed by a statutory standard and theoretically limited in scope, but far reaching in practice on account of the hopelessly broad and vague terms of that statutory standard. Influencing every detention hearing is the lack of placement alternatives other than detention and the lack of treatment alternatives within the detention placement.

A further problem regarding the fairness of the detention hearing arises from the role that the probation counselor is forced to play. Because the representative of the district attorney's office is rarely prepared to argue for or against detention, the counselor often appears to the child to be the prosecutor, especially since a determination to release the child would usually have been made prior to the detention hearing.

Most probation counselors are uncomfortable with their role as untrained legal adversaries of the child's attorney, but they believe that making recommendations about a child's detention or release is their responsibility. Whatever negative impressions are left with the child as a result of his perception of the probation counselor as prosecutor can be mitigated, they argue, by establishing the limits of the counselor-child relationship at an early stage. Rejected by each counselor interviewed as both deceptive and inefficient was the suggestion that a hearing officer, who could relate to the court the probation counselor's recommendations regarding detention, might serve to insulate the counselor from the negative reactions of his probationers.

The Code provides that "[n]othing in this section shall be construed as denying a child the right to bail." This broad statement is the only reference in the formal law [11] to the right to bail and must be read together with the vague standards for detention or release of the child. A conflict arises because a child who must be detained for his own welfare still has the right of bail, and if bond is posted, the child's welfare or best interest may be jeopardized. The court's solution has been to detain on the statutory authority and, if the setting of bail is requested, to set such an excessive amount that as a practical matter the child cannot be released. This practice is especially common in CHINS cases. Its effect is to abrogate the child's right to bail, which the Supreme Court has defined as intended only to assure the presence of the accused at further court hearings. Also, because the formal law and the Colorado Rules of Juvenile Procedure provide no standards for ascertaining the amount of bail calculated to meet this purpose, the court rarely inquires as to the financial status of the child or parent, previous appearances or lack of appearance at court hearings following release, and other factors relevant to fixing the amount of bail. In fact, one referee in the court, in response to counsel's argument for reduction of bail, stated that standards set by the United States Supreme Court did not apply.[12]

A final problem in the area of detention is the absence of a time limit for the filing of a petition against the child. The Code provides that "[n]o child shall be held in a detention or shelter facility longer than forty-eight hours * * * unless a petition has been filed, or the court determines that it would be contrary to the welfare of the child or of the community to release the child from detention." The court has utilized the latter basis for detaining children longer than 48 hours and has been generally diligent in bringing children before the court for detention hearings within the time limit. However, once it is determined that a child must be detained, there is no further time

---

[11] Colo.R.Juv.P. 59(c) states that "[i]f the court believes that release will be contrary to the welfare of the child or the community, the court may order further detention and shall support such order with appropriate findings of fact, subject, however, to the right of the child to bail."

[12] The presiding judge in the same case had initially set bail at $3,000, and then, upon advice from his clerk that perhaps it would be met, raised it to $5,000 and finally to $10,000, all without questioning the child or her parents. The girl was alleged to have run away from home.

period imposed by law within which a petition must be filed. In practice, the filing often takes as long as 10 days, and it is even longer until the plea hearing is held. The child's detention is not automatically reviewed by the court until 10 days after the detention hearing,[13] and even then there is no remedy for the child unless counsel can convince the court to order filing or release within a specified period of time.

The child detained following the detention hearing by then probably feels inexorably bound into the juvenile justice system. The child who is released to his parents or to a shelter facility may be just as involved, but the indices of freedom still exist for him. The decision of the probation department to file a formal petition, handle informally, or handle unofficially probably has the greatest impact on whether the released child is to be exposed to the entire system.

Meanwhile, the child detained in the living units of Denver Juvenile Hall waits—for a visit from his family or lawyer, for his next court appearance, for a chance to escape.

PABON, THE CASE FOR ALTERNATIVES TO DETENTION; 34 JUVENILE AND FAMILY COURT JOURNAL 37 (August 1983) *

Use of Secure Detention

Many observers have commented on the fact that the modern American strategy for correcting juveniles tends to rely on an emergent policy. The policy is: *offer more juveniles detention/jailing than any other correctional response.* In the United States, nearly 1 million children are admitted to detention facilities yearly. On any given day, about 12,000 youngsters are being held in more than 300 detention centers in the nation.[14] In New York state alone, 12,740 detention admissions were recorded in 1979; and 8,551 of these were admissions to secure detention.

There is a general consistency among various definitions of detention. Most definitions agree on three common elements: juvenile detention consists of (1) temporary care, (2) while awaiting court adjudication, placement or transfer to another jurisdiction, (3) in a physically restricting setting. However, specific definitions and conceptions of detention vary. For instance, New York state defines detention exactly as others except that, instead of stating that

---

[13] This 10-day review of detention is merely an administrative practice of the Denver Juvenile Hall, established following complaints of defense attorneys that children were getting "lost" up in the living units and many times continued to be detained even after the probation counselor had decided to file a formal petition.

* Copyright by the National Council of Juvenile and Family Court Judges.

[14] Rosemary Sarri, Under Lock and Key: Juvenile and Jails and Detention (Ann Arbor, Mich.: National Assessment of Juvenile Corrections, 1974).

detention is temporary care in a physically restricting facility, it uses the terms, "detention shall mean temporary care away from their homes of children held * * * pending court or return to another jurisdiction." [15] This definition allows the use of "non-secure" detention which is temporary care of children held for court in "a facility characterized by the absence of physically restricting construction, hardware and procedures."

Other states make provisions for detention in settings that are not physically restricting. Pennsylvania, California and Utah also provide for non-secure detention. Illinois, Ohio and Missouri allow delinquency and status offenders to be placed in foster homes or shelters during the court process. Florida has established a community detention program which combines intensive supervision during the court process with non-secure homes if needed. These alternative detention programs have probably diverted a large number of juveniles from physically restricting facilities where complete security was not necessary to insure court appearance or to protect community safety. Yet, we continue to use secure detention at an increasing level.

Recent data suggest that a greater emphasis on due process inside the courtroom and a verbal commitment to diversion and community-based programs have not halted the reliance on detention lockups. According to a recent report released by the National Center for the Assessment of Alternatives to Juvenile Justice Processing, approximately 520,000 juveniles were admitted annually to detention centers during the mid-1970s. In addition, approximately 120,000 juveniles were detained annually in adult jail during the same time period. In 1973 alone, according to one survey, an estimated 100,000 youngsters spent at least one day in an adult jail and nearly 500,000 other youths were admitted to local detention facilities. These figures represent an increase of 50 percent over the 1965 statistics and are certainly higher than the population at risk of detention.

On a local level, a recent study of detention practices in New York state indicated that, although secure detention admission totals have declined during the past five years, a notable increase in non-secure detention utilization shows more of a change in usage patterns than a significant decline in overall detention admissions. Since 1975, there has been a nearly 30 percent reduction in secure detention admissions in New York state. Much of this is attributable to the removal of status offenders from secure detention. An accurate assessment of the decrease in the use of secure detention must, therefore, include a consideration of non-secure usage.

It is estimated that there were 1,600 admissions in 1975 to non-secure facilities; by 1979, this figure had risen to 4,189 admissions. In 1975, only 12 percent of the total number of detention admissions

[15] NYS Division for Youth, Juvenile Detention in New York State: Policy and Practice (Albany, N.Y.: 1977), p. 11.

were to non-secure facilities; whereas in 1979, one-third of the admissions were to non-secure detention. This change was made possible by the dramatic increase in the availability of non-secure spaces. For example, in 1977, there were 280 certified non-secure beds; in 1979, there were 470 beds. The combined totals for the years 1975 and 1979 show a decrease of about 727 admissions, representing only a 5 percent decrease in the use of the detention system in general. Thus, the 30 percent decrease in the use of secure detention is largely compensated for by the increased use of non-secure facilities. While the use of non-secure detention is clearly an important reform, it must not be allowed to disguise the fact that large numbers of juveniles are still being brought into the residential detention system.

An Over-Reliance Correctional Response

According to Judge Carrell McGraw, who released the survey's findings, "children may be legally placed in jail only if they are over the age of 14 years and are charged with the commission of a violent felony or are males 16 years of age and older who are awaiting transfer to a correctional institution.

Of the 377 juveniles who were jailed from January 1 to June 30, 334 appear to have been locked up illegally. Only 43 of the incarcerations appeared to comply with the law, according to the survey. Thirty of those 43 were jailed for committing violent felonies and 17 were awaiting transfer.

Of the 334 illegal incarcerations, 160 of the youths were jailed for misdemeanors; seven for violations of probation; 51 for status offenses; 97 for non-violent felonies; and 15 for unspecified reasons.[16]

This demonstrated preference for short-term lockups has never been set forth in any written publication that I have been able to locate. It cannot be found in philosophical statements of "progressive" reforms, legislative preambles to 20th century juvenile court statutes, judicial opinions, court administrative guidelines, local police manuals or any other type of document. But this pervasive practice of using detention as "short-term lockups" or as an *unofficial correctional disposition* exist anyway.

While there is general agreement about the types of juveniles who should be detained, i.e., those who will run away before court or placement and those who will commit another crime, it is obvious that the criteria for detention are open to a variety of interpretations and encompass a wide area of discretion. They require what are predictive and often subjective judgments.

* * *

Furthermore, one might anticipate that the alleged present offense would predict the decision-making outcome. Yet, a recent

[16] Statewide Youth Advocacy, Institutions, 3, no. 12 (December 1980): 19.

study of detention admissions in New York state indicated that the majority of secure detention admissions are not charged with serious offenses. In 1979, less than 25 percent of the secure detention admissions were charged with serious offenses.

Moreover, the question of racism arises in the figures on ethnicity of detention admissions. For instance, minority admissions accounted for more than 70 percent of the secure detention totals in the above study. Minority representation in the detention population was substantially greater than in the general population.

In a cohort study carried out in Racine, Wis., it was found that "minorities make up a disproportionate number of those referred to the juvenile court because they have more police contacts, more contacts for more serious categories of behavior, and a disproportionate number are referred beyond what would be expected considering the categories of behavior into which their reasons for police contact fall * * *." [17] At the same time, this study found that "the idea of Blacks and Chicanos as the focal point of the delinquency and crime problem is not only distorted by the failure to consider the spatial distribution of minorities (their ecological status) but is to a considerable extent a fiction based on confusing contextually-derived behavior and the characteristics of groups * * *."

In accordance with most juvenile justice standards, the category of youth unnecessarily admitted to secure detention includes all those for whom a less restrictive form of restraint would suffice. The Juvenile Justice and Delinquency Prevention Act of 1974 calls for the use of the "least restrictive means" possible, consistent with public safety, for the detention of juveniles. Yet, secure detention statistics in New York state are evidence of the failure to comply with this principle. In 1979, less than 10 percent of the securely-detained youth population were given secure placement upon adjudication; more than two-thirds of all detention admissions were detained in secure facilities.

Today we usually refer to detained youngsters as being "under lock and key." From an historical perspective, detention emerged as a juvenile functional equivalent for local jails. That is why many of them have bars on the windows and secure architecture built into their designs. Living conditions may be less harsh than residence in a local jail, but that fact does not change its functioning as a "community-based social control" facility. Furthermore, if we treat a juvenile jailing as functionally equivalent to a detention, then it is possible to conceptualize this experience as also functioning as a *non-formal, but actual, dispositional tool*. For example, more than 50 percent of the total admissions to secure detention in 1979 in New York state were released in three days or less, and approximately 45 percent were released to their homes. This over-reliance on detention suggest its use as a disposition device by the juvenile justice system.

[17] Lyle W. Shannon, "Assessing the Relationship of Adult Criminal Careers to Juvenile Delinquency: A Study of the Three Birth Cohorts," Iowa Community Research Center, n.d., pp. 15–16.

The juvenile court's well-documented use of detention after arrest as a substitute for formal adjudication represents a troublesome social control issue. Perhaps the notion of using short-term lockups for this kind of additional social function is at odds with our self-proclaimed ideal image of providing "prevention" and "treatment." Historically, since the turn of the century, we have not had a legitimate, short-term custodial disposition separate and apart from a lengthy stay at a training school. Officials have apparently adapted to this system deficiency by creating a short-term lockup as the dominant correctional response to juvenile misdeeds—without explicitly calling it a type of disposition. The pervasive dominance of this correctional response indicates that it serves multiple social control functions for communities throughout the nation. Nationwide, detention is about seven times as frequent as post-adjudication commitment to secure facilities. As a result, this might explain why there has been a scarcity of service programs developed as alternatives to detention.

Danger to the Community or to the Youngster

The juvenile justice literature of the past 10 years contains many private and public organization and commission reports criticizing detention practices throughout the nation.

> The detention of juveniles * * * represents one of the most serious problems in the administration of juvenile justice. * * * (it is) caused or compounded by profound defects in the system of juvenile justice itself: in the inadequacy of the information and the decision making process that leads to detention; in the delays between arrest and ultimate dispositions; and in the lack of visibility and accountability that pervades the process.[18]

Yet, detention prior to adjudication is a part of the juvenile justice system which has received relatively little research attention. The decision to detain usually takes only a few minutes before a judge. Little information as to the necessity of detention is ordinarily available, limited mostly to what the youngster, arresting officer or complainant and probation officer can furnish. The object of pretrial detention in the adult court is to assure the alleged offender's presence at trial; but in the case of juveniles, the purpose is much broader because of the court's power to act in the "best interest of the child" and to provide services that the judge or staff deems necessary or desirable.

For many youngsters detention is their first institutional experience with juvenile justice. The majority of detained youngsters are not subsequently committed to the state correctional system, but in detention they acquire an inkling of what to expect if they continue to get into trouble. The sociopsychological effects of detention are not clear but may have a significant impact on a youth's self-image,

[18] Institute of Judicial Administration, American Bar Association Juvenile Justice Standards: Interim Status (Cambridge, Mass.: Ballinger Publishing Co., 1980), p. 12.

confidence or feeling of alienation. On the other hand it is possible that many juveniles are able to neutralize the effects of this experience in various ways. Equally or more important, however, detention signifies to others who must make decisions about him, that in the judgment of the court he must be separated from society while awaiting adjudication of his offense. Furthermore, the decision to place a juvenile in a secure detention facility as compared to a detention foster home or shelter care facility offers a basis for characterization which may profoundly influence subsequent decision-makers responsible for his care. The findings of a recent study indicated that 47 percent of the youths detained in custodial settings were subsequently placed in secure programs compared to 18 percent of the youth detained in treatment facilities and 9 percent in shelter care units. This might not be particularly surprising except for the fact that the study data also indicated: (1) that age (younger youths) and proximity of a detention facility were the variables most strongly related to the decision to detain in the first place; and (2) that decisions to detain in custodial, treatment or shelter care were most strongly related to the availability of alternatives to secure detention and to the youths' runaway histories. It raises the spectre of a "system" so inconsistent that it differentially handles a group of youths for the most part more similar than not. Moreover, the initial differences in where a youth is detained generate more serious dispositions later on at the hands of the same system.

The argument that many youngsters are unnecessarily detained and that they could be released without increasing the threat to the safety of the community or to the operation of the court process is more directly bolstered by a recent study.[19] The author chose two counties in which detention practices were generally in accord with the 1976 standards of the National Advisory Committee on Standards for the Administration of Juvenile Justice—Gloucester County, N.J., and Taos County, N.M.—and two counties in which detention practices were not—Salt Lake County, Utah, and Lenewee County, Mich. Gloucester and Salt Lake are primarily urban counties, and Taos and Lenewee are rural. In the counties studied, the author found not only the predictable variations in detention practices, but also the lack of relation between detention practices and the character of the court referral population. For instance, when he applied the national standards to the court records of Gloucester and Salt Lake counties, Gloucester County showed up with a more serious offender population. According to the standards, 17 percent of the court referrals in Gloucester could have been detained while only 8.3 percent of the court referrals in Salt Lake should have been. In practice, however, only 8 percent of the Gloucester referrals were detained but a full 14.1 percent of the referrals in Salt Lake were detained. This sort of discrepancy was even more dramatic in the case of the rural counties. Despite the fact that the application of the national criteria indicated that about the same percentage of the court referrals should have

---

[19] Richard Kihm, Standards for Pre-Trial Detention for Juveniles (University of Illinois, Community Research Forum, 1980).

been detained in the two counties, Taos County detained no young-sters for more than 12 hours between arrest and final disposition of the case while Lenewee County detained 30 percent.

What the study goes on to show is that Gloucester and Taos counties were able to release the arrested youth without any addition-al threat to the community's safety or the court process. Among these four counties, there were no significant differences in the rates at which youngsters failed to appear for subsequent judicial proceed-ings. Likewise, the rates at which youngsters were rearrested in the period between their initial contact with the courts and the final disposition of their cases was roughly similar, except for Salt Lake County—with its higher rate of detention—where 21.5 percent of the youngsters were rearrested before the final disposition of their first referral in contrast to 12.5 percent in Gloucester County.

* * *

NOTE

IJA–ABA Juvenile Justice Standards Project, Standards Relating to Interim Status: The Release, Control and Detention of Accused Juvenile Offenders Between Arrest and Disposition (1980) proposes the following guidelines for release by juvenile court intake personnel and for review of intake detention decisions by the judge of the juvenile court in a detention hearing:

6.6 * Guidelines for status decision

A. Mandatory release. The intake official should release the accused juvenile unless the juvenile:

1. is charged with a crime of violence which in the case of an adult would be punishable by a sentence of one year or more, and which if proven is likely to result in commitment to a security institution, and one or more of the following additional factors is present:

a. the crime charged is a class one juvenile offense;

b. the juvenile is an escapee from an institution or other placement facility to which he or she was sentenced under a previous adjudication of criminal conduct;

c. the juvenile has a demonstrable recent record of willful failure to appear at juvenile proceedings, on the basis of which the official finds that no measure short of detention can be imposed to reasonably ensure appearance; or

2. has been verified to be a fugitive from another jurisdiction, an official of which has formally requested that the juvenile be placed in detention.

B. Mandatory detention. A juvenile who is excluded from mandatory release under subsection A. should not, *pro tanto,* be automatically detained. No category of alleged conduct or background in and of itself should justify a failure to exercise discretion to release.

C. Discretionary situations.

1. Release vs. detention. In every situation in which the release of an arrested juvenile is not mandatory, the intake official should first consider and determine whether the juvenile qualifies for an available diversion program, or whether any form of control short of detention is available to reasonably reduce the risk of flight or misconduct. If no such measure will suffice, the official should explicitly state in writing the reasons for rejecting each of these forms of release.

2. Unconditional vs. conditional or supervised release. In order to minimize the imposition of release conditions on persons who would appear in court without them, and present no substantial risk in the interim, each jurisdiction should develop guidelines for the use of various forms of release based upon the resources and programs available, and analysis of the effectiveness of each form of release.

3. Secure vs. nonsecure detention. Whenever an intake official determines that detention is the appropriate interim status, secure detention may be selected only if clear and convincing evidence indicates the probability of serious physical injury to others, or serious probability of flight to avoid appearance in court. Absent such evidence, the accused should be placed in an appropriate form of nonsecure detention, with a foster home to be preferred over other alternatives.

7.7 * Guidelines for status decisions

A. Release alternatives. The court may release the juvenile on his or her own recognizance, on conditions, under supervision, including release on a temporary, non-overnight basis to the attorney if so requested for the purpose of preparing the case, or into a diversion program.

B. Mandatory release. Release by the court should be mandatory when the state fails to establish probable cause to believe the juvenile committed the offense charged or in any situation in which the arresting officer or intake official was required to release the juvenile but failed to do so, unless the court is in possession of additional information which justifies detention under these standards.

C. Discretionary situations. In all other cases, the court should review all factors that officials earlier in the process were required by these standards to have considered. The court should review with particularity the adequacy of the reasons for detention recorded by the police and the intake official.

D. Written reasons. A written statement of the findings of facts and reasons why no measure short of detention would suffice should be made part of the order and filed immediately after the hearing by any judge who declines to release an accused juvenile from detention. An order continuing the juvenile in detention should be construed as authorizing nonsecure detention only, unless it contains an express direction to the contrary, supported by reasons. If the court orders release under a form of control to which the juvenile objects, the court should upon request by the attorney for the juvenile, record the facts and reasons why unconditional release was denied.

* Reprinted with permission from Standards Relating to Interim Status, Copyright 1980, Ballinger Publishing Company.

A. PLACE AND CONDITIONS OF PRE-HEARING DETENTION

VERNON'S TEXAS CODES ANNOTATED, FAMILY CODE
(1983 Supp).

Sec. 51.12 Place and Conditions of Detention.

(a) Except after transfer to criminal court for prosecution under Section 54.02 of this code, a child shall not be detained in or committed to a compartment of a jail or lockup in which persons arrested for, charged with, or convicted of crime are detained or committed, nor be permitted contact or communication with such persons.

(b) The proper authorities in each county shall provide a suitable place of detention for children who are parties to proceedings under this subtitle, but the juvenile court shall control the conditions and terms of detention and shall permit visitation with the child at all reasonable times.

(c) In each county, the judge of the juvenile court and the members of the juvenile board, if there is one, shall personally inspect the detention facilities at least annually and shall certify in writing to the authorities responsible for operating and giving financial support to the facilities that they are suitable or unsuitable for the detention of children in accordance with:

(1) the requirements of Subsection (a) of this section;

(2) the requirements of Article 5115, Revised Civil Statutes of Texas, 1925, as amended, defining "safe and suitable jails," if the detention facility is a county jail; and

(3) recognized professional standards for the detention of children.

(d) A child detained in a facility that has not been certified under Subsection (c) of this section as suitable for the detention of children shall be entitled to immediate release from custody in that facility.

(e) If there is no certified place of detention in the county in which the petition is filed, the designated place of detention may be in another county.

The Juvenile Justice and Delinquency Prevention Act of 1974, the relevant sections of which are set out Chapter 8, Section B2, infra, severely limits the use of secure detention for juveniles charge but not yet adjudicated delinquent by requiring compliance with the Act's standards as a pre-condition to a state's receiving federal aid under the Act.

D.B. v. TEWKSBURY

United States District Court for the District of Oregon, 1982.
545 F.Supp. 896.

FRYE, DISTRICT JUDGE:

This is a civil rights action brought pursuant to 42 U.S.C. § 1983. Plaintiffs and members of plaintiffs' class are all children who are presently confined, or who are subject to confinement in the Columbia County Correctional Facility (CCCF), an adult jail, in St. Helens, Oregon. Plaintiffs challenge the constitutionality of defendants' actions in confining plaintiffs and members of their class in CCCF. Plaintiffs seek declaratory and injunctive relief.

SPECIAL FINDINGS OF FACT

The named plaintiffs are children, all of whom have been detained in CCCF. Plaintiffs and their next friend and next friend of the class, Susan F. Mandiberg, represent a class certified by the court as consisting of similarly situated children.

Defendant Graham Tewksbury is the Director of the Columbia County Juvenile Department. Defendants A.J. Ahlborn, Robert M. Hunt, and Marion Sahagian are commissioners of the Columbia County Board of Commissioners. Defendant Tom Tennant is the Sheriff of Columbia County. He is responsible for the general operation and supervision of the Sheriff's Department, including CCCF. Defendant Willard E. Jones is the corrections supervisor of CCCF. He is responsible for the general operation and supervision of CCCF and for carrying out the Sheriff's policies and procedures in CCCF. Defendant James D. Taylor is the assistant corrections supervisor of CCCF. Defendants James E. Cox, Dale Len Durant, Larry C. Knowles, and Dale R. Stubbs are corrections officers in CCCF.

In acting and/or failing to act and in maintaining the conditions in CCCF, defendants, and each of them, separately and in concert, have been and are acting under color of and pursuant to the statutes, ordinances, regulations, customs, and usages of the State of Oregon and in their capacities as heretofore stated. Children have been and continue to be detained in CCCF with the knowledge of all the defendants.

CCCF houses both adults and children in the same facility. Many adults are convicted prisoners serving time on sentences already imposed. All children held in CCCF are pretrial detainees, i.e., there has been no adjudication with regard to these children's acts, status, or behavior. They range in age from 12 to 18. Many of the children are "status offenders." Status offenders are children who, by virtue of their ages, are confined for being beyond parental control or running away from home. Of 101 children held at CCCF during a nine month period in 1980, 36 were held on status offense charges. The remaining children during this period were held for acts which, if they had been done by an adult, would constitute crimes. Sometimes children are placed in CCCF for shelter care: for example, a child who has been raped can be placed in CCCF.

Children do not stay in CCCF for long periods of time, but status offenders ordinarily are confined longer than those detained for criminal acts. In any event, 70 percent of the children who were confined in CCCF in 1981 were released within 24 hours. Nearly 75 percent of the children held in CCCF are released to their parents. A small number pose an immediate threat to community safety or their own safety or may flee from the court's jurisdiction. In 1980, of 124 children confined in CCCF, during a nine month period, only 25 required secure custody. The others could have been released without posing a serious threat to community safety, personal safety, or court jurisdiction.

CCCF is located on the ground floor of the Columbia County Courthouse in St. Helens, Oregon. It was built in 1962 and was altered in 1975. The offices of defendant Tewksbury and each of his three juvenile counselors are located in a building connected to the CCCF building.

Children detained in CCCF are usually placed in quarters consisting of multiple-occupancy cells with a common day space. They may be placed in isolation cells, however. Each multiple-occupancy cell contains steel bed frames, a toilet-sink installation, one overhead light, and a steel-barred wall with a sliding door. Children are locked inside the cells from 10 p.m. to 6 a.m.

The day room area, i.e., the common room, contains a metal picnic table, fluorescent lighting fixtures, and a single shower unit. There is no natural light in the cells occupied by children. Illumination is sufficient for overall visibility. All walls, floors, and ceilings are solid concrete or concrete block materials. The walls are painted blue.

Doors entering into these areas are either steel bars or solid metal. Each door contains a small viewing window and a food service slot. Children are detained in cells geared for as many as three children. Sometimes children ranging in age from 12 to 17 years are placed in the same cell.

Children held in CCCF are not issued sheets, mattress covers, or pillows. They sleep on mattresses covered with urethane and they are given a wool blanket. Occasionally children are not given mattresses. Those children placed in isolation cells sleep on cement floors.

Female children are not advised by matrons that sanitary napkins or tampons are available. If requested, however, they are made available. Matrons are not stationed within the secure detention area of CCCF. They are stationed in the front office area and are in the jail only to make checks on the female children. In order to obtain a sanitary napkin or tampon, female children must strike their cell doors or yell to attract the attention of a male corrections officer, who in turn contacts a matron. There are no full-time matrons available during night shifts, but if a female child is detained during the night, a part-time matron is called and is available.

There is no 24-hour a day intake screening process at CCCF. The intake process at CCCF is essentially an *admissions* process rather than a *screening* process. Part of the reason that children are detained at CCCF rather than being placed elsewhere is that there are no written criteria upon which to make decisions regarding who should be detained in CCCF. There is no policy as to *who* makes a decision when a child is to be lodged in jail. There is a phone list for jail staff to use to try to reach juvenile counselors, but counselors are sometimes unavailable. Children are then lodged based upon the decision of the corrections officer (jailer). If an arresting officer can locate a juvenile counselor, there is nothing in writing that tells the officer or the juvenile counselor when to lodge the child. For example, D.P. was arrested with a friend. D.P.'s friend was released to his parents who came to pick him up. D.P., however, was lodged in CCCF because his custodial grandmother did not have a car and therefore could not pick him up. Even if a juvenile counselor is available, the juvenile counselor does not speak directly with the child before he or she makes an intake decision. There are no written procedures for how to handle physically, mentally, or emotionally handicapped children. Jail personnel testified that none of these children are ever detained.

All clothing of children detained in CCCF is confiscated. Children are issued jail clothes which consist of jeans, a shirt, and socks for boys, and slacks, a blouse, and socks for girls. No child lodged in CCCF may have underwear.

Toilet facilities at CCCF are not screened from view and children using these toilet facilities are visible to other children and to corrections officers. The day room area has a shower which can be used at all times when the children are not locked in their cells. On occasion showers in CCCF are not equipped with shower curtains. Children showering are visible to other children and to corrections officers. Female children using the toilet or shower are visible to male corrections officers. Male children using the toilet or shower are visible to matrons.

Children in CCCF are sometimes placed in either of two isolation cells. These are $8' \times 8'$ windowless concrete block rooms, barren of all furniture and furnishings. Sometimes it is very cold in the isolation cells. Near the center of the isolation cell there is a sewer hole which is the only facility for urination and defecation.

Lighting and the mechanism for flushing the sewer hole for each isolation cell are controlled outside the cell by the corrections staff. Lights in the isolation cells are sometimes left on or off for long periods of time. Sometimes the sewer hole is not flushed for long periods. When the mechanism for the sewer hole is flushed by a corrections staff officer, water and sewage gushes onto the cell floor.

The isolation cells are located across a corridor from the adult male dormitory cell which holds up to 18 prisoners. For a child to be placed in isolation, that child must be moved down a corridor immediately outside the adult male dormitory cell. The child can see the adult male prisoners, and the adult male prisoners can see him or her. When the isolation cell door is closed, children in isolation and the adults in the dormitory cell can and do communicate by talking in loud voices. Children may also encounter adult inmates during the intake process.

There are no written standards for placement of children in isolation. There is no one designated to determine if and when a child should be placed in isolation. There is no absolute limit to the period of time that a child can be held in isolation. Isolation cells have been used when children were intoxicated or under the influence of drugs. Children have also been placed in isolation for perceived offenses or disputes between children held in the same cell. There is no psychological screening of children placed in isolation. No log is maintained when a child is placed in isolation.

Meals served to children are planned, prepared, and served by corrections officers. Corrections officers must prepare meals in addition to performing their other duties. Corrections officers are not trained in nutrition or food preparation. They are not supervised by a nutritionist or a dietitian. There are no written menus. Meals are prepared from foods available in storage. Food served to children is the same as that served to adult prisoners and to the corrections personnel themselves, except that children at CCCF are not allowed to buy food through the commissary, while adult prisoners are. Special dietary needs of children, or special dietary needs of a child such as a diabetic child are not considered.

No medical screening procedure is used for children admitted to CCCF other than a visual inspection by an untrained corrections officer. Children who are intoxicated or under the influence of drugs are admitted to CCCF. Corrections officers have no training in identifying or meeting the needs of intoxicated or drug dependent children. These children may be placed in isolation. For example, one of the plaintiffs, D.P., was arrested while intoxicated and was placed in isolation for uncooperative behavior. He received no counseling or assistance from anyone trained to deal with an intoxicated child. After shattering his finger and breaking out several teeth, he was transported to Dammasch Hospital.

K.K. was also detained at CCCF while intoxicated. Because of belligerent behavior, he was placed in a juvenile section in handcuffs. He received no medical screening, monitoring, or assistance, and was later found on his cell floor in a pool of vomit and urine. He was then taken to Columbia District Hospital where he was admitted for observation.

There is no daily sick call for children at CCCF. There is no regular program for a doctor or a registered nurse to visit the jail to identify or attend to the medical needs of children held in CCCF. Emergency medical equipment in the jail consists of a first aid kit and an oxygen tank.

Corrections officers determine whether a child needs medical treatment based upon perception, common sense, and experience. If a child believes he or she is ill, the child notifies a corrections officer, who decides whether the child should be taken to a doctor. There are no written criteria for corrections officers to follow in determining whether a child should see a doctor.

There are no special rules or procedures for the treatment of emotionally disturbed children who panic in a jail setting. There is no emergency medical health service. There are no psychiatrists, psychologists, or counselors on call. Frequently children in CCCF do not see their juvenile court counselors at all during their incarceration in the jail. There is no written log kept of juvenile court counselor visits to the jail.

There are no educational programs for children at CCCF. Children are not allowed to have books or magazines or pencils and paper. This policy is not the jail's policy, but the policy of the Juvenile Department. Corrections officers have been instructed by the Juvenile Department not to give children reading material or pencils and paper. It is also the policy of the sheriff. C.H., a juvenile, was twice jailed for truancy. Jailers refused to give him any of his school books.

There are no recreational programs, materials, or activities for children at CCCF. Children have no access to televisions, radios, or any other recreational material, including books, magazines, and pencils and paper.

There are no facilities or equipment for exercise. There is no exercise room and there are no organized exercise classes or programs for children, although children may exercise in the cells or in the day room area.

Children are treated considerably differently from adults. Adults have access to books, television, radio, cards, and other recreational materials; children do not. Adults are allowed to have underwear brought to them at CCCF; children are not. Adults have regular visitation and may visit with friends as well as families; children have no regularly scheduled visitation. Adults are allowed to send and receive mail; children are not allowed to send or receive mail. Adults are provided paper, writing material, envelopes, and stamps. Children are not allowed to have paper, writing material, envelopes, or stamps. Adults are allowed to make one phone call upon admission; children are not allowed to make a phone call upon admission. Adults are allowed to make phone calls during their period of incarceration. Children at CCCF, prior to the court entering its preliminary injunction dated June 10, 1981, were prohibited from making phone calls without Juvenile Department permission. When an attorney comes to CCCF to see an adult inmate, this visitation is allowed. If an attorney comes to CCCF to see a child, the attorney must go through the Juvenile Department to gain access to the child.[20] An inmate manual governs the conduct of adults held in CCCF. Children are not advised what behavior will result in disciplinary action or sanctions. There are no grievance procedures for children.

[20] An attorney appointed by a Juvenile Court Judge may have access to a child without permission of the Juvenile Department. All of the plaintiffs and presumably many of the class, had no appointed attorney while detained in CCCF.

Parents are not allowed to visit children confined in CCCF without permission of the Juvenile Department. Jailers do not have the authority to allow parent-child visitation. Visitation with children in CCCF is controlled by the Juvenile Department and not the jail. The visitation policy for children is not in writing. There are no standards within the Juvenile Department for granting or denying visits with children in CCCF. No contact visits are allowed. Parents and detained children must talk to one another by means of a telephone and are separated by shatter-proof glass. Jailers sometimes will not tell inquiring parents whether or not their child is, in fact, in jail.

There are no formal written policies and procedures pertaining to the care and treatment of juveniles at CCCF. The policies that do exist are developed informally and handed down verbally. Therefore, many policies are in a constant state of flux and/or confusion. Furthermore, it is impossible to determine which policies are promulgated by the Juvenile Department and which policies are promulgated by the Sheriff's Department. There is no written contract between the Juvenile Department and the Sheriff's Department or jail regarding confinement of children.

There are no written rules governing the conduct of children held in CCCF. Therefore, children are not notified of what behavior is expected of them. What behavior is expected of them is left to the individual whims and caprices of the various corrections officers in charge. For example, it is up to an individual officer's discretion to decide if a child should be locked in isolation. It is up to an individual officer's discretion what restraining physical tactic to employ in dealing with a child.

All full-time corrections officers at CCCF are men. There are three part-time matrons who are employed to handle female children. Matrons are not stationed within the security detention area of CCCF. The part-time matrons are not required to receive training that male corrections officers receive. If a female child wants to get the attention of a matron, she first must get the attention of a male guard, who in turn contacts the matron. Ordinarily, female children are not informed by jail staff as to how to get the attention of a matron. Frequently only one corrections officer staffs the jail.

Corrections officers at CCCF are basically jail staff. They have no training and little time to work with children. For example, if a child locked in a cell is screaming or yelling, the officer may go to the cell and yell, "Quiet down." The personnel at CCCF are not prepared or trained to treat children in other than a manner consistent with a maximum security lock-up facility.

Although there is no evidence to indicate physical abuse such as beatings, there is evidence that corrections personnel have made verbal threats toward detained children and have refused to tell them the time of day when requested. Since there is no natural light in the children's cells and since there are no clocks, children often become disoriented as to time.

Generally, the corrections staff has been insensitive to the needs of children in stressful situations. For example, when C.H. called for help when he and his brother were being harassed by older juveniles, the staff did not respond for a long time. One jailer told L.B. and other girls that they could bleed to death if they wanted to during an incident when the girls had broken a light bulb and were carving on their bodies. When D.B. called for help when he saw an adult inmate lying on the ground with slashed wrists, the corrections officer told him to "Shut up or go to the isolation cell." When D.P. refused to sign a paper during the booking process, a corrections officer grabbed D.P. by the hair and used an arm lock to pull D.P. to his cell. One corrections officer threatened to put D.P. in a cell with a "buck nigger" and showed D.P. a bloody shirt which the officer claimed indicated what happened to the last person who shared a cell with a "buck nigger."

Children in CCCF are allowed to see and hear adult inmates.[21] All entry ways, passages, and exits to and from the facility are the same for juveniles and adults. Children in both isolation and regular cells can and do communicate with adult inmates. Several of the plaintiffs have been subjected to sexually suggestive comments from adults. Corrections officers do not invite child-adult communication; however, they cannot prevent it.

In January, 1980, the Columbia County Circuit Judge appointed a special investigating Grand Jury to make a complete investigation into the conditions at CCCF. That Grand Jury inspected the jail and took testimony. In May, 1980, the Grand Jury found numerous deficiencies in the facility and specifically recommended that children not be kept in CCCF until these conditions were remedied. The Grand Jury further expressed "hope" that alternatives to confinement of children in CCCF would be developed.

After the Federal Defender for the District of Oregon investigated conditions in CCCF, the United States Marshals Service discontinued placement of federal prisoners in CCCF.

Columbia County has some cost-effective alternative facilities for housing children. Shelter care is available. Defendants agree that removal of children from CCCF could result in a potential financial saving to Columbia County. Facilities in Cowlitz County, Washington, and at the Multnomah County Juvenile Detention Facilities, in Portland, Oregon are available. Columbia County participates in the Juvenile Services Act and in the 1981–82 biennium received approximately $100,000 under that act. Columbia County has been negotiating for and could receive funds in the amount of $36,000 under the Boys and Girls Aid Jail Removal Initiative Proposal. Columbia County has a special fund of approximately $25,000 given as a bequest for the betterment of conditions for children.

[21] Although CCCF is in violation of the screening provisions of ORS 419.575, ORS 169.079 (1979) (amended 1981; re- numbered ORS 169.740), statutory violations at CCCF will not be addressed in this opinion.

Data from a contiguous county, Clackamas County, indicate that children requiring secure custody in Clackamas County are housed in Multnomah County's Juvenile Detention Facility and that this program does not cost Clackamas County any more money than putting children into jails. Columbia County can request free technical assistance through the Federal Office of Juvenile Justice and Delinquency Prevention. At no cost to Columbia County, procedures, practices, programs, and planning can be provided so that Columbia County has access to expertise and planning and monitoring skills of experts in the field of juvenile care. It would take approximately 30 days to effect a 100% removal of children from CCCF and set up alternatives.

Current literature in the field of juvenile justice indicates that behavior modification of socially-deviant children is best achieved when children are diverted from the criminal justice system and its jails and punishments whenever possible. Studies also indicate that whenever restraints of children are necessary for the protection of society or protection of the children themselves, these restraints are best carried out through diversion programs, home detention, shelter care, crisis or emergency centers, or through intensive counselling and monitoring. As a last resort, the literature indicates, children who need to be confined should be held—not in jails or dungeons—but in juvenile detention centers geared to meet the needs of these children.

The jailing of children in maximum security adult jails such as CCCF stigmatizes (or brands) them as criminals. This interferes with their relationships with their families, schools, and communities—and most of all with their ability to confront adolescent crises and emerge from those crises as *law-abiding* productive adults. It increases the chance that they will forever be "criminals." The fact that the confinement is brief does not reduce the harm.

The plaintiffs were credible witnesses. Details of their stories were corroborated by the testimony of defendants, themselves, the Columbia County Grand Jury report, the Federal Defender's report, the CCCF jail records (and absence of records), and the expert witnesses.

Defendant Tewksbury has publicly described CCCF as "pretty much a bare lockup, just like the adult jail, but the kids don't get the same privileges * * *. It's a boring place, a helluva place." He has further stated "Detention is punishment and I try to make it as unappetizing as possible. The last place a child wants to be."

GENERAL FACTUAL FINDINGS

CCCF is designed for the purpose of confinement, without regard for human dignity or need. Nothing over and above the basic minimums necessary for the maintenance of bodily functions is provided to children at CCCF. Nothing at CCCF is responsive to the emotional and physical needs of children in conflict with the law and their families. CCCF is a maximum security lock-up facility.

Placement of children within cells without regard to their ages or levels of maturity and without adequate supervision by trained corrections staff and without regard to the reasons why they are being held, increases antisocial behavior such as violence and physical abuse.

To require a female child to strike a cell door or to yell for assistance in order to receive sanitary napkins causes needless embarrassment and humiliation to such child. To require any child to go without underwear in a culture in which underwear is considered a requirement of dress causes needless embarrassment and humiliation for the child.

The requirement that children wear jail "uniforms," and the lack of privacy for the use of showers and bathrooms contribute to feelings of anxiety and loss of self-esteem which are counterproductive to the goals of the juvenile justice system. The failure to provide counseling or psychiatric care for children in CCCF is also counterproductive to these goals.

The lack of programs and the method of "treatment" reflect policies of the Juvenile Department and the institution, rather than inadequate resources. These policies result in harsher treatment for pretrial detainee children than for adult prisoners, many of whom have been convicted and sentenced. The denial of access to family and friends by way of regularly scheduled visits, use of telephone, and use of mail, needlessly creates or intensifies children's fears, hostilities, and rages, and is, again, counterproductive to the goals of the juvenile justice system.

The failure to have a written policy results in confusion, arbitrary decisions, and different treatment under similar situations. Without written rules children are at the mercy of the corrections staff and therefore subject to unnecessary anxieties about what to do or expect. There is nothing for children to do while confined at CCCF. This creates needless idleness, boredom, acute anxiety, fear, depression, and hostility. Idle, unattended, confined children present special supervisory problems. They frequently become destructive and cause physical harm to each other, themselves, or to their surroundings.

CCCF is inadequately staffed and the staff is inadequately trained to handle children. As a result, there is a lack of proper care of children. Jailers without special training in dealing with children under stress or emotionally distressed children are not qualified to provide the kind of counseling and therapy which is consistent with the goals of the juvenile justice system.

Confinement in CCCF is clearly and fundamentally intended to punish children. Punishment is the treatment of choice of Columbia County's Juvenile Department for its detained children. This "treatment" has little or nothing to do with simple detention, rehabilitation, or even the protection of society.

CONTENTIONS OF THE PARTIES

Plaintiffs contend *inter alia* that the conditions and restrictions imposed on plaintiffs and plaintiffs' class by defendants constitute punishment and thereby violate plaintiffs' rights as pretrial detainees not to be punished under the due process clause of the 14th Amendment to the United States Constitution.

Plaintiffs seek (1) a declaration that their federal constitutional rights have been violated, and (2) a permanent injunction enjoining defendants from confining plaintiffs and members of their class in CCCF or any other adult correctional facility. Plaintiffs request an award of attorney fees and costs, and any other relief that the court deems just and proper.

Defendants contend that they have acted pursuant to Oregon statutory provisions and that the Oregon statutory provisions pertaining to the detention of juveniles do not violate the United States Constitution.

This case requires the court to examine the federal due process rights of children detained prior to a hearing or adjudication in CCCF, an adult maximum security correctional facility.

CONFINEMENT IN CCCF AS PUNISHMENT

Oregon statutory law allows a child to be detained in local correctional facilities such as CCCF so long as the portion of the facility holding the child is screened from the sight and sound of adult prisoners. ORS 419.575, ORS 169.079 (1979) (amended 1981; renumbered ORS 169.740). Under Oregon law, then, plaintiffs may legitimately be incarcerated in CCCF prior to an adjudication of their status or guilt. It is the scope of their federal constitutional rights during this period of confinement before a hearing that is the focus of this case.

The Due Process Clause of the Fourteenth Amendment to the United States Constitution requires that a pretrial detainee not be punished. *Bell v. Wolfish*, 441 U.S. 520, 99 S.Ct. 1861, 60 L.Ed.2d 447 (1979). A state does not acquire the power to punish a person— adult or child (assuming a child is convicted of committing a crime)— until after it has secured a formal adjudication of guilt in accordance with due process of law. Not every disability imposed in preadjudication detention amounts to "punishment," however. The very fact of detention implies a measure of restriction of movement, choice, privacy, and comfort.

This court must determine whether the conditions imposed upon plaintiffs are imposed for the purpose of punishment or whether they are incidents of some other legitimate governmental purpose. In this case the determination is simple. Defendant Tewksbury has stated publicly and expressly that he intends to punish children detained in CCCF. It is the express intent of defendants that plaintiffs' confinements in CCCF be punishments. The intent to punish is carried out in the extraordinary conditions of confinement imposed on plaintiffs while confined in CCCF. Confinement of child pretrial detainees in CCCF as it now exists is punishment prior to an adjudication of guilt.

Defendants have violated plaintiffs' due process rights under the Fourteenth Amendment to be free from pretrial punishments by confining plaintiffs in CCCF. Those extraordinary conditions which alone and in combination constitute punishment are:

1. Failure to provide *any* form of work, exercise, education, recreation, or recreational materials.

2. Failure to provide minimal privacy when showering, using toilets, or maintaining feminine hygiene.

3. Placement of intoxicated or drugged children in isolation cells without supervision or medical attention.

4. Placement of younger children in isolation cells as a means of protecting them from older children.

5. Failure to provide adequate staff supervision to protect children from harming themselves and/or other children.

6. Failure to allow contact between children and their families.

7. Failure to provide an adequate diet.

8. Failure to train staff to be able to meet the psychological needs of confined children.

9. Failure to provide written institutional rules, sanctions for violation of those rules, and a grievance procedure.

10. Failure to provide adequate medical care.

CONFINEMENT IN JAILS AS PUNISHMENT FOR STATUS OFFENDERS

Plaintiffs also contend and ask the court to rule that even if the conditions of confinement at CCCF are corrected, plaintiffs and plaintiffs' class may not be detained in CCCF because the confinement of plaintiffs and plaintiffs' class in *any* adult jail constitutes punishment *per se* and is therefore unconstitutional. The court will address this contention first as it relates to status offenders, i.e., runaway children or children who are out of parental control.

The impact that a runaway child or a child out of the control of his or her parents has on the family and may have on the community causes alarm and often leads to the necessity for societal intervention. The runaway or out-of-control child can jeopardize the lives and property of other people as well as his own life. The question is: Does the *status* of such a child justify placing that child in a jail?

Society has historically used terror, confinement, and punishment as a means of dealing with "status." For example, insane people used to be beaten and imprisoned. Lepers were sent to remote and undesirable geographical areas. As recently as 1962 the legislature of the State of California enacted a law which made *being* a narcotic addict a crime for which punishment could be inflicted. That law was ruled unconstitutional by the United States Supreme Court. Robinson v. State of California, 370 U.S. 660, 82 S.Ct. 1417, 8 L.Ed.2d 758 (1962).

A child who has run away from home or is out of parental control is clearly a child in distress, a child in conflict with his family and his society. But nobody contends he is a criminal. A runaway child or a child out of control, as an addict or an insane person, may be confined for treatment or for the protection of society, but to put such a child in a jail—any jail—with its criminal stigma—constitutes punishment and is a violation of that child's due process rights under the Fourteenth Amendment to the United States Constitution. No child who is a *status* offender may be lodged constitutionally in an adult jail.

CONFINEMENT IN JAILS FOR CHILDREN ACCUSED OF COMMITTING CRIMES

The court must now turn to the issue of whether it is constitutionally permissible to lodge children who have been accused of committing crimes in adult jails pending adjudication of the charges against them. The court has above ruled that confining children in CCCF pending adjudication of crimes or status constitutes punishment, and the court has further ruled that detaining children in *any* jails on the basis of their status or condition constitutes punishment and is an unconstitutional deprivation of due process. The court must now deal with children charged with committing crimes and must suppose that the jails in which these children are lodged are modern, "enlightened" kinds of jails—ones which provide different methods of discipline, care, and treatment appropriate for individual children according to age, personality, and mental and physical condition. The court must further suppose that these jails are adequately staffed and provide reasonable measures of comfort, privacy, medical care, food, and recreation. Would it be constitutionally permissible to lodge children accused of committing crimes in these jails?

In deciding this issue, the court declines to rule on the "punishment" aspect of the due process clause of the 14th Amendment. Instead the court will rely on the "fundamental fairness" doctrine enunciated in In Re Gault, 387 U.S. 1, 87 S.Ct. 1428, 18 L.Ed.2d 527 (1967) and juvenile cases decided after the *Gault* decision.

Due process—or fundamental fairness—does not guarantee to children all the rights in the adjudication process which are constitutionally assured to adults accused of committing crimes. For example, children are not entitled to a jury trial, to indictment by Grand Jury, or to bail. In lieu of these constitutional rights, children are not to be treated or considered as criminals. An adjudication of a child as guilty does not have the effect of a conviction nor is such child deemed a criminal. Even upon a finding of "guilt" as to the criminal charges, the child may not be imprisoned in adult jails as punishment for his acts. ORS 419.507, 419.509.

Juvenile proceedings, in the State of Oregon as elsewhere, are in the nature of a guardianship imposed by the state as *parens patriae* to provide the care and guidance that under normal circumstances would be furnished by the natural parents.[22] It is, then, fundamentally fair—constitutional—to deny children charged with crimes rights available to adults charged with crimes if that denial is offset by a special solicitude designed for children.

But when the denial of constitutional rights for children is not offset by a "special solicitude" but by lodging them in adult jails, it is fundamentally unfair.[23] When children who are found *guilty* of committing criminal acts cannot be placed in adult jails, it is fundamentally unfair to lodge children *accused* of committing criminal acts in adult jails.

In 1966 the United States Supreme Court envisioned the problem confronting this court:

> "* * * There is evidence, in fact, that there may be grounds for concern that the child receives the worst of both worlds: that he gets neither the protections accorded to adults nor the solicitous care and regenerative treatment postulated for children."

Kent v. United States, 383 U.S. 541, 556, 86 S.Ct. 1045, 1054, 16 L.Ed. 2d 84 (1966).

The supervisors at jails are guards—not guardians. Jails hold convicted criminals and adults charged with crimes. Jails are prisons, with social stigmas. Children identify with their surroundings. They may readily perceive themselves as criminals, for who goes to jail except for criminals? A jail is not a place where a truly concerned natural parent would lodge his or her child for care and guidance. A jail is not a place where the state can constitutionally lodge its children under the guise of *parens patriae.*

To lodge a child in an adult jail pending adjudication of criminal charges against that child is a violation of that child's due process rights under the Fourteenth Amendment to the United States Constitution.

CONCLUSION

Plaintiffs are entitled to a permanent injunction and to reasonable attorneys' fees including reasonable attorneys' fees for the hearing on the motion for preliminary injunction. Plaintiffs' counsel shall submit to the court a proposed judgment order disposing of this case.

[22] ORS 419.474(2) provides that juvenile court proceedings "* * * shall be liberally construed to the end that a child coming within the jurisdiction of the court may receive such care, guidance and control, preferably within his own home, as will lead to the child's welfare and the best interests of the public, and that when a child is removed from the control of his parents the court may secure for him care that best meets the needs of the child."

[23] This opinion does not apply to children who are remanded to adult criminal courts and who are afforded all of the constitutional rights accorded to adults charged with crimes. This opinion also does not apply to children temporarily detained in police stations pending the obtaining of identifying information.

Plaintiffs' counsel shall at the same time file their claims for attorneys' fees with supporting data and a memorandum. Defendants' counsel shall have 20 days to object to the form of the judgment and to request a hearing on the amount of the attorneys' fees. If the court receives no objection or request for hearing, it will sign the judgment order and will allow such attorneys' fees as it deems reasonable in accordance with law.

B. THE PRE–ADJUDICATION LIBERTY INTEREST

1. RIGHT TO BAIL?

The statutes and cases which follow reflect varying judgments about the appropriateness of—indeed the constitutional necessity for—provisions for bail in the context of a juvenile release-detention system.

REVISED STATUTES OF NEBRASKA (1982 Cum.Supp.)

43–253. Temporary custody of juvenile; investigation; release; when. Upon delivery to the juvenile court or probation officer of a juvenile who has been taken into temporary custody under sections 43–248 and 43–250, the court or probation officer shall immediately investigate the situation of the juvenile and the nature and circumstances of the events surrounding his or her being taken into custody. Such investigation may be by hearing on the record before the court or by informal means when appropriate. The court or probation officer may immediately release such juvenile to the custody of his or her parent, guardian, relative, or other responsible person, or the court may admit such juvenile to bail by bond in such amount and on such conditions and security as the court, in its sole discretion, shall determine, or the court may proceed as provided in section 43–254. In no case shall the court or probation officer release such juvenile if it appears that further detention or placement of such juvenile is a matter of immediate and urgent necessity for the protection of such juvenile or the person or property of another or if it appears that such juvenile is likely to flee the jurisdiction of the court.

HAWAII REVISED STATUTES (1983 P.P.Supp.)

§ 571–32 Detention; shelter; release; notice. (a) If a child who is believed to come within section 571–11(1) or (2) is not released as provided in section 571–31 and is not deemed suitable for diversion, such child shall be taken without unnecessary delay to the court or to the place of detention or shelter designated by the court. If the court determines that the child requires care away from the child's own home but does not require secure physical restriction, such child shall be given temporary care in any available non-secure child caring institution, foster family home, or other shelter facility.

* * *

(h) Provisions regarding bail shall not be applicable to children detained in accordance with this chapter, except that bail may be allowed after a child has been transferred for criminal prosecution pursuant to waiver of family court jurisdiction.

CODE OF GEORGIA ANNOTATED (1982 Supp.)

24A–1402 Release, delivery to court, detention; bail; unruly child.

* * *

(d) Bail. All juveniles subject to the jurisdiction of the juvenile court and alleged to be delinquent or unruly, on application of the parent or guardian, shall have the same right to bail as adults; and the judge shall admit to bail all juveniles under his jurisdiction in the same manner and under the same circumstances and procedures as are applicable to adults accused of the commission of crimes.

L.O.W. v. THE DISTRICT COURT

Supreme Court of Colorado, 1981.
623 P.2d 1253.

DUBOFSKY, JUSTICE.

In response to a petition filed under C.A.R. 21, we issued a Rule to Show Cause why the respondent district court should not set bond for the petitioner. We now discharge the Rule.

Petitioner L.O.W., a child, was charged in a delinquency petition in Arapahoe County District Court with acts which would have constituted second-degree burglary, a class three felony, section 18–4–203, C.R.S. 1973 (now in 1978 Repl.Vol. 8), if the child had been an adult. At a detention hearing on October 23, 1980, the district court heard testimony from the investigating police officer and reviewed both a counselor's report and the petitioner's court history. The evidence disclosed that the petitioner twice had been adjudicated a delinquent child and was the subject of a reserved ruling in another case. He had previously failed to appear for a jury trial and revocation hearing in Arapahoe County and had missed a court appearance in Jefferson County. At the time of the detention hearing L.O.W. was on probation for carrying a concealed weapon. Delinquency petitions based on serious charges were pending against him in Denver and Jefferson Counties. He was also subject to probation revocation proceedings based on the allegations in this case.

The district court found that probable cause existed to believe that the petitioner had committed an act of delinquency and that it was in the best interests of the child and the community for him to remain in detention at the Arapahoe Youth Center. The trial court denied the petitioner's request that bond be set in a reasonable amount.

Because no new evidence was adduced at subsequent detention hearings held on October 29 and November 3, 1980, the court continued the petitioner's detention. The petitioner did not present evidence relevant to his request for bond at any of the hearings.[24]

The petitioner contends that the trial court's refusal to set bond contravenes U.S. Const., Amend. VIII and Colo.Const., Art. II, Sec. 20 [25] prohibiting excessive bail, and sections 16–4–101, C.R.S.1973 (1979 Supp.),[26] 16–4–102, C.R.S.1973 (1978 Repl.Vol. 8) [27] and 19–2–103(7), C.R.S.1973 (1978 Repl.Vol. 8).[28] We conclude that a child does not have an absolute constitutional or statutory right to bail pending adjudication of the charges filed against him in juvenile court. Because the respondent district court's findings in this case justified detention of L.O.W. without bail we discharge the Rule.

I.

We issued the Rule to Show Cause in this case on November 3, 1980, but, in order to avoid protracted juvenile court proceedings, we denied petitioner's request that the proceedings be stayed. On December 15, 1980, the petitioner appeared before the respondent court and admitted engaging in conduct which would have been aggravated motor vehicle theft if committed by an adult.[29] The court then detained the petitioner without bond until the dispositional hearing on January 5, 1981. * * *

II.

The Eighth Amendment to the United States Constitution provides that "[e]xcessive bail shall not be required * * *." * * *

Section 20 of Article II of the Colorado Constitution is identical to the Eighth Amendment. In addition, Section 19 of Article II of the Colorado Constitution provides that:

[24] C.R.J.P. 23 provides:

"(a) The court may, in its order admitting any child to bail, impose certain conditions, including who may post a bond for the child, with whom the child shall reside during the pendency of the proceedings, and any other conditions necessary for the child's welfare or safety.

(b) The court may order that any personal recognizance bond be secured by the personal obligation of the minor child and his parents, guardian, legal custodian, or other responsible adult."

See In re M., 3 Cal.3d 16, 473 P.2d 737, 89 Cal.Rptr. 33 (1970).

[25] See also Article II, Section 19 of the Colorado Constitution.

[26] Section 16–4–101 provides:

"All persons shall be bailable before conviction, except in a prosecution for a capital offense in which the proof is evident or the presumption great * * *."

[27] Section 16–4–102 provides:

"Any person who is in custody and for whom no bail has been set pursuant to the applicable rule of criminal procedure may advise any judge of a court of record in the county where he is being held of that fact with a request that bail be set * * *."

See also Crim.P. 46.

[28] Section 19–2–103(7) provides: "Nothing in this section shall be construed as denying a child the right to bail."

[29] The delinquency petition filed with the court after October 23, 1980, charged the petitioner with acts which, had they been committed by an adult, would constitute second-degree burglary of a dwelling, aggravated motor vehicle theft, and theft.

"All persons shall be bailable by sufficient sureties except for capital offenses, when the proof is evident or the presumption great."

We have interpreted Section 19 to confer an absolute right to bail in all except capital cases. * * * The purpose of bail is to ensure the defendant's presence at trial and not to punish him before he has been convicted. * * *

Rights provided to adult defendants in criminal proceedings, however, have not been made uniformly available to juveniles because the protective purposes of juvenile proceedings preponderate over their punitive function. * * * Although early decisions held that "the juvenile is not entitled to bail, to indictment by grand jury, to a public trial or to trial by jury," In re Gault, supra, 387 U.S. at 14, 87 S.Ct. at 1436, the "applicable due process standard in juvenile proceedings, as [since] developed by *Gault* and [In re] Winship [397 U.S. 358, 90 S.Ct. 1068, 25 L.Ed.2d 368 (1970)], is fundamental fairness." McKeiver v. Pennsylvania, supra, 403 U.S. at 543, 91 S.Ct. at 1985, 29 L.Ed.2d at 659.[30] * * *

The general thrust of these Supreme Court decisions has been to accommodate the goals and philosophies of the juvenile system within the due process framework of fundamental fairness. * * *

We have held that the fundamental fairness standard obligates trial courts to comply with statutory and constitutional speedy trial requirements in juvenile as well as adult proceedings, *P.V. v. District Court*, supra; that the standard of proof beyond a reasonable doubt which governs adult probation revocation proceedings also governs juvenile probation revocation proceedings, People in the Interest of C.B., 196 Colo. 362, 585 P.2d 281 (1978); and that the rule authorizing an adult defendant in a criminal proceeding to challenge for cause a prospective juror employed by a law enforcement agency is equally applicable to juvenile delinquency proceedings, People in the Interest of R.A.D., 196 Colo. 430, 586 P.2d 46 (1978).[31] However, Sections 19 and 20 of Article II of the Colorado Constitution have not heretofore been applied to juvenile preadjudication proceedings.

To determine whether a juvenile has a constitutional right to bail, we first must inquire whether consistently with fundamental fairness " 'the juvenile court's assumed ability to function in a unique manner,' McKeiver v. Pennsylvania, supra 403 U.S. at 547, 91 S.Ct. at 1987," Breed v. Jones, supra 421 U.S. at 533, 95 S.Ct. at 1787, justifies withholding from juveniles the constitutional right to bail. We must weigh the adverse impact of bail on informal pre-adjudica-

[30] The United States Supreme Court has declined to consider whether juveniles have a constitutional right to bail. In re Whittington, 391 U.S. 341, 88 S.Ct. 1507, 20 L.Ed.2d 625 (1968).

[31] Since July 1, 1980, the Colorado Rules of Juvenile Procedure have provided that delinquency proceedings are to be conducted in accordance with the Colorado Rules of Criminal Procedure except as otherwise provided by statute or the Rules of Juvenile Procedure. C.R.J.P. 1. Crim.P. 46 does not apply to admission to bail in juvenile proceedings to the extent it is inconsistent with the Children's Code and C.R.J.P. 23, * * *.

tion juvenile proceedings against the benefits to be anticipated from a right to bail. * * *

The use of bail in adult criminal proceedings has been criticized, * * * particularly because it disadvantages indigent defendants. * * * Observing that "to superimpose a provision for bail in the Juvenile Court would cause unexplored difficulties for most juveniles, particularly those who are indigent," In re M., supra 473 P.2d at 744, n. 17, 89 Cal.Rptr. at 40, n. 17, the California Supreme Court declined to decide whether juveniles have a constitutional right to bail. Instead the court ruled that the state's juvenile court law, which does not require that bond be posted, establishes an adequate system for the pre-hearing release of juveniles. Id. Few children are financially independent and their parents may be unwilling or unable to post bail. At the same time, commercial surety may be unavailable because minors' contracts are voidable. * * *

If children are detained too frequently, a right to bail will not remedy the practice. * * * It is more likely that, were it recognized, a right to bail would become a substitute for other, more appropriate forms of release. Commentary to American Bar Association's Juvenile Justice Standards Relating to Interim Status (1980) at 66.

Virtually every court which has considered the issue has found that juvenile code safeguards obviate the need for a right to bail in juvenile pre-adjudication proceedings. * * * The American Bar Association's Juvenile Justice Standards Relating to Interim Status, supra, recommend that "the use of bail bonds in any form as an alternative interim status should be prohibited." Section 4.7 at 24.[32] See also President's Commission on Law Enforcement and the Administration of Justice, Task Force Report: Juvenile Delinquency and Youth Crime at 36 (1967).

The United States Court of Appeals for the Ninth Circuit, refusing to overturn Oregon's statutory ban on bail for juveniles, noted that Oregon had enacted an elaborate statutory scheme governing pre-adjudication detention and called the statutory detention hearing a "critical stage" in the juvenile proceeding. * * * Unlike bail setting proceedings, informal detention hearings afford a judge an opportunity to consider the child's needs and welfare. * * * In some instances, the court may consider substitute care for the child if the parent is unwilling to have the child return home or the child does not wish to remain at home pending an adjudication hearing. * * *

Bail does not necessarily result in a juvenile's release from detention. When a juvenile's bail is not posted, the setting of bail alone does not effectuate the presumption of innocence, aid the child's preparation of a defense, or assure the child's presence at future court proceedings. The presumption of innocence and the child's participation in preparation of his defense may, however, be

[32] The Colorado "Standards of Juvenile Justice" (1974) make no reference to bail in juvenile proceedings.

effectuated by curtailing the use of pre-adjudication detention. And while monetary bail may, in some cases, provide an additional assurance of appearance if a child's inadequate ties to the community or record of past failures to appear militate against a personal recognizance bond, it is within the trial court's discretion to set bond for a child in such cases.

If the policy expressed in section 19–2–103(3)(a)(I) of the Children's Code—disapproving the use of detention except in cases satisfying the demanding statutory standards—is implemented, the need for bail will be minimized in juvenile proceedings. We therefore hold that there is no unqualified constitutional right to bail for a juvenile under the United States and Colorado Constitutions.[33] However, a trial court may detain a juvenile without bail only after giving due weight to a presumption that a juvenile should be released pending a dispositional hearing except in narrowly defined circumstances where the state establishes that detention is necessary to protect the child from imminent harm or to protect others in the community from serious bodily harm which the child is likely to inflict. Davis, Rights of Juveniles, § 3.10 at 3–39 (1980).

The trial court in this case applied the Children's Code standards for detention:

" * * * it would be contrary to the welfare of the child or of the community to release the child from detention."

See section 19–2–103(3)(a)(I).[34] These standards were first published in the "Standard Juvenile Court Act" in 1959 by the National Probation and Parole Association (predecessor of the National Council on Crime and Delinquency). The "Standard Juvenile Court Act" permitted detention if the child's "immediate welfare" or "the protection of the community requires that he be detained."

The standards for juvenile detention recommended recently by the American Bar Association are more precise:

"3.1   Restraints on the freedom of accused juveniles pending trial and disposition are generally contrary to public policy. The preferred course in each case should be unconditional release.

3.2   The imposition of interim control or detention on an accused juvenile may be considered for the purposes of:

A.   Protecting the jurisdiction and process of the courts;

B.   Reducing the likelihood that the juvenile may inflict serious bodily harm on others during the interim period; or

---

[33] The federal constitutional due process standard of fundamental fairness which balances the right to bail with the benefit "of fairness, of concern, of sympathy, and of paternal attention that the juvenile court system contemplates," McKeiver v. Pennsylvania, supra, 403 U.S. at 550, 91 S.Ct. at 1988; P.V. v. District Court, supra, guides our determination that a juvenile does not have a right to bail under the Colorado Constitution.

[34] " * * * The Children's Code contains very broad criteria for detention which are open to interpretation and are not adequately enforced." 1981 Juvenile Justice and Delinquency Prevention Plan, Colorado Department of Local Affairs, Division of Criminal Justice, August 31, 1980.

C. Protecting the accused juvenile from imminent bodily harm upon his or her request.

3.3 The interim control or detention should not be imposed on an accused juvenile:

A. To punish, treat, or rehabilitate the juvenile;

B. To allow parents to avoid their legal responsibilities;

C. To satisfy demands by a victim, the police, or the community;

D. To permit more convenient administrative access to the juvenile;

E. To facilitate further interrogation or investigation; or

F. Due to a lack of a more appropriate facility or status alternative.

* * *

4.2 The state should bear the burden at every stage of the proceedings of persuading the relevant decision maker with clear and convincing evidence that restraints on an accused juvenile's liberty are necessary, and that no less intrusive alternative will suffice.

4.3 Whenever a decision is made at any stage of the proceedings to adopt an interim measure other than unconditional release, the decision maker should concurrently state in writing or on the record the specificity of evidence relied upon for that conclusion, and the authorized purpose or purposes that justify that action."

American Bar Association, Juvenile Justice Standards Relating to Interim Status, supra at 50.

The transcript of the trial court's ruling includes specific findings that L.O.W. had avoided the jurisdiction and process of the court in the past [35] and had been in possession of a deadly weapon.[36] The court's findings and conclusions indicate that it gave due weight to the presumption that the petitioner should be released pending the dispositional hearing but found that there was a factual basis for detaining L.O.W. in order to protect others in the community from serious bodily harm which he was likely to inflict. * * * The trial court's findings here were sufficient to detain the child without bail.

---

[35] This, under our statute, is not alone sufficient for holding a child without bail. However, if a court does not have statutory grounds for detaining a child, but the child has avoided the jurisdiction and process of the court in the past, and the court concludes that there is a danger that the child will not appear for adjudication, the court may set bail to ensure the child's presence in court. See our opinion, infra at 1261.

[36] While we were not furnished with the record upon which the court based its determination, the court specifically found that the evidence was "clear and convincing."

III.

One issue remains to be resolved. Colorado is one of a handful of states which by statute provide for bail in juvenile court proceedings. * * *. The statutory predecessors of section 19–2–103(7), C.R.S.1973 (1978 Repl.Vol. 8), of the Children's Code provided that any delinquent child "shall also have the right now given by law to any person to give bond or other security for its appearance at the trial of such case * * *." L.03, page 181, § 6, R.S. 08, § 591; C.L. § 659; CSA C.33, § 58, C.R.S. '53, 22–8–6; C.R.S.1963, 22–8–6(3).[37] The same statutes provided that "no incarceration of the child proceeded against thereunder shall be made unless in the opinion of the judge of the court * * * it shall be necessary to insure his attendance in court at such time as shall be required * * *."

In 1967, the General Assembly adopted the Children's Code. In section 22–2–2(2), C.R.S.1963, the Children's Code provided that "[t]he child shall then be released to the care of his parents or other responsible adult, unless his immediate welfare or the protection of the community requires that he be detained * * *." The following section, 22–2–3(7), stated that "[n]othing in this section shall be construed as denying a child the right to bail." The 1973 recodification of the Colorado Revised Statutes consolidated the standards for detention and the bail provision in section 19–2–103. The standards for detention in section 19–2–103 were modified slightly by the General Assembly in 1978 and 1979, but the general detention standard, "contrary to the welfare of the child or of the community to release the child from detention," remained unchanged. Colo.Sess. Laws 1978, ch. 68, 19–2–103 at 364; Colo.Sess.Laws 1979, ch. 181, 19–2–103 at 761.

The detention criteria enumerated in section 19–2–103(3)(a)(I), C.R.S.1973 (1979 Supp.), and the statutory right to bail recodified in section 19–2–103(7), C.R.S.1973, appear to conflict. The trial court has discretion under subsection (3) to detain a juvenile, but under subsection (7), its discretion is subordinated to a juvenile's right to bail.

Our resolution of this apparent conflict is based on section 2–4–206, C.R.S.1973, which provides that:

"If statutes enacted at the same or different sessions of the general assembly are irreconcilable, the statute prevails which is latest in its effective date * * *."

and section 2–4–208, C.R.S.1973, which provides that:

"A statute which is re-enacted, revised, or amended is intended to be a continuation of the prior statute and not a new enactment, insofar as it is the same as the prior statute."

---

[37] Prior to the adoption of special provisions for juvenile court proceedings, a juvenile was legally responsible for his criminal conduct and punished as an adult. Under these circumstances, the legislature afforded juveniles adult procedural safeguards including the right to bail. * * *

Subsection (7) is a continuation of a statute originally adopted in 1903; subsection (3) is a continuation of the Children's Code provisions originally adopted in 1967. Subsection (3) is the later in effective date. Under the rules of statutory construction, subsection (3) will prevail if the statutes are irreconcilable. However, because we have a duty to construe the subsections to avoid inconsistency when possible, Alpert Corporation v. State Department of Highways, Colo., 603 P.2d 944 (1979); People v. James, 178 Colo. 401, 497 P.2d 1256 (1972), we construe subsection (7)'s provision for bail to be supplementary to the district court's authority to detain juveniles under subsection (3).

Our opinion here should not be construed to negate the availability of bail to juveniles in appropriate situations. For example, bail may be appropriate if a juvenile is subject to detention solely because of danger that he will not appear for adjudication.[38] In such situations bail should be considered as a viable, if not constitutionally mandated, alternative to detention. "Pre-Trial Detention of Juveniles," 6 Am.J.Crim.Law 137 (1978). We recognize that the option of setting monetary bail in a juvenile proceeding does not preclude a trial court from considering conditions of release which will be in the child's best interests. * * *

The trial judge here did not have a statutory or constitutional mandate to grant bail pending the juvenile delinquency adjudication. The court's reasons for detaining the petitioner justify denial of bail.

Rule discharged.

NOTES

1. In Doe v. State, 487 P.2d 47 (Alaska, 1971), the court discussed the right to release and the suitability of the bail system to juvenile cases, concluding that:

"We hold that a child has the right to remain free pending an adjudication that the child is delinquent, dependent, or in need of supervision, where the facts supporting the petition involve an act which, if committed by an adult, would be a crime, and where the court has been given reasonable assurance that the child will appear at future court proceedings. If the facts produced at the inquiry show that the child cannot return or remain at home, every effort must be made to place the child in a situation where his freedom will not be curtailed. Only if there is clearly no alternative available may the child be committed to a detention facility and deprived of his freedom."

* * *

Id. at 50–53.

2. In Morris v. D'Amario, 416 A.2d 137 (R.I.1980) the court rejected the juvenile's contention that detention pending adjudication proceedings constituted "imprisonment" under the Rhode Island Constitution.

[38] If the parent supplies the money for bail, the parent is likely to take steps to ensure the child's presence in court.

Article I, § 9 provides in pertinent part:

> "All persons imprisoned ought to be bailed by sufficient surety, unless for offenses punishable by death or by imprisonment for life, when the proof of guilt is evident or the presumption great."

This argument is without merit. The right to bail guaranteed by art. I, § 9 extends only to persons imprisoned; juveniles held pending delinquency proceedings are not so detained.

> On the contrary, it is well established that in juvenile delinquency proceedings the state, through the Family Court, acts in *parens patriae* rather than as prosecuting attorney and judge. * * * The principal concerns of the Family Court when determining the proper disposition of a child pending adjudication of his delinquency are the welfare of the child and the welfare of the community. * * * In deciding who should retain custody of the child, therefore, the court is exercising substitute parental control, not imposing imprisonment. * * * When the court grants custody of the child to the state, it is placing him in the care of surrogate parents who exercise parental authority, not penal authority; accordingly the right to bail guaranteed to adults, on whom the state cannot impose parental authority, is inapplicable to the Family Court detention decision. Cf. McKeiver v. Pennsylvania, 403 U.S. 528, 550–51, 91 S.Ct. 1976, 1989, 29 L.Ed.2d 647, 664 (1971) (Sixth Amendment right to trial by jury inapplicable to juvenile proceedings).

Id. at 139–40.

The court also rejected the juvenile's equal protection and due process claims. As to the former, the court concluded that the liberty interest of a child is not the same as that of an adult, and that the state's "* * * ability to place a child in an environment providing proper care and guidance is manifestly important to the goal of molding that child into a law-abiding citizen * * *." Id. at 140. Stressing flexibility in the administration of juvenile law, the court said:

> Indeed, when properly administered, a flexible placement procedure focusing on the welfare of both the child and the community will best serve the juvenile's emotional and familial needs.

Ibid.

The thrust of the juvenile's due process claim was a lack of detailed standards to guide the judge's decision to detain the juvenile. Using a flexible balancing approach, the court found adequate safeguards.

> We therefore conclude that due process does not require that rights similar to those required in the *Gault* context be afforded to juveniles with respect to pre-hearing-pre-detention determinations.

> Nevertheless, we believe that the juvenile possesses a liberty interest in the pre-hearing-placement procedure which, consistent with the concept of fundamental fairness pervading each stage of the juvenile process, should not be denied in the absence of minimum due-process safeguards. * * * Accordingly, we hold that prior to the time the juvenile is presented to the court for placement pending the delinquency adjudication, he and his parents must be notified in writing of the nature and possible consequences of the placement proceedings. We believe that written notice will afford the juvenile and his parent a reasonable opportunity to prepare for the proceedings, thereby safeguarding the child's liberty interest and the parents' custodial interest. * * * Furthermore, the child and his parents must also be notified that the

child has a right to the assistance of counsel at the proceedings and that, if the family is indigent, counsel will be appointed to represent the child. * * * If the court determines that detention in the custody of the court will best serve the interests of the child and the community, it must articulate in writing the facts and reasons on which it based its decision to detain the juvenile. * * * Finally, a record of the proceedings must be made so that appellate review of the decision might be obtained.

Id. at 141–42.

3. A number of statutes provide for bail in juvenile cases. Most of them make clear the preference that the child be released to the parent's custody where that is feasible. Occasionally the child's own promise to appear is recognized in statutory form as a basis for release.

260.171 Release or detention

Subdivision 1. If a child is taken into custody as provided in section 260.165, the parent, guardian, or custodian of the child shall be notified as soon as possible. Unless there is reason to believe that the child would endanger himself or others, not return for a court hearing, not remain in the care or control of the person to whose lawful custody he is released, or that the child's health or welfare would be immediately endangered, the child shall be released to the custody of his parent, guardian, custodian, or other suitable person. That person shall promise to bring the child to the court, if necessary, at the time the court may direct. If the person taking the child into custody believes it desirable he may request the parent, guardian, custodian, or other person designated by the court to sign a written promise to bring the child to court as provided above. The intentional violation of such a promise, whether given orally or in writing, shall be punishable as contempt of court.

The court may require the parent, guardian, custodian or other person to whom the child is released, to post any reasonable bail or bond required by the court which shall be forfeited to the court if the child does not appear as directed. The court may also release the child on his own promise to appear in juvenile court.

Minn.Stat.Ann. (1984 Supp.).

2. THE NECESSITY FOR INDIVIDUALIZED DECISION–MAKING

IN RE M.
Supreme Court of California, 1970.
3 Cal.3d 16, 89 Cal.Rptr. 33, 473 P.2d 737.

TOBRINER, JUSTICE. This case raises the basic issue of whether a juvenile court may refuse to consider specific facts supporting the release of a juvenile prior to a jurisdictional hearing and, instead, establish a rule that all juveniles accused of a specified type of offense should automatically be detained. We give the reasons why we have concluded that the juvenile court law protects the minor's right to an individualized detention hearing, in which the court may not dispose of cases by mechanical rules on a categorical basis.

1. *The facts*

On March 17, 1970, the supervising probation officer for the juvenile department of the superior court filed a petition alleging that William M., a minor, came within the provisions of section 602 of the Welfare and Institutions Code. (See Welf. & Inst.Code, § 650.) The petition specified that on January 28, 1970, the minor had violated Health and Safety Code section 11531 by selling marijuana to an officer of the police department. At 6 a.m. on March 19, 1970, an officer to whom William M. had allegedly sold marijuana took the youth into temporary custody pursuant to an arrest warrant. (Welf. & Inst.Code, § 625.) The officer did not release the minor on his promise, or the assurance of his parents, that he would appear for further proceedings.[39] Instead, the 16-year-old youth was taken to the county juvenile hall and remained there until the detention hearing. (See Welf. & Inst.Code, §§ 627–632.)

At 2 p.m., Thursday, March 19, William M., his parents, his attorney, a family friend who was also an attorney, and the probation officer appeared before the juvenile court for a detention hearing. The court opened the proceedings by reading the charges and the police report. The court then said: *"It looks like it is all pre-arranged, but anybody who sells marijuana or LSD is detained here until his regular hearing, for the safety of others."* (Italics added.) The youth's attorney offered to show that the young man was a good student at a local high school, that he had never had any school disciplinary problems, and that he had never before been arrested. The attorney described the minor's salutary home life with parents who were willing to provide care and guidance and capable of doing so. The attorney offered to show that under these circumstances the youth would not present an imminent danger to himself or others. On this offer of proof the trial court refused to release the juvenile.[40] The attorney then proposed, as an "officer of this court," "to take full responsibility for this boy and let him live in my home until the hearing." When the court rejected this suggestion the youth's attorney requested a one-day continuance of the detention

---

[39] Welfare and Institutions Code section 626: "An officer who takes a minor into temporary custody under the provisions of Section 625 shall thereafter proceed as follows: (a) He may release such minor; or (b) He may prepare in duplicate a written notice to appear before the probation officer of the county in which such minor was taken into custody at a time and place specified in the notice. * * * Upon the execution of the promise to appear, he shall immediately release such minor. * * * or (c) He may take such minor without unnecessary delay before the probation officer of the county * * *. *In determining which disposition of the minor he will make, the officer shall prefer the alternative which least restricts the minor's freedom of movement, provided such alter-* *native is compatible with the best interests of the minor and the community."* (Italics added.)

[40] The juvenile court explained: "Well, it is not a hard decision; it is an unhappy decision that I make, but your boy is going to stay here, and I have got twelve year old kids in here for doing the same thing that he did, and I am going to keep every kid in this place until they have their regular hearing that I catch selling marijuana, LSD, or pills. If you sat here every day and saw some of these kids who have been using this stuff—marijuana, LSD, what-have-you—and see what happens to them, then when I figure that anybody sells this stuff to anybody for a profit, I am not going to take any chance on what they will do between now and their regular hearing."

hearing. (Welf. & Inst. Code, § 638.) The court granted the continuance and observed, "you are just wasting your time. * * *"

On Friday the attorney recited to the court the standards for detention of juveniles under Welfare and Institutions Code section 635,[41] cited the relevant legislative history which prohibits detention for the sake of therapeutic effect,[42] presented the only relevant California appellate court opinion on the detention question, and marshalled the facts which in this case favored the young man's release.[43] Finally, the attorney expressed concern for the deleterious effect that detention might have on the youth and his education.

The court refused this offer of proof and did not permit William M. or his parents to testify. Although the court declared that it tried to avoid holding juveniles in custody, it further stated that it detained, pending a jurisdictional hearing, as a matter of "philosophy" or "policy," every child who was charged with the offense involved in the present case.[44] The court observed: "The Legislature must have thought it [the offense] was serious, it is five years to life if he were an adult." The attorney answered, "If he were an adult, he would be out on bail at this very moment." The court offered: "If you want to have him handled as an adult, I will certify him to adult court and you can bail him out * * *. But, as I have already told you, your

[41] Welfare and Institutions Code section 635: "The court will examine such minor, his parent, guardian, or other person having relevant knowledge, hear such relevant evidence as the minor, his parent or guardian or their counsel desires to present, and, *unless it appears* that such minor has violated an order of the juvenile court or has escaped from the commitment of the juvenile court or *that it is a matter of immediate and urgent necessity for the protection of such minor or the person or property of another that he be detained or that such minor is likely to flee the jurisdiction of the court, the court shall make its order releasing such minor from custody."* (Italics added.)

[42] Report of the Governor's Special Study Commission on Juvenile Justice, Part I—Recommendations for Changes in California's Juvenile Court Law (1960): "While detention may have a therapeutic effect in select cases, in the Commission's view, it is neither the function of law enforcement agencies nor probation departments to use it for this purpose. In our opinion, this is clearly and unmistakably a judicial responsibility which must be arrived at after juvenile court jurisdiction has been established." (P. 42.)

[43] The attorney read letters from the principal and class counselor of the boy's school, which described the boy as "courteous," "well mannered," "quiet," "con-cerned with his studies," "liked and accepted by his peer group," and willing to follow school rules and regulations. The attorney brought to the courtroom nine members of the community who knew the boy and who all would testify that "regardless of what this boy may be accused of having done, he is a boy who will abide by the wishes of this court. He will not be a danger to himself, to others, or to property; that the family and home situation is such that he will be supervised and he will be controlled."

[44] "The Court: However, when you see fifteen children killed a year ago [in this county] because of this substance abuse thing, and two have already been killed this year, I have made it a policy that anybody who sells or furnishes marijuana, sells LSD—you name it—to anyone and gets paid for it, then they are going to be detained until the next hearing. And whatever you want to call it, I will say it is because of the immediate and urgent necessity, for the protection of any person or the property of another, and that is my philosophy, and that is my basis for detaining this young man.

"* * *

"The Court: And there are about twenty-five others, so he is not alone. There are about twenty-five others in here, as I told you yesterday, from the age of, I think, thirteen or twelve year old girls, up to eighteen."

client is going to be detained, and there is not a thing you can do about it. You can go up and try to get a writ or something, test it, and that is your problem." The jurisdictional hearing [45] was set for April 7, 1970.[46]

William M. remained in juvenile hall over the weekend. On Monday the youth's father filed a petition for a writ of habeas corpus with the Court of Appeal. On the same day that court denied the petition without opinion. The father then filed a petition for hearing here; on March 26, 1970, we granted the petition, transferring the matter to this court. We issued an order "to show cause before this court when the matter is ordered on calendar why the relief prayed for should not be granted." Pending determination of the petition, we directed that the young man be released from custody until the jurisdictional hearing in the juvenile court. The youth was released to the custody of his parents on the same day, having spent a total of seven days in juvenile hall.

On April 6, 1970, the district attorney, respondent in proceedings before this court, filed a petition for an order staying further proceedings in the juvenile court against William M. We unanimously denied that petition in order to avoid the hardship that would be inflicted upon the boy by the protraction of proceedings pending against him. On April 7, 1970, the juvenile court found true the allegations of the petition filed March 17, 1970, under Welfare and Institutions Code section 602,[47] declared the juvenile a ward of the court, and placed him in the home of his parents under probation conditions and the supervision of the probation officer. The young man is now living at home with his parents and no further problem of delinquency has arisen.

2. *Since this case raises issues of grave public concern this court should resolve them rather than declare the case moot on its somewhat unusual factual background.*

[45] The California Juvenile Court Law provides for a jurisdictional hearing at which the juvenile court determines whether the facts of the case will support its jurisdiction to declare the minor to be a ward of the court.

[46] Welfare and Institutions Code section 636: "If it appears upon the hearing that such minor has violated an order of the juvenile court or has escaped from a commitment of the juvenile court or that it is a matter of immediate and urgent necessity for the protection of such minor or the person or property of another that he be detained or that such minor is likely to flee the jurisdiction of the court, the court may make its order that such minor be detained in the juvenile hall or other suitable place designated by the juvenile court for a period not to exceed 15 judicial days and shall enter said order together with its findings of fact in support thereof in the records of the court."

[47] At the jurisdictional hearing, the juvenile admitted the allegations of the affidavit of the complaining officer. That affidavit described the offense with which petitioner is charged: the sale of one "can" of marijuana to the affiant police officer for $10 and another one-half "can" to a second officer for $5. The sale allegedly took place in petitioner's bedroom, to which another juvenile, who was also present at the sale, had directed the officers. The second juvenile introduced the two officers, and a third "special" officer to petitioner, and all went to petitioner's room where petitioner produced a brown paper bag from his desk drawer. The two packets of marijuana were taken from this bag, passed to the other juvenile and the officers, and finally sold to the officers.

At the outset we are confronted with the district attorney's assertion that because the jurisdictional hearing has already occurred "the matter concerning the Writ of Habeas Corpus is now rendered moot." When this court issued its order directing that the youth be released from detention pending the jurisdictional hearing in juvenile court, we granted, as a practical matter, the habeas corpus relief which petitioner sought. But if a pending case poses an issue of broad public interest that is likely to recur, the court may exercise an inherent discretion to resolve that issue even though an event occurring during its pendency would normally render the matter moot.

* * *

The United States Supreme Court has recently suggested the importance of determining important issues which would not otherwise be decided because of the brevity of the sentence under review. "Many deep and abiding constitutional problems are encountered primarily at a level of 'low visibility' in the criminal process—in the context of prosecutions for 'minor' offenses which carry only short sentences. We do not believe that the Constitution contemplates that people deprived of constitutional rights at this level should be left utterly remediless and defenseless against repetitions of unconstitutional conduct." (Sibron v. New York (1968) 392 U.S. 40, 52–53, 88 S.Ct. 1889, 1897, 20 L.Ed.2d 917.)

The detention proceedings challenged in the present case occurred at a level of "low visibility" in a short period of time, and involved asserted errors which are not ordinarily reviewable on appeal. This case reached its present posture because we refused to stay the jurisdictional hearing in the juvenile court pending our consideration of the petition for habeas corpus. We denied that stay in order to protect the juvenile, because even a few weeks delay in the court proceedings would have hindered his proper care and guidance. We doubt that this court will soon be presented with another opportunity to resolve the important questions raised here as to prehearing detention. In the hope that we may provide much-needed guidance for "the orderly administration of justice * * *" we explain the grounds which we believe sustain the release of the youth.

3. *The juvenile court failed to consider the youth's case on its individual merits, and held him in custody under the court's policy that all those who had allegedly sold marijuana should be detained prior to the jurisdictional hearing.*

The architects of the Juvenile Court Law clearly sought to remove California's lamentable practices as to excessive detention. (See Witkin, Summary of Cal.Law (1969 Supp.) Parent and Child, §§ 171A–172A, at pp. 1394–1399.)[48] Welfare and Institutions Code

[48] Report of the Governor's Special Study Commission on Juvenile Justice, Part I—Recommendations for Changes in California's Juvenile Court Law (1960): "California has been severely criticized by national probation and child welfare organizations for excessive juvenile detention practices. The Commission's study, unfortunately, substantiates the validity of this criticism. * * * [In 1958] almost three-fourths of the delinquent juveniles referred to probation de-

section 502 declared the purpose of the law to be "to secure for each minor under the jurisdiction of the juvenile court such *care and guidance, preferably in his own home,* as will serve the spiritual, emotional, mental, and physical welfare of the minor and the best interests of the State; *to preserve and strengthen the minor's family ties* whenever possible, removing him from the custody of his parents only when his welfare or safety and protection of the public cannot be adequately safeguarded without removal. * * *" (Italics added.) To this end, the Legislature stated in section 635 * * * that after the detention hearing "the court *shall make its order releasing* such *minor from custody,*" "*unless* it appears * * * that it is a matter of *immediate and urgent necessity* for the protection of such minor or the person or property of another that he be detained or that such minor is likely to flee the jurisdiction of the court, * * *" (Italics added.) By requiring that the minor be released unless the case fell within one of the specified categories, the Legislature indicated its intention that detention be the exception, not the rule.[49]

If a child is not released by the arresting officer * * * or the probation officer, * * * the probation officer must immediately file a petition under Welfare and Institutions Code section 630 and a

partments by law enforcement agencies were detained in juvenile halls. In some communities, the ratio was even higher— virtually every juvenile referred by law enforcement officers to the probation department was detained, notwithstanding the fact that some minors were apprehended in error, many committed inconsequential offenses, and many others had responsible parents able to control the minor pending the juvenile court appearance.

"* * *

"The Commission is aware that some of the minors placed in detention facilities were already court wards. The Commission is also aware that a small proportion of those detained could not be immediately released either because a parent temporarily was not at home or for some equally appropriate reason. However, these unusual circumstances do not apply to the greater majority of detained juveniles.

"* * *

"Unnecessary detention is both costly and unwarranted. To reduce the large volume of juvenile detention in California, the Commission recommends a more conscientious, discriminating exercise of the detention screening decision by probation departments and early detention hearings. Otherwise, California's undistinguished reputation for excessive detention practices will persist." (Pp. 41–42.)

[49] The California Juvenile Court Law, as properly administered, provides an adequate system for the prehearing release of juveniles without the requirement of posting bail. (See Fulwood v. Stone (1967) 129 U.S.App.D.C. 314, 394 F.2d 939, 943; Baldwin v. Lewis (E.D.Wis. 1969) 300 F.Supp. 1220, 1233.) Hence, we decline to consider whether juveniles are constitutionally entitled to bail. In *Gault* the United States Supreme Court declared that "whatever may be their precise impact, neither the Fourteenth Amendment nor the Bill of Rights is for adults alone." But the court observed: "we are not here concerned with the procedures or constitutional rights applicable to the pre-judicial stages of the juvenile process * * *" and did not consider whether a child is entitled to bail. (In re Gault (1967) 387 U.S. 1, 13–14, 87 S.Ct. 1428, 1436, 18 L.Ed.2d 527.) The Juvenile Court Law and section 635, as properly construed, do not permit the detention of juveniles for the protection of society in situations in which an adult would be entitled to bail pending trial. Section 635, however, does provide ample authority for the detention of children for their own protection; to superimpose a provision for bail in the Juvenile Court would cause unexplored difficulties for most juveniles, particularly those who are indigent.

detention hearing must be held within one judicial day. * * * Welfare and Institutions Code section 635 provides that at the detention hearing "[t]he court will examine such minor, his parent, guardian, or other person having relevant knowledge, hear such relevant evidence as the minor, his parent or guardian or their counsel desires to present. * * *" If the court finds that detention is necessary, it may order him detained.

The procedure of the juvenile court in the instant case and its failure to release the minor resemble the situation in In re Macidon (1966) 240 Cal.App.2d 600, 49 Cal.Rptr. 861. There the juvenile court had notified the probation officer that a detention hearing was to be held in every case in which the juvenile was charged with the commission of a felonious act, whether or not the juvenile had theretofore been released by the police or a probation officer. The Macidon child had allegedly stolen a purse from a 12-year-old girl on December 17, 1965. Although the officers took the youth into temporary custody they immediately released him to his mother's custody upon her written assurance that he would appear in court.

The probation officer filed a request for young Macidon's detention which did not allege any factual basis to support it, aside from the alleged commission of the offense. At the detention hearing the court asked the minor only his name, age, and school. Merely ascertaining the presence of the boy's mother, the court did not ask any questions of her or of the minor or of the probation officer. Apparently predicating its ruling on the material contained in the police report and a statement of the probation officer for two of the five youths charged with the offense, the court failed to follow the mandate of section 635. On this record the Court of Appeal released the boy because: first, the juvenile court had failed properly to conduct the detention hearing required by section 635; second, the facts as set forth in the reports presented at the detention hearing failed to provide any basis for detaining the minor; third, the court failed to make the findings of fact required by section 636.[50]

Since the date of rendition of the *Macidon* decision the Legislature has amended Welfare and Institutions Code section 630 to read

---

[50] In its order detaining the youth the juvenile court in the instant case failed to state the specific ground upon which it relied: "WHEREAS, a hearing having been held this date, and the Court having considered the facts presented finds it is necessary for the protection of person or property of others that said minor be detained, pursuant to Section 635 of the Welfare and Institutions Code * * *." Welfare and Institutions Code section 636 contains alternative grounds for detention. Hence, the juvenile court must at least specify the ground which the facts support. In the absence of such findings the reviewing court may well be faced with great difficulty in determining the factual basis for detention. In the instant case the juvenile court, during the process of the detention hearing, did, however, set forth with repeated emphasis the basis for detention. The judge clearly indicated that, regardless of the facts of the individual case, all juveniles charged with the same offense as William M. would be detained pending the jurisdictional hearing. The conclusory findings are clarified by the judge's forthright comments which were recorded in the transcript of the proceeding submitted to this court. Hence, under these circumstances, we cannot conclude that the failure to state specific findings under Welfare and Institutions Code section 636 furnishes grounds for release of the youth.

in pertinent part: "In [the detention] hearing the minor has a privilege against self-incrimination and has a right to confrontation by, and cross-examination of, any person examined by the court as provided in Section 635." By granting the youth the right to remain silent and the right of confrontation in sections 630 and 635, the Legislature has now clearly indicated that the probation officer, at the detention hearing, is charged with the duty of adducing facts which will support detention under section 636.[51] The probation officer must present a prima facie case that the minor committed the alleged offense; otherwise the court will lack the "immediate and urgent necessity" for detention of a youth charged under section 602. In addition, the probation officer must state facts upon which he based his decision not to release the minor prior to the detention hearing (Welf. & Inst.Code, § 628).[52]

In the instant case the juvenile court failed to conduct the detention hearing in the manner prescribed by the *Macidon* decision and the subsequently amended Juvenile Court Law. The court did not even hear any testimony by the probation officer; it did not consider his report under Welfare and Institutions Code section 628. Failing to follow the requirements of section 635 the court did not examine the young man, his parents, or his character witnesses. The court merely asked the minor whether he understood the charges; the boy responded, "Yes, sir." Neither the court nor the probation officer asked any questions of the parents. On the other hand, the youth's attorney presented an extensive offer of relevant testimony and evidence which the court refused to admit or consider.

We recognize that the Legislature intended to create an atmosphere of compassionate informality in juvenile court proceedings; * * * we note, however, that in this case the juvenile law's concern

---

[51] "The detention hearing under California practice has tended to be pro forma. It frequently consisted of nothing more than a brief report by the probation officer and a cursory review of the police report. One salient change brought about by the 1967 amendments is the addition to section 630, which reads in part: 'In * * * [the detention] hearing the minor * * * has a right to confrontation by, and cross-examination of, witnesses.' This means that in a delinquency hearing the probation officer will be required to present a prima facie case that the minor committed the offense, since the 'immediate and urgent necessity' for detention is necessarily premised upon this assumption. This requirement for full evidentiary hearing, coupled with provision for appointment of counsel, should, in and of itself, do more than anything else to remedy California's over-detention practices." * * * (Boches, Juvenile Justice in California: A Re-evaluation, supra, 19 Hastings L.J. 47, 79.) Section 635 provides that all juveniles shall be released unless the case falls into one of the specified categories, and section 630 grants the right to remain silent during the detention hearing. Hence, the probation officer must assume the burden of showing that the child should be detained.

[52] In the present case the juvenile court read and considered the police report. The youth denied the charges, but his attorney did not challenge the facts set forth in the police officer's declaration insofar as they established a prima facie case that the youth committed the charged offense. The court on two occasions offered to order the police officers to testify; the attorney for the juvenile neither accepted the offer nor asserted his right to confrontation and cross-examination. Under these circumstances the court properly considered the police officer's affidavit in finding a prima facie case that the youth had committed the charged offense.

with the best interests of the minor was irretrievably lost in the very beginning of the hearing when the court adopted a steadfast posture that any young person charged with the alleged offense would, regardless of the facts of the case, be detained. As a consequence, the court permitted the youth's counsel to present a lengthy offer of proof in which the attorney attempted to show that the youth should not be detained.[53]

The nature of the charged offense cannot in itself constitute the basis for detention.[54]

The requirement for factual hearings prescribed by sections 630 and 635 would be pointless if the juvenile court could refuse to hear any facts at all in named categories of cases. Clearly, the Legislature intended that the court should exercise its discretion on the facts of the individual case, rather than enclose certain cases in tombs of silence.

In the present case the court's concern as to releasing any minor charged with the sale of marijuana centered in his fear that "these kids" would "be out, laughing at their parents and commercially selling narcotics between now and their regular hearing." The court refused to hear any evidence to show that the juvenile would not repeat his alleged offense during the short period between the detention and the jurisdictional hearings. The court refused to consider the fact that the young man had been living at home with his parents for nearly seven weeks between the time his offense came to the attention of the police and the filing of the petition for wardship.

Moreover, neither the probation officer nor anyone else offered a scintilla of evidence that the youth—a first offender—had been involved in any large purchase, possession, or sale of the forbidden commodity. The court ignored the fact that, once the parents were alerted to their son's conduct, they clearly demonstrated their willingness and ability to provide care and guidance for him. The court refused to consider the abundant testimony of the school officials and the other nine adults who could attest to the young man's good character and the family's cohesion and concern.

---

[53] The juvenile court, of course, may not assume guilt if the minor denies responsibility for the alleged offense. * * * Nor may the juvenile court condition the juvenile's release upon his waiver of his privilege against self-incrimination.

[54] "Although it is difficult to delineate what does justify detention of a minor, it is relatively easy to set forth a number of factors that do not constitute 'immediate and urgent necessity' and are not relevant to detention. (1) Public outcry against the offense allegedly committed by the minor; (2) The need to crack down generally on juveniles in the area; (3) The nature of the offense per se; (4) The belief that detention would have a salutary effect on the minor (the juvenile court does not have the right to exercise its jurisdiction over a minor for this purpose, if at all, until an adjudication of wardship or dependency has been made); (5) Convenience of the police, the probation officer, or the district attorney for investigation purposes; (6) Concern that the minor will fabricate a defense to his case; (7) Inability of the minor to show good cause why he should be released." (California Juvenile Court Practice (Cont.Ed. Bar 1968) § 41, at p. 52.)

The decision to take a minor away from his home, his parents, and his friends is fraught with such grave consequences [55] that the juvenile court cannot establish mechanical "policies" for automatic detention. The Legislature has indicated that children should be released except under certain specific conditions of "immediate and urgent necessity." We share the juvenile court's concern with the serious problem of drug abuse among juveniles, but concern cannot justify the elimination of elementary requirements of individualized justice and due process.

The basic predicate of the Juvenile Court Law is that each juvenile be treated as an individual. The whole concept of our procedure is that special diagnosis and treatment be accorded the psychological and emotional problems of each offender so that he achieves a satisfactory adjustment. Nothing could be further from the spirit of the law than the absorption of the individual into a stereotype. A mechanized, mass treatment of offenders not only violates our deep conviction that each individual should personally obtain the protection of due process of law but also thwarts the legislative objective of providing the troubled youth of today with particularized treatment directed toward rehabilitation.

The order to show cause, having served its purpose, is discharged, and the writ of habeas corpus is denied.

NOTES

1. In Commonwealth ex rel. Sprowal v. Hendrick, 438 Pa. 435, 265 A.2d 348 (1970) the Supreme Court of Pennsylvania articulated these procedures and criteria for the pretrial detention of juveniles:

> In the normal course of events, a juvenile who has not yet had an adjudicatory hearing is released into the custody of a responsible party, usually his or her parents. This is no doubt attributable at least in part to the fact that juveniles normally have only limited mobility, and we fully expect that there will be no reduction in the high percentage of

---

[55] An amicus describes some of the consequences which flow from the excessive use of pre-adjudicative detention: "Locking up children charged with or suspected of offenses, before adjudication, probably does more to contribute to the army of habitual criminals than any other procedure in what is called the juvenile justice system. It is difficult for an adult who has not been through the experience to realize the terror that engulfs a youngster the first time he loses his liberty and has to spend the night or several days or weeks in a cold, impersonal cell or room away from home or family. * * * the speed with which relatively innocent youngsters succumb to the infectious miasma of 'Juvy' and its practices, attitudes, and language * * * is not surprising. The experience tells the youngster that he is 'no good' and that society has rejected him.

So he responds to society's expectation, sees himself as a delinquent, and acts like one. In its 1967 report, The Challenge of Crime in a Free Society, page 80, the President's Commission on Law Enforcement and Administration of Justice defined this psychological response: 'Official action may actually help to fix and perpetuate delinquency in the child through a process in which the individual begins to think of himself as delinquent and organizes his behavior accordingly. That process itself is further reinforced by the effect of the labelling upon the child's family, neighbors, teachers, and peers, whose reactions communicate to the child in subtle ways a kind of expectation of delinquent conduct. The undesirable consequences of official treatment are maximized in programs that rely on institutionalizing the child.' "

juveniles who are currently so released. As with adults, however, certain restrictive or coercive measures may be proper if they are necessary to insure the appearance of the juvenile at subsequent proceedings. Such measures should be utilized, however, only when the hearing court reasonably determines that there is no other less coercive method whereby future attendance can be reasonably assured and places the reasons for this finding on the record.

Unlike an adult, however, a juvenile may be detained by the juvenile court for reasons other than the necessity of guaranteeing his presence at future proceedings. If a juvenile does not have a home with his parents or other responsible party, or is in need of protective custody, or is in need of psychiatric help or should have psychological testing and evaluation, he or she may be detained for such protective purposes before there is an adjudication of delinquency. The judge who orders such detention must, however, specifically find that the detention is necessary and must have support for the order in the record developed at the pre-adjudicatory hearing. Additionally, the detention must be tailored to the justification.

265 A.2d at 349–50.

2. In Kinney v. Lenon, 425 F.2d 209 (9th Cir.1970) the Court of Appeals ordered a juvenile released from pre-trial detention while refusing to decide the constitutionality of an Oregon statute prohibiting bail in juvenile cases:

Appellant is a minor child of seventeen years now detained in the Juvenile Detention Home in Multnomah County, Oregon, pending trial in Juvenile Court on charges arising out of a schoolyard fight.

Appellant alleges that there were many potential witnesses to the fight, that he cannot identify them by name but would recognize them by sight, that appellant's attorneys are white though he and the potential witnesses are black, that his attorneys would consequently have great practical difficulty in interviewing and lining up the witnesses, and that appellant is the sole person who can do so. His request to be released into the custody of his parents was denied by the Juvenile Court. Relief was sought and denied in the United States District Court for the District of Oregon, and application for an order restraining appellant's continued detention has been made to this court.

* * *

[W]e are of the opinion that, in the peculiar circumstances of this case, failure to permit appellant's release for the purpose of aiding the preparation of his defense unconstitutionally interfered with his due-process right to a fair trial.

The ability of an accused to prepare his defense by lining up witnesses is fundamental, in our adversary system, to his chances of obtaining a fair trial.

* * *

This is not a case where release from detention is sought simply for the convenience of the appellant. There is here a strong showing that the appellant is the only person who can effectively prepare his own defense. We may take notice, as judges and lawyers, of the difficulties often encountered, even by able and conscientious counsel, in overcoming the apathy and reluctance of potential witnesses to testify. It would require blindness to social reality not to understand that these difficulties may be exacerbated by the barriers of age and race. Yet the alternative to some sort of release for appellant is to cast the entire burden of assembling witnesses onto his attorneys, with almost certain prejudice to appellant's case.

The appellee suggests that appellant is properly detained in view of what are claimed to be previous instances of harassment of the state's witnesses. But the Juvenile Court is not without power to take appropriate measures to prevent any such misconduct, and our order so provides.

Id. at 210.

3. PREVENTIVE DETENTION

SCHALL v. MARTIN

Supreme Court of the United States, 1984.
__ U.S. __, 104 S.Ct. 2403, 81 L.Ed.2d 207.

JUSTICE REHNQUIST delivered the opinion of the Court.

Section 320.5(3)(b) of the New York Family Court Act authorizes pretrial detention of an accused juvenile delinquent based on a finding that there is a "serious risk" that the child "may before the return date commit an act which if committed by an adult would constitute a crime." [56] Appellees brought suit on behalf of a class of all juveniles detained pursuant to that provision. The district court struck down § 320.5(3)(b) as permitting detention without due process of law and ordered the immediate release of all class members. 513 F.Supp. 691 (1981). The Court of Appeals for the Second Circuit affirmed, holding the provision "unconstitutional as to all juveniles" because the statute is administered in such a way that "the detention period serves as punishment imposed without proof of guilt established according to the requisite constitutional standard." 689 F.2d 365, 373–374 (1982). We noted probable jurisdiction, 460 U.S. 1079, 103 S.Ct. 1765, 76 L.Ed.2d 340 (1983), and now reverse. We conclude that preventive detention under the Family Court Act serves a legitimate state objective, and that the procedural protections afforded pretrial detainees by the New York statute satisfy the requirements of the Due Process Clause of the Fourteenth Amendment to the United States Constitution.

I

Appellee Gregory Martin was arrested on December 13, 1977, and charged with first-degree robbery, second-degree assault, and

---

[56] Section 320.5 of the Family Court Act (FCA) provides, in relevant part:

"1. At the initial appearance, the court in its discretion may release the respondent or direct his detention.

"   * * *

"3. The court shall not direct detention unless it finds and states the facts and reasons for so finding that unless the respondent is detained;

"(a) there is a substantial probability that he will not appear in court on the return date; or

"(b) there is a serious risk that he may before the return date commit an act which if committed by an adult would constitute a crime." Appellees have only challenged pretrial detention under § 320.5(3)(b). Thus, the propriety of detention to ensure that a juvenile appears in court on the return date, pursuant to § 320.5(3)(a), is not before the Court.

criminal possession of a weapon based on an incident in which he, with two others, allegedly hit a youth on the head with a loaded gun and stole his jacket and sneakers. See Plaintiff's Exhibit 1. Martin had possession of the gun when he was arrested. He was 14 years old at the time and, therefore, came within the jurisdiction of New York's Family Court. The incident occurred at 11:30 at night, and Martin lied to the police about where and with whom he lived. He was consequently detained overnight.[57]

A petition of delinquency was filed, and Martin made his "initial appearance" in Family Court on December 14th, accompanied by his grandmother.[58] The Family Court judge, citing the possession of the loaded weapon, the false address given to the police, and the lateness of the hour, as evidencing a lack of supervision, ordered Martin detained under § 320.5(3)(b) * * *. A probable cause hearing was held five days later, on December 19th, and probable cause was found to exist for all the crimes charged. At the fact-finding hearing held December 27–29, Martin was found guilty on the robbery and criminal possession charges. He was adjudicated a delinquent and placed on two years' probation.[59] He had been detained pursuant to

[57] When a juvenile is arrested, the arresting officer must immediately notify the parent or other person legally responsible for the child's care. FCA § 305.2(3). Ordinarily, the child will be released to the custody of his parent or guardian after being issued an "appearance ticket" requiring him to meet with the probation service on a specified day. Id., at § 307.1(1). See n. 9, supra. If, however, he is charged with a serious crime, one of several designated felonies, see id., at § 301.2(8), or if his parent or guardian cannot be reached, the juvenile may be taken directly before the Family Court. Id., at § 305.2. The Family Court judge will make a preliminary determination as to the jurisdiction of the court, appoint a law guardian for the child, and advise the child of his or her rights, including the right to counsel and the right to remain silent.

Only if, as in Martin's case, the Family Court is not in session and special circumstances exist, such as an inability to notify the parents, will the child be taken directly by the arresting officer to a juvenile detention facility. Id., at § 305.2(4)(c). If the juvenile is so detained, he must be brought before the Family Court within 72 hours or the next day the court is in session, whichever is sooner. Id., at § 307.3(4). The propriety of such detention, prior to a juvenile's initial appearance in Family Court, is not at issue in this case. Appellees challenged only judicially ordered detention pursuant to § 320.5(3)(b).

[58] The first proceeding in Family Court following the filing of the petition is known as the initial appearance even if the juvenile has already been brought before the court immediately following his arrest. FCA § 320.2.

[59] The "fact finding" is the juvenile's analogue of a trial. As in the earlier proceedings, the juvenile has a right to counsel at this hearing. Id., at § 341.2. See In re Gault, 387 U.S. 1, 87 S.Ct. 1428, 18 L.Ed.2d 527 (1967). Evidence may be suppressed on the same grounds as in criminal cases, FCA § 330.2, and proof of guilt, based on the record evidence, must be beyond a reasonable doubt, id., at § 342.2. See In re Winship, 397 U.S. 358, 90 S.Ct. 1068, 25 L.Ed.2d 368 (1970). If guilt is established, the court enters an appropriate order and schedules a dispositional hearing. Id., at § 345.1.

The dispositional hearing is the final and most important proceeding in the Family Court. If the juvenile has committed a designated felony, the court must order a probation investigation and a diagnostic assessment. Id., at § 351.1. Any other material and relevant evidence may be offered by the probation agency or the juvenile. Both sides may call and cross-examine witnesses and recommend specific dispositional alternatives. Id., at § 350.4. The court must find, based on a preponderance of the evidence, id., at § 350.3(2), that the juvenile is delinquent and requires supervision, treatment or confinement. Id., at § 352.1. Otherwise, the petition is dismissed. Ibid.

If the juvenile is found to be delinquent, then the court enters an order of disposition. Possible alternatives include

§ 320.5(3)(b), between the initial appearance and the completion of the fact-finding hearing, for a total of fifteen days.

Appellees Luis Rosario and Kenneth Morgan, both age 14, were also ordered detained pending their fact-finding hearings. Rosario was charged with attempted first-degree robbery and second-degree assault for an incident in which he, with four others, allegedly tried to rob two men, putting a gun to the head of one of them and beating both about the head with sticks. See Plaintiff's Exhibit 2. At the time of his initial appearance, on March 15, 1979, Rosario had another delinquency petition pending for knifing a student, and two prior petitions had been adjusted.[60] Probable cause was found on March 21. On April 11, Rosario was released to his father, and the case was terminated without adjustment on September 25, 1979.

Kenneth Morgan was charged with attempted robbery and attempted grand larceny for an incident in which he and another boy allegedly tried to steal money from a 14-year-old girl and her brother by threatening to blow their heads off and grabbing them to search their pockets. See Plaintiff's Exhibit 3. Morgan, like Rosario, was on release status on another petition (for robbery and criminal possession of stolen property) at the time of his initial appearance on March 27, 1978. He had been arrested four previous times, and his mother refused to come to court because he had been in trouble so often she did not want him home. A probable cause hearing was set for March 30, but was continued until April 4, when it was combined with a fact-finding hearing. Morgan was found guilty of harassment and petit larceny and was ordered placed with the Department of Social Services for 18 months. He was detained a total of eight days between his initial appearance and the fact-finding hearing.

On December 21, 1977, while still in preventive detention pending his fact-finding hearing, Gregory Martin instituted a habeas corpus class action on behalf of "those persons who are, or during the

a conditional discharge; probation for up to two years; nonsecure placement with, perhaps, a relative or the division for youth; transfer to the commissioner of mental health; or secure placement. Id., at § 353.1–§ 353.5. Unless the juvenile committed one of the designated felonies, the court must order the least restrictive available alternative consistent with the needs and best interests of the juvenile and the need for protection of the community. Id., at § 352.2(2).

[60] Every accused juvenile is interviewed by a member of the staff of the probation department. This process is known as "probation intake." See Testimony of Mr. Benjamin (Supervisor, New York Dept. of Probation), J.A., at 142. In the course of the interview, which lasts an average of 45 minutes, the probation officer will gather what information he can about the nature of the case, the attitudes of the parties involved, and the child's past history and current family circumstances. Id., at 144, 153. His sources of information are the child, his parent or guardian, the arresting officer and any records of past contacts between the child and the Family Court. On the basis of this interview, the probation officer may attempt to "adjust," or informally resolve, the case. FCA § 308.1(2). Adjustment is a purely voluntary process in which the complaining witness agrees not to press the case further, while the juvenile is given a warning or agrees to counseling sessions or, perhaps, referral to a community agency. Id., at § 308.1 (Practice Commentary). In cases involving designated felonies or other serious crimes, adjustment is not permitted without written approval of the Family Court. Id., at § 308.1(4). If a case is not informally adjusted, it is referred to the "presentment agency."

pendency of this action, will be preventively detained pursuant to" § 320.5(3)(b) of the Family Court Act. Rosario and Morgan were subsequently added as additional named plaintiffs. These three class representatives sought a declaratory judgment that § 320.5(3)(b) violates the Due Process and Equal Protection Clauses of the Fourteenth Amendment.

In an unpublished opinion, the district court certified the class. The court also held that appellees were not required to exhaust their state remedies before resorting to federal habeas because the highest state court had already rejected an identical challenge to the juvenile preventive detention statute. See People ex rel. Wayburn v. Schupf, 39 N.Y.2d 682, 385 N.Y.S.2d 518, 350 N.E.2d 906 (1976). Exhaustion of state remedies, therefore, would be "an exercise in futility." J.A., at 26.

At trial, appellees offered in evidence the case histories of thirty-four members of the class, including the three named petitioners. Both parties presented some general statistics on the relation between pretrial detention and ultimate disposition. In addition, there was testimony concerning juvenile proceedings from a number of witnesses, including a legal aid attorney specializing in juvenile cases, a probation supervisor, a child psychologist, and a Family Court judge. On the basis of this evidence, the district court rejected the equal protection challenge as "insubstantial," [61] but agreed with appellees that pretrial detention under the Family Court Act violates due process.[62] The court ordered that "all class members in custody pursuant to Family Court Act Section [320.5(3)(b)] shall be released forthwith." J.A., at 93.

The Court of Appeals affirmed. After reviewing the trial record, the court opined that "the vast majority of juveniles detained under [§ 320.5(3)(b)] either have their petitions dismissed before an adjudication of delinquency or are released after adjudication." 689 F.2d, at 369. The court concluded from that fact that § 320.5(3)(b) "is

---

[61] The equal protection claim, which was neither raised on appeal nor decided by the Second Circuit, is not before us.

[62] The district court gave three reasons for this conclusion. First, under the FCA, a juvenile may be held in pretrial detention for up to five days without any judicial determination of probable cause. Relying on Gerstein v. Pugh, 420 U.S. 103, 114, 95 S.Ct. 854, 863, 43 L.Ed.2d 54 (1975), the district court concluded that pretrial detention without a prior adjudication of probable cause is, itself, a per se violation of due process. 513 F.Supp., at 717.

Second, after a review of the pertinent scholarly literature, the court noted that "no diagnostic tools have as yet been devised which enable even the most highly trained criminologists to predict reliably which juveniles will engage in violent crime." 513 F.Supp., at 708. *A fortiori,*

the court concluded, a Family Court judge cannot make a reliable prediction based on the limited information available to him at the initial appearance. Id., at 712. Moreover, the court felt that the trial record was "replete" with examples of arbitrary and capricious detentions. Id., at 713.

Finally, the court concluded that preventive detention is merely a euphemism for punishment imposed without an adjudication of guilt. The alleged purpose of the detention—to protect society from the juvenile's criminal conduct—is indistinguishable from the purpose of post-trial detention. And given "the inability of trial judges to predict which juveniles will commit crimes," there is no rational connection between the decision to detain and the alleged purpose, even if that purpose were legitimate. Id., at 716.

utilized principally, not for preventive purposes, but to impose punishment for unadjudicated criminal acts." Id., at 372. The early release of so many of those detained contradicts any asserted need for pretrial confinement to protect the community. The court therefore concluded that § 320.5(3)(b) must be declared unconstitutional as to all juveniles. Individual litigation would be a practical impossibility because the periods of detention are so short that the litigation is mooted before the merits are determined.[63]

II

There is no doubt that the Due Process Clause is applicable in juvenile proceedings. "The problem," we have stressed, "is to ascertain the precise impact of the due process requirement upon such proceedings." In re Gault, 387 U.S. 1, 13–14, 87 S.Ct. 1428, 1436–1437, 18 L.Ed.2d 527 (1967). We have held that certain basic constitutional protections enjoyed by adults accused of crimes also apply to juveniles. See In re Gault, supra, at 31–57, 87 S.Ct., at 1445–1459 (notice of charges, right to counsel, privilege against self-incrimination, right to confrontation and cross-examination); In re Winship, 397 U.S. 358, 90 S.Ct. 1068, 25 L.Ed.2d 368 (1970) (proof beyond a reasonable doubt); Breed v. Jones, 421 U.S. 519, 95 S.Ct. 1779, 44 L.Ed.2d 346 (1975) (double jeopardy). But the Constitution does not mandate elimination of all differences in the treatment of juveniles. See, e.g., McKeiver v. Pennsylvania, 403 U.S. 528, 91 S.Ct. 1976, 29 L.Ed.2d 647 (1971) (no right to jury trial). The State has "a *parens patriae* interest in preserving and promoting the welfare of the child," Santosky v. Kramer, 455 U.S. 745, 766, 102 S.Ct. 1388, 1401, 71 L.Ed.2d 599 (1982), which makes a juvenile proceeding fundamentally different from an adult criminal trial. We have tried, therefore, to strike a balance—to respect the "informality" and "flexibility" that characterize juvenile proceedings, In re Winship, supra, 397 U.S., at 366, 90 S.Ct., at 1073, and yet to ensure that such proceedings comport with the "fundamental fairness" demanded by the Due Process Clause. Breed v. Jones, supra, 421 U.S., at 531, 95 S.Ct., at 1786; McKeiver, supra, 403 U.S., at 543, 91 S.Ct., at 1985 (plurality opinion).

The statutory provision at issue in this case, § 320.5(3)(b), permits a brief pretrial detention based on a finding of a "serious risk" that an arrested juvenile may commit a crime before his return date. The question before us is whether preventive detention of juveniles pursuant to § 320.5(3)(b) is compatible with the "fundamental fairness" required by due process. Two separate inquiries are necessary to answer this question. First, does preventive detention under the New York statute serve a legitimate state objective? * * * And, second, are the procedural safeguards contained in the Family Court

[63] Judge Newman concurred separately. He was not convinced that the record supported the majority's statistical conclusions. But he thought that the statute was procedurally infirm because it granted unbridled discretion to Family Court judges to make an inherently uncertain prediction of future criminal behavior. 689 F.2d, at 377.

Act adequate to authorize the pretrial detention of at least some juveniles charged with crimes? See Mathews v. Eldridge, 424 U.S. 319, 335, 96 S.Ct. 893, 903, 47 L.Ed.2d 18 (1976); Gerstein v. Pugh, 420 U.S. 103, 114, 95 S.Ct. 854, 863, 43 L.Ed.2d 54 (1975).

A

Preventive detention under the Family Court Act is purportedly designed to protect the child and society from the potential consequences of his criminal acts. People ex rel. Wayburn v. Sckupf, 39 N.Y.2d 682, 385 N.Y.S.2d 518, 521–522, 350 N.E.2d 906, 910–911 (1976). When making any detention decision, the Family Court judge is specifically directed to consider the needs and best interests of the juvenile as well as the need for the protection of the community. FCA § 301.1; In re Craig S., 57 A.D.2d 761, 394 N.Y.S.2d 200 (1977). In Bell v. Wolfish, 441 U.S., at 534 n. 15, 99 S.Ct., at 1871 n. 15, we left open the question whether any governmental objective other than ensuring a detainee's presence at trial may constitutionally justify pretrial detention. As an initial matter, therefore, we must decide whether, in the context of the juvenile system, the combined interest in protecting both the community and the juvenile himself from the consequences of future criminal conduct is sufficient to justify such detention.

The "legitimate and compelling state interest" in protecting the community from crime cannot be doubted. * * * We have stressed before that crime prevention is "a weighty social objective," * * * and this interest persists undiluted in the juvenile context. See In re Gault, 387 U.S. 1, 20 n. 26, 87 S.Ct. 1428, 1440 n. 26, 18 L.Ed.2d 527 (1967). The harm suffered by the victim of a crime is not dependent upon the age of the perpetrator.[64] And the harm to society generally may even be greater in this context given the high rate of recidivism among juveniles. In re Gault, 387 U.S., at 22, 87 S.Ct., at 1440.

The juvenile's countervailing interest in freedom from institutional restraints, even for the brief time involved here, is undoubtedly substantial as well. See In re Gault, 387 U.S., at 27, 87 S.Ct., at 1443. But that interest must be qualified by the recognition that juveniles, unlike adults, are always in some form of custody. * * * Children, by definition, are not assumed to have the capacity to take care of themselves. They are assumed to be subject to the control of their parents, and if parental control falters, the State must play its part as *parens patriae*. * * * In this respect, the juvenile's liberty interest may, in appropriate circumstances, be subordinated to the State's "*parens patriae* interest in preserving and promoting the welfare of

[64] In 1982, juveniles under 16 accounted for 7.5 percent of all arrests for violent crimes, 19.9 percent of all arrests for serious property crime, and 17.3 percent of all arrests for violent and serious property crimes combined. 1982 Crime in the United States 176–177 (United States Dept. of Justice) ("violent crimes" include murder, non-negligent manslaughter, forcible rape, robbery and aggravated assault; "serious property crimes" include burglary, larceny-theft, motor vehicle theft and arson).

the child." Santosky v. Kramer, 455 U.S. 745, 766, 102 S.Ct. 1388, 1401, 71 L.Ed.2d 599 (1982).

The New York Court of Appeals, in upholding the statute at issue here, stressed at some length "the desirability of protecting the juvenile from his own folly." People ex rel. Wayburn v. Schupf, 39 N.Y.2d 682, 385 N.Y.S.2d 518, 520–521, 350 N.E.2d 906, 909–910 (1976).[65] Society has a legitimate interest in protecting a juvenile from the consequences of his criminal activity—both from potential physical injury which may be suffered when a victim fights back or a policeman attempts to make an arrest and from the downward spiral of criminal activity into which peer pressure may lead the child.

*   *   *

The substantiality and legitimacy of the state interests underlying this statute are confirmed by the wide-spread use and judicial acceptance of preventive detention for juveniles. Every State, as well as the United States in the District of Columbia, permits preventive detention of juveniles accused of crime. A number of model juvenile justice acts also contain provisions permitting preventive detention.[66] And the courts of eight States, including the New York Court of Appeals, have upheld their statutes with specific reference to protecting the juvenile and the community from harmful pretrial conduct, including pretrial crime.   *   *   *

[65] "Our society recognizes that juveniles in general are in the earlier stages of their emotional growth, that their intellectual development is incomplete, that they have had only limited practical experience, and that their value systems have not yet been clearly identified or firmly adopted * * *.

"For the same reasons that our society does not hold juveniles to an adult standard of responsibility for their conduct, our society may also conclude that there is a greater likelihood that a juvenile charged with delinquency, if released, will commit another criminal act than that an adult charged with crime will do so. To the extent that self-restraint may be expected to constrain adults, it may not be expected to operate with equal force as to juveniles. Because of the possibility of juvenile delinquency treatment and the absence of second-offender sentencing, there will not be the deterrent for the juvenile which confronts the adult. Perhaps more significant is the fact that in consequence of lack of experience and comprehension the juvenile does not view the commission of what are criminal acts in the same perspective as an adult * * *. There is the element of gamesmanship and the excitement of 'getting away' with something and the powerful inducement of peer pressures. All of these commonly acknowledged factors make the commission of criminal conduct on the part of juveniles in general more likely than in the case of adults." People ex rel. Wayburn v. Schupf, 39 N.Y.2d 682, 385 N.Y.S.2d 518, 520–521, 350 N.E.2d 906, 909–910 (1976).

[66] See United States Department of Justice, Office of Juvenile Justice and Delinquency Prevention, Standards for the Administration of Juvenile Justice, Report of the National Advisory Committee for Juvenile Justice and Delinquency Prevention (U.S.Gov. Printing Office, July 1980), at 294–296; Uniform Juvenile Court Act, § 14, 9A U.L.A. (National Conference of Commissioners on Uniform State Laws—1968); Standard Juvenile Court Act, Art. IV, § 16, proposed by the National Council on Crime and Delinquency (6th Ed.1959); W. Sheridan, Legislative Guide for Drafting Family and Juvenile Court Acts, § 20(a)(1) (Dept. of HEW, Children's Bureau, Pub. No. 472–1969); see also Standards for Juvenile and Family Courts, at 62–63 (Dept. of HEW, Children's Bureau, Pub. No. 437–1966). Cf. Institute of Judicial Administration/American Bar Association Juvenile Justice Standards Relating to Interim Status: The Release, Control, and Detention of Accused Juvenile Offenders Between Arrest and Disposition 3.2B (detention limited to "reducing the likelihood that the juvenile may inflict serious bodily harm on others during the interim").

"The fact that a practice is followed by a large number of states is not conclusive in a decision as to whether that practice accords with due process, but it is plainly worth considering in determining whether the practice 'offends some principle of justice so rooted in the traditions and conscience of our people as to be ranked as fundamental,'" * * * In light of the uniform legislative judgment that pretrial detention of juveniles properly promotes the interests both of society and the juvenile, we conclude that the practice serves a legitimate regulatory purpose compatible with the "fundamental fairness" demanded by the Due Process Clause in juvenile proceedings. Cf. McKeiver v. Pennsylvania, 403 U.S. 528, 548, 91 S.Ct. 1976, 1987, 29 L.Ed.2d 647 (1971) (plurality opinion).[67]

Of course, the mere invocation of a legitimate purpose will not justify particular restrictions and conditions of confinement amounting to punishment. It is axiomatic that "[d]ue process requires that a pretrial detainee not be punished." Bell v. Wolfish, 441 U.S., at 535 n. 16, 99 S.Ct., at 1872 n. 16. Even given, therefore, that pretrial detention may serve legitimate regulatory purposes, it is still necessary to determine whether the terms and conditions of confinement under § 320.5(3)(b) are in fact compatible with those purposes. Kennedy v. Mendoza-Martinez, 372 U.S. 144, 168–169, 83 S.Ct. 554, 567–568, 9 L.Ed.2d 644 (1963). "A court must decide whether the disability is imposed for the purpose of punishment or whether it is but an incident of some other legitimate governmental purpose." Bell v. Wolfish, supra, 441 U.S., at 538, 99 S.Ct., at 1873. Absent a showing of an express intent to punish on the part of the State, that determination generally will turn on "whether an alternative purpose to which [the restriction] may rationally be connected is assignable for it, and whether it appears excessive in relation to the alternative purpose assigned [to it.]" * * *

There is no indication in the statute itself that preventive detention is used or intended as a punishment. First of all, the detention is strictly limited in time. If a juvenile is detained at his initial appearance and has denied the charges against him, he is entitled to a probable cause hearing to be held not more than three days after the conclusion of the initial appearance or four days after the filing of

---

[67] Appellees argue that some limit must be placed on the categories of crimes that detained juveniles must be accused of having committed or being likely to commit. But the discretion to delimit the categories of crimes justifying detention, like the discretion to define criminal offenses and prescribe punishments, resides wholly with the state legislatures. Whalen v. United States, 445 U.S. 684, 689, 100 S.Ct. 1432, 1436, 63 L.Ed.2d 715 (1980); Rochin v. California, 342 U.S. 165, 168, 72 S.Ct. 205, 207, 96 L.Ed. 183 (1952). See also Rummel v. Estelle, 445 U.S. 263, 275, 100 S.Ct. 1133, 1139, 63 L.Ed.2d 382 (1980) ("the presence or absence of violence does not al-

ways affect the strength of society's interest in deterring a particular crime").

More fundamentally, this sort of attack on a criminal statute must be made on a case-by-case basis. United States v. Raines, 362 U.S. 17, 21, 80 S.Ct. 519, 522, 4 L.Ed.2d 524 (1960). The court will not sift through the entire class to determine whether the statute was constitutionally applied in each case. And, outside the limited First Amendment context, a criminal statute may not be attacked as overbroad. See New York v. Ferber, 458 U.S. 747, 102 S.Ct. 3348, 73 L.Ed.2d 1113 (1982).

the petition, whichever is sooner. FCA § 325.1(2).[68] If the Family
Court judge finds probable cause, he must also determine whether
continued detention is necessary pursuant to § 320.5(3)(b). Id., at
§ 325.3(3).

Detained juveniles are also entitled to an expedited fact-finding
hearing. If the juvenile is charged with one of a limited number of
designated felonies, the fact-finding hearing must be scheduled to
commence not more than fourteen days after the conclusion of the
initial appearance. Id., at § 340.1. If the juvenile is charged with a
lesser offense, then the fact-finding hearing must be held not more
than three days after the initial appearance.[69] In the latter case,
since the time for the probable cause hearing and the fact-finding
hearing coincide, the two hearings are merged.

Thus, the maximum possible detention under § 320.5(3)(b) of a
youth accused of a serious crime, assuming a three-day extension of
the fact-finding hearing for good cause shown, is seventeen days.
The maximum detention for less serious crimes, again assuming a
three-day extension for good cause shown, is six days. These time-
frames seem suited to the limited purpose of providing the youth
with a controlled environment and separating him from improper
influences pending the speedy disposition of his case.

The conditions of confinement also appear to reflect the regulatory purposes relied upon by the State. When a juvenile is remanded
after his initial appearance, he cannot, absent exceptional circumstances, be sent to a prison or lockup where he would be exposed to
adult criminals. FCA § 304.1(2). Instead, the child is screened by an
"assessment unit" of the Department of Juvenile Justice. Testimony
of Mr. Kelly (Deputy Commissioner of Operations, New York City
Department of Juvenile Justice), J.A., at 286–287. The assessment
unit places the child in either nonsecure or secure detention. Non-
secure detention involves an open facility in the community, a sort of
"halfway house," without locks, bars or security officers where the
child receives schooling and counseling and has access to recreational
facilities. Id., at 285; Testimony of Mr. Benjamin, J.A., at 149–150.

Secure detention is more restrictive, but it is still consistent with
the regulatory and *parens patriae* objectives relied upon by the
State. Children are assigned to separate dorms based on age, size
and behavior. They wear street clothes provided by the institution
and partake in educational and recreational programs and counseling
sessions run by trained social workers. Misbehavior is punished by
confinement to one's room. See Testimony of Mr. Kelly, J.A., at 292–
297. We cannot conclude from this record that the controlled environment briefly imposed by the State on juveniles in secure pretrial
detention "is imposed for the purpose of punishment" rather than as

---

[68] For good cause shown, the court
may adjourn the hearing, but for no more
than three additional court days. FCA
§ 325.1(3).

[69] In either case, the court may adjourn
the hearing for not more than three days

for good cause shown. FCA § 340.1(3).
The court must state on the record the
reason for any adjournment. Id., at
§ 340.1(4).

"an incident of some other legitimate government purpose." Bell v. Wolfish, 441 U.S., at 538, 99 S.Ct., at 1873.

The Court of Appeals, of course, did conclude that the underlying purpose of § 320.5(3)(b) is punitive rather than regulatory. But the court did not dispute that preventive detention might serve legitimate regulatory purposes or that the terms and conditions of pretrial confinement in New York are compatible with those purposes. Rather, the court invalidated a significant aspect of New York's juvenile justice system based solely on some case histories and a statistical study which appeared to show that "the vast majority of juveniles detained under [§ 320.5(3)(b)] either have their petitions dismissed before an adjudication or are released after adjudication." 689 F.2d, at 369. The court assumed that dismissal of a petition or failure to confine a juvenile at the dispositional hearing belied the need to detain him prior to fact finding and that, therefore, the pretrial detention constituted punishment. Id., at 373. Since punishment imposed without a prior adjudication of guilt is *per se* illegitimate, the Court of Appeals concluded that no juveniles could be held pursuant to § 320.5(3)(b).

There are some obvious flaws in the statistics and case histories relied upon by the lower court.[70] But even assuming it to be the case that "by far the greater number of juveniles incarcerated under [§ 320.5(3)(b)] will never be confined as a consequence of a disposition imposed after an adjudication of delinquency," 689 F.2d, at 371–372, we find that to be an insufficient ground for upsetting the widely-shared legislative judgment that preventive detention serves an important and legitimate function in the juvenile justice system. We are unpersuaded by the Court of Appeals' rather cavalier equation of detentions that do not lead to continued confinement after an adjudication of guilt and "wrongful" or "punitive" pretrial detentions.

Pretrial detention need not be considered punitive merely because a juvenile is subsequently discharged subject to conditions or put on probation. In fact, such actions reinforce the original finding that close supervision of the juvenile is required. Lenient but supervised disposition is in keeping with the Act's purpose to promote the

---

[70] For example, as the Court of Appeals itself admits, 689 F.2d, at 369 n. 18, the statistical study on which it relied mingles indiscriminately detentions under § 320.5(3)(b) with detentions under § 320.5(3)(a). The latter provision applies only to juveniles who are likely not to appear on the return date if not detained, and appellees concede that such juveniles may be lawfully detained. Brief for Appellees, at 93. Furthermore, the thirty-four case histories on which the court relied were handpicked by appellees' counsel from over a three-year period. Compare Plaintiff's Exhibit 19a (detention of Geraldo Delgado on March 5, 1976) with Plaintiff's Exhibit 35a (detention of James Ancrum on August 19, 1979). The Court of Appeals stated that appellants did not contest the representativeness of these case histories. 689 F.2d at 369 n. 19. Appellants argue, however, that there was no occasion to contest their representativeness because the case histories were not even offered by appellees as a representative sample, and were not evaluated by appellees' expert statistician or the district court in that light. See Brief for Intervenor-Appellant, at 24–25 n.* We need not resolve this controversy.

welfare and development of the child.[71] As the New York Court of Appeals noted:

> "It should surprise no one that caution and concern for both the juvenile and society may indicate the more conservative decision to detain at the very outset, whereas the later development of very much more relevant information may prove that while a finding of delinquency was warranted, placement may not be indicated." People ex rel. Wayburn v. Schupf, 39 N.Y.2d 682, 385 N.Y.S.2d 518, 522, 350 N.E.2d 906, 910 (1976).

Even when a case is terminated prior to fact finding, it does not follow that the decision to detain the juvenile pursuant to § 320.5(3) (b) amounted to a due process violation. A delinquency petition may be dismissed for any number of reasons collateral to its merits, such as the failure of a witness to testify. The Family Court judge cannot be expected to anticipate such developments at the initial hearing. He makes his decision based on the information available to him at that time, and the propriety of the decision must be judged in that light. Consequently, the final disposition of a case is "largely irrelevant" to the legality of a pretrial detention. Baker v. McCollan, 443 U.S. 137, 145, 99 S.Ct. 2689, 2695, 61 L.Ed.2d 433 (1979).

It may be, of course, that in some circumstances detention of a juvenile would not pass constitutional muster. But the validity of those detentions must be determined on a case-by-case basis. Section 320.5(3)(b) is not invalid "on its face" by reason of the ambiguous statistics and case histories relied upon by the court below.[72] We find no justification for the conclusion that, contrary to the express language of the statute and the judgment of the highest state court, § 320.5(3)(b) is a punitive rather than a regulatory measure. Preventive detention under the Family Court Act serves the legitimate state objective, held in common with every State in the country, of protecting both the juvenile and society from the hazards of pretrial crime.

---

[71] Judge Quinones testified that detention at disposition is considered a "harsh solution." At the dispositional hearing, the Family Court judge usually has "a much more complete picture of the youngster" and tries to tailor the least restrictive dispositional order compatible with that picture. Testimony of Judge Quinones, J.A., at 279–281.

[72] Several *amici* argue that similar statistics obtain throughout the country. See, e.g., Brief of the American Bar Association, at 23; Brief of the Association for Children of New Jersey, at 8, 11; Brief of the Youth Law Center and the Juvenile Law Center of Philadelphia, at 13–14. But even if New York's experience were duplicated on a national scale, that fact would not lead us, as *amici* urge, to conclude that every State and

the United States are illicitly punishing juveniles prior to their trial. On the contrary, if such statistics obtain nationwide, our conclusion is strengthened that the existence of the statistics in this case is not a sufficient ground for striking down New York's statute. As already noted: "The fact that a practice is followed by a large number of states is not conclusive in a decision as to whether that practice accords with due process, but it is plainly worth considering in determining whether the practice 'offends some principle of justice so rooted in the traditions and conscience of our people to be ranked as fundamental.' Snyder v. Massachusetts, 291 U.S. 97, 105 [54 S.Ct. 330, 332, 78 L.Ed. 674] (1934)." Leland v. Oregon, 343 U.S. 790, 798, 72 S.Ct. 1002, 1007, 96 L.Ed. 1302 (1952).

B

Given the legitimacy of the State's interest in preventive detention, and the nonpunitive nature of that detention, the remaining question is whether the procedures afforded juveniles detained prior to fact finding provide sufficient protection against erroneous and unnecessary deprivations of liberty. See Mathews v. Eldridge, 424 U.S. 319, 335, 96 S.Ct. 893, 903, 47 L.Ed.2d 18 (1976).[73] In Gerstein v. Pugh, 420 U.S. 103, 114, 95 S.Ct. 854, 863, 43 L.Ed.2d 54 (1975), we held that a judicial determination of probable cause is a prerequisite to any extended restraint on the liberty of an adult accused of crime. We did not, however, mandate a specific timetable. Nor did we require the "full panoply of adversary safeguards—counsel, confrontation, cross-examination, and compulsory process of witnesses." Id., at 119, 95 S.Ct., at 866. Instead, we recognized "the desirability of flexibility and experimentation by the States." Id., at 123, 95 S.Ct., at 868. *Gerstein* arose under the Fourth Amendment, but the same concern with "flexibility" and "informality," while yet ensuring adequate predetention procedures, is present in this context. * * *

In many respects, the Family Court Act provides far more predetention protection for juveniles than we found to be constitutionally required for a probable cause determination for adults in *Gerstein*. The initial appearance is informal, but the accused juvenile is given full notice of the charges against him and a complete stenographic record is kept of the hearing. See 513 F.Supp., at 702. The juvenile appears accompanied by his parent or guardian.[74] He is first informed of his rights, including the right to remain silent and the right to be represented by counsel chosen by him or by a law guardian assigned by the court. FCA § 320.3. The initial appearance may be adjourned for no longer than 72 hours or until the next court day, whichever is sooner, to enable an appointed law guardian or other counsel to appear before the court. Id., at § 320.2(3). When his counsel is present, the juvenile is informed of the charges against him and furnished with a copy of the delinquency petition. Id., at § 320.4(1). A representative from the presentment agency appears in support of the petition.

The nonhearsay allegations in the delinquency petition and supporting depositions must establish probable cause to believe the juvenile committed the offense. Although the Family Court judge is not required to make a finding of probable cause at the initial appearance, the youth may challenge the sufficiency of the petition on that ground. FCA § 315.1. Thus, the juvenile may oppose any

[73] Appellees urge the alleged lack of procedural safeguards as an alternative ground for upholding the judgment of the Court of Appeals. Brief for Appellees, at 62–75. The court itself intimated that it would reach the same result on that ground, 689 F.2d, at 373–374, and Judge Newman, in his concurrence, relied expressly on perceived procedural flaws in the statute. Accordingly, we deem it necessary to consider the question.

[74] If the juvenile's parent or guardian fails to appear after reasonable and substantial efforts have been made to notify such person, the court must appoint a law guardian for the child. FCA § 320.3.

recommended detention by arguing that there is not probable cause to believe he committed the offense or offenses with which he is charged. If the petition is not dismissed, the juvenile is given an opportunity to admit or deny the charges. Id., at § 321.1.[75]

At the conclusion of the initial appearance, the presentment agency makes a recommendation regarding detention. A probation officer reports on the juvenile's record, including other prior and current Family Court and probation contacts, as well as relevant information concerning home life, school attendance, and any special medical or developmental problems. He concludes by offering his agency's recommendation on detention. Opposing counsel, the juvenile's parents, and the juvenile himself may all speak on his behalf and challenge any information or recommendation. If the judge does decide to detain the juvenile under § 320.5(3)(b), he must state on the record the facts and reasons for the detention.[76]

As noted, a detained juvenile is entitled to a formal, adversarial probable cause hearing within three days of his initial appearance, with one three-day extension possible for good cause shown.[77] The burden at this hearing is on the presentment agency to call witnesses and offer evidence in support of the charges. Id., at § 325.2. Testimony is under oath and subject to cross-examination. Ibid. The accused juvenile may call witnesses and offer evidence in his own behalf. If the court finds probable cause, the court must again decide whether continued detention is necessary under § 320.5(3)(b). Again, the facts and reasons for the detention must be stated on the record.

In sum, notice, a hearing, and a statement of facts and reasons are given prior to any detention under § 320.5(3)(b). A formal probable cause hearing is then held within a short while thereafter, if the fact-finding hearing is not itself scheduled within three days. These flexible procedures have been found constitutionally adequate under the Fourth Amendment, see Gerstein v. Pugh, and under the

---

[75] If the child chooses to remain silent, he is assumed to deny the charges. FCA § 321.1. With the consent of the court and of the presentment agency, the child may admit to a lesser charge. If he wishes to admit to the charges or to a lesser charge, the court must, before accepting the admission, advise the child of his right to a fact-finding hearing and of the possible specific dispositional orders that may result from the admission. Ibid. The court must also satisfy itself that the child actually did commit the acts to which he admits. Ibid.

With the consent of the victim or complainant and the juvenile, the court may also refer a case to the probation service for adjustment. If the case is subsequently adjusted, the petition is then dismissed. Id., at § 320.6.

[76] Given that under Gerstein, 420 U.S., at 119–123, 95 S.Ct., at 865–868, a proba-

ble cause hearing may be informal and nonadversarial, a Family Court judge could make a finding of probable cause at the initial appearance. That he is not required to do so does not, under the circumstances, amount to a deprivation of due process. Appellees fail to point to a single example where probable cause was not found after a decision was made to detain the child.

[77] The Court in Gerstein indicated approval of pretrial detention procedures that supplied a probable cause hearing within five days of the initial detention. 420 U.S., at 124 n. 25, 95 S.Ct., at 868 n. 25. The brief delay in the probable cause hearing may actually work to the advantage of the juvenile since it gives his counsel, usually appointed at the initial appearance pursuant to FCA § 320.2(2), time to prepare.

Due Process Clause, see Kent v. United States, 383 U.S. 541, 557, 86 S.Ct. 1045, 1055, 16 L.Ed.2d 84 (1966). Appellees have failed to note any additional procedures that would significantly improve the accuracy of the determination without unduly impinging on the achievement of legitimate state purposes.[78]

Appellees argue, however, that the risk of erroneous and unnecessary detentions is too high despite these procedures because the standard for detention is fatally vague. Detention under § 320.5(3)(b) is based on a finding that there is a "serious risk" that the juvenile, if released, would commit a crime prior to his next court appearance. We have already seen that detention of juveniles on that ground serves legitimate regulatory purposes. But appellees claim, and the district court agreed, that it is virtually impossible to predict future criminal conduct with any degree of accuracy. Moreover, they say, the statutory standard fails to channel the discretion of the Family Court judge by specifying the factors on which he should rely in making that prediction. The procedural protections noted above are thus, in their view, unavailing because the ultimate decision is intrinsically arbitrary and uncontrolled.

Our cases indicate, however, that from a legal point of view there is nothing inherently unattainable about a prediction of future criminal conduct. Such a judgment forms an important element in many decisions,[79] and we have specifically rejected the contention, based on the same sort of sociological data relied upon by appellees and the district court, "that it is impossible to predict future behavior and that the question is so vague as to be meaningless." Jurek v. Texas, 428 U.S. 262, 274, 96 S.Ct. 2950, 2957, 49 L.Ed.2d 929 (1976) (opinion

---

[78] Judge Newman, in his concurrence below, offered a list of statutory improvements. These suggested changes included: limitations on the crimes for which the juvenile has been arrested or which he is likely to commit if released; a determination of the likelihood that the juvenile committed the crime; an assessment of the juvenile's background; and a more specific standard of proof. * * * there is no indication that delimiting the category of crimes justifying detention would improve the accuracy of the § 320.5(3)(b) determination in any respect.

[79] See Jurek v. Texas, 428 U.S. 262, 274–275, 96 S.Ct. 2950, 2957–2958, 49 L.Ed.2d 929 (1976) (death sentence imposed by jury); Greenholtz v. Nebraska Penal Inmates, 442 U.S. 1, 9–10, 99 S.Ct. 2100, 2104–2105, 60 L.Ed.2d 668 (1979) (grant of parole); Morrissey v. Brewer, 408 U.S. 471, 480, 92 S.Ct. 2593, 2599, 33 L.Ed.2d 484 (1972) (parole revocation).

A prediction of future criminal conduct may also form the basis for an increased sentence under the "dangerous special offender" statute, 18 U.S.C. § 3575 (1976 & Supp. V 1981). Under § 3575(f), a "dangerous" offender is defined as an individual for whom "a period of confinement longer than that provided for such [underlying] felony is required for the protection of the public from further criminal conduct by the defendant." The statute has been challenged numerous times on the grounds that the standard is unconstitutionally vague. Every Court of Appeals considering the question has rejected that claim. United States v. Davis, 710 F.2d 104, 108–109 (CA3), cert. denied, ___ U.S. ___, 104 S.Ct. 505, 78 L.Ed.2d 695 (1983); United States v. Schell, 692 F.2d 672, 675–676 (CA10 1982); United States v. Williamson, 567 F.2d 610, 613 (CA4 1977); United States v. Bowdach, 561 F.2d 1160, 1175 (CA5 1977); United States v. Neary, 552 F.2d 1184, 1194 (CA7), cert. denied, 434 U.S. 864, 98 S.Ct. 197, 54 L.Ed.2d 139 (1977); United States v. Stewart, 531 F.2d 326, 336–337 (CA6), cert. denied, 426 U.S. 922, 96 S.Ct. 2629, 49 L.Ed.2d 376 (1976).

of STEWART, POWELL and STEVENS, JJ.); id., at 279, 96 S.Ct., at 2959 (WHITE, J., concurring).

We have also recognized that a prediction of future criminal conduct is "an experienced prediction based on a host of variables" which cannot be readily codified. Greenholtz v. Nebraska Penal Inmates, 442 U.S. 1, 16, 99 S.Ct. 2100, 2108, 60 L.Ed.2d 668 (1979). Judge Quinones of the Family Court testified at trial that he and his colleagues make a determination under § 320.5(3)(b) based on numerous factors including the nature and seriousness of the charges; whether the charges are likely to be proved at trial; the juvenile's prior record; the adequacy and effectiveness of his home supervision; his school situation, if known; the time of day of the alleged crime as evidence of its seriousness and a possible lack of parental control; and any special circumstances that might be brought to his attention by the probation officer, the child's attorney, or any parents, relatives or other responsible persons accompanying the child. Testimony of Judge Quinones, J.A., at 254–267. The decision is based on as much information as can reasonably be obtained at the initial appearance. Ibid.

Given the right to a hearing, to counsel and to a statement of reasons, there is no reason that the specific factors upon which the Family Court judge might rely must be specified in the statute. As the New York Court of Appeals concluded, People ex rel. Wayburn v. Schupf, 39 N.Y.2d 682, 385 N.Y.S.2d 518, 522, 350 N.E.2d 906, 910 (1976), "to a very real extent Family Court must exercise a substitute parental control for which there can be no particularized criteria." There is also no reason, we should add, for a federal court to assume that a state court judge will not strive to apply state law as conscientiously as possible. Sumner v. Mata, 449 U.S. 539, 549, 101 S.Ct. 764, 770, 66 L.Ed.2d 722 (1981).

It is worth adding that the Court of Appeals for the Second Circuit was mistaken in its conclusion that "individual litigation * * * is a practical impossibility because the periods of detention are so short that the litigation is mooted before the merits are determined." 689 F.2d, at 373. In fact, one of the juveniles in the very case histories upon which the court relied was released from pretrial detention on a writ of habeas corpus issued by the state Supreme Court. New York courts also have adopted a liberal view of the doctrine of "capable of repetition, yet evading review" precisely in order to ensure that pretrial detention orders are not unreviewable.
*　*　*

The required statement of facts and reasons justifying the detention and the stenographic record of the initial appearance will provide a basis for the review of individual cases. Pretrial detention orders in New York may be reviewed by writ of habeas corpus brought in state Supreme Court. And the judgment of that court is appealable as of right and may be taken directly to the Court of Appeals if a constitutional question is presented. N.Y.Civil Practice Law § 5601(b)(2) (1978). Permissive appeal from a Family Court order may also be had to the appellate division. FCA § 365.2. Or a motion for reconsideration may be directed to the Family Court judge. Id., at § 355.1(1)(b). These postdetention procedures provide a sufficient mechanism for correcting on a case-by-case basis any erroneous detentions ordered under § 320.5(3). Such procedures may well flesh out the standards specified in the statute.

III

The dissent would apparently have us strike down New York's preventive detention statute on two grounds: first, because the preventive detention of juveniles constitutes poor public policy, with the balance of harms outweighing any positive benefits either to society or to the juveniles themselves, post, at 2424, 2433, and, second, because the statute could have been better drafted to improve the quality of the decision-making process, post, at 2431–2432. But it is worth recalling that we are neither a legislature charged with formulating public policy nor an ABA committee charged with drafting a model statute. The question before us today is solely whether the preventive detention system chosen by the State of New York and applied by the New York Family Court comports with constitutional standards. Given the regulatory purpose for the detention and the procedural protections that precede its imposition, we conclude that § 320.5(3)(b) of the New York Family Court Act is not invalid under the Due Process Clause of the Fourteenth Amendment.

The judgment of the Court of Appeals is

Reversed.

C. THE RIGHT TO A DETENTION HEARING

1. HOW SOON?

PEOPLE v. CLAYBORN

Illinois Appellate Court, First District, Third Division, 1980.
90 Ill.App.3d 1047, 46 Ill.Dec. 435, 414 N.E.2d 157.

SIMON, JUSTICE:

* * *

Darrell Clayborn was taken into custody on Friday, May 30, 1980 at about 2:00 p.m. A petition for adjudication of wardship was filed immediately. The next day he was taken before a judge who scheduled a detention hearing for Monday, June 2, 1980. On that day the State told the court that its witness, a police officer, was unavailable but could appear the next day. Over Clayborn's objection, the court continued the detention hearing until Tuesday, June 3, 1980.

Clayborn received a detention hearing on June 3, 1980, at about 11:20 a.m. Probable cause was found. The next day he filed a writ of habeas corpus which was denied after a hearing by the circuit court. Clayborn remained in custody. On June 17, 1980 an adjudicatory hearing was held at which Clayborn was found to be a delinquent. On July 16, 1980, he was released from custody and placed on one year's probation.

The pertinent provisions of the Juvenile Court Act provide:

"A law enforcement officer may, without a warrant, take into temporary custody a minor (a) whom the officer with reasonable cause believes to be [delinquent]. * * * A probation officer * * * shall immediately investigate the circumstances of the minor and the facts surrounding his being taken into custody. The minor shall be immediately released to the custody of his parent * * * unless the probation officer * * * finds that further detention is a matter of immediate and urgent necessity for the protection of the minor or of the person or property of another * * *.

The written authorization of [the probation officer] constitutes authority for the superintendent of a detention home or * * * a county or municipal jail to detain and keep a minor for up to 36 hours, excluding Saturdays, Sundays and court-designated holidays.

Unless sooner released, a minor * * * taken into temporary custody must be brought before a judicial officer within 36 hours, exclusive of Saturdays, Sundays and court-designated holidays, for a detention hearing * * * to determine whether he shall be further held in custody. * * *

When a parent * * * is present and so requests, the detention * * * hearing shall be held immediately if the court is in session, otherwise at the earliest feasible time. * * *

The minor must be released from custody at the expiration of the 36 * * * hour period * * * if not brought before a judicial officer within that period." (Ill.Rev.Stat.1979, ch. 37, pars. 703–1(1), 703–4, 703–5(1, 3, 4).)

The provisions must be interpreted in light of the purpose of the Act, which is to serve the welfare of the minor and the best interests of the community, to preserve family ties by giving preferential treatment to parental custody and to secure to the minor at least the procedural rights afforded adults. Ill.Rev.Stat.1979, ch. 37, par. 701–2.

The provisions for a prompt detention hearing fulfill the requirement imposed by Article I, section 7 of the Illinois Constitution of 1970. They offer the juvenile more protection than adults, for the Act mandates immediate release from custody when the right to a prompt probable cause review is denied. Where adults are concerned, however, there is no remedy for a violation of art. I, sec. 7. People v. Howell (1975), 60 Ill.2d 117, 123, 324 N.E.2d 403, 406.

The Juvenile Court Act defines with precision what constitutes a prompt detention hearing. A minor must be taken before a judge for a detention hearing within 36 hours of being taken into custody. The Act makes allowance for delays when the courts are not in session, and so in fact a juvenile might have to wait more than 36 hours for a detention hearing. In this case, for example, Clayborn might have properly been in custody for many more than 36 hours before his detention hearing, since he was in custody over a weekend. But the essential point of the statute is clear; a minor must be taken before a judge for a detention hearing within the first 36 hours the courthouse doors are open after he is taken into custody.

The State argues that any appearance before a judge satisfies the statute. But the Act does not require meaningless appearances in court. It requires that the minor be taken before a judge so that the circumstances of his detention can be reviewed and probable cause established. It requires a hearing. See Ill.Rev.Stat.1979, ch. 37, par. 703–6 for the specifics of the hearing.

The 36-hour limitation is not merely directory. The provision of the Juvenile Court Act that requires that the adjudicatory hearing be held within 30 days was found to be directory in In re Armour (1974), 59 Ill.2d 102, 319 N.E.2d 496. That provision states that the petition "shall be set for an adjudicatory hearing within 30 days." (Ill.Rev. Stat.1979, ch. 37, par. 704–2.) *Armour* noted that "shall" can mean either "may" or "must" and held that the legislature intended that it mean "may". No such analysis is possible here. The Act says that the minor *"must* be brought before a judicial officer within 36 hours." (Ill.Rev.Stat.1979, ch. 37, par. 703–5(4) (emphasis added).) The literal wording of the statute must be respected. In addition, unlike in *Armour*, there is a remedy provided for a violation of the mandate of this provision—"the minor must be released from custody." The existence of the remedy lends support to the conclusion that the 36-hour limitation is mandatory.

The State argues that literal compliance means that a detention hearing would have to have been held at 2:00 a.m. on June 3. No such result is required. The detention hearing does not have to be held at the end of 36 hours of custody, only before 36 hours have elapsed. The legislature did not mean to put the circuit court to an impossible task, but only to provide for prompt detention hearings. It felt that 36 hours was adequate time to prepare for and provide a detention hearing. The State's suggestion that substantial compliance with the limitation is enough if the delay beyond 36 hours is reasonable is not a sound interpretation of the statute.

Given the policy of the Act to keep the minor in parental custody, the constitutional requirement of a prompt hearing for any detention and the unavailability of bail in the juvenile court, there are strong policy arguments for strict compliance with the Act. There might be instances in which substantial compliance would have to be tolerated, such as where the normal functioning of the courts break down. But that is not the case here. The only reason for the continuance in this case was the temporary unavailability of the State's witness. The State concedes that its witness, a police officer, could have come to court the next day, but it gives no reason for his unavailability on the scheduled date of Clayborn's detention hearing. More than the convenience of the State's witnesses is required to justify a delay in a minor's detention hearing.

All that remains to consider is the proper remedy for the delay. The defendant argues that because the State failed to hold a detention hearing within the proper time it should not have been allowed to hold him in custody at all before the adjudicatory hearing. Significantly, the defendant does not challenge the juvenile court's jurisdiction to hold the adjudicatory hearing or place him on probation. It has already been held that violation of this statute does not deprive the court of jurisdiction over the minor. * * *

Instead, the defendant asks this court to interpret section 3–5(4) of the Act, providing that the minor "must be released from *custody*." (Ill.Rev.Stat.1979, ch. 37, par. 703–5(4) (emphasis added).) Custody is the important term. Two interpretations are possible: one is that the legislature intended that when a detention hearing is delayed too long, the juvenile is to be released but only until the delayed detention hearing is held. The second interpretation is that the legislature intended that the juvenile not be held in custody at all prior to the adjudicatory hearing.

The latter interpretation is the more reasonable. The Act nowhere authorizes a detention hearing after the 36-hour limitation has expired. Section 3–5(4), like sections 4–2 and 5–3(4), mandates a maximum period of time that a minor may be held in custody pending judicial action. (Daniels, at 977, 480.) To adopt the former interpretation would be to increase the amount of overall time a minor spends in custody while awaiting adjudication and disposition of the petition of wardship. The latter interpretation encourages the State to make up for the delay in holding a detention hearing. If the State wishes to keep a minor off the street, it will schedule the adjudicatory hearing at the earliest possible moment, thus vitiating the earlier delay in holding a detention hearing. The statutory policy favoring prompt juvenile proceedings is served by construing section 3–5(4) to ban any further detention after a violation of the 36-hour period of section 3–5(1).

When Clayborn petitioned for a writ of habeas corpus, he should have been released. The juvenile court erred in denying the petition. However, since then Clayborn's adjudicatory hearing has been held and he has been released from custody. The issue of his detention is therefore moot. This opinion, nevertheless, is authorized by the public interest exception to the general rule that a moot case will be immediately dismissed. * * * The detention of a juvenile is a matter of public concern and an authoritative determination of the issue will guide public officials and juvenile court judges who are likely to face the problem in the future. * * *

Appeal Dismissed.

MCGILLICUDDY, P.J., and MCNAMARA, J., concur.

NOTE

In In Re McCall, 108 Ill.App.3d 164, 63 Ill.Dec. 906, 438 N.E.2d 1269 (1982), the juvenile's detention hearing was held 45 hours instead of the required 36 hours after he was taken into custody. The juvenile argued that the appropriate remedy was dismissal of the case, claiming that to do otherwise was to deny him due process of law. The court conceded that a trial court has authority to dismiss a criminal indictment when due process has been denied, but only on a "clear showing of actual and substantial prejudice * * *." The court went on to hold that absent such a showing, the appropriate remedy was that mandated in *Clayborn*—release from custody prior to the adjudicatory hearing and not dismissal.

2. RIGHT TO PROBABLE CAUSE DETERMINATION

The student will recall that in Schall v. Martin, supra, the Court found no constitutional problem caused by a potential 3 day period beyond the time of the "initial appearance" and a separate "probable cause" determination. In particular, the Court found that a procedure so structured did not conflict with the requirements for adults laid down in the *Gerstein* case discussed both in *Schall* and in the following case.

R.W.T. v. DALTON

United States Court of Appeals for the Eighth Circuit, 1983.
712 F.2d 1225, cert. denied ___ U.S. ___, 104 S.Ct. 527, 78 L.Ed.2d 710.

Before ARNOLD and BENNETT,* CIRCUIT JUDGES, and HENLEY, SENIOR CIRCUIT JUDGE.

ARNOLD, CIRCUIT JUDGE.

In this case a class of juveniles allege that they were denied their constitutional rights when they were detained in Missouri county jails without being afforded probable-cause determinations. * * *

I.

The plaintiffs are a class of juveniles who have been, are, or may be detained in jails or detention centers by juvenile authorities * * *. The plaintiffs sought declaratory and injunctive relief on two issues. * * *

The second issue concerned the defendants' practice of detaining juveniles without affording them a preliminary hearing before a neutral and detached judicial officer to determine whether there was probable cause to believe that the juveniles had committed the acts with which they were charged. On October 14, 1980, the District Court granted summary judgment in favor of the plaintiffs on this issue, holding that the defendants' practice violated the plaintiffs' right to be free from unreasonable seizure under the Fourth and Fourteenth Amendments.[80] * * *

---

* The Hon. Marion T. Bennett, United States Circuit Judge for the Federal Circuit, sitting by designation.

[80] The District Court denied the plaintiffs' request that the probable-cause hearing be attended by full adversary

II.

Under Missouri law, the juvenile court has jurisdiction over both children who are charged with violating the criminal law—delinquents—and children who are charged with committing noncriminal acts which are considered dangerous to the welfare of the juvenile or others—status offenders. The jurisdictional statute reads in pertinent part:

> 1. * * * the juvenile court shall have exclusive original jurisdiction in proceedings:
>
> * * *
>
> (2) Involving any child * * * who is alleged to be in need of care and treatment because:
>
>> (a) The child while subject to compulsory school attendance is repeatedly and without justification absent from school; or
>>
>> (b) The child disobeys the reasonable and lawful directions of his parents or other custodian and is beyond their control; or
>>
>> (c) The child is habitually absent from his home without sufficient cause, permission, or justification; or
>>
>> (d) The behavior or associations of the child are otherwise injurious to his welfare or to the welfare of others; or
>>
>> (e) The child is charged with an offense not classified as criminal, or with an offense applicable only to children * * *.
>
> (3) Involving any child who is alleged to have violated a state law or municipal ordinance * * *.

Mo.Ann.Stat. § 211.031 (Vernon 1983). It is important to note that each of the five categories listed in paragraph (2) turns on some past act on the part of the juvenile charged.

Both delinquents and status offenders may be taken into judicial custody by law-enforcement officers or by the juvenile officer. Mo. Sup.Ct.R. 111.01.[81] The juvenile officer has authority to authorize detention of the child for 48 hours. Mo.Sup.Ct.R. 111.06(b). The juvenile can be detained for more than 48 hours only upon a court order to hold the juvenile for a detention hearing. Mo.Sup.Ct.R. 111.06(d). The detention hearing, at which the court determines "whether the juvenile is to be continued in detention or released," must be held within three days, excluding weekends and legal holi-

---

safeguards such as appointment of counsel and cross-examination, citing Gerstein v. Pugh, 420 U.S. 103, 95 S.Ct. 854, 43 L.Ed.2d 54 (1975), and Moss v. Weaver, 525 F.2d 1258 (5th Cir.1976). The plaintiffs do not contest this ruling on appeal.

[81] We set forth the procedure prescribed by the current Missouri Supreme Court Rules, which were amended to make detention hearings mandatory after January 1, 1982, over a year after the District Court rendered its decision. The amended rules are no more explicit with regard to the necessity for probable-cause hearings than were the former rules.

days, from the date of the court order.   Mo.Sup.Ct.R. 111.07(b).   At the hearing, "The court shall receive testimony and other evidence relevant only to the necessity for detention of the juvenile."   Mo.Sup. Ct.R. 111.08(b).   The court must release the child

unless the court finds that detention is required:

(1) to protect the juvenile; or

(2) to protect the person or property of others; or

(3) because the juvenile may flee or be removed from the juris-diction of the courts; or

(4) because the juvenile has no custodian or suitable adult to provide care and supervision for the juvenile and return the juvenile to the court when required; or

(5) because the juvenile is a fugitive from another jurisdiction and an official of that jurisdiction has required the juvenile be detained pending return to that jurisdiction.

Mo.Sup.Ct.R. 111.08(d).   As the Comment to the Rule emphasizes, "The detention hearing is to determine only whether a juvenile should be continued in detention, or released to his custodian."   The rule requires no inquiry into whether there is probable cause to believe that the child has committed any particular past act.   Sometime after the detention decision is made, the court holds a hearing on the merits of the charges against the juvenile and makes a disposition of the case.   Mo.Sup.Ct.R. 119.01–.07.

The District Court found that although sometimes the juvenile judge made a probable-cause determination before or shortly after the juvenile was incarcerated,

this is mainly the product of the juvenile court judge's reliance on the representation of the juvenile officer.   As such, even though a reasonable determination as to probable cause is made in some cases, no hearing is held before a neutral and detached judicial officer.

D.R. 147.   This finding is clearly supported by the record.   Judge David A. Dalton, who was currently serving as the juvenile court judge, testified:

Q   Is there a separate probable cause hearing at all that's held for juveniles?

A   For what purpose?

Q   Simply to determine whether or not there is probable cause to believe that the youth committed the act?

A   No.   All the statute requires is that a petition be filed and if the petition is filed, there has been a determination of some probable cause prior to that time.

Q   But is that a judicial determination or just a determina-tion made by your staff?

A   It's by the juvenile officer.

Deposition of Judge Dalton 15–16.

III.

The judges concede that juveniles who are accused of committing acts which violate the criminal law are entitled to probable-cause determinations by a neutral and detached judicial officer. They argue that status offenders are not entitled to probable-cause determinations, that the relief granted by the District Court did not extend to status offenders, and that the plaintiffs had no standing to bring this suit.

A.

We agree with the District Court that juveniles who are detained because they are suspected of committing criminal acts must be afforded a prompt probable-cause hearing.[82]   In Gerstein v. Pugh, 420 U.S. 103, 95 S.Ct. 854, 43 L.Ed.2d 54 (1975), the Court held that the Fourth Amendment requires the State to "provide a fair and reliable determination of probable cause as a condition for any significant pretrial restraint of liberty, and this determination must be made by a judicial officer either before or promptly after arrest." Id. at 125, 95 S.Ct. at 868–869. Although *Pugh* involved only the right of adults to a probable-cause hearing, we believe that the right must be extended to juveniles as well. *   *   *

The Court has declined to extend only one procedural right to juvenile offenders—the right to a jury trial. In McKeiver v. Pennsylvania, 403 U.S. 528, 91 S.Ct. 1976, 29 L.Ed.2d 647 (1971), the Court found that the benefits of a juvenile court's ability to function in a "unique manner" outweighed the fact-finding advantages of a jury trial. Id. at 547, 91 S.Ct. at 1987 (plurality opinion).

That requiring juvenile courts to hold probable-cause hearings will not impinge on their ability to function in a "unique manner" is evidenced by the number of decisions that have recognized that probable-cause hearings are fundamental to juveniles' rights to due process. *   *   * Experts in the field also view probable-cause hearings as crucial to procedural fairness. E.g., Juvenile Justice Standards Project, Institute of Judicial Administration-American Bar Association, Standards Relating to Interim Status § 7.6F, Standards Relating to Pretrial Court Proceedings §§ 4.1, 4.2 (1980); Paulsen & Whitebread, Juvenile Law and Procedure 120 (1974). The right not to be jailed for any substantial period of time without a neutral decision that there is probable cause is basic to a free society. Children should enjoy this right no less than adults.

B.

Nevertheless, the state argues that juveniles who are detained for committing acts which, if they were adults, would not be criminal

---

[82] Although the judges' counsel stated at oral argument that the District Court approved *ex parte* determinations of probable cause, the court's order makes clear that hearings are required. D.R. 144–45.

are not entitled to probable-cause hearings. Juvenile-court adjudications of status offenses are claimed to be essentially civil, not criminal.

We hold that juveniles who are detained for committing "status offenses," as that term is used by the parties in this case, are entitled to probable-cause hearings to the same extent as juveniles who are accused of committing criminal acts.

> [D]etermining the applicability of constitutional rights, in juvenile proceedings, requires that courts eschew "the 'civil' label-of-convenience which has been attached to juvenile proceedings," In re Gault, supra, 387 U.S. at 50, 87 S.Ct. at 1455 * * *. Breed v. Jones, supra, 421 U.S. at 529, 95 S.Ct. at 1785. * * * It would be anomalous to afford less protection to children who are accused of acts, such as running away, truancy, and the like, which do not present an immediate threat to society, than to children who are accused of such criminal acts as murder, robbery, and rape.[83] In either case, the juvenile court may not proceed unless there is probable cause to believe that the child has committed a proscribed act. As a practical matter, both classes of juveniles are subject to the same pre-trial deprivation of liberty: both accused delinquents and accused status offenders may be put in jail pending a judicial hearing on the merits of their cases. In fact, under Missouri law, status offenders are treated the same as delinquents except for certain restrictions on "sentencing." [84]

NOTES

1.   In Gerstein v. Pugh, 420 U.S. 103, 95 S.Ct. 854, 43 L.Ed.2d 54 (1975), the Court first held that a suspect in a criminal case who was arrested without a warrant and who was detained as a result was entitled to a prompt probable cause determination before a neutral and detached magistrate. The Court, however, reversed the Fifth Circuit determination that it should be a full adversary hearing.

"Both the District Court and the Court of Appeals held that the determination of probable cause must be accompanied by the full panoply of adversary safeguards—counsel, confrontation, cross-examination, and compulsory process for witnesses. A full preliminary hearing of this sort is modeled after the procedure used in many States to determine whether the evidence justifies going to trial under an information or presenting the case to a grand jury. See Coleman v. Alabama, 399 U.S. 1, 90 S.Ct. 1999, 26 L.Ed. 2d 387 (1970); Y. Kamisar, W. LaFave & J. Israel, Modern Criminal Procedure 957–967, 996–1000 (4th ed. 1974). The standard of proof required of the prosecution is usually referred to as "probable cause," but in some jurisdic-

---

[83] For purposes of this appeal, the category "status offenders" means juveniles accused of any of the specific past acts listed in Mo.Ann.Stat. § 211.031.1(2) (Vernon 1983), quoted ante at 6. Missouri juvenile courts also have jurisdiction over juveniles alleged to be in need of care and treatment because their parents are neglecting them, or because they are otherwise without proper care, custody, or support. Mo.Ann.Stat. § 211.031.1(1) (Vernon 1983). This last-described class of juveniles is not involved in this case.

[84] For example, status offenders cannot be committed to the Division of Youth Services for a first offense. Mo. Ann.Stat. § 211.181.2(2)(a) (Vernon 1983).

tions it may approach a prima facie case of guilt. A.L.I. Model Code of Pre-arraignment Procedure, Commentary on Article 330, at 90–91 (Tent.Draft No. 5, 1972). When the hearing takes this form, adversary procedures are customarily employed. The importance of the issue to both the State and the accused justifies the presentation of witnesses and full exploration of their testimony on cross-examination. This kind of hearing also requires appointment of counsel for indigent defendants. Coleman v. Alabama, supra. And, as the hearing assumes increased importance and the procedures become more complex, the likelihood that it can be held promptly after arrest diminishes. See A.L.I. Model Code of Pre-arraignment Procedure, supra, at 33–34.

"These adversary safeguards are not essential for the probable cause determination required by the Fourth Amendment. The sole issue is whether there is probable cause for detaining the arrested person pending further proceedings. This issue can be determined reliably without an adversary hearing. The standard is the same as that for arrest. That standard—probable cause to believe the suspect has committed a crime—traditionally has been decided by a magistrate in a nonadversary proceeding on hearsay and written testimony, and the Court has approved these informal modes of proof.

"Guilt in a criminal case must be proved beyond a reasonable doubt and by evidence confined to that which long experience in the common-law tradition, to some extent embodied in the Constitution, has crystalized into rules of evidence consistent with that standard. These rules are historically grounded rights of our system, developed to safeguard men from dubious and unjust convictions, with resulting forfeitures of life, liberty and property.

"   *   *   *

"In dealing with probable cause, however, as the very name implies, we deal with probabilities. These are not technical; they are the factual and practical considerations of everyday life on which reasonable and prudent men, not legal technicians, act. The standard of proof is accordingly correlative to what must be proved." Brinegar v. United States, 338 U.S. 160, 174–175, 69 S.Ct. 1302, 1310, 93 L.Ed. 1879 (1949).

Cf. McCray v. Illinois, 386 U.S. 300, 87 S.Ct. 1056, 18 L.Ed.2d 62 (1967).

"The use of an informal procedure is justified not only by the lesser consequences of a probable cause determination but also by the nature of the determination itself. It does not require the fine resolution of conflicting evidence that a reasonable-doubt or even a preponderance standard demands, and credibility determinations are seldom crucial in deciding whether the evidence supports a reasonable belief in guilt. See F. Miller, Prosecution: The Decision to Charge a Suspect with a Crime 64–109 (1969).[85] This is not

---

[85] In Morrissey v. Brewer, 408 U.S. 471, 92 S.Ct. 2593, 33 L.Ed.2d 484 (1972), and Gagnon v. Scarpelli, 411 U.S. 778, 93 S.Ct. 1756, 36 L.Ed.2d 656 (1973), we held that a parolee or probationer arrested prior to revocation is entitled to an informal preliminary hearing at the place of arrest, with some provision for live testimony. 408 U.S., at 487, 92 S.Ct., at 2603; 411 U.S., at 786, 93 S.Ct., at 1761. That preliminary hearing, more than the probable cause determination required by the Fourth Amendment, serves the purpose of gathering and preserving live testimony, since the final revocation hearing frequently is held at some distance from the place where the violation occurred. 408 U.S., at 485, 92 S.Ct., at 2602; 411 U.S., at 782–783 n. 5, 93 S.Ct., at 1759–1760. Moreover, revocation proceedings may offer less protection from initial error than the more formal criminal process, where violations are defined by statute and the prosecutor has a professional duty not to charge a suspect with crime unless he is satisfied of probable cause.

to say that confrontation and cross-examination might not enhance the reliability of probable cause determinations in some cases. In most cases, however, their value would be too slight to justify holding, as a matter of constitutional principle, that these formalities and safeguards designed for trial must also be employed in making the Fourth Amendment determination of probable cause.[86]

"Because of its limited function and its nonadversary character, the probable cause determination is not a "critical stage" in the prosecution that would require appointed counsel. The Court has identified as "critical stages" those pretrial procedures that would impair defense on the merits if the accused is required to proceed without counsel. Coleman v. Alabama, 399 U.S. 1, 90 S.Ct. 1999, 26 L.Ed.2d 387 (1970); United States v. Wade, 388 U.S. 218, 226–227, 87 S.Ct. 1926, 1931–1932, 18 L.Ed.2d 1149 (1967). In Coleman v. Alabama, where the Court held that a preliminary hearing was a critical stage of an Alabama prosecution, the majority and concurring opinions identified two critical factors that distinguish the Alabama preliminary hearing from the probable cause determination required by the Fourth Amendment. First, under Alabama law the function of the preliminary hearing was to determine whether the evidence justified charging the suspect with an offense. A finding of no probable cause could mean that he would not be tried at all. The Fourth Amendment probable cause determination is addressed only to pretrial custody. To be sure, pretrial custody may affect to some extent the defendant's ability to assist in preparation of his defense, but this does not present the high probability of substantial harm identified as controlling in *Wade* and *Coleman*. Second, Alabama allowed the suspect to confront and cross-examine prosecution witnesses at the preliminary hearing. The Court noted that the suspect's defense on the merits could be compromised if he had no legal assistance for exploring or preserving the witnesses' testimony. This consideration does not apply when the prosecution is not required to produce witnesses for cross-examination.

"Although we conclude that the Constitution does not require an adversary determination of probable cause, we recognize that state systems of criminal procedure vary widely. There is no single preferred pretrial procedure, and the nature of the probable cause determination usually will be shaped to accord with a State's pretrial procedure viewed as a whole. While we limit our holding to the precise requirement of the Fourth Amendment, we recognize the desirability of flexibility and experimentation by the States. It may be found desirable, for example, to make the probable cause determination at the suspect's first appearance before a judicial officer,[87] see

---

See ABA Code of Professional Responsibility, DR 7–103(A) (a prosecutor "shall not institute or cause to be instituted criminal charges when he knows or it is obvious that the charges are not supported by probable cause"); ABA Standards Relating to the Administration of Criminal Justice, The Prosecution Function, §§ 1.1, 3.4, 3.9 (1974); American College of Trial Lawyers, Code of Trial Conduct, rule 4(c) (1972).

[86] Criminal justice is already overburdened by the volume of cases and the complexities of our system. The processing of misdemeanors, in particular, and the early stages of prosecution generally are marked by delays that can seriously affect the quality of justice. A constitutional doctrine requiring adversary hearings for all persons detained pending trial could exacerbate the problem of pretrial delay.

[87] Several States already authorize a determination of probable cause at this stage or immediately thereafter. See Colo.Rev.Stat. § 39–2–3 (1965 Supp.); Hawaii Rev.Stat. § 708–9(5) (1968); Vt. Rules Crim.Proc. 3(b), 5(c) (1974). This Court has interpreted the Federal Rules of Criminal Procedure to require a determination of probable cause at the first appearance. Jaben v. United States, 381

McNabb v. United States, 318 U.S. 332, 342–344, 63 S.Ct. 608, 613–614, 87 L.Ed. 819 (1943), or the determination may be incorporated into the procedure for setting bail or fixing other conditions of pretrial release. In some States, existing procedures may satisfy the requirement of the Fourth Amendment. Others may require only minor adjustment, such as acceleration of existing preliminary hearings. Current proposals for criminal procedure reform suggest other ways of testing probable cause for detention.[88] Whatever procedure a State may adopt, it must provide a fair and reliable determination of probable cause as a condition for any significant pretrial restraint on liberty,[89] and this determination must be made by a judicial officer either before or promptly after arrest.

Id. at 119–26, 95 S.Ct. at 866–9, 43 L.Ed.2d at 68–72.

2. In Moss v. Weaver, 525 F.2d 1258 (5th Cir.1976) the Fifth Circuit affirmed the judgment of the District Court that detention of juveniles without a finding of probable cause was in violation of the Fourth Amendment. But the Court of Appeals, based upon the Supreme Court's opinion in Gerstein v. Pugh, reversed that portion of the District Court judgment requiring that the determination of probable cause be made in the context of an adversarial hearing:

> We know of no unique features of the juvenile courts by which *Gerstein's* reasoning could be distinguished. On the contrary, it is

U.S. 214, 218, 85 S.Ct. 1365, 1367, 14 L.Ed.2d 345 (1965); Mallory v. United States, 354 U.S. 449, 454, 77 S.Ct. 1356, 1359, 1 L.Ed.2d 1479 (1957).

[88] Under the Uniform Rules of Criminal Procedure (Proposed Final Draft 1974), a person arrested without a warrant is entitled, "without unnecessary delay," to a first appearance before a magistrate and a determination that grounds exist for issuance of an arrest warrant. The determination may be made on affidavits or testimony, in the presence of the accused. Rule 311. Persons who remain in custody for inability to qualify for pretrial release are offered another opportunity for a probable cause determination at the detention hearing, held no more than five days after arrest. This is an adversary hearing, and the parties may summon witnesses, but reliable hearsay evidence may be considered. Rule 344.

The A.L.I. Model Code of Pre-arraignment Procedure (Tent.Draft No. 5, 1972, and Tent.Draft No. 5A, 1973) also provides a first appearance at which a warrantless arrest must be supported by a reasonably detailed written statement of facts. § 310. The magistrate may make a determination of probable cause to hold the accused, but he is not required to do so and the accused may request an attorney for an "adjourned session" of the first appearance to be held within 2 "court days." At that session, the magistrate makes a determination of probable cause upon a combination of written and live testimony:

"The arrested person may present written and testimonial evidence and arguments for his discharge and the state may present additional written and testimonial evidence and arguments that there is reasonable cause to believe that he has committed the crime of which he is accused. The state's submission may be made by means of affidavits, and no witnesses shall be required to appear unless the court, in the light of the evidence and arguments submitted by the parties, determines that there is a basis for believing that the appearance of one or more witnesses for whom the arrested person seeks subpoenas might lead to a finding that there is no reasonable cause." § 310.2(2) (Tent.Draft No. 5A, 1973).

[89] Because the probable cause determination is not a constitutional prerequisite to the charging decision, it is required only for those suspects who suffer restraints on liberty other than the condition that they appear for trial. There are many kinds of pretrial release and many degrees of conditional liberty. See 18 U.S.C. § 3146; ABA Standards Relating to the Administration of Criminal Justice, Pretrial Release § 5.2 (1974); Uniform Rules of Criminal Procedure, Rule 341 (Proposed Final Draft 1974). We cannot define specifically those that would require a prior probable cause determination, but the key factor is significant restraint on liberty.

normally assumed that the distinctive advantages of juvenile tribunals derive from their informal nature. We are apprehensive that these advantages, to the extent that they now exist, might be lessened if juvenile proceedings were freighted with the requirements of trial-type procedures.

Id. at 1261. Finally, the Court of Appeals noted that the Supreme Court in *Gerstein* had found the probable cause determination not to be a critical stage requiring a right to counsel but in light of the practice of providing representation from the public defender's office, refused to decide that question.

3. RIGHT TO COUNSEL

Statutes now commonly provide for counsel at "all stages of any proceedings alleging delinquency, unruliness or deprivation." See Ga.Code Ann. § 24A–2001 (1982 Supp.), or "prior to the adjudicatory or transfer hearing by the court of any case involving a child * * * alleged to be in need of services or delinquent." See Va.Code Ann. § 16.1–266 (1984 Cum.Supp.). The question whether such general statutory language is applicable to detention hearings is raised in the *T.K.* case.

Standard 7.6 of the Standards Relating to Interim Status of the IJA–ABA Juvenile Justice Standards recommends that a juvenile have a right to an attorney at a "release hearing." A similar recommendation is made by the National Advisory Committee for Juvenile Justice and Delinquency Prevention. See Standards for the Administration of Juvenile Justice, Standard 3.132.

T.K. v. STATE

Georgia Court of Appeals, 1972.
126 Ga.App. 269, 190 S.E.2d 588.

CLARK, JUDGE. This case marks the third appeal to this court on questions of legal rights of juveniles under the new Juvenile Court Code of Georgia (Ga.L.1971, p. 709 et seq.; Code Ann. § 24A–101 et seq.) which became effective July 1, 1971. Even though we affirm the juvenile court's final decision in this appeal we find it necessary under the enumeration of error raising this question as well as for future guidance to determine whether our new statute entitles an accused to be represented by counsel at the stage known as "detention hearing."

In Reed v. State of Ga., 125 Ga.App. 568, 188 S.E.2d 392, we dealt with the notice requirement which the statute expressly makes a prerequisite to the conduct of any "transfer" hearing in which the juvenile court will consider relinquishing its jurisdiction and transferring the offense to another court for prosecution, e.g., superior court. We there ruled the notice to the accused and the accused's parents must state the specific purpose of the proposed "transfer" hearing.

In Mack v. State of Ga., 125 Ga.App. 639, 188 S.E.2d 828, this court was called upon to review a finding of delinquency at an "adjudication hearing" in which the evidence presented below included an incriminating statement by the juvenile to a detective at home in the presence of his mother after having been properly advised of his rights in the presence of his mother. The court was also required to consider the extent to which the juvenile court retains dispositional authority once a committal to the Division of Children and Youth has occurred.

In the case sub judice appellant appeals from an order finding him to be in a state of delinquency and committing him to the Division of Children and Youth for care, supervision and planning. The petition filed against appellant alleged, in effect, his participation on two occasions of vandalism of a junior high school and thereby committing the offenses of burglary and criminal damage to property.

The record reveals that on October 9, 1971, an officer of the Warner Robins Department of Public Safety responded to a call that somebody was in one of the buildings on the Warner Robins Junior High School campus. The officer saw and stopped two boys who started to leave on bicycles as he arrived. The boys, one of whom was appellant, were promptly delivered to a juvenile officer for Houston County. Any juvenile officer receiving custody of a child is required to make an immediate investigation and release the child unless it appears that detention is warranted or required. Code Ann. § 24A–1404. Such taking into custody is expressly stated to be "not an arrest, except for the purpose of determining its validity under the Constitution of this State or of the United States." Code Ann. § 24A–1301(b). The youngster was released to his parents with the family being requested to appear October 12 for a pre-hearing interview.

Upon explanation to them of their son's legal rights at the pre-hearing interview the parents stated their desire to have legal representation. This interview was followed immediately by the detention hearing at which the juvenile court judge explained its nature, pointing out it was "to determine probable cause and possible detention." Although the parents indicated their financial ability and desire to hire an attorney, the court did not postpone the hearing for this purpose but completed the proceedings with a formal order committing the accused to a detention home. He further ordered the petition which is required under Ch. 24A–16 to be filed immediately. This would have resulted in the "adjudication hearing" being held "not be later than 10 days after the filing of the petition" under the provisions of Code Ann. § 24A–1701 because of the detention. Otherwise there is a thirty day limitation. Code Ann. § 24A–1404(b).

A petition for release on bail was filed on October 15, by the attorney hired by the parents. This bail hearing took place October 20 and after hearing evidence the accused was released to his parents on his own recognizance. The requisite petition for scheduling the dispositive hearing was filed October 18 with the trial scheduled for October 26. This would have been within the statutory time of 30 days for one who is not in detention but was rescheduled upon the attorney's motion for continuance to November 23. The primary purpose for the postponement was a desire to have a psychological examination and time for defense preparation.

This adjudication hearing, referred to in the record as "Factual Investigation and Dispositional Phase," was a full scale trial with the district attorney representing the State and with the retained attorney competently and capably representing the accused. *Held:*

1. Code Ann. § 24A–1404(c) provides that prior to the commencement of a detention hearing, the parties shall be informed of their right to counsel and to appointed counsel if they are needy persons. Code Ann. § 24A–2001(a) provides: "[A] party is entitled to representation by legal counsel *at all stages of any proceedings alleging delinquency * * *.* If a party appears without counsel, the court shall ascertain whether he knows of his right thereto and to be provided with counsel by the court if he is a needy person. *The court may continue the proceeding to enable a party to obtain counsel * * *"* (Emphasis supplied.)

The record shows the required advice concerning counsel was given to the child's parents but not until *just before* the detention hearing (during a pre-detention hearing interview) and again *during* the hearing itself. It also appears that on both occasions the parents stated they *did* want to retain and be represented by counsel. The statutory directive and constitutional right to counsel includes "reasonable time and opportunity to secure counsel." Powell v. Alabama, 287 U.S. 45, 53 S.Ct. 55, 77 L.Ed. 158.

Appellee asserts the detention hearing is similar in nature to "the arrest stage" so that representation by a lawyer, even for adults who may be putative criminals, is not an essentiality. We disagree, particularly since the legislature here dealt separately with "taking into custody" (Code Ann. Ch. 24A–13), "detention" (Code Ann. Ch. 24A–14), and proceedings in connection with the "detention hearing". We submit the detention hearing serves a function analogous to a commitment hearing in the criminal process dealing with adults. The duty of a committing court "is simply to determine whether there is sufficient reason to suspect the guilt of the accused, to require him to appear and answer before the court competent to try him; and whenever such probable cause exists, it is the duty of the court to commit." Code § 27–407.

The new Juvenile Code obviously intends that procedural due process requirements established by In re Gault, 387 U.S. 1, 87 S.Ct. 1428, 18 L.Ed.2d 527 (1967) be observed. It also seeks nonconfinement, rehabilitation, and restoration to parental care wherever possible rather than punishment.

The legislature's recognition of the importance of the lawyer to the accused juvenile is shown in the fact that the Act refers to counsel in eight different portions of the Juvenile Court Code, §§ 24A–1404(c); 24A–1701(d); 24A–2001(a, b); 24A–2201(d); 24A–2501(a)(1); 24A–3401(a)(3); and 24A–3502(b).

Prior to the passage in 1971 of the Juvenile Court Code this court in Freeman v. Wilcox, 119 Ga.App. 325, 167 S.E.2d 163, had already recognized the importance of the juvenile's right to counsel at all adjudicative stages of juvenile proceedings.

The clear aim of the framers of our Juvenile Court Code was to emphasize non-confinement and fulfillment of parental responsibilities with rehabilitation of the accused but that if there is to be a formal hearing, whether it be detention or adjudicatory, then the child is entitled to counsel for such hearing.

2. In Coleman v. Alabama, 399 U.S. 1, 90 S.Ct. 1999, 26 L.Ed.2d 387, the United States Supreme Court ruled the preliminary or commitment hearing [90] to be a "critical stage" of the prosecution so that if one was held, then the accused is entitled to be represented by counsel. It therefore remanded the matter to the trial court (as was done by the Alabama court—see Coleman v. State, 46 Ala.App. 737, 239 So.2d 223) so that a hearing might be held and a finding made as to whether beyond a reasonable doubt lack of counsel did or did not result in harm or prejudice to his fair trial rights at the jury trial. This court followed that ruling in Mollins v. State, 122 Ga.App. 865, 179 S.E.2d 111 and exercised its authority under Code § 6–1610 with remand of the case for determination as to whether or not such deprivation of counsel caused defendant to suffer prejudice at the trial of the case.

In the present instance an examination of the record shows no harm to have resulted from the lack of counsel at that stage. The child and his parents were not deprived of any right to make any available defense on the merits at the "adjudicatory hearing" and nothing developed at the detention hearing was used in any manner against the child at this trial. In fact our review of the record and of the transcripts of the four hearings (detention, bail, continuance, and dispositional) demonstrated that the court and its officers acted throughout in absolute good faith towards the appellant and his parents. The obvious courtesy and understanding thus exhibited are to be commended, especially in view of the physical and mental pressures which come to bear upon a child and his parents when trouble occurs and with it the specter of separation from family and deprivation of freedom. The failure of the trial judge to delay the detention hearing on his own motion upon learning of the desire for legal representation occurred only because of the innovations of our new Code and a misunderstanding of some of its requirements.

Accordingly, we hold there was no harmful error in the failure to have counsel in this case at the detention hearing.

*   *   *

[90] Two Georgia Supreme Court decisions rendered since Coleman v. Alabama have ruled the holding of a commitment hearing is not a requisite to a trial for commission of a felony. Brown v. Holland, 228 Ga. 628, 187 S.E.2d 246 and Burston v. Caldwell, 228 Ga. 795, 187 S.E.2d 900. These dealt with adults and therefore should not be construed as ruling that the detention hearing required by our Juvenile Court Code may be dispensed with, particularly in view of Kent v. United States, 383 U.S. 541, 86 S.Ct. 1045, 16 L.Ed.2d 84.

NOTE

Would a juvenile detained on the basis of an underlying felony (murder) be entitled to call witnesses—indeed to testify himself—at a detention hearing? In State In the Interest of Morrison, 406 So.2d 246 (La.App., 1981), the court granted a writ of mandamus to allow the juvenile to present evidence. The court recognized that nothing in *Gault* or *Gerstein* compelled that conclusion, but found the absence of a denial of such a right in the Louisiana Code justified an inference as a matter of statutory construction that the juvenile had such a right.

D. ALTERNATIVES TO DETENTION

PABON, THE CASE FOR ALTERNATIVES TO DETENTION, 34 JUVENILE AND FAMILY COURT JOURNAL 37 at 42–44 (August, 1983) *

Yet, there are many examples of successful alternatives to secure detention for juveniles.

Home detention programs permit youths to reside with their parents while meeting with probation officer aides at least daily. Some jurisdictions emphasize the supervision and surveillance aspects of this approach, while others stress the service components.

Attention homes are group homes usually housing between five and 12 juveniles plus one set of live-in house parents. Frequently the home is a converted single-family dwelling in a residential neighborhood so that the juveniles can continue attending their schools. Social service workers are often available to the juveniles and to the adults providing care.

Runaway programs are also group residences, but they differ in certain respects from each other and from the attention homes. Admission is not limited to juveniles referred from detention intake, and the program emphasizes intensive counseling to resolve immediate crises, followed by referrals for longer term help if needed. Youths usually only stay a short time since the primary goal is to help them return to their natural parents.

Private residential foster homes can be quite different from one another. For example, one program might pay single women aged 20–30 to take one girl at a time into their homes for 24-hour care and supervision while agency staff develop full treatment plans. In contrast, another agency might set a network of foster homes (two beds each), group homes (five beds each) and a receiving unit group home (four beds). In addition to the foster parents and group home parents, small numbers of professional staff provide counseling and advocacy services.

In their careful analysis of home detention, attention homes, runaway programs and private residential homes, Pappenfort and Young found that upward of 90 percent of juveniles in programs providing alternatives to secure detention neither committed new offenses nor ran away. For the 14 programs studied the failure rate—i.e., proportion of youths allegedly committing new offenses or running away while in the program—ranged from 2.4 percent to 12.8 percent. The various program formats appear to be roughly equal in their ability to keep their charges out of trouble and available to the court. The higher rates of failures appear to be caused by factors outside the control of program employees, such as excessive lengths of stay caused by slow court processing.

Interestingly, the range of alternative to detention programs appears to be most scarce in metropolitan urban areas, i.e., New York City, where there are abundant resources for the development of such programs. This is especially the case in terms of implementing "tracking" or "big brother/sister" types of non-residential alternatives. For instance, there are numerous small local or indigenous social, welfare, fraternal and community organizations in every neighborhood in an urban city which could be utilized to provide home detention services to youngsters within their area. Two or three such organizations could be identified in a particular community planning board or neighborhood and contracted on a fee or voluntary basis for delivery of services to youngsters referred by the local detention authorities or court system. Where necessary, linkages could be established with major local agencies in each community planning board district, i.e., a multiservice center, to provide intensive social services to youngsters and their families, and to serve as supports to the indigenous organizations.

Neighborhoods and communities that may foster criminal character in youths also have many natural human resources that, if properly tapped, can be effective in addressing the community's most complex problems. A community can be a viable organism. When it suffers acute breakdown, it moves to fight off threats to its existence. Over the past decade, programs and activities in several cities throughout the country have been studied in which community members themselves are using their own resources to deal with the problems of youth. The apparent effectiveness of these neighborhood projects is impressive. Youths who were once anathema to community stability have reversed roles and are now acting as protectors of their own neighborhoods. The successes appear to be based on principles of youth development associated with a strong sense of "family," binding together adult supervisors and the youths to be changed.

In these programs a structure of primary relations among members support the possibility of cooperation and authentic mutual influence, as individual and community development proceed together. The importance of primary bonding in any person-changing process must be stressed. Socialization and development are influenced by contact with other socialized beings. In this, conformity is never total, and individuals observe some norms and ignore others. But the desire to be with people in gratifying ways leads the individual to compromise, and the gratification from finding needs met through encounters with others and the development of emotional and practical interdependence increase the individual's willingness to modify the self in group-approved directions.

The chance that anyone will genuinely subordinate learned adaptations to the influence of a new group and new norms depends on the degree to which the new group resembles or is in fact composed of already familiar people with whom the individual can readily find things in common. It seems probable that those with whom he may have associated all along—people from his own neighborhood, people of the same social, cultural and economic circumstances—could gain entrance to his deeper personal feelings and strivings more readily than professional helpers drawn from other social categories, educational levels or cultural orientations. The already-familiar neighborhood people are also more readily accepted in psychodramas of self-renovations than similar but unchosen associates.

Moreover, inner-city neighborhoods, where social and cultural identities are widely shared, have the potential for acting as true communities; that is, they are not mere aggregates of statistics of social problems and social disorganizations. There is the strong possibility that the residents will come together in conscious awareness of shared problems and relationships, forming communities of interest. They recognize the commonality of their life chances and adaptive styles and accept the responsibility to advance the common good. The involvement of local social, welfare, fraternal, religious and community groups and their residents in the development of non-residential and "family-style" alternatives to detention is an exceptional opportunity.

Epilogue

There will continue to be a steady, if irregular, need for secure detention for some juveniles charged with serious offenses. But the present indiscriminate use of detention after arrest as a substitute for formal adjudication represents a troublesome, and unjustified, social control device. Many private and public organization and commission reports have criticized detention practices throughout the nation. They have all indicated their bewilderment over the tendency to introduce factors beyond protecting the public safety and court process. At the same time, studies have demonstrated that many youngsters are unnecessarily detained and that they could be released without increasing the threat to the safety of the community or the operation of the court process. Unfortunately, the widespread use of detention can be explained by the realization that we have not had a legitimate, short-term custodial dispositional option separate and apart from a lengthy stay at a training school within our sentencing packages. Detention serves this purpose; it is an informal correctional response to juvenile misdeeds—without explicitly calling it a type of disposition.

There must be flexibility in handling juvenile offenders, so that the number of juveniles in secure settings is reduced. Flexibility must be evident not only in legislative and administrative criteria governing selection of youths for detention and in the decision as to whether youths are to be placed in secure detention or an alternative program, but there must be available a wide variety of alternative programs, including non-residential ones. The abundant "natural" resources of our communities must be involved in the development and implementation of these programs.

The pervasive dominance of secure detention as a correctional dispositional response and a recognition of the profound impact of the detention decision on future decisionmakers and dispositions underlies the importance of this correctional tool, and argues for the development of alternatives to an emergent policy that offers more juvenile jailing/detention than any other correctional response.

*

Chapter 6

THE DECISION WHETHER TO TREAT AS AN ADULT OR A CHILD

A. PROCEDURAL DUE PROCESS IN THE TRANSFER DECISION

KENT v. UNITED STATES

Supreme Court of the United States, 1966.
383 U.S. 541, 86 S.Ct. 1045, 16 L.Ed.2d 84.

MR. JUSTICE FORTAS delivered the opinion of the Court.

This case is here on certiorari to the United States Court of Appeals for the District of Columbia Circuit. The facts and the contentions of counsel raise a number of disturbing questions concerning the administration by the police and the Juvenile Court authorities of the District of Columbia laws relating to juveniles. Apart from raising questions as to the adequacy of custodial and treatment facilities and policies, some of which are not within judicial competence, the case presents important challenges to the procedure of the police and Juvenile Court officials upon apprehension of a juvenile suspected of serious offenses. Because we conclude that the Juvenile Court's order waiving jurisdiction of petitioner was entered without compliance with required procedures, we remand the case to the trial court.

Morris A. Kent, Jr., first came under the authority of the Juvenile Court of the District of Columbia in 1959. He was then aged 14. He was apprehended as a result of several housebreakings and an attempted purse snatching. He was placed on probation, in the custody of his mother who had been separated from her husband since Kent was two years old. Juvenile Court officials interviewed Kent from time to time during the probation period and accumulated a "Social Service" file.

On September 2, 1961, an intruder entered the apartment of a woman in the District of Columbia. He took her wallet. He raped her. The police found in the apartment latent fingerprints. They were developed and processed. They matched the fingerprints of Morris Kent, taken when he was 14 years old and under the jurisdiction of the Juvenile Court. At about 3 p.m. on September 5, 1961, Kent was taken into custody by the police. Kent was then 16 and therefore subject to the "exclusive jurisdiction" of the Juvenile Court. D.C.Code § 11–907 (1961), now § 11–1551 (Supp. IV, 1965). He was still on probation to that court as a result of the 1959 proceedings.

Upon being apprehended, Kent was taken to police headquarters where he was interrogated by police officers. It appears that he admitted his involvement in the offense which led to his apprehension and volunteered information as to similar offenses involving housebreaking, robbery, and rape. His interrogation proceeded from about 3 p.m. to 10 p.m. the same evening.[1]

Some time after 10 p.m. petitioner was taken to the Receiving Home for Children. The next morning he was released to the police for further interrogation at police headquarters, which lasted until 5 p.m.[2]

The record does not show when his mother became aware that the boy was in custody but shortly after 2 p.m. on September 6, 1961, the day following petitioner's apprehension, she retained counsel.

Counsel, together with petitioner's mother, promptly conferred with the Social Service Director of the Juvenile Court. In a brief interview, they discussed the possibility that the Juvenile Court might waive jurisdiction under D.C.Code § 11–914 (1961), now § 11–1553 (Supp. IV, 1965) and remit Kent to trial by the District Court. Counsel made known his intention to oppose waiver.

Petitioner was detained at the Receiving Home for almost a week. There was no arraignment during this time, no determination by a judicial officer of probable cause for petitioner's apprehension.[3]

During this period of detention and interrogation, petitioner's counsel arranged for examination of petitioner by two psychiatrists

[1] There is no indication in the file that the police complied with the requirement of the District Court that a child taken into custody, unless released to his parent, guardian or custodian, "shall be placed in the custody of a probation officer or other person designated by the court, or taken immediately to the court or to a place of detention provided by the Board of Public Welfare, and the officer taking him shall immediately notify the court and shall file a petition when directed to do so by the court." D.C.Code § 11–912 (1961), now § 16–2306 (Supp. IV, 1965).

[2] The elicited statements were not used in the subsequent trial before the United States District Court. Since the statements were made while petitioner was subject to the jurisdiction of the Juvenile Court, they were inadmissible in a subsequent criminal prosecution under the rule of Harling v. United States, 111 U.S.App. D.C. 174, 295 F.2d 161 (1961).

[3] In the case of adults, arraignment before a magistrate for determination of probable cause and advice to the arrested person as to his rights, etc., are provided by law and are regarded as fundamental. Cf. Fed.Rules Crim.Proc. 5(a), (b); Mallory v. United States, 354 U.S. 449, 77 S.Ct.

1356, 1 L.Ed.2d 1479. In Harling v. United States, supra, the Court of Appeals for the District of Columbia has stated the basis for this distinction between juveniles and adults as follows:

"It is, of course, because children are, generally speaking, exempt from criminal penalties that safeguards of the criminal law, such as Rule 5 and the exclusionary Mallory rule, have no general application in juvenile proceedings." 111 U.S.App.D.C., at 176, 295 F.2d, at 163.

In Edwards v. United States, 117 U.S. App.D.C. 383, 384, 330 F.2d 849, 850 (1964) it was said that: " * * * special practices * * * follow the apprehension of a juvenile. He may be held in custody by the juvenile authorities—and is available to investigating officers—for five days before any formal action need be taken. There is no duty to take him before a magistrate, and no responsibility to inform him of his rights. He is not booked. The statutory intent is to establish a non-punitive, non-criminal atmosphere."

We indicate no view as to the legality of these practices. Cf. Harling v. United States, supra, 111 U.S.App.D.C., at 176, 295 F.2d, at 163, n. 12.

and a psychologist. He thereafter filed with the Juvenile Court a motion for a hearing on the question of waiver of Juvenile Court jurisdiction, together with an affidavit of a psychiatrist certifying that petitioner "is a victim of severe psychopathology" and recommending hospitalization for psychiatric observation. Petitioner's counsel, in support of his motion to the effect that the Juvenile Court should retain jurisdiction of petitioner, offered to prove that if petitioner were given adequate treatment in a hospital under the aegis of the Juvenile Court, he would be a suitable subject for rehabilitation.

At the same time, petitioner's counsel moved that the Juvenile Court should give him access to the Social Service file relating to petitioner which had been accumulated by the staff of the Juvenile Court during petitioner's probation period, and which would be available to the Juvenile Court judge in considering the question whether it should retain or waive jurisdiction. Petitioner's counsel represented that access to this file was essential to his providing petitioner with effective assistance of counsel.

The Juvenile Court judge did not rule on these motions. He held no hearing. He did not confer with petitioner or petitioner's parents or petitioner's counsel. He entered an order reciting that after "full investigation, I do hereby waive" jurisdiction of petitioner and directing that he be "held for trial for [the alleged] offenses under the regular procedure of the U.S. District Court for the District of Columbia." He made no findings. He did not recite any reason for the waiver.[4] He made no reference to the motions filed by petitioner's counsel. We must assume that he denied, *sub silentio*, the motions for a hearing, the recommendation for hospitalization for psychiatric observation, the request for access to the Social Service file, and the offer to prove that petitioner was a fit subject for rehabilitation under the Juvenile Court's jurisdiction.[5]

Presumably, prior to entry of his order, the Juvenile Court Judge received and considered recommendations of the Juvenile Court staff, the Social Service file relating to petitioner, and a report dated September 8, 1961 (three days following petitioner's apprehension), submitted to him by the Juvenile Probation Section. The Social Service file and the September 8 report were later sent to the District Court and it appears that both of them referred to petitioner's mental condition. The September 8 report spoke of "a rapid deterioration of [petitioner's] personality structure and the possibility of mental ill-

[4] At the time of these events, there was in effect Policy Memorandum No. 7 of November 30, 1959, promulgated by the judge of the Juvenile Court to set forth the criteria to govern disposition of waiver requests. It is set forth in the Appendix. This Memorandum has since been rescinded. See United States v. Caviness, 239 F.Supp. 545, 550 (D.C.D.C. 1965).

[5] It should be noted that at this time the statute provided for only one Juvenile Court judge. Congressional hearings and reports attest the impossibility of the burden which he was supposed to carry. The statute was amended in 1962 to provide for three judges for the court.

ness." As stated, neither this report nor the Social Service file was made available to petitioner's counsel.

The provision of the Juvenile Court Act governing waiver expressly provides only for "full investigation." It states the circumstances in which jurisdiction may be waived and the child held for trial under adult procedures, but it does not state standards to govern the Juvenile Court's decision as to waiver. The provision reads as follows:

> "If a child sixteen years of age or older is charged with an offense which would amount to a felony in the case of an adult, or any child charged with an offense which if committed by an adult is punishable by death or life imprisonment, the judge may, after full investigation, waive jurisdiction and order such child held for trial under the regular procedure of the court which would have jurisdiction of such offense if committed by an adult; or such other court may exercise the powers conferred upon the juvenile court in this subchapter in conducting and disposing of such cases."

Petitioner appealed from the Juvenile Court's waiver order to the Municipal Court of Appeals, which affirmed, and also applied to the United States District Court for a writ of habeas corpus, which was denied. On appeal from these judgments, the United States Court of Appeals held on January 22, 1963, that neither appeal to the Municipal Court of Appeals nor habeas corpus was available. In the Court of Appeals' view, the exclusive method of reviewing the Juvenile Court's waiver order was a motion to dismiss the indictment in the District Court. Kent v. Reid, 114 U.S.App.D.C. 330, 316 F.2d 331 (1963).

Meanwhile, on September 25, 1961, shortly after the Juvenile Court order waiving its jurisdiction, petitioner was indicted by a grand jury of the United States District Court for the District of Columbia. The indictment contained eight counts alleging two instances of housebreaking, robbery, and rape, and one of housebreaking and robbery. On November 16, 1961, petitioner moved the District Court to dismiss the indictment on the grounds that the waiver was invalid. He also moved the District Court to constitute itself a Juvenile Court as authorized by D.C.Code § 11–914 (1961), now § 11–1553 (Supp. IV, 1965). After substantial delay occasioned by petitioner's appeal and habeas corpus proceedings, the District Court addressed itself to the motion to dismiss on February 8, 1963.

The District Court denied the motion to dismiss the indictment. The District Court ruled that it would not "go behind" the Juvenile Court judge's recital that his order was entered "after full investigation." It held that "The only matter before me is as to whether or not the statutory provisions were complied with and the Courts have held * * * with reference to full investigation, that that does not mean a quasi judicial or judicial hearing. No hearing is required."

On March 7, 1963, the District Court held a hearing on petitioner's motion to determine his competency to stand trial. The court determined that petitioner was competent.[6]

At trial, petitioner's defense was wholly directed toward proving that he was not criminally responsible because "his unlawful act was the product of mental disease or mental defect." Durham v. United States, 94 U.S.App.D.C. 228, 241, 214 F.2d 862, 875, 45 A.L.R.2d 1430 (1954). Extensive evidence, including expert testimony, was presented to support this defense. The jury found as to the counts alleging rape that petitioner was "not guilty by reason of insanity." Under District of Columbia law, this made it mandatory that petitioner be transferred to St. Elizabeths Hospital, a mental institution, until his sanity is restored. On the six counts of housebreaking and robbery, the jury found that petitioner was guilty.[7]

Kent was sentenced to serve five to 15 years on each count as to which he was found guilty, or a total of 30 to 90 years in prison. The District Court ordered that the time to be spent at St. Elizabeths on the mandatory commitment after the insanity acquittal be counted as part of the 30- to 90-year sentence. Petitioner appealed to the United States Court of Appeals for the District of Columbia Circuit. That court affirmed. 119 U.S.App.D.C. 378, 343 F.2d 247 (1964).

Before the Court of Appeals and in this Court, petitioner's counsel has urged a number of grounds for reversal. He argues that petitioner's detention and interrogation, described above, were unlawful. He contends that the police failed to follow the procedure prescribed by the Juvenile Court Act in that they failed to notify the parents of the child and the Juvenile Court itself, note 1, supra; that petitioner was deprived of his liberty for about a week without a determination of probable cause which would have been required in

[6] The District Court had before it extensive information as to petitioner's mental condition, bearing upon both competence to stand trial and the defense of insanity. The court had obtained the "Social Service" file from the Juvenile Court and had made it available to petitioner's counsel. On October 13, 1961, the District Court had granted petitioner's motion of October 6 for commitment to the Psychiatric Division of the General Hospital for 60 days. On December 20, 1961, the hospital reported that "It is the concensus [sic] of the staff that Morris is emotionally ill and severely so * * * we feel that he is incompetent to stand trial and to participate in a mature way in his own defense. His illness has interfered with his judgment and reasoning ability * * *." The prosecutor opposed a finding of incompetence to stand trial, and at the prosecutor's request, the District Court referred petitioner to St. Elizabeths Hospital for psychiatric observation. According to a letter from the Superintendent of St. Elizabeths of April 5, 1962, the hospital's staff found that petitioner was "suffering from mental disease at the present time, Schizophrenic Reaction, Chronic Undifferentiated Type," that he had been suffering from this disease at the time of the charged offenses, and that "if committed by him [those criminal acts] were the product of this disease." They stated, however, that petitioner was "mentally competent to understand the nature of the proceedings against him and to consult properly with counsel in his own defense."

[7] The basis for this distinction—that petitioner was "sane" for purposes of the housebreaking and robbery but "insane" for the purposes of the rape—apparently was the hypothesis, for which there is some support in the record, that the jury might find that the robberies had anteceded the rapes, and in that event, it might conclude that the housebreakings and robberies were not the products of his mental disease or defect, while the rapes were produced thereby.

the case of an adult; that he was interrogated by the police in the absence of counsel or a parent, cf. Harling v. United States, 111 U.S. App.D.C. 174, 176, 295 F.2d 161, 163, n. 12 (1961), without warning of his right to remain silent or advice as to his right to counsel, in asserted violation of the Juvenile Court Act and in violation of rights that he would have if he were an adult; and that petitioner was fingerprinted in violation of the asserted intent of the Juvenile Court Act and while unlawfully detained and that the fingerprints were unlawfully used in the District Court proceeding.

These contentions raise problems of substantial concern as to the construction of and compliance with the Juvenile Court Act. They also suggest basic issues as to the justifiability of affording a juvenile less protection than is accorded to adults suspected of criminal offenses, particularly where, as here, there is an absence of any indication that the denial of rights available to adults was offset, mitigated or explained by action of the Government, as *parens patriae*, evidencing the special solicitude for juveniles commanded by the Juvenile Court Act. However, because we remand the case on account of the procedural error with respect to waiver of jurisdiction, we do not pass upon these questions.

It is to petitioner's arguments as to the infirmity of the proceedings by which the Juvenile Court waived its otherwise exclusive jurisdiction that we address our attention. Petitioner attacks the waiver of jurisdiction on a number of statutory and constitutional grounds. He contends that the waiver is defective because no hearing was held, because no findings were made by the Juvenile Court, because the Juvenile Court stated no reasons for waiver; and because counsel was denied access to the Social Service file which presumably was considered by the Juvenile Court in determining to waive jurisdiction.

We agree that the order of the Juvenile Court waiving its jurisdiction and transferring petitioner for trial in the United States District Court for the District of Columbia was invalid. There is no question that the order is reviewable on motion to dismiss the indictment in the District Court, as specified by the Court of Appeals in this case. Kent v. Reid, supra. The issue is the standards to be applied upon such review.

We agree with the Court of Appeals that the statute contemplates that the Juvenile Court should have considerable latitude within which to determine whether it should retain jurisdiction over a child or—subject to the statutory delimitation—should waive jurisdiction. But this latitude is not complete. At the outset, it assumes procedural regularity sufficient in the particular circumstances to satisfy the basic requirements of due process and fairness, as well as compliance with the statutory requirement of a "full investigation." Green v. United States, 113 U.S.App.D.C. 348, 308 F.2d 303 (1962).[8]

8 "What is required before a waiver is, as we have said, 'full investigation.' * * * It prevents the waiver of juris- diction as a matter of routine for the purpose of easing the docket. It pre- vents routine waiver in certain classes of

The statute gives the Juvenile Court a substantial degree of discretion as to the factual considerations to be evaluated, the weight to be given them and the conclusion to be reached. It does not confer upon the Juvenile Court a license for arbitrary procedure. The statute does not permit the Juvenile Court to determine in isolation and without the participation or any representation of the child the "critically important" question whether a child will be deprived of the special protections and provisions of the Juvenile Court Act. It does not authorize the Juvenile Court, in total disregard of a motion for hearing filed by counsel, and without any hearing or statement or reasons, to decide—as in this case—that the child will be taken from the Receiving Home for Children and transferred to jail along with adults, and that he will be exposed to the possibility of a death sentence instead of treatment for a maximum, in Kent's case, of five years, until he is 21.

We do not consider whether, on the merits, Kent should have been transferred; but there is no place in our system of law for reaching a result of such tremendous consequences without ceremony—without hearing, without effective assistance of counsel, without a statement of reasons. It is inconceivable that a court of justice dealing with adults, with respect to a similar issue, would proceed in this manner. It would be extraordinary if society's special concern for children, as reflected in the District of Columbia's Juvenile Court Act, permitted this procedure. We hold that it does not.

1. The theory of the District's Juvenile Court Act, like that of other jurisdictions,[9] is rooted in social welfare philosophy rather than in the *corpus juris*. Its proceedings are designated as civil rather than criminal. The Juvenile Court is theoretically engaged in determining the needs of the child and of society rather than adjudicating criminal conduct. The objectives are to provide measures of guidance and rehabilitation for the child and protection for society, not to fix criminal responsibility, guilt and punishment. The State is *parens patriae* rather than prosecuting attorney and judge. But the admonition to function in a "parental" relationship is not an invitation to procedural arbitrariness.

2. Because the State is supposed to proceed in respect of the child as *parens patriae* and not as adversary, courts have relied on the premise that the proceedings are "civil" in nature and not criminal, and have asserted that the child cannot complain of the deprivation of important rights available in criminal cases. It has been asserted that he can claim only the fundamental due process

alleged crimes. It requires a judgment in each case based on 'an inquiry not only into the facts of the alleged offense but also into the question whether the *parens patriae* plan of procedure is desirable and proper in the particular case.' Pee v. United States, 107 U.S.App.D.C. 47, 50, 274 F.2d 556, 559 (1959)." Green v. United States, supra, at 350, 308 F.2d, at 305.

[9] All States have juvenile court systems. A study of the actual operation of these systems is contained in Note Juvenile Delinquents: The Police, State Courts, and Individualized Justice, 79 Harv.L.Rev. 775 (1966).

right to fair treatment.[10] For example, it has been held that he is not entitled to bail; to indictment by grand jury; to a speedy and public trial; to trial by jury; to immunity against self-incrimination; to confrontation of his accusers; and in some jurisdictions * * * that he is not entitled to counsel.

While there can be no doubt of the original laudable purpose of juvenile courts, studies and critiques in recent years raise serious questions as to whether actual performance measures well enough against theoretical purpose to make tolerable the immunity of the process from the reach of constitutional guaranties applicable to adults. There is much evidence that some juvenile courts, including that of the District of Columbia, lack the personnel, facilities and techniques to perform adequately as representatives of the State in a *parens patriae* capacity, at least with respect to children charged with law violation. There is evidence, in fact, that there may be grounds for concern that the child receives the worst of both worlds: that he gets neither the protections accorded to adults nor the solicitous care and regenerative treatment postulated for children.

This concern, however, does not induce us in this case to accept the invitation to rule that constitutional guaranties which would be applicable to adults charged with the serious offenses for which Kent was tried must be applied in juvenile court proceedings concerned with allegations of law violation. The Juvenile Court Act and the decisions of the United States Court of Appeals for the District of Columbia Circuit provide an adequate basis for decision of this case, and we go no further.

3. It is clear beyond dispute that the waiver of jurisdiction is a "critically important" action determining vitally important statutory rights of the juvenile. The Court of Appeals for the District of Columbia Circuit has so held. See Black v. United States, supra; Watkins v. United States, 119 U.S.App.D.C. 409, 343 F.2d 278 (1964). The statutory scheme makes this plain. The Juvenile Court is vested with "original and exclusive jurisdiction" of the child. This jurisdiction confers special rights and immunities. He is, as specified by the statute, shielded from publicity. He may be confined, but with rare exceptions he may not be jailed along with adults. He may be detained, but only until he is 21 years of age. The court is admonished by the statute to give preference to retaining the child in the custody of his parents "unless his welfare and the safety and protection of the public can not be adequately safeguarded without * * * removal." The child is protected against consequences of adult conviction such as the loss of civil rights, the use of adjudication against him in subsequent proceedings, and disqualification for public employment. D.C.Code §§ 11–907, 11–915, 11–927, 11–929 (1961).

The net, therefore, is that petitioner—then a boy of 16—was by statute entitled to certain procedures and benefits as a consequence

[10] Pee v. United States, 107 U.S.App. D.C. 47, 274 F.2d 556 (1959).

of his statutory right to the "exclusive" jurisdiction of the Juvenile Court. In these circumstances, considering particularly that decision as to waiver of jurisdiction and transfer of the matter to the District Court was potentially as important to petitioner as the difference between five years' confinement and a death sentence, we conclude that, as a condition to a valid waiver order, petitioner was entitled to a hearing, including access by his counsel to the social records and probation or similar reports which presumably are considered by the court, and to a statement of reasons for the Juvenile Court's decision. We believe that this result is required by the statute read in the context of constitutional principles relating to due process and the assistance of counsel.

The Court of Appeals in this case relied upon Wilhite v. United States, 108 U.S.App.D.C. 279, 281 F.2d 642 (1960). In that case, the Court of Appeals held, for purposes of a determination as to waiver of jurisdiction, that no formal hearing is required and that the "full investigation" required of the Juvenile Court need only be such "as is needed to satisfy *that* court * * * on the question of waiver." (Emphasis supplied.) The authority of Wilhite, however, is substantially undermined by other, more recent, decisions of the Court of Appeals.

In Black v. United States, decided by the Court of Appeals on December 8, 1965, the court held that assistance of counsel in the "critically important" determination of waiver is essential to the proper administration of juvenile proceedings. Because the juvenile was not advised of his right to retained or appointed counsel, the judgment of the District Court, following waiver of jurisdiction by the Juvenile Court, was reversed. The court relied upon its decision in Shioutakon v. District of Columbia, 98 U.S.App.D.C. 371, 236 F.2d 666 (1956), in which it had held that effective assistance of counsel in juvenile court proceedings is essential. * * * In Black, the court referred to the Criminal Justice Act, enacted four years after Shioutakon, in which Congress provided for the assistance of counsel "in proceedings before the juvenile court of the District of Columbia." * * * The Court held that "The need is even greater in the adjudication of waiver [than in a case like Shioutakon] since it contemplates the imposition of criminal sanctions." 122 U.S.App. D.C., at 395, 355 F.2d at 106.

In Watkins v. United States, 119 U.S.App.D.C. 409, 343 F.2d 278 (1964), decided in November 1964, the Juvenile Court had waived jurisdiction of appellant who was charged with housebreaking and larceny. In the District Court, appellant sought disclosure of the social record in order to attack the validity of the waiver. The Court of Appeals held that in a waiver proceeding a juvenile's attorney is entitled to access to such records. The court observed that

> "All of the social records concerning the child are usually relevant to waiver since the Juvenile Court must be deemed to consider the entire history of the child in determining waiver. The relevance of particular items must be construed generously.

Since an attorney has no certain knowledge of what the social records contain, he cannot be expected to demonstrate the relevance of particular items in his request.

"The child's attorney must be advised of the information upon which the Juvenile Court relied in order to assist effectively in the determination of the waiver question, by insisting upon the statutory command that waiver can be ordered only after 'full investigation,' and by guarding against action of the Juvenile Court beyond its discretionary authority." 119 U.S.App.D.C., at 413, 343 F.2d, at 282.

The court remanded the record to the District Court for a determination of the extent to which the records should be disclosed.

The Court of Appeals' decision in the present case was handed down on October 26, 1964, prior to its decisions in Black and Watkins. The Court of Appeals assumed that since petitioner had been a probationer of the Juvenile Court for two years, that court had before it sufficient evidence to make an informed judgment. It therefore concluded that the statutory requirement of a "full investigation" had been met. It noted the absence of "a specification by the Juvenile Court Judge of precisely why he concluded to waive jurisdiction." * * * While it indicated that "in some cases at least" a useful purpose might be served "by a discussion of the reasons motivating the determination," * * * it did not conclude that the absence thereof invalidated the waiver.

As to the denial of access to the social records, the Court of Appeals stated that "the statute is ambiguous." It said that petitioner's claim, in essence, is "that counsel should have the opportunity to challenge them, presumably in a manner akin to cross-examination." * * * It held, however, that this is "the kind of adversarial tactics which the system is designed to avoid." It characterized counsel's proper function as being merely that of bringing forward affirmative information which might help the court. His function, the Court of Appeals said, "is not to denigrate the staff's submissions and recommendations." * * * Accordingly, it held that the Juvenile Court had not abused its discretion in denying access to the social records.

We are of the opinion that the Court of Appeals misconceived the basic issue and the underlying values in this case. It did note, as another panel of the same court did a few months later in Black and Watkins, that the determination of whether to transfer a child from the statutory structure of the Juvenile Court to the criminal processes of the District Court is "critically important." We hold that it is, indeed, a "critically important" proceeding. The Juvenile Court Act confers upon the child a right to avail himself of that court's "exclusive" jurisdiction. As the Court of Appeals has said, "[I]t is implicit in [the Juvenile Court] scheme that non-criminal treatment is to be the rule—and the adult criminal treatment, the exception which must be governed by the particular factors of individual cases." Harling v. United States, 111 U.S.App.D.C. 174, 177–178, 295 F.2d 161, 164–165 (1961).

Meaningful review requires that the reviewing court should review. It should not be remitted to assumptions. It must have before it a statement of the reasons motivating the waiver including, of course, a statement of the relevant facts. It may not "assume" that there are adequate reasons, nor may it merely assume that "full investigation" has been made. Accordingly, we hold that it is incumbent upon the Juvenile Court to accompany its waiver order with a statement of the reasons or considerations therefor. We do not read the statute as requiring that this statement must be formal or that it should necessarily include conventional findings of fact. But the statement should be sufficient to demonstrate that the statutory requirement of "full investigation" has been met; and that the question has received the careful consideration of the Juvenile Court; and it must set forth the basis for the order with sufficient specificity to permit meaningful review.

Correspondingly, we conclude that an opportunity for a hearing which may be informal, must be given the child prior to entry of a waiver order. Under Black, the child is entitled to counsel in connection with a waiver proceeding, and under Watkins, counsel is entitled to see the child's social records. These rights are meaningless—an illusion, a mockery—unless counsel is given an opportunity to function.

The right to representation by counsel is not a formality. It is not a grudging gesture to a ritualistic requirement. It is of the essence of justice. Appointment of counsel without affording an opportunity for hearing on a "critically important" decision is tantamount to denial of counsel. There is no justification for the failure of the Juvenile Court to rule on the motion for hearing filed by petitioner's counsel, and it was error to fail to grant a hearing.

We do not mean by this to indicate that the hearing to be held must conform with all of the requirements of a criminal trial or even of the usual administrative hearing; but we do hold that the hearing must measure up to the essentials of due process and fair treatment.

With respect to access by the child's counsel to the social records of the child, we deem it obvious that since these are to be considered by the Juvenile Court in making its decision to waive, they must be made available to the child's counsel. This is what the Court of Appeals itself held in Watkins. There is no doubt as to the statutory basis for this conclusion, as the Court of Appeals pointed out in Watkins. We cannot agree with the Court of Appeals in the present case that the statute is "ambiguous." The statute expressly provides that the record shall be withheld from "indiscriminate" public inspection, "except that such records or parts thereof *shall* be made available by rule of court or special order of court to such persons * * * as have a *legitimate interest* in the protection * * * of the child * * *."[11] The Court of Appeals has held in Black, and we

---

[11] Under the statute, the Juvenile Court has power by rule or order, to subject the examination of the social records to conditions which will prevent misuse of the information. Violation of any such rule or order, or disclosure of

agree, that counsel must be afforded to the child in waiver proceedings. Counsel, therefore, have a "legitimate interest" in the protection of the child, and must be afforded access to these records.[12]

We do not agree with the Court of Appeals' statement, attempting to justify denial of access to these records, that counsel's role is limited to presenting "to the court anything on behalf of the child which might help the court in arriving at a decision; it is not to denigrate the staff's submissions and recommendations." On the contrary, if the staff's submissions include materials which are susceptible to challenge or impeachment, it is precisely the role of counsel to "denigrate" such matter. There is no irrebutable presumption of accuracy attached to staff reports. If a decision on waiver is "critically important" it is equally of "critical importance" that the material submitted to the judge—which is protected by the statute only against "indiscriminate" inspection—be subjected, within reasonable limits having regard to the theory of the Juvenile Court Act, to examination, criticism and refutation. While the Juvenile Court judge may, of course, receive *ex parte* analyses and recommendations from his staff, he may not, for purposes of a decision on waiver, receive and rely upon secret information, whether emanating from his staff or otherwise. The Juvenile Court is governed in this respect by the established principles which control courts and quasi-judicial agencies of the Government.

For the reasons stated, we conclude that the Court of Appeals and the District Court erred in sustaining the validity of the waiver by the Juvenile Court. The Government urges that any error committed by the Juvenile Court was cured by the proceedings before the District Court. It is true that the District Court considered and denied a motion to dismiss on the grounds of the invalidity of the waiver order of the Juvenile Court, and that it considered and denied a motion that it should itself, as authorized by statute, proceed in this case to "exercise the powers conferred upon the juvenile court." But we agree with the Court of Appeals in Black, that "the waiver question was primarily and initially one for the Juvenile Court to decide and its failure to do so in a valid manner cannot be said to be harmless error. It is the Juvenile Court, not the District Court, which has the facilities, personnel and expertise for a proper determination of the waiver issue." 122 U.S.App.D.C., at 396, 355 F.2d, at 107.[13]

the information "except for purposes for which * * * released," is a misdemeanor. D.C.Code § 11–929 (1961), now, without substantial change, § 11–1586 (Supp. IV, 1965).

[12] In Watkins, the Court of Appeals seems to have permitted withholding of some portions of the social record from examination by petitioner's counsel. To the extent that Watkins is inconsistent with the standard which we state, it cannot be considered as controlling.

[13] It also appears that the District Court requested and obtained the Social Service file and the probation staff's report of September 8, 1961, and that these were made available to petitioner's counsel. This did not cure the error of the Juvenile Court. Perhaps the point of it is that it again illustrates the maxim that while nondisclosure may contribute to the comfort of the staff, disclosure does not cause heaven to fall.

Ordinarily we would reverse the Court of Appeals and direct the District Court to remand the case to the Juvenile Court for a new determination of waiver. If on remand the decision were against waiver, the indictment in the District Court would be dismissed. * * * However, petitioner has now passed the age of 21 and the Juvenile Court can no longer exercise jurisdiction over him. In view of the unavailability of a redetermination of the waiver question by the Juvenile Court, it is urged by petitioner that the conviction should be vacated and the indictment dismissed. In the circumstances of this case, and in light of the remedy which the Court of Appeals fashioned in Black, supra, we do not consider it appropriate to grant this drastic relief.[14] Accordingly, we vacate the order of the Court of Appeals and the judgment of the District Court and remand the case to the District Court for a hearing *de novo* on waiver, consistent with this opinion.[15] If that court finds that waiver was inappropriate, petitioner's conviction must be vacated. If, however, it finds that the waiver order was proper when originally made, the District Court may proceed, after consideration of such motions as counsel may make and such further proceedings, if any, as may be warranted, to enter an appropriate judgment.

Reversed and remanded.

APPENDIX TO OPINION OF THE COURT

Policy Memorandum No. 7, November 30, 1959.

The authority of the Judge of the Juvenile Court of the District of Columbia to waive or transfer jurisdiction to the U. S. District Court for the District of Columbia is contained in the Juvenile Court Act (§ 11–914 D.C.Code, 1951 Ed.). This section permits the Judge to waive jurisdiction "after full investigation" in the case of any child "sixteen years of age or older [who is] charged with an offense which would amount to a felony in the case of an adult, or any child charged with an offense which if committed by an adult is punishable by death or life imprisonment."

The statute sets forth no specific standards for the exercise of this important discretionary act, but leaves the formulation of such criteria to the Judge. A knowledge of the Judge's criteria is important to the child, his parents, his attorney, to the judges of the U. S. District Court for the District of Columbia, to the United States Attorney and his assistants and to the Metropolitan Police Department, as well as to the staff of this court, especially the Juvenile Intake Section.

[14] Petitioner is in St. Elizabeths Hospital for psychiatric treatment as a result of the jury verdict on the rape charges.

[15] We do not deem it appropriate merely to vacate the judgment and remand to the Court of Appeals for reconsideration of its present decision in light of its subsequent decisions in Watkins and Black, supra. Those cases were decided by different panels of the Court of Appeals from that which decided the present case, and in view of our grant of certiorari and of the importance of the issue, we consider it necessary to resolve the question presented instead of leaving it open for further consideration by the Court of Appeals.

Therefore, the Judge has consulted with the Chief Judge and other judges of the U. S. District Court for the District of Columbia, with the United States Attorney, with representatives of the Bar, and with other groups concerned and has formulated the following criteria and principles concerning waiver of jurisdiction which are consistent with the basic aims and purpose of the Juvenile Court Act.

An offense falling within the statutory limitations (set forth above) will be waived if it has prosecutive merit and if it is heinous or of an aggravated character, or—even though less serious—if it represents a pattern of repeated offenses which indicate that the juvenile may be beyond rehabilitation under Juvenile Court procedures, or if the public needs the protection afforded by such action.

The determinative factors which will be considered by the Judge in deciding whether the Juvenile Court's jurisdiction over such offenses will be waived are the following:

1. The seriousness of the alleged offense to the community and whether the protection of the community requires waiver.

2. Whether the alleged offense was committed in an aggressive, violent, premeditated or willful manner.

3. Whether the alleged offense was against persons or against property, greater weight being given to offenses against persons especially if personal injury resulted.

4. The prosecutive merit of the complaint, i.e., whether there is evidence upon which a Grand Jury may be expected to return an indictment (to be determined by consultation with the United States Attorney).

5. The desirability of trial and disposition of the entire offense in one court when the juvenile's associates in the alleged offense are adults who will be charged with a crime in the U. S. District Court for the District of Columbia.

6. The sophistication and maturity of the juvenile as determined by consideration of his home, environmental situation, emotional attitude and pattern of living.

7. The record and previous history of the juvenile, including previous contacts with the Youth Aid Division, other law enforcement agencies, juvenile courts and other jurisdictions, prior periods of probation to this Court, or prior commitments to juvenile institutions.

8. The prospects for adequate protection of the public and the likelihood of reasonable rehabilitation of the juvenile (if he is found to have committed the alleged offense) by the use of procedures, services and facilities currently available to the Juvenile Court.

It will be the responsibility of any officer of the Court's staff assigned to make the investigation of any complaint in which waiver of jurisdiction is being considered to develop fully all available information which may bear upon the criteria and factors set forth above. Although not all such factors will be involved in an individual case, the Judge will consider the relevant factors in a specific case before reaching a conclusion to waive juvenile jurisdiction and transfer the case to the U. S. District Court for the District of Columbia for trial under the adult procedures of that Court.

MR. JUSTICE STEWART, with whom MR. JUSTICE BLACK, MR. JUSTICE HARLAN and MR. JUSTICE WHITE join, dissenting.

This case involves the construction of a statute applicable only to the District of Columbia. Our general practice is to leave undisturbed decisions of the Court of Appeals for the District of Columbia Circuit concerning the import of legislation governing the affairs of the District.

    * * * It appears, however, that two cases decided by the Court of Appeals subsequent to its decision in the present case may have considerably modified the court's construction of the statute. Therefore, I would vacate this judgment and remand the case to the Court of Appeals for reconsideration in the light of its subsequent decisions, Watkins v. United States, 119 U.S.App.D.C. 409, 343 F.2d 278, and Black v. United States, 122 U.S.App.D.C. 393, 355 F.2d 104.

NOTES

1. Appellate courts have divided on the question whether the Kent decision is based on the Constitution or on the District of Columbia juvenile code. Some courts regard Kent as a constitutionally-based decision in light of the Supreme Court's subsequent opinion in In re Gault.

2. Consider the applicability of the Kent decision to the following problems:

    a. The juvenile court has exclusive jurisdiction over a child under the age of 17 who is alleged to have engaged in criminal conduct. A child under 17 commits a robbery in which he murders the victim. He is adjudicated delinquent for the robbery and committed to the state training school. When he becomes 17, he is charged with murder and is returned to criminal court from training school to stand trial for that offense.

    b. The juvenile court has exclusive jurisdiction over a child under the age of 17 who is alleged to have engaged in criminal conduct. A child who is alleged to have committed a felony while over the age of 15 may be transferred to criminal court for prosecution after juvenile court proceedings that satisfy any constitutional requirements Kent may impose. If the juvenile court refuses to waive jurisdiction or if the juvenile court conducts an adjudication hearing, the child may never be prosecuted for any offense known to the juvenile court judge at the time of that proceeding. However, if the juvenile court takes no action at all, the child may be prosecuted when he becomes 17 years of age for an offense committed between the ages of 15 and 17.

    c. The juvenile court has exclusive jurisdiction over a child under the age of 15 who is alleged to have engaged in criminal conduct. The juvenile court and the criminal court have concurrent jurisdiction over a child between the ages of 15 and 17 who is alleged to have committed a criminal offense.

3. In State v. Scurlock, 35 Or.App. 579, 581 P.2d 986 (1978) the prosecutor delayed filing charges against the defendant for a period of eight

months until he achieved his 18th birthday. Under Oregon law, age at the time of filing of charges, rather than age at the time of the offense, was controlling. When criminal charges were filed without a juvenile transfer hearing, defendant objected on various constitutional grounds. The Oregon Court of Appeals set aside the trial court's dismissal of the indictment, commenting that defendant had not shown that the procedures employed prejudiced him in his defense of charges *in the criminal trial.*

The Oregon Supreme Court modified the decision of the Court of Appeals and remanded the defendant to juvenile court:

> This is not a case in which the delay in taking the defendant into custody was justified because there was a good faith investigation in progress. The State concedes that the delay was for the sole purpose of avoiding a remand proceeding under ORS 419.533. Under these circumstances, we hold that the defendant cannot initially be prosecuted as an adult in the circuit court.

State of Oregon v. Ronald E. Scurlock, 286 Or. 277, 282, 593 P.2d 1159, 1162 (1979).

4. IJA–ABA Juvenile Justice Standards Project, Standards Relating to Transfer Between Courts 1.1 (1980) recommends that, "No criminal court should have jurisdiction in any proceeding against any person whose alleged conduct would constitute an offense on which a juvenile court adjudication could be based if at the time the offense is alleged to have occurred such person was fifteen, sixteen or seventeen years of age, unless the juvenile court has waived its jurisdiction over that person." *

UNITED STATES v. BLAND

United States Court of Appeals, District of Columbia Circuit, 1972.
153 U.S.App.D.C. 254, 472 F.2d 1329, certiorari denied, 412 U.S. 909, 93
S.Ct. 2294, 36 L.Ed.2d 975 (1973).

WILKEY, CIRCUIT JUDGE: The United States as statutory appellant seeks review of a memorandum opinion and order of the United States District Court for the District of Columbia, holding 16 D.C. Code § 2301(3)(A) unconstitutional as (1) an arbitrary legislative classification and (2) a negation of the presumption of innocence. Section 2301(3)(A) provides:

> The term "child" means an individual who is under 18 years of age, except that the term "child" does not include an individual who is sixteen years of age or older and—
>
> > (A) charged by the United States Attorney with (i) murder, forcible rape, burglary in the first degree, robbery while armed, or assault with intent to commit any such offense, or (ii) an offense listed in clause (i) and any other offense properly joinable with such an offense. * * *

The appellee, born 30 July 1954, had been indicted pursuant to Section 2301(3)(A) as an adult (he was sixteen at the time of his arrest and indictment) on charges of armed robbery of a post office and related offenses on 8 February 1971. Appellee moved below to dismiss the indictment for lack of jurisdiction, asserting that the

---

* Reprinted with permission from Standards Relating to Transfer Between Courts, Copyright 1980, Ballinger Publishing Company.

statutory basis for prosecuting him as an adult was constitutionally deficient in that it failed to provide him with procedural due process. The District Court dismissed the indictment.

I. *The Legislative Background.*

Congress, pursuant to its constitutional authority to exercise exclusive jurisdiction over the District of Columbia, created the Family Division of the Superior Court of the District of Columbia. In defining the jurisdiction of the Family Division, Congress conferred on it exclusive jurisdiction of "proceedings in which a *child, as defined in section 16–2301,* is alleged to be delinquent, neglected, or in need of supervision." Thus, the Family Division's jurisdiction extends over a person—a child—alleged to have committed delinquent acts, a child being classified as a person not having yet reached the chronological age of 18 and not charged by the United States Attorney with certain specified crimes listed in 16 D.C.Code § 2301. As to any other individual, either one who has reached 18 or who has reached the age of 16 and has been charged by the United States Attorney with one or more of the enumerated felonies,[16] he is not a child and is to be prosecuted in the regular adult court system,

* * *

The legislative history accompanying 16 D.C.Code § 2301 reveals Congress' intent in enacting this legislation: To improve the operation of the juvenile justice system in the District of Columbia by removing from its jurisdiction certain individuals between the ages of 16 and 18 whom Congress concluded (1) were beyond rehabilitation in the juvenile justice system, and (2) whose presence in that system served as a negative influence on other juveniles. This represents a policy judgment of Congress, after gathering extensive appropriate evidence, as to how persons should be classified as "adult" and "child" for the purposes of rehabilitation following the commission of a criminal offense. We note that the policy judgment was both negative and positive: some previously classified as juveniles were beyond rehabilitation; others of the same chronological age were susceptible to special juvenile treatment, and for any chance of success these latter should be protected against the hard-core repeat offenders of the same chronological age.

While Congress easily could have established 16 as the age cutoff date (it is not clear what constitutional infirmities our dissenting colleague would have found in that less sympathetic approach), it

---

[16] D.C.Code § 2301(3) also provides:

(3) The term "child" means an individual who is under 18 years of age, except that the term "child" does not include an individual who is sixteen years of age or older and—

* * *

(B) charged with an offense referred to in subparagraph (A)(i) and convicted by plea or verdict of a lesser included offense; or

(C) charged with a traffic offense.

For purposes of this subchapter the term "child" also includes a person under the age of twenty-one who is charged with an offense referred to in subparagraph (A)(i) or (C) committed before he attained the age of sixteen or a delinquent act committed before he attained the age of eighteen.

concluded that some within the 16–18 age bracket were susceptible of rehabilitation, and determined that those age 16 and 17 whose offenses charged were minor were to be included within the juvenile system.   As the Department of Justice made clear in its Memorandum to the Senate Committee:

> The jurisdictional age for all juveniles was not lowered to 16 because there are still first offenders charged with minor offenses who may benefit from juvenile treatment up to the age of 18, and treating them as adults may be harsh and unnecessary. At the same time, experience has shown that in certain crime categories, juvenile treatment is unworkable.   Accordingly, the jurisdictional age has been lowered with respect to these crimes.

Under the initial Senate version of Section 2301, the jurisdiction of the Family Division

> extends, in general, to persons under the age of 18.   Excluded from the latter class, however, is any person 16 years of age or older in any case (1) where such person is formerly [sic] charged with the commission of one or more of certain enumerated grave offenses, and (2) where such persons has [sic] previously had the benefit of special juvenile disposition after being charged with serious misconduct committed after attaining the age of 15.

The Senate Committee on the District of Columbia, in revealing its rationale for excluding such persons from the jurisdiction of the Family Division, stated:

> The Committee has concluded that a juvenile can reliably be considered too well formed or sophisticated for, and beyond the reach of, mere juvenile therapy if the particular juvenile has already been exposed, in years of relative discretion, to the juvenile system and treated to the extent that his case required (as suggested by a prior finding of delinquency), and has nevertheless returned to serious misconduct (as suggested by a serious felony charge).[17]

The initial House version of Section 2301 provided that "a person, 16 years of age or older, who is charged by the United States attorney with an enumerated violent crime [a more extensive list than contained in the initial Senate version] is automatically subject to the jurisdiction of the adult court."   The House Committee on the District of Columbia, referring to the same statistics on serious offenses committed by juveniles and to the growing recidivist rate among this group cited by the Senate Committee, gave the following as the basis

---

[17] * * * The Committee also noted, however: "Conversely, the committee did not take so dim a view of juveniles in the 16- to 18-year old age group generally as to presume sophistication in every case involving serious misconduct—and especially in cases involving first offenders or where any previous offense was committed before the onset of a relatively significant degree of discretion." * * * As such, "[t]he committee was not inclined, therefore, to approve a lowering of the jurisdictional age limit (for the Family Division) in simple reaction to statistic indicating a greater incidence of crime committed by juveniles aged 16 to 18." * * *

for its exclusion of those 16 years of age or older charged with a certain serious crime from the Family Division's jurisdiction:

> Because of the great increase in the number of serious felonies committed by juveniles and because of the substantial difficulties in transferring juvenile offenders charged with serious felonies to the jurisdiction of the adult court under present law, provisions are made in this subchapter for a better mechanism for separation of the violent youthful offender and recidivist from the rest of the juvenile community.

As finally enacted, Section 2301 reflects a compromise between the initial Senate and House versions. It provides that the Family Division shall have jurisdiction over "persons under 18 except those 16 and older charged by the United States attorney with murder, forcible rape, robbery while armed, burglary in the first degree, or assault with intent to commit one of these offenses, or any such offense and a properly joinable offense." As such, it eliminates the previous finding of delinquency required under the initial Senate version and shortens the list of serious crimes contained in the initial House version.

II. *The Due Process and Equal Protection of the Law Issue.*

The District Court found Section 2301(3)(A) invalid as violative of due process of law:

> The determination that a child should be tried as an adult cannot be made without the safeguard of basic due process. Without a provision in the new statute that would require some determination, reached after a fair hearing, that an individual is beyond the help of the Family Division, that statute must fall as violative of due process.

To the Government's objection below that the statute specifically classifies those individuals who are at least 16 years of age and charged with certain enumerated crimes by the United States Attorney as exempt from the Family Division's jurisdiction, the District Court found no standards in the statute to guide the United States Attorney in making this determination, hence it held that the statute denies due process to those individuals so charged.

A.

In relation to this holding of the District Court, we note in the first place that legislative classifications are entitled to a strong presumption of validity and may be "set aside only if no grounds can be conceived to justify them."

* * *

As the discussion on the legislative background of Section 2301(3)(A), supra, indicates, Congress was well acquainted with the problems confronting the juvenile justice system in the District of Columbia; logically its definition of the Family Division's jurisdiction reflects its particular concern with the rise in the number of serious crimes committed by those 16 years of age and over coupled with the growing recidivist rate among this group.

Secondly, legislative exclusion of individuals charged with certain specified crimes from the jurisdiction of the juvenile justice system is not unusual. The Federal Juvenile Delinquency Act excludes offenses which are punishable by death or life imprisonment. Several states have similarly excluded certain crimes in defining the jurisdiction of their respective systems of juvenile justice,[18] while others vest concurrent jurisdiction over enumerated crimes in both their adult and juvenile courts.[19] Finally, the United States District Court for the District of Maryland, upheld by the Fourth Circuit, while it did find a geographic age distinction in the jurisdiction of the Maryland Juvenile Court violative of due process, found no difficulties with the exclusion of those 14 years of age and over charged with capital crimes from juvenile jurisdiction.

B.

The disagreement of our dissenting colleague arises almost solely from his fundamental unwillingness to accept Congress' power to define what is a "child." The words "child," "infant," and "minor" from early times in various legal systems have been susceptible to definition by statute; the critical "age" for specified purposes has varied, and differed between male and female. See Bouvier's Law Dictionary; Black's Law Dictionary. Before 1970 the District of Columbia Code (16 D.C.Code § 2301 (1967)), defined "child" as "a person under 18 years of age." Our dissenting colleague seems to consider this statute and its definition immutable, apparently because it was involved in Kent v. United States; we accept the fact that Congress has abolished this statutory definition and by statute substituted another, to which we simply give full effect.

We think the position of the appellee here would have more validity if it were possible to read (as apparently the dissenting opinion does) the word "child" as "child (as defined in the previous and now repealed statute)," but of course this is absurd. Yet it is necessary that the meaning of "child" be as defined in the repealed statute for the legal position of the appellee to be sustained. Believing that Congress has power to amend a statutory definition, we start with the definition of "child" currently on the statute books, and reach the legal conclusions set forth herein.

---

[18] * * * Challenges to these provisions as violative of due process and equal protection of the law have not prevailed. See State v. Ayers, Del., 260 A.2d 162 (1969), in which the court rejected a Fourteenth Amendment challenge to 11 Del.Code Ann. § 363(d) (an anti-riot statute), which provided that those over sixteen years of age and charged with violating this statute were to be tried as adults. See also, to the same effect, Prevatte v. Director, 5 Md. App. 406, 248 A.2d 170 (1968), and Davis v. State, Miss., 204 So.2d 270, rev'd on other ground, 394 U.S. 721, 89 S.Ct. 1394, 22 L.Ed.2d 676 (1969).

[19] 37 Ill.Ann.Stat. § 702–7(3), upheld in People v. Carlson, 108 Ill.App.2d 463, 247 N.E.2d 919 (1969). See also, DeBacker v. Sigler, 185 Neb. 352, 175 N.W.2d 912 (1970), and Mayne v. Turner, 24 Utah 2d 195, 468 P.2d 369 (1970), sustaining concurrent jurisdiction in their respective adult and juvenile courts over certain enumerated offenses.

Similarly, the appellee's argument on an alleged "waiver" of the jurisdiction of the Family Court is based on the now outmoded definition. The District of Columbia Code states clearly that the jurisdiction of the Family Division of the Superior Court in delinquency cases is limited to those who come within the statutory definition of "child." 11 D.C.Code § 1101 provides:

> The Family Division of the Superior Court shall be assigned, in accordance with chapter 9, exclusive jurisdiction of—
>
> (13) proceedings in which a *child, as defined in* 16–2301, is alleged to be a delinquent. * * * (Emphasis supplied.)

Until it is determined whether a person is a "child" within the statutory definition, there is no jurisdiction; therefore, *a fortiori* there can be no waiver of jurisdiction.

Nor is it true "a suspected juvenile remains a child until he is charged with an enumerated offense by the United States Attorney." There is just no classification of the person as a child or an adult until (1) his age is accurately ascertained, and (2) the decision on prosecution is made. Congress has incorporated more than one element in the definition of a "child." Until all the elements of the definition are ascertained, the status of the person is simply uncertain, just as under the 1967 definition the status of a person would be uncertain until his true age was established.

C.

The District Court's finding in the case at bar, and appellee's assertion to the same effect—that the exercise of the discretion vested by Section 2301(3)(A) in the United States Attorney to charge a person 16 years of age or older with certain enumerated offenses, thereby initiating that person's prosecution as an adult, violates due process—ignores the long and widely accepted concept of prosecutorial discretion, which derives from the constitutional principle of separation of powers. The Fifth Circuit, in holding that a court had no power to compel a United States Attorney to sign an indictment, stated:

> Although as a member of the bar, the attorney for the United States is an officer of the court, he is nevertheless an executive official of the Government, and it is as an officer of the executive department that he exercises a discretion as to whether or not there shall be prosecution in a particular case. It follows, as an incident of the constitutional separation of powers, that the courts are not to interfere with the free exercise of the discretionary powers of the attorneys of the United States in their control over criminal prosecutions.

While there may be circumstances in which courts would be entitled to review the exercise of prosecutorial discretion, these circumstances would necessarily include the deliberate presence of such factors as "race, religion, or other arbitrary classification," not found in the case at bar. For example, in the absence of such factors, this court has held that the exercise of prosecutorial discretion, even when it results in different treatment of codefendants originally charged in the same case with the same offense, does not violate due process or equal protection of the law.

The District Court and appellee in the case at bar point to the acknowledged significant effect of the United States Attorney's decision whether to charge an individual 16 years of age or older with certain enumerated offenses, and conclude that, in the absence of a hearing, due process is violated when such a decision is made. This, however, overlooks the significance of a variety of other common prosecutorial decisions, e.g., whether to charge one person but not another possible codefendant; whether to charge an individual with a misdemeanor or a felony; etc.[20] Furthermore, the decision whether to charge an individual with a misdemeanor or a felony has long determined the court in which that person will be tried.[21] We cannot accept the hitherto unaccepted argument that due process requires an adversary hearing before the prosecutor can exercise his age-old function of deciding what charge to bring against whom. Grave consequences have always flowed from this, but never has a hearing been required.

While the Supreme Court was presented with the precise question raised by this appeal on an earlier occasion, it declined to rule on the question because of "the barrenness of the record on this issue," including the failure of the Nebraska Supreme Court to pass on it, and the fact that "[s]o far as we have been made aware, this issue does not draw into question the validity of any Nebraska statute."[22] The Federal Juvenile Delinquency Act, however, presents an analo-

[20] Appellee's attempt to equate the United States Attorney's decision in the case at bar with the transfer of an individual from the jurisdiction of the juvenile court to that of adult court is unavailing. In contrast to such a situation, the case at bar involves *no* initial juvenile court jurisdiction; the United States Attorney's decision to charge an individual sixteen years of age or older with certain enumerated offenses operates automatically to exclude that individual from the jurisdiction of the Family Division. The cases cited by the appellee are equally inapposite: In re Gault, 387 U.S. 1, 87 S.Ct. 1428, 18 L.Ed.2d 527 (1967), did not involve the question of adult court jurisdiction over persons sixteen years of age or over; Kent v. United States, 383 U.S. 541, 86 S.Ct. 1045, 16 L.Ed.2d 84 (1966), Haziel v. United States, 131 U.S.App.D.C. 298, 404 F.2d 1275 (1968), and Black v. United States, 122 U.S.App.D.C. 393, 355 F.2d 104 (1965), all involved the "full investigation" requirement of 11 D.C. Code § 1553 (1967), the former local juvenile statute. Under former Section 1553, individual judgments were to be made by the Juvenile Court as to whether a particular youth should be "waived" for trial as an adult. The comparable transfer provision of the revised juvenile statute, 16 D.C.Code § 2307 (Supp. IV, 1971), is not at issue in the case at bar, which involves determination of which jurisdiction—adult or juvenile—attaches to appellee in the first instance. As such, it cannot involve a transfer from a nonexistent juvenile jurisdiction to adult court.

[21] Also, since 1 February 1971 in the District of Columbia, the decision of *which* felony to charge has similarly determined the court having jurisdiction. 11 D.C.Code §§ 502, 923 (Supp. IV, 1971).

[22] DeBacker v. Brainard, 396 U.S. 28, 32, 90 S.Ct. 163, 165, 24 L.Ed.2d 148 (1969), in which the Supreme Court dismissed the grant of certiorari as "improvidently granted." Id., at 33, 90 S.Ct. 163. In a subsequent case, the Nebraska Supreme Court considered the same question and found the exercise of such discretion did not violate due process. * * *

gous situation on which courts have passed judgment. Section 5032 of the Act provides in relevant part:

> A juvenile alleged to have committed one or more acts in violation of a law of the United States not punishable by death or life imprisonment, and not surrendered to the authorities of a state, shall be proceeded against as a juvenile delinquent if he consents to such procedure, unless the Attorney General, in his discretion, has expressly directed otherwise.

The discretion provided the Attorney General under this section can, of course, result in vastly different consequences for an individual subject to the Act since commitment of a juvenile adjudicated delinquent may continue under the Act, as under the comparable provision of the D.C.Code, only for the remainder of the youth's minority. Despite the significance of this decision, Judge Weinfeld of the District Court for the Southern District of New York stated:

> * * * under this section [§ 5032], which requires the juvenile's consent to such proceeding, the ultimate decision as to whether the Government will forego prosecution under the general criminal statutes rests in the sole discretion of the Attorney General. The Assistant Attorney General, who is authorized to exercise the Attorney General's discretion, has directed that this defendant be prosecuted under regular adult criminal procedures. The Court is without power to interfere with or overrule the exercise of this discretion.[23]

As such, judicial consideration of the legitimate scope of prosecutorial discretion clearly encompasses the exercise of such discretion where it has the effect of determining whether a person will be charged as a juvenile or as an adult. In the absence of such "suspect" factors as "race, religion, or other arbitrary classification," the exercise of discretion by the United States Attorney in the case at bar involves no violation of due process or equal protection of the law.

* * *

IV. *Conclusion.*

For these reasons, the order of the District Court dismissing appellee's indictment, on the basis of its opinion holding 16 D.C.Code § 2301(3)(A) unconstitutional as an arbitrary legislative classification and as a negation of the presumption of innocence, is accordingly reversed and the case remanded for trial.

Reversed and remanded.

J. SKELLY WRIGHT, CIRCUIT JUDGE, dissenting:

As a matter of abstract legal analysis, the opinion of my brethren might appear to some degree persuasive. But we do not sit to decide questions in the abstract, and we are not writing on a clean slate. In 1966 the Supreme Court spoke clearly and specifically

---

[23] United States v. Verra, 203 F.Supp. 87, 91 (S.D.N.Y.1962) (footnote omitted); accord, Ramirez v. United States, 238 F.Supp. 763, 764 (S.D.N.Y.1965).

about this area. See Kent v. United States, 383 U.S. 541, 86 S.Ct. 1045, 16 L.Ed.2d 84 (1966). It held, in unmistakable terms, that before a child under 18 can be tried in adult court the Constitution requires a hearing "sufficient in the particular circumstances to satisfy the basic requirements of due process and fairness * * *." Id. at 553, 86 S.Ct. at 1053.[24] I had not supposed that it was within our power as a lower federal court to change this mandate. Nor had I imagined that Congress could "overrule" this constitutional decision by a simple statutory enactment. Yet the majority holds that whereas before passage of the Court Reform Act of 1970 the Constitution required a hearing, after its passage the Constitution requires no such thing. While I must confess that this display of judicial legerdemain leaves me properly dazzled and mystified, I cannot quite persuade myself that the rabbit has really emerged from the hat. I would therefore hold that appellee is entitled to a hearing with counsel and a statement of reasons before he can be charged and tried as an adult.

I

From the majority's discussion of the statute's legislative history, one might assume that the definition of "child" in 16 D.C.Code § 2301(3)(A) (Supp. V. 1972) has remained unchanged from earliest times or that the story of how it took its present form is uninteresting and irrelevant. In fact, 16 D.C.Code § 2301(3)(A) is a fairly recent addition to the Code and its legislative history has a direct bearing on the proper resolution of this case.

Before 1970 the District of Columbia Code defined "child" as "a person under 18 years of age." See 16 D.C.Code § 2301 (1967). 11 D.C.Code § 1551(a)(1) (1967), in turn, granted "original and exclusive jurisdiction" to the Juvenile Court for the trial of children as defined in 16 D.C.Code § 2301. Thus initially any person under the age of 18 was to be tried in Juvenile Court. It did not necessarily follow, however, that such a trial always took place. Under the provisions of 11 D.C.Code § 1553 (1967), the Juvenile Court was permitted to "waive" jurisdiction over a child 16 years of age or older who was charged with a felony or over any child charged with a crime punishable by death or life imprisonment. While such a waiver was to be preceded by a "full investigation," the statute on its face prescribed no standards governing the waiver determination. In practice, the "full investigation" frequently proved cursory in nature, * * * although the procedural protections surrounding it were gradually expanded under the proddings of this court. See, e.g., Watkins v. United States, 119 U.S.App.D.C. 409, 343 F.2d 278 (1964) (juvenile entitled to access to his social records during waiver proceedings); Black v. United States, 122 U.S.App.D.C. 393, 355 F.2d 104 (1965) (juvenile entitled to counsel at waiver proceedings).

[24] In my judgment, nothing better illustrates my brethren's fundamental misunderstanding of the issues presented in this case than their failure to consider *Kent* in the body of the opinion for the court.

Matters stood at this point when, in 1966, the Supreme Court considered the statute in its landmark *Kent* decision. The Court began its analysis by observing that the waiver decision was vitally important to the accused—that, indeed, it could potentially mean the difference between a few years confinement and a death penalty.

* * *

In light of the obviously crucial nature of these rights, the Court affirmed the *Black-Watkins* requirements of access to social records and assistance of counsel during waiver proceedings. But it also held that the statute, when "read in the context of constitutional principles relating to due process and the assistance of counsel," 383 U.S. at 557, 86 S.Ct. at 1055, required more. Specifically, the juvenile was "entitled to a hearing *   *   * and to a statement of reasons for the Juvenile Court's decision." Ibid. This was because "there is no place in our system of law for reaching a result of such tremendous consequences without ceremony—without hearing, without effective assistance of counsel, without a statement of reasons. It is inconceivable that a court of justice dealing with adults, with respect to a similar issue, would proceed in this manner. It would be extraordinary if society's special concern for children, as reflected in the District of Columbia's Juvenile Court Act, permitted this procedure." 383 U.S. at 554, 86 S.Ct. at 1053.

Thus during the period immediately after *Kent* juveniles were afforded a wide range of procedural rights in connection with waiver proceedings. So matters stood until 1970 when, in conjunction with sweeping legislation to reform the District of Columbia judicial system, Congress made some innocuous sounding changes in the Juvenile Court's jurisdiction. The new legislation retained the basic waiver mechanism, although the statute now explicitly provided for a hearing and a statement of reasons and established some standards to guide the judge in making the waiver decision. See 16 D.C.Code § 2307 (Supp. V 1972). Similarly, the new statute continued to grant "exclusive jurisdiction" to the Family Court for "proceedings in which a child, as defined in section 16–2301, is alleged to be delinquent *   *   *." 11 D.C.Code § 1101(13) (Supp. V 1972). But whereas previously a "child" had been defined to include all persons 18 years of age or younger, the new 16 D.C.Code § 2301 excepted from the definition "an individual who is sixteen years of age or older and *   *   * charged by the United States Attorney with (i) murder, forcible rape, burglary in the first degree, robbery while armed, or assault with intent to commit any such offense, or (ii) an offense listed in clause (i) and any other offense properly joinable with such an offense." 16 D.C.Code § 2301(3)(A) (Supp. V 1972).

As a moment's reflection makes clear this so-called "definition" in fact establishes a second, parallel waiver procedure whereby a juvenile can be transferred from the Family Division to adult court. If the Government chooses, it may institute waiver proceedings in Family Court and attempt to convince the judge that under the standards enunciated in the Act the child could more appropriately be tried in adult court. It would be surprising if this procedure were much utilized in cases covered by 16 D.C.Code § 2301(3)(A), however, since under it the Government must observe the procedural rules mandated by *Kent.* Moreover, there is always the possibility that the Government will not carry its burden before the Family Court judge, in which case the waiver attempt would fail.

These risks and inconveniences can be avoided by following the second alternative. If the prosecutor simply charges the juvenile with one of the enumerated offenses, the juvenile ceases to be a "child" under 16 D.C.Code § 2301(3)(A) and, hence, the Family Court is automatically divested of jurisdiction.[25] Thus if the prosecutor follows the second alternative the waiver decision becomes his alone, and he is permitted to make it without the encumbrance of a hearing, the requirement that he state reasons, the inconvenience of bearing the burden of proof, or the necessity of appointing counsel for the accused.

I think it obvious that this second procedure was written into the Act in order to countermand the Supreme Court's decision in *Kent* as well as this court's rulings in *Watkins* and *Black.* Indeed, the House Committee primarily responsible for drafting the provision virtually admitted as much. The Committee Report explains 16 D.C.Code § 2301(3)(A) as follows:

> "Because of the great increase in the number of serious felonies committed by juveniles *and because of the substantial difficulties in transferring juvenile offenders charged with serious felonies to the jurisdiction of the adult court under present law,* provisions are made in this subchapter for a better mechanism for separation of the violent youthful offender and recidivist from the rest of the juvenile community."

H.Rep. 91–907, 91st Cong., 2d Sess., at 50 (1970). (Emphasis added.) While the surface veneer of legalese which encrusts this explanation need fool no one, a simultaneous translation into ordinary English might, perhaps, prove helpful. The "substantial difficulties * * * under present law" to which the Committee coyly refers are, of course, none other than the constitutional rights explicated in the *Kent* decision. And the "better mechanism" which the Committee proposes is a system for running roughshod over those rights in a

---

[25] I think the legislative history of 16 D.C.Code § 2301(3)(A) makes it abundantly plain that the section was intended to provide a parallel waiver procedure. See, e.g., H.Rep. 91–907, 91st Cong., 2d Sess., at 50 (1970):

"Present law provides that a child age 16 and older who is charged with a felony may be transferred to adult court. Under the definitions in this bill, a person, 16 years of age or older, who is charged by the United States attorney with an enumerated violent crime is automatically subject to the jurisdiction of the adult court. However, if the United States Attorney declines to prosecute for the felony, the arresting officer will take such action as necessary to place the case within the jurisdiction of the Family Division. The case may not thereafter be transferred to the Criminal Division for adult treatment."

manner which is unlikely to encourage those of us still committed to constitutionalism and the rule of law.[26]

This blatant attempt to evade the force of the *Kent* decision should not be permitted to succeed. The result in *Kent* did not turn on the particular wording of the statute involved or on the particular waiver mechanism there employed. Rather, as the Court itself made clear, the rights expounded in *Kent* are fundamental and immutable. "The right to representation by counsel is not a formality. It is not a grudging gesture to a ritualistic requirement. It is of the essence of justice." 383 U.S. at 561, 86 S.Ct. at 1057. I must confess, therefore, that I find myself unable to approach the majority's elaborate argumentation with an entirely open mind. As one who has long believed that our Constitution prohibits abrogations of due process "whether accomplished ingeniously or ingenuously," Smith v. Texas, 311 U.S. 128, 132, 61 S.Ct. 164, 85 L.Ed. 84 (1940), I react with a good deal of skepticism to an argument which supposes that "the essence of justice" can be defeated by a juggling of the definition of juvenile or a minor modification of Family Court jurisdiction. Nonetheless, I am willing to meet the majority on its own ground, since I am convinced that when its arguments are closely examined they must inevitably fall of their own weight.

II

I take it that my brethren and I begin our analysis of 16 D.C. Code § 2301(3)(A) with a common premise: nothing in the Constitution prevents Congress from shifting the waiver decision from the Family Court judge to the United States Attorney or from establishing a supplemental waiver proceeding before the United States Attorney to complement the Family Court proceeding. There may be some decisions which are so peculiarly judicial in nature that they may not be transferred to an executive officer without running afoul of the Constitution. See Coolidge v. New Hampshire, 403 U.S. 443, 91 S.Ct. 2022, 29 L.Ed.2d 564 (1971). Cf. Crowell v. Benson, 285 U.S. 22, 54–63, 52 S.Ct. 285, 76 L.Ed. 598 (1932). But, as the many cases cited by the majority demonstrate, this decision is simply not one of them.

* * *

[26] Normally, of course, it is the duty of a court to presume that Congress legislates with the Constitution in mind. See United States v. Rumely, 345 U.S. 41, 45, 73 S.Ct. 543, 97 L.Ed. 770 (1953). But surely there are limits beyond which this principle cannot be stretched. Cf. King v. Smith, 392 U.S. 309, 334–335, 88 S.Ct. 2128, 20 L.Ed.2d 1118 (1968) (Mr. Justice Douglas, concurring). One can glean something of the atmosphere in which this legislation was drafted by reading the introduction to the House Committee Report:

"Your Committee is not aware of any period in the Capital's history when crime was so rampant as now, when the police have been so shackled, when prosecutors because of technicalities, and courts because of unrealistic philosophies, and failure to go full speed ahead, have contributed to a major breakdown of law enforcement, and there has been such shocking failure in large part of the machinery of justice to bring to punishment admitted murderers, rapists and others guilty of aggravated assaults and robberies. This is a crime infested city; let there be no ignoring that fact!"

H.Rep. 91–907, supra note 2, at 3.

It should be readily apparent, however, that this observation does little to advance the argument. The issue in this case is not *whether* the prosecutor should be permitted to make waiver decisions, but rather *how* he should go about making those decisions.[27] Put slightly differently, the question is whether the shift in decision making responsibility from the court to the prosecutor eliminates the need for the procedural rights expounded in *Kent*. I would, of course, answer that question "no." The transfer of the waiver decision from the neutral judge to the partisan prosecutor increases rather than diminishes the need for due process protection for the child. In answering the question "yes" the Government and the majority here rely on essentially three lines of argument. Although these contentions are interrelated, for purposes of analysis they are best addressed *seriatim*.

A

' The Government first argues that the *Kent* decision should be limited to situations in which the Government attempts to retract some pre-existing right, and that this is not such a situation. One gets a hint, I think, as to the merit of this argument from the fact that the majority barely mentions it in its otherwise eclectic defense of the statutory scheme. Nonetheless, since it is the contention chiefly relied upon by the Government and most forcefully pressed at oral argument, I think it deserves a few words of rebuttal.

As the Government reads *Kent,* its holding is restricted to cases where the Family Court has exclusive jurisdiction *ab initio* and the prosecutor attempts to wrest this jurisdiction from it. After passage of the Court Reform Act, it is argued, the Family Court is no longer vested with exclusive jurisdiction over persons between 16 and 18 who are suspected of committing serious felonies. Rather, the Government contends, this jurisdiction is now concurrent, and the United States Attorney is vested with the authority to determine the forum in which to proceed. Since there is no longer a pre-existing right to juvenile treatment, there is no longer a necessity to observe the

[27] Once this distinction is grasped, it becomes plain that virtually every decision cited by the majority is inapposite to the issues in this case. The majority relies exclusively on cases holding that the prosecutor may constitutionally make waiver decisions, e.g., DeBacker v. Sigler, 185 Neb. 352, 175 N.W.2d 912 (1970), appeal dismissed, 403 U.S. 926, 91 S.Ct. 2258, 29 L.Ed.2d 706 (1971), or on cases holding that except in extreme situations prosecutorial discretion is not to be disturbed, e.g., Oyler v. Boles, 368 U.S. 448, 82 S.Ct. 501, 7 L.Ed.2d 446 (1962); United States v. Cox, 5 Cir., 342 F.2d 167, cert. denied, 381 U.S. 935, 85 S.Ct. 1767, 14 L.Ed.2d 700 (1965). My brethren fail to cite a single case where a prosecutorial waiver decision was challenged on the ground that the prosecutor failed to follow proper procedures before making the decision. So far as I have been able to determine, there is no such case. The only possible exception to this blanket statement is Gentry v. Neil, E.D. Tenn., 310 F.Supp. 791 (1970), where a federal district judge rejected a *habeas corpus* petitioner's claim that he was entitled to a hearing before an adult court could assert jurisdiction over him. A careful reading of that case, however, makes clear that the petitioner was asserting a constitutional right to a preliminary hearing *by the juvenile court* before waiver could be effected. See 310 F.Supp. at 792. The petitioner did not challenge, and the court did not decide, the constitutional validity of the procedure used by the *prosecutor* in deciding to try the case in adult court.

procedural formalities which, under *Kent,* must accompany divestiture of such a right.

Despite the superficial plausibility of this argument, I think it plainly fallacious. In the first place, I can find nothing in *Kent* which speaks to Platonic distinctions between divestiture of an existing right and failure to grant a right not already in existence. *Kent* rested, not on some fine point of metaphysics, but on the crucially important distinction between the treatment afforded children in an adult court and that granted them in Family Court. * * * Of course, that distinction is just as important whether the selection of the adult forum is spoken of as the divestiture of an existing, exclusive juvenile jurisdiction or as the initial choice of a concurrent adult jurisdiction. In either case, the consequences to the child are precisely the same and, hence, the procedural protections should be identical.

Moreover, even if one excepts the dubious vestiture-divestiture distinction as relevant, the Government's argument simply does not fit the contours of the statute. It is not true that the United States Attorney's decision to proceed in adult court negates no pre-existing right or that the Family Court lacks exclusive jurisdiction *ab initio.* In fact, the basic jurisdictional statute remains, for our purposes, unchanged since the Supreme Court's decision in *Kent.* Now, as then, the Juvenile Court is in terms granted *exclusive* jurisdiction over all children as defined in 16 D.C.Code § 2301. *Compare* 11 D.C. Code § 1551(a)(1) (1967) *with* 11 D.C.Code § 1101(13) (Supp. V 1972). True, the definition of child contained in 16 D.C.Code § 2301 has now been modified. But under the new definition, a suspected juvenile remains a child until he is charged with an enumerated offense by the United States Attorney.[28] It follows that under 11 D.C.Code § 1101 the Family Court retains exclusive jurisdiction until the United States Attorney ends the defendant's status as a child by charging him with an enumerated crime. Thus the United States Attorney's charge acts to divest the Juvenile Court of its pre-existing exclusive jurisdiction in precisely the same manner as does the juvenile judge's waiver

---

[28] Although the Government contests this point, a careful examination of the statute leaves no doubt as to its validity. The statute begins by defining a child as "an individual who is under 18 years of age." However, it then excepts from this definition individuals "charged by the United States attorney" with certain enumerated offenses. Obviously, a youth who has not yet been charged does not fall within this exception and, hence, remains a "child" until the charging decision is made.

This legislative arrangement leads, in turn, to an interesting quirk in the statute which has apparently gone unnoticed by both the Government and appellee. 16 D.C.Code § 2302(a) (Supp. V 1972) provides: "If it appears to a[n adult] court, during the pendency of a criminal charge and before the time when jeopardy would attach in the case of an adult, that a minor defendant was a child *at the time of an alleged offense,* the court shall forthwith transfer the charge against the defendant, together with all papers and documents connected therewith, to the [Family] Division." (Emphasis added.) Obviously, the defendant fits within the 16 D.C.Code § 2301 definition of a child "at the time of the alleged offense" unless *at that time* he had been charged with one of the enumerated offenses in conjunction with some unrelated proceeding. It follows that even under the majority's decision appellee may be able to secure a 16 D.C.Code § 2302(a) transfer to the Family Division.

decision.[29] Since the divestiture is the same, the procedural rights accompanying it should be the same, and we need look no farther than *Kent* to determine what those rights are.

B

The majority wisely eschews substantial reliance on the Government's divestiture argument to distinguish *Kent*. But in its stead my brethren adopt two other arguments which, to me at least, seem equally unconvincing. First, the majority seems to contend that *Kent* is inapposite because it applied to a judicial decision, whereas 16 D.C.Code § 2301 contemplates a prosecutorial decision. Thus the majority apparently concedes, as it must, that *Kent* continues to guarantee procedural rights when the waiver is effected by a judge. * * * But these rights do not attach when the same decision is made by a prosecutor, apparently because "the United States Attorney's decision * * * marks only the beginning of the process of adjudication of appellee's guilt, a process marked by the presence of all the traditional protections of procedural due process, followed by the extraordinarily liberal rehabilitation provisions of the Federal Youth Corrections Act." * * * This argument will not stand analysis.[30] The decision by a juvenile judge or by the United States Attorney to treat the child as an adult for prosecution purposes marks the beginning of precisely the same process of adjudication. And it cannot be doubted that the United States Attorney is certainly a less disinterested decision maker than the Juvenile Court judge. It would seem then that, in order to compensate for lack of neutrality, *compare* Shadwick v. City of Tampa, 407 U.S. 345, 92 S.Ct. 2119, 32 L.Ed.2d 783 (1972), *with* Coolidge v. New Hampshire, supra, procedural niceties should be *more* rather than less carefully observed when the prosecutor is the decision maker.

As long ago as 1935 the Supreme Court was presented with an argument that "the acts or omissions of the prosecuting attorney can [never] * * * amount either to due process of law or to a denial of due process of law." Mooney v. Holohan, 294 U.S. 103, 111–112, 55 S.Ct. 340, 341, 79 L.Ed. 791 (1935). That contention was rejected in no uncertain terms. "Without attempting at this time to deal with the question at length we deem it sufficient for the present purpose to say that we are unable to approve this narrow view of the requirement of due process. That requirement, in safeguarding the

[29] This interpretation of the statute is buttressed by the administrative practice of the D.C. police and corrections officials who, according to uncontested assertions in appellee's supplemental memoranda and affidavits, uniformly treat an arrested juvenile as a child until the U.S. Attorney divests him of that status by charging him with an enumerated offense.

[30] To the extent that it is premised on the assumption that "all the traditional protections of procedural due process" compensate for the lack of an initial *Kent* hearing, the argument simply has no basis in fact. The traditional due process guarantees surrounding trial may assure a fair determination of guilt or innocence, but they do nothing to assure a fair choice between juvenile and adult procedures. That choice is made long before the trial begins in the privacy of the prosecutor's office. * * *

liberty of the citizen against deprivation through the action of the State, embodies the fundamental conceptions of justice which lie at the base of our civil and political institutions." 294 U.S. at 112, 55 S.Ct. at 341. In light of all that has occurred since *Mooney* * * * it is surprising to say the least to see resurrected the notion that conduct which has "no place in our system of law" when engaged in by a judge, * * * is magically transformed into all the process which is due when engaged in by a prosecutor.

It should be clear, then, that the test for when the Constitution demands a hearing depends not on which government official makes the decision, but rather on the importance of that decision to the individual affected. "The extent to which procedural due process must be afforded * * * is influenced by the extent to which [an individual] may be 'condemned to suffer grievous loss.'" Goldberg v. Kelly, 397 U.S. 254, 262–263, 90 S.Ct. 1011, 1017, 25 L.Ed.2d 287 (1970). The test is not a precise one, and reasonable men may differ as to its application in close cases, but at least the underlying requirement is clear. "Certain principles have remained relatively immutable in our jurisprudence. One of these is that where governmental action seriously injures an individual, and the reasonableness of the action depends on fact findings, the evidence used to prove the Government's case must be disclosed to the individual so that he has an opportunity to show that it is untrue." * * *

All of these cases involved decision by executive, rather than judicial, officers. Yet in each case the Constitution was held to require a hearing, presumably because "the [individual's] interest in avoiding * * * loss outweigh[ed] the governmental interest in summary adjudication." * * * In *Kent* the Supreme Court weighed the grievous consequences of a waiver decision against the Government's relatively meager interest in summary procedures. In the end the Court struck the balance in favor of fair procedures, and that balance is good enough for me.

The argument for why appellee should be entitled to representation by counsel at his waiver hearing is somewhat more elaborate but, in the end, no less persuasive. To the extent the contention is grounded on the Sixth Amendment right to counsel, it must be conceded that the majority's position seems to have some force. In a recent decision, a plurality of the Supreme Court has held that a right to counsel accrues only "at or after the initiation of adversary *judicial* criminal proceedings—whether by way of formal charge, preliminary hearing, indictment, information, or arraignment." Kirby v. Illinois, 406 U.S. 682, 689, 92 S.Ct. 1877, 1882, 32 L.Ed.2d 411 (1972). (Emphasis added.)[31] Hence, even though *Kent* held the

[31] In fact, only 4 Justices joined the opinion containing the language quoted in text. Four other Justices thought that the principles announced in United States v. Wade, 388 U.S. 218, 87 S.Ct. 1926, 18 L.Ed.2d 1149 (1967), and Gilbert v. California, 388 U.S. 263, 87 S.Ct. 1951, 18 L.Ed.2d 1178 (1967), governed "critical" confrontations between the defendant and the government even if they occurred at a pretrial stage. See Kirby v. Illinois, 406 U.S. 682, 689–705, 92 S.Ct. 1877, 1882–1890 (1972). The deciding vote was cast by Mr. Justice Powell, who concurred in the result only with the cryptic comment that he "would not ex-

waiver determination to be a "critically important" stage of the prosecution when made by a judge, cf. Coleman v. Alabama, 399 U.S. 1, 90 S.Ct. 1999, 26 L.Ed.2d 387 (1970) Sixth Amendment rights may not attach if the decision is made by a nonjudicial officer at a precharge stage of the proceedings. *Compare* Kirby v. Illinois, supra, *with* United States v. Wade, 388 U.S. 218, 87 S.Ct. 1926, 18 L.Ed.2d 1149 (1967). But cf. Escobedo v. Illinois, 378 U.S. 478, 84 S.Ct. 1758, 12 L.Ed.2d 977 (1964).

If that were the end of the matter, *Kirby* might pose a significant obstacle to an extension of the *Kent* counsel requirement to prosecutorial waivers. But it must be remembered that *Kent* was not solely, or even primarily, a Sixth Amendment decision. As argued above, *Kent's* requirement of a hearing and a statement of reasons was premised on the Fifth Amendment guarantee of procedural due process, a guarantee which has nothing to do with "critical stages," or with judicial as opposed to prosecutorial decision making.[32]

Once the right to a hearing is established, it follows, I think, that appellee also has a right to counsel—not because the Sixth Amendment requires it, but because it is necessary to protect Fifth Amendment rights. Thus, in retrospect at least, it seems clear that there is no Sixth Amendment right to counsel during the precharge custodial interrogation discussed in Miranda v. Arizona, 384 U.S. 436, 86 S.Ct. 1602, 16 L.Ed.2d 694 (1966). Yet a lawyer was required nonetheless "not to vindicate the constitutional right to counsel as such, but * * * 'to guarantee full effectuation of the privilege against self-incrimination. * * *'" Kirby v. Illinois, supra, 406 U.S. at 689, 92 S.Ct. at 1882, quoting Johnson v. New Jersey, 384 U.S. 719, 729, 86 S.Ct. 1772, 16 L.Ed.2d 882 (1966). Similarly, it could not conceivably be argued that Sixth Amendment rights attach to welfare termination proceedings, which are not even criminal in nature. Yet the Supreme Court held that there was a right to counsel nonetheless because counsel was necessary to "help delineate the issues, present the factual contentions in an orderly manner, conduct cross-examination,

tend the *Wade-Gilbert per se* exclusionary rule." 406 U.S. at 691, 92 S.Ct. at 1883. Justice Powell's opinion is, of course, subject to a variety of interpretations. However, his refusal to join the plurality opinion might be taken as an indication that, although he believes there is a precharge substantive right to counsel, he "would not extend the * * * *per se* exclusionary rule." Ibid. Cf. Wolf v. Colorado, 338 U.S. 25, 69 S.Ct. 1359, 93 L.Ed. 1782 (1949). On this reading of the opinion, there are 5 votes on the Court for a precharge right to counsel at critical stages, although only 4 are for an extension of the *Wade-Gilbert* exclusionary rule to this situation. Since the waiver decision was held a "critically important" stage in *Kent*, see 383 U.S. at 556, 86 S.Ct. 1045, and since it involves

the exclusion of no evidence, *Kirby* arguably does not preclude a 6th Amendment right to counsel at a prosecutorial waiver proceeding. However, I find it unnecessary to reach a final judgment as to Justice Powell's meaning since in my view there are independent non-6th Amendment grounds for requiring counsel at prosecutorial waiver proceedings. * * *

[32] Indeed, *Kirby* itself makes abundantly clear that, although the counsel requirement of *Wade* and *Gilbert* does not apply to precharge lineups, the *Wade-Gilbert* due process standards are fully effective at this stage. See 406 U.S. at 690, 92 S.Ct. at 1883. See also Stovall v. Denno, 388 U.S. 293, 87 S.Ct. 1967, 18 L.Ed.2d 1199 (1967).

and generally safeguard the interests of the recipient." Goldberg v. Kelly, supra, 397 U.S. at 270–271, 90 S.Ct. at 1022.[33]

I think all the arguments which influenced the Court to require counsel in *Goldberg* and *Miranda* are fully applicable here. "The right to be heard would be, in many cases, of little avail if it did not comprehend the right to be heard by counsel," Powell v. Alabama, 287 U.S. 45, 68–69, 53 S.Ct. 55, 64, 77 L.Ed. 158 (1932), and nowhere is this more true than when the individual presenting his case is a frightened juvenile confronted with the sometimes impersonal machinery of justice.

Congress itself seems to have realized that a waiver hearing would be a mockery without the presence of counsel. 16 D.C.Code § 2304 (Supp. V 1972) provides: "A child alleged to be delinquent or in need of supervision is entitled to be represented by counsel at all critical stages of [Family] Division proceedings * * *." The Senate Committee explained this provision as follows:

> "The proposed section guarantees representation at 'all critical stages' of the proceedings, the concept used in Miranda v. Arizona, 384 U.S. 436 (1966). * * * Further detail is left to the courts, and the statute is cast in terms which will absorb future court decisions without necessitating statutory change."

S.Rep. 91–620, 91st Cong., 1st Sess., at 16 (1969). The citation to *Miranda* indicates that Congress did not use the term "critical stages" in its Sixth Amendment sense since, as argued above, *Miranda* was not a Sixth Amendment decision. Rather, Congress seems to have intended that counsel be provided the juvenile at all stages where critically important decisions affecting his case are made. *Kent* held that waiver proceedings are such a stage, and Congress was aware of the *Kent* decision when 16 D.C.Code § 2304 was drafted. I would therefore hold that counsel is required under statutory as well as constitutional compulsion.

C

Finally, the Government argues that extension of *Kent* to prosecutorial waivers would abrogate the ancient doctrine of prosecutorial discretion. It is, of course, still widely believed that prosecutors have a broad, unreviewable discretion to determine which offenders to charge and what crimes to charge them with, although even this notion is now widely challenged by the leading scholars. See, e.g., K. Davis, Discretionary Justice 188–214 (1969). But it should be readily apparent that usual notions of prosecutorial discretion have nothing to do with this case. The defendant does not ask us to review the substance of the prosecutor's charging decision or to place limits on the scope of his discretion. Bland directs his complaint to the

---

[33] True, the Supreme Court did not hold that counsel must be *provided* to indigent recipients at the pre-termination stage. But this was apparently because "the statutory [post-termination] 'fair hearing' will provide the recipient with a full administrative review." Goldberg v. Kelly, 397 U.S. 254, 266–267, 90 S.Ct. 1011, 1020, 25 L.Ed.2d 287 (1970).

procedures the prosecutor uses rather than to the *merits* of the decision ultimately reached. Reference to the Supreme Court's decision in *Kent* is again instructive. The *Kent* majority recognized that "the Juvenile Court should have considerable latitude within which to determine whether it should retain jurisdiction over a child" and that the court had "a substantial degree of discretion as to the factual considerations to be evaluated, the weight to be given them and the conclusion to be reached." 383 U.S. at 552–553, 86 S.Ct. at 1053. But, the Court continued, this admittedly broad discretion did not give the judge "a license for arbitrary procedure." * * * Similarly, I think it plain here that the prosecutor's broad authority to choose between juvenile and criminal procedures provides no argument for the power to exercise that authority in a manner which does not comport with procedural due process.

The majority's opinion suggests reliance on a broad appeal to prosecutorial discretion, but ultimately comes to rest on the more specialized argument that the prosecutor has unreviewable discretion as to whether or not to grant a hearing. As should be readily apparent, this formulation merely assumes the answer to the very question before us for decision. The assumption is made, moreover, on the basis of flimsy evidence and a fallacious analogy.

My brothers point to "the significance of a variety of other common prosecutorial decisions, e.g., whether to charge one person but not another possible codefendant; whether to charge an individual with a misdemeanor or a felony; etc. * * * Grave consequences have always flowed from this, but never has a hearing been required." * * * With all respect, one could just as easily infer from the lack of authority provided to support this proposition that never has a hearing been *requested*. But even if one assumes, *arguendo*, that a hearing is not necessary in these situations, it hardly follows that a child may be summarily deprived of his right to juvenile treatment without being heard. As the majority itself indicates, there are dramatically real differences between run-of-the-mill charging decisions and prosecutorial waiver of Family Court jurisdiction. A normal charging decision is "only the beginning of the process of adjudication of [defendant's] guilt, a process marked by the presence of all the traditional protections of procedural due process * * *." * * * A defendant has the opportunity to show that he was improperly charged—that is, that he is not guilty—at the preliminary hearing, at the trial itself, and, if necessary, on appeal.

In contrast, the waiver decision marks not only the beginning but also the end of adjudication as to the child's suitability for juvenile treatment. It is well established that, barring equal protection problems, a guilty person has no right not to be charged with a criminal offense. * * * But a "guilty" child may, under certain circumstances, have a right to be charged as a juvenile. * * * The question of juvenile treatment turns not on the issue of guilt, but on such factors as the maturity of the child and his susceptibility to rehabilitation. See Haziel v. United States, supra. These factors, unlike the question of guilt, drop out of the case once the initial waiver decision is made. Hence it is especially vital that the procedures be fair at the one point in the criminal process where these matters are considered. The very fact that the prosecutor's decision is largely unreviewable and therefore final argues for, rather than against, making certain that he has all the facts before him when he exercises his great responsibility.

Nor is the majority on firm ground when it compares prosecutorial waiver to the decision "whether to charge an individual with a misdemeanor or a felony [which] has long determined the court in which that person will be tried." * * * It trivializes the juvenile court system to suggest that it represents merely an alternative forum for the trial of criminal offenses. The Family Court is more than just another judicial body; it is another system of justice with different procedures, a different penalty structure, and a different philosophy of rehabilitation. * * * We play a cruel joke on our children by arguing that the juvenile system is a nonadversary, noncriminal, beneficent instrument of rehabilitation when determining whether criminal procedures are to be required at trial, see McKeiver v. Pennsylvania, supra, while at the same time maintaining that it is just another criminal court when determining the procedures which must accompany waiver.

III

It will not do to minimize or ignore the consequences of the decision reached today. The majority suggests that youths tried in adult court will still receive a measure of protection, since conviction may be "followed by the extraordinarily liberal rehabilitation provisions of the Federal Youth Corrections Act." * * * There is, however, more than a touch of irony in this suggestion. A similar point was made by District Judge Gesell in upholding 16 D.C.Code § 2301 in an unrelated case: "It should be noted that * * * in the event of convictions the extraordinarily flexible provisions of the Federal Youth Correction [*sic*] Act designed to create programs for limited incarceration and effective rehabilitation are completely available." * * * Yet Judge Gesell has also found that large numbers of eligible youths are being denied Youth Corrections Act treatment precisely because there presently are no youth facilities available, and that "[t]he pressures from overcrowding [have resulted] in a complete frustration of the Youth Corrections Act program." * * *

Thus I do not think we can escape the fact that after our decision today there will be many impressionable 16- and 17-year-olds who will be packed off to adult prisons where they will serve their time with hardened criminals. These children will be sentenced, moreover, without any meaningful inquiry into the possibility of rehabilitation through humane juvenile disposition. Sometimes I think our treatment of these hapless "criminals" is dictated by the age-old principle "out of sight—out of mind." Yet there is no denying the fact that we cannot write these children off forever. Some day they will grow up and at some point they will have to be freed from incarceration. We will inevitably hear from the Blands and Kents again, and the kind of society we have in the years to come will in no small measure depend upon our treatment of them now.

Perhaps I should add that I harbor no illusions as to the efficacy of our juvenile court system. I share Mr. Justice Fortas' view that "the highest motives and most enlightened impulses [have] led to a peculiar system for juveniles, unknown to our law in any comparable context. The constitutional and theoretical basis for this peculiar system is—to say the least—debatable. And in practice * * * the results have not been entirely satisfactory." * * * Nor do I believe that a fair and constitutional waiver system would rescue from the clutches of adult punishment every juvenile capable of rehabilitation in a more beneficent environment. As Chief Judge Bazelon has pointed out, "The job of saving the boy who has compiled a long juvenile record and then committed a serious offense after his sixteenth birthday may be so costly, or so difficult even if no cost were spared, that the [waiver procedures] required by statutes cannot but be a pious charade in many cases."

I must admit, then, to considerable uncertainty as to the ultimately proper disposition of a case such as Bland's, given our scarce societal resources, our limited knowledge of juvenile corrections, and the intractable nature of the root problems of poverty and social disintegration. I am certain of a few propositions, however. I am confident that a child is unlikely to succeed in the long, difficult process of rehabilitation when his teachers during his confinement are adult criminals. I am sure that playing fast and loose with fundamental rights will never buy us "law and order": constitutional rights for children won in *Kent,* like other constitutional rights, are protected from "sophisticated as well as simple-minded" modes of revision or repeal. * * * And I am convinced that the beginning of wisdom in this area, as in so many others, is a respect and concern for the individual—the kind of respect and concern which the due process clause guarantees. I would therefore hold that Congress may not abrogate a child's constitutional rights to a hearing, representation by counsel and a statement of reasons before he is charged and tried as an adult.

I must respectfully dissent.

Before BAZELON, CHIEF JUDGE, and WRIGHT, McGOWAN, TAMM, LEVENTHAL, ROBINSON, MacKINNON, ROBB, and WILKEY, CIRCUIT JUDGES.

ORDER

PER CURIAM.

On consideration of appellee's suggestion for rehearing *en banc,* it is

Ordered by the court, *en banc*, that appellee's aforesaid suggestion for rehearing *en banc* is denied.[a]

[a] Separate statements by various judges in support of their votes either to grant or to deny rehearing are omitted.

Three justices dissented from the Supreme Court's denial of the petition for certiorari.

MR. JUSTICE DOUGLAS, with whom MR. JUSTICE BRENNAN and MR. JUSTICE MARSHALL concur, dissenting.

* * *

The District of Columbia Act was modified after *Kent* so as to give the U.S. Attorney the power to remove a juvenile from the statutory category of "child" merely by charging him with a designated felony. The House Report No. 91–907, 91st Cong., 2d Sess., at 50, explains the reason for the change:

"Because of the great increase in the number of serious felonies committed by juveniles and because of the substantial difficulties in transferring juvenile offenders charged with serious felonies to the jurisdiction of the adult court under present law, provisions are made in this subchapter for a better mechanism for separation of the violent youthful offender, and recidivist from the rest of the juvenile community."

The "substantial difficulties" are obviously the constitutional rights explicated in *Kent* and in *Gault*. The "better mechanism" is the use of the short cut employed, *viz:* the discretion of the prosecutor. Two rather large questions are presented and they seem to me to be substantial.

First. A Juvenile or "child" is placed in a more protected position than an adult, not by the Constitution but by an Act of Congress. In that category he is theoretically subject to rehabilitative treatment. Can he on the whim or caprice of a prosecutor be put in the class of the run-of-the-mill criminal defendants, without any hearing, without any chance to be heard, without an opportunity to rebut the evidence against him, without a chance of showing that he is being given an invidiously different treatment than others in his group? *Kent* and *Gault* suggest that those are very substantial constitutional questions.

Second. The barricade behind which the prosecutor operates is that this, like other prosecutions, is committed to his informed discretion, which is beyond the reach of judicial intrusion. Justice Black and I said in dissent in Berra v. United States, 351 U.S. 131, 135, 140, 76 S.Ct. 685, 691, 100 L.Ed. 1013:

"* * * it is true that under our system Congress may vest the judge and jury with broad power to say how much punishment shall be imposed for a particular offense. But it is quite different to vest such powers in a prosecuting attorney. A judge and jury act under procedural rules carefully prescribed to protect the liberty of the individual. Their judgments and verdicts are reached after a public trial in which a defendant has the right to be represented by an attorney. No such protections are thrown around decisions by a prosecuting attorney. Substitution of the prosecutor's caprice for the adjudicatory process is an action I am not willing to attribute to Congress in the absence of clear command. Our system of justice rests on the conception of impersonality in the criminal law."

The Administrative Procedure Act, 5 U.S.C. § 701 et seq., gives the courts power to review "agency action" and to hold it unlawful, if found to be "contrary to constitutional right, power, privilege, or immunity." § 706(2)(B). This arguably is broad enough to reach the exercise of a prosecutor's discretion in a way that violates the standards of due process laid down in *Kent* and in *Gault*.

One needs no reminder that government too can be lawless, that government cannot lead the way in law and order when it is the great malefactor. The Administrative Procedure Act is indeed part of the citizen's arsenal against lawless government. As Kenneth Davis said in Discretionary Justice (1969) p. 210 "* * * under the Administrative Procedure Act judicial review of the exercise of executive discretion is the rule and unreviewability is the exception."

Respecting "the settled judicial tradition" not to interfere with the prosecuting function Kenneth Davis says:

"Is it because the tradition became settled during the nineteenth century when courts were generally assuming that judicial intrusion into any administration would be unfortunate? Is it because the tradition became settled while the Supreme Court was actuated by its 1840 remark that 'The interference of the Courts with the performance of the ordinary duties of the executive departments of the government, would be productive of nothing but

NOTES

1. Pendergrast, age 17, had an altercation with one Perry, which terminated when Pendergrast hit Perry on the head with a baseball bat. Instead of charging Pendergrast with assault with intent to kill as an adult, the prosecutor elected to petition him as a child in Family Court. Two and one-half months later Perry died of his wounds. The following day, the prosecutor charged him with second degree murder in the adult court. To Pendergrast's objection that because Family Court jurisdiction had attached, it could not be divested without a transfer hearing, the District of Columbia Court of Appeals responded:

> Appellant relies principally on Kent v. United States, * * * That case dealt with the construction of the pre-court reorganization predecessor of the present statute. The District of Columbia Juvenile Court Act, as it was then known, was interpreted as requiring a hearing prior to the Juvenile Court's waiver of jurisdiction over a juvenile. *Kent* thus was decided in the context of pre-court reorganization standards for determining when jurisdiction over a juvenile first attached.
>
> Prior to 1970, the Juvenile Court automatically acquired jurisdiction over anyone under 18 charged with an offense, since the term "child" then was defined simply as "a person under 18 years of age." Act of Dec. 23, 1963, Pub.L. No. 88–241, § 1, 77 Stat. 586. Jurisdiction attached to the person of the accused, and continued throughout his minority or until explicitly relinquished by the Juvenile Court. In re Lem, D.C.Mun.App., 164 A.2d 345, 348 (1960).
>
> In 1970, Congress enacted the District of Columbia Court Reorganization Act, which in part amended § 16–2301 of the D.C.Code. The amendment changed the definition of a "child" and, derivatively, altered the scope of Family Division jurisdiction. Section 16–2301(3)(A) now states:
>
>> The term "child" means an individual who is under 18 years of age, except that the term "child" does not include an individual who is sixteen years of age or older and—
>>
>>> (A) charged by the United States attorney with (i) murder, forcible rape, burglary in the first degree, robbery while armed, or assault with intent to commit any such offense, * * *

mischief"? Is it because the tradition became settled before the courts made the twentieth-century discovery that the courts can interfere with executive action to protect against abuses but at the same time can avoid taking over the executive function? Is it because the tradition became settled before the successes of the modern system of *limited* judicial review became fully recognized?

"On the basis of what the courts know today about leaving administration to administrators but at the same time providing an effective check to protect against abuses, should the courts not take a fresh look at the tradition that prevents them from reviewing the prosecuting function? Throughout the governmental system, courts have found that other administrative or executive functions are in need of a judicial check, with a limited scope of review. *The reasons for a judicial check of prosecutors' discretion are stronger than for such a check of other administrative discretion that is now traditionally reviewable.* Important interests are at stake. Abuses are common. The questions involved are appropriate for judicial determination. And much injustice could be corrected." *Id.*, 211–212.

These two questions are large questions and substantial ones. I would grant the petition for certiorari in order to resolve them.

The legislative history of the Act makes it clear that this change was meant to work a substantive contraction of the Juvenile Court's earlier jurisdiction. Congress stressed that:

> Because of the great increase in the number of serious felonies committed by juveniles and because of the substantial difficulties in transferring juvenile offenders charged with serious felonies to the jurisdiction of the adult court under present law, provisions are made in this subchapter for a better mechanism for separation of the violent youthful offender and recidivist from the rest of the juvenile community.

H.R.Rep. No. 907, 91st Cong., 2d Sess. 50 (1970). Additionally, Congress stated that under the new bill,

> a person, 16 years of age or older, who is charged by the United States Attorney with an enumerated violent crime is automatically subject to the jurisdiction of the adult court.

Ibid. Such language further conveys the intention of Congress that jurisdiction over a 16- or 17-year-old juvenile charged with one of the specified offenses is not to be exercised in the Family Division unless the United States Attorney elects not to charge such an accused as an adult. The House Report also states that a "person 16 years or older, charged by the U.S. Attorney with an enumerated violent crime * * * is an adult * * *." Id. at 149.

In an extensive footnote in his brief, appellant raises the question of the constitutionality of § 16–2301(3). In a post-court reorganization decision, the circuit court sustained the Statute's constitutionality. United States v. Bland, * * *. While that opinion is not binding upon us in our interpretation of the specific District of Columbia Code provision involved, we share and endorse the views expressed by the *Bland* majority. Congress may define who is a child for the purposes of the special treatment the juvenile statutes provide, and Congress has chosen to permit the exclusion of persons in a situation such as appellant's from such treatment. We conclude that Family Division jurisdiction attaches only if the United States Attorney declines to prosecute in a § 16–2301(3) case.

Finally, certain facts should be stressed. This is not a case in which the United States Attorney could have elected to charge appellant with murder on July 26, 1972. The opportunity for such action did not arise until 2½ months after the assault, when Perry died. On October 11, the offense charged was different from that which had been petitioned on July 26, both in its elements and in its magnitude. Certainly there was no dilatoriness in the charging process. When Perry's death occurred, the dismissal of the juvenile petition and the filing of the adult charge were accomplished promptly. There was no need for a transfer hearing, and there was proper jurisdiction for the trial of appellant for murder as an adult.

Pendergrast v. U.S., 332 A.2d 919 at 922–3 (D.C.Ct.App.1975).

2. Defendant, age 16, was indicted for arson, and no delinquency petition was ever filed against him. His counsel moved, pre-trial, that the prosecutor be required to seek leave of court as a pre-condition to prosecuting the defendant as an adult rather than a juvenile. The motion was denied and defendant was convicted. The Illinois Supreme Court reversed and remanded:

"The Juvenile Court Act specifies the duties to be performed by an officer who takes a minor into custody. Section 3–2 provides:

'A law enforcement officer who takes a minor into custody without a warrant under Section 3–1 shall immediately make a reasonable attempt to notify the parent * * *; and the officer shall without unnecessary delay take the minor to the nearest juvenile police officer designated for such purposes in the county of venue or shall surrender the minor to a juvenile police officer in the city or village where the offense is alleged to have been committed. The minor, if not released, shall be delivered without unnecessary delay to the court or to the place designated by rule or order of court for the reception of minors.' Ill.Rev.Stat.1971, ch. 37, par. 703–2.

"Section 2–7 of the Juvenile Court Act describes the duties of the prosecutor and the judge with respect to the prosecution of a juvenile under the criminal laws. In 1971 it provided:

" '(1) Except as provided in this Section, no boy who was under 17 years of age * * * at the time of the alleged offense may be prosecuted under the criminal laws of this state * * *.

" '(3) If a petition alleges commission by a minor 13 years of age or over of an act which constitutes a crime under the laws of this State, the State's Attorney shall determine the court in which that minor is to be prosecuted; however, if the Juvenile Court Judge objects to the removal of a case from the jurisdiction of the Juvenile Court, the matter shall be referred to the chief judge of the circuit for decision and disposition. If criminal proceedings are instituted, the petition shall be dismissed insofar as the act or acts involved in the criminal proceedings are concerned. Taking of evidence in an adjudicatory hearing in any such case is a bar to criminal proceedings based upon the conduct alleged in the petition.' Ill.Rev.Stat.1971, ch. 37, par. 702–7.

"The trial court was of the opinion that once the State's Attorney had obtained an indictment, and thus indicated his decision that the juvenile should be prosecuted criminally, the court had no power to interfere with that determination. The majority opinion of the appellate court approved that conclusion.

"We do not agree with this interpretation. The governing statute forbade the criminal prosecution of any boy under the age of 17 'Except as provided in this Section.' The discretion which the statute gave to the State's Attorney to decide in what manner to proceed against the juvenile was expressly conditioned upon the filing of a petition which alleged the commission of a crime: 'If a petition alleges commission * * * of an act which constitutes a crime under the laws of this State, the State's Attorney shall determine the court in which that minor is to be prosecuted; * * *.' (Ill.Rev.Stat.1971, ch. 37, par. 702–7.) The prohibition against criminal prosecution of juveniles continued until the juvenile had been brought before the juvenile 'unless the court in proceedings under this Act authorizes the judge to overrule the prosecutor's determination if the juvenile court judge objected to the transfer of the case for criminal prosecution. The legislative intention that the ultimate determination was to be a judicial one is emphasized by section 2–8, which prohibits law-enforcement officers from transmitting fingerprints or photographs of a juvenile 'unless the court in proceedings under this Act authorizes the transmission or enters an order under

Section 2–7 *permitting* the institution of criminal proceedings.' (Emphasis supplied.) Ill.Rev.Stat.1971, ch. 37, par. 702–8; see People v. McCalvin (1973), 55 Ill.2d 161, 167, 302 N.E.2d 342.

"Because of the failure to comply with the requirements of the Juvenile Court Act, the judgments of the circuit and appellate courts are reversed and the cause is remanded to the circuit court of Cass County." People v. Rahn, 59 Ill.2d 302, 303, 304–5, 319 N.E.2d 787, 788–9 (1974).

3. In People v. Putland, 102 Misc.2d 517, 423 N.Y.S.2d 999 (Crim.Ct. 1979), the court held that a statute requiring the consent of the district court before the minor could be transferred from the adult court to the juvenile court did not violate the doctrine of separation of powers.

IN RE K.W.S.

Texas Court of Civil Appeals, 1975.
521 S.W.2d 890.

KEITH, JUSTICE. This is an appeal from the County Court of Jefferson County at Law No. 2, sitting as a juvenile court, wherein the court waived its jurisdiction over appellant, K.W.S., as a juvenile, certified him as an adult for criminal proceedings, and transferred him to the Criminal District Court of Jefferson County for further proceedings. Tex.Family Code Ann. § 54.02 (1975), V.T.C.A.

Appellant's able appointed counsel, true to the tradition of effective advocacy, has presented the appeal with great care and precision, presenting thirteen points of error. Although we have considered each of such points carefully, we do not find it necessary to discuss each point in detail.

It is necessary, however, for a detailed statement to be made concerning the procedures employed in this instance so that we may have a proper basis for discussion of the procedural problems presented by the appeal. On June 4, 1974, the State filed its "Motion for Detention Order" seeking to detain appellant "pending trial of the above styled and numbered cause." As grounds therefor, the State alleged: "That said child should be detained because he is likely to abscond from the jurisdiction of the Court; further, suitable supervision is not being provided by a parent, guardian, custodian, or other person." The trial judge signed an order upon the same date authorizing his detention "for a period not to exceed ten (10) days, or until other arrangements can be made for said child." [34] Presumably, the orders were entered under the authority of § 54.01, but our record does not include the testimony, if any, introduced at the hearings required under the cited section.

The State filed other pleadings which we will summarize; and, for convenience in subsequent references, we will affix Roman numerals to such pleadings: I. Motion requesting juvenile court to waive its jurisdiction, filed June 4, following the several subdivisions

---

[34] The State filed, and the trial court entered, identical motions and orders upon the following dates, all in 1974: June 14; June 24; July 5; July 15; July 29; August 8; August 20; and August 29.

of § 54.02(f), charged robbery.[35]   II. First amended motion requesting waiver of jurisdiction, filed June 12, charging murder.[36]   III.
Original petition, filed June 14, charging that appellant had engaged
in delinquent conduct by causing the death of Jean Alexander by
shooting her with a gun on June 10, whereby the State sought his
adjudication as a delinquent child. The allegations followed those set
out in § 53.04(d). IV. Motion requesting juvenile court to waive its
jurisdiction, filed June 14, paragraph V charging murder as set out
* * * supra.

In the meanwhile, the trial court ordered diagnostic tests to be
made of appellant and appointed counsel to represent him in the
proceedings then pending.

On August 27, summons issued to the appellant, which was
served on him on August 28, commanding his appearance before the
court on September 3, "then and there to answer the Petition of The
State of Texas * * * wherein the said Petitioner alleges the following facts which he says constitutes the said [K.W.S.] a delinquent
child, to-wit: All as fully set out in accompanying true copy of the
Petition of the said Plaintiff, The State of Texas."

The original summons, an exhibit in our record, shows that this
summons had attached to it the first motion requesting waiver of
jurisdiction (pleading *I*, supra, charging robbery as set out * * *
supra), *and* pleading *III*, supra, charging that appellant was a juvenile delinquent and seeking his adjudication as such.

The summons did not mention that a hearing was to be held on
the State's motion for relinquishment of jurisdiction; the motion for
relinquishment which was attached did not mention murder, although
the petition to declare appellant a delinquent charged murder as the
ground for an adjudication of delinquency.[37]

At the very outset of the proceedings, counsel for appellant
raised the deficiencies in the summons. The Court's remarks in
calling the case are set out in the margin.[38] In answer to the Court's
question, counsel began by stating: "I think there is some confusion

[35] Paragraph III of this motion to
waive alleged: "That the alleged offense
is of the grade of felony, to-wit: That on
or about the *3rd* day of June, 1974, in the
County of Jefferson, State of Texas, the
said [K.W.S.] did then and there, while in
the course of committing theft of current
money of the United States, hereinafter
called 'the property,' from Jean Alexander, with intent to obtain and maintain
control of the property, using and exhib-
iting a deadly weapon, namely, a handgun, knowingly and intentionally cause
bodily injury to Jean Alexander, against
the peace and dignity of the State."

[36] Paragraph III of this motion to
waive alleged: "That the alleged offense
is of the grade of felony, to-wit: That on
or about the *10th* day of June, 1974, in
the County of Jefferson, State of Texas,

the said [K.W.S.] did then and there intentionally and knowingly cause the
death of Jean Alexander by shooting her
with a gun, against the peace and dignity
of the State."

[37] The child had been in detention at
least since June 4; the petition to adjudge him a delinquent had been on file
since June 14, yet the hearing was not
set until September 3. See § 53:05(b)(1),
requiring the hearing to be held not later
than ten days after the petition was filed.

[38] "The Court: Let the record also reflect that the State's attorney is present
and that this is a hearing upon a motion
to certify [K.W.S.] under Section 54.02 of
Title 3 of the Family Code. All right, is
that correct, Counsel?"

in the proceedings." He then mentioned that while he was not surprised at the fact that a certification hearing was to be held, rather than an adjudication hearing, the summons referred only to an adjudication hearing.[39]

Counsel stipulated that "the last time that this was slated" he had been advised that a certification hearing was to be conducted, and that he had ample time to prepare for either type of hearing. Finally, having been asked by the court if he still wanted "to assert your defense that the notice is not proper for the certification hearing," counsel agreed that the child had "ample notice" of the certification hearing. After the Court expressed some doubts as to the validity of the summons, counsel stated, "We'll waive that defect."

By point of error three, appellant contends that the summons was defective and "no waiver of said defect was *properly* obtained from said child"; point four contends that appellant was denied due process of law "on the issue of waiver of jurisdiction because the *child* was never given proper notice of the ultimate facts and specific issues to be confronted during the hearing." We sustain points three and four for the reasons now to be stated.

We hold that the summons served upon appellant did not conform to the mandatory requirements of § 54.02(b); thus, procedural due process was not afforded appellant. In re Gault, 387 U.S. 1, 13, 87 S.Ct. 1428, 18 L.Ed.2d 527, 538 (1967). For, as was said in Kent v. United States, 383 U.S. 541, 556, 86 S.Ct. 1045, 1055, 16 L.Ed.2d 84, 94 (1966): "It is clear beyond dispute that the waiver of jurisdiction is a 'critically important' action determining vitally important statutory rights of the juvenile."

A very recent case by the San Antonio Court is highly persuasive here. In R.K.M. v. State, 520 S.W.2d 878 (Tex.Civ.App.—San Antonio, 1975), the court had before it a summons which notified the minor of a transfer hearing: " 'The purpose of the hearing at the above date and time is to consider waiver of jurisdiction and discretionary transfer.' " No mention was made of the phrase "to criminal court" anywhere in the summons. In a well-reasoned opinion which we follow, Justice Klingeman said:

> "We see no reason not to adhere to the clear and unambiguous provisions of Section 54.02(b). The statute provides that the summons must state that the hearing is for the purpose of considering discretionary transfer to criminal court. The summons here did not do so. We are not inclined to hold that the word 'must' as used in the statute means 'perhaps,' 'maybe,' 'sometime,' or 'substantially.' It is an easy matter to track the

---

[39] In urging the deficiencies in the summons, counsel said: "I direct the Court's attention to Section 54.02, Your Honor, which states that the summons of this particular type proceeding, if this is what the Court is going on today, must state that the hearing is for the purpose of considering the transfer of jurisdiction to the Criminal Court, which this summons absolutely fails to do, Your Honor. And, quite on the contrary, Your Honor, gives the child and attorney for the child notice that it has elected to proceed on its written petition for adjudication."

language of the statute and to do so would not work a hardship on anyone." (520 S.W.2d p. 880)

Holding that the mandatory language of the statute must be followed, the cause was reversed and remanded to the trial court.

We have already noted that the summons in the instant case notified appellant of an adjudication hearing and no mention was made *anywhere in the summons* that the hearing was for the purpose of considering a discretionary transfer to a criminal court.

Moreover, the motion for relinquishment which was attached charged aggravated robbery and appellant was transferred to the district court to stand trial for murder. Thus, in our view, the summons was fatally defective. The waiver of jurisdiction can be upheld only by a valid waiver of the notice and we now turn our attention to the question of waiver.

* * *

[In the omitted part of the opinion the court held that a "waiver" made by counsel alone did not bind the child, and that the appearance of the child, under the circumstances, was not "voluntary" for purposes of finding a waiver.]

UNITED STATES v. J.D.

United States District Court, Southern District of New York, 1981.
517 F.Supp. 69.

SWEET, DISTRICT JUDGE.

On January 2, 1981, three youths, the defendants herein, were arrested and charged with having committed acts of juvenile delinquency, in violation of 18 U.S.C. §§ 5031–42. Specifically, the defendants were charged with the attempted robbery of a branch of the Manufacturers Hanover Trust Company located in the Bronx. Six days later, a four-count Juvenile Information was filed charging the defendants with various acts of juvenile delinquency, including conspiracy, attempted bank robbery, carrying of firearms during the commission of a felony and possession of an unregistered firearm in violation of 18 U.S.C. §§ 371, 2113(a), 924(c) and 26 U.S.C. § 5861(d).

The government seeks transfer of these defendants to adult status and permission to proceed against them by criminal indictment. In conjunction with that motion and as a preliminary step toward its consideration and determination, the government seeks an order pursuant to 18 U.S.C. § 5037(c) committing the defendants to the custody of the Attorney General for observation and study by an appropriate agency on an outpatient basis. The object of the proposed study would be "to ascertain as to each defendant his personal traits, his capabilities, his background, any previous delinquency or criminal experience, his present intellectual development and psychological maturity and any mental and physical defect." The agency would be charged with reporting its findings to the government, to defense counsel and to this court, for use in the hearing on and determination of the issues raised by the transfer motion. That

motion calls upon this court to make findings on certain factors
enumerated by the statute in order to determine whether the requested transfer would be in the "interest of justice." See 18 U.S.C.
§ 5032. Those factors are:

> the age and social background of the juvenile; the nature of the
> alleged offense; the extent and nature of the juvenile's prior
> delinquency record; the juvenile's present intellectual develop-
> ment and psychological maturity; the nature of past treatment
> efforts and the juvenile's response to such efforts; the availabili-
> ty of programs designed to treat the juvenile's behavioral prob-
> lems.

Id.

Counsel for all three defendants oppose the government's motion
for a commitment order. They argue that the statute under which
the motion is made, 18 U.S.C. 5037(c), as the government seeks to
have it applied, is unconstitutional because it would compel the
defendants to give potentially self-incriminatory testimony. They
also challenge the statute governing the transfer proceeding itself, 18
U.S.C. § 5032, arguing, in essence, that it articulates no clear standard to guide the judge in his determination of whether a transfer
would be in the interest of justice. That lack, they allege, works a
violation of due process.

I am not yet called upon to reach a decision on the transfer
motion itself. Because the facts to be developed and arguments to be
presented at the hearing on that motion presumably may relate to
and clarify the significance of the factors set forth in 18 U.S.C.
§ 5032, I reserve decision on the due process challenge to that statute
until consideration of the transfer motion itself.

However, I am persuaded by some of the arguments of defense
counsel pertaining to the Fifth Amendment implications of the government's construction of § 5037(c). Cognizant of my obligation to
interpret congressional enactments in a manner consistent with the
Constitution when such an interpretation is possible, I conclude that
the statute itself is constitutional but that the application sought by
the government here would violate the defendants' Fifth Amendment
rights. Therefore, although I have decided to grant the government's motion for a commitment order, I am imposing certain limitations on the government's reliance on the defendants as sources of
information about themselves, and, specifically, on the government's
use of the information that the defendants provide. Those limitations
and the reasons for their imposition are set forth below.

The government contends that ordering the defendants to submit
to the proposed study would not violate their Fifth Amendment
rights. It argues, first, that a transfer proceeding is not a criminal
case but an "intermediate step, designed to ascertain how the juvenile
should be treated in the interest of justice," and contends that
therefore the Fifth Amendment does not apply to this stage of a
juvenile action. Second, the Government takes the position that even

if the Fifth Amendment does apply, it would not be violated by the proposed study because the compulsion involved would not be used to elicit "incriminatory testimony," as those terms have been interpreted under authorities claimed to be relevant here.   The defense disputes both arguments, claiming, in essence, that they are based on fictions.

The government's argument that a transfer proceeding is only an "intermediate step" is beside the point.[40] Its irrelevance to the issue of whether the Fifth Amendment applies to transfer proceedings is revealed by the conclusion of the Supreme Court in In re Gault, 387 U.S. 1, 87 S.Ct. 1428, 18 L.Ed.2d 527 (1967). In *Gault*, the court ruled that juveniles are entitled to the Fifth Amendment's protection against self-incrimination in juvenile proceedings themselves, despite the non-criminal nature of those proceedings. The court emphasized that substance and not form controls in determining the applicability of the Fifth Amendment to proceedings that are not labeled "criminal," id. at 49–50, 87 S.Ct. at 1455–1456, and found that the Amendment does apply to juvenile proceedings, in part because the defendant's liberty is at stake. The court looked to the purposes of the privilege, and in particular its goal of preventing the state "whether by force or by psychological domination, from overcoming the mind and will of the person under investigation and depriving him of the freedom to decide whether to assist the state in securing his conviction." Id. at 47, 87 S.Ct. at 1454. Both of these grounds support the applicability of the Fifth Amendment to transfer proceedings as well as to juvenile proceedings themselves. The defendants would be open to a far longer period of incarceration if the transfer motion were to be successful than if they were to be proceeded against as juveniles. Their liberty is therefore very much at stake. Withholding Fifth Amendment protection from these defendants during this stage of these proceedings would deprive them of the freedom to choose whether to assist the state. Therefore, under *Gault*, I find the Fifth Amendment applicable to transfer proceedings under 18 U.S.C. § 5032.

The government's second argument raises more complex problems. Relying on a line of cases rejecting Fifth Amendment challenges to compelled psychiatric examinations in connection with defenses based on mental capacity, see United States v. Baird, 414 F.2d 700 (2d Cir.1969), cert. denied, 396 U.S. 1005, 90 S.Ct. 559, 24 L.Ed.2d 497 (1970), and sentencing proceedings, see Hollis v. Smith, 571 F.2d 685 (2d Cir.1978), the government contends that the statements sought to be elicited from the defendants here are neither "testimonial" nor "incriminating," and that therefore the Fifth Amendment

[40] Furthermore, although technically accurate, * * * the Government's position ignores reality. The reality is that the purpose of the proceeding is to determine the fundamentally important question of whether the defendants are to be open to criminal prosecution at all. Thus, though it may not in and of itself be a criminal proceeding, it is " 'a preliminary hearing in a criminal case,' " United States v. E.K., 471 F.Supp. 924, 929 (D.Or.1979); and in fact it is "the essential preliminary step in any criminal prosecution of the juvenile." Id. See generally United States v. Hill, 538 F.2d 1072 (4th Cir.1976) (distinctions between juvenile proceedings and criminal prosecutions).

does not block their compulsion. See generally Fisher v. United States, 425 U.S. 391, 409, 96 S.Ct. 1569, 1580, 48 L.Ed.2d 39 (1976) (Fifth Amendment proscribes "compelling a person to give 'testimony' that incriminates him.") This argument requires a review of the rationale behind the holdings of *Baird* and *Hollis.*

In *Baird,* defense counsel introduced psychiatric testimony to the effect that the defendant lacked the mental capacity to appreciate the wrongfulness of his conduct or to conform his conduct to the requirements of the law by reason of a mental disease or defect. As part of that testimony, the defense offered statements made by the defendant to a psychiatrist during the course of a psychiatric interview. It countered a hearsay objection with the argument that the defendant's statements were offered for the purpose of illuminating and providing a foundation for the psychiatrist's diagnosis, rather than for the truth of the matter asserted. That argument was accepted, then turned against the defense when the government moved to have the defendant examined by its own psychiatrist. The court ordered the defendant to submit to such an examination, but conditioned that order with an evidentiary ruling that allowed the government doctor to testify to those statements made by the defendant that related to the doctor's opinion of the defendant's mental capacity, but not to those statements directly relating to the defendant's income tax situation. That ruling was affirmed on appeal. The Second Circuit analogized the defendant's statements, admitted as they were as "verbal acts" and not for their truth, to real or physical evidence, the compelled taking of which is constitutionally permissible. See Schmerber v. California, 384 U.S. 757, 86 S.Ct. 1826, 16 L.Ed.2d 908 (1966). Subsequent cases have followed *Baird.* * * *.

In *Hollis,* supra, a similar issue arose in the context of a sentencing proceeding. There, the court ordered a convicted defendant to submit to a psychiatric examination in connection with a determination of whether the defendant should be sentenced to a determinate or an indeterminate term. The court rejected a Fifth Amendment challenge to that order, finding that the statements to be elicited from the defendant were neither testimonial nor incriminating. It based its conclusion regarding the non-testimonial aspect of the statements on *Baird* and similar cases, see, e.g. United States v. Albright, 388 F.2d 719 (4th Cir.1968), agreeing that, because of their proposed use as a foundation for diagnosis, the statements were to be considered as akin to real or physical evidence and not as communications or testimony. *Hollis,* supra, at 691. Its conclusion that the statements were not incriminating was also based on their intended use. Because they were not to enter into a determination of guilt or innocence or be utilized as leads to other offenses, the court concluded that these statements were not "incriminating" for Fifth Amendment purposes.

Although *Baird, Hollis,* and the cases that track them are relevant to the issues presented here, they are not controlling because the scope and purpose of the government's intended inquiry far exceeds the purposes of the inquiries engaged in in those cases. Those cases allow the government to compel statements to be used as verbal acts. Here, however, the government seeks to use the defendants not only as sources of diagnostic tools—"verbal acts"—but as sources of factual information of central importance to the determination of the transfer motion. It seeks information about each defendant's "personal traits, his capabilities, his background, any previous delinquency or criminal experience, his present intellectual development and psychological maturity and any mental and physical defect * * *." It appears from the government's papers that it would then seek to use the information supplied by the defendants to supply proof of the factors set forth in 18 U.S.C. § 5032, to be considered by the court in its determination of the transfer motion. Those factors, listed supra p. 70, include not only psychological traits, which, under the rationale of *Hollis*, *Baird* and related cases could be established legitimately through use of the defendants' statements as "verbal acts," but also such things as the social backgrounds and prior records of the defendants. As to those factors, the government would rely on the content of the defendants' statements to supply a factual predicate for a favorable disposition of the transfer motion. In other words, it would rely upon those statements for their testimonial significance. That proposed use differentiates this case from *Baird* and *Hollis*, and calls for a different result.

Furthermore, unlike the situations presented in *Baird*, *Hollis* and related cases in which the courts concluded that the statements were to be used for non-incriminatory purposes, here the statements are sought for a purpose directly relating to criminality. In *Baird*, the court refused to admit statements tending to show the guilt or innocence of the accused, and thereby sought to avoid the incrimination problem. In *Hollis*, the court concluded that because the statements were to be used for sentencing and not for a determination of guilt, their intended use was non-incriminatory. In other cases, statements admitted for the purpose of allowing a determination with respect to the defendants sanity were termed non-incriminatory because the issue of sanity was seen as distinct from the issue of guilt or innocence. See, e.g. United States v. Albright, supra. But cf. United States v. Alvarez, 519 F.2d 1036 (3d Cir.1975) (use of compelled statements to establish sanity, a matter going to guilt or innocence, raises Fifth Amendment problem). In all of the cases just discussed, the term "incriminatory" was used narrowly to mean relating to guilt or innocence. In all of those cases, the defendants were already subject to criminal prosecution. The present situation is different. Here, although it is true that the statements would not be used upon trial to determine the defendants' guilt or innocence, the government would use the defendants' statements to render them liable to criminal prosecution in the first instance. That proposed use calls for a somewhat broader view of the meaning of incrimination, for such use is "incriminatory" in a very practical sense, and a sense of fundamental importance to these defendants. The statute's prohibition against using the defendants' statements in any subsequent

criminal proceeding, 18 U.S.C. § 5032, does not negate that incriminatory effect.

Furthermore, unlike cases dealing with various psychological
defenses, which turned in part on notions of waiver or estoppel by the
defendant who injected psychiatric issues into the litigation, see, e.g.,
United States v. Baird, supra, the present case presents no waiver
question. The government seeks to compel the psychiatric examination; the defendants have raised no psychological defenses, and they
oppose the government's application.

I conclude that as to all areas of proposed inquiry with the
exception of the defendants' intellectual development, psychological
maturity and mental defects, insofar as the government seeks to rely
upon the defendants themselves to supply information relevant to the
transfer motion, the government seeks to compel incriminatory testimony in violation of the defendants' Fifth Amendment rights. Such
use will not be allowed. The commitment order itself, however, will
be granted upon the conditions outlined below.

The government is entitled to an order compelling the defendants
to submit to psychiatric evaluations designed to assess their psychological maturity and intellectual development and to ascertain whether they have any mental defects. As to all other areas of inquiry set
forth in 18 U.S.C. § 5037(c), and all other factors enumerated in 18
U.S.C. § 5032, the government must rely on other investigative
resources in marshalling evidence for a hearing on the transfer
motion. "[O]ur accusatory system of criminal justice demands that
the government seeking to punish an individual produce the evidence
against him by its own independent labors, rather than by the cruel,
simple expedient of compelling it from his own mouth." Miranda v.
Arizona, 384 U.S. 436, 460, 86 S.Ct. 1602, 1620, 16 L.Ed.2d 694 (1966).

It is all but inevitable that in the course of any psychiatric
evaluations of these defendants, the psychiatrists will inquire into the
defendants' social backgrounds, previous delinquency, criminal experience, and other matters. Such inquiry is not prohibited by this
opinion. What is prohibited is use of the defendants' statements
about those subjects, in this or any subsequent proceeding, as proof
of their content, rather than as verbal acts of diagnostic significance
in the psychiatrists' evaluations of the defendants' psychological
maturity, intellectual development, and possible mental defects. This
distinction precludes the use of the defendants' statements for their
testimonial significance, and requires the government to rely on other
sources of information and proof in the more biographical areas of
inquiry.

The government suggests in its papers that as to one of the
proposed areas of inquiry, the defendants' "previous delinquency or
criminal experience," the relevant records are unavailable to it because of the statute's prohibition against fingerprinting or
photographing juvenile defendants without the written consent of the
judge. 18 U.S.C. § 5038(d)(1). The government has not applied for
court consent to such processing here, nor has such consent been

denied. Any argument based on the supposed necessity of relying on the defendants as the sole available sources of the information sought must therefore fail. Cf. United States v. Cohen, 530 F.2d 43, 48 (5th Cir.), cert. denied, 429 U.S. 855, 97 S.Ct. 149, 50 L.Ed.2d 130 (1976) (without compelled psychiatric examination in case in which defense of insanity is raised, the government will lack a satisfactory method of meeting the defendant's proof on the issue of sanity). As to the remaining proposed areas of inquiry, other sources of information must be explored.

The language of the statute is not inconsistent with this determination. 18 U.S.C. § 5037(c) allows the court to order an accused juvenile committed to the custody of the Attorney General for "observation and study by an appropriate agency," and requires that agency to study and report on the enumerated factors. It does not state that the agency is to rely on the juvenile himself for all relevant information, and nothing in the overall statutory scheme requires such an interpretation. § 5032 says nothing about the source or form of proof to be adduced by the government and considered by the court in regard to the factors to be considered on the transfer motion. I therefore reach the conclusions set forth above regarding the permissible scope of the agency's and the prosecutor's use of the juvenile's own statements, in order to construe the statute in a manner consistent with the Constitution.

Finally, in order to safeguard the defendants' Fifth Amendment rights, the government must take stringent steps to ensure that no impermissible use of statements made by these defendants during psychiatric interviews is made. The measures to be taken toward that end properly extend beyond the statute's prohibition against the use of such statements in subsequent criminal prosecutions, see 18 U.S.C. § 5032, for that alone does not adequately protect against Fifth Amendment deprivations. The Government may compel speech for diagnostic use, but it could not force the defendants to supply either incriminatory testimony, see *Fisher*, supra, or investigative leads, see generally Kastigar v. United States, 406 U.S. 441, 92 S.Ct. 1653, 32 L.Ed.2d 212 (1972) (government may not rely on immunized testimony as investigative resource). Therefore, it must not use the statements to be compelled here for those other purposes. In order to ensure that the use of these statements is confined to the constitutional purposes for which they will be compelled, the Government should keep all records pertaining to the psychiatric interviews separate from its other investigatory files, and prevent the use of any of the information obtained during those interviews in the investigation or prosecution of any matters, including the present and all subsequent proceedings, concerning these defendants. Most immediately, these statements must not be used by the agency to which these juveniles are now committed for study in connection with that agency's investigation of the non-psychological factor to be explored. Agency employees charged with those areas of investigation are to have no access to the psychiatric files. The government will have the burden of proving that it has fulfilled this obligation. See id. (to insure that scope of immunity is co-extensive with the scope of Fifth Amendment privilege, prosecution must prove that evidence proposed to be used is derived from a legitimate source wholly independent of the compelled testimony).

Submit order on notice within ten (10) days. This opinion will be sealed, copies will be made available to counsel.

It is so ordered.

APPENDIX

On consent of all attorneys, this opinion is being submitted for publication with the defendants' names withheld.

NOTES

1. In A.D.P. v. State, 646 S.W.2d 568 (Tex.App.1983) the court rejected a contention that statements made during psychiatric testing pending a transfer hearing were not admissible at the transfer hearing unless the juvenile had been given *Miranda* warnings prior to the adjudication. In doing so, the court found Estelle v. Smith, 451 U.S. 454, 101 S.Ct. 1866, 68 L.Ed.2d 359 (1981) (such warnings required before responses could be used at the punishment phase of a [capital] case), inapplicable to juvenile certification proceedings.

2. In State v. Holland, 98 Wash.2d 507, 656 P.2d 1056 (1983), the court held that although such statements are inadmissible at the transfer hearing, they are admissible at his subsequent criminal trial in the absence of evidence that they were coerced or otherwise untrustworthy.

3. A number of courts have held that reliable confessions that would be inadmissible at a juvenile delinquency adjudication hearing for failure to give *Miranda* warnings are nevertheless admissible at a transfer hearing. See Winstead v. State, 371 So.2d 418 (Ala.1979); Marvin v. State, 95 Nev. 836, 603 P.2d 1056 (1979); In Interest of J.G., 119 Wis.2d 748, 350 N.W.2d 668 (1984).

4. In Texas even an alleged involuntary confession is admissible in a transfer hearing. See Matter of S.E.C., 605 S.W.2d 955 (Tex.Civ.App.1980).

IN THE MATTER OF DAVID B.
California Court of Appeals, 1977.
68 Cal.App.3d 931, 137 Cal.Rptr. 577.

POTTER, ASSOCIATE JUSTICE.

In this habeas corpus proceeding, the minor challenges the validity of an adjudication order of September 16, 1976, of the Riverside County Superior Court which was based upon the minor's admissions that he had committed violations of section 10852 of the Vehicle Code (tampering with a car) and section 449a of the Penal Code (arson). The validity of the admissions was attacked upon the dual grounds that the nature of the arson offense was not adequately explained and that the consequences of the admissions were insufficiently explained to the minor, who was not told either the nature of or the possible duration of the C.Y.A. commitment which might result.

After the adjudication in Riverside County, the juvenile proceeding was transferred to Los Angeles County. The minor's motion to return the matter to Riverside County for further proceedings was denied and at a disposition hearing of November 5, 1976, the referee made a disposition order committing the minor to the California Youth Authority. A de novo rehearing before the juvenile court judge was held on December 16, 1976. At this time the court ruled that it did not have jurisdiction to review the determination of wardship made by the Riverside court and thus found the admissions valid. The minor was again committed to the California Youth Authority.

Based on the petition to this court, an order to show cause was issued on February 2, 1977, commanding the juvenile court either to vacate the September 16, 1976 adjudication order and the December 16, 1976 commitment order and "in said matter, hold a new adjudication hearing" or, in the alternative, show cause why a writ of habeas corpus should not issue.

On March 4, 1977, the juvenile court conducted a hearing on the validity of the adjudication order. As a result of that hearing, the court found "that minor's constitutional waivers were defective and that said waivers failed to comply with *In re Tahl,*" and based on such invalidity the court ordered that the September 16, 1976 adjudication order and the December 16, 1976 order committing minor to the California Youth Authority "are vacated and set aside." On said date the court further ordered that a suitable placement order in another proceeding previously consolidated with the instant proceeding should remain in effect and the matter was continued to March 18, 1977, "for 15 day review."

By supplemental petition filed March 9, 1977, seeking a writ of mandate and/or prohibition, minor has called the court's attention to the fact that on March 7, 1977, in respondent court, a new petition alleging the same incidents involved in the Riverside petition was filed, the minor was arraigned on the new petition and the matter was set for adjudication on March 23, 1977. Contemporaneously, the district attorney filed a notice of fitness hearing and the fitness hearing was likewise set for March 23, 1977. The supplemental petition sought to restrain the court from conducting a new fitness hearing upon the basis (1) that the original fitness determination made in the Riverside proceeding, of which no review was sought, was res judicata, and (2) that the relitigation of the fitness question with the potential for increased incarceration should the minor be found not amenable to juvenile court treatment, violated due process of law guaranteed by the Constitution of the United States and the Constitution of California by the chilling effect which it placed upon the minor's right to review the jurisdictional determination.

The juvenile court's order of March 4, 1977, has rendered this proceeding moot insofar as it sought vacation of the September 16 adjudication order and the disposition order based thereon. The entire matter, however, is not moot inasmuch as the juvenile court has not carried out that portion of the order to show cause which specified that upon vacating the adjudication and disposition orders that said court "in said matter, hold a new adjudication hearing." The conduct of an adjudication hearing necessarily implies that the minor is amenable to juvenile court treatment; since January 1, 1976, Welfare and Institutions Code section 707 has prohibited the taking of a plea to the petition until any challenge of the minor's fitness is disposed of. The filing and consideration of a new petition and any consideration anew of the question of minor's amenability to juvenile court treatment constitutes circumvention of rather than compliance with the order to show cause. We must, therefore, consider what order of this court is appropriate to govern the further conduct of the original proceedings which are before this court on the petition for writ of habeas corpus.

The principles governing the propriety of permitting the district attorney to refile and to reopen the question of minor's amenability to juvenile court treatment are stated in the most recent opinion of the United States Supreme Court in dealing with such matters. In *Blackledge v. Perry* (1974) 417 U.S. 21, 94 S.Ct. 2098, 40 L.Ed.2d 628, the federal due process clause was held to preclude state action chilling a defendant's right to review a misdemeanor conviction by trial de novo in the superior court by the prosecutor adding a felony count based on the same incident. In so holding, the court said (417 U.S. at 27–29, 94 S.Ct. at 2102):

> "The lesson that emerges from *Pearce, Colten,* and *Chaffin* is that the Due Process Clause is not offended by all possibilities of increased punishment upon retrial after appeal, but only by those that pose a realistic likelihood of 'vindictiveness.' *Unlike the circumstances presented by those cases, however, in the situation here the central figure is not the judge or the jury, but the prosecutor.* The question is whether the opportunities for vindictiveness in this situation are such as to impel the conclusion that due process of law requires a rule analogous to that of the *Pearce* case. We conclude that the answer must be in the affirmative.

> "A prosecutor clearly has a considerable stake in discouraging convicted misdemeanants from appealing and thus obtaining a trial de novo in the Superior Court, since such an appeal will clearly require increased expenditures of prosecutorial resources before the defendant's conviction becomes final, and may even result in a formerly convicted defendant's going free. And, if the prosecutor has the means readily at hand to discourage such appeals—by 'upping the ante' through a felony indictment whenever a convicted misdemeanant pursues his statutory appellate remedy—the State can insure that only the most hardy defendants will brave the hazards of a de novo trial.

"There is, of course, no evidence that the prosecutor in this case acted in bad faith or maliciously in seeking a felony indictment against Perry. The rationale of our judgment in the *Pearce* case, however, was not grounded upon the proposition that actual retaliatory motivation must inevitably exist. Rather, we emphasized that 'since the fear of such vindictiveness may unconstitutionally deter a defendant's exercise of the right to appeal or collaterally attack his first conviction, due process also requires that a defendant be freed of apprehension of such a retaliatory motivation on the part of the sentencing judge.' [North Carolina v. Pearce,] 395 U.S. 711 at 725, 89 S.Ct. [2072], at 2080, 23 L.Ed.2d 656. We think it clear that the same considerations apply here. A person convicted of an offense is entitled to pursue his statutory right to a trial de novo, *without apprehension that the State will retaliate by substituting a more serious charge for the original one, thus subjecting him to a significantly increased potential period of incarceration.* Cf. United States v. Jackson, 390 U.S. 570, 88 S.Ct. 1209, 20 L.Ed.2d 138.

"Due process of law requires that such a potential for vindictiveness must not enter into North Carolina's two-tiered appellate process. We hold, therefore, that it was not constitutionally permissible for the State to respond to Perry's invocation of his statutory right to appeal by bringing a more serious charge against him prior to the trial de novo. [Fns. omitted.]" (Emphasis added.)

The same considerations apply in the case at bench. " * * * [N]either the Fourteenth Amendment nor the Bill of Rights is for adults alone." (Application of Gault (1967) 387 U.S. 1, 13, 87 S.Ct. 1428, 1436, 18 L.Ed.2d 527, 538.) As in *Blackledge,* here the "central figure is not the judge or the jury, but the prosecutor" who is "upping the ante" by filing a new petition and demanding a suitability hearing thereby ensuring that the minor risk far more serious consequences as a result of his successful review of the original jurisdictional order. Through the prosecutor, the State clearly has retaliated and thereby has exposed the minor to a "significantly increased potential period of incarceration." Such potential is manifest from the fact that the maximum period of incarceration to which a minor can be subjected, assuming C.Y.A. commitment, is different and more onerous in the case of a defendant tried as an adult than it is for persons committed by juvenile court. (Cf. Welf. & Inst.Code, §§ 1769, 1770, 1771.) Further, if minor were tried as an adult, he could be sentenced to prison for the term prescribed by law, a substantially more onerous disposition than permissible in juvenile court proceedings.

Accordingly, a peremptory writ shall issue commanding respondent court to hold a new adjudication hearing in said proceeding No. J 811640 and to conduct such other procedures as may then be required by law.

FORD, P.J., and ALLPORT, J., concur.

B.   CRITERIA FOR THE TRANSFER DECISION

To this point we have been concerned primarily with the strictly procedural requirements mandated by *Kent*—hearing, counsel (with access to the juvenile's social records) and a statement of reasons in support on any waiver order sufficient to permit meaningful appellate review of the decision. *Kent* did not, however, require that any particular set of criteria be used, nor did the *Kent* court speak to the question whether whatever standards are used must be set out in statutory form or, indeed, whether they must be announced in advance at all. *A fortiori* the Court did not tell us how specific the criteria must be, nor—if advance notice is necessary—whether a formal rule of court, or an established practice in a particular court was either necessary or sufficient. The next materials address themselves to what substantive requirements must be embodied in the criteria, however they may be expressed, coupled with an inquiry into methods for making those criteria meaningful in day-to-day application. In *Bland*, the issue was primarily one of who has discretion, particularly whether it may be lodged with the prosecutor relatively free of controls: In the materials which follow concentration is on control of discretion, assumed to be properly located in the juvenile judge.

The student should pay particular attention to Section 707 of the California Welfare and Institutions Code, reproduced below, because it reflects a growing tendency to treat relatively older juveniles who commit serious offenses as better candidates for trial as adults.

TEXAS CODES ANNOTATED—FAMILY CODE—TITLE III
(1972 & 1983 p. supp.)

§ 54.02.   Waiver of Jurisdiction and Discretionary Transfer to Criminal Court

(a) The juvenile court may waive its exclusive original jurisdiction and transfer a child to the appropriate district court or criminal district court for criminal proceedings if:

(1) the child is alleged to have violated a penal law of the grade of felony;

(2) the child was 15 years of age or older at the time he is alleged to have committed the offense and no adjudication hearing has been conducted concerning that offense; and

(3) after full investigation and hearing the juvenile court determines that because of the seriousness of the offense or the background of the child the welfare of the community requires criminal proceedings.

(b) The petition and notice requirements of Sections 53.04, 53.05, 53.06, and 53.07 of this code must be satisfied, and the summons must state that the hearing is for the purpose of considering discretionary transfer to criminal court.

(c) The juvenile court shall conduct a hearing without a jury to consider transfer of the child for criminal proceedings.

(d) Prior to the hearing, the juvenile court shall order and obtain a complete diagnostic study, social evaluation, and full investigation of the child, his circumstances, and the circumstances of the alleged offense.

(e) At the transfer hearing the court may consider written reports from probation officers, professional court employees, or professional consultants in addition to the testimony of witnesses. At least one day prior to the transfer hearing, the court shall provide the attorney for the child with access to all written matter to be considered by the court in making the transfer decision. The court may order counsel not to reveal items to the child or his parent, guardian, or guardian ad litem if such disclosure would materially harm the treatment and rehabilitation of the child or would substantially decrease the likelihood of receiving information from the same or similar sources in the future.

(f) In making the determination required by Subsection (a) of this section, the court shall consider, among other matters:

 (1) whether the alleged offense was against person or property, with greater weight in favor of transfer given to offenses against the person;

 (2) whether the alleged offense was committed in an aggressive and premeditated manner;

 (3) whether there is evidence on which a grand jury may be expected to return an indictment;

 (4) the sophistication and maturity of the child;

 (5) the record and previous history of the child; and

 (6) the prospects of adequate protection of the public and the likelihood of the rehabilitation of the child by use of procedures, services, and facilities currently available to the juvenile court.

(g) If the juvenile court retains jurisdiction, the child is not subject to criminal prosecution at any time for any offense alleged in the petition or for any offense within the knowledge of the juvenile court judge as evidenced by anything in the record of the proceedings.

(h) If the juvenile court waives jurisdiction, it shall state specifically in the order its reasons for waiver and certify its action, including the written order and findings of the court, and transfer the child to the appropriate court for criminal proceedings. On transfer of the child for criminal proceedings, he shall be dealt with as an adult and in accordance with the Texas Code of Criminal Procedure, 1965. The transfer of custody is an arrest. The examining trial shall be conducted by the court to which the case was transferred, which may remand the child to the jurisdiction of the juvenile court.

(i) If the child's case is brought to the attention of the grand jury and the grand jury does not indict for the offense charged in the complaint forwarded by the juvenile court, the district court or criminal district court shall certify the grand jury's failure to indict to the juvenile court. On receipt of the certification, the juvenile court may resume jurisdiction of the case.

(j) The juvenile court may waive its exclusive original jurisdiction and transfer a person to the appropriate district court or criminal district court for criminal proceedings if:

(1) the person is 18 years of age or older;

(2) the person was 15 years of age or older and under 17 years of age at the time he is alleged to have committed a felony;

(3) no adjudication concerning the alleged offense has been made or no adjudication hearing concerning the offense has been conducted; and

(4) the juvenile court finds from a preponderance of the evidence that after due diligence of the state it was not practicable to proceed in juvenile court before the 18th birthday of the person because:

(A) the state did not have probable cause to proceed in juvenile court and new evidence has been found since the 18th birthday of the person; or

(B) the person could not be found.

(k) The petition and notice requirements of Sections 53.04, 53.05, 53.06, and 53.07 of this code must be satisfied, and the summons must state that the hearing is for the purpose of considering waiver of jurisdiction under Subsection (j) of this section.

(l) The juvenile court shall conduct a hearing without a jury to consider waiver of jurisdiction under Subsection (j) of this section.

IJA–ABA Juvenile Justice Standards Project, Standards Relating to Transfer Between Courts (1980) proposes the following standards for making the decision whether to transfer a child from juvenile to criminal court:

2.2 * Necessary findings

A. The juvenile court should waive its jurisdiction only upon finding:

1. that probable cause exists to believe that the juvenile has committed the class one or class two juvenile offense [b] alleged in the petition; and

---

* Reprinted with permission from Standards Relating to Transfer Between Courts, Copyright 1980, Ballinger Publishing Company.

[b] IJA–ABA Juvenile Justice Standards Project, Standards Relating to Juvenile Delinquency and Sanctions 4.2 B 1 (1980) defines a "class one juvenile offense" as an offense punishable by death or imprisonment for life or for a term in excess of [twenty] years, and a class two offense as one punishable for a term of "in excess of [five] but not more than [twenty] years."

2. that by clear and convincing evidence the juvenile is not a proper person to be handled by the juvenile court.

B. A finding of probable cause to believe that a juvenile has committed a class one or class two juvenile offense should be based solely on evidence admissible in an adjudicatory hearing of the juvenile court.

C. A finding that a juvenile is not a proper person to be handled by the juvenile court must include determinations, by clear and convincing evidence, of:

1. the seriousness of the alleged class one or class two juvenile offense;

2. a prior record of adjudicated delinquency involving the infliction or threat of significant bodily injury;

3. the likely inefficacy of the dispositions available to the juvenile court as demonstrated by previous dispositions of the juvenile; and

4. the appropriateness of the services and dispositional alternatives available in the criminal justice system for dealing with the juvenile's problems and whether they are, in fact, available.

Expert opinion should be considered in assessing the likely efficacy of the dispositions available to the juvenile court. A finding that a juvenile is not a proper person to be handled by the juvenile court should be based solely on evidence admissible in a disposition hearing of the juvenile court.

D. A finding of probable cause to believe that a juvenile has committed a class one or class two juvenile offense may be substituted for a probable cause determination relating to that offense (or a lesser included offense) required in any subsequent juvenile court proceeding. Such a finding should not be substituted for any finding of probable cause required in any subsequent criminal proceeding.

CALIFORNIA WELFARE AND INSTITUTIONS CODE
(1984 Supp.)

§ 707. Determination of minor's fitness for treatment under juvenile court law: Investigation and submission of report: Criteria

(a) In any case in which a minor is alleged to be a person described in Section 602 by reason of the violation, when he or she was 16 years of age or older, of any criminal statute or ordinance except those listed in subdivision (b), upon motion of the petitioner made prior to the attachment of jeopardy the court shall cause the probation officer to investigate and submit a report on the behavioral patterns and social history of the minor being considered for a determination of unfitness. Following submission and consideration of the report, and of any other relevant evidence which the petitioner or the minor may wish to submit, the juvenile court may find that the minor is not a fit and proper subject to be dealt with under the juvenile court law if it concludes that the minor would not be amenable to the care, treatment, and training program available through the facilities of the juvenile court, based upon an evaluation of the following criteria:

(1) The degree of criminal sophistication exhibited by the minor.

(2) Whether the minor can be rehabilitated prior to the expiration of the juvenile court's jurisdiction.

(3) The minor's previous delinquent history.

(4) Success of previous attempts by the juvenile court to rehabilitate the minor.

(5) The circumstances and gravity of the offense alleged to have been committed by the minor.

A determination that the minor is not a fit and proper subject to be dealt with under the juvenile court law may be based on any one or a combination of the factors set forth above, which shall be recited in the order of unfitness. In any case in which a hearing has been noticed pursuant to this section, the court shall postpone the taking of a plea to the petition until the conclusion of the fitness hearing, and no plea which may already have been entered shall constitute evidence at such hearing.

(b) The provisions of subdivision (c) shall be applicable in any case in which a minor is alleged to be a person described in Section 602 by reason of the violation, when he or she was 16 years of age or older, of one of the following offenses:

(1) Murder.

(2) Arson of an inhabited building.

(3) Robbery while armed with a dangerous or deadly weapon.

(4) Rape with force or violence or threat of great bodily harm.

(5) Sodomy by force, violence, duress, menace, or threat of great bodily harm.

(6) Lewd or lascivious act as provided in subdivision (b) of Section 288 of the Penal Code.

(7) Oral copulation by force, violence, duress, menace, or threat of great bodily harm.

(8) Any offense specified in Section 289 of the Penal Code.

(9) Kidnapping for ransom.

(10) Kidnapping for purpose of robbery.

(11) Kidnapping with bodily harm.

(12) Assault with intent to murder or attempted murder.

(13) Assault with a firearm or destructive device.

(14) Assault by any means of force likely to produce great bodily injury.

(15) Discharge of a firearm into an inhabited or occupied building.

(16) Any offense described in Section 1203.09 of the Penal Code.

(17) Any offense described in Section 12022.5 of the Penal Code.

(18) Any felony offense in which the minor personally used a weapon listed in subdivision (a) of Section 12020 of the Penal Code.

(19) Any felony offense described in Section 136.1 or 137 of the Penal Code.

(20) Manufacturing, compounding, or selling one-half ounce or more of any salt or solution of a controlled substance specified in subdivision (e) of Section 11055 of the Health and Safety Code.

(c) With regard to a minor alleged to be a person described in Section 602 by reason of the violation, when he or she was 16 years of age or older, of any of the offenses listed in subdivision (b), upon motion of the petitioner made prior to the attachment of jeopardy the court shall cause the probation officer to investigate and submit a report on the behavioral patterns and social history of the minor being considered for a determination of unfitness. Following submission and consideration of the report, and of any other relevant evidence which the petitioner or the minor may wish to submit the minor shall be presumed to be not a fit and proper subject to be dealt with under the juvenile court law unless the juvenile court concludes, based upon evidence, which evidence may be of extenuating or mitigating circumstances, that the minor would be amenable to the care, treatment, and training program available through the facilities of the juvenile court based upon an evaluation of each of the following criteria:

(1) The degree of criminal sophistication exhibited by the minor.

(2) Whether the minor can be rehabilitated prior to the expiration of the juvenile court's jurisdiction.

(3) The minor's previous delinquent history.

(4) Success of previous attempts by the juvenile court to rehabilitate the minor.

(5) The circumstances and gravity of the offenses alleged to have been committed by the minor.

A determination that the minor is a fit and proper subject to be dealt with under the juvenile court law shall be based on a finding of amenability after consideration of the criteria set forth above, and findings therefor recited in the order as to each of the above criteria that the minor is fit and proper under each and every one of the above criteria. In making a finding of fitness, the court may consider extenuating or mitigating circumstances in evaluating each of the above criteria. In any case in which a hearing has been noticed pursuant to this section, the court shall postpone the taking of a plea to the petition until the conclusion of the fitness hearing and no plea which may already have been entered shall constitute evidence at the hearing.

(d) If, subsequent to a finding that a minor is an unfit subject to be dealt with under the juvenile court law, the minor is convicted in a court of criminal jurisdiction of any offense listed in subdivision (b) of Section 707, the finding of unfitness which preceded the conviction shall be applicable to any offense listed in subdivision (b) of Section 707 which is alleged to have been committed subsequent to the conviction. The probation officer shall not be required to investigate or submit a report regarding the fitness of a minor for any such subsequent charge. This subdivision shall not be construed to affect the right to appellate review of a finding of unfitness or the duration of the jurisdiction of the juvenile court as specified in Section 607 at the hearing.

In the Matter of Rickey Dale MATHIS, a child

STATE EX REL. JUVENILE DEPARTMENT OF DOUGLAS COUNTY v. MATHIS

Court of Appeals of Oregon, 1975.
21 Or.App. 740, 537 P.2d 148.

Before SCHWAB, C.J., and LANGTRY and FORT, JJ.

LANGTRY, JUDGE. This is a proceeding in which the district attorney of Douglas County moved that Mathis, age 16, be remanded to adult court. Mathis was then the subject of a juvenile court petition because of an alleged murder and robbery committed by him. The juvenile court ordered the remand and the juvenile appeals.

We can make no better a summary statement of the evidence than that in the following excerpts from the trial judge's findings with only one exception which will be noted later:

"Rickey Dale Mathis is 16 years of age. His birthdate was August 21, 1958. It is to be assumed as a fact Mathis committed the acts charged. (State v. Zauner, 250 Or. 101, 441 P.2d 83 (1968). These assumed facts would therefore be that decedent persuaded Mathis to engage in sexual perversity, in the midst of which Mathis set upon decedent stabbing him a number of times, attempting to beat him with a small hammer, and beating him with a skillet or frying pan, causing decedent's death. Mathis is also alleged to have robbed decedent of money and property (a car).

"*   *   *

"*   *   * Mathis has had, from the beginning of formal schooling, a continuing inability to progress in school in what shall be arbitrarily denominated a normal manner. His principal problem appears to be an inability to master reading, and perhaps spelling *   *   *.

"Mathis has had many advantages. It appears material needs (and at least all reasonable wants) have been more than adequately provided. On the other hand, he is the last of four children in a household wherein the parents and the other three children apparently succeeded easily in the areas he finds troublesome.

"Mathis has not previously been referred to juvenile authorities. He has, however, experimented with some drugs, has drank [sic] alcoholics, he smokes, and uses profane and obscene language. He has on numerous occasions been a truant and a school discipline problem. He has been suspended and was transferred from a 'progressive' school setting to a 'more conventional' school. He has twice been a runaway, the last time ending in the present charge.

"Mathis' problems at schools caused him to be transferred as mentioned and also to be referred for psychiatric help. He received evaluation and treatment by counseling on a weekly basis for about seven or eight months immediately prior to the offense alleged. This psychiatric therapy was given by an experienced doctor who appears to be eminently qualified in his field. The immediate and actual cause of the last runaway is not apparent. Another psychiatrist, engaged on behalf of Mathis, found him not to be mentally ill; however, found, in addition to the aforementioned school problems, that Mathis had a progressive history of temper tantrums, depressions, runaway, truancy, lying, swearing and resistance to authority.

"Paradoxically, Mathis was an active Boy Scout, excelling in achievement and scouting ability * * *.

"* * *

"Mathis has been an exemplary inmate during his confinement in detention. He is reported to have acted with maturity in matters involving custodial problems of other juvenile inmates with whom he has been associated during his confinement. He has been detained in jail areas reserved for juveniles. There is no evidence of association with adult jail inmates.

"Both psychiatrists who testified estimate Mathis will need counseling for three or four years.

"Testimony has been received from Mathis' parents, treating psychiatrist, teachers and other associates. Most of these witnesses favor retention of juvenile court jurisdiction. * * * [I]t appears the fact, that if kept in juvenile court jurisdiction and wardship established, commitment to State Children's Services Division (MacLaren) is, without doubt, the only available and appropriate placement."

The trial judge concluded:

"In the opinion of the court, the motion to remand should and must be granted. The movant's evidence was that which supports the offenses alleged. Almost all other witnesses favored retention of juvenile court jurisdiction * * *.

"It is urged on Mathis' behalf that he has not previously been adjudicated delinquent nor received the services available though [sic] counseling. His behavior pattern, however, is a familiar one. It seems most unlikely that any lack of prior juvenile court counseling service is of any persuasive significance in view of the extended efforts by schools to assist him, as well as the weekly psychiatric counseling he received over at least a seven months ['] period of time. In this regard, Mathis' reaction to 'crisis' (the truth of the charge being assumed) was of a kind and character weighing against retention of jevenile [sic] jurisdiction.

"Mathis is at the threshhold [sic] of maturity. He was a juvenile heretofore; he will not be hereafter. He would, if retained in juvenile court, enter the only facility available to him above the average age of other inmates. From the testimony, it is unlikely he would be retained beyond his 19th year, or, any more than three years. A longer period for any re-adjustment as well as a subsequent period of continued supervision seems clearly indicated. The public's interest cannot be otherwise reasonably recognized. On the other hand, he would, if convicted and sentenced to incarceration in adult court, enter an institution at the lowest age level. The former consideration outweighs the latter.

"There are other considerations. The factual circumstances which would be relied upon for conviction involve the decedent's reputation. Moreover, the offense chargeable carries lesser included offenses so that mens rea, that is, state of mind is very significant. *Indeed, one of the possible alternative results of proceedings in adult court is exoneration.*

"For all the foregoing reasons, the court is of the opinion that the best interests of Mathis and the public can be most properly served by granting the motion to remand." (Emphasis supplied.)

Mr. Graham, a program director at MacLaren School for Boys testified. He supervises about one-third of the boys committed to that institution. He stated that he had four students in his unit who were there because of homicides they had committed. One of them had been "administratively transferred" from Oregon Correctional Institution to MacLaren. Thus, it appears that for a situation like we have at bar, where the juvenile at first may need the type of juvenile care that MacLaren affords, but will outgrow it and may still need more institutional care, and undoubtedly more years of supervision of parole nature if not institutional care, the methods exist for meeting these various needs.

But the variety of the methods are only possible if the juvenile's case is tried in adult court with resultant commitment to the Corrections Division. See ORS 179.473, 179.476(3) and (4), and

420.011.[41] Perhaps, as the trial judge noted, an adult court criminal trial will result in exoneration. But if it does not, the juvenile can be served with his age group peers while still a juvenile if the facts justify it, and with the public still protected by his further confinement or supervision after juvenile age if the facts then justify that approach.

The trial judge thoroughly considered the legal alternatives, the alleged crime and the particulars relating to this juvenile, his welfare and public protection.

We have considered the dissenting opinion and recognize that it takes the opposite side in a close case. However, we feel that it incorrectly views some of the facts surrounding the killing. A tape recording of the boy's confession was heard by the court. It is not in the record we have reviewed. However, Officer Winningham reviewed in his testimony what the boy told him (and presumably it is identical with the taped confession). The boy did not testify. There were no other witnesses to the event. There was nothing in the officer's testimony or any other testimony we have reviewed about the boy's mounting the victim's back. The prosecutor in his opening statement said the stabbing was done with the boy's knife, and this statement was not challenged. There is nothing in Officer Winningham's testimony or any other testimony we have reviewed about a "switchblade knife extending from the victim's trouser pocket."

---

[41] ORS 179.473 provides:

"(1) Notwithstanding any other provision of law, whenever the welfare of the person transferred and the efficient administration of the institutions require the transfer, subject to ORS 179.476:

"* * *

"(b) * * * [A] division may make a permanent or nonpermanent transfer of a person from any institution under the jurisdiction of that division to any other institution under the jurisdiction of that same division.

"(2) A student of a juvenile training school may not be transferred to the Oregon State Penitentiary under subsection (1) of this section. A student of a juvenile training school who has been transferred to another institution may not be transferred from such other institution to the Oregon State Penitentiary.

"(3) A student of a juvenile training school may not be transferred to another institution under the supervision of the Corrections Division unless all of the following conditions are met:

"(a) The student is 16 years of age or older.

"(b) The behavior of the student at the training school is such as to endanger his own welfare or the welfare of others.

"(c) The student continues to receive, at the institution to which he is transferred, training of a type and degree at least as well suited for juveniles as that prescribed by ORS 420.120 or 420.320.

"(d) The consent of the committing court has been obtained after a hearing pursuant to ORS 419.498 [due process juvenile court hearing]."

ORS 179.476(3) and (4) provide:

"(3) An inmate who has been transferred from one of the institutions may be retransferred to that institution or, pursuant to ORS 179.473, to any other institution listed in ORS 179.321 [does not include juvenile training schools].

"(4) The duration of a transfer from a juvenile training school may not exceed the period of the original commitment. Any such individual must, prior to his release, be returned to the juvenile training school for release."

ORS 420.011 provides:

"(1) * * * [A]dmissions to the juvenile training schools are limited to persons between the ages of 12 and 18 years * * *. No child admitted to a juvenile training school shall be transferred by administrative process to any penal or correctional institution.

"(2) * * * [P]ersons under the age of 21 years who are committed to the custody of the Corrections Division [includes OCI] under ORS 137.124 may be assigned to a juvenile training school by the Corrections Division."

Rather, the officer said the boy told him that, when he returned with the oil to the room where the victim was, both were naked, the victim lying face down on the bed,

> "* * * he glanced down and he saw his pocketknife out of the—partially out of his pocket of his trousers that were lying on the floor. He said that he decided that he didn't want to go through with this, that he reached down very carefully and quietly, that he depressed the button on the side of the knife and opened the knife and subsequently started stabbing * * *.

> "* * *

> "* * * [B]y depressing the button he said it was quiet so **Mr.** * * * wouldn't hear anything. He held the button down so there was no click."

From this, we infer that the boy carried a springblade knife, and that under the stress of the situation, and desiring to acquire the victim's money, in a cool and calculated manner he proceeded with the assault.

The trial judge's decision is well buttressed with reason and we agree with it.

Affirmed.

FORT, JUDGE (dissenting).

This case presents the always difficult problem of whether a child should be remanded for trial as an adult. The alleged crime was committed four days after his 16th birthday.

As the majority points out, this boy, not yet in high school, had never previously been referred to a juvenile court. His school difficulties were not of major dimensions and in the six months prior to the crime charged they had greatly improved, as a result of a change in schools combined with weekly treatment by a fully qualified child psychiatrist. Nothing in his prior history remotely hints at violent tendencies.

In State ex rel. Juv. Dept. v. Cardiel, 18 Or.App. 49, 523 P.2d 1057 (1974), we considered a somewhat similar case involving a 16-year-old boy. There the boy was slightly older than Rickey Mathis, was for all practical purposes emancipated, and indeed was living with a girl whom he referred to as his wife, had been regularly employed, and at the time the offense occurred was enrolled in the Chicano Indian Study Center in a carpentry course. He had long been a school dropout. The charge there was attempted murder involving the repeated stabbing in the back of a man who was successfully resisting an effort by Cardiel's older brother to defeat him in a weaponless fight.

Unlike the case at bar, the victim did not die. In reversing the trial court, this court said:

> "Considering the circumstances surrounding the incident, that the alleged victim had Ralph's [appellant's] brother on the ground, which Ralph undoubtedly construed as threatening to his

brother, and considering all other things, we are inclined to think that, regardless of the viciousness of the attack, it was a 'one time thing.' We also consider Ralph's previous lack of contact with authorities, and his mother's testimony that he had been a good-natured and jovial child, one of the babies of the family. Her testimony is obviously prejudiced toward Ralph but it is some indication of a characteristic good nature on his part.

"The record supports a conclusion that Ralph is physically, emotionally and mentally immature for his age. There is definite potential for rehabilitation. In the adult prison system, he would be substantially more vulnerable to physical and sexual assaults due to his size and immaturity. We conclude that Ralph's and the public's interests would be best served by retaining him within the juvenile court system." 18 Or.App. at 53, 523 P.2d at 1059.

Here, this boy, four days past his 16th birthday, had run away from home on what was generally described as a vacation during the summertime. He was enticed into a homosexual situation by a man approximately 40 years of age at the latter's summer mountain cabin and paid $40, ostensibly to perform one and one-half hours' work. While the boy was so engaged, the man induced him to engage in oral sodomy and then sought to persuade him to perform an act of anal sodomy on him. After being sent from the man's bedroom to get some lubricating oil he returned to the bedroom, found the man lying naked, face down on the bed, his clothes still in a heap on the floor. When the boy mounted his back he saw on the floor a switchblade knife extending from the victim's trouser pocket. He reached over, having determined that he would not go through with the demanded act and, apparently repelled by the situation, picked up the knife and quietly opened it, and instead of proceeding to carry out the act of anal sodomy he stabbed the victim repeatedly in the back and, as he turned over, again in the chest. When the victim did not die the boy obtained a heavy frying pan and hammer and beat him over the head, fracturing his skull. After leaving the mountain cabin he later returned, took the man's wallet and car keys and fled in his car. In contrast to the *Cardiel* case where the boy fled the state and had to be returned from Arizona, this boy, even before leaving the mountain forest area, contacted officials and reported what he had done.

Here, the boy was still in school, although he had had a record of truancy and suspension for smoking prior to the school transfer above referred to.

Nothing in this record indicates any prior involvement whatever of a homosexual nature in the boy's life, nor any indication of violence. Like *Cardiel*, this, too, was clearly "a one time thing." Both psychiatrists who testified in this case, the juvenile department personnel, and representatives of the State Training School agreed that this boy was a better candidate for rehabilitation in the juvenile system than in the adult. The two psychiatrists estimated a maximum period of three to four years as necessary to his rehabilitation.

Unlike *Cardiel,* this boy comes from a strong family background. His mother is and has been a school teacher for many years, holding a Master's Degree. His father, a college graduate, is a highly successful engineer and has worked for more than 20 years in a responsible position for a major corporation. His older sister is a registered nurse. One of his two older brothers is a college graduate and the other is now attending college. Thus, unlike *Cardiel,* where the boy was completely emancipated and had no family strengths, this boy's family offers unusual strengths to aid in his rehabilitation. Here the trial court concluded that because of the viciousness of the crime it was unlikely that this boy could be rehabilitated before he is 21. No trained professional in either the social work, correctional or medical fields expressed such an opinion. Nor did anyone recommend that this boy should be remanded to the adult court or committed to an adult institution, or that either would be in the best interest of the public or of the boy.

From my examination of this record I conclude that the state has failed to establish, whether one applies the rule of preponderance of the evidence, clear and convincing evidence or proof beyond a reasonable doubt [42] that it is in the best interests either of the public or of

[42] The standard of proof required to support an order of remand remains today unclear. ORS 419.500(1) requires proof beyond a reasonable doubt "in the adjudicative phase of a hearing where a finding of jurisdiction may result in institutionalization," but otherwise "by a preponderance of * * * [the] evidence." Its 1971 amendment (Oregon Laws 1971, ch. 31, § 1, p. 44) doubtless reflected the mandate of McKeiver v. Pennsylvania, 403 U.S. 528, 91 S.Ct. 1976, 29 L.Ed.2d 647 (1971). ORS 419.533(1)(c) provides only that a remand may be ordered if "the juvenile court *determines* that retaining jurisdiction will not serve the best interests of the child and the public." (Emphasis supplied.)

Neither Kent v. United States, 383 U.S. 541, 86 S.Ct. 1045, 16 L.Ed.2d 84 (1966), nor In re Gault, 387 U.S. 1, 87 S.Ct. 1428, 18 L.Ed.2d 527 (1967), at the federal level, nor State v. Little, 241 Or. 557, 407 P.2d 627 (1965), cert. denied 385 U.S. 902, 17 L.Ed.2d 133 (1966), State v. Zauner, 250 Or. 105, 441 P.2d 85 (1968), nor Bouge v. Reed, 254 Or. 418, 459 P.2d 869 (1969), in our Supreme Court, have dealt with this question. On May 27, 1975, the United States Supreme Court in Breed v. Jones, 421 U.S. 519, 95 S.Ct. 1779, 44 L.Ed.2d 346, a case dealing primarily with double jeopardy in relation to juvenile remand proceedings, said:

"* * * In Kent v. United States, 383 U.S., at 562, 86 S.Ct. [1045], at 1057, the Court held that hearings under the statute there involved 'must measure up to the essentials of due process and fair treatment.' *However, the Court has never attempted to prescribe criteria for, or the nature and quantum of evidence that must support, a decision to transfer a juvenile for trial in adult court.* We require only that, whatever the relevant criteria and whatever the evidence demanded, a State determine whether it wants to treat a juvenile within the juvenile court system before entering upon a proceeding that may result in an adjudication that he has violated a criminal law and in a substantial deprivation of liberty, rather than subject him to the expense, delay, strain and embarrassment of two such proceedings." (Emphasis supplied, footnote omitted.) 421 U.S. at 538, 95 S.Ct. at 1790.

Breed in short reiterates the need for "fundamental fairness" earlier required in *Kent, Gault* and *McKeiver,* but declines to fill in the interstices between the intersections of that reticulated creation. Our own recent decisions shed no light on this question. *See:* State v. Weidner, 6 Or.App. 317, 484 P.2d 844, 487 P.2d 1385 (1971); State ex rel. Juv. Dept. v. Slack, 17 Or.App. 57, 520 P.2d 905, S.Ct. review denied (1974); State ex rel. Juv. Dept. v. Cardiel, 18 Or.App. 49, 523 P.2d 1057 (1974). Since, however, appellant here in his brief asserts only that the state failed to establish its case by a preponderance of the evidence, it is not necessary to reach the question here.

this child that he be remanded to adult court, let alone both of them, as ORS 419.533(1)(c) requires.

Accordingly, I respectfully dissent.

NOTES

1. In In Interest of Hobson, 6 Kan.App.2d 873, 636 P.2d 198 (1981), the court held that uncertainty in the mind of the judge conducting the waiver hearing about whether the juvenile would remain in the hands of Social and Rehabilitation Services until his psychiatric and psychological needs were met was not a proper ground to waive jurisdiction to the criminal court.

2. The student will recall that whether an "insanity" defense is available in a juvenile delinquency proceeding was considered in Chapter 2, supra. In In Interest of L.L., 165 Ga.App. 49, 299 S.E.2d 53 (1983) the Georgia court was faced with a similar problem in the context of a waiver hearing.

It is undisputed that L.L. is a moderate mental retardate with an IQ of 44 and a mental age of 8, who also suffers from schizophrenia which is in remission and is controllable by medication.

There is evidence that L.L. was not receiving adequate and appropriate care, training, education and other specialized services; and that he needs constant supervision and vocational and social training to assist in his own care in the future and to control his inappropriate behavior. The opinion of experts who had examined L.L. was that he should be placed in a mental retardation institution to provide the supervision, education and training he needs.

However, there is also evidence from which it could be inferred that L.L.'s needs could be handled by a combination of non-institutional schooling, sheltered workshop training and close parental supervision. In addition, there was testimony that it would be very difficult to find a mental retardation institution that would take L.L.

Accordingly, we find that there was some evidence to support the juvenile court's determination that L.L. was not committable to an institution for the mentally retarded or mentally ill and that the court did not abuse its discretion in making that determination.

Id. at 50, 299 S.E.2d at 54–55.

SUMMERS v. STATE

Supreme Court of Indiana, 1967.
248 Ind. 551, 230 N.E.2d 320.

PER CURIAM. This matter is before this Court on the petition of the appellee, State of Indiana, seeking a rehearing and reconsideration. We believe that the opinion filed by this Court on June 23, 1967 should be clarified and delineated. We are moved to this position by reason of the import and impact of the opinion in juvenile matters.

*   *   *

The statute, Ind.Ann.Stat. § 9–3214 (1966 Supp.), providing waiver of jurisdiction is as follows:

"If a child fifteen (15) years of age or older is charged with an offense which would amount to a crime if committed by an adult, the judge, after full investigation, may waive jurisdiction and order such child held for trial under the regular procedure of the court which would have jurisdiction of such offense if committed by an adult; or such court may exercise the powers conferred upon the juvenile court in this act (§§ 9–3201—9–3225) in conducting and disposing of such case: Provided, That the judges of the juvenile courts of this state who shall waive the jurisdiction of such child as provided herein may at the time of the waiver fix a recognizance bond for the person to answer the charge in the court which would have jurisdiction of such offense if committed by an adult."

§ 9–3214, supra, is identical in import to that considered by Supreme Court of the United States in Kent v. United States, 383 U.S. 541, 547–548, 86 S.Ct. 1045, 1050, 16 L.Ed.2d 84 (1966) and in such particulars reads as follows:

"If a child sixteen years of age or older is charged with an offense which would amount to a felony in the case of an adult, * * * the judge may, after full investigation, waive jurisdiction and order such child held for trial under the regular procedure of the court which would have jurisdiction of such offense if committed by an adult * * *."

Jurisdiction conferred upon juvenile courts is justified only under the *parens patriae* power of the state. Thus, the statutes must be interpreted to conform to the principles essential to the valid exercise of that power. Where the court's exclusive original jurisdiction extends to children, "the legal obligations due to them" as well as "from them" as the "basic purpose and principle" of its functions, must be adhered to. See Johnson v. State (concurring opinion), supra.

The Supreme Court of the United States in Kent, supra, 383 U.S. at 554–555, 86 S.Ct. at 1954, speaking of the *parens patriae* nature of juvenile court acts stated:

"* * * The State is *parens patriae* rather than prosecuting attorney and judge. But the admonition to function in a 'parental' relationship is not an invitation to procedural arbitrariness."

Because the State is supposed to proceed in respect to a child as *parens patriae* and not as an adversary, courts have relied on the premise that the proceedings are civil in nature and not criminal. It has been asserted that he can claim only the fundamental due process right to fair treatment. Pee v. United States, 107 U.S.App.D.C. 47, 274 F.2d 556 (1959).

In *Kent*, supra, there is a lengthy discussion and criticism of juvenile proceedings in general. Suffice it to say that in a decision on the question of waiver such as presented here, the court held that the determination of whether a waiver and transfer of the juvenile to the criminal processes of the District Court was a "critically important" proceeding. It was therefore declared that the scheme and purposes of juvenile proceedings were to be governed by not-criminal treatment "and the adult criminal treatment (was an) exception which must be governed by the particular factors of individual cases." The court there further stated that courts of appellate jurisdiction should conduct a "meaningful review" of the waiver and transfer proceedings. Review should not be remitted to assumptions. In order to engage in a meaningful review this court must have a statement of the juvenile court's reasons which motivated the waiver including, of course, a statement of the relevant facts. We may not assume that there are adequate reasons, nor should we merely assume that "full investigation has been made".

Accordingly we hold here as was held in *Kent,* supra, "that it is incumbent upon the Juvenile Court to accompany its waiver order with a statement of the reasons or considerations therefor". We, as the reviewing court, hold that the statement while not necessarily including a conventional finding of facts, should be sufficient to demonstrate unequivocally that the strict statutory requirement of a full investigation and hearing has been met and that a conscientious determination of the question of waiver has been made. We require that the reasons for the order of waiver should be stated with sufficient specificity to permit a meaningful review.

It is readily apparent from an examination of the waiver and transfer order before us that it is merely a printed order signed by the judge. It contains nothing but the words of the statute authorizing transfer. Under the rule in the *Kent* case it clearly is pregnant with the same defects as the order considered there and is only *pro forma.*

Further we hold in accordance with *Kent* that the appellant Summers should have a right to a full hearing in the Lake Juvenile Court. He should have the right to counsel at such hearing; the right to confrontation of the witnesses against him; and the right to present evidence, if any be available to him, of any circumstances that would entitle him to the benefits that might be afforded to him by the provisions of the Juvenile Act. And it is only after such a hearing that a waiver and order of transfer to the Lake Criminal Court may be lawfully made. Such order and transfer should be accompanied with an appropriate statement of reasons as hereinbefore indicated. Of course a record of such proceeding should be made for the criminal court and this court in determining the justification for the transfer and waiver.

Judge Draper speaking for this Court in the case of Cook v. State (1951), 231 Ind. 695, 701, 97 N.E.2d 625, 627, 110 N.E.2d 749 stated that " * * * [c]onstitutional rights should not be grudgingly extended. * * * " It is our belief that such a succinct rule of guidance should govern this court in the disposition of the matter before us. We should "not hesitate", and in fact should "hasten" to extend the appellant "fair treatment" under "due process" as has been mandated by the federal courts in the determination of rights of juveniles. It seems imperative that we should face the responsibility for delineating guidelines to be used by the trial courts in the determination of matters under our Juvenile Act. Failure to recognize the development of the "fair treatment" rule under "due process" as it has rapidly developed since 1959 has inevitably led to the rules enunciated in the *Kent* case, supra.   Any failure to do so now, in our opinion, would indicate an unwillingness and hesitancy to recognize and give credence and due weight to the judicial problems developing in many areas of juvenile jurisdiction.   More importantly we would fail in our responsibility to the trial courts.

Therefore, facing our responsibilities to delineate guidelines for the juvenile courts *re* waiver orders, we should clearly and unequivocally state that the reasons for such waiver to a criminal court must be something more than the mere state of mind of the judge.   They must be a matter of record after a full hearing.   In this regard, we would say that an offense committed by a juvenile may be waived to a criminal court if the offense has specific prosecutive merit in the opinion of the prosecuting attorney;   or if it is heinous or of an aggravated character, greater weight being given to offenses against the person than to offenses against property;   or, even though less serious, if the offense is part of a repetitive pattern of juvenile offenses which would lead to a determination that said juvenile may be beyond rehabilitation under the regular statutory juvenile procedures;   or where it is found to be in the best interest of the public welfare and for the protection of the public security generally that said juvenile be required to stand trial as an adult offender.   We do not necessarily limit the determinative factors to those stated above but we suggest them only as guidelines, any one of which might be determinative of the propriety for waiver in a given case.   Kent v. United States, supra.

We further hold that should the prosecuting attorney believe that a juvenile offense in a particular instance has specific prosecutive merit, he may, by petition and the presentment of information to the juvenile court, seek a hearing on the matter of waiver of jurisdiction of a juvenile pursuant to the provisions of §§ 9–3208 and 9–3214, supra.   Johnson v. State, supra, (concurring opinion).   The juvenile court may then determine whether a hearing on such matter is feasible or necessary under the circumstances presented by the information and make an order book entry consistent with such determination.   However, if a hearing be ordered then such hearing shall be conducted according to the rules hereinabove delineated.   Otherwise, the juvenile court may retain jurisdiction if in its judgment the same is warranted under the law and proceed to exercise the powers, duties and responsibilities conferred upon it by the Juvenile Act.

The foregoing holding and discussion relevant to the procedure by the prosecuting attorney is not to be construed to be the exclusive manner by which a waiver of jurisdiction may be effectuated.   We have discussed it as a feasible procedure in view of the responsibilities and duties exercised by the prosecutor's office.   The court has the power conferred upon it by § 9–3214, supra, to effect a valid waiver and transfer as a result of information furnished by a peace officer or citizen upon a full investigation and after hearing, however, such order shall be made consistent with the rules enunciated herein.

In summation we hold that the entire record of the proceedings in the Lake Juvenile Court demonstrates that the fair treatment required by due process of law was not sufficiently accorded this juvenile. Pee v. United States, supra; Kent v. United States, supra; In re Gault, 387 U.S. 1, 87 S.Ct. 1428, 18 L.Ed.2d 527 (1967).

For the foregoing reasons it is now ordered that this cause be remanded to the Lake Criminal Court with instructions to vacate and expunge any and all records heretofore made below, and to transfer this matter to the Lake Juvenile Court for further proceedings by that court in accordance with this opinion. It is further ordered that this opinion shall supersede the opinions heretofore filed June 23, 1967 and reported in 227 N.E.2d 680.

Rehearing granted.

ATKINS v. STATE

Supreme Court of Indiana, 1972.
259 Ind. 596, 290 N.E.2d 441.

DEBRULER, JUSTICE. This is an appeal from an order of the Juvenile Court of Marion County, Honorable Harold Fields, presiding, waiving jurisdiction of appellants to the Marion County Criminal Court for trial. On February 27, 1969, a group of twenty-one Shortridge High School students, including the seven appellants, were suspended from school for three days for participating in certain peaceful but disruptive protests, the details of which are not particularly relevant to this appeal. After the suspension the appellants, in apparent protest, proceeded to the front of the school building and sat on the steps near the flagpole where they began to chant. Mr. Green, the vice-principal, asked them to leave and go home because they were disturbing the school and warned them that if they did not leave the matter would be turned over to the police. Police Inspector Klein addressed the students telling them that if they did not leave the premises promptly they would be subject to arrest. The students did not leave but instead they locked arms and continued to chant. The appellants were arrested and charged with disorderly conduct in violation of I.C.1971, 35–27–2–1, being Burns § 10–1510. On October 20, 1969, the hearing on the prosecutor's petition for waiver of jurisdiction to criminal court was held and on November 8, 1969, the juvenile court entered the waiver order. Appellants contend that the order is invalid because it was not supported by sufficient evidence and was not set out with the required specificity.

The ultimate issue for the juvenile court at a waiver hearing is whether the juvenile should be waived to criminal court jurisdiction. The juvenile court has a choice—waive or retain the juvenile for disposition within the juvenile system. Indiana Code 1971, 31–5–7–14, being Burns § 9–3214. In the absence of statutory criteria, we derive the standards to be used in making this choice from the structure and purpose of the juvenile justice system itself. Schornhorst, "The Waiver of Juvenile Jurisdiction: Kent Revisited" (1968), 43 Ind.L.J. 583. The juvenile court had original exclusive jurisdiction over these appellants, I.C.1971, 33–12–2–3, being Burns § 9–3103, and they could not be proceeded against in the first instance by criminal indictment or affidavit. State ex rel. Atkins v. Juvenile Court of Marion County (1969), 252 Ind. 237, 247 N.E.2d 53. Only the juvenile court could, after hearing, relinquish jurisdiction over appellants. Indiana Code 1971, 31–5–7–1, being Burns § 9–3201, states the overall purpose of the juvenile justice system as follows:

> "The purpose of this act is to secure for each child within its provisions such care, guidance and control, *preferably in his own home*, as will serve the child's welfare and the best interests of the state; and when such child is removed from his own family, to secure for him custody, care and discipline *as nearly as possible equivalent to that which should have been given by his parents."* (Emphasis added.)

This statutory context creates a presumption in favor of disposing of juvenile matters *within* the juvenile system and makes waiver to criminal court jurisdiction a last resort to be used only when the juvenile court after full hearing determines that the range of dispositions available within the juvenile system are not adequate in the particular case to serve "the child's welfare and the best interests of the state." Waiver to criminal court is then to be the exception and as such is to be explicitly justified in the waiver order. That is the central teaching of Summers v. State (1967), 248 Ind. 551, 230 N.E.2d 320, where we said:

> " 'that it is incumbent upon the Juvenile Court to accompany its waiver order with a statement of the reasons or considerations therefor'. We, as the reviewing court, hold that the statement while not necessarily including a conventional finding of facts, should be sufficient to demonstrate unequivocally that the strict statutory requirement of a full investigation and hearing has been met and that a conscientious determination of the question of waiver has been made. We require that the reasons for the order of waiver should be stated with sufficient specificity to permit a meaningful review." 248 Ind. at 559–560, 230 N.E.2d at 325.

The waiver order in this case reads in pertinent part:

> "(Judge Harold N. Fields) CONDUCTED a full investigation of the matter and now finds:
>
> 1. The child is (was) over fifteen (15) years of age and under eighteen (18) years of age to wit: 17 years, at the time of the charged offense.
>
> 2. The offense charged would be a crime if committed by an adult, to wit: DISORDERLY CONDUCT.
>
> 3. The matter has specific prosecutive merit in the opinion of the Prosecutor if waived to a court of adult criminal jurisdiction.

4. That if the matter were to be retained in the juvenile jurisdiction and child adjudged to be delinquent, no disposition available to the Juvenile Court is reasonably calculated to effect rehabilitation in that: The case cannot be heard in Juvenile Court and disposition made until after the child has reached the age of eighteen (18) years, thus precluding commitment to a state institution."

We agree with appellants that the findings are not clear enough to permit meaningful review.

The first two findings are necessary, statutory conditions for waiver and are not at issue in this case. Burns § 9–3214, supra. Number 3 is a finding that in the *prosecutor's* opinion the case had "specific prosecutive merit." If that is intended to mean that the prosecutor has indicated his willingness to prosecute and his estimate that he can do so successfully, then it could well be a *necessary* requirement for waiver. However, those two factors could never by themselves be *sufficient* for a waiver order. The fact that the prosecutor thinks the case *can* be successfully prosecuted in criminal court does not mean that it *should* be so prosecuted and that is the central issue before the juvenile court on a waiver hearing. If the finding is intended to mean something else then it should be made known by the juvenile court. The point here is that the juvenile court finding number 3 is a conclusion of unknown meaning and thus does not permit an intelligent review by this Court required by *Summers*, supra.

This is also true of number 4. One minor point is that the juvenile court is in error in stating that appellants' being over eighteen years of age precludes him from committing them to "a state institution". The juvenile court is only precluded from committing persons over eighteen to the Boys School. Indiana Code 1971, 11–3–2–3, being Burns § 13–914a. Under I.C.1971, 31–5–7–15, being Burns § 9–3215, he could still commit them to "any suitable public institution or agency, which shall include, but is not limited to, the state institutions for feeble minded, epileptic, insane." Apparently those were not considered appropriate institutions in this case. The more important question is why the unavailability of commitment to the Boys School *requires* that the appellants should not be handled at all within the juvenile system. There are at least two different reasons the juvenile court *could* offer: (1) Although the juvenile court had not yet made a determination as to what disposition the facts of this case demanded, since the ultimate sanction within the juvenile system was not available this alone rendered all the other possible dispositions useless leaving waiver to criminal court as the only alternative. (2) The juvenile court *had* determined that the facts of this case required these appellants be committed to the Boys School and since that disposition was unavailable, waiver to criminal court jurisdiction was the only alternative. Under *Summers*, waiver order is to be such that this Court in reviewing the order is not to be "remitted to assumptions" concerning the reasons for the order.

That is precisely what we are doing in this case—assuming what were the juvenile court reasons for the waiver.

Even if we were to depart from the *Summers* case and *assume* the waiver order rests on one of the above reasons then the order is invalid because there is absolutely no evidence in the record to support waiver in this case on either of the two theories.

There is no reason offered by the juvenile court or the appellee for a conclusion that the other dispositions available to a juvenile court are worthless without the ultimate threat of commitment to the Boys School. Burns § 9–3215, supra, provides several alternative dispositions:

"(1) Place the child on a probation or under supervision in his own home or in the custody of a relative or other fit person, upon such terms as the court may determine;

"(2) Commit the child to any suitable public institution or agency, which shall include, but is not limited to, the state institutions for the feeble-minded, epileptic, insane, or any other hospital or institution for the mentally ill, or commit the child to a suitable private institution or agency incorporated or organized under the laws of the state, and authorized to care for children or to place them in suitable approved homes;

"(3) The court may make such child a ward of the court, a ward of the department of public welfare of the county, or a ward of any licensed child placing agency in the state willing to receive such wardship;

"(4) May take cause under advisement or postpone findings and judgment for a period not to exceed two years unless sooner requested by the party proceeded against in which event not to exceed ninety days;

"(5) Make such further disposition as may be deemed to be to the best interests of the child, except as herein otherwise provided."

See also 1971 O.A.G. 14. In addition, I.C.1971, 31–5–7–24, being Burns § 9–3223, in reference to juvenile proceedings, provides:

"Any person who wilfully violates, neglects or refuses to obey or perform any order of the court may be proceeded against for contempt."

See also I.C.1971, 33–12–2–7, being Burns § 9–3107, to the same effect. Several of these possible dispositions would appear to be sufficiently grave to take the place of commitment to the Boys School as an ultimate threat, e.g., commitment to a *private* boys home for juveniles of which there are several in this State.

In addition the juvenile court position is refuted by considering the case of a juvenile accused of an act of delinquency *not* amounting to a crime if committed by an adult, which juvenile is seventeen years, eleven months when the act is committed and over eighteen when the juvenile court obtains jurisdiction. Commitment to the

Boys School would be unavailable, as in this case, but that juvenile *cannot* be waived to criminal court. Would the juvenile court merely release the juvenile because the use of the lesser sanction would be futile? We think not. The court would use the tools available to it. The point is that this Court should not indulge a general assumption that the other dispositions available to a juvenile court are worthless in the absence of the ultimate threat of commitment to a state institution and there is nothing in this particular case to support such a conclusion.

The above cited statutory context, Burns § 9–3201, supra, in addition to creating a presumption in favor of disposing of juvenile matters within the juvenile system, also creates a presumption in favor of using the *least severe* disposition available to the juvenile court which will serve the needs of the case. Therefore commitment to the Boys School is to be resorted to only if the less severe dispositions are inadequate.

All seven of these appellants were duly enrolled in high school at the time of this incident. All seven appellants lived with at least one of their parents; three of them lived with mother and father; three lived with their mother and the father was deceased. All seven appellants voluntarily appeared with counsel at the initial hearing without summons and all but one appellant appeared with one or more of their parents. All the appellants had at least one parent who attended the waiver hearing and co-operated with the juvenile court by identifying their children for the record. Appellants are charged with a misdemeanor of disorderly conduct which was a completely nonviolent demonstration against the school for felt grievances. The appellants Atkins, Holt, Lewis, Marshall and Yowell had no previous record of trouble leading to involvement in the juvenile justice system. In the case of these five appellants there is no evidence that the less severe dispositions available within the juvenile system would be inadequate especially since the system had never been tried at all. Accordingly we hold the juvenile court erred in waiving these five appellants to the jurisdiction of the criminal court.

It appears that appellants Brown and Edmondson have a record of past juvenile offenses and therefore we remand those two appellants to the juvenile court for a redetermination of the waiver issue and to permit the juvenile court to weigh the significance of the prior offenses in light of the legal standards set forth in this opinion.

HUNTER and PRENTICE, JJ., concur.

ARTERBURN, C.J., dissents with opinion in which GIVAN, J., concurs.

ARTERBURN, CHIEF JUSTICE (dissenting).

I am unable to agree with the reasoning expressed in the majority opinion.

On February 26, 1969, a large group of students, including appellants, gathered in the office of Mr. Merrill, Dean of Men, at Shortridge High School in the City of Indianapolis, to discuss the previous day's occurrence in the school cafeteria. They demanded the right to hold a meeting in the school auditorium during the 4th period. Mr. Lloyd Green, the vice-principal, told them that they could not use the auditorium at the time requested, but that it would be available for their proposed use at 3:15 p.m. that day. At the beginning of the 4th period, between 10:30 and 10:40 a.m., the group nevertheless went to the auditorium. The doors of the auditorium were open, but it was unlighted. The students went in and attempted to entice other students to join in the forbidden meeting. The students were told to return to their classes, but that there would be a meeting at 3:15 p.m. There is evidence in the record that Mr. Green was pushed and shoved while in the auditorium. At the beginning of the 5th period the students went down the hall to the cafeteria singing "We will overcome." In the cafeteria they talked with other students for approximately ten minutes and then proceeded into the west corridor with a group of students. As they reached a point north of the library door they began to sing. At about 3:15 p.m. that same afternoon the appellants and a number of other students went to the auditorium and held the permitted meeting.

On February 27, 1969, the students again went to Mr. Merrill's office before 8:00 a.m. At that time, they were requested to proceed to their classes. During a performance of the Indianapolis Symphony Orchestra in the auditorium, the students stood up, proceeded to the nearest aisle, and walked out. They were accompanied out of the auditorium and into the cafeteria where they were told by three vice-principals that they were suspended from school for three days. The appellants then proceeded to the front of the school building and sat on the steps near the flagpole where they began a loud prolonged chant. Mr. Green asked them to leave and go home because they were disturbing the school and cautioned them that if they did not leave, the matter would be turned over to the police. There were several police officers present, and Inspector Klein addressed the appellants telling them that if they did not leave the premises promptly they would be subject to arrest. The students did not leave. Instead, they locked arms and continued to chant, whereupon they were arrested and charged with disorderly conduct. IC 1971, 35–27–2–1, Burns' Ind.Stat.Ann. § 10–1510 (1972 Supp.) provides:

> Whoever shall act in a loud, boisterous or disorderly manner so as to disturb the peace and quiet of any neighborhood or family, by loud or unusual noise, or by tumultous or offensive behavior, threatening, traducing, quarreling, challenging to fight or fighting, shall be deemed guilty of disorderly conduct, and upon conviction, shall be fined in any sum not exceeding five hundred dollars [$500] to which may be added imprisonment for not to exceed one hundred eighty [180] days.

This case is now here a second time. The appellants, Rodman Atkins, James R. Edmonson, Karen Lewis, Van Marshall, Darrick Holt, Derrick Yowell, and Jerome K. Brown, and 23 other students were indicted by the Marion County Grand Jury. The indictments were filed in Division I of Marion County Criminal Court and the judge transferred each case to juvenile court immediately. On March 5, 1969, the juvenile court noted the transfer and ordered a case filed against each defendant. On March 7, 1969, the prosecuting attorney of the 19th Judicial Circuit of Indiana, filed a petition for Waiver of Juvenile Jurisdiction in each case and the Court ordered a hearing on the petition for March 12, 1969. Each appellant then sought a Writ of Prohibition in this Court seeking to prohibit the Juvenile Court from acting on the ground that it had no jurisdiction. In that case, we granted the writ by a divided court. State ex rel. Atkins v. Juvenile Court of Marion Co. (1969), 252 Ind. 237, 247 N.E.2d 53. It should be noted that our decision in *Atkins*, supra, was handed down on May 6, 1969. Judge Fields, who presided during the proceedings below, had dismissed each of the cases on April 5, 1969, agreeing with the contention that juvenile jurisdiction was imperfectly obtained.[c]

On June 13, 1969, new petitions were filed in the Juvenile Court of Marion County against the appellants and others, and the Prosecuting Attorney immediately filed petitions for waiver of jurisdiction. On June 14, 1969, the hearing was continued after the appellants and their attorneys appeared, and appellants were ordered released to their parents. On July 2, summons were issued to the appellants and their parents to appear on July 17. On October 19, the cause was set for hearing on the petition for waiver. At that time, counsel for appellants and the State stipulated in open court that the record as it stood from the proceedings of March 12, 1969 and thereafter would be the record in its entirety for the present hearing and proceedings. The stipulation was accepted by the Court and entered of record. The cause was reset for oral argument and the defendant-appellants were again released to the custody of their parents. On October 20,

[c] "Jurisdiction shall be obtained in the following manner.

" 'A person subject to the jurisdiction of the juvenile court under this act may be brought before it by either of the following means and by no other: " '(a) By petition praying that the person be adjudged delinquent * * *.' Ind.Ann. Stat. § 9–3207 (1966 Supp.)

"The steps necessary to the juvenile court's exclusive original jurisdiction are set forth as follows:

" 'Any person may and any peace officer shall give to the court information * * * that there is within the county or residing within the county a * * * delinquent child. Thereupon, the court shall, as far as possible, make preliminary inquiry to determine whether * * * further action be taken. Whenever practicable such inquiry shall include a preliminary investigation of the home and environmental situation of the child, his previous history and the circumstances of the condition alleged and if the court shall determine that formal jurisdiction should be acquired, shall authorize a petition to be filed by the probation officer * * *.' Ind.Ann.Stat. § 9–3208 (1966 Supp.)

"It has been held that § 9–3208, supra, is implementive of § 9–3207, supra, and that it was the intent of the legislature in such cases that if the judge of the juvenile court believed that formal jurisdiction should be acquired, the judge should authorize a petition to be filed.

"Thus the exclusive original jurisdiction may only be obtained by the juvenile court as set forth above and unless such preliminary statutory procedural steps are taken there is no jurisdiction established. *A fortiori*, jurisdiction not obtained by the juvenile court cannot be waived to the criminal court." Summers v. State, 248 Ind. 551, 556–57, 230 N.E.2d 320, 323 (1967).

the hearing on petition for waiver of jurisdiction was held, and the proceedings of March 12, 1969, to March 19, 1969, which was the initial waiver hearing on the charges brought by indictment, were stipulated into the present record. The former hearing had lasted seven days during which time some 40 witnesses were called by the parties, and approximately 46 exhibits were offered. On November 8, 1969, the petition for waiver was granted by the Juvenile Court and an order to that effect was entered.

The Honorable Harold N. Fields, Judge of the Marion County Juvenile Court rendered the following Orders of Waiver of Jurisdiction, omitting purely formal parts (the Orders being identical as to each appellant except where noted otherwise):

"(Judge Harold N. Fields) CONDUCTED a full investigation of the matter and now finds:

1. The child is (was) over fifteen (15) years of age and under eighteen (18) years of age to wit: *17* years, at the time of the charged offense.

2. The offense charged would be a crime if committed by an adult, to wit: DISORDERLY CONDUCT.

3. The matter has specific prosecutive merit in the opinion of the Prosecutor if waived to a court of adult criminal jurisdiction.

4. That if the matter were to be retained in the juvenile jurisdiction and child adjudged to be delinquent, no disposition available to the Juvenile Court is reasonably calculated to effect rehabilitation in that: The case cannot be heard in Juvenile Court and disposition made until after the child has reached the age of eighteen (18) years, thus precluding commitment to a state institution.

(Additionally as to appellants Brown and Edmondson)

The offense charged is part of a repetitive pattern of juvenile offenses, to wit:

(As to Jerome K. Brown)

11–21–65 O.A.P.A. Theft

11–18–68 Robbery (Waived to Criminal Court)

(As to James R. Edmondson)

5–31–65 ROBBERY

AND THE COURT: NOW ORDERS

1. That the Court waive jurisdiction and order said child held for trial under regular procedures of the Criminal Court of Marion County on a charge that (name) is hereby alleged to be a delinquent child in this to wit: On or about February 27, 1969, at and in the County of Marion, State of Indiana, did then and there unlawfully act in a loud, boisterous, and disorderly manner, so as to disturb the peace and quiet of a certain neighborhood, to wit: Shortridge High School, and

34th and Meridian Streets at Shortridge High School, by loud
and unusual noise, then and there being contrary to the form
of the Statute in such case made and provided, and against
the peace and dignity of the State of Indiana.

2.   That pending trial on said charge in the Criminal Court of
Marion County, that said child be:

Released to his parents.

(or in the case of Jerome K. Brown) Remanded to the
custody of the Sheriff of Marion County with bond set in the
amount of $500.00."

In the case at bar, it is clear that a full and adequate hearing was
held on the question of waiver of jurisdiction, and that the trial judge
did more than just recite his conclusions or state of mind in the
waiver orders. Our concern in Summers v. State (1967), 248 Ind. 551,
230 N.E.2d 320, was to insure that the waiver determination would be
made on the basis of a full and adequate hearing. We did not mean
to limit the trial judge's discretion except to the extent that a
statement of reasons is required to permit a meaningful review. The
requirements set out in *Summers* were followed by the trial judge
here. The appellants were all very close to the age of eighteen at the
time of these proceedings. The offense for which they were charged
would be a crime if committed by an adult, i.e., disorderly conduct.
The trial judge found that the matter had specific prosecutive merit
in the opinion of the prosecutor. In addition, the judge found that
there was no disposition reasonably calculated to effect rehabilitation
in these cases since the appellants were so close to the age of
eighteen years, and by the time of trial they would be over eighteen
years of age and not subject to commitment to any juvenile institution. He was obviously of the belief that the dispositions available to
the Juvenile Court were not adequate in these cases. We see no
justification for disturbing that judgment. We find nothing to indicate that Judge Fields abused his discretion or acted in an arbitrary
manner with respect to these appellants. The waiver order contains
ample reasons to support waiver of jurisdiction as to these appellants.
Thus, the procedures used here are fully consistent with the guidelines we set out in *Summers*, supra, and the orders of waiver as to
these appellants are not contrary to law.

The substance of the majority opinion requires a fullfledged
hearing on a mere waiver of jurisdiction to the criminal court, in
order to determine the possible punishments under each set of
circumstances. If it is conceivably possible to use the remedies of
the juvenile system, then the trial court has no right to waive to a
criminal court. The trial court, however, must guess, since the
majority suggests that the Supreme Court decides whether or not the
remedies are adequate within the juvenile process. All of this comes
prior to the trial of the meritorious issues, thus creating two full
trials and a change of judge. I further point out that a juvenile
proceeding is not supposed to be a criminal proceeding, although I
realize that the United States Supreme Court, in the cases of In re

Gault (1967), 387 U.S. 1, 87 S.Ct. 1428, 18 L.Ed.2d 527, and Kent v. United States (1966), 383 U.S. 541, 86 S.Ct. 1045, 16 L.Ed.2d 84, has played havoc with our juvenile proceedings by imposing almost all the procedural requirements of the criminal process upon the juvenile system.

The majority speculates on situations in which juveniles are charged with conduct that does not constitute a crime for an adult. We do not have that situation here, since the so-called juveniles who now are more than 18 years of age are alleged to have committed a crime, although the majority opinion denominates their acts as "certain peaceful but disruptive protests" and "completely non-violent demonstrations against the school for felt grievances." As I read the record, disorderly conduct, when it takes the form of loud noises, running, blocking, singing and includes pushing and shoving, does violence to the rights of others who desire peace and quiet in order to pursue the legitimate goal of receiving an education. The crime for which the appellants are charged involves the infringement of important rights belonging to their fellow students by disrupting the educational processes at Shortridge High School. It is well settled that conduct which materially and substantially interferes with the operation of the public educational system may be prohibited even though expressive activity is involved. Tinker v. Des Moines Independent Community School District (1969), 393 U.S. 503, 89 S.Ct. 733, 21 L.Ed.2d 731. The appellants seek to assert rights under our Juvenile Code when, at the same time, they were unwilling to recognize and honor the rights of their classmates. We think the trial judge, considering their age, could reasonably refuse to treat such individuals as children under our statutes.

The appellants are all now over 18 years of age, and considering the slow progress that this case is making, having been before us twice and sent back for a rehearing, these appellants will be full grown men and women, still subject to the juvenile process as a result of the majority opinion. The purposes for which our juvenile system was created are lost in the jungle of court proceedings that the majority opinion compels in this case. We must have discipline in schools if we are going to have any success in meeting our educational goals. Schools should have the power to enforce discipline. What this Court is doing here by not supporting the trial court and the school authorities results in nothing but chaos in the school systems. In my opinion, Judge Fields explicitly stated, and with good cause, the reason why the juvenile court should not retain jurisdiction for these 18-year-old appellants who have the right to vote and who should be tried as adults for their crime in a criminal court.

GIVAN, J., concurs.

CLEMONS v. STATE

Court of Appeals of Indiana, 1974.

162 Ind.App. 50, 317 N.E.2d 859, cert. denied, 423 U.S. 859, 96 S.Ct. 113, 46 L.Ed.2d 86 (1975).

STATON, JUDGE. James Clemons was seventeen years old when a delinquency petition charging him with first degree burglary, transportation of stolen property across the state line, and possession of false selective service registration cards was filed in juvenile court. A second petition was filed by the prosecutor requesting that James Clemons be waived from juvenile court jurisdiction so that he could be tried as an adult pursuant to I.C.1971, 31–5–7–14 (Burns Code Ed.). After the waiver hearing, Clemons was waived by the juvenile court to the Porter Superior Court. Clemons pled guilty to a charge of third degree burglary and was sentenced to a term not to exceed one year on the Indiana State Farm. His appeal to this Court raises three issues:

Issue One: Is I.C.1971, 31–5–7–14 (Burns Code Ed.) unconstitutional for failure to provide standards for waiver?

Issue Two: Was Clemons denied procedural due process by the admission of hearsay at his waiver hearing?

Issue Three: Was there sufficient evidence to support the waiver order?

In our review of these three issues, we conclude that I.C.1971, 31–5–7–14, supra, is not unconstitutional, that Clemons was accorded a fair hearing fulfilling the requirements of due process and that there was sufficient evidence to support the waiver order. We affirm.

I.

Constitutionality

There is a strong presumption favoring the constitutionality of a statute. Cheaney v. State (1972), Ind., 285 N.E.2d 265, cert. denied 410 U.S. 991, 93 S.Ct. 1516, 36 L.Ed.2d 189 (1973); Hicks v. State (1967), 249 Ind. 24, 230 N.E.2d 757.

Clemons contends that I.C.1971, 31–5–7–14 is void for vagueness in violation of the Fourteenth Amendment to the United States Constitution and Article I, Section 12 of the Indiana Constitution. He relies upon People v. Fields (1972), 388 Mich. 66, 199 N.W.2d 217 which held a statute similar to the Indiana waiver statute to be an unconstitutional delegation of legislative power to the judiciary.

There has been some confusion between the non-delegation doctrine and procedural due process. This is understandable since the standards requirement in delegation cases is evolving into a protection of the individual from arbitrary or discriminatory exercises of discretion. See People v. Fields (1974), 391 Mich. 206, 216 N.W.2d 51, aff'd on rehearing (dissenting opinion); Warren v. Marion County (1960), 222 Or. 307, 314, 353 P.2d 257, 261; Davis, Administrative

Law Treatise § 2.00 (1970 Supp.). However, we have concluded that I.C.1971, 31–5–7–14 does not violate either the nondelegation doctrine or the due process clause.

We will treat the delegation of legislative power challenge solely as a challenge to separation of powers under Article 3, § 1 and Article 4, § 1 of the Indiana Constitution. Although the non-delegation doctrine in Indiana prohibits the legislature from delegating its power to make law, the legislature can delegate power to determine facts or the state of things upon which the application of the law depends. Kryder v. State (1938), 214 Ind. 419, 424, 15 N.E.2d 386; City of Aurora v. Bryant (1960), 240 Ind. 492, 165 N.E.2d 141; Noble v. City of Warsaw (1973), Ind.App., 297 N.E.2d 916; 16 Am.Jur.2d Constitutional Law § 256 (1964). The challenged statute, I.C.1971, 31–5–7–14 (Burns Code Ed.) provides:

> "If a child fifteen [15] years of age or older is charged with an offense which would amount to a crime if committed by an adult, the judge, after full investigation, may waive jurisdiction and order such child held for trial under the regular procedure of the court which would have jurisdiction of such offense if committed by an adult; or such court may exercise the powers conferred upon the juvenile court in this act [31–5–7–1—31–5–7–25] in conducting and disposing of such case: Provided, That the judges of the juvenile courts of this state who shall waive the jurisdiction of such child as provided herein may at the time of the waiver fix a recognizance bond for the person to answer the charge in the court which would have jurisdiction of such offense if committed by an adult."

As Justice DeBruler recognized in Atkins v. State (1972), Ind., 290 N.E.2d 441, the standards to be used by the juvenile judge in making the decision to either waive or retain jurisdiction are derived from the structure and purpose of the juvenile justice system itself. The overall purpose of the juvenile justice system is found in I.C.1971, 31–5–7–1 (Burns Code Ed.) as follows:

> "The purpose of this act [31–5–7–1—31–5–7–25] is to secure for each child within its provisions such care, guidance and control, preferably in his own home, as will serve the child's welfare and the best interests of the state; and when such child is removed from his own family, to secure for him custody, care and discipline as nearly as possible equivalent to that which should have been given by his parents."

Thus, under I.C.1971, 31–5–7–14, the juvenile court judge must determine if the child is 15 years or older, if he is charged with an offense which would amount to a crime if committed by an adult, and if waiver will serve the child's welfare and the best interests of the state. This is not lawmaking; it is an exercise of judicial discretion. We note that the Supreme Courts of Kansas, Massachusetts, Nevada and New Mexico have declared similar broad standards sufficient to overcome an unconstitutional delegation challenge. Only People v. Fields, supra, has held the Michigan waiver statute to be an unconstitutional delegation. In In re Juvenile, supra, 306 N.E.2d at 827 n. 7, the Supreme Court of Massachusetts expressly refused to follow the *Fields* case. The *Fields* opinion has been criticized. Note, Constitutional Law—Juvenile Waiver Statute—Delegation of Legislative Power to Judiciary, 1973 Wis.L.Rev. 259.[43]

We also refuse to follow the *Fields* case. We conclude that I.C. 1971, 31–5–7–14 does not delegate legislative authority to the judiciary.

The second constitutional argument by Clemons is that the lack of precise standards in I.C.1971, 31–5–7–14 results in a denial of due process in two ways: (1) the standards provided are so vague as to allow arbitrary, capricious or discriminatory decision-making and (2) the standards are so unclear that the juvenile cannot effectively prepare for the waiver hearing.[44] We hold that the standard for "the child's welfare and the best interests of the state" expressed in I.C. 1971, 31–5–7–1 is a sufficient guideline to save I.C.1971, 31–5–7–14 from being void on its face for vagueness. Similar general standards have been upheld in other jurisdictions answering attacks on their waiver statutes for being unconstitutionally vague. See Briggs v. United States (1955), 96 U.S.App.D.C. 392, 226 F.2d 350; L. v. Superior Court of Los Angeles County (1972), 7 Cal.3rd 592, 102 Cal. Rptr. 850, 498 P.2d 1098; Sherfield v. State (Okl.Cr.1973), 511 P.2d 598; In re Correia (1968), 104 R.I. 251, 243 A.2d 759; In re Salas (1974), Utah, 520 P.2d 874; In re F.R.W. (1973), 61 Wis.2d 193, 212 N.W.2d 130, certiorari denied 416 U.S. 974, 94 S.Ct. 2000, 40 L.Ed.2d 563 (1974). As the Supreme Court of Wisconsin stated in In re F.R.W., supra, 212 N.W.2d at 139, citing Miller v. Quatsoe (E.D.Wis. 1971), 332 F.Supp. 1269, 1275:

> " 'Unlike a typical criminal action, a juvenile waiver proceeding vests the judge with a wide amount of discretion in making his determination. In his decision making, the juvenile judge does not simply deal with a specific factual incident in the accused's life as does a criminal court judge, but rather the juvenile judge must consider the juvenile's past, his future, his mind, and his acts and then balance these factors against the safety, needs and demands of society. * * *' "

See also, Kent v. United States (1966), 383 U.S. 541, 552, 86 S.Ct. 1045, 16 L.Ed.2d 84. The Legislature has recognized the inherent difficulty in identifying the varied merit-factors to be considered by the juvenile court judge and the need for a consideration of each case on its own merit-factors.

[43] The Supreme Court of Michigan in an opinion on rehearing has expressed regret that the non-delegation doctrine was adopted as the vehicle for declaring their waiver statute unconstitutional. See People v. Fields (1974), 391 Mich. 206, 216 N.W.2d 51, 53.

[44] Clemons argues that I.C.1971, 31–5–7–14 is unconstitutionally vague for fail-ure to provide proper notice of the conduct proscribed by the statute or the probable consequences of engaging in the proscribed conduct. However, I.C. 1971, 31–5–7–14 does not describe criminal conduct but merely provides a procedure for the waiver of jurisdiction by the juvenile court.

The juvenile is protected from arbitrary, capricious or discriminatory decision-making by the safeguards enunciated in Summers v. State (1967), 248 Ind. 551, 230 N.E.2d 320; Atkins v. State (1972), Ind., 290 N.E.2d 441 and Kent v. United States, supra. Both Kent v. United States and Summers v. State, supra, recognize the necessity that a waiver order be accompanied by a statement of the reasons for the waiver order of sufficient specificity to permit meaningful review. Atkins v. State, supra, recognizes a presumption in favor of disposing of juvenile matters within the juvenile system. If the reasons given for waiver do not explicitly justify the waiver order in light of "the child's welfare and the best interests of the state" then such waiver order would be reversed on appeal. Appellate review has long been recognized as a check upon discretionary decision-making. Ritter v. Ritter (1839), 5 Blackf. (Ind.) 81.

The standard for "the child's welfare and the best interests of the state" is sufficient notice to the juvenile to enable preparation for the waiver hearing. Summers v. State, supra, specifically gives the juvenile the right to present evidence of any circumstances that would entitle him to the benefits inherent in the juvenile justice system. In determining what "the child's welfare and the best interests of the state" requires, the juvenile court judge must necessarily consider:

1. the nature of the offense

2. whether it is part of a repetitive pattern of juvenile offenses

3. whether the child is beyond rehabilitation under the juvenile justice system

4. whether waiver is necessary to protect the public security.[45]

Kent v. United States, supra, gives the juvenile's counsel access to social, probation or similar reports in preparing for the waiver hearing. A broad standard is constitutionally sound when proper safeguards are provided. We conclude that I.C.1971, 31–5–7–14 is not unconstitutionally vague on its face.[46]

II.

Hearsay

Clemons contends that he was denied "the procedural due process right of freedom from hearsay evidence." To support this contention, he urges that under the rationale of In re Gault (1967), 387 U.S. 1, 87 S.Ct. 1428, 18 L.Ed.2d 527, a juvenile is entitled to all the procedural rights afforded a criminal defendant. We reject the "total rights" concept of juvenile justice. The admission of hearsay

[45] We note that prosecutive merit was also a factor to be considered under the criteria set forth in the Appendix to Kent v. United States, supra, and under guidelines set out in Summers v. State, supra. However, this factor was held to be insufficient alone to support a waiver order in Atkins v. State, supra.

[46] Although we hold I.C.1971, 31–5–7–14 (Burns' Code Ed.) to be constitutional on its face, we do not foreclose the possibility that in some future case it may be found to have been unconstitutionally applied.

evidence at a juvenile waiver hearing is not a denial of due process per se.

Although recent decisions of the United States Supreme Court and the Supreme Court of Indiana have greatly expanded the rights of juveniles in juvenile proceedings, the total rights concept argued for by Clemons has not been adopted. McKeiver v. Pennsylvania (1971), 403 U.S. 528, 91 S.Ct. 1976, 29 L.Ed.2d 647; Bible v. State (1970), 253 Ind. 373, 254 N.E.2d 319. As the United States Supreme Court stated in McKeiver v. Pennsylvania, supra, 403 U.S. at 551, 91 S.Ct. at 1989:

> "If the formalities of the criminal adjudicative process are to be superimposed upon the juvenile court system, there is little need for its separate existence. Perhaps that ultimate disillusionment will come one day, but for the moment we are disinclined to give impetus to it."

The standard for determining what due process requires in a particular juvenile proceeding is "fundamental fairness." McKeiver v. Pennsylvania, supra, 403 U.S. at 543, 91 S.Ct. 1976; Bible v. State, supra, 253 Ind. at 385, 254 N.E.2d 319; Patterson v. Hopkins (N.D. Miss.1972), 350 F.Supp. 676.

In examining the question of whether "fundamental fairness" at a juvenile waiver hearing requires the exclusion of hearsay evidence, it is important to understand the nature of the waiver hearing.[47] Unlike the delinquency hearing, a waiver hearing is dispositional in nature. As the Supreme Court of Washington stated in State v. Piche (1968), 74 Wash.2d 9, 442 P.2d 632, 635, cert. denied 393 U.S. 1041, 89 S.Ct. 666, 21 L.Ed.2d 588 (1969).

> "In determining whether the essentials of due process and fair treatment were provided in the instant case, it is important to keep in mind the exact nature of a juvenile court transfer [waiver] hearing. Such a hearing does not result in a determination of delinquency. * * *; does not result in the determination of guilt as may a criminal trial; and does not directly result in confinement or other punishment as may both a delinquency hearing and a criminal proceeding. In short, the transfer hearing is not an adversary proceeding. Rather, the sole purpose of the transfer hearing, as we have recently said, is to determine 'whether best interests of the child and of society would be served by the retention of the juvenile court authority over him or whether the juvenile, under all the circumstances, should be transferred to be tried as an adult.' * * *."

* * * Also, it should be noted that the right to confrontation of witnesses extended to a juvenile at a waiver hearing in Summers v. State, supra, does not mandate application of the hearsay rules. * * *

---

[47] Several courts have recently held that hearsay is inadmissible in a juvenile delinquency hearing as a violation of due process. * * *

We conclude that fundamental fairness does not require the exclusion of hearsay in the waiver hearing setting. Just as in the judicial function of sentencing, consideration must be given to such factors as the previous record, background, and possibility for rehabilitation of the particular individual before the Court. The decision-making performed by the trial judge in sentencing is analogous to the waiver determination by a juvenile court judge. As we stated in Hineman v. State (1973), Ind.App., 292 N.E.2d 618, 624:

"* * * The strict rules of evidence applicable during trial are no longer applicable at sentencing where the precommitment report may be a dominate influence. This basic difference was drawn by the Supreme Court of the United States in Williams v. New York (1949), 337 U.S. 241, 246–247, 69 S.Ct. 1079, 1083, 93 L.Ed. 1337:

" '* * * Highly relevant—if not essential—to his selection of an appropriate sentence is the possession of the fullest information possible concerning the defendant's life and characteristics. And modern concepts individualizing punishment have made it all the more necessary that a sentencing judge not be denied an opportunity to obtain pertinent information by a requirement of rigid adherence to restrictive rules of evidence properly applicable to the trial.' "

Other jurisdictions have considered the applicability of the hearsay rules in juvenile waiver hearings. They have concluded that such hearings are dispositional and that the hearsay rules do not apply. See In re Murphy (1972), 15 Md.App. 434, 291 A.2d 867; State v. Piche, supra; State v. Carmichael, supra.

Clemons asserts that it was error to admit into evidence testimony by the investigating police officer regarding a confession by Clemons which would be inadmissible under the safeguards enunciated in Lewis v. State (1972), Ind., 288 N.E.2d 138. Clemons' argument is based, not on hearsay, but on denial of the Fifth Amendment right against self-incrimination. However, neither Lewis v. State, supra, involving the use of a juvenile confession in a subsequent criminal trial, nor the recent Bridges v. State (1973), Ind., 299 N.E.2d 616, involving use of a confession at a delinquency hearing, are applicable to the dispositional waiver hearing. Neither Kent v. United States nor Summers v. State, supra, expressly extend the Fifth Amendment right against self-incrimination to waiver hearings. Two other jurisdictions considering the admission of pre-hearing confessions at waiver hearings have refused to find such an admission reversible error. State v. Piche and State ex rel. Juvenile Dept. of Marion Cty. v. Johnson, supra. The juvenile's guilt or innocence is not at issue in a waiver hearing. None of the inadmissible confession evidence can be used against the juvenile in a later delinquency hearing or criminal trial. Lewis v. State; Bridges v. State, supra. If the juvenile's confession is considered at all by the waiver hearing judge, it can only be considered as it relates to "the child's welfare and the best interests of the state." [48] The Fifth Amendment privilege against self-incrimination is inapplicable in the waiver hearing setting where the confession may not be viewed as inculpatory and where it may not be used in a later criminal or delinquency adjudication.[49]

Other testimony by the investigating police officer involved statements made to him by the victim of the burglary and an opinion by the officer that there was probable cause to believe Clemons committed the burglary.[50] Even if the rules of hearsay applied to the above testimony, any error in admission would be harmless. It is well-settled in Indiana that a trial judge is presumed to know the rules of evidence and that he is presumed to have considered only the evidence properly before the court. King v. State (1973), Ind.App., 292 N.E.2d 843; City of Indianapolis v. Medenwald (1973), Ind.App., 301 N.E.2d 795.

The final hearsay objection involved a probation report prepared by the Porter County Probation Department. The report contained information from the LaPorte County Juvenile Office. Although the Porter County Probation Officer testified at the waiver hearing and was available for cross-examination, Clemons contends that he was denied his right to confront witnesses. As in the case of a sentencing hearing, to hold that the hearsay rules apply to exclude such evidence as psychological reports, probation reports and social reports would seriously impair the juvenile judge's ability to determine whether waiver was in "the child's welfare and the best interests of the state." [51] Clemons is protected from consideration of erroneous reports by his right to access to such reports under Kent v. United States, supra, and by his right to present evidence of any circumstances that would entitle him to the benefits of the juvenile system under Summers v. State, supra. As the United States Supreme Court stated in Kent v. United States, supra, 383 U.S. at 563, 86 S.Ct. at 1058:

[48] The court in State ex rel. Juvenile Dept. of Marion Cty. v. Johnson (1972), 11 Or.App. 313, 501 P.2d 1011, 1015:

" * * * We think a statement made by the boy shortly after he was taken into custody is relevant, not to establish whether or not he committed the acts alleged, though certainly it may have a tendency to do so, but to aid those qualified as experts to express an opinion concerning the ultimate question before the court—the determination of what is in the best interest of the child and of the public. For the same reason it has value to the court in making its determination. * * *"

[49] Unless the specific safeguards enunciated in Lewis v. State and Bridges v. State, supra, are observed, the juvenile's confession is clearly inadmissible at the delinquency hearing. We recognize that it may be fundamentally unfair for a juvenile court judge who has heard evidence of an invalid confession at a juvenile's waiver hearing to later adjudicate the issue of his delinquency for the same offense.

[50] The record discloses that the complained of testimony regarding statements by the victim was stricken by the court negating this contention of error. Transcript at 57.

[51] Tumbleson v. Tumbleson (1947), 117 Ind.App. 455, 73 N.E.2d 59 and Ford v. State (1952), 122 Ind.App. 315, 104 N.E.2d 406 cited by Clemons to support his contention that the juvenile judge could not consider probation office reports in making his waiver determination are distinguishable. They both involved adjudicatory hearings as opposed to the dispositional hearing involved in the case before this Court.

"* * * [I]f the staff's submissions include materials which are susceptible to challenge or impeachment, it is precisely the role of counsel to 'denigrate' such matter. There is no irrebuttable presumption of accuracy attached to staff reports. If a decision on waiver is 'critically important' it is equally of 'critical importance' that the material submitted to the judge—which is protected by the statute only against 'indiscriminate' inspection—be subjected, within reasonable limits having regard to the theory of the Juvenile Court Act, to examination, criticism and refutation. While the Juvenile Court judge may, of course, receive *ex parte* analyses and recommendations from his staff, he may not, for purposes of a decision on waiver, receive and rely upon secret information, whether emanating from his staff or otherwise. The Juvenile Court is governed in this respect by the established principles which control courts and quasi-judicial agencies of the Government."

III.

Sufficiency of the Evidence

Although the hearsay rules of evidence do not necessarily apply to waiver hearings, we recognize that the record may be devoid of evidence pertinent to "the child's welfare and the best interests of the state." Atkins v. State, supra. The juvenile judge in this case gave the following reasons for waiver:

"That the offense involved in this alleged delinquency hearing [has] specific prosecuting [sic] merit; also that the offense involved, if true, is a part of a reptative [repetitive] pattern and it is also the Court's finding that the Juvenile involved may very well be beyond rehabilitation upon Juvenile procedures and that it is in the best interests of the public welfare and public security that this Juvenile be waived over to stand trial as an adult offender.

"The Court specifically finds that there have been many previous offenses involving this Juvenile and that formal and informal probation in the past have been unable to rehabilitate said Juvenile.

"The Court further finds that said Juvenile has presented no evidence in this cause showing any circumstances that might entitle him to the benefits afforded him by the provisions of the Juvenile Act.

"IT IS THEREFORE, ORDERED, ADJUDGED AND DE-CREED by the Court that jurisdiction be waived and said Juvenile be held over for trial under the regular procedure of the Court which would have jurisdiction of the offense, if committed by an adult."

James Clemons was seventeen years old when the delinquency petition charging him with first degree burglary, transportation of stolen property across the state line, and possession of false selective service registration cards was filed in juvenile court. Clemons had an extensive record of previous trouble, including in part: vandalism—1966; theft—1969; assault and battery—1972; theft—1972; possession of stolen property—1972; vehicle taking—1972. Previous attempts to rehabilitate Clemons within the juvenile justice system included release to the custody of either his father or mother, who are divorced, probation and admittance to White's Institute. The probation officer's opinion was that neither probation nor release to Clemons' mother would be effective. He testified that Clemons had a history of running away and that he needed total supervision. The alternatives of the Boys' School or some other institution were explored, and the probation officer testified that such alternatives might or might not be effective in the case of James Clemons. Finally, the probation officer indicated that upon more than one occasion, Clemons stated that he would not stay anywhere that the court desired to place him. Clemons presented no evidence to refute the testimony of the probation officer or the probation report. He presented no evidence of circumstances that would entitle him to the benefits of the juvenile justice system. The reasons for waiver stated by the juvenile judge and the record in support thereof adequately demonstrate that rehabilitation within the juvenile justice system had been unsuccessful. There is sufficient evidence to support the trial court's waiver judgment.

We affirm.

HOFFMAN, C.J., and GARRARD, J., concur.

NOTE

Justice Levin, dissenting in the *Fields* case referred to in *Clemons*, wrote a particularly astute analysis of the unsuitability of the nondelegation doctrine.

> There are a large number of statutory provisions delegating discretionary power to judges without any express standard to guide its exercise. If we hold that a statute conferring on a judge discretionary power is necessarily invalid if guiding standards are not contained in the statute itself, it would necessarily foreshadow holding unconstitutional important provisions of the Code of Criminal Procedure.[52] Large segments of other statutes, e.g., the Revised Judicature Act and the Probate Code, would similarly fall.

[52] As the question before us is one of criminal procedure, we turned to the Code of Criminal Procedure for illustrations. The illustrations could be multiplied by reference to the Revised Judicature Act, the Probate Code, and countless other enactments.

Under the Code of Criminal Procedure, 1927 P.A. 175; M.C.L.A. chs. 760–776; M.S.A. ch. 287, the Legislature has conferred, without any standards whatsoever to guide their exercise, the following powers on judges or courts to be exer-

cised in the judge's or the court's "discretion":

(a) Whether to remand for preliminary examination after a defendant, not then represented by counsel, waives examination. M.C.L.A. § 767.42; M.S.A. § 28.982.

(b) Whether two or more defendants, jointly indicted, shall be tried separately or jointly. M.C.L.A. § 768.5; M.S.A. § 28.1028.

Especially pertinent is the Holmes Youthful Trainee Act which permits a court to "elect" to consider and assign to the status of a youthful trainee a youth who commits a criminal offense between his 17th and 20th birthdays or a youth waived to the court by the juvenile court. M.C.L.A. §§ 762.11, 762.15; M.S.A. §§ 28.853(11), 28.853(15). Many persons, by reason of the Holmes Act and the exercise of trial judge discretion,[53] have avoided criminal prosecution. If the Holmes Act were held to be unconstitutional because express standards are not stated, this beneficial diversion from the formal criminal process might come to an end.

The Legislature might not respond to a decision declaring the Holmes Act unconstitutional. If it were to add standards, little would be added to what is already known and we could ourselves attend to. We know the likely standards: consider the nature of

(c) Whether a sentence imposed for prison escape shall commence forthwith or upon termination of the term or terms the offender is serving. M.C.L.A. § 768.7a; M.S.A. § 28.1030(1).

(d) Whether members of a jury after they are sworn and before the cause is submitted, shall be kept together or permitted to separate. M.C.L.A. § 768.16; M.S.A. § 28.1039.

(e) Whether to exclude evidence of alibi or insanity if the defendant fails to file a notice of such a defense. M.C.L.A. § 768.21; M.S.A. § 28.1044.

(f) Whether to allow leading questions. M.C.L.A. § 768.24; M.S.A. § 28.1047.

(g) whether persons informed against as recidivists shall be sentenced to serve a term of up to 1½ times the longest term prescribed in the case of a second conviction (M.C.L.A. § 769.10; M.S.A. § 28.1082), of up to twice the longest term in the case of a third conviction (M.C.L.A. § 769.11; M.S.A. § 28.1083), of up to life imprisonment in the case of a fourth conviction (M.C.L.A. § 769.12; M.S.A. § 28.1084), or, rather, placed on probation.

(h) Where a crime is committed by a person confined in a penal institution, the preliminary examination may be held in the institution at the "option" of the magistrate. M.C.L.A. § 768.7; M.S.A. § 28.1030.

Other provisions conferring discretionary power without standards, that, like the waiver of juvenile jurisdiction provision, do not mention the word "discretion," are the following:

(a) The court may with the consent of a youth who commits a criminal offense between his 17th and 20th birthdays elect to consider and assign such youth to the status of a youthful trainee under the Holmes Youthful Trainee Act. M.C.L.A. § 762.11; M.S.A. § 28.853(11).

(b) Names of additional witnesses may be added to an information before or during the trial (M.C.L.A. § 767.40; M.S.A. § 28.980), and additional alibi or insanity defense witnesses may be added (M.C.L.A. § 768.20; M.S.A. § 28.1043), in both cases "by leave of the court and upon such conditions as the court shall determine."

(c) The court may at any time before, during or after trial amend the indictment. M.C.L.A. § 767.76; M.S.A. § 28.1016.

(d) A judge may grant a commission to examine material out of state witnesses. M.C.L.A. § 767.77; M.S.A. § 28.1017.

(e) On order of a judge, a defendant may have witnesses examined before a trial in his behalf "conditionally." M.C.L.A. § 767.79; M.S.A. § 28.1019.

(f) Courts are empowered to pronounce sentences of probation, fine or imprisonment, the only limitation being that the sentence cannot exceed the penalty prescribed by law. M.C.L.A. §§ 769.1, 769.8; M.S.A. §§ 28.1072, 28.1080.

(g) A person sentenced to life or any term of years may not be paroled under the lifer law (i.e., after 10 years or more of the sentence has been served) if the sentencing judge files written objections. M.C.L.A. § 791.234; M.S.A. § 28.2304.

(h) Special parole (i.e., release before service of the minimum term less good time) may only be granted with the "approval" of the sentencing judge. M.C.L.A. § 791.233; M.S.A. § 28.2303.

---

[53] The Court of Appeals has indicated that the decision whether a youth shall be tried in a criminal court or given the status of a youthful trainee will be made in the exercise of the trial judge's discretion. People v. Bandy, 35 Mich.App. 53, 58, 192 N.W.2d 115 (1971) (leave denied.)

the offense, the history of the offender, the likelihood of his responding favorably, and the like, standards very much like the criteria, now formalized in the court rule and statute, developed by probate judges for deciding whether to waive juvenile court jurisdiction to a court of general criminal jurisdiction.

The failure of the Legislature to promulgate standards does not gainsay the desirability of requiring guidelines for the exercise of discretionary power. But, surely, we would not hold unconstitutional the Holmes Act, the indeterminate sentence statute or the other statutory provisions mentioned * * * because of the absence of standards in the statute itself. The solution is to formalize sound criteria to govern in future cases now that the need and desirability of structuring the exercise of judicial discretion has been recognized.

XI

The prosecutor has a broad, totally unstructured discretion in charging that is rarely challenged and, with narrow exceptions, not subject to judicial review.[54]

The police also exercise an undefined but very real discretion in charging, releasing without charge many offenders, particularly youthful offenders.[55]

Two men are arrested for engaging in precisely the same criminal conduct. One may be charged and the other released without charge. The legislative proliferation of the common law crimes often means that criminal conduct constitutes more than one crime; this generally gives the prosecutor a choice of charges to lodge against an offender. Persons who engage in the same criminal conduct may be charged with committing different offenses—the possible penalties they face frequently depend on the charge brought by the prosecutor and not on the anti-social conduct in which they engage. The judiciary has declined invitations to control this enormous discretion.[56]

The powers of the prosecutor are not constitutionally established. His duties and powers are those "provided by law." Const. 1963, art. 7, § 4.

In the context of the prosecutor's almost unlimited discretion in charging, a power delegated to him by the Legislature, power which the Legislature manifestly could structure by more carefully defining the various penal offenses, power exercised without any of the safeguards that accompany the judicial process, it simply makes no sense to hold that an adjudication by a probate judge, guided by fundamentally the same highly generalized multi-choice standards

[54] See Miller, Prosecution: The Decision to Charge a Suspect With Crime, p. 154 et seq.; Miller & Remington, Procedures Before Trial, 339 Annals 111, 113–120 (1962); The President's Commission on Law Enforcement and Administration of Justice—Task Force Report: The Courts, pp. 5–8 (1967); Davis, Discretionary Justice, pp. 188–190; 224–225 (1969).

[55] See Packer, The Limits of the Criminal Sanction, p. 291 (1968); Davis, Discretionary Justice, pp. 188–190; 224–225 (1969).

[56] Compare Genesee Prosecutor v. Genesee Circuit Judge, 386 Mich. 672, 683, 194 N.W.2d 693 (1972); People v. Jackson, 29 Mich.App. 654, 185 N.W.2d 608 (1971); People v. Graves, 31 Mich.App. 635, 188 N.W.2d 87 (1971); contrast People v. Mire, 173 Mich. 357, 138 N.W. 1066 (1912).

now formalized by court rule and statute, was defective because the Legislature was unaware that its imprimatur should be added to the judicially-developed standards.

In contrast with the prosecutor's decision to charge Fields, the probate judge's decision to waive jurisdiction of Fields followed a judicial hearing after notice, Fields was represented by counsel, the proceedings were stenographically transcribed, the judge stated the standards by which he felt bound in reaching his decision, he explained the reasons for his decision, and there was an opportunity for judicial review of the waiver decision in the appellate courts.

XII

Standards—the standards added to the waiver of juvenile jurisdiction provision by the Legislature in response to our original opinion—will not eliminate errors in human judgment and in decision making. Standards cannot prevent the arbitrary exercise of power and unjustified discrimination in its administration.

While the standards promulgated by this Court and subsequently enacted by the Legislature are a useful guide for the judicial decision maker, there were few cases in which probate judges were asked to waive jurisdiction before formal standards were promulgated, and still fewer in which waiver orders were entered, where waiver could not have been sustained under the newly-promulgated standards.

The primary safeguards against abuse of discretion by agencies and judges alike—which is at the heart of the objections stated in the originally filed opinion, not delegation as such—are the rights to an evidentiary hearing after proper notice, to representation by counsel and to judicial review upon a transcribed record of the judge's decision elucidated with a statement of facts found and reasons for decision. These safeguards attended the juvenile waiver hearing in this case and have generally been observed in most probate jurisdictions in this state even before *Kent;* they are now formalized in the Juvenile Court Rules of 1969.

The means of protecting juveniles who are improvidently waived to a court of general criminal jurisdiction is appellate intervention. We can protect against unjustified discrimination in the exercise of the waiver power by encouraging the circuit courts and the Court of Appeals to exercise, and by ourselves exercising, thoughtful review on appeals from orders waiving jurisdiction. This means reading transcripts, weighing the testimony, scrutinizing the reasons advanced for ordering and sustaining the waiver, and, where unconvinced, unhesitating intervention.

We would affirm.

People v. Fields, 391 Mich. 206, 246–52, 216 N.W.2d 51, 68–71 (1974). People v. Fields was overruled by People v. Peters, 397 Mich. 360, 244 N.W.2d 898 (1976), cert. denied 429 U.S. 944, 97 S.Ct. 365, 50 L.Ed.2d 315 (1976).

ALABAMA CODE

§ 12-15-33. Transfer of cases to juvenile court from other courts.

(a) If it shall be ascertained during the pendency of a criminal or quasi-criminal charge that a defendant was a child, as defined in this chapter, at the time of the alleged offense, that court, which shall have the duty to ascertain such age, shall forthwith transfer the case, together with all the papers, documents and transcripts of any testimony connected therewith, to the juvenile court. The transferring court shall order that the juvenile be taken forthwith to the place of detention designated by the juvenile court or to the juvenile court itself or shall release him to the custody of his parent or guardian or other person legally responsible for him or under his own recognizance, to be brought before the court at a time designated by it. The accusatory pleading may serve in lieu of a petition in the juvenile court, unless that court directs the filing of a petition. The juvenile court shall then proceed as provided in this chapter. All action taken by the court prior to transfer of the case shall be deemed null and void unless the juvenile court transfers under section 12-15-34.

(b) Any court exercising jurisdiction over traffic offenses may transfer any case involving an alleged traffic offense by a child, as defined in this chapter, to the juvenile court for adjudication as an act of delinquency. (Acts 1975, No. 1205, § 5-112.)

VERMONT STATUTES ANNOTATED, TITLE 33, CHAPTER 12 (1980)

§ 635. Transfer from other courts

(a) If it appears to any court of this state in a criminal proceeding that the defendant was under the age of sixteen years at the time the offense charged was alleged to have been committed, that court shall forthwith transfer the case to the juvenile court under the authority of this chapter.

(b) If it appears to any court of this state in a criminal proceeding that the defendant was over the age of sixteen years and under the age of eighteen years at the time the offense charged was alleged to have been committed, that court may forthwith transfer the proceeding to the juvenile court under the authority of this chapter, and the minor shall thereupon be considered to be subject to this chapter as a delinquent child.

(c) Any such transfer shall include a transfer and delivery of a copy of the accusatory pleading and other papers, documents, and transcripts of testimony relating to the case. Upon any such transfer, that court shall order that the defendant be taken forthwith to a place of detention designated by the juvenile court or to that court itself, or shall release him to the custody of his parent or guardian or other person legally responsible for him, to be brought before the juvenile court at a time designated by that court. The juvenile court shall then proceed as provided in this chapter as if a petition alleging delinquency had been filed with the court under section 645 of this title on the effective date of such transfer. * * *

McKINNEY'S CONSOLIDATED LAWS OF NEW YORK
(1982 and 1983–4 Supp.), CRIMINAL
PROCEDURE LAW

§ 180.75 Proceedings upon felony complaint; juvenile offender

1. When a juvenile offender is arraigned before a local criminal court, the provisions of this section shall apply in lieu of the provisions of sections 180.30, 180.50 and 180.70 of this article.

2. If the defendant waives a hearing upon the felony complaint, the court must order that the defendant be held for the action of the grand jury of the appropriate superior court with respect to the charge or charges contained in the felony complaint. In such case the court must promptly transmit to such superior court the order, the felony complaint, the supporting depositions and all other pertinent documents. Until such papers are received by the superior court, the action is deemed to be still pending in the local criminal court.

3. If there be a hearing, then at the conclusion of the hearing, the court must dispose of the felony complaint as follows:

(a) If there is reasonable cause to believe that the defendant committed a crime for which a person under the age of sixteen is criminally responsible, the court must order that the defendant be held for the action of a grand jury of the appropriate superior court, and it must promptly transmit to such superior court the order, the felony complaint, the supporting depositions and all other pertinent documents. Until such papers are received by the superior court, the action is deemed to be still pending in the local criminal court; or

(b) If there is not reasonable cause to believe that the defendant committed a crime for which a person under the age of sixteen is criminally responsible but there is reasonable cause to believe that the defendant is a "juvenile delinquent" as defined in subdivision one of section 301.2 of the family court act, the court must specify the act or acts it found reasonable cause to believe the defendant did and direct that the action be removed to the family court in accordance with the provisions of article seven hundred twenty-five of this chapter; or

(c) If there is not reasonable cause to believe that the defendant committed any criminal act, the court must dismiss the felony complaint and discharge the defendant from custody if he is in custody, or if he is at liberty on bail, it must exonerate the bail.

4. Notwithstanding the provisions of subdivision two and three of this section, a local criminal court shall, at the request of the

district attorney, order removal of an action against a juvenile offender to the family court pursuant to the provisions of article seven hundred twenty-five of this chapter if, upon consideration of the criteria specified in subdivision two of section 210.43 of this chapter, it is determined that to do so would be in the interests of justice. Where, however, the felony complaint charges the juvenile offender with murder in the second degree as defined in section 125.25 of the penal law, rape in the first degree as defined in subdivision one of section 130.35 of the penal law, sodomy in the first degree as defined in subdivision one of section 130.50 of the penal law, or an armed felony as defined in paragraph (a) of subdivision forty-one of section 1.20 of this chapter, a determination that such action be removed to the family court shall, in addition, be based upon a finding of one or more of the following factors: (i) mitigating circumstances that bear directly upon the manner in which the crime was committed; or (ii) where the defendant was not the sole participant in the crime, the defendant's participation was relatively minor although not so minor as to constitute a defense to the prosecution; or (iii) possible deficiencies in proof of the crime.

5.   Notwithstanding the provisions of subdivision two, three, or four, if a currently undetermined felony complaint against a juvenile offender is pending in a local criminal court, and the defendant has not waived a hearing pursuant to subdivision two and a hearing pursuant to subdivision three has not commenced, the defendant may move in the superior court which would exercise the trial jurisdiction of the offense or offenses charged were an indictment therefor to result, to remove the action to family court. The procedural rules of subdivisions one and two of section 210.45 of this chapter are applicable to a motion pursuant to this subdivision. Upon such motion, the superior court shall be authorized to sit as a local criminal court to exercise the preliminary jurisdiction specified in subdivisions two and three of this section, and shall proceed and determine the motion as provided in section 210.43 of this chapter; provided, however, that the exception provisions of paragraph (b) of subdivision one of such section 210.43 shall not apply when there is not reasonable cause to believe that the juvenile offender committed one or more of the crimes enumerated therein, and in such event the provisions of paragraph (a) thereof shall apply.

6.   (a) If the court orders removal of the action to family court, it shall state on the record the factor or factors upon which its determination is based, and the court shall give its reasons for removal in detail and not in conclusory terms.

(b) The district attorney shall state upon the record the reasons for his consent to removal of the action to the family court where such consent is required. The reasons shall be stated in detail and not in conclusory terms.

(c) For the purpose of making a determination pursuant to subdivision four or five, the court may make such inquiry as it deems necessary. Any evidence which is not legally privileged may be introduced. If the defendant testifies, his testimony may not be introduced against him in any future proceeding, except to impeach his testimony at such future proceeding as inconsistent prior testimony.

(d) Where a motion for removal by the defendant pursuant to subdivision five has been denied, no further motion pursuant to this section or section 210.43 of this chapter may be made by the juvenile offender with respect to the same offense or offenses.

(e) Except as provided by paragraph (f), this section shall not be construed to limit the powers of the grand jury.

(f) Where a motion by the defendant pursuant to subdivision five has been granted, there shall be no further proceedings against the juvenile offender in any local or superior criminal court for the offense or offenses which were the subject of the removal order.

CERTIFICATION OF MINORS TO THE JUVENILE COURT: AN EMPIRICAL STUDY
8 San Diego L.Rev. 404, 410, 415–424 (1971).[*]

* * *

Almost all states have separate juvenile courts which take jurisdiction over offenders below a certain age, usually 16 or 18. In addition, most states have statutes which basically allow concurrent jurisdiction of offenders between the ages of 16 and 18. Details vary from one state to another, but the general scheme is for the juvenile court to have original jurisdiction of offenders under a certain age, usually 18 with a possibility of transferring any offender over a certain age, usually 14 or 16, to the adult court after a finding is made in the juvenile court that the offender is unfit for juvenile process. The process of transferring a case from juvenile to adult court is known as "waiver of jurisdiction" in most states, but the terms "certification" and "remand" are also common and are used in California. The adult courts generally have original jurisdiction over offenders over the age of 16 or 18 with authority to certify offenders under the age of 21 to the juvenile court for consideration of treatment as a juvenile where the minor would appear to benefit more from the services of the juvenile court. Although this study examines the practice in one county of California, the problem exists in every state and the local situation is considered reasonably representative of the national practice.

* * *

It appears that there are settled guidelines for certifying a minor from juvenile court to the adult court and yet no guidelines for certifying a minor from adult court to juvenile court other than the judge should not "abuse his discretion." The empirical study reported below seeks to determine what type of cases are, in fact, certified to the juvenile court and, just as important, what is done with these cases when they reach the juvenile court.

METHOD

The probation case folders of cases certified from the municipal and superior courts of San Diego County, California to the juvenile court were examined for four months during a one-year period after the final disposition of the case in the juvenile court. The four months were randomly chosen except that months with an unusually low or high amount of certifications were avoided to insure uniform sample size. All the cases that were certified in each month were examined except for a minimal number of cases each month that were not available because of misfiling or similar mechanical problems. The period covered was August 1969 to July 1970. The four months examined were October 1969, January 1970, March 1970 and July 1970, or one month in each quarter. The total number of cases examined was 231, which represented approximately one-third of the total of 742 cases certified during the period.

The cases were tabulated into different categories based on the criteria suggested in *Kent*, for example, the number and percentages of youth certified with extensive criminal records, serious offenses, emancipated status, et cetera. The final disposition of the juvenile court was also tabulated into four different categories reflecting either adult-oriented dispositions, such as court costs (basically a fine), or juvenile type dispositions, such as juvenile probation, juvenile work project, voluntary counseling, et cetera.

RESULTS

The individual factors, isolated as they are, must be viewed with caution since each case must be decided on its own merits taking the totality of factors into consideration on a case by case basis. However, certain general trends can be ascertained by using a statistical approach and for this purpose only the approach is valid.

TABLE I

Past Record

	October 1969	January 1970	March 1970	July 1970	Total Sample
Juvenile Record	(18) 37%	(15) 28%	(19) 30%	(23) 34%	(75) 32%
Adult Record	(7) 15%	(3) 6%	(4) 6%	(5) 7%	(19) 8%
Traffic Record (Extensive)	(4) 8%	(5) 9%	(6) 10%	(9) 13%	(24) 10%
Total Past Record	(29) 60%	(23) 46%	(29) 46%	(37) 55%	(118) 51%
	N = 48	N = 53	N = 63	N = 67	TN = 231

Table I shows the number and percentages of minors certified with past records. The juvenile record column included only cases serious enough to have a probation file opened and did not include minor offenses handled by the police on an informal basis. The adult record column included only convictions or prosecutions then pending in adult courts. Arrest records were not used. The traffic record column included only repeated violators and excluded non-moving violations.

From *Table I* we note that thirty-two percent of all certifications had previous juvenile records. While this factor alone might not indicate unfitness for juvenile court process, one wonders why the minor is suddenly in a position to take advantage of juvenile services because he is over the age of eighteen and has committed another offense after having previously had the advantage of juvenile services. It is a fact that the juvenile court is overloaded in almost every jurisdiction and that certifications which have already shown an inability to profit from the juvenile court process take time and resources away from juveniles who may better be able to profit from the experience. It is not suggested that a prior juvenile record be a bar to certification, but it is suggested that 32 percent is too high a percentage to believe that individual factors in each case outweighed the behavior pattern suggested by the previous record with the juvenile court. A much more likely theory is that the minors are being certified to the juvenile court in many cases with little, if any, consideration of their amenability to the juvenile court process.

The adult record column reveals that 19 minors, or 8 percent of all certifications, had either adult convictions, were on adult probation, or had prosecutions pending in adult court. Again, one wonders why a minor should now be handled in a juvenile court if his background had previously been found more appropriate for adult court process or if he in some cases was already on adult probation.

Another facet of the same problem is the effect of older, sophisticated offenders on younger, more impressionable youth. The older age and previous law violations may serve as a status symbol for a youth who may be on the brink of choosing a life of crime. Minors with adult and juvenile records together comprise 40 percent of all certifications. These statistics suggest more thought about the certification process from the vantage point of the adult court.

Individual cases may have additional factors which defeat the presumption of "adulthood," but the large percentage certified suggests that much judicial time and energy could be saved if more consideration of record were given at the adult court before certification.

Table II shows the number and percentage of minors certified charged with serious offenses. Statistics on the type of offense for the month of July 1970 were not available and the table covers three months with a total sample of 164 cases. Using the *Kent* criteria, these include mostly offenses against the person although burglary of $500 or more and sale of drugs were included as they are almost universally considered serious offenses. The sale of drugs column included only actual sales and almost all of these were admitted sales to undercover agents.

TABLE II

Serious Offenses

	October 1969	January 1970	March 1970	July 1970	Total Sample
Sale of Drugs	(3) 6%	(3) 6%	(10) 16%	—	(16) 10%
Burglary of $500+	(3) 6%	(1) 2%	(2) 3%	—	(6) 4%
Assault & Battery	(1) 2%	(1) 2%	0	—	(2) 1%
Robbery	(1) 2%	(1) 2%	0	—	(2) 1%
Murder & Manslaughter	0	(1) 2%	0	—	(1) 1%
Total Serious Offenses	(8) 17%	(7) 13%	(12) 19%	—	(27) 16%
	N = 48	N = 53	N = 63	—	TN = 164

TABLE III

Less Serious Offenses

	October 1969	January 1970	March 1970	Total Sample
Possession Marijuana	(11) 23%	(13) 25%	(17) 27%	(41) 25%
Possession Dangerous Drugs	(8) 17%	(6) 11%	(16) 25%	(30) 18%
Under Influence Drugs	(6) 13%	(8) 15%	(2) 3%	(16) 10%
Possession LSD	(3) 6%	(1) 2%	(6) 10%	(10) 6%
All Other Offenses	(12) 25%	(18) 34%	(10) 16%	(40) 24%
Total Less Serious Offenses	(40) 83%	(46) 87%	(51) 81%	(137) 84%
	N = 48	N = 53	N = 63	TN = 164

Table III shows the number and percentages of minors certified with less serious offenses. Although the offenses may seem serious to some and from a social and personal standpoint are serious indeed, they are categorized using the *Kent* standards and are offenses where the real victim is usually the offender and society at large.

Since the seriousness of the alleged offense is only one factor in the certification process and is a factor the courts appear to feel of less importance, *Table II* and *Table III* would seem to be of less significance. However, in view of the current drug problem, sale of drugs might be considered of special importance. Again, although individual case factors may defeat the presumption, it is hard to imagine a person over the age of 18 who sells drugs illegally for a profit as the type of individual who is best suited for handling by our juvenile courts. It is especially hard to entertain this belief for all 16 of the minors certified when they comprise 10 percent of the certification in the sample for the one-year period.

TABLE IV

Emancipation Factors

	October 1969	January 1970	March 1970	July 1970	Total Sample
Emancipated (Composite Score)	(6) 13%	(9) 17%	(8) 13%	(17) 25%	(40) 17%
Self-Supporting	(9) 19%	(8) 15%	(13) 21%	(18) 27%	(48) 21%
Married	0	(1) 2%	(2) 3%	(1) 1%	(4) 2%
Military	(3) 6%	(5) 9%	(1) 1%	(4) 6%	(13) 6%
College Student	(8) 17%	(5) 9%	(14) 22%	—	(27) 16%
Non-Resident	(5) 10%	(8) 15%	(13) 21%	(13) 19%	(39) 13%
	N = 48	N = 53	N = 63	N = 67	TN = 231

Table IV shows some factors used in considering whether a minor's life style is more like a juvenile living at home under the guidance of his parent or like an adult with independent status. The emancipated column is a composite score and represents the number and percentage of minors with three or more indicators of emancipation, such as not living at home, independent income, lack of guidance from parental figure, et cetera. The number of college students certified in the month of July was not available. Twenty-one percent of all the minors certified were self-supporting and 13 percent of all cases certified were non-residents, usually out of state transients. It might be asked what services the local juvenile court can offer a minor who lives two thousand miles away. Of course, courtesy supervision by an out-of-state juvenile court is a possibility, but practical problems arise because jurisdiction age differs from state to state and many juvenile courts are less than enthusiastic about supervising a 20-year-old for shoplifting a candy bar when the jurisdiction of their court ends at age 16.

TABLE V

Miscellaneous Factors

	October 1969	January 1970	March 1970	July 1970	Total Sample
Minor or Attorney Prefer Adult Ct	(1) 2%	(3) 6%	(2) 3%	(1) 1%	(7) 3%
Companion Handled in Adult Ct	(1) 2%	(3) 6%	(5) 8%	(10) 15%	(19) 8%
Probation Report Recommend Remand	(18) 38%	(13) 25%	(10) 16%	(12) 18%	(53) 23%
Actually Remanded to Adult Court	(10) 21%	(12) 23%	(5) 8%	(12) 18%	(39) 17%
	N = 48	N = 53	N = 63	N = 67	TN = 231

Table V shows miscellaneous factors associated with the transfer of cases between the adult or juvenile court. Seven minors wanted their cases to remain in adult court, possibly because a minor may receive a stricter disposition in juvenile court for some traffic matters where the statutes require automatic revocation of driving privileges for certain offenses committed by minors.

TABLE VI

Juvenile Court Dispositions

	October 1969	January 1970	March 1970	July 1970	Total Sample
Juvenile Type Disposition	(6) 13%	(7) 13%	(20) 32%	(17) 25%	(50) 21%
Adult Type Disposition (Court Costs & Dismiss)	(24) 50%	(28) 53%	(27) 43%	(31) 46%	(110) 48%
Dismiss, Lack of Evidence	(8) 17%	(6) 11%	(11) 17%	(7) 10%	(32) 14%
Remand to Adult Ct	(10) 21%	(12) 23%	(5) 8%	(12) 18%	(39) 17%
	N = 48	N = 53	N = 63	N = 67	TN = 231

Table VI shows the status of the cases after final disposition by the juvenile court. The column juvenile type disposition includes cases that were given a disposition of a nature not available to the adult court. Included in this category were juvenile probation, juvenile work project, haircuts, voluntary counseling programs, et cetera. Although probation is available to the adult court, it differs significantly from juvenile probation in that the latter involves more emphasis on family and community factors. Adult type dispositions consisted of court costs and dismissal of the juvenile court petition. The court costs ranged generally from twenty-five dollars to five hundred dollars. It would appear the court cost and dismissal action is essentially a fine which would also be available to the adult court with the important exception that the offender has only a juvenile record and no adult convictions when he is certified to the juvenile court. Thirty-two cases, which comprise 14 percent of all cases certified, were dismissed because of lack of evidence. It appears that some adult courts use certifications to the juvenile court as a convenient means of getting rid of cases which are either lacking in evidence or are of such minor consequence as not to justify court time. This is a minor point, but it was presumably the purpose of the legislature in setting up the juvenile court to provide specialized services for youthful offenders rather than provide disposal of adult cases where the charges were without merit.

Of more significance in *Table VI* is the fact that 110 minors, or 48 percent of all minors certified, were given adult type dispositions. These dispositions were court costs which appear to be a fine; a disposition also available to the adult court. The reason for these dispositions is apparent; what else can the juvenile court do with a minor who has already been on juvenile probation and failed, is not living at home under parental supervision, is self-supporting and lives out of state, et cetera. The remand column shows that a significant number of these minors are remanded (17 percent). In many cases, this is a waste of time for all concerned, since the adult court will likely give the minor a suspended sentence and a fine which, to the minor, is viewed the same as court costs in the juvenile court.

Indeed, a recent statistical study examined a total of 184 cases in Riverside County and concluded that there was no statistically significant difference between the success rates of the cases handled on juvenile probation and those handled on adult probation (Chi Square = .098 P > .70).[57]

> The results of the study indicate that among cases which were eligible to be considered for certification the likelihood for success was the same whether juvenile or adult probation was granted (85 percent and 82.4 percent). This could be the basis for an argument to either extend certification to many more individuals or to do away with it, depending on one's point of view.

[57] * * * *Chi Square* is a traditional test of statistical significance which in this case shows that the slight difference in the two groups is attributable to chance rather than to a meaningful difference between the groups.

It appears to be a misuse of judicial process to certify these gross cases in the first place, and an equal misuse of judicial process for the juvenile court to be forced to either give a fine or remand the case to the adult court.

Concerning California certification practices in general, it was further noted:

1. Most of the counties use differing guidelines to determine suitability for certification, and many of these guidelines are quite dissimilar.

2. Five counties do not accept certification cases in juvenile court, as a matter of policy. Larger counties are included, so that availability of probation supervision is not the determining factor in these policies.

3. Five counties generally accept certification in juvenile court, as a matter of policy, in order to prevent the client from having an adult conviction record.

4. Of the 46 counties which accept certifications, only three have special supervision programs for those clients, and only one has a specific treatment program which has organized rehabilitative services for them.

The question devolves to the difference between a juvenile record and an adult conviction. Many attorneys are quite frank in admitting that the reason they seek certification to the juvenile court is not because they feel their client is more amenable to the services of the juvenile court but because, in the spirit of advocacy, they are trying to get the best deal for their client and avoid the serious consequences of an adult conviction. The merits of this practice is the subject of another debate, but surely the legislature's purpose in creating the juvenile court was to provide specialized services for youthful offenders rather than save adults from the consequences of their own acts. This practice becomes further suspect when we re-examine *Table I* and note that many of these clients we are trying to save from the horrors of an adult conviction have already enjoyed the services of the juvenile court and have failed to benefit and some, in fact, already have adult convictions on their record. The practice only succeeds in mixing older offenders with younger offenders without providing any specialized treatment program for the older offender. An illusionary benefit is thus bought at a high price.

IV. CONCLUSION

The provisions of most state statutes for the transfer of cases of young offenders from the adult court to the juvenile court is necessary to avoid many injustices in individual cases. Unquestionably, the vast majority of cases certified to the juvenile courts result in greater justice and better service to the community. But a substantial minority of minors are either certified to the juvenile court without any consideration of their amenability to the juvenile court process or are certified for reasons in violation of the spirit of the juvenile court, such as avoidance of the stigma of an adult conviction or frivolity of the case against the minor. The results are a misuse of judicial process, a denial of the accused's right to a speedy trial, and an overburdening of both the adult and the juvenile court calendars.

An alternative might be, first, to give a brief consideration of the *Kent* factors at the adult level, perhaps by requiring the attorneys to include some type of brief information concerning the minor's background with the motion for certification and, second, to either eliminate or reduce to minor violations some of the unpopular laws which the adult courts are so hesitant to adjudicate. But the real significance of this problem is not the specific misuse of judicial process which it represents, but the dishonesty it reveals concerning the juvenile court process. At a time when many people are beginning to question the underlying assumptions of the juvenile court process, we see that attorneys are deliberately working against one of the basic goals of the juvenile court by mixing older sophisticated offenders with more impressionable youth in order to "get their client the best deal." We also see that to many people, being judged delinquent is synonymous with being "criminal." At this same critical period in juvenile court evolution, we see indications that probation officers do not consider a commitment to the Youth Authority as rehabilitative and statistics that strongly indicate that older youth do just as well when handled in the adult courts without the "benefits" of a certification to the juvenile court. Manipulation of the mechanics of a legal system to avoid evils which have entered that system is no substitute for honest recognition of the problems and a straight forward effort at solution.

NOTES

1. In several instances, prosecutors have attempted to appeal immediately an order of a juvenile judge refusing to certify a child to an adult criminal court. In some instances, the reason given for refusing to review the order is its interlocutory character. Welfare of A.L.J. v. State, 300 Minn. 542, 220 N.W.2d 303 (1974); State v. Valentine, 536 P.2d 1291 (Okl.Cr.App. 1975).

2. In other instances, children who have been certified have attempted to appeal the certification order immediately. For the most part, courts have interpreted their procedural statutes to require dismissal of the appeal on the ground that the order is interlocutory. Although under earlier Maryland statutes the order was final and so immediately appealable, the Maryland statute was later amended to make the order interlocutory. The matter is discussed in Aye v. State, 17 Md.App. 32, 299 A.2d 513 (1973); In re Trader, 20 Md.App. 1, 315 A.2d 528 (1974) reversed and remanded 272 Md. 364, 325 A.2d 398 (1974); In re Appeal No. 961 etc., 23 Md.App. 9, 325 A.2d 112 (1974). See also, Buchanan v. Commonwealth, 652 S.W.2d 87 (Ky.1983).

On the other hand the Supreme Court of Hawaii, following California and Idaho cases, held that the juvenile must appeal from the transfer order prior to the commencement of the criminal trial. State v. Stanley, 60 Haw. 527, 592 P.2d 422, (1979), cert. denied 444 U.S. 871, 100 S.Ct. 149, 62 L.Ed.2d 97 (1979).

3. The juvenile who is certified to and convicted in a criminal court may appeal from the judgment of conviction, assigning as one of his grounds the impropriety of the certification order. In re Appeal No. 961 etc., 23 Md.App. 9, 325 A.2d 112 (1974). The state, on the other hand, has been denied a right to appeal from an adjudication of delinquency even on the ground that certification should have occurred. State v. Valentine, 536 P.2d 1291 (Okl. Cr.App.1975) (based on statute); State v. Jump, 160 Ind.App. 1, 309 N.E.2d 148 (1974) (based on discretion of juvenile court). In any event, since the Supreme Court of the United States has held the double jeopardy clause of the federal constitution applicable to juvenile delinquency proceedings, the state would in any event be precluded from trying the child in a criminal proceeding. See Breed v. Jones, 421 U.S. 519, 95 S.Ct. 1779, 44 L.Ed.2d 346 (1975).

4. If, on the other hand, the juvenile court is without jurisdiction, prohibition is available to prevent that court from proceeding either by way of adjudicating the child a delinquent or by way of certifying him to the criminal court. State ex rel. Atkins v. Juvenile Court, 252 Ind. 237, 247 N.E.2d 53 (Sup.Ct.Ind.1969). See also, In re F.R.W., 61 Wis.2d 193, 212 N.W.2d 130, cert. denied 416 U.S. 974, 94 S.Ct. 2000, 40 L.Ed.2d 563 (1973), holding that the State could appeal directly to the Wisconsin Supreme Court from an order denying certification based on an incorrect holding that the Wisconsin certification statute was unconstitutional.

5. Dicta in People v. Morris, 57 Mich.App. 573, 226 N.W.2d 565 (1975), cert. denied, 423 U.S. 849, 96 S.Ct. 90, 46 L.Ed.2d 72 (1975) suggests that by entering a guilty plea in a criminal case, the defendant waives any defect in the certification hearing based on the use there of a confession which may have been obtained during a period of illegal detention.

Chapter 7

THE ADJUDICATION HEARING

A. THE SUPREME COURT'S FRAMEWORK

IN RE GAULT

Supreme Court of the United States, 1967.
387 U.S. 1, 87 S.Ct. 1428, 18 L.Ed.2d 527.

MR. JUSTICE FORTAS delivered the opinion of the Court.

This is an appeal under 28 U.S.C. § 1257(2) from a judgment of the Supreme Court of Arizona affirming the dismissal of a petition for a writ of habeas corpus. 99 Ariz. 181, 407 P.2d 760 (1965). The petition sought the release of Gerald Francis Gault, appellants' 15-year-old son, who had been committed as a juvenile delinquent to the State Industrial School by the Juvenile Court of Gila County, Arizona. The Supreme Court of Arizona affirmed dismissal of the writ against various arguments which included an attack upon the constitutionality of the Arizona Juvenile Code because of its alleged denial of procedural due process rights to juveniles charged with being "delinquents." The court agreed that the constitutional guarantee of due process of law is applicable in such proceedings. It held that Arizona's Juvenile Code is to be read as "impliedly" implementing the "due process concept." It then proceeded to identify and describe "the particular elements which constitute due process in a juvenile hearing." It concluded that the proceedings ending in commitment of Gerald Gault did not offend those requirements. We do not agree, and we reverse. We begin with a statement of the facts.

I.

On Monday, June 8, 1964, at about 10 a.m., Gerald Francis Gault and a friend, Ronald Lewis, were taken into custody by the Sheriff of Gila County. Gerald was then still subject to a six months' probation order which had been entered on February 25, 1964, as a result of his having been in the company of another boy who had stolen a wallet from a lady's purse. The police action on June 8 was taken as the result of a verbal complaint by a neighbor of the boys, Mrs. Cook, about a telephone call made to her in which the caller or callers made lewd or indecent remarks. It will suffice for purposes of this opinion to say that the remarks or questions put to her were of the irritatingly offensive, adolescent, sex variety.

At the time Gerald was picked up, his mother and father were both at work. No notice that Gerald was being taken into custody was left at the home. No other steps were taken to advise them that their son had, in effect, been arrested. Gerald was taken to the Children's Detention Home. When his mother arrived home at about 6 o'clock, Gerald was not there. Gerald's older brother was sent to look for him at the trailer home of the Lewis family. He apparently learned then that Gerald was in custody. He so informed his mother. The two of them went to the Detention Home. The deputy probation officer, Flagg, who was also superintendent of the Detention Home, told Mrs. Gault "why Jerry was there" and said that a hearing would be held in Juvenile Court at 3 o'clock the following day, June 9.

Officer Flagg filed a petition with the court on the hearing day, June 9, 1964. It was not served on the Gaults. Indeed, none of them saw this petition until the habeas corpus hearing on August 17, 1964. The petition was entirely formal. It made no reference to any factual basis for the judicial action which it initiated. It recited only that "said minor is under the age of eighteen years, and is in need of the protection of this Honorable Court; [and that] said minor is a delinquent minor." It prayed for a hearing and an order regarding "the care and custody of said minor." Officer Flagg executed a formal affidavit in support of the petition.

On June 9, Gerald, his mother, his older brother, and Probation Officers Flagg and Henderson appeared before the Juvenile Judge in chambers. Gerald's father was not there. He was at work out of the city. Mrs. Cook, the complainant, was not there. No one was sworn at this hearing. No transcript or recording was made. No memorandum or record of the substance of the proceedings was prepared. Our information about the proceedings and the subsequent hearing on June 15, derives entirely from the testimony of the Juvenile Court Judge, Mr. and Mrs. Gault and Officer Flagg at the habeas corpus proceeding conducted two months later. From this, it appears that at the June 9 hearing Gerald was questioned by the judge about the telephone call. There was conflict as to what he said. His mother recalled that Gerald said he only dialed Mrs. Cook's number and handed the telephone to his friend, Ronald. Officer Flagg recalled that Gerald had admitted making the lewd remarks. Judge McGhee testified that Gerald "admitted making one of these [lewd] statements." At the conclusion of the hearing, the judge said he would "think about it." Gerald was taken back to the Detention Home. He was not sent to his own home with his parents. On June 11 or 12, after having been detained since June 8, Gerald was released and driven home. There is no explanation in the record as to why he was kept in the Detention Home or why he was released. At 5 p.m. on the day of Gerald's release, Mrs. Gault received a note signed by Officer Flagg. It was on plain paper, not letterhead. Its entire text was as follows:

"Mrs. Gault:

"Judge McGHEE has set Monday June 15, 1964 at 11:00 A.M. as the date and time for further Hearings on Gerald's delinquency

"/s/ Flagg"

At the appointed time on Monday, June 15, Gerald, his father and mother, Ronald Lewis and his father, and Officers Flagg and Henderson were present before Judge McGhee. Witnesses at the habeas corpus proceeding differed in their recollections of Gerald's testimony at the June 15 hearing. Mr. and Mrs. Gault recalled that Gerald again testified that he had only dialed the number and that the other boy had made the remarks. Officer Flagg agreed that at this hearing Gerald did not admit making the lewd remarks. But Judge McGhee recalled that "there was some admission again of some of the lewd statements. He—he didn't admit any of the more serious lewd statements." Again, the complainant, Mrs. Cook, was not present. Mrs. Gault asked that Mrs. Cook be present "so she could see which boy that done the talking, the dirty talking over the phone." The Juvenile Judge said "she didn't have to be present at that hearing." The judge did not speak to Mrs. Cook or communicate with her at any time. Probation Officer Flagg had talked to her once—over the telephone on June 9.

At this June 15 hearing a "referral report" made by the probation officers was filed with the court, although not disclosed to Gerald or his parents. This listed the charge as "Lewd Phone Calls." At the conclusion of the hearing, the judge committed Gerald as a juvenile delinquent to the State Industrial School "for the period of his minority [that is, until 21], unless sooner discharged by due process of law." An order to that effect was entered. It recites that "after a full hearing and due deliberation the Court finds that said minor is a delinquent child, and that said minor is of the age of 15 years."

No appeal is permitted by Arizona law in juvenile cases. On August 3, 1964, a petition for a writ of habeas corpus was filed with the Supreme Court of Arizona and referred by it to the Superior Court for hearing.

At the habeas corpus hearing on August 17, Judge McGhee was vigorously cross-examined as to the basis for his actions. He testified that he had taken into account the fact that Gerald was on probation. He was asked "under what section of * * * the code you found the boy delinquent?"

His answer is set forth in the margin.[1] In substance, he concluded that Gerald came within ARS § 8–201, subsec. 6(a), which specifies that a "delinquent child" includes one "who has violated a law of the state or an ordinance or regulation of a political subdivision thereof." The law which Gerald was found to have violated is ARS § 13–377.

[1] "Q. All right. Now, Judge, would you tell me under what section of the law or tell me under what section of—of the code you found the boy delinquent?

"A. Well, there is a—I think it amounts to disturbing the peace. I can't give you the section, but I can tell you the law, that when one person uses lewd language in the presence of another person, that it can amount to—and I consider that when a person makes it over the phone, that it is considered in the presence, I might be wrong, that is one section. The other section upon which I consider the boy delinquent is Section 8–201, Subsection (d), habitually involved in immoral matters."

This section of the Arizona Criminal Code provides that a person who "in the presence or hearing of any woman or child * * * uses vulgar, abusive or obscene language, is guilty of a misdemeanor * * *." The penalty specified in the Criminal Code, which would apply to an adult, is $5 to $50, or imprisonment for not more than two months. The judge also testified that he acted under ARS § 8–201, subsec. 6(d) which includes in the definition of a "delinquent child" one who, as the judge phrased it, is "habitually involved in immoral matters."[2]

Asked about the basis for his conclusion that Gerald was "habitually involved in immoral matters," the judge testified, somewhat vaguely, that two years earlier, on June 2, 1962, a "referral" was made concerning Gerald, "where the boy had stolen a baseball glove from another boy and lied to the Police Department about it." The judge said there was "no hearing," and "no accusation" relating to this incident, "because of lack of material foundation." But it seems to have remained in his mind as a relevant factor. The judge also testified that Gerald had admitted making other nuisance phone calls in the past which, as the judge recalled the boy's testimony, were "silly calls, or funny calls, or something like that."

The Superior Court dismissed the writ, and appellants sought review in the Arizona Supreme Court. That court stated that it considered appellants' assignments of error as urging (1) that the Juvenile Code, ARS § 8–201 to § 8–239, is unconstitutional because it does not require that parents and children be apprised of the specific charges, does not require proper notice of a hearing, and does not provide for an appeal; and (2) that the proceedings and order relating to Gerald constituted a denial of due process of law because of the absence of adequate notice of the charge and the hearing; failure to notify appellants of certain constitutional rights including the rights to counsel and to confrontation, and the privilege against self-incrimination; the use of unsworn hearsay testimony; and the failure to make a record of the proceedings. Appellants further asserted that it was error for the Juvenile Court to remove Gerald from the custody of his parents without a showing and finding of their unsuitability, and alleged a miscellany of other errors under state law.

The Supreme Court handed down an elaborate and wide-ranging opinion affirming dismissal of the writ and stating the court's conclusions as to the issues raised by appellants and other aspects of the juvenile process. In their jurisdictional statement and brief in this

---

[2] ARS § 8–201, subsec. 6, the section of the Arizona Juvenile Code which defines a delinquent child, reads:

" 'Delinquent child' includes:

"(a) A child who has violated a law of the state or an ordinance or regulation of a political subdivision thereof.

"(b) A child who, by reason of being incorrigible, wayward or habitually disobedient, is uncontrolled by his parent, guardian or custodian.

"(c) A child who is habitually truant from school or home.

"(d) A child who habitually so deports himself as to injure or endanger the morals or health of himself or others."

Court, appellants do not urge upon us all of the points passed upon
by the Supreme Court of Arizona. They urge that we hold the
Juvenile Code of Arizona invalid on its face or as applied in this case
because, contrary to the Due Process Clause of the Fourteenth
Amendment, the juvenile is taken from the custody of his parents and
committed to a state institution pursuant to proceedings in which the
Juvenile Court has virtually unlimited discretion, and in which the
following basic rights are denied:

1. Notice of the charges;

2. Right to counsel;

3. Right to confrontation and cross-examination;

4. Privilege against self-incrimination;

5. Right to a transcript of the proceedings; and

6. Right to appellate review.

We shall not consider other issues which were passed upon by the
Supreme Court of Arizona. We emphasize that we indicate no
opinion as to whether the decision of that court with respect to such
other issues does or does not conflict with requirements of the
Federal Constitution.

II.

The Supreme Court of Arizona held that due process of law is
requisite to the constitutional validity of proceedings in which a court
reaches the conclusion that a juvenile has been at fault, has engaged
in conduct prohibited by law, or has otherwise misbehaved with the
consequence that he is committed to an institution in which his
freedom is curtailed. This conclusion is in accord with the decisions
of a number of courts under both federal and state constitutions.

This Court has not heretofore decided the precise question. In
Kent v. United States, 383 U.S. 541, 86 S.Ct. 1045, 16 L.Ed.2d 84
(1966), we considered the requirements for a valid waiver of the
"exclusive" jurisdiction of the Juvenile Court of the District of
Columbia so that a juvenile could be tried in the adult criminal court
of the District. Although our decision turned upon the language of
the statute, we emphasized the necessity that "the basic requirements of due process and fairness" be satisfied in such proceedings.
Haley v. State of Ohio, 332 U.S. 596, 68 S.Ct. 302, 92 L.Ed. 224 (1948),
involved the admissibility, in a state criminal court of general jurisdiction, of a confession by a 15-year-old boy. The Court held that the
Fourteenth Amendment applied to prohibit the use of the coerced
confession. Mr. Justice Douglas said, "Neither man nor child can be
allowed to stand condemned by methods which flout constitutional
requirements of due process of law." To the same effect is Gallegos
v. State of Colorado, 370 U.S. 49, 82 S.Ct. 1209, 8 L.Ed.2d 325 (1962).
Accordingly, while these cases relate only to restricted aspects of the
subject, they unmistakably indicate that, whatever may be their
precise impact, neither the Fourteenth Amendment nor the Bill of
Rights is for adults alone.

limited
only to adjudication stage — viel usually or Rehnquist

We do not in this opinion consider the impact of these constitutional provisions upon the totality of the relationship of the juvenile and the state. We do not even consider the entire process relating to juvenile "delinquents." For example, we are not here concerned with the procedures or constitutional rights applicable to the pre-judicial stages of the juvenile process, nor do we direct our attention to the post-adjudicative or dispositional process. We consider only the problems presented to us by this case. These relate to the proceedings by which a determination is made as to whether a juvenile is a "delinquent" as a result of alleged misconduct on his part, with the consequence that he may be committed to a state institution. As to these proceedings, there appears to be little current dissent from the proposition that the Due Process Clause has a role to play. The problem is to ascertain the precise impact of the due process requirement upon such proceedings.

* * *

In view of this, it would be extraordinary if our Constitution did not require the procedural regularity and the exercise of care implied in the phrase "due process." Under our Constitution, the condition of being a boy does not justify a kangaroo court. The traditional ideas of Juvenile Court procedure, indeed, contemplated that time would be available and care would be used to establish precisely what the juvenile did and why he did it—was it a prank of adolescence or a brutal act threatening serious consequences to himself or society unless corrected? Under traditional notions, one would assume that in a case like that of Gerald Gault, where the juvenile appears to have a home, a working mother and father, and an older brother, the Juvenile Judge would have made a careful inquiry and judgment as to the possibility that the boy could be disciplined and dealt with at home, despite his previous transgressions.[3] Indeed, so far as appears in the record before us, except for some conversation with Gerald about his school work and his "wanting to go to * * * Grand Canyon with his father," the points to which the judge directed his attention were little different from those that would be involved in determining any charge of violation of a penal statute. The essential difference between Gerald's case and a normal criminal case is that safeguards available to adults were discarded in Gerald's case. The summary procedure as well as the long commitment was possible because Gerald was 15 years of age instead of over 18.

[3] The Juvenile Judge's testimony at the habeas corpus proceeding is devoid of any meaningful discussion of this. He appears to have centered his attention upon whether Gerald made the phone call and used lewd words. He was impressed by the fact that Gerald was on six months' probation because he was with another boy who allegedly stole a purse—a different sort of offense, sharing the feature that Gerald was "along." And he even referred to a report which he said was not investigated because "there was no accusation" "because of lack of material foundation."

With respect to the possible duty of a trial court to explore alternatives to involuntary commitment in a civil proceeding, cf. Lake v. Cameron, 124 U.S.App. D.C. 264, 364 F.2d 657 (1966), which arose under statutes relating to treatment of the mentally ill.

If Gerald had been over 18, he would not have been subject to Juvenile Court proceedings. For the particular offense immediately involved, the maximum punishment would have been a fine of $5 to $50, or imprisonment in jail for not more than two months. Instead, he was committed to custody for a maximum of six years. If he had been over 18 and had committed an offense to which such a sentence might apply, he would have been entitled to substantial rights under the Constitution of the United States as well as under Arizona's laws and constitution. The United States Constitution would guarantee him rights and protections with respect to arrest, search, and seizure, and pretrial interrogation. It would assure him of specific notice of the charges and adequate time to decide his course of action and to prepare his defense. He would be entitled to clear advice that he could be represented by counsel, and, at least if a felony were involved, the State would be required to provide counsel if his parents were unable to afford it. If the court acted on the basis of his confession, careful procedures would be required to assure its voluntariness. If the case went to trial, confrontation and opportunity for cross-examination would be guaranteed. So wide a gulf between the State's treatment of the adult and of the child requires a bridge sturdier than mere verbiage, and reasons more persuasive than cliché can provide. As Wheeler and Cottrell have put it, "The rhetoric of the juvenile court movement has developed without any necessarily close correspondence to the realities of court and institutional routines."

In Kent v. United States, supra, we stated that the Juvenile Court Judge's exercise of the power of the state as *parens patriae* was not unlimited. We said that "the admonition to function in a 'parental' relationship is not an invitation to procedural arbitrariness." With respect to the waiver by the Juvenile Court to the adult court of jurisdiction over an offense committed by a youth, we said that "there is no place in our system of law for reaching a result of such tremendous consequences without ceremony—without hearing, without effective assistance of counsel, without a statement of reasons." We announced with respect to such waiver proceedings that while "We do not mean * * * to indicate that the hearing to be held must conform with all of the requirements of a criminal trial or even of the usual administrative hearing; but we do hold that the hearing must measure up to the essentials of due process and fair treatment." We reiterate this view, here in connection with a juvenile court adjudication of "delinquency," as a requirement which is part of the Due Process Clause of the Fourteenth Amendment of our Constitution.[4]

---

[4] The Nat'l Crime Comm'n Report recommends that "Juvenile courts should make fullest feasible use of preliminary conferences to dispose of cases short of adjudication." Id., at 84. See also D.C. Crime Comm'n Report, pp. 662–665. Since this "consent decree" procedure would involve neither adjudication of delinquency nor institutionalization, nothing we say in this opinion should be construed as expressing any views with respect to such procedure. The problems of pre-adjudication treatment of juveniles, and of post-adjudication disposition, are unique to the juvenile process; hence what we hold in this opinion with

We now turn to the specific issues, which are presented to us in the present case.

III.

NOTICE OF CHARGES

Appellants allege that the Arizona Juvenile Code is unconstitutional or alternatively that the proceedings before the Juvenile Court were constitutionally defective because of failure to provide adequate notice of the hearings. No notice was given to Gerald's parents when he was taken into custody on Monday, June 8. On that night, when Mrs. Gault went to the Detention Home, she was orally informed that there would be a hearing the next afternoon and was told the reason why Gerald was in custody. The only written notice Gerald's parents received at any time was a note on plain paper from Officer Flagg delivered on Thursday or Friday, June 11 or 12, to the effect that the judge had set Monday, June 15, "for further Hearings on Gerald's delinquency."

A "petition" was filed with the court on June 9 by Officer Flagg, reciting only that he was informed and believed that "said minor is a delinquent minor and that it is necessary that some order be made by the Honorable Court for said minor's welfare." The applicable Arizona statute provides for a petition to be filed in Juvenile Court, alleging in general terms that the child is "neglected, dependent or delinquent." The statute explicitly states that such a general allegation is sufficient, "without alleging the facts." There is no requirement that the petition be served and it was not served upon, given to, or shown to Gerald or his parents.

The Supreme Court of Arizona rejected appellants' claim that due process was denied because of inadequate notice. It stated that "Mrs. Gault knew the exact nature of the charge against Gerald from the day he was taken to the detention home." The court also pointed out that the Gaults appeared at the two hearings "without objection." The court held that because "the policy of the juvenile law is to hide youthful errors from the full gaze of the public and bury them in the graveyard of the forgotten past," advance notice of the specific charges or basis for taking the juvenile into custody and for the hearing is not necessary. It held that the appropriate rule is that "the infant and his parents or guardian will receive a petition only reciting a conclusion of delinquency. But no later than the initial hearing by the judge, they must be advised of the facts involved in the case. If the charges are denied, they must be given a reasonable period of time to prepare."

We cannot agree with the court's conclusion that adequate notice was given in this case. Notice, to comply with due process requirements, must be given sufficiently in advance of scheduled court proceedings so that reasonable opportunity to prepare will be af-

regard to the procedural requirements at the adjudicatory stage has no necessary applicability to other steps of the juvenile process.

forded, and it must "set forth the alleged misconduct with particularity." It is obvious, as we have discussed above, that no purpose of shielding the child from the public stigma of knowledge of his having been taken into custody and scheduled for hearing is served by the procedure approved by the court below. The "initial hearing" in the present case was a hearing on the merits. Notice at that time is not timely; and even if there were a conceivable purpose served by the deferral proposed by the court below, it would have to yield to the requirements that the child and his parents or guardian be notified, in writing, of the specific charge or factual allegations to be considered at the hearing, and that such written notice be given at the earliest practicable time, and in any event sufficiently in advance of the hearing to permit preparation. Due process of law requires notice of the sort we have described—that is, notice which would be deemed constitutionally adequate in a civil or criminal proceeding. It does not allow a hearing to be held in which a youth's freedom and his parents' right to his custody are at stake without giving them timely notice, in advance of the hearing, of the specific issues that they must meet. Nor, in the circumstances of this case, can it reasonably be said that the requirement of notice was waived.

IV.

RIGHT TO COUNSEL

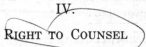

Appellants charge that the Juvenile Court proceedings were fatally defective because the court did not advise Gerald or his parents of their right to counsel, and proceeded with the hearing, the adjudication of delinquency and the order of commitment in the absence of counsel for the child and his parents or an express waiver of the right thereto. The Supreme Court of Arizona pointed out that "[t]here is disagreement [among the various jurisdictions] as to whether the court must advise the infant that he has a right to counsel." It noted its own decision in Arizona State Dept. of Public Welfare v. Barlow, 80 Ariz. 249, 296 P.2d 298 (1956), to the effect "that *the parents* of an infant in a juvenile proceeding cannot be denied representation by counsel of their choosing." (Emphasis added.) It referred to a provision of the Juvenile Code which it characterized as requiring "that the probation officer shall look after the interests of neglected, delinquent and dependent children," including representing their interests in court. The court argued that "The parent and the probation officer may be relied upon to protect the infant's interests." Accordingly it rejected the proposition that "due process requires that an infant have a right to counsel." It said that juvenile courts have the discretion, but not the duty, to allow such representation; it referred specifically to the situation in which the Juvenile Court discerns conflict between the child and his parents as an instance in which this discretion might be exercised. We do not agree. Probation officers, in the Arizona scheme, are also arresting officers. They initiate proceedings and file petitions which they verify, as here, alleging the delinquency of the child; and they testify, as here, against the child. And here the probation officer was also superintendent of the Detention Home. The probation officer cannot act as counsel for the child. His role in the adjudicatory hearing, by statute and in fact, is as arresting officer and witness against the child. Nor can the judge represent the child. There is no material difference in this respect between adult and juvenile proceedings of the sort here involved. In adult proceedings, this contention has been foreclosed by decisions of this Court. A proceeding where the issue is whether the child will be found to be "delinquent" and subjected to the loss of his liberty for years is comparable in seriousness to a felony prosecution. The juvenile needs the assistance of counsel to cope with problems of law, to make skilled inquiry into the facts, to insist upon regularity of the proceedings, and to ascertain whether he has a defense and to prepare and submit it. The child "requires the guiding hand of counsel at every step in the proceedings against him." Just as in Kent v. United States, supra, 383 U.S., at 561–562, 86 S.Ct., at 1057–1058, we indicated our agreement with the United States Court of Appeals for the District of Columbia Circuit that the assistance of counsel is essential for purposes of waiver proceedings, so we hold now that it is equally essential for the determination of delinquency, carrying with it the awesome prospect of incarceration in a state institution until the juvenile reaches the age of 21.[5]

During the last decade, court decisions, experts, and legislatures have demonstrated increasing recognition of this view. In at least one-third of the States, statutes now provide for the right of representation by retained counsel in juvenile delinquency proceedings, notice of the right, or assignment of counsel, or a combination of these. In other States, court rules have similar provisions.

The President's Crime Commission has recently recommended that in order to assure "procedural justice for the child," it is necessary that "Counsel * * * be appointed as a matter of course wherever coercive action is a possibility, without requiring any affirmative choice by child or parent."[6] As stated by the authoritative

---

[5] This means that the commitment, in virtually all cases, is for a minimum of three years since jurisdiction of juvenile courts is usually limited to age 18 and under.

[6] Nat'l Crime Comm'n Report, pp. 86–87. The Commission's statement of its position is very forceful:

"The Commission believes that no single action holds more potential for achieving procedural justice for the child in the juvenile court than provision of counsel. The presence of an independent legal representative of the child, or of his parent, is the keystone of the whole structure of guarantees that a minimum system of procedural justice requires. The rights to confront one's accusers, to cross-examine witnesses, to present evidence and testimony of one's own, to be unaffected by prejudicial and unreliable evidence, to participate meaningfully in the dispositional decision, to take an appeal have substantial meaning for the overwhelming majority of persons brought before the juvenile court only if they are provided with competent lawyers who can invoke those rights effectively. The most informal and well-intentioned of judicial proceedings are technical; few adults without legal training can influence or even understand them; certainly children cannot. Papers are drawn and charges expressed in legal language. Events follow one another in a manner that appears arbitrary and confusing to the uninitiated. Decisions, unexplained, appear too official to chal-

"Standards for Juvenile and Family Courts," published by the Children's Bureau of the United States Department of Health, Education, and Welfare:

> "As a component part of a fair hearing required by due process guaranteed under the 14th amendment, notice of the right to counsel should be required at all hearings and counsel provided upon request when the family is financially unable to employ counsel."   Standards, p. 57.

This statement was "reviewed" by the National Council of Juvenile Court Judges at its 1965 Convention and they "found no fault" with it.   The New York Family Court Act contains the following statement:

> "This act declares that minors have a right to the assistance of counsel of their own choosing or of law guardians in neglect proceedings under article three and in proceedings to determine juvenile delinquency and whether a person is in need of supervision under article seven.   This declaration is based on a finding that counsel is often indispensable to a practical realization of due process of law and may be helpful in making reasoned determinations of fact and proper orders of disposition."

The Act provides that "At the commencement of any hearing" under the delinquency article of the statute, the juvenile and his parent shall be advised of the juvenile's "right to be represented by counsel chosen by him or his parent * * * or by a law guardian assigned by

lenge.   But with lawyers come records of proceedings; records make possible appeals which, even if they do not occur, impart by their possibility a healthy atmosphere of accountability.

"Fears have been expressed that lawyers would make juvenile court proceedings adversary.   No doubt this is partly true, but it is partly desirable.   Informality is often abused.   The juvenile courts deal with cases in which facts are disputed and in which, therefore, rules of evidence, confrontation of witnesses, and other adversary procedures are called for.   They deal with many cases involving conduct that can lead to incarceration or close supervision for long periods, and therefore juveniles often need the same safeguards that are granted to adults. And in all cases children need advocates to speak for them and guard their interests, particularly when disposition decisions are made.   It is the disposition stage at which the opportunity arises to offer individualized treatment plans and in which the danger inheres that the court's coercive power will be applied without adequate knowledge of the circumstances.

"Fears also have been expressed that the formality lawyers would bring into juvenile court would defeat the therapeu-

tic aims of the court.   But informality has no necessary connection with therapy; it is a device that has been used to approach therapy, and it is not the only possible device.   It is quite possible that in many instances lawyers, for all their commitment to formality, could do more to further therapy for their clients than can the small, over-worked social staffs of the courts. * * *

"The Commission believes it is essential that counsel be appointed by the juvenile court for those who are unable to provide their own.   Experience under the prevailing systems in which children are free to seek counsel of their choice reveals how empty of meaning the right is for those typically the subjects of juvenile court proceedings.   Moreover, providing counsel only when the child is sophisticated enough to be aware of his need and to ask for one or when he fails to waive his announced right [is] not enough, as experience in numerous jurisdictions reveals.

"*The Commission recommends:*

"Counsel should be appointed as a matter of course wherever coercive action is a possibility, without requiring any affirmative choice by child or parent."

the court * * *." The California Act (1961) also requires appointment of counsel.

We conclude that the Due Process Clause of the Fourteenth Amendment requires that in respect of proceedings to determine delinquency which may result in commitment to an institution in which the juvenile's freedom is curtailed, the child and his parents must be notified of the child's right to be represented by counsel retained by them, or if they are unable to afford counsel, that counsel will be appointed to represent the child.

At the habeas corpus proceeding, Mrs. Gault testified that she knew that she could have appeared with counsel at the juvenile hearing. This knowledge is not a waiver of the right to counsel which she and her juvenile son had, as we have defined it. They had a right expressly to be advised that they might retain counsel and to be confronted with the need for specific consideration of whether they did or did not choose to waive the right. If they were unable to afford to employ counsel, they were entitled in view of the seriousness of the charge and the potential commitment, to appointed counsel, unless they chose waiver. Mrs. Gault's knowledge that she could employ counsel was not an "intentional relinquishment or abandonment" of a fully known right.[7]

V.

CONFRONTATION, SELF-INCRIMINATION, CROSS-EXAMINATION

Appellants urge that the writ of habeas corpus should have been granted because of the denial of the rights of confrontation and cross-examination in the Juvenile Court hearings, and because the privilege against self-incrimination was not observed. The Juvenile Court Judge testified at the habeas corpus hearing that he had proceeded on the basis of Gerald's admissions at the two hearings. Appellants attack this on the ground that the admissions were obtained in disregard of the privilege against self-incrimination. If the confession is disregarded, appellants argue that the delinquency conclusion, since it was fundamentally based on a finding that Gerald had made lewd remarks during the phone call to Mrs. Cook, is fatally defective for failure to accord the rights of confrontation and cross-examination which the Due Process Clause of the Fourteenth Amendment of the Federal Constitution guarantees in state proceedings generally.

Our first question, then, is whether Gerald's admission was improperly obtained and relied on as the basis of decision, in conflict with the Federal Constitution. For this purpose, it is necessary briefly to recall the relevant facts.

Mrs. Cook, the complainant, and the recipient of the alleged telephone call, was not called as a witness. Gerald's mother asked

---

[7] Johnson v. Zerbst, 304 U.S. 458, 464, 58 S.Ct. 1019, 1023, 82 L.Ed. 1461 (1938); Carnley v. Cochran, 369 U.S. 506, 82 S.Ct. 884, 8 L.Ed.2d 70 (1962); United States ex rel. Brown v. Fay, 242 F.Supp. 273 (D.C.S.D.N.Y.1965).

the Juvenile Court Judge why Mrs. Cook was not present and the judge replied that "she didn't have to be present." So far as appears, Mrs. Cook was spoken to only once, by Officer Flagg, and this was by telephone. The judge did not speak with her on any occasion. Gerald had been questioned by the probation officer after having been taken into custody. The exact circumstances of this questioning do not appear but any admissions Gerald may have made at this time do not appear in the record. Gerald was also questioned by the Juvenile Court Judge at each of the two hearings. The judge testified in the habeas corpus proceeding that Gerald admitted making "some of the lewd statements * * * [but not] any of the more serious lewd statements." There was conflict and uncertainty among the witnesses at the habeas corpus proceeding—the Juvenile Court Judge, Mr. and Mrs. Gault, and the probation officer—as to what Gerald did or did not admit.

We shall assume that Gerald made admissions of the sort described by the Juvenile Court Judge, as quoted above. Neither Gerald nor his parents were advised that he did not have to testify or make a statement, or that an incriminating statement might result in his commitment as a "delinquent."

The Arizona Supreme Court rejected appellants' contention that Gerald had a right to be advised that he need not incriminate himself. It said: "We think the necessary flexibility for individualized treatment will be enhanced by a rule which does not require the judge to advise the infant of a privilege against self-incrimination."

In reviewing this conclusion of Arizona's Supreme Court, we emphasize again that we are here concerned only with a proceeding to determine whether a minor is a "delinquent" and which may result in commitment to a state institution. Specifically, the question is whether, in such a proceeding, an admission by the juvenile may be used against him in the absence of clear and unequivocal evidence that the admission was made with knowledge that he was not obliged to speak and would not be penalized for remaining silent. In light of Miranda v. State of Arizona, 384 U.S. 436, 86 S.Ct. 1602, 16 L.Ed.2d 694 (1966), we must also consider whether, if the privilege against self-incrimination is available, it can effectively be waived unless counsel is present or the right to counsel has been waived.

It has long been recognized that the eliciting and use of confessions or admissions require careful scrutiny. Dean Wigmore states:

"The ground of distrust of confessions made in certain situations is, in a rough and indefinite way, judicial experience. There has been no careful collection of statistics of untrue confessions, nor has any great number of instances been even loosely reported * * * but enough have been verified to fortify the conclusion, based on ordinary observation of human conduct, that under certain stresses a person, especially one of defective mentality or peculiar temperament, may falsely acknowledge guilt. This possibility arises wherever the innocent person is placed in such a situation that the untrue acknowledgment of guilt is at the time the more promising of two alternatives between which he is obliged to choose; that is, he chooses any risk that may be in falsely acknowledging guilt, in preference to some worse alternative associated with silence.

* * *

"The principle, then, upon which a confession may be excluded is that it is, under certain conditions, *testimonially untrustworthy* * * *. [T]he essential feature is that the principle of exclusion is a testimonial one, analogous to the other principles which exclude narrations as untrustworthy * * *."

This Court has emphasized that admissions and confessions of juveniles require special caution. In Haley v. State of Ohio, 332 U.S. 596, 68 S.Ct. 302, 92 L.Ed. 224, where this Court reversed the conviction of a 15-year-old boy for murder, Mr. Justice Douglas said:

"What transpired would make us pause for careful inquiry if a mature man were involved. And when, as here, a mere child— an easy victim of the law—is before us, special care in scrutinizing the record must be used. Age 15 is a tender and difficult age for a boy of any race. He cannot be judged by the more exacting standards of maturity. That which would leave a man cold and unimpressed can overawe and overwhelm a lad in his early teens. This is the period of great instability which the crisis of adolescence produces. A 15-year-old lad, questioned through the dead of night by relays of police, is a ready victim of the inquisition. Mature men possibly might stand the ordeal from midnight to 5 a.m. But we cannot believe that a lad of tender years is a match for the police in such a contest. He needs counsel and support if he is not to become the victim first of fear, then of panic. He needs someone on whom to lean lest the overpowering presence of the law, as he knows it, crush him. No friend stood at the side of this 15-year-old boy as the police, working in relays, questioned him hour after hour, from midnight until dawn. No lawyer stood guard to make sure that the police went so far and no farther, to see to it that they stopped short of the point where he became the victim of coercion. No counsel or friend was called during the critical hours of questioning."

In *Haley*, as we have discussed, the boy was convicted in an adult court, and not a juvenile court. In notable decisions, the New York Court of Appeals and the Supreme Court of New Jersey have recently considered decisions of Juvenile Courts in which boys have been adjudged "delinquent" on the basis of confessions obtained in circumstances comparable to those in *Haley*. In both instances, the State contended before its highest tribunal that constitutional requirements governing inculpatory statements applicable in adult courts do not apply to juvenile proceedings. In each case, the State's contention was rejected, and the juvenile court's determination of delinquency was set aside on the grounds of inadmissibility of the confession. In Matters of W. and S., 19 N.Y.2d 55, 277 N.Y.S.2d 675,

224 N.E.2d 102 (1966) (opinion by Keating, J.), and In Interests of Carlo and Stasilowicz, 48 N.J. 224, 225 A.2d 110 (1966) (opinion by Proctor, J.).

The privilege against self-incrimination is, of course, related to the question of the safeguards necessary to assure that admissions or confessions are reasonably trustworthy, that they are not the mere fruits of fear or coercion, but are reliable expressions of the truth. The roots of the privilege are, however, far deeper. They tap the basic stream of religious and political principle because the privilege reflects the limits of the individual's attornment to the state and—in a philosophical sense—insists upon the equality of the individual and the state. In other words, the privilege has a broader and deeper thrust than the rule which prevents the use of confessions which are the product of coercion because coercion is thought to carry with it the danger of unreliability. One of its purposes is to prevent the state, whether by force or by psychological domination, from overcoming the mind and will of the person under investigation and depriving him of the freedom to decide whether to assist the state in securing his conviction.

It would indeed be surprising if the privilege against self-incrimination were available to hardened criminals but not to children. The language of the Fifth Amendment, applicable to the States by operation of the Fourteenth Amendment, is unequivocal and without exception. And the scope of the privilege is comprehensive. As Mr. Justice White, concurring, stated in Murphy v. Waterfront Commission, 378 U.S. 52, 94, 84 S.Ct. 1594, 1611, 12 L.Ed.2d 678 (1964):

> "The privilege can be claimed in *any proceeding*, be it criminal or civil, administrative or judicial, investigatory or adjudicatory. * * * it protects *any disclosures* which the witness may reasonably apprehend *could be used in a criminal prosecution or which could lead to other evidence that might be so used.*" (Emphasis added.)

With respect to juveniles, both common observation and expert opinion emphasize that the "distrust of confessions made in certain situations" to which Dean Wigmore referred in the passage quoted supra, at 1453, is imperative in the case of children from an early age through adolescence. In New York, for example, the recently enacted Family Court Act provides that the juvenile and his parents must be advised at the start of the hearing of his right to remain silent. The New York statute also provides that the police must attempt to communicate with the juvenile's parents before questioning him, and that absent "special circumstances" a confession may not be obtained from a child prior to notifying his parents or relatives and releasing the child either to them or to the Family Court. In In Matters of W. and S., referred to above, the New York Court of Appeals held that the privilege against self-incrimination applies in juvenile delinquency cases and requires the exclusion of involuntary confessions, and that People v. Lewis, 260 N.Y. 171, 183 N.E. 353, 86

A.L.R. 1001 (1932), holding the contrary, had been specifically overruled by statute.

The authoritative "Standards for Juvenile and Family Courts" concludes that, "Whether or not transfer to the criminal court is a possibility, certain procedures should always be followed. Before being interviewed [by the police], the child and his parents should be informed of his right to have legal counsel present and to refuse to answer questions or be fingerprinted if he should so decide."

Against the application to juveniles of the right to silence, it is argued that juvenile proceedings are "civil" and not "criminal," and therefore the privilege should not apply. It is true that the statement of the privilege in the Fifth Amendment, which is applicable to the States by reason of the Fourteenth Amendment, is that no person "shall be compelled in any *criminal case* to be a witness against himself." However, it is also clear that the availability of the privilege does not turn upon the type of proceeding in which its protection is invoked, but upon the nature of the statement or admission and the exposure which it invites. The privilege may, for example, be claimed in a civil or administrative proceeding, if the statement is or may be inculpatory.

It would be entirely unrealistic to carve out of the Fifth Amendment all statements by juveniles on the ground that these cannot lead to "criminal" involvement. In the first place, juvenile proceedings to determine "delinquency," which may lead to commitment to a state institution, must be regarded as "criminal" for purposes of the privilege against self-incrimination. To hold otherwise would be to disregard substance because of the feeble enticement of the "civil" label-of-convenience which has been attached to juvenile proceedings. Indeed, in over half of the States, there is not even assurance that the juvenile will be kept in separate institutions, apart from adult "criminals." In those States juveniles may be placed in or transferred to adult penal institutions after having been found "delinquent" by a juvenile court. For this purpose, at least, commitment is a deprivation of liberty. It is incarceration against one's will, whether it is called "criminal" or "civil." And our Constitution guarantees that no person shall be "compelled" to be a witness against himself when he is threatened with deprivation of his liberty—a command which this Court has broadly applied and generously implemented in accordance with the teaching of the history of the privilege and its great office in mankind's battle for freedom.

In addition, apart from the equivalence for this purpose of exposure to commitment as a juvenile delinquent and exposure to imprisonment as an adult offender, the fact of the matter is that there is little or no assurance in Arizona, as in most if not all of the States, that a juvenile apprehended and interrogated by the police or even by the Juvenile Court itself will remain outside of the reach of adult courts as a consequence of the offense for which he has been taken into custody. In Arizona, as in other States, provision is made for Juvenile Courts to relinquish or waive jurisdiction to the ordinary criminal courts. In the present case, when Gerald Gault was interrogated concerning violation of a section of the Arizona Criminal Code, it could not be certain that the Juvenile Court Judge would decide to "suspend" criminal prosecution in court for adults by proceeding to an adjudication in Juvenile Court.

It is also urged, as the Supreme Court of Arizona here asserted, that the juvenile and presumably his parents should not be advised of the juvenile's right to silence because confession is good for the child as the commencement of the assumed therapy of the juvenile court process, and he should be encouraged to assume an attitude of trust and confidence toward the officials of the juvenile process. This proposition has been subjected to widespread challenge on the basis of current reappraisals of the rhetoric and realities of the handling of juvenile offenders.

In fact, evidence is accumulating that confessions by juveniles do not aid in "individualized treatment," as the court below put it, and that compelling the child to answer questions, without warning or advice as to his right to remain silent, does not serve this or any other good purpose. In light of the observations of Wheeler and Cottrell, and others, it seems probable that where children are induced to confess by "paternal" urgings on the part of officials and the confession is then followed by disciplinary action, the child's reaction is likely to be hostile and adverse—the child may well feel that he has been led or tricked into confession and that despite his confession, he is being punished.

Further, authoritative opinion has cast formidable doubt upon the reliability and trustworthiness of "confessions" by children. This Court's observations in Haley v. State of Ohio are set forth above. The recent decision of the New York Court of Appeals referred to above, In Matters of W. and S. deals with a dramatic and, it is to be hoped, extreme example. Two 12-year-old Negro boys were taken into custody for the brutal assault and rape of two aged domestics, one of whom died as the result of the attack. One of the boys was schizophrenic and had been locked in the security ward of a mental institution at the time of the attacks. By a process that may best be described as bizarre, his confession was obtained by the police. A psychiatrist testified that the boy would admit "whatever he thought was expected so that he could get out of the immediate situation." The other 12-year-old also "confessed." Both confessions were in specific detail, albeit they contained various inconsistencies. The Court of Appeals, in an opinion by Keating, J., concluded that the confessions were products of the will of the police instead of the boys. The confessions were therefore held involuntary and the order of the Appellate Division affirming the order of the Family Court adjudging the defendants to be juvenile delinquents was reversed.

A similar and equally instructive case has recently been decided by the Supreme Court of New Jersey. In Interests of Carlo and Stasilowicz, supra. The body of a 10-year-old girl was found. She had been strangled. Neighborhood boys who knew the girl were questioned. The two appellants, aged 13 and 15, confessed to the police, with vivid detail and some inconsistencies. At the Juvenile Court hearing, both denied any complicity in the killing. They testified that their confessions were the product of fear and fatigue due to extensive police grilling. The Juvenile Court Judge found that the confessions were voluntary and admissible. On appeal, in an extensive opinion by Proctor, J., the Supreme Court of New Jersey reversed. It rejected the State's argument that the constitutional safeguard of voluntariness governing the use of confessions does not apply in proceedings before the Juvenile Court. It pointed out that under New Jersey court rules, juveniles under the age of 16 accused of committing a homicide are tried in a proceeding which "has all of the appurtenances of a criminal trial," including participation by the county prosecutor, and requirements that the juvenile be provided with counsel, that a stenographic record be made, etc. It also pointed out that under New Jersey law, the confinement of the boys after reaching age 21 could be extended until they had served the maximum sentence which could have been imposed on an adult for such a homicide, here found to be second-degree murder carrying up to 30 years' imprisonment. The court concluded that the confessions were involuntary, stressing that the boys, contrary to statute, were placed in the police station and there interrogated; that the parents of both boys were not allowed to see them while they were being interrogated; that inconsistencies appeared among the various statements of the boys and with the objective evidence of the crime; and that there were protracted periods of questioning. The court noted the State's contention that both boys were advised of their constitutional rights before they made their statements, but it held that this should not be given "significant weight in our determination of voluntariness." Accordingly, the judgment of the Juvenile Court was reversed.

In a recent case before the Juvenile Court of the District of Columbia, Judge Ketcham rejected the proffer of evidence as to oral statements made at police headquarters by four juveniles who had been taken into custody for alleged involvement in an assault and attempted robbery. In the Matter of Four Youths, Nos. 28–776–J, 28–778–J, 28–783–J, 28–859–J, Juvenile Court of the District of Columbia, April 7, 1961. The court explicitly stated that it did not rest its decision on a showing that the statements were involuntary, but because they were untrustworthy. Judge Ketcham said:

> "Simply stated, the Court's decision in this case rests upon the considered opinion—after nearly four busy years on the Juvenile Court bench during which the testimony of thousands of such juveniles has been heard—that the statements of adolescents under 18 years of age who are arrested and charged with violations of law are frequently untrustworthy and often distort the truth."

We conclude that the constitutional privilege against self-incrimination is applicable in the case of juveniles as it is with respect to adults. We appreciate that special problems may arise with respect to waiver of the privilege by or on behalf of children, and that there may well be some differences in technique—but not in principle—depending upon the age of the child and the presence and competence of parents. The participation of counsel will, of course, assist the police, Juvenile Courts and appellate tribunals in administering the privilege. If counsel was not present for some permissible reason when an admission was obtained, the greatest care must be taken to assure that the admission was voluntary, in the sense not only that it was not coerced or suggested, but also that it was not the product of ignorance of rights or of adolescent fantasy, fright or despair.

The "confession" of Gerald Gault was first obtained by Officer Flagg, out of the presence of Gerald's parents, without counsel and without advising him of his right to silence, as far as appears. The judgment of the Juvenile Court was stated by the judge to be based on Gerald's admissions in court. Neither "admission" was reduced to writing, and, to say the least, the process by which the "admissions," were obtained and received must be characterized as lacking the certainty and order which are required of proceedings of such formidable consequences. Apart from the "admission," there was nothing upon which a judgment or finding might be based. There was no sworn testimony. Mrs. Cook, the complainant, was not present. The Arizona Supreme Court held that "sworn testimony must be required of all witnesses including police officers, probation officers and others who are part of or officially related to the juvenile court structure." We hold that this is not enough. No reason is suggested or appears for a different rule in respect of sworn testimony in juvenile courts than in adult tribunals. Absent a valid confession adequate to support the determination of the Juvenile Court, confrontation and sworn testimony by witnesses available for cross-examination were essential for a finding of "delinquency" and an order committing Gerald to a state institution for a maximum of six years.

The recommendations in the Children's Bureau's "Standards for Juvenile and Family Courts" are in general accord with our conclusions. They state that testimony should be under oath and that only competent, material and relevant evidence under rules applicable to civil cases should be admitted in evidence. The New York Family Court Act contains a similar provision.

As we said in Kent v. United States, 383 U.S. 541, 554, 86 S.Ct. 1045, 1053, 16 L.Ed.2d 84 (1966), with respect to waiver proceedings, "there is no place in our system of law for reaching a result of such tremendous consequences without ceremony * * *." We now hold that, absent a valid confession, a determination of delinquency and an order of commitment to a state institution cannot be sustained in the absence of sworn testimony subjected to the opportunity for cross-examination in accordance with our law and constitutional requirements.

Holding

VI.

APPELLATE REVIEW AND TRANSCRIPT OF PROCEEDINGS

Appellants urge that the Arizona statute is unconstitutional under the Due Process Clause because, as construed by its Supreme Court, "there is no right of appeal from a juvenile court order * * *." The court held that there is no right to a transcript because there is no right to appeal and because the proceedings are confidential and any record must be destroyed after a prescribed period of time. Whether a transcript or other recording is made, it held, is a matter for the discretion of the juvenile court.

This Court has not held that a State is required by the Federal Constitution "to provide appellate courts or a right to appellate review at all." In view of the fact that we must reverse the Supreme Court of Arizona's affirmance of the dismissal of the writ of habeas corpus for other reasons, we need not rule on this question in the present case or upon the failure to provide a transcript or recording of the hearings—or, indeed, the failure of the Juvenile Judge to state the grounds for his conclusion. Cf. Kent v. United States, supra, 383 U.S., at 561, 86 S.Ct., at 1057, where we said, in the context of a decision of the juvenile court waiving jurisdiction to the adult court, which by local law, was permissible: "* * * it is incumbent upon the Juvenile Court to accompany its waiver order with a statement of the reasons or considerations therefor." As the present case illustrates, the consequences of failure to provide an appeal, to record the proceedings, or to make findings or state the grounds for the juvenile court's conclusion may be to throw a burden upon the machinery for habeas corpus, to saddle the reviewing process with the burden of attempting to reconstruct a record, and to impose upon the Juvenile Judge the unseemly duty of testifying under cross-examination as to the events that transpired in the hearings before him.

For the reasons stated, the judgment of the Supreme Court of Arizona is reversed and the cause remanded for further proceedings not inconsistent with this opinion. It is so ordered.

Judgment reversed and cause remanded with directions.

MR. JUSTICE BLACK, concurring.

The juvenile court laws of Arizona and other States, as the Court points out, are the result of plans promoted by humane and forward-looking people to provide a system of courts, procedures, and sanctions deemed to be less harmful and more lenient to children than to adults. For this reason such state laws generally provide less formal and less public methods for the trial of children. In line with this policy, both courts and legislators have shrunk back from labeling these laws as "criminal" and have preferred to call them "civil." This, in part, was to prevent the full application to juvenile court cases of the Bill of Rights safeguards, including notice as provided in the Sixth Amendment, the right to counsel guaranteed by the Sixth, the right against self-incrimination guaranteed by the Fifth, and the right to confrontation guaranteed by the Sixth. The Court here holds, however, that these four Bill of Rights safeguards apply to protect a juvenile accused in a juvenile court on a charge under which he can be imprisoned for a term of years. This holding strikes a well-nigh fatal blow to much that is unique about the juvenile courts in the Nation. For this reason, there is much to be said for the position of my Brother STEWART that we should not pass on all these issues until they are more squarely presented. But since the majority of the Court chooses to decide all of these questions, I must either do the same or leave my views unexpressed on the important issues determined. In these circumstances, I feel impelled to express my views.

The juvenile court planners envisaged a system that would practically immunize juveniles from "punishment" for "crimes" in an effort to save them from youthful indiscretions and stigmas due to criminal charges or convictions. I agree with the Court, however, that this exalted ideal has failed of achievement since the beginning of the system. Indeed, the state laws from the first one on contained provisions, written in emphatic terms, for arresting and charging juveniles with violations of state criminal laws, as well as for taking juveniles by force of law away from their parents and turning them over to different individuals or groups or for confinement within some state school or institution for a number of years. The latter occurred in this case. Young Gault was arrested and detained on a charge of violating an Arizona penal law by using vile and offensive language to a lady on the telephone. If an adult, he could only have been fined or imprisoned for two months for his conduct. As a juvenile, however, he was put through a more or less secret, informal hearing by the court, after which he was ordered, or more realistically, "sentenced," to confinement in Arizona's Industrial School until he reaches 21 years of age. Thus, in a juvenile system designed to lighten or avoid punishment for criminality, he was ordered by the State to six years' confinement in what is in all but name a penitentiary or jail.

Where a person, infant or adult, can be seized by the State, charged, and convicted for violating a state criminal law, and then ordered by the State to be confined for six years, I think the Constitution requires that he be tried in accordance with the guarantees of all the provisions of the Bill of Rights made applicable to the States by the Fourteenth Amendment. Undoubtedly this would be true of an adult defendant, and it would be a plain denial of equal protection of the laws—an invidious discrimination—to hold that others subject to heavier punishments could, because they are children, be denied these same constitutional safeguards. I consequently agree with the Court that the Arizona law as applied here denied to the parents and their son the right of notice, right to counsel, right against self-incrimination, and right to confront the witnesses against young Gault. Appellants are entitled to these rights, not because "fairness, impartiality and orderliness—in short, the essentials of due process"—require them and not because they are "the procedural rules which have been fashioned from the generality of due process," but because they are specifically and unequivocally granted by provisions of the Fifth and Sixth Amendments which the Fourteenth Amendment makes applicable to the States.

A few words should be added because of the opinion of my BROTHER HARLAN who rests his concurrence and dissent on the Due Process Clause alone. He reads that clause alone as allowing this Court "to determine what forms of procedural protection are necessary to guarantee the fundamental fairness of juvenile proceedings" "in a fashion consistent with the 'traditions and conscience of our people.'" Cf. Rochin v. People of California, 342 U.S. 165, 72 S.Ct. 205, 96 L.Ed. 183. He believes that the Due Process Clause gives this Court the power, upon weighing a "compelling public interest," to impose on the States only those specific constitutional rights which the Court deems "imperative" and "necessary" to comport with the Court's notions of "fundamental fairness."

I cannot subscribe to any such interpretation of the Due Process Clause. Nothing in its words or its history permits it, and "fair distillations of relevant judicial history" are no substitute for the words and history of the clause itself. The phrase "due process of law" has through the years evolved as the successor in purpose and meaning to the words "law of the land" in Magna Charta which more plainly intended to call for a trial according to the existing law of the land in effect at the time an alleged offense had been committed. That provision in Magna Charta was designed to prevent defendants from being tried according to criminal laws or proclamations specifically promulgated to fit particular cases or to attach new consequences to old conduct. Nothing done since Magna Charta can be pointed to as intimating that the Due Process Clause gives courts power to fashion laws in order to meet new conditions, to fit the "decencies" of changed conditions, or to keep their consciences from being shocked by legislation, state or federal.

And, of course, the existence of such awesome judicial power cannot be buttressed or created by relying on the word "procedural." Whether labeled as "procedural" or "substantive," the Bill of Rights safeguards, far from being mere "tools with which" other unspecified "rights could be fully vindicated," are the very vitals of a sound constitutional legal system designed to protect and safeguard the most cherished liberties of a free people. These safeguards were written into our Constitution not by judges but by Constitution makers. Freedom in this Nation will be far less secure the very moment that it is decided that judges can determine which of these safeguards "should" or "should not be imposed" according to their notions of what constitutional provisions are consistent with the "traditions and conscience of our people." Judges with such power, even though they profess to "proceed with restraint," will be above the Constitution, with power to write it, not merely to interpret it, which I believe to be the only power constitutionally committed to judges.

There is one ominous sentence, if not more, in my BROTHER HARLAN'S opinion which bodes ill, in my judgment, both for legislative programs and constitutional commands. Speaking of procedural safeguards in the Bill of Rights, he says:

"These factors in combination suggest that legislatures may properly expect only a cautious deference for their procedural judgments, but that, conversely, courts must exercise their special responsibility for procedural guarantees with care to permit ample scope for achieving the purposes of legislative programs. * * * [T]he court should necessarily proceed with restraint."

It is to be noted here that this case concerns Bill of Rights Amendments; that the "procedure" power my BROTHER HARLAN claims for the Court here relates solely to Bill of Rights safeguards; and that he is here claiming for the Court a supreme power to fashion new Bill of Rights safeguards according to the Court's notions of what fits tradition and conscience. I do not believe that the Constitution vests any such power in judges, either in the Due Process Clause or anywhere else. Consequently, I do not vote to invalidate this Arizona law on the ground that it is "unfair" but solely on the ground that it violates the Fifth and Sixth Amendments made obligatory on the States by the Fourteenth Amendment. Cf. Pointer v. State of Texas, 380 U.S. 400, 412, 85 S.Ct. 1065, 1072, 13 L.Ed.2d 923 (Goldberg, J., concurring). It is enough for me that the Arizona law as here applied collides head-on with the Fifth and Sixth Amendments in the four respects mentioned. The only relevance to me of the Due Process Clause is that it would, of course, violate due process or the "law of the land" to enforce a law that collides with the Bill of Rights.

MR. JUSTICE WHITE, concurring.

I join the Court's opinion except for Part V. I also agree that the privilege against compelled self-incrimination applies at the adjudicatory stage of juvenile court proceedings. I do not, however, find an adequate basis in the record for determining whether that privilege was violated in this case. The Fifth Amendment protects a person from being "compelled" in any criminal proceeding to be a witness against himself. Compulsion is essential to a violation. It may be that when a judge, armed with the authority he has or which people think he has, asks questions of a party or a witness in an adjudicatory hearing, that person, especially if a minor, would feel compelled to answer, absent a warning to the contrary or similar information from some other source. The difficulty is that the record made at the habeas corpus hearing, which is the only information we have concerning the proceedings in the juvenile court, does not directly inform us whether Gerald Gault or his parents were told of Gerald's right to remain silent; nor does it reveal whether the parties were aware of the privilege from some other source, just as they were already aware that they had the right to have the help of counsel and to have witnesses on their behalf. The petition for habeas corpus did not raise the Fifth Amendment issue nor did any of the witnesses focus on it.

I have previously recorded my views with respect to what I have deemed unsound applications of the Fifth Amendment. See, for example, Miranda v. State of Arizona, 384 U.S. 436, 526, 86 S.Ct. 1602, 1654, 16 L.Ed.2d 694, and Malloy v. Hogan, 378 U.S. 1, 33, 84 S.Ct. 1489, 1506, 12 L.Ed.2d 653, dissenting opinions. These views, of course, have not prevailed. But I do hope that the Court will proceed with some care in extending the privilege, with all its vigor, to proceedings in juvenile court, particularly the nonadjudicatory stages of those proceedings.

In any event, I would not reach the Fifth Amendment issue here. I think the Court is clearly ill-advised to review this case on the basis of Miranda v. State of Arizona, since the adjudication of delinquency took place in 1964, long before the Miranda decision. See Johnson v. State of New Jersey, 384 U.S. 719, 86 S.Ct. 1772, 16 L.Ed.2d 882. Under these circumstances, this case is a poor vehicle for resolving a difficult problem. Moreover, no prejudice to appellants is at stake in this regard. The judgment below must be reversed on other grounds and in the event further proceedings are to be had, Gerald Gault will have counsel available to advise him.

For somewhat similar reasons, I would not reach the questions of confrontation and cross-examination which are also dealt with in Part V of the opinion.

Mr. Justice Harlan, concurring in part and dissenting in part.

Each of the 50 States has created a system of juvenile or family courts, in which distinctive rules are employed and special consequences imposed. The jurisdiction of these courts commonly extends both to cases which the States have withdrawn from the ordinary processes of criminal justice, and to cases which involve acts that, if performed by an adult, would not be penalized as criminal. Such courts are denominated civil, not criminal, and are characteristically said not to administer criminal penalties. One consequence of these systems, at least as Arizona construes its own, is that certain of the rights guaranteed to criminal defendants by the Constitution are withheld from juveniles. This case brings before this Court for the first time the question of what limitations the Constitution places upon the operation of such tribunals.[8] For reasons which follow, I have concluded that the Court has gone too far in some respects, and fallen short in others, in assessing the procedural requirements demanded by the Fourteenth Amendment.

I.

I must first acknowledge that I am unable to determine with any certainty by what standards the Court decides that Arizona's juvenile

---

[8] Kent v. United States, 383 U.S. 541, 86 S.Ct. 1045, 16 L.Ed.2d 84, decided at the 1965 Term, did not purport to rest on constitutional grounds.

courts do not satisfy the obligations of due process. The Court's premise, itself the product of reasoning which is not described, is that the "constitutional and theoretical basis" of state systems of juvenile and family courts is "debatable"; it buttresses these doubts by marshaling a body of opinion which suggests that the accomplishments of these courts have often fallen short of expectations.[9] The Court does not indicate at what points or for what purposes such views, held either by it or by other observers, might be pertinent to the present issues. Its failure to provide any discernible standard for the measurement of due process in relation to juvenile proceedings unfortunately might be understood to mean that the Court is concerned principally with the wisdom of having such courts at all.

If this is the source of the Court's dissatisfaction, I cannot share it. I should have supposed that the constitutionality of juvenile courts was beyond proper question under the standards now employed to assess the substantive validity of state legislation under the Due Process Clause of the Fourteenth Amendment. It can scarcely be doubted that it is within the State's competence to adopt measures reasonably calculated to meet more effectively the persistent problems of juvenile delinquency; as the opinion for the Court makes abundantly plain, these are among the most vexing and ominous of the concerns which now face communities throughout the country.

The proper issue here is, however, not whether the State may constitutionally treat juvenile offenders through a system of specialized courts, but whether the proceedings in Arizona's juvenile courts include procedural guarantees which satisfy the requirements of the Fourteenth Amendment. Among the first premises of our constitutional system is the obligation to conduct any proceeding in which an individual may be deprived of liberty or property in a fashion consistent with the "traditions and conscience of our people." Snyder v. Commonwealth of Massachusetts, 291 U.S. 97, 105, 54 S.Ct. 330, 332, 78 L.Ed. 674. The importance of these procedural guarantees is doubly intensified here. First, many of the problems with which Arizona is concerned are among those traditionally confined to the processes of criminal justice; their disposition necessarily affects in the most direct and substantial manner the liberty of individual citizens. Quite obviously, systems of specialized penal justice might permit erosion, or even evasion, of the limitations placed by the Constitution upon state criminal proceedings. Second, we must recognize that the character and consequences of many juvenile court proceedings have in fact closely resembled those of ordinary criminal trials. Nothing before us suggests that juvenile courts were intended as a device to escape constitutional constraints, but I entirely

[9] It is appropriate to observe that, whatever the relevance the Court may suppose that this criticism has to present issues, many of the critics have asserted that the deficiencies of juvenile courts have stemmed chiefly from the inadequacy of the personnel and resources available to those courts. See, e.g., Paulsen, Kent v. United States: The Constitutional Context of Juvenile Cases, 1966 Sup. Ct.Rev. 167, 191–192; Handler, The Juvenile Court and the Adversary System: Problems of Function and Form, 1965 Wis.L.Rev. 7, 46.

agree with the Court that we are nonetheless obliged to examine with circumspection the procedural guarantees the State has provided.

The central issue here, and the principal one upon which I am divided from the Court, is the method by which the procedural requirements of due process should be measured. It must at the outset be emphasized that the protections necessary here cannot be determined by resort to any classification of juvenile proceedings either as criminal or as civil, whether made by the State or by this Court. Both formulae are simply too imprecise to permit reasoned analysis of these difficult constitutional issues. The Court should instead measure the requirements of due process by reference both to the problems which confront the State and to the actual character of the procedural system which the State has created. The Court has for such purposes chiefly examined three connected sources: first, the "settled usages and modes of proceeding," Den ex dem. Murray v. Hoboken Land & Improvement Co., 18 How. 272, 277, 15 L.Ed. 372; second, the "fundamental principles of liberty and justice which lie at the base of all our civil and political institutions". Hebert v. State of Louisiana, 272 U.S. 312, 316, 47 S.Ct. 103, 104, 71 L.Ed. 270 and third, the character and requirements of the circumstances presented in each situation. FCC v. WJR, The Goodwill Station, 337 U.S. 265, 277, 69 S.Ct. 1097, 1104, 93 L.Ed. 1353; Yakus v. United States, 321 U.S. 414, 64 S.Ct. 660, 88 L.Ed. 834. See, further, my dissenting opinion in Poe v. Ullman, 367 U.S. 497, 522, 81 S.Ct. 1752, 1765, 6 L.Ed.2d 989, and compare my opinion concurring in the result in Pointer v. State of Texas, 380 U.S. 400, 408, 85 S.Ct. 1065, 1070. Each of these factors is relevant to the issues here, but it is the last which demands particular examination.

The Court has repeatedly emphasized that determination of the constitutionally required procedural safeguards in any situation requires recognition both of the "interests affected" and of the "circumstances involved." FCC v. WJR, The Goodwill Station, supra, 337 U.S. at 277, 69 S.Ct. at 1104. In particular, a "compelling public interest" must, under our cases, be taken fully into account in assessing the validity under the due process clauses of state or federal legislation and its application. See, e.g., Yakus v. United States, supra, 321 U.S. at 442, 64 S.Ct. at 675; Bowles v. Willingham, 321 U.S. 503, 520, 64 S.Ct. 641, 650, 88 L.Ed. 892; Miller v. Schoene, 276 U.S. 272, 279, 48 S.Ct. 246, 247, 72 L.Ed. 568. Such interests would never warrant arbitrariness or the diminution of any specifically assured constitutional right, Home Bldg. & Loan Assn. v. Blaisdell, 290 U.S. 398, 426, 54 S.Ct. 231, 235, 78 L.Ed. 413, but they are an essential element of the context through which the legislation and proceedings under it must be read and evaluated.

No more evidence of the importance of the public interests at stake here is required than that furnished by the opinion of the Court; it indicates that "some 601,000 children under 18, or 2% of all children between 10 and 17, came before juvenile courts" in 1965, and that "about one-fifth of all arrests for serious crimes" in 1965 were of juveniles. The Court adds that the rate of juvenile crime is steadily rising. All this, as the Court suggests, indicates the importance of these due process issues, but it mirrors no less vividly that state authorities are confronted by formidable and immediate problems involving the most fundamental social values. The state legislatures have determined that the most hopeful solution for these problems is to be found in specialized courts, organized under their own rules and imposing distinctive consequences. The terms and limitations of these systems are not identical, nor are the procedural arrangements which they include, but the States are uniform in their insistence that the ordinary processes of criminal justice are inappropriate, and that relatively informal proceedings, dedicated to premises and purposes only imperfectly reflected in the criminal law, are instead necessary.

It is well settled that the Court must give the widest deference to legislative judgments that concern the character and urgency of the problems with which the State is confronted. Legislatures are, as this Court has often acknowledged, the "main guardian" of the public interest, and, within their constitutional competence, their understanding of that interest must be accepted as "well-nigh" conclusive. Berman v. Parker, 348 U.S. 26, 32, 75 S.Ct. 98, 102, 99 L.Ed. 27. This principle does not, however, reach all the questions essential to the resolution of this case. The legislative judgments at issue here embrace assessments of the necessity and wisdom of procedural guarantees; these are questions which the Constitution has entrusted at least in part to courts, and upon which courts have been understood to possess particular competence. The fundamental issue here is, therefore, in what measure and fashion the Court must defer to legislative determinations which encompass constitutional issues of procedural protection.

It suffices for present purposes to summarize the factors which I believe to be pertinent. It must first be emphasized that the deference given to legislators upon substantive issues must realistically extend in part to ancillary procedural questions. Procedure at once reflects and creates substantive rights, and every effort of courts since the beginnings of the common law to separate the two has proved essentially futile. The distinction between them is particularly inadequate here, where the legislature's substantive preferences directly and unavoidably require judgments about procedural issues. The procedural framework is here a principal element of the substantive legislative system; meaningful deference to the latter must include a portion of deference to the former. The substantive-procedural dichotomy is, nonetheless, an indispensable tool of analysis, for it stems from fundamental limitations upon judicial authority under the Constitution. Its premise is ultimately that courts may not substitute for the judgments of legislators their own understanding of the public welfare, but must instead concern themselves with the validity under the Constitution of the methods which the legislature has selected. See e.g., McLean v. State of Arkansas, 211 U.S. 539,

547, 29 S.Ct. 206, 208, 53 L.Ed. 315; Olsen v. State of Nebraska, 313 U.S. 236, 246–247, 61 S.Ct. 862, 865, 85 L.Ed. 1305. The Constitution has in this manner created for courts and legislators areas of primary responsibility which are essentially congruent to their areas of special competence. Courts are thus obliged both by constitutional command and by their distinctive functions to bear particular responsibility for the measurement of procedural due process. These factors in combination suggest that legislatures may properly expect only a cautious deference for their procedural judgments, but that, conversely, courts must exercise their special responsibility for procedural guarantees with care to permit ample scope for achieving the purposes of legislative programs. Plainly, courts can exercise such care only if they have in each case first studied thoroughly the objectives and implementation of the program at stake; if, upon completion of those studies, the effect of extensive procedural restrictions upon valid legislative purposes cannot be assessed with reasonable certainty, the court should necessarily proceed with restraint.

The foregoing considerations, which I believe to be fair distillations of relevant judicial history, suggest three criteria by which the procedural requirements of due process should be measured here: first, no more restrictions should be imposed than are imperative to assure the proceedings' fundamental fairness; second, the restrictions which are imposed should be those which preserve, so far as possible, the essential elements of the State's purpose; and finally, restrictions should be chosen which will later permit the orderly selection of any additional protections which may ultimately prove necessary. In this way, the Court may guarantee the fundamental fairness of the proceeding, and yet permit the State to continue development of an effective response to the problems of juvenile crime.

II.

Measured by these criteria, only three procedural requirements should, in my opinion, now be deemed required of state juvenile courts by the Due Process Clause of the Fourteenth Amendment: first, timely notice must be provided to parents and children of the nature and terms of any juvenile court proceeding in which a determination affecting their rights or interests may be made; second, unequivocal and timely notice must be given that counsel may appear in any such proceeding in behalf of the child and its parents, and that in cases in which the child may be confined in an institution, counsel may, in circumstances of indigency, be appointed for them; and third, the court must maintain a written record, or its equivalent, adequate to permit effective review on appeal or in collateral proceedings. These requirements would guarantee to juveniles the tools with which their rights could be fully vindicated, and yet permit the States to pursue without unnecessary hindrance the purposes which they believe imperative in this field. Further, their imposition now would later permit more intelligent assessment of the necessity under the

Fourteenth Amendment of additional requirements, by creating suitable records from which the character and deficiencies of juvenile proceedings could be accurately judged. I turn to consider each of these three requirements.

The Court has consistently made plain that adequate and timely notice is the fulcrum of due process, whatever the purposes of the proceeding. See, e.g., Roller v. Holly, 176 U.S. 398, 409, 20 S.Ct. 410, 413, 44 L.Ed. 520; Coe v. Armour Fertilizer Works, 237 U.S. 413, 424, 35 S.Ct. 625, 628, 59 L.Ed. 1027. Notice is ordinarily the prerequisite to effective assertion of any constitutional or other rights; without it, vindication of those rights must be essentially fortuitous. So fundamental a protection can neither be spared here nor left to the "favor or grace" of state authorities. Central of Georgia Ry. v. Wright, 207 U.S. 127, 138, 28 S.Ct. 47, 51, 52 L.Ed. 134; Coe v. Armour Fertilizer Works, supra, 237 U.S. at 425, 35 S.Ct. at 628.

Provision of counsel and of a record, like adequate notice, would permit the juvenile to assert very much more effectively his rights and defenses, both in the juvenile proceedings and upon direct or collateral review. The Court has frequently emphasized their importance in proceedings in which an individual may be deprived of his liberty, see Gideon v. Wainwright, 372 U.S. 335, 83 S.Ct. 792, 9 L.Ed. 2d 799, and Griffin v. People of State of Illinois, 351 U.S. 12, 76 S.Ct. 585, 100 L.Ed. 891; this reasoning must include with special force those who are commonly inexperienced and immature. See Powell v. State of Alabama, 287 U.S. 45, 53 S.Ct. 55, 77 L.Ed. 158. The facts of this case illustrate poignantly the difficulties of review without either an adequate record or the participation of counsel in the proceeding's initial stages. At the same time, these requirements should not cause any substantial modification in the character of juvenile court proceedings: counsel, although now present in only a small percentage of juvenile cases, have apparently already appeared without incident in virtually all juvenile courts; [10] and the maintenance of a record should not appreciably alter the conduct of these proceedings.

The question remains whether certain additional requirements, among them the privilege against self-incrimination, confrontation, and cross-examination, must now, as the Court holds, also be imposed. I share in part the views expressed in my BROTHER WHITE'S concurring opinion, but believe that there are other, and more deep-seated, reasons to defer, at least for the present, the imposition of such requirements.

Initially, I must vouchsafe that I cannot determine with certainty the reasoning by which the Court concludes that these further requirements are now imperative. The Court begins from the premise, to which it gives force at several points, that juvenile courts need not satisfy "all of the requirements of a criminal trial." It

[10] The statistical evidence here is incomplete, but see generally Skoler & Tenney, Attorney Representation in Juvenile Court, 4 J.Fam.Law 77. They indicate that some 91% of the juvenile court judges whom they polled favored representation by counsel in their courts. Id., at 88.

therefore scarcely suffices to explain the selection of these particular procedural requirements for the Court to declare that juvenile court proceedings are essentially criminal, and thereupon to recall that these are requisites for a criminal trial. Nor does the Court's voucher of "authoritative opinion," which consists of four extraordinary juvenile cases, contribute materially to the solution of these issues. The Court has, even under its own premises, asked the wrong questions: the problem here is to determine what forms of procedural protection are necessary to guarantee the fundamental fairness of juvenile proceedings, and not which of the procedures now employed in criminal trials should be transplanted intact to proceedings in these specialized courts.

In my view, the Court should approach this question in terms of the criteria, described above, which emerge from the history of due process adjudication. Measured by them, there are compelling reasons at least to defer imposition of these additional requirements. First, quite unlike notice, counsel, and a record, these requirements might radically alter the character of juvenile court proceedings. The evidence from which the Court reasons that they would not is inconclusive,[11] and other available evidence suggests that they very likely would.[12] At the least, it is plain that these additional requirements would contribute materially to the creation in these proceedings of the atmosphere of an ordinary criminal trial, and would, even if they do no more, thereby largely frustrate a central purpose of these specialized courts. Further, these are restrictions intended to conform to the demands of an intensely adversary system of criminal justice; the broad purposes which they represent might be served in juvenile courts with equal effectiveness by procedural devices more consistent with the premises of proceedings in those courts. As the Court apparently acknowledges, the hazards of self-accusation, for example, might be avoided in juvenile proceedings without the imposition of all the requirements and limitations which surround the privilege against self-incrimination. The guarantee of adequate notice, counsel, and a record would create conditions in which suitable alternative procedures could be devised; but, unfortunately, the Court's haste to impose restrictions taken intact from criminal procedure may well seriously hamper the development of such alternatives. Surely this illustrates that prudence and the principles of the

---

[11] Indeed, my Brother BLACK candidly recognizes that such is apt to be the effect of today's decision. * * * The Court itself is content merely to rely upon inapposite language from the recommendations of the Children's Bureau, plus the terms of a single statute.

[12] The most cogent evidence of course consists of the steady rejection of these requirements by state legislatures and courts. The wide disagreement and uncertainty upon this question are also reflected in Paulsen, Kent v. United States: The Constitutional Context of Juvenile Cases, 1966 Sup.Ct.Rev. 167, 186, 191.

See also Paulsen, Fairness to the Juvenile Offender, 41 Minn.L.Rev. 547, 561–562; McLean, An Answer to the Challenge of Kent, 53 A.B.A.J. 456, 457; Alexander, Constitutional Rights in Juvenile Court, 46 A.B.A.J. 1206; Shears, Legal Problems Peculiar to Children's Courts, 48 A.B.A.J. 719; Siler, The Need for Defense Counsel in the Juvenile Court, 11 Crime & Delin. 45, 57–58. Compare Handler, The Juvenile Court and the Adversary System: Problems of Function and Form, 1965 Wis.L.Rev. 7, 32.

Fourteenth Amendment alike require that the Court should now impose no more procedural restrictions than are imperative to assure fundamental fairness, and that the States should instead be permitted additional opportunities to develop without unnecessary hindrance their systems of juvenile courts.

I find confirmation for these views in two ancillary considerations. First, it is clear that an uncertain, but very substantial number of the cases brought to juvenile courts involve children who are not in any sense guilty of criminal misconduct. Many of these children have simply the misfortune to be in some manner distressed; others have engaged in conduct, such as truancy, which is plainly not criminal.[13] Efforts are now being made to develop effective, and entirely noncriminal, methods of treatment for these children. In such cases, the state authorities are in the most literal sense acting *in loco parentis;* they are, by any standard, concerned with the child's protection, and not with his punishment. I do not question that the methods employed in such cases must be consistent with the constitutional obligation to act in accordance with due process, but certainly the Fourteenth Amendment does not demand that they be constricted by the procedural guarantees devised for ordinary criminal prosecutions. Cf. State of Minnesota ex rel. Pearson v. Probate Court, 309 U.S. 270, 60 S.Ct. 523, 84 L.Ed. 744. It must be remembered that the various classifications of juvenile court proceedings are, as the vagaries of the available statistics illustrate, often arbitrary or ambiguous; it would therefore be imprudent, at the least, to build upon these classifications rigid systems of procedural requirements which would be applicable, or not, in accordance with the descriptive label given to the particular proceeding. It is better, it seems to me, to begin by now requiring the essential elements of fundamental fairness in juvenile courts, whatever the label given by the State to the proceeding; in this way the Court could avoid imposing unnecessarily rigid restrictions, and yet escape dependence upon classifications which may often prove to be illusory. Further, the provision of notice, counsel, and a record would permit orderly efforts to determine later whether more satisfactory classifications can be devised, and if they can, whether additional procedural requirements are necessary for them under the Fourteenth Amendment.

Second, it should not be forgotten that juvenile crime and juvenile courts are both now under earnest study throughout the country. I very much fear that this Court, by imposing these rigid procedural requirements, may inadvertently have served to discourage these efforts to find more satisfactory solutions for the problems of juvenile crime, and may thus now hamper enlightened development of the

---

[13] Estimates of the number of children in this situation brought before juvenile courts range from 26% to some 48%; variation seems chiefly a product both of the inadequacy of records and of the difficulty of categorizing precisely the conduct with which juveniles are charged. See generally Sheridan, Juveniles Who Commit Noncriminal Acts: Why Treat in a Correctional System? 31 Fed.Probation 26, 27. By any standard, the number of juveniles involved is "considerable." Ibid.

systems of juvenile courts. It is appropriate to recall that the Fourteenth Amendment does not compel the law to remain passive in the midst of change; to demand otherwise denies "every quality of the law but its age". Hurtado v. People of State of California, 110 U.S. 516, 529, 4 S.Ct. 111, 117, 28 L.Ed. 232.

III.

Finally, I turn to assess the validity of this juvenile court proceeding under the criteria discussed in this opinion. Measured by them, the judgment below must, in my opinion, fall. Gerald Gault and his parents were not provided adequate notice of the terms and purposes of the proceedings in which he was adjudged delinquent; they were not advised of their rights to be represented by counsel; and no record in any form was maintained of the proceedings. It follows, for the reasons given in this opinion, that Gerald Gault was deprived of his liberty without due process of law, and I therefore concur in the judgment of the Court.

Mr. Justice Stewart, dissenting.

The Court today uses an obscure Arizona case as a vehicle to impose upon thousands of juvenile courts throughout the Nation restrictions that the Constitution made applicable to adversary criminal trials. I believe the Court's decision is wholly unsound as a matter of constitutional law, and sadly unwise as a matter of judicial policy.

Juvenile proceedings are not criminal trials. They are not civil trials. They are simply not adversary proceedings. Whether treating with a delinquent child, a neglected child, a defective child, or a dependent child, a juvenile proceeding's whole purpose and mission is the very opposite of the mission and purpose of a prosecution in a criminal court. The object of the one is correction of a condition. The object of the other is conviction and punishment for a criminal act.

In the last 70 years many dedicated men and women have devoted their professional lives to the enlightened task of bringing us out of the dark world of Charles Dickens in meeting our responsibilities to the child in our society. The result has been the creation in this century of a system of juvenile and family courts in each of the 50 States. There can be no denying that in many areas the performance of these agencies has fallen disappointingly short of the hopes and dreams of the courageous pioneers who first conceived them. For a variety of reasons, the reality has sometimes not even approached the ideal, and much remains to be accomplished in the administration of public juvenile and family agencies—in personnel, in planning, in financing, perhaps in the formulation of wholly new approaches.

I possess neither the specialized experience nor the expert knowledge to predict with any certainty where may lie the brightest hope for progress in dealing with the serious problems of juvenile delinquency. But I am certain that the answer does not lie in the Court's opinion in this case, which serves to convert a juvenile proceeding into a criminal prosecution.

The inflexible restrictions that the Constitution so wisely made applicable to adversary criminal trials have no inevitable place in the proceedings of those public social agencies known as juvenile or family courts. And to impose the Court's long catalog of requirements upon juvenile proceedings in every area of the country is to invite a long step backwards into the nineteenth century. In that era there were no juvenile proceedings, and a child was tried in a conventional criminal court with all the trappings of a conventional criminal trial. So it was that a 12-year-old boy named James Guild was tried in New Jersey for killing Catharine Beakes. A jury found him guilty of murder, and he was sentenced to death by hanging. The sentence was executed. It was all very constitutional.[14]

A State in all its dealings must, of course, accord every person due process of law. And due process may require that some of the same restrictions which the Constitution has placed upon criminal trials must be imposed upon juvenile proceedings. For example, I suppose that all would agree that a brutally coerced confession could not constitutionally be considered in a juvenile court hearing. But it surely does not follow that the testimonial privilege against self-incrimination is applicable in all juvenile proceedings.[15] Similarly, due process clearly requires timely notice of the purpose and scope of any proceedings affecting the relationship of parent and child. Armstrong v. Manzo, 380 U.S. 545, 85 S.Ct. 1187, 14 L.Ed.2d 62. But it certainly does not follow that notice of a juvenile hearing must be framed with all the technical niceties of a criminal indictment. See Russell v. United States, 369 U.S. 749, 82 S.Ct. 1038, 8 L.Ed.2d 240.

In any event, there is no reason to deal with issues such as these in the present case. The Supreme Court of Arizona found that the

---

[14] State v. Guild, 5 Halst. 163, 10 N.J.L. 163, 18 Am.Dec. 404.

"Thus, also, in very modern times, a boy of ten years old was convicted on his own confession of murdering his bedfellow, there appearing in his whole behavior plain tokens of a mischievous discretion; and as the sparing this boy merely on account of his tender years might be of dangerous consequence to the public, by propagating a notion that children might commit such atrocious crimes with impunity, it was unanimously agreed by all the judges that he was a proper subject of capital punishment." 4 Blackstone, Commentaries 23 (Wendell ed. 1847).

[15] Until June 13, 1966, it was clear that the Fourteenth Amendment's ban upon the use of a coerced confession is constitutionally quite a different thing from the Fifth Amendment's testimonial privilege against self-incrimination. See, for example, the Court's unanimous opinion in Brown v. State of Mississippi, 297 U.S. 278, at 285–286, 56 S.Ct. 461, 464–465, 80 L.Ed. 682, written by Chief Justice Hughes and joined by such distinguished members of this Court as Mr. Justice Brandeis, Mr. Justice Stone, and Mr. Justice Cardozo. See also Tehan v. United States ex rel. Shott, 382 U.S. 406, 86 S.Ct. 459, 15 L.Ed.2d 453, decided January 19, 1966, where the Court emphasized the "contrast" between "the wrongful use of a coerced confession" and "the Fifth Amendment's privilege against self-incrimination". 382 U.S., at 416, 86 S.Ct., at 465. The complete confusion of these separate constitutional doctrines in Part V of the Court's opinion today stems, no doubt, from Miranda v. State of Arizona, 384 U.S. 436, 86 S.Ct. 1602, a decision which I continue to believe was constitutionally erroneous.

parents of Gerald Gault "knew of their right to counsel, to subpoena and cross examine witnesses, of the right to confront the witnesses against Gerald and the possible consequences of a finding of delinquency." 99 Ariz. 181, 185, 407 P.2d 760, 763. It further found that "Mrs. Gault knew the exact nature of the charge against Gerald from the day he was taken to the detention home." 99 Ariz., at 193, 407 P.2d, at 768. And, as MR. JUSTICE WHITE correctly points out, p. 1463, ante, no issue of compulsory self-incrimination is presented by this case.

I would dismiss the appeal.

IN RE WINSHIP

Supreme Court of the United States, 1970.
397 U.S. 358, 90 S.Ct. 1068, 25 L.Ed.2d 368.

MR. JUSTICE BRENNAN delivered the opinion of the Court.

Constitutional questions decided by this Court concerning the juvenile process have centered on the adjudicatory stage at "which a determination is made as to whether a juvenile is a 'delinquent' as a result of alleged misconduct on his part, with the consequence that he may be committed to a state institution." In re Gault, 387 U.S. 1, 13, 87 S.Ct. 1428, 1436, 18 L.Ed.2d 527 (1967). *Gault* decided that, although the Fourteenth Amendment does not require that the hearing at this stage conform with all the requirements of a criminal trial or even of the usual administrative proceeding, the Due Process Clause does require application during the adjudicatory hearing of "the essentials of due process and fair treatment." * * * This case presents the single, narrow question whether proof beyond a reasonable doubt is among the "essentials of due process and fair treatment" required during the adjudicatory stage when a juvenile is charged with an act which would constitute a crime if committed by an adult.[16]

Section 712 of the New York Family Court Act defines a juvenile delinquent as "a person over seven and less than sixteen years of age who does any act which, if done by an adult, would constitute a crime." During a 1967 adjudicatory hearing, conducted pursuant to § 742 of the Act, a judge in New York Family Court found that appellant, then a 12-year-old boy, had entered a locker and stolen

---

[16] Thus, we do not see how it can be said in dissent that this opinion "rests entirely on the assumption that all juvenile proceedings are 'criminal prosecutions,' hence subject to constitutional limitations." As in *Gault*, "we are not here concerned with * * * the pre-judicial stages of the juvenile process, nor do we direct our attention to the post-adjudicative or dispositional process." * * * In New York, the adjudicatory stage of a delinquency proceeding is clearly distinct from both the preliminary phase of the juvenile process and from its disposition-al stage. * * * Similarly, we intimate no view concerning the constitutionality of the New York procedures governing children "in need of supervision." * * * Nor do we consider whether there are other "elements of due process and fair treatment" required during the adjudicatory hearing of a delinquency proceeding. Finally, we have no occasion to consider appellant's argument that § 744(b) is a violation of the Equal Protection Clause, as well as a denial of due process.

$112 from a woman's pocketbook. The petition which charged appellant with delinquency alleged that his act, "if done by an adult, would constitute the crime or crimes of Larceny." The judge acknowledged that the proof might not establish guilt beyond a reasonable doubt, but rejected appellant's contention that such proof was required by the Fourteenth Amendment. The judge relied instead on § 744(b) of the New York Family Court Act which provides that "[a]ny determination at the conclusion of [an adjudicatory] hearing that a [juvenile] did an act or acts must be based on a preponderance of the evidence." [17] During a subsequent dispositional hearing, appellant was ordered placed in a training school for an initial period of 18 months, subject to annual extensions of his commitment until his 18th birthday—six years in appellant's case. The Appellate Division of the New York Supreme Court, First Judicial District, affirmed without opinion * * * The New York Court of Appeals then affirmed by a four-to-three vote, expressly sustaining the constitutionality of § 744(b), 24 N.Y.2d 196, 299 N.Y.S.2d 414, 247 N.E.2d 253 (1969). We noted probable jurisdiction. * * * We reverse.

* * *

[In the portion of the opinion omitted here, the Court concluded that the "proof beyond a reasonable doubt" standard was constitutionally mandated in criminal cases].

II

We turn to the question whether juveniles, like adults, are constitutionally entitled to proof beyond a reasonable doubt when they are charged with violation of a criminal law. The same considerations which demand extreme caution in factfinding to protect the innocent adult apply as well to the innocent child. We do not find convincing the contrary arguments of the New York Court of Appeals, *Gault* rendered untenable much of the reasoning relied upon by that court to sustain the constitutionality of § 744(b). The Court of Appeals indicated that a delinquency adjudication "is not a 'conviction' (§ 781); that it affects no right or privilege, including the right to hold public office or to obtain a license (§ 782); and a cloak of protective confidentiality is thrown around all the proceedings (§§ 783–784)." * * * The court said further: "The delinquency status is not made a crime; and the proceedings are not criminal. There is, hence, no deprivation of due process in the statutory provision [challenged by appellant] * * *." * * * In effect the Court of Appeals distinguished the proceedings in question here from a criminal prosecution by use of what *Gault* called the " 'civil' label-of-convenience which has been attached to juvenile proceedings." * * * But *Gault* expressly rejected that distinction as a reason for

---

[17] The ruling appears in the following portion of the hearing transcript:

Counsel: "Your Honor is making a finding by the preponderance of the evidence."

Court: "Well, it convinces me."

Counsel: "It's not beyond a reasonable doubt, Your Honor."

Court: "That is true * * * Our statute says a preponderance and a preponderance it is."

holding the Due Process Clause inapplicable to a juvenile proceeding. * * * The Court of Appeals also attempted to justify the preponderance standard on the related ground that juvenile proceedings are designed "not to punish, but to save the child." * * * Again, however, *Gault* expressly rejected this justification. * * * We made clear in that decision that civil labels and good intentions do not themselves obviate the need for criminal due process safeguards in juvenile courts, for "[a] proceeding where the issue is whether the child will be found to be 'delinquent' and subjected to the loss of his liberty for years is comparable in seriousness to a felony prosecution." * * *

Nor do we perceive any merit in the argument that to afford juveniles the protection of proof beyond a reasonable doubt would risk destruction of beneficial aspects of the juvenile process. Use of the reasonable-doubt standard during the adjudicatory hearing will not disturb New York's policies that a finding that a child has violated a criminal law does not constitute a criminal conviction, that such a finding does not deprive the child of his civil rights, and that juvenile proceedings are confidential. Nor will there be any effect on the informality, flexibility, or speed of the hearing at which the factfinding takes place. And the opportunity during the post-adjudicatory or dispositional hearing for a wide-ranging review of the child's social history and for his individualized treatment will remain unimpaired. Similarly, there will be no effect on the procedures distinctive to juvenile proceedings which are employed prior to the adjudicatory hearing.

The Court of Appeals observed that "a child's best interest is not necessarily, or even probably, promoted if he wins in the particular inquiry which may bring him to the juvenile court." * * * It is true, of course, that the juvenile may be engaging in a general course of conduct inimical to his welfare which calls for judicial intervention. But that intervention cannot take the form of subjecting the child to the stigma of a finding that he violated a criminal law [18] and to the possibility of institutional confinement on proof insufficient to convict him were he an adult.

We conclude, as we concluded regarding the essential due process safeguards applied in *Gault*, that the observance of the standard of proof beyond a reasonable doubt "will not compel the States to abandon or displace any of the substantive benefits of the juvenile process." Finally, we reject the Court of Appeals' suggestion that there is, in any event, only a "tenuous difference" between the reasonable-doubt and preponderance standards. The suggestion is singularly unpersuasive. In this very case, the trial judge's ability to distinguish between the two standards enabled him to make a finding of guilt which he conceded he might not have made under the standard of proof beyond a reasonable doubt. Indeed, the trial

---

[18] The more comprehensive and effective the procedures used to prevent public disclosure of the finding, the less the danger of stigma. As we indicated in *Gault*, however, often the "claim of secrecy * * * is more rhetoric than reality."

judge's action evidences the accuracy of the observation of commentators that "the preponderance test is susceptible to the misinterpretation that it calls on the trier of fact merely to perform an abstract weighing of the evidence in order to determine which side has produced the greater quantum, without regard to its effect in convincing his mind of the truth of the proposition asserted." *   *   *

III

In sum, the constitutional safeguard of proof beyond a reasonable doubt is as much required during the adjudicatory stage of a delinquency proceeding as are those constitutional safeguards applied in *Gault*—notice of charges, right to counsel, the rights of confrontation and examination, and the privilege against self-incrimination. We therefore hold, in agreement with Chief Judge Fuld in dissent in the Court of Appeals, "that, where a 12-year-old child is charged with an act of stealing which renders him liable to confinement for as long as six years, then, as a matter of due process *   *   * the case against him must be proved beyond a reasonable doubt." *   *   *

Reversed.

MR. JUSTICE HARLAN, concurring.

No one, I daresay, would contend that state juvenile court trials are subject to *no* federal constitutional limitations. Differences have existed, however, among the members of this Court as to *what* constitutional protections do apply. *   *   *

The present case draws in question the validity of a New York statute which permits a determination of juvenile delinquency, founded on a charge of criminal conduct, to be made on a standard of proof which is less rigorous than that which would obtain had the accused been tried for the same conduct in an ordinary criminal case. While I am in full agreement that this statutory provision offends the requirement of fundamental fairness embodied in the Due Process Clause of the Fourteenth Amendment, I am constrained to add something to what my BROTHER BRENNAN has written for the Court, lest the true nature of the constitutional problem presented become obscured or the impact on state juvenile court systems of what the Court holds today be exaggerated.

I

Professor Wigmore, in discussing the various attempts by courts to define how convinced one must be to be convinced beyond a reasonable doubt, wryly observed: "The truth is that no one has yet invented or discovered a mode of measurement for the intensity of human belief. Hence there can be yet no successful method of communicating intelligently *   *   * a sound method of self-analysis for one's beliefs," 9 Wigmore, Evidence 325 (1940).

Notwithstanding Professor Wigmore's skepticism, we have before us a case where the choice of the standard of proof has made a difference: the juvenile judge below forthrightly acknowledged that he believed by a preponderance of the evidence, but was not convinced beyond a reasonable doubt, that appellant stole $112 from the complainant's pocketbook. Moreover, even though the labels used for alternative standards of proof are vague and not a very sure guide to decisionmaking, the choice of the standard for a particular variety of adjudication does, I think, reflect a very fundamental assessment of the comparative social costs of erroneous factual determinations.

To explain why I think this so, I begin by stating two propositions, neither of which I believe can be fairly disputed. First, in a judicial proceeding in which there is a dispute about the facts of some earlier event, the factfinder cannot acquire unassailably accurate knowledge of what happened. Instead, all the factfinder can acquire is a belief of what *probably* happened. The intensity of this belief— the degree to which a factfinder is convinced that a given act actually occurred—can, of course, vary. In this regard, a standard of proof represents an attempt to instruct the factfinder concerning the degree of confidence our society thinks he should have in the correctness of factual conclusions for a particular type of adjudication. Although the phrases "preponderance of the evidence" and "proof beyond a reasonable doubt" are quantitatively imprecise, they do communicate to the finder of fact different notions concerning the degree of confidence he is expected to have in the correctness of his factual conclusions.

A second proposition, which is really nothing more than a corollary of the first, is that the trier of fact will sometimes, despite his best efforts, be wrong in his factual conclusions. In a lawsuit between two parties, a factual error can make a difference in one of two ways. First, it can result in a judgment in favor of the plaintiff when the true facts warrant a judgment for the defendant. The analogue in a criminal case would be the conviction of an innocent man. On the other hand, an erroneous factual determination can result in a judgment for the defendant when the true facts justify a judgment in plaintiff's favor. The criminal analogue would be the acquittal of a guilty man.

The standard of proof influences the relative frequency of these two types of erroneous outcomes. If, for example, the standard of proof for a criminal trial were a preponderance of the evidence rather than proof beyond a reasonable doubt, there would be a smaller risk of factual errors that result in freeing guilty persons, but a far greater risk of factual errors that result in convicting the innocent. Because the standard of proof affects the comparative frequency of these two types of erroneous outcomes, the choice of the standard to be applied in a particular kind of litigation should, in a rational world, reflect an assessment of the comparative social disutility of each.

When one makes such an assessment, the reason for different standards of proof in civil as opposed to criminal litigation becomes apparent. In a civil suit between two private parties for money damages, for example, we view it as no more serious in general for there to be an erroneous verdict in the defendant's favor than for there to be an erroneous verdict in the plaintiff's favor. A preponderance of the evidence standard therefore seems peculiarly appropriate for, as explained most sensibly, it simply requires the trier of fact "to believe that the existence of a fact is more probable than its nonexistence before [he] may find in favor of the party who has the burden to persuade the [judge] of the fact's existence."

In a criminal case, on the other hand, we do not view the social disutility of convicting an innocent man as equivalent to the disutility of acquitting someone who is guilty. As Mr. Justice Brennan wrote for the Court in Speiser v. Randall, 357 U.S. 513, 525–526, 78 S.Ct. 1332, 1341–1342, 2 L.Ed.2d 1460:

> "There is always in litigation a margin of error, representing error in fact-finding, which both parties must take into account. Where one party has at stake an interest of transcending value— as a criminal defendant his liberty—this margin of error is reduced as to him by the process of placing on the other party the burden * * * of persuading the fact-finder at the conclusion of the trial of his guilt beyond a reasonable doubt."

In this context, I view the requirement of proof beyond a reasonable doubt in a criminal case as bottomed on a fundamental value determination of our society that it is far worse to convict an innocent man than to let a guilty man go free. It is only because of the nearly complete and long-standing acceptance of the reasonable-doubt standard by the States in criminal trials that the Court has not before today had to hold explicitly that due process, as an expression of fundamental procedural fairness, requires a more stringent standard for criminal trials than for ordinary civil litigation.

II

When one assesses the consequences of an erroneous factual determination in a juvenile delinquency proceeding in which a youth is accused of a crime, I think it must be concluded that, while the consequences are not identical to those in a criminal case, the differences will not support a distinction in the standard of proof. First, and of paramount importance, a factual error here, as in a criminal case, exposes the accused to a complete loss of his personal liberty through a state-imposed confinement away from his home, family, and friends. And, second, a delinquency determination, to some extent at least, stigmatizes a youth in that it is by definition bottomed on a finding that the accused committed a crime.[19] Al-

---

[19] The New York statute was amended to distinguish between a "juvenile delinquent"—i.e., a youth "who does any act which, if done by an adult, would constitute a crime," N.Y.Family Ct.Act § 712 (1963), and a "[p]erson in need of supervision" [PINS] who is a person "who is an habitual truant or who is incorrigible, ungovernable or habitually disobedient and beyond the lawful control of parent or other lawful authority." The PINS category was established in order to avoid the stigma of finding someone to be a "juvenile delinquent" unless he committed a criminal act. The Legislative Committee report stated: " 'Juvenile delinquent' is now a term of disapproval. The judges of the Children's Court and the Domestic Relations Court of course are aware of this and also aware that

though there are no doubt costs to society (and possibly even to the youth himself) in letting a guilty youth go free, I think here, as in a criminal case, it is far worse to declare an innocent youth a delinquent. I therefore agree that a juvenile court judge should be no less convinced of the factual conclusion that the accused committed the criminal act with which he is charged than would be required in a criminal trial.

III

I wish to emphasize, as I did in my separate opinion in *Gault*, 387 U.S. 1, 65, 87 S.Ct. 1428, 1463, that there is no automatic congruence between the procedural requirements imposed by due process in a criminal case, and those imposed by due process in juvenile cases.[20] It is of great importance, in my view, that procedural strictures not be constitutionally imposed that jeopardize "the essential elements of the State's purpose" in creating juvenile courts, id., at 72, 87 S.Ct. at 1467. In this regard, I think it worth emphasizing that the requirement of proof beyond a reasonable doubt that a juvenile committed a criminal act before he is found to be a delinquent does not (1) interfere with the worthy goal of rehabilitating the juvenile, (2) make any significant difference in the extent to which a youth is stigmatized as a "criminal" because he has been found to be a delinquent, or (3) burden the juvenile courts with a procedural requirement which will make juvenile adjudications significantly more time consuming, or rigid. Today's decision simply requires a juvenile judge to be more confident in his belief that the youth did the act with which he has been charged.

With these observations, I join the Court's opinion, subject only to the constitutional reservations expressed in my opinion in *Gault*.

MR. CHIEF JUSTICE BURGER, with whom MR. JUSTICE STEWART joins, dissenting.

The Court's opinion today rests entirely on the assumption that all juvenile proceedings are "criminal prosecutions," hence subject to constitutional limitations. This derives from earlier holdings, which like today's holding, were steps eroding the differences between juvenile courts and traditional criminal courts. The original concept of the juvenile court system was to provide a benevolent and less formal means than criminal courts could provide for dealing with the

government officials and private employers often learn of an adjudication of delinquency." N.Y.Jt. Legislative Committee on Court Reorganization, The Family Court Act, Pt. 2, at 7 (1962). Moreover, the powers of the police and courts differ in these two categories of cases. See id., at 7–9. Thus, in a PINS type case, the consequences of an erroneous factual determination are by no means identical to those involved here.

[20] In Gault, for example, I agree with the majority that due process required (1) adequate notice of the "nature and terms" of the proceedings; (2) notice of the right to retain counsel, and an obligation on the State to provide counsel for indigents "in cases in which the child may be confined"; and (3) a written record "adequate to permit effective review." 387 U.S., at 72, 87 S.Ct., at 1467. Unlike the majority, however, I thought it unnecessary at the time of *Gault* to impose the additional requirements of the privilege against self-incrimination, confrontation, and cross-examination.

special and often sensitive problems of youthful offenders. Since I see no constitutional requirement of due process sufficient to overcome the legislative judgment of the States in this area, I dissent from further strait-jacketing of an already overly-restricted system. What the juvenile court systems need is not more but less of the trappings of legal procedure and judicial formalism; the juvenile system requires breathing room and flexibility in order to survive, if it can survive the repeated assaults from this Court.

Much of the judicial attitude manifested by the Court's opinion today and earlier holdings in this field is really a protest against inadequate juvenile court staffs and facilities; we "burn down the stable to get rid of the mice." The lack of support and the distressing growth of juvenile crime have combined to make for a literal breakdown in many if not most juvenile courts. Constitutional problems were not seen while those courts functioned in an atmosphere where juvenile judges were not crushed with an avalanche of cases.

My hope is that today's decision will not spell the end of a generously conceived program of compassionate treatment intended to mitigate the rigors and trauma of exposing youthful offenders to a traditional criminal court; each step we take turns the clock back to the pre-juvenile court era. I cannot regard it as a manifestation of progress to transform juvenile courts into criminal courts, which is what we are well on the way to accomplishing. We can only hope the legislative response will not reflect our own by having these courts abolished.

MR. JUSTICE BLACK, dissenting [omitted].

NOTE

Winship was held to apply retroactively in Ivan v. City of New York, 407 U.S. 203, 92 S.Ct. 1951, 32 L.Ed.2d 659 (1972).

McKEIVER v. PENNSYLVANIA

Supreme Court of the United States, 1971.
403 U.S. 528, 91 S.Ct. 1976, 29 L.Ed.2d 647.

MR. JUSTICE BLACKMUN announced the judgment of the Court and an opinion in which The CHIEF JUSTICE, MR. JUSTICE STEWART, and MR. JUSTICE WHITE join.

These cases present the narrow but precise issue whether the Due Process Clause of the Fourteenth Amendment assures the right to trial by jury in the adjudicative phase of a state juvenile court delinquency proceeding.

I

The issue arises understandably, for the Court in a series of cases already has emphasized due process factors protective of the juvenile:

1.　Haley v. Ohio, 332 U.S. 596, 68 S.Ct. 302, 92 L.Ed. 224 (1948), concerned the admissibility of a confession taken from a 15-year-old boy on trial for first-degree murder.　It was held that, upon the facts there developed, the Due Process Clause barred the use of the confession.　Mr. Justice Douglas, in an opinion in which three other Justices joined, said, "Neither man nor child can be allowed to stand condemned by methods which flout constitutional requirements of due process of law."　332 U.S. at 601, 68 S.Ct. at 304, 92 L.Ed. at 229.

2.　Gallegos v. Colorado, 370 U.S. 49, 82 S.Ct. 1209, 8 L.Ed.2d 325, 87 A.L.R.2d 614 (1962), where a 14-year-old was on trial, is to the same effect.

3.　Kent v. United States, 383 U.S. 541, 86 S.Ct. 1045, 16 L.Ed.2d 84 (1966), concerned a 16-year-old charged with housebreaking, robbery, and rape in the District of Columbia.　The issue was the propriety of the juvenile court's waiver of jurisdiction "after full investigation," as permitted by the applicable statute.　It was emphasized that the latitude the court possessed within which to determine whether it should retain or waive jurisdiction "assumes procedural regularity sufficient in the particular circumstances to satisfy the basic requirements of due process and fairness, as well as compliance with the statutory requirement of a 'full investigation.' "　383 U.S., at 553, 86 S.Ct., at 1053, 16 L.Ed.2d at 93.

4.　In re Gault, 387 U.S. 1, 87 S.Ct. 1428, 18 L.Ed.2d 527 (1967), concerned a 15-year-old, already on probation, committed in Arizona as a delinquent after being apprehended upon a complaint of lewd remarks by telephone.　Mr. Justice Fortas, in writing for the Court, reviewed the cases just cited and observed,

"Accordingly, while these cases relate only to restricted aspects of the subject, they unmistakably indicate that, whatever may be their precise impact, neither the Fourteenth Amendment nor the Bill of Rights is for adults alone."　387 U.S. at 13, 87 S.Ct., at 1436, 18 L.Ed.2d at 538.

The Court focused on "the proceedings by which a determination is made as to whether a juvenile is a 'delinquent' as a result of alleged misconduct on his part, with the consequence that he may be committed to a state institution" and, as to this, said that "there appears to be little current dissent from the proposition that the Due Process Clause has a role to play."　P. 13, 18 L.Ed.2d p. 538.　Kent was adhered to: "We reiterate this view, here in connection with the juvenile court adjudication of 'delinquency,' as a requirement which is part of the Due Process Clause of the Fourteenth Amendment of our Constitution."　Pp. 30–31, 18 L.Ed.2d p. 548.　Due process, in that proceeding, was held to embrace adequate written notice; advice as to the right to counsel, retained or appointed; confrontation; and cross-examination.　The privilege against self-incrimination was also held available to the juvenile.　The Court refrained from deciding whether a State must provide appellate review in juvenile cases or a transcript or recording of the hearings.

5. DeBacker v. Brainard, 396 U.S. 28, 90 S.Ct. 163, 24 L.Ed.2d 148 (1969), presented, by state habeas corpus, a challenge to a Nebraska statute providing that juvenile court hearings "shall be conducted by the judge without a jury in an informal manner." However, because that appellant's hearing had antedated the decisions in Duncan v. Louisiana, 391 U.S. 145, 88 S.Ct. 1444, 20 L.Ed.2d 491 (1968), and Bloom v. Illinois, 391 U.S. 194, 88 S.Ct. 1477, 20 L.Ed. 2d 522 (1968), and because Duncan and Bloom had been given only prospective application by DeStefano v. Woods, 392 U.S. 631, 88 S.Ct. 2093, 20 L.Ed.2d 1308 (1968), DeBacker's case was deemed an inappropriate one for resolution of the jury trial issue. His appeal was therefore dismissed. Mr. Justice Black and Mr. Justice Douglas, in separate dissents, took the position that a juvenile is entitled to a jury trial at the adjudicative stage. Mr. Justice Black described this as "a right which is surely one of the fundamental aspects of criminal justice in the English-speaking world," 396 U.S., at 34, 90 S.Ct., at 166, 24 L.Ed.2d at 154, and Mr. Justice Douglas described it as a right required by the Sixth and Fourteenth Amendments "where the delinquency charged is an offense that, if the person charged were an adult, would be a crime triable by jury." 396 U.S., at 35, 90 S.Ct., at 167, 24 L.Ed.2d at 155.

6. In re Winship, 397 U.S. 358, 90 S.Ct. 1068, 25 L.Ed.2d 368 (1970), concerned a 12-year-old charged with delinquency for having taken money from a woman's purse. The Court held that "the Due Process Clause protects the accused against conviction except upon proof beyond a reasonable doubt of every fact necessary to constitute the crime with which he is charged," 397 U.S., at 364, 90 S.Ct., at 1073, 25 L.Ed.2d at 375, and then went on to hold, p. 368, 90 S.Ct., at 1075, 25 L.Ed.2d p. 377, that this standard was applicable, too, "during the adjudicatory stage of a delinquency proceeding."

From these six cases—Haley, Gallegos, Kent, Gault, DeBacker and Winship—it is apparent that:

1. Some of the constitutional requirements attendant upon the state criminal trial have equal application to that part of the state juvenile proceeding that is adjudicative in nature. Among these are the rights to appropriate notice, to counsel, to confrontation and to cross-examination, and the privilege against self-incrimination. Included, also, is the standard of proof beyond a reasonable doubt.

2. The Court, however, has not yet said that *all* rights constitutionally assured to an adult accused of crime also are to be enforced or made available to the juvenile in his delinquency proceeding. Indeed, the Court specifically has refrained from going that far:

"We do not mean by this to indicate that the hearing to be held must conform with all of the requirements of a criminal trial or even of the usual administrative hearing; but we do hold that the hearing must measure up to the essentials of due process and fair treatment." *Kent*, 383 U.S., at 562, 86 S.Ct., at 1057, 16 L.Ed.2d at 97, 98; *Gault*, 387 U.S., at 30, 87 S.Ct., at 1445, 18 L.Ed.2d at 548.

3. The Court, although recognizing the high hopes and aspirations of Judge Julian Mack, the leaders of the Jane Addams School [21] and the other supporters of the juvenile court concept, has also noted the disappointments of the system's performance and experience and the resulting widespread disaffection. *Kent,* 383 U.S., at 555–556, 86 S.Ct., at 1054–1055, 16 L.Ed.2d at 94; *Gault,* 387 U.S., at 17–19, 87 S.Ct., at 1438–1439, 18 L.Ed.2d at 540, 541. There have been, at one and the same time, both an appreciation for the juvenile court judge who is devoted, sympathetic, and conscientious, and a disturbed concern about the judge who is untrained and less than fully imbued with an understanding approach to the complex problems of childhood and adolescence. There has been praise for the system and its purposes, and there has been alarm over its defects.

4. The Court has insisted that these successive decisions do not spell the doom of the juvenile court system or even deprive it of its "informality, flexibility or speed." Winship, 397 U.S., at 366–367, 90 S.Ct., at 1074, 25 L.Ed.2d at 377. On the other hand, a concern precisely to the opposite effect was expressed by two dissenters in Winship. 397 U.S., at 375–376, 90 S.Ct., at 1078–1079, 25 L.Ed.2d at 381, 382.

II

With this substantial background already developed, we turn to the facts of the present cases:

No. 322. Joseph McKeiver, then age 16, in May 1968 was charged with robbery, larceny, and receiving stolen goods (felonies under Pennsylvania law, 18 P.S. §§ 4704, 4807, and 4817) as acts of juvenile delinquency. At the time of the adjudication hearing he was represented by counsel.[22] His request for a jury trial was denied and his case was heard by Judge Theodore S. Gutowicz of the Court of Common Pleas, Family Division, Juvenile Branch, of Philadelphia County, Pennsylvania. McKeiver was adjudged a delinquent upon findings that he had violated a law of the Commonwealth. 11 P.S. § 243(4)(a). He was placed on probation. On appeal, the Superior Court affirmed without opinion. In re McKeiver, 215 Pa.Super. 760, 255 A.2d 921 (1969).

Edward Terry, then age 15, in January 1969 was charged with assault and battery on a police officer and conspiracy (misdemeanors under Pennsylvania law, 18 P.S. §§ 4708 and 4302) as acts of juvenile delinquency. His counsel's request for a jury trial was denied and his case was heard by Judge Joseph C. Bruno of the same Juvenile Branch of the Court of Common Pleas of Philadelphia County. Terry was adjudged a delinquent on the charges. This followed an adjudi-

---

[21] See Mr. Justice Fortas' article, Equal Rights—For Whom? 42 N.Y.U.L.Rev. 401, 406 (1967).

[22] At McKeiver's hearing his counsel advised the court that he had never seen McKeiver before and "was just in the middle of interviewing him." The court allowed him five minutes for the interview. Counsel's office, Community Legal Services, however, had been appointed to represent McKeiver five months earlier. Appendix 2.

cation and commitment in the preceding week for an assault on a teacher. He was committed, as he had been on the earlier charge, to the Youth Development Center at Cornwalls Heights. On appeal, the Superior Court affirmed without opinion. In re Terry, 215 Pa.Super. 762, 255 A.2d 922 (1969).

The Supreme Court of Pennsylvania granted leave to appeal in both cases and consolidated them. The single question considered, as phrased by the court, was "whether there is a constitutional right to a jury trial in juvenile court." The answer, one justice dissenting, was in the negative. In re Terry, 438 Pa. 339, 265 A.2d 350 (1970). We noted probable jurisdiction. 399 U.S. 925, 90 S.Ct. 2271, 26 L.Ed. 2d 791 (1970).

The details of the McKeiver and Terry offenses are set forth in Justice Roberts' opinion for the Pennsylvania court, 438 Pa., at 341–342 nn. 1 and 2, 265 A.2d, at 351 nn. 1 and 2, and need not be repeated at any length here. It suffices to say that McKeiver's offense was his participating with 20 or 30 youths who pursued three young teenagers and took 25 cents from them; that McKeiver never before had been arrested and had a record of gainful employment; that the testimony of two of the victims was described by the court as somewhat inconsistent and as "weak"; and that Terry's offense consisted of hitting a police officer with his fists and with a stick when the officer broke up a boys' fight Terry and others were watching.

No. 128. Barbara Burrus and approximately 45 other black children, ranging in age from 11 to 15 years,[23] were the subjects of juvenile court summonses issued in Hyde County, North Carolina, in January 1969.

The charges arose out of a series of demonstrations in the county in late 1968 by black adults and children protesting school assignments and a school consolidation plan. Petitions were filed by North Carolina state highway patrolmen. Except for one relating to James Lambert Howard, the petitions charged the respective juveniles with wilfully impeding traffic. The charge against Howard was that he wilfully made riotous noise and was disorderly in the O.A. Peay School in Swan Quarter; interrupted and disturbed the school during its regular sessions; and defaced school furniture. The acts so charged are misdemeanors under North Carolina law. N.C.Gen. Stats. §§ 20.174.1, 14–132(a), 14–273.

The several cases were consolidated into groups for hearing before District Judge Hallett S. Ward, sitting as a juvenile court. The same lawyer appeared for all the juveniles. Over counsel's objection, made in all except two of the cases, the general public was excluded. A request for a jury trial in each case was denied.

The evidence as to the juveniles other than Howard consisted solely of testimony of highway patrolmen. No juvenile took the

---

[23] In North Carolina juvenile court procedures are provided only for persons under the age of 16. N.C.Gen.Stat. §§ 7A–277 and 7A–278(1) (1969).

stand or offered any witness. The testimony was to the effect that on various occasions the juveniles and adults were observed walking along Highway 64 singing, shouting, clapping, and playing basket-ball. As a result, there was interference with traffic. The marchers were asked to leave the paved portion of the highway and they were warned that they were committing a statutory offense. They either refused or left the roadway and immediately returned. The juveniles and participating adults were taken into custody. Juvenile petitions were then filed with respect to those under the age of 16.

The evidence as to Howard was that on the morning of December 5, he was in the office of the principal of the O.A. Peay School with 15 other persons while school was in session and was moving furniture around; that the office was in disarray; that as a result the school closed before noon; and that neither he nor any of the others was a student at the school or authorized to enter the principal's office.

In each case the court found that the juvenile had committed "an act for which an adult may be punished by law." A custody order was entered declaring the juvenile a delinquent "in need of more suitable guardianship" and committing him to the custody of the County Department of Public Welfare for placement in a suitable institution "until such time as the Board of Juvenile Correction or the Superintendent of said institution may determine, not inconsistent with the laws of this State." The court, however, suspended these commitments and placed each juvenile on probation for either one or two years conditioned upon his violating none of the State's laws, upon his reporting monthly to the County Department of Welfare, upon his being home by 11 p.m. each evening, and upon his attending a school approved by the Welfare Director. None of the juveniles has been confined on these charges.

On appeal, the cases were consolidated into two groups. The North Carolina Court of Appeals affirmed. In re Burrus, 4 N.C.App. 523, 167 S.E.2d 454 (1969); In re Shelton, 5 N.C.App. 487, 168 S.E.2d 695 (1969). In its turn the Supreme Court of North Carolina deleted that portion of the order in each case relating to commitment, but otherwise affirmed. In re Burrus, 275 N.C. 517, 169 S.E.2d 879 (1969). Two justices dissented without opinion. We granted certiorari. 397 U.S. 1036, 90 S.Ct. 1379, 25 L.Ed.2d 647 (1970).

It is instructive to review, as an illustration, the substance of Justice Roberts' opinion for the Pennsylvania court. He observes, 265 A.2d, at 352, that "For over sixty-five years the Supreme Court gave no consideration at all to the constitutional problems involved in the juvenile court area"; that Gault "is somewhat of a paradox, being both broad and narrow at the same time"; that it "is broad in that it evidences a fundamental and far-reaching disillusionment with the anticipated benefits of the juvenile court system"; that it is narrow because the court enumerated four due process rights which it held applicable in juvenile proceedings, but declined to rule on two other claimed rights, p. 353; that as a consequence the Pennsylvania court was "confronted with a sweeping rationale and a carefully tailored holding"; that the procedural safeguards "Gault specifically made applicable to juvenile courts have already caused a significant 'constitutional domestication' of juvenile court proceedings," p. 354; that those safeguards and other rights, including the reasonable doubt standard established by Winship, "insure that the juvenile court will operate in an atmosphere which is orderly enough to impress the juvenile with the gravity of the situation and the impartiality of the tribunal and at the same time informal enough to permit the benefits of the juvenile system to operate" (footnote omitted); that the "proper inquiry, then, is whether the right to a trial by jury is 'fundamental' within the meaning of Duncan in the context of a juvenile court which operates with *all* of the above constitutional safeguards"; and that his court's inquiry turned "upon whether there are elements in the juvenile process which render the right to a trial by jury less essential to the protection of an accused's rights in the juvenile system than in the normal criminal process."

Justice Roberts then concluded that such factors do inhere in the Pennsylvania juvenile system: (1) Although realizing that "faith in the quality of the juvenile bench is not an entirely satisfactory substitute for due process," p. 355, the judges in the juvenile courts "do take a different view of their role than that taken by their counterparts in the criminal courts." (2) While one regrets its inadequacies, p. 355, "the juvenile system has available and utilizes much more fully various diagnostic and rehabilitative services" that are "far superior to those available in the regular criminal process." (3) Although conceding that the post-adjudication process "has in many respects fallen far short of its goals, and its reality is far harsher than its theory," the end result of a declaration of delinquency "*is* significantly different from and less onerous than a finding of criminal guilt" and "we are not yet convinced that the current practices do not contain the seeds from which a truly appropriate system can be brought forth." (4) Finally, "of all the possible due process rights which could be applied in the juvenile courts, the right to trial by jury is the one which would most likely be disruptive of the unique character of the juvenile process." It is the jury trial that "would probably require substantial alteration of the traditional practices." The other procedural rights held applicable to the juvenile process "will give the juvenile sufficient protection" and the addition of the trial by jury "might well destroy the traditional character of juvenile proceedings."

The court concluded, p. 356, that it was confident "that a properly structured and fairly administered juvenile court system can save our present societal needs without infringing on individual freedoms."

IV

The right to an impartial jury "[i]n all criminal prosecutions" under federal law is guaranteed by the Sixth Amendment. Through the Fourteenth Amendment that requirement has now been imposed upon the States "in all criminal cases which—were they to be tried in a federal court—would come within the Sixth Amendment's guarantee." This is because the Court has said it believes "that trial by jury in criminal cases is fundamental to the American scheme of justice." Duncan v. Louisiana, 391 U.S. 145, 149, 88 S.Ct. 1444, 1447, 20 L.Ed. 2d 491, 496 (1968); Bloom v. Illinois, 391 U.S. 194, 210–211, 88 S.Ct. 1477, 1486–1487, 20 L.Ed.2d 522, 533, 534 (1968).

This, of course, does not automatically provide the answer to the present jury trial issue, if for no other reason than that the juvenile court proceeding has not yet been held to be a "criminal prosecution," within the meaning and reach of the Sixth Amendment, and also has not yet been regarded as devoid of criminal aspects merely because it usually has been given the civil label. *Kent*, 383 U.S., at 554, 86 S.Ct., at 1054, 16 L.Ed.2d at 93; *Gault*, 387 U.S., at 17, 49–50, 87 S.Ct., at 1438, 18 L.Ed.2d at 540, 558; *Winship*, 397 U.S., at 365–366, 90 S.Ct., at 1073–1074, 25 L.Ed.2d at 375, 376.

Little, indeed, is to be gained by any attempt simplistically to call the juvenile court proceeding either "civil" or "criminal." The Court carefully has avoided this wooden approach. Before Gault was decided in 1967, the Fifth Amendment's guarantee against self-incrimination had been imposed upon the state criminal trial. Malloy v. Hogan, 378 U.S. 1, 84 S.Ct. 1489, 12 L.Ed.2d 653 (1964). So, too, had the Sixth Amendment's rights of confrontation and cross-examination. Pointer v. Texas, 380 U.S. 400, 85 S.Ct. 1065, 13 L.Ed.2d 923 (1965), and Douglas v. Alabama, 380 U.S. 415, 85 S.Ct. 1074, 13 L.Ed. 2d 934 (1965). Yet the Court did not automatically and peremptorily apply those rights to the juvenile proceeding. A reading of Gault reveals the opposite. And the same separate approach to the standard of proof issue is evident from the carefully separated application of the standard, first to the criminal trial, and then to the juvenile proceeding, displayed in Winship. 397 U.S., at 361 and 365, 90 S.Ct., at 1071 and 1073, 25 L.Ed.2d at 373, and 375.

Thus, accepting "the proposition that the Due Process Clause has a role to play," *Gault*, 387 U.S., at 13, 87 S.Ct., at 1436, 18 L.Ed.2d at 538, our task here with respect to trial by jury, as it was in Gault with respect to other claimed rights, "is to ascertain the precise impact of the due process requirement."

V

The Pennsylvania juveniles' basic argument is that they were tried in proceedings "substantially similar to a criminal trial." They say that a delinquency proceeding in their State is initiated by a petition charging a penal code violation in the conclusory language of an indictment; that a juvenile detained prior to trial is held in a building substantially similar to an adult prison; that in Philadelphia juveniles over 16 are, in fact, held in the cells of a prison; that counsel and the prosecution engage in plea bargaining; that motions to suppress are routinely heard and decided; that the usual rules of evidence are applied; that the customary common law defenses are available; that the press is generally admitted in the Philadelphia juvenile courtrooms; that members of the public enter the room; that arrest and prior record may be reported by the press (from police sources, however, rather than from the juvenile court records); that, once adjudged delinquent, a juvenile may be confined until his majority in what amounts to a prison (see In re Bethea, 215 Pa.Super. 75, 76, 257 A.2d 368, 369 (1969), describing the state correctional institution at Camp Hill as a "maximum security prison for adjudged delinquents and youthful criminal offenders"); and that the stigma attached upon delinquency adjudication approximates that resulting from conviction in an adult criminal proceeding.

The North Carolina juveniles particularly urge that the requirement of a jury trial would not operate to deny the supposed benefits of the juvenile court system; that the system's primary benefits are its discretionary intake procedure permitting disposition short of adjudication, and its flexible sentencing permitting emphasis on rehabilitation; that realization of these benfits does not depend upon dispensing with the jury; that adjudication of factual issues on the one hand and disposition of the case on the other are very different matters with very different purposes; that the purpose of the former is indistinguishable from that of the criminal trial; that the jury trial provides an independent protective factor; that experience has shown that jury trials in juvenile courts are manageable; that no reason exists why protection traditionally accorded in criminal proceedings should be denied young people subject to involuntary incarceration for lengthy periods; and that the juvenile courts deserve healthy public scrutiny.

VI

All the litigants here agree that the applicable due process standard in juvenile proceedings, as developed by Gault and Winship, is fundamental fairness. As that standard was applied in those two cases, we have an emphasis on factfinding procedures. The requirements of notice, counsel, confrontation, cross-examination, and standard of proof naturally flowed from this emphasis. But one cannot say that in our legal system the jury is a necessary component of accurate factfinding. There is much to be said for it, to be sure, but we have been content to pursue other ways for determining facts. Juries are not required, and have not been, for example, in equity cases, in workmen's compensation, in probate, or in deportation cases. Neither have they been generally used in military trials. In Duncan the Court stated, "We would not assert, however, that every criminal trial—or any particular trial—held before a judge alone is unfair or that a defendant may never be as fairly treated by a judge as he would be by a jury." 391 U.S., at 158, 88 S.Ct., at 1452, 20 L.Ed.2d at 501. In DeStefano, for this reason and others, the Court refrained from retrospective application of Duncan, an action it surely would have not taken had it felt that the integrity of the result was seriously at issue.   And in Williams v. Florida, 399 U.S. 78, 90 S.Ct. 1893, 26 L.Ed.2d 446 (1970), the Court saw no particular magic in a 12-man jury for a criminal case, thus revealing that even jury concepts themselves are not inflexible.

We must recognize, as the Court has recognized before, that the fond and idealistic hopes of the juvenile court proponents and early reformers of three generations ago have not been realized.   The devastating commentary upon the system's failure as a whole, contained in the Task Force Report: Juvenile Delinquency and Youth Crime (President's Commission on Law Enforcement and the Administration of Justice (1967)), pp. 7–9, reveals the depth of disappointment in what has been accomplished.   Too often the juvenile court judge falls far short of that stalwart, protective and communicating figure the system envisaged.[24]   The community's unwillingness to provide people and facilities and to be concerned, the insufficiency of time devoted, the scarcity of professional help, the inadequacy of dispositional alternatives, and our general lack of knowledge all contribute to dissatisfaction with the experiment.[25]

The Task Force Report, however, also said, page 7, "To say that juvenile courts have failed to achieve their goals is to say no more than what is true of criminal courts in the United States.   But failure is most striking when hopes are highest."

Despite all these disappointments, all these failures, and all these shortcomings, we conclude that trial by jury in the juvenile court's adjudicative stage is not a constitutional requirement.   We so conclude for a number of reasons:

1.   The Court has refrained, in the cases heretofore decided, from taking the easy way with a flat holding that all rights constitutionally assured for the adult accused are to be imposed upon the state juvenile proceeding.   What was done in Gault and in Winship is

---

[24] "A recent study of juvenile court judges * * * revealed that half had not received undergraduate degrees; a fifth had received no college education at all; a fifth were not members of the bar." Task Force Report, p. 7.

[25] What emerges, then, is this: In theory the juvenile court was to be helpful and rehabilitative rather than punitive. In fact the distinction often disappears, not only because of the absence of facilities and personnel but also because of the limits of knowledge and technique. In theory the court's action was to affix no stigmatizing label. In fact a delinquent is generally viewed by employers, schools, the armed services—by society generally—as a criminal. In theory the court was to treat children guilty of criminal acts in noncriminal ways. In fact it labels truants and runaways as junior criminals.

"In theory the court's operations could justifiably be informal, its findings and

decisions made without observing ordinary procedural safeguards, because it would act only in the best interest of the child.

In fact it frequently does nothing more nor less than deprive a child of liberty without due process of law—knowing not what else to do and needing, whether admittedly or not, to act in the community's interest even more imperatively than the child's. In theory it was to exercise its protective powers to bring an errant child back into the fold. In fact there is increasing reason to believe that its intervention reinforces the juvenile's unlawful impulses. In theory it was to concentrate on each case the best of current social science learning. In fact it has often become a vested interest in its turn, loathe to cooperate with innovative programs or avail itself of forward-looking methods." Task Force Report, p. 9.

aptly described in Commonwealth v. Johnson, 211 Pa.Super. 62, 74, 234 A.2d 9, 15 (1967):

"It is clear to us that the Supreme Court has properly attempted to strike a judicious balance by injecting procedural orderliness into the juvenile court system. It is seeking to reverse the trend [pointed out in Kent, 383 U.S., at 556, 86 S.Ct., at 1045, 16 L.Ed.2d at 94] whereby 'the child receives the worst of both worlds * * *.' "

2. There is a possibility, at least, that the jury trial, if required as a matter of constitutional precept, will remake the juvenile proceeding into a fully adversary process and will put an effective end to what has been the idealistic prospect of an intimate, informal protective proceeding.

3. The Task Force Report, although concededly pre-Gault, is notable for its not making any recommendation that the jury trial be imposed upon the juvenile court system. This is so despite its vivid description of the system's deficiencies and disappointments. Had the Commission deemed this vital to the integrity of the juvenile process, or to the handling of juveniles, surely a recommendation or suggestion to this effect would have appeared. The intimations, instead, are quite the other way. Task Force Report, 38. Further, it expressly recommends against abandonment of the system and against the return of the juvenile to the criminal courts.[26]

4. The Court specifically has recognized by dictum that a jury is not a necessary part even of every criminal process that is fair and equitable. Duncan v. Louisiana, 391 U.S. at 149–150 n. 14, and at 158, 88 S.Ct., at 1447, and 1452, 20 L.Ed.2d at 496, and, at 501.

5. The imposition of the jury trial on the juvenile court system would not strengthen greatly, if at all, the factfinding function, and would, contrarily, provide an attrition of the juvenile court's assumed ability to function in a unique manner. It would not remedy the

[26] "Nevertheless, study of the juvenile courts does not necessarily lead to the conclusion that the time has come to jettison the experiment and remand the disposition of children charged with crime to the criminal courts of the country. As trying as are the problems of the juvenile courts, the problems of the criminal courts, particularly those of the lower courts, which would fall heir to much of the juvenile court jurisdiction, are even graver; and the ideal of separate treatment of children is still worth pursuing. What is required is rather a revised philosophy of the juvenile court based on the recognition that in the past our reach exceeded our grasp. The spirit that animated the juvenile court movement was fed in part by a humanitarian compassion for offenders who were children. That willingness to understand and treat people who threaten public safety and security should be nurtured, not turned aside as hopeless sentimentality, both be-cause it is civilized and because social protection itself demands constant search for alternatives to the crude and limited expedient of condemnation and punishment. But neither should it be allowed to outrun reality. The juvenile court is a court of law, charged like other agencies of criminal justice with protecting the community against threatening conduct. Rehabilitating offenders through individualized handling is one way of providing protection, and appropriately the primary way in dealing with children. But the guiding consideration for a court of law that deals with threatening conduct is nonetheless protection of the community. The juvenile court, like other courts, is therefore obliged to employ all the means at hand, not excluding incapacitation, for achieving that protection. What should distinguish the juvenile from the criminal courts is greater emphasis on rehabilitation, not exclusive preoccupation with it." Task Force Report, p. 9.

defects of the system. Meager as has been the hoped-for advance in the juvenile field, the alternative would be regressive, would lose what has been gained, and would tend once again to place the juvenile squarely in the routine of the criminal process.

6. The juvenile concept held high promise. We are reluctant to say that, despite disappointments of grave dimensions, it still does not hold promise, and we are particularly reluctant to say, as do the Pennsylvania petitioners here, that the system cannot accomplish its rehabilitative goals. So much depends on the availability of resources, on the interest and commitment of the public, on willingness to learn, and on understanding as to cause and effect and cure. In this field, as in so many others, one perhaps learns best by doing. We are reluctant to disallow the States further to experiment and to seek in new and different ways the elusive answers to the problems of the young, and we feel that we would be impeding that experimentation by imposing the jury trial. The States, indeed, must go forward. If, in its wisdom, any State feels the jury trial is desirable in all cases, or in certain kinds, there appears to be no impediment to its installing a system embracing that feature. That, however, is the State's privilege and not its obligation.

7. Of course there have been abuses. The Task Force Report has noted them. We refrain from saying at this point that those abuses are of constitutional dimension. They relate to the lack of resources and of dedication rather than to inherent unfairness.

8. There is, of course, nothing to prevent a juvenile court judge, in a particular case where he feels the need, or when the need is demonstrated, from using an advisory jury.

9. "The fact that a practice is followed by a large number of states is not conclusive in a decision as to whether that practice accords with due process, but it is plainly worth considering in determining whether the practice 'offends some principle of justice so rooted in the traditions and conscience of our people as to be ranked as fundamental.' Snyder v. Massachusetts, 291 U.S. 97, 105, 54 S.Ct. 330, 332, 78 L.Ed. 674 (1934)." Leland v. Oregon, 343 U.S. 790, 798, 72 S.Ct. 1002, 96 L.Ed. 1302, 1308 (1952). It therefore is of more than passing interest that at least 29 States and the District of Columbia by statute deny the juvenile a right to a jury trial in cases such as these. The same result is achieved in other States by judicial decision. In 10 States statutes provide for a jury trial under certain circumstances.

10. Since Gault and since Duncan the great majority of States, in addition to Pennsylvania and North Carolina, that have faced the issue have concluded that the considerations that led to the result in those two cases do not compel trial by jury in the juvenile court.

*   *   *

11. Stopping short of proposing the jury trial for juvenile proceedings are the Uniform Juvenile Court Act, § 24(a), approved in July 1968 by the National Conference of Commissioners on Uniform

State Laws; the Standard Juvenile Court Act, Article V, § 19, proposed by the National Council on Crime and Delinquency (see W. Sheridan, Standards for Juvenile and Family Courts 73 (1968)); and the Legislative Guide for Drafting Family and Juvenile Court Acts § 29(a) (1969) (issued by the Children's Bureau, Social and Rehabilitation Service, United States Department of H.E.W.).

12. If the jury trial were to be injected into the juvenile court system as a matter of right, it would bring with it into that system the traditional delay, the formality and the clamor of the adversary system and, possibly, the public trial. It is of interest that these very factors were stressed by the District Committee of the Senate when, through Senator Tydings, it recommended, and Congress then approved, as a provision in the District of Columbia Crime Bill, the abolition of the jury trial in the juvenile court. S.Rep. No. 91–620, 91st Cong., 1st Sess., 1969, pp. 13–14.

13. Finally, the arguments advanced by the juveniles here are, of course, the identical arguments that underlie the demand for the jury trial for criminal proceedings. The arguments necessarily equate the juvenile proceeding—or at least the adjudicative phase of it—with the criminal trial. Whether they should be so equated is our issue. Concern about the inapplicability of exclusionary and other rules of evidence, about the juvenile court judge's possible awareness of the juvenile's prior record and of the contents of the social file; about repeated appearances of the same familiar witnesses in the persons of juvenile and probation officers and social workers—all to the effect that this will create the likelihood of prejudgment—chooses to ignore, it seems to us, every aspect of fairness, of concern, of sympathy, and of paternal attention that the juvenile court system contemplates.

If the formalities of the criminal adjudicative process are to be superimposed upon the juvenile court system, there is little need for its separate existence. Perhaps that ultimate disillusionment will come one day, but for the moment we are disinclined to give impetus to it.

Affirmed.

MR. JUSTICE WHITE, concurring.

Although the function of the jury is to find facts, that body is not necessarily or even probably better at the job than the conscientious judge. Nevertheless, the consequences of criminal guilt are so severe that the Constitution mandates a jury to prevent abuses of official power by insuring, where demanded, community participation in imposing serious deprivations of liberty and to provide a hedge against corrupt, biased, or political justice. We have not, however, considered the juvenile case a criminal proceeding within the meaning of the Sixth Amendment and hence automatically subject to all of the restrictions normally applicable in criminal cases. The question here is one of due process of law and I join the Court's opinion holding that the States are not required by that clause to afford jury trials in juvenile courts where juveniles are charged with acts.

The criminal law proceeds on the theory that defendants have a will and are responsible for their actions. A finding of guilt establishes that they have chosen to engage in conduct so reprehensible and injurious to others that they must be punished to deter them and others from crime. Guilty defendants are considered blameworthy; they are branded and treated as such, however much the State also pursues rehabilitative ends in the criminal justice system.

For the most part, the juvenile justice system rests on more deterministic assumptions. Reprehensible acts by juveniles are not deemed the consequence of mature and malevolent choice but of environmental pressures (or lack of them) or of other forces beyond their control. Hence the state legislative judgment not to stigmatize the juvenile delinquent by branding him a criminal; his conduct is not deemed so blameworthy that punishment is required to deter him or others. Coercive measures, where employed, are considered neither retribution nor punishment. Supervision or confinement is aimed at rehabilitation, not at convincing the juvenile of his error simply by imposing pains and penalties. Nor is the purpose to make the juvenile delinquent an object lesson for others, whatever his own merits or demerits may be. A typical disposition in the juvenile court where delinquency is established may authorize confinement until age 21, but it will last no longer and within that period will last only so long as his behavior demonstrates that he remains an unacceptable risk if returned to his family. Nor is authorization for custody until 21 any measure of the seriousness of the particular act which the juvenile has performed.

Against this background and in light of the distinctive purpose of requiring juries in criminal cases, I am satisfied with the Court's holding. To the extent that the jury is a buffer to the corrupt or overzealous prosecutor in the criminal law system, the distinctive intake policies and procedures of the juvenile court system to a great extent obviate this important function of the jury. As for the necessity to guard against judicial bias, a system eschewing blameworthiness and punishment for evil choice is itself an operative force against prejudice and short-tempered justice. Nor where juveniles are involved is there the same opportunity for corruption to the juvenile's detriment or the same temptation to use the courts for political ends.

Not only are those risks that mandate juries in criminal cases of lesser magnitude in juvenile court adjudications, but the consequences of adjudication are less severe than those flowing from verdicts of criminal guilt. This is plainly so in theory, and in practice there remains a substantial gulf between criminal guilt and delinquency, whatever the failings of the juvenile court in practice may be. Moreover, to the extent that current unhappiness with juvenile court performance rests on dissatisfaction with the vague and overbroad grounds for delinquency adjudications, with faulty judicial choice as to disposition after adjudication or with the record of rehabilitative custody, whether institutional or probationary, these shortcomings are in no way mitigated by providing a jury at the adjudicative stage.

For me there remain differences of substance between criminal and juvenile courts. They are quite enough for me to hold that a jury is not required in the latter. Of course, there are strong arguments that juries are desirable when dealing with the young, and States are free to use juries if they choose. They are also free, if they extend criminal court safeguards to juvenile court adjudications, frankly to embrace condemnation, punishment, and deterrence as permissible and desirable attributes of the juvenile justice system. But the Due Process Clause neither compels nor invites them to do so.

MR. JUSTICE BRENNAN, concurring in No. 322 and dissenting in No. 128.

I agree with the plurality opinion's conclusion that the proceedings below in these cases were not "criminal prosecutions" within the meaning of the Sixth Amendment. For me, therefore, the question in these cases is whether jury trial is among the "essentials of due process and fair treatment," In re Gault, 387 U.S. 1, 30, 87 S.Ct. 1428, 1445, 18 L.Ed.2d 527, 548 (1967), required during the adjudication of a charge of delinquency based upon acts which would constitute a crime if engaged in by an adult. See In re Winship, 397 U.S. 358, 359, and n. 1, 90 S.Ct. 1068, 1070, 25 L.Ed.2d 368, 372 (1970). This does not, however, mean that the interests protected by the Sixth Amendment's guarantee of jury trial in all "criminal prosecutions" are of no importance in the context of these cases. The Sixth Amendment, where applicable, commands that these interests be protected by a particular procedure, that is, trial by jury. The Due Process Clause commands not a particular procedure, but only a result: in my Brother Blackmun's words, "fundamental fairness * * * in factfinding." In the context of these and similar juvenile delinquency proceedings, what this means is that the States are not bound to provide jury trials on demand so long as some other aspect of the process adequately protects the interests that Sixth Amendment jury trials are intended to serve.[27]

In my view, therefore, the due process question cannot be decided upon the basis of general characteristics of juvenile proceedings, but only in terms of the adequacy of a particular state procedure to "protect the [juvenile] from oppression by the Government," Singer v. United States, 380 U.S. 24, 31, 85 S.Ct. 783, 788, 13 L.Ed.2d 630, 636 (1965), and to protect him against "the compliant, biased, or

---

[27] "A criminal process which was fair and equitable but used no juries is easy to imagine. It would make use of alternative guarantees and protections which would serve the purposes that the jury serves in the English and American systems." Duncan v. Louisiana, 391 U.S. 145, 150 n. 14, 88 S.Ct. 1444, 1448, 20 L.Ed.2d 491, 497 (1968). This conclusion is, of course, inescapable in light of our decisions that petty criminal offenses may be tried without a jury notwithstanding the defendant's request. E.g., District of Columbia v. Clawans, 300 U.S. 617, 57 S.Ct. 660, 81 L.Ed. 843 (1937).

eccentric judge." Duncan v. Louisiana, 391 U.S. 145, 156, 88 S.Ct. 1444, 1451, 20 L.Ed.2d 491, 500 (1968).

Examined in this light, I find no defect in the Pennsylvania cases before us. The availability of trial by jury allows an accused to protect himself against possible oppression by what is in essence an appeal to the community conscience, as embodied in the jury that hears his case. To some extent, however, a similar protection may be obtained when an accused may in essence appeal to the community at large, by focusing public attention upon the facts of his trial, exposing improper judicial behavior to public view, and obtaining if necessary executive redress through the medium of public indignation. Of course the Constitution, in the context of adult criminal trials, has rejected the notion that public trial is an adequate substitute for trial by jury in serious cases. But in the context of juvenile delinquency proceedings, I cannot say that it is beyond the competence of a State to conclude that juveniles who fear that delinquency proceedings will mask judicial oppression may obtain adequate protection by focusing community attention upon the trial of their cases. For however much the juvenile system may have failed in practice, its very existence as an ostensibly beneficent and noncriminal process for the care and guidance of young persons demonstrates the existence of the community's sympathy and concern for the young. Juveniles able to bring the community's attention to bear upon their trials may therefore draw upon a reservoir of public concern unavailable to the adult criminal defendant. In the Pennsylvania cases before us, there appears to be no statutory ban upon admission of the public to juvenile trials.[28] Appellants themselves, without contradiction, assert that "the press is generally admitted" to juvenile delinquency proceedings in Philadelphia.[29] Most important, the record in these cases is bare of any indication that any person whom appellants sought to have admitted to the courtroom was excluded. In these circumstances, I agree that the judgment in No. 322 must be affirmed.

The North Carolina cases, however, present a different situation. North Carolina law either permits or requires exclusion of the general public from juvenile trials.[30] In the cases before us, the trial judge "ordered the general public excluded from the hearing room and stated that only officers of the court, the juveniles, their parents or guardians, their attorney and witnesses would be present for the

---

[28] The generally applicable statute, Pa. Stat.Ann. § 11–245 (1965), merely provides that juvenile proceedings shall be "separate" from regular court business. Pa.Stat.Ann. § 11–269–402 (1970), requiring exclusion of the general public from juvenile hearings, applies only to Allegheny County. Both of the instant cases were tried in Philadelphia County.

[29] The judges of the Philadelphia Juvenile Court exercise varying degrees of control over admission to the courtroom, but the press is generally admitted * * *." Brief for Appellants, at 9 n. 9.

[30] N.C.Gen.Stat. § 110–24 (1966), as in force at the time of these trials, appears on its face to permit but not require such exclusion, as does the identical language of the present statute, N.C.Gen.Stat. § 7A–285 (1969). The North Carolina Supreme Court in the present cases has read these statutes as a legislative determination "that a public hearing is [not] in the best interest of the youthful offender." In re Burrus, 275 N.C. 517, 530, 169 S.E.2d 879, 887 (1969).

hearing." In re Burrus, 4 N.C.App. 523, 525, 167 S.E.2d 454, 456 (1969), notwithstanding petitioners' repeated demand for a public hearing. The cases themselves, which arise out of a series of demonstrations by black adults and juveniles who believed that the Hyde County, North Carolina, school system unlawfully discriminated against black schoolchildren, present a paradigm of the circumstances in which there may be a substantial "temptation to use the courts for political ends." Opinion of Mr. Justice White, ante, at 1990, 29 L.Ed.2d at 665. And finally, neither the opinions supporting the judgment nor the respondent in No. 128 has pointed to any feature of North Carolina's juvenile proceedings that could substitute for public or jury trial in protecting the petitioners against misuse of the judicial process. Cf. Duncan v. Louisiana, 391 U.S. 145, 188, 193, 88 S.Ct. 1444, 1469, 20 L.Ed.2d 491, 518, 520 (1968) (Harlan, J., dissenting) (availability of resort to "the political process" is an alternative permitting States to dispense with jury trials). Accordingly, I would reverse the judgment in No. 128.

MR. JUSTICE HARLAN, concurring in the judgments.

If I felt myself constrained to follow Duncan v. Louisiana, 391 U.S. 145, 88 S.Ct. 1444, 20 L.Ed.2d 491 (1968), which extended the Sixth Amendment right of jury trial to the States, I would have great difficulty, upon the premise seemingly accepted in my Brother Blackmun's opinion, in holding that the jury trial right does not extend to state juvenile proceedings. That premise is that juvenile delinquency proceedings have in practice actually become in many, if not all, respects criminal trials. But see my concurring and dissenting opinion in In re Gault, 387 U.S. 1, 65, 87 S.Ct. 1428, 1463, 18 L.Ed.2d 527, 567 (1967). If that premise be correct, then I do not see why, given Duncan, juveniles as well as adults would not be constitutionally entitled to jury trials, so long as juvenile delinquency systems are not restructured to fit their original purpose. When that time comes I would have no difficulty in agreeing with my Brother Blackmun, and indeed with my Brother White, the author of Duncan, that juvenile delinquency proceedings are beyond the pale of Duncan.

I concur in the judgments in these cases however, on the ground that criminal jury trials are not constitutionally required of the States, either as a matter of Sixth Amendment law or due process. See my dissenting opinion in Duncan and my concurring opinion in Williams v. Florida, 399 U.S. 78, 118–119, 90 S.Ct. 1893, 1915–1916, 26 L.Ed.2d 446, 463, 464 (1970).

MR. JUSTICE DOUGLAS, with whom MR. JUSTICE BLACK and MR. JUSTICE MARSHALL concur, dissenting.

These cases from Pennsylvania and North Carolina present the issue of the right to a jury trial for offenders charged in juvenile court and facing a possible incarceration until they reach their majority. I believe the guarantees of the Bill of Rights, made applicable to the States by the Fourteenth Amendment, require a jury trial.

In the Pennsylvania cases one of the appellants was charged with robbery (18 Pa.Stat.Ann. § 4704), larceny (18 Pa.Stat.Ann. § 4807), and receiving stolen goods (18 Pa.Stat.Ann. § 4817) as acts of juvenile delinquency. 11 Pa.Stat.Ann. § 246. He was found a delinquent and placed on probation. The other appellant was charged with assault and battery on a police officer (18 Pa.Stat.Ann. § 4708) and conspiracy (18 Pa.Stat.Ann. § 4302) as acts of juvenile delinquency. On a finding of delinquency he was committed to a youth center. Despite the fact that the two appellants, aged 15 and 16, would face potential incarceration until their majority, 11 Pa.Stat.Ann. § 250, they were denied a jury trial.

In the North Carolina cases petitioners are students, from 11 to 15 years of age, who were charged under one of three criminal statutes: (1) "disorderly conduct" in a public building, N.C.Gen.Stat. § 14–132 (1969); (2) "wilful" interruption or disturbance of a public or private school, N.C.Gen.Stat. § 14–273; or (3) obstructing the flow of traffic on a highway or street, N.C.Gen.Stat. § 20–174.1.

Conviction for each of these crimes would subject a person, whether juvenile or adult, to imprisonment in a state institution. In the case of these students the possible term was six to 10 years; it would be computed for the period until an individual reached the age of 21. Each asked for a jury trial which was denied. The trial judge stated that the hearings were juvenile hearings, not criminal trials. But the issue in each case was whether they had violated a state criminal law. The trial judge found in each case that the juvenile had committed "an act for which an adult may be punished by law" and held in each case that the acts of the juvenile violated one of the criminal statutes cited above. The trial judge thereupon ordered each juvenile to be committed to the state institution for the care of delinquents and then placed each on probation for terms from 12 to 24 months.

We held in In re Gault, 387 U.S. 1, 13, 87 S.Ct. 1428, 1436, 18 L.Ed.2d 527, 538, that "neither the Fourteenth Amendment nor the Bill of Rights is for adults alone." As we noted in that case, the Juvenile Court movement was designed to avoid procedures to ascertain whether the child was "guilty" or "innocent" but to bring to bear on these problems a "clinical" approach. Id., at 15, 16, 87 S.Ct., at 1437, 1438, 18 L.Ed.2d at 539. It is of course not our task to determine as a matter of policy whether a "clinical" or "punitive" approach to these problems should be taken by the States. But where a State uses its juvenile court proceedings to prosecute a juvenile for a criminal act and to order "confinement" until the child reaches 21 years of age or where the child at the threshold of the proceedings faces that prospect, then he is entitled to the same procedural protection as an adult. As Mr. Justice Black said in In re Gault, supra, at 61, 87 S.Ct., at 1461, 18 L.Ed.2d at 565 (concurring):

> "Where a person, infant or adult, can be seized by the State, charged, and convicted for violating a state criminal law, and then ordered by the State to be confined for six years, I think the

Constitution requires that he be tried in accordance with the guarantees of all the provisions of the Bill of Rights made applicable to the States by the Fourteenth Amendment. Undoubtedly this would be true of an adult defendant, and it would be a plain denial of equal protection of the laws—an invidious discrimination—to hold that others subject to heavier punishments could, because they are children, be denied these same constitutional safeguards."

Just as courts have sometimes confused delinquency with crime, so have law enforcement officials treated juveniles not as delinquents but as criminals. As noted in the President's Crime Commission Report:

"In 1965, over 100,000 juveniles were confined in adult institutions. Presumably most of them were there because no separate juvenile detention facilities existed. Nonetheless it is clearly undesirable that juveniles be confined with adults."

President's Commission on Law Enforcement, Challenge of Crime 179 (1967). Even when not incarcerated with adults the situation may be no better. One Pennsylvania correctional institution for juveniles is a brick building with barred windows, locked steel doors, a cyclone fence topped with barbed wire and guard towers. A former juvenile judge described it as "a maximum security prison for adjudged delinquents." In re Bethea, 215 Pa.Super. 75, 76, 257 A.2d 368, 369.

In the present cases imprisonment or confinement up to 10 years was possible for one child and each faced at least a possible five-year incarceration. No adult could be denied a jury trial in those circumstances. Duncan v. Louisiana, 391 U.S. 145, 162, 88 S.Ct. 1444, 1454, 20 L.Ed.2d 491, 503. The Fourteenth Amendment which makes trial by jury provided in the Sixth Amendment applicable to States speaks of denial of rights to "any person," not denial of rights to "any adult person"; and we have held indeed that where a juvenile is charged with an act that would constitute a crime if committed by an adult, he is entitled to trial by jury with proof beyond a reasonable doubt. In re Winship, 397 U.S. 358, 90 S.Ct. 1068, 25 L.Ed.2d 368.

In De Backer v. Brainard, 396 U.S. 28, 33, 90 S.Ct. 163, 24 L.Ed. 2d 148, 153, Mr. Justice Black and I dissented from a refusal to grant a juvenile, who was charged with forgery, a jury trial merely because the case was tried before Duncan v. Louisiana, 391 U.S. 145, 88 S.Ct. 1444, 20 L.Ed.2d 491, was decided. Mr. Justice Black, after noting that a juvenile being charged with a criminal act was entitled to certain constitutional safeguards, viz. notice of the issues, benefit of counsel, protection against compulsory self-incrimination, and confrontation of the witnesses against him, added:

"I can see no basis whatsoever in the language of the Constitution for allowing persons like appellant the benefit of those rights and yet denying them a jury trial, a right which is surely one of the fundamental aspects of criminal justice in the English-speaking world." 396 U.S., at 34, 90 S.Ct., at 166, 24 L.Ed.2d at 154.

I added that by reason of the Sixth and Fourteenth Amendments the juvenile is entitled to a jury trial: "* * * as a matter of right where the delinquency charged is an offense that, if the person were an adult, would be a crime triable by jury. Such is this case, for behind the facade of delinquency is the crime of forgery." Id., at 35, 90 S.Ct., at 167, 24 L.Ed.2d at 155.

Practical aspects of these problems are urged against allowing a jury trial in these cases.[31] They have been answered by Judge De Ciantis of the Family Court of Providence, Rhode Island, in a case entitled In the Matter of McCloud, decided January 15, 1971. A juvenile was charged with the rape of a 17-year-old female and Judge De Ciantis granted a motion for a jury trial in an opinion, a part of which I have attached as an appendix to this dissent. He there concludes that "the real traumatic" experience of incarceration without due process is "the feeling of being deprived of basic rights." He adds:

"The child who feels that he has been dealt with fairly and not merely expediently or as speedily as possible will be a better prospect for rehabilitation. Many of the children who come before the court come from broken homes, from the ghettos; they often suffer from low self-esteem; and their behavior is frequently a symptom of their own feelings of inadequacy. Traumatic experiences of denial of basic rights only accentuate the past deprivation and contribute to the problem. Thus, a general societal attitude of acceptance of the juvenile as a person entitled to the same protection as an adult may be the true beginning of the rehabilitative process."

Judge De Ciantis goes on to say that "Trial by jury will provide the child with a safeguard against being prejudged" by a judge who

[31] The Public Defender Service for the District of Columbia and the Neighborhood Legal Services Program of Washington, D.C., have filed a brief amicus in which the results of a survey of jury trials in delinquency cases in the 10 States requiring jury trials plus the District of Columbia are set forth. The cities selected were mostly large metropolitan areas. Thirty juvenile courts processing about 75,000 juvenile cases a year were canvassed: "* * * we discovered that during the past five and a half years, in 22 out of 26 courts surveyed, cumulative requests for jury trials totaled 15 or less. In the remaining five courts in our sample, statistics were unavailable. During the same period, in 26 out of 29 courts the cumulative number of jury trials actually held numbered 15 or less, with statistics unavailable for two courts in our sample. For example, in Tulsa, Oklahoma, counsel is present in 100% of delinquency cases, but only one jury trial has been requested and held during the past five and one-half years. In the Juvenile Court of Fort Worth, Texas, counsel is also present in 100% of the cases, and only two jury trials have been requested since 1967. The Juvenile Court in Detroit, Michigan, reports that counsel is appointed in 70–80% of its delinquency cases, but thus far in 1970, it has had only four requests for a jury. Between 1965 and 1969 requests for juries were reported as 'very few.'

"In only four juvenile courts in our sample has there clearly been a total during the past five and one-half years of more than 15 jury trial requests and/or more than 15 such trials held."

The four courts showing more than 15 requests for jury trials were Denver, Houston, Milwaukee, and Washington, D.C.

may well be prejudiced by reports already submitted to him by the police or caseworkers in the case. Indeed the child, the same as the adult, is in the category of those described in the Magna Carta:

> "No freeman may be * * * imprisoned * * * except by the lawful judgment of his peers, or by the law of the land."

These cases should be remanded for trial by jury on the criminal charges filed against these youngsters.

APPENDIX TO DISSENT IN NO. 128

(Douglas, J.)

De Ciantis, J.: The defendant, who will hereinafter be referred to as a juvenile, on the sixth day of September, 1969, was charged with Rape upon a female child, seventeen years old, in violation of Title 11, Chapter 37, Section 1, of the General Laws of 1956. * * *

TRAUMA

The fact is that the procedures which are now followed in juvenile cases are far more traumatic than the potential experience of a jury trial. Who can say that a boy who is arrested and handcuffed, placed in a lineup, transported in vehicles designed to convey dangerous criminals, placed in the same kind of a cell as an adult, deprived of his freedom by lodging him in an institution where he is subject to be transferred to the state's prison and in the "hole" has not undergone a traumatic experience?

The experience of a trial with or without a jury is meant to be impressive and meaningful. The fact that a juvenile realizes that his case will be decided by twelve objective citizens would allow the court to retain its meaningfulness without causing any more trauma than a trial before a judge who perhaps has heard other cases involving the same juvenile in the past and may be influenced by those prior contacts. To agree that a jury trial would expose a juvenile to a traumatic experience is to lose sight of the real traumatic experience of incarceration without due process. The real traumatic experience is the feeling of being deprived of basic rights. In the matter of Reis, this Court indicated the inadequacies of the procedure under which our court operates. A judge who receives facts of a case from the police and approves the filing of a petition based upon those facts may be placed in the untenable position of hearing a charge which he has approved. His duty is to adjudicate on the evidence introduced at the hearing and not be involved in any pre-adjudicatory investigation.

It is contrary to the fundamental principles of due process for the court to be compelled, as it is in this state, to act as a one-man grand jury, then sit in judgment on its own determination arising out of the facts and proceedings which he conducted. This responsibility belongs with a jury.

BACKLOG

An argument has been made that to allow jury trials would cause a great backlog of cases and, ultimately, would impair the functioning of the juvenile court. The fact however is that there is no meaningful evidence that granting the right to jury trials will impair the function of the court. Some states permit jury trials in *all* juvenile court cases; a few juries have been demanded, and there is no suggestion from these courts that jury trials have impeded the system of juvenile justice.

In Colorado, where jury trials have been permitted by statute, Judge Theodore Rubin of the Denver Juvenile Court has indicated that jury trials are an important safeguard and that they have not impaired the functioning of the Denver Juvenile Courts. For example, during the first seven months of 1970, the two divisions of the Denver Juvenile Court have had fewer than two dozen jury trials, in both delinquency and dependency-neglect cases. In Michigan, where juveniles are also entitled to a jury trial, Judge Lincoln of the Detroit Juvenile Court indicates that his court has had less than five jury trials in the year 1969 to 1970.

The recent Supreme Court decision of Williams v. Florida, 399 U.S. 78, 90 S.Ct. 1893, 26 L.Ed.2d 446 (June 22, 1970), which held that the constitutional right to trial by jury in criminal cases does not require a twelve-member jury, could be implemented to facilitate the transition to jury trials. A jury of less than twelve members would be less cumbersome, less "formal," and less expensive than the regular twelve-member jury, and yet would provide the accused with objective factfinders.

In fact the very argument of expediency, suggesting "supermarket" or "assembly-line" justice is one of the most forceful arguments in favor of granting jury trials. By granting the juvenile the right to a jury trial, we would, in fact, be protecting the accused from the judge who is under pressure to move the cases, the judge with too many cases and not enough time. It will provide a safeguard against the judge who may be prejudiced against a minority group or who may be prejudiced against the juvenile brought before him because of some past occurrence which was heard by the same judge.

There have been criticisms that juvenile court judges, because of their hearing caseload, do not carefully weigh the evidence in the adjudicatory phase of the proceedings. It is during this phase that the judge must determine whether in fact the evidence has been established beyond a reasonable doubt that the accused committed the acts alleged in the petition. Regardless of the merit of these criticisms they have impaired the belief of the juveniles, of the bar and of the public as to the opportunity for justice in the juvenile court. Granting the juvenile the right to demand that the facts be determined by a jury will strengthen the faith of all concerned parties in the juvenile system. * * *

It is important to note, at this time, a definite side benefit of granting jury trials, i.e., an aid to rehabilitation. The child who feels that he has been dealt with fairly and not merely expediently or as speedily as possible will be a better prospect for rehabilitation. Many of the children who come before the court come from broken homes, from the ghettos; they often suffer from low self-esteem; and their behavior is frequently a symptom of their own feelings of inadequacy. Traumatic experiences of denial of basic rights only accentuate the past deprivation and contribute to the problem. Thus, a general societal attitude of acceptance of the juvenile as a person entitled to the same protection as an adult may be the true beginning of the rehabilitative process.

PUBLIC TRIAL

Public trial in the judgment of this Court does not affect the juvenile court philosophy.

In re Oliver [32] Mr. Justice Black reviews the history of the public trial. Its origins are obscure, but it seems to have evolved along with the jury trial guarantee in English common law and was then adopted as a provision of the Federal Constitution as well as by most state constitutions. Among the benefits of a public trial are the following:

    1. "Public trials come to the attention of key witnesses unknown to the parties. These witnesses may then voluntarily come forward and give important testimony."

    2. "The spectators learn about their government and acquire confidence in their judicial remedies."

    3. "The knowledge that every *criminal* trial is subject to contemporaneous review in the form of public opinion is an effective restraint on possible abuse of judicial power." (P. 270, 68 S.Ct. p. 506, 92 L.Ed. 692.)

Justice Black has nothing to say on the question of whether a public trial acts as a deterrent to crime, but it is clear that he believes *publicity to improve the quality of criminal justice, both theoretically and practically.*

As for the juvenile trial issue, he writes:

"Whatever may be the classification of juvenile court proceedings, they are often conducted without admitting all the public. But it has never been the practice to wholly exclude parents, relatives, and friends, or to refuse juveniles the benefit of counsel." (P. 266, 68 S.Ct. p. 504, 92 L.Ed. 690.)

In fact, the juvenile proceedings as presently conducted are far from secret. Witnesses for the prosecution and for the defense, social workers, court reporters, students, police trainees, probation counselors, and sheriffs are present in the courtroom. Police, the Armed Forces, the Federal Bureau of Investigation obtain informa-

---

[32] 333 U.S. 257, 68 S.Ct. 499, 92 L.Ed. 682.

tion and have access to the police files. There seems no more reason to believe that a jury trial would destroy confidentiality than would witnesses summoned to testify.

The Court also notes the report of the PRESIDENT'S COMMISSION OF LAW ENFORCEMENT AND ADMINISTRATION OF JUSTICE, THE CHALLENGE OF CRIME IN A FREE SOCIETY 75 (1967), wherein it is stated:

> "A juvenile's adjudication record is required by the law of most jurisdictions to be private and confidential; in practice the confidentiality of those reports is often violated." Furthermore, "[s]tatutory restrictions almost invariably apply only to court records, and even as to those the evidence is that many courts routinely furnish information to the FBI and the military, and on request to government agencies and even to private employers."

JUDGE'S EXPERTISE

The Court is also aware of the argument that the juvenile court was created to develop judges who were experts in sifting out the real problems behind a juvenile's breaking the law; therefore, to place the child's fate in the hands of a jury would defeat that purpose. This will, however, continue to leave the final decision of disposition solely with the judge. The role of the jury will be only to ascertain whether the facts, which give the court jurisdiction, have been established beyond a reasonable doubt. The jury will not be concerned with social and psychological factors. These factors, along with prior record, family and educational background, will be considered by the judge during the dispositional phase.

Taking into consideration the social background and other facts, the judge, during the dispositional phase, will determine what disposition is in the best interests of the child and society. It is at this stage that a judge's expertise is most important, and the granting of a jury trial will not prevent the judge from carrying out the basic philosophy of the juvenile court.

Trial by jury will provide the child with a safeguard against being prejudged. The jury clearly will have no business in learning of the social report or any of the other extraneous matter unless properly introduced under the rules of evidence. Due process demands that the trier of facts should not be acquainted with any of the facts of the case or have knowledge of any of the circumstances, whether through officials in his own department or records in his possession. If the accused believes that the judge has read an account of the facts submitted by the police or any other report prior to the adjudicatory hearing and that this may prove prejudicial, he can demand a jury and insure against such knowledge on the part of the trier of the facts.

WAIVER OF JURY TRIAL

Counsel also questions whether a child can waive his right to a jury trial or, in fact, whether a parent or counsel may waive.

When the waiver comes up for hearing, the Court could, at its discretion, either grant or refuse the juvenile's waiver of a jury trial, and/or appoint a guardian or legal counsel to advise the child.

My experience has shown that the greatest percentage of juveniles who appear before the court in felony cases have lived appalling lives due to parental neglect and brutality, lack of normal living conditions, and poverty. This has produced in them a maturity which is normally acquired much later in life. They are generally well aware of their rights in a court of law. However, in those cases where a child clearly needs guidance, the court-appointed guardian or attorney could explain to him the implications of a waiver. The juvenile's rights and interests would thus be protected every bit as stringently as they are today before he is allowed to plead guilty or not guilty to a complaint. A guilty plea is, after all, a waiver of the right to trial altogether.

Counsel is placed with the responsibility of explaining to the juvenile the significance of guilty and nolo contendere pleas, of instructing the juvenile on the prerogative to take the witness stand, and is expected to advise his client in the same manner as he would an adult to stand trial. And now counsel suggests to the Court that counsel is not capable of explaining and waiving the right to a jury trial. The Court fails to see the distinction between this waiver and the absolute waiver, to wit, a guilty plea. Counsel should act in the best interest of his client, even if this may be in conflict with the parents. On a number of occasions this Court has appointed counsel for a juvenile whose parents could not afford to retain private counsel, and where the parents' interests were in conflict with those of the child. This procedure will be continued and the Court will continue to rely on the good judgment of the bar.

The Court could easily require that a waiver of a jury trial be made in person by the juvenile in writing, in open court, with the consent and approval of the Court and the attorney representing both the juvenile and the state. The judge could ascertain as to whether the juvenile can intelligently waive his right and, if necessary, appoint counsel to advise the youth as to the implications connected with the waiver. This could be accomplished without any difficulty through means presently available to the Court.

JURY OF PEERS

One of the most interesting questions raised is that concerning the right of a juvenile to a trial by his peers. Counsel has suggested that a jury of a juvenile's peers would be composed of other juveniles, that is, a "teenage jury." Webster's Dictionary, Second Edition, 1966, defines a peer as an equal, one of the same rank, quality, value.

The word "peers" means nothing more than citizens, In re Grilli, 110 Misc. 45, 179 N.Y.S. 795, 797. The phrase "judgment of his peers" means at common law, a trial by a jury of twelve men, State v. Simon, 61 Kan. 752, 60 P. 1052. "Judgment of his peers" is a term expressly borrowed from the Magna Charta, and it means a trial by jury, Ex parte Wagner, 58 Okl.Cr. 161, 50 P.2d 1135. The Declaration of Independence also speaks of the equality of *all* men. Are we now to say that a juvenile is a second-class citizen, not equal to an adult? The Constitution has never been construed to say women must be tried by their peers, to wit, by all-female juries, or Negroes by all-Negro juries.

The only restriction on the makeup of the jury is that there can be no systematic exclusion of those who meet local and federal requirements, in particular, voting qualifications.

The Court notes that presently in some states 18-year-olds can vote. Presumably, if they can vote, they may also serve on juries. Our own legislature has given first passage to an amendment to the Constitution to permit 18-year-olds to vote. Thus, it is quite possible that we will have teenage jurors sitting in judgment of their so-called "peers."

CRIMINAL PROCEEDING

The argument that the adjudication of delinquency is not the equivalent of criminal process is spurious. This Court has discussed the futility of making distinctions on the basis of labels in prior decisions. Because the legislature dictates that a child who commits a felony shall be called a delinquent does not change the nature of the crime. Murder is murder; robbery is robbery—they are both criminal offenses, not civil, regardless and independent of the age of the doer. * * *

It is noteworthy that in our statute there is not an express statutory provision indicating that the proceedings are civil. Trial by jury in Rhode Island is guaranteed to *all* persons, whether in criminal cases or in civil cases. That right existed prior to the adoption of the Constitution; and certainly whether one is involved in a civil or criminal proceeding of the Family Court in which his "liberty" is to be "taken" "imprisoned" "outlawed" and "banished" he is entitled to a trial by jury. (Henry v. Cherry & Webb, 30 R.I. 13, at 30, 73 A. 97).

This Court believes that although the juvenile court was initially created as a social experiment, it has not ceased to be part of the judicial system. In view of the potential loss of liberty at stake in the proceeding, this Court is compelled to accord due process to all the litigants who come before it; and, therefore, all of the provisions of the Bill of Rights, including trial by jury, must prevail.

The Court concludes that the framers of our Constitution never intended to place the power in any one man or official, and take away the "protection of the law from the rights of an individual." It meant "to secure the blessings of liberty to themselves and posterity." The Constitution was written with the philosophy based upon a composite of all of the most liberal ideas which came down through the centuries. The Magna Charta, the Petition of Rights, the Bill of Rights and the Rules of Common Law; and the keystone is the preservation of individual liberty. All these ideas were carefully inserted in our Constitution.

The juvenile is constitutionally entitled to a jury trial.

B. COMPETENCY TO STAND TRIAL

MATTER OF WELFARE OF S.W.T.

Supreme Court of Minnesota, 1979.
277 N.W.2d 507.

WAHL, JUSTICE.

This is a combined appeal, pursuant to Minn.St. 260.291, subd. 1, by two juveniles, S.W.T. and N.R.S., from an order of the Hennepin County District Court, Juvenile Division, determining after a joint hearing that appellants committed delinquent acts, aiding and abetting manslaughter in the second degree, in violation of Minn.St. 609.205(1) by shooting a rifle across the Mississippi River, causing the death of a young man on the other bank. We affirm as to N.R.S., reverse as to S.W.T., and remand.

The issues raised on appeal are: (1) whether the juvenile court erred in denying S.W.T.'s request for a competency hearing; * * *

* * *

Counsel for S.W.T. filed a motion on October 28, 1976 to stay the adjudicatory hearing on the ground that S.W.T. was incapable of understanding the proceedings and participating in his own defense. This motion was heard by a referee of the juvenile court on November 1, 1976, immediately prior to the adjudicatory hearing, and denied as untimely, based upon an order entered by the juvenile court on October 4, 1976, requiring "counsel to advise the court by October 15th of any constitutional or pretrial motions or be barred from making any motion which could be raised by then." * * * [T]he referee found that the boys had violated Minn.St. 609.205(1) and, therefore, had committed a delinquent act.

* * * Without addressing the issue of competency, the juvenile court then affirmed the referee's decision. This appeal followed.

1. We address first the issue of whether the trial court erred in denying S.W.T.'s request for a competency hearing prior to undergoing adjudicatory proceedings. On October 28, 1976, counsel for S.W.T. moved to stay the adjudicatory hearing on the grounds that S.W.T. was incapable of understanding the proceedings and participating in his own defense. The motion was to have been supported by evidence from S.W.T.'s psychologist and juvenile detention record. The referee denied the motion as untimely on the basis of an order entered at the omnibus hearing on October 4, 1976, which required "counsel to advise the court by October 15th of any constitutional or

pre-trial motions or be barred from making any motion which could be raised by then."

The competency of an accused is generally defined as his ability to understand the nature of the proceedings against him and to participate in his own defense. See, Dusky v. United States, 362 U.S. 402, 80 S.Ct. 788, 4 L.Ed.2d 824 (1960); Rule 20.01, subd. 1, Rules of Criminal Procedure. Although the general area of competency is usually discussed in connection with adult criminal proceedings, we regard the right not to be tried or convicted while incompetent to be a fundamental right, even in the context of a juvenile delinquency adjudicatory proceeding. Under the circumstances presented in this case, we conclude that it was error for the court to fail to conduct a preliminary evaluation of S.W.T.'s competency to proceed with the adjudicatory phase of the proceedings.

The record indicates that counsel for S.W.T. received a psychological evaluation on September 29, 1976. Copies were furnished to the state and the juvenile court at the omnibus hearing on October 4, 1976. Contained in that report was a statement which raised the issue of competency:

> "Given the intellectual and personality liabilities, and inflexibility of this young man, he in no manner comprehends the gravity of the total implications of, nor the total proceedings facing him."

Psychological testing and examination continued until the November 1 adjudicatory hearing, and counsel intended to introduce additional psychological information amassed during the period from October 24 to October 29.

The contents of the original report were sufficient to raise substantial doubt and put the juvenile court and the parties on notice that a potential question would be raised regarding S.W.T.'s competency. While it would have been preferable to move the court at the omnibus hearing to stay further proceedings pending further examination, or to formally advise the court that such a motion was contemplated, the failure to do so does not preclude the assertion of lack of competency. Because the court has a continuing obligation to inquire into a juvenile's fitness for trial where substantial information or the juvenile's observed demeanor raises doubts as to his competency,[33] the juvenile court erred in denying S.W.T. a competency hearing. The uncontradicted opinion of the psychologist was that S.W.T. did not comprehend, nor was he able to participate in, the proceedings. On the record before us we find that S.W.T. was not competent to be subjected to adjudicatory hearing in November 1976. Therefore, we reverse and remand S.W.T.'s appeal.

* * *

[33] Cf., Drope v. Missouri, 420 U.S. 162, 179, 95 S.Ct. 896, 907, 43 L.Ed.2d 103, 117 (1975); Pate v. Robinson, 383 U.S. 375, 385, 86 S.Ct. 836, 842, 15 L.Ed.2d 815, 822 (1966); State v. Jensen, 278 Minn. 212, 215, 153 N.W.2d 339, 341 (1967).

STATE EX REL. DANDOY v. SUPERIOR COURT IN AND FOR THE COUNTY OF PIMA

Supreme Court of Arizona, 1980.
127 Ariz. 184, 619 P.2d 12.

HOLOHAN, VICE CHIEF JUSTICE.

Petitioners brought a special action in the Court of Appeals, Division Two, challenging the authority of the Respondent Juvenile Court Judge to order the continued involuntary hospitalization of the respondent minor (real party in interest). The Court of Appeals determined that the juvenile court had exceeded its jurisdiction and ordered that the juvenile be discharged from the hospital and released to the custody of either the Pima County Sheriff or a Pima County probation officer. The respondent judge petitioned this court to review the decision of the Court of Appeals. * * * We granted review. Opinion of the Court of Appeals is vacated.

The respondent juvenile is the subject of three petitions filed in the juvenile court, alleging that she has committed delinquent acts.

After the filing of the petitions, the juvenile was referred to two psychiatric facilities for testing and evaluation, but she escaped from both units. When the juvenile was apprehended after her second escape, she was taken back to the second facility for emergency treatment and completion of her evaluation. After the evaluation was completed she was held in custody at the Pima County Juvenile Court Detention Center.

As a result of the juvenile's actions, the juvenile's court-appointed attorney filed a motion for a "Court ordered psychiatric examination as mandated by A.R.S. 8–242A."

A hearing on the juvenile's mental health was held on October 30, 1979. Testimony and evidence were taken, after which the respondent judge order the juvenile "committed to the Arizona State Hospital for evaluation and treatment" for "no less than thirty days." The court made four findings:

"(1) THAT the minor at present is a danger to herself and others;

"(2) THAT the minor is unable to assist in her defense;

"(3) THAT the minor is unable to fully comprehend all of the legal proceedings in the Court at this time;

"(4) THAT the minor needs additional evaluation and treatment."

It was further ordered that the hospital advise the court, the juvenile's attorney and her mother when she was ready for release or discharge. A review hearing was set for November 27, 1979.

The state hospital's "Discharge Summary," dated November 24, 1979, reported the hospital staff's conclusion that the juvenile's problems were consistent with a character disorder, that she could assist in her own defense and that she was capable of understanding the legal proceedings. The hospital staff recommended that she be discharged to the court immediately following her court hearing on November 27, 1979.

At the review hearing on November 27, 1979, the juvenile's attorney advised the court that he did not feel the juvenile was able to assist in her defense. The court found that "the minor is still dangerous to herself or others, based on the reports submitted to the Court and filed in the social file." The court ordered that the juvenile remain at the state hospital for continued treatment and that a review of the matter be held on December 20, 1979.

On December 3, 1979, the state hospital advised the respondent judge by letter that the juvenile was not mentally ill and was not in need of inpatient psychiatric care. The representatives of the hospital felt that they could not clinically or legally justify the continued hospitalization of the juvenile, and the child was to be discharged on December 7, 1979. The respondent judge replied on December 5, 1979, that the juvenile appeared to be a danger to herself, requiring institutional care and ordered that she remain in the custody of the state hospital.

The Attorney General upon behalf of the petitioners challenges both the authority of the respondent judge to commit the juvenile to the state hospital in the manner done in this case and to continue her involuntary hospitalization.

The petitioners question the authority of the juvenile court to commit a juvenile to the state hospital under A.R.S. § 8–242 before the juvenile has been adjudicated delinquent, dependent, or incorrigible. It is conceded that the juvenile has never been adjudicated delinquent, dependent, or incorrigible.

From our reading of the statute it appears clear that the section in question applies only to the disposition of juveniles who have been adjudicated by the juvenile court to be delinquent, dependent, or incorrigible. See In re Maricopa County Appeal, 15 Ariz.App. 536, 489 P.2d 1238 (1971). A.R.S. § 8–242 did not authorize the action taken by the juvenile court.

It is contended that the juvenile court had authority under the Mental Health Services Act, particularly A.R.S. § 36–520 et seq. and A.R.S. § 36–533 et seq., to order the juvenile committed for treatment.

Although the juvenile court made an express finding that the juvenile was a danger to herself, the court did not act in full compliance with the procedures set forth in the Mental Health Services Act. It must also be noted that under the Mental Health Services Act the person committed may be released by the medical director of the treating agency. A.R.S. § 36–543. The term of treatment is a medical decision, not a judicial one. The juvenile court's action in ordering the continued hospitalization of the juvenile was not authorized by the Mental Health Services Act.

Throughout the tortured path of this case there remains the issue of how does the juvenile court determine the mental competency of a juvenile? There is no rule of procedure nor method specified for determining a juvenile's competency prior to adjudication in either the statutes concerning the juvenile court, A.R.S. § 8–201 et seq., or in the Rules of Procedure for the Juvenile Court, 17A A.R.S.

The United States Supreme Court held in Application of Gault, 387 U.S. 1, 87 S.Ct. 1428, 18 L.Ed.2d 527 (1967), that a juvenile must be accorded due process protections in the adjudication of charges against him. In an adult criminal prosecution it would be a violation of due process to convict a mentally incompetent accused. State v. Wagner, 114 Ariz. 459, 561 P.2d 1231 (1977). As the Supreme Court stated in Drope v. Missouri, 420 U.S. 162, 95 S.Ct. 896, 43 L.Ed.2d 103 (1975):

> "It has long been accepted that a person whose mental condition is such that he lacks the capacity to understand the nature and object of the proceedings against him, to consult with counsel, and to assist in preparing his defense may not be subjected to a trial.
>
> * * *
>
> "[T]he prohibition is fundamental to an adversary system of justice." 95 S.Ct. at 903, 904.

In the context of a juvenile delinquency adjudicatory proceeding, the right not to be tried or convicted while incompetent has been held to be a fundamental right. In re Welfare of S.W.T., 277 N.W.2d 507 (Minn.1979).

Gault establishes that due process requires that a juvenile have notice of the charges against him and the right to assistance of counsel would be meaningless if the juvenile, through mental illness, was unable to understand the charges or assist in her own defense.

The requirements of due process necessitate the conclusion that the juvenile court must have the power to inquire into a juvenile's mental competency prior to adjudication.

Generally the procedure followed in adult prosecution is not applicable to juvenile proceedings. In re Appeal in Maricopa County Juvenile Action No. J–86715, 122 Ariz. 300, 594 P.2d 554 (App.1979); In re Appeal in Yavapai County, Juvenile Action No. 7707, 25 Ariz. App. 397, 543 P.2d 1154 (1975). There have been occasions, however, when reference has been made to the adult system and made applicable to the juvenile system. See In re Anonymous, Juvenile Court No. 6358–4, 14 Ariz.App. 466, 484 P.2d 235 (1971); In re Appeal in Maricopa County, Juvenile Action No. J–72804, 18 Ariz.App. 560, 504 P.2d 501 (1972) and again, in In re Appeal in Pima County, Juvenile Action No. J–47735–1, 26 Ariz.App. 46, 546 P.2d 23 (1976). It appears that the determination of mental competency of a juvenile for trial is one of those instances where the procedure followed in adult prosecution must be applied to juvenile cases. The adult procedure is set forth in Rule 11 of the Rules of Criminal Procedure, 17 A.R.S.

It must be noted that the medical authorities at the state hospital conducted an examination and made a report which would comply with the provisions of Rule 11. The medical authorities advised the respondent court that the juvenile was not mentally ill and that she was able to understand the proceedings and assist her counsel. Nothing further could have been achieved by keeping the juvenile in the state hospital. See also Rule 11.3(d) Rules of Criminal Procedure.

The difficulty in this case occurred primarily because there was confusion in differentiating between the procedure to determine mental competency prior to adjudication and the procedure for making a disposition of a mentally ill child after adjudication. The procedure to be followed in the former situation is that provided in Rule 11 of the Criminal Rules, and the procedure to be followed in the latter situation, after adjudication, is that provided in A.R.S. § 8–242.

The relief sought by the petitioners is granted.

STRUCKMEYER, C.J., and HAYS, CAMERON and GORDON, JJ., concur.

NOTES

1. Arizona Rule of Criminal Procedure 11 is as follows.

Rule 11.1   Definition and effect of incompetency

A person shall not be tried, convicted, sentenced or punished for a public offense while, as a result of a mental illness or defect, he is unable to understand the proceedings against him or to assist in his own defense.

Rule 11.2   Motion to have defendant's mental condition examined

At any time after an information is filed or indictment returned, any party may move for an examination to determine whether a defendant is competent to stand trial, or to investigate his mental condition at the time of the offense. The motion shall state the facts upon which the mental examination is sought.

Rule 11.5   Hearing and orders

a. Hearing. When the examinations have been completed, the court shall hold a hearing to determine the defendant's competency. The parties may introduce other evidence regarding the defendant's mental condition, or by written stipulation, submit the matter on the experts' reports.

b. Orders. After the hearing:

(1) If the court finds that the defendant is competent, proceedings shall continue without delay.

(2) If the court determines that the defendant is incompetent and that there is no substantial probability that he will become competent within a reasonable period of time, it shall

(i) Order him civilly committed if it finds that his condition warrants such commitment according to the standards provided by law; or

(ii) Release him forthwith.

(3) If the court determines that the defendant is incompetent, but that there is a substantial probability that he will be restored to competency within a reasonable period of time, it shall order him committed to the

supervision of an institution authorized to receive him for an indefinite period not to exceed six months or his earlier attainment of competency.

c. Modification of Order. The court may modify any order under Rule 11.5(b)(3) at any time.

d. Reports. The court may order any person responsible for a defendant's treatment under Rule 11.5(b)(2) or (3) to submit periodic reports on his status to the court and prosecutor.

2. In In re Jeffrey C., 81 Misc.2d 651, 366 N.Y.S.2d 826 (N.Y.Fam.Ct. 1975), the court also held that the nature of the required competency hearing must be the same in juvenile delinquency cases as in adult criminal cases. The case poignantly demonstrates the difficulties inherent in a system whose original characteristics have been substantially changed but whose philosophical underpinnings remain largely intact. In *Jeffrey C.*, a boy of 15 with a record of a dozen arrests, 6 formal appearances before the juvenile court and a history of mental illness going back to age 7, was before the court on a petition charging delinquency based on his having shot someone four times. In granting his motion for the full-blown competency hearing, the judge pointed out that Jeffrey had "escaped" from non-secure facilities on several occasions, and on each of them the formal record showed that the mental health authorities had marked his record "discharged." The case also, as does *Dandoy*, supra, demonstrates the tragic consequences when authority is divided among personnel with strangely different ideas about the appropriateness of various kinds of legal actions—even assuming that a dishonest record entry is within the discretion of the mental health officials.

C. DOUBLE JEOPARDY

BREED v. JONES

Supreme Court of the United States, 1975.
421 U.S. 519, 95 S.Ct. 1779, 44 L.Ed.2d 346.

MR. CHIEF JUSTICE BURGER delivered the opinion of the Court.

We granted certiorari to decide whether the prosecution of respondent as an adult, after juvenile court proceedings which resulted in a finding that respondent had violated a criminal statute and a subsequent finding that he was unfit for treatment as a juvenile, violated the Fifth and Fourteenth Amendments to the United States Constitution.

On February 9, 1971, a petition was filed in the Superior Court of California, County of Los Angeles Juvenile Court, alleging that respondent, then 17 years of age, was a person described by Cal. Welf. & Inst'ns Code § 602,[34] in that, on or about February 8, while armed with a deadly weapon, he had committed acts which, if committed by an adult, would constitute the crime of robbery in

---

[34] As of the date of filing of the petition in this case, Cal.Welf. & Inst'ns Code § 602 (West 1966) provided:

"Any person under the age of 21 years who violates any law of this State or of the United States or any ordinance of any city or county of this State defining crime or who, after having been found by the juvenile court to be a person de-

scribed by Section 601, fails to obey any lawful order of the juvenile court, is within the jurisdiction of the juvenile court, which may adjudge such person to be a ward of the court."

An amendment in 1971, not relevant here, lowered the jurisdictional age from 21 to 18. C. 1748, § 66, 1871 Cal.Stats. 3766.

violation of Cal.Penal Code § 211. The following day, a detention hearing was held, at the conclusion of which respondent was ordered detained pending a hearing on the petition.[35]

The jurisdictional or adjudicatory hearing was conducted on March 1, pursuant to Cal.Welf. & Inst'ns Code § 701.[36] After taking testimony from two prosecution witnesses and respondent, the Juvenile Court found that the allegations in the petition were true and that respondent was a person described by § 602, and it sustained the petition. The proceedings were continued for a dispositional hearing,[37] pending which the court ordered that respondent remain detained.

At a hearing conducted on March 15, the Juvenile Court indicated its intention to find respondent "not * * * amenable to the care, treatment and training program available through the facilities of the

[35] See Cal.Welf. & Inst'ns Code §§ 632, 635, 636 (West 1966). The probation officer was required to present a prima facie case that respondent had committed the offense alleged in the petition. In re William M., 3 Cal.3d 16, 89 Cal.Rptr. 33, 473 P.2d 737 (1970). Respondent was represented by court-appointed counsel at the detention hearing and thereafter.

[36] At the time of the hearing, Cal.Welf. & Inst'ns Code § 701 (West 1966) provided:

"At the hearing, the court shall first consider only the question whether the minor is a person described by Section 600, 601, or 602, and for this purpose, any matter or information relevant and material to the circumstances or acts which are alleged to bring him within the jurisdiction of the juvenile court is admissible and may be received in evidence; however, *a preponderance of evidence*, legally admissible in the trial of criminal cases, must be adduced to support a finding that the minor is a person described by Section 602, and a preponderance of evidence, legally admissible in the trial of civil cases must be adduced to support a finding that the minor is a person described by Sections 600 or 601. When it appears that the minor has made an extra judicial admission or confession and denies the same at the hearing, the court may continue the hearing for not to exceed seven days to enable the probation officer to subpoena witnesses to attend the hearing to prove the allegations of the petition. If the minor is not represented by counsel at the hearing, it shall be deemed that objections that could have been made to the evidence were made." (Emphasis added.)

A 1971 amendment substituted "proof beyond a reasonable doubt supported by

evidence" for the language in italics. C. 934, § 1, 1971 Cal.Stats. 1832. Respondent does not claim that the standard of proof at the hearing failed to satisfy due process. See In re Winship, 397 U.S. 358, 90 S.Ct. 1068, 25 L.Ed.2d 368 (1970); DeBacker v. Brainard, 396 U.S. 28, 31, 90 S.Ct. 163, 165, 24 L.Ed.2d 148 (1969).

Hereafter, the § 701 hearing will be referred to as the adjudicatory hearing.

[37] At the time, Cal.Welf. & Inst'ns Code § 702 (West Supp.1968) provided:

"After hearing such evidence, the court shall make a finding, noted in the minutes of the court, whether or not the minor is a person described by Sections 600, 601, or 602. If it finds that the minor is not such a person, it shall order that the petition be dismissed and the minor be discharged from any detention or restriction theretofore ordered. If the court finds that the minor is such a person, it shall make and enter its findings and order accordingly and shall then proceed to hear evidence on the question of the proper disposition to be made of the minor. Prior to doing so, it may continue the hearing, if necessary, to receive the social study of the probation officer or to receive other evidence on its own motion or the motion of a parent or guardian for not to exceed 10 judicial days if the minor is detained during such continuance, and if the minor is not detained, it may continue the hearing to a date not later than 30 days after the date of filing of the petition. The court may, for good cause shown continue the hearing for an additional 15 days, if the minor is not detained. The court may make such order for detention of the minor or his release from detention, during the period of the continuance, as is appropriate."

juvenile court" under Cal.Welf. & Inst'ns Code § 707.[38] Respondent's counsel orally moved "to continue the matter on the ground of surprise," contending that respondent "was not informed that it was going to be a fitness hearing." The court continued the matter for one week, at which time, having considered the report of the probation officer assigned to the case and having heard her testimony, it declared respondent "unfit for treatment as a juvenile," [39] and ordered that he be prosecuted as an adult.[40]

Thereafter, respondent filed a petition for a writ of habeas corpus in Juvenile Court, raising the same double jeopardy claim now presented. Upon the denial of that petition, respondent sought habeas corpus relief in the California Court of Appeal, Second Appellate District. Although it initially stayed the criminal prosecution pending against respondent, that court denied the petition. In re Gary Steven J., 17 Cal.App.3d 704, 95 Cal.Rptr. 185 (1971). The Supreme Court of California denied respondent's petition for hearing.

After a preliminary hearing respondent was ordered held for trial in Superior Court, where an information was subsequently filed accusing him of having committed robbery, in violation of Cal.Penal

[38] At the time, Cal.Welf. & Inst'ns Code § 707 (West Supp.1967) provided:

"At any time during a hearing upon a petition alleging that a minor is, by reason of violation of any criminal statute or ordinance, a person described in Section 602, when substantial evidence has been adduced to support a finding that the minor was 16 years of age or older at the time of the alleged commission of such offense and that the minor would not be amenable to the care, treatment and training program available through the facilities of the juvenile court, or if, at any time after such hearing, a minor who was 16 years of age or older at the time of the commission of an offense and who was committed therefor by the court to the Youth Authority, is returned to the court by the Youth Authority pursuant to Section 780 or 1737.1, the court may make a finding noted in the minutes of the court that the minor is not a fit and proper subject to be dealt with under this chapter, and the court shall direct the district attorney or other appropriate prosecuting officer to prosecute the person under the applicable criminal statute or ordinance and thereafter dismiss the petition or, if a prosecution has been commenced in another court but has been suspended while juvenile court proceedings are held, shall dismiss the petition and issue its order directing that the other court proceedings resume.

"In determining whether the minor is a fit and proper subject to be dealt with under this chapter, the offense, in itself, shall not be sufficient to support a find-

ing that such minor is not a fit and proper subject to be dealt with under the provisions of the Juvenile Court Law.

"A denial by the person on whose behalf the petition is brought of any or all of the facts or conclusions set forth therein or of any interference to be drawn therefrom is not, of itself, sufficient to support a finding that such person is not a fit and proper subject to be dealt with under the provisions of the Juvenile Court Law.

"The court shall cause the probation officer to investigate and submit a report on the behavioral patterns of the person being considered for unfitness."

[39] The Juvenile Court noted:

"This record I have read is one of the most threatening records I have read about any Minor who has come before me.

"We have, as a matter of simple fact, no less than three armed robberies, each with a loaded weapon. The degree of delinquency which that represents, the degree of sophistication which that represents and the degree of impossibility of assistance as a juvenile which that represents, I think is overwhelming * * *" App. 33.

[40] In doing so, the Juvenile Court implicitly rejected respondent's double jeopardy argument, made at both the original § 702 hearing and in a memorandum submitted by counsel prior to the resumption of that hearing after the continuance.

Code § 211, while armed with a deadly weapon, on or about February 8, 1971. Respondent entered a plea of not guilty, and he also pleaded that he had "already been placed once in jeopardy and convicted of the offense charged, by the judgment of the Superior Court of the County of Los Angeles, Juvenile Court, rendered * * * on the 1st day of March, 1971." App. 47. By stipulation, the case was submitted to the court on the transcript of the preliminary hearing. The court found respondent guilty of robbery in the first degree under Cal.Penal Code § 211a and ordered that he be committed to the California Youth Authority.[41] No appeal was taken from the judgment of conviction.

On December 10, 1971, respondent, through his mother as guardian *ad litem,* filed the instant petition for a writ of habeas corpus in the United States District Court for the Central District of California. In his petition he alleged that his transfer to adult court pursuant to Cal.Welf. & Inst'ns Code § 707 and subsequent trial there "placed him in double jeopardy." App. 13. The District Court denied the petition, rejecting respondent's contention that jeopardy attached at his adjudicatory hearing. It concluded that the "distinctions between the preliminary procedures and hearings provided by California law for juveniles and a criminal trial are many and apparent and the effort of [respondent] to relate them is unconvincing," and that "even assuming jeopardy attached during the preliminary juvenile proceedings * * * it is clear that no new jeopardy arose by the juvenile proceeding sending the case to the criminal court." 343 F.Supp. 690, 692 (CD Cal.1972).

The Court of Appeals reversed, concluding that applying double jeopardy protection to juvenile proceedings would not "impede the juvenile courts in carrying out their basic goal of rehabilitating the erring youth," and that the contrary result might "do irreparable harm to or destroy their confidence in our judicial system." The court therefore held that the Double Jeopardy Clause "is fully applicable to juvenile court proceedings." 497 F.2d 1160, 1165 (CA9 1974).

Turning to the question whether there had been a constitutional violation in this case, the Court of Appeals pointed to the power of the Juvenile Court to "impose severe restrictions upon the juvenile's liberty," ibid., in support of its conclusion that jeopardy attached in respondent's adjudicatory hearing.[42] It rejected petitioner's conten-

---

[41] The authority for the order of commitment derived from Cal.Welf. & Inst'ns Code § 1731.5 (West Supp.1970). At the time of the order, Cal.Welf. & Inst'ns Code § 1771 (West 1966) provided:

"Every person convicted of a felony and committed to the authority shall be discharged when such person reaches his 25th birthday, unless an order for further detention has been made by the committing court pursuant to Article 6 (commencing with Section 1800) or unless a

petition is filed under Article 5 of this chapter. In the event such a petition under Article 5 is filed, the authority shall retain control until the final disposition of the proceeding under Article 5."

[42] In reaching this conclusion, the Court of Appeals also relied on Fain v. Duff, 488 F.2d 218 (CA 5 1973), cert. pending, No. 73–1768, and Richard M. v. Superior Court, 4 Cal.3d 370, 93 Cal.Rptr. 752, 482 P.2d 664 (1971), and it noted that "California concedes that jeopardy at-

tion that no new jeopardy attached when respondent was referred to Superior Court and subsequently tried and convicted, finding "continuing jeopardy" principles advanced by petitioner inapplicable. Finally, the Court of Appeals observed that acceptance of petitioner's position would "allow the prosecution to review in advance the accused's defense and, as here, hear him testify about the crime charged," a procedure it found offensive to "our concepts of basic, even-handed fairness." The court therefore held that once jeopardy attached at the adjudicatory hearing, a minor could not be retried as an adult or a juvenile "absent some exception to the double jeopardy prohibition," and that there "was none here." 497 F.2d, at 1168.

We granted certiorari because of a conflict between courts of appeals and the highest courts of a number of States on the issue presented in this case and similar issues and because of the importance of final resolution of the issue to the administration of the juvenile court system.

I

The parties agree that, following his transfer from Juvenile Court, and as a defendant to a felony information, respondent was entitled to the full protection of the Double Jeopardy Clause of the Fifth Amendment, as applied to the States through the Fourteenth Amendment. See Benton v. Maryland, 395 U.S. 784, 89 S.Ct. 2056, 23 L.Ed.2d 707 (1969). In addition, they agree that respondent was put in jeopardy by the proceedings on that information, which resulted in an adjudication that he was guilty of robbery in the first degree and in a sentence of commitment. Finally, there is no dispute that the petition filed in Juvenile Court and the information filed in Superior Court related to the "same offence" within the meaning of the constitutional prohibition. The point of disagreement between the parties, and the question for our decision, is whether, by reason of the proceedings in Juvenile Court, respondent was "twice put in jeopardy."

II

Jeopardy denotes risk. In the constitutional sense, jeopardy describes the risk that is traditionally associated with a criminal prosecution. See Price v. Georgia, 398 U.S. 323, 326, 329, 90 S.Ct. 1757, 1759, 26 L.Ed.2d 300 (1970); Serfass v. United States, 420 U.S. 377, 95 S.Ct. 1055, 43 L.Ed.2d 265 (1975). Although the constitutional language, "jeopardy of life or limb," suggests proceedings in which only the most serious penalties can be imposed, the Clause has long been construed to mean something far broader than its literal language. See Ex parte Lange, 85 U.S. (18 Wall.) 163, 170–173, 21 L.Ed. 872 (1873).[43] At the same time, however, we have held that the risk

taches when the juvenile is adjudicated a ward of the court." 497 F.2d at 1166.

[43] Distinctions which in other contexts have proved determinative of the constitutional rights of those charged with offenses against public order have not similarly confined the protection of the Double Jeopardy Clause. Compare

to which the Clause refers is not present in proceedings that are not "essentially criminal." Helvering v. Mitchell, 303 U.S. 391, 398, 58 S.Ct. 630, 632, 82 L.Ed. 917 (1938). See United States ex rel. Marcus v. Hess, 317 U.S. 537, 63 S.Ct. 379, 87 L.Ed. 498 (1943); One Lot Emerald Cut Stones v. United States, 409 U.S. 232, 93 S.Ct. 489, 34 L.Ed.2d 438 (1972). See also J. Sigler, Double Jeopardy 60–62 (1969).

Although the juvenile court system had its genesis in the desire to provide a distinctive procedure and setting to deal with the problems of youth, including those manifested by antisocial conduct, our decisions in recent years have recognized that there is a gap between the originally benign conception of the system and its realities. With the exception of McKeiver v. Pennsylvania, 403 U.S. 528, 91 S.Ct. 1976, 29 L.Ed.2d 647 (1971), the Court's response to that perception has been to make applicable in juvenile proceedings constitutional guarantees associated with traditional criminal prosecutions. In re Gault, 387 U.S. 1, 87 S.Ct. 1428, 18 L.Ed.2d 527 (1967); In re Winship, 397 U.S. 358, 90 S.Ct. 1068, 25 L.Ed.2d 368 (1970). In so doing the Court has evinced awareness of the threat which such a process represents to the efforts of the juvenile court system, functioning in a unique manner, to ameliorate the harshness of criminal justice when applied to youthful offenders. That the system has fallen short of the high expectations of its sponsors in no way detracts from the broad social benefits sought or from those benefits that can survive constitutional scrutiny.

We believe it is simply too late in the day to conclude, as did the District Court in this case, that a juvenile is not put in jeopardy at a proceeding whose object is to determine whether he has committed acts that violate a criminal law and whose potential consequences include both the stigma inherent in such a determination and the deprivation of liberty for many years.[44] For it is clear under our cases that determining the relevance of constitutional policies, like determining the applicability of constitutional rights, in juvenile proceedings, requires that courts eschew "the 'civil' label-of-convenience which has been attached to juvenile proceedings," In re Gault, supra, 387 U.S. at 50, 87 S.Ct. at 1455, and that "the juvenile process * * * be candidly appraised." 387 U.S. at 21, 87 S.Ct. at 1440. See In re Winship, supra, 397 U.S. at 365–366, 90 S.Ct. at 1073.

As we have observed, the risk to which the term jeopardy refers is that traditionally associated with "actions intended to authorize criminal punishment to vindicate public justice." United States ex rel. Marcus v. Hess, supra, 317 U.S. at 548–549, 63 S.Ct. at 388.

Robinson v. Neil, 409 U.S. 505, 93 S.Ct. 876, 35 L.Ed.2d 29 (1973), with Baldwin v. New York, 399 U.S. 66, 90 S.Ct. 1886, 26 L.Ed.2d 437 (1970), and Argersinger v. Hamlin, 407 U.S. 25, 92 S.Ct. 2006, 32 L.Ed.2d 530 (1972). For the details of Robinson's trial for violating a city ordinance, see Robinson v. Henderson, 268 F.Supp. 349 (E.D.Tenn.1967), aff'd, 391 F.2d 933 (CA 6 1968).

[44] At the time of respondent's dispositional hearing, permissible dispositions included commitment to the California Youth Authority until he reached the age of 21 years. See Cal.Welf. & Inst'ns Code §§ 607, 731 (West 1966). Petitioner has conceded that the "adjudicatory hearing is, in every sense, a court trial." Tr. of Oral Arg. 4.

Because of its purpose and potential consequences, and the nature and resources of the State, such a proceeding imposes heavy pressures and burdens—psychological, physical, and financial—on a person charged. The purpose of the Double Jeopardy Clause is to require that he be subject to the experience only once "for the same offence." See Green v. United States, 355 U.S. 184, 187, 78 S.Ct. 221, 223, 2 L.Ed.2d 199 (1957); Price v. Georgia, 398 U.S., at 331, 90 S.Ct. at 1762; United States v. Jorn, 400 U.S. 470, 479, 91 S.Ct. 547, 554, 27 L.Ed.2d 543 (1971).

In In re Gault, supra, 387 U.S. at 36, 87 S.Ct. at 1448, this Court concluded that, for purposes of the right to counsel, a "proceeding where the issue is whether the child will be found to be 'delinquent' and subjected to the loss of his liberty for years is comparable in seriousness to a felony prosecution." See In re Winship, supra, 397 U.S. at 366, 90 S.Ct. at 1073. The Court stated that the term "delinquent" had "come to involve only slightly less stigma than the term 'criminal' applied to adults," In re Gault, supra, 387 U.S. at 24, 87 S.Ct. at 1441; see In re Winship, supra, 397 U.S. at 367, 90 S.Ct. at 1074, and that, for purposes of the privilege against self-incrimination, "commitment is a deprivation of liberty. It is incarceration against one's will, whether it is called 'criminal' or 'civil.'" In re Gault, supra, 387 U.S. at 50, 87 S.Ct. at 1455. See 387 U.S., at 27, 87 S.Ct. at 1443; In re Winship, supra, 397 U.S. at 367,[45] 90 S.Ct. at 1074.

Thus, in terms of potential consequences, there is little to distinguish an adjudicatory hearing such as was held in this case from a traditional criminal prosecution. For that reason, it engenders elements of "anxiety and insecurity" in a juvenile, and imposes a "heavy personal strain." See Green v. United States, supra, 355 U.S. at 187, 78 S.Ct. at 223; United States v. Jorn, supra, 400 U.S. at 479, 91 S.Ct. at 554; Snyder, The Impact of the Juvenile Court Hearing on the Child, 17 Crime & Delinquency 180 (1971). And we can expect that, since our decisions implementing fundamental fairness in the juvenile court system, hearings have been prolonged, and some of the burdens incident to a juvenile's defense increased, as the system has assimilated the process thereby imposed. See Note, Double Jeopardy and the Waiver of Jurisdiction in California's Juvenile Courts, 24 Stan.L.Rev. 874, 902 n. 138 (1972). Cf. Canon and Kolson, Rural Compliance with Gault; Kentucky, A Case Study, 10 J.Fam.L. 300, 320–326 (1971).

We deal here, not with "the formalities of the criminal adjudicative process," McKeiver v. Pennsylvania, 403 U.S., at 551, 91 S.Ct. at 1989, but with an analysis of an aspect of the juvenile court system in terms of the kind of risk to which jeopardy refers. Under our

---

[45] Nor does the fact "that the purpose of the commitment is rehabilitative and not punitive * * * change its nature. * * * Regardless of the purposes for which incarceration is imposed, the fact remains that it is incarceration. The rehabilitative goals of the system are admirable, but they do not change the drastic nature of the action taken. Incarceration of adults is also intended to produce rehabilitation." Fain v. Duff, 488 F.2d, at 225. See President's Commission on Law Enforcement and Administration of Justice, Task Force Report: Juvenile Delinquency and Youth Crime 8–9 (1967).

decisions we can find no persuasive distinction in that regard between the proceeding conducted in this case pursuant to Cal.Welf. & Inst'ns Code § 701 and a criminal prosecution, each of which is designed "to vindicate [the] very vital interest in enforcement of criminal laws." United States v. Jorn, supra, 400 U.S. at 479, 91 S.Ct. at 554. We therefore conclude that respondent was put in jeopardy at the adjudicatory hearing. Jeopardy attached when respondent was "put to trial before the trier of the facts," ibid., that is, when the Juvenile Court, as the trier of the facts, began to hear evidence. See Serfass v. United States, 420 U.S. at 377, 95 S.Ct. 1055.[46]

III

Petitioner argues that, even assuming jeopardy attached at respondent's adjudicatory hearing, the procedure by which he was transferred from Juvenile Court and tried on a felony information in Superior Court did not violate the Double Jeopardy Clause. The argument is supported by two distinct, but in this case overlapping, lines of analysis. First, petitioner reasons that the procedure violated none of the policies of the Double Jeopardy Clause or that, alternatively, it should be upheld by analogy to those cases which permit retrial of an accused who has obtained reversal of a conviction on appeal. Second, pointing to this Court's concern for "the juvenile court's assumed ability to function in a unique manner," McKeiver v. Pennsylvania, supra, 403 U.S. at 547, 91 S.Ct. at 1987, petitioner urges that, should we conclude traditional principles "would otherwise bar a transfer to adult court after a delinquency adjudication," we should avoid that result here because it "would diminish the flexibility and informality of juvenile court proceedings without conferring any additional due process benefits upon juveniles charged with delinquent acts."

A

We cannot agree with petitioner that the trial of respondent in Superior Court on an information charging the same offense as that for which he had been tried in Juvenile Court violated none of the policies of the Double Jeopardy Clause. For, even accepting petitioner's premise that respondent "never faced the risk of more than one punishment," we have pointed out that "the Double Jeopardy Clause * * * is written in terms of potential or risk of *trial* and conviction, not punishment." Price v. Georgia, 398 U.S. at 329, 90 S.Ct. at 1761. (Emphasis added.) And we have recently noted:

> "The policy of avoiding multiple trials has been regarded as so important that exceptions to the principle have been only grudgingly allowed. Initially, a new trial was thought to be unavailable after appeal, whether requested by the prosecution or the defendant. * * * It was not until 1896 that it was made

---

[46] The same conclusion was reached by the California Court of Appeal in denying respondent's petition for a writ of habeas corpus. In re Gary Steven J., 17 Cal. App.3d, at 710, 95 Cal.Rptr., at 189.

clear that a defendant could seek a new trial after conviction, even though the Government enjoyed no similar right. * * * Following the same policy, the Court has granted the Government the right to retry a defendant after a mistrial only where 'there is a manifest necessity for the act, or the ends of public justice would otherwise be defeated.' United States v. Perez, 9 Wheat. (22 U.S.) 579, 580, 6 L.Ed. 165 (1824)." United States v. Wilson, 420 U.S. 332, 343, 95 S.Ct. 1013, 1022, 43 L.Ed.2d 232 (1975). (Footnote omitted.)

Respondent was subjected to the burden of two trials for the same offense; he was twice put to the task of marshaling his resources against those of the State, twice subjected to the "heavy personal strain" which such an experience represents. United States v. Jorn, 400 U.S., at 479, 91 S.Ct., at 554. We turn, therefore, to inquire whether either traditional principles or "the juvenile court's assumed ability to function in a unique manner," McKeiver v. Pennsylvania, supra, 403 U.S. at 547, 91 S.Ct. at 1987, support an exception to the "constitutional policy of finality" to which respondent would otherwise be entitled. United States v. Jorn, supra.

B

In denying respondent's petitions for writs of habeas corpus, the California Court of Appeal first, and the United States District Court later, concluded that no new jeopardy arose as a result of his transfer from Juvenile Court and trial in Superior Court. See In re Gary Steven J., 17 Cal.App.3d, at 710, 95 Cal.Rptr. at 189; 343 F.Supp., at 692. In the view of those courts, the jeopardy that attaches at an adjudicatory hearing continues until there is a final disposition of the case under the adult charge. See also In re Juvenile, Mass., 306 N.E.2d 822 (1974). Cf. Bryan v. Superior Court, 7 Cal.3d 575, 102 Cal.Rptr. 831, 498 P.2d 1079 (1972), cert. denied, 410 U.S. 944, 93 S.Ct. 1380, 35 L.Ed.2d 610 (1973).

The phrase "continuing jeopardy" describes both a concept and a conclusion. As originally articulated by Mr. Justice Holmes in his dissent in Kepner v. United States, 195 U.S. 100, 134–137, 24 S.Ct. 797, 806, 49 L.Ed. 114 (1904), the concept has proved an interesting model for comparison with the system of constitutional protection which the Court has in fact derived from the rather ambiguous language and history of the Double Jeopardy Clause. See United States v. Wilson, supra, at 351–52, 95 S.Ct. 1013. Holmes' view has "never been adopted by a majority of this Court." United States v. Jenkins, 420 U.S. 358, 369, 95 S.Ct. 1006, 1013, 43 L.Ed.2d 250 (1975).

The conclusion, "continuing jeopardy," as distinguished from the concept, has occasionally been used to explain why an accused who has secured the reversal of a conviction on appeal may be retried for the same offense. See Green v. United States, 355 U.S., at 189, 78 S.Ct. at 224; Price v. Georgia, 398 U.S., at 326, 90 S.Ct. at 1759; United States v. Wilson, supra, at 343–44, n. 11, 95 S.Ct. at 1022. Probably a more satisfactory explanation lies in analysis of the respective interests involved. See United States v. Tateo, 377 U.S. 463, 465–466, 84 S.Ct. 1587, 1589, 12 L.Ed.2d 448 (1964); Price v. Georgia, supra, 398 U.S. at 329 n. 4, 90 S.Ct. at 1761; United States v. Wilson, supra. Similarly, the fact that the proceedings against respondent had not "run their full course," Price v. Georgia, supra, 398 U.S. at 326, 90 S.Ct. at 1759, within the contemplation of the California Welfare and Institutions Code, at the time of transfer, does not satisfactorily explain why respondent should be deprived of the constitutional protection against a second trial. If there is to be an exception to that protection in the context of the juvenile court system, it must be justified by interests of society, reflected in that unique institution, or of juveniles themselves, of sufficient substance to render tolerable the costs and burdens, noted earlier, which the exception will entail in individual cases.

C

The possibility of transfer from Juvenile Court to a court of general criminal jurisdiction is a matter of great significance to the juvenile. See Kent v. United States, 383 U.S. 541, 86 S.Ct. 1045, 16 L.Ed.2d 84 (1966). At the same time, there appears to be widely shared agreement that not all juveniles can benefit from the special features and programs of the juvenile court system and that a procedure for transfer to an adult court should be available. See, e.g, National Advisory Commission on Criminal Justice Standards and Goals, Report on Courts, Commentary to Standard 14.3, at 300–301 (1973). This general agreement is reflected in the fact that an overwhelming majority of jurisdictions permits transfer in certain circumstances.[47] As might be expected, the statutory provisions differ in numerous details. Whatever their differences, however, such transfer provisions represent an attempt to impart to the juvenile court system the flexibility needed to deal with youthful offenders who cannot benefit from the specialized guidance and treatment contemplated by the system.

We do not agree with petitioner that giving respondent the constitutional protection against multiple trials in this context will diminish flexibility and informality to the extent that those qualities relate uniquely to the goals of the juvenile court system.[48] We agree that such a holding will require, in most cases, that the transfer decision be made prior to an adjudicatory hearing. To the extent that evidence concerning the alleged offense is considered relevant,[49] it

---

[47] See generally Task Force Report, supra, * * * at 24–25. See also Rudstein, Double Jeopardy in Juvenile Proceedings, 14 Wm. & Mary L.Rev. 266, 297–300 (1972); Carr, The Effect of the Double Jeopardy Clause on Juvenile Proceedings, 6 U.Tol.L.Rev. 1, 21–22 (1974).

[48] That the flexibility and informality of juvenile proceedings are diminished by the application of due process standards is not open to doubt. Due process standards inevitably produce such an effect, but that tells us no more than that the Constitution imposes burdens on the functioning of government and especially of law enforcement institutions.

[49] Under Cal.Welf. & Inst'ns Code § 707 (West 1972), the governing criterion with respect to transfer, assuming the juvenile is 16 years of age is charged with a violation of a criminal statute or ordinance, is amenability "to the care,

may be that, in those cases where transfer is considered and rejected, some added burden will be imposed on the juvenile courts by reason of duplicative proceedings. Finally, the nature of the evidence considered at a transfer hearing may in some States require that, if transfer is rejected, a different judge preside at the adjudicatory hearing.[50]

We recognize that juvenile courts, perhaps even more than most courts, suffer from the problems created by spiraling caseloads unaccompanied by enlarged resources and manpower. See President's Commission on Law Enforcement and Administration of Justice, Task Force Report: Juvenile Delinquency and Youth Crime 7–8 (1967). And courts should be reluctant to impose on the juvenile court system any additional requirements which could so strain its resources as to endanger its unique functions. However, the burdens that petitioner envisions appear to us neither qualitatively nor quantitatively sufficient to justify a departure in this context from the fundamental prohibition against double jeopardy.

A requirement that transfer hearings be held prior to adjudicatory hearings affects not at all the nature of the latter proceedings. More significant, such a requirement need not affect the quality of decisionmaking at transfer hearings themselves. In Kent v. United States, 383 U.S., at 562, 86 S.Ct. at 1057, the Court held that hearings under the statute there involved "must measure up to the essentials of due process and fair treatment." However, the Court has never attempted to prescribe criteria for, or the nature and quantum of evidence that must support, a decision to transfer a juvenile for trial in adult court. We require only that, whatever the relevant criteria, and whatever the evidence demanded, a State determine whether it wants to treat a juvenile within the juvenile court system before entering upon a proceeding that may result in an adjudication that he has violated a criminal law and in a substantial deprivation of liberty,

treatment and training program available through the facilities of the juvenile court." The section further provides that neither "the offense, in itself" nor a denial by the juvenile of the facts or conclusions set forth in the petition shall be "sufficient to support a finding that [he] is not a fit and proper subject to be dealt with under the provisions of the Juvenile Court Law." * * * The California Supreme Court has held that the only factor a juvenile court must consider is the juvenile's "behavior pattern as described in the probation officer's report," Jimmy H. v. Superior Court, 3 Cal.3d 709, 714, 478 P.2d 32, 35 (1970), but that it may also consider, inter alia, the nature and circumstances of the alleged offense. See id., at 716, 478 P.2d, at 36.

In contrast to California, which does not require any evidentiary showing with respect to the commission of the offense, a number of jurisdictions require a finding of probable cause to believe the juvenile committed the offense before transfer is permitted. See Rudstein, supra, * * * at 298–299; Carr, supra, * * * at 21–22. In addition, two jurisdictions appear presently to require a finding of delinquency before the transfer of a juvenile to adult court. Ala.Code, Tit. 13, § 364 (1958) [see Rudolph v. State, 286 Ala. 189, 238 So.2d 542 (1970)]; W.Va. Code Ann. § 49–5–14 (1966).

[50] See, e.g., Fla.Stat.Ann. § 39.09(2)(g) (1974); Tenn.Code Ann. § 37–234(c) (Supp.1974); Wyo.Stat. § 14–115.38(c) (Supp.1973); Uniform Juvenile Court Act, § 34(e), approved in July 1968 by the National Conference of Commissioners on Uniform State Laws. See also Donald L. v. Superior Court, 7 Cal.3d 592, 598, 498 P.2d 1098, 1101 (1972).

rather than subject him to the expense, delay, strain and embarrassment of two such proceedings.[51]

Moreover, we are not persuaded that the burdens petitioner envisions would pose a significant problem for the administration of the juvenile court system. The large number of jurisdictions that presently require that the transfer decision be made prior to an adjudicatory hearing,[52] and the absence of any indication that the juvenile courts in those jurisdictions have not been able to perform their task within that framework, suggest the contrary. The likelihood that in many cases the lack of need or basis for a transfer hearing can be recognized promptly reduces the number of cases in which a commitment of resources is necessary. In addition, we have no reason to believe that the resources available to those who recommend transfer or participate in the process leading to transfer decisions are inadequate to enable them to gather the information relevant to informed decision prior to an adjudicatory hearing. See generally State v. Halverson, 192 N.W.2d 765, 769 (Iowa 1971); Rudstein, Double Jeopardy in Juvenile Proceedings, 14 Wm. & Mary L.Rev. 266, 305–306 (1972); Note, 24 Stan.L.Rev., at 897–899.[53]

To the extent that transfer hearings held prior to adjudication result in some duplication of evidence if transfer is rejected, the burden on juvenile courts will tend to be offset somewhat by the cases in which, because of transfer, no further proceedings in Juvenile Court are required. Moreover, when transfer has previously been rejected, juveniles may well be more likely to admit the commission of the offense charged, thereby obviating the need for adjudicatory hearings, than if transfer remains a possibility. Finally, we note that those States which presently require a different judge to preside at an adjudicatory hearing if transfer is rejected also permit waiver of that requirement.[54] Where the requirement is not waived, it is

[51] We note that nothing decided today forecloses States from requiring, as a prerequisite to the transfer of a juvenile, substantial evidence that he committed the offense charged, so long as the showing required is not made in an adjudicatory proceeding. See Collins v. Loisel, 262 U.S. 426, 429, 43 S.Ct. 618, 625, 67 L.Ed. 1062 (1923); Serfass v. United States, 420 U.S. 377, 95 S.Ct. 1055, 43 L.Ed.2d 265 (1975). The instant case is not one in which the judicial determination was simply a finding of, e.g., probable cause. Rather, it was an adjudication that respondent had violated a criminal statute.

[52] See Rudstein, supra, n. 14, at 299–300; Carr, supra, n. 14, at 24, 57–58. See also Uniform Juvenile Court Act §§ 34(a), (c); Model Rules for Juvenile Courts, Rule 9 (National Council on Crime and Delinquency 1969); Legislative Guide for Drafting Family and Juvenile Court Acts §§ 27, 31(a) (Dept. of HEW, Children's Bureau Pub. No. 472–1969). In contrast, apparently only three States presently require that a hearing on the juvenile petition or complaint precede transfer. Ala.Code, Tit. 13, § 364 (1958) [see Rudolph v. State, 286 Ala. 189, 238 So.2d 542]; Mass.Gen.Laws Ann. c. 119, § 61 (1969) [see In re Juvenile, Mass., and n. 10, 306 N.E.2d 822, 829–830 and n. 10 (1974)]; W.Va.Code Ann. § 49–5–14 (1966).

[53] We intimate no views concerning the constitutional validity of transfer following the attachment of jeopardy at an adjudicatory hearing where the information which forms the predicate for the transfer decision could not, by the exercise of due diligence, reasonably have been obtained previously. Cf., e.g., Illinois v. Somerville, 410 U.S. 458, 93 S.Ct. 1066, 35 L.Ed.2d 425 (1973).

[54] * * *

"The reason for this waiver provision is clear. A juvenile will ordinarily not want to dismiss a judge who has refused to transfer him to a criminal court.

difficult to see a substantial strain on judicial resources. See Note, 24 Stan.L.Rev., at 900–901.

Quite apart from our conclusions with respect to the burdens on the juvenile court system envisioned by petitioner, we are persuaded that transfer hearings prior to adjudication will aid the objectives of that system. What concerns us here is the dilemma that the possibility of transfer after an adjudicatory hearing presents for a juvenile, a dilemma to which the Court of Appeals alluded. * * * Because of that possibility, a juvenile, thought to be the beneficiary of special consideration, may in fact suffer substantial disadvantages. If he appears uncooperative, he runs the risk of an adverse adjudication, as well as of an unfavorable dispositional recommendation.[55] If, on the other hand, he is cooperative, he runs the risk of prejudicing his chances in adult court if transfer is ordered. We regard a procedure that results in such a dilemma as at odds with the goal that, to the extent fundamental fairness permits, adjudicatory hearings be informal and nonadversary. See In re Gault, 387 U.S., at 25–27, 87 S.Ct. at 1442; In re Winship, 397 U.S., at 366–367, 90 S.Ct. at 1074; McKeiver v. Pennsylvania, 403 U.S., at 534, 550, 91 S.Ct. at 1981. Knowledge of the risk of transfer after an adjudicatory hearing can only undermine the potential for informality and cooperation which was intended to be the hallmark of the juvenile court system. Rather than concerning themselves with the matter at hand, establishing innocence or seeking a disposition best suited to individual correctional needs, the juvenile and his attorney are pressed into a posture of adversary wariness that is conducive to neither. Cf. Kay and Segal, The Role of the Attorney in Juvenile Court Proceedings: A Non-Polar Approach, 61 Geo.L.J. 1401 (1973); Carr, The Effect of the Double Jeopardy Clause on Juvenile Proceedings, 6 U.Tol.L.Rev. 1, 52–54 (1974).[56]

IV

We hold that the prosecution of respondent in Superior Court, after an adjudicatory proceeding in Juvenile Court, violated the Double Jeopardy Clause of the Fifth Amendment, as applied to the

There is a risk of having another judge assigned to the case who is not as sympathetic. Moreover, in many cases, a rapport has been established between the judge and the juvenile, and the goal of rehabilitation is well on its way to being met." Brief for National Council of Juvenile Court Judges as Amicus Curiae, at 38.

[55] Although denying respondent's petition for a writ of habeas corpus, the judge of the Juvenile Court noted: "If he doesn't open up with a probation officer there is of course the danger that the probation officer will find that he is so uncooperative that he cannot make a recommendation for the kind of treatment you think he really should have and, yet,

as the attorney worrying about what might happen as [sic] the disposition hearing, you have to advise him to continue to more or less stand upon his constitutional right not to incriminate himself. * * *" App. 38. See Note, 24 Stan.L. Rev., at 902 n. 137.

[56] With respect to the possibility of "making the juvenile proceedings confidential and not being able to be used against the minor," the judge of the Juvenile Court observed: "I must say that doesn't impress me because if the minor admitted something in the Juvenile Court and named his companions nobody is going to eradicate from the minds of the district attorney or other people the information they obtained." App. 41–42.

States through the Fourteenth Amendment. The mandate of the Court of Appeals, which was stayed by that court pending our decision, directs the District Court "to issue a writ of habeas corpus directing the state court, within 60 days, to vacate the adult conviction of Jones and either set him free or remand him to the juvenile court for disposition." Since respondent is no longer subject to the jurisdiction of the California Juvenile Court, we vacate the judgment and remand the case to the Court of Appeals for such further proceedings consistent with this opinion as may be appropriate in the circumstances.

So ordered.

Judgment vacated and case remanded.

SWISHER v. BRADY

Supreme Court of the United States, 1978.
438 U.S. 204, 98 S.Ct. 2699, 57 L.Ed.2d 705.

MR. CHIEF JUSTICE BURGER delivered the opinion of the Court.

This is an appeal from a three-judge District Court for the District of Maryland. Nine minors, appellees here, brought an action under 42 U.S.C. § 1983, seeking a declaratory judgment and injunctive relief to prevent the State from filing exceptions with the Juvenile Court to proposed findings and recommendations made by masters of that court. The minors' claim was based on an alleged violation of the Double Jeopardy Clause of the Fifth Amendment, as applied to the States through the Fourteenth Amendment. The District Court's jurisdiction was invoked under 28 U.S.C. §§ 1343, 2281, and 2284 (as then written); this Court's jurisdiction, under 28 U.S.C. § 1253.

I

In order to understand the present Maryland scheme for the use of masters in juvenile court proceedings, it is necessary to trace briefly the history both of antecedent schemes and of this and related litigation.

Prior to July 1975, the use of masters in Maryland juvenile proceedings was governed by Rule 908.e, Maryland Rules of Procedure. It provided that a master "shall hear such cases as may be assigned to him by the court." The Rule further directed that, at the conclusion of the hearing, the master transmit the case file and his "findings and recommendation" to the Juvenile Court. If no party filed exceptions to these findings and recommendations, they were to be "promptly * * * confirmed, modified or remanded by the judge." If, however, a party filed exceptions—and in delinquency hearings, only the State had the authority to do so—then, after notice, the Juvenile Court judge would "hear the entire matter or such specific matters as set forth in the exceptions *de novo.*"

In the city of Baltimore, after the State filed a petition alleging that a minor had committed a delinquent act, the clerk of the Juvenile

Court generally would assign the case to one of seven masters.[57]   In the ensuing unrecorded hearing, the State would call its witnesses and present its evidence in accordance with the rules of evidence applicable in criminal cases.   The minor could offer evidence in defense.   At the conclusion of the presentation of evidence, the master usually would announce his findings and contemplated recommendations.   In a minority of those cases where the recommendations favored the minor's position, the State would file exceptions, whereupon the Juvenile Court judge would try the case *de novo.*[58]

In 1972, a Baltimore City master concluded, after a hearing, that the State had failed to show beyond a reasonable doubt that a minor, William Anderson, had assaulted and robbed a woman.   His recommendation to the Juvenile Court judge reflected that conclusion.   The State filed exceptions.   Anderson responded with a motion to dismiss the notice of exceptions, contending that Rule 908.e, with its provision for a *de novo* hearing, violated the Double Jeopardy Clause. The Juvenile Court judge ruled that juvenile proceedings as such were not outside the scope of the Double Jeopardy Clause.   He then held that the proceeding before him on the State's exceptions would violate Anderson's right not to be twice put in jeopardy and, on that basis, granted the motion to dismiss.   The judge granted the same relief to similarly situated minors, including several who later initiated the present litigation.

The State appealed and the Court of Special Appeals reversed. In re Anderson, 20 Md.App. 31, 315 A.2d 540 (1974).   That court assumed, for purposes of its decision, that jeopardy attached at the commencement of the initial hearing before the master.   It held, however, that

> "there is *no adjudication* by reason of the master's findings and recommendations.   The proceedings before the master and his findings and recommendations are simply the first phase of the hearing which continues with the consideration by the juvenile judge.   Whether the juvenile judge, in the absence of exceptions, accepts the master's findings or recommendations, modifies them or remands them, or whether, when exceptions are filed, he hears the matter himself de novo, there is merely a continuance of the hearing and the initial jeopardy.   In other words, *the hearing,* and the jeopardy thereto attaching, terminate only upon a valid adjudication *by the juvenile judge,* not upon the findings and recommendations of the master."   Id., at 47, 315 A.2d, at 549 (footnotes omitted;   emphasis added).

On this basis, the court concluded that the *de novo* hearing was not a second exposure to jeopardy.

[57] In 1974, of 5,345 delinquency hearings conducted in the Juvenile Court, 5,098 were held before masters.   The remaining 247 were assigned in the first instance to the judge.

[58] In 1974, the Juvenile Court judge conducted 80 *de novo,* or "exceptions," hearings in delinquency matters.   All hearings before the judge were recorded.

On appeal by the minors, the Court of Appeals affirmed, although on a rationale different from that of the intermediate appellate court. In re Anderson, 272 Md. 85, 321 A.2d 516 (1974). It held that "a hearing before a master is not such a hearing as places a juvenile in jeopardy." Central to this holding was the court's conclusion that masters in Maryland serve only as ministerial assistants to judges; although authorized to hear evidence, report findings and make recommendations to the judge, masters are entrusted with none of the judicial power of the State, including the *sine qua non* of judicial office—the power to enter a binding judgment.

In November 1974, five months after the Court of Appeals' decision, nine juveniles sought federal habeas corpus relief, contending that by taking exceptions to masters' recommendations favorable to them the State was violating their rights under the Double Jeopardy Clause. These same nine minors also initiated a class action under 42 U.S.C. § 1983 in which they sought a declaratory judgment and injunctive relief against the future operation of Rule 908.e. The sole constitutional basis for their complaint was, again, the Double Jeopardy Clause. A three-judge court was convened to hear this matter, and it is the judgment of that court we now review.

Before either the three-judge District Court or the single judge reviewing the habeas corpus petitions could act, the Maryland Legislature enacted legislation which, for the first time, provided a statutory basis for the use of masters in juvenile court proceedings. In doing so, it modified slightly the scheme previously operative under Rule 908.e. The new legislation required that hearings before a master be recorded and that, at their conclusion, the master submit to the Juvenile Court judge written findings of fact, conclusions of law, and recommendations. Either party was authorized to file exceptions and could elect a hearing on the record or a *de novo* hearing before the judge. The legislature specified that the masters' "proposals and recommendations for juvenile causes do not constitute orders or final action of the court." Accordingly, the judge could, even in the absence of exceptions, reject a master's recommendations and conduct a *de novo* hearing or, if the parties agreed, a hearing on the record. Maryland Courts and Judicial Proceedings Ann. § 3–813 (Supp.1977).

In June 1975, within two months of the enactment of § 3–813 and before its July 1, 1975 effective date, the single-judge United States District Court held that the Rule 908.e provision for a *de novo* hearing on the State's exceptions violated the Double Jeopardy Clause. Aldridge v. Dean, 395 F.Supp. 1161 (Md.1975). In that court's view, a juvenile was placed in jeopardy as soon as the State offered evidence in the hearing before a master. The court also concluded that to subject a juvenile to a *de novo* hearing before the Juvenile Court judge was to place him in jeopardy a second time. Accordingly, it granted habeas corpus relief to the six petitioners already subjected by the State to a *de novo* hearing. The petitions of the remaining three, who had not yet been brought before the

Juvenile Court judge, were dismissed without prejudice as being premature.

In response to both the enactment of § 3–813 and the decision in Aldridge v. Dean, supra, the Maryland Court of Appeals, in the exercise of its rulemaking power, promulgated a new rule, and the one currently in force, Rule 911, to govern the use of masters in juvenile proceedings. Rule 911 differs from the statute in significant aspects. First, in order to emphasize the nonfinal nature of a master's conclusions, it stresses that all of his "findings, conclusions, recommendations or * * * orders" are only *proposed*. Second, the State no longer has power to secure a *de novo* hearing before the Juvenile Court judge after unfavorable proposals by the master. The State still may file exceptions, but the judge can act on them only on the basis of the record made before the master and "such additional, [relevant] evidence * * * to which the parties raise no objection." The judge retains his power to accept, reject or modify the master's proposals, to remand to the master for further hearings, and to supplement the record for his own review with additional evidence to which the parties do not object.[59]

[59] Rule 911, in its entirety, provides:

"a. Authority

"1. Detention or Shelter Care.

"A master is authorized to order detention or shelter care in accordance with Rule 912 (Detention or Shelter Care) subject to an immediate review by a judge if requested by any party.

"2. Other Matters.

"A master is authorized to hear any cases and matters assigned to him by the court, except a hearing on a waiver petition. The findings, conclusions and recommendations of a master do not constitute orders or final action of the court.

"b. Report of the Court.

"Within ten days following the conclusion of a disposition hearing by a master, he shall transmit to the judge the entire file in the case, together with a written report of his proposed findings of fact, conclusions of law, recommendations and proposed orders with respect to adjudication and disposition. A copy of his report and proposed order shall be served upon each party as provided by Rule 306 (Service of Pleadings and Other Papers).

"c. Review by Court if Exceptions Filed.

"Any party may file exceptions to the master's proposed findings, conclusions, recommendations or proposed orders. Exceptions shall be in writing, filed with the clerk within five days after the master's report is served upon the party, and shall specify those items to which the party excepts, and whether the hearing is to be *de novo* or on the record. A copy shall be served upon all other parties pursuant to Rule 306 (Service of Pleadings and Other Papers).

"Upon the filing of exceptions, a prompt hearing shall be scheduled on the exceptions. An excepting party other than the State may elect a hearing *de novo* or a hearing on the record. If the State is the excepting party, the hearing shall be on the record, supplemented by such additional evidence as the judge considers relevant and to which the parties raise no objection. In either case the hearing shall be limited to those matters to which exceptions have been taken.

"d. Review by Court in Absence of Exceptions.

"In the absence of timely and proper exceptions, the master's proposed findings of fact, conclusions of law and recommendations may be adopted by the court and the proposed or other appropriate orders may be entered based on them. The court may remand the case to the master for further hearings, or may, on its own motion, schedule and conduct a further hearing supplemented by such additional evidence as the court considers relevant and to which the parties raise no objection. Action by the court under this section shall be taken within two days after the expiration of the time for filing exceptions."

Thus, Rule 911 is a direct product of the desire of the State to continue using masters to meet the heavy burden of juvenile court caseloads while at the same time assuring that their use not violate the constitutional guarantee against double jeopardy. To this end, the Rule permits the presentation and recording of evidence in the absence of the only officer authorized by the state constitution, see In re Anderson, supra, 272 Md., at 104–105, 321 A.2d, at 526–27, and by statute, § 3–813, to serve as the factfinder and judge.

After the effective date of Rule 911, July 1, 1975, the plaintiffs in the § 1983 action amended their complaint to bring Rule 911 within its scope. They continued to challenge the state procedure, however, only on the basis of the Double Jeopardy Clause. Other juveniles intervened as the ongoing work of the juvenile court brought them within the definition of the proposed class. Their complaints in intervention likewise rested only on the Double Jeopardy Clause.

The three-judge District Court certified the proposed class under Fed.Rule Civ.Proc. 23(b)(2) to consist of all juveniles involved in proceedings where the State had filed exceptions to a master's proposed findings of nondelinquency. That court then held that a juvenile subjected to a hearing before a master is placed in jeopardy, even though the master has no power to enter a final order. It also held that the Juvenile Court judge's review of the record constitutes a "second proceeding at which [the juvenile] must once again marshal whatever resources he can against the State's and at which the State is given a second opportunity to obtain a conviction." Brady v. Swisher, 436 F.Supp. 1361, 1369 (Md.1977). Accordingly, the three-judge District Court enjoined the defendants-state officials from taking exceptions to either a master's proposed finding of nondelinquency or his proposed disposition.

We noted probable jurisdiction solely to determine whether the Double Jeopardy Clause prohibits state officials, acting in accordance with Rule 911, from taking exceptions to a master's proposed findings. 434 U.S. 963, 98 S.Ct. 501, 54 L.Ed.2d 449 (1977).

II

The general principles governing this case are well-established.

"A State may not put a defendant in jeopardy twice for the same offense. Benton v. Maryland, 395 U.S. 784, 89 S.Ct. 2056, 23 L.Ed.2d 707. The constitutional protection against double jeopardy unequivocally prohibits a second trial following an acquittal. The public interest in the finality of criminal judgments is so strong that an acquitted defendant may not be retried even though 'the acquittal was based upon an egregiously erroneous foundation.' * * * If the innocence of the accused has been confirmed by a final judgment, the Constitution conclusively presumes that a second trial would be unfair.

"Because jeopardy attaches before the judgment becomes final, the constitutional protection also embraces the defendant's 'valued right to have his trial completed by a particular tribunal.' * * * Consequently, as a general rule, the prosecutor is entitled to one, and only one, opportunity to require an accused to stand trial." Arizona v. Washington, 434 U.S. 497, 503, 98 S.Ct. 824, 829, 55 L.Ed.2d 717 (1978) (footnotes omitted).

In the application of these general principles, the narrow question here [60] is whether the State in filing exceptions to a master's proposals, pursuant to Rule 911, thereby "require[s] an accused to stand trial" a second time. We hold that it does not. Maryland has created a system with Rule 911 in which an accused juvenile is subjected to a single proceeding which begins with a master's hearing and culminates with an adjudication by a judge.

Importantly, a Rule 911 proceeding does not impinge on the purposes of the Double Jeopardy Clause. A central purpose "of the prohibition against successive trials" is to bar "the prosecution [from] another opportunity to supply evidence which it failed to muster in the first proceeding." Burks v. United States, 437 U.S. 1, at 10–12, 98 S.Ct. 2141, at 2147, 57 L.Ed.2d 1 (1978). A Rule 911 proceeding does not provide the prosecution that forbidden "second crack." The State presents its evidence once before the master. The record is then closed, and additional evidence can be received by the Juvenile Court judge only with the consent of the minor.

The Double Jeopardy Clause also precludes the prosecutor from "enhanc[ing] the risk that an innocent defendant may be convicted," Arizona v. Washington, supra, at 503, 98 S.Ct., at 829 by taking the question of guilt to a series of persons or groups empowered to make binding determinations. Appellees contend that in its operation Rule 911 gives the State the chance to persuade two such factfinders: first the master, then the Juvenile Court judge. In support of this contention they point to evidence that juveniles and their parents sometimes consider the master "the judge" and his recommendations "the verdict." Within the limits of jury trial rights, see McKeiver v. Pennsylvania, 403 U.S. 528, 91 S.Ct. 1976, 29 L.Ed.2d 647 (1971), and other constitutional constraints, it is for the State, not the parties, to designate and empower the factfinder and adjudicator. And here Maryland has conferred those roles only on the Juvenile Court judge. Thus, regardless of which party is initially favored by the master's

[60] The State contends that jeopardy does not attach at the hearing before the master. Our decision in Breed v. Jones, 421 U.S. 519, 95 S.Ct. 1779, 44 L.Ed.2d 346 (1975), however, suggests the contrary conclusion. "We believe it is simply too late in the day to conclude * * * that a juvenile is not put in jeopardy at a proceeding whose object is to determine whether he has committed acts that violate a criminal law and whose potential consequences include both the stigma inherent in such a determination and the deprivation of liberty for many years."

Id., at 529, 95 S.Ct., at 1785. The California juvenile proceeding reviewed in *Breed* involved the use of a referee, or master, and was not materially different—for purposes of analysis of attachment of jeopardy—from a Rule 911 proceeding. See generally In re Edgar M., 14 Cal.3d 727, 537 P.2d 406 (1975); cf. Jesse W. v. Superior Court, 20 Cal.3d 893, 576 P.2d 963 (1978).

It is not essential to decision in this case, however, to fix the precise time when jeopardy attaches.

proposals, and regardless of the presence or absence of exceptions, the judge is empowered to accept, modify or reject those proposals.

Finally, there is nothing in the record to indicate that the procedure authorized under Rule 911 unfairly subjects the defendant to the embarrassment, expense and ordeal of a second trial proscribed in Green v. United States, 355 U.S. 184, 78 S.Ct. 221, 2 L.Ed. 2d 199 (1957). Indeed, there is nothing to indicate that the juvenile is even brought before the judge while he conducts the "hearing on the record," or that the juvenile's attorney appears at the "hearing" and presents oral argument or written briefs. But even if there were such participation or appearance, the burdens are more akin to those resulting from a judge's permissible request for post-trial briefing or argument following a bench trial than to the "expense" of a full-blown second trial contemplated by the Court in *Green.*

In their effort to characterize a Rule 911 proceeding as two trials for double jeopardy purposes, appellees rely on two decisions of this Court, Breed v. Jones, 421 U.S. 519, 95 S.Ct. 1779, 44 L.Ed.2d 346 (1975), and United States v. Jenkins, 420 U.S. 358, 95 S.Ct. 1006, 43 L.Ed.2d 250 (1975).

In *Breed,* we held that a juvenile was placed twice in jeopardy when, after an adjudicatory hearing in juvenile court on a charge of delinquent conduct, he was transferred to adult criminal court, tried and convicted for the same conduct. All parties conceded that jeopardy attached at the second proceeding in criminal court. The State contended, however, that jeopardy did not attach in the juvenile court proceeding, although that proceeding could have culminated in a deprivation of the juvenile's liberty. We rejected this contention and also the contention that somehow jeopardy "continued" from the first to the second trial. *Breed* is therefore inapplicable to the Maryland scheme, where juveniles are subjected to only one proceeding, or "trial."

Appellees also stress this language from *Jenkins:*

"[I]t is enough for purposes of the Double Jeopardy Clause * * * that further proceedings of some sort, devoted to the resolution of factual issues, going to the elements of the offense charged, would have been required upon reversal and remand. *Even if the District Court were to receive no additional evidence, it would be necessary for it to make supplemental findings.* * * * [To do so] would violate the Double Jeopardy Clause." 420 U.S., at 370, 95 S.Ct., at 1013 (emphasis added).

Although we doubt that the Court's decision in a case can be correctly identified by reference to three isolated sentences, any language in *Jenkins* must now be read in light of our subsequent decision in United States v. Scott, 437 U.S. 82, 98 S.Ct. 2187, 57 L.Ed. 2d 65 (1978). In *Scott* we held that it is not all proceedings requiring the making of supplemental findings that are barred by the Double Jeopardy Clause but only those that follow a previous trial ending in an acquittal, in a conviction either not reversed on appeal or reversed because of insufficient evidence, see Burks v. United States, supra, or in a mistrial ruling not prompted by "manifest necessity," see Arizona v. Washington, supra. A Juvenile Court judge's decision terminating a Rule 911 proceeding follows none of those occurrences. Furthermore, *Jenkins* involved appellate review of the final judgment of a trial court fully empowered to enter that judgment. Nothing comparable occurs in a Rule 911 proceeding. See n. 15, supra.

To the extent the Juvenile Court judge makes supplemental findings in a manner permitted by Rule 911—either *sua sponte*, in response to the State's exceptions, or in response to the juvenile's exceptions, and either on the record or on a record supplemented by evidence to which the parties raise no objection—he does so without violating the constraints of the Double Jeopardy Clause.

Accordingly, we reverse and remand for further proceedings consistent with this opinion.

It is so ordered.

MR. JUSTICE MARSHALL, with whom MR. JUSTICE BRENNAN and MR. JUSTICE POWELL join, dissenting [omitted].

––––––––

STATE IN THE INTEREST OF J.J.

Juvenile and Domestic Relations Court of Camden County, 1975.
132 N.J.Super. 464, 334 A.2d 80.

KING, J.C.C., Temporarily Assigned.

The juvenile was charged with the offense of breaking and entering into and larceny from a public school building on January 6, 1974. He appeared in the Camden County Juvenile and Domestic Relations Court at an informal hearing with his parents and without counsel on March 13, 1974 and admitted the allegations charged in the petition. The trial judge adjudicated the juvenile delinquent and placed him on probation for one year. His probation was conditioned upon obtaining entry into the Job Corps and in the interim attending weekly sessions at the probation office.

In July, 1974 a violation of probation was filed against the juvenile because he failed to fulfill the conditions of probation. A hearing on the violation of probation was scheduled. The original hearing court also scheduled a formal hearing on the original breaking and entering and larceny charges and required counsel to be present in the event that if an adjudication of delinquency resulted following formal hearing a disposition of commitment could be entertained as a possible alternative. See R. 5:3–3, In re Gault, 387 U.S. 1, 87 S.Ct. 1428, 18 L.Ed.2d 527 (1967). The original trial judge then recused himself on his own motion because of his previous familiarity with the matter.

Juvenile now moves before this successor court to dismiss the charges on the ground that a second and formal hearing, with the implication of possible commitment, would violate his rights to due process of law and would place him twice in jeopardy for the same offense, contrary to the State and Federal Constitutions, and the provisions of the statute, N.J.S.A. 2A:4–60. No suggestive or controlling precedent is available for the resolution of this problem.

A similar situation was considered in State in the Interest of G.J., 108 N.J.Super. 186, 260 A.2d 513 (App.Div.1969), cert. den. 55 N.J. 447, 262 A.2d 702 (1970). There the juvenile was not represented by counsel in the original informal proceeding at which she was adjudicated delinquent and placed on probation for chronic truancy. Subsequently, juvenile's absence from school persisted and she was charged with a violation of probation. At a formal hearing with *Gault* safeguards, including counsel, the court found that her continued truancy from school constituted a probation violation and her disposition was a commitment to the State Home for Girls. On appeal the juvenile urged that the commitment was illegal because it was based on a violation of probation resulting from her original determination of delinquency occurring at an informal hearing without counsel. The Appellate Division rejected that argument, reasoning that the commitment to the State Home was actually based on a new substantive finding of delinquency resulting from continuing truancy, rather than on a finding of a violation of probation. The fact that the matter came before the court on a violation of probation was not determinative so long as the underlying offense, chronic truancy, was sufficient in itself to support an adjudication and subsequent commitment.

In the present case the alleged violations of probation—failing to obtain entry into the Job Corps and failing to attend weekly counselling sessions as ordered—could not support an independent adjudication of delinquency. The case of *G.J.* indicates that a court may not commit a juvenile for violation of probation alone, regardless of need for commitment or representation by counsel at the probation violation, if the original probation emanated from an uncounselled informal adjudication. The only possible way this present court may consider all of the options available in the treatment of this juvenile, including commitment or the threat of commitment if probation is not successful, would be to conduct a formal hearing on the original charges with all of the *Gault* safeguards, including counsel.

The pertinent section of the statute reads as follows:

> All defenses available to an adult charged with a crime, offense or violation shall be available to a juvenile charged with committing an act of delinquency.

> All cases arising under this act not referred as provided by sections 7 or 8 shall be heard and decided by the juvenile and domestic relations court without a jury. The right to be secure from unreasonable searches and seizures, the right not to be placed twice in jeopardy for the same offense, and the right of due process of law shall be applicable in cases arising under this act as in cases of persons charged with crime. [N.J.S.A. 2A:4–60]

This provision became effective on March 1, 1974 as part of the so-called "JINS" law (Juveniles In Need of Supervision), N.J.S.A. 2A:4–42 et seq., which concerns jurisdiction and proceedings in the juvenile court. A review of the legislative history available to the court is not enlightening as to any special intent or design to be implied by the inclusion of the proscription against double jeopardy in the legislation. In the absence of any special mention the court can only conclude a legislative intent to restate the historic common law and constitutional concept of jeopardy as a reminder that they pertain to our juvenile justice system. This court has no doubt that our State Supreme Court and Federal Supreme Court would find traditional concepts of double jeopardy "selectively incorporated" into a juvenile justice system if faced with the issue, and this court premises its opinion on such an anticipated ruling.

* * *

The constitutional and statutory safeguards against double jeopardy assure that the State with its great resources and awesome power will not be permitted to harass and oppress the individual citizen with multiple prosecutions or punishments for the same offense. State v. Currie, 41 N.J. 531, 535, 197 A.2d 678 (1964); State v. Sims, 65 N.J. 359, 371, 322 A.2d 809 (1974). The *Currie* decision emphasized that "in applying the prohibition against double jeopardy, the emphasis should be on underlying policies rather than technisms. The primary purpose should be fairness and fulfillment of reasonable expectations in the light of the constitutional and common law goals." 41 N.J. at 539, 197 A.2d at 683.

In the present case the elements of harassment and oppression do not appear involved. The initial informal hearing afforded a somewhat minimally restrictive mode of treatment for the situation without any possible exposure to the serious consequence of incarceration. This initial informal hearing approach was not one required of the State but was afforded to the juvenile in the best spirit of *parens patriae*, hopefully to provide a less harsh remedy to resolve what the initial trial judge sincerely believed to be a budding and potentially serious problem. Certainly in dealing with all juvenile problems the court initially resorts to the least severe and restrictive feasible measure in an effort to find a solution. But that measure did not work here. As a result of the informal adjudication the juvenile was never in danger of a custodial disposition. His exposure to a formal hearing and its potential for an actual or suspended custodial sentence arises not from any capricious, whimsical or malicious activity by the State but from his own failure to fulfill the consensual terms of his probation.

The creation of the two types of hearings, formal and informal (essentially the requirement of counsel distinguishes the two), was an immediate consequence of *Gault* and was formalized by prior court rule, R. 5:9–1(c)–(e) (1967 rule amended in 1974). The dichotomy has since been deleted from the rules, but the practice continues in effect, both at the adjudicative level as well as at the initial intake level.

The informal hearing allows the court to deal with each case in a uniquely flexible, speedy and individualized fashion. This procedure is similar to the pretrial diversionary program under R. 3:28 and the motion-to-suspend-proceeding in controlled dangerous substance possession cases under N.J.S.A. 24:21–27 where the matter is returned to court if the adult offender does not comply with the program. Jeopardy should not attach simply because the State agrees to the less onerous procedure.

Following an informal hearing the court may order any disposition specified in N.J.S.A. 2A:4–61 except commitment. Subsection (c) enables the court to place a delinquent juvenile on probation for a period not to exceed three years "upon such written conditions as the court deems will aid rehabilitation of the juvenile." Obviously the court must have some means by which to encourage compliance with the conditions of probation, or the entire process may become farcical and ineffective. To accept juvenile's position here would be to render the court powerless in its efforts to deal with a potentially serious social problem. Indeed, if further indifference to probation persists, a suspended sentence following a formal adjudication with the realistic alternative of incarceration may in many instances be sufficient to motivate cooperation with the probation program by the otherwise indifferent juvenile. Once the court's acknowledged impotent posture is publicized through the "grapevine" the entire process of informally adjudicated probation, so often to the benefit of the juvenile and society is jeopardized and demoralized. Havoc could be created in the probation programs presently being utilized; general disrespect or the dilution of institutional morale in the probation department could follow.

A finding here in favor of juvenile's contention of double jeopardy would effectively oust the court of any meaningful jurisdiction over the child and deprive the State of any chance of helping the juvenile unless he commits another serious offense. This approach is not consistent with the historical philosophy of the juvenile court or the legislative intent. An institutional result would be the requirement of formal hearings in all cases in order to insure the meaningful enforcement of probation in the few where such enforcement is necessary. The court does not feel that compelling the juvenile to appear now at a first formal hearing, protected by the safeguards of *Gault* and its progeny, violates any fundamental right of the juvenile. Certainly any inculpatory statements made by the juvenile at the initial uncounselled informal hearing would not be admissible at the formal hearing. Cf. State v. Boone, 66 N.J. 38, 327 A.2d 661 (1974). On balance, the interests of the juvenile are well protected at all stages by this result.

It should be added that if the juvenile desires to urge prejudice as a result of a delay in his formal adjudicative hearing, this court will be alert to his contentions and give consideration to such an application within the confines of the principles as stated in Barker v. Wingo, 407 U.S. 514, 92 S.Ct. 2182, 33 L.Ed.2d 101 (1972); State v.

Davis, 131 N.J.Super. 484, 330 A.2d 601 (App.Div.1974), and State v. Smith, 131 N.J.Super. 354, 330 A.2d 29 (App.Div.1974), insofar as they relate to the juvenile justice system. Motion to dismiss is denied and the matter will be promptly listed for a formal hearing before a judge unacquainted with the matter.

NOTE

To what extent, if at all, do the protections against double jeopardy apply to in need of supervision (non-delinquency) proceedings? In In the Interest of R.L.K., 67 Ill.App.3d 451, 23 Ill.Dec. 737, 384 N.E.2d 531 (1978) a MINS (minor in need of supervision) petition was filed which was dismissed by the juvenile court after hearing on failure of proof. The state then filed a delinquency petition alleging law violations arising out of the same transaction. The Illinois court held that the state criminal code provisions dealing with compulsory joinder and principles of double jeopardy prevented the state from proceeding on the delinquency petition. The court noted that the sole dispositional difference between MINS and delinquency cases is that only in the latter may the respondent be committed to the Juvenile Division of the Department of Corrections. The court then concluded:

> Thus, because the potential consequences of a MINS and a delinquency determination are substantially similar—including the stigma associated with both proceedings—the protection afforded delinquents by the compulsory adjoinder and double jeopardy provisions of the Criminal Code should be applied to MINS children. * * * Moreover, the double jeopardy clause embodied in the fifth amendment of the United States Constitution and applied to the states through the due process clause of the fourteenth amendment also should apply in MINS cases as well as juvenile delinquency proceedings.

Id. at 534–35.

D. NOTICE OF CHARGES

1. SPECIFICITY

IN INTEREST OF BRYANT

Illinois Appellate Court, 1974.
18 Ill.App.3d 887, 310 N.E.2d 713.

ADESKO, PRESIDING JUSTICE: A petition for adjudication of a minor as a delinquent was filed on August 26, 1972, against Bobby Bryant, respondent in this appeal, charging that he had committed the offenses of battery upon Officer Robert Brennan and aggravated assault upon Officer Michael Duffin. After a hearing on November 21, 1972, the court made a finding of delinquency on both counts and a social investigation was called for by the court. Respondent appeals this finding and contends that:

> (1) The petition for the adjudication of a minor as a delinquent failed to allege that the officer was engaged in the execution of his official duties and was, therefore, insufficient to charge aggravated battery;

* * *

The petition asking that Bobby Bryant be adjudicated a delinquent charges him as follows regarding the aggravated battery:

"In that Bobby A. Bryant has on 25 August 1972 at Cook County, Illinois, committed the offense of Aggravated Battery in that he knowing Robert Brennan to be a Chicago Policeman Peace Officer did intentionally, without legal justification caused bodily harm by striking Officer Brennan in the mouth with a broom handle knocking out three teeth of Officer Brennan without legal justification, in violation of Chapter 38, Section 12–4(b) (6) Illinois Revised Statutes."

Respondent submits that this charge fails to include an essential element of the offense of aggravated battery in that it is not stated that the officer was "engaged in the execution of any of his official duties." (Ill.Rev.Stat.1971, ch. 38, par. 12–4(b)(6).) In support of this position, respondent submits the case of People v. Bailey, 10 Ill.App. 3d 191, 293 N.E.2d 186. In *Bailey* a conviction for aggravated battery brought under an indictment similar to the aggravated battery charge in the instant case was reversed due to the insufficiency of the indictment. The court there stated:

"On appeal, defendant's sole contention is that the indictment is void. In pertinent part the indictment charged:

" '* * * that Johnny Bailey * * * committed the offense of *Aggravated Battery* in violation of Paragraph 12–4, Chapter 38, Illinois Revised Statutes, 1969, in that he, the defendant, knowing one Paul Nusbaum to then and there be a police officer of the City of Dixon, Illinois, did intentionally and knowingly without legal justification, cause bodily harm to the said Paul Nusbaum by kicking him * * *.'

"Although no subsection of Section 12–4 is set forth in the indictment, we presume from the verbiage used that defendant was charged under Section 12–4(b)(6), which provides that a person is guilty of aggravated battery who:

" '* * * in committing a battery * * * knows the individual harmed to be a peace officer * * * engaged in the execution of any of his official duties * * *.'

"According to this statute, a simple battery inflicted upon a police officer constitutes an aggravated battery only if the officer is 'engaged in the execution of any of his official duties.' See People v. Spears, 106 Ill.App.2d 430, 435–436, 245 N.E.2d 544 (1969).

"The instant indictment does not set forth an essential element of the offense in that there is no allegation that the police officer was engaged in the execution of his official duties. This element cannot be inferred, as the State alleges, from the wording 'knowing one Paul Nusbaum, to then and there be a police officer.' " (10 Ill.App.3d 192, 293 N.E.2d 186.)

If we were dealing with an adult criminal proceeding, the above case would quite clearly be dispositive of this issue. The State does not dispute this, but rather argues that since the instant case involved a juvenile proceeding, that the petition in regards to the aggravated battery was sufficient.

The Juvenile Court Act provides that a minor may be adjudicated a delinquent for the violation or attempted violation of any federal or state law or municipal ordinance. (Ill.Rev.Stat.1971, ch. 37, par. 702–2.) The State, based on this provision, argues that a delinquency petition is sufficient if it charges a minor with any act which, if proven, would allow the court to adjudicate the minor a delinquent. In the instant case, it is argued that the petition is sufficient to properly charge respondent with "lesser included offense of battery." The State further submits that these petitions are "quasi-criminal" in nature and should not be "construed with the same narrow scope as applied to the sufficiency of a criminal information, complaint, or indictment." We disagree.

This question is controlled by the opinion of the United States Supreme Court, In re Gault, 387 U.S. 1, 87 S.Ct. 1428, 18 L.Ed.2d 527. Mr. Justice Fortas, delivering the opinion of the court in that case, discussed the type of notice that due process requires be given in a juvenile petition:

"* * * Notice, to comply with due process requirements, must be given sufficiently in advance of scheduled court proceedings so that reasonable opportunity to prepare will be afforded, and it must '*set forth the alleged misconduct with particularity.*' [note]

"* * * Notice at that time is not timely; and even if there were a conceivable purpose served by the deferral proposed by the court below, *it would have to yield to the requirements that the child and his parents or guardian be notified, in writing, of the specific charge or factual allegations to be considered at the hearing, and that such written notice be given at the hearing*, and that such written notice be given at the earliest practicable time, and in any event sufficiently in advance of the hearing to permit preparation. *Due process of law requires notice of the sort we have described—that is, notice which would be deemed constitutionally adequate in a civil or criminal proceeding.* [note] *It does not allow a hearing to be held in which a youth's freedom and his parents' right to his custody are at stake without giving them timely notice, in advance of the hearing, of the specific issues that they must meet.*" (387 U.S. 33–34, 87 S.Ct. 1446, emphasis added.)

The Illinois Supreme Court, in the case In re Urbasek, 38 Ill.2d 535, 232 N.E.2d 716, adopted the reasoning of the *Gault* decision. Based on *Gault* the court held, *inter alia*, that due process in a juvenile court delinquency proceeding required "adequate advance notice of the charges, the right to counsel, the privilege against self-incrimination and the right to confrontation and cross-examination of witnesses." (38 Ill.2d 540, 232 N.E.2d 719.) The State's argument that notice and other aspects of a juvenile proceeding need not be construed in the same "narrow" manner as an adult criminal proceeding cannot stand in light of the decision in *Gault*. (Though cited and thoroughly discussed by respondent in his brief as the principal support for his argument, the *Gault* decision is not distinguished or discussed by the State in its answering brief.) The "quasi-criminal" concept and the related justification for procedural shortcomings, that the proceedings were "for the protection of the child", were rejected by the court in *Gault*. As was stated in *Urbasek:*

> "We note that this interpretation of the *Gault* decision is in direct conflict with the ruling of the District of Columbia Court of Appeals in In re Wylie, (D.C.App.) 231 A.2d 81, which refused to depart from its earlier decision in In re Bigesby, D.C.App., 202 A.2d 785, where it held that the injection of the criminal law concept of guilty beyond a reasonable doubt into 'civil' delinquency proceedings would be 'both unnecessary and improper.' (202 A.2d at 786.) We believe, however, that the reasoning of that court does not comport with the recurrent theme of the majority in *Gault* which equated many aspects of a delinquency adjudication with a criminal conviction." (38 Ill.2d 540, 232 N.E.2d 719.)

Due process of law requires that a juvenile, in the same manner as an adult, be notified of the charges against him. The charges must "set forth with particularity the misconduct upon which the delinquency petition was based", so that the juvenile will be able to prepare a proper defense and conduct "such investigation [of the charges] as may be necessary." (In re Interest of Carson, 10 Ill.App. 3d 387, 389, 294 N.E.2d 75, 77.) In the instant case, the part of the petition relating to the alleged aggravated battery is clearly inadequate in this regard and the finding that respondent committed the offense is hereby reversed. It is not necessary, therefore, for us to consider respondent's other contention, that the State failed to prove the offense of aggravated battery beyond a reasonable doubt.

* * *

NOTES

1. "We reaffirm our position that a petition which institutes a youth court proceeding must recite factual allegations specific and definite enough to fairly apprise the juvenile, his parents, custodians or guardians of the particular act or acts of misconduct or the particular circumstances which will be inquired into at the adjudicatory proceedings.

"We further hold that in those cases where a charge of delinquency is based upon the violation of a criminal law, the petition must charge the offense with the same particularity required in a criminal indictment. The petition in this case fails to meet these standards and is therefore insufficient to support the committal of Dennis to a training school."

In re Interest of Dennis, 291 So.2d 731, 733 (Miss.1974).

2. "The first question raised is whether the petition was insufficient because of its failure to state with particularity the charges against the three youths. In substance, the petition charged that (1) on or about May 11, 1973, the minors involved were attending the Philadelphia Public Schools and were involved in an assault and battery on school officials and others;

(2) the minors are guilty of acts which make them delinquent children and wayward children; and (3) on other occasions the minors have engaged in assaults and been unruly children.

"These indefinite allegations are wholly insufficient to invoke the limited jurisdiction of the Youth Court. See In Interest of Dennis, a Minor, Miss., 291 So.2d 731 (1974)."

In re Triplett, 292 So.2d 171, 172 (Miss.1974).

3. Does a petition alleging that a youth

"did wilfully, unlawfully, feloniously, take, steal and carry away on the dates hereinafter mentioned the property hereinafter described: 8/23/72, a 1968 Ford Pickup; 8/25/72, a 1967 Mustang; on 8/28/72, a Malibu, all of a value of $2,000.00."

meet the specificity requirements of *Dennis*, supra? See In Interest of Burnworth, 293 So.2d 461, 462 (Miss.1974). Held: Not sufficient.

4. Contrast People v. Longley, 16 Ill.App.3d 405, 306 N.E.2d 527 (1973):

"Respondent contends that 'assuming that the State meant to charge Respondent with a violation of Ch. 38, Sec. 24–1, that Section called Unlawful Use of Weapons, the charge is still inadequate.' Respondent argues that the only part of this statute which could conceivably fit the factual situation of this case is Sec. 24–1(a)(4) which states:

" '(a) A person commits the offense of unlawful use of weapons when he knowingly:

" '(4) Carries concealed *   *   * on or about his person except when on his land or in his own abode or fixed place of business any pistol, revolver or other firearm; *   *   *' "

"Respondent contends that because the allegation of concealment was not made in the petition, the petition was ineffective.

"The petition which was filed in the Circuit Court of Cook County recited in relevant part that 'Gary Longley knowingly carried on or about his person a pistol.'

"We are of the opinion that it is not an absolute requirement for this statute to use the word 'concealed' because the phrase 'On or about his person' refers to carrying a weapon readily available for use. People v. Hunt, 272 Ill.App. 496.

"In addition, the offense of 'Unlawful Use of Weapons' can now, contrary to respondent's contention, be proved by Chapter 38, Paragraph 24–1(a)(10) (Ill.Rev.Stat.1972 Supp., ch. 38, par. 24–1(a)(10)) which provides:

" '(a) A person commits the offense of unlawful use of weapons when he knowingly:

" 'Carries or possesses in a vehicle or on or about his person within the corporate limits of a city, village or incorporated town, except when on his land or in his own abode or fixed place of business, any loaded pistol, revolver or other firearm.'

"We believe that it is significant to observe that Chapter 38, Paragraph 24–1(a)(10) requires no allegation of 'concealment.'

"Moreover, it is not necessary that a petition contain all the language of the statute on the subject. It is sufficient if it states the offense in the terms and language of the statute creating the offense or states the offense in language sufficiently explicit that the defendant may know the nature of the charge against him. People v. Love, 310 Ill. 558, 142 N.E. 204.

"In the present case the petition adequately advised respondent of the nature of the charge against him. Therefore respondent's contention is without merit."

Id. at 409–10, 306 N.E.2d at 530–1.

5. Some defects or inaccuracies are disregarded both in criminal and juvenile cases. Consider *Longley*, supra:

On February 2, 1972, a petition for adjudication of Wardship was filed in the Circuit Court of Cook County alleging that respondent, Gary Darwin Longley, a minor, had committed the offense of Unlawful Use of Weapons. Specifically the petition alleged that respondent "knowingly carried on or about his person a pistol, Meltor .25 caliber automatic pistol serial 259178–265494, in violation of Chapter 38, Section 24–124 (sic), Illinois Revised Statutes." On March 2, 1972, at the conclusion of a hearing conducted concerning the petition, respondent was adjudged to be a delinquent. He appeals.

When this case was called for hearing on March 1, 1972, the Assistant State's Attorney informed the trial judge that the People were ready to proceed and that the petition alleged a violation of Unlawful Use of Weapons, "Chapter 38, Section 24–1–4." Respondent's counsel stated that he was "ready for trial" and requested that the trial judge hear the respondent's motion to suppress.

Respondent contends that the petition for adjudication of Wardship failed to allege a violation of law. The petition for adjudication of Wardship filed in the Circuit Court of Cook County on February 2, 1972, states in relevant part as follows:

"In that Gary Darwin Longley has on, or about 1 Feb. 72 at Cook County, Illinois, committed the offense of Unlawful Use of Weapons in that he, knowingly carried on or about his person a pistol; Meltor .25 Cal. automatic pistol serial 259178–265494, in violation of Chapter 38, Section 24–124 (sic), Illinois Revised Statutes."

Respondent contends that the failure of the People to specify the correct section, namely Ill.Rev.Stat.1971, ch. 38, par. 24–1(a) 4, is reversible error. Both parties to this appeal are in agreement that the allegations in the petition for adjudication of Wardship must meet the requirements of an indictment.

We are of the opinion that the incorrect citation in the petition is a formal defect and cannot be considered reversible error. Ill.Rev.Stat. 1971, ch. 38, par. 111–5; People v. Hampton, 105 Ill.App.2d 228, 245 N.E.2d 47.

Respondent also contends that the petition advised him that he has violated a "non-existent statute" (Chapter 38, Section 24–124 (sic)) and there was no way to prepare a defense to such a charge.

We are of the opinion that respondent was apprised with reasonable certainty of the offense with which he was being charged. The petition specifically stated that the respondent was being charged with "Unlawful Use of Weapons," and there was a full description of the pistol and the date of the offense. Moreover, on March 1, 1972, at the hearing on respondent's motion to suppress, the Assistant State's Attorney indicated the statute upon which the People were proceeding. In the presence of respondent's counsel, the Assistant State's Attorney stated to the court: "Your Honor, this is a petition alleging Unlawful Use of Weapon; Chapter 38, Section 24–1–4, [24–1(a)(4)]. The State is ready for trial."

Respondent's counsel stated, "The defendant (respondent) is ready for trial at this time * * *." The preceding colloquy indicates that there was adequate notice of the charge being adjudicated with full acceptance and understanding by respondent's counsel before the trial commenced.

We are of the opinion that the respondent was fully informed of the charge and he has no solid ground upon which to complain.

Id. at 406–09, 306 N.E.2d at 529–30.

2. VARIANCE AND AMENDMENT

D.P. v. STATE

Georgia Court of Appeals, 1973.
129 Ga.App. 680, 200 S.E.2d 499.

SYLLABUS OPINION BY THE COURT

STOLZ, JUDGE. The appellant, a juvenile, was brought before the Juvenile Court of Fulton County on a petition alleging his delinquency in that he had committed the offense of burglary. Upon hearing the evidence, the court found that the evidence failed to show beyond a reasonable doubt that the juvenile had committed burglary. The court did find that the juvenile had committed the offense of theft by receiving stolen goods. The court adjudicated the juvenile a delinquent in need of supervision and rehabilitation, and placed him on probation, from which judgment the juvenile appeals. *Held:*

* * *

2. The appellant contends that there is a fatal variance between the offense *alleged* as the basis for delinquency (burglary) and the offense *found* as the basis for the adjudication of his delinquency (receiving stolen goods).

While cases in the juvenile court are not criminal proceedings, Code Ann. § 24A–2401 (Ga.L.1971, pp. 709, 736), due process must always be scrupulously adhered to.

The statutory contents of petitions alleging delinquency are set out in Code Ann. § 24A–1603 (Ga.L.1971, pp. 709, 726). Here it should be noted that former Code Ann. § 24–2411 (Ga.L.1951, pp. 291, 299; 1968, pp. 1013, 1022), which was repealed by Ga.L.1971, pp. 709, 756, and concerned itself with the same subject matter, contained the following: "In addition, the petition shall set forth, with specificity, the Federal, State or local law or municipal ordinance alleged to have been violated or attempted to have been violated, either in the terms and language of the particular code, or so plainly that the nature of the offense charged may easily be understood by the child and his parents or guardian."

The offense of receiving known stolen goods is "an offense wholly dissimilar from burglary in its nature and characteristics. One is accomplished by the presence and use of active force * * * whilst in the other is an utter absence of every element of burglary, as well as a transaction totally distant in time, place, circumstances, grade and punishment; one a felony, the other a misdemeanor."

Gilbert v. State, 65 Ga. 449, 451. "Under the Criminal Code of Georgia, Section 26–1806, theft by receiving stolen property (a misdemeanor) requires a receiving, disposing or retaining of stolen property which the accused knows or should know was stolen (Ga.L.1968, pp. 1249, 1292; 1969, pp. 857, 859) while the offense of burglary (Criminal Code § 26–1601) requires an entering or remaining in a building without authority with intent to commit a felony or theft therein. Nowhere is there an allegation of receiving, disposing or retaining of stolen property." Gearin v. State, 127 Ga.App. 811, 812, 195 S.E.2d 211, 212.

We must now address ourselves to the resolution of two questions: (1) Since Code Ann. § 24A–1603 requires only "a statement that it is in the best interest of the child and the public that the proceeding be brought and, if delinquency or unruly conduct is alleged, that the child is in need of supervision, treatment or rehabilitation, as the case may be", is the allegation that the juvenile committed burglary merely surplusage? (2) Must the petition set forth with specificity the alleged violation of law either in the language of the particular code, or so plainly that the nature of the offense charged may be easily understood by the child and his parents or guardian?

Question (1) is answered in the negative. Question (2) is answered in the affirmative.

In In re Gault, 387 U.S. 1, 87 S.Ct. 1428, 1446, 18 L.Ed.2d 527, the landmark Arizona juvenile case, the petition recited only that " * * * said minor is a delinquent minor and that it is necessary that some order be made by the Honorable Court for said minor's welfare."

The Arizona statute specifically provided for such a general allegation, and the Arizona Supreme Court held that the petition need recite only a conclusion of delinquency. In Gault, supra, p. 33, 87 S.Ct. p. 1446, the United States Supreme Court rejected these contentions, stating: "Notice, to comply with due process requirements, must be given sufficiently in advance of scheduled court proceedings so that reasonable opportunity to prepare will be afforded, and it must *set forth the alleged misconduct with particularity.* * * * Due process of law requires notice of the sort we have described— that is, notice which would be deemed constitutionally adequate in a civil or criminal proceeding. It does not allow a hearing to be held in which a youth's freedom and his parents' right to his custody are at stake without giving them timely notice, in advance of the hearing, of the *specific issues* that they must meet." (Emphases supplied.)

In the case at bar, the constitutionality of the statute (Code Ann. § 24A–1603, supra) is not attacked. If it had been, the Supreme Court, not this court, would have jurisdiction of this appeal. However, the appellant does contend, with justification, that he had no notice that the charge upon which his delinquency might be based would be changed from burglary to receiving stolen goods. Consequently, the defendant did not subpoena a material witness in defending the receiving stolen goods charge because the witness had no knowledge of the alleged burglary offense. As previously shown, the offense of receiving stolen goods is not a lesser included offense within the crime of burglary. Gearin v. State, supra.

Consequently, there was insufficient notice to the juvenile of the offense alleged to be the basis for his delinquency, and the judgment of the trial court must be reversed.

Judgment reversed.

EBERHARDT, P.J., and PANNELL, J., concur.

STATE IN THE INTEREST OF SIMON

Louisiana Court of Appeals, 1974.
295 So.2d 473.

Before FRUGÉ, HOOD and WATSON, JJ.

WATSON, JUDGE. This is an appeal from the judgment of a juvenile court, appellate jurisdiction being vested in this court by Article 7, Section 29 of the Louisiana Constitution of 1921, as amended.

Following a hearing in the juvenile court, the appellant was committed to the Department of Corrections, State of Louisiana, under a judgment which reads as follows:

"It is therefore ordered, adjudged and decreed that James Lynell Simon, a minor born the 23rd day of September, 1959, is adjudged a child who has committed an offense not classified as criminal but who is in need of supervision, care and rehabilitation and is committed to the care of the Department of Corrections, State of Louisiana, for an indefinite period not to exceed his majority." (Tr. 5).

On appeal, counsel for the appellant contends that the juvenile court erred in committing appellant. The specific argument is that, when the state failed to establish that appellant had violated the specific statute with which he was charged, the juvenile court made the commitment on another ground, as stated in the judgment quoted above.

A juvenile proceeding is initiated by the filing of a petition under LSA–R.S. 13:1574. This statute outlines the methods by which juvenile proceedings are commenced and provides for the contents of the petition, including the following requirements:

C. The petition shall set forth with specificity:

1. The facts which bring the child within the provisions of this chapter, together with a statement, when delinquency is alleged, that the child is in need of supervision, care, or rehabilitation. If a violation of law is the basis for filing the petition, the petition shall cite the statute or municipal ordinance which the child is alleged to have violated;

In the case before us a petition was filed on March 15, 1974 by the District Attorney of the Thirty-first Judicial District. It is not contended that the petition is defective. Appellant's claim is that the petition sets forth the information required by LSA–R.S. 13:1574, but that he was committed for some other charge or offense. The portion of the petition which is pertinent to the contention being made by appellant, reads as follows:

"* * * said child is within the provisions of Title 13, Sections 1569, et seq., and is a child in need of supervision, care, and rehabilitation for having committed the following delinquent act, to-wit: On or about January 18, 1974, James L. Simon did unlawfully commit the crime of receiving stolen things by receiving one ring, valued at $250.00, property of Mrs. Wade Lormand, under circumstances which indicate that the said James L. Simon knew or had good reason to believe that the said ring was the subject of a theft, in violation of L.R.S. 14:69."

Facts

The facts surrounding the alleged offense, as developed by the hearing in juvenile court, are that the appellant was given a ring to hold by another youth during a physical education class. The appellant, according to the testimony of the other youth, put the ring in his pocket, and later in the day, the appellant was requested to return the ring. The appellant, again according to the other youth, said he did not have the ring so the other youth complained to the school principal. The appellant was summoned from his class and instructed to get the ring from his locker. When appellant returned from the locker area, he told the principal that he had lost the ring coming up the stairs. The youth who gave appellant the ring later searched for it, but, according to his testimony, he was unable to find the ring. On cross-examination, it was developed that the youth had not told appellant that the ring was stolen. He apparently led appellant to believe that he had purchased the ring.

The school principal confirmed that he had called appellant in, that appellant informed him that the ring was in his locker and that appellant was instructed to bring it to the office. The principal testified further that when appellant came back, he reported that he had lost the ring.

Another witness was a thirteen year old youth who testified that appellant had asked him to help look for the ring. He indicated that he did not actually search for it because he was in a hurry.

The only other witness to testify was a State Juvenile Probation and Parole Officer, Joe Fairfield. This officer testified that he knew appellant and that he had consulted with him about the loss of the ring. He testified that he had also discussed the matter with appellant's parents. Mr. Fairfield also described his search for the ring at the school building, which actually appears to have been an attempt to duplicate the loss of the ring or determine the likelihood of an occurrence such as appellant had described previously to the probation officer.　The substance of Mr. Fairfield's testimony was that the story told to him by appellant as to how the ring was lost was improbable.

Appellant did not testify but invoked his constitutional privilege not to do so.　Clearly, a juvenile is not required to testify if he chooses to remain silent and this is not to be construed against him. Amendment V, United States Constitution; LSA–R.S. 13:1579.

*　*　*

Reasons for Judgment

After hearing the witnesses whose testimony is reviewed above, the juvenile court signed a judgment in the terms previously quoted. However, to fully state the decision of the juvenile court it is necessary to also quote the reasons assigned in open court for the judgment rendered and the exchange in court between the juvenile judge and the attorney for appellant.　It was as follows:

"THE COURT: The Court is going to rule in the matter that this child is in need of supervision, care, and rehabilitation.　The Court does not feel that he had knowledge of the fact that he was receiving stolen things, but the Court does feel that he was at fault in taking this ring and not returning it.

"The Court does not believe that the ring was lost; the Court does believe that he either still has this ring, or that he has disposed of it at his own—at his own ends.　And for this reason, The Court feels that he is in need of supervision, care, and rehabilitation and will assign him to the diagnostic center.

"MR. GUIDRY: Your Honor, we understand the ruling.　As I understand, the Defendant was charged specifically with receiving stolen goods and that it is the ruling of the Court that he is not guilty of—

"THE COURT: He's not guilty of this, but he is in need of supervision for the reason that he did know that this ring did not belong to him; he took the ring, he did not return it.　It was in his locker; he said he lost it.　Mr. Fairfield has testified that he could not have lost it where he said he lost it.　The Court feels that the child did not tell the truth.　The child claimed the right against self incrimination; he would not talk to the Court.　This is a juvenile hearing and the Court thinks that under these circumstances, he certainly is in need of supervision of the State."

As to the charge of violating LSA–R.S. 14:69, Receiving Stolen Things, the juvenile judge obviously concluded that appellant did not know or have good reason to believe the ring was stolen.　He therefore held correctly that appellant had not violated the criminal statute; an essential element was not proved.　In re Glassberg, 230 La. 396, 88 So.2d 707 (1956); State v. Melanson, 259 So.2d 609 (La. App. 4 Cir.1972).

Issues

The issues thus presented for our determination are: (1) whether appellant was committed to the Department of Corrections, State of Louisiana, on a charge other than that specified by the petition filed against him; and (2) if so, is there a violation of his constitutional or statutory rights which would require that the commitment be set aside.

As to the first issue, a mere reading of the quoted portions of the judgment, the reasons for judgment, and the charge in the petition is sufficient to answer the first issue affirmatively. Appellant was found not to have committed the criminal offense alleged in the petition, but he was committed as being in need of supervision.

We have reflected on the question of whether the appellant was charged with being delinquent or merely in need of supervision, care or rehabilitation under the terms of LSA–R.S. 13:1569. We have concluded that appellant was in fact charged with delinquency even though it is not clear from the wording of the petition. Significant in this connection is the wording of the petition which refers to a "delinquent act" and which referred to a specific criminal law which was alleged to have been violated. Therefore, we determine that appellant was charged with being delinquent.

The second issue is whether in committing appellant, as being a child in need of supervision for having committed some other offense, the statutory and constitutional rights of the child were violated.

Notice of the specific charges against an accused, whether adult or juvenile, is fundamental to the law of the State of Louisiana and that of the United States. The Louisiana Constitution of 1921 requires an accused to be informed of the nature and cause of the accusation against him. Article 1, Section 10. Louisiana statutory law requires that a juvenile and his parents be informed of a specific charge against the youth. LSA–R.S. 13:1574, 13:1575. This is in accord with the notions of due process of law as provided by the Fourteenth Amendment of the Constitution of the United States. The United States Supreme Court, speaking of due process, has said:

> "It does not allow a hearing to be held in which a youth's freedom and his parents' right to his custody are at stake without giving them timely notice, in advance of the hearing, of the specific issues that they must meet." Application of Gault, supra, 87 S.Ct. 1428 at 1447.

This rule has been recognized in Louisiana. Judge Ellis writing for the First Circuit in In re State in Interest of Hampton, 257 So.2d 459 (La.App. 1 Cir.1972), summarized the requirement as follows:

> "* * * a juvenile may not be adjudged delinquent unless his guilt of the specific charges against him is shown in accordance with the foregoing principles. That is, a judge may not make a finding of delinquency based on misconduct other than that which is set forth in the petition. This would violate the constitu-

tional right of the juvenile to be notified of the charges against him." 257 So.2d 459 at 460.

It is important to note that appellant is only fourteen years of age. Under the terms of his commitment he could be held in an institution until age eighteen, a period of almost four years.

Our Louisiana courts have realized the serious consequences of commitment by a juvenile court. In State in Interest of Ogletree, 244 So.2d 288 (La.App. 4 Cir.1971), it was declared:

"The requirements of proof must be stringent if severe consequences flow from a finding of delinquency based on this proof. A juvenile should not be subjected to possibility of institutional confinement on proof insufficient to convict him if he were an adult. In re Winship, 397 U.S. 358, 90 S.Ct. 1068, 25 L.Ed.2d 368 (1970)." 244 So.2d 290.

We find that there was a violation of appellant's rights which requires setting aside the commitment.

* * *

HOOD, JUDGE (dissenting).

I am unable to concur in the majority opinion.

My colleagues have found that the juvenile, James L. Simon, "was in fact charged with delinquency." I do not agree. The petition seeks only to have him declared to be "a child in need of supervision, care and rehabilitation." There is no prayer in the petition that he be decreed to be delinquent, and the judgment rendered by the court does not find him to be delinquent. On the contrary, the court specifically decreed that he committed an offense *"not classified as criminal,"* and that because of the non-criminal offense which he committed, he is *"in need of supervision, care and rehabilitation."*

Under the provisions of LSA–R.S. 13:1561–1599, and particularly LSA–R.S. 13:1569 and 1579.1, proceedings may be instituted in a juvenile court to have a child declared to be any one of the following:

(a) Delinquent;

(b) Neglected or dependent;

(c) In need of supervision;

(d) In need of the protection of the state; or

(e) Abandoned.

A "delinquent child" is defined in LSA–R.S. 13:1569, as follows:

"14. 'Delinquent child' means a child who has committed a delinquent act and is in need of care or rehabilitation."

A "child in need of supervision" is defined in the same section as:

"15. 'Child in need of supervision' means a child who:

"a. Being subject to compulsory school attendance, is habitually truant from school; or "b.   habitually disobeys the reasonable and lawful demands of his parents, tutor, or other custodian, and is ungovernable and beyond their control; or

"c.   *has committed an offense not classified as criminal or one applicable only to children;* and

"d.   in any of the foregoing, is in need of care or rehabilitation."   (Emphasis added).

In this case the petition alleges and seeks to have the juvenile declared to be only a "child in need of supervision." It is true that the grounds alleged for seeking that relief are that he committed a criminal act, that is, receiving stolen property. I see no objection to alleging the commission of an offense which is more serious than necessary in order to support the prayer of the petition. And I believe that in this case, because of the allegation and prayer of the petition, the court could *not* have declared the child to be delinquent, even if all of the elements of the criminal offense of receiving stolen property had been proved. I do not subscribe to the view that since the petition alleges a criminal act as the basis for the relief sought, any judgment rendered by the court in response to that petition must be regarded as a declaration that the child is delinquent, and that the court cannot consider and grant the relief actually sought based on a lesser included offense.

The evidence produced at the hearing established that the child did receive a stolen ring, although he was not aware of the fact that it was stolen, that he knew that it was not his ring, and that he nevertheless kept the ring or disposed of it for his own use, and thus failed or refused to return it to the person who had intrusted it to him. In my opinion the boy committed an "offense," within the meaning of LSA–R.S. 13:1569(15), and the evidence thus is sufficient to support the decree of the trial court declaring him to be in need of supervision.

Actually, I think the evidence shows that the child committed the crime of "theft," as defined in LSA–R.S. 14:67. I concede that in criminal law the crime of theft may not be a lesser included criminal offense to the crime of receiving stolen things, but as will be pointed out later in this dissent, this case must be governed by the Code of Civil Procedure rather than procedures applied in criminal law. LSA–C.C.P. art. 891 provides that the petition shall contain a short, clear and concise statement of the object of the demand and of the material facts upon which the cause of action is based. The petition in this case sets out clearly all of the facts which were actually proved and on which the trial court based its decision. All of the requirements of the Code of Civil Procedure thus were met. In my view, the "offense" which was shown to have been committed by the boy was a lesser offense than the one alleged in the petition, and I think it clearly was included in the more serious one.

There certainly can be no objection to the trial judge's holding that the boy committed an "offense not classified as criminal," when he might properly have held that the offense actually committed was criminal in nature. Such a holding benefited the child, and the appellant thus has no right to complain of it.

Our laws make a distinction between a proceeding which seeks to have a child declared to be "delinquent" and a proceeding which seeks only to have him declared to be "in need of supervision." LSA–R.S. 13:1579, relating to hearings in the juvenile court, provides that, "The hearing shall be conducted in accordance with the general rules of procedure used in civil proceedings. * * *" LSA–R.S. 13:1579.1 provides:

> "The rules of evidence prevailing in proceedings governed by the Code of Civil Procedure shall be applicable to a proceeding to declare a child *delinquent*, neglected or dependent, *in need of supervision*, in need of the protection of the state or abandoned; provided, however, no child shall be adjudged to be *delinquent* in the absence of proof beyond a reasonable doubt that such condition exists." (Emphasis added).

It is apparent that in all juvenile proceedings, including those seeking to have a child declared to be delinquent, the rules of Civil Procedure are applicable, and it is only when a child is to be adjudged "delinquent" that the proof must be beyond a reasonable doubt.

The majority cites several cases as authority for their conclusion that the decree of the trial court must be reversed. The principal ones relied on are In re State in Interest of Hampton, 257 So.2d 459 (La.App. 1 Cir.1972); and State in Interest of Ogletree, 244 So.2d 288 (La.App. 4 Cir.1971). I find that none of those cases are applicable. Every case cited, except one, involved a judgment decreeing a child to be "delinquent." The case which did not involve such a circumstance was In re State In the Interest of Elliott, 206 So.2d 802 (La.App. 2 Cir.1968), but that case involved a proceeding against an adult. In the instant case the child was not found to be delinquent, and the petition never alleged or prayed that he be declared to be such.

IN RE APPEAL IN MARICOPA COUNTY, JUVENILE ACTION NO. J–75755

Supreme Court of Arizona, 1974.
111 Ariz. 103, 523 P.2d 1304.

LOCKWOOD, JUSTICE. This petition for review was filed on behalf of the State of Arizona pursuant to Rule 28(a), 17A A.R.S. by the Maricopa County Attorney. We have been asked to review the decision of the Court of Appeals in the Matter of the Appeal in Maricopa County Juvenile Action No. J–75755, 21 Ariz.App. 542, 521 P.2d 641 (1974). In that decision the Court of Appeals reversed an adjudication of delinquency by the juvenile court based on a finding that the juvenile had committed criminal trespass.

On April 9, 1973, a petition was filed in the juvenile court alleging that on or about March 30, 1973, the juvenile had committed burglary on the dwelling house of Lydia Gonzales and stole three dollars from her purse. On July 5, 1973 the hearing was held. The evidence presented at the hearing indicated that two other boys went into the house and took the money. The juvenile refused to accept any of the money. The juvenile took the stand in his own defense and testified concerning what transpired in the following manner:

"A. Well, we was walking along and then Ralph asked us, did we want to go break in this house. And we said: Well, we ain't going to break in; we ain't going to take nothing; we are just going to walk in, you know.

"And Ralph said, 'Well, I will take something,' and he went inside. Cory, he stayed outside. I went inside and then a purse was laying on the thing and then Ralph picked it up and took all the money out, and then he told me to come in and help him check the house over; and I said, 'No, I'm going back out.'

"Then he called me chicken and then I went back out, and then he started checking the house over. He went until he was through."

The court granted a motion for a directed verdict for the juvenile as to the charge of petty theft. In addition the court found that there was no burglary but found that there was sufficient evidence to support a charge of "trespass". Accordingly the court adjudicated the juvenile delinquent. On appeal the adjudication was reversed on the ground that trespass was not a lesser included offense of burglary.

The first issue raised by the petitioner is whether the crime of trespass for which the juvenile was found to have committed is a lesser included offense of burglary with which he was originally charged. The general rule is that the accused may be convicted of an offense different from that which he was charged only if it is an included offense. * * * This may occur under two circumstances: (1) the included offense is by its very nature always a constituent part of the major offense charged; or (2) the terms of the charging document describe the lesser offense even though the lesser offense would not always form a constituent part of the major offense charged. State v. Woody, 108 Ariz. 284, 496 P.2d 584 (1972).

The test to determine if an offense is a lesser included offense is whether the first (greater) offense cannot be committed without necessarily committing the second (lesser). * * *

Criminal trespass is defined by A.R.S. § 13–712(9) as:

"Loitering or prowling upon the private property of another, without the consent of or lawful business with the owner or occupant thereof."

Burglary is defined by A.R.S. § 13–302(A) as:

"* * * entering a building, dwelling house * * * with intent to commit grand or petty theft, or any felony, * * *."

Under certain circumstances a burglary can be committed where the accused had the permission of the owner of the property to be there. For example where the defendant had general permission to pass through the room of the victim in order to have access to his own room, but entered the victim's room with the intent to steal and did steal the victim's watch, he was guilty of burglary. The elements of breaking and unlawful entry were not essential to the statute. In McCreary v. State, 25 Ariz. 1, 212 P. 336 (1923) the court pointed out the distinction between statutory and common law burglary:

> "Much of the reasoning upon which this appeal is based is due to a misunderstanding of the meaning and scope of the statute defining burglary. The statutory burglary is widely different from the common-law crime of the same name, and the reasoning and decisions of the courts cited by appellant have to do with the common-law burglary, which involves a breaking, and have little application to the offense in which braking is not an element. The statutory offense involves no unlawfulness of entry, except as the entry becomes unlawful by reason of the felonious or larcenous intent of the person entering. If appellant entered the room of the complaining witness under general permission to do so for the purpose of going to and from his own room, but with larcenous intent, the burglary of the statute was committed. The courts of other states have many times applied statutes in which breaking is not an element of burglary to conditions similar to the facts of this case. In the case of People v. Barry, 94 Cal. 481, 29 P. 1026, decided in 1892, a larceny was committed in a grocery store during business hours, by a person who entered under the general invitation to the public to visit the store on lawful errands." 25 Ariz. at 2, 212 P. at 336.

Thus the fact that the defendant had permission to go in and out of a service station was no defense to statutory burglary of the station if he subsequently entered with intent to steal the cash register. State v. Owen, 94 Ariz. 354, 385 P.2d 227 (1963).

In State v. Miller, 108 Ariz. 441, 501 P.2d 383 (1972), this court held that because the burglary statute does not contain the common law requirement of breaking and entering and only requires a showing that the person entering the building with intent to commit theft or any felony, forcible trespass, A.R.S. § 13–711, is not a lesser included offense of burglary.

On the other hand the elements of trespass are loitering or prowling, on the property of another, and without the owner's permission. Thus it is apparent from the foregoing that the elements of the two offenses are different and that one is not a lesser included offense of the other.

Nevertheless the adjudication of delinquency may still be upheld. Rule 4(b), Rules of Procedure for the Juvenile Court, 17A A.R.S. provides that "A petition may be amended by order of the court at any time on its own motion or in response to the motion of any interested party before an adjudication; provided the parties are notified and granted sufficient time to meet the new allegations."

After hearing all the evidence presented by both sides, the juvenile court judge made the following statement:

"I think clearly there was a trespass and I think I perhaps stretch reasonable doubt when I say there was not a burglary here, as I think that is probably what the evidence discloses. But for reasons which I deem sufficient and wise, there will not be an adjudication of burglary. But I do find that there was a trespass and under the facts of this case, a lesser included offense. Accordingly, the Court finds and adjudicates [the juvenile] delinquent for that trespass."

It is apparent from the foregoing that the court had in effect amended the petition alleging acts of delinquency on the part of the juvenile. Under the circumstances of the case brought out by the testimony presented in court this was the proper response on the part of the juvenile court. However it appears from the record that the court should have permitted the parties sufficient opportunity to meet the new allegations. Therefore it is necessary to remand the case to the juvenile court in order to permit the parties an opportunity to address themselves to the allegation that the juvenile had committed trespass.

* * *

* * * [T]he opinion of the Court of Appeals is vacated and the case is remanded to the Juvenile Court for further proceedings not inconsistent with this opinion.

HAYS, C.J., CAMERON, V.C.J. and STRUCKMEYER and HOLOHAN, JJ., concur.

3. NOTICE TO PARENTS

UNITED STATES v. WATTS

United States Court of Appeals for the Tenth Circuit, 1975.
513 F.2d 5.

Before SETH, HOLLOWAY, and BARRETT, CIRCUIT JUDGES.

BARRETT, CIRCUIT JUDGE. Duane Watts (Watts) appeals from the Trial Court's judgment finding him guilty of involuntary manslaughter and adjudging him to be a Juvenile Delinquent under the provisions of the Federal Juvenile Delinquency Act, 18 U.S.C. §§ 5031–5037.

Watts, an Indian and a minor aged 17 at the time of the alleged offense, was initially charged by complaint with the offense of murder arising from the stabbing death of his brother, Calvert Watts. He was thereafter indicted for voluntary manslaughter. Subsequently, upon failure of the United States Department of Justice to consent to Watts' being charged as an adult, and with the consent of Watts and his counsel, the prior indictment was dismissed and an Information, charging Juvenile Delinquency-Manslaughter, was filed. At trial Watts attempted, unsuccessfully, to establish that he had acted in self defense in stabbing his brother during an altercation.

On this appeal Watts contends: (1) that his right to due process was violated by reason of the failure of adequate notice being provided to his parents; * * *

I.

Watts' chief allegation, i.e., that he was denied due process because his parents were not given notice of the charges against him, nor were they advised of his right to counsel, etc., is premised solely upon the Supreme Court's landmark decision in In re Gault, 387 U.S. 1, 87 S.Ct. 1428, 18 L.Ed.2d 527 (1967). While Watts baldly claims that the federal courts have consistently followed the Supreme Court's mandate in this regard, he has cited no cases squarely holding on this point, nor have we, through our own research, uncovered any such authority. The question of whether the failure of notice to a juvenile's parents, standing alone, constitutes sufficient grounds for the reversal of a determination of juvenile delinquency under the Federal Act, we find to be of first impression before this court.

In establishing standards for the type of notice which would comport with due process requirements for juvenile delinquency proceedings, the Court in *Gault* held:

> Notice, to comply with due process requirements, must be given sufficiently in advance of scheduled court proceedings so that reasonable opportunity to prepare will be afforded, and it must "set forth the alleged misconduct with particularity." * * * even if there were a conceivable purpose served by the deferral proposed by the court below, it would have to yield to the requirements that the child *and his parents* or guardian be notified, *in writing*, of the specific charge or factual allegations to be considered at the hearing, and that such written notice be given at the earliest practicable time, and in any event sufficiently in advance of the hearing to permit preparation. Due process of law requires notice of the sort we have described—that is, notice which would be deemed constitutionally adequate in a civil or criminal proceeding. It does not allow a hearing to be held in which a youth's freedom and *his parents' right to his custody* are at stake without giving *them* timely notice, in advance of the hearing, of the specific issues that they must meet. (Emphasis supplied). 387 U.S. at 33–34, 87 S.Ct. at 1446.

While *Gault*, supra, dealt specifically with the constitutionality of a state scheme for juvenile proceedings, the rights enumerated by that decision are based upon protections afforded by the United States Constitution and, consequently, we view them to be equally applicable to federal proceedings dealing with juvenile offenders under the Federal Juvenile Delinquency Act.[61]

Although the express language in *Gault* requiring that notice be given to both the juvenile and his parents is unequivocal, we are not convinced that the failure of such notice to the parents must lead in all cases to the automatic reversal of the juvenile's adjudication as a delinquent.

Our review of the decision in *Gault* and our search of other authorities does not convince us that there exists a separate and independent due process right to notice of delinquency proceedings belonging to the parents of the juvenile defendant, Watts.[62] Howev-

[61] While the U.S. Attorney correctly pointed out in his brief that at the time of these proceedings the Federal Act did not require that notice be given to the juvenile's parents, we deem it significant to note that such a requirement has been included in a recent amendment to that Act. Section 503 of the Juvenile Justice and Delinquency Prevention Act of 1974 (P.L. 93–415; 88 Stat. 1109) amended Section 5033 of Title 18 U.S.C. to read:

Whenever a juvenile is taken into custody for an alleged act of juvenile delinquency, the arresting officer shall immediately advise such juvenile of his legal rights * * * and shall immediately notify the Attorney General and *the juvenile's parents,* * * * of such custody. The arresting officer *shall also notify the parents,* * * * *of the rights of the juvenile and of the nature of the alleged offense.* (Emphasis added).

We further note the implicit recognition by the Congress that from the time of the decision in In Re Gault, the Federal Juvenile Delinquency Act has been deficient in providing for those safeguards which the court there mandated:

Finally, it is necessary to amend the Federal Juvenile Delinquency Act to guarantee certain basic procedural and constitutional protections to juveniles under Federal jurisdiction. The Committee believes that the Act should provide for the unique characteristics of a juvenile proceeding and the constitutional safeguards fundamental to our system of justice. Six years after the Supreme Court in In Re Gault, decried the lack of certain due process protections in juvenile proceedings, the Federal Juvenile Delinquency Act *has not been changed to reflect those due process rights.* (Emphasis added).

Senate Report No. 93–1011; 1974 U.S. Code Cong. and Admin.News, p. 5312 (October 15, 1974).

[62] In this regard, we note that while parents must be given notice in proceedings wherein custody is at stake, Armstrong v. Manzo, 380 U.S. 545, 85 S.Ct. 1187, 14 L.Ed.2d 62 (1965), and while the Court in *Gault* spoke in terms of the "interest" of parents in retaining custody of the juvenile as partial justification for their being given notice, we also take notice of certain distinctions between this case and those in which the right to notice has been clearly afforded parents. For example, unlike custody proceedings between divorced parents, or those in which the state is attempting to take custody from parents on charges of non-support, etc., here there is no direct attack upon the parents' right to custody. Rather, any effect upon custody is purely incidental to the main function of the proceedings, i.e., to determine delinquency. Secondly, any deprivation suffered by parents following a delinquency proceeding will not necessarily be in the nature of a permanent deprivation of all parental rights, as is relied upon as justification for notice in *Armstrong*, supra. We further observe that the due process standards set forth in *Gault* (including the right to notice) were specifically held to apply only to that part of the juvenile proceedings in which *delinquency* is determined and not to that stage of the proceedings in which the *disposition* of the delinquent child is at issue, *Gault*, supra, 387 U.S. at 27, 87 S.Ct. 1428. It is only at this latter stage that the matter of custody is actually determined. It would therefore seem that any right to notice belonging to the parents based upon the contention that custody is at stake would be applicable, if at all, only to this latter stage of the proceedings, and hence, *Gault* would not seem to be a reliable authority for a claim of such right.

Finally, we recognize that there are several cases holding that the Federal Constitution does not require that a minor's parents be notified prior to the commencement of criminal proceedings against him (even though, presumably,

er, because the parents are not parties to the present action we need not now decide whether such a right exists, and if so whether it has been violated. Further, we do not and need not decide what remedy may be available or appropriate.

Instead, our concern on this appeal is solely with whether a violation of the standard established in *Gault* requiring that notice be given to a juvenile's parents constitutes such a deprivation of the *juvenile's right* to due process as to, per se, require a reversal of the determination of his delinquency.

Preliminarily, we note the following language from the Supreme Court's recent decision in Goss v. Lopez, 419 U.S. 565, 95 S.Ct. 729, 42 L.Ed.2d 725 (1975), which concerned the type of due process notice which must be given students prior to their suspension:

> * * * the interpretation and application of the Due Process Clause are intensely practical matters and * * * "the very nature of due process *negates any concept of inflexible procedures universally* applicable to every imaginable situation." Cafeteria Workers v. McElroy, 367 U.S. 886, 895 [81 S.Ct. 1743, 6 L.Ed.2d 1230] (1961). (Emphasis added).

> 419 U.S. at 578, 95 S.Ct. at 738.

Similarly, we find applicable the Court's statement in *Gault* that the due process standards established therein are to be "intelligently and not ruthlessly administered." 387 U.S. at 21, 87 S.Ct. 1428.

In Michigan v. Tucker, 417 U.S. 433, 94 S.Ct. 2357, 41 L.Ed.2d 182 (1974), the Supreme Court recognized that certain procedural safeguards (in that case the *Miranda* warnings) were not themselves rights protected by the Constitution but were, instead, prophylactic measures laid down to insure that basic rights were not violated. This being so, where only the prophylactic safeguard has been violated but the basic right has not, reversal is not necessarily required.

In Holloway v. Wainwright, supra, the Court stated that the purpose underlying statutes requiring notice to parents is to "furnish a safeguard to minors accused of crimes by requiring that the opportunity be made available for consultation and advice with the individuals, who, society must assume, are those most vitally concerned with the minor's best interests." 451 F.2d at 151. The basic right protected by such safeguards is that of the child to be made aware of the charges against him and to be assured a reasonable opportunity to prepare his defense. Kemplen v. State of Maryland, 428 F.2d 169 (4th Cir.1970). In this regard, the parents' function would seem to be similar to that of legal counsel.

Watts has made no contention that he was not made fully aware of the charges against him or that he was in any way prejudiced in

"custody" of the child is as much at stake in those proceedings as it is in delinquency proceedings). See, Adams v. Wainwright, 445 F.2d 832 (5th Cir.1971), certiorari denied 404 U.S. 860, 92 S.Ct. 160, 30 L.Ed.2d 103 (1971); Holloway v. Wainwright, 451 F.2d 149 (5th Cir.1971).

preparing his case due to the failure of notice being given to his parents. There is no allegation here that Watts was denied the opportunity to confront and cross-examine all adverse witnesses or to secure the presence of favorable witnesses or present evidence in his own defense. Unlike the factual situation in *Gault*, the record here reveals that Watts himself had adequate written notice of the precise charges against him well in advance of the hearing and was at all material times represented by competent counsel.[63] Furthermore, Watts' mother and his stepfather were obviously available to assist him with his defense, as evidenced by the fact that they were present at trial and testified in his behalf.

We do not intend hereby to condone the Government's failure to notify, or even attempt to notify, the juvenile's parents. Such notification may often be the only practical method of insuring that a juvenile is accorded fundamental due process rights mandated by In re Gault. Where, as here, however, it is clear that the juvenile has not, *in fact*, been denied due process (even though there has been a technical violation of a prophylactic safeguard established to protect that right), we see no need for a per se rule requiring reversal. Cf., In Re State in Interest of Harrell, 254 La. 963, 229 So.2d 63 (1969).

The law cannot realistically require that officers investigating serious crimes make no errors whatsoever, and before such error will be penalized it must be determined that such sanction serves a valid and useful purpose. Michigan v. Tucker, supra. There is no allegation here that the investigating officers' failure to notify Watts' parents was willful.[64] Further, there has been no showing made that the Government's case was in any way enhanced by its failure to supply such notice. A "deterrence" argument is not, therefore, applicable here. Nor are we convinced that a reversal, under the circumstances presented by this case, would in anywise enhance the "fact finding process." See, McKeiver v. Pennsylvania, 403 U.S. 528, 543, 91 S.Ct. 1976, 29 L.Ed.2d 647 (1971).

Finally, we agree with the conclusion of the District Court in Walker v. State of Florida, 328 F.Supp. 620 (S.D.Fla.1971), aff'd 466 F.2d 485 (5th Cir.1972):

> *Gault* established that in "loss of liberty proceedings" the juvenile, with respect to certain constitutional rights, is to be treated as an adult. * * * No more was required, no less was offered.

328 F.Supp. at 624.

Under the total circumstances of this case, we agree with the conclusion of the trial court and hold that Watts was not denied the fundamental "fair treatment" mandated by In Re Gault.

---

[63] We are not unmindful of the fact that Watts' own counsel presumably had it within his own power to notify the juvenile's parents had he felt strongly that his client would have been materially benefited by their being so informed. His failure to do so may have been a trial tactic to preserve technical error.

[64] Indeed, their reliance upon the Federal Act's lack of such a requirement seems reasonable in light of the fact that Congress had not changed the Act to include such a requirement until some 7 years after the decision in In Re Gault.

* * *

We affirm.

HOLLOWAY, CIRCUIT JUDGE (concurring in result):

I concur fully in Part II of the court's opinion. As to Part I, I agree with the result reached but am unable to agree with the analysis of the due process requirements laid down by In Re Gault, 387 U.S. 1, 87 S.Ct. 1428, 18 L.Ed.2d 527. I cannot agree that the failure to give notice to the parents may be viewed a mere technical violation of a prophylactic safeguard, and not a constitutional infringement.

The Supreme Court spoke in plain terms of the due process requirements involved in Gault, 387 U.S. 1, 33, 87 S.Ct. 1428, 1446, 18 L.Ed.2d 527. The Court recognized the requirements that:

the child and his parents or guardian be notified, in writing, of the specific charge or factual allegations to be considered at the hearing, and that such written notice be given at the earliest practicable time, and in any event sufficiently in advance of the hearing to permit preparation. *Due process of law requires notice of the sort we have described—that is, notice which would be deemed constitutionally adequate in a civil or criminal proceeding.* (Emphasis added).

Again, as to the nature of the requirement of parental notice, the Court made it unmistakably clear that "* * * the Due Process Clause of the Fourteenth Amendment requires that * * * the child and his parents must be notified of the child's right to be represented by counsel * * *" Id. at 41, 87 S.Ct. at 1451.

In McKeiver v. Pennsylvania, 403 U.S. 528, 532, 91 S.Ct. 1976, 1980, 29 L.Ed.2d 647, the plurality opinion reaffirmed the constitutional stature of the notice requirements spelled out by *Gault*, stating that "Due Process, in that proceeding, was held to embrace adequate written notice. * * * "

In Armstrong v. Manzo, 380 U.S. 545, 550, 85 S.Ct. 1187, 1190, 14 L.Ed.2d 62, the Court had earlier stressed the fundamental nature of the due process requirement of notice:

An elementary and fundamental requirement of due process in any proceeding which is to be accorded finality is notice reasonably calculated, under all the circumstances, to apprise interested parties of the pendency of the action and afford them an opportunity to present their objections.[65]

Moreover, as the majority opinion in the instant case notes, * * * the Congress recognized that the 1974 amendment to the Federal Juvenile Delinquency Act prescribing notice to the parents was necessary "to guarantee certain basic procedural and constitutional protections to juveniles under Federal jurisdiction," Senate Report No. 93–1011, 1974 United States Code Congressional and

[65] The Court restated this proposition from Mullane v. Central Hanover Trust Co., 339 U.S. 306, 314, 70 S.Ct. 652, 94 L.Ed. 865.

Administrative News, p. 4264. The Report stated that the Act had not been changed since *Gault* " *   *   * to reflect those due process rights." Id.

Thus, we are not dealing here with a procedural gloss, but with the essence of due process. Due process consists, in large part, of procedure.

Moreover the notice to the parents, along with other essentials, is not merely for protection of their right to custody, see *Gault*, supra, 387 U.S. at 34, 87 S.Ct. 1428, but is notice required for the juvenile's benefit to insure that the parents may have a reasonable opportunity to participate in preparing and presenting the juvenile's case. Cf. Brown v. Cox, 467 F.2d 1255, 1261 (4th Cir.). Such notice therefore is an essential ingredient of due process guaranteed for the juvenile's protection, and the failure to afford it was a constitutional infringement of his rights.

Recognizing that a constitutional error was involved, there remains the question whether the error was harmless beyond a reasonable doubt. Harrington v. California, 395 U.S. 250, 254, 89 S.Ct. 1726, 23 L.Ed.2d 284; Chapman v. California, 386 U.S. 18, 24, 87 S.Ct. 824, 17 L.Ed.2d 705. I feel the omission must be viewed under this test, applied in light of the purpose of the parental notice requirement.

The record does not show whether the parents were able to give assistance in the preparation of the juvenile's case before trial. However the case was not complicated. It is clear that the defendant had the assistance of retained counsel at the arraignment on March 22, 1974, when the delinquency proceeding was commenced with defendant's consent, and at trial on April 10, 1974. Further, the defendant was 17½ years of age [66] and had the ability and opportunity to discuss preparation with trial counsel.

Moreover at the trial, both the defendant's mother and stepfather [67] participated in the presentation of defendant's case at trial by giving testimony tending to support the position of self-defense developed by the defendant and his counsel. The mother brought to the trial parts of a broken bottle said to have been used by the deceased brother in the fight between him and defendant Watts.

[66] Of course, this age factor cannot excuse the lack of the required notices but, in a proper case, I feel it may be considered as a relevant factor in determining whether such a constitutional error was harmless.

[67] The stepfather lived in Buena Vista and the mother at Towaoe at the time of trial. While the record does not show the facts, defendant's brief states that his natural father lives on the Ute Reservation in Southwest Colorado. Brief of Appellant, p. 4. The defendant testified he had lived with his stepfather in the

summer of 1973, after getting out of school in Albuquerque and that he lived with his grandmother at Towaoe from September, 1973, through January 1974.

The trial court determined at the time of arraignment on March 22, 1974, that defendant should be released on his own recognizance on the condition he not leave the near vicinity of the stepfather in Buena Vista. Thus, the stepfather and the mother appear to be the appropriate persons that these facts cause us to consider in connection with the parental notice requirement.

On consideration of the record as a whole, I conclude that the constitutional error was harmless beyond a reasonable doubt, and agree that the trial court's determination should be affirmed.

THOMAS v. STATE

Florida District Court of Appeals, 1974.
301 So.2d 487.

HOBSON, ACTING CHIEF JUDGE. Appellant, Steven Thomas, entered a plea of nolo contendere to a charge of escape in violation of § 944.40 F.S., was adjudged guilty and sentenced to ten years imprisonment.

On May 1, 1973, when Thomas appeared before the lower court for appointment of counsel, he informed the court that he was 18 years old, had never been married, and that his parents' names were Mr. and Mrs. James E. Thomas. He gave the court the address of his parents, which was recorded by the court reporter as being 123 North Linville, West Lane, Michigan. The next day Assistant State Attorney Aulls sent the notice required by the provisions of § 925.07 F.S. to James E. Thomas, 123 North Linville, Westland, Michigan.

On May 15, 1973, at a hearing before the court Mr. Aulls stated that he had sent the required notice to the address in Westland given him by Thomas, but had received no reply or proof that the notice had been received. The trial judge made inquiry into the matter, and was twice assured by Thomas that the notice had been sent to the correct address in Westland. The trial judge found it appeared that reasonable notice had been given to the parents, and upon Thomas' request, named his attorney as his guardian and postponed arraignment. On May 21, 1973, Thomas entered a plea of nolo contendere, and before accepting the plea, the court questioned him regarding the voluntariness of his plea.

On this direct appeal Thomas' counsel contends that the State has failed to comply with the notice requirements of § 925.07 F.S.

The record before us does not show that at the time Thomas entered his plea on May 21, 1973, timely notice had actually been given to his parents; Collins v. Wainwright, Fla.1962, 146 So.2d 97. The State did not produce a return receipt showing the receipt of the notice; Cf. Johnson v. Cochran, Fla.1960, 124 So.2d 488, or any other proof showing that Thomas' parents had actual knowledge of the charge. Nor was it shown that the court or other responsible official asked Thomas to designate some relative or friend for the purpose of receiving such notice. The failure to comply with any of the alternatives in the statute renders the judgment and sentence void. Kinard v. Cochran, Fla.1959, 113 So.2d 843; State v. Cochran, Fla.1961, 126 So.2d 883. A minor's conviction must be reversed if the record does not affirmatively show that the court fulfilled its duty under the statute. Warren v. State, Fla.App.1st, 1972, 266 So.2d 114.

The judgment and sentence are reversed, and the cause remanded for further proceedings on the information filed against the appellant.

Reversed and remanded.

GRIMES, J., concurs.

BOARDMAN, J., dissents with opinion.

BOARDMAN, JUDGE (dissenting).

The uncontroverted facts show that notice was mailed to appellant's parents by certified mail at the address he provided the court. A return receipt was not received, neither, however, was the letter returned as undelivered. In a similar situation in Snell v. Mayo, Fla. 1956, 84 So.2d 581, our supreme court held:

> * * * presumptively at least, the notice reached the destination to which it was addressed and sent in due course of mail. (84 So. 2d 581, 582).

I am of the opinion that the presumption exists that the letter in the case sub judice likewise reached its destination.

Further, the trial judge, after ascertaining that no reply was received from the parents and that appellant knew of no other address, appointed the public defender as the appellant's guardian.

For the foregoing reasons, I respectfully dissent and would affirm the decision of the trial court.

E. EVIDENTIARY LIMITATIONS

1. HEARSAY

MISSISSIPPI CODE ANNOTATED § 43–21–203(4)
(1983 Supp.)

All hearings shall be conducted under such rules of evidence and rules of court as may comply with applicable constitutional standards.

CALIFORNIA WELFARE AND INSTITUTIONS CODE,
(1979 ed. & 1983–4 Supp.)

§ 701. Question to be determined: Admissibility and sufficiency of evidence: Procedure on minor's denial of extrajudicial admission or confession: Objections where minor not represented by counsel

At the hearing, the court shall first consider only the question whether the minor is a person described by Section 300, 601, or 602. The admission and exclusion of evidence shall be pursuant to the rules of evidence established by the Evidence Code and by judicial decision. Proof beyond a reasonable doubt supported by evidence, legally admissible in the trial of criminal cases, must be adduced to support a finding that the minor is a person described by Section 602, and a preponderance of evidence, legally admissible in the trial of civil cases must be adduced to support a finding that the minor is a person described by Section 300 or 601. When it appears that the minor has made an extrajudicial admission or confession and denies the same at the hearing, the court may continue the hearing for not to exceed seven days to enable the prosecuting attorney to subpoena witnesses to attend the hearing to prove the allegations of the petition. If the minor is not represented by counsel at the hearing, it shall be deemed that objections that could have been made to the evidence were made.

§ 300. Persons subject to jurisdiction of juvenile court

Any person under the age of 18 years who comes within any of the following descriptions is within the jurisdiction of the juvenile court which may adjudge such person to be a dependent child of the court:

(a) Who is in need of proper and effective parental care or control and has no parent or guardian, or has no parent or guardian willing to exercise or capable of exercising such care or control, or has no parent or guardian actually exercising such care or control. No parent shall be found to be incapable of exercising proper and effective parental care or control solely because of a physical disability, including, but not limited to, a defect in the visual or auditory functions of his or her body, unless the court finds that the disability prevents the parent from exercising such care or control.

(b) Who is destitute, or who is not provided with the necessities of life, or who is not provided with a home or suitable place of abode.

(c) Who is physically dangerous to the public because of a mental or physical deficiency, disorder or abnormality.

(d) Whose home is an unfit place for him by reason of neglect, cruelty, depravity, or physical abuse of either of his parents, or of his guardian or other person in whose custody or care he is.

(e) Who has been freed for adoption from one or both parents for 12 months by either relinquishment or termination of parental rights and for whom an interlocutory decree has not been granted pursuant to Section 224n of the Civil Code or an adoption petition has not been granted.

§ 601. Same: Persons subject to adjudication as ward of court for refusal to obey orders of parents, etc.

(a) Any person under the age of 18 years who persistently or habitually refuses to obey the reasonable and proper orders or directions of his parents, guardian, or custodian, or who is beyond the control of such person, or who is under the age of 18 years when he violated any ordinance of any city or county of this state establishing a curfew based solely on age is within the jurisdiction of the juvenile court which may adjudge such person to be a ward of the court.

(b) If a school attendance review board determines that the available public and private services are insufficient or inappropriate to correct the habitual truancy of the minor, or to correct the minor's persistent or habitual refusal to obey the reasonable and proper orders or directions of school authorities, or if the minor fails to respond to directives of a school attendance review board or to services provided, the minor is then within the jurisdiction of the juvenile court which may adjudge such person to be a ward of the court; provided, that it is the intent of the Legislature that no minor who is adjudged a ward of the court pursuant solely to this subdivision shall be removed from the custody of the parent or guardian except during school hours.

§ 602. Person subject to adjudication as ward of court for violation of law, or ordinance defining crime

Any person who is under the age of 18 years when he violates any law of this state or of the United States or any ordinance of any city or county of this state defining crime other than an ordinance establishing a curfew based solely on age, is within the jurisdiction of the juvenile court, which may adjudge such person to be a ward of the court.

TEXAS FAMILY CODE—VERNON'S TEXAS CODES ANNOTATED, Title 3, § 54.03(d), (1972 ed. & 1983 Supp.).

"Only material, relevant, and competent evidence in accordance with the requirements for the trial of civil cases may be considered in the adjudication hearing * * *."

NEW YORK FAMILY COURT ACT—McKinney's Consolidated Laws of New York Ann., (1983 ed. & 1984 Supp.).

§ 744(a).

"Only evidence that is competent, material, and relevant may be admitted in a fact-finding hearing."

NOTES

1. In In re Farms, 216 Pa.Super. 445, 268 A.2d 170 (1970), the court was faced with an effort by the defendant to get a witness to testify about the contents of a statement made to him by another witness, on the theory that the prior statement was inconsistent with the testimony of the latter witness at the hearing. The court concluded that were this an adult trial, the defendant would have been entitled to have the evidence admitted, and so reversed and remanded for a new adjudicatory hearing.

Juvenile proceedings have, from their inception, been more relaxed than trials of adults. Many, sometimes too many, of the procedural rights accorded adults were denied to juveniles. *Gault* decided that, before a juvenile could be stigmatized a delinquent and deprived of his liberty, due process at least required notice of charges, counsel, the right to confront and crossexamine accusing witnesses, and the privilege against self-incrimination. In re Gault, 387 U.S. 1, 87 S.Ct. 1428, 18 L.Ed.2d 527 (1967). *Winship* decided that, when a juvenile is charged with a violation of criminal law and could be similarly stigmatized and incarcerated as a result of a finding of violation, then the finding must be upon proof beyond a reasonable doubt. In re Winship, 397 U.S. 358, 90 S.Ct. 1068, 25 L.Ed.2d 368 (1970).

But the rationale of *Gault* and *Winship* was that only certain essentials of due process were required. The Court was clear, however, that due process did not require abandonment of "the informality, flexibility, [and] speed" of the juvenile procedure if the juvenile's interest in a fair adjudication was not overcome thereby. In re Winship, supra, 397 U.S. at 366, 90 S.Ct. at 1074.

In nonjury cases, strict adherence to the technicalities of the rules of hearsay does not necessarily lead to the most just finding. "The jury-trial system of rules of Evidence is *not* the only safe system of investigation in matters of liberty and property * * *. Nor is it correct to assume that the general wisdom of experience which is represented in the system at large is represented in all the detailed rules rigidly enforced * * *. What is commonly forgotten is that most of the rules * * * are merely rules of caution, i.e., they are based upon a *possibility* of error; so that the failure to observe the rule is perfectly consistent with a high probability of truth." 1 J. Wigmore, Evidence § 4(b), pp. 35–36 (3rd ed. 1940). "The main direction of the federal case law is toward the view that in nonjury trials a finding may be based on 'the kind of evidence on which responsible persons are accustomed to rely in serious affairs,' whether or not the evidence is technically inadmissible as hearsay." Davis, op. cit., note 2 [a] supra at 1368, quoting in part from NLRB v. Remington Rand, 94 F.2d 862, 873 (2d Cir.), cert. denied, 304 U.S. 576, 58 S.Ct. 1046, 82 L.Ed. 1540 (1938).

In juvenile cases, where the judge sits alone as the trier of fact and where it is his duty to become as knowledgeable and inquisitive as reasonably possible, it is better for him to admit hearsay "for what it's worth." He can make the determination whether responsible people would rely upon it in serious affairs when he makes his findings. He, by his experience in dealing with thousands of juveniles, being exposed to their statements, both forthright and delusive, will not be swayed, as a jury would, by hearsay which is not to be relied upon.

Of course, we would not allow an adjudication of delinquency based on hearsay. Such a result would be in violation of a juvenile's right of confrontation. In re Gault, supra, 387 U.S. at 56–57, 87 S.Ct. at 1459. But, when a matter as important as the prior statement of a witness is brought to the court's attention, it should be permitted to consider it, whether or not it technically is an exception to the hearsay rule.

[a] The footnote 2 referred to in the text follows:

It should be noted moreover that hearsay in nonjury cases has not, in practice, been subject to the restrictive technical rulings that are more common in jury cases. Judges sitting as the trier of fact usually admit hearsay "for what it's worth", without ruling on its admissibility. Professor Davis has suggested that the Committee on Rules of Practice and Procedure of the Judicial Conference of the United States re-examine its proposed Federal Rules of Evidence to consider whether "(1) a rule that apparently useful hearsay may be admitted in a nonjury case even if it would be inadmissible in a jury case and (2) a rule that a finding in a nonjury case may be based on the kind of evidence on which responsible persons are accustomed to rely in serious affairs even if the evidence would be excluded as hearsay in a jury case." Davis, Hearsay in Nonjury Cases, 83 Harv. L.Rev. 1362, 1368 (1970).

Id. at 450, 268 A.2d at 174.

As appellant's counsel in this Court so aptly put it: "If the statement of Richard Hines was in fact substantially identical with his testimony, what had the Commonwealth to fear from the disclosure of his statement? In fact, testimony that the statement was consistent would have served only to bolster the Commonwealth case." It was the kind of statement that, once brought to the court's attention by counsel, would be helpful to the court in deciding what the true history of the incident was.

In summary, the prior inconsistent statement was clearly admissible in the trial of an adult. In juvenile proceedings, where we should not quarrel over the technical niceties of the hearsay rule, a *fortiori* it should have been admitted. To do otherwise, was error and denied appellant a fair adjudicatory proceeding.

Id. at 452–54, 268 A.2d at 174–6.

2. Do *Gault* and its successors require that hearsay evidence be excluded from the adjudication phase of delinquency determinations? Does it, in conjunction with *Winship*, require that there be sufficient non-hearsay evidence to support a finding of delinquency beyond a reasonable doubt? Or, instead that there be some non-hearsay evidence that, when added to hearsay evidence, meets the burden? Consider the following:

"The adjudication must be reversed. The only evidence presented by the State as to the automobile being a stolen vehicle was the testimony of arresting officer Paz. While he was being cross-examined by D.C.'s counsel, the trial judge asked Paz whether he had checked out ownership of the car. When he answered that he had, the judge inquired, 'What was it?' Counsel's immediate objection that this was not competent testimony was overruled, and Paz then said that he had called headquarters which, in turn, 'called NCIC for a look-up on the vehicle and they found it was stolen out of Rutherford, your Honor.'

"This double hearsay should not have been permitted. Evidence Rule 63. Whatever the informalities that are tolerated in formal hearings of juvenile matters, hearsay of a kind so fundamental to the State's case as here should not be allowed. In re Gault, 387 U.S. 1, 87 S.Ct. 1428, 18 L.Ed.2d 527 (1967), which held that juvenile court proceedings are subject to the constitutional requirements of due process of law, requires no less. * * * The double hearsay testimony of Paz struck at the heart of due process."

State in the Interest of D.C., 114 N.J.Super. 499, 501, 277 A.2d 402, 403 (1971).

"In the trial court, Alvin Chaplin, Donald's probation officer, over objection, reviewed the juvenile's social history. He stated that Donald had previously been sent to a foster home by the State Department of Welfare and Institutions but had run away. Chaplin also testified that Donald had twice been involved in driving an automobile without an operator's permit and had run away from home on several occasions. The source of the latter information was Donald's mother who was present in court but did not testify. He further testified that Donald had admitted to him stealing alcoholic beverages and becoming inebriated.

"Donald offered no evidence, and the trial court ruled that it was committing Donald to the State Department of Welfare and Institutions because he was already on probation, because he had committed various offenses including intoxication and driving without a permit, and because the school authorities could not 'handle' him.

"The question for decision is whether the hearsay portions of Chaplin's testimony were inadmissible and prejudicial in a juvenile proceeding.

"In Lewis v. Commonwealth, Va., 198 S.E.2d 629 (1973), decided this day, we considered the nature of a juvenile proceeding and held that a due process standard of fundamental fairness governed juvenile court procedure. The record in the case at bar shows that the trial court, in finding that Donald was incorrigible, was influenced by Chaplin's hearsay testimony, to which there was proper objection. We hold that the admission of such evidence violated the due process standard of fundamental fairness required in a juvenile proceeding, and its admission was prejudicial error."

Gilbert v. Commonwealth, 214 Va. 142, 142–3, 198 S.E.2d 633, 633–4 (1973).

"Respondent contends that the court's findings were based upon hearsay evidence. It is true that some of the testimony offered was hearsay. However, respondent, who was represented by counsel at the hearing, made no objection or motion to strike. The testimony was therefore competent and could be considered. Abbitt v. Bartlett, 252 N.C. 40, 112 S.E.2d 751; State v. Davis, 8 N.C.App. 589, 174 S.E.2d 865.

"Moreover, there was other competent evidence to support the court's findings. The victim of the assault testified that he was sitting on the commode in the boy's bathroom of Louisburg High School when respondent and some other students came in and turned off the lights. The lights remained off for a minute or more and during that time the witness was kicked in the neck. When the lights came back on respondent was seen walking toward the door. The witness testified, 'I am able to say which one kicked me. David Dunston. He was the only one near enough to do it.'

"The findings and conclusions of the Juvenile Court are specific and are technically sound. We have reviewed the complete record and conclude that no prejudicial error appears therein."

In re Dunston, 12 N.C.App. 33, 34, 182 S.E.2d 9, 9–10 (1971).

2. REVIEWING SOCIAL STUDY REPORT PRIOR TO ADJUDICATION

IN RE R

Supreme Court of California, 1970.
83 Cal.Rptr. 671, 464 P.2d 127, 1 Cal.3d 855.

TOBRINER, JUSTICE. Gladys R., a 12-year-old girl, appeals from a judgment declaring her a ward of the court and committing her to the custody of the probation officer for private institutional placement. For the reasons we shall point out, the court committed reversible error in reviewing the social study report before the jurisdictional hearing.

* * *

The Santa Clara County Superior Court, sitting as a juvenile court, found that the appellant's conduct brought her within the terms of Welfare and Institutions Code section 602 [68] because she committed an act proscribed by Penal Code section 647a (annoying or molesting a child under 18). Immediately after accepting factual allegations that the child committed acts which could invoke the jurisdiction of the court under section 602, the juvenile court proceeded: "Now, we come to the question of what action should be taken, and in this connection, the Court has been supplied with a special report called a social study, which is ordered admitted in evidence at this time *and which has been thoroughly reviewed by the Court.* The social study tells the Court whether the child has a prior record, where the child is now, what the child told the probation officer when interviewed, what the parents told the probation officer when interviewed, the child's school report, welfare report, juvenile hall report, psychological, psychiatric and medical reports, personal history and family backgrounds, and last of all the probation officer evaluates that information and data and makes a recommendation to the Court." (Italics added.)

The quoted comments clearly indicate that the court examined the social study report prior to its determination of whether appellant had committed an act that would warrant the court's declaration of a wardship. The report contains matter not relevant to the jurisdiction of the court and therefore inadmissible at the hearing on that issue.

* * *

1. *The court committed reversible error in reviewing the social study report before the determination of the issue of jurisdiction.*

The history of Welfare and Institutions Code sections 701,[69] 702,[70] and 706 [71] clearly indicates that the Legislature intended to create a bifurcated juvenile court procedure in which the court would first determine whether the facts of the case would support the jurisdiction of the court in declaring a wardship and *thereafter* would consider the social study report at a hearing on the appropriate disposition of that ward.[72] This procedure affords a necessary pro-

---

[68] Welfare and Institutions Code section 602 reads: "Any person under the age of 21 years who violates any law of this State * * * defining crime * * * is within the jurisdiction of the juvenile court, which may adjudge such person to be a ward of the court." References hereinafter to section 602, without mention of any code, are to the quoted section.

[69] Section 701 provides that "the court shall first consider only the question whether the minor [comes within the court's jurisdiction], and *for this purpose,* any matter or information relevant and material to the circumstances or acts which are alleged to bring him within the jurisdiction of the juvenile court is admissible and may be received in evidence * * *." (Italics added.)

[70] Section 702 provides that "if the court finds that the minor is [within its jurisdiction], it shall make and enter its findings and order accordingly and shall *then* proceed to hear evidence on the question of the proper disposition to be made of the minor. Prior to doing so, it may continue the hearing, if necessary, to receive the social study of the probation officer * * *." (Italics added.)

[71] Section 706 provides that: "*After* finding [the minor comes within its jurisdiction], the court shall hear evidence on the question of the proper disposition to be made of the minor. The court shall receive in evidence the social study of the minor made by the probation officer * * *." (Italics added.)

[72] In 1959 the Governor of California appointed a Special Study Commission on

tection against the premature resolution of the jurisdictional issue on the basis of legally incompetent material in the social report.

A prohibition of review of the social report before a determination of the jurisdictional issue does not hinder the creation of a court atmosphere conducive to a just consideration of the juvenile's case. We recognize that the juvenile court in this case acted entirely within its view of the best interest of the child. It undoubtedly believed that its perusal of the report prior to a decision on the jurisdictional issue would provide helpful background information.[73] We hold, however, that Welfare and Institutions Code sections 701, 702, and 706 prohibit the judge from reading the social report before the jurisdictional hearing.

A recent decision of the Court of Appeal correctly holds that the construction given in *Corey* to the new statutory scheme of Welfare and Institutions Code sections 701, 702, and 706 must apply to all juvenile proceedings, including the instant case, initiated since the 1961 amendments. (In re Steven F., supra, 270 A.C.A. 643, 75 Cal. Rptr. 887.)[74]   *Corey* did not involve a new constitutional rule that

Juvenile Justice to undertake a comprehensive study of the California Juvenile Court Law. The commission strongly criticized the juvenile courts because they "do not distinguish between the jurisdictional facts and the social data at the hearing. Consequently, wardship is sometimes decided on issues that evolve from a social investigation even though the jurisdictional facts have not been clearly substantiated.

"In our opinion, a two-stage hearing procedure is essential. This will serve to differentiate more sharply between legal proof and treatment knowledge and will result in the application of each to the appropriate question for court decision.

"We also realize that any increase in the number of hearings may further reduce the time available to hear such case. Therefore, we recommend that both hearings be permitted to be held on the same day, provided the probation report and treatment recommendations are available. The sequence, however, should be preserved in any event." (Report of the Governor's Special Study Commission on Juvenile Justice (1960) p. 28.)

The commission thus recommended new statutory language which, with modifications not at issue in this case, the Legislature enacted as Welfare and Institutions Code sections 701, 702, and 706.

[73] Actually, the juvenile and his family might be reluctant to cooperate fully with the probation officer if they thought that the results of the social investigation would become available to the judge prior to the jurisdictional hearing. The probation officer would thus be prevented

from submitting to the trial court a social report which contained a complete review of the facts relevant to the ward's disposition. In addition, if the juvenile believed that the probation officer's report would be reviewed prior to the jurisdictional hearing, the important and close relationship between the juvenile and the probation officer might be jeopardized.

[74] The Attorney General also claims that In re Corey, supra, 266 Cal.App.2d 295, 72 Cal.Rptr. 115, announces a "new rule" that should be applied prospectively because *Corey* will adversely affect the administration of justice by encouraging attacks upon previous adjudications. The Attorney General points to a 1965 survey indicating that a majority of California judges continued to read the social study before the jurisdictional hearing (see Edwin M. Lemert, The Juvenile Court—Quest and Realities, Task Force Report: Juvenile Delinquency and Youth Crime; The President's Commission on Law Enforcement and Administration of Justice (1967) p. 101) and to certain comments by B.E. Witkin: "The statutes suggest, if they do not prescribe, a document separate from the probation report, and for a good reason: The data will be in great part irrelevant to and highly prejudicial on the issue of jurisdiction, and the study should not therefore be offered in evidence until the hearing on disposition. [Citations.] But in practice the social study is not held close to the deputy's vest and formally offered in evidence at the proper time. It just sort of appears on the judge's desk, and he knows it is there. May he read it before the first hearing? Should he read it?

overturned prior decisions * * * but rather interpreted statutory provisions whose interpretation had previously remained unsettled. Furthermore, the failure of the minor's attorney to object at the juvenile court hearing to the court's premature use of the social study does not bar the consideration of this issue on appeal; we cannot expect an attorney to anticipate that an appellate court will later interpret the controlling sections in a manner contrary to the apparently prevalent contemporaneous interpretation.

We must hold that the court's review of the social study prior to the jurisdictional hearing constituted prejudicial error. Both In re Corey, supra, 266 Cal.App.2d 295, 299, 72 Cal.Rptr. 115, 118, and In re Steven F., supra, 270 A.C.A. 643, 645, 75 Cal.Rptr. 887, state: "Where the commission of a crime is alleged as the jurisdictional fact and the allegation is disputed, the court's error in [reviewing] the social study before the jurisdictional hearing goes so directly to the fairness of the hearing that the resulting adjudication is not saved by article VI, section 13, of the California Constitution." The court's review of the social report in advance of the jurisdictional hearing would perhaps not require reversal in a case in which the contents of the social study entirely favored the minor and his home environment. But in the present case the social study showed some inquiry into appellant's intent under section 647a and some negative indications about appellant's home environment. Hence, the court's review of the social study prior to the jurisdictional hearing, at which the jurisdictional facts were far from conclusive, constituted prejudicial error.

NOTE

In re Ernest J., 52 Md.App. 56, 447 A.2d 97 (1982) held erroneous (though harmless) the admission of juvenile services officer's testimony as to juvenile's prior contacts with juvenile services.

3. CORROBORATION

IN RE R.C.[b]

California Court of Appeal, 1974.
39 Cal.App.3d 887, 114 Cal.Rptr. 735.

CHRISTIAN, ASSOCIATE JUSTICE. R.C. appeals from an order of the juvenile court committing him to the Youth Authority after it had

Can he run an efficient bifurcated hearing from beginning to end without reading it in advance? Those questions are not for me to answer; but if, as I am reliably informed, he does make a practice of reading it before the first hearing, he must in that hearing totally blank out his memory of the wholly inadmissible evidence of other offenses and misconduct, bad reputation, and derogatory opinions of neighbors [and others]." (See Proceedings of the Third Annual Institute for Juvenile Court Judges and Referees, Sponsored by the Judicial Council of California (1964) pp. 124, 141–142.)

The Attorney General's dire predictions have not proved accurate. Following the *Corey* decision on October 1, 1968, and the *Steven F.* decision on March 12, 1969, no great flood of habeas corpus petitions have raised this issue.

[b] The California Supreme Court reached the same conclusion in In re Mitchell P., 22 Cal.3d 946, 151 Cal.Rptr.

been determined that he had set fire to two structures; appellant was found to be a minor within the provisions of Welfare and Institutions Code section 602.

The evidence is not in conflict. At about 3:40 a.m., February 26, 1973, two police officers patrolling the area of O'Farrell and Fillmore Streets, in San Francisco, observed a young man standing in the partly opened doorway of a building and looking inside. The young man turned and walked across the street where he joined another boy. The officers stopped them, asked for their names, dates of birth and addresses, and asked what they were doing. After the boys had identified themselves as R.C. and J.J., the officers placed them in the back of the police vehicle and explained that they were being detained while the officers checked further into what they had been doing. Appellant had been identified to one of the officers earlier that evening as a possible suspect in a series of fires that had been set in the Fillmore area.

Inspecting the doorway where J.J. had first been seen, the officers observed fresh scratches and impressions indicating that the door had been forced open. The officers then checked the lot across the street, where they had seen appellant making a tossing motion; a knife was found. The officers then took the boys into custody.

On arrival at the Hall of Justice, the two boys were placed in separate rooms for questioning concerning a fire in which two deaths had occurred. J.J. convincingly denied knowledge of that fire, but admitted that he, D.B. and appellant were members of "the Flames" and were responsible for 14 or 15 other fires in the Western Addition area. As a result of this conversation, the officers concluded that the boys were not responsible for the arson-homicide which had been the primary focus of investigation. Appellant refused to talk.

It was stipulated at the hearing on the petition against appellant that fires set at 935 Webster Street and 1437–39 Golden Gate Avenue were incendiary in origin. It was also stipulated that if minors D.B. and J.J. were called to the stand, both would testify that they, along with appellant had set fire to vacant buildings at 1437–39 Golden Gate Avenue and 935 Webster Street, with the intent to burn the buildings. Appellant did not testify.

Counsel for appellant moved to strike the petition on the ground that Penal Code section 1111 required corroboration of the stipulated testimony of D.B. and J.J., who were accomplices in the offense charged against appellant. The motion was denied.

Appellant points out that he was found to have violated a state law and was thereby brought within the jurisdiction of the juvenile court (Welf. & Inst.Code, § 602), solely on the testimony of two accomplices. Penal Code section 1111 provides that a *"conviction* can not be had upon the testimony of an accomplice unless it be corroborated by such other evidence as shall tend to connect the

330, 587 P.2d 1144 (1978), cert. den. sub.
nom Ponting v. Cal. 444 U.S. 845, 100
S.Ct. 90, 62 L.Ed.2d 59 (1979).

defendant with the commission of the offense; * * * " (Emphasis added.) According to the strict language of the statute, there was corroboration in that the two accomplices supported each other. But it has been held that the testimony of one accomplice cannot corroborate that of another. * * *

Appellant first contends that Penal Code section 1111 should by its own terms be construed as applying to a juvenile proceeding. Proof that a juvenile has violated a state law must be "supported by evidence, legally admissible in the trial of criminal cases, * * * " (Welf. & Inst.Code, § 701.) Historically, accomplice testimony was inadmissible, but the rule of exclusion was replaced in the British courts as early as the 18th Century (7 Wigmore on Evidence (3d ed. 1940) § 2056). Courts in this state have also repeatedly held that Penal Code section 1111, requiring corroboration, does not go to the admissibility of evidence, but to the effect to be given that testimony. * * *

Penal Code section 1111 by its own terms applies only to criminal *convictions*, while Welfare and Institutions Code section 503 provides that an "order adjudging a minor to be a ward of the juvenile court shall *not be deemed a conviction of a crime for any purpose*, nor shall a proceeding in the juvenile court be deemed a criminal proceeding." (Emphasis added.) To apply Penal Code section 1111 to a juvenile proceeding would thus be contrary to the intention expressed in the statute.

It is argued, however, that the determination of wardship on the basis of uncorroborated accomplice testimony was a deprivation of due process. It is true that proceedings to determine whether a minor is a delinquent must comport with the essentials of due process and fair treatment. (In re Gault (1967) 387 U.S. 1, 30–31, 87 S.Ct. 1428, 18 L.Ed.2d 527; Kent v. United States (1966) 383 U.S. 541, 553, 86 S.Ct. 1045, 16 L.Ed.2d 84.) Where a juvenile is charged with an act which would constitute a crime if committed by an adult, "proof beyond a reasonable doubt" at the adjudicatory stage is one of these essentials. (In re Winship (1970) 397 U.S. 358, 368, 90 S.Ct. 1068, 25 L.Ed.2d 368; Richard M. v. Superior Court (1971) 4 Cal.3d 370, 378, 93 Cal.Rptr. 752, 482 P.2d 664; see also Welf. & Inst.Code, § 701.)

Appellant bases his due process contention on a New York decision which reversed an adjudication of delinquency where the sole evidence connecting the juvenile to acts of arson and burglary consisted of testimony by the accomplice to those acts. (In re M. (1970) 34 A.D.2d 761, 310 N.Y.S.2d 399.) The New York court reversed on the basis of In re Winship, supra, 397 U.S. 358, 90 S.Ct. 1068, reasoning that proof beyond a reasonable doubt requires corroboration of accomplice testimony. (In re M., supra, 310 N.Y.S.2d at pp. 400–401.) However, that application of *Winship* appears to be questionable. As the concurring opinion in *In re M.* noted: "In the instant case the rule in question limiting the effect of accomplice testimony is obviously not an essential of due process as is shown by the fact that it is not the rule in the United States courts and in the vast majority of states [citations]." (In re M., supra, 310 N.Y.S.2d at pp. 401–402.) [75] The federal courts do not require corroboration of accomplice testimony in federal prosecutions. Instead, federal juries are instructed that accomplice testimony is to be received with caution and weighed with great care. * * * The California requirement that accomplice testimony be corroborated is a legislative refinement; it is not a rule included within the traditional concepts of due process. * * * If corroboration of accomplice testimony is not an essential of due process in criminal cases, it similarly is not required in juvenile cases.

An alternative ground for the New York holding in *In re M.*, and a contention advanced by appellant in this case, is that application of Penal Code section 1111 in juvenile court proceedings is required by the equal protection clause of the Fourteenth Amendment to the United States Constitution. The claim is that all the rules of evidence and standards of proof applied in criminal cases must be extended to juvenile proceedings because in either type of proceeding the accused or the juvenile faces the possibility of a substantial loss of freedom.

Both the United States Constitution and the Constitution of California require similar treatment of persons similarly situated, allowing discrimination between one class and another only on the basis of distinctions reasonably related to the proper purposes of the law. A classification which results in differences of treatment "must not be arbitrary, but must be based upon some differences in the classes having a substantial relation to a legitimate object to be accomplished." * * *

It is established that the differing needs and characteristics of adult offenders and juveniles justify the maintenance of a separate and different system of justice for each of the two classes. * * * It remains to be determined whether differences between the adult criminal justice system and the juvenile system reasonably justify withholding application of the accomplice rule in juvenile proceedings. Differences between the two systems will be examined, and decisions which have upheld or rejected different treatment of adults and juveniles will be analyzed to provide a context for our decision.

A difference often advanced to justify disparate treatment of juveniles and adults is that juvenile cases are "civil" while adult cases are "criminal." But those simple labels do not suffice; deeper analysis of the characteristics and purposes of the two systems is required. (See McKeiver v. Pennsylvania, supra, 403 U.S. 528, 544, 91 S.Ct. 1976, 29 L.Ed.2d 647.)

Some of the reasoning which has been used to support different treatment of juveniles will not withstand such analysis. Thus, the purpose of Penal Code section 1111 does not, of itself, support limitation of the accomplice rule to adult cases. The requirement

---

[75] Nevertheless, the rule of *In re M.* has been followed in subsequent New York cases. (See In re L. (1973) 41 A.D.2d 674, 340 N.Y.S.2d 1001 [corroboration of accomplice required]; In the Matter of Eric R. (1970) 34 A.D.2d 402, 312 N.Y.S.2d 447 [corroboration of complainant required in rape case].)

that accomplice testimony be corroborated is designed to guard against testimony from tainted sources which has been given in the hope of leniency or immunity. (People v. Wallin (1948) 32 Cal.2d 803, 808, 197 P.2d 734.) There is no indication that accomplice testimony is more trustworthy, or less likely to be given in hope of leniency, simply because the person charged with an offense is a juvenile. Similarly, respondent's contention is not conclusive, that to apply Penal Code section 1111 to juvenile proceedings which do not involve juries "is to say that a judge may not fairly consider the weight and value to be given the testimony of an accomplice in light of all of the surrounding facts and circumstances of the case." The statute applies to adult criminal cases tried before a judge as well as to those tried before a jury. Thus, the absence of a jury in a juvenile case is not a full answer to appellant's equal protection claim.

Respondent suggests that withholding application of the accomplice rule of Penal Code section 1111 to juvenile court proceedings is justified by the fact that unavailability of corroborative testimony would in some cases block judicial intervention which might serve the welfare of the juvenile by providing rehabilitation. The United States Supreme Court rejected a similar contention in deciding that due process requires adjudication of delinquency to be supported by proof beyond a reasonable doubt, saying: "It is true, of course, that the juvenile may be engaging in a general course of conduct inimical to his welfare that calls for judicial intervention. But that intervention cannot take the form of subjecting the child to the stigma of a finding that he violated a criminal law and to the possibility of institutional confinement on proof insufficient to convict him were he an adult." (In re Winship, supra, 397 U.S. at p. 367, 90 S.Ct. at p. 1074.) Yet *Winship*'s conclusions as to due process do not foreclose the question whether the rule of Penal Code section 1111, which is not required by due process, may be withheld in juvenile cases.

The different purposes of the juvenile system may nevertheless justify reasonable differences in procedure so long as due process standards are met. In an equal protection analysis it is not insignificant that juries are never used in the juvenile court. It is not unreasonable to suppose that a judge conducting a juvenile hearing is less likely than a jury would be, to accept accomplice testimony uncritically. It is also significant that the consequences of a criminal conviction may be more severe than the consequences of an adjudication of delinquency. Although in a particular case the peculiarities of the juvenile commitment process may cause a juvenile offender to be confined longer than one prosecuted as an adult for the same conduct, the juvenile system does not employ any commitments paralleling the severe maximum sentences provided for adults convicted of major crimes. Although Penal Code section 1111 protects not only adults charged with major offenses but also adults charged with minor offenses carrying light punishments, it is not unreasonable to give some weight to the relative severity of possible consequences in comparing the adult and juvenile systems.

Several specific safeguards of the adult criminal system are held not to have been mandated for juvenile offenders by the requirements of equal protection. The right to bail has not extended to juvenile cases. (See In re William M. (1970) 3 Cal.3d 16, 26, n. 17, 89 Cal.Rptr. 33, 473 P.2d 737; In re Magnuson (1952) 110 Cal.App.2d 73, 74, 242 P.2d 362 [no right to bail on appeal].) Similarly, the protections afforded by preliminary hearings or grand juries are not required in juvenile cases. (See In re T.R.S. (1969) 1 Cal.App.3d 178, 181, 81 Cal.Rptr. 574.)

The unavailability of the adult court procedure for dismissal of a charge after successful completion of probation (Pen.Code, § 1203.4) does not deny equal protection to juveniles. (In re S.A., supra, 6 Cal. App.3d 241, 245, 85 Cal.Rptr. 775.) Neither does the 5-year waiting period before juvenile records may be sealed. (T.N.G. v. Superior Court, supra, 4 Cal.3d 767, 94 Cal.Rptr. 813, 484 P.2d 981.) Although due process includes the right to trial by jury in state criminal proceedings (Duncan v. Louisiana (1968) 391 U.S. 145, 88 S.Ct. 1444, 20 L.Ed.2d 491), equal protection does not require that the juvenile courts use juries. (See McKeiver v. Pennsylvania, supra, 403 U.S. 528, 91 S.Ct. 1976, 29 L.Ed.2d 647.) The absence of a jury is a difference far more important than the inapplicability of Penal Code section 1111. Yet it was held to be permissible because if jury trial were required as a matter of constitutional right, the juvenile proceeding would be remade into a full adversary process. "If the jury trial were to be injected into the juvenile court system as a matter of right, it would bring with it into that system the traditional delay, the formality, and the clamor of the adversary system and, possibly, the public trial." (Id. at p. 550, 91 S.Ct. at p. 1988.) Similarly, the rule that accomplice testimony must be corroborated, if applied to juvenile proceedings, would tend toward formality and an adversary atmosphere in the juvenile system.

We recognize that many protections of the criminal system have been extended to juveniles charged with violating the law. Thus the statutes provide that in a proceeding under Welfare and Institutions Code section 602, a minor must be advised of his constitutional rights (Welf. & Inst.Code, § 627.5); he is protected by a double jeopardy provision (Welf. & Inst.Code, § 606); and he has a right to counsel (Welf. & Inst.Code, §§ 633, 634, 679), a right to notice of the charges against him (Welf. & Inst.Code, § 633), a right to confront and cross-examine witnesses (Welf. & Inst.Code, §§ 630, 702.5), a privilege against self-incrimination (Welf. & Inst.Code, §§ 630, 702.5), a right to appeal, and a right to a free transcript on appeal if he cannot afford counsel (Welf. & Inst.Code, § 800).

Similarly, other protections have been extended as a matter of due process. The exclusionary rules relating to illegally seized evidence apply (In re Robert T. (1970) 8 Cal.App.3d 990, 88 Cal.Rptr. 37), as do the rules for unconstitutional pretrial identification. (In re Carl T. (1969) 1 Cal.App.3d 344, 351, 81 Cal.Rptr. 655.) An explicit waiver of rights prior to a judicial admission as in Boykin v. Alabama

(1969) 395 U.S. 238, 89 S.Ct. 1709, 23 L.Ed.2d 274, is required in juvenile proceedings (In re Michael M. (1970) 11 Cal.App.3d 741, 96 Cal.Rptr. 887), and statements obtained from juveniles in violation of *Miranda* are inadmissible. (In re Roderick P. (1972) 7 Cal.3d 801, 811, 103 Cal.Rptr. 425, 500 P.2d 1.) The bar on multiple prosecutions (Pen.Code, § 654) applies to juvenile delinquency proceedings. (In re Benny G. (1972) 24 Cal.App.3d 371, 373, 101 Cal.Rptr. 28.) Violation of a criminal statute must be proved beyond a reasonable doubt before a court can exercise jurisdiction over a juvenile pursuant to Welfare and Institutions Code section 602. (Welf. & Inst.Code, § 701; see also In re Winship, supra, 397 U.S. 358, 90 S.Ct. 1068.) An appeal on the insufficiency of the evidence is subject to the same standards which govern review of criminal convictions generally. (In re Roderick P., supra, 7 Cal.3d 801, 809, 103 Cal.Rptr. 425, 500 P.2d 1.)

But these protections have not been based on concepts of equal protection; they have either been created by statute or recognized as being required by due process. The purposes and structure of the juvenile system are different from the adult criminal justice system. Hence when due process has been satisfied reasonable differences in procedure are not unconstitutional.

The order is affirmed.

CALDECOTT, P.J., concurs.

RATTIGAN, ASSOCIATE JUSTICE (dissenting).

I dissent.

Appellant has been subjected to wardship of the juvenile court upon its factual determination, reached on the basis of uncorroborated accomplice testimony only, that he had "violate[d] * * * [a] * * * law of this state" (Welf. & Inst.Code, § 602) in that he had committed the crime of arson proscribed by Penal Code section 447a.

I agree with the majority that the adjudication did not operate to deprive appellant of due process of law, as guaranteed him under the Fourteenth Amendment, by reason of its having been based upon such testimony alone. (See Lisenba v. California (1941) 314 U.S. 219, 226–227, 62 S.Ct. 280, 86 L.Ed. 166; In re M. (1970) 34 A.D.2d 761, 310 N.Y.S.2d 399, 401–402 [concurring opinion].) I do not agree with the full import of the majority's statements (1) that "[t]he different purposes of the juvenile system may * * * justify reasonable differences in procedure so long as due process standards are met," or (2) that "[t]he purposes and structure of the juvenile system are different from the adult criminal justice system. Hence when due process has been satisfied reasonable differences in procedure are not unconstitutional." In my view, the justification of such "differences," upon the sole basis that "due process standards are met" or that "due process has been satisfied," ignores the affected juvenile's constitutional right to equal protection of the laws, as distinguished from his right to due process but as also guaranteed him by the

Fourteenth Amendment. (See, e.g., Douglas v. California (1963) 372 U.S. 353, 356–358, 83 S.Ct. 814, 9 L.Ed.2d 811.)

Appellant has invoked his right to equal protection on the ground that the uncorroborated accomplice testimony, upon which the adjudication of his wardship is based, would have been insufficient to support the *conviction* of an *adult* of the same crime (arson, in violation of Pen.Code, § 447a) by reason of the provisions of Penal Code section 1111.[76]

The decisions cited by the majority, in which comparable equal-protection claims by juveniles have been denied, rest upon one or both of the alternative premises that the disparity of treatment accorded to juveniles is justified (1) because a contrary holding would subvert the essential difference between juvenile and adult prosecutions by equating them as adversary proceedings (see, e.g., McKeiver v. Pennsylvania (1971) 403 U.S. 528, 550–551, 91 S.Ct. 1976, 29 L.Ed.2d 647 [trial by jury]); or (2) because the specific, disparate treatment in question otherwise operated to serve the best interests of the affected juvenile or of the system of juvenile justice generally. (See, e.g., T.N.G. v. Superior Court (1971) 4 Cal.3d 767, 783, 94 Cal.Rptr. 813, 484 P.2d 981; In re S.A. (1970) 6 Cal.App.3d 241, 246, 85 Cal.Rptr. 775.)

I am not persuaded that corroboration of accomplice testimony, if exacted in a juvenile proceeding pursuant to Penal Code section 1111, would escalate such proceeding to the adversary dimensions which attend the prosecution of an adult (compare McKeiver v. Pennsylvania, supra, 403 U.S. 528 at pp. 550–551, 91 S.Ct. 1976, 29 L.Ed.2d 647), nor that withholding the statute's benefits in such proceeding has the effect of serving the interests of the affected juvenile or of the system of juvenile justice generally. (Compare T.N.G. v. Superior Court, supra, 4 Cal.3d 767 at p. 783, 94 Cal.Rptr. 813, 484 P.2d 981; In re S.A., supra, 6 Cal.App.3d 241 at p. 246, 85 Cal.Rptr. 775.)

I am unable to find any other rational basis for the differentiated treatment which was accorded appellant in terms of Penal Code section 1111. It therefore appears to me that he falls squarely within the meaning of the United States Supreme Court's declaration (quoted by the majority) that judicial intervention in a juvenile's conduct "cannot take the form of subjecting the child to the stigma of a finding that he violated a criminal law and to the possibility of institutional confinement *on proof insufficient to convict him were he an adult.*" (In re Winship (1970) 397 U.S. 358, 367, 90 S.Ct. 1068, 1074, 25 L.Ed.2d 368 [italics added].)

I conclude that the adjudication of appellant's wardship, upon the basis of uncorroborated accomplice testimony which would have been

[76] "1111. A conviction can not be had upon the testimony of an accomplice unless it be corroborated by such other evidence as shall tend to connect the defendant with the commission of the offense; and the corroboration is not sufficient if it merely shows the commission of the offense or the circumstances thereof. An accomplice is hereby defined as one who is liable to prosecution for the identical offense charged against the defendant on trial in the cause in which the testimony of the accomplice is given."

insufficient to convict an adult of the crime with which he (appellant) was essentially charged, operated to deny him equal protection of the laws under the Fourteenth Amendment. I would therefore reverse the juvenile court's order accordingly.

NOTES

1. It is our opinion that the traditional concept of requirement of corroboration of an accomplice's testimony afforded to a person being prosecuted for a criminal offense should also be afforded a juvenile at the adjudicatory stage of a juvenile proceeding. This Court recognizes no constitutional requirement for the same but finds as a matter of policy it is necessary in the preservation of the integrity of the evidence in such a proceeding to require an accomplice's testimony at the adjudicatory stage to be corroborated. We therefore find that an accomplice's testimony must always be corroborated with legally sufficient evidence before a juvenile may be adjudicated a delinquent.

Smith v. State, 525 P.2d 1251, 1253–4 (Okla.Cr.1974).

2. If an out-of-court confession requires corroboration in a criminal case, should corroboration also be required in a juvenile case? In re R, 79 Cal.Rptr. 247 (1969) imposed such a requirement. A Georgia statute says that "[a] confession validly made by a child out of court is insufficient to support an adjudication of delinquency unless it is corroborated in whole or in part by other evidence." Ga.Code Ann. § 24A–2002(b) (1981 & 1983 Supp.).

3. In criminal cases containing corpus delicti issues, the problem of corroboration of an extra-judicial statement is usually, though not invariably, involved. Is the corpus delicti rule per se now a part of juvenile law? See In re State in the Interest of W.J., 116 N.J.Super. 462, 282 A.2d 770 (1971).

4. CONFRONTATION

IN RE APPEAL NO. 977 FROM CIRCUIT COURT OF BALTIMORE CITY

Maryland Court of Special Appeals, 1974.
22 Md.App. 511, 323 A.2d 663.

MOYLAN, JUDGE. This case involves the applicability of the confrontation clause of the Sixth Amendment, as fleshed out in Bruton v. United States, 391 U.S. 123, 88 S.Ct. 1620, 20 L.Ed.2d 476 (1968), to a delinquency hearing in the Juvenile Court of Baltimore City. The juvenile affected is the appellant, who shall be known herein as "John Doe." He and a companion, who shall be known herein as "Richard Roe," were charged with being delinquent by virtue of having committed acts which, had they been perpetrated by adults, would have constituted the crimes of 1) attempted robbery with a deadly weapon, 2) the use of a handgun in the commission of a crime of violence, and 3) assault with intent to murder. At a joint adjudicatory hearing, both respondents were found delinquent on the robbery and handgun charges and not delinquent on the assault charge by Judge Joseph L. Carter.

The robbery attempt in question occurred on September 18, 1973, at approximately 5:30 p.m. Four black males, apparently at the same time, entered Roman's Food Market. Richard Roe drew a gun upon Louis Roman, the owner. Mr. Roman fled toward the back of the store, pulling an audible burglar alarm as he did so. Richard Roe fired and a bullet struck the rear wall above Mr. Roman's head.

Richard Roe fled and was apprehended by the police after a short chase. The gun was recovered from some bushes near the store, where Roe had thrown it. Richard Roe was also positively identified by Dennis Lucas, a customer in the store at the time of the offense.

The case against the appellant was more tenuous. Lucas, the customer, made no observations pertaining to the appellant and did not identify him in any fashion, either at the trial or at the arrest scene. Officer Santivasci, who responded to the alarm, saw the appellant run from the store, although he also stated that he gave the appellant scant notice because he was busy pursuing Richard Roe. When Richard Roe was run down and brought back to the crime scene, the appellant was standing, unbothered by police, victim, or witness, in a crowd that had gathered. Only after an accusation had been made by Richard Roe and the appellant had been arrested, did Mr. Roman identify the appellant to the police officers as "part of the four that came into the store." At the trial, Mr. Roman could not identify the appellant.

The damning evidence against the appellant was a statement made by Richard Roe. As Richard Roe was being led back to the store, he pointed to the appellant who was standing in the gathered crowd and said, "I am not going for this myself. The other guy was with me is over there."

At the joint trial, Richard Roe elected not to testify. When the judge admitted the statement made by Richard Roe admitting his own guilt even as he accused the appellant of sharing that guilt, he appeared initially to be admitting it only as against Richard Roe and not as against the appellant. It is clear, however, that the statement was not so limited once it had been loosed upon the trial.

At the close of the evidence, the court asked for argument. The assistant state's attorney first summarized the case against Richard Roe. He concluded that phase of his argument, " * * * and I ask the Court to find the respondent, Richard Roe, delinquent of all three, and certainly if not of the lesser offense, as well as the other two petitions [sic]."

He then turned distinctly to the evidence against the appellant:

> "As far as [John Doe], I feel that [John Doe], along with the other two, who we do not know to this date who they were, was acting in concert with [Richard Roe]. [John Doe] was another thing, if Your Honor please. There was only one gun involved, and [Richard Roe] was the wielder of that weapon. [John Doe] was in the store. [John Doe] was running from the scene immediately thereafter. [John Doe] was in the vicinity at the apprehension, *and [John Doe] was pointed out by [Richard*

Roe], *who, when he was caught, said he was not going down the drain by himself."* (Emphasis supplied.)

The court's curiosity was immediately piqued:

"THE COURT: Which one said that?"

The assistant state's attorney not only again identified the out-of-court declarant but again drove home the hearsay accusation:

"[Richard Roe] said to Officer Cohen as a spontaneous statement [a theory not theretofore urged and untenable in any event] that he is not going by himself, that he was with me, and referred to [John Doe], and I ask Your Honor to find [John Doe] as culpable as [Richard Roe]."

The defense, in closing argument, attempted to remove the sting of the hearsay accusation:

" * * * we would like to go back and point out that the primary evidence submitted by the State is a piece of evidence which is—again it is inadmissible against our client, because it is an admission by [Richard Roe], and again, in Markley v. State, 173 Md. 309 [196 A. 95], that an admission or a confession of a co-defendant is not admissible for use against the co-defendant."

No statement followed from the court as to any limitation on the use of the Richard Roe statement and the final fact-finding by the court in arriving at its verdict indicates no such limiting:

"The next charge is that [John Doe] in company with [Richard Roe] unlawfully did, with a dangerous and deadly weapon, attempt to rob Louis Roman. I think that—and, of course, *you have got one definite piece of evidence here, which standing alone might not be enough, but* he was seen, that is to say, [*John Doe*] *was seen running from the store.* I think the testimony of the officer that Mr. Roman identified [John Doe] at the scene, or shortly thereafter is admissible. *I think the other statement of [Richard Roe] is admissible. Taken together, I think it is sufficient.* I have no doubts of *his* participation in this affair and *his* guilt, so I find both of them delinquent as to that particular charge." (Emphasis supplied.)

The above fact-finding is clearly as to the appellant and not, as the State urged upon at argument, a composite fact-finding weaving back and forth between the cases against both accused. There is no mention of the gun or its recovery, the chase of Richard Roe or his identification by Lucas. The court was clearly summarizing the case against the appellant.

Although we are dealing for the first time with the application of this particular Sixth Amendment protection to the juvenile forum, the guiding principles give clear direction. Pointer v. Texas, 380 U.S. 400, 85 S.Ct. 1065, 13 L.Ed.2d 923 (1965), established that the confrontation clause of the Sixth Amendment was absorbed into the due process clause of the Fourteenth Amendment and, therefore, applicable to the states. Bruton v. United States, supra, established that, in a jury trial at least, the admission of a co-defendant's confession implicating the defendant constituted reversible error where the confessing co-defendant did not take the stand. The undergirding principle is that such a procedure denies a defendant his Sixth Amendment right to confront, via cross-examination, his accuser.

Maryland had anticipated the *Bruton* decision, at least as to the literal non-admissibility of the confession of a non-testifying co-defendant against a non-confessing defendant. Malcolm v. State, 232 Md. 222, 192 A.2d 281 (1963). Since the decision in *Bruton*, we have applied its principle in a number of cases, both jury and non-jury.
* * *

In the present case, of course, we are dealing with a juvenile delinquency adjudicatory hearing, and not a criminal trial. In re Gault, 387 U.S. 1, 87 S.Ct. 1428, 18 L.Ed.2d 527 (1967), however, is completely dispositive. In applying various constitutional protections to the "quasi-criminal" proceedings in the adjudication of delinquency, the Supreme Court specifically included:

1.   Notice of charges;

2.   Right to counsel;

3.   Right to confrontation and cross-examination; and

4.   The privilege against compulsory self-incrimination.

On cross-examination, the Court was very explicit, at 387 U.S. 57, 87 S.Ct. 1459:

> "We now hold that, absent a valid confession, a determination of delinquency and an order of commitment to a state institution cannot be sustained in the absence of sworn testimony subjected to the opportunity for cross-examination in accordance with our law and constitutional requirements."

The applicability to juvenile delinquency adjudicatory hearings of the Sixth Amendment confrontation clause generally and the *Bruton* doctrine specifically cannot be doubted. We hold that they do apply.

It is, furthermore, clear in the instant case that none of the recognized exceptions to the *Bruton* doctrine bar its utilization here. The exclusionary rule of *Bruton*, for instance, is not required where the confessing co-defendant takes the stand and the right to confrontation, through cross-examination, is therefore satisfied. * * * Such is not the case here. The exclusionary rule of *Bruton* has been held to be inapplicable where the co-defendant's confession does not directly implicate the defendant. * * * Such is not the case here. The exclusionary rule of *Bruton* has been held to be inapplicable where the questioned confession merely corroborates and makes more credible the testimony of an adverse witness, * * * or where the references to the defendant are either neutral or favorable. * * * Neither is the case here. The exclusionary rule of *Bruton* has been held to be inapplicable when the co-defendant's out-of-court confession is adopted by the defendant, * * * or where it merely "interlocks" with the defendant's own statements. * * * Such is not the case here.

The State takes ultimate refuge in reading overbroadly a perfectly valid dictum of Judge Powers for this Court in Bowman, Brooks and Harris v. State, supra, at 16 Md.App. 388, 297 A.2d n. 3: "In view of the basis of the *Bruton* holding, and the role of a judge in a non-jury trial as discussed by the Court of Appeals in State v. Hutchinson, 260 Md. 227, 271 A.2d 641, it would seem that there could be no *Bruton* error in a non-jury trial in Maryland." *Hutchinson*, the predicate case, established simply that when a trial judge announces that he is factoring an admittedly inadmissible piece of evidence out of his decisional equation, we will indulge in the presumption that he, unlike a jury of laymen, is able to so compartmentalize his thought process. Judge Powers' dictum, correct in the limited context that a jury cannot be relied upon to sort out the contaminating chaff of the inadmissible from the hygienic wheat of the admissible even upon proper instruction, simply did not speak to the situation where the judge himself misperceives the admissibility question in the first instance.[77] In the court trial, we initially presume that the judge, unlike the lay jury, is able to follow his own instructions in terms of careful discrimination. The presumption is rebutted, however (or, more properly, it does not even arise), where the judge's instructions to himself are discernibly erroneous. In the instant case, we do not question the capacity of the judge to discount the Richard Roe admission, had he indicated an inclination so to discount. The record reveals, however, that he affirmatively chose to consider and gave it a pivotal weight. That, we hold, was error.

It remains only to be seen whether the error was harmless. Our considered use of the adjective "pivotal" in the preceding paragraph betrays our answer to that question. *Bruton* errors, of course, may be harmless. Schneble v. Florida, 405 U.S. 427, 92 S.Ct. 1056, 31 L.Ed.2d 340 (1972) (where "the properly admitted evidence of guilt is so overwhelming, and the prejudicial effect of the codefendant's admission is so insignificant by comparison, that it is clear beyond a reasonable doubt that the improper use of the admission was harmless error"); Harrington v. California, 395 U.S. 250, 89 S.Ct. 1726, 23 L.Ed.2d 284 (1969) (where a *Bruton* error was found harmless because the testimony of other eyewitnesses made the questioned confession of a co-defendant relatively insignificant and cumulative). The acid test for harmless error was enunciated in Chapman v. California, 386 U.S. 18, at 24, 87 S.Ct. 824, at 828, 17 L.Ed.2d 705 (1967):

> "[B]efore a federal constitutional error can be held harmless, the court must be able to declare a belief that it was harmless beyond a reasonable doubt."

[77] In *Bowman*, as in *Hutchinson*, the trial court affirmatively excluded the questioned evidence.

We are not satisfied in the present case beyond a reasonable doubt that the *Bruton* error did not contribute to the appellant's adjudication of delinquency. Indeed, we are satisfied that quite the reverse was true. In this belief, we are reinforced by In re Ingram, 15 Md.App. 356, 291 A.2d 78 (1972). In *Ingram*, the judge was held to have improperly considered in a waiver hearing a prior criminal court conviction which had been voided. In reversing, we noted the inapplicability of the *Hutchinson* rationale because of the trial court's "obvious reliance" upon the voided criminal proceedings. The "obvious reliance" upon Richard Roe confession in the instant case was manifest and explicit.

In view of our disposition of the case upon this issue, it is unnecessary to address the two other contentions raised by the appellant.

Judgment reversed; case remanded for new hearing.

5. SELF–INCRIMINATION

IN RE SPALDING

Maryland Court of Appeals, 1975.
273 Md. 690, 332 A.2d 246.

Argued before MURPHY, C.J., and SINGLEY, SMITH, DIGGES, LEVINE, ELDRIDGE and O'DONNELL, JJ.

LEVINE, JUDGE. In the landmark decision of In re Gault, 387 U.S. 1, 87 S.Ct. 1428, 18 L.Ed.2d 527 (1967), the Supreme Court held, for the first time, that various of the federal constitutional guarantees accompanying ordinary criminal proceedings are applicable, in certain instances, to state juvenile delinquency cases. Those safeguards, all embraced within fundamental procedural due process, are: Notice of charges; the right to counsel; confrontation and cross-examination; and the privilege against self-incrimination. Appellant seeks to extend that holding—with specific reference to self-incrimination—to another area of juvenile court jurisdiction in Maryland, known as "Children in Need of Supervision" (CINS).

The Court of Special Appeals in Matter of Carter and Spalding, 20 Md.App. 633, 318 A.2d 269 (1974), upheld the decision of the Circuit Court for Baltimore County sitting as a Juvenile Court rejecting appellant's claim. We granted certiorari to consider whether statements made to the police by appellant—then 13 years of age—should have been suppressed; whether she was denied her constitutional right to refuse to testify; and whether she should have been permitted to cross-examine a police officer with regard to both voluntariness of the statements made to him and the warnings mandated by Miranda v. Arizona, 384 U.S. 436, 86 S.Ct. 1602, 16 L.Ed.2d 694, 10 A.L.R.3d 974 (1966).

In the early morning hours of January 31, 1973, Officer Joseph W. Price, a member of the Baltimore County Police Department assigned to the Dundalk station, responded on instructions from his headquarters to a call from City Hospital to investigate a possible rape and overdose of narcotics. There, he was met by a Mr. Carter, who advised him that his daughter, age 11, had taken a white tablet which had impaired her speech, had caused a loss of equilibrium and had dilated her pupils. She had also admitted to her parents that she had engaged in sexual intercourse with an adult male on January 29 in an apartment immediately below that occupied by her family. She contrived this visit by climbing down from her bedroom window. When questioned by the police officer, the child acknowledged the episode of the 29th, and added that on the same occasion she had engaged in sexual acts with others who were present including two women. The Carters had brought their daughter to the hospital because they wanted her examined for possible sexual intercourse and treated for the drug.

Later that morning, at approximately 6:30 A.M., Officer Price again met with the Carter family at the Dundalk police station. Also there in response to a phone call from the officer were appellant and her mother. The minister of the church attended by both families was also present. Officer Price and one of his superiors then proceeded to interrogate both girls under somewhat disorganized conditions. Much of this appears to have resulted from interference by both the minister, who exercised considerable influence over the girls, and the parents. Ultimately, with permission of the latter, Officer Price obtained written statements from both girls. The officer later testified that the parents had " * * * insisted on the girls giving the information. They were at sometime, they were [sic] some yelling at the girls and the girls being upset, crying, they were trying to calm them down. They were trying to help and assist getting all the information they could."

In her oral and written statements to the police that morning, as well as in her statements subsequently given to Juvenile Bureau detectives, appellant admitted her participation in the same events of the 29th as had been described by the Carter youngster. In doing so, she supplied the names of all those who had been in attendance on that occasion. She also recounted additional episodes of similar sexual activity in the basement of her home with male boarders residing there; and at a number of other "parties" in the apartment below that occupied by the Carters. She was able to attend these early-morning functions amounting to nothing less than orgies at which adults and juveniles were in heavy attendance, by placing a sleeping pill in her mother's coffee. She was furnished the pills, and was driven to those bizarre parties by one Sheldon B. Coon, who apparently was the impresario of the "sex ring." He gave a pill to the girls on each occasion immediately before they departed from their residences, and again before they engaged in sexual inter-course. This seems to have had a narcotic-like influence on them.

After the police had struggled through their various interroga-tion procedures on the 31st, they took the girls to the Parkville police station, with the approval of the Department of Juvenile Services, where they were detained overnight. This step was taken because the statements furnished by the girls disclosed assaults upon them by Coon, who threatened to kill them if they ever revealed information to anyone concerning the parties. The official report filed by the police specified "protective custody" as the reason for the detention. Once the police had completed the interviews, they immediately sought arrest warrants for the large number of adults identified by the girls. The men in this group were charged with "statutory rape" and the women with "unnatural and perverted sexual practices." In both instances, the two girls were listed as victims.

On the following morning, February 1, 1973, both girls were brought before Juvenile Master Kahl pursuant to petitions of the Department of Juvenile Services, which charged each with being a "delinquent child" and "in need of supervision,[78] within the meaning and intent of Section 70–2 of Article 26 of the Annotated Code of Maryland." The Master found both girls to be in need of care and treatment, but, significantly, did not find them to be "delinquent." [79] His memorandum, dated February 1, 1973, is quoted here:

> "Police investigation indicates that these young girls have been *victimized* by a group of adults in the Dundalk area and elsewhere, for purposes of sexual abuse and drug experimentation. It is not known at this point just how much damage has already been done, physically and psychologically, to these girls. The situation is one of the most serious that I have encountered in my four years with the Juvenile Court.
>
> "Both girls are in need of medical treatment immediately, and notwithstanding whatever wishes the parents of the girls may have at this time, *I find them to be Children In Need Of Supervision* and am committing them to the Department of Juvenile Services for placement, with the intention that they shall be immediately admitted to the University Hospital *for medical evaluation and treatment.*
>
> "On February 7, 1973, they are to be transported to the Maryland Children's Center for evaluation and return to Court one month thereafter." (emphasis added).

During the ensuing month, extensive psychiatric and family studies were conducted at the Maryland Children's Center.

On March 7, 1973, immediately upon their return from the Children's Center, the girls attended a hearing before Juvenile Master Peach. Armed with the thorough reports and comprehensive

---

[78] The reasons assigned for these allegations are:

" * * * investigation by the Baltimore County Police Department revealed that the respondent had consumed controlled and prohibitive [sic] narcotics and engaged in acts of sexual intercourse and sexual perversion with an unknown number of male and female adults for a period of more than one year. The respondent is ungovernable and beyond the control of her parent, deports herself in such a manner as to be a danger to herself and others and is in need of care and treatment."

[79] In fact, the petition previously referred to above appears to contain the only official suggestion of delinquency in the record. Ironically, the "complaint" form of the Department of Juvenile Services, apparently completed on either the 31st or 1st, lists "child in need of supervision" as the sole "offense description."

recommendation of the Children's Center, he adjudicated each girl to be "a child in need of supervision" and "in need of care and treatment." He therefore "committed both of them to the Department of Juvenile Services for placement and planning so that they can receive some therapy to help them cope with the problems which I am sure lie ahead for both of them." Exceptions to the findings and recommendations of the Master were duly noted on behalf of each juvenile, accompanied by a request for a *de novo* hearing before the court.

Pursuant to the exceptions and requests, the cases came on for trial on May 3, 1973, before the Circuit Court for Baltimore County sitting as a Juvenile Court (Jenifer, J.), where extensive testimony and argument ensued in accordance with Maryland Rule 908. Shortly before the trial commenced, a written motion was filed on behalf of appellant aimed at suppressing the statements made by her to the police, to the Juvenile Service workers and to the staff of the Children's Center. At the outset of the trial, the court announced that it would reserve its ruling on that motion.

During the course of the trial, objections to the admissibility of those statements were renewed on the grounds that the fourfold *Miranda* warnings had not been given by any of the interrogating officers prior to or during any questioning.[80] Officer Price, however, had announced to all those assembled at the police station that "anything they said could be used against them in a court of law if they were charged." This colloquy also appears in the testimony:

> "MR. MEOLA: Your Honor, I would like to question the officer about what warning he did give these children.
>
> "THE COURT: I don't think he has to give any warning. *They were not in custody for the commission of a crime or for a delinquency petition at this time.* They were volunteered statements given with the consent at the insistence of the parents. The *Miranda* warning doesn't apply to these statements, gentlemen." (emphasis added).

It is this refusal that laid the groundwork for one of the three questions framed by the Writ of Certiorari.

Later in the trial, when asked by the court to describe how he elicited the statements from the girls, Officer Price stated "They volunteered all of this information to begin with, and it was so bizarre I started asking questions to try to pinpoint dates and time and individuals." The confusion which reigned at the police station and the abbreviated warning announced by Officer Price are demonstrated in this excerpt from his testimony:

> "Q Okay, you stated earlier the parents were shouting at the girls?
>
> "A Everybody was yelling at each other trying to get information, specifically from Elaine [Carter], because she was

---

[80] Only the statements made to the police are included within the ambit of our review pursuant to the Writ of Certiorari.

still under the influence of drugs, trying to get through to her. The parents were upset.

"Q   You stated earlier the girls were crying?

"A   Yes, I did, from the yelling of the parents.

"Q   Whom did you make the statement to the statement they made would be used against them, to whom did you make that statement?

"A   I made it to everyone in the room there, anything they said could be used against them in a court of law.

"THE COURT: Did you go any further?

"A   Yes, sir, if they were charged with a crime, named offense.

"Q   Was this while they were quiet or were they still yelling?

"A   Everybody was milling around. I had a little bit of trouble with Reverend Gatling there. I had to threaten to arrest him just to keep him quiet.

"Q   Do you know for certain that the parents heard that statement?

"A   I cannot be certain anybody heard anything."

In the course of their testimony, Officer Price and the detectives from the Juvenile Bureau were permitted, over objection, to state what the girls had said during the various interviews. Then, an announcement by the prosecuting attorney that he proposed to call appellant to the stand as a witness drew a vigorous objection from counsel on the ground of self-incrimination. Prior to any definitive ruling by the court, however, she was shown her written statement given to Officer Price on January 31, and confirmed the truth of its contents. She also acknowledged on her direct testimony that she knew Coon and certain of the other persons for whom adult warrants had been issued. When asked by her own counsel whether anyone at the police station had informed her that she was not required to make any statements, she replied:

"A   Well, we more or less made it on our own. We figured we could save some more kids, but they gave us no rights or anything.

"THE COURT: Give you what?

"A   Any kind of rights, we thought we were doing the State a favor.

"THE COURT: Well, as I understand that you said you made the statement on your own?

"A   Yes."

At the conclusion of the trial, the court rendered its decision orally, finding that the evidence overwhelmingly had established the girls to be in need of supervision because they had "deported themselves so as to injure or endanger themselves or others" and there-

fore required "guidance, treatment, or rehabilitation." These findings were incorporated into written orders, which also committed the
girls to the jurisdiction of the Department of Juvenile Services for
placement in foster homes with prescribed visitation rights granted to
their parents. It is from those orders that the appeal was taken to
the Court of Special Appeals.

The contentions that the statements made to the police should
have been suppressed at the court hearing and that cross-examination
of the police officer should have been permitted regarding the voluntariness of those statements and the *Miranda* warnings were rejected by the Court of Special Appeals on the basis that the questioning of the police at the hospital and at the police station was not
custodial interrogation within the meaning of *Miranda*.

In holding that appellant's compelled testimony did not violate
her privilege against self-incrimination, the Court of Special Appeals
carefully traced the enactment of the jurisdictional category, "Child
in Need of Supervision," created by Chapter 432 of the Laws of 1969.
As Judge Moore noted for the court, such a child refers to one who is:

" '(1) Subject to compulsory school attendance who is habitually
and without justification truant from school;

" '(2) Without substantial fault on the part of his parents, guardian, or other custodian, who is habitually disobedient, *ungovernable,* and beyond their control;

" '(3) *Who so deports himself as to injure or endanger himself
or others;* or

" '(4) Who has committed an offense applicable only to children;
and

" '(5) Requires guidance, treatment or rehabilitation.' " (emphasis
added). 20 Md.App. at 649, 318 A.2d at 278.

This classification, therefore, stands in marked contrast to a "Delinquent child," defined as one " 'who commits a delinquent act and who
requires supervision, treatment or rehabilitation.' [Subject to the
provisions of Art. 26, § 70–2(d)] a 'Delinquent act' was defined in
§ 70–1(g) as 'an act which is in violation of Article 66½ of this Code,
any other traffic violation, or an act *which would be a crime if done
by a person who is not a child.'* " (Emphasis in original). 20 Md.
App. at 649–650, 318 A.2d at 279.

Essentially, then, the Court of Special Appeals stressed the basic
statutory distinctions between the delinquency and CINS categories,
taking particular care to emphasize the differences in disposition
which are prescribed for each. For example, Code (1957, 1966 Repl.
Vol., 1972 Supp.) Art. 26, § 70–19, applicable at all times material to
these proceedings, provided:

"(a) If a child is found to be neglected, delinquent, in need of
supervision, mentally handicapped, or dependent, the court may
make disposition as most suited to the physical, mental, and
moral welfare of the child; but *no child (except a delinquent*

child) may be confined in an institution or other facility designed or operated for the benefit of delinquent children, provided that this prohibition shall not apply to facilities designated by the State Department of Juvenile Services of the Department of Health and Mental Hygiene.

"(b) If an adequate facility required by this section has not been established, the court may approve a facility under the supervision and control of the State departments of juvenile services, social services, mental hygiene and other appropriate child-care agencies, for temporary use as such facility; but the use of a facility which does not meet the requirement of this section may not continue beyond January 1, 1975." (emphasis added).

And § 70–21 also provided, in relevant part, that "No child shall be committed or transferred to a penal institution or other facility used primarily for the execution of sentences of persons convicted of a crime." [81]

The Court of Special Appeals summed it all up in stating:

"It is evident, we think, that an important purpose of the legislative revision of the juvenile code was to insulate certain forms of juvenile misconduct from the consequences of an adjudication of delinquency as described in *Gault.* The creation of the category of CINS reflects a studied design of the legislature to insure that treatment of children guilty of misconduct peculiarly reflecting the propensities and susceptibilities of youth, will acquire none of the institutional, quasi-penal features of treatment that in *Gault's* view had been the main difference between the theory and the practice of the juvenile court system. * * *" 20 Md.App. at 653, 318 A.2d at 281.

Thus, it "decline[d] to go further and hold that in a proceeding upon a CINS petition due process requires that the child be permitted, on Fifth Amendment grounds, to have relevant evidence excluded and to refuse to testify." *Id.* at 654, 318 A.2d at 281.

We shall affirm, finding it necessary, however, to decide only that the Fifth Amendment privilege against self-incrimination is inapplicable to this proceeding. Because we so hold, the related questions of *Miranda* warnings and voluntariness are subsumed within that holding. "The privilege against self-incrimination is, of course, related to the question of the safeguards necessary to assure that admissions or confessions are reasonably trustworthy, that they are not the mere fruits of fear or coercion, but are reliable expressions of the truth." In re Gault, supra, 387 U.S. at 47, 87 S.Ct. at 1454.

Since this case derives its impetus from *Gault*, we pause for a careful examination of the relevant facts on which that decision is

---

[81] Both appellee and the Court of Special Appeals have noted that in the 1974 recodification, § 3–832 added a prohibition against confinement "in a juvenile training school or any similar institution" for all categories except delinquency. This was not effective, however, in May 1973.

bottomed. The conduct which precipitated the police action there consisted of "lewd or indecent remarks" allegedly made during a telephone call to the female complainant. As a consequence, Gault was charged with being, and was found by a juvenile court judge to be, a "delinquent child."

Under the Arizona Juvenile Code, not unlike its Maryland counterpart, the definition of a "delinquent child" includes one "who has violated a law of the state * * *." The Arizona Criminal Code provided "that a person who 'in the presence or hearing of any woman or child * * * uses vulgar, abusive or obscene language, is guilty of a misdemeanor. * * *' The penalty specified in the Criminal Code, which would apply to an adult, is $5 to $50, or imprisonment for not more than two months." 387 U.S. at 8–9, 87 S.Ct. at 1434. Gault, who was then 15, was committed as a juvenile delinquent to the State Industrial School "'for the period of his minority [that is, until 21], unless sooner discharged by due process of law.'" 387 U.S. at 7–8, 87 S.Ct. at 1433 (brackets in original).

Although some disagreement existed over what had transpired at the juvenile court hearing, there being no transcript or recording of those proceedings, it is apparent that *Gault* was predicated on alleged admissions made in response to questions propounded by the juvenile court judge. Since the complainant did not appear, the adjudication of delinquency appears to have rested solely on those admissions. Neither Gault nor his parents were advised that he was not required to testify or make a statement, or that an incriminating statement might result in his commitment as a "delinquent." As we have already intimated, Gault was not represented by counsel.

In *Gault*, the Court did not deal with the totality of the relationship between the juvenile and the state; indeed, it did not even consider the entire process applicable to juvenile "delinquents."

" * * * We consider only the problems presented to us by this case. These relate to the proceedings by which a determination is made as to whether a juvenile is a 'delinquent' as a result of alleged misconduct on his part, with the consequence that he may be committed to a state institution. As to these proceedings, there appears to be little current dissent from the proposition that the Due Process Clause has a role to play. * * *" 387 U.S. at 13, 87 S.Ct. at 1436.

Turning to the issue of self-incrimination, the Court again emphasized that it was " * * * concerned only with a proceeding to determine whether a minor is a 'delinquent' and which may result in commitment to a state institution." 387 U.S. at 44, 87 S.Ct. at 1452. This same emphasis was repeated in even stronger terms when the Court said that " * * * juvenile proceedings to determine 'delinquency,' which may lead to commitment to a state institution, must be regarded as 'criminal' for purposes of the privilege against self-incrimination." 387 U.S. at 49, 87 S.Ct. at 1455. Thus, the scope of *Gault* is clear. When the Supreme Court " * * * conclude[d] that the constitutional privilege against self-incrimination is applicable in the case of juveniles as it is with respect to adults," 387 U.S. at 55, 87 S.Ct. at 1458, it was referring to a proceeding to determine "delinquency," viz., " * * * an act which would be a crime if done by a person who is not a child," which is the statutory definition in Maryland. The test enunciated in *Gault*, however, is two-pronged. In addition, the "delinquency" must be such that it may result in commitment to a state institution.

That *Gault* must be so read is confirmed, we think, by subsequent decisions of the Supreme Court. To the panoply of constitutional safeguards extended by *Gault* has subsequently been added the requirement of proof beyond a reasonable doubt, In re Winship, 397 U.S. 358, 90 S.Ct. 1068, 25 L.Ed.2d 368 (1970). "The Court held in In Re Winship * * * that proof beyond a reasonable doubt is among the essentials of due process and fair treatment that must be afforded at the adjudicatory stage *when a juvenile is charged with an act that would constitute a crime if committed by an adult.*" Ivan V. v. City of New York, 407 U.S. 203, 92 S.Ct. 1951, 32 L.Ed.2d 659 (1972) (applying *Winship* retroactively) (emphasis added). See McKeiver v. Pennsylvania, 403 U.S. 528, 537, 91 S.Ct. 1976, 29 L.Ed. 2d 647 (1971).

Whatever else is established by *Gault*, it is clear that labels are not controlling in determining the applicability of the Due Process Clause to juvenile proceedings. In regard to the first "prong" of the test, for example, it is doubtful that the *Gault* result would have been different had merely the title of the proceedings been changed from "delinquency" to "CINS," and all else had remained the same. The essential element is that the juvenile be charged with an act which would be a crime if committed by an adult. In In re Winship, supra, the Court relied on *Gault* in answering affirmatively the question "whether proof beyond a reasonable doubt is among the 'essentials of due process and fair treatment' required during the adjudicatory stage *when a juvenile is charged with an act which would constitute a crime if committed by an adult.*" 397 U.S. at 359, 90 S.Ct. at 1070 (emphasis added). The Court later added that " * * * intervention [by a juvenile court] cannot take the form of subjecting the child to the stigma of a finding that he violated a criminal law and to the possibility of institutional confinement on proof insufficient to convict him were he an adult." Id. at 367, 90 S.Ct. at 1074. See Ivan V. v. City of New York, supra, 407 U.S. at 203, 92 S.Ct. 1951.

Labels are equally unimportant in terms of the second "prong," confinement in a state institution. As the Court said:

> " * * * A boy is charged with misconduct. The boy is committed to an institution where he may be restrained of liberty for years. It is of no constitutional consequence—and of limited practical meaning—that the institution to which he is committed is called an Industrial School. The fact of the matter is that, however euphemistic the title, a 'receiving home' or an 'industrial school' for juveniles is an institution of confinement in which the

child is incarcerated for a greater or lesser time. His world becomes 'a building with whitewashed walls, regimented routine and institutional hours * * *.' Instead of mother and father and sisters and brothers and friends and classmates, his world is peopled by guards, custodians, state employees, and 'delinquents' confined with him for anything from waywardness to rape and homicide." In re Gault, supra, 387 U.S. at 27, 87 S.Ct. at 1443.

"A proceeding where the issue is whether the child will be found to be 'delinquent' and subjected to the loss of his liberty for years is comparable in seriousness to a felony prosecution." 387 U.S. at 36, 87 S.Ct. at 1448. Finally, the Court added: "For this purpose, at least, commitment is a deprivation of liberty. It is incarceration against one's will, whether it be called 'criminal' or 'civil.'" 387 U.S. at 50, 87 S.Ct. at 1455.

In sum, then, Due Process requires that various of the federal constitutional guarantees accompanying ordinary criminal proceedings, specifically including the privilege against self-incrimination, be made applicable at the adjudicatory stage of those juvenile proceedings in which the act charged would constitute a crime if committed by an adult *and* which may result in confinement of the child to a state institution.

Other state courts that have considered the question of which proceedings should invoke an application of the *Gault* rights have reached similar conclusions. For example, California's statutory scheme is quite similar to Maryland's, an apparent difference, however, being that delinquent and CINS children may be sent to the same institutions under the California Code. In that state, "[j]uveniles are entitled to the fundamental protection of the Bill of Rights in proceedings that may result in confinement or other sanctions, whether the state labels these proceedings 'criminal' or 'civil.' (citations omitted)." M. v. Superior Court of Shasta County, 4 Cal.3d 370, 375, 93 Cal.Rptr. 752, 756, 482 P.2d 664, 668 (1971).

The California courts have consistently held that CINS children are entitled to the same guarantees as delinquent children when they are charged with an act which would be a crime if committed by an adult, M. v. Superior Court of Shasta County, supra, 93 Cal.Rptr. at 758, 482 P.2d at 670 (" * * * juveniles, like adults, are constitutionally entitled under the Due Process Clause to proof beyond a reasonable doubt at the adjudicatory stage when they are charged with an act which would constitute a crime if committed by an adult."); [82] In re D, 23 Cal.App.3d 1045, 100 Cal.Rptr. 706, 708 (1972) ("Since the minors are not accused of wrongdoing [under § 600] the constitutional mandates applicable to hearings pursuant to Welfare and Institutions Code sections 601 and 602 * * * have no relevancy."); In re R, 274 Cal.App.2d 749, 79 Cal.Rptr. 247, 250 (1969) ("Where, however, the proof of the allegation rests solely upon the admissions of the

---

[82] Section 702.5 of the California Welfare and Institutions Code specifically gives the right against self-incrimination to § 601 and § 602 children, but this statutory provision has not been the rationale of these cases.

minor, ＊ ＊ ＊ the minor may rightly contend that proof of such allegations of the commission of a felony must be under the same standards as if the petition were under section 602 [delinquency] ＊ ＊ ＊ "); In re Rambeau, 266 Cal.App.2d 1, 72 Cal.Rptr. 171, 176–77 (1968) (juvenile protected against self-incrimination "where the essential finding of the court is that a felony ＊ ＊ ＊ has been committed.")

Illustrative of the label fallacy is In re H, 5 Cal.App.3d 781, 85 Cal.Rptr. 359 (1970). In that case, a juvenile was charged under § 602 [delinquency] with assault with a deadly weapon and manslaughter. The sole evidence against him was his confession that he struck the child for whom he was babysitting. The confession was suppressed, as having been illegally obtained, and the petition was dismissed. The trial judge, on his own motion, however, promptly amended the petition to charge the juvenile with being "in danger of leading an idle, dissolute, lewd, or immoral life" under § 601 [CINS]; and then admitted the confession and sustained the petition, since the defendant was no longer charged with "delinquency." The Court of Appeal reversed, holding:

> "Even though the amended petition was filed under section 601 [CINS], the minor rightly may demand that proof of the allegation of the *commission of felonies* must meet the same standards as if the petition was brought under section 602 [delinquency], namely, a preponderance of evidence legally admissible in the trial of *criminal* cases. ＊ ＊ ＊ 'Thus, a confession illegally obtained cannot be relied upon to support a finding that a minor committed a crime.' (citations omitted)." 85 Cal. Rptr. at 366. (emphasis in original).

In Florida, the reasonable doubt standard is applied in the adjudicatory phase of a delinquency proceeding where the act of delinquency charged is one which would constitute a crime if committed by an adult. State v. V.D.B., 270 So.2d 6 (Fla.1972). "Despite the fact that the courts have with consistency recognized the civil character of juvenile proceedings, nonetheless, it is now well established that in delinquency proceedings based upon a charge of violation of criminal law (which if proved could lead to loss of liberty) criminal due process standards apply ＊ ＊ ＊." In Interest of E.P., 291 So.2d 238, 239 (Fla.App.1974).

Similarly, the Rhode Island Supreme Court has held: "Where the state attempts to have a juvenile declared wayward or delinquent because he violated a state criminal statute, the state must prove beyond a reasonable doubt each and every element of the offense charged." In re Pereira, 306 A.2d 821, 823 (R.I.1973). On the other hand, *Gault* rights have been held not to apply "in a juvenile proceeding where no public offense is charged." In re Henderson, 199 N.W.2d 111, 119 (Iowa 1972); In re D, supra, 23 Cal.App.3d 1045, 100 Cal.Rptr. at 708.

We turn then to Cindy Ann Spalding. The state contends that the *Gault* rights do not apply to CINS because of the significant differences between those proceedings and delinquency cases. It cites these dissimilarities: CINS children may not be confined in institutions designed or operated for the benefit of delinquent children; CINS children may not be placed in detention;[83] and CINS children may not be waived to adult criminal courts. Also, in the teeth of the *Gault* teaching that labels are of little consequence, the State nevertheless argues that the label "CINS" bears significantly less stigma than "delinquent." Finally, the State claims that, having been placed in a foster home, appellant was not committed to a "state institution" because shelter care and foster homes are not in that category.

Understandably enough, appellant maintains that "CINS" children, though treated differently in certain respects, are the same as "delinquent" children for the purpose of applying *Gault* rights. She emphasizes that at the time of her hearing, she conceivably could have been confined with delinquent children; that she could have been committed to a "state institution," and thus compelled to leave her home with a resulting curtailment of her freedom; that she is now one step closer to incarceration; and that she was charged with violating a criminal statute. Although there is much to commend these arguments, we need not decide whether the second prong of the *Gault* test, i.e., potential confinement of the child to a state institution, mandated an application of the privilege against self-incrimination in this case. We reach this conclusion because, in any event, we think that appellant was not *charged* in this proceeding with an act which would constitute a crime if committed by an adult.

As we noted earlier, the petition filed on February 1, 1973, did allege that appellant was both a "delinquent child" and a "child in need of supervision." The reasons assigned for these allegations were the consumption of narcotics, the acts of sexual intercourse and perversion practiced upon her, and her ungovernability. But, in the context of all the material events, which ensued during the critical period, since she was, in fact, a victim, the charge of "delinquency" in the petition must be regarded as simply an unexplained anomaly.

The testimony describing the circumstances at the hospital and the police station clearly depicts the girls as victims of "sex" crimes committed by the adults. That this was the position of the police is borne out not merely by their subsequent testimony, but also by their immediate application for adult arrest warrants listing the girls as victims; the overnight detention for the purpose of "protective custody"; and the total absence of suggested criminality on the part of the girls in any police records.

[83] Code (1974), § 3–823 of the Courts and Judicial Proceedings Article, effective January 1, 1974, so provides; but as we have already observed, it is the statutory scheme applicable in May 1973 that governs this case. At that time, Art. 26, § 70–12 permitted detention of CINS children, but not in a jail or other facility used for detention of adults charged with a criminal offense and children adjudicated or alleged to be delinquent. Moreover, even this statutory prohibition was riddled with exceptions.

Even within the Department of Juvenile Services, the "delinquency" charge is out-of-step with every other official record or entry pertaining to the girls. Its own complaint form, completed on the same day as the petition, lists "child in need of supervision" as the single "offense description." Again, on that same day, February 1, the Master referred to the girls as having "been victimized by a group of adults," found them to be "in Need of Supervision" and omitted any mention of "delinquency." Nothing in their four-week commitment to Maryland Children's Center for psychiatric evaluation was inconsistent with this official attitude. Nor do the reports and recommendations of that institution reflect a contrary view.

In sum, with the elimination of the delinquency "charge" by the Master on February 1, the claims of alleged "criminal" conduct, on which it was premised, vanished with it. What remained was the single allegation that appellant " * * * is ungovernable and beyond the control of her parent, deports herself in such a manner as to be a danger to herself and others and is in need of care and treatment." From that time forward, at least, appellant was not charged in this proceeding with any acts which would constitute a crime if committed by an adult.

As we have said, we do not find it necessary to rest our decision on the second prong of the test laid down by *Gault*, pertaining to possible confinement in a "state institution." It is sufficient to hold that since appellant was not charged with an act which, in the circumstances of this case, would constitute a crime if committed by an adult, the privilege against self-incrimination is not applicable to these proceedings.

Judgment affirmed; appellant to pay costs.

ELDRIDGE, JUDGE (dissenting):

The majority's decision in this case cannot be reconciled with In re Gault, 387 U.S. 1, 87 S.Ct. 1428, 18 L.Ed.2d 527 (1967), and later Supreme Court cases dealing with the constitutional rights to be accorded accused children in juvenile proceedings. * * *

The majority opinion, in my view, correctly construes *Gault*, and the subsequent Supreme Court cases, as setting forth a two-pronged test for determining whether the Fifth Amendment privilege against self-incrimination is applicable to a juvenile proceeding. The test is: (1) whether the juvenile "is charged with an act that would constitute a crime if committed by an adult," * * * and (2) whether the child may be "subjected to the loss of his liberty," or whether the proceedings "may result in commitment to a state institution," * * *.

Moreover, as the majority opinion in this case seems initially to acknowledge, labels are not controlling as to either aspect of the test. It does not matter whether the name of the proceedings is "delinquency" or "child in need of supervision" ("CINS"), or whether the loss of liberty may be commitment to an "industrial school" or a "receiving home." * * * The child's entitlement to the protection of the privilege against self-incrimination depends upon the substance of the matter, namely whether he or she is charged with an act that would be a crime if committed by an adult and whether the proceedings could result in a deprivation of liberty.

Despite an apparent recognition of these principles by the majority in this case, and specifically a recognition that labels are not controlling, the majority opinion goes on to make the labels "victim" and "CINS" determinative. Although the acts by petitioner Cindy Ann Spalding which caused these proceedings, and her subsequent deprivation of liberty, would have been criminal acts if committed by an adult, the majority labels her the "victim" of "sex crimes." Based upon this label, and the fact that the charge and title of the proceedings were later limited to a "child in need of supervision," the majority denies petitioner the constitutional right not to incriminate herself and upholds the action of the trial court in compelling her to take the witness stand and testify against herself.

There can be no question in this case about the fact that the original basis for the charges against petitioner, and one of the grounds for the ultimate adjudication of a "child in need of supervision," was her commission of acts which would have constituted crimes if committed by an adult. In the petition to the juvenile court, filed February 1, 1973, Cindy Ann Spalding was charged with being a delinquent child and a child in need of supervision. The only specific facts alleged in the petition as a basis for the charges were that "respondent has consumed controlled and prohibited narcotics and engaged in acts of sexual intercourse and sexual perversion with an unknown number of male and female adults for a period of more than one year." It was also alleged, without any additional supporting facts being set forth, that Cindy Ann Spalding was "ungovernable and beyond the control of her parent" and was "a danger to herself and others."

The juvenile court master, Mr. Kahl, on February 1, 1973, signed a "Commitment Order," which recited that Cindy Ann Spalding has been adjudged a child in need of supervision and which committed her to the custody of the Department of Juvenile Services. The "Memorandum" of Master Kahl which accompanied that order stated, "Police investigation indicates that these young girls have been victimized by a group of adults in the Dundalk area and elsewhere, for purposes of sexual abuse and drug experimentation." Other than a reference to the fact that the girls needed medical treatment, the sexual conduct and drug abuse constituted the only facts or basis set forth in the memorandum for the commitment order.

On March 7, 1973, petitioner was returned from the Maryland Children's Center and was committed to the custody of the Department of Juvenile Services by Juvenile Court Master Peach. In Master Peach's memorandum accompanying the order committing petitioner, he referred to her "participation in unbelievable sex orgies" and the use of drugs. While the master also referred to the fact that petitioner had not been attending school and had been in the habit of sleeping until two or three o'clock in the afternoon, there is no doubt that the behavior which furnished in large part the basis for the commitment order was engaging in "sex orgies" and drug abuse.

At the juvenile court trial itself, testimony offered by the prosecution to sustain the charge of "child in need of supervision" largely related to the girls' use of narcotics, to petitioner's having "drugged" her mother, and to the "sex orgies." The trial judge, in his opinion delivered at the end of the trial adjudicating petitioner and her codefendant to be "children in need of supervision," found as a fact that the girls "have been associated in immoral sexual activities" and have "indulged" in the taking of "drugs of a narcotic nature." While the trial judge also placed some weight upon petitioner's failure to attend school, there is no question but that the sexual and drug abuse activities furnished the principal factual basis for the judge's adjudication and commitment order.

Of course, using "controlled and prohibited narcotics" and engaging in "acts of * * * sexual perversion," to use the language of the petition against Cindy Ann Spalding, are serious crimes in Maryland. Maryland Code (1971 Repl.Vol., 1974 Cum.Supp.), Art. 27, § 554, punishes "unnatural or perverted sexual practices" of the type which petitioner was alleged to have committed, by a maximum sentence of ten years in the penitentiary. Art. 27, § 276 et seq., the "Controlled Dangerous Substances" law sets forth various criminal penalties for the use of prohibited narcotic drugs. Petitioner was clearly "charged with * * * act[s] which would constitute * * * crime[s] if committed by an adult," * * *, and these acts furnished a large part of the basis for the ultimate "CINS" adjudication and commitment.

The majority opinion states that there is a "marked contrast" between the "delinquent" classification and the "CINS" or "child in need of supervision" classification.[84] However, as this case illustrates, criminal conduct may furnish the factual basis for the "CINS" adjudication. For example, "CINS" includes children who are "habitually disobedient, ungovernable, and beyond [their parents'] control." Code (1974), § 3–801(f)(2) of the Courts and Judicial Proceedings Article. The evidence of such characteristics, as in this case, may be criminal acts. "CINS" also includes a child who "[d]eports himself so as to injure or endanger himself or others," § 3–801(f)(3) of the Courts and Judicial Proceedings Article. Of course, a child who commits criminal acts such as using narcotic drugs or "drugging" someone else, is deporting herself "so as to injure or endanger" herself or others. This is why "labels" should not be, and under the Supreme Court's decisions are not, controlling.

While not dealt with in the majority opinion, the other "prong" or requirement of the *Gault* test was also met in this case. While petitioner was in fact committed to a "foster home" instead of an

---

[84] Actually, as the opinion of the Court of Special Appeals in this case points out, much of what is now contained in the "CINS" definition was formerly included in the definition of a "delinquent" child. Matter of Carter and Spalding, 20 Md. App. 633, 650, 318 A.2d 269 (1974).

"institution," forced living for a period of years in a "foster home" and away from one's own home and family is a "loss of his liberty," Gault, supra, 387 U.S. at 36, 87 S.Ct. 1428. Moreover, even if commitment to a foster home, and against the will of the child and her parents, would not be deemed to meet the second requirement of the *Gault* test, petitioner was subjected to the possibility of commitment to an institution. Code (1972 Repl.Vol., 1974 Cum.Supp.) Art. 52A, § 5(c), specifically authorizes a juvenile court judge to commit a "CINS" child "to any public or private institution * * *." As to limitations upon this authority, the pertinent statute in effect at the time of petitioner's trial, Code (1966 Repl.Vol., 1972 Cum.Supp.), Art. 26, § 70–19, authorized confinement of a "CINS" child in an institution provided that the institution were not designed or operated for the benefit of delinquent children. There were exceptions even to that proviso. The present statute, Code (1974), § 3–832(c) of the Courts and Judicial Proceedings Article, adds the further limitation to the authority to commit "CINS" children to institutions, requiring that such institutions may not be juvenile training schools or something similar to juvenile training schools. Limitations upon the nature of the institutions to which "CINS" children may be committed do not change the fact that under Maryland law, a child adjudicated to be in need of supervision may be committed to "an institution of confinement in which the child is incarcerated for a greater or lesser time." Gault, supra, 387 U.S. at 27, 87 S.Ct. at 1443.

The two-pronged test of *Gault* was therefore met in this case. Petitioner was charged with acts that would be crimes if committed by adults, and petitioner was subjected to the prospect of a loss of liberty or confinement in an institution. Consequently, under *Gault*, the Fifth Amendment privilege against self-incrimination was fully applicable to this proceeding.

There can be no doubt in this case that the petitioner's Fifth Amendment rights were violated. At no time were the warnings required by Miranda v. Arizona, 384 U.S. 436, 86 S.Ct. 1602, 16 L.Ed. 2d 694, 10 A.L.R.3d 974, rehearing denied 385 U.S. 890, 87 S.Ct. 11, 17 L.Ed.2d 121 (1966), given. Both the trial court and the Court of Special Appeals stated that petitioner was not yet in custody when her incriminating statements were first made to the police on January 31, 1973, and therefore under *Miranda* warnings were not required. This view of what constitutes "custody" is a dubious one. The Supreme Court in *Miranda* defined custodial interrogation as "questioning initiated by law enforcement officers after a person has been taken into custody or otherwise deprived of his freedom of action in any significant way." 384 U.S. at 444, 86 S.Ct. at 1612. Here, petitioner was brought to the police station by her mother at 6:30 a.m. on January 31, 1973, following a phone call from the investigating police officer and a request from the officer that she be brought to the station. As far as the record shows, she has never been at liberty to return home since that time. She was interrogated during the day at the station, gave a written statement, and was then taken to another police station where, with the approval of the Department of Juvenile Services, she was "detained" overnight. On the following morning, February 1, 1973, petitioner was formally charged and committed to the custody of the Department of Juvenile Services. To say that petitioner was not in custody from and after the morning of January 31, 1973, is to be unrealistic. Moreover, even if it be assumed *arguendo* that petitioner was not yet in custody on January 31st, the record shows that after the first hearing before the juvenile master and the commitment order on February 1st, petitioner was interrogated further by the police and the juvenile authorities, gave information to them, and no *Miranda* warnings were given at those times either.

[handwritten margin note: Custodially interrogated w/out Miranda warning]

Finally, wholly apart from the matter of *Miranda* warnings, petitioner's Fifth Amendment rights were violated when at the trial she was compelled, over her attorney's objection, to take the witness stand and testify against herself. At the trial, after several prosecution witnesses testified the following took place:

"MR. NEWELL [prosecuting attorney]: I call Cindy Ann Spalding to the stand.

"MR. MEOLA [petitioner's attorney]: Objection.

"THE COURT: Well—

"MR. MEOLA: I instruct my witness not to testify at all. She may be—

"THE COURT: All right, take the stand, Cindy, step up to the stand. All right, you'll be sworn first."

Petitioner was then examined extensively by the trial judge and the prosecuting attorney. Objections made by her attorney to incriminating questions were ignored or overruled. The language of the Fifth Amendment is that "No person * * * shall be compelled in any criminal case to be a witness against himself * * *." No more clear-cut violation of that provision could be imagined than what occurred at petitioner's trial.

The majority opinion in this case could have significant consequences. Because Cindy Ann Spalding is labelled a "victim," and because the proceedings are called "CINS" instead of "delinquent," she is deemed not entitled to those constitutional rights which the Supreme Court has held are applicable in juvenile proceedings. However, if petitioner was a "victim," anytime a juvenile is engaged in criminal activity with adults, the juvenile could be said to be a "victim." A teenager might be enticed by an adult into engaging in a series of armed robberies with the adult, and could be viewed as a "victim." Turning to the name of the proceeding, since criminal acts may be the basis for "CINS" proceedings, and since an adjudication that a child is in need of supervision may lead to confinement in an institution for as long a period as an adjudication that he is delinquent, virtually all juvenile proceedings could be labelled "CINS" by the authorities without significant consequences. Thus by using the right labels, i.e., "victim" and "CINS," the police and juvenile authorities will be able to bypass the requirements laid down by the Supreme Court in *Gault.*

NOTES

1. In Ellery C. v. Redlich, 32 N.Y.2d 588, 347 N.Y.S.2d 51, 300 N.E.2d 424 (1973), the New York Court of Appeals held invalid any commitment of a PINS to an institution in which juvenile delinquents are confined, whether or not that be a state training school. Furthermore, lower New York courts have given full retroactive effect to the *Ellery C.* decision. See, In re Evelyn M., 43 A.D.2d 563, 349 N.Y.S.2d 400 (1973); People ex rel. Soffer v. Luger, 75 Misc.2d 70, 347 N.Y.S.2d 345 (1973). For the response of the Division of Youth to *Ellery C.,* see Chapter 9, infra.

Against this background consider New York Family Court Act section 741, which applies to both delinquency and PINS proceedings:

> (a) At the initial appearance of a respondent in a proceeding and at the commencement of any hearing under this article, the respondent and his parent or other person legally responsible for his care shall be advised of the respondent's right to remain silent and of his right to be represented by counsel chosen by him or his parent or other person legally responsible for his care, or by a law guardian assigned by the court under part four of article two.

2. In In re Grand Jury Proceedings, 160 U.S.App.D.C. 249, 491 F.2d 42 (1974), the court held that the "use immunity" granted by 18 U.S.C. section 6002 to witnesses testifying in grand jury proceedings extends to use of the testimony of a juvenile should he later be the object of a delinquency proceeding. The juvenile, therefore, may be compelled to testify before the grand jury. Quaere. If the conduct testified to would serve as the basis for a PINS though not a delinquency petition, may the juvenile be required to testify? Does the answer depend on whether the privilege against self-incrimination is available to PINS?

F. BURDEN OF PROOF

The Supreme Court's decision in *In re Winship,* supra, is, of course, a limited one. In later chapters of this book, we will consider whether it is applicable to stages of the juvenile justice process other than the hearing at which a determination of delinquency is made. Our present concerns are whether there are procedures peculiar to the juvenile justice process which dilute the impact of *Winship* even at the adjudicative stage and whether the principle is applicable in non-delinquency proceedings.

TEXAS FAMILY CODE, VERNON'S TEXAS CODES ANN.
TITLE 3, SECTION 54.03(f) (1972 & 1983 Supp.).

" * * * The child shall be presumed to be innocent of the charges against him and no finding that a child has engaged in delinquent conduct or conduct indicating a need for supervision may be returned unless the state has proved such beyond a reasonable doubt * * *."

UNIFORM JUVENILE COURT ACT

Section 29. [*Hearing—Findings—Dismissal.*]

(a) After hearing the evidence on the petition the court shall make and file its findings as to whether the child is a deprived child, or if the petition alleges that the child is delinquent or unruly, whether the acts ascribed to the child were committed by him. If the court finds that the child is not a deprived child or that the allegations of delinquency or unruly conduct have not been established it shall dismiss the petition and order the child discharged from any detention or other restriction theretofore ordered in the proceeding.

(b) If the court finds on proof beyond a reasonable doubt that the child committed the acts by reason of which he is alleged to be delinquent or unruly it shall proceed immediately or at a postponed hearing to hear evidence as to whether the child is in need of treatment or rehabilitation and to make and file its findings thereon. In the absence of evidence to the contrary evidence of the commission of acts which constitute a felony is sufficient to sustain a finding that the child is in need of treatment or rehabilitation. If the court finds that the child is not in need of treatment or rehabilitation it shall dismiss the proceeding and discharge the child from any detention or other restriction theretofore ordered.

(c) If the court finds from clear and convincing evidence that the child is deprived or that he is in need of treatment or rehabilitation as a delinquent or unruly child, the court shall proceed immediately or at a postponed hearing to make a proper disposition of the case.

Do you perceive any constitutional problems lurking in this pre-*Winship* draft?

IN INTEREST OF WHEELER

Supreme Court of Iowa, 1975.
229 N.W.2d 241.

REYNOLDSON, JUSTICE. This appeal is from a district court judgment finding Phillip James Wheeler, age 15, a delinquent and committing him to the Iowa Training School for Boys, Eldora, Iowa. We affirm.

Phillip's juvenile problems became apparent when he was seven years of age. His father is in prison. His mother's parental rights were severed by court order and he was placed in legal custody of Dallas county department of social welfare. Thereafter Phillip was in a number of foster homes, YMCA Boy's Home, Johnston, Iowa, and Boy's Town at Omaha, Nebraska. Testimony indicated Phillip ran off many times from YMCA Boy's Home and at least once from Boy's Town.

August 20, 1971, a petition alleging Phillip's delinquency was filed. The proceeding came before the court and was continued on several subsequent occasions. An answer was filed October 15, 1973, raising constitutional issues. Meanwhile the county department became discouraged and asked to be relieved of custody. The juvenile court then placed custody in the fifth judicial district juvenile probation office with authority for that office to place Phillip in his mother's home. The matter was again continued.

August 27, 1974, an amended petition was filed. It was alleged Phillip was a delinquent child under § 232.2(13), The Code, 1973. Specific allegations asserted he 1) had violated State law [§ 232.2(13) (a)] by breaking and entering with intent to commit a public offense (§ 708.8) and 2) had habitually deported himself in a manner injurious to himself or others [§ 232.2(13)(d)] by breaking and entering and committing lascivious acts with a minor. An amended answer denied all these allegations, incorporated the prior answer, and raised additional constitutional questions.

Upon pre-hearing motion for adjudication of law points the constitutional objections were overruled. At hearing evidence was introduced to show Phillip and another juvenile had broken into a swimming pool building and taken candy. The boys had been drinking beer. The "lascivious act" was proved by a mother who testified she had found Phillip in his mother's apartment engaged in sexual intercourse with her 11-year-old daughter.

A "Family Record" compiled by the juvenile probation office was admitted into evidence, as was testimony of the Dallas county sheriff concerning jail cell damage which Phillip may have caused just prior to the hearing.

The appeal to this court seeks review of the following issues: 1) Is § 232.31, The Code, unconstitutional on its face and as applied because it allows determination of delinquency on "clear and convincing" evidence? * * *

I. Section 232.31, The Code, provides, *inter alia:*

> "The court's finding with respect to neglect, dependency, and delinquency shall be based upon clear and convincing evidence under the rules applicable to the trial of civil cases * * *.*"

Phillip asserts when a finding of delinquency is grounded upon commission of an act which would constitute a crime if committed by an adult it is constitutionally impermissible to apply the "clear and convincing" standard of proof rather than the requirement of proof beyond a reasonable doubt. We do not agree with the State's contention this ground was not raised below.

The State now concedes when the basis of a delinquency charge is an alleged public offense due process requires proof beyond a reasonable doubt. * * *

Assuming, although its order does not so disclose, the juvenile court here used the lesser standard, reversal is not required if in our *de novo* review the evidence satisfies the reasonable doubt standard and requires delinquency adjudication. * * *

We hold evidence of the breaking and entering charge convinces beyond a reasonable doubt. Each element of the crime was established. The only "sufficiency" challenge made by Phillip relates to his specific intent in light of some evidence of drinking. See State v. Sill, 199 N.W.2d 47, 49 (Iowa 1972). Baker, the boy who was with Phillip, testified he did not know how much beer Phillip drank but thought he was intoxicated. But he also testified Phillip told him he wanted to get some candy and then entered the building and got candy. A law officer who observed Phillip after his apprehension the same evening noted nothing which would indicate he was not in full control of his mental and physical faculties. He opined Phillip was not under influence of an alcoholic beverage. We are not persuaded by Baker's testimony.

Phillip also argues the juvenile court applied the same unconstitutional standard of proof with respect to the "habitual deportment" subsection of § 232.2(13). He also argues the allegation of lascivious acts charged a crime (required to be proved beyond a reasonable doubt) despite being subsumed under the "habitual deportment" allegation.

We are not required to resolve either of these contentions. Although in a colloquy from the bench immediately following the testimony the court stated it was "going" to find Phillip a delinquent for violating the State breaking and entering law and also for drinking intoxicating liquors and engaging in sexual intercourse with a minor, this was not his ultimate order. The "Order of Court" subsequently written and filed September 4, 1974, specified the only ground for delinquency was breaking and entering. It did not purport to incorporate, even by reference, the court's prior remarks.

* * *

In our *de novo* review we find the juvenile court was right in its determination and the cause is affirmed.

Affirmed.

NOTES

1. In In Interest of Potter, 237 N.W.2d 461 (Iowa 1976) the appellant was adjudicated a delinquent and committed to training school for violating a statute (since repealed) defining a delinquent as one "who habitually deports himself in a manner that is injurious to himself or others." In response to appellant's contention that her right to due process had been violated by the juvenile court's application of the statutorily required standard of clear and convincing evidence in her case the court responded, "Where, however, the basis for the proceeding is conduct potentially 'injurious to the juvenile or others' and not 'commission of a public offense,' due process is satisfied by application of the 'clear and convincing evidence' standard of proof, rather than 'beyond a reasonable doubt.'" Id. at 461–62.

2. In In the Matter of K., 26 Or.App. 451, 554 P.2d 180 (1976) the court held that a finding that an eleven year old had engaged in behavior "such as to endanger his own welfare or the welfare of others" need not be supported by evidence beyond a reasonable doubt because no one under age twelve could be committed to a juvenile training school under state law.

G. JURY TRIAL

In McKeiver v. Pennsylvania, the Supreme Court of the United States held that a jury trial was not an element of due process of law in a juvenile proceeding. What it did not hold is also important:

"If, in its wisdom, any State feels the jury trial is desirable in all cases, or in certain kinds, there appears to be no impediment to its installing a system embracing that feature. * * * "

403 U.S. at 547, 91 S.Ct. at 1987, 29 L.Ed.2d at 662 (1971).

IJA–ABA Juvenile Justice Standards Project, Standards Relating to Adjudication (1980) takes the position that jury trials should be available in juvenile cases:

4.1 Trial by jury *

A. Each jurisdiction should provide by law that the respondent may demand trial by jury in adjudication proceedings when respondent has denied the allegations of the petition.

B. Each jurisdiction should provide by law that the jury may consist of as few as six persons and that the verdict of the jury must be unanimous.

In fact, as the following material discloses, juveniles do get jury trials in a number of situations.

JUVENILE RIGHT TO JURY TRIAL—POST McKEIVER
1971 Wash.U.L.Q. 605, 605–14.**

* * *

The state juvenile codes provide varying bases for a right to a jury trial. Generally the right arises in six situations: (1) when the juvenile has committed a crime outside the scope of the juvenile court's jurisdiction; (2) when the criminal court has concurrent jurisdiction over the juvenile and exercises it; (3) when the juvenile court exercises a discretionary power to waive the juvenile to the criminal court; (4) if a right to a jury trial is provided within the juvenile court proceeding; (5) if a right to a jury trial is afforded on appeal; or (6) if a right to a jury trial is afforded in the criminal court after a judge has waived jurisdiction at the request of the juvenile.

Within these broad categories the right to a jury trial exists in various forms. Despite apparent language to the contrary, *McKeiver* may not foreclose future challenges to state experimentation with the juvenile's right to a jury trial. Consequently, this note analyzes the statutory provisions a juvenile could utilize should he desire a jury trial and the implications of exercising that choice. The discussion of these implications focuses on the dispositional provisions a juvenile exposes himself to if he opts for a jury trial. Finally the note

---

* Reprinted with permission from Standards Relating to Adjudication, Copyright 1980, Ballinger Publishing Company.

** Copyright 1971 by Washington University.

examines the interplay of these provisions and suggests possible constitutional infirmities remaining after the *McKeiver* decision.

II. SURVEY OF JUVENILE RIGHT TO JURY TRIAL

A. *Right to Jury Trial Within Juvenile System*

In fifteen of the fifty-one jurisdictions, juveniles have a right to a trial by jury in the juvenile court proceedings. Ten of these jurisdictions provide jury trial by statute and five by judicial mandate. In Alaska, Iowa, New Mexico, Rhode Island and Tennessee, the state courts have held the due process clause of the federal constitution, the state constitution or both mandate the right to a jury trial. After *McKeiver*, the continuing existence of the right to a jury trial seems questionable in Tennessee where only the federal constitution was relied on. In New York and Iowa, on the other hand, the effect of *McKeiver* is uncertain since the specific constitutional provisions relied on are unclear. In New Mexico, Rhode Island and Alaska the state, as well as federal, constitutions were relied on. In these states the state constitutions should still support the decisions.

Among the states that provide for jury trials in the juvenile court, only nine grant the right to every juvenile who comes before them. Alaska, Iowa, New Mexico and Rhode Island grant jury trials only to those juveniles who commit a crime. In Tennessee, jury trials are available only to juveniles who commit felonies. In South Dakota, a jury trial is available to every juvenile if the judge, in his discretion, deems it appropriate.

Since juveniles in these fifteen jurisdictions receive jury trials within the juvenile system, they receive the same disposition as others before the juvenile court. There is no difference in confinement or treatment, and the consequence of requesting a jury is limited to the formalizing of the adjudicatory phase of the juvenile proceedings.

B. *Right to Jury Trial Outside Juvenile System*

Although the other jurisdictions do not permit a jury trial in the juvenile court, a juvenile might be able to obtain a jury trial after appealing an unfavorable decision to another court or after the juvenile court waives jurisdiction. In three jurisdictions, the juvenile can request a jury trial when he appeals to the circuit or superior court following an unfavorable decision in the juvenile court.

In Massachusetts the superior court assumes original jurisdiction over the proceeding just as if the case had originated there. In Delaware and Kentucky, on the other hand, the superior or circuit courts exercise appellate jurisdiction.

If appellate courts exercise original jurisdiction, presumably they could dispose of the juvenile either as an adult or as a juvenile. The Massachusetts statute, however, requires Massachusetts superior courts to utilize juvenile dispositional facilities in these instances. Since the Delaware and Kentucky courts exercise appellate jurisdiction, their dispositional powers should also be derived from the juvenile court; however, there is no clear statutory limitation as in Massachusetts.

In jurisdictions where a jury trial is unavailable within the juvenile court or on appeal, a juvenile might receive a jury trial if the juvenile court waives jurisdiction to the criminal court. However, in four of these states, the jurisdiction of the juvenile court is exclusive without any provision for waiver. In thirteen others, the court is without authority to waive its exclusive jurisdiction for juveniles under a certain age. Including these thirteen, however, there are still thirty jurisdictions where juvenile-initiated or court-initiated waiver provisions offer some way to obtain a jury trial.

In five of these thirty jurisdictions, juveniles (or an interested party) have a statutory right to request a waiver of jurisdiction to the criminal court. This right takes various forms. Any child in Florida who commits an act that would be a crime may request waiver; however, only juveniles over 13 in Illinois, 16–17 in New Jersey and 18–21 in Nevada may do so. In Kansas, any juvenile who commits an act that would be a felony may request waiver.

These five jurisdictions disagree as to whether the juvenile loses his right to a juvenile disposition by requesting and receiving waiver of the juvenile court's jurisdiction. In New Jersey and Nevada, where only older juveniles may request waiver, the juveniles are treated as adults for dispositional purposes. In Illinois and Kansas, juveniles are sent to juvenile dispositional facilities. In Florida, where there is no age limitation, juveniles are sent either to prison or to its juvenile dispositional facilities.

If a juvenile does not have a statutory right to request waiver, some states place waiver in the discretion of the juvenile court judge. There are twenty-six states with court-initiated waiver provisions in which a juvenile might receive a jury trial if he is unable to do so by the previously discussed processes. In these twenty-six jurisdictions there are four categorical guidelines for determining whether waiver should be exercised. First, if the juvenile is unamenable to a juvenile disposition and there is reasonable cause to believe he is delinquent or has committed a crime, six jurisdictions may waive him; secondly, if the juvenile is unamenable to the juvenile process, has committed a crime, is sane and waiver would be in his best interests and the best interests of the community, six jurisdictions authorize waiver; thirdly, eight jurisdictions leave waiver to the discretion of the judge if the juvenile has committed a felony (or sometimes any crime); and fourthly, if a juvenile has committed a felony (or sometimes any crime) and it is in his best interest and that of the community, then six jurisdictions authorize waiver to the criminal court.

Since the waiver of jurisdiction in these instances is discretionary, the question arises whether a juvenile can request to be waived to the criminal court if he desires a jury trial. Although such a request might be granted, counsel may find himself in the precarious position of arguing that his client was unamenable to the juvenile process.

Responses to inquiries to a number of juvenile court judges indicate that statutes in the first two of the above categories, which contain provisions such as "unamenable to a juvenile disposition", will not be construed to waive a juvenile over for criminal prosecution simply because the juvenile desires a jury trial. A juvenile is waived only if he is "unamenable"—not because of his request.

In the third and fourth categories, great discretion is afforded the judge. Judges from states utilizing the fourth category, in which "the best interests of the child and community" is a guideline, indicate a willingness to waive jurisdiction if a request is made for purposes of a jury trial. Judges from states utilizing the third category, in which the discretion of the judge is untrammeled, indicate a propensity to read an "unamenable" provision into the statute and achieve the same result as in the first two categories; this result, however, is not universal.

If discretionary waiver provisions are utilized to obtain a jury trial, consideration should be given to the possible dispositional consequences. Discretionary waiver statutes were enacted for juveniles who could not benefit by the juvenile process. Once jurisdiction is waived the criminal court accepts jurisdiction and, if found guilty, the juvenile is sentenced according to the penal statute which he has violated. Six states, however, indicate that the criminal courts may have the power to utilize the juvenile facilities to dispose of the juvenile.

A second possible consequence to be considered prior to a request for waiver is the possibility that waiver might be binding on all future offenses, particularly if the waiver is based on a finding of "unamenability". The majority of judges have indicated, however, that each time a juvenile comes before the court the issue of waiver is reconsidered in total.

McKeiver seemingly sanctions this multitude of statutory schemes under the rubric of "experimentation".

* * *

NOTES

1. In People v. Superior Court, 15 Cal.3d 271, 124 Cal.Rptr. 47, 539 P.2d 807 (1975), the Supreme Court of California considered the question whether an advisory jury could be empaneled in a juvenile proceeding.

"We recognize that the use of advisory juries in juvenile court proceedings will inevitably involve problems of a practical nature relating to the empanelment and supervision of such juries, including matters of challenges and instructions. We believe, however, that pending any future legislative or judicial developments, problems of this kind are best left to the sound discretion of the juvenile court judge who chooses to empanel an advisory jury to assist in the ascertainment of jurisdictional facts. Few difficulties are likely to arise in this area in light of the fact that the advisory jury by its nature is merely an adjunct to the juvenile court in its function as the ultimate fact-finder pursuant to sections 701 and 702.

"Having concluded that the broad provisions of section 680 include a discretionary power on the part of the juvenile court to empanel an advisory jury to assist in the determination of jurisdictional issues, we now turn to the question whether it was an abuse of discretion to order such a jury to be empanelled in the instant case.

"In its Recommendation No. 11 (set forth in substance in fn. 4, ante) the Commission, in a sentence to which we have adverted above, expressed the frame of reference which it considered fundamental to the sound administration of juvenile justice. "The problem in attempting to establish acceptable juvenile court procedures is to attain a working balance between two essential objectives—first, preserving the guarantee of due process to the minor; and second, establishing an informal court atmosphere so that potentially harmful effects of the proceedings are minimized and the minor's receptivity to treatment is encouraged." It is this "working balance" which must concern the juvenile court in the exercise of the discretionary powers vested in it by section 680.

"In the instant case, the juvenile court expressed its full awareness of the subject principle and specifically based its determination upon it. Thus, in making its oral order, the court stated: "In determining whether to exercise such power [i.e., the power to empanel an advisory jury], the court should be guided by and be first satisfied that it would serve the interests of justice to invoke such a procedure without serious impairment of the overall salutary purposes of the non-adversary juvenile court proceedings."

"In arriving at its determination in light of this principle, the court considered six specific factors. First, it was noted that the charges against the minor, which had been denied by him, were of a very serious nature—involving among them the murder and sexual abuse of a four-year-old child. Second, it was anticipated that the adjudicatory hearing might involve as many as 40 witnesses, including expert witnesses. Third, the evidence to be presented by the People was to be largely circumstantial in nature. Fourth, the incidents which had given rise to the hearing had received substantial coverage in the various news media, and the minor had been identified by name as a suspect. Fifth, the "potential period of wardship placement" was substantial. And sixth, the hearing was estimated to require from four to five days. On the basis of these considerations the court, making clear reference to the language of section 680, concluded: "In considering the special facts and circumstances in this case presented it appears to this court that the most effective and expeditious ascertainment of facts occurring during the adjudicative stage can best be accomplished by empanelment of a jury to render any [sic] advisory verdict to aid and assist the court during the adjudicative stage only." The court went beyond this finding, however, to relate its determination to the guiding principle to which we have adverted. "[T]o the extent that the use of such advisory jury would inject an additional adversary flavor it is the finding of this court that its potential effect is greatly outweighed by the substantial benefit afforded to the court in utilizing an advisory verdict of the jury under the special facts and circumstances postured in this case."

"We are satisfied that the juvenile court in this case made a proper and informed decision and that no abuse of discretion has been shown. In arriving at its determination to empanel an advisory jury, the court addressed itself to considerations which fall into three general categories: (a) the nature and relative difficulty of the factfinding task in the particular case, (b) the seriousness of the charges from the point of view of probable disposition of the minor if they were sustained, and (c) the extent to which any salutary effects attendant upon an informal proceeding remained possible of achievement in the circumstances. Essentially it weighed the considerations in the first two categories against those in the third. On the one hand, the fact that serious charges were to be disputed by a great deal of largely circumstantial evidence indicated that the advantages to be derived from the use of an advisory jury were great. On the other hand, in light of the broad areas of factual and legal dispute, which necessarily would have to be resolved in an adversary setting—and also in light of the loss of confidentiality which had already occurred—any benefits normally attendant upon an informal proceeding had been rendered speculative. In these circumstances the court was well within its discretion in empanelling the advisory jury. We uphold its order.

"We emphasize in closing that our determination today should not operate to render the use of an advisory jury commonplace in section 602 proceedings. In the normal case, where the disputed jurisdictional issues are few and can be resolved with relative ease, the balance may continue to be struck in favor of an informal proceeding without the assistance of a jury. Only in the exceptional case, where the benefits to be derived from the use of an advisory jury far outweigh any benefits of informality and confidentiality which can be achieved in the circumstances, will sound judicial discretion choose to empanel an advisory jury to aid the court. The case before us is such an exceptional case."

Id. at 283–285, 124 Cal.Rptr. at 55–56, 539 P.2d at 815–16.

2. In People ex rel. Carey v. White, 65 Ill.2d 193, 2 Ill.Dec. 345, 357 N.E.2d 512 (1976), the Supreme Court of Illinois issued a writ of mandamus directing a juvenile court judge to expunge orders directing that jury trials be granted minors in pending delinquency proceedings. The Court found that the legislature had made clear its intent that the judge alone should make the factual findings under the Juvenile Court Act. After noting some of the reasons set out in *McKeiver* why jury trials, might be undesirable in juvenile cases, the Court felt that the use of even an advisory jury "would offend the spirit and policies underlying the Juvenile Court Act * * *" and that the "same considerations which persuaded the General Assembly that a conventional trial by jury would be detrimental in the handling of juveniles would apply to advisory juries. It would certainly tend to introduce into this system the adversary process, and its accompanying formalities and delays." Id. at 516.

3. In People in Interest of R.A.D., 196 Colo. 430, 586 P.2d 46 (1978) the court held that the same rights to challenge for cause must be extended to juvenile delinquency proceedings as are available in criminal prosecutions.

H.   RIGHT TO A PUBLIC TRIAL

When *McKeiver*, supra, came before the Supreme Court, it was consolidated with In re Burrus, 275 N.C. 517, 169 S.E.2d 879, affirmed 403 U.S. 528, 91 S.Ct. 1976, 24 L.Ed.2d 647 (1969). Mr. Justice Brennan, dissenting in the *Burrus* case, found the absence of *both* the jury trial and public trial safeguards left the North Carolina juvenile procedures bereft of any substitute means of protecting juveniles "against misuse of the judicial process." 403 U.S. at 556,

91 S.Ct. at 1992, 29 L.Ed.2d at 667. It may be important that the *Burrus* case involved 46 Black children protesting school assignments and a school consolidation plan.

In RLR v. State, 487 P.2d 27 (Alaska, 1971), the Alaska Supreme Court addressed the question of the child's right to have the public included:

"The Federal and Alaska's Constitutions provide that '[i]n all criminal prosecutions, the accused shall enjoy ["have" in Alaska's Constitution] the right to a * * * public trial * * *.' The sentence guaranteeing the right also guarantees the rights to speedy trial and an impartial jury. The leading case on public trial, Re Oliver, holds that the Due Process Clause of the Fourteenth Amendment prohibits secret trials in criminal proceedings. *Oliver* says that the traditional Anglo-American distrust for secret trials has been attributed to the despotism of the Spanish Inquisition, the English Court of Star Chamber, and the French lettre de cachet, and quotes Bentham's charge that secret proceedings produce 'indolent and arbitrary' judges, unchecked no matter how 'corrupt' by recordation and appeal. The court cites as values of a public trial that it safeguards against attempts to employ the courts as instruments of persecution, restrains abuse of judicial power, brings the proceedings to the attention of key witnesses not known to the parties, and teaches the spectators about their government and gives them confidence in their judicial remedies. In a concurring opinion in Estes v. Texas, Justice Harlan says that

" '[e]ssentially, the public-trial guarantee embodies a view of human nature, true as a general rule, that judges, lawyers, witnesses, and jurors will perform their respective functions more responsibly in an open court than in secret proceedings. * * * A fair trial is the objective, and "public trial" is an institutional safeguard for attaining it.

'Thus the right of "public trial" is not one belonging to the public, but one belonging to the accused, and inhering in the institutional process by which justice is administered.'

"Appellant argues that he was denied his constitutional right to a public trial by AS 47.10.070. That statute provides in relevant part that

" '[t]he public shall be excluded from the hearing, but the court, in its discretion, may permit individuals to attend a hearing, if their attendance is compatible with the best interest of the minor.'

"Rules of Children's Procedure 12(d)(2) provides that

" '[c]hild hearings shall not be open to the general public. The court may, however, in its discretion after due consideration for the welfare of the child and of the public interest, admit particular individuals to the hearing.'

"The federal constitutional guarantee has not been construed to mean that all judicial proceedings must be open to any interested member of the public at any time. Some authorities hold that the right to public trial belongs to the public as well as the defendant so public trial is not subject to defendant's waiver, while others hold that the guarantee is for the benefit of the accused, and may be asserted or waived only by him. In both the federal and Alaska's constitutions, the right to public trial is part of a list of rights explicitly stated to be rights of the accused. Some jurisdictions hold that the general public may be excluded consistently with the public trial guarantee so long as the defendant has an opportunity to designate those whom he desires to have present. Others take the view that the general public cannot be excluded in this way. Where the right has been denied, no prejudice need be shown, since such a showing would be almost impossible to make. The right may be waived. We held in Flores v. State that unintentional brief exclusion of a newspaper reporter from part of the reading back to the jury of a section of testimony previously given, when at least one other spectator was present, did not deny the right to public trial.

"In re Burrus holds that despite *Gault*, juveniles are not constitutionally entitled to public trial. It is weak authority, however, since it so concludes merely by labeling delinquency proceedings noncriminal, rather than by analyzing the purposes of the public trial requirement to see whether they would be served by applying the right to delinquency proceedings. Many authorities favor a policy in delinquency proceedings of avoiding total secrecy by admitting persons with a special interest in the case or the work of the court, including perhaps the press, but prohibiting disclosure of juveniles' names and excluding the general public. Various reasons are given for this policy. It is said that permitting an audience to attend the hearing would interfere with the 'case work relationship' between the judge and the child. Publicity is condemned on the grounds that it is an additional and excessive punishment to that prescribed by the court, or in the alternative that it encourages delinquency by permitting a youngster to 'flaunt his unregeneracy.' Publication of names of juvenile delinquents is condemned on the ground that it confirms the child in his delinquent identity and impedes his integration into law-abiding society by reducing his ability to obtain legitimate employment, qualify for licenses and bonds, and join the armed services. An important commentator on this subject recommends that the general public be excluded from juvenile hearings, but that the press should be admitted, though prohibited from publishing data which would identify particular juveniles; if he so desires, however, the juvenile should have a public hearing. These social policy considerations are based on empirical propositions which may be false and have not been tested. Some commentary favors open court proceedings for juveniles on the grounds that secrecy and the informality engendered thereby hinders rehabilitation partly by misleading juveniles and their parents into underestimating the seriousness of delinquency. Recent commentary tends to be critical of secrecy because it screens from public view arbitrariness and lawlessness by juvenile courts.

"Just as alleged, bad motives of the legislature cannot be considered in determining constitutionality and construction of statutes, so we cannot withhold application of federal and state constitutional provisions on the grounds that those who created various systems of governmental activity such as the juvenile court acted from benevolent motives. Nor will constitutional problems be ignored in deference to untested empirical propositions about what sorts of judicial proceedings succeed in rehabilitating persons charged with misconduct; as between these sorts of prescriptions for what is good for society and constitutional prescriptions, the latter are authoritative. The reasons for the constitutional guarantees of public trial apply as much to juvenile delinquency proceedings as to adult criminal proceedings. Delinquency proceedings as much as adult criminal prosecutions can be used as instruments of persecution, and may be subject to judicial abuse. The appellate process is not a sufficient check on juvenile courts for problems of mootness and the cost of prosecuting an appeal screen most of what goes on from appellate court scrutiny. We cannot help but notice that the children's cases appealed to this court have often shown much more extensive and fundamental error than is generally found in adult criminal cases and wonder whether secrecy is not fostering a judicial attitude of casualness toward the law in children's proceedings. In any event,

"'civil labels and good intentions do not themselves obviate the need for criminal due process safeguards in juvenile courts, for "[a] proceeding where the issue is whether the child will be found to be 'delinquent' and subjected to the loss of his liberty for years is comparable in seriousness to a felony prosecution."'

"Therefore, we hold that children are guaranteed the right to a public trial by the Alaska Constitution.

"One additional facet of the child's right to a public trial remains to be considered. AS 47.10.070 [85] and the similar Children's Rule 12(d)(2), provide for the exclusion of the public from children's hearings. Rules of Children's Procedure 12(d)(2), which governs, provides that,

"'Child hearings shall not be open to the general public. The court may, however, in its discretion after due consideration

---

[85] AS 47.10.070 provides in part that:

The public shall be excluded from the hearing, but the court, in its discretion, may permit individuals to attend a hearing, if their attendance is compatible with the best interests of the minor.

The statute providing for exclusion of the public from juvenile hearings is procedural, so is outside the scope of legislative authority unless two-thirds of each house of the legislature votes to change the rule promulgated by the supreme court in this matter. Alaska Const. art. IV, sec. 15. Children's proceedings are among the "civil and criminal cases in all courts" over which this constitutional provision gives this court rule-making authority which is intended to be plenary and not capable of reduction by re-labeling of proceedings. Cf. Silverton v. Marler, 389 P.2d 3 (Alaska 1964).

The statute making criminal the publication by newspapers, radio stations, and television stations of juvenile delinquents' names, AS 47.10.090(b), and the similar rule, Rules of Children's Procedure 26, are not challenged in this appeal.

for the welfare of the child and of the public interest, admit particular individuals to the hearing.'

"This flexible rule must be interpreted and applied in a manner consistent with the child's constitutional right to public trial. The evils of secrecy may be avoided by permitting the child to open the adjudicative and dispositive hearings to any individuals. Where the child's choice may be adverse to his own interests, a guardian ad litem may be appointed under the principles discussed in the preceding section dealing with the right to trial by jury. It is an abuse of discretion for the court to refuse admittance to individuals whose presence is favored by the child, except in special circumstances such as the unavailability of a courtroom sufficiently large to hold all the individuals whose presence is sought. If the child or his guardian ad litem wants the press, friends, or others to be free to attend, then the hearing must be open to them. The area of discretion in the rule, where the court may refuse to open the hearing, involves persons whose presence is not desired by the child. Since we have determined that the case must be reversed on other grounds, we find it unnecessary to decide whether the denial of a public trial in the adjudicative stage in the case at bar was plain error."

Id. at 35–9.

The reader will note the suggestion in *RLR*, supra, that the judge has discretion whether to exclude persons whose presence is not desired by the child. Compare: In re Jones, 46 Ill.2d 506, 263 N.E.2d 863 (1970).

"On January 3, 1969, a petition was filed in the circuit court of Champaign County alleging that respondent Kimmel Jones, then 16-years-of-age, was a delinquent minor in that on December 24, 1968, he committed the offense of reckless conduct (Ill.Rev.Stat.1967, ch. 38, par. 12–5) by placing an explosive device in a mail box at the home of Everett Smith. The petition was signed by Delmar Dawkins, stating that he knew "the contents thereof and that the same are true to the best of his knowledge, information and belief."

"Summons was properly served directing respondent's appearance on January 22, 1969. The adjudicatory hearing was continued until January 27, 1969. On January 23, 1969, pursuant to leave of court, Jones filed his motion to dismiss in which he argued that the petition was insufficient in that it was "verified on information and belief, contrary to the Illinois Constitution. Article II, Section 6 [S.H.A.]." The motion was denied. Respondent then requested a jury trial, which was denied.

"At the adjudicatory hearing, respondent moved for the exclusion from the court room of all witnesses, the general public, and representatives of the news media. Specifically, respondent waived 'the right to have * * * any form of a public hearing.' No objection being interposed by the State, the court ordered the exclusion of witnesses, the general public and the press. Jones also filed a motion for a preliminary conference with a probationary officer (Ill.

Rev.Stat.1967, ch. 37, par. 703–8), and a motion for change of venue because of adverse publicity, both of which were denied. After the rulings and a short recess, the judge informed counsel that certain representatives of the news media had formally requested to be readmitted to the court room during the proceedings. Over respondent's objection, the judge allowed the newsmen to be present in the court room, subject, however, to the condition that nothing be published regarding what transpired in the proceedings until further order of the court.

"Thereafter, the State's Attorney made an opening statement of the facts of the case. Contending that he wished to avoid further adverse publicity, respondent made a judicial admission of the facts as presented by the State. The court then entered a finding that respondent was a delinquent minor and adjudged him a ward of the court.

"Respondent has appealed directly to this court raising several constitutional issues. First, he claims that he was deprived of his constitutional right to a jury trial. However, in In re Fucini, 44 Ill.2d 305, 255 N.E.2d 380, we held that neither the Illinois nor the United States constitution requires a jury trial in proceedings under the Juvenile Court Act. (Ill.Rev.Stat.1967, ch. 37, par. 701–1 et seq.) Accordingly, the trial court's action in denying respondent's jury demand was proper.

"It is next argued that the trial court erred in admitting the members of the news media to the adjudicatory hearing. Essentially, he contends that the sixth amendment right to a public trial is a personal right of the accused which can be waived. Section 1–20(6) of the Juvenile Court Act (Ill.Rev.Stat.1969, ch. 37, par. 701–20(6)) provides that "The general public except the news media shall be excluded from any hearing and, except for persons specified in this Section, only persons, including representatives of agencies and associations, who in the opinion of the court have a direct interest in the case or in the work of the court shall be admitted to the hearing." However, it is clear that the legislature intended that openness should prevail throughout the proceedings. We are of the opinion that section 1–20(6) serves the dual function of not only protecting a respondent's right to a "public trial" but also preserves the right of the general populace to know what is transpiring in *its* courts.

"In Singer v. United States (1965), 380 U.S. 24, 34–35, 85 S.Ct. 783, 790, 13 L.Ed.2d 630, 638, Mr. Chief Justice Warren, speaking for a unanimous court stated: 'The ability to waive a constitutional right does not ordinarily carry with it the right to insist upon the opposite of that right. For example, although a defendant can, under certain circumstances, waive his constitutional right to a public trial, he has no absolute right to compel a private trial * * *.' The right of the public to know what is transpiring in the courts so they may properly evaluate the work of their servants—judge, prosecutor, sheriff and clerk—is equally as important as guaranteeing to the defendant a fair and impartial trial. (Bridges v. California (1941), 314 U.S. 252, 62

S.Ct. 190, 86 L.Ed. 192; Pennekamp v. Florida (1946), 328 U.S. 331, 66 S.Ct. 1029, 90 L.Ed. 1295; Estes v. Texas (1965), 381 U.S. 532, 85 S.Ct. 1628, 14 L.Ed.2d 543.)

"In the case at bar, no hint of prejudice to the respondent can be found by the action of the trial court in modifying its exclusion order. This was a hearing tried before a judge, and, in compliance with the statute, all members of the general public, with the exception of the press, were excluded. No suggestion is made that the court was prejudiced against respondent, and indeed a reading of the record indicates the hearing was impartial. We find no error in the court refusing respondent a purely 'private' trial."

* * *

In L. Loble and M. Wylie, Delinquency Can be Stopped (1967) it was argued that permitting public access to court hearings and encouraging the printing of the names of juveniles in newspapers is an effective device for delinquency prevention. A number of states responded by enacting so-called "Loble laws" requiring that certain juvenile court hearings be open to the public. Tex.Rev.Civ.Stat. Art. 2338–1, § 15–A (Vernon's 1970 Supp.): "If a child has been charged with the violation of a penal law of the grade of felony and if the child has previously been declared delinquent, officials concerned with the case shall release upon request information as to the name and address of the child and the alleged offense. Hearings on the case in the juvenile court shall be open to persons having a legitimate interest in the proceedings, including representatives of the news media; and juvenile court records shall be open to inspection by representatives of the news media." (This statute was repealed as part of the general revision of the Texas Juvenile Court Act.)

See also the Montana Youth Court Act, Mont.Rev.Codes, section 10–1220(5) (Supp.1974).

"In a hearing on a petition under this section, the general public shall be excluded and only such persons admitted as have a direct interest in the case; except that when a hearing in the court is held on a written petition charging the commission of a felony, persons with a legitimate interest in the proceeding, including representatives of public information media, shall not be excluded from the hearing." (This statute was also repealed) Why?

SMITH v. DAILY MAIL PUBLISHING CO.
Supreme Court of the United States, 1979.
443 U.S. 97, 99 S.Ct. 2667, 61 L.Ed.2d 399.

Mr. Chief Justice Burger delivered the opinion of the Court.

We granted certiorari to consider whether a West Virginia statute violates the First and Fourteenth Amendments of the United States Constitution by making it a crime for a newspaper to publish, without the written approval of the juvenile court, the name of any youth charged as a juvenile offender.

(1)

The challenged West Virginia statute provides:

"[N]or shall the name of any child, in connection with any proceedings under this chapter, be published in any newspaper without a written order of the court * * *." W.Va.Code § 49–7–3 (1976).

and

"A person who violates * * * a provision of this chapter for which punishment has not been specifically provided, shall be guilty of a misdemeanor, and upon conviction shall be fined not less than ten nor more than one hundred dollars, or confined in jail not less than five days nor more than six months, or both such fine and imprisonment." § 49–7–20.

On February 9, 1978, a 15-year-old student was shot and killed at Hayes Junior High School in St. Albans, W.Va., a small community located about 13 miles outside of Charleston, W.Va. The alleged assailant, a 14-year-old classmate, was identified by seven different eye witnesses and was arrested by police soon after the incident.

The Charleston Daily Mail and the Charleston Daily Gazette, respondents here, learned of the shooting by monitoring routinely the police band radio frequency; they immediately dispatched reporters and photographers to the Junior High School. The reporters for both papers obtained the name of the alleged assailant simply by asking various witnesses, the police and an assistant prosecuting attorney who were at the school.

The staffs of both newspapers prepared articles for publication about the incident. The Daily Mail's first article appeared in its February 9 afternoon edition. The article did not mention the alleged attacker's name. The editorial decision to omit the name was made because of the statutory prohibition against publication, without prior court approval.

The Daily Gazette made a contrary editorial decision and published the juvenile's name and picture in an article about the shooting that appeared in the February 10 morning edition of the paper. In addition, the name of the alleged juvenile attacker was broadcast over at least three different radio stations on February 9 and 10. Since the information had become public knowledge, the Daily Mail decided to include the juvenile's name in an article in its afternoon paper on February 10.

On March 1, an indictment against the respondents was returned by a grand jury. The indictment alleged that each knowingly published the name of a youth involved in a juvenile proceeding in violation of W.Va.Code § 49–7–3 (1976). Respondents then filed an original jurisdiction petition with the West Virginia Supreme Court of Appeals, seeking a writ of prohibition against the prosecuting attorney and the circuit court judges of Kanawha County, petitioners here. Respondents alleged that the indictment was based on a statute that violated the First and Fourteenth Amendments of the United States Constitution and several provisions of the State's constitution and requested an order prohibiting the county officials from taking any action on the indictment.

The West Virginia Supreme Court issued the writ of prohibition. Relying on holdings of this Court, it held that the statute abridged the freedom of the press. The court reasoned that the statute operated as a prior restraint on speech and that the State's interest in protecting the identity of the juvenile offender did not overcome the heavy presumption against the constitutionality of such prior restraints.

We granted certiorari. 439 U.S. 963, 99 S.Ct. 448, 58 L.Ed.2d 420 (1978).

(2)

Respondents urge this Court to hold that because § 49–7–3 requires court approval prior to publication of the juvenile's name it operates as a "prior restraint" on speech. See Nebraska Press Association v. Stuart, 427 U.S. 539, 96 S.Ct. 2791, 49 L.Ed.2d 683 (1976); New York Times Co. v. United States, 403 U.S. 713, 91 S.Ct. 2140, 29 L.Ed.2d 822 (1971); Organization for a Better Austin v. Keefe, 402 U.S. 415, 91 S.Ct. 1575, 29 L.Ed.2d 1 (1971); Near v. Minnesota ex rel. Olson, 283 U.S. 697, 51 S.Ct. 625, 75 L.Ed. 1357 (1931). Respondents concede that this statute is not in the classic mold of prior restraint, there being no prior injunction against publication. Nonetheless, they contend that the prior approval requirement acts in "operation and effect" like a licensing scheme and thus is another form of prior restraint. See Near v. Minnesota ex rel. Olson, supra, at 708, 51 S.Ct., at 628. As such, respondents argue, the statute bears "a 'heavy presumption' against its constitutional validity." Organization for a Better Austin v. Keefe, supra, 402 U.S., at 419, 91 S.Ct., at 1578. They claim that the State's interest in the anonymity of a juvenile offender is not sufficient to overcome that presumption.

Petitioners do not dispute that the statute amounts to a prior restraint on speech. Rather, they take the view that even if it is a prior restraint the statute is constitutional because of the significance of the State's interest in protecting the identity of juveniles.

(3)

The resolution of this case does not turn on whether the statutory grant of authority to the juvenile judge to permit publication of the juvenile's name is, in and of itself, a prior restraint. First Amendment protection reaches beyond prior restraints, Landmark Communications, Inc. v. Virginia, 435 U.S. 829, 98 S.Ct. 1535, 56 L.Ed.2d 1 (1978); Cox Broadcasting Corp. v. Cohn, 420 U.S. 469, 95 S.Ct. 1029, 43 L.Ed.2d 328 (1975), and respondents acknowledge that the statutory provision for court approval of disclosure actually may have a less oppressive effect on freedom of the press than a total ban on the publication of the child's name.

Whether we view the statute as a prior restraint or as a penal sanction for publishing lawfully obtained, truthful information is not dispositive because even the latter action requires the highest form of state interest to sustain its validity. Prior restraints have been accorded the most exacting scrutiny in previous cases. See Nebraska Press Association v. Stuart, supra, 427 U.S., at 561, 96 S.Ct., at 2803; Organization for a Better Austin v. Keefe, supra, 402 U.S., at 419, 91 S.Ct., at 1577; Near v. Minnesota ex rel. Olson, supra, 283 U.S., at 716, 51 S.Ct., at 631. See also Southeastern Promotions, Ltd. v. Conrad, 420 U.S. 546, 95 S.Ct. 1239, 43 L.Ed.2d 448 (1975). However, even when a state attempts to punish publication after the event it must nevertheless demonstrate that its punitive action was necessary to further the state interests asserted. Landmark Communications, Inc. v. Virginia, supra, 435 U.S., at 843, 98 S.Ct., at 1543. Since we conclude that this statute cannot satisfy the constitutional standards defined in *Landmark Communications, Inc.,* we need not decide whether, as argued by respondents, it operated as a prior restraint.

Our recent decisions demonstrate that state action to punish the publication of truthful information seldom can satisfy constitutional standards. In *Landmark Communications* we declared unconstitutional a Virginia statute making it a crime to publish information regarding confidential proceedings before state judicial review commission that heard complaints about alleged disabilities and misconduct of state court judges. In declaring that statute unconstitutional, we concluded:

> "[T]he publication Virginia seeks to punish under its statute lies near the core of the First Amendment, and the Commonwealth's interests advanced by the imposition of criminal sanctions are insufficient to justify the actual and potential encroachments on freedom of speech and of the press which follow therefrom." Id., at 838, 98 S.Ct., at 1541.

In Cox Broadcasting Corp. v. Cohn, supra, we held that damages could not be recovered against a newspaper for publishing the name of a rape victim. The suit had been based on a state statute that made it a crime to publish the name of the victim; the purpose of the statute was to protect the privacy right of the individual and the family. The name of the victim had become known to the public through official court records dealing with the trial of the rapist. In declaring the statute unconstitutional, the Court, speaking through Mr. Justice White, reasoned:

> "By placing the information in the public domain on official court records, the State must be presumed to have concluded that the public interest was thereby being served. * * * States may not impose sanctions on the publication of truthful information contained in official court records open to public inspection." Id., 420 U.S., at 495, 95 S.Ct., at 1046.

One case that involved a classic prior restraint is particularly relevant to our inquiry. In Oklahoma Publishing Co. v. District Court, 430 U.S. 308, 97 S.Ct. 1045, 51 L.Ed.2d 355 (1976), we struck down a state court injunction prohibiting the news media from publishing the name or photograph of an 11-year-old boy who was being tried before a juvenile court. The juvenile judge had permitted reporters and other members of the public to attend a hearing in the case, notwithstanding a state statute closing such trials to the public. The court then attempted to halt publication of the information obtained from that hearing. We held that once the truthful information was "publicly revealed" or "in the public domain" the court could not constitutionally restrain its dissemination.

None of these opinions directly controls this case; however, all suggest strongly that if a newspaper lawfully obtains truthful information about a matter of public significance then state officials may not constitutionally punish publication of the information, absent a need to further a state interest of the highest order. These cases involved situations where the government itself provided or made possible press access to the information. That factor is not controlling. Here respondents relied upon routine newspaper reporting techniques to ascertain the identity of the alleged assailant. A free press cannot be made to rely solely upon the sufferance of government to supply it with information. See Houchins v. KQED, Inc., 438 U.S. 1, 11, 98 S.Ct. 2588, 2595, 57 L.Ed.2d 553 (1978) (plurality opinion); Branzburg v. Hayes, 408 U.S. 665, 681, 92 S.Ct. 2646, 2656, 33 L.Ed.2d 626 (1972). If the information is lawfully obtained, as it was here, the state may not punish its publication except when necessary to further an interest more substantial than is present here.

(4)

The sole interest advanced by the State to justify its criminal statute is to protect the anonymity of the juvenile offender. It is asserted that confidentiality will further his rehabilitation because publication of the name may encourage further antisocial conduct and also may cause the juvenile to lose future employment or suffer other consequences for this single offense. In Davis v. Alaska, 415 U.S. 308, 94 S.Ct. 1105, 39 L.Ed.2d 347 (1974), similar arguments were advanced by the State to justify not permitting a criminal defendant to impeach a prosecution witness on the basis of his juvenile record. We said there that "[w]e do not and need not challenge the State's interest as a matter of policy in the administration of criminal justice to seek to preserve the anonymity of a juvenile offender." Id., at 319, 94 S.Ct., at 1112. However, we concluded that the State's policy must be subordinated to the defendant's Sixth Amendment right of confrontation. Ibid. The important rights created by the First Amendment must be considered along with the rights of defendants guaranteed by the Sixth Amendment. See Nebraska Press Association v. Stuart, 427 U.S. 539, 561, 96 S.Ct. 2791, 2803, 49 L.Ed.2d 683

(1976). Therefore, the reasoning of *Davis* that the constitutional right must prevail over the State's interest in protecting juveniles applies with equal force here.

The magnitude of the State's interest in this statute is not sufficient to justify application of a criminal penalty to respondents. Moreover, the statute's approach does not satisfy constitutional requirements. The statute does not restrict the electronic media or any form of publication, except "newspapers," from printing the names of youths charged in a juvenile proceeding. In this very case, three radio stations announced the alleged assailant's name before the Daily Mail decided to publish it. Thus, even assuming the statute served a state interest of the highest order, it does not accomplish its stated purpose.

In addition, there is no evidence to demonstrate that the imposition of criminal penalties is necessary to protect the confidentiality of juvenile proceedings. As Respondents' Brief points out at page 29 n. **, all 50 states have statutes that provide in some way for confidentiality, but only five, including West Virginia, impose criminal penalties on nonparties for publication of the identity of the juvenile. Although every state has asserted a similar interest, all but a handful have found other ways of accomplishing the objective. See Landmark Communications, Inc. v. Virginia, 435 U.S. 829, 843, 98 S.Ct. 1535, 1543, 56 L.Ed.2d 1 (1978).

(5)

Our holding in this case is narrow. There is no issue before us of unlawful press access to confidential judicial proceedings, see Cox Broadcasting Corp. v. Cohn, 420 U.S. 469, 496 n. 26, 95 S.Ct. 1029, 1046 n. 26, 43 L.Ed.2d 328 (1975); there is no issue here of privacy or prejudicial pretrial publicity. At issue is simply the power of a state to punish the truthful publication of an alleged juvenile delinquent's name lawfully obtained by a newspaper: The asserted state interest cannot justify the statute's imposition of criminal sanctions on this type of publication. Accordingly, the judgment of the West Virginia Supreme Court of Appeals is

Affirmed.

MR. JUSTICE POWELL took no part in the consideration or decision of this case.

MR. JUSTICE REHNQUIST, concurring in the judgment.

Historically, we have viewed freedom of speech and of the press as indispensable to a free society and its government. But recognition of this proposition has not meant that the public interest in free speech and press always has prevailed over competing interests of the public. "Freedom of speech thus does not comprehend the right to speak on any subject at any time," American Communications Assn. v. Douds, 339 U.S. 382, 394, 70 S.Ct. 674, 682, 94 L.Ed. 925 (1950), and "the press is not free to publish with impunity everything and anything it desires to publish." Branzburg v. Hayes, 408 U.S.

665, 683, 92 S.Ct. 2646, 2658, 33 L.Ed.2d 626 (1972); see Near v. Minnesota ex rel. Olson, 283 U.S. 697, 708, 716, 51 S.Ct. 625, 628, 631, 75 L.Ed. 1357 (1931). While we have shown a special solicitude for freedom of speech and of the press, we have eschewed absolutes in favor of a more delicate calculus that carefully weighs the conflicting interests to determine which demands the greater protection under the particular circumstances presented. E.g., Landmark Communications, Inc. v. Virginia, 435 U.S. 829, 838, 843, 98 S.Ct. 1535, 1541, 1543, 56 L.Ed.2d 1 (1978); Nebraska Press Assn. v. Stuart, 427 U.S. 539, 562, 96 S.Ct. 2791, 2804, 49 L.Ed.2d 683 (1976); American Communications Assn. v. Douds, supra, 339 U.S., at 400, 70 S.Ct., at 684.

The Court does not depart from these principles today. * * * Instead, it concludes that the asserted state interest is not sufficient to justify punishment of publication of truthful, lawfully obtained information about a matter of public significance. * * * So valued is the liberty of speech and of the press that there is a tendency in cases such as this to accept virtually any contention supported by a claim of interference with speech or the press. See Jones v. Opelika, 316 U.S. 584, 595, 62 S.Ct. 1231, 1238, 86 L.Ed. 1691 (1942). I would resist that temptation. In my view, a State's interest in preserving the anonymity of its juvenile offenders—an interest that I consider to be, in the words of the Court, of the "highest order"—far outweighs any minimal interference with freedom of the press that a ban on publication of the youth's name entails.

It is a hallmark of our juvenile justice system in the United States that virtually from its inception at the end of the last century its proceedings have been conducted outside of the public's full gaze and the youths brought before our juvenile courts have been shielded from publicity. See H. Lou, Juvenile Courts in the United States 131–133 (1927); Geis, Publicity and Juvenile Court Proceedings, 30 Rky.Mt.L.Rev. 101, 102, 116 (1958). This insistence on confidentiality is born of a tender concern for the welfare of the child, to hide his youthful errors and "bury them in the graveyard of the forgotten past." In re Gault, 387 U.S. 1, 24–25, 87 S.Ct. 1428, 1442, 18 L.Ed.2d 527 (1967). The prohibition of publication of a juvenile's name is designed to protect the young person from the stigma of his misconduct and is rooted in the principle that a court concerned with juvenile affairs serves as a rehabilitative and protective agency of the State. National Advisory Comm. on Criminal Justice Standards and Goals, Juvenile Justice and Delinquency Protection, Standard 5.13, at 224–225 (1976); see Davis v. Alaska, 415 U.S. 308, 319, 94 S.Ct. 1105, 1111, 39 L.Ed.2d 347 (1974); Kent v. United States, 383 U.S. 541, 554–555, 86 S.Ct. 1045, 1053–1054, 16 L.Ed.2d 84 (1966). Publication of the names of juvenile offenders may seriously impair the rehabilitative goals of the juvenile justice system and handicap the youths' prospects for adjustment in society and acceptance by the public. E. Eldefonso, Law Enforcement and the Youthful Offender 166 (3d ed. 1978). This exposure brings undue embarrassment to the families of youthful offenders and may cause the juvenile to lose employment opportunities or provide the hard core delinquent the kind of attention he seeks, thereby encouraging him to commit further antisocial acts. Davis v. Alaska, supra, 415 U.S., at 319, 94 S.Ct., at 1111. Such publicity also renders nugatory States' expungement laws, for a potential employer or any other person can retrieve the information the States seek to "bury" simply by visiting the morgue of the local newspaper. The resultant widespread dissemination of a juvenile offender's name, therefore, may defeat the beneficent and rehabilitative purposes of a State's juvenile court system.[86]

By contrast, a prohibition against publication of the names of youthful offenders represents only a minimal interference with freedom of the press. West Virginia's statute, like similar laws in other States, prohibits publication only of the name of the young person. See W.Va.Code § 49–7–3. The press is free to describe the details of the offense and inform the community of the proceedings against the juvenile. It is difficult to understand how publication of the youth's name is in any way necessary to performance of the press' "watchdog" role. In those rare instances where the press believes it is necessary to publish the juvenile's name, the West Virginia law, like the statutes of other States, permits the juvenile court judge to allow publication. The juvenile court judge, unlike the press, is capable of determining whether publishing the name of the particular young person will have a deleterious effect on his chances for rehabilitation and adjustment to society's norms.[87]

Without providing for punishment of such unauthorized publications it will be virtually impossible for a State to ensure the anonymi-

[86] That publicity may have a harmful impact on the rehabilitation of a juvenile offender is not mere hypothesis. Recently, two clinical psychologists conducted an investigation into the effects of publicity on a juvenile. They concluded that publicity "placed additional stress on [the juvenile] during a difficult period of adjustment in the community, and it interfered with his adjustment at various points when he was otherwise proceeding adequately." Howard, Grisso & Neems, Publicity and Juvenile Court Proceedings, 11 Clearinghouse Rev. 203, 210 (1977). Publication of the youth's name and picture also led to confrontations between the juvenile and his peers while he was in detention. Ibid. While this study obviously is not controlling, it does indicate that the concerns that prompted enactment of state laws prohibiting publication of the names of juvenile offenders are not without empirical support.

[87] The Court relies on Davis v. Alaska, 415 U.S. 308, 94 S.Ct. 1105, 39 L.Ed.2d 347 (1974). * * * But Davis, which presented a clash between the interests of the State in affording anonymity to juvenile offenders and the defendant's Sixth Amendment right of confrontation,

does not control the disposition of this case. In Davis, where the defendant's liberty was at stake, the Court stated that "[s]erious damage to the strength of the State's case would have been a real possibility had petitioner been allowed to pursue this line of inquiry [related to the juvenile offender's record]." Id., at 319, 94 S.Ct., at 1112. The State also could have protected the youth from exposure by not using him to make out its case. Id., at 320, 94 S.Ct., at 1112. By contrast, in this case the State took every step that was in its power to protect the juvenile's name, and the minimal interference with the freedom of the press caused by the ban on publication of the youth's name can hardly be compared with the possible deprivation of liberty involved in Davis. Because in each case we must carefully balance the interest of the State in pursuing its policy against the magnitude of the encroachment on the liberty of speech and of the press that the policy represents, it will not do simply to say, as the Court does, that the "important rights created by the First Amendment must be considered along with the rights of defendants guaranteed by the Sixth Amendment." * * *

ty of its juvenile offenders. Even if the juvenile court's proceedings and records are closed to the public, the press still will be able to obtain the child's name in the same manner as it was acquired in this case. * * * Thus, the Court's reference to effective alternatives for accomplishing the State's goals is a mere chimera. The fact that other States do not punish publication of the names of juvenile offenders, while relevant, certainly is not determinative of the requirements of the Constitution.

Although I disagree with the Court that a state statute punishing publication of the identity of a juvenile offender can never serve an interest of the "highest order" and thus pass muster under the First Amendment, I agree with the Court that West Virginia's statute "does not accomplish its stated purpose." * * * The West Virginia statute prohibits only newspapers from printing the names of youths charged in juvenile proceedings. Electronic media and other forms of publication can announce the young person's name with impunity. In fact, in this case three radio stations broadcast the alleged assailant's name before it was published by The Charleston Daily Mail. * * * This statute thus largely fails to achieve its purpose. It is difficult to take very seriously West Virginia's asserted need to preserve the anonymity of its youthful offenders when it permits other, equally, if not more, effective means of mass communication to distribute this information without fear of punishment. See Branzburg v. Hayes, 408 U.S., at 700, 92 S.Ct., at 2666; Bates v. Little Rock, 361 U.S. 516, 525, 80 S.Ct. 412, 417, 4 L.Ed.2d 480 (1960). I, therefore, join in the Court's judgment striking down the West Virginia law. But for the reasons previously stated, I think that a generally effective ban on publication that applied to all forms of mass communication, electronic and print media alike, would be constitutional.

NOTE

For detailed studies of the impact of the new Supreme Court cases relating to press access to various phases of the criminal process see Katz, The Grim Reality of Open Juvenile Delinquency Hearings, 28 N.Y.L. Sch. L. Rev. 101 (1983) and Note, The Right to Access and Juvenile Delinquency Hearings: The Future of Confidentiality, 16 Ind. L. Rev. 911 (1983). The student should also consider the principal case as well as the above commentary in connection with chapter 11, infra.

I. RIGHT TO A SPEEDY TRIAL

The Supreme Court has held that the Speedy Trial Guarantee of the Sixth Amendment is binding on the states in criminal prosecutions. The scope of the limitation has been most completely developed in Barker v. Wingo, 407 U.S. 514, 92 S.Ct. 2182, 33 L.Ed.2d 101 (1972). In In The Interest of C.T.F., the Iowa Supreme Court held that the speedy trial guarantees, whatever they may be, apply equally in adult criminal prosecutions and in juvenile delinquency adjudicatory hearings, 316 N.W.2d 865, 868 (Iowa 1982). In State v. Barksdale, immediately infra, the court explained both the nature of the test in adult cases as well as how it is applied in a juvenile delinquency proceeding.

STATE v. BARKSDALE

Family Court of Delaware, 1982.
451 A.2d 1174.

GALLAGHER, JUDGE:

Respondent has moved the court for an order dismissing the charges of terroristic threatening (81–8–65–4) and reckless endangering in the first degree (81–8–65–2) because of the failure of the State to provide him with a speedy trial. The charges against respondent are quite serious. With respect to reckless endangering in the first degree the charge is that respondent attacked his brother with a wooden statue and a six-inch knife and forced him from the house with the same. With respect to terroristic threatening the charge is that respondent threatened to kill his brother while holding an open knife. Both of these offenses are alleged to have occurred on August 3, 1981.

Complaints alleging the above offenses were received in Family Court on August 4, 1981. The petitions alleging the offenses were executed on December 1, 1981. The petitions were scheduled for case review on January 7, 1982, and since no plea agreement was reached they were set down for trial. On January 7, 1982, respondent moved for an order dismissing all pending charges because of the failure of the State to provide him with a speedy trial. The State argued that the motion should be denied because six months had not elapsed since the alleged incident date. The motion was denied on January 7, 1982. On January 25, 1982, all pending charges were scheduled for trial. None of the State's witnesses, including the alleged victim, appeared for trial. Respondent who had had transportation arranged through the Division of Social Services did not appear because the transporting vehicle was stuck in the ice. The following day, January 26, 1982, the parties were before the court and all pending charges other than those here involved were disposed of by a plea agreement. Respondent received a suspended commitment on January 26, 1982, to Ferris School with a year's supervised probation. According to the disposition the State reserved the right to go to trial on the remaining two charges.

Nothing further happened with respect to the above petitions after January 26, 1982, until respondent moved for dismissal of the petitions on July 6, 1982. They have not been scheduled for hearing by the scheduling department as they should have been. The State has done nothing to encourage the scheduling department to schedule these petitions for trial. Neither has respondent. Respondent asserts that he wishes to apply for acceptance in the Job Corps, the wish he entertained when his first motion was denied on January 7, 1982. He complains that he is barred from the Job Corps while these charges are pending.

Eleven months have elapsed since the alleged incident date. Over seven months have elapsed since the petitions were executed. Almost six months have elapsed since the one scheduled trial date. Almost six months have elapsed since the State reserved the right to go to trial on the remaining charges.

If delay were the only factor to be considered when deciding the pending motion, clearly respondent would be entitled to a dismissal. Delay, however, is only one of the factors meriting consideration. *See* State v. Michael Bush, Del.Super., IN–81–06–0503 FC *et seq.*, Bifferato, J. (June 24, 1982).

The leading case is Barker v. Wingo, 407 U.S. 514, 92 S.Ct. 2182, 33 L.Ed.2d 101 (1972). In that case the court rejected two suggestions as to what the Constitution should require as to a speedy trial: (1) that there be a specified time period within which defendant is to be offered trial; and (2) failure of the defendant to demand trial gives rise to a presumption of waiver. The court, instead, opted for the balancing test in which the conduct of both the prosecution and the defendant are weighed in relation to each other. (407 U.S. 530). Stating that this test compels an *ad hoc* approach in determining speedy trial questions, the court then identified four factors, namely "length of delay, the reason for the delay, the defendant's assertion of his right, and prejudice to the defendant." (407 U.S. at 530, 92 S.Ct. at 2192). The balancing factors will now be considered.

LENGTH OF DELAY

As we have seen eleven months have elapsed since the alleged incidents, and over seven months have elapsed since the petitions were executed. Almost six months have elapsed since the last scheduled trial date. The length of delay is significant. It is a triggering mechanism. But length of delay is not an all governing factor. The alleged offenses here are quite serious. We are not considering an ordinary street crime. Therefore, because of the seriousness of these offenses more delay is tolerable.

REASON FOR DELAY

Respondent argues that the State is responsible for the delay because it has a prosecutorial duty to see that petitions are brought to trial expeditiously. But neither party can simply ignore a pending petition in the hope that someone in the scheduling department will schedule a hearing. For better or for worse the State does rely on the scheduling department for this function and does not keep track of petitions that have not gone to trial. While the State certainly has a responsibility in this area, respondent is not without responsibility. There is nothing in the record to suggest that respondent has been seeking the intervention of the scheduling department to fix a trial date. Even if the court were to look exclusively to the State for responsibility in seeing that these petitions were scheduled for trial, the most that can be said is that the State was negligent in its duty, since no one has suggested a deliberate attempt to delay trial in order to hamper the defense.

RESPONDENT'S ASSERTION OF HIS RIGHT

Respondent has done nothing since January, 1982, to bring about a disposition of the pending charges, except for the filing of this motion. Certainly as I have just pointed out, respondent has a clear responsibility in this regard, which he has not bothered to undertake.

PREJUDICE TO RESPONDENT

There are three interests to be considered under this heading:

(1) To prevent oppressive pretrial incarceration;

(2) To minimize anxiety and concern of the accused; and

(3) To limit the possibility that the defense will be impaired.

Oppressive pretrial incarceration is not a factor. While respondent might have been committed to the custody of the Department of Correction for other charges to which he pled guilty on January 26, 1982, the fact is that he received a suspended commitment and has been on probation since that date and continues on probation to the present time. He was never incarcerated on these charges.

With respect to minimizing the anxiety and concern of the accused, it is true that respondent has been anxious to enter the Federal Job Corps program. However, while it has been alleged that the pendency of these charges affects his ability to be accepted in the Job Corps, this allegation has not been proven and there is no assurance that respondent would be accepted in the Job Corps even if the pending charges were disposed of.

The most important factor is limiting the possibility that the defense will be impaired. There has been no allegation by respondent of any impairment in his ability to conduct his defense. So this is not a factor.

The court has carefully considered the balancing test factors and on balance concludes that the State has not failed at this juncture to provide respondent with a speedy trial. Therefore, respondent's motion to dismiss the pending charges for that reason is denied. However, the scheduling department is directed with the cooperation of both the State and respondent to fix a trial date for the two pending charges within the next two weeks before this Judge on an emergency basis so that these charges can be disposed of.

It is so ordered.

NOTE

Whether there is a constitutional right to a speedy trial in juvenile proceedings or not, the problem remains whether the presence or absence of pre-trial detention has any bearing on the length of time that may pass without an adjudication hearing.

"This writ of habeas corpus must be sustained and the alleged juvenile delinquent discharged from custody under her pending detention resulting from the proceedings taken in the Family Court with reference to the juvenile delinquency petition dated December 2, 1964.

"On that day her law guardian requested an adjournment to procure witnesses. The court, having inquired at that point and been informed that there was a prior record, directed that she be remanded to Youth House with bail set at $1,000. Then the question of the length of the adjournment was discussed. The law guardian requested an adjournment of one day. The petitioner police officer suggested nine days and the court thereupon adjourned the matter for nine days. The relator has in the meantime been in detention in the Youth House.

"The Family Court Act provides for two separate hearings—a 'fact-finding hearing' and a 'dispositional hearing'. To prevent unreasonable delay in holding the fact-finding hearing, section 747 provides: 'A fact-finding hearing shall commence not more than three days after the filing of a petition under this article if the respondent is in detention.' Section 748 deals with the adjournment of a fact-finding hearing and provides: '(a) If the respondent is in detention, the court may adjourn a fact-finding hearing (i) on its own motion or on motion of the petitioner for good cause shown for not more than three days; (ii) on motion on behalf of the respondent * * * for a reasonable period of time.'

"It is clear that, since relator was being placed in detention, the Family Court did not have the authority to adjourn the fact-finding hearing for more than three days on the motion of the petitioner police officer. Any adjournment for a longer period of time could be done only on motion or consent of the person representing the alleged juvenile delinquent. Here the law guardian vigorously opposed a lengthy adjournment.

"The fact that bail was set does not negate the holding that the relator was placed in detention and has in fact been in detention during this period of more than three days.

"The purpose and spirit of the Family Court Act for a prompt fact-finding hearing where a respondent is in detention, would be frustrated were this court to hold otherwise.

"Relator's discharge is from the detention resulting from the proceedings taken with reference to the petition dated December 2, 1964."

Geller, Justice, in People v. Poland, 44 Misc.2d 769 at 769–70, 255 N.Y.S.2d 5 at 6 (1964).

J. RIGHT TO COUNSEL

It is clear from *Gault*, alone, that if counsel is required in the kind of proceeding in question, both the juvenile and his parents must be notified of their right to retain counsel, and, if they are indigent, to have counsel appointed for them. There is less certainty about the kind of proceedings to which the counsel right extends. The first problem, whether it extends to procedures other than adjudication, is considered along with discussion of those other stages. The second problem, whether it extends to PINS proceedings is less clear.

In many states commitment to a training school is a dispositional option in PINS type proceedings, though in others it is not. Should the counsel line be drawn between Delinquency and PINS cases, or between Delinquency and those PINS cases in which commitment is a possibility on the one hand, and PINS and perhaps Neglect or Dependency cases where it is not? Consider this question both in its constitutional aspects and independently of them. For example, the new Texas statute, Texas Family Code in section 54.03(b), provides for counsel in both PINS and Delinquency cases, although training school is a possible disposition only in Delinquency cases.

Two other problems are what role counsel is to play in a juvenile proceeding and what are the standards by which a waiver of counsel can be effected.

IN RE WALKER

Supreme Court of North Carolina, 1972.
282 N.C. 28, 191 S.E.2d 702.

On 2 August 1971 Mrs. Katherine Walker, mother of Valerie Lenise Walker, filed a petition in the district court alleging in pertinent part:

"1. That the above named child is less than sixteen years of age and resides in the district at the address shown above, or was found in the district as alleged herein.

"2. That the names and addresses of the child's parents * * * are as follows:

Name: Mr. & Mrs. John Walker
Relation or Title: Parents.
Address: 541 E. Bragg Street,
      Greensboro, North Carolina.

"3. Said child is an undisciplined child as defined by G.S. 7A–278 in that she has been regularly disobedient to her parents during the last six months; that the said child will not mind and obey; that the child goes and comes as she pleases and keeps late hours; that the child associates with persons of questionable character and frequents places not approved by the parents; further, that the child is almost beyond the control of her parents.

"Petitioner prays the court to hear the case to determine whether the allegations are true and whether the child is in need of the care, protection or discipline of the State."

A juvenile summons was thereupon issued and served upon Valerie Lenise Walker and her parents on 9 August 1971, summoning them to appear in juvenile court for a hearing on the allegations in the petition, copy of which was served with the summons.

The matter came on for hearing before Judge Gentry on 17 August 1971. Valerie was present with her mother and the court counselor, Mrs. Ann M. Jones. Valerie was not represented by an attorney at this hearing. Judge Gentry heard evidence and found (a) that Valerie Lenise Walker, born 14 April 1957, is a child under sixteen years of age in the custody and under the supervision and control of her parents, Mr. and Mrs. John Walker; (b) that Valerie has been regularly disobedient to her parents in that she goes and comes without permission, keeps late hours, associates with persons that her parents object to, and goes to places where her parents tell her not to go; and (c) that Valerie is an undisciplined child and in need of the discipline and supervision of the State. This order was signed on 19 August 1971.

Based on the foregoing findings, it was ordered, adjudged and decreed that Valerie was an undisciplined child within the meaning of the law. She was placed on probation subject to the following conditions:

"1. That she be of good behavior and conduct herself in a law-abiding manner;

"2. That she mind and obey her parents and not leave home without permission and then to go only to places that she has permission to go and return as directed;

"3. That she attend school regularly during the school year and obey the school rules and regulations;

"4. That she report to the court counselor as directed, truthfully answer questions put to her concerning her conduct, behavior, associates and activities and carry out requests given her concerning such;

"5. That this matter be reopened for further orders on March 22, 1972 at 2:00 p.m.

"This matter is retained for further orders of the court."

Thereafter, on 21 September 1971, Ann M. Jones, Court Counselor, filed a verified petition and motion in the cause for further consideration and review of the case, alleging:

"That the said child is a delinquent child as defined by G.S. § 7A–278(2) in that the said child has violated Conditions No. 1, 2, and 3 of the probation order dated August 19, 1971, in that the said child continuously disobeys her parents in that she goes and comes as she pleases; keeps late hours; and frequents places not approved by her parents; further, the said child refuses to obey school rules and regulations in that she misbehaves in the classroom and is disrespectful to school officials; further, the said child is beyond the control of her parents."

A juvenile summons was thereupon issued and served upon Valerie and her parents, notifying them to appear in juvenile court for a further hearing upon the matters alleged in the motion, copy of which was served with the summons on 22 September 1971.

Prior to the hearing the public defender of the Eighteenth Judicial District was appointed to represent Valerie, and the matter came on for hearing before Judge Gentry on 15 October 1971. At that time Valerie was present with her mother and was represented by Wallace C. Harrelson and J. Dale Shepherd, Public Defenders.

Present representing the State was Thaddeus A. Adams, III, Assistant Solicitor.

Prior to the introduction of evidence, Valerie's counsel moved to vacate the order dated 19 August 1971 finding that Valerie was an undisciplined child and placing her on probation for that she was not represented by counsel at that time and was unable to defend herself on the charge that she was an undisciplined child, resulting in a denial of due process. Her counsel further moved to dismiss the petition and motion in the cause filed 21 September 1971 by Ann M. Jones, Court Counselor, for that G.S. § 7A–278 violates the Equal Protection Clause of the Fourteenth Amendment in that the statute provides for an adjudication of delinquency when the respondent has violated none of the laws of the State of North Carolina. Both motions were denied and respondent duly excepted.

Katherine Walker, mother of Valerie, testified that she lives with her husband and seven small children, including Valerie; that she and her husband both work and that Valerie is usually not at home when she returns from work; that Valerie fails to do the chores which have been assigned to her, such as cleaning her room, the bathroom, and taking her turn washing dishes; that when Valerie comes home she usually says she has been at Mrs. Cunningham's house with Vanessa Cunningham; that Valerie has been told not to leave home without telling her mother where she is going but she continues to disobey in that respect; that Valerie keeps late hours and sometimes comes in at eleven, twelve, one and two o'clock at night; that Valerie has been to Paradise Inn in violation of parental instructions; that Paradise Inn sells beer and has a bad reputation and is no place for a fourteen-year-old girl; that during Valerie's nocturnal absences her parents do not know where she is.

Mrs. Walker further testified that she is the mother of ten children; that Valerie is lazy and disobedient; that Valerie signed for a registered letter from school officials, addressed to her mother, and then destroyed the letter. Mrs. Walker said: "All I want her to do is to behave like a fourteen year old should."

Howard King, Assistant Principal at Mendenhall Junior High School, testified that Valerie came to his school on September 8, 1971, and was placed in special education with a group of students who had similar defects in adjusting; that from September 8 to September 21 he saw Valerie in his office many times on referral from all of her teachers except one for disrupting the class; that he had numerous conferences with Valerie and specifically recalls one problem which arose due to Valerie's refusal to dress out in the physical education class; that she refused to dress for physical education practically every day and gave no reason for her refusal; that he could not communicate very well with Valerie because she sucked her thumb, did not talk for a while, "and when she does start talking it's almost impossible to keep her from talking and it doesn't have any meaning to what we're talking about when she comes to the office. * * * It was not something that was relevant."

Mr. King further testified that Valerie was large for her age and as compared to the other children in the class; that Valerie was sent by her teachers to the office practically every day, does not fit into the classroom and disrupts whatever the teachers try to do; that he would have suspended her each day but had no way to get her home; that he simply required her to sit in the office and occasionally she would leave the office without permission; that Valerie does not respond to any methods of discipline available at the school.

The probation officer testified that Valerie had problems at her previous school similar to those described by Mr. King; that her attitude was bad toward her probation officer as well as others and that her behavior has not shown improvement; that Valerie does not have a receptive attitude toward her probation officer or the school or her mother in regard to discipline.

The respondent elected to offer no evidence and moved to dismiss the proceeding at the close of all the evidence. The motion was denied, and under date of 27 October 1971 Judge Gentry signed an order providing in pertinent part as follows:

"The court finds, upon hearing evidence, that the child was before the court on August 17, 1971 and that she was adjudged to be an undisciplined child and placed on probation, one of the conditions of probation being that she be of good behavior and conduct herself in a law-abiding manner; another condition being that she mind and obey her mother and not be away from home without permission. Another condition was that she attend school regularly and obey the school rules and regulations. The court finds that the said child did not obey her parents in that she left home without permission and did keep late hours at night. That she went to places that she was told not to go to by her parents and that she failed to do chores assigned to her by her mother. The court further finds that the child was sent out of the classroom in school a number of times for disobeying the teachers and disturbing the class. That she also refused to dress for her Physical Education classes without giving any reasons for doing so. The court finds that these acts of the child constitute a violation of the conditions of probation and that she is a delinquent child for having violated the conditions of probation and that she is in need of the discipline and supervision of the state. Court further finds that since September 21, 1971, the said child has been a constant behavior problem in school and has not responded to disciplinary actions taken and that she continues to disobey her mother. The court finds that she is in need of more discipline and supervision than can be provided for her within Guilford County.

"IT IS NOW THEREFORE ORDERED, ADJUDGED AND DECREED THAT Valerie Walker, having been found to be a delinquent child, that the said child is hereby committed to the North Carolina Board of Juvenile Correction and is to be in the custody and under the control and supervision of the officials thereof until discharged, in keeping with the requirements of law. That she is to remain in the temporary custody of the court until she can be delivered to the designated correction school by Court Counselor Mrs. Jones.

"This the 27th day of October, 1971.

B. GORDON GENTRY
JUDGE PRESIDING".

From the foregoing order respondent appealed to the Court of Appeals which found no error, 14 N.C.App. 356, 188 S.E.2d 731. Respondent thereupon appealed to the Supreme Court, allegedly as of right, asserting involvement of substantial constitutional questions arising under the Constitution of the United States and of this State.

* * *

HUSKINS, JUSTICE: Appellant Valerie Walker contends that she had a constitutional right to counsel at the hearing on the initial petition alleging her to be an *undisciplined* child. We first consider whether the Constitution affords her such right.

In In re Gault, 387 U.S. 1, 87 S.Ct. 1428, 18 L.Ed.2d 527 (1967), the United States Supreme Court held, *inter alia,* that "the Due Process Clause of the Fourteenth Amendment requires that in respect of proceedings to determine delinquency which may result in commitment to an institution in which the juvenile's freedom is curtailed, the child and his parents must be notified of the child's right to be represented by counsel retained by them, or if they are unable to afford counsel, that counsel will be appointed to represent the child." A similar statutory right to counsel for indigent juveniles at a hearing which could result in commitment to an institution is afforded by G.S. § 7A–451(a)(8).

The initial petition alleging that Valerie was an *undisciplined* child was heard on August 17, 1971. At that time the 1969 version of Article 23, Chapter 7A of the North Carolina General Statutes (Jurisdiction and Procedure Applicable to Children) was in effect. It was not until September 1, 1971, that the present version of that article became effective. See 1971 Session Laws, ch. 1180. Therefore, we must consult the 1969 version to determine whether the hearing of the "undisciplined child" petition was a proceeding "which may result in commitment to an institution in which the juvenile's freedom is curtailed."

The 1969 version of Article 23 of Chapter 7A of the General Statutes, in relevant part, contains the following definitions in G.S. § 7A–278:

"(1) 'Child' is any person who has not reached his sixteenth birthday.

"(2) 'Delinquent child' includes any child who has committed any criminal offense under State law or under an ordinance of local government, including violations of the motor vehicle laws or a child who has violated the conditions of his probation under this article.

* * *

"(5) 'Undisciplined child' includes any child who is unlawfully absent from school, or who is regularly disobedient to his parents or guardian or custodian and beyond their disciplinary control, or who is regularly found in places where it is unlawful for a child to be, or who has run away from home."

G.S. § 7A–286 (1969), after requiring the judge to select the disposition which provides for the protection, treatment, rehabilitation or correction of the child, as may be appropriate in each case, makes the following alternatives available to any judge exercising juvenile jurisdiction: "(4) In the case of any child who is delinquent or undisciplined, the court may: a. Place the child on probation * * *; or b. Continue the case * * *; or, *if the child is delinquent*, the court may c. Commit the child to the care of the North Carolina Board of Juvenile Correction. * * *" (Emphasis added.)

Despite the somewhat awkward structure of G.S. § 7A–286, (1969), it is clear that under its terms no judge exercising juvenile jurisdiction had any authority upon finding the child to be *undisciplined* to commit such child to the Board of Juvenile Correction for assignment to a State facility in which the juvenile's freedom is curtailed. The statute permitted incarceration of *delinquent* children only. A contrary holding by the Court of Appeals in In re Martin, 9 N.C.App. 576, 176 S.E.2d 849 (1970), is apparently based on a misconstruction of the statute and is not authoritative. We emphasize that there was no authority under G.S. § 7A–286 (1969) for the commitment of an *undisciplined* child to the North Carolina Board of Juvenile Correction where the child may be assigned to a State facility in which the juvenile's freedom is curtailed.

Therefore, we hold that neither *Gault*, supra, nor G.S. § 7A–451(a)(8) afforded Valerie Walker the right to counsel at the hearing on the initial petition alleging her to be an undisciplined child, for under the wording of G.S. § 7A–286(4) (1969) that hearing could not result in her commitment to an institution in which her freedom would be curtailed. Nor would there be such a right under the statute as presently written. See G.S. § 7A–286(5) (1971).

Appellant would have this Court go further than *Gault* requires. She argues for the right to counsel at the hearing of an *undisciplined child* petition on the theory that such a hearing is a critical stage in the juvenile process since it subjects the child to the risk of probation and since a violation of probation means that the child is *delinquent* and subject to commitment. In such fashion appellant seeks to engraft upon the juvenile process the "critical stage" test used by the United States Supreme Court in determining the scope of the Sixth Amendment right to counsel in *criminal prosecutions*. * * * We find no authority for such engraftment. Whatever may be the proper classification for a juvenile proceeding in which the child is alleged to be undisciplined, it certainly is not a criminal prosecution within the meaning of the Sixth Amendment which guarantees the assistance of counsel "in all criminal prosecutions."

* * *

The right to counsel delineated in *Gault* has not been extended to other procedural steps in juvenile proceedings. Neither this Court nor the United States Supreme Court has ever applied the "critical stage" test to the juvenile process. Accordingly, we hold that counsel is not constitutionally required at the hearing on an *undisciplined child* petition. See In re Gault, supra (n. 48) in which it is stated: "[W]hat we hold in this opinion with regard to the procedural requirements at the adjudicatory stage has no necessary applicability to other steps of the juvenile process."

The fact that a child initially has been found to be undisciplined and placed on probation is merely incidental to a later petition and motion alleging delinquency based on violation of the terms of probation. The initial finding can never legally result in commitment to an institution in which the juvenile's freedom is curtailed. It is only the latter petition and motion, and the finding that the child is a *delinquent* child by reason of its conduct since the initial hearing, that may result in the child's commitment. * * *

Appellant makes the further contention that North Carolina's statutory scheme, G.S. §§ 7A–278(5), 7A–285 and 7A–286(2) and (4), allowing a child to be adjudged *undisciplined* and placed on probation *without benefit of counsel*, while at the same time requiring counsel before a child may be adjudged *delinquent*, denies equal protection of the laws to the undisciplined child.

This argument has no merit and cannot be sustained. The Equal Protection Clause is offended only if the classifications of "undisciplined" and "delinquent" rest on grounds wholly irrelevant to the achievement of the State's objective. "State legislatures are presumed to have acted within their constitutional power despite the fact that, in practice, their laws result in some inequality. A statutory discrimination will not be set aside if any state of facts reasonably may be conceived to justify it." McGowan v. Maryland, 366 U.S. 420, 81 S.Ct. 1101, 6 L.Ed.2d 393 (1961). In seeking solutions which provide in each case for the protection, treatment, rehabilitation and correction of the child, it is impellingly relevant to the achievement of the State's objective that distinctions be made between undisciplined children on the one hand and delinquent children on the other. The one may need protection while the other needs correction. In our opinion, the statutes under attack embody no violation of the Equal Protection Clause. In a procedural context, as here, the Equal Protection Clause requires no more than the Due Process Clause requires.

* * *

Affirmed.

BOBBITT, CHIEF JUSTICE (dissenting).

* * *

For present purposes, I accept as valid the conditions of probation and the sufficiency of the evidence to support Judge Gentry's findings that Valerie's conduct subsequent to August 19th was in violation of the conditions of her probation.

The applicable statutory provisions quoted below appear in G.S. Volume 1B, Replacement 1969.

* * *

G.S. § 7A–285 includes the following: "The juvenile hearing shall be a simple judicial process designed to adjudicate the existence or nonexistence of any of the conditions defined by G.S. 7A–278(2) through (5) which have been alleged to exist, and to make an appropriate disposition to achieve the purposes of this article. In the adjudication part of the hearing, the judge shall find the facts and shall protect the rights of the child and his parents in order to assure due process of law, including the right to written notice of the facts alleged in the petition, the right to counsel, the right to confront and cross-examine witnesses, and the privilege against self-incrimination. In cases where the petition alleges that a child is delinquent *or* undisciplined *and* where the child *may* be committed to a State institution, the child shall have a right to assigned counsel as provided by law in cases of indigency." (Our italics.)

Valerie was found delinquent and committed solely on the ground she had violated certain of the probation conditions imposed when she was adjudicated an "undisciplined child" on August 19th. The adjudication that she was an "undisciplined child" was absolutely essential to a valid commitment for violation of probation conditions. The Court holds that she was entitled to assigned counsel *only at the final hearing* to determine whether the probation conditions had been violated. In my opinion, she was equally entitled to assigned counsel at the earlier hearing to determine whether she should be adjudged an "undisciplined child."

Here a fourteen-year-old girl was brought before the juvenile court upon the complaint of her mother. Absent counsel, she stood alone before the court. In addition to the statutory requirement, it is my opinion that due process required that counsel be assigned to represent her at any hearing which might result in an adjudication prejudicial to her.

For the reasons indicated, I would reverse the decision of the Court of Appeals, vacate Judge Gentry's order of October 27, 1971, and remand the cause with direction that a plenary hearing be conducted when Valerie is represented by counsel for *de novo* consideration and determination of the charge in the original petition that she is an "undisciplined child."

SHARP, J., joins in this dissenting opinion.

NOTES

1. The right to counsel in both juvenile and adult cases includes the right to effective assistance of counsel. The Supreme Court of California in In re F., 11 Cal.3d 249, 113 Cal.Rptr. 170, 520 P.2d 986 (1974) held that a juvenile's attorney must be allowed to make closing arguments in a juvenile delinquency adjudication. The right to effective assistance of counsel for an indigent can also include funds to employ an investigator, Johnny S. v. Superior Court, 90 Cal.App.3d 826, 153 Cal.Rptr. 550 (1979).

2. Relying on Holloway v. Arkansas, 435 U.S. 475, 98 S.Ct. 1173, 55 L.Ed.2d 426 (1978) the Illinois Appellate Court held that the same considerations which cause constitutional problems when a single attorney represents codefendants in an adult criminal trial are also present in a juvenile delinquency proceeding. See In Interest of V.W., 112 Ill.App.3d 587, 67 Ill.Dec. 965, 445 N.E.2d 445 (1983).

KAY AND SEGAL, THE ROLE OF THE ATTORNEY IN JUVENILE COURT PROCEEDINGS: A NON–POLAR APPROACH

61 Georgetown Law Journal 1401, 1409–15 (1973).[*]

ADJUDICATION

An attorney representing a child in a juvenile court hearing has a number of undisputed special responsibilities. Since the child who becomes entangled in the juvenile system finds himself in an alien and apparently unfriendly environment, the juvenile's lawyer clearly can serve a useful purpose merely by acting as an adult figure whom the child may trust and on whom he may rely. The lawyer can give the child a feeling that he can communicate and have his needs made known to the court. The lawyer also can translate the requirements and procedures of the system to the juvenile. In this way there is further assurance that the child will receive the maximum benefit from the proceeding itself.

The nature of the lawyer's professional responsibility in the adjudicatory stage of juvenile proceedings becomes more clouded as it begins to manifest a basic conflict between the adversary tradition and the juvenile court system itself: to what extent should the lawyer act in a traditional adversary role in an attempt to prevent the adjudication of his client as a delinquent child? As with every other client the lawyer is of course obliged to represent a juvenile "zealously within the bounds of the law." In adult criminal trials this obligation demands that, within the bounds of professional ethics, the lawyer use all his skill and resources in order to establish his client's innocence. It is not at all clear that the attorney is under a similar duty to work as single-mindedly against a finding of delinquency for his client in juvenile proceedings.

The role difference between the two contexts is explained by the fundamentally different character of both the court proceedings and the clients involved. An adult criminal trial is a means of ascertaining the facts about the alleged criminal conduct of the defendant. The adversary process is firmly established as the preferred factfinding system in ordinary criminal courts. This system of fact-finding, however, has been expressly rejected as the optimum method in the case of juvenile offenders; there, cooperation, consultation and investigation have been deemed the most sensible ways of arriving at the truth. The non-adversary nature of the juvenile system has remained intact even after the Supreme Court decisions requiring due process for juveniles.

The nature of the client also radically affects the lawyer's professional responsibility in a juvenile adjudication proceeding. An adult defendant is presumably capable of determining his own interest; an attorney who represents him should work on behalf of that interest. While conclusive weight may be given to an adult's decision that it is not in his best interest to be convicted, it is not surprising that such weight might not be given to a similar decision by a juvenile. A child's attorney may feel that the best interest of his client is served not so much by attempting to spare him from an adjudication of delinquency, as by presenting the court with sufficient information to allow the court to exercise its own judgment as to the issue of the child's delinquency. As distinguished from the adult situation, the juvenile attorney may feel permitted—indeed obligated—to act on a conviction that non-criminal sanctions and paternal guidance are the best thing for the child he is representing.

If the attorney believes the child to be innocent of the charges upon which a finding of delinquency may be based, an adversary course of action is fairly clear. Using every tool made available by the requirements of due process the attorney should zealously resist any finding of delinquency. The only problem presented by this case is where the lawyer is aware of other aspects of a child's behavior which indicate that the child could benefit from probation, state custody or counseling. In such a situation the attorney might conclude that he is not representing the juvenile's best interests by seeking a non-delinquency determination. The juvenile court system was founded on the assumption that it was not designed so much to react to specific actions of a child as to assist him when he exhibited a tendency toward improper conduct. This preventive aspect of the rationale behind juvenile courts is reflected in the extremely broad categories of behavior which may serve as a basis for declaring a child delinquent. Nevertheless, if the attorney does believe the child to be innocent of the charges against him, the attorney's feeling that the child could benefit from treatment should not dim his adversary posture; any other posture would come dangerously close to urging the court to render a finding of "delinquent" where, as a statutory matter, the child is not believed to be delinquent.

A far more difficult problem arises when the attorney personally is convinced that the child, in fact, did commit the offense for which the hearing is to be held. Many lawyers may feel that in this circumstance the proper course of conduct is to act in a non-adversary fashion and to reveal their belief in their client's guilt to the judge and thus assure the benefits of rehabilitation to the child. Adopting a less extreme position, other attorneys, while feeling such a total abandonment of the adversary role in juvenile proceedings to be improper, may nevertheless believe that at least some of the more technical methods of securing acquittal should not be employed. To a greater or lesser extent both groups of attorneys view the lawyer's duty in this situation as one of ensuring that the court receive all the factual information necessary to make its own determination on the issue of a client's delinquency. This commitment to provide full information is clearly at odds with the traditional criminal advocacy role. The ordinary criminal advocate would attempt to prevent disclosure to the court and prosecuting authorities of information unfavorable to the verdict he seeks. A few examples provide illustrations of situations in which a juvenile attorney might depart from this practice.

In re Gault assured juveniles the right to refuse to give self-incriminating testimony. However, *Gault* itself applied only to the adjudicatory stage, leaving open the question whether the child's privilege against self-incrimination should apply to all phases of the juvenile process, including preliminary interviews with police intake officers and social workers. An adult's attorney is almost certain to advise a client to remain silent in such a situation rather than to reveal facts which might lead to conviction. Some commentators have maintained that this advice is even more important for a juvenile since the child may be more vulnerable to an adult's threats or promises and thus more likely to give incriminating information or even a confession. Others could of course argue that only complete openness with, say, a social worker will maximize a child's chance of being rehabilitated.

A similar problem arises when juvenile authorities attempt to use evidence which has been obtained in some constitutionally defective way. Should the juvenile's lawyer move to suppress such evidence? Several basic objections can be made to suppression attempts by the attorney in a juvenile court. First, such strategy could encourage the child to lie and to conceal his activities, when the very purpose of the juvenile system is to teach the child moral values. Secondly, by attempting to suppress relevant evidence, the lawyer is blocking the presentation of complete and accurate information to the court. The decision whether to declare the child delinquent will be made more difficult, and the risk of an incorrect decision will be increased. One critic of such tactics has claimed that a lawyer who uses them "possesses no social conscience, or is constitutionally contentious or vainly legalistic or mentally myopic."

It should be noted that practical considerations may call for the juvenile's attorney to shun the adversary role even when he would be otherwise committed to obtaining a finding of no delinquency. Despite the Supreme Court decisions discussed above, the personnel and philosophy of most juvenile courts remain largely unchanged from the pre-*Gault* era. The lawyer still is considered an intruder in such courts and may be particularly unwelcome if he brings "the clamor of the adversary system" into court with him. Concerned that a juvenile judge's distaste for adversary methods may have adverse effects on his client, a lawyer may properly believe the child's best interest requires the presentation of his client's case without the aid of such tactics. By cooperating with the judge he can hope to earn a more desirable disposition for the child.

When the lawyer feels that use of exclusionary tactics can block a justifiable finding of delinquency, it may well be appropriate for him to evaluate the child and the probability of various dispositions resulting from a finding of delinquency. The lawyer who believes from personal knowledge of the child, the child's family, and past history that a finding of delinquency with its resulting disposition will be beneficial, may be more willing to allow otherwise excludable information to be introduced. For example, the attorney may feel that a juvenile who has experienced his first trouble with the law because of unfortunate associations may benefit from a supervised probation period or that a child who has shown a long record of offenses requires institutional help to break a behavior pattern.

This type of judgment of course calls for the lawyer's calculated guess as to the probability of the various dispositions the court might order. While the vast majority of adjudications result in no more than probation, the attorney's familiarity with the court and its past practices obviously is a critical factor influencing his final decision. Such an approach also calls upon the attorney to evaluate the various facilities available for treatment of juvenile offenders in the event of a finding of delinquency. While the attorney may consider probation to be a harmless burden on the child, he should be much more wary in cases where institutional confinement is a possible result. The failures and even the dangers of juvenile institutions have been extensively recognized. Even an attorney who feels that his client has committed the offense in question and is in serious need of professional help may feel justified in using every power at his disposal to prevent a result which he considers extremely harmful to his client.

The decision-making process just described raises very serious problems with respect to the competence of lawyers to evaluate the complex factors which contribute to or detract from a child's well being. The juvenile court and its professional staff have been established precisely to provide such expertise. The lawyer might be said to usurp the court's function when he makes an *a priori* decision as to what outcome is desirable and then tailors his tactics to achieve that result. However, where substantial doubt exists as to whether the juvenile court is making optimal decisions for the child's welfare, this allegation would seem to be unjustified. If the lawyer has good reason to believe that the juvenile court often makes the wrong determination and that the treatment it prescribes is often harmful, then abandonment of the adversary role in every case would be directly counter to the child's welfare. Similarly when the attorney believes that by a full presentation of the facts his client is likely to receive treatment which would be in the child's best interests, it would certainly be improper to deprive the child of that benefit by use of strict adversary tactics. So long as the juvenile court fails to function completely along the lines of the rehabilitation model which it was designed to approximate, an attorney has no choice but to make the difficult evaluations suggested.

The lawyer's duty to his client is to represent his best interests. When the client is unable to make that determination for himself, it has been recognized that the lawyer may sometimes make it for him. The adversary method of factfinding is only one possible means of achieving what is best for the client. In an ideal juvenile court with an enlightened judge and expert social workers, the adversary approach would probably not be the most appropriate. In the highly imperfect real world of juvenile courts and juvenile corrections—and to the extent that the juvenile rehabilitation model is not met in reality—the surest technique of achieving the child's best interest and the use of advocacy often will coincide.[c]

IN RE APPEAL NO. 544 SEPT. TERM, 1974, CIRCUIT COURT, CECIL CTY.

Maryland Court of Special Appeals, 1975.
25 Md.App. 26, 332 A.2d 680.

Argued before ORTH, C.J., and DAVIDSON and MELVIN, JJ.
ORTH, CHIEF JUDGE.

* * *

THE FACTS

The Pleadings

On 19 June 1974 two petitions were filed in the Circuit Court for Cecil County sitting as a Juvenile Court showing that appellant was a delinquent child. Petition No. 3370 gave as reason that "on or about September 12, and September 14, 1973" appellant broke into a certain dwelling house with intent to steal personal property and that he "unlawfully did, or did attempt to, steal, take, and carry away" designated personal goods of the value of less than $100. Petition No. 3371 gave as reason that "on April 30 and May 3, 1974" appellant broke into the same dwelling house with the same intent and "unlawfully did, or did attempt to, steal, take and carry away" certain designated personal goods of the value of less than $100. The petitioner was Robert G. Ellis, whose "relationship or concern" was

---

[c] Lawrence, The Role of Legal Counsel in Juveniles' Understanding of their Rights, 34 Juv. & Fam.L.J. (No. 4) 49, contains a valuable study of the difficul- ties in getting juveniles to understand their rights and makes suggestions about how to make counsel more effective in communicating those rights.

given as "Investigating Officer" of the Maryland State Police. The petitions were authorized by R. Darrell King, whose title was given as "Juvenile Probation Officer," Department of Social Services.

On 24 June 1974 identical answers were filed to the petitions. Each "Answer" consists of a printed form, designated as "Form 38", on which it is stated "To be prepared by: Agency authorizing filing of petition." Apparently, therefore, each was prepared by the Department of Juvenile Services. It is addressed to the Judges of the Juvenile Court, and the first part reads:

"In answer to the petition filed in the above entitled case, we, the undersigned, hereby state that the following facts are true:

" '1. We have received a copy of the petition, have read the petition, have had the allegations explained to us and are satisfied that we understand the statements contained in the petition.

" '2. We have been advised that should the Court make a finding of delinquency ["child in need of supervision" crossed out] the Court could take jurisdiction and make such disposition as the Court feels is most suitable.

" '3. We have been advised that we have a constitutional right to be represented by an attorney in the case.

" '4. We have been advised that we have the right to be represented by a Public Defender if we are unable to afford an attorney.

" '5. We have been advised that we have a right to a full hearing on the petition, and that in the event of a finding of delinquency ["child in need of supervision" crossed out] we have a right of appeal to the Court of Special Appeals of Maryland.

" '6. In filing this Answer we have not been offered any promise of favor or reward, and we have not been threatened or made afraid by any person representing or employed by any government agency.' "

This statement follows:

"WHEREFORE, being satisfied that we have received fair notice of the allegations in the petition and that we understand the allegations and our rights as set forth above, we, the undersigned, voluntarily and of our own free will:

" '1. (x) waive the right to be represented by an attorney.

" '2. (x) waive the right to a hearing on the allegations in the petition; admit that the statements in the petition are true and correct; and, consent to have the Court make a finding of delinquency ["child in need of supervision" crossed out] and make an appropriate disposition in this case.' "

The "x" indicating that 1. and 2. applies is typed in. Each Answer is signed by appellant and his mother and witnessed by King over the title, "Juvenile Counselor."

The Adjudicatory Hearing

The petitions came on for hearing on 27 June 1974 in the Circuit Court for Cecil County sitting as a Juvenile Court. An assistant State's attorney appeared in behalf of the petitioner. Appellant was not represented. The judge was informed that the petitions had been answered, identified appellant and his parents, and said he was "going through this because I see you are here without a lawyer and I want to protect your Constitutional rights." He explained the allegations thus:

"[A]ppellant] is charged with breaking into the dwelling house of Michael Fabiucci of Charlestown on the 12th and 14th of September last year and stealing alcoholic beverages plus some other things valued at less than $100.00. He's also charged with—that first was Juvenile 3370.

The second is Juvenile 3371, which he's charged doing just about the same thing, breaking into the dwelling house of the same person and the same things. This occurred on the 30th of April and again on the 3rd of May, 1974."

He made inquiry about the Answers:

"Do you recall signing that?

"[Mother]: (Nods in assent.)

"THE COURT: You know in that case that [appellant] admits doing both these things? You understand that, * * *?

"[Appellant]: (Nods in assent.)

"THE COURT: And also you are willing to proceed here this morning without a lawyer. You have a Constitutional right to a lawyer if you want one. Is that understood?

"[Appellant]: (Nods in assent.)"

Thereupon, the judge entered "a finding of delinquency", and stated: "[W]e will have a few facts from the Department of Juvenile Services and we will find a delinquency in law, after which we will go ahead and decide what ought to be done." King testified. Examined by the Assistant State's Attorney he said that he had done "intake counseling work" with appellant in connection with the petitions and was familiar with the "factual background" of them. He said he was prepared, based on his counseling, to tell whether appellant was in need of care, treatment and rehabilitation. The judge interjected: "In order to be legal about it, let's split your presentation to telling us why he needs care and I'll make the adjudication * * *." King gave three reasons why appellant was in need of guidance, treatment and rehabilitation. He had been found to be delinquent in November of 1973 and placed on probation which was still open. The offense then was the same type as now charged—breaking into a residence or store and stealing alcoholic beverages. There were "some problems at home with [him], specifically in the area of drinking, the use of alcoholic beverages, coming in late at night, and then lying to his parent about his activities." The last factor "is that there is a somewhat disturbing development and medical history, which may indicate some problems for [him]." No more specificity with respect to any of the reasons was offered or requested. The Judge said: "Enter a finding of delinquency, Mr. Clerk".[88]

The Disposition Hearing

A disposition hearing followed immediately. Courts Art. § 3–829(b).[89] The judge made further inquiry of King, received information from him and made disposition:

"The disposition in this case shall be that [appellant], first of all, shall make restitution in the amount of $38.50 in Juvenile 3370, and that he shall make restitution in the amount of $247.31 in Juvenile 3371, that amount in the last case be reduced by whatever [three others involved in the offenses] might happen to wind up paying. And that his parents, * * *, being present in this Court today, are likewise charged with making these payments and I would urge contempt citations if these payments are not made in accordance with Juvenile Services—with his parents and Juvenile Services.

And, further, that he be committed to the Maryland Training School for Boys for an indefinite period and, as part of that program, that he be processed in the Maryland Children's Center for whatever evaluation and help he can gain by such processing.

And he is committed to the custody of the Sheriff or Juvenile Services, or however you want to handle it for transportation to the Maryland Training School for Boys."

King asked if appellant was to go to the Maryland Training School for Boys. The judge replied: "Whatever's the most convenient except I don't want him in the community. I want him institutionalized. He's committed to the Maryland Training School for Boys, yes."

[88] Those proceedings are reflected in the docket entries as follows:

"Hearing. * * *

Waived right to an attorney.

Finding: Delinquent in Fact.

Witnesses sworn. Testimony heard and taken.

Finding: Delinquent."

[89] As we have indicated, to be found delinquent a child must be shown to (1) have committed a delinquent act, and (2) require supervision, treatment or rehabil-itation. Courts Art. § 3–801(k). "Disposition hearing" is defined to mean "a hearing to determine (1) Whether the child is in need of supervision, treatment, or rehabilitation; and if so, (2) The nature of the supervision, treatment, or rehabilitation." Courts Art. § 3–801(n). Thus, there appears to be an overlapping. To be delinquent, a child must be in need of supervision, treatment, or rehabilitation. This, therefore, has already been determined at the adjudicatory hearing before the disposition hearing is held.

DECISION

Assistance of Counsel

By legislative enactment, a party in a juvenile case "is entitled to representation by legal counsel at every stage of any proceeding under this subtitle [8, Juvenile Causes]." Courts Art. § 3–830(d), "Right to Counsel." Rule 918, § a provides: "The parties may be represented by counsel retained by them in all proceedings." Section b reads: "Unless knowingly and intelligently waived, an indigent child shall be entitled to have counsel appointed by the court to represent him in a waiver, adjudicatory or disposition hearing or a hearing under Rule 915 ["Modification, Vacation or Renewal of Orders"] if his parents are also indigent or unwilling to employ counsel. In all cases not involving delinquency, the right to have counsel appointed shall apply only to those proceedings which are contested." By ch. 209, Acts 1971, which created the position of Public Defender in Maryland, the legislature declared that it was the policy of the State and the legislative intent "to provide for the realization of the constitutional guarantees of counsel in the representation of indigents, including related necessary services and facilities, in criminal and *juvenile* proceedings within the State, and to assure effective assistance and continuity of counsel to indigent accused taken into custody and indigent defendants in criminal and *juvenile* proceedings before the courts of the State of Maryland, and to authorize the Office of Public Defender to administer and assure enforcement of the provisions of this article in accordance with its terms." (emphasis added). Code, Art. 27A, § 1. The Act imposed the duty on the Public Defender to provide legal representation for indigent defendants, in certain proceedings, Code, Art. 27A, § 4, including, "In any criminal or juvenile proceeding constitutionally requiring the presence of counsel prior to presentment before a commissioner or judge," subsection (b)(1); "Criminal or juvenile proceedings, where the defendant is charged with a serious crime, before the District Court of Maryland, the Supreme Bench of Baltimore City, the various circuit courts within the State of Maryland, the Court of Special Appeals of Maryland, and the Court of Appeals of Maryland," subsection (b)(2); and "Any other proceeding where possible incarceration pursuant to a judicial commitment of individuals in institutions of a public or private nature may result," subsection (b)(5).

It is clear that appellant was entitled to representation by legal counsel with regard to the petitions filed against him. This includes legal assistance not only at the adjudicatory hearing but also with regard to the signing of the Answers. The effect of the Answers, if valid, would be to determine the matter of appellant's delinquency with little more ado. By them, he not only waived representation of counsel, but relinquished his entitlement to a hearing, surrendered his right to have the allegations proved beyond a reasonable doubt, dispensed with the need to be confronted by the witnesses against him, gave up the guarantee against self-incrimination, confessed that he committed the offenses charged, consented to be found delinquent and agreed to have the court make "an appropriate disposition," all without the benefit of counsel. See Freeman v. Wilcox, 119 Ga.App. 325, 167 S.E.2d 163 (1969).

If appellant was indigent, and if his parents were either indigent or unwilling to employ counsel for him, it was the duty of the Public Defender to represent him. It cannot be ascertained from the record whether he was entitled to the services of the Public Defender because we find no inquiry concerning the matter. Apparently reliance was had on the bald statement of waiver in the Answers.[90] Therefore, whether appellant and his parents were indigent or not, or whether his parents, financially able to employ counsel, were unwilling to do so or not, is not material at this point. The initial question is whether there was an effective waiver of the right to the assistance of counsel.

The Court of Appeals has carefully delineated the procedure to be followed with respect to waiver of counsel in a criminal proceeding. Its Rule 719, § c, entitled "Waiver Inquiry", prescribes:

> "If, at any stage of the proceeding, an accused indicates a desire or inclination to waive representation, the court shall not permit such a waiver, unless it determines, after appropriate questioning in open court, that the accused fully comprehends: (i) the nature of the charges and any lesser-included offenses, the range of allowable punishments, and that counsel may be of assistance to him in determining whether there may be defenses to the charges or circumstances in mitigation thereof; (ii) that the right to counsel includes the right to the prompt assignment of an attorney, without charge to the accused if he is financially unable to obtain private counsel; (iii) that even if the accused intends to plead guilty, counsel may be of substantial value in developing and presenting material which could affect the sentence; and (iv) that among the accused's rights at trial are the right to call witnesses in his behalf, the right to confront and cross-examine witnesses, the right to obtain witnesses by compulsory process, and the right to require proof of the charges beyond a reasonable doubt."

Section f requires the docket entries or transcript affirmatively to show compliance with the Rule. The Rule implements the constitutional mandates enunciated in Gideon v. Wainwright, 372 U.S. 335, 83 S.Ct. 792, 9 L.Ed.2d 799; Johnson v. Zerbst, 304 U.S. 458, 58 S.Ct. 1019, 82 L.Ed. 1461, and Carnley v. Cochran, 369 U.S. 506, 82 S.Ct. 884, 8 L.Ed.2d 70. It has been consistently held that the requirements of the Rule are mandatory, and that compliance with them is

---

[90] At the adjudicatory hearing the extent of inquiry of appellant by the court concerning an attorney was, as we have indicated, the question: "And you are willing to proceed here this morning without a lawyer. You have a Constitutional right to have a lawyer if you want

one. Is that understood?" The record shows only that appellant "Nods in assent."

We note that on appeal, appellant was represented by an attorney assigned by the Public Defender.

required irrespective of the type of plea entered, or the lack of an affirmative showing of prejudice to the accused. * * * Although Rule 719 is applicable only to criminal cases, Rule 1 a 2, and a juvenile adjudicatory hearing is not technically a criminal case, although endowed with many of the incidents of a criminal trial, see supra, we believe no less is required for a knowing and intelligent waiver of counsel in a delinquency proceeding involving children than is required in a criminal proceeding, ordinarily involving adults. To have a less strict standard for an effective waiver of counsel by a child than by an adult would be completely incongruous. The Supreme Court of the United States observed in North Carolina v. Alford, 400 U.S. 25, 37, 91 S.Ct. 160, 167, 27 L.Ed.2d 162, that " * * * the Constitution is concerned with the practical consequences, not the formal categorizations, of state law."

With the provisions of Rule 719 as the criterion, we find, on the record before us, that the court should not have permitted the waiver of representation. We hold that, due to the lack of counsel, the waivers and admissions in the Answers were invalid and ineffective and the adjudicatory hearing was void. The judgment is reversed.

NOTE

IJA–ABA Juvenile Justice Standards Project, Standards Relating to Pretrial Court Proceedings 6.1 (1980) takes the position that "a juvenile's right to counsel may not be waived."

K. THE "GUILTY PLEA" PROCESS

Most juvenile cases, like most criminal cases, are uncontested, that is, the defendant admits all the facts necessary to permit the court to enter an order adjudicating him a delinquent. Defendant's admission may be formally made in an answer to the complaint or the defendant may stipulate that the testimony of certain witnesses would establish the court's jurisdiction. In other cases, witnesses may testify, but with the understanding that the defendant will not cross-examine them nor offer testimony in defense. In all "uncontested cases" a jury is, of course, waived. The effect of these practices is the juvenile equivalent of the plea-of-guilty system in criminal cases. What accounts for the large number of uncontested cases in juvenile court? Which of the following might be important? (1) The purpose of the juvenile process is to help the defendant, not punish him. (2) The juvenile court has broad discretion in disposition and is not limited by the charges brought or mandatory sentences. (3) Prosecutors traditionally have played a small role in juvenile court. (4) The juvenile court judge dominates the juvenile process more than the criminal court judge does the criminal process. (5) Most juvenile court dispositions place the juvenile on probation; a disposition that commits him to a training school is comparatively more rare than a prison sentence by a criminal court. (6) The very most serious juvenile cases are likely to be transferred to criminal court for prosecution. (7) There is usually very substantial pre-trial screening of cases by court staff so that usually only the repeated offender reaches the juvenile court hearing stage.

CHILDREN IN NEED: OBSERVATIONS OF PRACTICES OF THE DENVER JUVENILE COURT.*

F. Plea Hearing

I would guess about 90% of the delinquency cases in juvenile court are bargained out.[91] But the pleas are better from the DA's point of view because the kids plead out to offenses as alleged on the petition—the original charge—instead of to a lesser included charge, as occurs in the adult system.

> Deputy District Attorney in
> the Denver Juvenile Court

Although hundreds of children in the Denver Juvenile Court participate each year in the tactic of plea bargaining, very few understand the process. Plea bargaining in the juvenile system results in substantially less benefit to the accused than it does in the adult system, where a guilty plea nearly always reduces the potential extent of the punishment. Under the Code, however, almost exactly the same dispositional alternatives are open to the court, regardless of the number or types of offenses admitted.

The negotiating positions of the participants in the plea bargaining process are comparable in both the adult and juvenile systems. The district attorney usually is unwilling to dismiss several charges if one allegation will be admitted for three reasons: 1) his perceived responsibility to the police department, to victims of juvenile offenses, and to society as to prosecute all wrongdoers on all charges filed; 2) his opportunity to use a lengthy record of admissions by a juvenile to argue at the dispositional stage for commitment to the Department of Institutions or more harsh sanctions, or if the juvenile reappears before the court, for a transfer of jurisdiction to the adult system; and 3) his belief that mass dismissals contribute to a diminishing respect among juveniles for the legal system.

Defense counsel participate in the practice of plea bargaining to limit the severity of the disposition of each case and to thwart possible attempts by the district attorney to have juvenile court jurisdiction transferred later. Some defense counsel also believe that parole can be obtained more quickly if there are fewer admitted offenses, although this has not been substantiated. Finally, many counsel, especially private counsel, conclude that if they get half or

---

* Permission to reprint the following article written by Hufnagel and Davidson has been obtained from the Denver Law Journal, University of Denver (Colorado Seminary), College of Law. This article appeared in Volume 51 of the Denver Law Journal at pages 377 through 382. Copyright 1974 by the Denver Law Journal, University of Denver (Colorado Seminary), College of Law.

[91] In fiscal year 1971–72, 1,817 petitions were filed in the Denver Juvenile Court as CHINS, revocation of CHINS probation, delinquency and revocation of delinquency probation. Of these, only 176, just under 10 percent, resulted in trials, 50 to a jury (all delinquency) and 126 to the court (123 delinquency).

more of the charges in each case dismissed, the child-client will perceive that he has been well represented.

Most children are represented at plea hearings by the public defender or by an attorney or student from the Legal Aid Society. The attorney may not have represented the child at the detention hearing, and, in any event, counsel usually does not receive a copy of the petition sufficiently in advance of the hearing to conduct an investigation or to speak with the child prior to the morning on which a plea must be entered.

Counsel generally asks the child if he has seen a copy of the petition. Most answer "no," indicating that they have not seen it, do not remember it, or do not know what a petition is. After the petition is shown to the child and the charges explained, counsel advises the child of his rights and explains the purpose of the plea hearing,[92] making clear that whether or not the charges are true, the child may insist that the district attorney prove them. If the child wishes to admit one or more of the allegations in the petition, counsel advises the child that probation, removal from his family, or commitment may be the consequence of entering an admission.[93] If the child persists in his desire to enter a plea of admission, counsel then probes the voluntariness of the plea.[94]

The voluntariness of pleas of admission in the Denver Juvenile Court is often questionable, primarily because of the involvement of probation counselors in planning the disposition. The child's attorney must carefully explain that while the probation counselor may already have made some plans, they are only recommendations and the judge or referee is free to reject them.[95] If the child is entering an admission based on a perceived disposition, the plea is involuntary.

[92] A typical and understandable explanation might be worded:

"In the hearing today, the referee just wants to know whether you admit the charges (or the burglary, runaway, etc.) or whether you deny the charges and want the district attorney to prove it beyond a reasonable doubt. He would have to call witnesses to prove that the charges are true, and we could ask those witnesses questions and have our own witnesses to show that the charges are not true. We could have a jury trial or we could just let the judge decide. Even if you think that the charges are true, you don't have to admit them—you don't have to help the district attorney out; you have a right to have them proved against you. Can you decide what you want to do?"

[93] Counsel might utilize the following format:

"You know that if you admit this charge, that will give the court power over you for 2 years or maybe even longer. The referee (or judge) could put you on probation which means that you

would have to visit with a probation counselor probably once a week or so, and he or she would be keeping an eye on you. The court could also take you away from your family and put you someplace else to live—like in a group home or on a ranch. The court could even lock you up for 2 years at Mountview or Lookout. The court can't do any of these things unless you admit the charges or unless they're proved against you in a trial. Do you still think you want to admit the charges?"

[94] "You know you don't have to admit the charges? Do you think anyone made you decide to admit them? Has your probation officer or anyone else promised you anything if you admit? Is this what you want to do even though you know what could happen?"

[95] Whenever delinquency allegations are involved, Colo.Rev.Stat.Ann. § 22–1–8(1)(b) (Supp.1967) forbids probation department investigation and study of possible dispositional recommendations prior to adjudication or entry of a plea of admission. However, it is broadly known

A concept which is a source of difficulty for children is the right of having charges proved against them, particularly if the children know the allegations are true or know that they were involved in the alleged offense. Most children feel that if they "did it," denying the allegations is lying. Often a child can be educated if his attorney will explain that a denial of allegations really means that the child wants to have the charges proved in trial. Counsel might briefly describe trial procedure. Nevertheless, even after such an explanation, some children never understand their right to trial.

If the child wishes to deny the charges, counsel questions him more thoroughly about the alleged offense and begins to evaluate possible defenses. On account of their shortened preparation time, some attorneys deny all allegations in each petition so that an investigator can establish the facts prior to the omnibus hearing. Others proceed with whatever a child tells them and willingly enter admissions at the plea hearing.

Because most children desire to admit guilt, because many already have incriminated themselves in conversations with their probation counselors, because the majority of attorneys or law students are inexperienced in practicing in Denver Juvenile Court, and because some attorneys view probation as an inconsequential punishment, it is possible that some children admit allegations despite the availability of a valid legal defense. It is also common for prosecutors and defenders to cooperate in gaining a conviction because "the kid needs some help." The legal ethics of these positions are certainly questionable.

When counsel and the child have agreed to the plea that will be entered, they proceed to a hearing before a referee. The plea hearing is generally very short and routinized. The referee or probation counselor introduces the case by identifying the parties present and stating that the hearing is for the purpose of entering a plea. Generally counsel for the child waives both a formal advisement of the child's rights by the court and a reading of the petition. The judicial officer then asks whether the child is prepared to enter a plea. Unless counsel requests either a continuance based on lack of notice or a need for further investigation, or a dismissal based on insufficiency of service, he enters the child's plea. If a denial is entered, the case is set for an omnibus hearing before a judge. Unless the issues of detention or bond are raised and argued, that terminates the plea hearing.

If an admission of one or more of the charges is entered, the referee should inquire into the voluntariness of the plea. The format which should be used is similar to that suggested for use by counsel for the child. However, some judicial officers either do not inquire into voluntariness or perfunctorily ask if the admission is being made under any threat, promise, or coercion. Most children will say "no," even if they do not understand the question. Once the judicial officer

and frankly admitted by probation counselors that planning for disposition begins probably at the filing stage, but certainly before adjudication.

is satisfied as to the voluntariness of the plea and some disposition has been made of any remaining counts,[96] he accepts the plea and sets the case for dispositional hearing.

Ninety percent of the children named in petitions filed in the Denver Juvenile Court enter admissions of guilt. It is impossible to determine how many of these have an informed understanding of their rights and the consequences of their admissions. Most are represented by legal counsel, advised of their rights, and formally questioned as to the voluntariness of their admissions. Although the statutory requirements are met, it is debatable, in view of the uncomprehending acquiescence of some children, whether the constitutional requirements of due process are also satisfied.

The Code, Rules of Juvenile Procedure, Colorado case law, and administrative guidelines promulgated by the Denver Juvenile Court are silent as to the plea hearing. The drafters of the Code and Rules apparently contemplated one or, at the most, two hearings for an alleged CHINS or juvenile delinquent. The adjudicatory hearing was established to determine "whether the allegations of the petition are admitted or, if contested, are supported by evidence beyond a reasonable doubt." Once the allegations had been established beyond a reasonable doubt, whether through admissions of the child or proof at trial, the court was directed by the Code to "sustain the petition, and * * * make an order of adjudication * * *." The court could then proceed with the dispositional hearing or continue the hearing on the motion of any interested party. Early in 1971, however, the Denver Juvenile Court began to split the adjudicatory and dispositional hearings.

The plea hearing is an appropriate time for counsel to make procedural objections concerning the petition itself or the legitimacy of court jurisdiction over the child. However, because there is no right in a plea hearing to proceed before a judge in the first instance, and because such issues are still timely if raised at the omnibus hearing, most defense attorneys prefer to raise them before a judge at that time.

NOTES

1. IJA–ABA Juvenile Justice Standards Project, Standards Relating to Pretrial Court Proceedings (1980) makes the following recommendations with respect to allocation of responsibility among the juvenile, counsel and others with respect to waiver of rights in the juvenile process:

[96] If only one or two of several allegations is admitted to, defense counsel will move for the dismissal of the other count. If those other counts are CHINS allegations, the court will usually dismiss them forthwith. If they are delinquency allegations, the concurrence of the district attorney's representative is usually required. If that concurrence is not forthcoming, the remaining charges will be set for omnibus hearing, usually in a couple of weeks.

6.1 Waiver of the juvenile's rights: in general *

A. Any right accorded to the respondent in a delinquency case by these standards or by federal, state, or local law may be waived in the manner described below. A juvenile's right to counsel may not be waived.

B. For purposes of this part:

1. A "mature respondent" is one who is capable of adequately comprehending and participating in the proceedings;

2. An "immature respondent" is one who is incapable of adequately comprehending and participating in the proceedings because of youth or inexperience. This part does not apply to determining a juvenile's incapacity to stand trial or otherwise participate in delinquency proceedings by reason of mental disease or defect.

C. Counsel for the juvenile bears primary responsibility for deciding whether the juvenile is mature or immature. If counsel believes the juvenile is immature, counsel should request the court to appoint a guardian *ad litem* for the juvenile.

D. A mature respondent should have the power to waive rights on his or her own behalf, in accordance with Standard 6.2. Subject to Standard 6.3, the rights of an immature respondent may be waived on his or her behalf by the guardian *ad litem*.

6.2 Waiver of the rights of mature respondents *

A. A respondent considered by counsel to be mature should be permitted to act through counsel in the proceedings. However the juvenile may not personally waive any right:

1. except in the presence of and after consultation with counsel; and

2. unless a parent has first been afforded a reasonable opportunity to consult with the juvenile and the juvenile's counsel regarding the decision. If the parent requires an interpreter for this purpose, the court should provide one.

B. The decision to waive a mature juvenile's privilege against self-incrimination; the right to be tried as a juvenile or as an adult where the respondent has that choice; the right to trial, with or without a jury; and the right to appeal or to seek other postadjudication relief should be made by the juvenile. Counsel may decide, after consulting with the juvenile, whether to waive other rights of the juvenile.

6.3 Waiver of the rights of immature respondents *

A. A respondent considered by counsel to be immature should not be permitted to act through counsel, nor should a plea on behalf of an immature respondent admitting the allegations of the petition be accepted. The court may adjudicate an immature respondent delinquent only if the petition is proven at trial.

B.   The decision to waive the following rights of an immature respondent should be made by the guardian *ad litem*, after consultation with the respondent and counsel: the privilege against self-incrimination; the right to be tried as a juvenile or as an adult, where the respondent has that choice; the right to a jury trial; and the right to appeal or seek other postadjudication relief. Subject to subsection A. of this standard, other rights of an immature respondent should be waivable by counsel after consultation with the juvenile's guardian *ad litem*.

6.4   Recording *

A.   Express waivers should be executed in writing and recorded. When administering a waiver of the juvenile's right, the judge or other official should:

1.   ascertain whether the waiver is being made by the juvenile or by the guardian *ad litem* on the juvenile's behalf;

2.   if the juvenile is waiving a right on his or her own behalf, require counsel to affirm belief in the juvenile's capacity to do so, and affirm that counsel has otherwise complied with the requirements of this part; and

3.   ascertain that the juvenile or guardian *ad litem*, as the case may be, is voluntarily and intelligently waiving the right in the presence of and after advice of counsel.

B.   Waivers should be executed in the dominant language of the waiving party or, if executed in English and the waiving party's dominant language is not English, should be accompanied by a translator's affidavit certifying that he or she has faithfully and accurately translated all conversations between the juvenile, parent[s], guardian *ad litem*, counsel, and the court with respect to the waiver decision. The affidavit should be recorded.

2.   IJA–ABA Juvenile Justice Standards Project, Standards Relating to Adjudication (1980) takes the position that plea bargaining in juvenile cases should either be recognized and regulated (much as it is in criminal cases) or efforts should be made to eliminate plea bargaining in all its forms in juvenile cases:

3.1   Capacity to plead *

A.   The juvenile court should not accept a plea admitting an allegation of the petition without determining that the respondent has the mental capacity to understand his or her legal rights in the adjudication proceeding and the significance of such a plea.

B.   In determining whether the respondent has the mental capacity to enter a plea admitting an allegation of the petition, the juvenile court should inquire into among other factors:

1.   the respondent's chronological age;

2.   the respondent's present grade level in school or the highest grade level achieved while in school;

3.   whether the respondent can read and write; and

---

* Reprinted with permission from Standards Relating to Pretrial Court Proceedings, Copyright 1980, Ballinger Publishing Company.

* Reprinted with permission from Standards Relating to Adjudication, Copyright 1980, Ballinger Publishing Company.

    4. whether the respondent has ever been diagnosed or treated for mental illness or mental retardation.

3.2 Admonitions before accepting a plea admitting an allegation of the petition *

The judge of the juvenile court should not accept a plea admitting an allegation of the petition without first addressing the respondent personally, in language calculated to communicate effectively with the respondent, and:

    A. determining that the respondent understands the nature of the allegations;

    B. informing the respondent of the right to a hearing at which the government must confront respondent with witnesses and prove the allegations beyond a reasonable doubt and at which respondent's attorney will be permitted to cross-examine the witnesses called by the government and to call witnesses on the respondent's behalf;

    C. informing the respondent of the right to remain silent with respect to the allegations of the petition as well as of the right to testify if desired;

    D. informing the respondent of the right to appeal from the decision reached in the trial;

    E. informing the respondent of the right to a trial by jury;

    F. informing the respondent that one gives up those rights by a plea admitting an allegation of the petition; and

    G. informing the respondent that if the court accepts the plea, the court can place respondent on conditional freedom for (——) years or commit respondent to (the appropriate correctional agency) for (——) years.

3.3 Responsibilities of the juvenile court judge with respect to plea agreements *

    A. Subject to the qualification contained in subsection B. of this standard, the juvenile court judge should not participate in plea discussions.

    B. If a plea agreement has been reached that contemplates entry of a plea admitting an allegation of the petition in the expectation that other allegations will be dismissed or not filed, or that dispositional concessions will be made, the juvenile court judge should require disclosure of the agreement and the reasons therefor in advance of the time for tender of the plea. Disclosure of the plea agreement should be on the record in the presence of the respondent. The court should then indicate whether it will concur in the proposed agreement. If the court concurs, but later decides not to grant the concessions contemplated by the plea agreement, it should so advise the respondent and then call upon the respondent either to affirm or withdraw the plea.

    C. When a plea admitting an allegation of the petition is tendered as a result of a plea agreement, the juvenile court judge should give the agreement due consideration, but notwithstanding its existence, should reach an independent decision whether to grant the concessions contemplated in the agreement.

3.4 Determining voluntariness of a plea admitting the allegations of the petition *

A. The juvenile court should not accept a plea admitting an allegation of the petition without determining that the plea is voluntary.

B. By inquiry of the attorneys for the respondent and for the government, the juvenile court should determine whether the tendered plea is the result of a plea agreement and, if so, what agreement has been reached.

C. If the attorney for the government has agreed to seek concessions that must be approved by the court, the court should advise the respondent personally that those recommendations are not binding on the court and follow the procedures provided in Standard 3.3 B.

D. The court should then address the respondent personally and determine whether any other promises or inducements or any force or threats were used to obtain the plea.

3.5 Determining accuracy of a plea admitting the allegations of the petition *

The juvenile court should not accept a plea admitting an allegation of the petition without making an inquiry and satisfying itself that the allegation admitted is true. The inquiry should be conducted:

A. by requiring the attorney for the government to describe the proof that the government would expect to produce if the case were tried; or

B. by personally questioning the respondent as to respondent's conduct in the case.

3.6 Inquiry concerning effectiveness of representation *

A. The juvenile court should not accept a plea admitting an allegation of the petition unless it determines that the respondent was given the effective assistance of an attorney.

B. The juvenile court should make that determination upon tender of a plea admitting an allegation of the petition and should do so by inquiring:

    1. of the respondent and respondent's attorney concerning the number and length (but not the content) of conferences the attorney has had with respondent;

    2. of the attorney for the respondent concerning the factual investigation, if any, that the attorney conducted in the case;

    3. of the attorney for the respondent concerning the legal preparation, if any, that the attorney made on behalf of respondent;

4. of the respondent and respondent's attorney concerning what advice the attorney gave respondent concerning whether to admit or deny the allegations of the petition;

5. of the respondent and respondent's attorney concerning whether there has been any conflict between them as to whether respondent should admit an allegation of the petition, and if there was, subject to the attorney-client privilege, the nature of that conflict.

3.7 Parental participation in uncontested cases *

A. Except when a parent is the complainant, the judge of the juvenile court should not accept a plea admitting an allegation of the petition without inquiring of the respondent's parent or parents who are present in court whether they concur in the course of action the respondent has chosen.

B. The judge of the juvenile court should consider the responses of the respondent's parents to the court's inquiry in exercising discretion on whether to reject the tendered plea.

Alternate 3.3 Responsibilities of officials to prohibit plea bargaining *

A. Each jurisdiction should provide by law that its public policy is to prohibit plea bargaining in all forms in the juvenile courts of that jurisdiction and should endeavor to implement that policy by mandating the measures recommended in subsections B. through L. of this standard.

B. The juvenile court should not permit its disposition of a case to be affected by whether the respondent tendered a plea admitting an allegation of the petition.

C. The judge of the juvenile court should use all reasonable means to prevent the recommendations or contents of social history reports from being affected by whether the respondent tendered a plea admitting an allegation of the petition.

D. The attorney for the government should not permit a recommendation of a disposition of a case or the representations made in a dispositional hearing to be affected by whether the respondent entered a plea admitting an allegation of the petition.

E. The attorneys for the respondent and the government should not discuss with each other any disposition of the case contemplating that the respondent will enter a plea admitting an allegation of the petition.

F. The attorney for the respondent should not advise or suggest to the respondent or respondent's family that the disposition of the case may be affected by whether the respondent tenders a plea admitting an allegation of the petition.

G. The attorney for the government should not refrain from filing allegations or refrain from prosecuting allegations already filed in the

---

expectation that the respondent will thereby be induced to tender a plea admitting an allegation of the petition.

H.   The attorney for the government should not file or threaten to file a motion to transfer a case to criminal court for prosecution of respondent as an adult or refrain from pressing such a motion or move to dismiss such a motion in the expectation that the respondent will thereby be induced to tender a plea admitting an allegation of the petition.

I.   The attorney for the government may move to dismiss a petition or to strike an allegation in a petition, but should not move to dismiss or strike in the expectation that the respondent will thereby be induced to enter a plea admitting a remaining allegation.

J.   The attorney for the government may move to amend a petition in accordance with Standard 2.2, but should not move to amend to allege less serious conduct in the expectation that the respondent will thereby be induced to enter a plea admitting an allegation of the amended petition.

K.   The judge of the juvenile court should require the attorney for the government to state the reasons for moving to dismiss a petition, to strike an allegation in a petition, or to amend a petition to allege less serious conduct and should scrutinize such motions and statements of reasons with particular care to determine their compliance with the jurisdiction's policy of prohibiting plea bargaining.

L.   If the juvenile court determines that a motion to dismiss a petition, to strike an allegation in a petition, or to amend a petition to allege less serious conduct was made in the expectation that the respondent would thereby be induced to enter a plea admitting a remaining or amended allegation, it should deny the motion.

Alternate 3.4   Determining voluntariness of a plea admitting the allegations of the petition *

A.   The juvenile court should not accept a plea admitting the allegations of the petition without determining whether the plea is voluntary.

B.   The juvenile court should address the respondent personally and determine whether any promises or inducements or any force or threats were used to obtain the plea.

C.   The juvenile court should address the respondent personally and inform the respondent that the disposition of the case, if there is an adjudication, will not be affected by whether respondent admits or denies the allegations of the petition.

D.   By inquiry of the respondent and the attorneys for the respondent and the government, the juvenile court should determine whether there have been plea discussions or a plea agreement and, if so, the nature of the discussions or agreement.

E.   If the juvenile court determines that the tendered plea is the result of plea discussions or a plea agreement, it should reject the plea, enter a plea for the respondent denying the allegations of the petition, and set the matter for trial.

IN RE M.

District Court of Appeal of California, 1970.
11 Cal.App.3d 741, 96 Cal.Rptr. 887.

ELKINGTON, ASSOCIATE JUSTICE.

A petition filed with the Contra Costa County Juvenile Court under the provisions of article 7, sections 650–664, Welfare and Institutions Code, alleged that Michael M., a minor, aged 17, "did sell a restricted dangerous drug, to wit: a hallucinagen known as lysergic acid diethylamide (LSD) * * * thereby violating section 11912 of the Health and Safety Code of California" and that he therefore came "within the provisions of section 602 of the Juvenile Court law [Welf. & Inst.Code]."

The juvenile court thereafter found the allegations of the petition to be true and committed Michael to the California Youth Authority. The proceedings on which the finding and commitment were based were the following: "THE COURT: The reason for this hearing this morning is that a petition was filed in the Juvenile Court, stating that Michael comes within Section 602 of the Juvenile Court Law, in that on or about May 7, 1969, he did sell a restricted dangerous drug, LSD, without a written prescription, thereby violating Section 11912 of the Health and Safety Code. Counsel, does your client admit or deny that? [COUNSEL]: My client admits that, Your Honor. THE COURT: Michael, is that true? THE MINOR: Yes."; also Michael made certain admissions immediately thereafter in open court in the presence of, and without objection by, his attorney, as to the details of his offense.

On his appeal Michael contends that the foregoing proceedings were tantamount to a plea of guilty; that he did not knowingly and intelligently waive his constitutional rights of confrontation and against self-incrimination; and that the rule of Boykin v. Alabama, 395 U.S. 238, 89 S.Ct. 1709, 23 L.Ed.2d 274, requiring a recorded showing of waiver of such rights on a plea of guilty to a criminal charge, is applicable to his case.

There can be little doubt that Michael's admissions to the court were, in their practical effect, equivalent to a plea of guilty to a charge of felonious possession of a restricted dangerous drug. As a result he could be, and was, committed to a state institution, the California Youth Authority, where he may be confined until age 21 (see Welf. & Inst.Code, § 1769), and, under some conditions, even longer (see Welf. & Inst.Code, § 1800).

It is now well established law that juvenile court proceedings, where a minor may be adjudged a delinquent and subjected to detention as here imposed, " 'must measure up to the essentials of due process.' " (In re Gault, 387 U.S. 1, 30, 87 S.Ct. 1428, 1445, 18 L.Ed.2d 527; Kent v. United States, 383 U.S. 541, 562, 86 S.Ct. 1045, 16 L.Ed.2d 84.) Among these "essential" constitutional rights are those of *confrontation* and against *self-incrimination*. (In re Winship, 397 U.S. 358, 90 U.S. 1068, 1075, 25 L.Ed.2d 368, 377–378; In re Gault, supra, 387 U.S. pp. 42–57, 87 S.Ct. 1428.)

It is noted that California's Welfare and Institutions Code, section 702.5, enacted 1967, provides that in a hearing taken to determine whether a minor comes within the provisions of section 602 of that code, "the minor has a privilege against self-incrimination and has a right to confrontation by, and cross-examination of, witnesses."

Boykin v. Alabama, supra, 395 U.S. 238, 243, 89 S.Ct. 1709, 1712, 23 L.Ed.2d 274, holds that before a plea of guilty may be accepted in a criminal case the defendant, among other things, must affirmatively waive: (1) his "privilege against compulsory self-incrimination guaranteed by the Fifth Amendment and applicable to the States by reason of the Fourteenth" and (2) the "right to confront one's accusers." Such a waiver must be "spread upon the record" by the prosecution; it will not be presumed from a silent record (pp. 242, 243, 89 S.Ct. 1709). A clear implication of *Boykin* is that no inference of waiver may be drawn from the presence of, or statements by defendant's counsel; it must appear to have been understandingly made by defendant himself. And the question whether there has been an effective waiver of the pertinent constitutional rights "is of course governed by federal standards." (P. 243, 89 S.Ct. p. 1712.)

The strictures of *Boykin* reasonably, and under the compulsion of Kent v. United States, supra, In re Gault, supra, and In re Winship, supra, are equally applicable to juvenile court proceedings where the minor is liable to a substantial term of institutional detention.

Boykin is to "be given prospective application only, i.e., to those cases in which pleas were entered subsequent to the effective date of that decision." (In re Tahl, 1 Cal.3d 122, 135, 81 Cal.Rptr. 577, 586, 460 P.2d 449, 458.) The instant juvenile court proceedings took place on July 31, 1969, almost two months after the announcement of *Boykin* on June 2, 1969; its rule therefore is clearly applicable.

From the foregoing discussion it becomes clear that the rule of *Boykin* must be applied to the case at bench. Michael, in what was equivalent to a plea of guilty resulting in his commitment to a state institution, did not affirmatively waive his constitutional rights to confrontation and against self-incrimination.

No merit is seen in Michael's contention that even under proper constitutional procedures his commitment to the California Youth Authority under the facts of his case would be an abuse of the juvenile court's authority.

There is no reason to believe that other complained of errors will recur in such future proceedings as may be held; we therefore do not consider them.

The commitment to the California Youth Authority is reversed; the juvenile court will take such further proceedings as are not inconsistent with the views here expressed.

MOLINARI, P.J., and SIMS, J., concur.

———

A.E.K. v. STATE

District Court of Appeal of Florida, Third District, 1983.
432 So.2d 720.

Before HENDRY, NESBITT and DANIEL S. PEARSON, JJ.

DANIEL S. PEARSON, JUDGE.

We hold that where counsel, for the avowed and singular purpose of preserving his client's right to appeal the trial court's denial of a motion to suppress the juvenile's confession, stipulates that the court determine the juvenile's guilt solely on facts proffered by the prosecutor; and where such proffered facts, to which no legal defense is made, establish beyond dispute the juvenile's guilt of the crime charged in the petition for delinquency; the proceedings, which predictably and immediately concluded with an adjudication of delinquency, are a mere substitution for, and the functional equivalent of, a nolo contendere plea, requiring, therefore, that in accordance with *Boykin v. Alabama*, 395 U.S. 238, 89 S.Ct. 1709, 23 L.Ed.2d 274 (1969), the record reflect that the juvenile was informed of and knowingly and intelligently waived the constitutional rights normally incident to a trial.

The operative facts are these. The court denied the juvenile's motion to suppress his confession and physical evidence obtained as a result of the confession. Counsel for the juvenile then announced that his client would be entering a plea of nolo contendere to the charge, expressly reserving the right to appeal the suppression ruling. He immediately thought better of his precipitousness and brought the problem to the attention of the prosecutor, who, in turn, brought it to the attention of the court.

"[PROSECUTOR]: Your Honor, at this time, we'd like to seek some guidance from the Bench. The Defense seems to be between the proverbial rock and a hard place. I believe, they're willing to enter a nolo plea, but, feel that in so doing, they will lose their right to appeal.

*   *   *

"THE COURT: Well, I want them to appeal. I think, that's a very interesting point that the Public Defender's made. And, I think, it ought to be appealed. Why are you losing your right to appeal?

"[DEFENSE COUNSEL]: Your Honor, in the case of Brown v. State, there's a—motion to deny suppression of a confession. It's never dispositive of the case, and, therefore, a nolo contendere plea is not appropriate preserving that right.

* * *

"THE COURT: I can't give you advice, then, if that's—you've got a legal problem, that you have to—even if I gave you advice, it could be bad advice.

"[PROSECUTOR]: Judge, may I point—Judge, may I proffer to the Court, if the State were to proffer after the—after the denial of the motion to suppress, if the State would proffer the facts, would his Honor make a determination, based on the facts proffered, that they're offering facts sufficient to warrant finding of guilt?

"THE COURT: Well, it doesn't make any difference to me. It's their problem, not mine.

"[DEFENSE COUNSEL]: Your Honor, I think the solution would be, if the State would proffer the facts, we will stipulate to them. Then, if we could argue our motion for judgment of acquittal, then the Court can rule as to whether or not there's sufficient evidence, and finding the Defendant guilty, or not guilty.

"THE COURT: Okay. You want to proffer the facts, and then, you're going to argue; okay? Is that all right?"

The prosecutor thereupon proffered the facts:

"[PROSECUTOR]" Your Honor, the facts in this—facts in this case are that [A.E.K.] was employed as a dish washer in a Holiday Inn. On, or about his work shift, on that day was three to eleven. The—his supervisor, and the general manager of the Holiday Inn would testify that, after his work shift, very—in the early hours of the morning, he was seen walking around in an area of the Holiday Inn, where band and musical equipment was kept. The victims in the case, Mr. Parker, and Mr. Givens would testify that when they returned on that following day—same day, to play a musical engagement there, that most of their musical equipment was missing. Mr. Felton, the manager would testify that he called Mr. Givens into the office, and, as a result of conversation with—I'm sorry. Called [A.E.K.] into the office. As a result of the conversation with [A.E.K.], [A.E.K.] took the two musicians to a house where the equipment was ransomed back for forty dollars. Some time, thereafter, [A.E.K.'s] father came to Mr. Felton, and gave him a paper bag containing microphones, he said, 'Here is the rest of the equipment.' Those would be the facts, Judge."

Defense counsel stipulated to the foregoing facts, renewed his motion to suppress, and moved for a judgment of acquittal, asserting, without argument, that the State "has not proven a prima facie case." The defense then rested and renewed its motions, now asserting that the State "has not proven their case beyond a reasonable doubt." The trial court found the juvenile guilty of theft, and adjudicated him to be delinquent.

At the outset, we recognize that there are instances in which a defendant through counsel may waive the penumbra of rights associated with a full-blown trial without his actions being considered the equivalent of pleading guilty or nolo contendere, so as to invoke the concomitant requirement that it be affirmatively shown that his waiver was intelligently and voluntarily made. Thus, courts have held that where the defendant's agreement to stipulate to the facts (in effect a waiver of the right to confront and cross-examine witnesses and to compel the attendance of witnesses to testify on the defendant's behalf) is found to be attributable to a legitimate trial tactic calculated to enhance the defendant's chance of acquittal, no affirmative showing that the waiver was intelligently and voluntarily made is necessary. See, e.g., Application of Reynolds, 397 F.2d 131 (3d Cir.1968). And this same conclusion has been reached where it can be fairly said that, notwithstanding the stipulation to the facts, the defendant continues to assert a viable defense to the charges, the adversary nature of the proceeding continues, and the factfinder, be it jury or court, is required to determine a genuinely contested issue.[97]　*　*　*

Where, however, as in the present case, no viable defense offering an even arguable chance for acquittal existed or, otherwise stated, the stipulated facts were dispositive of the defendant's guilt; the defense motions for judgment of acquittal were perfunctory in nature, calculated not to evoke a favorable decision on a genuinely disputed issue, but rather to preserve the record for appeal [98] and the defendant's maintenance of his not guilty position in conjunction with the stipulated facts was expressly an alternative to a nolo contendere plea; we consider that, under the totality of the circumstances, the proceedings below were the functional equivalent of a nolo contendere plea requiring an affirmative showing that this plea, masquerading as a trial, was intelligently and voluntarily made by the defendant himself with full understanding of the rights being waived. See Brookhart v. Janis, 384 U.S. 1, 86 S.Ct. 1245, 16 L.Ed.2d 313 (1966); United States v. Brown, 428 F.2d 1100 (D.C.Cir.1970); Julian v. United States, 236 F.2d 155 (6th Cir.1956); People v. Sutton, 169 Cal.Rptr. 656, 113 Cal.App.3d 162 (1980); Bunnell v. Superior Court of Santa Clara Cty., 13 Cal.App.3d 592, 119 Cal.Rptr. 302, 531 P.2d 1086 (1975); In re Steven H., 130 Cal.App.3d 449, 181 Cal.Rptr. 719 (1982); Glenn v. United States, 391 A.2d 772 (D.D.C.1978); Sutton v.

[97] Some courts have held that a totally uncontested trial based on stipulated facts can never be considered tantamount to a nolo contendere or guilty plea, since a trial, in any form, unlike a nolo contendere or guilty plea, does not foreclose an appeal. See United States v. Sanza, 519 F.Supp. 26 (D.C.Md.1980); People v. Garrett, 104 Ill.App.3d 178, 60 Ill.Dec. 406, 432 N.E.2d 1305 (1982). Since in Florida appeals can be taken from nolo contendere pleas where the right to appeal an issue is expressly reserved, there exists no impediment to our considering the proceedings below as the functional equivalent of, at least, a nolo contendere plea.

[98] Presumably, defense counsel's motions for judgment of acquittal made at the conclusion of the State's proffer and the entire case were designed solely to preserve the defendant's right to contest the sufficiency of the remaining evidence in the event that the appellate court were to overturn the trial court's denial of the motion to suppress the juvenile's statement and the fruits thereof. * * *

State, 289 Md. 360, 424 A.2d 755 (1981); Commonwealth v. Duquette, 386 Mass. 834, 438 N.E.2d 334 (1982).

Accordingly, since the record is totally lacking in any showing that the juvenile was informed of and knowingly and intelligently waived the constitutional rights attendant to a trial, we reverse the adjudication of delinquency and remand the cause for further proceedings consistent with this opinion.

IN RE GREEN
Ohio Court of Appeals, 1982.
4 Ohio App.3d 196, 447 N.E.2d 129.

McCormac, Judge.

Delisa Green, appellant herein, age fourteen, was charged with an act of delinquency in Franklin County Juvenile Court for commission of the offense of aggravated murder. Prior to trial, her attorney filed a motion to suppress statements made by her to Columbus Police Department officers. The motion was overruled.

An adjudicatory hearing was held on August 20, 1981, at which time the state moved to amend the charge of aggravated murder to one of murder and to strike the factual allegations in the complaint that defendant caused Donald Smith's death while attempting to commit robbery, which amendment was permitted. The state then discovered that a key witness had not appeared and they could not secure her presence by capias. On the basis of the absence of that witness, the state moved the court to amend the complaint of murder to one of voluntary manslaughter, alleging "that the child, while under extreme emotional stress, brought on by serious provocation reasonably sufficient to incite her to use deadly force, did knowingly cause the death of another." The second amended complaint was accepted by the court without objection.

The following procedure then took place in disposition of the complaint:

"Mr. Martin, it is my understanding that, based on this amendment to the affidavit, that your client now wishes to amend her plea to this charge from one of not guilty to guilty?

"MR. MARTIN: Your Honor, in discussing the matter with the Prosecutor and discussing it with my client, we have agreed to enter a no contest plea to the charge of voluntary manslaughter. I have advised Delisa that she has the right to a trial and has the right to have the State prove her guilty beyond a reasonable doubt and has the right to present witnesses and the right to remain silent. If she enters a no contest plea, she admits the allegations contained in the complaint. She realizes this and she realizes she will not have a formal trial, and that the likelihood—the probable result would be a permanent commitment to the Ohio Youth Commission where they could keep her up until age 21.

"THE COURT: Are you willing to waive the hearsay rule and the rule of sworn testimony and permit the party to proceed on the police report?

"MR. MARTIN: Yes, we are, Your Honor. We have agreed with Mr. Belli to present no mitigating circumstances.

"THE COURT: Does the Prosecutor have the police report?

"MR. BELLI: Yes, Your Honor. There is a summary and an extensive investigation in that folder.

"THE COURT: The Court, at this time, will make a finding of guilty on the charge of voluntary manslaughter under Section 2903.03 of the Ohio Revised Code."

The court committed Delisa Green permanently to the Ohio Youth Commission.

Delisa Green has appealed, asserting that the trial court erred in overruling her motion to suppress her statements to the police. Her assignments of error deal only with the correctness of the court's ruling on the motion to suppress.

The state argues that the no contest plea of appellant constituted an admission of the allegations of the second amended complaint and a waiver of any error in the ruling of the trial court on the pretrial motion to suppress.

Juv.R. 29(C) provides as follows:

"*Entry of admission or denial.* The court shall request each party against whom allegations are made in the complaint to admit or deny the allegations. A failure or refusal to admit the allegations shall be deemed a denial."

There is no provision in the Juvenile Rules for guilty, not guilty, or no contest pleas. The only response to the allegations of a juvenile complaint are admission or denial of the allegations.

Juv.R. 29(D) and (E) provide as follows:

"(D) *Initial procedure upon entry of an admission.* The court may refuse to accept an admission and shall not accept an admission without addressing the party personally and determining that:

"(1) He is making the admission voluntarily with understanding of the nature of the allegations and the consequences of the admission; and

"(2) He understands that by entering his admission he is waiving his rights to challenge the witnesses and evidence against him, to remain silent and to introduce evidence at the adjudicatory hearing.

"The court may hear testimony, review documents, or make further inquiry, as it deems appropriate, or it may proceed directly to the action required by subdivision (F).

"(E) *Initial procedure upon entry of a denial.* If a party denies the allegations, the court shall:

"(1) Direct the prosecuting attorney or another attorney-at-law to assist the court by presenting evidence in support of the allegations of a complaint;

"(2) Order the separation of witnesses, upon request of any party;

"(3) Take all testimony under oath or affirmation in either question-answer or narrative form; and

"(4) Determine the issues by proof beyond a reasonable doubt in juvenile traffic offense, delinquency, and unruly proceedings, by clear and convincing evidence in dependency, neglect, and child abuse proceedings, and by a preponderance of the evidence in all other cases."

The procedure for pleas in juvenile court in relation to a delinquency complaint differs substantially from the pleas provided by Crim.R. 11 in an adult criminal proceeding. Crim.R. 11 expressly authorizes guilty, no contest and not guilty pleas. A plea of guilty is a complete admission of the defendant's guilt. Crim.R. 11(B)(1). A plea of no contest is not an admission of defendant's guilt, but is an admission of the truth of the facts alleged in the indictment. Crim.R. 11(B)(2). There is no statement in Crim.R. 11 that a no contest plea results in a waiver of a defendant's right to challenge evidence against him as is specifically provided for by Juv.R. 29(D)(2) in relation to an admission of allegations of the complaint. Instead, Crim.R. 12(H) specifically preserves the right of defendant to appeal an erroneous ruling on a pretrial motion to suppress. There is no comparable provision in the Juvenile Rules. Moreover, there is no provision in Juv.R. 29 that a plea of guilty is a complete admission of the defendant's guilt which would require no further production of evidence as is provided by Crim.R. 11. Despite an admission of the allegations of the complaint, the court may hear testimony or make further inquiry.

Juv.R. 29(C) provides that a failure or refusal to admit the allegations shall be deemed a denial. An "admission" of the nature provided by the adult of a no contest plea constitutes something less than a total admission of the allegations of the complaint without any right to challenge the evidence to be used, including evidence which the trial court has refused to suppress at a pretrial motion hearing as is contemplated by Juv.R. 29.

Apparently, although it is not completely clear from the transcript, the no contest plea was entered on the basis that appellant would be able to appeal the trial court's ruling on the pretrial motion to suppress as would be true in an adult criminal case. However, juvenile procedure is clearly different and there are different ramifications for admissions in a juvenile case than in an adult case. The trial court failed to inquire of appellant personally to determine whether the "no contest plea," a plea not recognized by the Juvenile Rules, was intended to be an admission and, if so, that appellant understood that she was waiving her rights to challenge all evidence used against her.

Consequently, the trial court erroneously disposed of the case based upon the no contest plea. The no contest plea was not the unequivocal admission of the allegations of the complaint contemplated by Juv.R. 29(D). Being something less than an admission, it must be construed as a denial. The court was required to have the prosecuting attorney prove the issues of delinquency beyond a reasonable doubt. Juv.R. 29(E).

It is premature for us to rule upon the assignments of error raised in appellant's brief, which relate only to the correctness of the trial court's ruling on the motion to suppress. The appellant has established, by direct appeal, that the procedure used by the trial court was prejudicial to her rights in being construed as an admission of the allegations of the complaint which negated the obligation of the state to prove the allegations beyond a reasonable doubt.

The case is remanded to juvenile court for further procedure consistent with this decision.

Judgment reversed and case remanded.

WHITESIDE, P.J., and STRAUSBAUGH, J., concur.

IN RE D.

Supreme Court of New York, Appellate Division, 1970.
34 A.D.2d 41, 310 N.Y.S.2d 82.

GABRIELLI, JUSTICE.

* * *

On January 29, 1969 appellant, then 15 years of age, was charged with being a juvenile delinquent in having intentionally shot and killed his father. The accusation and petition filed, further charged that the described acts, "if done by an adult, would constitute the crime * * * of Murder (Violation of Section 125.25 of the Penal Law of the State of New York)".

Following his arraignment, extended argument was had upon his motion for a jury trial. This application was denied by written decision on March 10, 1969. On the following day the court, by written decision and order, also denied appellant's motion for an order to require the County Attorney "to establish that the respondent (appellant herein) committed the acts stated in the petition" by proof beyond a reasonable doubt. The court then directed that the fact-finding hearing be commenced two days later. In the interim, appellant was denied a stay by a member of this court and, on the following day (the day set for the hearing), his application for an adjournment to obtain a Federal Court review of the constitutional questions, was denied by the court below. Appellant again unsuccessfully renewed his motions for a jury trial or, in the alternative, for a ruling that without a jury trial he could not be subjected to a sentence of greater than 1 year. A brief recess was then taken during which there was an off-the-record conference between counsel for appellant, the court and the Assistant County Attorney.

Following the conference the latter announced that if appellant would admit the allegations of a new petition charging him with an act which, if performed by an adult would be a violation of Section 120.25 of the Penal Law, he would thereafter move for a dismissal of the old petition. Section 120.25 of the Penal Law provides that the crime of reckless endangerment in the first degree is committed when one engages in conduct which creates grave risk of death to another, the punishment for which is a maximum of 7 years' imprisonment, if committed by an adult. Upon his admission of this charge, appellant was subsequently adjudged a juvenile delinquent and committed to the New York State Agricultural and Industrial School for a period not to exceed three years. Appeal is taken from this adjudication and order of commitment. It is well to note here that upon a finding of juvenile delinquency the possible punishment on the withdrawn charge is commitment to Elmira Reception Center for a similar term. (Family Court Act, § 758[b], [c]).

In denying appellant's motion for a direction regarding the burden of proof the court held that there is no requirement "to establish that the respondent committed the acts alleged in the petition by proof beyond a reasonable doubt but (only) as required by section 744–b by a preponderance of the evidence". Section 744(b) of the Family Court Act, in pertinent part provides that:

"Any determination at the conclusion of a fact-finding hearing that a respondent did an act or acts must be based on a preponderance of the evidence."

In so holding, the court erroneously deprived appellant of a fundamental right which has now been held by the Supreme Court to be constitutionally protected, requiring the burden of proof to be beyond a reasonable doubt. (In the Matter of Winship, 397 U.S. 358, 90 S.Ct. 1068, 25 L.Ed.2d 368 [dec. March 31, 1970]). Section 744(b) of the Family Court Act, insofar as it requires a quantum of proof by a mere preponderance of the evidence is, therefore, declared unconstitutional.

It is urged that the admission of the acts alleged in the second petition was the result of a bargain made by this 15 year old boy and, therefore, he may not now disclaim this voluntary "plea". The dissenting justice has bottomed his conclusion and reasoning on the argument that "appellant's admission of the allegations of the new petition and his commitment should be sustained on the ground that it was sought by him and freely taken as a part of a bargain which was struck for his benefit". We are unable to subscribe to any theory or suggestion that a youth of this age has the capacity to waive or "bargain" away any of his constitutional rights or, indeed, that such a theory could be adopted under the circumstances so glaringly present in this case. Of equally compelling importance, the record clearly shows that neither the second petition nor appellant's admission was considered until after the denial of the last of his several motions for a jury trial. Significantly the first petition, to which appellant's motions were originally addressed, was not dismissed until after the second petition was acted on. Additionally, we reach the inescapable conclusion that appellant was effectively denied his fundamental right of a hearing under a constitutionally protected right to a jury trial as well as rules requiring that proof of the commission of the charged acts be beyond a reasonable doubt and, therefore, his admission of the acts contained in the substituted petition was extracted in an impermissible manner. (cf. Nieves v. United States, 280 F.Supp. 994, 1001).

In the light of all of the described circumstances the admission, then, was not voluntarily made but rather was the result of the denial of his motions for a jury trial, the denial of adjournments prior to his "admission" of the charges and the ruling as to the required burden of proof, all of which effectively constituted instruments of coercion as to his admission of the acts alleged in the second petition. As we view the totality of these proceedings, we conclude that appellant has been denied the essentials of due process and was deprived of these constitutional rights.

Holding!

* * *

The order should be reversed and the proceeding remitted to the Onondaga Family Court for further proceedings not inconsistent with this opinion.

Motion to dismiss appeal denied. Order reversed on the law and facts and matter remitted to Onondaga County Family Court for further proceedings not inconsistent with the Opinion by GABRIELLI, J.

All concur, except HENRY, J., who dissents and votes to affirm, in an Opinion.

HENRY, JUSTICE (dissenting).

When appellant appeared with his attorney in Family Court on March 13, 1969 to answer the petition dated January 29, 1969, charging him with acts which if committed by an adult would be in violation of Section 125.25 of the Penal Law constituting the crime of Murder, the Court, in response to a question asked by appellant's attorney, correctly stated that on the allegations of the petition appellant could be committed to Elmira Reception Center for a period up to three years. Appellant's attorney thereupon requested an adjournment for the purpose of having a discussion with the Court and the County Attorney. After the discussion the County Attorney stated:

> " * * * it is the recommendation of our office that a new petition be filed and this petition would be an allegation that Daniel Richard * * * performed an act which if performed by an adult would be a Violation of Section 120.25 of the Penal Law of the State of New York. (reckless endangerment) It is further our recommendation that upon the appropriate arraignment of this Court and upon Respondent being represented by

counsel and by being properly advised by the Court, if he admits the allegations of the new petition that at that time I would move for dismissal of the old petition ＊ ＊ ＊ ".

The Court received the new petition. It was read to appellant. The Court then stated to appellant and his attorney "you can admit or deny the petition." Appellant's attorney said, "He admits the petition". The Court asked appellant, "Do you admit the allegations of the petition?" and appellant answered, "Yes, your Honor". The record shows, and appellant does not claim otherwise, that appellant's answer to the new petition was voluntarily and understandingly made. He did not then, nor does he now, ask to withdraw or change his answer admitting the allegations. The order appealed from committed appellant to the New York State Agricultural and Industrial School at Industry for an indefinite period not to exceed three years.

The original petition charged acts which if committed by an adult would constitute a Class A felony (Penal Law § 125.25). Upon an adjudication thereunder commitment could be to Elmira Reception Center (Family Court Act, § 758(b)), whereas under the new petition appellant could not be so committed. Appellant's admission of the allegations of the new petition and his commitment should be sustained on the ground that it was sought by him and freely taken as part of a bargain which was struck for his benefit. (People v. Foster, 19 N.Y.2d 150, 154, 278 N.Y.S.2d 603, 606, 225 N.E.2d 200, 202). Reversal is not required by our decision in People v. Sawyer, 33 A.D.2d 242, 306 N.Y.S.2d 494, where we held that a youthful offender was entitled to a trial by jury notwithstanding his written consent to be tried without a jury, because his consent was extracted in an impermissible manner. He was required to consent to a non-jury trial as a prerequisite to consideration for adjudication as a youthful offender. In the case at bar no objection was made to the new petition. The answer admitting its allegations was voluntarily and understandingly made, and the allegations being admitted there was no issue to be tried.

The order should be affirmed.

IN RE D.

New York Court of Appeals, 1970.
27 N.Y.2d 90, 313 N.Y.S.2d 704, 261 N.E.2d 627, appeal dismissed, cert. denied D. v. Onondaga County, 403 U.S. 926, 91 S.Ct. 2244, 29 L.Ed.2d 705.

SCILEPPI, JUDGE.

＊   ＊   ＊

[The Court of Appeals reversed the rulings that juveniles were entitled to a jury trial and that *Winship* should be applied retroactively.]

＊   ＊   ＊

Moreover, a reversal is mandated on the further ground that respondent's voluntary and intelligent admission, by pleading guilty to the allegations of the second petition, accomplished an effective waiver and abandonment of all of the arguments urged on this appeal. The majority in the Appellate Division held that a 15-year-old lacked capacity to waive or bargain away any of his rights; however, Justice Henry, in dissent, took a different view: "The Court received the new petition. It was read to appellant. The Court then stated to appellant and his attorney 'you can admit or deny the petition.' Appellant's attorney said, 'He admits the petition'. The Court asked appellant, 'Do you admit the allegations of the petition?' and appellant answered, 'Yes, your Honor'. The record shows, and appellant does not claim otherwise, that appellant's answer to the new petition was voluntarily and understandingly made. He did not then, nor does he now, ask to withdraw or change his answer admitting the allegations. The order appealed from committed appellant to the New York State Agricultural and Industrial School at Industry for an indefinite period not to exceed three years.

"The original petition charged acts which if committed by an adult would constitute a Class A felony (Penal Law § 125.25). Upon an adjudication thereunder commitment could be to Elmira Reception Center (Family Court Act, § 758, (b)), whereas under the new petition appellant could not be so committed. Appellant's admission of the allegations of the new petition and his commitment should be sustained on the ground that it was sought by him [the off-the-record conference was requested by his attorney] and freely taken as part of a bargain which was struck for his benefit." (34 A.D.2d 49, 310 N.Y.S.2d 90–91).

We agree with Justice Henry, as there is no cogent reason why a 15-year-old, represented by counsel, cannot admit the allegations of a petition against him. While this appears to be a question of first impression in this court, such a practice is not, in our opinion, offensive to any of our notions of fairness and public policy.[99] In the case before us, there was no objection to the new petition and it is clear that respondent's admission was freely and intelligently made. Numerous motions addressed to the original petition had been made and when they were denied, respondent's attorney found it in the best interest of his client, after conferring with respondent and his family, to seek a new petition charging a lesser offense (see People v. Foster, 19 N.Y.2d 150, 278 N.Y.S.2d 603, 225 N.E.2d 200).

Since the admission to the allegations of the new petition was free from infirmity, the next question for our consideration deals with its effect. We believe that an admission to a juvenile delinquency petition should have the same force and effect as a plea of guilty

[99] Under section 2186 of the former Penal Law there was specific statutory authority permitting a 15-year-old, charged with a crime punishable by death or life imprisonment, to plead guilty to a lesser offense. This section was not continued into the current Penal Law which exempts those under 16 from criminal responsibility (§ 30.00) and defers these matters to juvenile delinquency proceedings in the Family Court.

to a criminal charge in a criminal case. "A plea of guilty is more than a confession which admits that the accused did various acts; it is itself a conviction; nothing remains but to give judgment and determine punishment" (Boykin v. Alabama, 395 U.S. 238, 242, 89 S.Ct. 1709, 1711, 23 L.Ed.2d 274). There are grave consequences which attach to a guilty plea as it is a surrender of substantial constitutional rights, including the privilege against self incrimination, the right of confrontation and the right to a trial by jury (Boykin v. Alabama, supra, at p. 242, 89 S.Ct. 1709; Brady v. United States, 397 U.S. 742, 90 S.Ct. 1463, 25 L.Ed.2d 747; McMann v. Richardson, 397 U.S. 759, 90 S.Ct. 1441, 25 L.Ed.2d 763).

Respondent in the instant case was in a position similar to the defendant in People v. Reyes, 26 N.Y.2d 97, 308 N.Y.S.2d 833, 257 N.E.2d 21 where we recently said (at p. 100, 308 N.Y.S.2d at p. 835, 257 N.E.2d at p. 23) that a "defendant after being informed that he has the right to a hearing [on his addiction to narcotics who] freely admits his addiction with the aid of counsel, * * * is in effect stating that no judicial inquiry is necessary and, therefore, it is irrelevant whether that inquiry would have been made with or without a jury".

Accordingly, the order appealed from should be reversed, the order of the Family Court, Onondaga County, reinstated and the certified question should be answered in the negative.

BREITEL, JUDGE (dissenting in part).

I agree that not all the procedural rights afforded adults under due process are necessarily applicable to juvenile delinquency proceedings, and that jury trials are not constitutionally required for adjudication of juvenile delinquency. Unlike youthful offender adjudication, which merely affords an alternative procedure for those subject to the criminal laws and penalties, these proceedings deal exclusively with children recognized as not criminally responsible.

On the issue of weight of the evidence, however, the United States Supreme Court's decision in In re Winship, 397 U.S. 358, 90 S.Ct. 1068, 25 L.Ed.2d 368, is controlling. Its determination that guilt must be proven beyond a reasonable doubt, and that that standard applies in juvenile delinquency proceedings, goes directly to the integrity of the fact-finding process. Retroactivity should, therefore, be extended the *Winship* case, at least, as here, to cases on direct appeal.

Nor does the plea of guilty to the petition, alleging an act which if committed by an adult would constitute reckless endangerment, suggest a convincing waiver of his rights. Although respondent's treatment would be the same regardless of whether he was found guilty before trial or upon his plea to either petition, by pleading guilty he did more than avoid the unpleasantness of a trial. By his plea to facts constituting reckless endangerment he avoided the alternatives of admitting to patricide or running the risk of such a declaration. Moreover, having asserted his right to a trial based on proof beyond a reasonable doubt, his unwillingness to risk a finding of guilt based on a lesser standard should not imply abandonment of his rights. Certainly proceeding to trial could in no way further clarify the issue raised by respondent and rejected by the trial court.

Accordingly, I dissent and vote that the order appealed from be modified to limit the hearing directed by the Appellate Division to one before the court alone.

NOTE

In In Re James B., 54 Md.App. 270, 458 A.2d 847 (1983), the state sought a transfer to adult criminal court. At the waiver hearing the prosecutor and juvenile informed the judge that they had reached an agreement embodying the following elements: (1) juvenile would admit certain allegations (which would establish that he committed the underlying offense); (2) the State would abandon the waiver effort; (3) the State would recommend referral to a "community supervision program;" (4) the State would not seek restitution.

The judge agreed to the first three, but rejected the fourth and ordered restitution in a particular amount. At a subsequent hearing on the issue of restitution, the judge increased the amount to cover an item not previously considered. The juvenile did not seek to have any aspect of the adjudication or disposition set aside except for the award of restitution. The appellate court found that the juvenile would have been entitled to withdraw his plea, but that he chose not to do so. Because the juvenile judge never acceded to the "non-restitution" part of the agreement between the State and the juvenile, there was no breach of the agreement. The appellate court, however, set aside, on the grounds of lack of notice, the part of the restitutionary award which went beyond the original disposition and remanded for a further evidentiary hearing on that issue.

*

Chapter 8

THE DISPOSITION DECISION

Perceptions about the appropriateness of the juvenile justice system as a whole have extended to attitudes toward the legitimacy of various objectives to be accomplished in choosing dispositions of adjudicated delinquents. Mr. Justice Fortas' brief description of the history and theory of the system is set out in the extract from *Gault*, reprinted in Chapter 1, supra. The student should re-read that extract now.

STATE EX REL. D.D.H. v. DOSTERT
Supreme Court of Appeals of West Virginia, 1980.
269 S.E.2d 401.

NEELY, CHIEF JUSTICE:

In this case we shall endeavor, with some apprehension, to clarify the proper procedures at the dispositional stage of a juvenile proceeding. The facts of these three consolidated cases [1] provide an excellent opportunity to explore the nature of the juvenile disposition. Indeed this particular child's journey into the juvenile justice system constitutes a veritable primer on how a juvenile should *not* be handled by the courts under either our prior rulings or the applicable sections of Chapter 49 of the W.Va.Code.

On 25 April 1979, a delinquency petition was filed against petitioner, then a twelve-year-old female, charging her with four crimes that would be felonious had they been committed by an adult. A detention hearing was held on 27 April 1979, after which the court ordered petitioner detained at the Jefferson County Juvenile Detention Center, a section of the county jail that is reserved for juvenile offenders.[2] On that same day, the court appointed J. Wendell Reed to represent the petitioner.

---

[1] The three consolidated cases are: 14602, a habeas corpus requesting that petitioner be removed from the Industrial Home for Girls which was issued by the Court 3 August 1979 releasing petitioner from Salem and directing her placement in the Odyssey Group Home in Morgantown or some other comparable facility; 14603, a writ of prohibition against Judge Pierre Dostert for his contempt proceeding against appointed counsel and removal of appointed counsel, J. Wendell Reed; and, 14769, an appeal from the adjudication and disposition of petitioner. While we draw on all the material presented to this Court in writing this opinion, our decision on the appeal, 14769, is dispositive of all the issues raised in each case with the exception of the writ of prohibition which we grant.

[2] Petitioner devoted a major portion of her argument to her detention in a common county jail for a combined period of almost 40 days. Petitioner would have us reverse the disposition on this basis alone for the court's blatant denial of the mandate in our law that juveniles are not to be housed in common county jails as set forth in State ex rel. R.C.F. v. Wilt, W.Va., 252 S.E.2d 168 (1979); however, we have chosen to reverse on the errors at trial. We condemn the actions of the circuit court in housing the juvenile in a common county jail and reserve the right to reverse for this illegality in the future. We note that under W.Va.Code, 49-2-16 [1980], "[t]he state department of welfare shall provide care in special boarding homes for children needing detention pending disposition by

721

While in detention, a preliminary hearing was held 3 May 1979 at which two counts of the petition were dismissed and probable cause was found on the other two, namely, breaking and entering an A & P store on 20 February 1979 and grand larceny of a pickup truck on 14 April 1979. Petitioner was subsequently released into the custody of her mother, but when she missed school she was returned to the detention center without a hearing. Counsel obtained her release two days later. On 12 June 1979 petitioner was again arrested for allegedly stealing an automobile, and she was detained in the Morgan County Jail, forty miles from her home. There is no record or hearing from that detention, save the summary order which included no findings of fact.

While we will focus upon the dispositional phase of the juvenile proceeding *sub judice*, we must first address the numerous errors committed at the adjudicatory stage. A formal juvenile petition was prepared which charged petitioner with delinquency for having committed grand larceny of a pickup truck and breaking and entering of an A & P store. On 15 June 1979, an adjudicatory hearing was held and petitioner was found delinquent on both counts. We must reverse this case because neither count was supported by sufficient, admissible evidence to sustain the charges.

* * *

Having determined that the delinquency conviction must be reversed, we turn to the dispositional stage of the proceeding so that upon remand a proper record can be made. Petitioner, who was thirteen years old at the time of the disposition and had never been adjudicated delinquent, was committed to the most restrictive alternative available, the Industrial Home for Girls in Salem, West Virginia. At the dispositional hearing, which was held 5 July 1979, the court relied primarily on the testimony of a social worker for the Department of Welfare, Joseph Corbin, who recommended that the petitioner be placed in the West Virginia Industrial School. He testified that he contacted two other less restrictive alternatives, namely, the Burlington United Methodist Home for Children and Youth, and Davis-Stuart, Inc., both of which refused to accept petitioner. Upon cross-examination, it became clear that counsel for petitioner had suggested the Odyssey House, a group home in Morgantown, to Mr. Corbin, but that he had not pursued that possibility because he was unfamiliar with the facility. Testimony was also received from a police officer, Raymond Burcker, who said that he had seen the petitioner out late at night standing outside a bar on at least two occasions. Petitioner's mother appeared as a witness, and she testified that she had been very sick during the past year and that she had sought the aid of the Welfare Department to place petitioner in a foster home. Apparently the Welfare Department did not respond.[3]

a court having juvenile jurisdiction * * *."

[3] The Department of Welfare has been clearly assigned the responsibility of providing care, support and protective services for children who are in need of public service under W.Va.Code, 49–2–16 [1980]. Under W.Va.Code, 49–5B–4 [1979] the Welfare Department has been directed to establish programs and services designed to prevent future juvenile

The court relied upon the recommendation of Dr. Bradley Soulé that petitioner "has a lot more potential to develop were she in a more highly structured environment than she has been in the past." While concluding that she had an extremely chaotic family life and a number of behavioral problems such as truancy, car theft, and drug abuse, Dr. Soulé also found petitioner to be "alert, articulate, behaviorally appropriate, and * * * cooperative * * * throughout the interview." The recommendation for a structured environment [4] was seconded by Dr. Roberts, a clinical psychologist who tested petitioner.

The Court also considered the report on petitioner completed by the social service worker, Joseph Corbin. He reported that: petitioner's home should have been condemned as unfit for human habitation; petitioner's mother had been hospitalized for several weeks during the winter of 1979 with cervical cancer; petitioner's stepfather deserted the family as soon as the medical problem appeared; petitioner's stepfather had a drinking and drug problem which prompted him physically to abuse the petitioner; petitioner's father deserted her mother three weeks after petitioner was born; petitioner's mother had been a welfare client since D.D.H. was born; and, although petitioner had missed over 100 days of school her only major behavioral problem was stealing on one occasion.

I

At the outset it is important to recognize that the juvenile law in West Virginia has been in substantial turmoil since this Court's decision in State ex rel. Harris v. Calendine, W.Va., 233 S.E.2d 318 (1977) which, among other things, prompted an entire revision of the statutory juvenile law.[5] Historically, protecting society from juvenile delinquency and helping juvenile offenders modify their behavior have been seen as complementary goals of the juvenile law; however, it is now generally recognized that caring for the juvenile and controlling the juvenile are often quite contradictory processes.[6]

delinquency. Denying the request of petitioner's mother to have petitioner placed under temporary care does not comply with the goal of diverting juveniles from the juvenile justice system.

[4] We have previously voiced grave reservations about the rehabilitative programs available at the West Virginia Industrial School for Boys (known as "Pruntytown") and have recommended that "incarceration of young people in the school should be limited to those who will clearly benefit from institutionalization or to those who are dangerous to themselves or others," State ex rel. K.W. v. Werner, W.Va., 242 S.E.2d 907 (1978). We have not been presented with a record of the industrial schools that "demonstrate[s] in detail the abuses and inadequacies," as Justice Miller recognized in his concurring opinion in *Werner*, supra

at 917; however, we heard discussion about dispositional alternatives during an extraordinary proceeding held on 4 June 1980. That discussion was similar to a "Brandeis Brief" in that it provided background information. Our reservations about available rehabilitation are not based on a study of our State facilities, but rather on a study of national authorities on juvenile justice which are discussed, *infra*.

[5] The Legislature has substantially rewritten the juvenile Code section every year since 1977 until this year (1980).

[6] Justice Fortas expressed skepticism about attaining these twin goals and suggested that, "[t]here is evidence, in fact, that there may be grounds for concern that the child receives the worst of both worlds: that he gets neither the protections accorded to adults nor the solicitous

Much of our juvenile law at the moment is predicated upon a healthy skepticism about the capacity of the State and its agents to help children when they are incarcerated in one of the juvenile detention facilities.[7] Thus, the control of juveniles and the treatment of juveniles (if that expression can be used without conjuring Kafkaesque images) are frequently irreconcilable goals. Furthermore, children can be dangerous, destructive, abusive, and otherwise thoroughly anti-social, which prompts an entirely understandable expectation in society of protection, even if we have matured beyond expecting retribution.

The dispositional stage of a juvenile proceeding is designed to do something which is almost impossible, namely, to reconcile: (1) society's interest in being protected from dangerous and disruptive children; (2) society's interest in nurturing its children in such a way that they will be productive and successful adults; (3) society's interest in providing a deterrent to other children who, but for the specter of the juvenile law, would themselves become disruptive and unamenable to adult control; (4) the citizens' demand that children be responsible for invasion of personal rights; and, (5) the setting of an example of care, love, and forgiveness by the engines of the state in the hope that such qualities will be emulated by the subject children.[8] While retribution is considered an unhealthy instinct and, conceivably, an

care and regenerative treatment postulated for children." Kent v. United States, 383 U.S. 541, 556, 86 S.Ct. 1045, 1054, 16 L.Ed.2d 84 (1966). Many others have recognized the difficulty in maintaining this Janus-faced role. See, e.g., V.L. Streib, Juvenile Justice in America 51 (1978).

[7] The cry for reform in the juvenile justice area has been growing louder over the past fifteen years. Edwin M. Lemert, writing for the Task Force in Delinquency in 1967, first argued that the grandiose models of the juvenile court should be brought into a more practical perspective. He argued that, "if there is a defensible philosophy for the juvenile court it is one of nonintervention. It is properly an agency of last resort for children, holding to a doctrine analogous to that of appeal courts which require that all other remedies be exhausted before a case will be considered." Task Force on Delinquency, President's Commission on Law Enforcement and Administration of Justice, U.S. Government Printing Office 96 (1967). His recommendation has been followed by a number of commentators arguing for nonintervention. See, e.g., V.L. Streib, Juvenile Justice in America (1978); Marticorena, "Take My Child, Please—A Plea for Radical Nonintervention," 6 Pepperdine L.Rev. 639 (1978–79); and, Chase, "Questioning the Juvenile Commitment: Some Notes on Method and

Consequences," 8 Ind.L.Rev. 373 (1974–75).

[8] Many states have been wrestling with some statutory reconciliation of these competing goals. In this regard it is interesting to compare the 1977 amendment to W.Va.Code, 49–1–1(a), the purpose clause for the child welfare chapter, with the 1978 amendment to the same section. The difference is subtle, but it demonstrates a recognition that child welfare cannot be completely "child centered." W.Va.Code, 49–1–1(a) [1977] says:

The purpose of this chapter is to provide a comprehensive system of child welfare throughout the State which will assure to each child such care and guidance, preferably in his own home, as will serve the spiritual, emotional, mental and physical welfare of the child; preserve and strengthen the child's family ties whenever possible with recognition to the fundamental rights of parenthood and with recognition of the state's responsibility to assist the family in providing the necessary education and training and protect the welfare of the general public. In pursuit of these goals it is the intention of the legislature to provide for removing the child from the custody of parents only when the child's welfare or the safety and protection of the public cannot be adequately safeguarded without removal; and, when the

immoral instinct in an enlightened society, nonetheless, State imposed retribution has historically been the *quid pro quo* of the State's monopoly of force and its proscription of individual retribution. Retribution is merely another way of saying that children are to be treated as responsible moral agents.

II

It is possible to make the dispositional stage of a juvenile proceeding so burdensome in requiring exhaustive examination of all "less restrictive alternatives," no matter how speculative, that we, in effect, direct lower courts to abandon all hope of confining a child.[9] That is not the clear purport, however, of W.Va.Code, 49–5–13(b) [1978] which says:

> In disposition the court shall not be limited to the relief sought in the petition and shall give precedence to the least restrictive of the following alternatives *consistent with the best interests and welfare of the public and the child * * *.*

[Emphasis supplied by the Court.]

W.Va.Code 49–5–13(b)(5) [1978] says:

> Upon a finding that no less restrictive alternative would accomplish the requisite rehabilitation of the child, and upon an adjudication of delinquency pursuant to subdivision (1), section four [§ 49–1–4], article one of this chapter, commit the child to an industrial home or correctional institution for children. Commitments shall <u>not exceed the maximum term</u> for which an adult could have been sentenced for the same offense, with discretion

child has to be removed from his own family, to secure for him custody, care and discipline as nearly as possible equivalent to that which should have been given by his parents, consistent with the child's best interests.

W.Va.Code, 49–1–1(a) [1978] says:

The purpose of this chapter is to provide a comprehensive system of child welfare throughout the State which will assure to each child such care and guidance, preferably in his own home, as will serve the spiritual, emotional, mental and physical welfare of the child; preserve and strengthen the child's family ties whenever possible with recognition to the fundamental rights of parenthood and with recognition of the state's responsibility to assist the family in providing the necessary education and training *and to reduce the rate of juvenile delinquency and to provide a system for the rehabilitation or detention of juvenile delinquents and protect the welfare of the general public.* In pursuit of these goals it is the intention of the legislature to provide for removing the

child from the custody of parents only when the child's welfare or the safety and protection of the public cannot be adequately safeguarded without removal; and, when the child has to be removed from his own family, to secure for him custody, care and discipline *consistent with the child's best interests and other goals herein set out.* [Emphasis supplied by the Court]

[9] Our Court has recently examined the procedures that must be followed before a juvenile may be properly committed to a juvenile correctional facility in State ex rel. S.J.C. v. Fox, W.Va., 268 S.E.2d 56 (1980). We followed the same procedure established in State ex rel. E.D. v. Aldredge, W.Va., 245 S.E.2d 849 (1978) which required that the court set forth a finding on the record that no less restrictive alternative was available before a transfer to criminal jurisdiction could be effected. *Fox,* supra analyzes all our previous dispositional decisions; however, none of the decisions discussed the philosophical underpinnings of the dispositional stage of the juvenile proceeding.

as to discharge to rest with the director of the institution, who may release the child and return him to the court for further disposition; * * *.

As David Dudley Field, author of the Field Code, once pointed out, substantive law can be "gradually secreted in the interstices of procedure." Consequently, it is important to explain exactly what the elaborate procedure at the dispositional stage is designed to do. Unless there are clear, understandable standards, procedure becomes confounding at best and disguised legislation at worst.

Chapter 49 of the W.Va.Code covering child welfare is clearly committed to the rehabilitative model. As we noted in State ex rel. Harris v. Calendine, W.Va., 233 S.E.2d 318, 325 (1977).

> The Legislature could choose to punish children guilty of criminal conduct in the same manner as it punishes adults, but as a matter of public policy the Legislature provided instead for a comprehensive system of child welfare. The aim of this system is to protect and rehabilitate children, not to punish them.

The rehabilitative model requires a great deal of information about the child at the dispositional hearing. Much of that information must necessarily focus on the critical issue of whether it is *possible* for the State or other social service agencies to help the child. Although helping the child is the first concern of the juvenile law, it is not the only concern, since at the *operational* rather than *theoretical* level, the rehabilitative approach has dramatic limitations, preeminent among which is that it interferes both with the deterrence of other children and the protection of society. While Code, 49–5–13(b) explicitly recognizes this problem, we have not yet refined an approach which intelligently uses procedure to arrive at sufficient information to permit a balancing of the child's liberty interest with society's need for protection and deterrence.

III

There is no alternative in our efforts to reconcile the competing goals of the juvenile justice system but to enter reluctantly into a brief discussion of the age-old philosophical controversy about free will and determinism.[10] Neither this Court nor anyone else in the world will ever definitively answer the question of whether mankind is determined or is possessed of free will. The philosophy of the law has generally accepted that at times people are determined while at other times they have free will. Pragmatically our legal tradition has answered the question by rules which recognize that men are guided

[10] The U.S. Supreme Court has steered clear of this controversy and only Justice White is on record for acknowledging that, "[f]or the most part, the juvenile justice system rests on more deterministic assumptions. Reprehensible acts by juveniles are not deemed the consequence of mature and malevolent choice but of environmental pressures (or lack of them) or of other forces beyond their control. Hence the state legislative judgment not to stigmatize the juvenile delinquent by branding him a criminal; his conduct is not deemed so blameworthy that punishment is required to deter him or others." McKeiver v. Pennsylvania, 403 U.S. 528, 551–52, 91 S.Ct. 1976, 1989, 29 L.Ed.2d 647 (1970).

entirely neither by external forces nor by free will; every person is influenced by both but is never totally controlled by either.

As perplexing as the philosophical argument over free will versus determinism may be, no single concept is as critical to the dispositional stage of a juvenile proceeding. The facts of the case before us clearly show a child whose sorrows are largely the result of external forces.[11] That she is difficult, ungovernable, and unmanageable is not disputed in the elaborate record before us, yet she was to the social forces around her the "wingless fly in the hands of small boys." On the other hand, hypothetically, we can envisage a child from a perfect middle class background, selling drugs to other children for no apparent reason other than the allure of enormous profits. To speculate that deep inside that child's psyche there is some hidden, predetermining factor is not adequate for the "deterrent" or "responsibility" purposes of the juvenile law. Furthermore, it is a negation of our entire tradition to say that every social transgression is the result of "illness." Many a very sane and well adjusted person has found the allure of illegal profits compelling. Children can, and often do, engage in delinquent conduct for no better reason than that they prefer having money to not having money.

Some things we have enough knowledge to treat and other things we do not have enough knowledge to treat. Broken homes, uncaring parents, learning disabilities, Dickensian poverty, parental abuse, and an unhealthy environment are all things which the State, "solicitous of the welfare of its children but also mindful of other demands upon the State budget for humanitarian purposes," State ex rel. Harris v. Calendine, W.Va., 233 S.E.2d 318, 331 (1977) can begin to cure. Where, however, no factor or factors can be isolated which we can treat, or which our over-all view of the State's role in providing social justice deems not worthy of a *treatment approach*, we must, for want of any other reasonable alternative, accept the

---

[11] A determinist pattern is evident in testimony about the petitioner offered by Sandra Lucht, Jefferson County School Board psychologist:

I have a feeling along the lines of her social maladjustment having not been caused by serious emotional disturbance but being caused by the conditions under which she had lived, modeling of her environment and her mother and people around her, her friends and I believe she is probably acting in a very natural way as to how she has learned to survive so when you look at all those factors and her problems and her behavior problems and her difficulty in going along with the norm set for people to act by, I have seen no evidence of what I term serious emotional disturbance which would imply to me great problem with control of emo-

tions, some neurotic tendencies of disordering thought processes or something along that line; * * *

Her home as reported by Joseph Corbin, the social worker, also paints a grim picture:

* * * The complex, if not, should have been condemned several years ago as unfit for human habitation. Charles Town has shut off all city services and water to the apartments due to non-payment of bills.

As far as sanitary conditions, one goes outdoors in the weeds, which have all but taken over the area.

Not only is Mrs. _____ and her three children living in the apartment, she is also allowing her brother, _____ _____ and his female companion to reside there also.

free will model, the goals of which are deterrence and juvenile responsibility.

IV

At the dispositional stage of the juvenile proceeding there are a number of actors whose roles have been established by statute. The first major actor is obviously the judge who, according to W.Va.Code, 49–5–13(a) [1978], is entitled to request the juvenile probation officer or State department worker to make an investigation of the environment of the child and the alternative dispositions possible. The second actor is the probation officer or State department worker who must fulfill this obligation, and the third actor is the counsel for the petitioner who is entitled to review any report made by the probation officer or welfare worker seventy-two hours before the dispositional hearing. In addition there is the child and his parents, guardian, or adult relatives, and the representatives of any social service agencies, including the schools, which have been involved in the case. Since the threshold question at any dispositional hearing is whether the child is delinquent because of his own free will or for environmental reasons which society can attack directly, all of the actors in the dispositional drama should concentrate their attention initially on that one subject. Obviously this is a question which the trial judge has always answered in his own mind. However, the thrust of the formal procedural model which has been evolving is that this question be developed on the record and reasons for determining a particular disposition be articulated for appellate review. We shall now focus on the role of each major actor.

THE ROLE OF COURT APPOINTED COUNSEL:

The dispositional stage of any juvenile proceeding may be the most important stage in the entire process; [12] therefore, it is the obligation of any court appointed or retained counsel to continue active and vigorous representation of the child through that stage. We have already held that counsel has a duty to investigate all resources available to find the least restrictive alternative, State ex rel. C.A.H. v. Strickler, W.Va., 251 S.E.2d 222 (1979), and here we confirm that holding. Court appointed counsel must make an independent investigation of the child's background. Counsel should present to the court any facts which could lead the court to conclude that the child's environment is a major contributing factor to his misbehavior. In this regard counsel should investigate the child's performance in school, his family background, the level of concern and leadership on the part of his parents, the physical conditions under which the child is living, and any health problems. Counsel

---

[12] "Since the majority of juvenile delinquency hearings involve pleas of guilty, * * * the disposition decision may be the most critical stage of all and the one most urgently requiring an advocate for the child," Skoler, "The Right to Counsel and the Role of Counsel in Juvenile Court Proceedings," 43 Ind.L.J. 558, 569 (1968).

must also inform himself in detail about the facilities both inside and outside the State of West Virginia which are able to help children.[13]

Armed with adequate information, counsel can then present the court with all reasonable alternative dispositions to incarceration and should have taken the initial steps to secure the tentative acceptance of the child into those facilities. It is not sufficient to suggest upon the record as an abstract proposition that there are alternatives; it is the affirmative obligation of counsel to advise the court of the exact terms, conditions, and costs of such alternatives, whether the Department of Welfare or any other source can pay for such alternative, and under what conditions any alternative facilities would be willing to accept the child.

The faithful discharge of these duties requires substantial industry; however, appointed counsel is entitled to be compensated for his time up to the statutory limit set for the criminal charges fund. Furthermore, energetic advocacy implies that the court must accommodate an adversarial proceeding at the disposition stage. In the case at bar, the court reacted to the legitimate efforts of the appointed attorney to arrange an alternative disposition by finding him in contempt and removing him from his appointment. Such practices are obviously condemned since it is envisaged that the child shall have an advocate who will make a record.[14]

The court undermined the efforts of counsel from the outset of the trial: counsel was given approximately thirty minutes to prepare before the first detention hearing, after which petitioner was placed in the Jefferson County Jail; after counsel obtained release of petitioner she was again placed in the Jefferson County Jail for failing to attend school and counsel received no notice of the second detention hearing; after counsel obtained release of petitioner she was arrested and taken before the court who placed her in the Morgan County Jail again without notice or presence of the child's counsel and with no record save the summary order; after petitioner was adjudicated delinquent, counsel represented the willingness of the Odyssey House in Morgantown to take petitioner for a trial period but the court refused all less restrictive alternatives; and, after placement in the Industrial Home for Girls counsel continued actively to pursue probation for petitioner to which the court reacted by withdrawing the appointment of counsel and requiring his appearance at a contempt hearing. This conduct is so unjustifiable that the State chose not even to address the validity of the contempt citation

[13] The Department of Welfare must prepare a descriptive catalogue of its juvenile programs and services at least once a year and those catalogues are to be readily available under W.Va.Code, 49–5B–7 [1979]. Furthermore, the West Virginia Child Care Association (WVCCA) publishes a Residential Child Care Directory which describes available services. In addition, the WVCCA maintains a Resource Center with a statewide telephone information service designed to assist social workers, agencies, lawyers and others in placing young people in the most appropriate group home or group child care agency. Their office is open Monday-Friday, 8:30 a.m.–5:00 p.m. and their telephone number is (304) 335-6211.

[14] For a cogent analysis of the defense counsel's role in dispositions, see IJA/ABA Juvenile Justice Standards Project, Standards Relating to Juvenile Counsel for Private Parties, pp. 168–87 (1977).

in its brief. We grant the writ of prohibition in connection with the contempt charges.

THE ROLE OF THE PROBATION OFFICER OR WELFARE WORKER:

The probation officer or welfare worker when requested by the judge is also responsible for discovering whether there are forces which are at work upon the child which either the Department of Welfare or other social service agencies can correct. In the case before us it is obvious that the petitioner had no adult supervision whatsoever and that she was left to fend for herself in the back streets. Obviously, before incarcerating a first offender like the petitioner it would have been incumbent upon the Department of Welfare to find a suitable environment for her. The record amply demonstrates from the history of the petitioner *after* this Court released her from the industrial school, that the petitioner is a somewhat unmanageable and ungovernable child who, at the time, would not remain in a juvenile refuge.[15] Nonetheless, absent at least one predisposition incidence of flight from a reasonable alternative, it was quite improper for the court to place her in the first instance in the industrial school. Upon remand the court must focus on her level of cooperation at the time she is again considered for disposition at the remand. Syl. pt. 3, State ex rel. S.J.C. v. Fox, W.Va., 268 S.E.2d 56 (1980).

The record before us also demonstrates that the Department of Welfare did not intervene with this child upon her initial arrest, although any inquiry into her background would have disclosed at the detention hearing that she was in need of help. The appropriate time for the Department of Welfare or the juvenile probation officer to intervene is at the first sign of trouble.

THE ROLE OF THE COURT:

It is the obligation of the court to hear all witnesses who might shed light upon the proper disposition of a child and before incarcerating a child, to find facts upon the record which would lead a reasonable appellate court to conclude in the words of the statute, either that "no less restrictive alternative would accomplish the requisite rehabilitation of the child * * *" or "the welfare of the public" requires incarceration. Where the court directs incarceration, he should affirmatively find upon the record either that the child's behavioral problem is not the result of social conditions beyond the child's control, but rather of an intentional failure on the part of the child to conform his actions to the law, or that the child will be dangerous if any other disposition is used, or that the child will not cooperate with any rehabilitative program absent physical restraint.

---

[15] Petitioner was placed in the Odyssey House, a group home, after her petition for a writ of habeas corpus was granted by this Court and she ran away from that placement. Evidence that is before our Court, but which was not before the circuit court, indicates that petitioner was apprehended in a stolen car on at least two other occasions after her initial disposition.

Where the court concludes that simple punishment will be a more effective rehabilitative device than anything else, the conclusion is certainly legitimate and within the discretion of the trial court; nonetheless, the trial court must elaborate on the record his reasons for that conclusion.

If the proceeding is merely the last in a long series involving the same child, the court should set forth any "less restrictive alternatives" which have already been tried and the actions of the child after those alternatives were implemented. Even when the child's behavior results from environmental factors, the court may find the child to pose an imminent danger to society because he will flee from all but secure facilities and, therefore, conclude that incarceration is the only reasonable alternative. *But must set forth reasons for incarceration!*

The court has a duty to insure that the child's social history is reviewed intelligently so that an individualized treatment plan may be designed when appropriate. This information also insures that the disposition decision is not made simply by reference to the very misbehavior which is the ground for the juvenile proceeding. The effectiveness of treatment is disputed to say the least, and this is particularly true whenever commitment to an institution is involved. Therefore, the judge making the dispositional determination should not place a child who is not dangerous and who can be accommodated elsewhere in an institution under the guise of "treating" the child.

While in the hearing before this Court it appeared that progress has been made in providing basic education and counseling in the State's industrial schools, the fact that these schools have improved does not make them the proper place for "rehabilitation" unless it appears that the child is either dangerous or must be restrained in a secure facility in order to prevent his flight.

THE ROLE OF THE CHILD:

When we are dealing with children between the ages of twelve and eighteen it must be recognized that no placement plan short of a secure, prison-like facility is capable of having a beneficial effect without the cooperation of the child. Therefore, it is impossible to avoid the conclusion that there is an affirmative obligation on the part of the child to cooperate.[16] Certainly one instance of a child failing to follow some Rhadamanthine ruling of a circuit court does not justify instant removal to an industrial school, but a consistent course of noncooperation, particularly when combined with a predilection to commit dangerous or destructive acts does justify the court in resorting to commitment.[17] This rule must be tempered, however, by

[16] That, indeed, may be the single most important factor regarding petitioner. Dr. Bradley Soulé, who examined her before the dispositional proceeding, concluded that the Alternative School Program at the Eastern Panhandle Mental Health Center might have benefited petitioner greatly but that "major obstacles were foreseen in terms of D.D.H.'s cooperation with attending such a program."

[17] Certain individuals must be punished and it is folly to think that judgments of juveniles do not serve as deterrents to at least a portion of juvenile society, not because juveniles fear rehabilitation, but because they fear punishment and incar-

the conclusion that where the agents of the State are gross incompetents and where the treatment and rehabilitative programs prescribed for the child are unreasonable, this Court will not permit incarceration where the true fault lies with the State and not with the child.[18]

When however, there is a consistent pattern of noncooperation which makes alternative rehabilitative programs impossible, the court should set forth the facts upon the record so that this Court will understand why the trial court concludes that there are no alternatives to placement in an institution.[19]

V

In reaching the conclusion that rehabilitation alone does not exhaust the goals of a juvenile disposition, and that responsibility and deterrence are also important elements in our juvenile philosophy, we have not simply embraced a conservative theory that juvenile delinquents need to be punished. Liberals and conservatives alike may find solace in this opinion because we acknowledge what has been an unspoken conclusion: our treatment looks a lot like punishment. At first glance an agreement among commentators at both philosophical

ceration. Despite all protestations to the contrary the label "juvenile delinquent" does carry stigma, and it is not always confidential. State ex rel. Daily Mail Publishing Co. v. Smith, W.Va., 248 S.E. 2d 269 (1978), affd., 443 U.S. 97, 99 S.Ct. 2667, 61 L.Ed.2d 399 (1979). Certainly the movement toward a punitive philosophy has been recognized in the criminal courts, see J. Andenaes, Punishment and Deterrence, 129–151 (1974); N. Morris, The Future of Imprisonment (1974); and, in the juvenile field see Fox, "The Reform of Juvenile Justice: Children's Right to Punishment," 25 Juv.Justice 2 (1974).

[18] In State ex rel. K.W. v. Werner, W.Va., 242 S.E.2d 901, 913 (1978) we said that "[j]uveniles are *constitutionally entitled* to the least restrictive alternative treatment that is consistent with the purpose of their custody." As we noted earlier, an adequate record has not been developed to determine if petitioner and others receive adequate treatment, and therefore, we leave that issue for another day.

[19] Some states have been more specific in rewriting their purpose clauses to reflect the legislative determination that rehabilitation alone does not exhaust the purposes of the juvenile justice system. For example, California added the underlined sections to its purpose clauses:

(a) The purpose of this chapter is to secure for each minor under the jurisdiction of the juvenile court such care and guidance, preferably in his own home, as will serve the spiritual, emotional, mental, and physical welfare of the minor and the best interests of the state; *to protect the public from criminal conduct by minors; to impose on the minor a sense of responsibility for his own acts;* to preserve and strengthen the minor's family ties whenever possible, removing him from the custody of his parents only when necessary for his welfare or for the safety and protection of the public * * * and, when the minor is removed from his own family, to secure for him custody, care, and discipline as nearly as possible equivalent to that which should have been given by his parents. This chapter shall be liberally construed to carry out these purposes.

(b) *The purpose of this chapter also includes the protection of the public from the consequences of criminal activity, and to such purpose probation officers, peace officers, and juvenile courts shall take into account such protection of the public in their determinations under this chapter.* Cal. [Welf. & Inst.] Code, § 202 [1977]. (Emphasis added.)

In Virginia the old purpose clause focused solely on the welfare of the child, Va.Code § 16.1–140 [1956], while the revised statute includes the purpose of "protect[ing] the community against those acts of its citizens which are harmful to others and * * * reduc[ing] the incidence of delinquent behavior." Va. Code, § 16.1–227 [1977].

poles may appear strange; however, both share the conclusion that treatment is often disguised punishment. Liberals are pleased that juvenile courts must exercise restraint in resorting to questionable "treatments" at the dispositional stage and conservatives are pleased that it has been admitted that punishment can be a viable goal of any given juvenile disposition.

While the conservatives talk about punishment as "retribution" and the cornerstone of "responsibility," the liberal, child advocates speak in terms of the "right to punishment." [20]　Once the rehabilitative model is accepted, the next fight is always to show that "treatment" is often a caricature—something worthy of a story of Kafka or a Soviet mental hospital. Therefore, while the conservatives throw up their hands because they believe punishment works better than treatment, the juvenile advocates return increasingly to punishment on the grounds that punishment is much less punishing than "treatment." [21]　Therefore, while our opinion in this case is hardly definitive, it is designed to give guidance concerning the factors to be developed in the record. In the final analysis, since we are dealing with a love of things irreconcilable, the successful implementation of the juvenile law must rest in the sound discretion of the trial court. A record which discloses conclusively that the trial court has considered all relevant factual material and dispositional theories will permit us to make an intelligent review, keeping in mind that discretionary, dispositional decisions of the trial courts should only be reversed where they are not supported by the evidence or are wrong as a matter of law.

Accordingly, for the reasons set forth above, the writ of habeas corpus heretofore issued is discharged as moot; the judgment of the Circuit Court of Jefferson County adjudging petitioner delinquent is reversed and the case is remanded for further proceedings consistent with this opinion; and, the writ of prohibition for which petitioner prays is awarded.

14602: Dismissed as moot;

14603: Writ awarded, and

14769: Reversed and remanded.

[20] Schur, Radical Nonintervention, Rethinking and the Delinquency Problem (1973); H. James, *Children in Trouble—A National Scandal* (1971); Fox, "The Reform of Juvenile Justice: Children's Right to Punishment," 25 Juv. Justice 2 (1974); ———, "Philosophy and the Principles of Punishment in the Juvenile Court," 8 Fam.L.Q. 373 (1974); Simpson, "Rehabilitation as the Justification of a Separate Juvenile Justice System," 64 Cal.L.Rev. 984 (1976); Marticorena, "Take My Child Please—A Plea for Radi-cal Nonintervention," 6 Pepperdine L.Rev. 639 (1978–79).

[21] In "A Time for Skepticism," 20 Crime & Delinq., 20, 22 (1974), Martin Gold asserts: "The best data at hand demonstrates that we have not yet solved the problem of the effective treatment of delinquency." See also "Corrections and Simple Justice," 64 J.Crim.L.C. 208, 209 (1973), and Lehman, "The Medical Model of Treatment," 18 Crime & Delinquency 204 (1972).

A. PROCEDURES AT INITIAL DISPOSITION HEARINGS

TEXAS FAMILY CODE VERNON'S TEXAS CODES ANNOTATED, TITLE 3 (1972)

§ 54.04. Disposition Hearing

(a) The disposition hearing shall be separate, distinct, and subsequent to the adjudication hearing. There is no right to a jury at the disposition hearing.

(b) At the disposition hearing, the juvenile court may consider written reports from probation officers, professional court employees, or professional consultants in addition to the testimony of witnesses. Prior to the disposition hearing, the court shall provide the attorney for the child with access to all written matter to be considered by the court in disposition. The court may order counsel not to reveal items to the child or his parent, guardian, or guardian ad litem if such disclosure would materially harm the treatment and rehabilitation of the child or would substantially decrease the likelihood of receiving information from the same or similar sources in the future.

(c) No disposition may be made under this section unless the court finds that the child is in need of rehabilitation or that the protection of the public or the child requires that disposition be made. If the court does not so find, it shall dismiss the child and enter a final judgment without any disposition.

* * *

(f) The court shall state specifically in the order its reasons for the disposition and shall furnish a copy of the order to the child. If the child is placed on probation, the terms of probation shall be written in the order.

* * *

(h) At the conclusion of the dispositional hearing, the court shall inform the child of his right to appeal, as required by Section 56.01 of this code.

IJA–ABA JUVENILE JUSTICE STANDARDS, STANDARDS RELATING TO DISPOSITIONAL PROCEDURES (1980).

6.3 * Conduct of the hearing.

As soon as practicable after the adjudication and any predisposition conference that may be held, a full disposition hearing should be conducted at which the judge should:

A. be advised as to any stipulations or disagreements concerning dispositional facts;

---

* Reprinted with permission from Standards Relating to Dispositional Procedures, Copyright 1980, Ballinger Publishing Company.

B.   allow the juvenile prosecutor and the attorney for the juvenile to present evidence, in the form of written presentations or by witnesses, concerning the appropriate disposition;

C.   afford the juvenile and the juvenile's parents or legal guardian an an opportunity to address the court;

D.   hear argument by the attorney for the juvenile and the juvenile prosecutor concerning the appropriate disposition;

E.   allow both attorneys to question any documents and cross-examine any witnesses;

F.   allow both attorneys to examine any person who prepares any report concerning the juvenile, unless the attorney expressly waives that right.

7.1   * Findings and formal requisites.

A.   The judge should determine the appropriate disposition as expeditiously as possible after the dispositional hearing, and when the disposition is imposed,

1.   make specific findings on all controverted issues of fact, and on the weight attached to all significant dispositional facts in arriving at the disposition decision;

2.   state for the record, in the presence of the juvenile, the reasons for selecting the particular disposition and the objective or objectives desired to be achieved thereby;

3.   when the disposition involves any deprivation of liberty or any form of coercion, indicate for the record those alternative dispositions, including particular places and programs, that were explored and the reason for their rejection;

4.   state with particularity the precise terms of the disposition that is imposed, including credit for any time previously spent in custody; and

5.   advise the juvenile and the juvenile's attorney of the right to appeal and of the procedure to be followed if the appellant is unable to pay the cost of an appeal.

1.   NOTICE AND HEARING
NEW YORK—McKINNEY'S FAMILY COURT ACT

§ 741.   Notice of rights; general provision

(a) At the initial appearance of a respondent in a proceeding and at the commencement of any hearing under this article, the respondent and his parent or other person legally responsible for his care shall be advised of the respondent's right to remain silent and of his right to be represented by counsel chosen by him or his parent or other person legally responsible for his care, or by a law guardian assigned by the court under part four of article two. Provided,

* Reprinted with permission from Standards Relating to Dispositional Procedures, Copyright 1980, Ballinger Publishing Company.

however, that in the event of the failure of the respondent's parent or other person legally responsible for his care to appear, after reasonable and substantial effort has been made to notify such parent or responsible person of the commencement of the proceeding and such initial appearance, the court shall appoint a law guardian and shall, unless inappropriate also appoint a guardian ad litem for such respondent, and in such event, shall inform the respondent of such rights in the presence of such law guardian and any guardian ad litem.

(b) The general public may be excluded from any hearing under this article and only such persons and the representatives of authorized agencies admitted thereto as have a direct interest in the case.

(c) At any hearing under this article, the court shall not be prevented from proceeding by the absence of the respondent's parent or other person responsible for his care if reasonable and substantial effort has been made to notify such parent or responsible person of the occurrence of the hearing and if the respondent and his law guardian are present. The court shall, unless inappropriate, also appoint a guardian ad litem who shall be present at such hearing and any subsequent hearing.

§ 746. Sequence of hearings

Upon completion of the fact-finding hearing the dispositional hearing may commence immediately after the required findings are made.

IN RE WILSON

Supreme Court of Pennsylvania, 1970.
438 Pa. 425, 264 A.2d 614.

ROBERTS, JUSTICE.   Late in the afternoon of June 2, 1968, Charles Laverne Wilson and several other youths became involved in an inter-racial street fight in Lancaster, Pennsylvania. No one was seriously injured in the course of the affray, and Wilson's participation was apparently confined to having thrown a few punches. Juvenile delinquency proceedings, however, were brought against Wilson as a result of the incident.

Wilson's case came on for a hearing at 9:30 a.m. on July 24, 1968. His counsel, whom he met for the first time that morning, entered no plea in Wilson's behalf and agreed that Wilson had participated in the fight. After the testimony was taken the following colloquy occurred:

> "Mr. Hummer [defense counsel]; Your Honor, I would like to say one thing. I think it is obvious from his testimony that this is not one of the leaders in whatever this gang consisted of, or whatever occurred here, and I don't even believe he was one of the main perpetrators. I think he was perhaps along with them, and as his own testimony was, he admitted that he did participate in the fracas.

"The Court: Well, of course he has been in trouble before. In 1965 he was charged with burglary and placed on probation. You also have some trouble going to school, don't you?

"Defendant: Yes, sir.

"The Court: Were you suspended from school also? You seem to be in need of some stricter discipline. Isn't that about right?

"Defendant: I don't know.

"The Court: You don't know. Well, if you don't know, the court so finds from the testimony in this case and from your prior conduct. The court adjudges Charles Laverne Wilson a delinquent and commits him to the State Correctional Institution at Camp Hill, Pennsylvania * * *." [22]

Wilson's appeal to the Superior Court resulted in an opinionless per curiam affirmance, with Judge Hoffman and Judge Spaulding dissenting in an opinion written by the former. We granted allocatur.

* * *

Wilson alleges that he was denied the right to "adequate and timely notice" mandated by In re Gault, 387 U.S. 1, 87 S.Ct. 1428, 18 L.Ed.2d 527 (1967), wherein the Supreme Court said that Due Process " * * * does not allow a hearing to be held in which a youth's freedom and his parents' right to his custody are at stake without giving them timely notice, in advance of the hearing, of the specific issues that they must meet." * * * Of course, the juvenile need not have notice of every factor which might be relevant in his hearing; but he must have notice of those factors upon which the adjudication will be based and of any other consideration which may be used to justify imposition of a sentence longer than the criminal maximum. It is quite clear that the hearing judge in this case drew no distinction between those issues which were relevant to the adjudication and those which were important only in determining the length of commitment. Rather, he obviously based the adjudication of delinquency on two previous incidents in which Wilson had been involved, a school suspension and a "burglary," as well as on the finding that he had participated in the street fight that led to the initiation of the proceedings. Neither Wilson, nor his parents, nor his counsel were alerted to the fact that these prior occurrences were going to be considered, and were therefore not prepared to either offer testimony or to argue the seriousness or relevance of these past

---

[22] " * * * the Juvenile Court based its commitment order on a limited inquiry which failed to present a complete and accurate picture of Wilson's needs. No testimony was solicited from Wilson or his mother, who was present throughout the hearing, as to his home life. Further no psychiatric examination was ordered nor did any probation officer testify as to Wilson's background. In short, the commitment order rested solely upon the fact that Wilson had participated in a street fight and that he had a prior record which was before the court at the hearing." Wilson Appeal, 214 Pa.Super. 160, 169, 251 A.2d 671, 675 (1969) (dissenting opinion).

events. In short, Wilson was not really given an opportunity to try several major aspects of his case.

The invidiousness of the procedure becomes obvious when one reads the dissenting opinion of Judge Hoffman who, unlike the hearing judge, had an opportunity to consider these events with the benefit of arguments from opposing counsel and with a greater leisure. He concluded that:

> "My own reading of Wilson's probation record, secured from the Juvenile Court of Lancaster County, however, negates the seriousness of this past conduct. The 'burglary' mentioned by the lower court refers to an incident which occurred when Wilson was 13 years old. At that time he broke a window in a public school, ran water in the school's toilet bowls and knocked a soap dispenser from the wall for a total damage of $8. He was placed on 14 months probation, and from the record, his conduct appears to have been satisfactory in that interval.

> "Wilson was also expelled from school for a reason omitted from his record * * * and * * * he was accused of, but never prosecuted for, using profane language in a diner."

Wilson Appeal, 214 Pa.Super. 160, 169, 251 A.2d 671, 676 (1969) (dissenting opinion).

From this summary of Wilson's record it is clear that the past conduct mentioned by the hearing judge was not of a serious nature, and that Wilson's inability to argue the importance of these factors probably contributed to the length of the commitment imposed.

* * *

Order of Superior Court reversed, adjudication and commitment vacated and case remanded for further proceedings consistent with this opinion.

HILL v. STATE

Court of Civil Appeals of Texas, 1970.
454 S.W.2d 429.

KLINGEMAN, JUSTICE. This is an appeal from a judgment of the District Court of Bexar County sitting as a juvenile court, finding appellant to be a delinquent child and ordering him committed to the care, custody and control of the Texas Youth Council to be placed in the Gatesville State School for Boys.

Appellant complains that the trial court erred in committing him to the Texas Youth Council for confinement in the Gatesville State School for Boys for an indeterminate period of time not extending beyond his 21st birthday, instead of committing him to the custody of his parents, without hearing any evidence as to how appellant's welfare and the best interests of the State would best be served.

Under the provisions of Article 2338–1, Sec. 13, Vernon's Ann. Civ.St., the Juvenile Court has certain alternatives once it has determined a child to be delinquent.[23]   In Sec. 1 of Article 2338–1, the Legislature expressed a preference that a child adjudged to be delinquent be placed in the care, custody and control, of its parents.[24]

Settled practices recognize three stages in juvenile proceedings, (1) the intake, (2) the adjudicatory hearing, and (3) the disposition. The first stage is the pre-judicial or intake stage, at which time juvenile authorities are confronted with and handle, for varying periods of time, cases of all kinds—truancy, insolence, smoking, runaways, morals, misdemeanors, felonies. The second stage is that of adjudication, the purpose of which is to determine judicially the truth of the allegations in a petition in delinquency. The third stage, disposition, is the process in reaching a considered judgment of the best method for handling the child adjudged a delinquent. * * *

We are concerned here only with the third stage, disposition.

Appellant, a boy eleven years of age, was charged with burglarizing a dry cleaning plant. Trial was before the court without a jury. The trial court filed findings of fact and conclusions of law finding that appellant committed a burglary in violation of the penal laws of the State of Texas and that he is a delinquent child. Appellant does not attack these findings and does not complain of the adjudication by the court that appellant is a delinquent child. We therefore deem it unnecessary to discuss the evidence pertaining to the offense committed. However, we have carefully examined the entire record, and find nothing therein pertaining to any inquiry or evidence as to how the child's welfare and best interest of the State would be served under the alternatives provided for by Article 2338–1, Sec. 13, after a child has been found to be delinquent. There is no evidence in the record indicating that the parents of appellant are not proper persons to have the care, custody and control of their minor son, Ronald. Nor is there any evidence that appellant had ever been in trouble before, or that his home conditions are detrimental to his welfare and best interests.

We have found only one Texas case which appears to be directly in point. This Court in Cantu v. State, 207 S.W.2d 901 (1948), stated: "It is error for a trial court to commit a delinquent child to others than the child's parents in the absence of evidence that such parents are not proper persons to have the care, guidance and custody of

---

[23] "(1) place the child on probation or under supervision in his own home or in the custody of a relative or other fit person, upon such terms as the court shall determine;

"(2) commit the child to a suitable public institution or agency, or to a suitable private institution or agency authorized to care for children; or to place them in suitable family homes or parental homes for an indeterminate period of time, not extending beyond the time the child shall reach the age of twenty-one (21) years;

"(3) make such further disposition as the court may deem to be for the best

interest of the child, except as herein otherwise provided."

[24] "Section 1. The purpose of this Act is to secure for each child under its jurisdiction such care, guidance and control, *preferably in his own home*, as will serve the child's welfare and the best interest of the state; and when such child is removed from his own family, to secure for him custody, care and discipline *as nearly as possible equivalent to that which should have been given him by his parents*. (Emphases added.)

such minor, or that it is for the best interest of such minor and the State that he be committed to the custody of others than his own parents."

We sustain appellant's sole point of error. Appellant here is a boy only eleven years of age, and there is no evidence in the record that he had ever been in trouble before. Under the record, we hold the trial court was in error in ordering appellant committed to the Gatesville State School for Boys without hearing any evidence as to how the best interests of the child and the State will be served. That part of the judgment finding appellant to be a delinquent child is affirmed, but the judgment is reversed insofar as it orders appellant committed to the care, custody, and control of the Texas Youth Council for commitment to the Gatesville State School for Boys, and remanded to the trial court for a hearing to establish whether the child's welfare and best interests of the State will best be served by placing the child under supervision of his parents in his own home, or by the other alternatives provided for under Article 2338–1, Sec. 13.

NOTES

1. Despite the lack of definitive federal cases, it seems clear that the child has a right to counsel at a disposition hearing. See In re F., 30 A.D.2d 933, 293 N.Y.S.2d 873 (1968); A.A. v. State, 538 P.2d 1004 (Alaska 1975). Indeed, In re F., supra, involved a PINS proceeding. Because it is clear that in an adult criminal proceeding the defendant is entitled to counsel at sentencing, Mempa v. Rhay, 389 U.S. 128, 88 S.Ct. 254, 19 L.Ed.2d 336 (1967), it would indeed be surprising if the Constitution did not require counsel for a group generically less able to manage their own affairs with respect to a decision of such overriding importance. Furthermore, as more and more juvenile codes are revised, the problem may become only theoretical, for modern codes almost invariably provide for counsel at this stage. See the New York statute, printed supra. See also Standards for the Administration of Juvenile Justice, Report of the National Advisory Committee for Juvenile Justice and Delinquency Prevention, Commentary for section 3.132 (1980).

2. In the adult system, the defendant is present at sentencing. Is it necessary in the juvenile system that the child, whether a delinquent or a PINS, be present when the disposition decision is made? Some of the arguments are reflected in the following.

JASEN, J., dissenting in In re Cecilia R., 36 N.Y.2d 317, 367 N.Y.S.2d 770, 327 N.E.2d 812 (1975):

> There can be little doubt, as the majority concedes, that a Family Court Judge has considerable discretion, especially during a dispositional hearing, to exclude a juvenile from the courtroom for limited periods of time. This is especially true when the nature of the testimony to be presented, as it was in this case, involved a recital of no fewer than 23 rejections of placement by private agencies made on her behalf. It should be perfectly obvious how emotionally devastating such rejection testimony would have been upon this young 13-year-old girl. Unlike a fact-finding hearing where a determination must be made whether or not a juvenile is in need of supervision, the dispositional hearing is held, after an inquiry similar to a probation investigation in criminal proceedings, for the purpose of determining whether the juvenile should be

placed under supervision or treatment. Certainly, Cecilia's presence during this part of the dispositional hearing would not assist the court in its determination whether to impose supervision or treatment. Had Cecilia been present at the time the testimony of the long list of rejections was offered, there can be no doubt that the Judge not only could have, but should have, excluded her from the courtroom. In any event, Cecilia's law guardian was present throughout the dispositional hearing and was aware of his client's absence from the courtroom, without any objection.

I would also note that there is absolutely no indication in the record that there existed any basis for refuting any of the testimony offered during the dispositional hearing, or that Cecilia would have had anything to say that she did not say to the court when she returned immediately following the testimony of the social worker. In ordering a new dispositional hearing in this case, the court is engaging in an exercise of utter futility as it is not seriously suggested by anyone that the ultimate disposition will be any different.

Id. at 323–324, 367 N.Y.S.2d at 776, 327 N.E.2d at 816.

In reversing and remitting for further proceedings, the majority, in an opinion by FUCHSBERG, J., held that the absence of the PINS at the disposition hearing was a denial of due process.

It cannot be said with certainty that, if Cecilia had been present even throughout her dispositional hearing, her placement would have been any different. But then she at least would have had the opportunity, for example, to react to testimony, reports or colloquy, to be available to testify, to make suggestions or requests to counsel, to clarify misunderstandings. Indeed, the record here contains indicia of just such possibilities. The social worker, Ms. Hudson, testified that Cecilia needed a 'one-to-one relationship' to help her mature, and thought Cecilia's disturbing behavior 'a normal response' to parental rejection. Those statements were not further developed. She also reported how one private agency which had rejected Cecilia after an overnight visit complained she had been 'popping pills all night' when it turned out that Cecilia had had a throat infection.

Perhaps Cecilia could have shed light on other things as well, such as the circumstances that produced the discouraging litany of her rejections by other nonsecure agencies.[25] An opportunity to probe behind them was a matter of no small importance in this proceeding, since the Family Court Act reflects a deliberate and calculated plan to place ' "persons in need of supervision" ' in authorized agencies for treatment and rehabilitation and not to commit them to penal institutions. (Matter of Anonymous, 43 Misc.2d 213, 215, 250 N.Y.S.2d 395, 397.)

---

[25] Cecilia's probation officer reported that she had been rejected by at least 23 such agencies. Of those, 19 rejected her because no vacancies existed, because of her age, residence or without giving a reason. Only four thought her not a suitable candidate because of her personal problems and needs. The officer's recital calls attention to the societal problems posed by the nonavailability of facilities for certain neglected children which impedes even heroic efforts by our courts to place them in authorized non-secure agencies before commitment to more controlled settings (see, generally, Polier, A View From the Bench, 12). It need hardly be added that, under such circumstances, creating pressures for dispositions dehors the merits, the dispositional hearing can become an even more crucial factor in salvaging a young life.

The Family Court Judge who presided at the dispositional hearing here did not lack conscientiousness, concern or sensitivity. Nor does it appear that Cecilia's absence was the consequence of any positive intent on the court's part to exclude her. And, while it has been urged that the law guardian acquiesced in the exclusion, we find no clear showing of that in the record. Cecilia's absence appears rather to be the result of the happenstance of a series of events permitted to come about by themselves.

Nonetheless, the fact is that, without sufficient legal cause, Cecilia, except for the time it took for a very brief announcement of the *result* of the hearing, was deprived of her right to be present at her dispositional hearing, an integral part of her PINS proceeding. Therefore, the disposition must be vacated.

We wish to make it clear, however, that, by this opinion, we do not say that Judges may never exclude PINS respondents from any part of a dispositional hearing. '[Due process] varies with the subject-matter and the necessities of the situation.' (Moyer v. Peabody, 212 U.S. 78, 84, 29 S.Ct. 235, 236, 53 L.Ed. 410 [Holmes, J.].)

The sociolegal nature of the problems with which Family Court Judges deal requires the exercise of considerable discretion. No two cases are the same, though they all concern troubled lives. Tender years, mental health, behavior in the courtroom, the need to shield some children from the emotional trauma certain disclosures would be likely to produce, these are not the kind of considerations which Family Court Judges must or should ignore. Bench conferences out of the hearing of the youngsters involved may be required. Circumstances maybe indeed exist to justify limited exclusion from the courtroom. However, the norm must be inclusion. Where there is absence, or exclusion is directed on the court's own motion or on application of the law guardian, its justification must be capable of expression and rationalization and should be recorded contemporaneously. Further, such absence or exclusion, where necessary, should be no broader than circumstances require.

Accordingly, the order should be reversed and a new dispositional hearing held, along with such other proceedings, if any, as the Family Court may deem appropriate in view of the passage of time since the original disposition.

Id. at 321–323, 367 N.Y.S.2d at 774–76, 327 N.E.2d at 814–15.

3. Although the dispositional hearing may follow the adjudication hearing "immediately" (see New York statute, printed supra, and In the Interest, of J.E.J., 419 So.2d 1032 (Miss.1982)) the hearings must be separate in function.

In the case at bar, the court continued the adjudicatory hearing and then held a hybrid hearing, not contemplated by the Act, after which it made decisions as to both adjudication and disposition. Besides the fact that such a procedure flouted the clear mandates of the Act, it created possibilities of evidentiary problems. At an adjudicatory hearing, the usual rules of evidence in criminal proceedings apply. But at a dispositional hearing, the court can consider all evidence helpful in determining the question of disposition, including evidence not competent for purposes of the adjudicatory hearing. Thus, a combined hearing presents the probability that evidence will be presented which is incompetent for purposes of adjudication, though it would properly be considered in making a dispositional decision.

In the Interest of L.H., 102 Ill.App.3d 169, 57 Ill.Dec. 714, 429 N.E.2d 612 (1981).

2. WHO MUST DECIDE?

The normal expectation in adult criminal cases is that the judge (or the jury where jury sentencing occurs) who tries the case imposes the sentence. It is clear, however, that adequate intervening circumstances — such as the death or resignation of the judge who tried the case — would not prevent a successor judge from imposing sentence. The problem becomes more complicated when the judge who accepted a guilty plea based on a plea bargain is not the judge who imposed sentence. The leading case is People v. Arbuckle, 22 Cal.3d 749, 150 Cal.Rptr. 778, 587 P.2d 220 (1978), holding that sentencing by the judge who accepted the plea bargain is an implied condition of the bargain. State v. Carson, 597 P.2d 862 (Utah 1979), on the other hand, required only that the sentencing judge be sufficiently familiar with the presentence report and any available presentence evaluations. While these same issues would seem to inhere — perhaps even more importantly — in the juvenile process, there is an additional complication — a referee or commissioner system is commonly in use.

IN RE MARK L.

Supreme Court of California, 1983.
34 Cal.2d 171, 193 Cal.Rptr. 165, 666 P.2d 22.

GRODIN, JUSTICE.

In juvenile court, Mark L., a minor, entered a no contest (Cal. Rules of Court, rule 1354(f)) before a San Mateo Superior Court Commissioner to an allegation that he committed felony burglary. (Pen.Code, § 459.) At a subsequent dispositional hearing, the commissioner declared Mark a court ward and released him to his parents' custody under a strict county probation program. Acting on his own motion, a juvenile court judge ordered rehearing (Welf. & Inst.Code, § 253), overturned the commissioner's dispositional order, and directed Mark's placement in the California Youth Authority (YA) for a 90-day diagnostic evaluation. (Id., § 704.) Mark seeks a writ of habeas corpus, asserting that the YA commitment is void, because the juvenile judge had no power to alter the commissioner's disposition. Under the circumstances of this case, we conclude that the contention has merit.

* * *

On October 7, 1982, the parties appeared before James Browning, a superior court commissioner. By prior agreement, Mark was prepared to enter a no contest to count IV, burglary of the Pickart home, in return for dismissal of the remaining counts of the petition. Under the terms of the bargain, disposition was left open.

While advising Mark of the consequences of his plea, Browning twice noted that disposition of the case would be "solely up to the Court." The commissioner cautioned that "the maximum disposition, I'm not saying the Court is going to impose this maximum, but the maximum the Court could impose on this Count would be six years in custody."

After Mark entered his plea and the remaining charges were dismissed, Browning announced the parties' agreement that disposition be continued for further psychiatric and probation reports on Mark's suitability for the county Placement Intervention Program. The commissioner emphasized that "the boy has a right to have the same judicial officer who received the no contest plea impose the disposition," but there were scheduling problems because Browning's normal court assignment was in Redwood City. After discussion, a dispositional hearing was set for October 22, a date convenient to Browning.

The dispositional hearing took place as scheduled. Browning indicated he had read the new report of Dr. Fricke, the court-appointed psychiatrist. It disclaimed a sexual motive in Mark's conduct and recommended he be returned to the community with "intensified treatment efforts" including restitution and apologies to the victims. The deputy district attorney, on the other hand, recommended a maximum 35-day commitment to YA for further diagnostic evaluation.

Browning declined to take that route. He adjudged Mark a court ward, referred him to the Placement Intervention Program for 90 days, specified separate psychiatric therapy for Mark and his parents, and imposed additional restrictions on Mark's movements and associations. Further proceedings were scheduled for January 21, 1983, and Mark was released to the physical custody of his parents under the conditions set in the order.

On October 29, Presiding Juvenile Judge Capaccioli advised Mark's counsel that he had ordered a rehearing of Commissioner Browning's disposition. Counsel lodged no objection on the record, and the rehearing was held on November 2. Both Fricke and Mark's probation officer testified that the YA setting was unsuitable, disruptive, and physically dangerous for Mark. Nonetheless, Judge Capaccioli placed Mark in YA for a 90-day diagnostic evaluation, ordered him immediately detained in juvenile hall, and continued final disposition in the meantime.

Mark sought a writ of habeas corpus in this court, and we issued an order to show cause. On November 16, we stayed the YA commitment pending resolution of his petition. On November 24, we directed that Mark be released in the interim to his parents' custody "under the terms and conditions" of the October 22 disposition by Commissioner Browning.

* * *

3. *Validity of Order on Rehearing.*

The Juvenile Court Law provides that many matters may be heard and decided in the first instance by referees rather than judges. (§§ 247–250.) [26] However, referees, sitting as such, are but "subordinate" judicial officers with limited powers. (Cal.Const., art. VI, § 22; In re Edgar M. (1975) 14 Cal.3d 727, 732, 122 Cal.Rptr. 574, 537 P.2d 406.) All their findings and orders are subject to rehearing de novo by a juvenile court judge, either at the minor's request or on the judge's own motion. (§§ 248–254.)

Nonetheless, Mark argues that the rehearing order in this case was beyond Judge Capaccioli's power. He contends, among other things, that the rehearing violated his right to disposition by the same judicial officer who took his negotiated plea. We agree and find the claim dispositive.

In People v. Arbuckle (1978) 22 Cal.3d 749, 150 Cal.Rptr. 778, 587 P.2d 220 this court held that "whenever a judge accepts a plea bargain and retains sentencing discretion under the agreement, an implied term of the bargain is that sentence will be imposed by that judge. Because of the range of dispositions available to a sentencing judge, the propensity in sentencing demonstrated by a particular judge is an inherently significant factor in the defendant's decision to enter a guilty plea. [Citations.]" Thus, the sentence imposed by a judge other than the one who took the plea "cannot be allowed to stand. [Citations.] * * *" (Pp. 756–757, 150 Cal.Rptr. 778, 587 P.2d 220.)

Arbuckle has been extended to dispositions by judges in juvenile cases. * * * The only issue remaining is whether it applied to the bargained plea in this case, since the plea was entered before a juvenile court officer other than a regular judge.

We emphasize that here, as in *Arbuckle*, the record indicates an actual assumption by the court and parties that the officer taking the plea would have final and exclusive dispositional authority. Browning made repeated references to the dispositions "the Court" could or might impose, "though I'm not saying" what the court "is going to" do. In context, Browning's interchangeable use of the personal pronoun with the phrase "the Court" implied that he and "the Court" were one and the same. (Compare *Arbuckle*, supra, 22 Cal.3d at p. 756, fn. 4, 150 Cal.Rptr. 778, 587 P.2d 220.)

If any doubt on that score remained, Browning laid it to rest by announcing Mark's right to have "the same judicial officer" who took the plea handle the disposition. That was an obvious reference to *Arbuckle*, and the deputy district attorney did not object. Despite Browning's usual assignment elsewhere, considerable effort was

---

[26] The Juvenile Court Law makes no provision for the use of *commissioners* in juvenile court. They have no power as juvenile referees unless appointed as such by the presiding judge of the juvenile court. (§ 247; In re Edgar M., supra, 14 Cal.3d 727, 733, fn. 6, 122 Cal. Rptr. 574, 537 P.2d 406.) The limited record before us does not disclose Browning's appointment as a juvenile referee, although the parties do not dispute Browning's authority to sit in that capacity.

expended to ensure that he, rather than some other judge or referee, would act at the dispositional phase. There seems ample basis to conclude "that the plea bargain herein was entered in expectation of and reliance upon [disposition] being imposed by the same [judicial officer]." (Id., at p. 756, 150 Cal.Rptr. 778, 587 P.2d 220.)

Yet any attempt by a referee, sitting as such, to make a final or binding disposition exempt from review by a juvenile judge would violate express statutory provisions (§§ 250–254); arguably it would contravene the "subordinate judicial duties" clause of the Constitution (art. VI, § 22, supra) as well. (See, e.g., People v. Oaxaca (1974) 39 Cal.App.3d 153, 158–159, 114 Cal.Rptr. 178.) The question arises whether those facts defeat the otherwise apparent *Arbuckle* bargain, either because such a bargain would be unenforceable, or because no *reasonable* expectation or reliance on Browning's final authority could have arisen. The Attorney General argues further that, even if the plea bargain did include an *Arbuckle* condition, Judge Capaccioli had the power to disregard it; the remedy for his breach of the bargain is simply to allow Mark to withdraw his plea.

The answer to these concerns seems relatively simple. The parties may stipulate to a hearing before a temporary judge. * * * Both commissioners and referees may, if the parties properly stipulate, act as temporary judges. * * * A temporary judge has full judicial powers, and his orders are as final and nonreviewable as those of a permanent judge. * * * We conclude that the parties' conduct in this case constituted a sufficient stipulation that Browning was acting as a temporary judge."

* * *

The District Attorney of San Mateo County initiated this section 602 proceeding. Through his deputy, he willingly appeared before Browning, raising no objection when that officer announced he was proceeding under an *Arbuckle* condition and later entered a disposition on that basis. Such conduct, we think, was "tantamount to a stipulation" that Browning, by virtue of his status as a commissioner was acting as a temporary judge rather than a referee.

It follows that Browning's dispositional order had the same force as that of any other juvenile judge. It could not be reheard in the juvenile court, and Judge Capaccioli's subsequent order on rehearing is therefore void. In effect, Browning's order was never superseded; it stands as the juvenile court's last determination of Mark's status.[27]

---

[27] Our analysis is consistent with the rule that breach of an *Arbuckle* condition entitles the minor to be resentenced by the original judge unless court procedures make that "impossible." (22 Cal. 3d at p. 757, 150 Cal.Rptr. 778, 587 P.2d 220.) Mark, of course, *was* "sentenced" by the judge who took the plea; another judge simply purported to vacate that order and enter a different disposition. The obvious solution is to reinstate the first, proper dispositional order.

Respondent suggests that Browning rendered no "final" disposition in any event, since the referral to the Placement Intervention Program was subject to review in 90 days. But all dispositions are expressly subject to the "further order of the court" in its continuing jurisdiction over the minor, its ward. (§ 727, subd. (a).) Such final dispositions subject to "further order" are distinguishable from the temporary YA diagnostic commitment, which is intended only to produce a

A word of caution is in order. We do not hold that every bargained plea entered before a juvenile referee is subject to *Arbuckle*. As we have seen, the rules may preclude the recognition of "implied" or "tantamount" stipulations conferring final dispositional authority on noncommissioner referees. (Ante, fn. 5.) In any event, the referee may state on the record that his judicial status is subordinate and that he has no power to make a binding disposition. If he does so, no inference of temporary judgeship can arise, and no reasonable reliance on an *Arbuckle* condition can be found.

Contrary circumstances exist in this case, however, and we have decided it accordingly. Our conclusion that an enforceable *Arbuckle* bargain arose makes it unnecessary to consider Mark's remaining contentions.

* * *

MOSK, RICHARDSON, KAUS, BROUSSARD and REYNOSO, JJ., concur.

BIRD, CHIEF JUSTICE, dissenting. (omitted)

3. EVIDENTIARY LIMITATIONS

In adult criminal trials many kinds of evidence are admissible at sentencing hearings which would not be admissible at trial. Clearly a presentence report would not be admissible at the trial stage of an adult criminal proceeding, although it would be—subject to requirements of disclosure to the accused—at the sentencing hearing. Hearsay rules are relaxed in adult criminal proceedings. The New York statute printed below indicates the same conclusion should be reached in juvenile disposition hearings. Similar problems are presented in connection with the use of unconstitutionally obtained evidence at sentencing in adult cases and in juvenile cases.

NEW YORK—McKINNEY'S FAMILY COURT ACT

§ 745. Evidence in dispositional hearings; required quantum of proof

(a) Only evidence that is material and relevant may be admitted during a dispositional hearing.

(b) An adjudication at the conclusion of a dispositional hearing must be based on a preponderance of the evidence.

COURT SUMMARY [a]

NAME OF CHILD: D,	Docket No. J–9328
James (Bobby)	Worker Mr. E.L. Somoskey
Age 13 Race W Sex M	Hearing Date February 14, 1969

11:30 A.M.

recommendation on future treatment. (§ 704.) In any event, the flaw here is Judge Capaccioli's usurpation of Browning's dispositional authority, which the parties intended as *exclusive*.

[a] This material was provided by Mr. William Anderson, Chief Juvenile Probation Officer, Travis County, Texas. It has been altered only to the extent neces-

* * *

PLEADED OFFENSE:

On January 17, 1969, James was referred to Gardner House [b] by Austin Police for possession of stolen property. James was taken before Corporation Court Judge Roy Martin and given the magistrate's warning. Information surrounding the alleged offense:

Around midnight on 1–16–69, James sneaked out of his home after his mother had retired for the evening. James had removed his mother's car keys from her purse and took her 1965 Oldsmobile station wagon for a joyride, without her knowledge or permission. While riding around he picked up Richard J, WM–13, Steve B, WM–14, Marc A, WM–14, James & John O, WM–15 & 16, and Gregory L, WM–14. After the seven boys rode around for awhile they proceeded to Walnut Motel, where six cases of empty soft drink bottles were taken and sold at Minit Mart, 7–11, and U'Totem Stores in North Austin. The money was spent for gasoline and refreshments. Mrs. Bryan R, Manager of the motel, was contacted and the theft was confirmed.

Later Gregory L and Richard J told James of burglarizing 3 local churches and having the loot hidden underneath Ridgetop Elementary School. After agreeing to attempt to sell part of the loot, James drove to Ridgetop School where he received one National Hawaiian guitar, one Silvertone Electric guitar, and one Silvertone amplifier. The total value of the three items is approximately $700.00. Other items were available but left underneath the school. Shortly thereafter, James took Gregory L, Richard J, and James B home. Around 1:30 A.M. James was observed driving through the Spartan Department Store parking area by Officer Brantley, Austin Police Department. Brantley felt the situation looked suspicious and stopped the car. James admitted the amplifier and guitars had been stolen, that he had no driver's license, and the car had been taken without permission. All seven boys were subsequently processed through the Austin Police Department and referred to Gardner House.

The amplifier and guitars were identified by Richard R, member Grace Assembly Church, as having been taken from the church during a burglary on or about December 14, 1968.

Travis County Welfare Unit was active with the family at this time but due to continued delinquency behavior by James his case was transferred to this department. A delinquency petition was filed and a hearing set for February 14, 1969.

During two separate office interviews while James was at Gardner House he emphatically denied being involved in any other offenses. However, on January 21, 1969, Deputy Ischy, Travis County Sheriff's Department, reported Michael S, WM–13, had implicated James in a burglary. Deputy Ischy confronted James with a written statement by S and James freely admitted the following facts. On or

sary to disguise the identities of those involved.

[b] Gardner House is the juvenile detention home in Travis County, Texas.

about January 11, 1969, James had spent the night with his friend, S, Route 8, on Lake Travis by Lakeway Inn. During the following morning the boys took Michael's shotgun and rifle down by the lake to shoot at bottles, cans, etc. The boys happened by a lake house with two old cars parked in front. From one car the boys took a fishing reel and a skidometer. At the house the boys kicked a basement door forcing it open, forced open a trap door onto an upper porch and broke a window to gain entry. From the house was taken one pair of binoculars, two hand warmers, one cigarette lighter, one tackle box, and one set of assorted keys. The approximate value of property is $50.00. Upon leaving the lake house each boy shot a hole in the windshield of one of the cars. The stolen property was recovered and returned to the rightful owner, Mrs. Grace B.

On January 24, 1969, James was released to his mother pending his hearing. He was instructed, should he not conduct himself properly at home until the hearing, he would be detained at Gardner House until legal disposition of the case was complete. On January 27, 1969, Officer Wisian, Austin Police Department reported James was in custody as a burglary suspect. James was transferred to this department by Sgt. Flores as a burglary suspect, for taking his mother's car without permission and further on the request of this officer.

Information surrounding this referral is as follows: On January 26, 1969, around midnight, James, his brother, Jay, and Scott T, WM–15, a friend spending the night at the D home, all sneaked out of the house with the car key and went joyriding in Mrs. D's station wagon. The boys first attended a movie at Show Town U.S.A. in North Austin. Around 3:00 A.M. the boys drove to the Holiday Inn, for no special reason, according to James. The boys were observed by the night porter, Mr. Alvin A, parked in the extreme rear of the Inn near room 402. Mr. A felt the situation looked suspicious and took down the car's license number. Shortly thereafter, Mr. Vincent C reported to Austin Police his room no. 402 had been burglarized. Two suitcases, one valise, and one over-night case, all filled with clothing had been taken. Also one ladies wallet containing approximately $15.00 in cash, several credit cards and other credentials along with a small container filled with jewelry had been stolen. Mr. C indicated the entrance door may have been left unlocked. Police checked out the license number provided by Mr. A and learned that the car was registered to Mrs. Frances D, 5102 B. Around 10:00 A.M. on January 27, 1969, Officer Wisian, Austin Police Department brought James to police headquarters for questioning. After several interviews with police and this officer, James continues to emphatically deny any knowledge of this offense.

James has been detained at Gardner House since January 27, 1969, pending his delinquency hearing.

OTHER OFFENSES:

(1) On September 21, 1965, James and Darlene D, a sister, were referred to Gardner House by Travis County Sheriff's Department

for disturbing the peace. On this day Deputy Guinn conferred with officers of this department in regards to several complaints the Sheriff's Department had received by Mr. L. H, involving James D and confederates. Officers Somoskey, Bowie and Deputy Guinn went by the H residence to explore the complaints. From the H living picture window we observed James, his sister Darlene, James H, WM–10, and Terry S, WM–12, harass Mr. H as they walked home from school. The children came upon the H yard, pushed and kicked at Mr. H, became verbally abusive and blew a whistle in the complainant's ears. Mr. H is an elderly man who donned himself in ragged clothing and appears on the border of senility. He is a perfect target for the kids and in a way contributes to the situation by fully participating in the near daily disturbances.

Deputy Guinn took the four youngsters in custody and referred them to Gardner House. Guinn further indicated that several complaints had been received from others in the neighborhood in regards to various acts of vandalism, theft, destruction of private property, and malicious mischief by James D and his siblings. Deputies reportedly made several efforts to quieten the situation. According to Guinn, the children generally denied being involved in neighborhood misconduct and the parents tended to minimize and suggest the behavior as quite normal for youngsters.

Mr. & Mrs. D were interviewed by Intake Officer, Mr. Charles Smith, and were advised in front of James and his sister, Darlene, to put an immediate stop to the situation before something serious happened. However, the following day Mr. H, the complainant, reported to Travis County Sheriff's Department, that on the evening of release from Gardner House, the parents and children came by his house and seriously threatened him for having reported the children to the authorities.

(2) On September 27, 1965, James was referred to Gardner House by Travis County Sheriff's Department charged with four counts of burglary.

On September 25, 1965, Mr. James Bryant, Principal, Walnut Creek School, reported to Travis County Sheriff's Department that he had in custody four youngsters caught inside the school building. Deputy Frank Bukowsky investigated and identified the boys as James D, Terry S, James H and Scott M. The four admitted breaking into the school, by forcing open a door. The four further admitted to breaking into and entering the school on at least four other occasions. Mr. Bryant confirmed that the school had been burglarized on several occasions over the past few months. James claims the first few times he entered the school building the boys only ran about the hallways and classrooms for fun and nothing was taken from the building. However, on or about September 17, 1965, the boys had forced entry into the school by prying open the front door and took candy, ice cream, milk, fruit, masking tape, and a teacher's name plate valued at approximately $5.00. Bukowsky transferred the boys to Gardner House, where they were interviewed by Intake Officer, Charles Smith. Mr. Smith noted that James had an extremely bad attitude and cleverly concealed the truth. James was assigned to E.L. Somoskey for an immediate work-up to help determine appropriate action. After several months of interviews with James and his parents and through numerous contacts with the school, the police, and the neighbors, a serious trend toward family disintegration was observed. Mrs. D is seriously "paranoid" in attitude. Without reason she emotionally accuses everyone and every agency of harassing her children or being out to get them. Complaints from neighbors in regards to the children continued. Neighbors report the D children throw all sorts of projectiles from rocks to rotten eggs at houses, cars, and pedestrians. The children also reportedly drift about the neighborhood at all hours of the night.

Mr. D also showed signs of severe emotional stress. He made unscheduled visits with Mr. Anderson, Chief Probation Officer, Judge Chas. Betts, Juvenile Judge and the Travis County Child Welfare Unit seeking advice on family problems and possible assistance for care and custody for his children. Both parents tended to make "loud noise" during intense family crisis but were unable to follow through with any plan.

(3) On November 17, 1967, Mrs. Donna H, reported James and his brother, William, to police for peeking into her windows around 9:30 P.M. Mrs. H reported to police that James and his siblings were serious problems in the whole neighborhood. She indicated further that the youngsters were seen walking the streets at unreasonable hours. Sgt. Keirsey, Austin Police Department discussed the complaint with Mrs. D and the children. Keirsey encouraged the mother to provide proper supervision, cautioned the children about further complaints and closed the case at police level.

(4) On March 30, 1968, Mr. Glenn A. Z, filed a neighborhood disturbance complaint with the police in regards to the D children.

Mr. Z reported to police the D children continued to commit a series of incidents involving prowling, object throwing, and vandalism in the neighborhood. The complainant indicated James had been seen pulling a knife on other children, striking other youngsters with baseball bats as well as his fists with little or no provocation. Mr. Z further indicates the children are left unsupervised for prolonged periods of time. The children have been seen roaming around the neighborhood at very late hours of the night, often after midnight. The mother allegedly goes out at night returning in the wee hours of the morning. One neighbor reported having seen the children on the streets as late as 4:00 A.M. and observed the mother coming in at 5:30 A.M. Sgt. Keirsey again talked to Mrs. D and the children and submitted a copy of the report to the Travis County Child Welfare Unit for their information.

(5) The following day, March 31, 1968, Mr. Z reported to police further malicious mischief by the D children.

Mr. Z reported sometime after midnight he heard a noise outside, investigated and saw James, Darlene and two of the smaller D children running from his yard. Further checking revealed James had thrown a light bulb and broken it against the house. Around 3:00 A.M. Mrs. Donna H again reported James was seen peeking into her bedroom window. After 3:00 A.M. the children were seen on the next street throwing eggs at several houses. Three individuals on that street filed complaints with the police. Mr. Z staying up the remainder of the night, observed Mrs. D coming home around 5:30 A.M. He further indicated attempts to reason with Mrs. D had been made but she appeared emotionally disturbed and was most unreasonable. Mr. Z indicated to police that he had been chosen as the neighborhood spokesman and suggested that something be done. The problem has become the concern of the entire neighborhood for their property and their children's safety. Again Sgt. Keirsey investigated, talked to the Ds and referred the complaint to the Child Welfare Unit.

(6) On August 19, 1968, around 9:00 A.M. Mr. Robert B. M caught two youngsters prowling inside his Willys jeep. Mr. M pursued the two youngsters to their home and notified the police. Sgt. Williams investigated and learned that James and William had stolen from the jeep an eight foot tow chain and a twin chrome oil pressure gauge. Also, on the morning of 8–18–68 Mr. M had seen William and Darlene in the jeep and they had taken a pair of forged U.S. pliers. The property was recovered and returned to the owner. Sgt. Williams discussed the matter with Mrs. Eva H, the children's grandmother who indicated her grandchildren are allowed to prowl the neighborhood all hours of the night, sometimes running until 4:00 A.M. The Child Welfare Unit handled the referral.

(7) On August 20, 1968, James was referred to Gardner House by Austin Police for theft of soft drink bottles. Mrs. H.D. L reported to police that around 11:00 A.M. on this day, James and William D had been observed by Mrs. Paul R taking 3 six packs of empty soft drink bottles from her garage. Police investigated and the boys admitted taking the bottles. Mr. Eugene L, 7–11 Manager, identified James as the youngster having sold him 3 six packs of empty Coke bottles. Police also questioned Mrs. D about a gold color Stingray bicycle James was riding and she indicated it was probably stolen. Police confiscated the bicycle. Child Welfare Unit handled the referral.

(8) On September 29, 1968, James was referred to Gardner House by Austin Police for theft of a motorcycle.

Department of Public Safety officer Jack Hopper informed the police that he had observed three subjects on a motorcycle behind Gulf Mart and he had grown suspicious. The subjects identified themselves as James & William D and Bruce C, WM–15. When Hopper found that none of the trio had a driver's license he had James walk the motorcycle from the Gulf Mart to his home. James had claimed the motorcycle belonged to him. Upon arrival at home,

Mrs. D informed Mr. Hopper the motorcycle did not belong to her son. Bruce C then admitted that he had stolen the motorcycle and was letting James use it. The owner was notified and the motorcycle returned. The 1967 Yamaha motorcycle had been damaged extensively according to the owner, James S.

This officer called Mrs. Linda Sullivan, Child Welfare worker, to determine exactly what was being planned for the D children. She indicated several children's institutions and Boys Ranches had been written and hopefully James would be placed outside the home soon. Mrs. Sullivan had applications pending at this time with Buckner's, Cal Farley's, West Texas, and Abilene Boy's Ranches. Child Welfare handled the referral and continued with the case.

(9) On October 11, 1968, James was handled by Austin Police for theft of milk. Mrs. Norman J notified police that a 1968 Ford Mustang was following a milk truck in her neighborhood with the lights off and the occupants were stealing milk from the porches as the milkman put the milk out. Officer Talley stopped the Ford in the 5500 block of Oakley. James D was driving and indicated the car belonged to his mother and that he had taken it without her permission. His confederate was Richard J. The boys had four gallons of milk in the car but informed the police they did not know where the milk had come from. The milk was released to the neighborhood milkman. James and Richard were taken to the police station where they were interrogated and released to their parents.

(10) On October 31, 1968, James was involved in a siphoning of gasoline case. Raymond M reported to police that two youngsters were siphoning gasoline from his automobile. Officer Lopez, Austin Police Department, made immediate investigation and observed two youngsters running from the vehicle. Lopez was able to corner one boy identified as Allen W, WM–17, who admitted that he and James D were siphoning gasoline for his 1957 Chevrolet which was located at the scene. Officer Lopez notified several other units in the area which converged on the D residence. Several officers reportedly saw James run into his home. Mrs. D reported to the officer at the front door that James was not home. However, officers were stationed around the house and saw no one leave. After about 30 minutes of police persuasion Mrs. D still denied that James was in the house. Mrs. D was taken into custody and transported to police headquarters. After a long counselling session, Mrs. D agreed to bring James by the police station the following day. However, she failed to do so.

(11) On November 1, 1968, James was referred to Gardner House by Austin Police for possession of stolen property. Around 1:40 A.M. this date Officer Brantley stopped a 1965 Buick station wagon for routine check. James was driving and again admitted he had taken his mother's car without her permission to joyride. Brantley observed a navy blue purse on the front seat and inquired. James insisted it belonged to his sister. Upon checking the purse out, it was discovered to have been stolen from a car. The purse and its contents were valued at approximately $30.00 in addition to the

various personal papers. The station wagon was placed on the pound at the police station and the mother was notified. Child Welfare handled the referral.

(12) On November 21, 1968, James was referred to Gardner House by Austin Police for traffic warrants. Around 1:00 A.M. on this date Officer Lewis received a call in regards to a juvenile driving a station wagon in and out of driveways in the 7800 block of Rutgers. Upon investigation Lewis learned that James D and Dan C, WM–16, were driving the car and neither had a driver's license. James has 6 outstanding traffic warrants against him. Child Welfare handled the referral. This officer recently checked with Corporation Court Judge Roy Martin in regards to disposition of the traffic warrants and learned that Mrs. Sullivan along with Mrs. D and James had appeared before him in a "tearful" state and indicated James was soon to be placed on a Boy's Ranch. With this information Judge Martin dismissed the warrants.

COMMUNITY RESOURCE INVOLVEMENT:

The D family first became known to this agency in 1964 when William was referred to Gardner House for arson. Child & Family disturbance was indicated and the case was referred to the Travis County Child Welfare Unit. On September 27, 1965, James and Jay were referred to Gardner House for burglary. This department then became active in conjunction with Child Welfare in an effort to provide assistance and supervision to these two boys. After observing severe family problems the case was referred to the Austin Child Guidance Clinic on January 26, 1966. Several appointments were scheduled but missed. Repeated efforts to get the family involved at the Guidance Clinic failed. On September 29, 1967, Dr. Boston, Psychiatrist, did an evaluation on Jay to assist in determining his needs. During November 1967, Father F. Carlin of the *Big Brothers* Program made contact with the family but was unable to accomplish anything. On January 22, 1968, a probation department conference was held and the case was assigned to Mr. Doug Johnson, graduate social work student from the University of Texas to conduct a thorough work-up and explore placement. Mr. Johnson felt there was hope for the family and obtained assistance by activating the Child & Family Services Agency. In June 1968, Mr. Johnson left the department and the case was transferred in total to the Child Welfare Unit, hoping the children could all be placed outside the home.

On October 11, 1968, Mrs. D voluntarily surrendered legal custody of James to the Child Welfare Unit for placement purposes. Mrs. Linda Sullivan, Child Welfare worker, applied with several institutions and boy's ranches without finding placement. Reasons given were generally no space available or unable to meet the child's needs. James was transferred back to the Probation Department on January 17, 1969, after continued acting out. On several occasions Mrs. D promised relatives in Houston or California would take James. Nothing ever materialized, however, on one occasion James was taken to

Houston but only stayed one weekend and then returned home. Mrs. D has retained Attorney Andy Vandygriff and Carol Larson has been assigned as Guardian ad litem.

SOCIAL HISTORY:

Mrs. D married the children's father in 1940 when she was only 14 years of age. The couple separated while he was in the military service during World War II and were divorced in 1946. After the divorce, both parents remarried. However, in 1948 the two divorced and re-married. It appears the couple's marriages have been riddled by conflict and infidelity.

In 1965 the family was living in a fashionable brick home. Mr. D, a plumbing contractor, earned a very good income and his wife thoroughly enjoyed spending it. Mrs. D often had a full time maid to do the bulk of her work. However, due to Mrs. D's continued inability to manage money and her drive to achieve social status, the home was lost. Shortly thereafter, the parents separated and Mrs. D moved. Again, Mrs. D refused to manage her household adequately. The home soon fell below the standard of the neighborhood with littered yard, broken windows and cluttered interior. During the summer of 1967, the parents went back together. However, in October 1967, Mr. D, at the age of 44 died of a cerebral hemorrage. In early 1968, after several financial settlements from her husband's death, Mrs. D moved into another fashionable home. She is currently receiving Veteran's Benefits and Social Security totaling approximately $525.00 per month. However, she continues her impulsive spending and is always in debt and pressed by bill collectors. Her current mode of living will in all likelihood collapse in the near future. Mr. D carried two life insurance policies. One is reported to be under contest by the insurance company. The other policy lists the children as the beneficiaries, therefore, Mrs. D has not received any life insurance payments. However, she indicates taking possible legal action to receive a share of her children's proceeds.

If verbalizing would solve Mrs. D's problems she would have none. She incessantly talks about what she is going to do and never does anything. When unable to talk herself out of a stressful situation she behaves in a paranoid fashion condemning her neighbors, the police, the schools, and others she feels are persecuting her and her family.

James is a very large and rugged looking boy for his age. He has average ability but is lazy and refuses to achieve. He will not obey his mother or do any work around the house. He bullies smaller children and generally terrorizes the neighborhood. In 1962, Jay suffered some brain damage resulting from an automobile accident. In 1961, Jay had an I.Q. score of 101 and in 1965 he tested a total I.Q. 58. He has been for the past few years in Special Education but is not achieving. He was recently suspended from school for the remainder of the year due to excessive and unexcused tardiness and truancy. Mrs. Linda Sullivan, Child Welfare worker indicates she plans to do a thorough work-up on Jay to determine what his needs are at this point. Jay has also been handled by the police department and referred to this department on several occasions mainly due to being encouraged by James. Darlene and William are also experiencing serious problems at school and have been handled by police and referred to Gardner House. The two youngest children, Debbie and Diane are not problems at this time. All the children are to some degree overweight.

SCHOOL REPORT:

Mr. Henley, Vice-Principal Burnet Jr. High School reports that James has not been in school since the 26th of September, 1968. Checking with Mr. Arthur Cunningham, Director Pupil Personnel and Special Services, revealed that on October 11, 1968, Mrs. Sullivan had been given permission to allow James to remain out of school in that he refused to attend and his mother was unable to make him attend. Mrs. Sullivan reported that several applications had been filed with Boy's Ranches and hopefully James would be placed outside the home soon. Since, James has made no effort to return to school and continues to behave without regard to laws of the community. During the 14 days of school James attended this year, he was referred to the Principal's office on four separate occasions for classroom disturbances. Mr. Henley reports on one occasion, James broke into the Anderson Lane Baptist Church, removed a fire extinguisher and sprayed a school bus. James attended Pierce Jr. High School in the 7th grade during the 1967 school year and was present 139 days and absent 37 days. The last semester at Pierce James flunked every class except Social Studies in which he received a C. James has an average I.Q. but maintains an extremely poor attitude towards school. School personnel have long been concerned about James and have worked diligently without success.

SPECIAL REPORT:

See attached copy of psychological evaluation dated October 22, 1968 by Dr. D.L. Bell, Psychologist.

OBSERVATION:

All parties involved with James and his family have over-extended themselves in an effort to help without any sign of hope. Due to James' continued outrageous conduct in the community, it is respectfully recommended that he be committed to the Texas State School for Boys at Gatesville.

PSYCHOLOGICAL EVALUATION

NAME: D, James (Bobby)	CASE NO.:
BORN: 7–8–55	DATE TESTED: 10–22–68
AGE: 13	EXAMINER: Donald Fox, M.A.
SEX: Male	AGENCY: MH–MR Center

REFERRAL: The client was referred by Linda Sullivan, Child Welfare, for intellectual and personality assessment as part of determining the feasibility of enrolling the client in a boys' ranch.

BEHAVIORAL OBSERVATIONS: Physically, Bobby appeared an average Caucasian male, 13-years old, of age-appropriate stature, but somewhat overweight, with no grossly observable abnormalities. Bobby performed all tasks requested of him by the examiner quickly and efficiently but did not spontaneously initiate any activity or conversation. Throughout the session he kept his eyes downcast, rarely looking at the examiner, frequently yawning, stretching and shifting about in his chair. At times, he appeared to be on the verge of tears. In the pretest interview, Bobby professed ignorance of the purpose of the interview when asked by the examiner. He was told that it was to help him with the decision to enroll him at the ranch and give ranch personnel some idea of what he was like. Questioning elicited his feelings that he had not been told anything about the kind of place the ranch was, did not want to go, and had no idea of what his mother thought about the idea. Bobby made no comment to the suggestion that he discuss the ranch more fully with both his mother and his caseworker.

ASSESSMENTS ADMINISTERED:

      (1) Drawings (house-tree-person)

      (2) Weschsler Intelligence Scale for Children (WISC)

      (3) Thematic Apperception Test (cards 1, 2, 6BM, 14, 8BM, 186F, 7BM, 7BM) Rotter

      (4) Incomplete Sentences (High School Form)

TEST RESULTS AND INTERPRETATION: With a Verbal IQ of 92, a Performance IQ of 92, and a Full Scale IQ of 91, Bobby is currently functioning at the lower end of the Average Intelligence Range. No marked strengths were noted. The four subtests showing below-average performance are those associated to some degree with the ability to differentiate and deal appropriately with the relevant and irrelevant factors in a situation. Since no other test data indicate either organicity or psychosis, the above finding is tentatively suggestive of either marked situational anxiety or a long history of confusing and inconsistent environmental (home) conditions, or both.

Due to Bobby's reticence little definitive information could be gained from personality test data and any inferences drawn from them are more than usually speculative. Currently, Bobby seems to be experiencing considerable anxiety that is realistically associated with his problems with the law. This anxiety is expressed in apprehension about what will happen to him in the future and in moralistic concern ("how to do right"). It is likely from Bobby's social case history that this concern is rooted in ineffective learning of impulse control coupled with demands by his mother to assume responsibilities not usually assigned to a boy of his age. Aware of these inadequacies, Bobby may frequently experience feelings of depression, helplessness, and self-degradation. He may try to control his depression through denial. His episodic anti-social behavior is probably an attempt to counteract his helplessness and low self-esteem. Bobby also shows some considerable need to establish a warm and loving relationship with someone, preferably an adult. Admittedly a subjective opinion, the examiner feels that although there seems little, if any, opportunity in Bobby's present environment for such a meaningful relationship, the boy still has the capacity to develop one. In this light, Bobby's unacceptable behavior may be viewed also as a means of gaining attention as a substitute for love.

SUMMARY: James (Bobby) D, a 13-year old, healthy Caucasian male, with a history of repeated anti-social behavior, is presently functioning in the range of Average Intelligence (WISC=91), with no obvious organic or psychotic signs. The boy was withdrawn, anxious and reticent during testing, providing little definitive personality test data. Tentatively, he appears to suffer from feelings of rejection and lovelessness (from mother and others), helplessness, inadequacy, guilt and moralistic concern, and poor impulse control. He may rely mainly on denial to control depression and employ anti-social behavior to counteract his low self-esteem and to gain attention in lieu of love. His problems are seen as environmentally based and not indicative of sociopathy; he still appears capable of developing meaningful interpersonal relationships under the proper circumstances.

RECOMMENDATIONS: Bobby should be placed in an environment that can provide:

(1) A clearly defined, consistent structure with firm limits;

(2) A sharply delineated, age-appropriate role within the environment that Bobby may assume and through which he may develop a more positive self-concept;

(3) A supportive, accepting, but firm, adult male to satisfy Bobby's affectional needs and provide a model for Bobby's socialization.

Insofar as the proposed placement in the boys' ranch can fulfill these requirements, the move would appear both realistic and highly desirable. Such placement would probably require a minimum of two years residency to insure stable personality development. Bobby's initial reaction to any placement will probably be increased depression and destructive anti-social behavior (possibly involving repeated runaways) until he has thoroughly tested the limits of his new environment and established some concept of his role there.

Donald Fox, M.A.　　　　　　　D.L. Bell, Ph.D.
Psychologist　　　　　　　　　Psychologist

NOTES

1. Is it proper for the probation officer to include neighbors' accusations against the defendant or his family in the Court Summary? Should accounts of criminal conduct be included when defendant was never adjudicated to have engaged in that conduct? Should it matter whether the

defendant admitted the offense to police, an intake officer or a probation officer?

2. Consider the following in the light of that portion of Kent v. U.S., supra, that deals with disclosure of social service records to defense counsel at a waiver of jurisdiction hearing.

> Appellant next contends the court erred in refusing to comply with 10 O.S. § 1115(b) during the dispositional portion of the hearing. That hearing followed directly the adjudication hearing and the transcript reflects one hearing ended and the other began on the same page. A ten minute recess was allowed for counsel to read the social summary and recommendation.

> Section 1115(b) provides:

> " 'Before making an order of disposition, the court shall advise the District Attorney, the parents, guardian, custodian or responsible relative, or their counsel, of the factual contents and the conclusion of reports prepared for the use of the court and considered by it, and afford fair opportunity, if requested, to controvert them.'

> "The record reflects the court not only refused to advise the parents of the contents of the report, he refused to allow the parents to see it and told counsel for appellant they were not entitled to view it.

> Counsel for appellant objected and stated the statute allows review and a fair opportunity to controvert such reports and the court stated:

> " 'By the Court: They are not entitled to know anything. Some of that report is from neighbors and from other sources the Court does not desire to be disseminated. You can read it and you can recite from it. I have no control over your telling them what you think is in it, but the Court does object to your giving that to anyone except where you got it, the Court.'

> Once again, the record makes it abundantly clear the court, for no cause shown, good or otherwise, denied the parents of appellant a right clearly set out in the Statutes."

Sorrels v. Steele, 506 P.2d 942, 945 (Okla.Cr.1973).

In S.C.H. v. State, 404 So.2d 811 (Fla.App.1981), the court quoted with approval the Florida Rules of Juvenile Procedure which entitled the child, his attorney and parents to disclosure " * * * except those portions classified as confidential by the submitting person or agency."

3. Must a court obtain a social investigation as a precondition to making a disposition? In Green v. United States, 446 A.2d 402 (D.C.App. 1982), the court held that if the trial court otherwise had sufficient data, a formal study would not be necessary to sustain a sentence under the Federal Youth Correction Act.

4. Suppose a juvenile testifies under a grant of immunity at a preliminary hearing in a criminal case. May his immunized testimony be used at the disposition phase of a subsequent juvenile delinquency case? The Wisconsin Court of Appeals said "no." State v. J.H.S., Jr., 90 Wis.2d 613, 280 N.W.2d 356 (App.1979).

5. The use of illegally obtained evidence other than at the trial stage has generally been approved in adult criminal cases. The issue is also present in the disposition stage of juvenile delinquency proceedings.

> At the disposition hearing, the People were allowed to bring to the attention of the court a statement (amounting to a confession)

made by the minor in a previous case in which the charge had been burglary and murder. In that case, that confession had been held inadmissible as being the fruit of an illegal arrest. The facts concerning that arrest and the obtaining of the confession were described in detail to the commissioner sitting in this case. The commissioner admitted the prior confession as part of the record in the disposition hearing. In so doing, he relied, and the People rely here, on In re Martinez (1970) 1 Cal.3d 641, 83 Cal.Rptr. 382, 463 P.2d 734, and People v. Rafter (1974) 41 Cal.App.3d 557, 116 Cal. Rptr. 281. In *Martinez*, the Supreme Court held that the Adult Authority, in a parole revocation proceeding, properly could consider statements obtained from Martinez in violation of *Dorado;* in *Rafter*, a similar holding was made as to the consideration of illegally obtained evidence at a probation revocation hearing. In spite of defendant's attempt to distinguish those cases, we find that the commissioner properly relied on the confession herein involved. Like parole and probation revocation proceedings, the issue before a juvenile court on a disposition hearing is the character of the person involved; the fact that the juvenile court law provides for separate hearings on adjudication and on disposition was enacted because the legislature recognized that much evidence, inadmissible on the issue of adjudication, will be relevant and material on the issue of the proper disposition of an adjudicated minor. The exception recognized by the cited cases, making inadmissible statements obtained by police methods that shook the conscience of the court, is not herein involved since the commissioner expressly found that the facts given to him did not show such conduct.

Defense counsel argues here that, if the use of illegally obtained evidence can be presented at a disposition hearing, police may be tempted to obtain such evidence, knowing that it cannot be used in the case under investigation, but with the hope that it may become useful, at some future date, in connection with some new charge. That same possibility exists in the parole and probation cases, but did not induce either of the two courts to reject the evidence. We recognize that a similar argument was found persuasive by the Supreme Court in People v. Disbrow (1976) 16 Cal.3d 101, 113, 127 Cal.Rptr. 360, 545 P.2d 272. However, as the court there stated (at p. 112, 127 Cal.Rptr. at p. 367, 545 P.2d at p. 279) its principal objection to the use of illegally obtained evidence for the purpose of impeachment was "[t]he considerable potential that a jury, even with the benefit of a limiting instruction, will view prior inculpatory statements as substantive evidence of guilt rather than merely reflecting on the declarant's veracity." No such risk exists in cases such as the one now before us, where the issue of "guilt" has, already, been adjudicated in a separate proceeding. Another difference exists between *Disbrow* and this case: the temptation on police to use improper methods to secure a confession for use in the very case under investigation is far stronger than the mere hope that an illegally obtained confession, filed away, may become useful in some future and then unknown case.

We conclude that the commissioner properly considered the earlier confession made in the burglary-murder case. That conclusion is reinforced by the decisions in Lockridge v. Superior Court (1970) 3 Cal.3d 166, 89 Cal.Rptr. 731, 474 P.2d 683, and in People v.

McInnis (1972) 6 Cal.3d 821, 100 Cal.Rptr. 618, 494 P.2d 690, where the Supreme Court held that evidence illegally obtained might still be used, in a later and disconnected case. As the Court said in *McInnis* (at p. 826, 100 Cal.Rptr. at p. 621, 494 P.2d at p. 693), to prevent the use in such a disconnected case "would in effect be giving a crime insurance policy in perpetuity to all persons once illegally arrested." In the case at bench, the minor cannot hide behind the illegality of his former arrest to prevent the juvenile court from obtaining a full picture of his character and need for rehabilitative treatment.

In the Matter of Peter B., 84 Cal.App.3d 583, 148 Cal.Rptr. 762 (1978). Because a hearing was granted by the California Supreme Court, the opinion quoted from appears only in the California Reporter, and, under California Supreme Court rules has no precedential value. It would seem significant to the student, if not to California lawyers, that the appeal was ultimately dismissed.

B. DISPOSITIONAL ALTERNATIVES

KANSAS STATUTES ANNOTATED, KANSAS JUVENILE OFFENDERS' CODE

38–1663. Dispositional alternatives. When a respondent has been adjudged to be a juvenile offender, the judge may select from the following alternatives:

(a) Place the juvenile offender on probation for a fixed period, subject to the terms and conditions the court deems appropriate, including a requirement of making restitution as required by subsection (h).

(b) Place the juvenile offender in the custody of a parent or other suitable person, subject to the terms and conditions the court orders, including a requirement of making restitution as required by subsection (h).

(c) Place the juvenile offender in the custody of a youth residential facility, subject to the terms and conditions the court orders.

(d) Place the juvenile offender in the custody of the secretary.

(e) Impose any appropriate combination of subsections (a) and (b), subsection (c) or subsection (d) and make other orders directed to the juvenile offender as the court deems appropriate.

(f) Commit the juvenile offender, if 13 years of age or older, to a state youth center if the juvenile offender:

(1) Has had a previous adjudication as a juvenile offender under this code or as a delinquent or miscreant under the Kansas juvenile code; or

(2) has been adjudicated a juvenile offender as a result of having committed an act which, if done by a person 18 years of age or over, would constitute a class A, B or C felony as defined by the Kansas criminal code.

(g) In addition to any other order authorized by this section, the court may order the juvenile offender to attend counseling sessions as the court directs. The costs of any counseling may be assessed as expenses in the case. No mental health center shall charge a fee for court-ordered counseling greater than that the center would have charged the person receiving the counseling if the person had requested counseling on the person's own initiative.

(h) Whenever a juvenile offender is placed pursuant to subsection (a) or (b), the court, unless it finds compelling circumstances which would render a plan of restitution unworkable, shall order the juvenile offender to make restitution to persons who sustained loss by reason of the offense. The restitution shall be made either by payment of an amount fixed by the court or by working for the persons in order to compensate for the loss. If the court finds compelling circumstances which would render a plan of restitution unworkable, the court may order the juvenile offender to perform charitable or social service for organizations performing services for the community.

Nothing in this subsection shall be construed to limit a court's authority to order a juvenile offender to make restitution or perform charitable or social service under circumstances other than those specified by this subsection or when placement is made pursuant to subsection (c) or (d).

* * *

The range of alternative dispositions considered in this chapter has certain characteristics. First, we are considering only dispositions made *after* an adjudication decision has been reached. At earlier points in the book we considered the many alternatives available to intake workers, or even to the police, either informally or as a result of formal statutory authorization. A formal diversion statute is an example, and, indeed, a lecture by a policeman ending all contact with the system is another. Second, we are grouping together some things that in some respects have different consequences. Specifically, we are treating under the same heading certain dispositions whether they are imposed directly, as, for example, restitution under the Washington statute we reproduce, infra, or indirectly as a condition of probation as in State in the Interest of D.G.W., also reproduced, infra. Similarly we treat alike training school commitments whose execution is suspended while the juvenile is on probation, and dispositions in which probation is directly ordered without any "backup" alternative. Although in the adult criminal system, the difference may be of considerable importance if and when the conditions of probation are violated and probation is revoked, it is difficult to find comparable juvenile law. In the adult system, if there is no sentence previously imposed, revocation of probation would require a new sentence, always assuming that result is the one desired, while if there is a suspended sentence, revocation of probation could simply be followed by execution of that sentence. It seems likely, though we are not certain, that when probation is ordered in juvenile cases, there is not likely to be a "back-up sentence." To return to the other problem, when a sanction such as restitution is directly ordered rather than made a condition of probation, there is no probation to revoke as well as—assuming the correctness of our assumptions—no "back-up" disposition. In the latter situation, use of some form of contempt procedure would seem to be necessary. In this regard, pay careful attention to Section 13.40.200 of the Washington Juvenile Justice Act, reproduced, infra.

1. DISPOSITIONS WITHIN THE COMMUNITY

a. Probation

IJA–ABA JUVENILE JUSTICE STANDARDS, STANDARDS RELATING TO DISPOSITIONS (1980)

3.2 Conditional. *

The court may sentence the juvenile to comply with one or more conditions, which are specified below, none of which involves removal from the juvenile's home. Such conditions should not interfere with the juvenile's schooling, regular employment, or other activities necessary for normal growth and development.

A. Suspended sentence.

The court may suspend imposition or execution of a more severe, statutorily permissible sentence with the provision that the juvenile meet certain conditions agreed to by him or her and specified in the sentencing order. Such conditions should not exceed, in severity or duration, the maximum sanction permissible for the offense.

B. Financial.
   1. Restitution.
   a. Restitution should be directly related to the juvenile's offense, the actual harm caused, and the juvenile's ability to pay.

   b. The means to carry out a restitution order should be available.

   c. Either full or partial restitution may be ordered.

   d. Repayment may be required in a lump sum or in installments.

   e. Consultation with victims may be encouraged but not required. Payments may be made directly to victims, or indirectly, through the court.

   f. The juvenile's duty of repayment should be limited in duration; in no event should the time necessary for repayment exceed the maximum term permissible for the offense.

   2. Fine.
   a. Imposition of a fine is most appropriate in cases where the juvenile has derived monetary gain from the offense.

    b. The amount of the fine should be directly related to the seriousness of the juvenile's offense and the juvenile's ability to pay.

    c. Payment of a fine may be required in a lump sum or installments.

    d. Imposition of a restitution order is preferable to imposition of a fine.

    e. The juvenile's duty of payment should be limited in duration; in no event should the time necessary for payment exceed the maximum term permissible for the offense.

    3. Community service.

    a. In sentencing a juvenile to perform community service, the judge should specify the nature of the work and the number of hours required.

    b. The amount of work required should be related to the seriousness of the juvenile's offense.

    c. The juvenile's duty to perform community service should be limited in duration; in no event should the duty to work exceed the maximum term permissible for the offense.

C. Supervisory.
    1. Community supervision.

    The court may sentence the juvenile to a program of community supervision, requiring him or her to report at specified intervals to a probation officer or other designated individual and to comply with any other reasonable conditions that are designed to facilitate supervision and are specified in the sentencing order.

    2. Day custody.

    The court may sentence the juvenile to a program of day custody, requiring him or her to be present at a specified place for all or part of every day or of certain days. The court also may require the juvenile to comply with any other reasonable conditions that are designed to facilitate supervision and are specified in the sentencing order.

D. Remedial.
    1. Remedial programs.

    The court may sentence the juvenile to a community program of academic or vocational education or counseling, requiring him or her to attend sessions designed to afford access to opportunities for normal growth and development. The duration of such programs should not exceed the maximum term permissible for the offense.

    2. Prohibition of coercive imposition of certain programs.

    This standard does not permit the coercive imposition of any program that may have harmful effects. Any such program should comply with the requirements of Standard 4.3 concerning informed consent.

In the Matter of GERALD B.

California Court of Appeal, 1980.
105 Cal.App.3d 119, 164 Cal.Rptr. 193.

RACANELLI, PRESIDING JUSTICE.

This appeal raises two issues: (1) whether a juvenile court may impose regular school attendance as a condition of probation following a wardship adjudication under section 602 of the Welfare and Institutions Code; and (2) whether such condition may validly require summary detention in the event of noncompliance. We conclude that while school attendance is an appropriate condition of probation, its violation may not be summarily enforced.

On February 28, 1979, Gerald, then 16 years of age, was adjudicated a ward of the court pursuant to the provisions of section 602. The offense charged was petty theft (a bottle of whiskey). On March 14, 1979, a dispositional hearing was held. The probation report considered by the court revealed prior contacts with authorities for curfew violation and public intoxication as well as an unspecified criminal charge pending in another jurisdiction; the report further disclosed a record of irregular school attendance and marked academic underachievement. The probation department recommended that Gerald be placed on formal probation for a period of six months in the custody of his mother, subject to alcohol abuse and family counseling and regular school attendance pursuant to a "special school order" imposing limited juvenile hall confinement in the event of one or more unexcused school absences. Following declaration of wardship, the juvenile court placed Gerald on probation subject to the recommended conditions, including the questioned order.[28] In granting probation, the court stated that the special order would become self-executing without further hearing.

At a subsequent hearing clarifying the manner in which the order would be enforced, it was established that the probation department routinely monitored similar orders by periodically contacting the schools involved and obtaining a list of those affected juveniles with unexcused absences. In the event of such absence, the juvenile is advised to spend the following weekend in juvenile hall; if there has been a second absence, the juvenile is arrested and—without benefit of prior notice to counsel (if any) or hearing—taken directly to juvenile hall to spend the remainder of the week. The parents are routinely notified and responsible for providing any existing medical excuse.

Gerald renews his challenge below based upon the statutory and constitutional grounds discussed herein.

* * *

[28] The challenged order provides: "SPECIAL SCHOOL ORDER: If you cut all or any part of a school day without a valid doctor's excuse, you will spend the following weekend in Juvenile Hall. Further, if you cut all or any part of a school day more than once during the week, you will spend the remainder of the week plus the weekend in Juvenile Hall."

Validity of School Attendance as a Probation Condition

Gerald first argues that the special order conflicts with the statutory scheme implementing a preliminary school board review of habitual truancy. (§§ 601, subd. (b), 601.1; Ed.Code, § 48263.) The argument must be rejected.

While it is relatively clear that truants are no longer subject to the original jurisdiction of the juvenile court under the amended provisions of section 601 * * * the basis of wardship jurisdiction herein was not Gerald's truancy but rather the determination of a *penal* violation under the provisions of section 602—a wholly independent basis of jurisdiction. * * * Thus, the statutory directives of prior referral to the local school attendance review board are inapplicable.

Upon an adjudication of wardship under section 602, the court may place the juvenile in parental custody subject to the supervision of the probation officer (see §§ 727, 730) and may impose "any and all reasonable conditions that it may determine fitting and proper" in the interests of justice and successful rehabilitation (§ 730; cf. Pen. Code, § 1203.1). Such a condition is valid and enforceable unless it bears no reasonable relationship to the underlying offense or prohibits conduct neither itself criminal in nature nor related to future criminality. * * * In light of the minor's history of irregular school attendance, his disobedience of a previous court order to enroll in school and the fact that the theft occurred during normal school hours, we conclude that the section 602 probation order requiring school attendance was both "fitting and proper" and reasonably calculated to serve the ends of justice and to enhance the likelihood of "reformation and rehabilitation of the ward." (§ 730; cf. § 731 [mandatory professional counseling]; Health & Saf.Code, §§ 11373 and 11376 [compulsory attendance in educational programs by narcotics offender].) Nor does Gerald contend otherwise.

Gerald next argues that the special order violates the statutory provision prohibiting locked detention for noncriminal conduct. (§ 207, subd. (b).) [29] He argues that the net effect of the order is to convert a section 601 status offense into a section 602 criminal offense by impermissibly "bootstrapping" an unexcused school absence into a punishable violation. * * * We find the argument unconvincing.

The limitation on secured detention contained in section 207, subdivision (b) applies where the minor is "taken into custody *solely*

---

[29] Section 207, subdivision (b) provides in pertinent part:

"Notwithstanding the provisions of subdivision (a), no minor shall be detained in any jail, lockup, juvenile hall, or other secure facility who is taken into custody solely upon the ground that he is a person described by Section 601 or adjudged to be such or made a ward of the juvenile court solely upon that ground, except as provided in subdivision (c). If any such minor, other than a minor described in subdivision (c), is detained, he shall be detained in a sheltered-care facility or crisis resolution home as provided for in Section 654, or in a nonsecure facility provided for in subdivision (a), (b), (c), or (d) of Section 727."

upon the ground that he is a person described by Section 601 or adjudged to be such or made a ward of the juvenile court *solely* upon that ground, * * *'' (Emphasis added.) As noted, Gerald was made a ward of the court by virtue of his criminal conduct under section *602;* his potential confinement to juvenile hall arises not from the fact of truancy alone, but as the result of a condition of probation stemming from such criminal conduct. And it is generally recognized that there is no legal impediment to the imposition of brief periods of juvenile hall detention *as a condition of probation* in section 602 proceedings.

*   *   *

Summary Enforcement

Gerald's principal challenge is directed to the provisions of the order calling for summary detention in juvenile hall on account of a reported absence from school. Relying upon an analogy to establish principles applicable to revocation proceedings (see Gagnon v. Scarpelli (1973) 411 U.S. 778, 93 S.Ct. 1756, 36 L.Ed.2d 656; Morrissey v. Brewer (1972) 408 U.S. 471, 92 S.Ct. 2593, 33 L.Ed.2d 484; People v. Vickers (1973) 8 Cal.3d 451), Gerald claims that the self-executing order invoking automatic confinement without opportunity for hearing is in flagrant disregard of fundamental principles of due process. The analogy is misplaced since the potential confinement herein is based not upon probation *revocation* or modification proceedings but upon the summary *implementation* of a condition involving an otherwise appropriate subject matter of probation. Yet the *effect* of such implementation resulting in a term of involuntary confinement with almost mechanical certitude solely by reason of an uncharged, unproved and noncriminal act is of doubtful validity.[30] * * * Had the order of probation been limited to compulsory school attendance without more, the prescribed statutory procedure in the event of noncompliance would have been a modification or revocation proceeding "subject to * * * procedural requirements" (§ 775), including the filing of a supplemental petition and a noticed hearing to determine whether the previous order of disposition has proven ineffectual. * * * Moreover, if the juvenile court thereafter concluded that probation should be revoked, the court would have been expressly prohibited from ordering the minor's *commitment* to the county juvenile hall unless a less restrictive facility was unavailable. * * * Thus, the special order would operate to completely circumvent the statutory procedural requirements by triggering *automatic* juvenile hall confinement merely upon a reported unexcused absence from school. Such summary disposition and resultant incarceration would indirectly nullify the legislative intent that juvenile hall detention be employed as a last resort (§ 730) and in principle would tend to frustrate the parallel legislative scheme which accords prior non-

---

[30] Conceivably, both the recalcitrant truant as well as the minor who possessed other plausible explanations justifying any absences nonetheless could be peremptorily subjected to periodic detention throughout the entire term of probation.

custodial treatment to habitual truants. * * * We therefore conclude that the challenged order, insofar as it purports to authorize automatic confinement in the county juvenile hall simply upon a reported school absence without medical excuse, is invalid and must be stricken.

We reverse and remand for such further proceedings as may be appropriate consistent with the views expressed herein.

NEWSOM and GRODIN, JJ., concur.

IN RE LITDELL

Supreme Court of Mississippi, 1970.
232 So.2d 733.

SMITH, JUSTICE. This is an appeal from an order of the Youth Court of Montgomery County revoking the probation of John Henry Litdell, a delinquent minor.

In May of 1968, the court had adjudged Litdell to be a delinquent within the meaning of Mississippi Code 1942 Annotated section 7185–09 (1952). He was not discharged but was placed on probation, in the custody of his mother.

In February of 1969, The District Attorney for Montgomery County petitioned the court to revoke Litdell's probation upon the grounds that he had failed to report, as required by the court's earlier decree, and that he had committed acts which would have constituted felonies if done by an adult. It developed that the requirement for reporting had been withdrawn and that charge was not considered and was not a factor in subsequent proceedings.

The matter was set for hearing on March 31, 1969, but on that date Litdell's mother informed the court that they were without counsel. The hearing was postponed and set for April 17, 1969, in order to afford them an opportunity to employ an attorney.

On April 2, 1969, 15 days prior to the date set for the hearing, the mother reported to the court that she and her son had been unable to obtain funds with which to employ counsel and were indigent; whereupon the court appointed a member of the Montgomery County Bar to represent them.

On April 17, 1969, the court convened for the purpose of conducting the hearing. Before the hearing commenced, Litdell's counsel moved to have the petition made more definite and certain and this motion was sustained. An amended petition was filed, after which the attorney announced ready, and an evidentiary hearing ensued. At the conclusion of the evidence and argument of counsel, the court revoked Litdell's probation and directed that he be sent to a state training school.

The principal arguments advanced by appellant for reversal are (1) Litdell and his mother did not have adequate notice of the April 17 hearing; and (2) no violation was shown of any condition set forth in Litdell's probation.

As to the first of these contentions, appellant relies upon In re Gault, 387 U.S. 1, 87 S.Ct. 1428, 18 L.Ed.2d 527 (1967). In an article in Note, Constitutional Law—Application of Basic Constitutional Guarantees to Juveniles, 39 Miss.L.J. 121, 129 (1967), the author points out that the requirement of notice in Mississippi Youth Court proceedings antedates *Gault.* In *Gault* there had been a flagrant omission of notice. In the present case, the petition was filed 48 days prior to the actual hearing on the merits. The youth and his mother attended on March 31, the date originally set, and the case was passed to April 17 to allow them to obtain the services of counsel. On April 2, these people reported to the court that they had been unable financially to employ an attorney to contest the petition, and were indigent. The court then appointed an attorney for them. This was 15 days before the hearing, which had been scheduled previously for April 17.

When the court convened on April 17, after counsel for Litdell had obtained an amendment making the petition more definite and certain, he announced ready, and the hearing proceeded without objection.

Due process requires only that *reasonable* notice be given.
 *   *   *

The presence of the mother and youth at the April 17 hearing was the third time that they had appeared before the court in connection with the petition to revoke Litdell's probation, having been present on March 31, the date on which the matter had been set originally, on which date the case was continued and set for April 17, and again on April 2, when appointment of counsel had been obtained. The attorney had been appointed 15 days prior to the hearing, and the record leaves no doubt that he gave appellant vigorous, conscientious and capable representation throughout. Following his appointment, the attorney had 15 days within which to investigate and prepare the case. In announcing ready, it must be assumed that he did so advisedly, and with the understanding that the hearing would proceed. We do not think that, under the circumstances, there was a denial of due process because of inadequate notice.

As to the second ground urged for reversal, that no violation of a condition of the probation was shown, it is conceded that there had been no violation of any express condition.

The court's view, expressed in its opinion, was that "if, in misbehaving as the undisputed record shows (Litdell) did since May of last year, he did not violate any written parole or probationary condition, the court considers that it is implicit in every order wherein it is not explicit, that if the child is paroled, he is paroled for some reason, and not discharged; and that if he is paroled *   *   * there is the meaning that there may be another day *   *   * as long as he was on parole and not discharged, the court would have the authority to revoke the parole and to do something else for the boy's good as long as it was justified, in the court's opinion, by proof of the boy's misconduct."

Appellant's position, however, is that since there had been no violation of any express condition of his probation, and he had not actually been convicted of any criminal offense, the court was without power to revoke the probation or to change its conditions.

The State's response to this proposition is, in effect, that the youth court's probation of any youth adjudged to be a delinquent carries with it an implied condition of good behavior.

The principle of implied conditions is well grounded in the law. For example, in Note, Legal Aspects of Probation Revocation, 59 Colum.L.Rev. 311, 315 (1959), there is a discussion of implied conditions in cases of probation:

> Further, it seems clear that some minimal restraints on a probationer's behavior may be implied in the nature and purposes of the probation system. *Thus, courts have found implied conditions that the probationer must not commit a felony and that he must obey reasonable directions and orders of the trial judge or a probation officer. Apparently, conditions are implied only as to conduct which the probationer clearly should have realized might result in revocation.* (Emphasis added).

In People v. Perez, 243 Cal.App.2d 528, 52 Cal.Rptr. 514, 517 (1966) the California court relied on implied conditions:

> Although the terms and conditions of the probation order are not disclosed by the record, *it is an implicit condition of every such order that the probationer refrain from engaging in any criminal activity or becoming "abandoned to improper associates or a vicious life."* (Emphasis added).

The proof here showed that Litdell, while on probation, had been taken into custody on numerous occasions by law officers in connection with various acts of misconduct, which included "car prowling," shoplifting, two incidents of assault and battery, and creating a public disturbance.

It is to be borne in mind that the Mississippi Youth Court Act [Mississippi Code 1942 Annotated section 7185–09 (Supp.1968)] provides that disposition of the child, *after adjudication*, is made by the court upon the basis of an *investigation*.

> In all cases, *after the adjudication thereof*, whenever it may appear for the best interest of said child so to do, *and after an investigation concerning said child has been made*, and subject to such conditions and supervision as the court may order, *the court may change the custody of said child*, or may dismiss the petition, or may terminate its jurisdiction over said child. (Emphasis added).

Obviously, the youth court might have directed the placement of Litdell in a training school at the time of his adjudication as a delinquent. The court did not do this. But neither did the court "terminate its jurisdiction." Rather, the court imposed the least restraint and the mildest supervision upon Litdell in the hope that this would be sufficient. The youth court's jurisdiction of youth adjudged to be delinquent is a continuing one, with a continuing power to alter the terms of the probation if, in the interests of the child, the original arrangement proves inadequate or to have been ill advised. Without this flexibility the court no longer would be in such an advantageous position to give a delinquent youth "another chance" as an initial measure, at least, by granting probation upon terms of the least possible restraint and the mildest supervision as was done in this case.

We have concluded that, under the circumstances in the record, appellant was not denied due process and that the court had jurisdiction, as well as power, to alter the arrangement originally made in order to provide necessary supervision and control of appellant, the original arrangement having proven inadequate in both respects.

Affirmed.

NEW YORK—McKINNEY'S FAMILY COURT ACT 1983

§ 757. Probation

(a) Rules of court shall define permissible terms and conditions of probation.

(b) The maximum period of probation shall not exceed one year. If the court finds at the conclusion of the original period that exceptional circumstances require an additional year of probation, the court may continue probation for an additional year.

IN THE MATTER OF WESTBROOKS

Supreme Court of South Carolina, 1982.
277 S.C. 410, 288 S.E.2d 395.

PER CURIAM:

Appellant was adjudicated delinquent as a result of a shoplifting charge filed against her in Family Court. The judge ordered her to perform thirty (30) hours of community service and placed her on indefinite probation. Appellant contends the lower court erred by placing her on indefinite probation. We disagree and affirm.

Section 14–21–620 of the 1976 Code sets forth the alternative dispositions available to a family court judge after a minor has been adjudicated delinquent. When a child is adjudicated delinquent by the Family Court, he may be punished only as prescribed by the Family Court Act. In re Skinner, 272 S.C. 135, 249 S.E.2d 746 (1978).

According to Section 14–21–620, the court may place the child on probation or under supervision in his own home or in the custody of a suitable person, upon such conditions as the court may determine. Section 14–21–620 further provides that probation shall be ordered and administered as a measure for the protection, guidance and well-being of the child and his family.

The family court is vested with broad discretion in imposing the conditions of probation. 43 C.J.S. Infants Section 78(b) (1978). The length of the probationary period constitutes a condition of probation within the lower court's discretion. We find no abuse of that discretion. Clearly, the court could not impose probation to extend beyond appellant's twenty-first birthday because the jurisdiction of the Family Court terminates when a child becomes twenty-one. See Section 14–21–510 S.C.Code of Laws (1976, as amended). Therefore, the probationary period would end on appellant's twenty-first birthday.

While we find no abuse of discretion in this instance, we are of the opinion that the better practice would be to set a definite period of probation. The order of the lower court is affirmed.

NOTES

1. May a juvenile delinquent be placed on probation for a longer term than an adult who committed the offense which supported the adjudication of delinquency? In In re John R., 92 Cal.App.3d 566, 155 Cal.Rptr. 78 (1979), the court distinguished the leading California case of People v. Olivas, 17 Cal.3d 236, 131 Cal.Rptr. 55, 551 P.2d 375 (1976), [discussed in In re Eric J., supra chapter 1, and in State v. J.K., infra this chapter] on the ground that "being home on probation" involves "no such deprivation of liberty" as is involved in physical confinement.

2. In In re L.L.W., 626 S.W.2d 261 (Mo.App.1981), the court reversed an order of "shock probation"—confinement in the county jail for a period of seven days—as illegal "for whatever time or reason."

3. Suppose a young woman adjudicated a juvenile delinquent had imposed as a condition of probation that she submit to "deprogramming" and that she avoid any contact with members of the religious cult of which she was a member when she engaged in the conduct that resulted in the delinquency adjudication. The entire opinion in In the Matter of A.H., a/k/a M.J., 459 A.2d 1045 (D.C.App.1983), follows:

Before KELLY, NEBEKER and FERREN, ASSOCIATE JUDGES.

JUDGMENT

PER CURIAM.

This appeal, taken pursuant to D.C.Code § 16–2328 (1981), came on for consideration on the pleadings of the respective parties and was argued by counsel. The appeal is from an order releasing the child into the custody of a parent plus a condition, imposed to protect the child's best interests, that he stay away from the Islamic Center at 2500 Massachusetts Avenue, N.W. (where he was arrested in connection with recent incidents of violence). Appellant's contention is that the stay-away order violates the First Amendment to the Constitution of the United States. On consideration of the foregoing, it is

Ordered and Adjudged that the order on review be, and hereby is, affirmed. See Brown v. Fogel, 387 F.2d 692, 696 (4th Cir.1967).

b. OTHER FORMS OF COMMUNITY DISPOSITIONS

WEST'S REVISED CODE WASHINGTON ANN.

13.40.020. Definitions

For the purposes of this chapter:

* * *

(2) "Community service" means compulsory service, without compensation, performed for the benefit of the community by the offender as punishment for committing an offense;

(3) "Community supervision" means an order of disposition by the court of an adjudicated youth. A community supervision order for a single offense may be for a period of up to one year and include one or more of the following:

(a) A fine, not to exceed one hundred dollars;

(b) Community service not to exceed one hundred fifty hours of service;

(c) Attendance of information classes;

(d) Counseling; or

(e) Such other services to the extent funds are available for such services, conditions, or limitations as the court may require which may not include confinement;

* * *

(17) "Restitution" means financial reimbursement by the offender to the victim, and shall be limited to easily ascertainable damages for injury to or loss of property, actual expenses incurred for medical treatment for physical injury to persons, and lost wages resulting from physical injury. Restitution shall not include reimbursement for damages for mental anguish, pain and suffering, or other intangible losses. Nothing in this chapter shall limit or replace civil remedies or defenses available to the victim or offender;

* * *

13.40.190. Disposition order—Restitution for loss—Waiver or modification of restitution

(1) In its dispositional order, the court shall require the respondent to make restitution to any persons who have suffered loss or damage as a result of the offense committed by the respondent. In addition, restitution may be ordered for loss or damage if the offender pleads guilty to a lesser offense or fewer offenses and agrees with the prosecutor's recommendation that the offender be required to pay restitution to a victim of an offense or offenses which, pursuant to a plea agreement, are not prosecuted. The payment of restitution shall be in addition to any punishment which is imposed pursuant to the other provisions of this chapter. The court may determine the amount, terms, and conditions of the restitution. If the respondent participated in the crime with another person or other persons, all such participants shall be jointly and severally responsible for the payment of restitution. The court may not require the respondent to

pay full or partial restitution if the respondent reasonably satisfies the court that he or she does not have the means to make full or partial restitution and could not reasonably acquire the means to pay such restitution. In cases where an offender has been committed to the department for a period of confinement exceeding fifteen weeks, restitution may be waived.

(2) A respondent under obligation to pay restitution may petition the court for modification of the restitution order.

13.40.200. Violation of order of restitution, community supervision, fines, penalty assessments, or confinement—Modification of order after hearing—Scope—Rights—Use of fines

(1) When a respondent fails to comply with an order of restitution, community supervision, penalty assessments, or confinement of less than thirty days, the court upon motion of the prosecutor or its own motion, may modify the order after a hearing on the violation.

(2) The hearing shall afford the respondent the same due process of law as would be afforded an adult probationer. The court may issue a summons or a warrant to compel the respondent's appearance. The state shall have the burden of proving by a preponderance of the evidence the fact of the violation. The respondent shall have the burden of showing that the violation was not a wilful refusal to comply with the terms of the order. If a respondent has failed to pay a fine, penalty assessments, or restitution or to perform community service hours, as required by the court, it shall be the respondent's burden to show that he or she did not have the means and could not reasonably have acquired the means to pay the fine, penalty assessments, or restitution or perform community service.

(3)(a) If the court finds that a respondent has wilfully violated the terms of an order pursuant to subsections (1) and (2) of this section, it may impose a penalty of up to thirty days confinement.

(b) If the violation of the terms of the order under (a) of this subsection is failure to pay fines, penalty assessments, complete community service, or make restitution, the term of confinement imposed under (a) of this subsection shall be assessed at a rate of one day of confinement for each twenty-five dollars or eight hours owed.

(4) If a respondent has been ordered to pay a fine or monetary penalty and due to a change of circumstance cannot reasonably comply with the order, the court, upon motion of the respondent, may order that the unpaid fine or monetary penalty be converted to community service. The number of hours of community service in lieu of a monetary penalty or fine shall be converted at the rate of the prevailing state minimum wage per hour. The monetary penalties or fines collected shall be deposited in the county general fund. A failure to comply with an order under this subsection shall be deemed a failure to comply with an order of community supervision and may be proceeded against as provided in this section.

STATE IN THE INTEREST OF D.G.W.

Supreme Court of New Jersey, 1976.
70 N.J. 488, 361 A.2d 513.

Hughes, C.J.

D.G.W., a juvenile, was charged with participating in 1973 and 1974 with three others in four instances of breaking and entering certain residences and school buildings and with theft and destruction of property therein worth thousands of dollars. If found guilty of these offenses, D.G.W. could be adjudicated a juvenile delinquent and incur statutory sanctions under N.J.S.A. 2A:4–14 et seq., now N.J. S.A. 2A:4–42 et seq.

Pleas of guilty to three of the charges were entered by agreement and one charge was dismissed.

The Juvenile and Domestic Relations Court judge placed the appellant on probation for one year, which he had authority to do under the statute, N.J.S.A. 2A:4–61(c). He determined, over the objection of defense counsel, to apply as a condition to such grant of probation the making of restitution to a victim of the offense.

The court ordered that the specific amount of restitution (as related to the damages caused by the juvenile misdeeds) be "worked out" with the probation department of the county. The judge further announced his availability to settle any dispute.

Thereafter (as indicated in an expanded record ordered by the Appellate Division), the probation department assembled a list of specific items of damage at one of the school buildings totaling $626. Since four individuals had taken part in the depredations, D.G.W. was ordered to be responsible for one-fourth of the total damage or $156.50. This pro rata distribution did not originate with the Court, but was suggested by the probation department. The estimated values of the damaged items of property were "based on the cost of repairing damaged machines plus the cost of materials and overtime estimated by their maintenance supervisor for damages to the building." No further verification of the amounts was requested by any of the four culprits. Accordingly D.G.W. neither requested nor received a hearing which would have permitted him to challenge the probation department's determination of the amount of restitution in his case.

Having failed to convince the Juvenile and Domestic Relations Court of its lack of jurisdictional authority to order restitution, D.G.W. appealed to the Appellate Division. While his appeal was pending there unheard, we granted certification, 68 N.J. 497, 348 A.2d 538 (1975), primarily to examine the jurisdictional capacity *vel non* of the court to attach a condition of restitution to a probationary term granted a juvenile offender. Should that question be answered in the affirmative, the further question arises as to the due process rights of the juvenile incident to determination of the extent and terms of the restitution order.

The Attorney General joined as *amicus* to assist the Court in deciding the primary question of the power and jurisdiction of the Juvenile and Domestic Relations Court to order restitution in such manner, particularly in view of this Court's decisions in State v. Mulvaney, 61 N.J. 202, 293 A.2d 668 (1972) and State in Interest of M.L., 64 N.J. 438, 317 A.2d 65 (1974). In *Mulvaney* the defendant was ordered to pay as a condition of probation one-fourth of the State's prosecution expenses. This Court vacated the imposition of these cost, *qua* costs, under N.J.S.A. 2A:168–2, to the extent that they exceeded the amounts allowed under the specific statute dealing with costs in criminal causes, N.J.S.A. 22A:3–1 to 6. And this result was reached in the face of a statutory authorization to a court, N.J. S.A. 2A:168–2, to include as a condition of probation that the probationer " * * * shall pay a fine or the costs of the prosecution, or both, * * *." This Court was unable to find in such language " * * * a grant of authority to *originate* a liability for costs which is not authorized by another statute." State v. Mulvaney, supra, 61 N.J. at 204, 293 A.2d at 669 (emphasis added).

Following the doctrine of *Mulvaney*, Justice Sullivan wrote for this Court in *M.L.* that "the provision in the general probation and parole law authorizing a court to require *payment* of a fine as a condition of probation does not confer upon a court the power to *impose* a fine. It only authorizes the court to require payment of a fine as a condition of probation where a fine is otherwise provided for by law. This is clear from our decision in State v. Mulvaney * * *." State in Interest of M.L., supra, 64 N.J. at 443, 317 A.2d at 67 (emphasis in original). And since the Legislature had never provided for the imposition of a fine on a juvenile offender, this Court determined that the Juvenile and Domestic Relations Court had no power to impose one, even as a condition of probation.

The bases of the holdings in *Mulvaney* and *M.L.* were primarily matters of statutory interpretation. In *Mulvaney* the Court recognized that the broad terms of N.J.S.A. 2A:168–2 must be read *in pari materia* with the statutory limitation on costs in criminal causes reflected in N.J.S.A. 22A:3–1 to 6. In *M.L.*, the Court was unable to discern in the legislative plan with regard to the correction of juveniles a source of the power to impose a fine as a condition of probation or otherwise. *Contra*, the power to commit to an institution or make other disposition authorized by statute. N.J.S.A. 2A:4–61.

The omission by the Legislature of the sanction of a fine against a juvenile offender seems clearly responsive to the general legislative purpose. Fines are essentially punitive in nature, State v. DeBonis, 58 N.J. 182, 192, 276 A.2d 137 (1972), whereas the statutory policy with respect to juveniles is to correct and rehabilitate rather than punish. * * *

* * *

It is against this background that we must determine the threshold question;—whether restitution in its broad sense, including the concept of reparation, may be a valid condition of probation imposed upon a juvenile offender;—or whether it, in essence, would come within the Court's reasoning in *Mulvaney* and *M.L.*, supra, as being discordant with the legislative purpose.

Beyond the validity of the restitution condition itself and the procedural due process necessary for the determination of the extent and terms of restitution to be made, are subsumed other questions raised by appellant. Where several participants are involved in a joint act of theft or vandalism, and all are required to make restitution, is a *pro rata* distribution of its burden appropriate? What is the relationship between indigency or ability to make restitution and the enforceability of the remedy of compelling restitution? What is the status of such remedy in the face of actual or potential claim for such damages in a civil action?

I.

As to the disposition of juvenile delinquency cases, the statute provides:

N.J.S.A. 2A:4–61. *Disposition of delinquency cases.*

If a juvenile is adjudged delinquent the juvenile and domestic relations court may order any of the following dispositions:

* * *

c. Place the juvenile on probation to the chief probation officer of the county or to any other suitable person who agrees to accept the duty of probation supervision for a period not to exceed 3 years *upon such written conditions as the court deems will aid rehabilitation of the juvenile;* or

* * *

i. Such other disposition not inconsistent with this act as the court may determine. [emphasis added].

The general statute dealing with the power of courts to suspend sentence and place offenders on probation provides:

N.J.S.A. 2A:168–1. *Power of courts to suspend sentence and place on probation; period of probation.*

* * *

The courts having jurisdiction over juvenile or domestic relations cases, when it shall appear that the best interests of the public as well as of the person adjudged guilty of any offense * * * before such court will be subserved thereby, shall have power to place the defendant on probation for a period of not less than 1 year nor more than 5 years. Such courts shall also have the power to place on probation under the same conditions children who shall come within the jurisdiction of the court.

* * *

The statute authorizing the fixing of conditions of probation provides:

N.J.S.A. 2A:168–2. *Conditions of probation.*

The court shall determine and may, at any time, modify the conditions of probation, and may, among others, include any of the following: That the probationer shall avoid injurious, immoral or vicious habits; shall avoid places or persons of disreputable or harmful character; shall report to the probation officer as directed by the court or probation officer; shall permit the probation officer to visit him at his place of abode or elsewhere; shall answer all reasonable inquiries on the part of the probation officer; shall work faithfully at suitable employment; shall not change his residence without the consent of the court or probation officer; shall pay a fine or the costs of the prosecution, or both, in one or several sums; *shall make reparation or restitution to the aggrieved parties for the damage or loss caused by his offense;* shall support his dependents. [emphasis added].

The court rule emphasizes, as does N.J.S.A. 2A:4–61, the rehabilitative purpose of probation:

R. 5:9–3. *Manner of Disposition.*

The court may make the following disposition of juvenile matters:

*   *   *

(2) Make an adjudication and

*   *   *

(C) Place the juvenile on probation to the chief probation officer of the county or to any other suitable person who agrees to accept the duty of probation supervision upon such *written conditions as the court deems will aid rehabilitation of the juvenile;* [emphasis added].

It is thus apparent that the legislative purpose would accommodate reparation or restitution (for brevity we shall hereafter include both concepts within the term "restitution") as a probation condition. Given its viability as a rehabilitative tool, imposition of restitution would also be permitted under the court rule.

We are bound to think, then, that unless restitution has to be considered primarily as punishment and little or nothing else, and thus discordant with the legislative plan (*Monahan,* supra), its use as a condition of probation would not fall within the interdiction of *Mulvaney* or *M.L.,* supra, both of which holdings we re-affirm today.

The dichotomy of punitive and rehabilitative purpose and effect implicit in probation was recognized by Chief Justice Weintraub in In re Buehrer, 50 N.J. 501, 509, 236 A.2d 592, 596 (1967):

The argument assumes that punishment and rehabilitation are somehow incompatible. Of course they are not. * * * Punishment and rehabilitation are not antagonists.

Probation assumes the offender can be rehabilitated without serving the suspended jail sentence. But this is not to say that probation is meant to be painless. Probation has an inherent sting, and restrictions upon the freedom of the probationer are realistically punitive in quality. * * * Probation is meant to serve the overall public interest as well as the good of the immediate offender. Thus N.J.S.A. 2A:168–1 authorizes the use of probation "[w]hen it shall appear that the best interests of the public as well as of the defendant will be subserved thereby." [footnote omitted].

It is significant that the same test is expressed by the Legislature with regard to probation for the juvenile offender,—"when it shall appear that the best interests of the public as well as of the person adjudged guilty * * * will be subserved thereby * * *." And if probation is to be granted for the accomplishment of the rehabilitative goals outlined by the statute, we think it follows, unless otherwise interdicted, that restitution as a condition thereof must be weighed in the same balance. Restitution manifestly serves the interest of the public for it is not right that either victim or the public should bear the whole burden, let us say, of loss from extensive juvenile vandalism. *Quaere:* does an order for restitution so clearly disserve the "best interests" of the juvenile offender that it must be abandoned as a rehabilitative tool? We think not.

We again advert to the words of Chief Justice Weintraub who, concurring in State in Interest of Carlo, 48 N.J. 224, 244, 225 A.2d 110, 121 (1966), noted that "[t]he object of the juvenile process is to make men out of errant boys." That truism underlay the decision of the court in State in Interest of O.W., 110 N.J.Super. 465, 266 A.2d 142 (App.Div.1970), upholding the right of the Juvenile and Domestic Relations Court to impose against the juvenile offender an order for the support of his illegitimate child:

> Under the second point, O.W. states that the Juvenile and Domestic Relations Court is a creature of the Legislature, with limited powers and jurisdiction. He argues that the scope of disposition available to it with respect to a juvenile offender is limited by N.J.S.A. 2A:4–37 (probation or commitment to some institution or to the State Board of Child Welfare), and by N.J. S.A. 2A:4–39, which provides that no adjudication upon the status of a child under 18 "shall operate to impose any of the civil disabilities ordinarily imposed by conviction * * *." Therefore, since neither statute mentions support payment by a juvenile, the order below was improper.
>
> The argument is specious and reflects a very restricted view of the Juvenile and Domestic Relations Court's jurisdiction. That court clearly has the power to award support in a bastardy proceeding, N.J.S.A. 9:17–12, and the statutes *in pari materia* should be construed together as a "unitary and harmonious whole, in order that each may be fully effective." City of Clifton v. Passaic County Board of Taxation, 28 N.J. 411, 421, 147 A.2d 1 (1958). To deny the court the exercise of its inherent power would be to thwart the rehabilitative object of the juvenile process—"to make men out of errant boys." State in the Interest of Carlo, 48 N.J. 224, 244, 225 A.2d 110 (1966) (Weintraub,

C.J. concurring). Indeed, In re El, 26 N.J.Misc. 285, 290, 60 A.2d 893 (Cty.Ct.1948), held that the Juvenile and Domestic Relations Court has exclusive jurisdiction in a bastardy proceeding against a juvenile. [Id. at 468, 266 A.2d at 143].

Here we see no barrier to application of the rule that, as in *O.W.,* supra, whenever possible statutes should be considered *in pari materia* so that each may be given effect. As we have noted, N.J. S.A. 2A:168–2 specifically recognizes restitution as a valid condition of probation, and N.J.S.A. 2A:168–1 extends the probation concept to the juvenile offender, as does N.J.S.A. 2A:4–61. Likewise, the imposition of probation upon a juvenile offender, as upon an adult, is associated with "the best interests of the public as well as of the" offender. No disharmony in the statutes is apparent. If, then, one of the purposes of restitution is rehabilitation of the offender (and we think it is, as argued by much of the professional commentary on the subject [31]), we can determine the primary question.

We hold that a just and fair order as to restitution is a valid and may indeed be a salutary condition of a term of probation. In the case here reviewed the imposition of that condition was proper, but its effectuation, as we shall point out, was procedurally deficient.

II.

Having thus determined that imposition of restitution as a condition of probation is within the jurisdictional authority of the Juvenile

[31] "There would seem to be sound reasons for the stipulation [i.e., restitution] in given cases. It is not only that aggrieved persons are recompensed. Unlike a fine as a condition of probation, or service of a jail term prior to supervision, restitution has an understandable logic. It is directly related to the offense and the attitude of the offender. There is a reality involved: society does not sanction fraud or other forms of theft; it does not approve injury inflicted upon an innocent person. Society wants to make sure the offender realizes the enormity of his conduct, and it asks him to demonstrate this by making amends to the individual most affected by the defendant's depredations.

* * *

"Restitution may have a positive casework connotation. It offers the individual something within reason that he can do here and now, within the limits of his ability to demonstrate to *himself* that he is changing. A fine is punitive. A jail sentence is retributive. But restitution makes sense. It is every man's obligation to meet responsibilities of this sort in civil life." [D. Dressler, Practice and Theory of Probation and Parole 176–77 (1959) (emphasis in original)].

Similar sentiment is expressed elsewhere:

"Another common pecuniary condition of probation is the requirement that the probationer make restitution for the damage or injury caused by his crime. *It is necessary that the amount and other terms of restitution or reparation be fixed by the court* (or whatever agency is responsible for fixing the conditions); *this function may not be delegated to a probation officer.* The power to fix such a condition is generally upheld, although it is clearer where the statute specifically authorizes it. The restitution or reparation required may not go beyond the actual loss or damage as established in the prosecution and must be directly related to the crime. Restitution serves the purposes of rehabilitation, if used to support a healthy attitude by the offender. It also serves to restore the loss (although partially) to the victim of the crime. * * * When reparation is a condition of probation, it is part of the defendant's rehabilitative effort, not a sentence." [S. Rubin, the Law of Criminal Correction 200–01 (1963) (emphasis added) (footnotes omitted)].

Cf. a more skeptical view,—Comment, "Juvenile Probation: Restrictions, Rights and Rehabilitation," 16 St. Louis U.L.J. 276, 280 (1971).

and Domestic Relations Court, we now consider whether the procedure here followed violated the juvenile's right to due process of law. In this regard we must address two distinct questions: first, is the right of due process applicable here and second, if it is, what procedure must be followed to safeguard it. E.g., Morrissey v. Brewer, 408 U.S. 471, 481, 92 S.Ct. 2593, 2600, 33 L.Ed.2d 484, 494 (1972); Avant v. Clifford, 67 N.J. 496, 518–22, 341 A.2d 629 (1975).

At the outset we note the recent expansion of due process protections to liberty and property interests, some not previously thought to be so protected. * * * Essentially due process rights are found whenever an individual risks governmental exposure to a "grievous loss." * * *

In the case before us we need not pause to distinguish between the application of due process protections to property interests and to liberty interests since both are implicated where restitution is imposed as a condition of probation. The juvenile has an obvious "property" interest in his earnings or other income to be paid over in satisfaction of the restitutionary amount. Additionally he has an obvious "liberty" interest in his continued probationary "freedom" which is subject to termination upon his unjustified failure or refusal to meet the restitutionary condition.

We are satisfied that deprivation of these interests triggers the juvenile's entitlement to due process and it remains only to decide what process is due. Avant v. Clifford, supra, 67 N.J. at 522, 341 A.2d 629.

The requirements of due process are, of necessity, flexible, calling for such procedural protections as the situation demands. Simply put, "not all situations calling for procedural safeguards call for the same kind of procedure." Morrissey v. Brewer, supra, 408 U.S. at 481, 92 S.Ct. at 2600, 33 L.Ed.2d at 494. To determine the precise procedures to be followed in cases such as this and to give specific guidance to the Juvenile and Domestic Relations Court judges, we begin by looking at "the precise nature of the government function involved as well as * * * the private interest that has been affected by governmental action." Cafeteria & Restaurant Workers Local 473 v. McElroy, 367 U.S. 886, 895, 81 S.Ct. 1743, 1748–49, 6 L.Ed.2d 1230, 1236 (1961).

To protect his interest in his earnings and income and his interest in continued liberty the juvenile, minimally, is concerned about (1) the amount of damage he will be held responsible for, (2) the method of determining the value, (3) his pro rata share where several defendants are involved and (4) a reasonable method of repayment which realistically assesses his ability to pay.

Balanced against these concerns is the State's interest in maintaining a disposition procedure which, while always preserving the offender's right to be heard, is not unduly encumbered. We are satisfied that a balance can be struck short of a full-blown adversarial procedure, something more in the nature of a summary proceeding than in, for instance, the plenary hearing held necessary in State v.

Horne, 56 N.J. 372, 267 A.2d 1 (1970) to justify classification of a convicted criminal defendant to sentencing under the Sex Offender Act, N.J.S.A. 2A:164–3 et seq.

III.

Once the court decides to impose restitution as a condition of probation (and unless, of course, the extent of damages and responsibility therefor are admitted by the offender), it should direct the probation department to conduct an investigation of the incident(s) contained in the complaint in order to determine the nature and extent of personal or property damages or other losses (e.g. *financial*) which were caused by the offender. The results of this investigation would then be summarized in a report similar to a presentence report for use by the court in setting the terms of probation. In this regard, the probation department is merely acting as a factfinder and an extension of the power of the court. This role is in accord with its statutorily delineated responsibility. See N.J.S.A. 2A:168–3 and 11. However, the final decision on the amount of restitution to be made and the terms thereof is within the sole province of the trial judge. It is noted here that other courts have disapproved of judicial abdication of this function as an improper delegation of responsibility. E.g., People v. Gallagher, 55 Mich.App. 613, 223 N.W.2d 92 (1974); People v. Frink, 68 N.Y.S.2d 103 (Cty.Ct.1947); Cox v. State, 445 S.W.2d 200 (Tex.Cr.App.1969). Case law in New Jersey has similarly recognized this limitation on the delegation of the court's responsibility to the probation department in determining the amount of support payments in a divorce action, see Plath v. Plath, 99 N.J. Super. 394, 396, 240 A.2d 171 (App.Div.1968), and the principle is equally applicable to the case here. Therefore, the trial judge below should not have left the conditions of restitution entirely in the hands of the probation department.

Contained in the report shall be the method used for determining the value of the losses incurred. Any recognized method of valuation may be utilized including, but not restricted to, cost of repair or replacement, market value or other reliable indicia (e.g. appraisals). Where feasible, verification of this information shall be provided in the report in the form of affidavits from contractors, materialmen or suppliers of goods taken or destroyed containing the cost of repairs or replacement; alternatively where other measures of value are used, affidavits shall be provided which describe the basis for the value given.

Also pertinent is the amount of money which the offender can or will be able to pay. The probation statute, N.J.S.A. 2A:168–2, does not specify that that factor is to be considered by the trial court in setting the conditions of probation, although it has been made explicit in other states. * * *

Nonetheless other jurisdictions whose statutes (like ours) do not expressly list ability to pay as a consideration conduct hearings on this issue. * * * In any case, regardless of the procedural device relied upon, the principle seems settled that the statutory power to impose restitution as a condition of probation must be exercised reasonably. See People v. Tidwell, 33 Ill.App.3d 232, 338 N.E.2d 113 (1975); In Matter of Edwards, 18 N.C.App. 469, 197 S.E.2d 87 (1973). Therefore, in addition to the other information to be supplied, the probation department shall also furnish the court with sufficient details as to the offender's present and probable future ability to repay the damages caused, in order for it to properly fix the amount to be imposed.[32]

Prior to the time of the sentencing the contents of the probation report would be made available to the juvenile as in the case of a presentence report. State v. Kunz, 55 N.J. 128, 144–45, 259 A.2d 895 (1969). And at the sentencing hearing, the juvenile may object to any of the material statements of fact contained therein and may present such evidence on his own behalf as the trial judge in his discretion deems necessary to the proper resolution of the issue. Cf. Morrissey v. Brewer, 408 U.S. 471, 487, 92 S.Ct. 2593, 2603, 33 L.Ed.2d 484, 497–98 (1972). In *Morrissey*, Chief Justice Burger mentioned these minimum requirements of due process:

> (a) written notice of the claimed violations [relevant facts] * * *; (b) disclosure * * * of evidence * * *; (c) opportunity to be heard in person and to present witnesses and documentary evidence; (d) the right to confront and cross-examine adverse witnesses (unless the hearing officer specifically finds good cause for not allowing confrontation); (e) a "neutral and detached" hearing body * * * members of which need not be judicial officers or lawyers; and (f) a written statement by the factfinders as to the evidence relied on and reasons [for acting]. [Id. at 488–89, 92 S.Ct. at 2604, 33 L.Ed.2d at 498–99].

Further, the *Morrissey* court emphasized that there was "no thought to equate this [procedural pattern] to a criminal prosecution in any sense. It is a narrow inquiry; the process should be flexible enough to consider evidence including letters, affidavits, and other material that would not be admissible in an adversary criminal trial." Id. at 489, 92 S.Ct. at 2604, 33 L.Ed.2d at 499.

The utility and fairness of such flexibility are apparent when one considers the situation in the present appeal. Here a plea of guilty was entered by agreement, and with advice of counsel, to several charges of theft and vandalism involving thousands of dollars; a pro rata allocation of a small portion of that damage was charged against appellant in the amount of $156.50; no challenge was ever voiced to

---

[32] In fixing the terms of restitution, the court will be aware that, in case of later default, in no event may the juvenile offender be institutionalized, or probation be terminated, solely because of *inability* to pay. Cf. Tate v. Short, 401 U.S. 395, 91 S.Ct. 668, 28 L.Ed.2d 130 (1971); Williams v. Illinois, 399 U.S. 235, 90 S.Ct. 2018, 26 L.Ed.2d 586 (1970); State v. DeBonis, supra. Consequently a restitution order against a school boy, for instance, without any prospect of even part-time employment (particularly under present economic conditions) might be a meaningless gesture. The judge however, being mindful of the rehabilitation factor, might suggest a search for part-time employment as bearing on good faith amends.

the specification of such damage items nor request made for their verification. While, as we hold here, the juvenile should have had access to the summary type of hearing which we describe, it would be a true distortion of due process requirements for him to be able to insist upon the production for cross-examination of contractors, engineers, education department officials and other witnesses, particularly where there is not the slightest indication of denial of responsibility for the damage specified, nor of its extent.

This is not to say that under other circumstances the same flexibility should not be available to a judge conducting such a hearing. A vast amount of damage, let us say by vandalism, minor implication of the particular juvenile involved, perhaps his domination by a juvenile gang "leader" primarily responsible for the damage, or other factors would have to be considered by the court if projected. Thus even though the less implicated juvenile offender might be appropriately adjudged as delinquent, his relative culpability for the damage inflicted should be considered by the court.

The appellant raises for the first time on this appeal an objection to the pro rata assessment of damages against him as one of the four persons involved on the basis that there was no express finding that he was personally responsible for one-quarter of the damages. Although the appellant admitted committing the acts of vandalism alleged in the complaint and did not initially challenge the amount of reparation fixed by the probation department, we nonetheless will consider the viability of appellant's claim in view of our decision to remand for further proceedings below, as an aid to the trial judge in making his determination. While the issue of how to properly allocate repayment among multiple offenders in a (damages-type) criminal action or juvenile matter apparently has not previously arisen in this state, some courts which have considered restitutionary conditions have ordered joint and individual liability for all defendants. See, e.g., People v. Flores, 197 Cal.App.2d 611, 17 Cal.Rptr. 382, 385 (Dist.Ct.App.1961); People v. Peterson, 62 Mich.App. 258, 233 N.W.2d 250, 255–56 (Ct.App.1975). In People v. Kay, 36 Cal.App. 3d 759, 111 Cal.Rptr. 894 (Ct.App.1973), the court reversed a trial court order of a pro rata assessment of damages against five defendants arrested during a student demonstration. That decision is distinguishable since the record there indicated that 123 persons were involved in the demonstration, and 18 who were convicted in municipal court were not required to pay anything; nor was there any evidence that the defendants had damaged any property since they were convicted of assault. As indicated, the record here discloses that four persons participated in the vandalism of certain high school facilities and that D.G.W. admitted his role therein. In the circumstances here, had there been a summary hearing, the trial judge would not have been remiss in finding a rebuttable presumption of proportionate liability against the juvenile before him, with the proviso that the juvenile would be afforded the opportunity to challenge this assessment.   See People v. Scherr, 9 Wis.2d 418, 101 N.W.2d 77, 80–81 (1960).[33]

Moreover, in the summary type of hearing which we project the judge will not be unmindful that in imposing the sanctions of the law, consideration is to be given to the offender as well as the offense involved.   State v. Ward, 57 N.J. 75, 82, 270 A.2d 1 (1970);   State v. Ivan, 33 N.J. 197, 201–02, 162 A.2d 851 (1960).   Bearing in mind the rehabilitative purpose of probation restitution he may distinguish between culprit "A," let us say, existing in the most meager poverty, whose restitution, if any, will be rehabilitative because earned by the sweat of his brow;   whereas as to culprit "B," perhaps the scion of a wealthy and supportive family, the same restitution requirement would be meaningless as a rehabilitative tool.   In the latter case reparation in kind might be deemed more effective.   In any event, a judge must not by inadvertence forget the lesson of Anatole France's cynical observation, commenting upon

> the majestic equality of the laws, which forbid rich and poor alike to sleep under the bridges, to beg in the streets, and to steal their bread. ["Le Lys Rouge," 5 Works of Anatole France 91 (W. Stephens transl. 1924)].

Finally, regarding the possible exposure of the juvenile offender to damages in a civil suit, since any amount collected and paid a victim by the probation department would be set off, we regard this issue as *de minimis* in the present case.

We remand to the Juvenile and Domestic Relations Court for reestablishment of the restitution amount upon which appellant's probation was conditioned, and for the completion of proceedings not inconsistent with this opinion.

So ordered.

For remandment: CHIEF JUSTICE HUGHES, JUSTICES MOUNTAIN, SULLIVAN, PASHMAN, CLIFFORD and SCHREIBER and JUDGE CONFORD—7.

Opposed—None.

NOTES

1.   What if the court finds that a juvenile is not "in need of assistance, guidance, treatment, or rehabilitation" and, therefore, is not delinquent, but nonetheless orders that the juvenile make restitution to the victim of the breaking and entering?   In In re Herbert B., 58 Md.App. 24, 472 A.2d 95, 98 (1984), the Court of Special Appeals said:

> It is significant that Section 3–829(a) does *not* require, as a predicate for ordering restitution, that the child be adjudicated a delinquent, i.e., that the court make the second finding that the child is in need of court assistance, guidance, treatment or rehabilitation. The only prerequisite in this regard is a finding that he committed a delinquent act and that the property of another was stolen, dam-

---

[33] We do not wish to be understood as implying that there might not be circumstances justifying imposition upon multiple delinquents of a joint obligation to pay the entire amount, or some portion thereof, of the damage caused.

aged or destroyed. Those findings were made at the adjudicatory hearing, and the record reflects that there was sufficient evidence to support them. Therefore the court did not err in ordering the appellant to make restitution to the proprietor of the laundromat for the damage that had been done.

2. Are there circumstances under which reparation in kind would be more appropriate? Suppose the reparation consisted of replanting a flower bed vandalized by the delinquent? Would it be important (controlling) that the victim preferred either money restitution or some form of community service which avoided contact between the victim and the delinquent?

3. Suppose a statute authorizes a judgment of restitution against the parent of an adjudicated delinquent who has inflicted injury on his victim or who has damaged his victim's property during the commission of the delinquent act. In In re James D., 295 Md. 314, 455 A.2d 966 (1983), the Court of Appeals held that the Maryland statute paraphrased, supra, does not apply to a parent who does not have actual custody and control over the child at the time of the delinquent act. And in In re Arnold M., 298 Md. 515, 471 A.2d 313 (1984), the same court held merely because the state may stand *in loco parentis* does not mean that the state is a parent within the meaning of the statute.

4. The California Court of Appeals in People v. Timothy Walter E., 99 Cal.App.3d 349, 160 Cal.Rptr. 256 (1979), agreed with the New Jersey court in State in the Interest of D.G.W., supra, that the disposition could not take the form of a fine without specific statutory authorization. The student, at this point, should consider IJA–ABA Standard 3.2, supra, as well as West's Revised Code Washington Annotated § 13.40.200, supra.

5. The Kansas statute set out at the beginning of this section authorizes an order to "attend Counseling sessions as the court directs." But see IJA–ABA Standard 3.2.

6. In In the Matter of the Welfare of Erickson, 24 Wash.App. 808, 604 P.2d 513 (1979), the delinquent contended that forced community service authorized under the Washington statute constituted "involuntary servitude" in violation of the Thirteenth Amendment. The general rule is that involuntary servitude is permissible only for those convicted of a crime. Should the juvenile's contention be sustained?

2. DISPOSITIONS OUTSIDE THE COMMUNITY

Obviously more serious liberty interests are implicated when the disposition results in confinement outside the community. It should not be surprising, then, that special problems arise when that alternative is being considered. It is even more likely that special problems will arise if a determinate commitment scheme is used, a problem that will be exacerbated if information not normally known to the judge at adjudication is systematically made known to him at that time or if commitment is mandatory rather than discretionary.

Additionally special problems may arise with respect to secure confinement of so-called status offenders, especially outside the community. And once again the problem is exacerbated if status offenders are "mixed in" with persons adjudicated delinquents on the basis of conduct that would be criminal if engaged in by an adult. All of these issues are addressed in this section.

IN RE ALINE D.

Supreme Court of California, 1975.
14 Cal.3d 557, 121 Cal.Rptr. 817, 536 P.2d 65.

RICHARDSON, JUSTICE.   We consider the question whether a minor who has previously been adjudicated a ward of the juvenile court and then placed, with unsuccessful results, in various local treatment facilities, may thereafter be committed to the California Youth Authority ("CYA") despite the expressed doubt of the court, acting through its referee, that she would benefit from such a commitment.   The record before us reflects that the referee ordered the CYA commitment solely because there appeared to be no other available placement facility.   We have concluded that, under the existing statutory scheme, and particularly Welfare and Institutions Code section 734, the commitment was improper and, accordingly, that the cause should be remanded to the juvenile court for reconsideration.

We recite pertinent portions of the troubled history of the minor, Aline D.   At the time of her commitment to CYA, she was 16, her father was absent from the family home and her mother had rejected her.   She had an I.Q. of 67 and a behavioral history of assaultive conduct and association with juvenile gangs.   She was originally placed in a family treatment program at juvenile hall, for reasons not specified in the record.   This placement continued from February 23, 1972, to May 1, 1972, and, according to a probation report, was "singularly unsuccessful."   Thereafter, she was released to the care of her mother but, one week later, ran away from home.   An attempt was made to place her in a probation department community day-care program, but her limited intellectual potential disqualified her.   On September 25, 1972, Aline was placed at the McKinnon Girls Home in Los Angeles, but soon thereafter the Home reported that she was having "problems with stealing, shoplifting, * * * refusal to attend school," and was participating in a juvenile gang.   Her placement with the Home terminated a few weeks later when she was arrested following an incident at a high school campus.   Aline was returned to juvenile court on allegations that she had violated Education Code section 13560 (wilful insult and abuse of teacher) and Penal Code section 653g (unlawful loitering about a school).   Following a hearing, the first charge was sustained and, on November 10, 1972, Aline's wardship was continued and "suitable placement" ordered for her.

Thereafter, on November 20, 1972, Aline was placed at the Penny Lane residential school in Los Angeles where she remained for ten days after which time her placement was terminated for various reasons, including her use of marijuana, bullying of associates, and membership in a juvenile gang.

On December 14, 1972, Aline was placed at the Detroit Arms Home, where she remained until January 10, 1973.   Her placement there was terminated as a result of her "active association" with the gang. A probation report, describing the circumstances of her association with the gang, reported that Aline let in eight or nine boy members of the gang who thereafter took three or four girls and left for two days, causing considerable difficulties.

Aline was returned to juvenile hall, pending further efforts to place her. A report of the foregoing placement efforts summarizes as follows: "Since this current detention on January 10, 1973 all efforts to place minor have met with defeat. Placements are not willing to handle the kinds of behavior minor has displayed in former placements." The responsible placement coordinator indicated that Los Angeles County has had no facilities capable of coping with the minor other than the Las Palmas Girls School.

On February 13, 1973, Las Palmas rejected Aline as unsuitable, because of her record of "assaultive behavior." The Las Palmas officials by letter recommended a commitment to CYA "where she would have the structure she obviously needs and also vocational training." On March 1, 1973, the probation officer filed a supplemental petition in juvenile court, alleging that Aline is not acceptable for placement in Los Angeles County institutions or facilities.

On May 21, 1973, a hearing was held before a juvenile court referee. The referee heard testimony from Mrs. Holt, a probation officer, and considered the contents of her placement report as well as letters and evaluations from psychiatrists regarding Aline's situation. The officer described her investigation of all conceivable placements available to Aline, including her mother and potential foster parents. The investigation included seven different facilities. Each placement was found unsuitable for Aline, although Mrs. Holt learned that Penny Lane eventually planned to establish a "closed setting for girls." According to Mrs. Holt, Aline, as a "severely delinquent young girl," requires a "closed facility" (by which is meant one with locked doors and limited visitation privileges), similar to county camps available for the placement of delinquent boys. If Aline were male, rather than female, Mrs. Holt would have recommended a camp community placement rather than CYA.

The reports of two psychiatrists and a clinical psychologist were before the court but have not been filed with us. The record does, however, contain their recommendations that Aline not be committed to CYA. One psychiatrist stated his opinion that Aline is not truly delinquent and that involvement with more delinquent and criminally oriented youths may adversely influence her. Near the conclusion of the hearing, the referee noted his lack of options. He observed that Aline could not simply be left in juvenile hall, as that facility serves only as a temporary detention facility. He explained his reluctance to order the proceedings dismissed, for Aline's mother had refused to accept her, and Aline would be back "on the streets." He agreed with Aline's counsel that it would be "very unwise to commit this minor to the California Youth Authority for the sole reason that it does not seem that there is anything else." Moreover, the referee acknowledged that "The fact remains, nevertheless, that all agree, including two psychiatrists, a clinical psychologist, Mrs. Holt, *all agree that she's not an appropriate subject for commitment to the youth authority, but that it is being done only because that seems to be the only recourse.*" (Italics added.)

After suspending the hearing temporarily to determine whether Aline might be eligible for placement by the Department of Public Social Services, and after learning that such placement would be refused, the referee concluded that he must order Aline committed to CYA, since " * * * the only other alternative that seems available to me now would be to dismiss this case and turn this lady out in the street, and I'm not going to do that." Counsel's motion to dismiss the proceedings, and for a rehearing, were denied, and Aline was ordered committed to CYA. Aline appeals.

Although the referee, following the hearing, signed a written form which contained a printed "finding" to the effect that the ward probably would benefit from the CYA commitment, our review of the record, summarized above, leads us to conclude that the referee ordered Aline committed to CYA solely because there appeared to be no other suitable placement for her. The motivation of the referee appears in his conclusion that "it seems that we are powerless" to avoid a CYA commitment. As we will develop below the provisions of the Juvenile Court Law do not permit a CYA commitment under such circumstances.

Preliminarily, we note the provisions of Welfare and Institutions Code section 502, which express in broad terms the general purposes of the Juvenile Court Law. These are to "secure for each minor * * * such care and guidance, preferably in his own home, as will serve the * * * welfare of the minor and the best interests of the State; * * * and, when the minor is removed from his own family, to secure for him custody, care, and discipline as nearly as possible equivalent to that which should have been given by his parents." The Juvenile Court Law is to be liberally construed to carry out the foregoing purposes.

In specific amplification of the foregoing purposes and with particular reference to the matter before us, section 734 of the Welfare and Institutions Code provides that "No ward of the juvenile court shall be committed to the Youth Authority unless the judge of the court is *fully satisfied* that the mental and physical condition and qualifications of the ward are such as to render it *probable that he will be benefited* by the reformatory educational discipline or other treatment provided by the Youth Authority." (Italics added.)

The foregoing language makes it clear that a CYA commitment may not be made for the sole reason that suitable alternatives do not exist. Instead, the court must be "fully satisfied" that a CYA commitment probably will benefit the minor. In the instant case, the referee's in-court statements, far from indicating that he was "fully satisfied," disclosed instead a substantial *dissatisfaction* with a CYA commitment. The requirements of section 734 not having been met, the commitment order must be reversed.

The rationale underlying section 734 becomes clear upon consideration of certain other sections of the Juvenile Court Law pertaining to the disposition of juvenile court wards. A review of these sections discloses a carefully conceived pattern affording the juvenile court a wide variety of choices at the dispositional phase of juvenile proceedings. Thus, a minor adjudged a "dependent child" under section 600 as one needing parental care and control or being destitute, or mentally or physically deficient, or whose home is unfit, may, under section 727, be placed in the care of (a) some reputable person of good moral character, (b) some association organized to care for such minors, (c) the probation officer for purposes of placement, or (d) any other public agency organized to provide care for needy or neglected children.

If the child is adjudged a ward of the court under section 601 because he refuses parental authority, or is beyond parental control, or is a truant or in danger of leading an immoral life, " * * * the court may order any of the types of treatment referred to in Section 727, and as an additional alternative, may commit the minor to a juvenile home, ranch, camp or forestry camp. If there is no county juvenile home, ranch, camp or forestry camp within the county, the court may commit the minor to the county juvenile hall. * * * Such [a] ward may be committed to the Youth Authority only upon a proceeding for the modification of an order of the court conducted pursuant to the provisions of Section 777 [requiring the filing of a supplemental petition in order to change placement to CYA]." (Id., § 730.)

Finally, when a minor is adjudged a ward of the court under section 602, i.e., the minor has committed a criminal offense or having been adjudged a ward under section 601 fails to obey an order of the juvenile court, " * * * the court may order any of the types of treatment referred to in Sections 727 and 730, and as an additional alternative, may commit the minor to the Youth Authority."

We may assume that Aline's wardship presently derives from a finding, under section 602, that she had either committed a criminal offense or had failed to obey an order of the juvenile court, by reason of a *nunc pro tunc* order to that effect entered on June 27, 1973. In any event, Aline's counsel does not suggest otherwise.

Under section 732, "Before a minor is conveyed to any state or county institution pursuant to this article, it shall be ascertained from the superintendent thereof that the person can be received." Likewise section 1736 provides in part that CYA "may in its discretion accept such [juvenile court] commitments." While sections 732 and 1736 suggest that CYA is vested with a measure of discretion to accept or reject juvenile court commitments, section 736, subdivision (a), indicates that such discretion is a limited one. Section 736, subdivision (a), provides that "The Youth Authority *shall* accept a person committed to it pursuant to this article if it believes that the person can be materially benefited by its reformatory and educational discipline, and if it has adequate facilities to provide such care. * * * " (Italics added; * * *.)

As properly observed by Justice Kingsley in the opinion by the Court of Appeal in this case, "The statutory scheme * * * as now embodied in section 730 et seq. of the Welfare and Institutions Code, contemplates a progressively restrictive and punitive series of disposition orders in cases such as that now before us—namely, home placement under supervision, foster home placement, placement in a local treatment facility and, as a last resort, Youth Authority placement."

As is evident from the applicable statute, "Commitments to the California Youth Authority are made only in the most serious cases and only after all else has failed." (Thompson, California Juvenile Court Deskbook, § 9.15, p. 123.) This concept is well established and has been expressed by the CYA itself. In light of the general purposes of juvenile commitments expressed in Welfare and Institutions Code section 502, discussed above, " * * * commitment to the Youth Authority is generally viewed as *the final treatment resource* available to the juvenile court and which least meets the description in the above provision [§ 502]. Within the Youth Authority system, there is gathered from throughout the State the most severely delinquent youths which have exhausted local programs." (Italics added; California Youth Authority, Criteria and Procedure for Referral of Juvenile Court Cases to the Youth Authority (1971) p. 1.)

We find of some significance the expressed guidelines and criteria prepared by the CYA itself in the above referenced publication which juvenile courts may use in CYA referrals. The "Criteria" lists (at p. 2) several "inappropriate cases" for commitment, including (1) *youths who are dependent or primarily placement problems*—"For these youths in need of a home and peer acceptance, as well as accepting adults, life in an institution might be totally fulfilling, resulting in an orientation to an institutional existence"; (2) *unsophisticated, mildly delinquent youths*, "for whom commingling with serious delinquents who make up the bulk of the Youth Authority population might result in a negative learning experience and serious loss of self-esteem"; and (3) *mentally retarded or mentally disturbed youths*, "for whom the probable benefits of treatment within the mental health system exceed those of programs within the Youth Authority. The Youth Authority has no programs for the mentally retarded nor psychiatric treatment programs for the mentally ill." The foregoing classifications in combination approach a behavioral profile of Aline, for in addition to her dependency and placement problems and delinquency, the record suggests that she is "borderline" mentally retarded.

Furthermore, statistics compiled by CYA indicate that at Ventura School for Girls (the only suitable CYA institution for Aline), Aline would be placed in the company of girls who had committed serious criminal offenses, including 16 homicides, 31 robberies and 38 assaults. (Department of the Youth Authority, Characteristics of California Youth Authority Wards (1974) Table 1E, p. 7.) According to the CYA's 1973 annual report, 85 percent of all youths committed to CYA had three or more delinquency "contacts," and 35 percent had eight or more such contacts. (Department of the Youth Authority, 1973 Annual Report, p. 11.)

In sum, the record before the juvenile court discloses that CYA may not be a suitable placement facility for Aline, and that the referee himself, acting for the juvenile court, entertained very substantial doubt in the matter. The record does not disclose that the court was, in the language of the statute, "fully satisfied that the * * * condition and qualifications of the ward are such as to render it probable that he will be benefitted" by the discipline or treatment available at CYA.

In order to assist the juvenile court in its reconsideration of the cause, we note a few possible alternative dispositions. Our suggestions should not be considered exhaustive of the possibilities, and the court should explore, of course, any other placement opportunities which the parties or the probation officer may suggest.

If the report indicates that Aline would not benefit from the treatment she would receive at CYA, and if no appropriate alternative placement exists at that time, then the proceedings should be dismissed. (Welf. & Inst.Code, § 782.) Section 888 of the Welfare and Institutions Code provides in pertinent part that, "Any county establishing such juvenile home, ranch, or camp under the provisions of this article [to place §§ 601 or 602 wards] may, by mutual agreement, accept children committed to such home, ranch, or camp by the juvenile court of another county in the State and the State shall reimburse the county maintaining the home, ranch, or camp to the amount of one-half the administrative cost of maintaining each child so committed. * * * "

Second, reference was made at the May 1973 hearing to the anticipated establishment of closed facilities at the Penny Lane school where Aline had once been placed. Mrs. Holt seemed to believe that such closed facilities might be a suitable placement for Aline.

Third, testimony at Aline's hearing described facilities in Los Angeles County for *boys* of the type appropriate for minors such as Aline. Although appearing to be the least promising alternative, conceivably some arrangement could be made to provide care and treatment for Aline at these facilities under some segregated arrangement.

Fourth, the record indicates that Aline may be a "borderline" mentally retarded child. Under Welfare and Institutions Code sections 6550 et seq. provision is made for the commitment to state hospital of juvenile court wards found (following evaluation and report) to be mentally retarded or mentally disordered. (See also § 6512.)

Finally, if on reconsideration the court determines that no appropriate alternative placement exists, but also finds that Aline probably would benefit from a CYA commitment under present circumstances, the court could consider the possibility of a temporary 90-day CYA commitment for purposes of observation and diagnosis, with provision for a report by the director of CYA concerning Aline's amenability to treatment. (See Welf. & Inst.Code, § 704.) If the report indicates that Aline is not benefiting from the treatment she is receiving at CYA, and if no appropriate alternative placement exists at that time, then the proceedings should be dismissed. (Welf. & Inst.Code, § 782.)

Juvenile commitment proceedings are designed for the purposes of rehabilitation and treatment, not punishment. * * * We fully recognize that in some cases, as in that before us, the question of appropriate placement poses to the appropriate officials seemingly insurmountable difficulties. Budgetary limitations, varying from county to county, may well preclude the maintenance of those specialized facilities otherwise necessary to provide the minor with optimum care and treatment. Even if such facilities exist, the minor's past conduct may itself require his or her exclusion therefrom. Nevertheless, under the present statutory scheme, supported by sound policy considerations, a commitment to CYA must be supported by a determination, based upon substantial evidence in the record, of probable benefit to the minor. The unavailability of suitable alternatives, standing alone, does not justify the commitment of a nondelinquent or marginally delinquent child to an institution primarily designed for the incarceration and discipline of serious offenders.

The order of commitment is reversed and the cause remanded for further proceedings consistent with this opinion.

WRIGHT, C.J., and TOBRINER, MOSK and SULLIVAN, JJ., concur.

CLARK, JUSTICE (dissenting).

I dissent.

Welfare and Institutions Code section 734 precludes neither a judge's expression of sorrow when required to commit a juvenile ward to the California Youth Authority, nor his expression of regret when less restrictive alternatives are unobtainable. Instead, section 734 only requires that the juvenile court find CYA commitment to be the most beneficial disposition available. The record reveals this statutory requirement has been more than satisfied.

Aline's history of delinquency includes shoplifting, theft, smoking marijuana and assaulting a grandmother. Her behavior has frequently been characterized as "assaultive," leading her probation officer to describe her as "a severely delinquent young girl * * * in terms of being a public menace."

Exhaustive efforts—all unsuccessful—were made to place Aline within the community. The first placement, in a family treatment program, was regarded as "singularly unsuccessful" and terminated after two months. Admission in a community day care program was then denied the ward due to her low intelligence. McKinnon Girls Home released Aline in two weeks because of "problems with stealing, shoplifting, bedwetting, refusal to attend school" and the claim she was a leader of a local street gang, the Cripts.

Aline's fourth placement, at Penny Lane School, lasted only 10 days because she "[s]moked grass at a concert—is muscle of the resistive kids—threatens weaker girls—girls are terrified as she leans on being a member of the Cript gang. About five Cript boys came to Penny Lane to see her—'freaked out' staff as one got into the house." Her fifth disposition, at the Detroit Arms, was terminated when Aline "let in eight or nine Cripts in the placement who took three or four girls and split for two days."

At this point the Los Angeles County placement coordinator concluded the county had no facility capable of coping with Aline, "other than possibly Las Palmas Girls School." However, Las Palmas declined to enroll the ward, concluding her assaultive behavior, low intelligence level and nonacceptance of responsibility revealed Aline "could not benefit from either our school or group therapy[,] the two main aspects of our program." Las Palmas recommended she be committed to the CYA "where she could have the structure she obviously needs and also vocational training."

Before Aline's commitment to the Youth Authority *seven* additional placement alternatives were investigated, all proving unsatisfactory. The commitment hearing itself was recessed to give the probation officer time to explore placement with the Department of Public Social Services. However, like previous efforts, this proved fruitless.

The record clearly reveals that all parties at the hearing—including Aline's counsel—agreed that every conceivable placement alternative had been exhausted, the only remaining disposition being to either completely dismiss Aline's wardship or to commit her to the CYA.[34] Since Aline's mother has refused to accept her back into the home, dismissal would place this child in the streets and under the influence of her gang. In these circumstances, release would provide Aline nothing but the opportunity to qualify more fully for CYA commitment—hardly a course of action to be recommended to the juvenile court system.

In contrast, CYA commitment offers Aline foreseeable benefit through treatment and training. The authority is empowered "to make use of law enforcement, detention, probation, parole, medical, educational, correctional, segregative and other facilities, institutions and agencies, whether public or private, within the State." (Welf. & Inst.Code, § 1753.) Its director is authorized to "enter into agreements with the appropriate public officials for separate care and special treatment in existing institutions for persons subject to the control of the Authority." (Welf. & Inst.Code, § 1753.) Finally, it can even train its own specialists. (Welf. & Inst.Code, § 1752.6.)

---

[34] From the juvenile court hearing to the present time, neither appellant nor the majority has specified any county facility suitable for Aline. Their contention that such a placement alternative *perhaps* exists is of no help to the lower court.

Far from being a single "placement facility," [35] the CYA is an *administration* comprised of *many* facilities, capable of providing individualized treatment where necessary.

The propriety of a CYA commitment under these circumstances cannot be negated by a juvenile court judge's expression of concern and regret. Such expression is not uncommon and should be commended—not masked by judicial indifference. Aline and her unfortunate circumstances understandably frustrated the judge. But while he no doubt was sorry that the ward's misconduct was sufficiently serious to "force the system to the wall," his statements were intended to make Aline realize that, in ordering commitment, he was doing only what her circumstances and conduct compelled. Such communication increases the minor's understanding for the system, improving his or her chance for rehabilitation and accountability to society.

Moreover, although the juvenile court judge commonly fears commitment may prove counterproductive, such fear is not prohibited by section 734. The code only requires the court's satisfaction that the conditions and qualifications of the ward "render it *probable* that he will be benefited" by commitment.[36] (Italics added.) It is unreasonable to interpret this section to require full satisfaction that successful treatment will not be jeopardized by adverse influences.

Finally, the majority's holding will stifle communication between judge and ward, replacing it with the formalism characteristic of the adult criminal trial. This is unfortunate. The closer a juvenile hearing moves toward becoming an adversarial proceeding, the more a child tends to view the law as either his oppressor or his fool—depending on who "wins the contest."

In conclusion, Aline must be characterized as an aggressive, assaultive delinquent who may benefit from CYA training and discipline. Disposition of her case should not rest on a judge's expression of sorrow or dismay. If it does, we fail both Aline and the juvenile justice system.

I would affirm the judgment of the juvenile court.

McComb, J., concurs.

---

[35] * * * Similarly, the majority's description of the authority as "punitive" is misconceived. California juvenile law has specifically rejected the concept of punishment: "The purpose of [the chapter establishing the CYA] is to protect society more effectively by substituting for retributive punishment methods of training and treatment * * *." (Welf. & Inst.Code, § 1700.) "Care and guidance" are the fundamental principles around which the juvenile justice system is fashioned. (Welf. & Inst.Code, § 502.) Treatment is not punitive even though the ward's mobility is curtailed. (Cf. In re De La O (1963) 59 Cal.2d 128, 28 Cal. Rptr. 489, 378 P.2d 793.)

[36] The judge here entered a *written finding* specifically stating that commitment to the CYA would be beneficial to Aline. However, the majority chooses to reject this finding and to reverse this case on the basis of explanatory remarks clearly intended by the juvenile judge to benefit the child.

NOTES

1. The New York Court of Appeals, in In re Ellery C. v. Redlich, 32 N.Y.2d 588, 347 N.Y.S.2d 51, 300 N.E.2d 424 (1973), held that a PINS could not be confined in the same institutions as children adjudged delinquent. Dean Monrad Paulsen commented on the response of the Division of Youth to Ellery C., and the subsequent treatment of that response by the New York Court of Appeals:

New York's Division for Youth responded to the Court of Appeals judgment by establishing four PINS facilities and four facilities for delinquents. New York University's Institute of Judicial Administration completed a study in September of 1975 which looked into the impact of "Ellery C", especially into the question whether a difference could be observed between PINS institutions and those housing delinquents. "On most items," the study concluded, " * * * the training schools surveyed were found to be very much alike. The study took into account, intake processes, physical living conditions, regulations and rules, education, recreation, treatment, discipline and some legal issues.

The study further indicated that the decision did not noticeably affect the ways PINS cases are approached by the Family Court. For example, there has been no change in the frequency with which PINS offenders are diverted from the judicial process. All in all, "Ellery C" caused the establishment of two programs for youngsters in trouble which were substantially identical. One wonders in what respect segregation of those adjudicated according to type of adjudication can be called "vital." Surely it ought to be possible to develop differential programs for children based on demonstrated psychological and social differences that could be carried out in the same institution irrespective of the training school's legal designation. It seems likely that an excellent program could benefit both PINS and delinquents.

In short, segregation of children in trouble in accordance with legal categories does not (in this experience at least) improve treatment although it is barely possible that a PINS' reputation suffers a bit less because others in the same place of confinement have not been found to have committed a criminal offense.

The reach of "Ellery C" was considered by the Court of Appeals in July 1974. Matter of Lavette M., 35 N.Y.2d 136, 316 N.E.2d 314, spoke of two cases each involving a thirteen year old child who had been adjudicated a person who needed supervision. Each child apparently was beyond the control of a parent or guardian. Further the two children, having been placed on probation, violated probationary terms by running away, twice in one case and several times in the other. Expert testimony was heard by the Family Court Judge that each child should be placed in a secure residential setting. Lawyers for the youngsters raised the point that the confinement of a PINS in a training school was unlawful in the light of "Ellery C" and that the PINS training schools would not provide "adequate and appropriate treatment," given the needs of these children. The Court of Appeals disagreed, saying "it is the confinement of PINS children in a *prison atmosphere* along with juveniles convicted of committing criminal acts that is proscribed, not the characterization of a facility as a training school, that is determinative." (italics supplied)

The opinion explained that the Court was "well aware of the current preference for expanding use of community agencies, community residential centers and similar shelters" for PINS but "absent a clear showing that the treatment provided at a training school is significantly inadequate," training school placement is not unlawful. The Court could not say that the "initiative to establish a fully adequate program * * * will not be carried to fruition," but warned that if, at a later time it appeared the program had not reached a satisfactory level of treatment performance "a different question will be presented."

The Court of Appeals, of course, did not have the studies of the Institute of Judicial Administration to which we have referred. Obviously the PINS training schools, in theory, could offer (so long as the training school did not maintain a "prison atmosphere") "adequate and appropriate" treatment even though the same program is available to delinquents in other, separate, institutions. Yet the finding of the Institute might have moved the Court to take a closer look at the program offered in the PINS training schools.

In deciding that the New York Division for Youth deserved a chance to implement a program undertaken in response to "Ellery C", *Lavette* looked largely at the facts that the schools are coeducational and employ some versions of the "cottage concept," that regular and remedial education programs are offered, that a psychiatrist and psychologists are available on a limited basis and more staffing is to be added pursuant to a Model Staffing Plan.

It is fair to say that the Court looked at the highly visible, *objective* matters of housing and personnel. It made no inquiry into the essential quality of the program in respect to meeting the special needs of an individual treatment.

The Court, however, was aware of this latter issue. At one point in the opinion it is acknowledged that there are practical limitations on the power of courts to determine the adequacy and effectiveness of treatment afforded PINS children. "By what yardstick are we to measure?" the opinion asks. The formulation of criteria to measure the effectiveness of treatment facilities is not "an exclusively judicial function." The Court should not determine what is the "best possible treatment" or to espouse "an ideal of a perhaps unattainable standard." Its role should rather be "to assure the presence of a bona fide treatment program."

Given this limitation of the Court's function, the opinion proceeds to define the right to treatment which has been recognized: "there must be a bona fide effort to adequately treat the child in need of supervision in the light of present knowledge." Training school commitments must be for "the purpose of individualized treatment and not mere custodial care." The failure to supply such treatment cannot be excused by "lack of staffing and facilities."

The treatment right includes "a requirement of initial diagnosis and of periodic reassessment so that treatment can be revised as diagnosis develops." Judge Jasen, the author of the opinion, concluded by saying: "Beyond this, we need not go at this time."

A short news-note such as this does not permit a detailed critical comment on these cases. But we can respond to them briefly. It is to be assumed that the opinion in *Lavette* is grounded on an idea of "treatment" which when applied to a troubled child improves behavior through an improvement in character. In the PINS cases presented here, does such treatment exist? Is it available at any cost? In the case of *Maurice C.* (a companion case to *Lavette* and dealt with in the same opinion) the child had a long history of running away from fosters homes, indeed he absconded three times to cities far from New York between the time of the PINS adjudication and his dispositional hearing. The court appointed psychiatrist stated that Maurice had poor judgment and was unable to get along with companions. This psychiatrist and a psychiatric report by another recommended that Maurice be placed in a secure, residential setting.

Does the present state of knowledge include knowing how to change Maurice except to place him in a training school and expose him to an opportunity for education? What is the likelihood of improvement for Maurice if he were given access to extensive psychiatric care or treatment by a clinical psychiatrist? It may well be that given present knowledge a training school not involving a "prison atmosphere," is the best way to treat Maurice until he is old enough to go his own way.

The opinion makes no mention of costs. Suppose there were effective treatments which could change Maurice for the better but the costs are $50,000 per year? Should such money be spent? Surely there are many uses for the funds which might serve higher values or will assist more persons than one. Does the Court truly mean that dubious and expensive "treatment" must be undertaken as the price for the state's placing a troubled, perhaps rebellious young teenager, in a training school. Some, I know, will agree that thirteen year olds ought to run their own lives. If one does not agree, some disposition must be made of the youngster which is both realistic and does not involve excessive expenditure.

Paulsen, PINS and the Right to Treatment—Two New York Cases, 2 All From the Family (A.A.L.S. Newsletter, Fam. & Juv.L. Section, December, 1975) 3–5.

2. Certo v. State, 53 A.D.2d 971, 385 N.Y.S.2d 824 (1976) provides the following sequel to *Ellery C.:*

In 1971, Ellery Coleman was adjudged a person in need of supervision (hereinafter "PINS") pursuant to article 7 of the Family Court Act and he was thereafter placed in a State training school. This disposition was reversed by the Court of Appeals on the ground that a training school was not a suitable location for a person never convicted of a crime (Matter of Ellery C., 32 N.Y.2d 588, 347 N.Y.S.2d 51, 300 N.E.2d 424), and the matter was remanded to Family Court for further proceedings. While under the supervision of that court, and on December 3, 1973, he stabbed and killed Mario Certo, a 14-year-old. This claimant, decedent's father, now seeks to hold the State liable in negligence for failing in its duty to provide suitable facilities to implement article 7 of the Family Court Act in that (1) it did not offer rehabilitative supervision but improperly confined him in a place where, in fact, he received criminal education, and (2) it failed to protect the public from a PINS.

It must be noted that the statutory scheme of article 7 of the Family Court Act is designed to benefit a PINS, not to protect the general public from him (Family Court Act, § 720, subds. [b] and [c], §§ 724,

756, 782). Having committed no criminal act (Family Court Act, § 712), a PINS cannot be categorized as a direct threat to society. Clearly, the acts for which the claimant seeks to hold the State responsible are inherently governmental in nature and do not constitute the type of activity for which the State has waived its immunity * * *. Accordingly, the claim was properly dismissed.

Id. at 825.

3. May a juvenile judge order a disposition not recommended by experts? For an affirmative answer, see In Interest of Duck, 323 Pa.Super. 456, 470 A.2d 1008 (1984). For a negative answer, see Egan v. M.S., 310 N.W.2d 719 (N.D. 1981) and People v. Carl B., 24 Cal.3d 212, 155 Cal.Rptr. 189, 594 P.2d 14 (1979).

The Juvenile Justice and Delinquency Prevention Act of 1974, as amended by the Juvenile Justice Amendments of 1977, 42 U.S.C.A. §§ 5601, et seq. (West 1977 and Supp.1979), mandates the deinstitutionalization of status and non-offenders.

42 U.S.C.A. § 5633(a)(12)(A) provides:

* * * juveniles who are charged with or who have committed offenses that would not be criminal if committed by an adult or offenses which do not constitute violations of valid court orders, or such nonoffenders as dependent or neglected children, shall not be placed in secure detention facilities or secure correctional facilities;

42 U.S.C.A. § 5633(c) provides:

* * * Failure to achieve compliance with the requirement of subsection (a)(12)(A) of this section within the three-year time limitation shall terminate any State's eligibility for funding under this subpart unless the Administrator determines that the State is in substantial compliance with the requirement, through achievement of deinstitutionalization of not less than 75 per centum of such juveniles, and has made, through appropriate executive or legislative action, an unequivocal commitment to achieving full compliance within a reasonable time not exceeding two additional years.

To enable the states to determine if a facility is a juvenile detention or correctional facility within the meaning of 42 U.S.C.A. § 5633(a)(12)(A), criteria were promulgated. A juvenile detention or correctional facility is:

(a) Any *secure* public or private *facility* used for the *lawful custody* of *accused* or *adjudicated juvenile offenders* or *nonoffenders;* or

(b) Any public or private facility, secure or nonsecure, which is also used for the lawful custody of accused or convicted adult *criminal offenders;* or

(c) Any nonsecure public or private facility that has a *bed capacity* for more than 20 accused or adjudicated *juvenile offenders* or *nonoffenders* unless:

1.   The facility is community based and has a bed capacity of 40 or less; or

2.   The facility is used *exclusively* for the lawful custody of *status offenders* or *nonoffenders.*

Definitions relating to the above criteria:

(a) *Juvenile offender.*—An individual subject to the exercise of juvenile court jurisdiction for purposes of adjudication and treatment based on age and offense limitations as defined by State law.

(b) *Criminal-type offender.*—A juvenile who has been charged with or adjudicated for conduct which would, under the law of the jurisdiction in which the offense was committed, be a crime if committed by an adult.

(c) *Status offender.*—A juvenile who has been charged with or adjudicated for conduct which would not, under the law of the jurisdiction in which the offense was committed, be a crime if committed by an adult.

(d) *Nonoffender.*—A juvenile who is subject to the jurisdiction of the juvenile court, usually under abuse, dependency, or neglect statutes for reasons other than legally prohibited conduct of the juvenile.

(e) *Accused juvenile offender.*—A juvenile with respect to whom a petition has been filed in the juvenile court alleging that such juvenile is a criminal-type offender or is a status offender and no final adjudication has been made by the juvenile court.

(f) *Adjudicated juvenile offender.*—A juvenile with respect to whom the juvenile court has determined that such juvenile is a criminal-type offender or is a status offender.

(g) *Facility.*—A place, an institution, a building or part thereof, set of buildings or an area whether or not enclosing a building or set of buildings which is used for the lawful custody and treatment of juveniles and may be owned and/or operated by public or private agencies.

(h) *Facility, secure.*—One which is designed and operated so as to insure that all entrances and exits from such facility, whether or not the person being detained has freedom of movement within the perimeters of the facility or which relies on locked rooms and buildings, fences, or physical restraint in order to control behavior of its residents.

(i) *Facility, nonsecure.*—A facility not characterized by the use of physically restricting construction, hardware and procedures and which provide its residents access to the surrounding community with minimal supervision.

(j) *Community-based.*—Facility, program, or service means a small, open group home or other suitable place located near the juvenile's home or family, and programs of community supervision and service which maintain community and consumer participation in the planning, operation, and evaluation of their programs which may include, but are not limited to, medical, educational, vocational, social, and psychological guidance, training, counseling, alcoholism treatment, drug treatment, and other rehabilitative services. This definition is from section 103(1) of the JJDP Act. For purposes of clarification the following is being provided:

(1) *Small:* Bed capacity of 40 or less.

(2) *Near:* In reasonable proximity of the juvenile's family and home community which allows a child to maintain family and community contact.

(3) *Consumer participation:* Facility policy and practice facilitates the involvement of program participants in planning, problem solving, and decision making related to the program as it affects them.

(4) *Community participation:* Facility policy and practice facilitates the involvement of citizens as volunteers, advisors, or direct service providers; and provide for opportunities for communication with neighborhood and other community groups.

(k) *Lawful custody.*—The exercise of care, supervision and control over a juvenile offender or nonoffender pursuant to the provisions of the law or of a judicial order or decree.

(*l*) *Exclusively.*—As used to describe the population of a facility, the term "exclusively" means that the facility is used only for a specifically described category of juvenile to the exclusion of all other types of juveniles.

(m) *Criminal offender.*—An individual, adult or juvenile, who has been charged with or convicted of a criminal offense in a court exercising criminal jurisdiction.

(n) *Bed capacity.*—The maximum population which has been set for day to day population and, typically, is the result of administrative policy, licensing or life safety inspection, court order, or legislative restriction.

43 Fed.Reg. 36402, 36407 (1978).

In 1981 24 states reported full compliance with the Act and 25 additional states reported at least 75% compliance, 1981 Annual Report of the Attorney General. The 1981 level of funding to the states was 62 million dollars, a figure reduced to 43 million dollars in 1982. 1982 Report of the Attorney General. By 1984 the total funding under the Juvenile Justice and Delinquency Prevention Act— including appropriations for grants to states and for individual research, contracts, cooperative agreements and other assistance as authorized by the Act was 70 million dollars. Public Law 98–166, Nov. 28, 1983.

STATE EX REL. HARRIS v. CALENDINE

Supreme Court of Appeals of West Virginia, 1977.
160 W.Va. 172, 233 S.E.2d 318.

NEELY, JUSTICE.

This habeas corpus proceeding calls into question the constitutional validity of West Virginia's classification and disposition of juvenile offenders. The Court does not find unconstitutional W.Va. Code, 49–1–4 [1941], which defines a "delinquent child," or W.Va. Code, 49–5–11 [1975], which authorizes certain methods of disposition for children adjudged delinquent; nevertheless, we find that definite guidelines are needed to prevent these statutes from being unconstitutionally applied in violation of W.Va.Const., art. III, § 10, the due process clause, and W.Va.Const., art. III, § 5, the cruel and unusual punishment clause.

The petitioner, Gilbert Harris, is a 16 year old boy now confined in the Davis Center, a forestry camp for boys, pursuant to an order of the Calhoun County Juvenile Court adjudging the petitioner delinquent because he had been absent from school for 50 days.

On April 9, 1976, the Director of Supportive Services for the Calhoun County Board of Education petitioned the juvenile court to find Mr. Harris either neglected or delinquent because of his irregular school attendance. A summons was served on petitioner's mother and stepfather stating that they were required to appear before the Calhoun County Juvenile Court, and after several continuances a hearing was finally held on May 17, 1976 at which the petitioner, his attorney, and petitioner's mother appeared. At the hearing the petitioner did not deny the allegations against him and was adjudicated a delinquent child. The juvenile court committed the petitioner to the care, custody, and control of the Commissioner of Public Institutions for the State of West Virginia for assignment to the Industrial School for Boys at Pruntytown until the petitioner became 16 years old in July 1976. Upon reaching age 16, petitioner was to be reassigned to a Youth Center for the balance of a one year period, after which he was to be remanded to the custody of the Calhoun County Juvenile Court. Petitioner had never been charged with a delinquent act before the bringing of the petition now under review and had never previously appeared before the juvenile court. Furthermore, petitioner was nearly 16 at the time he was adjudged delinquent for truancy, and he was ordered incarcerated for almost a year past the legal age when school attendance is required. W.Va. Code, 18–8–1 [1951].

Petitioner lived in a remote, rural section of Calhoun County and had some difficulty getting to school during the winter months. More importantly, however, it appears that the petitioner was ridiculed and shunned by his classmates because he suffered from a facial disfigurement and was mildly retarded. Petitioner had been enrolled in a special education class during junior high school and high school, but the record does not disclose any details about those classes in the local schools or the programs offered by either the industrial school at Pruntytown or the Forestry Camp at Davis.

* * *

The primary question presented by this proceeding is whether W.Va.Code, 49–1–4 [1941] and W.Va.Code, 49–5–11 [1975] establish methods for handling juvenile offenders which are inherently unconstitutional. These West Virginia statutes, which indiscriminately combine status offenders with criminal offenders, present an enormous potential for abuse and unconstitutional application. Nonetheless, under the doctrine of the least obtrusive remedy, this Court will avoid striking down legislation whenever " * * * there is an adequate remedy to prevent such legislation from being unconstitutionally applied." Point 4, Syllabus, State ex rel. Alsop v. McCartney, W.Va., 228 S.E.2d 278 (1976). To save these statutes from constitutional infirmity and to assure that they will be constitutionally applied, this Court will discuss the perimeters dictated by the Constitution of the State of West Virginia which circumscribe their application.

W.Va.Code, 49–1–4 [1941] establishes the conditions under which a child may be adjudicated delinquent. That Section provides:

"Delinquent child" means a person under the age of eighteen years who:

(1) Violates a law or municipal ordinance;

(2) Commits an act which if committed by an adult would be a crime not punishable by death or life imprisonment;

(3) Is incorrigible, ungovernable, or habitually disobedient and beyond the control of his parent, guardian, or other custodian;

(4) Is habitually truant;

(5) Without just cause and without the consent of his parent, guardian, or other custodian, repeatedly deserts his home or place of abode;

(6) Engages in an occupation which is in violation of law;

(7) Associates with immoral or vicious persons;

(8) Frequents a place the existence of which is in violation of law;

(9) Deports himself so as to wilfully injure or endanger the morals or health of himself or others.

Once a child has been adjudicated delinquent the methods of court disposition are set forth by W.Va.Code, 49–5–11 [1975] which provides as follows:

With a view to the welfare and interest of the child and of the State, the court or judge may, after the proceedings, make any of the following dispositions:

(1) Treat the child as a neglected child, in which case the provisions of article six [§ 49–6–1 et seq.] of this chapter shall apply;

(2) Order the child placed under the supervision of a probation officer;

(3) If the child be over sixteen years of age at the time of the commission of the offense the court may, if the proceedings originated as a criminal proceeding, enter an order showing its refusal to take jurisdiction as a juvenile proceeding and permit the child to be proceeded against in accordance with the laws of the State governing the commission of crimes or violation of municipal ordinances;

(4) Commit the child to an industrial home or correctional institution for minors;

(5) Commit the child to any public or private institution or agency permitted by law to care for children;

(6) Commit the child to the care and custody of some suitable person who shall be appointed guardian of the person and custodian of the child;

(7) Enter any other order which seems to the court to be in the best interest of the child.

Both of these statutes must be interpreted and applied in conformity with W.Va. Const., art. III, § 10, which provides "No person shall be deprived of life, liberty, or property, without due process of law, and the judgment of his peers" and W.Va. Const., art. III, § 5, which provides in part, "Excessive bail shall not be required, nor excessive fines imposed, nor cruel and unusual punishment inflicted * * *."

Inherent in the due process clause of the State Constitution are both the concept of substantive due process and the concept of equal protection of the laws. In order for the statutory scheme concerning juvenile delinquents to withstand constitutional scrutiny under the substantive due process standard, it must appear that the means chosen by the Legislature to achieve a proper legislative purpose bear a rational relationship to that purpose and are not arbitrary or discriminatory. Furthermore, under the equal protection standard it must appear that the statutes do not invite invidious discrimination based on race, color, creed, sex, national origin, or social class.

The cruel and unusual punishment standard requires that no person be punished unless he has done something which is generally recognized as deserving of punishment. Furthermore, as we implied in State ex rel. Hawks v. Lazaro, W.Va., 202 S.E.2d 109 (1974), the state cannot punish a person in fact while alleging to rehabilitate or otherwise help him.

The statutes under consideration, in the absence of guidelines for their application, fail to meet the equal protection, substantive due process, and the cruel and unusual punishment standards because they permit the classification and treatment of status offenders in the same manner as criminal offenders.

II

We are not concerned with whether a child may be committed to a state correctional facility such as Pruntytown or the Davis Center when, in the language of subsections 1 and 2 of Code, 49–1–4 [1941], the child either violates a law or municipal ordinance or commits an act which if committed by an adult would be a crime not punishable by death or life imprisonment. These subsections provide for both punishment and rehabilitation of those children who commit criminal acts which have long been recognized at common law.

We are, however, concerned with incarceration of children for status offenses. Particularly in the language of subsections 3 through 6 and subsection 8 of Code, 49–1–4 [1941] we are concerned with a child who is incorrigible, ungovernable, habitually disobedient and beyond the control of his parents, truant, repeatedly deserts his home or place of abode, engages in an occupation which is in violation of law, or frequents a place the existence of which is in violation of law. The Legislature has vested the juvenile court with jurisdiction over children who commit these status offenses so that the court may enforce order, safety, morality, and family discipline within the community. The intention of the law is laudable; however, the means employed to accomplish these ends are unconstitutional insofar as they result in the commitment of status offenders to secure, prison-like facilities which also house children guilty of criminal conduct, or needlessly subject status offenders to the degradation and physical abuse of incarceration.

At the outset the Court should make clear that we are not impressed with euphemistic titles used to disguise what are in fact secure, prison-like facilities. We define a secure, prison-like facility, regardless of whether it be called a "home for girls," "industrial school," "forestry camp," "children's shelter," "orphanage," or other imaginative name, as a place which relies for control of children upon locked rooms, locked buildings, guards, physical restraint, regimentation, and corporal punishment. Somehow, it appears to us that if the State's purpose is to develop a society characterized by peace and love, that our institutions for children should reflect those qualities and not their opposite. In fact, as we shall develop shortly, the status offender has a constitutional right, if not to love, at least to the absence of hate.

W.Va.Code, 49–5–11 [1975] provides a number of methods of disposition for juvenile offenders, including placing the delinquent child under supervised probation, committing the child to a public or private institution or agency, committing the child to the care and custody of some suitable person, entering any other order which would appear to be in the best interest of the child, and then finally committing the child to an industrial home or correctional institution for minors, i.e., a secure, prison-like facility. It is parsimony which circumscribes our courts' ability to treat status offenders constitutionally, not the absence of statutory authority.

The Equal Protection Standard

We find that with regard to the status offender the procedure for disposition set forth in Code, 49–5–11 [1975] can be applied in a manner repugnant to the basic principles of equal protection because it discriminates invidiously against children based upon social class, sex, and geographic location. It is obvious that a child from a family with financial resources will have an opportunity to use private institutional facilities which are far less restrictive, less dangerous, and less degrading than public correctional institutions. What would have happened to the petitioner in the case before us if he had come from an upper middle-class family in a city such as Charleston or Wheeling? He certainly would have had an opportunity to go to a private school. In the case before us we may reasonably infer that the Calhoun County Juvenile Court committed petitioner to a reform school because of the lack of a reasonable alternative which would have existed if petitioner had been from a different area or belonged to a different socio-economic class.

Furthermore, the status offender is inherently in a different class from the criminal offender. The Legislature could choose to punish children guilty of criminal conduct in the same manner as it punishes adults, but as a matter of public policy the Legislature provided instead for a comprehensive system of child welfare. The aim of this system is to protect and rehabilitate children, not to punish them. See State ex rel. Slatton v. Boles, 147 W.Va. 674, 130 S.E.2d 192 (1963); State ex rel. Browning v. Boles, 147 W.Va. 878, 132 S.E.2d 505 (1963). It has always been assumed that the Legislature can at any time withdraw some or all the benefits of this system from children guilty of criminal conduct. There is no such prospect for status offenders, however, since without the child welfare legislation they are guilty of no crimes cognizable and punishable by courts. This explains why status offenders have a special position within the current system, despite the fact that technically they are not distinguished from children guilty of actual criminal conduct. Since the class to which status offenders belong has been created under authority of the State's inherent and sovereign *parens patriae* power, Warner Bros. Pictures v. Brodel, 179 P.2d 57 (Cal.App.1947); Johnson v. State, 18 N.J. 422, 114 A.2d 1 (1955), and not under the plenary powers of the State to control criminal activity and punish criminals, Barker v. People, 3 Cow.(N.Y.) 686 (1824), status offenders must be treated in a fashion consistent with the *parens patriae* power, namely, they must be helped and not punished, State ex rel. Slatton v. Boles, supra; otherwise their classification becomes invidious, and accordingly, unconstitutional.

Finally, it should be noted that status offender legislation discriminates invidiously against females. It is apparent that status offense petitions can easily be used to bring under control young women suspected by their parents or by other authorities of promiscuous behavior. Our society tends to condemn female promiscuity more severely than male promiscuity, and this tendency may explain why females often are unfairly classified and treated as status offenders. This Court offers no explanation for this phenomenon, nor do we make any normative judgments regarding the wisdom of such a distinction; however, we recognize its existence and its discriminatory effect on female status offenders.[37] The control of sexual behavior may be accomplished by other means.

The Substantive Due Process Standard

Furthermore the Court finds no rational connection between the legitimate legislative purposes of enforcing family discipline, protecting children, and protecting society from uncontrolled children, and the means by which the State is permitted to accomplish these purposes, namely incarceration of children in secure, prison-like facilities.

It is generally recognized that the greatest colleges for crime are prisons and reform schools.[38] The most egregious punishment inflicted upon a child incarcerated in a West Virginia penal institution is not

[37] A recent study (December 1976) by the Division of Corrections, West Virginia Department of Public Institutions, indicates that female status offenders comprise a much larger percentage of the total number of their sex committed to secure, prison-like facilities than male status offenders comprise of theirs. This study identified 138 status offenders out of the total number of 477 children committed at that time to West Virginia's secure, prison-like facilities. Overall then, 29% of the children committed were status offenders.

There were 404 males in the sample population, of whom 72 were status offenders, or approximately 18% . On the other hand there were 73 females in the sample population, of whom 66 were status offenders, or approximately 90%.

The study provides additional evidence of the uneven treatment of females. Of the 72 males committed for status offenses, 41, or about 57%, had a prior history of criminal conduct. Although this prior history by itself would be insufficient, under the guidelines of this opinion, to justify the commitment of these male status offenders to secure, prison-like facilities, the figures do suggest that juvenile courts are giving some attention to the severity of male status offenders' behavioral problems before committing them to secure, prison-like facilities. On the other hand, only 12, or about 18%, of the 66 females committed for status offenses had a history of prior criminal conduct.

The inequities of the present commitment process are all the more alarming because male and female status offenders are being referred to juvenile courts in approximately equal numbers. According to the West Virginia Department of Welfare statistics, 1974 referrals for status offenses were divided 48% males, 52% females; 1975 referrals for status offenses were divided 47% males, 53% females; and 1976 referrals were 49.7% males, 50.3% females. Therefore, it appears that the present system manifests its sexual bias not in the mere referral of status offenders to the authorities, but rather in the failure to accord even-handed treatment at the stage where a determination is made to commit status offenders to secure, prison-like facilities.

[38] Among others, the United States Senate Judiciary Subcommittee to Investigate Juvenile Delinquency has recognized that juvenile penal institutions provide novice criminals a rich education in the ways of crime. The Chairman of the Subcommittee, the Honorable Birch Bayh, noted the particular folly of allowing status offenders to receive an education in crime at public expense: " * * * I have heard testimony from countless juveniles who have been incarcerated for acts which would not have been crimes for adults, and who have emerged from institutions embittered and highly sophisticated in the ways of crime." Bayh, Juveniles and the Law: An Introduction, 12 Am.Crim.L.Rev. 1 (1974). * * *

the deprivation of his liberty but rather his forced association with reprehensible persons. Prisons, by whatsoever name they may be known, are inherently dangerous places. Sexual assaults, physical violence, psychological abuse and total degradation are the likely consequences of incarceration. If one hopes to find rehabilitation in a penal institution, his hopes will be confounded.

This Court held in the case of State ex rel. Hawks v. Lazaro, supra, that the doctrine of *parens patriae* "has been suspect from the earliest times" and that when the State is proceeding under color of its *parens patriae* authority, it must actually have fair prospects of achieving a beneficent purpose, otherwise the reason for the authority fails. *Hawks,* supra, concerned the constitutional validity of West Virginia's mental health commitment statutes which this Court found to be violative of due process. In *Hawks* this Court subjected the State's incarceration of the mentally ill to a substantive due process test. The Court said at 202 S.E.2d 120:

> The theoretical beneficence of the state with regard to its citizens has been used in justification of state custody or guardianship from the medieval period to our own day, although the disparity between the theory of beneficence and the practice of cruelty and inhumanity has often been the subject of literature (see, Dickens, Oliver Twist; Bronte, Jane Eyre.) There is persuasive evidence that the alleged improvement in treatment in modern state facilities from medieval times to our own is more myth than reality, see, Wyatt v. Stickney, 325 F.Supp. 781 (D.C. Ala.1971) and that at the current low level of sociological and psychological knowledge, combined with the current parsimonious level of governmental support for state institutions, the state and its officers have a limited therapeutic role and a predominantly custodial role.

> In recognition of the conditions which exist at state institutions, numerous courts have recently required the state to demonstrate a reasonable relationship between the alleged harm which a person is likely to do to himself and the treatment designed to ameliorate the illness which may cause that harm. For example, in Darnell v. Cameron, 121 U.S.App.D.C. 58, 348 F.2d 64 (1965) the Court stated that mandatory confinement rests

---

In an effort to remedy the serious problems documented before his subcommittee, Senator Bayh, along with Senator Marlow Cook, introduced in Congress the Juvenile Justice and Delinquency Prevention Act. Passed in 1974 as Public Law 93–415, this act is in part concerned with the exposure of status offenders in juvenile correctional institutions to other juveniles guilty of criminal conduct. In response to this particular problem Congress has by law provided financial incentives to states and localities which are willing to remove status offenders from juvenile detention or correctional facilities and place them in shelter facilities or community based treatment programs. See 42 U.S.C. § 5601 et seq.

For a concurring view of the problem of common custody, see The Report of the California Assembly Interim Committee on Criminal Procedure, Juvenile Justice Processes (1974) at 14 which states that " * * * if any of them [status offenders] were ever on the verge of committing a criminal act, they have been brought to the right place [i.e. joint custody with juvenile delinquents] for a final push."

upon the supposition of the necessity for treatment, and that if there is no treatment, a committed individual can bring a *habeas corpus* proceeding to question the constitutionality of his involuntary hospitalization; also, in Medberry v. Patterson, 188 F.Supp. 557 (D.C.Colo.1960) the Court held that an involuntarily committed patient is entitled to treatment and lack of such treatment cannot be justified by a lack of staff or facilities. Accordingly the ancient doctrine of *parens patriae* is in full retreat on all fronts except in those very narrow areas where the state can demonstrate, as a matter of fact, that its care and custody is superior to any available alternative. In re Gault, 387 U.S. 1, 87 S.Ct. 1428, 18 L.Ed.2d 527 (1967); In re Simmons Children, 154 W.Va. 491, 177 S.E.2d 19 (1970); In re Willis, W.Va., [207 S.E.2d 129] (decided December 11, 1973). Therefore, in determining whether there is any justification under the doctrine of *parens patriae* for deviation from established due process standards, it is appropriate for this Court to consider that the State of West Virginia offers to those unfortunates who are incarcerated in mental institutions Dickensian squalor of unconscionable magnitudes.

We apply the same substantive due process standards to the commitment of children for status offenses, since such commitment has always been justified on the same *parens patriae* grounds as commitment of the mentally ill. In theory, the commitment of the mentally ill has been to protect them from themselves as well as to protect society from their actions. Essentially the same rationale exists for commitment of juvenile status offenders. That is, they must not be permitted to injure themselves, and society must protect itself from their actions. We find with regard to status offenders the same fact we found in *Hawks*, supra, with regard to the mentally ill, that the State means, namely incarceration in secure, prison-like facilities, except in a limited class of cases, bears no reasonable relationship to legitimate State purposes, namely, rehabilitation, protection of the children, and protection of society.

In view of the foregoing, and in view of the fact that there are numerous alternatives to incarceration for status offenders we hold that the State must exhaust every reasonable alternative to incarceration before committing a status offender to a secure, prison-like facility. Furthermore, for those extreme cases in which commitment of status offenders to a secure, prison-like facility cannot be avoided, the receiving facility must be devoted solely to the custody and rehabilitation of status offenders. In this manner status offenders can be spared contact under degrading and harmful conditions with delinquents who are guilty of criminal conduct and experienced in the ways of crime.

However, this does not limit the authority of the juvenile court to house and educate status offenders and criminal offenders together in shelter homes, residential treatment centers, and other modern facilities staffed by well trained, attentive, and dedicated people, where the atmosphere is characterized by love and concern rather than physical violence, corporal punishment and physical restraint of liberty, provided the court determines there is no danger to the physical safety or emotional health of the status offender.

The Cruel and Unusual Punishment Standard

In the case before us we are confronted with a child who was obviously in need of help, and yet the State chose to degrade him, to humiliate him, and to punish him by sending him to institutions which fail to meet his needs and cannot help him.

At the outset this Court acknowledges that the cruel and unusual punishment standard cannot easily be defined and certainly is not fixed; consequently, we feel the standard tends to broaden as society becomes more enlightened and humane. See State ex rel. Pingley v. Coiner, 155 W.Va. 591, 186 S.E.2d 220 (1972). The standard ought to be especially broad in its application to status offenders, whom the State has pledged *not* to punish at all, but rather, to protect and rehabilitate. Furthermore, status offenders are not guilty of the criminal conduct which ordinarily serves to make society's exercise of the penal sanction legitimate.

A good starting point for applying the cruel and unusual punishment standard to West Virginia's treatment of status offenders is the concept of disproportionality. This concept is explicitly recognized in W.Va. Const., art. III, § 5, "Penalties shall be proportioned to the character and degree of the offence" and is implicit in the Eighth Amendment to the United States Constitution, which originates in the same tradition as our own constitutional provision. See Weems v. United States, 217 U.S. 349, 30 S.Ct. 544, 54 L.Ed. 793 (1910), and Ralph v. Warden, 438 F.2d 786 (4th Cir.1970). A recent federal case, overturning the application of West Virginia's habitual offender law to a particular defendant, discussed the concept of disproportionality and identified three objective factors which can be useful in determining whether certain punishment is constitutionally disproportionate. These factors are: (1) the nature of the offense itself; (2) the legislative purpose behind the punishment; and (3) what punishment would have been applied in other jurisdictions. Hart v. Coiner, 483 F.2d 136 (4th Cir.1973).

As the preceding sections of this opinion have made clear, this Court is concerned with the class of offenders known as status offenders. By definition, the nature of the class of offenses committed by status offenders is non-criminal. Accordingly, the status offender is located on the extreme end of a spectrum of juvenile misconduct running from most serious to least serious offenses. The nature of their offenses thus tends to indicate that status offenders incarcerated in secure, prison-like facilities, along with children guilty of criminal conduct, are suffering a constitutionally disproportionate penalty.

The second consideration, the legislative purpose behind the punishment, has already been discussed at length in the substantive due process section of this opinion. To reiterate, this Court is unable to discern any rational connection between the legitimate legislative purposes of enforcing family discipline, protecting children, and protecting society from uncontrolled children and the incarceration of status offenders in secure, prison-like facilities along with children guilty of criminal conduct. We, like the court in Hart v. Coiner, supra, are in accord with Mr. Justice Brennan's observation: "If there is a significantly less severe punishment to achieve the purposes for which the punishment is inflicted, the punishment inflicted is unnecessary and therefore excessive." Hart v. Coiner, supra at 141.

Finally, we perceive that a "better rule" is emerging in other progressive jurisdictions, which eliminates or significantly limits the juvenile court's power to commit status offenders to secure, prison-like facilities along with children guilty of criminal conduct. New York's approach has been discussed in footnote 8 above.ᶜ Other jurisdictions, typical of those which do not incarcerate status offenders in secure, prison-like facilities along with children guilty of criminal conduct, include Massachusetts and Maryland. See Massachusetts General Laws Annotated, 119 § 39G [1973] and Annotated Code of Maryland § 3–832 [1973]. The nature of status offender punishment in other jurisdictions, which is by no means uniform, cannot, of course, control the outcome of this case. Nevertheless, in deciding in what direction an enlightened and humane society should move, this Court is entitled under W.Va. Const., art. III, § 5 to consider the response of other jurisdictions to the common problem which is presented here.

For all of the foregoing reasons, we conclude that the incarceration of status offenders in secure, prison-like facilities along with children guilty of criminal conduct inflicts a constitutionally disproportionate penalty upon status offenders, and as such violates W.Va. Const., art. III, § 5.

III

Accordingly, we hold that a status offender may still be adjudged delinquent under W.Va.Code, 49–1–4 [1941]; however, before he may be committed to a penal institution pursuant to the provisions of W.Va.Code, 49–5–11(4) [1975], there must be evidence on the record which clearly supports the conclusion, and the juvenile court must specifically find as a matter of fact, that no other reasonable alternative either is available or could with due diligence and financial commitment on the part of the State be made available to help the child, and that the child is so totally unmanageable, ungovernable, and anti-social that he or she is amenable to no treatment or restraint short of incarceration in a secure, prison-like facility. Furthermore, to reiterate in this context what we said above, no status offender in any event, regardless of incorrigibility, may be incarcerated in a

ᶜ The "footnote 8" referred to in the text, but omitted here, contains a discussion of material to be found in the Casebook at pp. 796–99.

secure, prison-like facility which is not devoted exclusively to the custody and rehabilitation of status offenders. We emphasize here that State parsimony is no defense to an allegation of deprivation of constitutional rights. The State may not punish a person not deserving of punishment merely because such action serves the State's interest in convenience of frugality. See Lavette M. v. Corporation Counsel of City of N.Y., 35 N.Y.2d 136, 359 N.Y.S.2d 20, 316 N.E.2d 314 (1974) and Rouse v. Cameron, 125 U.S.App.D.C. 366, 373 F.2d 451 (1966).

Consequently, the standard which the juvenile court must apply is not a standard of what facilities are *actually* available in the State of West Virginia for the treatment of juvenile status offenders, but rather a standard which looks to what facilities *could reasonably be made* available in an enlightened and humane state solicitous of the welfare of its children but also mindful of other demands upon the State budget for humanitarian purposes. We recognize that problems may arise, as for example, when a court is located in a rural part of West Virginia which lacks child-care facilities, and the court has no place to send a status offender except a correctional facility. Nevertheless, in such cases, if rehabilitation of the status offender could be accomplished by his commitment to a well-run, centralized state residential treatment center, or a local shelter facility where a small number of children live with professionally trained house parents, or by any other reasonable method, then the juvenile judge, as a matter of state constitutional law, must make a disposition under *Code* 49–5–11 [1975] which does not involve commitment to a secure, prison-like facility, or he must discharge the defendant.

For the foregoing reasons the writ of habeas corpus for which the petitioner prays is awarded and it is ordered that the petitioner be discharged forthwith from custody and restored to his liberty. Children currently committed to State facilities in violation of the guidelines enunciated in this opinion may bring actions in habeas corpus in the local circuit courts. It is further ordered that the Clerk of this Court shall send three copies of this opinion to the superintendents of each and every correctional facility in which juvenile offenders are committed together with an order of this court that those copies be posted in conspicuous places.

Writ awarded.

NOTE

In State ex rel. C.A.H. v. Strickler, Judge, 162 W.Va. 535, 251 S.E.2d 222 (1979), the Supreme Court of Appeals prohibited a juvenile judge from committing a status offender to a secure facility housing only girls adjudicated delinquent for committing criminal offenses even though no other secure facility was available in the state.

STATE EX REL. R.S. v. TRENT

Supreme Court of Appeals of West Virginia, 1982.
289 S.E.2d 166.

McGRAW, JUSTICE:

The petitioner, a sixteen-year-old male currently incarcerated in the West Virginia Industrial School for Boys, seeks a writ of habeas corpus to compel his release from the institution and a writ of mandamus to compel the committing court to place him in an appropriate residential treatment facility to meet his individual rehabilitative needs. He contends that his incarceration is illegal in that: (1) the committing court failed to receive him into its custody upon the recommendation of the Superintendent of the Industrial School; (2) he has demonstrated a history of mental illness; and (3) he was not accorded the least restrictive dispositional alternative. The petitioner also contends that he is entitled to receive individual treatment consistent with his therapeutic needs. We find merit in the petitioner's contentions and we grant the writ of mandamus prayed for. The writ of habeas corpus is conditionally awarded.

The petitioner has a history of delinquent and maladaptive behavior since the age of eight. He was expelled from school in the third grade and never returned. He has a history of severe drug and alcohol abuse since the age of eleven and may have been the subject of child abuse. He has been charged with numerous instances of breaking and entering, destruction of property, shoplifting and auto theft and has spent a good deal, if not the majority, of his youth in mental health facilities, detention centers and correctional institutions. Periodic psychological evaluations of the petitioner have led to diagnoses that he suffers from organic brain syndrome with behavioral reaction, emerging antisocial personality disturbance, borderline mental retardation and possible learning disabilities, all generally characterized as being within the mild to moderate range of impairment. Prognoses vary from below average to poor.

On April 21, 1980, the petitioner was committed to the Industrial School for Boys by the Circuit Court of Ohio County, after being adjudged delinquent on a charge of breaking and entering. He remained incarcerated there until April 7, 1981, at which time he was released from custody upon the recommendation of the Superintendent of the Industrial School, who had determined that continued incarceration of the petitioner at the school would be of no benefit to him. The petitioner was released into the custody of his mother but was placed with an aunt until his mother could move into a mobile home. On April 10, 1981, the petitioner was arrested for stealing a car and was incarcerated in the Ohio County Jail until April 12, 1981. On April 15, 1981, he was again arrested and incarcerated for the theft of a motor home.

Upon motion of counsel for the petitioner, the circuit court ordered that the petitioner undergo psychological testing and evaluation. The tests were conducted from April 29, 1981 to May 4, 1981.

On May 8, 1981, the petitioner was adjudged delinquent and was committed to the Industrial School for Boys for a term of not less than six months nor more than one year. On August 19, 1981, the Superintendent of the Industrial School, respondent herein, wrote a letter to the committing court recommending that the petitioner be returned to the custody of the court and that the Department of Welfare be directed to locate immediately an alternative facility for disposition of the petitioner. The Superintendent's stated reason for this recommendation was that incarceration of the petitioner at the Industrial School would not achieve his rehabilitation and was not in the petitioner's best interests. On August 26, 1981, Judge George Spillers of the First Judicial Circuit wrote a letter to Mr. Ronald Klug, the Supervisor of the Department of Welfare in Ohio County, directing him to implement the recommendations of Superintendent Trent. On November 5, 1981, Superintendent Trent wrote another letter to the circuit court indicating that he had received no response to his previous letter of August 19, 1981.

On December 1, 1981, Superintendent Trent again wrote to the committing court stating that the petitioner's placement at the school was not effective and again recommended that the petitioner be returned to the custody of the court for placement in an alternative facility. The Superintendent also suggested two out-of-state facilities which might be suited to the petitioner's needs. The petition in this case was filed on December 14, 1981.

The petitioner contends that his continued incarceration at the Industrial School following the Superintendent's recommendation that he be discharged into the custody of the committing court was illegal in that the committing court was required by law to comply with the Superintendent's recommendation. The petitioner also contends that his commitment was illegal in the first instance because the circuit court did not afford him the least restrictive dispositional alternative available which was consistent with the purpose of his custody and because he had made a showing of mental illness. Finally, the petitioner asserts that not only is his present incarceration unlawful for the above-stated reasons, but that he is entitled to receive individual treatment consistent with his therapeutic needs. On this ground the petitioner demands a writ of mandamus.

I.

We turn first to the petitioner's contention that his commitment to the Industrial School by the circuit court on May 8, 1981, was unlawful in the first instance. W.Va.Code § 49–5–13(b) (1980 Replacement Vol.) requires the juvenile court at the dispositional stage of delinquency proceedings to "give precedence to the least restrictive" of the enumerated dispositional alternatives "consistent with the best interests and welfare of the public and the child." See State ex rel. C.A.H. v. Strickler, W.Va., 251 S.E.2d 222 (1979). Moreover, juveniles are constitutionally entitled to the least restrictive treatment that is consistent with the purpose of their custody. State ex rel. K.W. v. Werner, W.Va., 242 S.E.2d 907 (1978). A juvenile against whom delinquency proceedings are brought as the result of the child's commission of an act which would be a crime if committed by an adult may be committed to an industrial home or correctional facility "[u]pon a finding that no less restrictive alternative would accomplish the requisite rehabilitation of the child * * *" W.Va. Code § 49–5–13(b)(5); State ex rel. S.J.C. v. Fox, W.Va., 268 S.E.2d 56 (1980).

In State ex rel. D.D.H. v. Dostert, W.Va., 269 S.E.2d 401 (1980), however, we held that a court having jurisdiction of juvenile proceedings "cannot justify incarceration in a secure, prison-like facility on the grounds of rehabilitation alone." Syl. pt. 5, in part. Rather the court's decision to commit the juvenile to an industrial school or correctional facility must be grounded on a number of factors indicating that incarceration is the appropriate disposition.

> In this regard the court should specifically address the following: (1) the danger which the child poses to society; (2) all other less restrictive alternatives which have been tried either by the court or by other agencies to whom the child was previously directed to avoid formal juvenile proceedings; (3) the child's background with particular regard to whether there are pre-determining factors such as acute poverty, parental abuse, learning disabilities, physical impairments, or any other discrete, causative factors which can be corrected by the State or other social service agencies in an environment less restrictive than an industrial school; (4) whether the child is amenable to rehabilitation outside an industrial school, and if not, why not; (5) whether the dual goals of deterrence and juvenile responsibility can be achieved in some setting less restrictive than an industrial school and if not, why not; (6) whether the child is suffering from no recognizable, treatable determining force and therefore is entitled to punishment; (7) whether the child appears willing to cooperate with the suggested program of rehabilitation; and, (8) whether the child is so uncooperative or so ungovernable that no program of rehabilitation will be successful without the coercion inherent in a secure facility. Id. Syl. pt. 4, in part.

Before ordering the incarceration of the child, the juvenile court is required to set forth upon the record the facts which lead to the conclusion that no less restrictive alternative is appropriate. The record must affirmatively show

> that the child's behavioral problem is not the result of social conditions beyond the child's control, but rather of an intentional failure on the part of the child to conform his actions to the law, or that the child will be dangerous if any other disposition is used, or that the child will not cooperate with any rehabilitative program absent physical restraint. Id. at 413–414.

Upon reviewing the circuit court's order committing the petitioner to the Industrial School, we find that the court made the following "specific findings":

1.   Every reasonable alternative with regard to placement has been explored.

2.   Due to his continuous violent and destructive behavior, [the petitioner] presents a danger to himself and to others.

3.   There is at this time no less restrictive alternative available or appropriate for [the petitioner] than placement into the custody of the Commissioner of Institutions of West Virginia, for placement at the Industrial School for Boys.

The circuit court made no recitation of facts to support the findings. There is no mention of the alternatives explored by the court and the reasons for their rejection. There is no indication of other less restrictive disposition alternatives already tried by the court or by social service agencies. There are no factual findings with regard to the extensive psychiatric and psychological evaluations of the petitioner nor any mention of the results of the court-ordered psychological examination of the petitioner which was conducted shortly before the dispositional hearing. The circuit court did not make a sufficient record in light of the guidelines set forth in State ex rel. D.D.H. v. Dostert, supra, which would enable this Court to review the reasons for the circuit court's determination that the petitioner's rehabilitation could be accomplished by no less restrictive alternative than incarceration at the Industrial School.

The other exhibits presented by the petitioner and the respondents, which should have been before the circuit court at the time of the dispositional hearing,* reveal facts that might support the circuit court's conclusions. The psychiatric evaluations of the petitioner over a period of three years indicated that he required a structured, secure environment where he could be taught forced acceptance of responsibility in order to conform his behavior to the law. The staff psychologists at the mental health facilities where the petitioner was hospitalized were of the opinion that hospitalization at those facilities was not conducive to the petitioner's rehabilitation. The petitioner's repeated delinquent behavior was indicative of the fact that past rehabilitative efforts had proved unsuccessful. On at least one occasion the petitioner had run away from the facility to which he had been committed and had committed a delinquent act.

The circuit court made no mention of these factors in its dispositional order, however. Moreover, it is uncontested that the petitioner had been incarcerated on a prior occasion at the Industrial School and had been released upon the assertion of the Superintendent that that facility was unable to fulfill the petitioner's rehabilitative needs. Since we have no record which would enable us to determine the factors that led to the conclusion that incarceration was the least restrictive appropriate alternative and to decide whether that conclusion was justified, we award a writ of habeas corpus in accordance

* W.Va.Code § 49–7–23 (1980 Replacement Vol.) requires the Department of Welfare to file of record and preserve "[t]he proceedings, records, reports, case histories, and all other papers or documents of or received by the State department in the administration of" Chapter 49.

with our decision in State ex rel. D.D.H. v. Dostert, supra, and order the petitioner discharged from the custody of the Superintendent of the Industrial School.

The petitioner also contends that his incarceration was unlawful in the first instance in that he had demonstrated a history of mental illness. W.Va.Code § 28–1–2(c) (1981 Cum.Supp.) provides in pertinent part, "[n]o youth who is mentally ill or significantly mentally retarded shall be committed to, or retained by, the commissioner of corrections, but shall be returned to the committing court for further disposition * * *." "Mental illness" is defined, for purposes of Chapter 27, as "a manifestation in a person of significantly impaired capacity to maintain acceptable levels of functioning in the areas of intellect, emotion and physical well-being." W.Va.Code § 27–1–2 (1980 Replacement Vol.).

Prior to the dispositional hearing the circuit court, upon request of the petitioner's counsel, ordered psychological examinations of the petitioner. The examinations occurred over a period of four days and consisted of psychological testing, interviews and observation of the petitioner by psychologists in private practice. The report of the results of the examination traced the petitioner's medical history and his background. The report concluded that the petitioner suffered from learning disabilities, a memory dysfunction and mental retardation in the mild to moderate range of impairment. The petitioner was also diagnosed as suffering from an organic brain disorder related to epilepsy which resulted in explosive behavior, but it appeared that drug treatment was successful in containing the petitioner's seizures. The report concluded that the petitioner's behavioral problems were more the result of an "anti-social personality disorder" than of "mental illness" or "organic disorders" and that the petitioner did not exhibit psychotic or neurotic behavior. The petitioner was found to be capable of understanding the proceedings against him and competent in assisting in his own defense. To this extent the court-ordered evaluation of the petitioner was in accord with prior evaluations of the petitioner's conduct. Earlier examinations, however, had also indicated that the petitioner tended to act to satisfy his immediate desires without reflection upon the inappropriateness of consequences of his behavior, and that he manifested hostility and suspicion of others and that he tended to respond to stressful situations with anger, lack of control and violence. It was on the basis of these observations that the prior evaluations recommended the petitioner's placement in a secure, supervised setting where his behavior could be modified. The court-ordered evaluation recommended that the petitioner be placed in a vocational rehabilitation program where his deficiencies in social learning and academic achievement could be corrected, but noted reservations as to the ability of such a program to provide adequate security.

We recognize, as the State asserts, that none of the psychological evaluations before the circuit court made a finding of mental illness in the petitioner's case. Indeed, the psychologists and psychiatrists who examined the petitioner cautiously avoided diagnosing the petitioner's behavioral problems as being the result of mental illness, attributing his delinquent behavior instead to an antisocial personality disorder which was not amenable to treatment in the setting of a conventional mental health facility. The medical reports show, however, that the petitioner is a disturbed child prone toward socially unacceptable behavior which he is unable to control.

We are of the opinion that the distinction between a troubled child who exhibits dangerous antisocial behavior which he is unable to control and a child who displays a "traditional" mental illness may be too subtle to be traced definitively by the judicial mind. We hold that a child who is mentally incapable of conforming his conduct to prescribed legal norms and who cannot restrain himself from committing proscribed antisocial acts, thereby presenting a danger to himself or to others, comes within the definition of "mental illness" and shall be treated accordingly. The petitioner here may fall within that category. While earlier evaluations indicated that in certain situations the petitioner is unable to control his behavior, the court-ordered evaluation conducted prior to the dispositional hearing was somewhat more favorable in its diagnosis. While the circuit court made a finding that the petitioner presented a danger to himself and to others, it should have posited that finding in mental incapacity. We think that where a question is raised as to the mental capacity of a child adjudged delinquent, the juvenile court is obliged to develop the matter and to state its findings upon the record so that the conclusion of the juvenile court as to the child's capacity may properly be reviewed in a subsequent proceeding. The court's investigation should involve multi-professional evaluations by those connected or employed by such agencies as the Department of Health, the County Board of Education, the Department of Welfare and the Department of Corrections, who are able to evaluate the child's abilities and disabilities.

II.

The petitioner also contends that his continued incarceration at the Industrial School after the Superintendent recommended that he be discharged and returned to the custody of the circuit court for placement in another facility was unlawful. The petitioner contends that upon receipt of the Superintendent's recommendation, the circuit court was required to discharge him from incarceration and receive him into custody pursuant to W.Va.Code § 49–5–13(b)(5).

W.Va.Code § 49–5–13(b)(5) reads in material part:

Commitments shall not exceed the maximum term for which an adult could have been sentenced for the same offense, *with discretion as to discharge to rest with the director of the institution, who may release the child and return him to the court for disposition;* * * *. (Emphasis added.)

In State ex rel. Washington v. Taylor, W.Va., 273 S.E.2d 84 (1980), we held that under this provision a circuit court did not have the authority to decline to receive a child whose release has been recommended by the director of the institution to which the child had been committed. In that case the Superintendent of the Industrial School had concluded that the child had successfully completed the institution's rehabilitation program and that his continued progress would not be served by further incarceration. The circuit court refused to accept custody, however, until the child had completed the minimum term of incarceration imposed at the dispositional hearing. We concluded that permitting the court to override the discretion of the institution's director and to require the child to remain incarcerated for a minimum term would undermine the institution's rehabilitation program.

Here, the Superintendent's recommendation that the petitioner be discharged from his custody was motivated by his conclusion that the Industrial School's treatment program was inadequate to achieve the petitioner's rehabilitation. In his letters to the circuit court, the Superintendent explained that the Industrial School's program was designed to use long term reinforcement, in the form of earning time towards early release, to achieve rehabilitation of the residents and that this treatment, when combined with the privileges available in a maximum security facility, was insufficient to motivate the petitioner. The Superintendent stated that the petitioner was suffering from a disorder that the facility was unable to treat; that the petitioner was interfering with the rehabilitation of other residents; that the petitioner was influenced by other residents of the institution to engage in unacceptable behavior; and that the petitioner's behavior had grown progressively worse even though he had been placed in the school's most intensive treatment unit. Superintendent Trent stated that further incarceration at the school or at any other similar facility with limited resources would be detrimental to the petitioner's health and well-being and recommended the petitioner's immediate placement in one of several out-of-state facilities which might be better able to meet the petitioner's needs.

The State contends that since the Superintendent's recommendation that the petitioner be discharged from his custody was not based on any determination that the petitioner had successfully completed the institution's treatment program, but rather on his conclusion that the petitioner had failed to respond to the treatment offered at the school, *Washington* is not applicable here. The State would have us hold that the Superintendent's recommendations are entitled to credence only when they are based on the conclusion that the child should be returned to the community. We do not think the discretion vested by W.Va.Code § 49–5–13(b)(5) in the director of a juvenile correctional institution is so limited.

The Legislature obviously bestowed upon the director of a correctional facility the discretion to recommend the return of an incarcerated child to the custody of the committing court in recognition of the fact that the director is the person best able to judge the progress of the child within the institution's rehabilitative program. If, after observing and evaluating the child's involvement in the institution's program, the director concludes that continued incarceration is not in the child's best interest, the circuit court is obliged to give credence to the director's professional judgment. It is irrelevant for purposes of W.Va.Code § 49–5–13(b)(5) whether the director's recommendation that custody be transferred is based on the success or failure of the institution's program to accomplish the rehabilitation of the child. Rather, the paramount consideration is the negative effect continued incarceration is likely to have either upon the child or upon the institution's effective treatment of other children. Consequently, where the director of a correctional institution to which a delinquent child has been committed determines that continued incarceration will not accomplish the rehabilitation of the child and recommends that the child be returned to the custody of the committing court for placement in another facility better suited to meet the needs of the child, the court to which such recommendation is directed is required by W.Va.Code § 49–5–13(b)(5) to defer to the discretion of the director and to take steps to implement an appropriate alternative disposition.

The State argues, however, that even if the circuit court was required by the statute to take custody of the petitioner, there is no basis for granting the habeas corpus relief sought by the petitioner because the Superintendent did not recommend the immediate release of the child, but only requested that the committing court take custody of the child and locate an alternative treatment facility. The State asserts that the circuit court did in fact accept custody of the petitioner and that the Superintendent voluntarily retained the petitioner at the Industrial School until a suitable treatment facility could be found.

The evidence shows that on August 19, 1981 Superintendent Trent requested the *immediate* transfer of the petitioner to an alternative treatment facility. The circuit court promptly requested the Department of Welfare to implement the recommendation. There is nothing on the record to indicate any action on the part of the court or the Department of Welfare for the next several months to secure the petitioner's placement in a more suitable facility. On November 5, 1981, the Superintendent informed the circuit court that he had received no response to his request. At the end of November the social service worker conducting the petitioner's case stated to the child's counsel that she was attempting to place the petitioner at the Davis center and had not considered out-of-state placement. On December 1, 1981, the Superintendent again contacted the circuit court requesting that it take custody of the child and named several out-of-state facilities that might be able to help the petitioner. It was not until the day after the petition was filed in this case that the Department of Welfare informed the circuit court that it was attempting to place the petitioner in one of two out-of-state facilities.

We do not think these facts support the State's contentions. Although the circuit judge promptly ordered the Department of

Welfare to locate an appropriate alternative facility in which to place the petitioner, the evidence shows that little, if any, action was taken by the Department of Welfare to implement the Superintendent's recommendation until approximately four months later after the petition was filed in this case. There is no evidence that the circuit court attempted to prod the Department of Welfare into action. Nor is there any indication that the Superintendent was notified that alternative placement was being sought for the petitioner. Indeed, the Superintendent's letters of November 5 and December 1, 1981, indicate that no response at all had been made to his original recommendation that custody of the petitioner be returned to the circuit court, much less a notification of compliance therewith.

We think it is clear from these facts that the Superintendent retained custody of the petitioner, not as an accommodation to the circuit court pending the location of an alternate facility, but rather because the circuit court did not order the petitioner transferred from the custody of the Department of Corrections. The circuit court must act affirmatively and in good faith to secure proper custody of a juvenile whom the director of a correctional institution has determined to be unamenable to treatment by further incarceration. As the record here shows no such effort by the circuit court with regard to the petitioner, we must conclude that the court has not yet complied with the Superintendent's request that the petitioner be returned to the custody of the court, and we award the writ of habeas corpus on this ground.

III.

The petitioner's final prayer is that a writ of mandamus issue to compel the circuit court to afford the petitioner appropriate treatment which will promote his rehabilitation. We think there is little question that a child adjudged delinquent and committed to the custody of the State has both a constitutional and a statutory right to treatment. We have noted on numerous occasions that the purpose of our juvenile justice system is to provide for the rehabilitation of delinquent children. State ex rel. D.D.H. v. Dostert, supra; State ex rel. Harris v. Calendine, W.Va., 233 S.E.2d 318 (1977). The rehabilitative goal of the juvenile justice system is embodied in the statement of purpose contained in W.Va.Code § 49–1–1(a) in (1981 Cum.Supp.):

> The purpose of this chapter is to provide a comprehensive system of child welfare throughout the State which will assure to each child such care and guidance, preferably in his or her home, and will serve the spiritual, emotional, mental and physical welfare of the child; preserve and strengthen the child's family ties whenever possible with recognition of the fundamental rights of parenthood and with recognition of the State's responsibility to assist the family in providing necessary education and training and to reduce the rate of juvenile delinquency and to provide a system for the rehabilitation or detention of juvenile delinquents and the protection of the welfare of the general public. In

pursuit of these goals it is the intention of the legislature to provide for removing the child from the custody of parents only when the child's welfare or the safety and protection of the public cannot be adequately safeguarded without removal; and, when the child has to be removed from his or her family, to secure for the child custody, care and discipline consistent with the child's best interests and other goals herein set out.

The child welfare law clearly contemplates that the rehabilitation of delinquent children shall be accomplished by a program of individualized care and treatment directed towards the ultimate goal of reintegrating such children into society so that they no longer pose a threat to themselves or to the public.

Moreover, since the State has defined its interest in taking custody of delinquent children as rehabilitation, due process requires that the nature of the child's custody bear a relation to that rehabilitative purpose. Jackson v. Indiana, 406 U.S. 715, 92 S.Ct. 1845, 32 L.Ed.2d 435 (1972).

The basis for commitment—to rehabilitate and re-establish the juvenile in society—is clearly grounded in a *parens patriae* rationale. Thus, under the *parens patriae* theory, the juvenile must be given treatment lest the involuntary commitment amount to an arbitrary exercise of governmental power proscribed by the due process clause.

Morales v. Turman, 383 F.Supp. 53, 71 (E.D.Tex.1974); rev'd on other grds., 535 F.2d 864 (5th Cir.1976). * * * This Court recognized the juvenile's constitutional right to treatment in State ex rel. K.W. v. Werner, supra.

To accomplish the rehabilitative goal of the juvenile justice system, all officers and employees of the State charged with implementing the provisions of the juvenile law are required to act in the best interests of the child and the public in establishing an individualized program of treatment which is directed toward the needs of the child and likely to result in the development of the child into a productive member of society.

Without a program of individualized treatment the result may be that the juveniles will not be rehabilitated, but warehoused, and that at the termination of detention they will likely be incapable of taking their proper places in free society; their interests and those of the state * * * thereby being defeated.

Nelson v. Heyne, 491 F.2d at 360.

The child welfare statutes clearly set forth the officers and agencies upon whom this obligation falls. The Department of Welfare is required to develop standards of child care and to advise, cooperate with, assist and supervise all child welfare agencies which care for delinquent children, W.Va.Code § 49–2–3 (1980 Replacement Vol.); to provide care, support and protective services for children in need of public services, W.Va.Code § 49–2–16 (1980 Replacement Vol.); to investigate alternative dispositions appropriate for delinquent children upon request of the court, W.Va.Code § 49–5–13(a) (1980 Replacement Vol.); to investigate the child's background and furnish information and assistance to the juvenile court, W.Va.Code § 49–5–15 (1980 Replacement Vol.); to establish rules and regulations governing juvenile correctional, detention and other facilities, W.Va. Code § 49–5–16a (1980 Replacement Vol.); to encourage alternatives within the juvenile justice system, W.Va.Code § 49–5B–4(a) (1980 Replacement Vol.); and to provide an individualized program of treatment for each child adjudged delinquent. W.Va.Code § 49–5B–4(b). The Department of Health is required to cooperate with and assist the Department of Welfare in its formulation of standards for child care and services for children, W.Va.Code § 49–2–3, and to conduct a physical and mental examination of wards of the court upon request of the court. W.Va.Code § 49–5–4 (1980 Replacement Vol.). The Commissioner of Corrections is required, upon request of the court, to accept custody of delinquent children, to have diagnostic and medical tests conducted and to submit a report of the results of such tests to the juvenile court, W.Va.Code § 49–5–13a (1980 Replacement Vol.), and to formulate rules and regulations governing the operation of juvenile correctional institutions. W.Va.Code § 49–5–16a. The juvenile court is required to protect wards of the court, W.Va.Code § 49–5–4; to hear all witnesses who might shed light upon the proper disposition of the child and give precedence to the least restrictive alternative disposition consistent with the best interests of the child and the public, W.Va.Code § 49–5–13(b); and to exercise continuing jurisdiction over children under the age of eighteen. W.Va.Code § 49–5–2 (1980 Replacement Vol.).

The statutory provisions clearly anticipate a cooperative effort on the part of the named officers and agencies to develop a comprehensive program of individualized treatment for juvenile offenders. This Court has recognized this purpose of the child welfare law. In State ex rel. D.D.H. v. Dostert, supra, we set forth in detail the respective roles of the court, the probation officer or welfare worker, the child and the child's counsel at the dispositional stage. In addition to those responsibilities specifically enumerated by statute, we concluded that the juvenile court is required to review intelligently the child's social history so that an individualized treatment plan may be devised and to order incarceration only when it appears that the child is dangerous or must be restrained in order to prevent flight, and the Department of Welfare is required to attempt to find a suitable alternative to incarceration. Counsel for the child is also required to participate actively at the dispositional stage and has a duty to make an independent investigation of the child's background; to inform himself in detail of the facilities both within and without the State which are suited to the child's needs and able to treat him; to take the initial steps to secure tentative acceptance of the child by appropriate facilities; and to advise the juvenile court of the terms and conditions under which such facilities will accept the child. The child's role in the process is to cooperate in the treatment program geared toward his rehabilitation and re-entry into society.

Of course, the respective obligations of these officers and agencies is most often discussed with respect to the disposition of the juvenile in the first instance. Certainly at that point those who are charged with effecting the purposes of the juvenile law are expected to act in concert to design a treatment program which can be reasonably predicted to facilitate the rehabilitation of the child and serve the interest of society. This responsibility does not end with the juvenile court's determination of the proper disposition. "Treatment and rehabilitation represent * * * a continuum measured by the period of time the juvenile offender remains in the state's custody." Nelson v. Heyne, 355 F.Supp. at 459. Those into whose care the child is placed have a responsibility to monitor and evaluate the progress of the child. If it becomes apparent that the child is unable to respond to the rehabilitative model of the caretaker institution, it is the responsibility of the director of the institution to report the failure of the ordered treatment to effect the rehabilitation of the child to the committing juvenile court and to recommend alternative treatment. The court should then require an immediate reevaluation of the alternatives appropriate for treatment of the juvenile, involving the appropriate agencies and officials in the process, and order the child placed in an environment better suited to his rehabilitative needs. As there does not appear to have been any affirmative effort on the part of the circuit court and the Department of Welfare to evolve, with the cooperation of other state agencies, a comprehensive individualized program of treatment with respect to the petitioner in the face of the Superintendent's recommendations, we grant the writ of mandamus prayed for and order the circuit court to supervise the development of such a program.

As a final matter, we note that juvenile courts and the Department of Welfare are not limited by statute to relying solely upon their own resources to develop individualized treatment programs for juvenile offenders. The Department of Welfare has the express authority to enter into cooperative ventures with private or State agencies in order to establish and implement rehabilitative alternatives for juveniles. W.Va.Code § 49–5B–4(c). Thus, the Department of Welfare is at liberty to call upon the expertise of the Department of Health, the Department of Education and county boards of education, as well as that of private agencies and organizations, to design and put into operation individualized treatment programs that will address the problems and needs of delinquent children, thereby fulfilling the interests of society. The juvenile courts and state agencies involved in the treatment process should draw upon these valuable resources to effect the rehabilitative purposes of the juvenile justice system.

For the reasons stated in this opinion, we award the writ of habeas corpus prayed for and order the petitioner discharged from the custody of the Superintendent of the Industrial School for Boys and remanded to the custody of the Circuit Court of Ohio County. A writ of mandamus will issue to compel the circuit court, in cooperation with the Department of Welfare and other agencies, to secure immediately the petitioner's placement in an appropriate juvenile rehabilitation and treatment facility whose program is designed to meet the petitioner's individual needs, in accordance with the principles enunciated herein.

Writs awarded.

IJA–ABA JUVENILE JUSTICE STANDARDS, STANDARDS RELATING TO JUVENILE DELINQUENCY AND SANCTIONS (1980).

5.2 Classes of juvenile offenses *

A.   Offenses within the criminal jurisdiction of the juvenile court should be classified as class one through class five juvenile offenses.

B.   Where, under a criminal statute or ordinance made applicable to juveniles pursuant to Standard 2.2, the maximum sentence authorized upon conviction for such offense is

    1.   death or imprisonment for life or for a term in excess of twenty years, it is a class one juvenile offense;

    2.   imprisonment for a term in excess of five but not more than twenty years, it is a class two juvenile offense;

    3.   imprisonment for a term in excess of one year but not more than five years, it is a class three juvenile offense;

    4.   imprisonment for a term in excess of six months but not more than one year, it is a class four juvenile offense;

    5.   imprisonment for a term of six months or less, it is a class five juvenile offense;

    6.   not prescribed, it is a class five juvenile offense.

6.2 Limitations on type and duration of sanctions *

A.   The juvenile court should not impose a sanction more severe than,

    1.   where the juvenile is found to have committed a class one juvenile offense,

        a.   confinement in a secure facility or placement in a nonsecure facility or residence for a period of twenty-four months, or

        b.   conditional freedom for a period of thirty-six months;

    2.   where the juvenile is found to have committed a class two juvenile offense,

a. confinement in a secure facility or placement in a nonsecure facility or residence for a period of twelve months, or

b. conditional freedom for a period of twenty-four months;

3. where the juvenile is found to have committed a class three juvenile offense,

a. confinement in a secure facility or placement in a nonsecure facility or residence for a period of six months, or

b. conditional freedom for a period of eighteen months;

4. where the juvenile is found to have committed a class four juvenile offense,

a. confinement in a secure facility for a period of three months if the juvenile has a prior record, or

b. placement in a nonsecure facility or residence for a period of three months, or

c. conditional freedom for a period of twelve months;

5. where the juvenile is found to have committed a class five juvenile offense,

a. placement in a nonsecure facility or residence for a period of two months if the juvenile has a prior record, or

b. conditional freedom for a period of six months.

B. For purposes of this standard, a juvenile has a "prior record" only when he or she has been formally adjudged previously to have committed:

1. an offense that would amount to a class one, two, or three juvenile offense, as defined in Standard 5.2, within the twenty-four months preceding the commission of the offense subject to sanctioning; or

2. three offenses that would amount to class four or five juvenile offenses, as defined in Standard 5.2, at least one of which was committed within the twelve months preceding the commission of the offense subject to sanctioning.

6.3   Multiple juvenile offenses *

A. When a juvenile is found to have committed two or more juvenile offenses during the same transaction or episode, the juvenile court should not impose a sanction more severe than the maximum sanction authorized by Standard 6.2 for the most serious such offense.

B. When, in the same proceeding, a juvenile is found to have committed two or more offenses during separate transactions or episodes, the juvenile court should not impose a sanction

---

* Reprinted with permission from Standards Relating to Juvenile Delinquency and Sanctions, Copyright 1980, Ballinger Publishing Company.

1.   more severe in nature than the sanction authorized by Standard 6.2 for the most serious such offense; or

2.   longer in duration than a period equal to one and a half times the period authorized by Standard 6.2 for the most serious such offense.

C.   When, at the time a juvenile is charged with an offense, the charging authority or its agents have evidence sufficient to warrant charging such juvenile with another juvenile offense, committed within the court's jurisdiction, the failure jointly to charge such offense should thereafter bar the initiation of juvenile court delinquency proceedings based on such offense.

6.4   Termination of orders imposing sanctions *

A juvenile court order imposing sanctions should terminate no later than the twenty-first birthday of the juvenile subject to such order.

IN MATTER OF FELDER

Family Court, Onondaga County, 1978.
93 Misc.2d 369, 402 N.Y.S.2d 528.

EDWARD J. MCLAUGHLIN, JUDGE.

This juvenile delinquency proceeding involves a designated felony pursuant to the Juvenile Justice Reform Act of 1976, (L.1976, ch. 878) N.Y. Family Court Act §§ 711–767, 29A McKinney's Consolidated Laws 1977.   It presents a case of first impression for this court. Respondent, a boy of fifteen, allegedly committed a robbery in the first degree, Penal Law § 160.15, a designated felony.   FCA § 712(h). When the case came before the Court, the Respondent moved for a jury trial, asserting that under Baldwin v. New York, 399 U.S. 66, 90 S.Ct. 1886, 26 L.Ed.2d 437 (1970), an individual charged with a crime where the penalty could exceed six months imprisonment is entitled to a jury trial.   The respondent alleged that since he can be confined in a secure facility for a period of time up to twelve months, pursuant to section 753–a(4)(a)(ii) of the Family Court Act, the *Baldwin* doctrine applied, and he is entitled to a trial by jury.

On the other hand, the petitioner alleged that the United States Supreme Court decision in McKeiver v. Pennsylvania, 403 U.S. 528, 91 S.Ct. 1976, 29 L.Ed.2d 647 (1971), is controlling.   *McKeiver* holds that a juvenile charged with a delinquency, which precludes, by definition, criminal consequences and tried in a civil court, does not have a due process right to a jury trial.   Petitioner further alleged that while New York is not constitutionally precluded from granting a jury trial under *McKeiver*, it has determined not to do so, citing In re Daniel G., 27 N.Y.2d 90, 313 N.Y.S.2d 704, 261 N.E.2d 627 (1970) and Matter of George S., 44 A.D.2d 352, 355 N.Y.S.2d 143 (1st Dept., 1974).

---

* Reprinted with permission from Standards Relating to Juvenile Delinquency and Sanctions, Copyright 1980, Ballinger Publishing Company.

The issue before the court, then, is whether the instant proceeding is controlled by *McKeiver* or by *Baldwin*. Specifically, the question turns on whether this is a juvenile proceeding within the meaning of *McKeiver*, or, whether so many of the attributes of a juvenile proceeding have been discarded that the proceeding is in effect "criminal" in nature and thus within the ambit of *Baldwin*.

A. IS A DESIGNATED FELONY PROCEEDING A JUVENILE PROCEEDING?

The concept of designated felony was created as a part of the Juvenile Justice Reform Act of 1976. * * *

The Legislature has chosen to label this new "designated felony concept" as a "juvenile" proceeding. It is axiomatic that this court is not bound by that designation if, in fact, the new proceeding is indeed a criminal proceeding. * * *

* * *

B. BACKGROUND OF THE JUVENILE JUSTICE SYSTEM

The fundamental substantive distinction between a juvenile proceeding and a criminal proceeding is that a juvenile disposition is limited to treatment, while a criminal proceeding may impose punishment regardless of whether the punishment results in retribution and, or, deterrence. The view that the difference between criminal and juvenile proceedings is the difference between retribution and deterrence, on the one hand, and treatment, on the other, is confirmed by an examination of the history of the juvenile court system. This examination will also show that a denial of a juvenile's full exercise of his constitutional rights can only be predicated upon the presence of the treatment principle of the juvenile justice system.

* * *

This historical examination of the origins of the juvenile justice system shows that the informality, flexibility, and, concomitantly, the absence of constitutional safeguards at juvenile proceedings was justified on the ground that the juvenile was to be treated and rehabilitated. Conversely, when the juvenile proceeding was primarily for retributive and deterrent purposes, it was considered criminal in nature, and hence subject to all of the limitations of a regular criminal proceeding. Sometimes referred to as the "exchange principle of juvenile law", the trading of the constitutional protections of a criminal proceeding for rehabilitation still remains today the *sine qua non* of juvenile proceedings. * * *

* * *

It is against this background that McKeiver v. Pennsylvania, supra, must be viewed. It is true that *McKeiver* stated that in a juvenile proceeding trial by jury is not a constitutional requirement. The Court specifically refused to abandon the salutary goals of the juvenile system and rejected the jury trial because it could "tend once again to place the juvenile squarely in the routine of the criminal process." 403 U.S., at 547, 91 S.Ct. at 1987. Indeed, the Court acknowledged that when a child is adjudicated as a juvenile, but treated as a criminal, an inconsistency results, for the Court stated: "Of course, there have been abuses. * * * We refrain from saying at this point that these abuses are of a constitutional dimension." Id., at 547–48, 91 S.Ct. at 1987. In effect, the Court deferred until a more appropriate occasion the determination of when a juvenile disposition fails to meet the rehabilitative premise of the juvenile system. The determination in *McKeiver* that in a juvenile proceeding a jury trial is not required, is, therefore, necessarily limited to those proceedings that are juvenile in nature. Thus, there is no requirement of a jury trial in family court where the disposition is rehabilitative and non-penal. When, however, the protections provided to the juvenile criminal offender have been so eroded away that what is actually a punishment is characterized as a treatment, an abuse of constitutional dimension has occurred, and, a jury trial is required before punishment, although appropriate, may be inflicted.

C. BACKGROUND OF THE 1976 ACT

In response to the reported increase in the frequency and severity of crimes committed by juveniles, the Legislature in the 1976 session enacted the Juvenile Justice Reform Act. * * * This bill significantly amended Article 7 of the Family Court Act. The express purpose of Article 7 was redefined to include, for the first time, consideration of the needs of the community: "In any juvenile procedure under this article, the court shall consider the needs and best interests of the respondent as well as the need for protection of the community." FCA § 711. To this end, the Legislature created restrictive placement. Rejecting proposals to transfer seriously violent juveniles to the adult criminal system, the Legislature adopted restrictive placement as a method of dealing with the juveniles within the juvenile system. * * *

The amendments to Article 7 define four new terms—designated felony act,[39] designated Class A felony act,[40] secure facility,[41] and restrictive placement. * * * Further, the amendments allow the County Attorney to be assisted by members of the District Attor-

[39] FCA § 712(h) " 'Designated felony act.' An act committed by a person fourteen or fifteen years of age which, if done by an adult, would be a crime (i) defined in sections 125.27 (murder in the first degree); 125.25 (murder in the second degree); 135.25 (kidnapping in the first degree); or 150.20 (arson in the first degree) of the penal law; (ii) defined in sections 120.10 (assault in the first degree); 125.20 (manslaughter in the first degree); 130.35 (rape in the first degree); 130.50 (sodomy in the first degree); 135.20 (kidnapping in the second degree), but only where the abduction involved the use or threat of use of deadly force; 150.15 (arson in the second degree); or

160.15 (robbery in the first degree) of the penal law; or (iii) defined in the penal law as an attempt to commit murder in the first or second degree or kidnapping in the first degree."

[40] FCA § 712(i) "Designated class A felony act." A designated felony act defined in clause (i) paragraph (h) of this section.

[41] FCA § 712(j) "Secure facility." A residential facility in which the juvenile delinquent may be placed under this article, which is characterized by physically restricting construction, hardware and procedures, and is designated a secure facility by the division for youth.

ney's staff, FCA § 254(c); provides that the probation service may not attempt to adjust some cases without the prior written approval of a judge, FCA § 734(a)(ii); requires that, with a few exceptions, the judge presiding at the fact finding hearing shall preside at the dispositional hearing, FCA § 742; and, eliminates in designated felony cases the judge's discretionary right to prevent disclosure of portions of the juvenile's reports and histories to either the respondent or the petitioner. FCA § 570.

D. AN ANALYSIS OF THE 1976 ACT

A significant change made by the Juvenile Justice Reform Act is the requirement that restrictive placement may be ordered for a juvenile found to have committed a designated felony, when the court determines that a juvenile requires such restrictive placement. FCA § 753–a. Once restrictive placement is ordered by the court, the delinquent must remain in the placement for twelve months, if the placement results from an adjudication on a Class A designated felony, or for six months, if the placement results from the adjudication of any designated felony. FCA § 753–a(3)(a)(ii); (4)(a)(ii). Further, during the period of restrictive placement, the right to petition the court to stay the execution, to set aside, modify, or vacate the disposition is suspended. It is this suspension of the provisions of part six, Article 7, of the Family Court Act which distinguishes a restrictive placement disposition from all other dispositions under Article 7. Thus, the Legislature has created a definite sentence of placement nearly indistinguishable from definite sentences imposed upon adults under section 70.20(2) of the Penal Law.

Further, in mandating the minimum period of restrictive placement, when restrictive placement has been found to be needed at all, the Legislature has introduced two other concepts of the criminal justice process previously unknown in the juvenile system. First, the length of the commitment is determined by the act committed rather than by the needs of the child, and second, the sentence is mandatory. In effect, the Legislature has determined that a child who at the time of his dispositional hearing requires restrictive placement will continue to require restrictive placement for the entire period of the minimum sentence. Prior to the enactment of this statute, the court was only required to determine that at the time of the dispositional hearing the needs of the child were for placement in an institution and that at any time during that initial period, if the child was successfully rehabilitated, he was entitled to release. Consistent with this philosophy of treatment was the provision that if at the end of the initial placement the child was not successfully rehabilitated, then, the period of placement could be extended. In effect, once the court makes a finding that restrictive placement is needed at the time of the disposition, the act then mandates a minimum sentence, a result which is more harsh on the juvenile than is the criminal procedure for the adult who is entitled to an indeterminate sentence in nearly all cases. PL § 70.00.

The distinction between indeterminate and determinate sentencing is not semantic, but indicates fundamentally different public policies. Indeterminate sentencing is based upon notions of rehabilitation, while determinate sentencing is based upon a desire for retribution or punishment.

In his vigorous dissent In re Gault, 387 U.S. 1, 87 S.Ct. 1428, 18 L.Ed.2d 527 (1967), Mr. Justice Stewart succinctly distinguished the purpose and mission of the juvenile system of justice from the purpose and mission of the criminal system. "The object of the one [juvenile] is correcting a condition. The object of the other [criminal] is conviction and punishment for a criminal act." 387 U.S., at 79, 87 S.Ct., at 1470. By mandating restrictive placement in a secure facility for a minimum of six months, the Legislature has created a disposition that more nearly resembles a punishment than a treatment and, thereby, has blurred the clearly distinct objectives of the juvenile justice system with those of the criminal justice system.

The thinly disguised intent of the Legislature to punish an adjudicated designated felon, based upon the criminal act and upon the characteristics of the victim of the criminal act, as opposed to rehabilitating and treating a juvenile offender is revealed by the 1977 amendment to section 753–a of the Family Court Act which states:

> * * * the court shall order a restrictive placement in any case where the respondent is found to have committed a designated felony act in which the respondent inflicted serious physical injury * * * upon another person who is sixty-two years of age or more. FCA § 753–a(2–a).

This court does not deny that punishment may be appropriate for certain designated felons. This court does insist, however, that deprivation of liberty for purposes of punishment based on the nature of criminal acts committed must be surrounded by constitutional protections not now available in family court proceedings.

The very heart of the rehabilitative nature of the juvenile justice system in New York is the array of remedies provided in part six of Article 7 of the Family Court Act, for it is these remedies that have protected the right of a juvenile to an indeterminate sentence. Cf. In the Matter of Ilone I., 64 Misc.2d 878, 316 N.Y.S.2d 356. (Family Court, Queens County, 1970). It is the indeterminate quality of a juvenile disposition that makes the disposition rehabilitative. To refuse to allow a part six motion (Family Ct. Act §§ 761–768) to modify or to terminate a placement gives the disposition clearly criminal characteristics.

E. TREATMENT

The Juvenile Justice Reform Act requires that treatment be available at restrictive placement facilities. The availability and quality of treatment available to the respondent is not at issue here. What is at issue is the mandatory time period required for treatment. FCA § 753–a.

Analogies may be made between the treatment of persons confined because of mental illness and juveniles confined because of delinquency. Serious consideration has been given recently to the constitutional rights of persons involuntarily committed to mental hospitals following non-criminal dispositions. In identifying treatment as a right for the mentally ill, for instance, a court concluded that at the least an institution must make a *bona fide* effort to cure, since the purpose of the involuntary hospitalization is treatment, not punishment. Rouse v. Cameron, 125 U.S.App.D.C. 366, 373 F.2d 451 (1966). Similarly, another federal district court found that non-criminal procedures for commitment which lacked constitutional safeguards were valid only for treatment and not for punishment. Wyatt v. Stickney, 325 F.Supp. 781 (M.D.Ala.1971). Cf. O'Connor v. Donaldson, 422 U.S. 563, 95 S.Ct. 2486, 45 L.Ed.2d 396 (1975); Jackson v. Indiana, 406 U.S. 715, 92 S.Ct. 1845, 32 L.Ed.2d 435 (1972).

Juveniles also have a right to treatment. Martarella v. Kelley, 349 F.Supp. 575 (S.D.N.Y.1972); Inmates of Boys' Training School v. Affleck, supra; M. v. M., 71 Misc.2d 396, 336 N.Y.S.2d 304 (Family Court, Bronx County, 1972). Moreover, one court has found that " 'the right to treatment' includes the right to *individualized* care and treatment." Nelson v. Heyne, 491 F.2d 352, at 360 (7th Cir.), cert. den. 417 U.S. 976, 94 S.Ct. 3183, 41 L.Ed.2d 1146 (1974) (emphasis in the original). The reasoning of the court in *Nelson* is helpful in analyzing time limited restrictive placement:

> Because children differ in their need for rehabilitation, individual need for treatment will differ. * * * Without a program of individual treatment the result may be that the juveniles will not be rehabilitated, but warehoused, and that at the termination of detention they will likely be incapable of taking their proper places in free society; their interests and those of the state thereby being defeated. Id.

Clearly, treatment may result in a cure in six days, or in six weeks, or in six months, or in one year, or never! By setting a mandatory minimum time period for restrictive placement, treatment becomes indistinguishable from punishment.

* * *

H. THE NEED FOR A JURY TRIAL

The revision of the Family Court Act by the Juvenile Justice Reform Act of 1976 transformed a purely rehabilitative juvenile statute into a statute that mirrors a retributive criminal statute, but fails to reflect the constitutional protections presumed to apply to such statutes. This transformation is most particularly evidenced by the requirement of restrictive placement in a secure facility for a definite period of time for a person found to have committed a designated felony and to be in need of restrictive placement with no provision for changing the placement if rehabilitation of the juvenile offender is found to have occurred. Other aspects of the revision also indicate that the designated felony proceeding is in its very essence a criminal proceeding, although labeled a juvenile proceeding. Since it is essentially a criminal proceeding, it is required that all the safeguards mandated by the United States Constitution be afforded the accused.

The particular constitutional safeguard now before the court is the Sixth Amendment right to a trial by jury. Since it is the conclusion of this court that the designated felony portions of the Juvenile Justice Reform Act of 1976 are fundamentally criminal in nature, the respondent is entitled to a trial by jury for a criminal prosecution.

Were it possible to extend this right to the respondent, no serious problem would arise. Unfortunately, it is not possible for this court to have the facts determined by a jury, since the law in this state is clear that no court may conduct a trial by jury unless such proceeding is authorized by statute. People v. Carroll, 7 Misc.2d 581, 161 N.Y.S.2d 339 (Kings County, County Court, 1957); In re Daniel G., supra.

The quandary thus created for the court is, may it proceed in this case given its inability to extend a right to a trial by jury? And further, if it may so proceed, how does it protect the rights of the respondent and the rights of society?

It is the determination of this court that it is entitled to proceed to the fact finding hearing on this alleged act of delinquency without a jury, provided that prior to the taking of any testimony the court advises the respondent that regardless of the outcome, this court will not order restrictive placement, and this it now does. Baldwin v. New York, supra.

If the alleged facts are proven, thereby giving this court jurisdiction to make a disposition, and if at that dispositional hearing it is determined that placement is necessary, such disposition will be ordered and the respondent may be placed for an initial period of eighteen months. If the treatment is not completed at the end of such time, placement will be extended within the provisions of the law and, accordingly, the right of society to be protected from further depredations will be as effectively insured as if a restrictive placement were ordered, and at the same time the right of the respondent to modification of that disposition as soon as he responds to treatment will be preserved.

Accordingly, motion for trial by jury is denied.

STATE v. J.K.

Supreme Court of Delaware, 1977.
383 A.2d 283, cert. denied 435 U.S. 1009, 98 S.Ct. 1882,
56 L.Ed.2d 392 (1978).

DUFFY, JUSTICE:

This certification proceeding arises from an appeal to the Superior Court of a Family Court order determining that the Juvenile

Mandatory Commitment Act, 10 Del.C. § 937, which became effective on July 30, 1976, is unconstitutional.

I

The facts before us are few and undisputed. J.K., a minor, was adjudged a delinquent in the Family Court for conduct which, if engaged in by an adult, is burglary in the second degree, 11 Del.C. § 825. Based on his personal history, the State contended that sentencing under the Act was *prima facie* required, but the Court declared the Act unconstitutional for vagueness and for violation of Equal Protection Standards.

Juvenile R.T. was also adjudged delinquent in the Family Court for committing two separate acts which violate 11 Del.C. § 825, if done by an adult. The Court again held the Act unconstitutional and, for that reason, refused to sentence him under its terms.

The Superior Court granted the State's motion to appeal from the Family Court orders and consolidated the two cases. The following questions were then certified and accepted by this Court:

* * *

"4. Does the Mandatory Commitment Act deny juveniles sentenced in Family Court under it equal protection as guaranteed by the Fourteenth Amendment since juveniles found non-amenable, can receive probation in Superior Court for the same offenses?

5. Do Sections (c)(6) and (c)(8) of the Mandatory Commitment Act satisfy the due process clause of the Fourteenth Amendment's prohibition against vagueness?

6. Does the Mandatory Commitment Act deny juveniles sentenced under it their Sixth Amendment guarantee of a right to a jury trial in capital [sic] cases because of the possibility of being incarcerated for longer than six months?"

The Act mandates certain fixed terms of commitment to the Department of Corrections of a "delinquent child" aged 14 years or older, who commits two or more specified offenses, not in the same transaction, within specified time periods. 10 Del.C. § 937(c)(1)–(5). The mandatory commitment is subject to the Court's discretionary power to suspend all commitment in excess of six months. Section 937(c)(6).

* * *

III

The fourth question certified is whether the Act denies equal protection to juveniles sentenced under its terms since non-amenable juveniles may receive probation in Superior Court for the same conduct.

On this issue the Family Court held that the Act denies equal protection of the laws to juveniles adjudged delinquent in Family Court.

The Court found that although the designation of juveniles as a classification (as distinguished from adults) is reasonable, the Act results in treating unequally persons within that classification. In more specific terms, the Court found determinative the fact that the Act mandates fixed terms of commitment for juveniles adjudged delinquent in Family Court, while juveniles declared non-amenable to the Family Court processes and bound over to Superior Court may be accorded probation for virtually all offenses included in the Act.

A.

In testing the equal protection guarantees, as they apply to a child under the Statute, we must examine State policy and place the issue in the juridical context in which it arises, and that requires some review of the Family Court's history.

The Family Court, from its creation in 1945, 45 Del.L. ch. 241, § 2, has had (with some exceptions) exclusive jurisdiction over a child charged with a violation of State law. See 10 Del.C. § 921 and its predecessors. The proceedings against a child are not criminal in concept or in practice. Indeed, the child is not even charged with a "crime," no matter what the conduct. See 10 Del.C. § 931. In the Family Court the charge is a general one of "delinquency." § 921(1), (2)a. Although the term "delinquency" is not defined by the Code, its meaning is made clear by the statutory definition of "delinquent child" which appears at § 901(7):

> " 'Delinquent child' means a child who commits an act which if committed by an adult would constitute a crime or, who is uncontrolled by his custodian or school authorities or who habitually so deports himself as to injure or endanger the morals or health of himself or others."

See also § 921(2)a which reads:

> "Any child charged in this State with delinquency by having committed any act or violation of any laws of this State or any subdivision thereof, except: * * * "

State policy in a proceeding against a child in the Family Court is to make it entirely a part of the Court's "civil jurisdiction," § 921, governed by a purpose stated as follows in § 902:

> "(a) In the firm belief that compliance with the law by the individual and preservation of the family as a unit are fundamental to the maintenance of a stable, democratic society, the General Assembly intends by enactment of this chapter that 1 court shall have original statewide civil and criminal jurisdiction over family and child matters and offenses as set forth herein. The court shall endeavor to provide for each person coming under its jurisdiction such control, care, and treatment as will best serve the interests of the public, the family, and the offender, to the

end that the home will, if possible, remain unbroken and the family members will recognize and discharge their legal and moral responsibilities to the public and to one another.

(b) This chapter shall be liberally construed that these purposes may be realized."

Since 1947, State policy has also included a "non-amenability" concept in the Family Court proceedings. 46 Del.L. ch. 209, § 1. Under the present Statute, a child is held to be "non-amenable," and therefore not subject to Family Court jurisdiction, when the Family Court determines that the child will not benefit from the "rehabilitative processes of the Court," after considering the following six non-exclusive criteria:

"(1) Whether, in view of the age and other personal characteristics of the child, the people of Delaware may best be protected and the child may best be made a useful member of society by some form of correctional treatment which the Family Court lacks power to assign; or

(2) Whether it is alleged death or serious personal injury was inflicted by the child upon anyone in the course of commission of the offense or in immediate flight therefrom; or

(3) Whether the child has been convicted of any prior criminal offense; or

(4) Whether the child has previously been subjected to any form of correctional treatment by the Family Court; or

(5) Whether it is alleged a dangerous instrument was used by the child; or

(6) Whether other participants in the same offense are being tried as adult offenders."

10 Del.C. § 938(c).

If the Court determines that the child is amenable, it proceeds to hear the case. If the Court decides that he is not amenable, the child is referred for trial as an adult to the Superior Court or to any other Court with jurisdiction over the offense. § 938(c).

From the statutory history, we conclude that Delaware public policy in dealing with minors charged with violations of State law is to divide them into two classes on the basis of the offenses charged. First, those charged with first degree murder, rape, kidnapping or certain motor vehicle offenses are, in effect, prosecuted as adults; second, those charged with any other offense are proceeded against, civilly, in the Family Court. After that Court has taken jurisdiction of an alleged offense of the second category, it is processed, no matter what the conduct, under the general charge of "delinquency." The Court's duty is to proceed in the child's interest, and that of his family and the public, § 902, unless and until there is a determination that he is not amenable. § 938(c).

So much for background and general policy. Let us now focus on these cases.

B.

As we understand its ruling, the Family Court determined that the Act denied equal protection to juveniles found to be "amenable," and hence subject to mandatory commitment, because non-amenable juveniles bound over for the Superior Court might be placed on probation for committing the same acts.

Although the constitutionality of the Amenability Statute, § 938, is not questioned directly, its validity is indirectly challenged by the attack upon the Mandatory Commitment Act, § 937.

The classic test of equal protection was announced by the United States Supreme Court in F.S. Royster Guano Co. v. Commonwealth of Virginia, 253 U.S. 412, 40 S.Ct. 560, 64 L.Ed. 989 (1920), wherein it was said:

> " * * * [T]he classification must be reasonable, not arbitrary, and must rest upon some ground of difference having a fair and substantial relation to the object of the legislation, so that all persons similarly circumstanced shall be treated alike."

* * *

The classification of minors for adult and/or juvenile disposition, based upon the amenability tests discussed herein, does not involve "inherently suspect" distinctions as do those based on alienage, nationality or race. See Graham v. Richardson, 403 U.S. 365, 91 S.Ct. 1848, 29 L.Ed.2d 534 (1971). Hence, the traditional principles of equal protection apply, requiring a reasonable basis for the classification.[42]

We emphasize that the classes under review here are not those of children and adults. The classifications are those of minors only, that is, between minors who are amenable to the Family Court rehabilitative processes and those who are not. We recognize that there is not in this lawsuit a direct attack on such classifications, but that is what underlays the surface criticism of possible difference in consequences for a minor who remains in the Family Court, and one who is bound over for Superior Court for engaging in the same conduct.

The non-amenability classification of a child is made by judicial decision under the statutory guidelines stated in § 938(c). Those are applicable, in the first instance only, (1) after a child has attained age 16 and is thereafter charged with being delinquent and (2) when a motion is made by the Attorney General or by the Court *sua sponte.* They are applicable also after a child has attained age 14 and is

---

[42] The minors have also argued that 10 Del.C. § 937(c) requires strict judicial scrutiny because it provides for mandatory incarceration. While a number of courts have declared that the right of personal liberty is a fundamental right, cf. People v. Olivas, Cal.Supr., 17 Cal.3d 236, 131 Cal.Rptr. 55, 551 P.2d 375 (1976), In re W, Cal.Supr., 5 Cal.3d 296, 96 Cal. Rptr. 1, 486 P.2d 1201 (1971), Bolling v. Manson, D.Conn., 345 F.Supp. 48 (1972), we are unaware of any case which supports the thesis argued by the minors and we decline to adopt it in this case.

thereafter charged in accordance with 10 Del.C. § 937(c)(5). Then a hearing is conducted to determine amenability.

Clearly, the object of the classification is to sort out any minors who, because of their personal characteristics and prior criminal conduct, and considering the allegations as to death or serious personal injuries to anyone during commission of the offense, and other relevant factors, are not judged suitable for the rehabilitative processes available in the Family Court. The non exclusive criteria used to make the determination of amenability consists of a consideration of the six factors listed in 10 Del.C. § 938(c), supra, an investigation of "the child's social, educational, psychological, psychiatric and delinquency records, his previous correctional treatment, his criminal propensities, and the police investigation relating to the charge," Family Court Rule 170(c) and the record made at a "transfer" hearing at which the minor is represented by retained or appointed counsel.

In our judgment, a distinction drawn by a Family Court Judge in the decisional process, after having properly applied these extensive criteria, cannot be said to be arbitrary or irrational. Only after it clearly appears to the Court that a reasonable difference exists between two juveniles so as to classify one as amenable and one as non-amendable [sic], may the Court bind each of them over to different treatment.

We find the classifications drawn by the amenability process to be reasonable, and we also find that they rest upon a basis of difference bearing a fair and substantial relation to legitimate goals. In this respect, we note that the object of the legislation, rehabilitation, particularly as to youthful offenders, is a compelling State interest. And while some of the gloss has been rubbed off the rationale discussed in Carter v. United States, D.C.Cir., 113 U.S.App. D.C. 123, 306 F.2d 283 (1962) (that is, the rehabilitative purpose is a *quid pro quo* for confining a juvenile offender for a longer period than an adult), see the critique of the *Carter* opinion in People v. Olivas, supra, the commitment aspect of the rehabilitative process is but one of many factors to be considered in the Delaware plan. The legislative judgment is that an attempt to salvage something in a juvenile who has committed the equivalent of two separate felonies in one year, § 938, should begin with a mandatory commitment for a six-month minimum.

While we do not for one minute underestimate the significance of loss of liberty for even one day, we cannot say that the State's plan in such cases is so unreasonable that it violates Equal Protection norms.

In sum, we find § 938 to be constitutionally sound.

C.

Having established that § 938 is constitutional, we now consider a principal contention made by the minors, namely, that a minor in similar circumstances bound over for Superior Court may receive probation. We pause to note that neither of the minors before us argues that he is not amenable to the Family Court processes and should be tried in the Superior Court.

We agree that, under the arguments made, the Superior Court "might" place on probation a minor found guilty of the same conduct as that charged to these minors. The State does not contend that the Court is without power to do so. But this one possibility loses much of its significance when one compares the difference in treatment between an amenable and a non-amenable juvenile.

Thus a non-amenable juvenile will not necessarily receive probation in the Superior Court, but instead may be subjected to a much longer prison term than the mandatory commitment period received by an amenable juvenile for the same conduct. In these cases, for example, the conduct alleged to have been committed by each minor is burglary in the second degree, a felony in violation of 11 Del.C. § 825 for which the maximum period of incarceration is twenty years. See 11 Del.C. § 4205(b)(3). A non-amenable juvenile is subject to a public trial in Superior Court and, if convicted, is adjudged guilty of a felony and thereafter loses the right of suffrage. Del. Const. Art. V, § 2. And a conviction may be used as evidence against him in future judicial proceedings.

In sharp contrast, in Family Court an amenable juvenile is afforded judicial treatment in his own best interest, 10 Del.C. § 902(a); he may have expunged from the Family Court records all evidence of arrest and adjudication, including fingerprints and photographs, § 930; he is not deemed a criminal nor charged with or prosecuted for a crime in any other court, § 931; the Family Court has varying dispositional alternatives, §§ 931, 937; the Family Court has discretion to order treatment for a juvenile, § 970; and § 972 assures the juvenile privacy and informality in the Family Court proceedings. * * *

The minors rely on People v. Olivas, supra, in which the California Supreme Court held that a State statute authorizing a Youth Authority to maintain control over misdemeanants for any period in excess of the maximum jail term provided for adults for the same offense, violated the equal protection requirements of both its own and the Federal constitutions. While there appear to be some similarities between the California and Delaware statutes under which a juvenile may be referred for prosecution as an adult, see the footnotes at 131 Cal.Rptr. at 57, 551 P.2d at 377, *Olivas* involved a factually different situation from the one before us. The California case involved a statutory scheme which discriminated in sentences between misdemeanants aged 16 to 21 and those older than 21 who committed identical acts. To the time of sentencing the two classes were each prosecuted as adults, and convicted as adults. Indeed, that is what the California Supreme Court found to be constitutionally unsound, i.e., that:

" * * * despite the fact that they are treated in the same manner as any competent adult during the process which results

in their convictions, such persons may be subjected to significantly greater terms of incarceration as a result of those convictions
solely by reason of their age * * *. [S]uch a sentencing
scheme constitutes a denial of equal protection * * *."

Olivas, supra, 131 Cal.Rptr. at 59, 551 P.2d at 379.

The *Olivas* Court expressly recognized that which it was not
deciding:

> "We are not confronted by a situation in which a juvenile
> adjudged under the *Juvenile Court Law as a juvenile* contends
> that his term of involuntary confinement may exceed that which
> might have been imposed on * * * [a] juvenile who committed
> the identical unlawful act and was thereafter convicted *in the
> criminal courts."* (Emphasis supplied.)

Olivas, 131 Cal.Rptr. at 59, 551 P.2d footnote 11 at 379.

The Delaware scheme creates a classifying technique, the amenability process, which results from the outset in treating two classes of
juveniles differently, processing one through the Family Court as a
juvenile, and one through the criminal courts as an adult. The plan
contemplates different treatment for amenable and non-amenable
juveniles, respectively, not merely at the sentencing stage, but from
the very early stages of a juvenile's encounter with the State.

In sum, we decide not merely an issue of enlarged sentencing nor
sentencing alone, but rather an issue which involves a broad spectrum of values in the disposition of juvenile offenders. While the
careful and detailed reasoning of the California Court is persuasive
as addressed to the issue raised in *Olivas,* we do not find it helpful in
deciding this appeal.

Traditionally when the decision was reached to commit the juvenile to a training school, the commitment was for an indeterminate
period of time. The New York change involved in *Felder,* supra, of
course represents a significant departure from that tradition. And
the mandatory feature of the Delaware code, discussed in *J.K.,* supra,
represents a still more extreme departure. In each instance, courts
have been forced to rethink the extent to which the *parens patriae*
principle can co-exist with these changes.

The Washington material which follows represents a further
evolution in thinking about dispositions in the juvenile system. In
part it reflects a recent development in the thinking about adult
sentencing procedures as reflected in the newer Minnesota and
Pennsylvania statutes (see Martin, Interests and Politics in Sentencing Reform: The Development of Sentencing Guidelines in Minnesota
and Pennsylvania, 29 Vill.L.Rev. 21 (1983). For a general discussion
of the advantages and disadvantages of sentencing guidelines, see
Coffee, Repressed Issues of Sentencing, Accountability, Predictabili-
ty, and Equality in the Era of the Sentencing Commission, 66 Geo.L.J.
975 (1978) and Zalman, Making Sentencing Guidelines Work: A

Response to Professor Coffee, 67 Geo.L.J. 1005 (1979)) and in part to reflect a new role for the juvenile court—to be an instrument of justice rather than a provider of services. Becker, Washington State's New Juvenile Code: An Introduction, 14 Gonz.L.Rev. 289, 307–08 (1979). Whether such an explicit denigration of the traditional *parens patriae* role causes additional problems at the constitutional law level should be of interest to students.

WEST'S REVISED CODE WASHINGTON ANN.
§§ 13.40.010, .020, .030, .160 (1984–85 Supp.)

13.40.010 Short title—Legislative intent—Chapter purpose

(1) This chapter shall be known and cited as the Juvenile Justice Act of 1977.

(2) It is the intent of the legislature that a system capable of having primary responsibility for, being accountable for, and responding to the needs of youthful offenders, as defined by this chapter, be established. It is the further intent of the legislature that youth, in turn, be held accountable for their offenses and that both communities and the juvenile courts carry out their functions consistent with this intent. To effectuate these policies, it shall be the purpose of this chapter to:

(a) Protect the citizenry from criminal behavior;

(b) Provide for determining whether accused juveniles have committed offenses as defined by this chapter;

(c) Make the juvenile offender accountable for his or her criminal behavior;

(d) Provide for punishment commensurate with the age, crime, and criminal history of the juvenile offender;

(e) Provide due process for juveniles alleged to have committed an offense;

(f) Provide necessary treatment, supervision, and custody for juvenile offenders;

(g) Provide for the handling of juvenile offenders by communities whenever consistent with public safety;

(h) Provide for restitution to victims of crime;

(i) Develop effective standards and goals for the operation, funding, and evaluation of all components of the juvenile justice system and related services at the state and local levels; and

(j) Provide for a clear policy to determine what types of offenders shall receive punishment, treatment, or both, and to determine the jurisdictional limitations of the courts, institutions, and community services.

13.40.020 Definitions

For the purposes of this chapter:

(1) "Serious offender" means a person fifteen years of age or older who has committed an offense which if committed by an adult would be:

(a) A class A felony, or an attempt to commit a class A felony;

(b) Manslaughter in the first degree, rape in the first degree, or rape in the second degree; or

(c) Assault in the second degree, extortion in the first degree, indecent liberties, kidnaping in the second degree, robbery in the second degree, burglary in the second degree, statutory rape in the first degree, or statutory rape in the second degree, where such offenses include the infliction of grievous bodily harm upon another or where during the commission of or immediate withdrawal from such an offense the perpetrator uses a deadly weapon or firearm as defined in RCW 9A.04.110;

* * *

(12) "Manifest injustice" means a disposition that would either impose an excessive penalty on the juvenile or would impose a serious, and clear danger to society in light of the purposes of this chapter;

(13) "Middle offender" means a person who has committed an offense and who is neither a minor or first offender nor a serious offender;

(14) "Minor or first offender" means a person sixteen years of age or younger whose current offense(s) and criminal history fall entirely within one of the following categories:

(a) Four misdemeanors;

(b) Two misdemeanors and one gross misdemeanor;

(c) One misdemeanor and two gross misdemeanors;

(d) Three gross misdemeanors;

(e) One class C felony and one misdemeanor or gross misdemeanor;

(f) One class B felony except: Any felony which constitutes an attempt to commit a class A felony; manslaughter in the first degree; rape in the second degree; assault in the second degree; extortion in the first degree; indecent liberties; kidnapping in the second degree; robbery in the second degree; burglary in the second degree; statutory rape in the second degree; vehicular homicide; or arson in the second degree.

For purposes of this definition, current violations shall be counted as misdemeanors.

* * *

13.40.030. Disposition standards for offenses—Establishment, procedure—Scope—Legislative review

(1)(a) The juvenile disposition standards commission shall propose to the legislature no later than November 1st of each even-numbered year disposition standards for all offenses. The standards shall establish, in accordance with the purposes of this chapter, ranges which may include terms of confinement and/or community supervision established on the basis of a youth's age, the instant offense, and the history and seriousness of previous offenses, but in no case may the period of confinement and supervision exceed that to which an adult may be subjected for the same offense(s). Standards proposed for offenders listed in RCW 13.40.020(1) shall include a range of confinement which may not be less than thirty days. No standard range may include a period of confinement which includes both more than thirty, and thirty or less, days. Disposition standards proposed by the commission shall provide that in all cases where a youth is sentenced to a term of confinement in excess of thirty days the department may impose an additional period of parole not to exceed eighteen months. Standards of confinement which may be proposed may relate only to the length of the proposed terms and not to the nature of the security to be imposed. In developing proposed disposition standards between July 24, 1983 and June 30, 1985, the commission shall consider the capacity of the state juvenile facilities and the projected impact of the proposed standards on that capacity through June 30, 1985.

(b) The secretary shall submit guidelines pertaining to the nature of the security to be imposed on youth placed in his or her custody based on the age, offense(s), and criminal history of the juvenile offender. Such guidelines shall be submitted to the legislature for its review no later than November 1st of each even-numbered year. At the same time the secretary shall submit a report on security at juvenile facilities during the preceding two-year period. The report shall include the number of escapes from each juvenile facility, the most serious offense for which each escapee had been confined, the number and nature of offenses found to have been committed by juveniles while on escape status, the number of authorized leaves granted, the number of failures to comply with leave requirements, the number and nature of offenses committed while on leave, and the number and nature of offenses committed by juveniles while in the community on minimum security status; to the extent this information is available to the secretary. The department shall include security status definitions in the security guidelines it submits to the legislature pursuant to this section.

(2) If the commission fails to propose disposition standards as provided in this section, the existing standards shall remain in effect and may be adopted by the legislature or referred to the commission for modification as provided in subsection (3) of this section. If the standards are referred for modification, the provisions of subsection (4) shall be applicable.

(3) The legislature may adopt the proposed standards or refer the proposed standards to the commission for modification. If the legislature fails to adopt or refer the proposed standards to the commission by February 15th of the following year, the proposed standards shall take effect without legislative approval on July 1st of that year.

(4) If the legislature refers the proposed standards to the commission for modification on or before February 15th, the commission shall resubmit the proposed modifications to the legislature no later than March 1st. The legislature may adopt or modify the resubmitted proposed standards. If the legislature fails to adopt or modify the resubmitted proposed standards by April 1st, the resubmitted proposed standards shall take effect without legislative approval on July 1st of that year.

(5) In developing and promulgating the permissible ranges of confinement under this section the commission shall be subject to the following limitations:

(a) Where the maximum term in the range is ninety days or less, the minimum term in the range may be no less than fifty percent of the maximum term in the range;

(b) Where the maximum term in the range is greater than ninety days but not greater than one year, the minimum term in the range may be no less than seventy-five percent of the maximum term in the range; and

(c) Where the maximum term in the range is more than one year, the minimum term in the range may be no less than eighty percent of the maximum term in the range.

13.40.160. Disposition order—Court's action prescribed—Disposition outside standard range, when—Right of appeal, when

(1) When the respondent is found to be a serious offender, the court shall commit the offender to the department for the standard range of disposition for the offense.

If the court concludes, and enters reasons for its conclusion, that disposition within the standard range would effectuate a manifest injustice the court shall impose a disposition outside the standard range. The court's finding of manifest injustice shall be supported by clear and convincing evidence.

A disposition outside the standard range shall be determinate and shall be comprised of confinement or community supervision, or a combination thereof. When a judge finds a manifest injustice and imposes a sentence of confinement exceeding thirty days, the court shall sentence the juvenile to a maximum term, and the provisions of RCW 13.40.030(5), as now or hereafter amended, shall be used to determine the range. A disposition outside the standard range is appealable under RCW 13.40.230, as now or hereafter amended, by the state or the respondent. A disposition within the standard range is not appealable under RCW 13.40.230 as now or hereafter amended.

(2) Where the respondent is found to be a minor or first offender, the court shall order that the respondent serve a term of community supervision. If the court determines that a disposition of community supervision would effectuate a manifest injustice the court may impose another disposition. A disposition other than a community supervision may be imposed only after the court enters reasons upon which it bases its conclusions that imposition of community supervision would effectuate a manifest injustice. When a judge finds a manifest injustice and imposes a sentence of confinement exceeding thirty days, the court shall sentence the juvenile to a maximum term, and the provisions of RCW 13.40.030(5), as now or hereafter amended, shall be used to determine the range. The court's finding of manifest injustice shall be supported by clear and convincing evidence.

Any disposition other than community supervision may be appealed as provided in RCW 13.40.230, as now or hereafter amended, by the state or the respondent. A disposition of community supervision may not be appealed under RCW 13.40.230 as now or hereafter amended.

(3) Where a respondent is found to have committed an offense for which the respondent declined to enter into a diversion agreement, the court shall impose a term of community supervision limited to the conditions allowed in a diversion agreement as provided in RCW 13.40.080(2) as now or hereafter amended.

(4) If a respondent is found to be a middle offender:

(a) The court shall impose a determinate disposition within the standard range(s) for such offense: *Provided,* That if the standard range includes a term of confinement exceeding thirty days, commitment shall be to the department for the standard range of confinement; or

(b) The court shall impose a determinate disposition of community supervision and/or up to thirty days confinement in which case, if confinement has been imposed, the court shall state either aggravating or mitigating factors as set forth in RCW 13.40.150 as now or hereafter amended.

(c) Only if the court concludes, and enters reasons for its conclusions, that disposition as provided in subsection (4)(a) or (b) of this section would effectuate a manifest injustice, the court shall sentence the juvenile to a maximum term, and the provisions of RCW 13.40.030(5), as now or hereafter amended, shall be used to determine the range. The court's finding of manifest injustice shall be supported by clear and convincing evidence.

(d) A disposition pursuant to subsection (4)(c) of this section is appealable under RCW 13.40.230, as now or hereafter amended, by the state or the respondent. A disposition pursuant to subsection (4)(a) or (b) of this section is not appealable under RCW 13.40.230 as now or hereafter amended.

(5) Whenever a juvenile offender is entitled to credit for time spent in detention prior to a dispositional order, the dispositional order shall specifically state the number of days of credit for time served.

(6) In its dispositional order, the court shall not suspend or defer the imposition or the execution of the disposition.

(7) In no case shall the term of confinement imposed by the court at disposition exceed that to which an adult could be subjected for the same offense.

STATE OF WASHINGTON JUVENILE DISPOSITION SENTENCING STANDARDS—Effective July 1, 1983.

INTRODUCTION:

It is the responsibility of the Juvenile Disposition Standards Commission to propose sentencing standards which establish determinant ranges of sanctions based on the offender's age, current offense seriousness, and prior criminal history.

The court's options in sentencing offenders vary by type of offender.

For *serious offenders* the court has two options: (A) Ordering the standard range, or (B) Declaring a manifest injustice and imposing a disposition outside the standard range.

For *middle offenders* the court has three options: (A) Sentencing to the standard range, (B) Sentencing to community supervision (maximum of $100 fine, 150 hours community service, one year of community supervision and after stating aggravating/mitigating circumstances, up to 30 days confinement), or (C) Declaring a manifest injustice and sentencing to a maximum term of confinement.

For *minor/first offenders*, the court has three options: (A) Sentencing to the standard range, (B) Sentencing to a term of community supervision (maximum of $100 fine, one year supervision, and/or 150 hours community service), or (C) Declaring a manifest injustice and sentencing to a maximum term of confinement.

INSTRUCTIONS:

After computing the points for each current offense using Sentencing Schedules A, B and C, use the following steps to determine the offender's disposition:

    1. Using the most serious current offense, determine whether the offender is a *serious, middle,* or *minor/first* offender.

    2. Select the schedule (D–1, D–2, or D–3) appropriate to the offender category (minor/first, middle, or serious).

    3. Select one of the sentencing options from the appropriate schedule.

* * *

We have selected a small but representative part of Sentencing Schedule A to illustrate the way in which the system works. Schedule A covers several pages and all relevant offenses.

* * *

SCHEDULE A

DJR Code, Description and Offense Category

Juvenile Disposition Offense Category	DJR Code	Description	Juvenile Disposition Category For Attempt, Bailjump, Conspiracy or Solicitation
		* * *	
		Homicide	
A+	9A32030	Murder 1	A
A+	9A32050	Murder 2	B+
B+	9A32060	Manslaughter 1	C+
C+	9A32070	Manslaughter 2	D+
B+	4661520	Negligent Homicide by Motor Vehicle	C+

* * *

SCHEDULE B

PRIOR OFFENSE INCREASE FACTOR

For use when all CURRENT OFFENSES occurred on or after July 1, 1981, i.e., amended standards apply.

TIME SPAN			
Offense Class	**0–12 Months**	**13–24 Months**	**25 and Over**
A+	.9	.8	.7
A	.9	.8	.6
B+	.9	.7	.4
B	.9	.6	.3
C+	.6	.3	.2
C	.5	.2	.2
D+	.3	.2	.1
D	.2	.1	.1
E	.1	.1	.1

Prior history—Any offense in which a diversion agreement or counsel and release form was signed, or any offense which has been adjudicated by the court to be correct prior to the commission of the current offense(s).

SCHEDULE C

CURRENT OFFENSE POINTS

For use when all CURRENT OFFENSES occurred on or after July 1, 1981, i.e., amended standards apply.

Offense Class	AGE					
	12 & Under	13	14	15	16	17
A+	STANDARD RANGE 125–156 Weeks					
A	250	300	350	375	375	375
B+	110	110	120	130	140	150
B	45	45	50	50	57	57
C+	44	44	49	49	55	55
C	40	40	45	45	50	50
D+	16	18	20	22	24	26
D	14	16	18	20	22	24
E	4	4	4	6	8	10

SCHEDULE D-1

This schedule may only be used for Minor/First Offenders. After the determination is made that a youth is a minor/first offender, the court has the discretion to select sentencing option A, B or C.

MINOR/FIRST OFFENDER

OPTION A.

STANDARD RANGE

Points	Community Supervision	Community Service Hours		Fine
1–9	0–3 months	&/or	0–8	&/or 0–$10
10–19	0–3 months	&/or	0–8	&/or 0–$10
20–29	0–3 months	&/or	0–16	&/or 0–$10
30–39	0–3 months	&/or	8–24	&/or 0–$25
40–49	3–6 months	&/or	16–32	&/or 0–$25
50–59	3–6 months	&/or	24–40	&/or 0–$25
60–69	6–9 months	&/or	32–48	&/or 0–$50
70–79	6–9 months	&/or	40–56	&/or 0–$50
80–89	9–12 months	&/or	48–64	&/or 0–$50
90–109	9–12 months	&/or	56–72	&/or 0–$50

OR

OPTION B.

STATUTORY OPTION

0–12 Mo. Community Supervision
0–150 Hrs. Community Service
0–100 Fine

A term of community supervision with a maximum of 150 hours, $100.00 fine and 12 months supervision and no confinement.

OR

OPTION C.

MANIFEST INJUSTICE

When a term of community supervision would effectuate a Manifest Injustice, another disposition may be imposed. When a judge imposes a sentence of confinement exceeding 30 days, the court shall sentence the juvenile to a maximum term and the provisions of RCW 13.40.030(5), as now hereafter amended, shall be used to determine the range.

[D2485]

SCHEDULE D-2

This schedule may only be used for Middle Offenders. After the determination is made that a youth is a middle offender, the court has the discretion to select sentencing option A, B or C.

MIDDLE OFFENDER

OPTION A.	OPTION B.	OPTION C.

OPTION A. — STANDARD RANGE

Points	Community Supervision	Community Service Hours	Fine	Confinement Days	Confinement Weeks
1–9	0–3 months	&/or 0–8	&/or 0–$10	&/or 0	
10–19	0–3 months	&/or 0–8	&/or 0–$10	&/or 0	
20–29	0–3 months	&/or 0–16	&/or 0–$10	&/or 0	
30–39	0–3 months	&/or 8–24	&/or 0–$25	&/or 2–4	
40–49	3–6 months	&/or 16–32	&/or 0–$25	&/or 2–4	
50–59	3–6 months	&/or 24–40	&/or 0–$25	&/or 5–10	
60–69	6–9 months	&/or 32–48	&/or 0–$50	&/or 5–10	
70–79	6–9 months	&/or 40–56	&/or 0–$50	&/or 10–20	
80–89	9–12 months	&/or 48–64	&/or 0–$50	&/or 10–20	
90–109	9–12 months	&/or 56–72	&/or 0–$50	&/or 15–30	
110–129					8–12
130–149					13–16
150–199					21–28
200–249					30–40
250–299					52–65
300–374					80–100
375+					103–129

Middle offenders with more than 110 points do not have to be committed. They may be assigned community supervision under Option B.

OPTION B. — COMMUNITY SUPERVISION AND/OR DETENTION

0–12 Mo. Community Supervision
0–150 Hrs. Community Service
0–100 Fine

OR

The court may impose a determinate disposition of community supervision and/or up to 30 days confinement; in which case, if confinement has been imposed, the court shall state either aggravating or mitigating factors as set forth in RCW 130.40.150, as now or hereafter amended.

OR

OPTION C. — MANIFEST INJUSTICE

If the court determines that a disposition under A and B would effectuate a Manifest Injustice, the court shall sentence the juvenile to a maximum term and the provisions of RCW 13.40.030(5), as now or hereafter amended, shall be used to determine range.

[D2486]

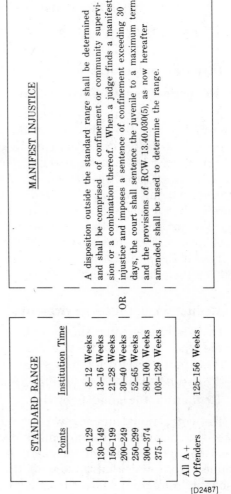

SCHEDULE D–3

This schedule may only be used for Serious Offenders. After the determination is made that a youth is a serious offender, the court has the discretion to select sentencing option A, or B.

SERIOUS OFFENDER

OPTION A.

STANDARD RANGE

Points	Institution Time
0–129	8–12 Weeks
130–149	13–16 Weeks
150–199	21–28 Weeks
200–249	30–40 Weeks
250–299	52–65 Weeks
300–374	80–100 Weeks
375+	103–129 Weeks
All A+ Offenders	125–156 Weeks

OR

OPTION B.

MANIFEST INJUSTICE

A disposition outside the standard range shall be determined and shall be comprised of confinement or community supervision or a combination thereof. When a judge finds a manifest injustice and imposes a sentence of confinement exceeding 30 days, the court shall sentence the juvenile to a maximum term, and the provisions of RCW 13.40.030(5), as now hereafter amended, shall be used to determine the range.

[D2487]

NOTES

1. Minor changes in the Standards will be found in the proposed standards which will become effective July 1, 1985. The most significant of them attaches the appropriate criminal code citation to the relevant offense listed in Schedule A, raises the prior offense increase factor for the A+ offense category and increases the standard range for institution time for all A+offenses. State of Washington Disposition Sentencing Standards, effective July 1, 1985.

2. The only constitutional challenges to the new system that we have been able to discover are not general attacks on it, but, instead, are on particular aspects of it. In State v. Bryan, 93 Wash.2d 177, 606 P.2d 1228 (1980), the court rejected a challenge to the statute as an unconstitutional delegation of legislative or judicial power. And in State v. Rhodes, 92 Wash. 2d 755, 600 P.2d 1264 (1979), the court held that the "manifest injustice" exception to the sentencing standards was not unconstitutionally vague.

C. MODIFICATION OF DISPOSITIONS

IJA—ABA JUVENILE JUSTICE STANDARDS, STANDARDS RELATING TO DISPOSITIONS (1980)

Dispositional orders may be modified as follows.

5.1 Reduction because disposition inequitable.*

A juvenile, his or her parents, the correctional agency with responsibility for the juvenile, or the sentencing court on its own motion may petition the sentencing court (or an appellate court) at any time during the course of the disposition to reduce the nature or the duration of the disposition on the basis that it exceeds the statutory maximum; was imposed in an illegal manner; is unduly severe with reference to the seriousness of the offense, the culpability of the juvenile, or the dispositions given by the same or other courts to juveniles convicted of similar offenses; or if it appears at the time of the application that by doing so it can prevent an unduly harsh or inequitable result.

5.2 Reduction because services not provided.*

The sentencing court should reduce a disposition or discharge the juvenile when it appears that access to required services is not being provided, pursuant to Standards 4.1 D.

5.3 Reduction for good behavior.*

The correctional agency with responsibility for a juvenile may reduce the duration of the juvenile's disposition by an amount not to exceed [5] percent of the original disposition if the juvenile has refrained from major infractions of the dispositional order or of the reasonable regulations governing any facility to which the juvenile is assigned.

5.4 Enforcement when juvenile fails to comply.*

The correctional agency with responsibility for a juvenile may petition the sentencing court if it appears that the juvenile has willfully failed to comply with any part of the dispositional order. In the case of a remedial sanction, compliance is defined in terms of attendance at the specified program, and not in terms of performance.

If, after a hearing, it is determined that the juvenile in fact has not complied with the order and that there is no excuse for the noncompliance, the court may do one of the following:

* Reprinted with permission from Standards Relating to Dispositions Copyright 1980, Ballinger Publishing Company.

* Reprinted with permission from Standards Relating to Dispositions Copyright 1980, Ballinger Publishing Company.

* Reprinted with permission from Standards Relating to Dispositions Copyright 1980, Ballinger Publishing Company.

* Reprinted with permission from Standards Relating to Dispositions Copyright 1980, Ballinger Publishing Company.

A. Warning and order to comply.

The court may warn the juvenile of the consequences of failure to comply and order him or her to make up any missed time, in the case of supervisory, remedial, or custodial sanctions or community work; or missed payment, in the case of restitution or fines.

B. Modification of conditions and/or imposition of additional conditions.

If it appears that a warning will be insufficient to induce compliance, the court may modify existing conditions or impose additional conditions calculated to induce compliance, provided that the conditions do not exceed the maximum sanction permissible for the offense. The duration of the disposition should remain the same, with the addition of any missed time or payments ordered to be made up.

C. Imposition of more severe disposition.

If it appears that there are no permissible conditions reasonably calculated to induce compliance, the court may sentence the juvenile to the next most severe category of sanctions for the remaining duration of the disposition. The duration of the disposition should remain the same, except that the court may add some or all of the missed time to the remainder of the disposition.

D. Commission of a new offense.

Where conduct is alleged that constitutes a willful failure to comply with the dispositional order and also constitutes a separate offense, prosecution for the new offense is preferable to modification of the original order. The preference for separate prosecution in no way precludes the imposition of concurrent dispositions.

1. REQUIRED FINDINGS AND SOME POSSIBLE LIMITATIONS

IN THE MATTER OF JAMES S.

California Court of Appeals, 1978.
81 Cal.App.3d 198, 144 Cal.Rptr. 893.

STEPHENS, ASSOCIATE JUSTICE.

This appeal follows a commitment of James to the California Youth Authority.[43] In October 1976, James was found to come within the provisions of Welfare and Institutions Code section 602 in that he committed attempted forcible rape. The victim was James' sister. Following a Youth Authority diagnostic study, James was declared a ward of the court on March 29, 1977, and ordered suitably placed. The court was under the impression that placement at Pride House was possible; that placement was strongly recommended.

On May 24, 1977, a supplemental petition pursuant to Welfare and Institutions Code section 777 was filed alleging that the "suitable placement" disposition therefore made had not been effective in James' rehabilitation in that: "* * * Eight placements, among

---

[43] A writ of habeas corpus (No. 32049) is before us at the same time raising the same issue as the appeal. An order to show cause has been issued.

them those present at the screening for difficult-to-place wards, have rejected minor, indicating that due to minor's legal history and his lack of motivation to help himself they cannot rehabilitate him." [44]

James demurred to the petition; it was overruled. The allegations of the petition were denied. Following the taking of testimony in support of the petition, James moved for a dismissal of the petition under Penal Code section 1118. The motion was denied. Additional evidence was introduced and, following argument, the petition was sustained.

There is no contention that James did not do the acts alleged in the original section 602 petition. Nor is there any question about the "placement" facilities refusing to accept James under the original disposition order. In addition to the eight facilities referred to in the petition, the bulk of 43 other placement facilities had been contacted without success or ruled out as not available to a youth of James' age (he was then approximately 18 years old).

The trial judge articulated the issue when he said: "The fact that the minor can't be placed insofar as I am concerned is the crucial issue here." Section 777 of Welfare and Institutions code, so far as relevant here, states: "An order changing * * * a previous order * * * by directing commitment to the Youth Authority shall be made only after noticed hearing upon a supplemental petition. (a) The supplemental petition shall be filed by the probation officer in the original matter and shall contain a concise statement of facts sufficient to support the conclusion that the previous disposition has not been effective in the rehabilitation or protection of the minor."

The crux of the problem facing us is to decide whether a 777 modification *requires* some misconduct upon the part of the minor or whether the inability of the juvenile court to effectuate its own disposition permits the escalation of restriction. Where the court concludes that the best disposition would be "suitable placement" it makes such an order in a conditional sense, i.e., provided a placement which is suitable can be obtained. To impose an "absolute" upon such a disposition by the juvenile court would cause hesitancy to try a *possible* adequate disposition.

When the premise of the juvenile court corrective system is weighed against the all-or-nothing reading of section 777 as requested by the public defender, the scale quickly tilts to afford the court the opportunity to obtain placement in lieu of a more structured confinement. When thwarted in this effort of effecting rehabilitation because of inability to obtain a suitable placement, the court properly returned the ward to court and imposed the appropriate commitment as the facts were then known to the judge.

We do not read In re Arthur N. (1976) 16 Cal.3d 226, 127 Cal. Rptr. 641, 545 P.2d 1345 as prohibitive of the procedure utilized in the instant case. True, in the customary type of case, a section 777

---

[44] The argument that placements were not exhausted is not persuasive. The probation department and the court need not spin its wheels doing what is known to be fruitless through experience.

hearing would be triggered by some act on the part of the ward causing ineffectiveness in his rehabilitation. When, however, the preferred disposition is in fact nonexistent, i.e., there exists no "suitable placement" facility, then certainly *that disposition* has failed of effectiveness within the meaning of the section. The juvenile court law does not demand the impossible, but rather is buttressed by hope and even expectation. The judges who are faced with the difficult task of reorienting youth into society's requirement of lawful behavior should not be hindered from applying the lightest hand cognizable with the realities of the situation before them. This is our case and we find no error in, first, the *attempted* order for suitable placement, and, second, upon finding that that disposition was nonexistent and, hence, ineffective, to reassess the dispositional alternatives. Under all of the facts before the court, after a full and fair hearing, we cannot say, as a matter of law, that the commitment ordered was either inappropriate or beyond the powers of the court.[45]

The order of commitment of the California Youth Authority is affirmed. The order to show cause heretofore issued having served its purpose and now being subsumed within this appeal and affirmance, is discharged.

KAUS, P.J., and HASTINGS, J., concur.

IN RE P.

Supreme Court of New York, Appellate Division, 1970.
34 A.D.2d 661, 310 N.Y.S.2d 125.

MEMORANDUM BY THE COURT. In a proceeding under article 7 of the Family Court Act in which appellant has been adjudged to be in need of supervision and placed on probation for one year by order of the Family Court, Kings County, dated October 15, 1969, the appeal is from a further order of said court dated March 5, 1970 which revoked the direction for probation and ordered appellant placed in the New York State Training School for 18 months.

Order modified, on the law and the facts and in the exercise of discretion, (1) by striking therefrom the decretal paragraph which orders appellant placed at the New York Training School for 18 months and (2) by substituting therefor a direction that appellant is remanded to the care and custody of the Commissioner of Social Services for placement in a suitable environment (Family Court Act, § 756, subd. [a]). As so modified, order affirmed, without costs.

In our opinion the Family Court improvidently exercised its discretion in ordering the placement of appellant in the New York State Training School, in view of the unchallenged report of Dr. Rodriguez which stated that placement in state training schools

---

[45] Reliance upon In re Aline D. (1975) 14 Cal.3d 557, 121 Cal.Rptr. 817, 536 P.2d 65, is misplaced. There the California Youth Authority was found to be inappropriate. That is not the instant case; here there were two choices, each deemed appropriate. The first was found unworkable and therefore the second ordered.

would be "a poor choice and possibly a risk." We appreciate the dilemma in which the Family Court found itself in the instant case. This case points up again the increasingly urgent need for proper facilities to provide adequate supervision and treatment for infants found to be persons "in need of supervision" pursuant to subdivision (b) of section 712 of the Family Court Act (see Matter of Lloyd, 33 A.D.2d 385, 308 N.Y.S.2d 419 [1st Dept., dec. Mar. 10, 1970]).

Although placement in state training schools has been permanently authorized as a proper disposition under the Family Court Act of persons found to be in need of supervision (L.1968, ch. 874), "the legislature has long recognized that the state training schools are hardly a beneficial haven for young people in need of supervision and such disposition was first interdicted (see Second Report of the Joint Legislative Committee, McKinney's Sess.Laws 1962, 3435) and then allowed as a stopgap measure for three years (L.1964, ch. 518; L. 1965, ch. 126; L.1966, ch. 705) until it was finally made permanent" (Matter of Lloyd, 33 A.D.2d 385, 308 N.Y.S.2d 419, supra [1st Dept., dec. Mar. 10, 1970]).

"The fact of the matter is that, however euphemistic the title, a 'receiving home' or an 'industrial school' for juveniles is an institution of confinement in which the child is incarcerated for a greater or lesser time. His world becomes 'a building with whitewashed walls, regimented routine and institutional hours * * *.' Instead of mother and father and sisters and brothers and friends and classmates, his world is peopled by guards, custodians, state employees, and 'delinquents' confined with him for anything from waywardness to rape and homicide" (In re Gault, 387 U.S. 1, 27, 87 S.Ct. 1428, 1443, 18 L.Ed.2d 527).

The creation of the additional designation of "person in need of supervision", pursuant to subdivision (b) of section 712 of the Family Court Act, represents enlightened legislative recognition of the difference between youngsters who commit criminal acts and those who merely misbehave in ways which, frequently, would not be objectionable save for the fact that the actor is a minor (e.g., running away from home, keeping late hours, truancy, etc.). However, the distinction becomes useless where, as here, the treatment accorded the one must be identical to that accorded the other solely because no other adequate alternative has been provided.

In the instant case the record contains positive evidence that placement in the Training School would be harmful to appellant. We recognize the difficulties facing the Commissioner of Social Services in the instant matter. However, "[t]he court is authorized to seek the cooperation of * * * all societies or organizations, public or private, having for their object the protection or aid of children * * *, to the end that the court may be assisted in every reasonable way to give the children * * * within its jurisdiction such care, protection and assistance as will best enhance their welfare" (Family Court Act, § 255).

IN RE G.G.D.

Supreme Court of Wisconsin, 1980.
97 Wis.2d 1, 292 N.W.2d 853.

DAY, JUSTICE.

G.G.D., a minor, seeks a review of a decision of the court of appeals summarily affirming an order of the county court for Milwaukee County, Children's Division, remanding his custody to the Department of Health and Social Services, Division of Corrections for placement at the Wisconsin School for Boys at Wales.

The relevant issues on review are:

1. May a juvenile's probation be revoked for violations of the conditions and restrictions placed on his liberty, when he was not informed of those conditions and the conditions were of a noncriminal nature? and,

2. Did the juvenile court abuse its discretion in revoking G.G.D.'s probation and remanding his custody to the Department of Health and Social Services, Division of Corrections?

* * *

1. MAY A JUVENILE'S PROBATION BE REVOKED FOR VIOLATIONS OF THE CONDITIONS AND RESTRICTIONS PLACED ON HIS LIBERTY, WHEN HE WAS NOT INFORMED OF THOSE CONDITIONS AND THE CONDITIONS WERE OF A NONCRIMINAL NATURE?

The state agrees that a juvenile who is placed on probation is entitled to notice of the conditions of his probation. However, the question of whether a juvenile is entitled to prior notice of the conditions of his probation before probation may be revoked is a matter of first impression in this jurisdiction. Consequently, we analyze whether notice must be given and if so, the form and extent of the notice required.

The question is presented in terms of whether G.G.D. is entitled under the Fourteenth Amendment due process clause to prior notice of the conditions which would lead to a revocation of his probation. We have not been cited, and we have not found a provision in the Children's Code, Chapter 48, effective at the time this case arose, that required a juvenile be given notice of the conditions of his probation. It has been held, independently of any constitutional requirement, that it is an abuse of the discretion of the authority responsible for probation revocation to revoke probation based on a condition of a non-criminal nature, where the individual was not given prior notice that violation of the condition would lead to a loss of liberty. United States v. Foster, 500 F.2d 1241 (9th Cir.1974). We conclude there is a more fundamental due process right to adequate notice of the conditions upon which the revocation of probation may be premised.

The basis for determining whether the treatment of juveniles in the adjudicatory and dispositional phases of a delinquency proceeding meets the requirements of due process is whether the procedure is fundamentally fair. McKeiver v. Pennsylvania, 403 U.S. 528, 543, 91 S.Ct. 1976, 1985, 29 L.Ed.2d 647 (1971). Even in those cases involving adults, the probation revocation proceeding is not a stage of the criminal prosecution to which the full panoply of procedural protections apply. Gagnon v. Scarpelli, 411 U.S. 778, 782, 93 S.Ct. 1756, 1759, 36 L.Ed.2d 656 (1973). Still, there results a substantial loss of liberty when probation is revoked and therefore, a probationer is entitled to certain procedural protections before this liberty interest may be denied.

Just as the principles of due process and fair play apply in parole revocation proceedings, Snajder v. State, 74 Wis.2d 303, 313, 246 N.W.2d 665 (1976), so too do they apply to probation revocation proceedings. See, Gagnon v. Scarpelli, 411 U.S. 778, 93 S.Ct. 1756, 36 L.Ed.2d 656 (1973). This Court has likewise held that there is "* * * no essential constitutional difference between a parole of an adult and 'liberty under supervision' of a juvenile * * *." State ex rel. Bernal v. Hershman, 54 Wis.2d 626, 630, 196 N.W.2d 721 (1972). Neither are there sufficient constitutional differences between the revocation of a juvenile's "supervision" and the revocation of an adult's probation to warrant divergent standards regarding notice. In State ex rel. Bernal, 54 Wis.2d at 630, 196 N.W.2d 721, 724 this Court stated that when there is no essential constitutional differences between the status of adults and juveniles in the criminal justice system, the procedures should be uniform so far as is practical. There is no reason in policy or practice to warrant the application of a lesser standard of notice to juveniles on probation than is granted to adult probationers. The juvenile suffers a loss of liberty and therefore is entitled to certain due process rights before he may be deprived of his liberty. See generally, In re Gault, 387 U.S. 1, 87 S.Ct. 1428, 18 L.Ed.2d 527 (1967); In re Winship, 397 U.S. 358, 90 S.Ct. 1068, 25 L.Ed.2d 368 (1970).

The assertion that the safeguards of due process apply, does not resolve the question of what process is due. Once probation has been granted "* * * this conditional liberty can be forfeited only by breaching the conditions of probation." State v. Tarrell, 74 Wis.2d 647, 653–654, 247 N.W.2d 696 (1976). The fact that the juvenile's liberty hinges upon his compliance with conditions which are not applicable to the public at large or other juveniles, renders the sufficiency of notice of these conditions crucial to the basic fairness of the system. When the juvenile authorities allege that a condition of probation has been violated, a basic requirement to insure "fundamental fairness" in the system must be that the juvenile has been given some warning in advance that particular conduct could lead to the revocation of probation. Just as there is an essential requirement that a criminal statute give fair warning of the conduct subject to punishment, * * * so too must a probationer be given "some fair warning" of the conditions upon which his continued right to probation depends. "It is an essential component of due process that individuals be given fair warning of those acts which may lead to a loss of liberty. * * * This is no less true whether the loss of liberty arises from a criminal conviction or the revocation of probation." United States v. Dane, 570 F.2d 840, 843 (9th Cir.1977) cert. denied, 436 U.S. 959, 98 S.Ct. 3075, 57 L.Ed.2d 1124 (1978).

Under the recently revised Children's Code, it is now required that when a child is adjudged delinquent, he may be placed under the supervision of an agency or the Department of Health and Social Services with "* * * conditions prescribed by the judge including reasonable rules for the child's conduct and the conduct of the child's parent, guardian or legal custodian, designed for the physical, mental and moral well-being and behavior of the child." Sec. 48.34(2), Stats. (1977). Although not explicitly provided for, we think that along with the duty to prescribe conditions comes the corresponding requirement that the juvenile receive notice of those conditions, either from the judge himself or the agency in charge of supervision. Nevertheless, it should be emphasized that certain conditions of probation are so basic that knowledge of them will be imputed to the probationer. Knowledge of the criminal law is one such condition. * * * At the revocation proceeding G.G.D. acknowledged that he knew he could not violate the law and remain on probation.

G.G.D.'s probation was revoked for noncriminal activity. In this situation the liberty of the probationer cannot be forfeited unless fair warning has been given to him. When probation is revoked based on a condition not formally given, the record must be closely examined to determine whether adequate notice was given to constitute fair warning. * * *

2. DID THE JUVENILE COURT ABUSE ITS DISCRETION IN REVOKING G.G.D.'S PROBATION AND REMANDING HIS CUSTODY TO THE DEPARTMENT OF HEALTH AND SOCIAL SERVICES, DIVISION OF CORRECTIONS?

The state, acknowledging that G.G.D. was entitled to a list of conditions of his probation, asserts that the juvenile had actual notice that cooperation with the caseworker from the Milwaukee County Department of Public Welfare was a condition of his probation. The juvenile court orally found that the juvenile "violated that trust the court placed him in [sic] through his manipulation, and continues to be a danger to himself and others; and I will find that he has violated his probation. It was clear to him that he had a special status at that time and that he would have to cooperate."

The only arguable support in the record for the above finding cited by the state is the following colloquy between the judge and the juvenile:

"Q. All right. What did you think of when you were placed on probation? What did you think you were supposed to do?

"A. I don't know.

"Q. You were placed on a stay of commitment. That means I sent you to the Boys School but held you back. What do you mean you don't know?

"A.   On probation?

"Q.   Right.

"A.   Just thought that, you know, if I broke the law I would be put away.

"Q.   You can do anything else you wanted to?

"A.   Well, no; but doing the things I did do, I was told to do.

"Q.   You are talking about going to Florida, but not then cooperating with placement by Mr. Parsons?

"A.   That, well—

"Q.   Isn't it a fact that everything—you wanted everything your way; right?

"A.   Well, I would like it that way; but it's not that— everything."

From this excerpt, and our independent examination of the record, we cannot perceive any basis for the finding that the juvenile knew that he was required to cooperate with placement or his probation would be revoked.

We do not determine whether in fact G.G.D. failed to cooperate. We merely determine that the juvenile court's finding that G.G.D. knew that his continued status as a probationer depended on his cooperation with the authorities, was against the great weight and clear preponderance of the evidence. This is the appropriate standard of review on appeals involving determinations of fact made by the juvenile court.[46] * * * Applying this standard, we overturn the juvenile court's finding that G.G.D. had known that he was to cooperate with his caseworker upon pain of probation revocation. While G.G.D.'s statement would be consistent with a finding that he knew he could not violate the law, knowledge which as noted earlier, would in any event be imputed to him, G.G.D. cannot be said to have had prior fair warning that his cooperation with his caseworker was a condition of his probation. Given the lack of notice, the revocation of G.G.D.'s probation violated his right to due process of law. Thus, revocation in this instance would be an abuse of the discretion of the juvenile court, since the court's discretion is necessarily limited by the requirement that the decision be consonant with the purposes of established law. * * *

The decision of the court of appeals is reversed. The order of the county court revoking probation is vacated and cause remanded to the circuit court for further proceedings not inconsistent with this opinion.

[46] The state erroneously assumes that the appropriate standard of review is whether the decision is "arbitrary and capricious," which is the standard employed by this Court when review is made by a writ of certiorari of a determination of the Department of Health & Social Services in adult probation and parole revocation proceedings. See, e.g., State ex rel. Johnson v. Cady, 50 Wis.2d 540, 550, 185 N.W.2d 306 (1971).

IN RE RONALD S.

California Court of Appeals, Fourth District, 1977.
69 Cal.App.3d 866, 138 Cal.Rptr. 387.

GARDNER, PRESIDING JUSTICE.

In this case we are called upon to review the well-intentioned efforts of the Legislature to afford justice in the juvenile court to the so-called status offender and to the equally well-intentioned efforts of a juvenile court judge to deal with certain unanticipated problems resulting from that legislative effort. We conclude that the effort of each was disastrous. Unhappily, in explaining our reasons for reaching this conclusion, it becomes necessary to inflict upon the reader an unconscionably long opinion. Some situations simply do not lend themselves to brevity.

BACKGROUND

To the cynic it might appear that no legislative session would be complete without a thoroughgoing and often confusing revision of the Juvenile Court Law. Tested by those standards, that same cynic would pronounce 1976 a vintage year. However, to the serious student of the Juvenile Court Law, such a blanket charge of legislative irresponsibility is unfair.

The Juvenile Court Law is, and has been, a battleground of divergent and often warring social and legal philosophies. On the one hand, we find those who believe thoroughly in the *parens patriae* philosophy of the original Juvenile Court Law. On the other hand, we find those who believe that blind obedience to that philosophy and its resulting disregard of constitutional rights of young people has, in many respects, reduced the juvenile court to little more than a kangaroo court for young people. We also have a battle to the death between those who, at the risk of oversimplification, believe in the lock-the-kids-up-and-throw-the-key-away philosophy and those who, again at the same risk of oversimplification, insist that every underage criminal, no matter how vicious, is but a misguided child and is to be treated as such. These conflicts have, from time to time, resulted in a hodge-podge of legislation.

Between 1903, when California created its first juvenile court until the late 1950's, the juvenile court picture in this state had become a checkerboard of inconsistent practices and procedures varying from county to county and judge to judge. The law had become a jumble of amendments and amendments to amendments. In 1961, the Legislature enacted that which has become known as the 1961 Juvenile Court Law. This was indeed a legislative milestone. The 1961 law appeared to satisfactorily bridge the gap between the feuding social and legal philosophies. It was simple, workable, understandable and relatively uncomplicated. However, the handing down of certain United States Supreme Court decisions (Breed v. Jones, 421 U.S. 519, 95 S.Ct. 1779, 44 L.Ed.2d 346; In re Winship, 397 U.S. 358, 90 S.Ct. 1068, 25 L.Ed.2d 368; In re Gault, 387 U.S. 1, 87

S.Ct. 1428, 18 L.Ed.2d 527; Kent v. United States, 383 U.S. 541, 86 S.Ct. 1045, 16 L.Ed.2d 84) necessitated certain changes in the law. (See Gardner, Gault and California, 19 Hastings Law Journal 527.) As a result, each legislative session since 1961 has resulted in some legislative tinkering with the basic law. Also, the 1976 offering appears to have been a major effort aimed at a reconciliation between the competing social and legal forces and theories. While it has many interesting facets, we address ourselves but to one—the handling of the status offender under the 1976 law.

THE STATUS OFFENDER

Everyone in the legal and judicial world is aware that the clientele of the juvenile court is divided, as was Caesar's Gaul, into three parts—Welfare & Institutions Code §§ 600, 601 and 602. (Hereafter all code sections are those of the Welfare and Institutions Code unless otherwise designated.)

Section 600 covers dependent children—the victims of cruelty, abuse, neglect, or depravity. No serious conflict exists as to the legislative and judicial handling of these tragic victims of social forces beyond their control. (All sections pertaining to dependent children have been renumbered in the 1976 law and now are in the 300 category.)

Section 602 covers underage law violators. Real conflicts still rage as to the proper handling of this category of minors. The 1976 legislation addressed itself at length to the problem. However, a judicial review of these changes must wait for another court and another day.

Section 601's have always been a major headache to the juvenile court. They fall between the chairs, so to speak. They are not the dependent children who are clearly entitled to the full protection of the juvenile court. Neither are they law breakers entitled to whatever firm or lenient treatment the law or individual judge feels appropriate for such offenders. For years, there has been wide spread unease with the problem of the 601.

CRITICISM OF THE PRE–1976 LAW

(A) Overbreadth.

As originally enacted the all-encompassing and vaguely defined sweep of the law was somewhat disturbing. As originally written, 601 covered a multitude of sins plus considerable behavior which the most strait-laced individual would have difficulty defining as sinful. Included within 601 were:

(1) The incorrigible.

An incorrigible is defined as a minor who persistently or habitually refuses to obey the reasonable and proper orders and directions of a parent or guardian or who is beyond the control of that parent or guardian.

(2) The truant.

(3) The curfew violator.

(4) And that greatest of all catchalls "* * * one who for any cause is in danger of leading an idle, dissolute, lewd or immoral life." Judicial history does not record that anyone ever beat that rap. A saint would have difficulty avoiding jeopardy under that provision during any given 24 hour period.

As a result of all of this overbreadth, the juvenile court often found itself acting as a glorified babysitter, a woefully inadequate substitute parent, a frustrated judicial truant officer, a reluctant enforcer of curfew laws which were often of doubtful validity, the involuntary warden of institutions crammed with fleet-footed but unsuccessful runaways and the guardian of the sexual mores of a large group of uncooperative young ladies who allegedly were in danger of leading idle, lewd, dissolute or immoral lives when they came into court and were not much better off when they left.

The 601 was a judicial nightmare. He resented being in court. He had violated no law. He usually just did not get along with his parents and, when one met the parents, this was often completely understandable. He was often severely maladjusted presenting bleak hope of effective treatment. Just as often he was a time-consuming minor nuisance some inadequate parent was trying to fob off on the court. While service in the juvenile court is one of the most challenging and rewarding of judicial services, it is often a most frustrating experience—particularly with 601's.

(B) The intermingling of 601's and 602's.

Under the pre-1976 law, both 601's and 602's were wards of the court (as distinguished from dependent children who were always rigidly segregated) and were detained in and often committed to the same institutions. Thus, the youngster whose only offense against society was that he could not get along with his parents, found himself cheek by jowl with the underage rapist, robber or heroin peddler.

(C) Bootstrapping.

One of the most persistent complaints about the pre-1976 law was the ease with which a 601 could become a 602 and conceivably end up in the CYA. The procedure went something like this: All dispositions available for a 602 were available for a 601 except one—commitment to the Youth Authority. This was reserved for 602's. However, it was quite simple for a 601 to become a 602 because one of the grounds for becoming a 602 was that after having been declared a 601 the juvenile "failed to obey a lawful order of the juvenile court." Thus, without breaking any law, a 601 could, by simply walking out of a foster home, become a 602 and could eventually be well on his way to the CYA.

Actually, the same thing could happen to a 600. For example, a 600 is taken from his parents because of their cruelty or depravity. He is often quite a disturbed youngster by the time the court gets him. So, he runs away from placement. This makes him a 601 because he is not obeying the reasonable directions of his foster parent. Again, he runs away from placement and thus becomes a 602 for failing to obey a lawful order of the court. Eventually, he could find himself in the Youth Authority for (1) being the victim of cruelty or depravity, and (2) not getting along with the system. Bootstrapping was a vicious practice.

THE 1976 AMENDMENTS

The first thing the 1976 Legislature did was to cut down on the breadth of the law by deleting entirely from section 601 the "* * * from any cause in danger of leading an idle, dissolute, lewd or immoral life" provision. For the truant there is a new section— 601(b)—which established new procedures not here pertinent. As a result there is left under section 601 only the incorrigible and curfew violator. Thus, overbreadth was corrected.

The next thing it did was to preclude contact between 601's and 602's by providing that 601's were to be detained in or committed to only sheltered-care facilities in the community or crisis resolution homes. No longer were they to be detained in juvenile halls or committed to institutions with underage criminal offenders. (§ 507(a)(b); 654; 727(1)(a)(b)(c); 4 Ops.Cal.Atty.Gen. (Jan. 18, 1977) CR. 76/62 I.L.)

Then to avoid the bootstrapping operation it removed from 602 the proviso that one could become a 602 by violating an order of the court when a 601.

So far, so good. It appeared that the Legislature had faced up to its responsibilities admirably.

THE 1976 PROBLEM

However, one small cloud, the size of a delinquent child's hand, immediately appeared on the judicial horizon.

In its zeal to afford treatment for 601's which would be removed from that available to underage criminals, the law provided that sheltered-care facilities and crisis resolution homes were not to be secure, i.e. they were not to be locked. The idea was that 601's were to be removed from the traditional juvenile court system and placed in community based service systems including temporary out-of-the-home care in open settings.

The trouble with this philosophy is that the 601's are often somewhat irresponsible, not to say nomadic. As a matter of fact, the overwhelming number of 601's are runaways. An immediate result of the 1976 amendment was that while the authorities were doing the preliminary paperwork at the front door of a nonsecure home for a runaway, the runaway was simply running away again out the backdoor. Placing a runaway in a nonsecure environment is something of an exercise in futility. To put it quite as succinctly as possible, 601's began to scatter like a covey of quail. As a result, the juvenile court judges of this state lost control of the situation and as an inevitable result, parents, police and the public became increasingly irate.

JUDGE VINCENT'S SOLUTION

Judge Raymond Vincent, one of the finest juvenile court judges in Orange County's history, faced with the above unfortunate turn of events made it a court policy that, when ordering a 601 detained at a crisis resolution home or sheltered-care facility, he was also ordered to stay put. Then when he did not, a petition was filed alleging a violation of Penal Code § 166(4), contempt of court. This being a criminal offense, he was elevated to a 602 status and could then be securely placed in juvenile hall—for the time being at least.

All of which, at long last, brings us to Ronald A.S., a 13 year old who had become a ward of the juvenile court under 601. Sent to a crisis center and ordered to stay there, he promptly left—the day he arrived. A petition under 602 was filed—violation of Penal Code § 166(4). The facts in the petition were found to be true and Ronald was ordered detained at the juvenile hall. By writ of habeas corpus he contests the 602 finding and his resulting incarceration in the juvenile hall.

THE DECISION

Unfortunately, while we sympathize with Judge Vincent and thoroughly understand his problem and the impossible situation in which the 1976 legislation has placed him and all the other juvenile court judges in the state, we must disapprove his solution for the fleet-footed 601's. While it may seem ridiculous to place a runaway in a nonsecure setting, nevertheless, that is what the Legislature has ordained. The Legislature has determined that 601's shall not be detained in or committed to secure institutions even if this makes juvenile court judges look ridiculous. The procedures established by Judge Vincent clearly are an inappropriate basis for a 602 petition. If they were, a deletion of language in section 602 would become meaningless and we would simply revert to the bootstrapping operation again. The court would be doing by indirection that which cannot be done directly. As the law now stands, the Legislature has said that if a 601 wants to run, let him run. While this may be maddening, baffling and annoying to the juvenile court judge, ours is not to question the wisdom of the Legislature.

We must grant the petition for writ of habeas corpus.

However, before leaving this matter, we feel a responsibility to address ourselves to the subject of possible legislative reaction.

It appears to us that the Legislature must make a clear-cut decision in this field. We have no suggestions as to just what that decision should be but point out that the field apparently is limited to three alternatives.

First, the Legislature can decide that 601's are no business of the state and step out of the field entirely. This could be done on the basis that parent and child relationships are no concern of the state and in the case of an alleged incorrigible, parent and child are simply going to have to work out their problem without state help or intervention. A necessary corollary to this would be that if a youngster wants to run away from home, that is his business.

Second, the Legislature can decide that state intervention is desirable in these matters, remove the 601 problem from the courts and place it in some other governmental agency which does not have the coercive power of a court. Thus, the state could provide facilities to which runaways would come voluntarily—where shelter, food, medical care, advice and counsel could be obtained. In other words, the state would maintain youth hostels with counseling services. However, once the state determines to do this, the juvenile court should be out of the picture because, as we will explain, it is intolerable to expect a court to administer such a program.

Third, if the Legislature determines that 601's are to remain under the protection of the juvenile court, section 507 must be amended to provide that in the proper case, a runaway may be detained in a secure setting. This could be done without the old procedure by which the minor could leapfrog into 602 status. It could also be done without placing the minor in contact with 602's simply by providing that in some instances a sheltered-care facility or crisis center be a secure establishment. If the juvenile court is to be saddled with the responsibility for 601's, it must also be afforded the tools and authorities to handle those cases. Courts must have coercive authority or they cease being courts. A judge does not suggest to a defendant that he go to prison, he sentences him to prison. A judge does not ask a parent to support his child, he orders him to do so. When a judge gives a money judgment or other relief to a litigant, procedures exist for the enforcement of that judgment. It is simply not fair to a juvenile court judge to whom the community looks for help to so restrict him that he cannot put his orders or decisions into effect. Certainly not all 601's need to be placed in secure facilities. However, some do and in these cases the juvenile court judge must have the authority to detain in a secure facility—if 601's are to remain in the juvenile court.

Petition for writ of habeas corpus granted.

TAMURA and KAUFMAN, JJ., concur.

NOTES

1. After *In re Ronald S.*, the California legislature amended the juvenile court law to allow for the secure detention of a status offender in a limited number of situations:

(c) A minor taken into custody upon the ground that he is a person described in Section 601, or adjudged to be a ward of the juvenile court solely upon that ground, may be held in a secure facility, other than a facility in which adults are held in secure custody, in any of the following circumstances:

(1) For up to 12 hours after having been taken into custody for the purpose of determining if there are any outstanding wants, warrants, or holds against the minor in cases where the arresting officer or probation officer has cause to believe that such wants, warrants, or holds exist.

(2) For up to 24 hours after having been taken into custody, in order to locate the minor's parent or guardian as soon as possible and to arrange the return of the minor to his parent or guardian.

(3) For up to 24 hours after having been taken into custody, in order to locate the minor's parent or guardian as soon as possible and to arrange the return of the minor to his parent or guardian, whose parent or guardian is a resident outside of the state wherein the minor was taken into custody, except that such period may be extended to no more than 72 hours when the return of the minor cannot reasonably be accomplished within 24 hours due to the distance of the parents or guardian from the county of custody, difficulty in locating the parents or guardian, or difficulty in locating resources necessary to provide for the return of the minor.

(d) Any minor detained in juvenile hall pursuant to subdivision (c) may not be permitted to come or remain in contact with any person detained on the basis that he has been taken into custody upon the ground that he is a person described in Section 602 or adjudged to be such or made a ward of the juvenile court upon that ground.

(e) Minors detained in juvenile hall pursuant to Sections 601 and 602 may be held in the same facility provided they are not permitted to come or remain in contact within that facility.

(f) Every county shall keep a record of each minor detained under subdivision (c), the place and length of time of such detention, and the reasons why such detention was necessary. Every county shall report, on a monthly basis, this information to the Department of the Youth Authority, on forms to be provided by that agency.

The Youth Authority shall not disclose the name of the detainee, or any personally identifying information contained in reports sent to the Youth Authority under this subdivision.

California Welfare and Institutions Code § 207.

2. The Alaska Supreme Court in L.A.M. v. State, 547 P.2d 827 (Alaska 1976), stated:

Runaway children of L.A.M.'s age are generally incapable of providing for or protecting themselves. As a result, police spend a substantial amount of time protecting these youths from those who would prey upon them, as well as protecting the community from those who are ultimately driven to criminal activity to provide themselves with the necessities of life.

*   *   *

The lower court determined that L.A.M. would not abide by any orders it entered regarding her supervision under AS 47.10.080(j). This behavior constitutes willful criminal contempt of the court's authority; were she an adult, her actions would be characterized as a "crime" under Alaska statutes. She was, therefore, properly declared a delinquent and subject to those sanctions available for the correction of a delinquent minor's behavior. Certainly, conciliation should precede coercion; and if coercion is necessary, mild sanctions should first be tried before more severe sanctions are imposed. However, where mild sanctions fail, the court's orders must be enforced and severe sanctions should be imposed if necessary. In the instant case, all available sanctions, save institutionalization, were tried and found unsuccessful. Thus, the lower court determined that it had no choice but to order L.A.M. institutionalized.

Id. at 834–36.

3. In K.K.B. v. State, 609 S.W.2d 824 (Tex.Civ.App.1980), the juvenile had been adjudicated a CINS, and found to be in need of supervision. She was placed on probation, with an express condition being, "Reside in the home of the person or persons to whom you are released and obey all of their instructions." Id. at 825. After three weeks she was returned to the Department of Human Resources and a case was filed alleging violation of the above condition on the sole basis that she refused to do her homework. Texas Family Code provides that violation of a reasonable and lawful order of the juvenile court constitutes delinquent conduct, and the Code permits commitment to the Texas Youth Council if the adjudication is based on delinquent conduct. The court approved the commitment.

> We also find that the condition of probation which required appellant to obey the instructions of the foster parent was not fatally vague or ambiguous and that it did give appellant fair notice of her obligations. The condition is actually quite specific. Appellant was required to obey all of the instructions of the foster parent. Of course, if the evidence revealed that those instructions were ambiguous, conflicting, or unreasonable, we would not affirm a finding of delinquent conduct based on violations of them, but the evidence shows without dispute that the rules and instructions were clear and specific, and that they were fully explained to and understood by the juvenile. The evidence further shows that the violations were knowing and deliberate. While the actual infractions might be considered to be minor, the trial court obviously gave careful consideration to the ramifications and implications of the child's contumacious attitude, and decided that her welfare in such circumstances required that she receive the protection and rehabilitative services of the Texas Youth Council. We cannot say that the trial court abused its discretion in making that decision.

Id. at 826.

2. PROCEDURES

VERNON'S TEXAS CODE ANNOTATED, FAMILY CODE

§ 54.05. Hearing to Modify Disposition

(a) Any disposition, except a commitment to the Texas Youth Commission, may be modified by the juvenile court as provided in this section until:

(1) the child reaches his 18th birthday; or

(2) the child is earlier discharged by the court or operation of law.

(b) All dispositions automatically terminate when the child reaches his 18th birthday.

(c) There is no right to a jury at a hearing to modify disposition.

(d) A hearing to modify disposition shall be held on the petition of the child and his parent, guardian, guardian ad litem, or attorney, or on the petition of the state, a probation officer, or the court itself. Reasonable notice of a hearing to modify disposition shall be given to all parties. When the petition to modify is filed under Section 51.03(a)(2) of this code, the court must hold an adjudication hearing and make an affirmative finding prior to considering any written reports under Subsection (e) of this section.

(e) After the hearing on the merits or facts, the court may consider written reports from probation officers, professional court employees, or professional consultants in addition to the testimony of other witnesses. Prior to the hearing to modify disposition, the court shall provide the attorney for the child with access to all written matter to be considered by the court in deciding whether to modify disposition. The court may order counsel not to reveal items to the child or his parent, guardian, or guardian ad litem if such disclosure would materially harm the treatment and rehabilitation of the child or would substantially decrease the likelihood of receiving information from the same or similar sources in the future.

(f) A disposition based on a finding that the child engaged in delinquent conduct may be modified so as to commit the child to the Texas Youth Commission if the court after a hearing to modify disposition finds beyond a reasonable doubt that the child violated a reasonable and lawful order of the court.

(g) A disposition based solely on a finding that the child engaged in conduct indicating a need for supervision may not be modified to commit the child to the Texas Youth Commission. A new finding in compliance with Section 54.03 of this code must be made that the child engaged in delinquent conduct as defined in Section 51.03(a) of this code.

(h) A hearing shall be held prior to commitment to the Texas Youth Commission as a modified disposition. In other disposition modifications, the child and his parent, guardian, guardian ad litem, or attorney may waive hearing in accordance with Section 51.09 of this code.

(i) The court shall specifically state in the order its reasons for modifying the disposition and shall furnish a copy of the order to the child.

NOTES

1. The Texas Family Code provides for jury trial at the adjudication hearing both in Delinquency and CINS proceedings. § 54.03. In In re E.B., 525 S.W.2d 543, (1975), cert. denied 424 U.S. 917, 96 S.Ct. 1119, 47 L.Ed.2d 323 (1976) the Court of Civil Appeals affirmed an order modifying the disposition of one previously adjudicated a delinquent and placed on probation, the new disposition being a commitment to the Youth Council, the agency which administers the training schools. The court rejected the argument that denying the juvenile probationer a jury trial at the disposition modification hearing was a denial of Equal Protection.

It is apparent that these statutes demonstrate a public policy of the state that no child shall be committed to the custody of the Texas Youth Council unless and until the child is found to be a child engaged in *delinquent conduct*—conduct of the more serious nature than that "indicating a need for supervision." No contention is made by the appellant in this case that he was deprived of his right to jury trial in the original adjudication hearing.

Id. at 545.

2. Cases are not in agreement as to the appropriate standard of proof for revocation of juvenile probation. Compare In re Arthur N., 16 Cal.3d 226, 127 Cal.Rptr. 641, 545 P.2d 1345 (1976) (proof beyond a reasonable doubt required) with In re the Welfare of Ames, 16 Wash.App. 239, 554 P.2d 1084 (1976) ("evidence which reasonably satisfied the court that the probationer has violated the law or some other condition of probation") and In the Matter of the Appeal in Maricopa County, Juvenile Action No. J–82718–S, 116 Ariz. 232, 568 P.2d 1130 (1977) (preponderance of the evidence).

PROBATION REVOCATION PROCEEDINGS CONCERNING RICHARD R

(1) SUPPLEMENTARY REPORT [d]

PROBATION OFFICER: DATE OF HEARING
MR. DAVID JASO   7/24/69
                                                                     9:30 A.M.

On 7/11/69, Richard R appeared before the Travis County Juvenile Court on the charge of breaking and entering a motor vehicle without the consent of the owner and was declared a delinquent child. Present in Court with Richard were his mother, sister, and Attorney. Dispositional hearing was set for 7/24/69 at 9:30 A.M.

The worker has known Richard since his case was assigned on 4/4/69. A social history form has been completed and is attached.[e]

In observing Richard and in discussing his case with school authorities, the worker is of the opinion that he is a shy and limited youngster. He is no doubt a follower and is easily led by others. The records indicate that he comes from a poor and large family and that he has been living with his mother and family at 960 M in far East Austin.

Richard's school record and accomplishments during the 1968–69 school year leaves much to be desired. In early September, 1968, Richard went to Allan Jr. High School and told authorities that he was entering the 8th grade at Dolores Catholic School. According to Mr. Gress, the principal of Dolores, Richard appeared at school in mid October, 1968 and stating that he was transferring from Allan Jr.

---

[d] This report, and the following four documents (rules of probation, police offense report, second supplemental report, and motion to revoke suspended commitment) were provided by Mr. William Anderson, Chief Juvenile Probation Officer, Travis County, Texas. These documents have been altered only to the extent necessary to disguise the identities of the persons involved.

[e] The social history form, consisting of biographical, health, educational, employment, and religious information about the defendant and his family, is omitted.

High. He was accepted into school but developed a bad case of truancy. He was counselled a great deal but to no avail. In December, 1968, Richard told Mr. Gress that he had entered Allan Jr. High and when this was checked out was found to be untrue. In February, 1969, Mrs. R spoke with Mr. Gress about Richard returning to school but Richard never showed up. On 4/9/69, the worker spoke with Mr. Gress about Richard returning to school and he agreed to accept him providing that Richard's eyes and ingrown toe nail were seen by a doctor. This was done and Richard did attend Dolores from mid April 1969 to the end of May, 1969.

On 7/1/69, at 4:30 A.M., Richard was referred by Police for theft from an auto. Also referred for the same offense was Daniel C. According to the police reports, Richard, Daniel and two other subjects, were seen by Officer J. Broaders as they prowled cars at 2215 Leon. When they saw the officer, they ran and were later apprehended. Because the worker was on vacation, Richard was released to his mother on 7/1/69. Richard was later interviewed by the worker and he freely admitted his involvement in the alleged offense by saying that he had met Daniel and Mario V in the evening of 6/30/69 and agreed to go riding with them. In doing so, he was later asked to go car prowling and did.

Despite that Richard has been hindered by his lack of parental supervision, school attendance and choice of associates, his attitude seems good. He has expressed his regret for getting involved in delinquent acts and seems to realize how serious the situation has become. He has asked for an opportunity to show that he can stay out of trouble and to show that he will adjust to probation rules. In view of this, it is respectfully recommended that Richard be placed on suspended commitment to the Texas Youth Council.

(2) RULES OF PROBATION

Richard R

1. I will report in person to my probation officer at the Travis County Juvenile Court on the 1st Tuesday of each month.

2. I will remain within the limits of Travis County, Texas. I will leave the limits of Travis County, Texas, only after receiving *written* permission from a probation officer of the Travis County Juvenile Court.

3. I will notify in writing the Travis County Juvenile Probation Department of any change of address, school or of employment.

4. I will attend school regularly and will notify a probation officer of the Travis County Juvenile Court when absent from school.

5. I will not operate a motor vehicle without *written* permission from a probation officer of the Travis County Juvenile Court.

6.   I will be at home each evening by 9:00 P.M., unless I am in the company of my parents and/or guardian; or with written permission from a probation officer of the Travis County Juvenile Court.

OTHER RULES:

7.

8.

I understand that any violation of my rules of probation by me can result in the revocation of my probation.

DATE:	8–5–69	PROBATIONER:	Richard R.
FATHER:	Deceased	MOTHER:	
PROBATION		APPROVED:	Chas. O. Betts
OFFICER:	David Jaso		Judge Presiding
GUARDIAN:			

(3) AUSTIN POLICE DEPARTMENT GENERAL OFFENSE REPORT

*   *   *

9–22–69   *   *   *

While on routine patrol, this officer observed a green 1963 Chevrolet circle the area of the Lexington Apartments at 3300 Manor Road. At about 0148 this vehicle stopped at the intersection of Manor Road and Anchor Lane where three subjects ran from the parking lot of the Lexington Apartments through the wooded area and got into the vehicle. This officer followed the vehicle to the Kayo Service Station at 1198 Airport where it was stopped. Found the vehicle to be driven by a Thomas G, LM DOB 8–11–49, of 6201 F, who also owned the vehicle. Also, in the front seat found a Rafael R, LM DOB 9–23–49, of 1418 M. Found the three subjects who were observed getting into the rear seat of the auto to be a Richard R, LM DOB 8–12–54 of 6800 C, a Louis T, LM DOB 7–22–54, of 6117 F and a Tony R, LM DOB 7–24–54 of 4905 P. The driver of the auto, Thomas G stated they were stealing auto parts. All five subjects were arrested for loitering and SPO burglary of auto.

In the trunk of the auto a Chevrolet stereo tape deck. In the front seat found a Titan reverb unit and four stereo tapes. Property tagged and left in central records with Sgt. Hodge.

*   *   *

Thomas G stated they had stolen the tape deck this date and the reverb unit this date also. Thomas G and Rafael R were placed in jail. Richard R, Louis T, and Tony R were taken to Gardner House.

Thomas G also has another tape deck mounted in his auto, which he claims to have purchased.

(4) SECOND SUPPLEMENTAL REPORT

PROBATION OFFICER: DATE OF HEARING:
MR. JASO   10/9/69
                                                     9:45 A.M.

On 7/11/69, Richard R appeared before the Travis County Juvenile Court on the charge of breaking and entering a motor vehicle without the consent of the owner and was declared a delinquent child. He subsequently appeared before the Court on 7/24/69 for his dispositional hearing. Present at the hearings with Richard were his mother, sister, brother, and Attorney.

At the dispositional hearing, Richard was placed on a suspended commitment to the Texas Youth Council. The Court ordered that he be placed on probation under the supervision of the Probation Officer but in the custody of his brother and sister-in-law, Mr. and Mrs. Pedro R, 6800 C Street, Austin, Texas. After the hearing, Richard's probation rules were explained and signed. A copy of the rules is attached.

Since being placed on probation, Richard has failed to abide to probation rules 3, 4, 5, and 6. From 9/16/69 to 9/21/69, Richard lived at 960 M without notifying the court. According to the school records, Richard entered school on 9/2/69 and as of 9/25/69, was absent 16 days without excuses or written notification to a probation officer. On 9/22/69, at about 2 A.M., Richard was arrested by the Austin Police for loitering and on suspicion of burglary of an auto. Richard did not have permission to be away from home after 9 P.M. nor was he in the company of his parents or guardian.

Because Richard has failed to adjust to probation, it is felt that his future progress will only become more unsatisfactory. Therefore, it is respectfully recommended that his suspended commitment be revoked and that he be committed to the Texas Youth Council.

(5) MOTION TO REVOKE SUSPENDED COMMITMENT

RICHARD R
8/12/54

TRAVIS COUNTY, TEXAS,
SITTING AS THE JUVENILE
COURT IN SAID COUNTY,
ON THIS, THE 30TH DAY
OF SEPTEMBER, A.D. 1969.

TO THE HONORABLE JUDGE OF SAID COURT:

Now comes Ray Grill, Juvenile Court Attorney, and moves that the suspended commitment of the above-named child be revoked for the following reasons:

I.

On the 11th day of July, 1969, Richard R was adjudged a delinquent child by this Court.

II.

On July 24, 1969, a dispositional hearing was heard and he was committed to the Texas Youth Council but said commitment was suspended pending his good behavior in the community.

III.

Said Respondent, Richard R, has failed to make an adequate adjustment while on probation in that he has been absent from school since September 2, 1969, in excess of seven days. Further, petitioner would allege that on September 22, 1969, in Austin, Travis County, Texas, Richard R was out beyond the curfew hours stated in his terms of probation, to-wit: he was at or near 1198 Airport Boulevard at 1:48 A.M. without the permission of his probation officer and without being in the company of his parents or guardian.

WHEREFORE, Petitioner would pray to the Court that the suspended commitment be revoked and that Richard R be committed to the Texas Youth Council.

QUESTIONS

What accounts for the differences between the probation violations alleged by the probation officer in the Second Supplemental Report and those alleged by the juvenile court attorney in the Motion to Revoke? Would you expect a juvenile court judge to revoke probation in this case if all that was shown was a single curfew violation and truancy in excess of seven days? Would you expect a juvenile court judge to revoke probation in this case unless he believed or strongly suspected that the defendant had continued his practice of stealing auto parts? Should the law require that if probation is to be revoked for criminal acts committed while on probation those acts must be proved or admitted in the probation revocation hearing, rather than being alleged, but unproved, in a report given to the judge? Should an attorney for the defendant have the right to see the Second Supplemental Report before the revocation hearing? The General Offense Report?

NAVES v. STATE

Supreme Court of Nevada, 1975.
91 Nev. 106, 531 P.2d 1360.

BATJER, JUSTICE. On August 23, 1971, appellant was found to be a delinquent child within NRS 62.040, and ordered committed to the care of the Nevada Youth Training Center. Execution of the order was immediately suspended and he was placed on probation.

Almost two years later, after a hearing in juvenile court, appellant was determined to be in violation of probation and ordered to the youth center. At the probation revocation hearing, appellant was not represented by counsel, and neither he nor his parents were advised that they could retain counsel or have counsel appointed.

Subsequently, appellant petitioned the district court for a writ of habeas corpus alleging that the juvenile court's failure to advise him of his right to counsel amounted to a denial of due process. This petition was denied.

Appellant now contends that he had an absolute right to counsel at the probation revocation hearing, because it was a critical stage of the proceedings. In support of this contention he cites Powell v. Sheriff, 85 Nev. 684, 462 P.2d 756 (1969) and In re Gault, 387 U.S. 1, 87 S.Ct. 1428, 18 L.Ed.2d 527 (1967). Neither of those cases is concerned with a probation revocation proceeding, and neither provides direct support for appellant's argument.

Gault extends to juveniles the right to counsel in delinquency proceedings which may result in commitment to an institution in which the juveniles' freedom is curtailed. In that case the High Court noted that such proceedings were comparable in seriousness to adult felony prosecutions.

We must now consider whether the right to counsel was required to be extended to appellant at his probation revocation hearing. Although adults enjoy no absolute right to counsel at probation revocation hearings, they may retain counsel or the court may appoint counsel under certain circumstances. In Gagnon v. Scarpelli, 411 U.S. 778, 93 S.Ct. 1756, 36 L.Ed.2d 656 (1973), the High Court determined that the need for counsel for an indigent probationer should be made on a case-by-case basis, and held that an appointment should be made in cases where the probationer makes a colorable claim that probation has not been violated or, even if there was a violation, claims such substantial mitigating circumstances as to render revocation inappropriate.[47] In Fairchild v. Warden, 89 Nev. 524, 516 P.2d 106 (1973), we concluded that the appointment of counsel was not required. Fairchild, an indigent probationer, had admitted violation of his probation and neither claimed nor suggested any mitigating circumstances.

Here, appellant (who made no claim of indigency or request for counsel) has admitted petty theft which was one of the allegations of probation violation, and has suggested no circumstances in mitigation. Although appellant did contest the allegation that he moved without notifying his probation officer, and suggested reasons for such conduct, the theft alone justifies revocation. Had the appellant been an adult indigent and the *Gagnon* test been applied, he would not have been entitled to the appointment of counsel. As a juvenile he is entitled to no greater rights at a probation revocation hearing than those afforded an adult.

The petition for writ of habeas corpus was properly denied by the lower court.

[47] Gagnon v. Scarpelli, supra, expressly reserved any decision on the right to retained counsel for non-indigents.

Affirmed.

GUNDERSON, C.J., and ZENOFF, MOWBRAY and THOMPSON, JJ., concur.

K.E.S. v. STATE

Georgia Court of Appeals, 1975.
134 Ga.App. 843, 216 S.E.2d 670.

CLARK, JUDGE. "Oh, for the wisdom of Solomon!" That plea is frequently heard from juvenile court judges when seeking a solution which will hopefully prevent a child from becoming a problem adult. Such omniscience is indeed desired in a case such as is now on appeal involving a fifteen-year-old girl, the product of an unstable home environment including tragic family deaths and a mother who has been married six times. Appellate judges also need and make the same prayer for Solomon-like sagacity, but we are limited in action because we serve as a court for the correction of legal errors. Whereas the trial court has direct contact with human beings, we must decide in the abstract: our task is to ascertain from the statutes and adjudicated cases the applicable controlling legal principles.

The instant appeal represented the third juvenile court appearance for appellant and her mother. The first two occasions resulted in the appellant being denominated "an unruly child" as defined in Code Ann. § 24A–401(g)(4). These previous instances involved the child running away from home. Despite prescribed probations during which court personnel used community rehabilitative resources their corrective efforts proved unsuccessful and the unhappy family situation remained. During one of the run-away periods the girl had married in Alabama by falsifying her age. Finally, as a result of the mother's report to the court of her daughter's defaults the court set a hearing for both parent and child in which the charge was made that the child was in violation of her probation on five counts. At that time the daughter was under treatment in a hospital psychiatric ward after she and a named older man with whom she had been living became " 'strung out' on drugs (marijuana)." (R. 67).

The record shows that on each of the three occasions when mother and daughter appeared for hearings, they had signed a court form which is under attack in this appeal. This document acknowledged receipt of a written copy of charges and written notice to appear, stated the right to have representation by a lawyer, that if funds were lacking an attorney would be furnished, and that they had the right to waive such representation by a lawyer. At this point the form also stated in capital letters: DO YOU WANT A LAWYER? YES _____ or NO _____. A check mark appears at the negative location on each of the three forms signed by both of them. The document also explained that "You have a right, to remain silent until you have a lawyer represent you" and the right to cross examine the witnesses. Furthermore, "Your child does not have to make any statement which would tend to incriminate him/her or amount to an admission by him/her of a crime, or amount to an admission of an act of juvenile delinquency." It also explained that "This court can dismiss the charges, place the juvenile on probation, in a Youth Development Center or transfer to Adult Court for disposition in that court."

On that same date a plea of guilty to violation of probation was entered and the court then adjudged the child "to be in a state of delinquency and in need of correction, treatment, care and rehabilitation." Accordingly, the child was committed to the Division of Family and Children Services of the Department of Human Resources.

Legal counsel thereafter entered this case and this appeal followed.

1. The first enumeration urges error in the failure to appoint an attorney to represent the child because "appellant, a minor girl, was represented only by a parent whose interest conflicted with appellant's in that said parent was the same person who brought the charges of violation of probation to the Court's attention and caused a petition demanding adjudication of those charges to be filed." Appellee argues absence of merit to this contention is twofold: (a) there is no right to counsel in probation revocation hearings; and (b) even if entitled to counsel as an absolute right, there was an effective waiver by the voluntary signatures in open court of both mother and child.

(A) We deal first with the right of counsel in revocation of probation hearings because of appellee's reliance upon the recent Georgia Supreme Court decision of Mercer v. Hopper, 233 Ga. 620, 212 S.E.2d 799 with counsel quoting from the majority opinion the categorical statement that "there is no right to counsel at a probation revocation hearing in Georgia." If this appeal involved an adult, then we would of course accept this judicial fiat from our supreme tribunal. This would be our duty by constitutional mandate. Code Ann. § 2–3708, Const. art. VI, § I, par. 8. Since, however, the instant case deals with our Juvenile Court Code, we examine its provisions to determine the manner in which our legislature has dealt with the subject and if a different rule applies in juvenile court.

That examination discloses that juvenile revocation of probation proceedings is not analogous to adult probation revocation hearings. As is pointed out in the Comment in the Annotated Code under § 24A–401, "The [Juvenile Court] Code distinguishes between a delinquent act and a delinquent child and between a delinquent child and a[n] unruly child." Section 24A–2801(b) provides that "An order granting probation to a child found to be delinquent or unruly may be revoked on the ground that the conditions of probation have not been observed." Then, in § 24A–401(e)(2) we find that the definition of a "delinquent act" includes "the act of disobeying the terms of supervision contained in a court order which has been directed to a child who has been adjudicated delinquent or unruly * * *." Therefore, a hearing in juvenile court seeking termination of probation must be treated as a delinquency trial. Accordingly, the trial judge here acted properly in ruling the child to have been delinquent.

Our conclusion that such revocation of probation proceedings under the Juvenile Court Code differs from that involving adults leads us to the further decision that in the juvenile court the child is of right entitled to counsel at a hearing which covers a determination by the court concerning the existence of delinquency by reason of violation of probation conditions. This is certainly the intent of the General Assembly in providing in § 24A–2001(a) that a juvenile "is entitled to representation by legal counsel at all stages of any proceedings alleging delinquency, unruliness and deprivation * * *." This statutory requirement of representation by an attorney in formal hearings, whether it be detention or adjudicatory, was recognized by our court in T.K. v. State of Ga., 126 Ga.App. 269, 274(1), 190 S.E.2d 588.

(B) We next consider whether there was a valid waiver of counsel. Right to representation by an attorney for juveniles derives from the famed Supreme Court decision of In re Gault, 387 U.S. 1, 87 S.Ct. 1428, 18 L.Ed.2d 527. The drafters of our enlightened 1971 Juvenile Court Code stated in their foreword that this decision "virtually demanded that Georgia's then-existing juvenile court laws be examined with the view toward engrafting adult due process requirements into the procedures for juveniles charged with delinquency." Section 24A–2001 of that Code legislates that right to counsel, as noted previously in this opinion.

Paragraph (a) of that section concludes with two sentences pertinent to our present considerations. The first is that "Counsel must be provided for a child not represented by his parent, guardian, or custodian." Our court, in A.C.G. v. State of Ga., 131 Ga.App. 156(1), 205 S.E.2d 435 ruled that this could be waived unless the child is "not represented by his parent, guardian, or custodian." The second sentence reads that "If the interests of two or more parties conflict, separate counsel shall be provided for each of them."

Under the facts of the instant case we have concluded that the waiver of counsel by the mother does not satisfy statutory standards. "The right to representation by counsel is not a formality. It is not a grudging gesture to a ritualistic requirement. It is of the essence of justice." Kent v. United States, 383 U.S. 541, 561, 86 S.Ct. 1045, 1057, 16 L.Ed. 84, 97. As this court noted in T.K. v. State of Ga., 126 Ga.App. 269, 274, 190 S.E.2d 588, 592: "The legislature's recognition of the importance of the lawyer to the accused juvenile is shown in the fact that the Act refers to counsel in eight different portions of the Juvenile Court Code. [Cits.]"

We cannot equate physical presence of a parent with meaningful representation. Daniels v. State, 226 Ga. 269, 273, 174 S.E.2d 422 ruled a waiver by a mother of her son's Miranda rights was not valid because she was under the influence of whiskey. That decision and Code Ann. § 24A–2001 means that the mother who waives the child's rights must be an unbiased mother, free of interests conflicting with the needs of her daughter whom she undertakes to represent—an ally, not an adversary. As complainant here on three occasions, the mother must legally be considered to be in conflict with the appellant daughter. The mother's waiver of counsel here, therefore, is not binding upon the child.

2. The accused also purportedly "waived" her personal right to counsel by signing a printed form with seven questions or statements thereon, bearing a check mark ($\checkmark$) beside the printed word "no" appearing as an answer to the question "Do you want a lawyer?" The State argues that this is a complete and sufficient waiver to her right to counsel. At the two previous hearings identical forms and answers are on file. It is this probation revocation hearing by which she was committed with which this appeal is concerned. There is no transcript of the proceedings and testimony by which we can determine on this review that the accused understood the meaning of her "waiver." Be that as it may, "the right to counsel may be waived * * *, *unless the child is 'not represented by his parent*, guardian, or custodian.' " (Emphasis supplied). A.C.G. v. State of Georgia, 131 Ga.App. 156(1), 205 S.E.2d 435, supra. "Counsel *must* be provided for a child not represented by his parent * * *" Code Ann. § 24A–2001. (Emphasis supplied.) Certainly here there was no competent representation of this girl by her mother, and the young girl's waiver was therefore ineffective. Additionally, the circumstances here of the child's psychiatric problems with her recent hospitalization and continuance of medications weakens the effect of the child's waiver in the absence of any transcript as to the court's investigation of this situation.

3. The court erred in not properly warning the accused that any incriminating statement could be used against her. This error was entwined in the failure to appoint counsel. The mimeographed or printed form referred to in Division 1 contains the phrase "You have the right to remain silent until you have a lawyer represent you," and also this recital: "Your child does not have to make any statement which would tend to incriminate him/her or amount to an admission by him/her of a crime, or amount to an admission of an act of juvenile delinquency." Nowhere is there a warning on that form provided by the court, nor is there anything in the record to indicate an explanation by the court to the accused, that anything she said could and would be used against her.

"The warning of the right to remain silent must be accompanied by the explanation that anything said can and will be used against the individual in court. This warning is needed in order to make him aware not only of the privilege, but also of the consequences of foregoing it. It is only through an awareness of these consequences that there can be any assurance of real understanding and intelligent exercise of the privilege. Moreover, this warning may serve to make the individual more acutely aware that he is faced with a phase of the adversary system—that he is not in the presence of persons acting solely in his interest." Miranda v. Arizona, 384 U.S. 436, 469, 86

S.Ct. 1602, 1625, 16 L.Ed.2d 694, 721. This "[C]onstitutional privilege against self-incrimination is applicable in the case of juveniles as it is with respect to adults." In re Gault, 387 U.S. 1, 55, 87 S.Ct. 1428, 1458, supra. To the same effect are Code Ann. § 24A–2002(b) and Freeman v. Wilcox, 119 Ga.App. 325, 327, 167 S.E.2d 163.

There is nothing to indicate that the accused was so warned.

4. Error was committed by the juvenile court by failure to cause the proceedings to be recorded by stenographic notes or by electronic, mechanical or other appropriate means, such not having been waived by the appellant.

Our Juvenile Court Code provides clearly that as to all hearings, "Unless waived by the juvenile and his parent, guardian or attorney, the proceedings *shall* be recorded by stenographic notes or by electronic, mechanical, or other appropriate means." Code Ann. § 24A–1801(b). (Emphasis supplied.) There was no waiver, and in the absence thereof the statute simply and plainly mandates a recording of the proceedings.

This court should not disregard the crystal clear intent of the legislature as expressed in the statute, requiring a stenographic record of the proceedings, or a record by other appropriate means, the absence of which was both error and harmful to the rights of the accused.

Judgment reversed.

PANELL, P.J., and QUILLIAN, J., concur.

PEOPLE IN THE INTEREST M.H.

Supreme Court of Colorado, 1983.
661 P.2d 1173.

ERICKSON, JUSTICE.

This appeal was taken by the district attorney following the entry of an order dismissing without prejudice certain petitions for revocation of M.H.'s probation. We affirm the district court.

M.H. was adjudicated a juvenile delinquent on January 30, 1981. Following adjudication, the district attorney, in three different petitions, alleged that M.H. had committed crimes which required that his probation be revoked. Before the petitions were heard and while an investigation of the charges by the probation department was pending, the district attorney filed new delinquency petitions asserting that M.H. was a juvenile delinquent based upon the commission of the same acts which were charged in the three probation revocation proceedings. More than a year's delay occurred between the filing of one of the petitions for revocation of probation and the filing of new charges based upon the same criminal acts.

When the matter was presented to the district court, the court concluded that the child required mental health treatment and should not be required to defend both the petitions to revoke probation and the new juvenile delinquency petitions which were based on the same acts. Defense counsel sought an order requiring that the juvenile be placed in the Aurora Day Resource Center for treatment. Treatment was not available without a court order. Accordingly, an order was entered requiring participation and treatment in the Aurora mental health program as a condition for the continuation of probation. In our view, the court had authority to modify the terms and conditions of probation.[48] Thereafter, the court, in attempting to expedite determination of whether the juvenile committed the alleged criminal acts, ordered the prosecution to proceed on the newly filed delinquency petitions to prevent the juvenile from having to defend both a revocation petition and a delinquency petition at the same time. The district judge then advised the child of his rights under the newly filed delinquency petitions and ordered that the cases be set for pretrial pursuant to C.R.J.P. 10, and dismissed without prejudice the petitions for revocation which were based on the same criminal episodes. The court's dismissal was predicated on the identical criminal charges being made in the petitions for revocation of probation and in the delinquency petitions. The district attorney appealed the dismissal of the petitions for revocation.

We have previously declared that in a criminal case when a petition to revoke probation is pending and new criminal charges are filed relating to the same transaction, the trial court may, in its discretion, determine whether it will first hear the revocation proceedings or the new criminal charges. * * * In our view, the same rule should be followed in juvenile proceedings.

* * *

A dismissal without prejudice allows the action to be refiled at a later date. The district court order merely directed the district attorney to prosecute the delinquency petitions without delay. A trial court's order of dismissal without prejudice will not be overturned unless there is an abuse of discretion in granting the order. * * * There is ample evidence in the record to support the trial court's conclusion that the best interests of the child would be served by immediate mental health treatment and an early determination of the criminal charges alleged. In view of the broad discretion granted district courts to dispose of juvenile matters, we affirm the court's order of dismissal without prejudice.

DUBOFSKY, J., concurs in the result only.

[48] See C.R.J.P. 11 and 12:

Rule 11 provides:

"(a) The court may modify the terms and conditions of probation at any time, without a hearing, except that, when a violation of the terms and conditions of probation is alleged or when the effect of a modification thereof may result in a change of legal custody, a hearing shall be held.

"(b) The child, his parents, guardian, or other legal custodian shall be provided with a copy of any modification of the terms and conditions of probation."

Rule 12 provides:

"When a petition is filed alleging a child has violated the terms and conditions of his probation, the court may make a preliminary investigation and may dismiss the petition if it finds that the grounds alleged therein, if proven, would not affect the prior terms and conditions of probation as ordered by the court."

D. APPELLATE REVIEW OF DISPOSITIONS

IN RE WALTER

Supreme Court of North Dakota, 1969.
172 N.W.2d 603.

TEIGEN, CHIEF JUSTICE. We are involved here with two appeals under Chapter 27–16, N.D.C.C., which provides that appeals may be taken from Juvenile Court orders determining and adjudging the transfer of care, custody and control of delinquent children. Both appeals are disposed of in this opinion.

The two boys in these titles were sixteen and seventeen years old, and both were found delinquent because, jointly, they had committed violations of State law by committing grand larceny. No issue is raised on their appeals nor in the proceedings below with respect to the finding of delinquency. Delinquency is admitted. No issue is raised as to the accusatory stages in the respective proceedings.

The issue raised on these appeals involves the disposition stage of the proceedings in the Juvenile Court. Both boys were committed to the State Industrial School by the Juvenile Court, and the contention is made on these appeals that such disposition was not justified under the evidence in either case.

These proceedings were held under the provisions of Chapter 27–16, N.D.C.C., which was in effect prior to the effective date of the Uniform Juvenile Court Act, codified as Chapter 27–20 and contained in the 1969 pocket supplement to the North Dakota Century Code. An appeal taken under either Act is triable anew in this court.

The question of disposition in juvenile proceedings has been considered by this court in several cases. In State v. Smith, 75 N.D. 29, 25 N.W.2d 270, this court held:

> "Where it is shown that the minor is a delinquent child, and that the parent having his custody is unfit to have charge of his training, upbringing and person, the court may commit him to the state training school for discipline, training and control, where there is nothing in the record to show any other alternative."

In Hardy v. Cunningham (N.D.), 167 N.W.2d 508, we held:

> "In juvenile proceedings the order with respect to custody shall be made solely upon the consideration of the welfare of the juvenile and the good of the State."

In discussing the problem this court, in State v. Myers, 74 N.D. 297, 22 N.W.2d 199, stated:

> "We realize that proper disposition of cases of juvenile delinquency requires a delicate balancing of mixed considerations and that even the most careful weighing of pertinent factors can only result in conclusions that are speculative to the extent that they attempt to predict the course of future events. Confidence that a correct conclusion has been reached must of necessity rest

upon hope founded in experience, rather than on certainty. We think therefore that the problem should be approached in a spirit of optimism and that drastic remedies should not be invoked where we can have reasonable hope that lesser ones will have an equal if not a complete success.

"What then are the factors to be considered and what relative weight is to be given to each? To what extent is the welfare of an individual delinquent to be counterbalanced by the good of the state? In one sense, a decision, which will help quiet public indignation over a scandalous condition which has arisen in a community, or which, because of its severity, will act as a forbidding example to other youngsters, may be said to be for the good of the state. But we do not think that, as used in the juvenile act, the phrase can be given such a broad interpretation. Considerations of expediency, the satisfaction of public indignation, or example are contrary to the whole spirit of the juvenile act. They are dependent on publicity to be effective for any purpose and all proceedings in juvenile court are declared by statute to be 'confidential'. Section 27–1606, R.C.1943. We therefore hold that the good of the State requires a child to be removed from a community only when his delinquency is such that he has become a danger to society either because of his own conduct or his influence upon others."

The decisions harmonize with the statute which allows the Juvenile Court a wide latitude in making disposition. Section 27–16–21, N.D.C.C.

The Juvenile Court, in its findings, found both boys to be delinquents and that it was for their best interests and the State's best interests that each be committed to the State Industrial School until each reaches his majority, with a recommendation for earlier discharge under described circumstances.

We shall now consider the question in light of our rulings and the statutes: Were the orders committing these two boys to the State Industrial School for their respective best interests and for the best interests of the State of North Dakota?

The evidence indicates that both juveniles turned themselves in to the police, admitting their part in the offense, the day after the offense was committed. All of the stolen merchandise was returned, except for a pair of gloves and a screwdriver. Restitution for any damage to the stolen goods has been arranged to the satisfaction of all parties involved.

At the juvenile hearing both boys testified, a parent of each of the boys testified, and their respective pastors testified. The Juvenile Commissioner and the State's Attorney also gave their recommendations.

The testimony at the hearing indicated that both boys acknowledged they had done wrong, each showed remorse, and each expressed the resolve to avoid such conduct in the future. The testimo-

ny further revealed that neither boy had been in trouble before
except that one of the boys had received a traffic ticket for riding as
a passenger on a motorcycle without a helmet; both were good
students at the high school and both intended to attend college after
high school. Both pastors testified that the boys were from good
families, and expressed their willingness to sponsor the youths if
probation were granted and assist in their rehabilitation in every way
possible.

The family situation in both cases indicates that the boys had not
been a discipline problem for their parents. In the present case there
is no evidence that either of the boys involved was in need of
treatment or rehabilitation other than that which he could receive in
the family home. In fact, the evidence is to the contrary. All of the
evidence indicates that the boys can, and will be, rehabilitated in their
own homes if given the opportunity.

The written recommendations of the State's Attorney, in both
cases, are as follows:

"1. Defendant is a good student and amenable to vested authority.

"2. This is the first criminal charge against the defendant.

"3. Restitution can and will be made.

"4. Rehabilitation could best be achieved in a home, familial,
societal environment.

"5. Defendant has not established a criminal behavioral syndrome.

"6. One (1) year deferred imposition of sentence is recommended, as rehabilitation, in all probability, would be best
achieved in a familial, *conselled* environment, rather than an
institutional situation."

The Juvenile Commissioner strongly recommended probation:

"These boys, I feel, as I mentioned when I first started, have
many, many things going for them. They are 'B' and 'A'
students, they are active in community affairs, they are active in
school affairs, and they are no discipline problem. They have no
prior record, as far as my office is concerned, with the exception
of one prior, minor traffic situation. They are cooperative, they
are not belligerent; and they are actually real good candidates, I
feel, to become productive members of society.

"In light of all I have said, I would recommend probationary
status rather than commitment to the State Industrial School."
Transcript, p. 108.

We think it is clear from the record that the lower court has
failed to follow the guidelines set out in previous decisions by this
court, supra. Recommendations for probation were made by the
State's Attorney, the Juvenile Commissioner, and the two ministers.
No one at the hearing recommended confinement in the Industrial
School.

The lower court's decision is based on the premise that it "will help quiet public indignation over a scandalous condition which has arisen in a community, or which because of its severity, will act as a forbidding example to other youngsters * * *." We said, in State v. Myers, supra, that this is not a factor to be taken into consideration in determining disposition in a juvenile case.

The good of the State requires a child to be removed from a community only when his delinquency is such that he has become a danger to society either because of his own conduct or his influence upon others. There is no indication, unless one indulges in the exact opposite of the "spirit of optimism" which this court has directed to be used, that these boys will ever again be a danger to society.

The lower court's attitude of satisfaction of public indignation, and its intent to set an example for purposes of deterrence, have resulted in a disregard of the intent of the statute which is characterized by its confidential proceedings and its concern with the welfare of the individual delinquent. The lower court was in error in giving the statute the broad interpretation which this court has refused to give it.

The orders committing these boys to the State Industrial School are, therefore, reversed and the two cases are remanded to the Juvenile Court of Morton County for the entry of appropriate orders in accordance with the philosophy of the law as expressed in this opinion.

NOTE

Review of decisions by juvenile courts varies considerably from jurisdiction to jurisdiction, ranging from full de novo review to review for abuse of discretion only. Additionally, the procedures vary from a need to resort to the extraordinary writs to appeal. See Bowman, Appeals From Juvenile Courts, 11 Crime & Delinquency 63 (1965).

There has been very little separate consideration of the reviewability of disposition decisions. Mr. Bowman, supra, suggests that skill and expertise on the part of juvenile judges are particularly significant at the disposition stage ("* * * training in related fields such as sociology and psychology, his daily contact with youthful offenders, and his staff of caseworkers and professional assistants would seem calculated to produce dispositions of unimpeachable fairness and rectitude.") and so would make appellate review of them inappropriate.

Although appellate review of sentences in criminal cases has received increased attention, indeed, is established law in many jurisdictions, there seems to be little comparable attention paid to the problem in the juvenile area. Do you think that juvenile judges are somehow more able to make appropriate dispositions than judges in criminal cases? (Remember, you may be talking about the same human being!) Would your answer be different if it turned out that many juvenile judges were not lawyers? Suppose most juvenile judges were social workers? (They are not.)

*

Chapter 9

TRAINING SCHOOLS

A. NATURE OF TRAINING SCHOOLS

THE PRESIDENT'S COMMISSION ON LAW ENFORCEMENT
AND ADMINISTRATION OF JUSTICE, TASK FORCE REPORT:
CORRECTIONS 141–47 (1967)

3. Juvenile Institutions

A juvenile training facility is normally part of a system separate from other State and local juvenile correctional services, which usually include, at a minimum, the courts, juvenile probation, and supervision (aftercare) of those released from the training facility. Together these services provide resources for the differential treatment required for juvenile offenders committing offenses from various levels of motivation.

I. INTRODUCTION

A. Purpose Served by Training Facilities

The role of the training school is to provide a specialized program for children who must be held to be treated. Accordingly, such facilities should normally house more hardened or unstable youngsters than should be placed, for example, under probation supervision.

The juvenile institutional program is basically a preparation and trial period for the ultimate test of returning to community life. Once return has been effected, the ultimate success of the facility's efforts is highly dependent on good aftercare services. These are needed to strengthen changes started in the institution; their value can be proved only in the normal conditions of community life.

* * *

C. Working Philosophies

The term "school of industry" or "reformatory" often designated the early juvenile training facilities, thus reflecting the relatively simple philosophies upon which their development was based. Their reform programs sought chiefly to teach the difference between right and wrong. Teaching methods were primarily on a precept level, tending to emphasize correct behavior, formal education, and, where possible, the teaching of a trade so that the trainee would have the skills to follow the "right."

To a large extent these elements continue to bulwark many programs, but the efficacy of the old methods has been increasingly questioned, and working philosophies now are moving in new directions, primarily for two reasons.

First, although statistics vary from school to school and can be differently interpreted, most experts agree that about half of the persons released from juvenile training facilities can be expected to be reincarcerated.

Second, they agree that if treatment is to produce lasting change, it must (regardless of technique) touch upon the personal reasons for delinquency. Like most people, juveniles caught in the "wrong" usually find it more comfortable to justify themselves as "right" than to acknowledge responsibility for being wrong and seeking to change. For the delinquent this means that, from the view he has of himself, he does not act out of "evil" but out of "good" which makes sense and can be justified. Delinquent behavior may be a satisfying experience to a youngster, especially if it meets his emotional needs. The approach, therefore, cannot be merely an appeal for a change in behavior that is offensive to the school; it must be concerned with what the behavior means to the youngster himself. Therefore, according to this view, the function of a training facility is to help a minor look honestly at his own attitudes and see to what degree they create difficulties in the sense that "as ye sow so shall ye reap." Having seen this, a minor then has a personal reference point for change that is connected with his own perception of "good"; he can arrive at personally responsible behavior because he feels this personal connection.

Evidence of the practicality of this viewpoint is found in observations common among training school youngsters themselves, who are quite capable of pointing out those in their group who are "really doing good" and those who are "just playing it cool." If the training school makes conformity the hallmark of progress, it teaches duplicity because, in so doing, it is suggesting that the real problem to be met is not "genuine change of feelings" but only change of "appearances," simply doing whatever the outer situation demands to "get by." The implications of this for further involvement in trouble are clear.

II. SURVEY FINDINGS

The survey findings are organized around three factors that significantly affect the operation of juvenile training facilities—(1) the presence of working philosophies that are consistent with what makes change possible; (2) a use of juvenile institutions by the courts and related groups that allows a program focused on change to operate; and (3) the presence of personnel, physical facilities, administrative controls, and other resources tailored to the job of producing change.

A. WORKING PHILOSOPHY

A good working philosophy clearly relates the institution's activities to its purpose and to the problems it must meet in serving this purpose.

Such a relationship between purpose and program is clearly outlined in the operations of some facilities. As a general matter, however, the absence of a clear working philosophy that ties programs to the achievement of more responsible attitudes is a significant weakness crucial to the problem of improving services.

Lack of understanding concerning the practicality of newer philosophies is a major problem. The difficulty of securing their acceptance is clearly illustrated by developments in the issue of discipline. For some years standards have declared that "corporal punishment should not be tolerated in any form in a training school program." The misbehaving youngster should see, to the greatest degree possible, the reason for a rule and its meaning for the particular brand of difficulty he encounters on the "outs." In this way discipline can become an avenue to new behavior having the force of personal meaning. The use of force shifts the emphasis away from the youngster and onto the smooth running of the institution. For someone with antagonistic attitudes, hitching behavior to the good of something he dislikes can be expected to have little lasting effect.

Thus, apart from the issue of whether physical abuse results, use of corporal punishment can reasonably be taken as a rough statistical indicator of the degree to which treatment viewpoints are actually operating. The survey found that corporal punishment is authorized in juvenile institutions in 10 States.

Another indicator of working philosophy is found in an institution's answer to the question, "How much security?" The institution's need to develop the youngsters' self-control often collides with the public's concern over escapes. Caught between the two, the administrator may set up a system of tight management which, he rationalizes, is for the youngsters' "own good." Thus the juvenile is used to serve the institution instead of the other way around.

A solution can be achieved by public and professional education. Though public expectations toward training facilities are often unrealistic, they must be met by the administrator if he wants to hold his job. Therefore, maximum efficiency—doing the best that current knowledge will allow—cannot be reached until this blurring effect is looked at honestly. If training facilities are to change youngsters, they must be allowed to operate out of philosophies consistent with this purpose. The public needs to learn that treatment approaches which allow "breathing room" are not naive but are, on the contrary, extremely practical. Properly conceived, they are directed at getting the trainee to assume more responsibility for his life rather than assigning it later to the police.

B. Uses Being Made of Training Schools

In theory, training schools are specialized facilities for changing children relatively hardened in delinquency. In practice, as the survey shows, they house a nonselective population and are primarily used in ways which make the serving of their theoretical best purpose, that of "change," beside the point.

This is not to say that other purposes being served by the typical training facility are not important in themselves. Rather, the point is whether they can best be served by a training facility, and, if they cannot, the effect of this extraneousness on the facility's prime reason for existence, the basic job for which it is intended. The extent to which its ability to do this job is diminished becomes clear from the following list of its "other" expedient purposes:

> Use as a detention or holding facility for youngsters awaiting completion of other plans for placement.

> Providing basic housing for youngsters whose primary need is a foster home or residential housing.

> Housing large numbers of youngsters whose involvement in trouble is primarily situational rather than deep-seated and who could be handled more efficiently under community supervision.

> Caring for mentally retarded youngsters committed to the training school because there is no room in a mental retardation facility or because no such institution exists.

> Providing care for youngsters with severe psychiatric problems who are committed to the training school because of no juvenile residential treatment program.

> Use of girls' facilities to provide maternity services.

The problem of varied intake is further complicated by differences in court commitment philosophies, each of which is a working view of "the best purpose a training facility should ideally serve." In summary, the effects of the diverse elements cited contribute to training facilities wherein no one is best served and most are served in default.

Variations in use of training schools are found among the states as a whole, as well as among the counties of a single State, and further show that many reference points other than "change" are the determiners of practice. If juvenile institutions were actually working in allegiance to a common "best use," statistics which reflect practice would have some uniformity of meaning. That this is not true is revealed by some of the statistical sketches below. For example, length-of-stay statistics do not now reflect differences in time needed to effect "change." If they did, one system's length of stay could be compared with another's, as a guideline for the efficacy of a given program. Rather, the data show that length of stay reflects some extraneous factor such as "overcrowding," or a population whose primary need is "housing," or children awaiting unavailable placements, or children who, though better suited to a probation program, must be held "long enough" to avoid court or community problems.

C. RESOURCES TO PRODUCE CHANGE

1. *Capacity*

The survey covers 220 State-operated juvenile institutional facilities in all States, Puerto Rico, and the District of Columbia. These facilities, constituting 86 percent of the juvenile training capacity in the United States, had a total capacity of 42,423 in 1965 and a total average daily population of 42,389, which was 10.7 percent more than the population reported to the Children's Bureau in 1964 by 245 State and local facilities.

The overcrowding suggested by daily population figures is not uniform. In 17 jurisdictions, in programs housing total average daily populations of 7,199 children (17 percent of the total), the average daily population is more than 10 percent below each system's capacity. Conversely, in 11 States, in programs housing 9,165 children (22 percent of the total reported by all 52 jurisdictions), the average daily population is 10 percent or more above their respective systems' capacities.

In many States the capacity of State and locally run training facilities is extended through use of private facilities. In some instances these are publicly subsidized, but control of the program remains in private hands. During the survey, 31 States reported using private facilities for the placement of delinquents. An estimate of the use of private facilities was not possible in eight of these States. The 23 States submitting estimates reported they had placed 6,307 youngsters in private facilities in 1965.

Concern about the increasing numbers of delinquents being housed in training facilities is growing. Only eight States at present have no plans for new construction which would increase the capacity of their institutional programs. Construction under way in 17 States will add space for 4,164 youngsters at a cost of $41,164,000. Thirty-one States report that they have $70,090,000 of construction authorized for an additional capacity of 7,090. Projecting still further ahead, 21 States report plans for additional capacity of 6,606 by 1975 at an anticipated cost of $66,060,000.

Thus, new construction, under way or authorized, will increase the present capacity (42,423 in State-run facilities) by 27 percent. By 1975, planned new construction will have increased present capacity by slightly over 42 percent.

2. Program

(a) *Diversification.* In contrast to the diversified program "balance" recommended by the standard, juvenile training facilities in most States present limited diversity of programs. Six of the larger jurisdictions now have nine or more facilities, but 8 States have only one facility serving juveniles and 14 States have only two facilities—a boys' school and a girls' school, a pattern that characterized State juvenile institutional systems for many years * * *

(b) *Average stay.* The length of stay for children committed to State training facilities ranges from 4 to 24 months; the median length of stay is 9 months. The number of children at the extremes of the range is relatively small * * *. Five State systems, housing 3 percent of the total, report an average length of stay of 6 months or less; eight State systems, housing 8 percent of the total, report average lengths of stay of more than 12 months. The remainder of the State systems—three-fourths of the total, housing nine-tenths of the institutional population—have an average length of stay of 6 months to a year.

Reception centers which serve primarily placement diagnostic purposes and do not include a treatment program for segments of their population report a surprisingly uniform average length of stay, ranging from 28 to 45 days.

* * *

(c) *Actual availability of service.* Services that look the same "on paper" are revealed by the survey to differ widely in quality. For example, 96 percent of the facilities contacted report the provision of medical services, and 94 percent report that dental services are provided. In fact, however, examination of operating practice in each jurisdiction shows major differences in the quality of these services. Where medical and dental services represent an especially expensive drain on hardpressed budgets, as is true in many programs, the decision that treatment is "needed" may be reached less quickly than where services are routinely available and "paid for." Thus quality differences are born.

Similar differences between what is available "on paper" and what is available "in fact" are to be found among other services offered by training facilities * * * The survey data indicate that nearly all programs (95 percent) provide recreational services; 88 percent educational programs; 86 percent, casework, and 79 percent, counseling services; and 75 percent, psychological, and 71 percent, psychiatric services. The question of concern, however, is not their provision "on paper" but their adequacy for the problems being faced. From this viewpoint, with the possible exception of education, improvement of all types of services seems badly needed. Support for this view is based on the existing ratios of treatment personnel to training school population (see chart 1).

3. Staff

The impact of a program upon children is largely determined by adequacy of staff, both quantitatively and qualitatively.

In 1965, State-run juvenile facilities employed 21,247 staff in programs housing an average daily population of 42,389 trainees.

(a) *Treatment personnel.* Of the total number employed, 1,154 were treatment personnel—psychiatrists, psychologists, and social caseworkers.

The standard calls for a minimum of 1 full-time psychiatrist for 150 children. On the basis of the average daily population of 42,389 in 1965, the number of psychiatrists required is 282.

The survey data show that the equivalent of 46 psychiatrists served the 220 State-operated facilities. More than half of them are found in only 5 States, with 1 State having the equivalent psychiatric time of 10 out of the total of 46 psychiatrists. Each of 37 States has less than the equivalent of 1 full-time psychiatrist available to its juvenile institution population. Only 4 States have enough psychiatric service available to satisfy the required 1:150 ratio.

To meet the requirements nationally, juvenile institutions need a total of 236 more psychiatrists than they now have.

The standard calls for a minimum of 1 full-time psychologist for 150 children. On the basis of the average daily population, the number of psychologists required is 282.

The survey data show that the equivalent of 182 psychologists work in the State-run juvenile facilities. However, as with psychiatrists, psychologists are found to be unequally distributed among the States: 106 (almost 60 percent of the total) are found in 9 States. Each of 21 States had the equivalent of not more than 1 psychologist. Only 12 States come up to the standard ratio.

To meet the requirements nationally, juvenile institution systems need a total of 100 more psychologists than they now have.

The standard declares that under ordinary conditions, a full-time caseworker in a juvenile institution should be assigned not more than 30 children. On the basis of the average daily population, the number of caseworkers required is 1,413.

The survey data show, in the 220 institutions, a total of 926 caseworkers, or 66 percent of the number required. To meet the requirements nationally, juvenile institution systems need a total of 487 more caseworkers than they now have.

Because the lack or absence of clinical personnel in many programs made comprehensive assessment uncertain, the survey established a general treatment potential index by stating the number of psychiatrists, psychologists, and caseworkers found in a system, combined in one category called professional personnel, in proportion to the number of trainees in the system. Since no single ratio was available as a national standard for such an index, the existing standards applicable to psychiatrists (1:150), psychologists (1:150), and caseworkers (1:30) were combined, making a total of 7 professional personnel per 150 trainees, or a ratio of 1:21.43 as a guideline.

Chart 1 shows that the range of indexes for 50 States is from 1:30 to 1:522. The average index is 1:64; the median is 1:33. In all, 14 State systems have treatment ratios better than the 1:21 suggested. Among the 38 jurisdictions with ratios poorer than this guideline, 22 have ratios of 1:42.9 (double the suggested guideline) or more.

(b) Teachers. The standard calls for a teacher-pupil ratio not exceeding 1:15.

Standards bearing on teacher ratios in training facilities are difficult to apply to survey data. Where public school systems assume a portion of the training system's academic burden, their teachers were not counted as institutional employees for purposes of the survey.

There were 2,495 teachers in the 220 institutions, an overall teacher-pupil ratio of 1:17 (see ch. 2). In 24 States, the teacher-pupil ratio is better than the 1:15 standard cited, and in 36 States it is better than 1:20. Moreover, in the remaining States several jurisdictions have ratios that are high because of the reasons cited above.

The general picture given by the survey data is consistent with experienced observation: The established standard for training facilities is met to a far greater degree in teaching than it is in the casework or psychological counseling function. The reason is probably that, in many facilities, academic teaching has been the traditional mainstay of programing; also, the teaching role is better understood, and training for teachers is well established. In those facilities where there aren't enough teachers, the problem is more likely to be budget than an insufficient supply of trained teachers. Even where salaries are competitive the training school is handicapped in recruiting the good teacher because its working conditions are usually less attractive than the public school's.

* * *

(e) Salaries. In general, salaries in merit-covered systems are higher than in nonmerit systems for comparable positions. * * * Table 7 shows beginning salaries according to position and the number of institutions paying that salary.

Table 7.—Beginning Salaries of Juvenile Institutional Personnel, by Number of Agencies

	Psychiatrist	Superintendent	Psychologist	Caseworker	Academic teacher	Vocational teacher	Cottage staff
Under $1,500	0	0	0	0	0	0	0
$1,501–$2,400	0	0	0	0	1	0	3
$2,401–$3,000	1	0	0	0	1	0	6
$3,001–$4,000	0	0	0	3	2	3	24
$4,001–$5,000	1	1	0	6	14	15	12
$5,001–$6,000	0	3	1	14	22	18	4
$6,001–$7,000	0	2	8	19	5	6	1
$7,001–$8,000	1	4	12	4	2	1	0
$8,001–$9,000	0	8	4	1	1	1	1
$9,001–$10,000	0	11	2	0	0	0	0
$10,001–$11,000	1	7	5	0	0	0	0
$11,001–$12,000	1	8	0	0	0	0	0
$12,001–$13,000	6	3	0	0	0	0	0
$13,001–$14,000	1	3	0	0	0	0	0
$14,001–$15,000	1	1	0	0	0	0	0
$15,001–$16,000	2	0	0	0	0	0	0
$16,001–$17,000	2	0	0	0	0	0	0
$17,001–$18,000	0	0	0	0	0	0	0
Over $18,000	2	0	0	0	0	0	0
Total	19	51	32	47	48	44	51

[D2488]

* * *

(g) Educational qualifications. The standard calls for the superintendent to have completed graduate training in the behavioral sciences or related fields of child development.

The survey found substantial variation among systems on educational requirements for the position (see table 8). Twelve jurisdictions require the superintendent to have a graduate degree; 28

require a college background; 10 have no formally established educational requirements—but this does not necessarily mean that trained persons are not sought. A number of systems recruit by trying to get the best person possible without formulating the requirements.

The standard calls for the caseworker to have graduated from an accredited school of social work.

Only three jurisdictions have failed to establish requirements for this position. Thirty-six require a college background; 11 require, in addition, a graduate degree.

The cottage staff in charge of the living unit, where most of the minor's time is spent, is the backbone of the training facility program. The key to effectiveness for this classification is ability to relate to children, emotional maturity, and flexibility in adapting to new situations.

No standard for this position has been offered. The traditional standard has been a high school education. Particularly in more sophisticated systems, graduation from college would be the preferred qualification.

Under present salary schedules for the cottage staff position, college graduates, or even persons having not more than a high school education (as required in 25 States) are virtually unattainable. Salaries are so low that establishing educational requirements is beside the point; * * * 25 States set no requirement for the position. One State reports that some of its cottage staff are on public welfare.

KM, A PROFILE OF WISCONSIN'S KETTLE MORAINE BOYS SCHOOL PLYMOUTH, WISCONSIN

General Information

The Kettle Moraine Boys School, under the jurisdiction of the Division of Corrections, is a training school for delinquent boys. Commitments are made by juvenile courts of the State of Wisconsin, to the Department of Health and Social Services. Provisions within the law provide that after a period of favorable adjustment, a boy may be released to aftercare supervision.

All boys found to be delinquent are sent to the Reception Center—Wisconsin School of Boys, located at Wales, Wisconsin—(one section of that institution has been designated as the reception center for all newly committed boys). Following approximately a month's stay at the reception center, where each boy receives a complete diagnostic evaluation, the Juvenile Review Board decides which institution, or plan, can best serve the needs of a particular boy. He is then transferred to one of the three juvenile facilities—(1) Wisconsin School for Boys—Wales; (2) Kettle Moraine Boys School; (3) Black River Camp; or (4) returned to the community, under field supervision.

The Kettle Moraine Boys School is an entirely new minimum security facility, without walls, fences, or bars, constructed to replace the hundred-year old school located in the City of Waukesha. It was officially dedicated on October 9, 1962, and comprises 480 acres in the beautiful Kettle Moraine State Forest, in Sheboygan County, approximately 12 miles west of the City of Plymouth, on Highway 67, and 15 miles east of the City of Fond du Lac, south of Highway 23.

The plant consists of 12 cottages, arranged about the campus in neighborhood clusters of four, each named after a Wisconsin River, and housing 25 boys in individual rooms; a beautiful all-faiths chapel; an administration building; a food service building; a school complex (known as the Forest Hills High School) consisting of a high school, grade school, pre-vocational school, a large gymnasium, an outdoor swimming pool and a general maintenance shop.

* * *

Redirecting Young Lives

New boys, received from the reception center at Wales are assigned to our orientation cottage, where they have an opportunity to meet with, and talk to the superintendent of the institution, the assistant superintendents, the school principal and other key personnel, such as the social workers and chaplains. These interviews take place during the first three days after arrival. During this time they receive basic information regarding the treatment program, including group and individual counselling, school attendance, the rating system, recreational opportunities, procedures and regulations of the school. They are shown the various buildings and given daily instructions in cottage housekeeping, making beds, proper grooming and dress, care of their clothing, and other routine tasks.

Physical examinations are given at the reception center, however, follow-up treatment including certain innoculations, is administered by our school physician. Boys are also referred to our full time dentist, for a complete dental checkup, and scheduled for future appointments, if necessary.

At the conclusion of the orientation period, an overall plan is implemented to meet the needs of each individual boy. He is then transferred from the orientation cottage and assigned to a regular cottage, beginning participation in the overall institution program.

Community Living

Emphasis is placed upon making community living a meaningful life experience. Each boy is expected to do his share of housekeeping and groundskeeping work. A boy's day begins when he arises at 6:30 a.m. After breakfast he cleans his room, and either attends school, or goes to his work assignment. Upon completion of the school day there is a period of extracurricular activities, i.e., band, chorus, varsity sports, crafts, group counselling, and so forth.

Every cottage has a television set, a pool table, a ping-pong table and ample small games, for boys to enjoy in their leisure time. They are encouraged to read good books, which are provided in every cottage and to write letters to members of their families. They are also expected to bring their "home work" from school as they have private rooms in which to read and study.

Youth counsellors supervise the boys while in the cottages; they work in shifts of eight hours per day. One senior counsellor is assigned the administrative duties in each of the twelve cottages.

Motivation by Reward

Every member of our staff who has direct supervision of a boy, including our cottage counsellors, work supervisors and our teachers, has an opportunity to rate a boy either I, II, or III. These ratings are based on conduct only. When a boy attains a class III rating, he is entitled to additional privileges, such as furloughs away from the institution to visit his family; indoor swimming at a neighboring community; special off-grounds movies; and attendance at athletic events. In addition, we have a school "scholastic honor roll", as well as special awards for various other activities. Boys strive to attain these rewards and, as a result, are conscious of their behavior.

Education

Boys under the age of 18 are expected to attend school full time. Regardless of age, all boys are encouraged to continue in school.

Boys who are enrolled in the formal educational program at the Kettle Moraine Boys School (and this includes the majority of the boys) take the same basic courses normally pursued in their community school. Graded classes, from 7th through 12th, are offered, with a full four year high school curriculum. Elementary school diplomas are issued to those who complete their eighth grade work during their enrollment at our school. High school credits earned here are transferred to, and accepted by, their home school, which issues high school diplomas in those cases where the requirements are completed by boys during their stay here.

We also have a special education class, for boys who have not achieved to the seventh grade level. Here they receive more individual attention, and help, thus giving them more of an opportunity to progress according to individual capabilities. A remedial reading teacher conducts daily sessions for boys who have a reading comprehension problem. Boys who are in the work program, as well as those who are enrolled in full time school may benefit from this program. All boys enrolled in the full time school program are required to attend physical education classes for one hour, five days a week. Instrumental and vocal music instructions are included in the curriculum.

In addition to the regular academic program, there is a prevocational program, consisting of printing, general metals, welding, machine shop, automotive shop, drafting, woodworking, arts and crafts, and driver education.

The non-school boy, or part time school boy, is assigned to the institutional work program which, wherever possible, is geared to provide vocational on-the-job training.

In general, life at the Kettle Moraine Boys School is comfortable, pleasant and, within limits, approximates that found in any good boarding school. The school is strict with boys who run away, and for older boys this may result in a transfer to a more secure institution. Disciplinary problems are dealt with mainly by deprivation of privileges. Corporal punishment, of course, is prohibited in Wisconsin institutions. A firm expectation that boys will adhere to rules and regulations, and the utilization of the disciplinary measures mentioned above, maintain the desired order within the institution.

Social Service

Social workers have the responsibility of trying to help each boy with his personal problems, whether it be difficulty with his institutional adjustment, interpersonal relations, or release planning. The most essential ingredient needed to help a boy is the formation of a constructive relationship, so that a boy can view his social worker as a person he can trust, confide in and emulate. Many of the boys have experienced harmful relationships with adults and it is necessary for the entire staff to provide a different kind of adult picture; one that is steady, fair and understanding.

Case workers spend a portion of their working hours circulating within the institution, interviewing boys individually, or in groups, exchanging information with teachers, counsellors and other staff. Group counselling is part of the total treatment program, used to make a rehabilitative impact on boys and to encourage them to examine and criticize their values as well as the values of others. Small discussion groups give each boy the opportunity to share his ideas with others and to test them against those of his peer group or against the facts presented by the group leader.

The services of a psychiatrist or psychologist are available to a boy when needed. Boys in residence, may be referred to the Wisconsin General Hospital, at Madison, for varied types of treatment, by our physician or dentist. Emergency surgery and minor surgery are performed at the Plymouth Hospital. For specialized treatment of eye (including glasses), ear and nose, the school has the medical services of a specialist, in Fond du Lac, who through pre-arranged appointments sees our boys in his office.

Religion

The religious program of the school is supervised by two full time chaplains; one for Protestants and one for Catholics. They conduct church services on Sundays and other religious days. Both chaplains also provide individual religious counselling and instructions.

Recreation

Adjacent to each cottage is an outside play area, where boys may take part in basketball, volleyball, tetherball, and horseshoe.

In addition to the program at the cottages, the school maintains a recreation program, utilizing facilities away from the cottage area. Boys have the use of a large gym, an auxiliary gym with gymnast equipment, and an outdoor swimming pool. In winter months much use is made of the surrounding rolling terrain, for activities such as skiing, tobogganing and ice skating.

Movies are provided at the school once a week. Intramural league competition in all team sports is held between cottages. This includes touch football, basketball, softball, volleyball, swimming, ping-pong, and baseball. Varsity football and basketball competition is carried on with neighboring schools.

* * *

BARTOLLAS AND SIEVERDES, COEDUCATIONAL TRAINING SCHOOLS: ARE THEY A PANACEA FOR JUVENILE CORRECTIONS? 34 JUVENILE AND FAMILY COURT JOURNAL 15 (August, 1983) *

Training schools have had many enemies. These institutions have been accused of being unsafe and violent settings in which the strong exploit the weak in every possible way, schools for crime because residents were socialized into peer cultures that encouraged them to become more informed about and committed to delinquent careers, inhumane, debilitating to the growth and development of a healthy personality and prohibitively expensive. Critics cited the high recidivism rates of juvenile correctional institutions as further evidence of their ineffectiveness. In the late 1960s and early 1970s, spurred on by blue ribbon national commissions and such abolitionists as Jerome Miller, critics even blissfully predicted that the disastrous 150–year experiment with training schools was finally coming to a close.

However, two groups have rallied to the defense of training schools: hard-liners, or "get-tough-with-kids" advocates; and moderates, who point to a number of improvements in state training schools the past decade. Hard-liners claim that training schools are needed for those hardened delinquents who refuse to respect the rights and property of citizens in the community. These predatory youngsters are seen as needing punishment and secure detention because it is obvious that they are exploiting the permissiveness of the juvenile justice system. Moderates defend the use of training schools because of the following humane practices instituted in the past decade: the removal of status offenders from these long-term facilities; the trend among state correctional systems to convert single-sex institutions into coeducational facilities; the dramatic reduction in staff brutality in these institutions, the much-improved training programs for all levels of staff; the growing use of grievance procedures for residents; and the tendency throughout the country to reduce the size of training schools and the length of institutional stay. Moderates give credit for these improvements both to court-mandated reforms, such as Morales v. Thurman, and to the in-house reforms generated by correctional administrators.

The purpose of this paper is to examine the quality of inmate life and the attitudes of residents in six coeducational training schools. Because of a report to the legislature documenting abuse and brutality of residents, widespread reforms were instituted in this state's training schools: the single-sex facilities were converted to coeducational; striking a resident for any reason became grounds for dismissal; staff training at a state corrections training center was required; and a group therapy program was established in all the training schools. This state juvenile correctional system, therefore, has become a good test of whether training schools with these more humane characteristics do generate a more positive response from residents.

* * *

In this paper the impact of these coeducational training schools is appraised by the answers to the following questions: How safe do residents feel? What is their social structure like? What are their attitudes toward the staff? How do residents feel about confinement? How do residents cope with institutional life? Because sex and race variables influenced how these questions are answered, the answers to each question are further evaluated according to sex and race.

Findings

Overall, the data show that residents in coeducational institutions were no more positive in their response to institutionalization than residents in single-sex training schools. In other words, this more humane approach to juvenile confinement did not eliminate the debilitating features of institutional processing.

* * *

Discussion

This study of six coeducational institutions in a southeastern state did not find residents much more positive about their institutional experiences than those inmates in more restrictive and custodially oriented settings. Although these coeducational institutions are somewhat more humane than the typical state training school, residents still developed a we-they mental set against the staff and the strong-will-survive culture with peers.

However, it can be claimed with some justification that the we-they mental set in these coeducational training schools is not as antagonistic toward staff as that found by Bartollas et al. and Feld in their studies of all-male training schools. Approximately one-third of these residents in these juvenile institutions felt antagonistic toward staff, thought the staff viewed them as troublemakers, indicated that they liked to "push" and "hassle" the staff and questioned whether the staff cared if they lived or died. Significantly, the longer residents were in these training schools, the less they trusted the staff; similarly, the more security-oriented the training school, the less the residents trusted the staff.

The social system of residents in these coeducational institutions also shows much in common with those reported in other studies of training schools. In respect to the seven argot roles found in these facilities, the inmates who adopted dominant and aggressive roles were at the top of the social order and those in the passive roles were at the bottom. White males, white females and American Indian females were the victims in these institutions and more often took the passive social roles. Black males, black females and American Indian males, meanwhile, more often took the aggressive and dominant roles. Moreover, the strong became the exploiters, and the weak became the victims. More than one-half of these youths were involved in an exploitation matrix in which they were exploiters or victims or exploiters in some situations and victims in others. Unfortunately, even in a state juvenile correctional system that attempted to establish a more humane approach to confinement, nearly one-tenth of these youths were sexually exploited. In other words, a high percentage of these institutionalized youths not only did not feel safe about their confinement but, indeed, were not safe.

It is also significant that an inmate code or conduct norm was present in these training schools and that residents in the minimum and maximum security facilities had a high compliance to these inmate conduct norms. In an institution or a state correctional system where there is solidarity in opposing staff norms, the anti-social values and behaviors of those residents who are more deep-seated in delinquency will shape the prevailing code. Thus, a cohesive peer culture will tend to have a much greater criminogenic impact upon residents than a culture which is splintered into various social groups.

There was little evidence of the positive impact of treatment or rehabilitation in these training schools. No interviewed staff members, whether social workers or youth counselors, indicated that they were having a positive impact upon residents. Nor did any group leader speak glowingly about the positive impact of group interaction. All staff members seemed to agree with one in a medium security institution who said, "It takes all our time to control these youths. We don't have time for anything else." Furthermore, not one interviewed resident mentioned treatment programs in their evaluation of the institutional experience.

This study also looked at two other indicators of the efficacy of juvenile institutionalization—how females felt about their confinement and how satisfied residents were with institutionalization.

White girls clearly felt like victims, but approximately 80 percent of all female residents found institutional life was not as bad as they had anticipated. More than 80 percent also found "doing time" easy. In terms of satisfaction with institutionalization, both male and female residents tended to look upon their confinement as time lost in their lives. They were, in effect, in jail, and the main task became one of enduring this punishment-oriented and deprived institutional experience. A large number of residents, especially whites, found institutionalization so painful that they chose to escape on one or more occasions.

Summary

This study of six coeducational institutions examining a great many variables leads to the conclusion that a quarter of the residents never felt safe; that is, they were nervous or scared all of the time. Moreover, 80 percent were scared at least some of the time. Residents also reported that: the most dominant and aggressive peers controlled the peer culture; that residents were basically resistant to staff; that institutionalization was, perhaps, easier than they thought it would be but certainly was not constructive by any means; and that most of the ways they chose to cope with institutionalization were anything but therapeutic. It can be argued with some justification that these institutions did less harm to residents than those described in Bartollas et al., Feld and other studies. Yet, these institutions clearly fall far short of offering humane and positive experiences for those juveniles confined in them.

Now, more than ever before, there is probably a better opportunity to reform juvenile correctional institutions. Since status offenders in most states are no longer being institutionalized with delinquents, training schools now hold a more homogenous population. Within this more homogenous population, the challenge is to make institutions safe and humane for all offenders, break up the negative and anti-social peer culture, provide the services that are needed and employ staff who will respond in positive ways to residents. Too many training schools are still schools of crime. It is imperative that an environment be created in these closed settings that will encourage youths to respond to confinement in more constructive and therapeutic ways.

B. ADMINISTRATION OF TRAINING SCHOOLS

1. SUBSTANTIVE RIGHTS OF JUVENILES AND LIMITS ON THEM

STANDARDS FOR THE ADMINISTRATION OF JUVENILE JUSTICE, REPORT OF THE NATIONAL ADVISORY COMMITTEE FOR JUVENILE JUSTICE AND DELINQUENCY PREVENTION. (U.S. Department of Justice, 1980).

4.41 Mail and Censorship

A juvenile should have the right to send mail without prior censorship or prior reading. A juvenile should also have the right to receive mail without prior reading or prior censorship. However, if the facility suspects the delivery of contraband or cash, it may require the juvenile to open the mail in the presence of a staff member.

A juvenile should have the right to mail a minimum of two letters per week at agency expense and any number of additional letters at his/her own expense.

All cash sent to juveniles should be retained by the juveniles or held for their benefit in accordance with the procedures of the facility. However, such procedures should be in writing and approved by the agency.

Packages should be exempt from these provisions and be subject to inspection at the discretion of the facility.

4.42 Dress Codes

Juveniles should have the right to wear their personal clothing if they so choose, or wear combinations of their own clothing and clothing issued by the facility in cases where their own clothing does not meet all of their clothing needs. Clothing issued by the facility should be available to those children lacking personal clothing or who choose to wear issued clothing.

Juveniles should also have the right to wear items of jewelry. However, reasonable restrictions may be imposed which prohibit juveniles from possessing items of clothing or jewelry that could be used to inflict bodily harm on themselves or others. Any time a restriction is placed upon the wearing of jewelry or clothing, a report should be forwarded to the ombudsman.

4.43 Personal Appearance

Restrictions on the right of juveniles to determine the length and style of their hair should be prohibited, except in individual cases where such restrictions are necessary for reasons of physical health or safety.

Restrictions on the right of students to grow facial hair should be prohibited, except in individual cases where such restrictions are necessary for reasons of physical health or safety.

Students should be required to observe reasonable precautions where the length and style of their hair could possibly pose a physical health or safety problem unless prescribed precautions are taken.

Before facility staff can remove head or facial hair against the wishes of any juvenile, an automatic grievance hearing shall be conducted as provided in Standard 4.81.

4.44 Visitation

A juvenile should have the right to receive any and all visitors at the times fixed for visits. However, a facility may deny access by a visitor if the visit would present a substantial danger to the health of the juvenile or the safety of the facility. Whenever a visitor is denied access, a written report should be prepared describing the dangers which the visit would pose and the basis for believing that the danger exists. The report should be kept on file, a copy should be given to the juvenile, and a copy should be sent to the ombudsman.

4.45 Religious Freedom

All facilities should afford the juveniles placed therein the right and the opportunity to participate in the religious observances of their choice.

Counseling to members of their faith by authorized representatives of religious denominations should be permissible at all facilities. However, the use of physical force, punishment, or coercion to compel attendance or participation in religious observances or rehabilitation programs predicated on religious beliefs should be prohibited.

4.48 Searches

Indiscriminant searches should be prohibited. Whenever there is reason to believe that the security of a facility is endangered or that contraband or objects which are illegal to possess are present in the facility, a search of a room, locker, or possessions of a juvenile may be conducted.

Whenever possible, a juvenile's physical presence should be assured prior to a search. When it is impossible to obtain the juvenile's physical presence the juvenile should be given prompt written notice of the search and of any article taken. Written reports of all searches should be given to the ombudsman.

4.49 Work Assignments

Juveniles may be required to perform work functions as part of their rehabilitative program. However, juveniles should not be required to do work:

    a.   Which is unreasonably arduous or demeaning;

    b.   Which is not an integral part of the rehabilitation program;

    c.   Which cannot be shown to be a benefit to the juveniles; or

    d.   Which has as its primary purpose monetary benefit to the facility or agency.

Juveniles subject to compulsory education laws should be required to work no more than four hours per day. Juveniles not subject to or exempted from such laws should not be required to work more than eight hours per day.

Juveniles should receive compensation for work which confers a substantial benefit upon the facility or oversight agency. However, such compensation may be less than that provided in the minimum-wage provisions of the Fair Labor Standards Act.

4.410 Right to Care and Treatment

Juveniles in residential facilities should have the right to a basic level of services, including but not limited to: an adequate and varied diet; varied recreation and leisure-time activities; preventive and immediate medical/dental care; remedial, special, vocational, and academic educational services; protection against physical and mental abuse; freedom to develop individuality; opportunity to participate or not participate in religious observances; clean, safe, adequately heated and lighted accommodations; and maximum feasible contact with family, friends, and community.

Juveniles in residential facilities have a right to a maximum level of treatment services, in accordance with their needs, including individual and group counseling, psychiatric and psychological services, and casework services. In addition, juveniles should not be subjected to treatment methods such as psychosurgery, electric stimulation of the brain, behavior modification involving excessive deprivation of personal liberties, or any other treatment which is cruel, demeaning, or dangerous.

While services are ordinarily most effective when participation is voluntary, juveniles should have an obligation to be physically available for services ordered by the family court during the dispositional period.

Physical force and other forms of punishment described in Standard 4.51 should never be used to compel participation. However, failure to be physically available for services may be considered in determining whether to recommend a change in disposition, although it should not be used as a basis for extending the dispositional period, except as specified in Standards 3.1810 and 3.1811.

4.411 Denial of Enumerated Rights

The rights enumerated in Standards 4.41–4.410 should be inalienable and should not be diminished or denied for disciplinary reasons.

4.51 Corporal Punishment and Use of Physical Restraint

Corporal punishment should be prohibited. However, use of physical force should be permitted:

a. For self-protection;

b. To separate juveniles who are fighting;

c. To restrain juveniles in danger of inflicting harm to themselves or others; or

d. To restrain juveniles who have absconded or who are in the process of absconding.

When use of physical force is authorized, the least force necessary under the circumstances should be employed.

Staff members of residential and nonresidential programs who are assigned to work with juveniles should receive written guidelines on the use of physical force, and written notice that corporal punishment is prohibited and that, in accordance with staff disciplinary procedures, loss of employment may result if use of corporal punishment is proven.

4.52 Room Confinement

Juveniles should be placed in room confinement only when no less restrictive measure is sufficient to protect the safety of the facility and the persons residing or employed therein. No juvenile should be placed in room confinement for more than one hour unless the procedures set forth in Standard 4.54 have been followed. Room confinement for more than twenty-four hours should never be imposed.

Ordinarily the place of confinement should be the juvenile's own room. When this is not possible, the place of confinement should be lighted, heated, cooled, and ventilated the same as other living areas in the facility and should be furnished with the items necessary for the juvenile's health and comfort. Juveniles placed in room confinement in facilities other than a foster home should be examined at least once during the day by a physician, visited at least twice during the day by a childcare worker or other member of the treatment staff, and be provided with educational materials and other services as needed. Juveniles placed in room confinement in foster homes should be visited periodically by the foster parent.

Juveniles placed in room confinement for more than twelve hours should be provided with at least thirty minutes of recreation and exercise outside of the room in which they are confined. No child placed in room confinement should be denied the rights set forth in Standards 4.41–4.410.

4.53 Loss of Privileges

The temporary suspension of a privilege enjoyed by a juvenile who is detained or subject to the dispositional authority of the family court should be an authorized form of discipline. A juvenile should be advised of the privileges subject to suspension and a list of such privileges should be posted in each residential facility. No juveniles should have a privilege suspended unless the procedures set forth in Standard 4.54 have been followed. In any event no privilege should be suspended for a period of more than fourteen consecutive days.

Food, including snacks, toiletries, and other items necessary for a minimum quality of life, as well as the rights enumerated in Standards 4.41–4.410, should not be diminished or denied for disciplinary purposes.

4.61 Mechanical Restraints

Mechanical restraints should be used only when a juvenile is uncontrollable and constitutes a serious and evident danger to him/herself or to others, or during transportation when necessary for public safety. Use of mechanical restraints except during transportation should not be imposed for more than a half hour. When in restraints, a juvenile should not be attached to any furniture or fixture.

4.62 Medical Restraints

For the purposes of these standards, medical restraints are medication administered either by injection or orally for the purposes of quieting an uncontrollable juvenile.

Medical restraints should be administered only in situations in which a juvenile is so uncontrollable that no other means of restraint can prevent the juvenile from harming him/herself. Medical restraints should be authorized only by a physician and should be administered only by a physician or a registered nurse.

Orders authorizing registered nurses to administer prescribed psychiatric medication at their own discretion for purposes of crisis intervention, should only be issued by a psychiatrist who has examined the juvenile and determined that such an order is required by the juvenile's ongoing treatment needs. A report should accompany each such order explaining the facts and reasons underlying it and providing specific instructions. The order should be re-examined weekly to determine whether the order is still necessary. If the order is continued, a written report explaining the facts and reasons underlying the continuation should be prepared monthly. A copy of reports explaining the issuance or continuance of such orders should be provided to the director of the facility and placed in the juvenile's file.

NOTE

The Standards set out above represent only one example of efforts to respond to criticisms of training schools. The IJA–ABA Standards in the Corrections Administration volume set out comparable standards. The interested student can find much enlightenment in the careful commentary to both the Department of Justice Standards and to the IJA–ABA Standards. And, of course, reference back to the descriptive and empirical material at the beginning of this chapter should once again be considered. Finally, the section on judicial intervention, infra, will provide still further help in judging the quality and effectiveness of training schools as at least some of them are currently administered.

2. PROCEDURAL PROTECTIONS

STANDARDS FOR THE ADMINISTRATION OF JUVENILE JUSTICE, REPORT OF THE NATIONAL ADVISORY COMMITTEE FOR JUVENILE JUSTICE AND DELINQUENCY PREVENTION. (U.S. Department of Justice, 1980).

4.46 Responsibility for Control and Apprehension of Juveniles

The control of juveniles placed in a residential facility should be solely a staff responsibility. Under no circumstances should residents of the facility be used to control other juveniles.

The return to a facility of juveniles who leave without authorization should be the responsibility of staff and law enforcement agencies. However, the staff should be authorized to allow residents of the facility to assist in carrying out this responsibility if:

a. The presence of the resident would aid in inducing the juvenile to return voluntarily;

b. The resident is accompanied by a staff member at all times; and

c. The use of physical force by the resident to secure the absent juvenile's return is prohibited.

4.47 Notice of Rules

The rules and regulations to be enforced against or on behalf of a juvenile placed in a residential facility should be posted in each living area of that facility.

4.54 Disciplinary Procedures

A chronological record of all disciplinary actions taken against juveniles placed in residential facilities should be maintained. This record should contain the name of the juvenile disciplined, the name of the person imposing the discipline, and the date of, the duration of, the actions leading to, and the reasons for the disciplinary action.

Before juveniles placed in a residential facility other than a foster home may be confined in a room, including their own room, for more than one hour, or have a privilege suspended for more than twenty-four hours, they should be given notice of the alleged infraction, access to the facility ombudsman or to a person in an equivalent capacity, and opportunity to respond to the allegations.

Before juveniles placed in any residential facility including a foster home may have a privilege suspended for more than seven days, there should be a hearing to determine whether the allegations are true and whether the sanction is appropriate. In conjunction with that hearing, the juvenile should be entitled:

a. To written notice of the rule violated and date, time, place, and nature of the alleged violation on which the hearing is based;

b. To adequate time to prepare;

c. To representation by the facility ombudsman, a member of the facility staff other than the ombudsman, another juvenile, or a volunteer from an established volunteer program;

d. To present evidence and testify;

e. To confront and cross-examine witnesses;

f. To an impartial hearing officer or board;

g. To have the hearing tape-recorded, the tape maintained by the agency for a two-year period, and access to the tape or a transcript thereof; and

h. To review of the decision by the agency director or an agency official above the level of facility director who reports to the agency director, or by an independent review board.

4.81 Grievance Procedures

Written grievance procedures should be established for all residential and nonresidential programs. Each juvenile should be provided with an explanation and a copy of these procedures at the time the juvenile is admitted to the facility.

Although the form of grievance procedures may vary, all such procedures should provide for:

a. Review of grievances by an agency official above the level of the facility director, and by an independent review board, or an impartial individual not employed by the agency;

b. Time limits for resolution of the grievance; and

c. Involvement of staff and juveniles

4.82 Ombudsman Programs

In addition to the grievance procedures described in Standard 4.81, juveniles placed in residential or nonresidential programs should have access to an ombudsman.

The ombudsman should investigate matters adversely affecting juveniles under agency supervision which are not raised in grievance procedures, and whenever possible should serve on the assessment team for juveniles placed in training schools. Ombudsmen should report to the director of ombudsmen or, if such a position has not been created, to an agency official above the level of facility director who should not be administratively responsible for the program in which the ombudsman is assigned to serve.

Ombudsmen should have substantial experience in the area of juvenile law, youth services, and investigation.

In order to encourage residents, staff, and administrators to communicate freely with the ombudsman, statements made to the ombudsman should be statutorily protected as privileged communication. The privilege may be waived by the person providing the information.

Ombudsman reports should not form the basis for agency disciplinary action. However, based upon information brought to light by the ombudsman, the agency should initiate its own independent investigations which may give rise to agency action.

COMMENT, THE ROLE OF THE ATTORNEY IN THE TREATMENT PHASE OF THE JUVENILE COURT PROCESS

12 St.L.U.L.J. 659, 670–78 (1968).*

An institutional care program

Perhaps even more significant to the child in the treatment scheme is the extent of his rights in the institutional setting where the deprivation of liberty is most severe. In the adult area it has been recognized that conviction of crime does not result in the denuding of the criminal of all rights. * * * Obviously, these observations are true a fortiori in the juvenile area where the only justification for incarceration is treatment rather than punishment. It will be useful, therefore, to examine the rights of the adult offender in the institutional setting and to consider to what extent the juvenile enjoys analogous rights.

* * *

It seems quite clear that courts should be even more zealous in enforcing the guarantee against cruel and unusual punishment in the juvenile area. Any infliction of corporal punishment which is not absolutely necessary for the maintenance of order should be prohibited.

Solitary confinement is a disciplinary procedure which may be of value in maintaining order. If used reasonably it is a device which may even be used on a juvenile with impunity. * * * It is obvious, however, that solitary confinement may be subject to abuse. Isolation for long periods of time without sufficient reason clearly may constitute cruel and unusual punishment. Similarly, isolation of a juvenile in unventilated or unsanitary cells is totally without justification and could bring about permanent psychological damage.

Another common form of discipline is deprivation. In the field of adult corrections this * * * may run the gamut from deprivation of rather insignificant privileges to deprivation of the means to fulfill rather basic needs. For example, in some states reduction of diet is authorized by statute as a disciplinary measure. * * * Similarly, loss of visiting and correspondence privileges is a common punishment. * * *

The total absurdity of such disciplinary procedures in juvenile institutions is readily apparent. Although deprivation of some privileges may be an effective disciplinary device, any deprivation which prevents the juvenile from fulfilling basic needs should be totally unacceptable.

* * *

While useful, productive work in connection with a program of education and counseling is a basic element in rehabilitation it can be abused as where the work is dangerous, extremely difficult, or where the hours are unreasonably long. * * * [T]here should be no question that an individual incarcerated in a juvenile institution should be provided with basics of adequate food and water, sanitary living quarters and provision of necessary medical attention. Any other approach would be totally inconsistent with the goals of treatment and rehabilitation. * * * It seems clear that, particularly in juvenile facilities, there can be no justification for a policy of racial discrimination, nor for denial of the inmate's first amendment right of freedom of religion. * * *

Inmate Communication

    *   *   * The prisoners' most unrestricted [first amendment] right of communication is found when the communication is for the purpose of gaining access to the courts. *   *   * As an adjunct to this rule is the requirement by some courts that prisoners be allowed access to legal materials necessary for the preparation of such documents. This rule will have little applicability to juvenile inmates due to the relatively short duration of their terms of confinement and their lack of familiarity with the legal process. It is, therefore, likely that, even were the institutions to allow access to the courts, juvenile inmates would likely make but infrequent use of the privilege.

    Perhaps even more important, at least in the eyes of the juvenile, is his right to communication of a personal nature—with his family, his friends or his attorney. It is clear that continued communication with the outside world is essential in the rehabilitative scheme. It seems, however, that even in the juvenile area, courts will uphold the rights of the institution's administrators to examine and read mail sent or received by the juvenile. One particularly touchy area is the right of unrestricted communication between the juvenile and his attorney. Since communication between the juvenile and his attorney is subject to a legal privilege, reading by the staff of the institution of the juvenile's mail might constitute a breach of the privilege. *   *   *

Juvenile's Right to Treatment

    Most significant *   *   * is the fact that, in addition to all the other rights retained by the juvenile who is institutionalized, it is possible that he has another right not enjoyed by adults—the right to treatment. *   *   * The entire emphasis of the juvenile courts is on treatment and, as a consequence, certain due process requirements have been relaxed. It seems to follow that if the juvenile is not receiving rehabilitative treatment his incarceration is invalid. *   *   * It seems likely, however, that relief will be available only in the most blatant cases, as where, for example, the child is confined in a facility intended primarily as a place to detain and punish adult offenders. *   *   *

Termination of Institutional Care

    The attorney may have an important role to play in securing for the juvenile release from the institution. *   *   * The attorney will have this opportunity but infrequently, since, as a practical matter, the child is ordinarily confined for a relatively short period of time in most circumstances. *   *   * Nevertheless, cases may arise in which a change in circumstances shortly after disposition would indicate that the disposition is no longer acceptable. *   *   *

3. JUDICIAL "CHECKS"

NELSON v. HEYNE

United States Court of Appeals for the Seventh Circuit, 1974.
491 F.2d 352, cert. denied, 417 U.S. 976, 94 S.Ct. 3183,
41 L.Ed.2d 1146 (1974).

Before KILEY, SENIOR CIRCUIT JUDGE, and FAIRCHILD and SPRECHER, CIRCUIT JUDGES.

KILEY, SENIOR CIRCUIT JUDGE.

The district court in this class civil rights action enjoined defendants from implementing alleged unconstitutional practices and policies in conducting the Indiana Boys School under their administration; and declared the practices and policies unconstitutional. In Appeal No. 72–1970 defendants challenge the validity of the judgment granting the injunction, and in Appeal No. 73–1446 challenge the declaratory judgment. We affirm.

The School, located in Plainfield, Indiana, is a medium security state correctional institution for boys twelve to eighteen years of age, an estimated one-third of whom are non-criminal offenders. The boys reside in about sixteen cottages. The School also has academic and vocational school buildings, a gymnasium and an administrative building. The average length of a juvenile's stay at the School is about six and one-half months. Although the School's maximum capacity is less than 300 juveniles, its population is generally maintained at 400. The counselling staff of twenty individuals includes three psychologists with undergraduate academic degrees, and one part-time psychiatrist who spends four hours a week at the institution. The medical staff includes one part-time physician, one registered nurse, and one licensed practical nurse.

The complaint alleged that defendants' practices and policies violated the 8th and 14th Amendments rights of the juveniles under their care. Plaintiffs moved for a temporary restraining order to protect them from, inter alia, defendants' corporal punishment and use of control-tranquilizing drugs. After hearing, the district court denied the motion and set the date for hearing on the merits. Defendants' answer generally denied plaintiffs' allegations. Trial briefs were filed upon the issue whether defendants deprived plaintiffs of their alleged right to adequate rehabilitative treatment.

The court found that it had jurisdiction and that the corporal punishment and the method of administering tranquilizing drugs by defendants constituted cruel and unusual punishment in violation of plaintiffs' 8th and 14th Amendment rights. The judgment restraining the challenged practices followed. The court thereafter, in a separate judgment, declared plaintiffs had the right to adequate rehabilitative treatment.

I—CRUEL AND UNUSUAL PUNISHMENT

A.

It is not disputed that the juveniles who were returned from escapes or who were accused of assaults on other students or staff members were beaten routinely by guards under defendants' supervision. There is no proof of formal procedures that governed the beatings which were administered after decision by two or more staff members. Two staff members were required to observe the beatings.

In beating the juveniles, a "fraternity paddle" between ½" and 2" thick, 12" long, with a narrow handle, was used. There is testimony that juveniles weighing about 160 pounds were struck five blows on the clothed buttocks, often by a staff member weighing 285 pounds. The beatings caused painful injuries.[1] The district court found that this disciplinary practice violated the plaintiffs' 8th and 14th Amendment rights, and ordered it stopped immediately.

We recognize that the School is a correctional, as well as an academic, institution.[2] No case precisely in point has been cited or found which decided whether supervised beatings in a juvenile reformatory violated the "cruel and unusual" clause of the 8th Amendment.[3] However, the test of "cruel and unusual" punishment has

---

[1] The trial record indicates that one juvenile was struck with such force that it caused him to sleep on his face for three days, with black, blue and numb buttocks. One juvenile testified that he bled after receiving five blows on his buttocks. Another, Daniel Roberts testified that once he pleaded, to no avail, with staff personnel not to be beaten until after certain blisters on his buttocks ceased to cause him pain.

[2] (a) The law appears to be well settled in both state and federal jurisdictions that school officials do not violate 8th Amendment proscriptions against cruel and unusual punishment where the punishment is reasonable and moderate. Ware v. Estes, 328 F.Supp. 657 (N.D.Tex. 1971); Sims v. Board of Education, 329 F.Supp. 678 (D.C.N.M.1971); Tinkham v. Kole, 252 Iowa 1303, 110 N.W.2d 258 (1961); Carr v. Wright (Ky.) 423 S.W.2d 521 (1968); Houeye v. St. Helen Parish School Board, 223 La. 966, 67 So.2d 553 (1953). In Ware there was evidence of beatings usually administered by hitting the student on his buttocks with a paddle. The paddle was wooden, 2′ long, ¼″ to ½″ thick, 6″ wide, used under a written rule which proscribed corporal punishment without parents' permission. The district court found that "some of the seven thousand" teachers in the public school district abused the policy, but that that fact, and nothing more, would

not make the policy itself unconstitutional. In Sims, the court found that beatings by school officials did not constitute cruel and unusual punishment where the plaintiff student received three blows with a paddle on the buttocks and experienced slight physical harm. In our case, there is ample evidence that the beatings caused severe injury. See generally 68 Am.Jur.2d Schools § 258 (1973).

(b) The courts in recent years have frowned upon the use of corporal punishment in penal and correctional institutions. See generally 60 Am.Jur.2d Penal and Correctional Institutions § 43 (1972). Corporal punishment has not been used for years in federal prisons. Jackson v. Bishop, 404 F.2d 571, 575 (8th Cir.1968). Courts have enjoined prison personnel from inflicting corporal punishment including the use of a strap for whipping. Talley v. Stephens, 247 F.Supp. 683 (E.D. Ark.1965); Jackson v. Bishop, supra. In Talley the court did not hold prison whippings are per se unconstitutional, but stated that they will be enjoined if excessive, and not applied under recognizable standards. In Jackson the 8th Circuit held that use of a strap in Arkansas penitentiaries was cruel and unusual punishment. * * *

[3] The court in Lollis v. New York, 322 F.Supp. 473 (S.D.N.Y.1970), involving the constitutionality of solitary confinement

been outlined. In his concurring opinion in Furman v. Georgia, 408 U.S. 238, 279, 92 S.Ct. 2726, 2747, 33 L.Ed.2d 346 (1971), Justice Brennan stated that:

> The final principle inherent in the [Cruel and Unusual Punishment] Clause is that a severe punishment must not be excessive. A punishment is excessive under this principle if it is unnecessary: The infliction of a severe punishment by the State cannot comport with human dignity when it is nothing more than the pointless infliction of suffering. If there is a significantly less severe punishment adequate to achieve the purposes for which the punishment is inflicted, the punishment inflicted is unnecessary and therefore excessive. (Citations omitted.)

Expert evidence adduced at the trial unanimously condemned the beatings. The uncontradicted authoritative evidence indicates that the practice does not serve as useful punishment or as treatment, and it actually breeds counter-hostility resulting in greater aggression by a child. For these reasons we find the beatings presently administered are unnecessary and therefore excessive. We think, under the test of *Furman*, that the district court did not err in deciding that the disciplinary beatings shown by this record constituted cruel and unusual punishment.[4]

The 8th Amendment prohibition against cruel and unusual punishment is binding on the states through the 14th Amendment. * * * The meaning of cruel and unusual punishment in law has varied through the course of history, and as the Court observed in Trop v. Dulles, 356 U.S. 86, 101, 78 S.Ct. 590, 598, 2 L.Ed.2d 630 (1958):

> The [8th Amendment] must draw its meaning from the evolving standards of decency that mark the progress of a maturing society.

The district court's decision meets tests that have been applied in decisions to determine whether the standards of decency in a maturing society have been met, i.e.: whether the punishment is disproportionate to the offense, Weems v. United States, 217 U.S. 349, 30 S.Ct. 544, 54 L.Ed. 793 (1910); and whether the severity or harshness of the punishment offends "broad and idealistic concepts of dignity, civilized standards, humanity, and decency." Jackson v. Bishop, 404 F.2d 571 (8th Cir.1968). The record before us discloses that the beatings employed by defendants are disproportionate to the offenses for which they are used, and do not measure up to contemporary standards of decency in our contemporary society.

There is nothing in the record to show that a less severe punishment would not have accomplished the disciplinary aim. And

---

in juvenile institutions, obliquely considered the binding and handcuffing of an inmate. Inmates of Boys' Training School v. Affleck, 346 F.Supp. 1354 (D.C. R.I.1972), also concerned the question of whether isolation of juvenile inmates constitutes cruel and unusual punishment.

[4] We do not hold that all corporal punishment in juvenile institutions or reformatories is per se cruel and unusual.

it is likely that the beatings have aroused animosity toward the School and substantially frustrated its rehabilitative purpose. We find in the record before us, to support our holding, general considerations similar to those the court in *Jackson* found relevant: (1) corporal punishment is easily subject to abuse in the hands of the sadistic and unscrupulous, and control of the punishment is inadequate; (2) formalized School procedures governing the infliction of the corporal punishment are at a minimum; (3) the infliction of such severe punishment frustrates correctional and rehabilitative goals; and (4) the current sociological trend is toward the elimination of all corporal punishment in all correctional institutions.

The Indiana Supreme Court decision in Indiana State Personnel Board v. Jackson, 244 Ind. 321, 192 N.E.2d 740 (1963), cited by the defendants, is of no aid to set aside the district court decision. There the court held, inter alia, under the *parens patriae* doctrine, that a public school teacher, in proper cases and proportions, may administer corporal punishment.[5] We agree with that decision.

B.

Witnesses for both the School and the juveniles testified at trial that tranquilizing drugs, specifically Sparine and Thorazine, were occasionally administered to the juveniles, not as part of an ongoing psychotherapeutic program, but for the purpose of controlling excited behavior.[6] The registered nurse and licensed practical nurse prescribed intramuscular dosages of the drugs upon recommendation of the custodial staff under standing orders by the physician.[7] Neither before nor after injections were the juveniles examined by medically competent staff members to determine their tolerances.

The district court also found this practice to be cruel and unusual punishment. Accordingly the court ordered the practice stopped immediately, and further ordered that no drug could be administered intramuscularly unless specifically authorized or directed by a physician in each case, and unless oral medication was first tried, except where the staff was directed otherwise by a physician in each case.

We agree with defendants that a judge lacking expertise in medicine should be cautious when considering what are "minimal medical standards" in particular situations. However, practices and

[5] There the dismissed teacher disciplined a fourteen year old girl in the classroom and in his office by striking her, in the presence of witnesses, very lightly and without anger, across the buttocks with a belt, and only after persuasion and other means had been tried and had failed.

[6] Plaintiff Steven Hegg testified that on one occasion while he was recuperating from a blow to the nose inflicted upon him by another student, his nose began to bleed profusely and he began to vomit and "holler for help." The nurse told him there was nothing seriously wrong with him; but when Steven continued to request help, she became infuriated and injected him with a tranquilizing drug. Eric Nelson testified to the effect that he was given shots of tranquilizing drugs on several occasions for the purpose of preventing him from running away from the School.

[7] The standing order provided that an emotionally upset boy under 116 pounds be given a half cc or 25 milligrams of Sparine. Above that weight he was to be given one cc or 50 milligrams of Sparine.

policies in the field of medicine, among other professional fields, are within judicial competence when measured against requirements of the Constitution. We find no error in the competent district court's determination here that the use of tranquilizing drugs as practiced by defendants was cruel and unusual punishment.

We are not persuaded by defendants' argument that the use of tranquilizing drugs is not "punishment." Experts testified that the tranquilizing drugs administered to the juveniles can cause: the collapse of the cardiovascular system, the closing of a patient's throat with consequent asphyxiation, a depressant effect on the production of bone marrow, jaundice from an affected liver, and drowsiness, hemotological disorders, sore throat and ocular changes.[8]

The interest of the juveniles, the School, and the state must be considered in determining the validity of the use of the School's tranquilizing drugs policy. The interest of the state appears to be identical more or less with the interest of the maladjusted juveniles committed to the School's care, i.e., reformation so that upon release from their confinement juveniles may enter free society as well adjusted members. The School's interest is in the attainment and maintenance of reasonable order so that the state's purpose may be pursued in a suitable environment. The School's interest, however, does not justify exposing its juveniles to the potential dangers noted above. Nor can Indiana's interest in reforming its delinquent or maladjusted juveniles be so compelling that it can use "cruel and unusual" means to accomplish its benevolent end of reformation.

We hold today only that the use of disciplinary beatings and tranquilizing drugs in the circumstances shown by this record violates plaintiffs' 14th Amendment right protecting them from cruel and unusual punishment. We do not intend that penal and reform institutional physicians cannot prescribe necessary tranquilizing drugs in appropriate cases. Our concern is with actual and potential abuses under policies where juveniles are beaten with an instrument causing serious injuries, and drugs are administered to juveniles intramuscularly by staff, without trying medication short of drugs and without adequate medical guidance and prescription.[9]

[8] Dr. James W. Worth, psychologist with the Mental Health Center of St. Joseph County, Indiana, also testified as follows:

I think the use of major tranquilizing drugs without intelligent and informed medical observation have no place * * * in the institution. These are serious drugs. They have serious effect on the individual. * * * [I]f this is not done with a full medical understanding of this individual with a physician present, harm could occur and furthermore, I think it tends to be degrading to an individual.

[9] Experts testified that the following minimum medical safeguards should be followed in the use of tranquilizing drugs:

(1) The individual administered the drug should be observed, during the duration of the drug's effect, by trained medical personnel, familiar with the possible adverse and harmful side effects of the drug used.

(2) The person receiving an IM (intramuscular) injection of a major tranquilizing drug should first receive a diagnosis or prescription authorizing the use of said drug by a qualified medical doctor, child psychiatrist, psychologist or physician.

(3) IM injections should only be administered by a physician or intern and only

II—THE RIGHT TO REHABILITATIVE TREATMENT

The School staff-to-juvenile ratio for purposes of treatment is approximately one to thirty. The sixteen counselors are responsible for developing and implementing individualized treatment programs at the institution, but the counselors need have no specialized training or experience. Administrative tasks ("paper work") occupy more than half of the counselors' time. The duties of the staff psychiatrist are limited to crises. He has no opportunity to develop and manage individual psychotherapy programs. The three staff psychologists do not hold graduate degrees and are not certified by Indiana. They render, principally, diagnostic services, mostly directed toward supervising in-take behavior classifications.

In June, 1971, the School adopted what was described as a differential treatment program, bottomed mainly on the Quay Classification System. Under the Quay System, upon their admission to the School, juveniles are classified with respect to four personality and behavior types on the basis of standardized tests: the inadequate, the neurotic, the aggressive, and the sub-cultural. Each of the sixteen cottages at the School houses twenty to thirty juveniles, with common personality and behavior patterns. Each cottage is served by a staff comprising a house manager, a counselor, an educator, and a consulting psychologist. The cottage staff meets weekly for evaluation of the rehabilitation program of each inmate. Upon admission to a cottage, each juvenile agrees to improve his behavior in four areas of institutional life: "cottage," "recreation," "school," and "treatment." Correspondingly, each has responsibility for physical maintenance of the residential area, social and athletic activities, specified levels of academic or vocational skills, and improved personality goals. With success in each of the four areas, the juvenile earns additional privileges, ultimately culminating in a parole date.

The district court decided that both Indiana law and the federal Constitution secure for juvenile offenders a "right to treatment," and that the School failed to provide minimal rehabilitative treatment. Defendants contend that there exists no right to treatment under the Constitution or Indiana law, and that if there is the right, the Quay Classification System used at the School did not violate the right. We hold, with the district court, that juveniles have a right to rehabilitative treatment.

after all attempts have failed to get the individual to take the drug orally.

(4) Major tranquilizing drugs, such as Thorazine and Sparine, should not be administered IM, unless given in a hospital where there is an intensive care unit and emergency facilities which could deal with possible adverse effects from the use of said drugs.

(5) Major tranquilizing drugs should only be used to control psychotic or pre-psychotic breakdowns or as a followup in assisting a schizophrenic patient from having a recurrence of a psychotic breakdown.

(6) Major tranquilizing drugs should not be used merely to induce sleep or unconsciousness for a period of time, but only as a part of a psychotherapeutic program of treatment.

The right to rehabilitative treatment for juvenile offenders has roots in the general social reform of the late nineteenth century, was nurtured by court decisions throughout the first half of this century, and has been established in state and federal courts in recent years. In re Gault, 387 U.S. 1, 15–16, 87 S.Ct. 1428, 1437, 18 L.Ed.2d 527 (1967), the Court stated:

> The early reformers were appalled by adult procedures and penalties, and by the fact that children could be given long prison sentences and mixed in jails with hardened criminals * * *. The child was to be "treated" and "rehabilitated" and the procedures, from apprehension through institutionalization, were to be "clinical" rather than punitive.

Since the beginning, state courts have emphasized the need for "treatment" in their Juvenile Court Acts. * * *

The United States Supreme Court has never definitively decided that a youth confined under the jurisdiction of a juvenile court has a constitutionally guaranteed right to treatment. But the Court has assumed, in passing on the validity of juvenile proceedings, that a state must provide treatment for juveniles. In Kent v. United States, 383 U.S. 541, 86 S.Ct. 1045, 16 L.Ed.2d 84 (1966), the Court reversed the district court's conviction of a sixteen year old after the District of Columbia Juvenile Court had waived its jurisdiction. Justice Fortas there, writing for the Court, commented on the theory and practice of juvenile courts:

> There is evidence, in fact, that there may be grounds for concern that the child receives the worst of both worlds: that he gets neither the protections accorded to adults nor the solicitous care and regenerative treatment postulated for children. 383 U.S. at 556, 86 S.Ct. at 1054.

Later, in In re Gault, supra, Justice Fortas "reiterate[d] the view" of *Kent* that the juvenile process need not meet the constitutional requirements of an adult criminal trial, but must provide essential "due process and fair treatment." This view has been continued subsequent to *Gault* in the Supreme Court decisions involving juvenile court procedures. * * *

It is true that the Supreme Court cases discussed above deal with procedural due process and not the right to rehabilitative treatment, but several recent state and federal cases, out of concern—based upon the *parens patriae* doctrine underlying the juvenile justice system—that rehabilitative treatment was not generally accorded in the juvenile reform process, have decided that juvenile inmates have a constitutional right to that treatment. * * *

In *Martarella* the court found a clear constitutional right to treatment for juveniles based on the 8th and 14th Amendments:

> What we have said, although the record would justify more, is sufficient to establish that, however benign the purposes for which members of the plaintiff class are held in custody, and whatever the sad necessities which prompt their detention, they

are held in penal condition. Where the State, as parens patriae, imposes such detention, it can meet the Constitution's requirement of due process and prohibition of cruel and unusual punishment *if, and only if, it furnishes adequate treatment to the detainee.* 349 F.Supp. at 585. (Emphasis supplied, footnotes omitted.)

After an historical analysis of the development of the right, the court concluded:

In sum, the law has developed to a point which justifies the assertion that: "A new concept of substantive due process is evolving in the therapeutic realm. This concept is founded upon a recognition of the concurrency between the state's exercise of sanctioning powers and its assumption of the duties of social responsibility. Its implication is that effective treatment must be the *quid pro quo* for society's right to exercise its *parens patriae* controls. Whether specifically recognized by statutory enactment or implicitly derived from the constitutional requirements of due process, the right to treatment exists." 349 F.Supp. at 600. (Footnotes omitted.)

In a most recent case, Morales v. Turman, 364 F.Supp. 166 (E.D.Tex. 1973), a federal district court specifically found that juveniles at Texas' six juvenile training schools have both a statutory and constitutional right to treatment.

We hold that on the record before us the district court did not err in deciding that the plaintiff juveniles have the right under the 14th Amendment due process clause to rehabilitative treatment.[10]

III—ADEQUACY OF TREATMENT

Experts testified at the trial, and the defendants admit, that the Quay System of behavior classification is not treatment. And case histories of maladjusted juveniles show that use of the System falls far short of its improved personality goals. Mrs. Betty Levine, resident instructor in sociology at the University of Indiana, testified that the School lacks the individual treatment given in the Indiana Girls School. The record shows very little individual treatment programmed, much less implemented, at the School; and it is unclear exactly how much time is spent in individual counselling. We conclude that the district court could properly infer that the Quay System as used in the School failed to provide adequate rehabilitative treatment.

We leave to the competent district court the decision: what is the minimal treatment required to provide constitutional due process,

---

[10] We note that the district court additionally determined that a right to treatment in this case has a statutory basis in view of the "custody, *care,* and discipline" language of the Indiana Juvenile Court Act, Burns Ind.Stat.Ann. § 9–3201, IC 1971, 31–5–7–1. (Emphasis supplied.)

We agree with this conclusion. Since we have today determined that the federal Constitution affords juveniles a right to treatment, any interpretation of the Indiana Act which would find no such right to exist would itself be unconstitutional.

having in mind that the juvenile process has elements of both the criminal and mental health processes.[11]

In our view the "right to treatment" includes the right to minimum acceptable standards of care and treatment for juveniles and the right to *individualized* care and treatment. Because children differ in their need for rehabilitation, individual need for treatment will differ. When a state assumes the place of a juvenile's parents, it assumes as well the parental duties, and its treatment of its juveniles should, so far as can be reasonably required, be what proper parental care would provide. Without a program of individual treatment the result may be that the juveniles will not be rehabilitated, but warehoused, and that at the termination of detention they will likely be incapable of taking their proper places in free society; their interests and those of the state and the school thereby being defeated.

We therefore affirm the judgment of the district court in each appeal, and remand only for the limited purpose of further proceedings in No. 73–1446 with respect to the right to rehabilitative treatment.

NOTES

1. In addressing itself to the criterion to be applied in evaluating a juvenile's confinement, the Court of Appeals in Creek v. Stone, 379 F.2d 106, 109 (D.C.Cir.1967) declared:

> * * * Juvenile Court legislation rests, in various aspects, on the premise that the state is undertaking in effect to provide for the child the kind of environment he should have been receiving at home, and that it is because of this that the appropriate officials * * * are permitted to take and retain custody of the child without affording him all the various procedural rights available to adults suspected of crime.

In the "construction and purpose" section of the Juvenile Court Act, Congress has provided that its provisions

> shall be liberally construed so that, with respect to each child coming under the court's jurisdiction:
>
> * * *
>
> (3) when the child is removed from his own facility, the court shall secure for him custody, care, and discipline as nearly as possible equivalent to that which should have been given him by his parents. 16 D.C.Code § 2316(3) (Supp. V, 1966).

The Congressional objective comprehends psychiatric care in appropriate cases. * * *

[11] The juvenile justice process can be understood to be a hybrid between the criminal system and the mental health process.

* * *

* * * Finally, the arguments for the right to treatment in both processes rely heavily upon the medical services, especially psychiatry and psychology. Note, A Right to Treatment for Juveniles, 1973 Wash.U.L.Q. 157, 160.

See also, N. Kittrie, Can the Right to Treatment Remedy the Ills of the Juvenile Process? 57 Geo.L.J. 848, 860–861 (1969); Note, The Courts, the Constitution and Juvenile Institutional Reform, 52 B.U.L.Rev. 33, 42–49 (1972).

See also Fulwood v. Stone, 394 F.2d 939, 944 (D.C.Cir.1967). Is this an adequate or appropriate standard for judicial evaluation of the adequacy of an institutionalized juvenile's "treatment"? If not, how might a better standard be phrased?

2. In Morales v. Turman, 562 F.2d 993 (5th Cir.1977) the Court of Appeals remanded for further taking of evidence a case in which the District Court had ordered extensive changes in the training schools operated by the Texas Youth Council. In doing so, it expressed serious reservations about the right to treatment rationale employed by the District Court and about the detailed requirements that court had imposed upon the administrative agency:

> Although the District Court has only ordered the parties to negotiate a plan for final relief, negotiations between the parties could not adequately incorporate these changes in the operation of TYC. To guide the negotiations the District Court has set forth extremely detailed minimum standards for the operation of TYC's facilities. Under these standards, for example, TYC must: (1) administer to all youths newly committed to their care Leiter and Weschler IQ tests standardized for blacks and Mexican Americans, Morales v. Turman, supra, 383 F.Supp. at 88; (2) have each student assessed by a language pathologist, id. at 90; (3) provide a coeducational living environment, id. at 100, and (4) provide a psychological staff with psychologists holding either masters or doctorates in psychology and experienced in work with adolescents, id. at 105. Many other similar requirements may be found in the District Court opinion. Because of this detail, TYC will lack the opportunity to show during negotiations that the changes they have initiated now satisfy constitutional standards even if all the specific requirements of the District Court opinion have not been met. Since the proper treatment of juveniles is a matter of dispute, the standards set forth by the District Court cannot be said to be the only constitutional method for rehabilitating juveniles. Therefore, the District Court must examine the new operations since only those aspects that continue to fail constitutional standards can be enjoined.

> For the reasons stated above, we find it necessary to remand this case for further evidentiary hearings. Since additional hearings may influence the relief granted we do not now decide the legal issues presented. We do, however, have reservations concerning the right to treatment theory relied on by the District Judge. In order to expedite a final disposition of this action, our difficulties with this theory are set out below.

> A right to treatment for juvenile offenders has not been firmly established. Only in recent years have courts discussed such a right. See, e.g., Rouse v. Cameron, 1966, 125 U.S.App.D.C. 366, 373 F.2d 451 (Bazelon, J.). This right has been defended on two grounds. First, supporters of the doctrine argue that a permissible governmental goal must justify any nontrivial abridgement of a person's liberty. For instance, exercise of the state's *parens patriae* power to provide care or supervision is assumed as the permissible goal for committing juveniles or the mentally incompetent. Treatment must therefore be provided to prevent the exercise of the *parens patriae* power from merely being a pretext for arbitrary governmental action. Second, the right to treatment is

viewed as a *quid pro quo* for reduced procedural protections. Whenever the state detains a person not in retribution for a specific offense, for an unlimited period of time or without the full procedural safeguards of a criminal trial, proponents of this right claim that due process requires that the person deprived of his liberty be in return entitled to treatment. To date most of the cases embracing this theory have involved the civil commitment of the mentally ill. See, e.g., Wyatt v. Aderholt, 5 Cir., 1974, 503 F.2d 1305; Donaldson v. O'Connor, 5 Cir., 1974, 493 F.2d 507, aff'd on other grounds, 422 U.S. 563, 95 S.Ct. 2486, 45 L.Ed.2d 396 (1975); Stachulak v. Coughlin, N.D.Ill., 1973, 364 F.Supp. 686.

These rationales for a right to treatment for the mentally ill raise serious problems. The civil commitment of the mentally ill without treatment is not necessarily an impermissible exercise of governmental power. The Constitution does not specify in what manner a state may exercise its *parens patriae* power. Historically, the states merely provided custodial care for the incompetent or mentally ill. See O'Connor v. Donaldson, 422 U.S. 563, 582–83, 95 S.Ct. 2486, 2497, 45 L.Ed.2d 396 (1975) (citing A. Deutsch, The Mentally Ill in America, 38–54, 114–131 [2d ed. 1949]) (Burger, C.J., concurring). The second basis for the right to treatment doctrine, i.e., compensation for reduced procedural protections, is also questionable. The interests of the individual and of society in the particular situation determine the standards for due process. See, e.g., Morrissey v. Brewer, 408 U.S. 471, 480–84, 92 S.Ct. 2593, 2599–601, 33 L.Ed.2d 484 (1972); McKeiver v. Pennsylvania, 403 U.S. 528, 543, 91 S.Ct. 1976, 1985, 29 L.Ed.2d 647 (1971). A state should not be required to provide the procedural safeguards of a criminal trial when imposing a quarantine to protect the public against a highly communicable disease. See Jacobson v. Massachusetts, 197 U.S. 11, 29–30, 25 S.Ct. 358, 362, 49 L.Ed. 643 (1905). Finally, treatment of the mentally ill is an extremely delicate task. Even experts in the field disagree as to the appropriate treatment and indeed if any treatment will be successful for a given patient. See Szasz, The Right to Health, 57 Geo.L.J. 734, 741 (1969). To attempt to specify the type of treatment that should be provided may well be beyond the competence of federal judges.

The case law has not universally accepted a right to treatment for the mentally ill. Further, in a recent case involving the right to treatment for the mentally ill, the Supreme Court held only that a nondangerous person could not be confined without treatment. O'Connor v. Donaldson, 422 U.S. 563, 95 S.Ct. 2486, 45 L.Ed.2d 396 (1975). The Court did not, however, decide whether a nondangerous person could be confined with treatment or if a dangerous person could be confined without treatment. Id. 422 U.S. at 572, 95 S.Ct. at 2492.

The argument for a right to treatment is even less strong as related to juvenile offenders. Many of the detained juveniles will have committed acts that clearly pose a danger to society. *Donaldson* left open the appropriateness of confining such individuals without treatment. Id. In addition, since many of the acts that result in a juvenile's detention would be crimes if committed by adults and since adult offenders do not have a right to treatment, a right to treatment for juveniles may be less appropriate than a similar right for the mentally ill. Of course, as a matter of social policy choosing a policy of rehabilitating juvenile offenders may be desirable.

While a right to treatment is doubtful, any constitutional abuses that may be found in the Texas juvenile program can be corrected without embracing such doctrine in this case. The eighth amendment prohibition of cruel and unusual punishment as the constitutional standard for the conditions of imprisonment can adequately remedy the conditions in TYC's institutions. For instance, the physical abuse of the students and degrading work assignments could be eliminated as cruel and unusual without adopting the questionable doctrine of a right to treatment. Admittedly the eighth amendment will not require the state to provide extensive vocational training, detailed personality assessments or coeducational facilities. The choice of providing these services properly remains with the State of Texas herein.

Finally, even if some form of right to treatment doctrine exists the minimum requirements established by the District Court are excessively detailed.[12] A court is not in a position to monitor day-by-day changes that affect rehabilitation programs. New treatments and testing techniques will inevitably develop. A rigid set of requirements for the state will not enable the TYC to adequately adjust to these changes. The passage of time will render obsolete many of the requirements found in the District Court opinion."

Id. at 997–99.

After rehearing was denied (565 F.2d 1215 [5th Cir.1977]) the parties proposed a settlement. The district court held the settlement needed more "working out." (569 F.Supp. 332 [D.Tex.1983]).

INMATES OF BOYS' TRAINING SCHOOL v. AFFLECK

United States District Court for the District of Rhode Island, 1972.
346 F.Supp. 1354.

PETTINE, CHIEF JUDGE. The indignities suffered by juveniles who did not respond well to their confinement to the Boys Training School and the attempts of Training School officials to cope with the disciplinary and running-away problems presented by such juveniles lead to the institution of this Civil Rights action. Confinement of these juveniles in the maximum security Adult Correctional Institution, in the resuscitated relic of a former women's prison, in dim and cold steel cellblocks, and in a wing of the adult medium security prison is argued to violate plaintiffs' constitutional rights to due process, and equal protection, and to constitute cruel and unusual punishment.

---

[12] Detailed standards have been used in some cases involving prison conditions. See e.g., Williams v. Edwards, 5 Cir., 1977, 547 F.2d 1206. But detailed standards may be more appropriate in the context of eighth amendment relief than in the context of a right to treatment. An order that guards stop beating prisoners or that inmates be adequately protected in their cell blocks will prevent cruel and unusual punishment of prisoners. But a court cannot be sure of achieving rehabilitation by requiring, for example, a state to give all juveniles the Weschler IQ test adjusted for minority youths.

Five named plaintiffs, for themselves and on behalf of a class, seek a preliminary injunction stopping confinement of juveniles in the Adult Correctional Institution Maximum Security building; in the solitary confinement cells of the Medium-Minimum Security building of the A.C.I.; and in Annex B, the old women's reformatory. They also seek to stop transfers of juveniles to the Youth Correctional Center (Annex C) of the Medium-Minimum Security Building and isolation of any juvenile in a room for more than two hours without a psychiatrist's certificate, and in any event, for more than 24 hours within a seven-day period. They also seek to define certain minimum requirements for conditions of confinement. While they do not seek to close Annex C immediately, they seek the return to the Training School of those juveniles transferred there without a judicial hearing.

Further prayers for relief raise, at the outside, important questions of the philosophy of treatment of juvenile offenders and, at base, vital questions of what rights juveniles retain in their confinement at state correctional centers. Arguing that these juveniles have a right to rehabilitative treatment, plaintiffs seek institution of vocational training, a drug rehabilitation program, and a psychiatric counseling program at the Boys' Training School. They also seek a full day of schooling for juveniles under age of sixteen, three hours of outdoors athletics, and the right of the juveniles to obtain food daily from the canteen unless a meal is served after six p.m. daily.

Jurisdiction exists on 28 U.S.C. § 1343. This has been certified as a class action.

The Court has viewed all of the involved places of confinement. A temporary restraining order was entered in January 1972, prohibiting the use of Annex B, the old Women's Reformatory, prohibiting the administrative transfer of further juveniles to the maximum security Adult Correctional Institution (A.C.I.), and conditioning the use of Annex C and its cellblock. Plaintiffs have moved for a preliminary injunction based primarily on evidence produced at hearing, stipulations, and affidavits. The motion for preliminary injunctive relief seeks support also from this Court's order of March 30, 1972 invoking its Rule 37, Fed.R.Civ.P., powers to sanction defendants for their consistent failure to comply with both the discovery rules and this Court's orders under the Federal Rules of Civil Procedure. See Hodgson v. Mahoney, 460 F.2d 326 (1st Cir.1972).

Defendants in this action are John Affleck, Director of the Rhode Island Department of Social and Rehabilitative Services; Anthony Orabone, Assistant Director of the Department in charge of the Division of Children and Youth Services; John Sharkey, Assistant Director of the Department in charge of the Division of Correctional Services; Francis Howard, Warden of the Adult Correctional Institution; Joseph Devine, Superintendent of the Boys Training School; the Board of Regents for Education for Rhode Island; Frederick Burke, the Commissioner of Education; William Robinson, the Director of the Division of Elementary and Secondary Education, Rhode Island Department of Education; and Edward Costa, the Title I Coordinator of the Division of Elementary and Secondary Education, Rhode Island Department of Education.

Preliminary Procedural Points

Defendants have sought dismissal of this action for failure to state a claim on which relief may be granted. Rule 12(b)(6), Fed.R. Civ.P. They have also asked that this Court abstain from decision.

This action raises questions of substantial constitutional import and will not be dismissed. As the Supreme Court recently held in Haines v. Kerner, 404 U.S. 519, 92 S.Ct. 594, 30 L.Ed.2d 652 (1972), summary placement of an inmate in solitary confinement states a cause of action under 42 U.S.C.A. § 1983. This law suit goes to the conditions of confinement of juveniles and, as such, is well within the jurisdiction of the federal courts. See Urbano v. McCorkle, 334 F.Supp. 161 (D.N.J.1971).

The intercession of a federal court into a state correctional system is a matter of much gravity and is not done here lightly. The Court, having entered a consent decree recently in a case concerning conditions at the Rhode Island Adult Correctional Institutions, was hopeful that the issues in this case could be similarly resolved, and accordingly, has encouraged the parties to negotiate their differences. Such efforts were unavailing; rather, as the record in this action demonstrates, this Court has had great difficulty in securing compliance from defendants with even customary discovery orders. In the circumstances of this case, the Court finds no equitable reason to withhold from ruling.

Nor does the Court find any justification in precedent to apply the abstention doctrine here. This case does not present issues of state law, the clarification of which would "obviate the need for a federal constitutional decision or would present the federal constitutional issue in significantly altered light." Wulp v. Corcoran, 454 F.2d 826 (1 Cir.1972). To defer this case to adjudication elsewhere would be to cause unnecessary delay and injury to these plaintiffs, and is not required by precedent. Cluchette v. Procunier, 328 F.Supp. 767 (N.D.Cal.1971). As this Court has previously indicated, it will not defer adjudication in respect to the unacceptable "hands-off" doctrine which denies that inmates have enforceable rights. Palmigiano v. Travisono, 317 F.Supp. 776 (D.R.I.1970).

Exhaustion of administrative remedies is not a prerequisite to a § 1983 suit attacking conditions of confinement. Rodriguez v. Mc-Ginnis, 456 F.2d 79 (2d Cir.1972); Edwards v. Schmidt, 321 F.Supp. 68 (W.D.Wis.1971). Even if it were, there do not appear to be any administrative remedies available here.

Finally, in terms of comity, I would note that for the most part this law suit does not attack actions taken by the state legislature or by the state judiciary. Primarily under attack are conditions resulting from decisions made in the administrative discretion of those defendants who are officials of the Boys Training School. It would be well to take heed of what Kenneth Culp Davis teaches:

" 'Where law ends tyranny begins.' I think that in our system of government, where law ends tyranny need not begin. Where law ends, discretion begins, and the exercise of discretion may mean either beneficence or tyranny, either justice or injustice, either reasonableness or arbitrariness."

Davis, Discretionary Justice, 3 (1969)

Of course, defendants have made these administrative decisions in light of the resources the legislature has made available to them.

Findings of Fact

The class of inmates at the Boys Training School may be divided into five sub-classes, depending on the reason for commitment: 1) those voluntarily committed by their parents. R.I.G.L. § 13-4-8; 2) those awaiting trial; 3) those convicted of delinquency, R.I.G.L. § 13-4-9, § 14-1-36; 4) those adjudicated wayward, R.I.G.L. § 14-1-36; and 5) those found to be dependent or neglected, R.I.G.L. § 14-1-34.

Most of the boys at the Training School are housed in cottages on the School grounds. For reasons concerned mostly with discipline and escape problems, some boys have been transferred from the cottages to functionally distinct and geographically separate institutions, known as Annex B, Annex C, Annex C cellblock, and the Maximum Security building of the Adult Correctional Institution (ACI). Some juveniles in Annex C and its cellblock were transferred there directly pursuant to court proceedings. As stipulated by the parties, juveniles otherwise are transferred to Annex B, Annex C and its cellblock, and Maximum Security without judicial hearing. It has been the past practice of defendants to effectuate these transfers without administrative hearing or prior notice. There are no specific rules or regulations which indicate what offenses will result in transfer of a juvenile to Maximum Security.

A registered nurse and a licensed practical nurse, located in the main building at the BTS, are on duty from 6:30 a.m. to 3 p.m. on weekdays, and on call for emergencies until 10 p.m. There is no psychiatrist or clinical psychologist on the BTS staff. A routine physical examination is given on entrance of a boy to the Training School. There is evidence, and I so find, of at least two probable suicide attempts by boys who received no medical or psychiatric care proximately following the attempts. The response of BTS supervisors to these suicide attempts was solitary confinement. There is other evidence indicating that the boys have not received adequate medical care; however, there is also contradicting evidence.

The decisions to transfer juveniles to the Maximum Security Building of the ACI is made by the Superintendent of the BTS, subject to the approval of the Assistant Director for Correctional Services R.I.G.L. § 13-4-12. Administrative transfers to Annex C are made on the decision of the Superintendent of the BTS alone. Boys detained at the BTS pending a court hearing have been administratively transferred both to the ACI and to Annex C. Boys confined to the BTS for truancy have been administratively transferred to Annex C.

Annex B

Annex B is a wing of the old women's reformatory built in 1863 and contains dingy cement rooms, approximately six feet by eight feet. Each room is furnished only with a bed, a sink, and a toilet. The toilet is flushed from outside the room by BTS personnel. The only opening in these cells is a barred window on the far wall, which opens onto a catwalk from which the inmate is observed.

Two of these cells are stripped isolation cells, containing nothing but a toilet, and a mattress on the floor. The cells have, at times, not had artificial lighting. In one of the cells, the window is boarded over, rendering it completely dark at times. These cells are known as "bug-out" rooms and are used for solitary confinement of boys.

The boys confined to Annex B are never allowed to go outside and exercise. Indeed they are almost never allowed out of their cells. They are allowed out of their cells only to take daily showers and to get meal trays. Meals are eaten in the rooms. Some boys, who have been in Annex B for a specified period of time, are allowed out of their cells to watch television for a short time. There are a few magazines and books available. A teacher provides one and a half hours daily of education to some boys. This education consists chiefly of working math problems.

No nurse or doctor is on duty at Annex B. Medical care for an inmate must first be requested by a staff member. Even when medical care was so requested in Annex B, it was usually not forthcoming.

Boys are confined to Annex B for periods ranging from a few days to two and a half months. No visitors, and this includes parents, are allowed.

The solitary confinement cells in Annex B are used to punish infractions by boys committed after they are confined to Annex B. Boys have been kept in these "bug-out" rooms a maximum of three to seven days. One inmate testified, and I accept his testimony as true, that he was confined to the solitary confinement cell for a week, wearing only his underwear. The room was dark and was cold. He was not given toilet paper, soap, sheets, blanket, or change of clothes. He was not allowed to leave the room. His testimony is corroborated by similar testimony from other boys who have been confined there. Boys do not receive a physical or psychiatric examination either prior to, during, or after confinement in the "bug-out" room.

There is no psychiatrist or clinical psychologist on the Training School staff or engaged in regular counseling at the school. Psychiatric help has been requested for inmates by staff members and not received. There is an obvious need for psychiatric aid as the following incident demonstrates.

A staff member testified, and I accept his testimony as true, that while on duty at Annex B he observed a boy attempting to hang himself. He managed to get the boy down. Requesting instructions and assistance from his superiors, the staff member was told to put the boy in the "bug-out" room. He did. Once in the room the boy started banging his head into the wall. The staff member removed the hysterical boy from the room. Assistance arrived in the form of two employees of the BTS, one a truck driver. They stayed and talked to the boy for a short period of time then instructed the staff member to put the boy back in the "bug-out" room. Disobeying these instructions, the staff member talked with the boy in his office for several hours until the boy was calmer. No trained psychiatric help was given.

During the past year, Annex B, including the two isolation rooms has enjoyed full occupancy. This Court ordered Annex B closed in January, 1972, by temporary restraining order. Defendants have agreed to continue the restraining order and have not since used Annex B.

Annex B was considered to be less severe confinement than Annex C by Training School officials.

Annex C

Annex C, which is a closed-off wing of the Medium-Minimum Security building of the Adult Correctional Institution, is a series of rooms on either side of a long corridor. One or two boys occupy a room, secured by a locked door. The windows are barred and many are broken, rendering the rooms cold. Some windows and the bars on the windows have been broken by boys in escape attempts. Annex C is far from escape proof.

Annex C contains 16 rooms, 15 are used for the boys and one room is used for staff. There is also a shower room and a recreation room. Access is had to an outdoors fenced-in yard. The basic furnishings of each room are a desk, a chair, beds, and a small table. There is a small window in the door of the cell. Clothing, bedding, and toilet articles are issued.

Meals are taken in the adult cafeteria where the boys have some contact with adult inmates, although this contact is generally limited by BTS personnel. Breakfast is at 7 a.m.; lunch, at 11 a.m.; and dinner at 3 p.m. After 3 p.m. candy is available at the canteen for some of the boys. For those without the canteen privileges there is nothing to eat for the 16 hour period between 3 p.m. and 7 a.m.

In spite of the presence of the exercise yard, it appears that the boys are rarely allowed outside for exercise. It is alleged that boys have not used the yard since Summer of 1971. There is no nurse and no doctor on duty in Annex C, nor do they make regular visits there. There is a locked medicine chest available, but the boys complain that their medicine is not given to them.

There is a "level" program at Annex C, that is, depending on his progress, a boy may be advanced to a different level with more privileges. One variant with the different levels is the amount of time a boy is allowed out of his cell. When not in their cells, the primary recreational activities in which the boys engage are watching television, roaming the hall, playing cards or doing calisthenics.

Boys under sixteen years of age are required to receive some educational training. A teacher comes for two hours a day. He teaches two groups, each of which receives an hour of education. Education primarily consists of doing mathematics problems. There are no math textbooks but there is a history book on which tests but not lessons are given. It is unclear whether boys over 17 years of age are allowed to participate in this education. There are inmates who have surpassed the level of education taught at Annex C so find it useless. Students have been, at times, excluded from this schooling by BTS officials.

There is no vocational training. A counsellor comes regularly, but, as testified, the plaintiffs may individually see him for only ten minutes weekly or less. The visitors allowed other than the counsellor are professionals such as attorneys. There are no activities such as arts or crafts, nor are there individualized programs. There is a ping-pong table some of the inmates are allowed to use. While defendants have submitted a schedule indicating there are "Human Relations" sessions, the overwhelming weight of the evidence to date is that there have not been any such sessions.

I accept as true the statement in plaintiffs' affidavits that boys are locked in their rooms for 24 hour periods for such offenses as inability to perform an exercise during calisthenics, "kidding around" with roommates, and making noise to get the guards to let them out to go to the bathroom. I also accept as true that guards sometimes ignore the boys' requests to go to the toilet or to open the window.

Transfers to Annex C are frequently grounded on escape attempts, and are accomplished without notice or hearing. There is evidence that the Assistant Director for Youth Services and the Superintendent of the BTS consider Annex C to be in need of change.

Annex C Cellblock

Located on the floor above Annex C is a series of small, dimly lit, steel-barred cells used for solitary confinement. Each cell is approximately eight feet by four feet, containing a metal slab bed and mattress, sink, and toilet. Boys confined there are released only to take showers, about twice a week. They get no exercise. The inmate's attorney, but not his family, is allowed to visit him there. Because windows on the wall opposite the cellblock are broken, the cells are cold. There is a small hole in the bars, through which meals, sometimes cold, are passed.

At times reading materials and toilet articles are given to the boys, at times they are withheld. Confinement to the cellblock is frequently for 15 day maximum periods. Clean sheets or underwear is not provided during the stay.

The offenses for which a boy is confined to the cellblock include running away, fighting, assault on guards, and homosexual behaviour.

There is no nurse or doctor on duty or who makes regular visits. A staff member testified, and I find as true, that on one occasion on coming on duty in the cellblock he discovered that a boy had slit his wrists, which were still bleeding and covered with bloody towels. Notifying other staff of this and requesting medical care for the boy, he was told they already knew of it. No doctor came to attend the boy during the next eight hours, nor was any other care forthcoming.

Maximum Security

Juveniles have been transferred from the Boys Training School to cells amidst the adult population of sections of the Maximum Security Building at the ACI. The juveniles are subject to the same rules, punishments, and opportunities as the adult inmates. While rehabilitative programs are generally available, the juveniles have not participated in them.

They have continual contact with adult inmates and learn from these inmates the tricks of the trade of crime. They have been the subject of homosexual overtures and threats from adult inmates.

The ACI contains adult male convicts who are convicted of felonies or misdemeanors and adults accused of committing felonies and misdemeanors.

Plaintiffs

I find it necessary to preserve the vitality of these findings of fact by more detailed findings about particular plaintiffs.

Bernard Humes was sent to a cell in Maximum Security from Annex C. He escaped from Annex C in October of 1971 and was put in the Annex C cellblock when he was caught. He was visited there by Mr. DeLorenzo, Mr. Gorman, and Mr. Pendergast who told him he would have to remain in the cellblock for fifteen days. He remained there thirty days, until November 18, 1971. His cell lacked hot water and was cold. He did not have enough blankets to keep warm. He was only let out to shower, which took five or ten minutes, two or three times a week. On November 18, 1971, two Training School officials visited him and told him to gather his things, he was going to maximum security. He received no prior notice of this transfer.

Humes had been transferred to the ACI Maximum Security once earlier in his Training School career. His response to whether he then learned anything from the adults was, "Well, nothing that can be used in society, I mean, how to steal something bigger, like, before I went there, maybe."

Humes had earlier been confined to Annex B for running away, an activity in which he frequently engaged, and had spent time in the

Annex B isolation room because "Somebody threw some soapy water in my eyes, and I bugged out because the supervisor wouldn't let me go and wash it out of my eyes."

Plaintiff James Young has been confined to the maximum security ACI. Prior to this, he had been locked in the cellblock of Annex C for 21 or 22 days for running away. He was given no prior notice or hearing, just told that he was confined for running away. He was only allowed out of the cell to take showers, two or three times a week. During most of his days in the cellblock there was no light in his cell, all of the bulbs being broken. The only visitor he was allowed was his attorney. Because of broken windows his cell was cold at night.

On November 18, 1971, without notice or judicial or administrative hearing, he was transferred to the maximum security section of the ACI. He is held in a cellblock with adult inmates. When asked whether he had learned anything at the ACI, he testified that he had learned how to do "better" B & E's (breaking and enterings) and to do armed robberies.

He testified that he had been in Annex B five to nine times, and had twice been put in Annex B's solitary cells, once for two or three days, and once for seven to ten days. The solitary cell was completely dark and was cold with winter air coming in through the knocked out window. He had no toilet paper, soap, sheets, blanket, or change of clothes. The only clothing he had was underwear. The covering on the mattress was worn through and he lay on the springs. He was never allowed out of the cell.

Plaintiff, General Jordan, age 17, was sent to Annex B after he ran away from the Boys Training School. For two and a half months he languished in a small cell. Eventually he was released from his cell to watch television. He was never given any exercise during this period, or allowed outside. He did not read because he had read all of the books there and he did not participate in the classes because he had advanced beyond the level of arithmetic being taught. He got to see his counsellor, on his own request, three times during this period.

On December 1, 1971, the day he expected to return to Family Court for a hearing, he was instead transferred to Annex C. He testified that his room was cold at night because the window was broken; that when he wasn't in his cell, he watched television; and that he was allowed out of his cell from 9:30 a.m. to 12 noon, and from 3:30 p.m. to 9:30 p.m.

Plaintiff Stephen Griffiths is let out of his room in Annex C for six hours a day and then usually watches television or plays cards. He testified that in September, 1971 he asked to go to church and was told that was not allowed. He also testified that he was denied access to medical facilities to treat swollen throat glands.

He was placed in solitary confinement in the cellblock above Annex C. The only times during his 15 day confinement he was released from his cell were to take showers, once or twice a week.

His request for reading materials and writing paper while in the cellblock was denied.

Conclusions of Law

This suit is concerned with the rights of boys confined to the Boys Training School. Not all of these boys have been convicted of violation of the criminal laws. Some are there because they are "wayward" children. R.I.G.L. § 14–1–3. Among such "wayward" boys, are boys who are found to be truants from schools, disobedient boys, and boys who have run away from home "without good or sufficient cause." Parents may voluntarily commit their sons to the Training School. R.I.G.L. § 13–4–8. Boys may be sent there because of "idleness." R.I.G.L. § 14–1–4. Other boys may end up at the Training School because they have been found to be "dependent" or "neglected" by their parents. R.I.G.L. § 14–1–34. It is possible for a boy to be committed to the BTS not for something he does, but for what he is, that is, "neglected." Furthermore, boys who have been accused of "delinquency" but who have not been tried before the Family Court of Rhode Island may be committed to the Training School. All of these boys, without distinction as to how they came to the Training School, have been subject to the Superintendent's discretion to transfer them to Annex B, and Annex C and its cellblock, and the Maximum Security Building of the ACI.

The purpose of removing a juvenile from his family enunciated by the Rhode Island legislature is "to secure for him custody, care and discipline as nearly as possible equivalent to that which should have been given by his parents." R.I.G.L. § 14–1–2. He is to be removed from his parents only when "his welfare or the safety and protection of the public cannot be safeguarded without such removal." R.I.G.L. § 14–1–2.

The purpose of confinement of juveniles under Rhode Island law is "instruction and reformation," not punishment. R.I.G.L. §§ 13–4–1, 13–4–13, 13–4–15. An adjudication upon a juvenile does not have the effect of a conviction nor is such a child deemed a criminal. R.I. G.L. § 14–1–40.

Juvenile adjudicative proceedings must be conducted in compliance with the standards of Due Process of law, because, as was held by the United States Supreme Court in In Re Gault, 387 U.S. 1, 27–28, 87 S.Ct. 1428, 1443–1444, 18 L.Ed.2d 527 (1967):

> "Ultimately, however, we confront the reality of that portion of the Juvenile Court process with which we deal in this case. A boy is charged with misconduct. The boy is committed to an institution where he may be restrained of liberty for years. It is of no constitutional consequence—and of limited practical meaning—that the institution to which he is committed is called an Industrial School. The fact of the matter is that, however euphemistic the title, a 'receiving home' or an 'industrial school' for juveniles is an institution of confinement in which the child is incarcerated for a greater or lesser time. His world becomes 'a

building with whitewashed walls, regimented routine and institutional hours * * *.' Instead of mother and father and sisters and brothers and friends and classmates, his world is peopled by guards, custodians, state employees, and 'delinquents' confined with him for anything from waywardness to rape and homicide.

"In view of this, it would be extraordinary if our Constitution did not require the procedural regularity and the exercise of care implied in the phrase 'due process.'"

As the Rhode Island Supreme Court has so aptly noted, "There is no age limitation contained in the constitutional guarantee of due process." In Re Holley, 268 A.2d 723 (R.I.1970). Due process does not guarantee to juveniles *all* rights in the adjudicative process which are constitutionally assured to an adult accused of a crime. It was the judgment of the Supreme Court in McKeiver v. Pennsylvania, 403 U.S. 528, 91 S.Ct. 1976, 29 L.Ed.2d 647 (1971) that due process does not require a jury trial in state juvenile delinquency hearings. The opinion of Justice Blackmun, in which three justices joined, found that imposition of the jury trial requirement would subvert the special nature of juvenile proceedings and that the states should be allowed to experiment toward accomplishment of the juvenile system's rehabilitative goals. 403 U.S. at 547, 91 S.Ct. 1976.

Thus, the constitutional validity of present procedural safeguards in juvenile adjudications, which do not embrace all of the rigorous safeguards of criminal court adjudications, appears to rest on the adherence of the juvenile justice system to rehabilitative rather than penal goals. See State ex rel. Londerholm v. Owens, 197 Kan. 212, 416 P.2d 259, 269 (1966). The Rhode Island legislature, in establishing its juvenile justice system, has specifically directed that it have rehabilitative, non-penal goals.

Rehabilitation, then, is the interest which the state has defined as being the purpose of confinement of juveniles. Due process in the adjudicative stages of the juvenile justice system has been defined differently from due process in the criminal justice system because the goal of the juvenile system, rehabilitation, differs from the goals of the criminal system, which include punishment, deterrence and retribution. Thus due process in the juvenile justice system requires that the post-adjudicative stage of institutionalization further this goal of rehabilitation. And whatever deviations, if any, from this goal of rehabilitation which might be tolerated as to those incarcerated juveniles convicted of violations of the criminal laws, such deviations are far less tolerable for the other classes of children incarcerated by the state. See Rozecki v. Gaughan, 459 F.2d 6 (1st Cir.1972).

As to at least one of the sub-classes of inmates at the BTS, those adjudicated juvenile delinquents, society also has an interest in being protected against their anti-social acts. As was said in Kent v. United States, 130 U.S.App.D.C. 343, 401 F.2d 408, 411–412 (1968):

"Parens patriae requires that the juvenile court to what is best for the child's care and rehabilitation so long as this disposition provides adequate protection for society. * * * But it is clear that society can be protected without departing from civilized standards for the prompt and adequate care of disturbed children."

It is in this context that plaintiffs' claims are considered. See also Note, The Courts, The Constitution and Juvenile Institutional Reform, 52 B.U.L.Rev. 33 (1972).

Annex B

Although defendants have voluntarily closed Annex B, the issue of confinement of juveniles at Annex B is not moot. In closing Annex B defendants did not concede any unconstitutionality or illegality in its operation. Because the situation may again be changed, the issue is not moot. Nolan v. Fitzpatrick, 451 F.2d 545, 551 (1st Cir.1971).

Conditions at Annex B were deplorable, as defendants themselves must have recognized in stopping its use. Lest defendants find themselves pressing Annex B into use again because of lack of adequate facilities elsewhere, this Court enjoins the use of Annex B and orders that it be closed.

The entire Annex, and most particularly its inhuman solitary confinement cells fit well the language used in Jones v. Wittenberg, 323 F.Supp. 93, 99 (N.D.Ohio 1971) aff'd 456 F.2d 854 (6th Cir.1972):

"We may suppose that the constitutional provision against cruel and unusual punishment was directed against such activities. In any event, when the total picture of confinement * * * is examined, what appears is confinement in cramped * * * quarters, lightless, airless, damp and filthy with * * * deprivation of most human contacts, except with others in the same subhuman state, no exercise or recreation, little if any medical attention, no attempt at rehabilitation, and for those who in despair or frustration lash out at their surroundings, confinement, stripped of clothing and every last vestige of humanity, in a sort of oubliette."

"The constitutional prohibition against cruel and unusual punishment 'is not fastened to the obsolete, but may acquire meaning as public opinion becomes enlightened by a humane justice.' Weems v. United States, 217 U.S. 349, 378, 30 S.Ct. 544, 553, 54 L.Ed. 793 (1910). If the constitutional provision against cruel and unusual punishment has any meaning, the evidence in this case shows that it has been violated. The cruelty is a refined sort, much more comparable to the Chinese water torture than to such crudities as breaking on the wheel."

Jones v. Wittenberg involved adult inmates; the instant case involves juveniles, who may not be treated like convicted criminals.

The fact that there is only some evidence of physical abuse of the boys does not immunize defendants from condemnation under the Eighth Amendment. The conditions in Annex B are insidiously destructive of the humanity of these boys. There were no or pitifully few "facilities or personnel for social services, exercise, recreation, reading, rehabilitation, or any other human resources to meet human needs." *Jones,* supra, at 97. To confine a boy without exercise, always indoors, almost always in a small cell, with little in the way of education or reading materials, and virtually no visitors from the outside world is to rot away the health of his body, mind, and spirit. To then subject a boy to confinement in a dark and stripped confinement cell with inadequate warmth and no human contact can only lead to his destruction.

The prohibition on cruel and unusual punishment is not a static concept " * * * but may acquire meaning as public opinion becomes enlightened by a humane justice." Weems v. United States, 217 U.S. 349, 378, 30 S.Ct. 544, 553, 54 L.Ed. 793 (1910). The fact that juveniles are *in theory* not punished, but merely confined for rehabilitative purposes, does not preclude operation of the Eighth Amendment. The reality of confinement in Annex B is that it is punishment. It is punishment imposed on obdurate boys by defendant administrators of the Training School. The legislature could not constitutionally, and has not, directly authorized confinement of juveniles to the "bug-out" rooms of Annex B. Defendants cannot do, in their administrative discretion, that which the legislature could not constitutionally authorize. See Kautter v. Reid, 183 F.Supp. 352 (D.D.C.1960); Comment, 84 Harv.L.Rev. 456, 459 (1970).

The Eighth Amendment draws its meaning from the evolving standards of decency that mark the progress of a maturing society. Trop v. Dulles, 356 U.S. 86, 101, 78 S.Ct. 590, 2 L.Ed.2d 630 (1958). It is binding on the states through the Fourteenth Amendment. Robinson v. California, 370 U.S. 660, 82 S.Ct. 1417, 8 L.Ed.2d 758 (1962). Affidavits submitted by plaintiffs' experts on the damaging effects of such solitary confinement are set out below:

Dr. Jerome Miller, Commissioner, Department of Youth Services for the Commonwealth of Massachusetts:

> "My experience in penology led me to conclude that isolation can never constitute rehabilitation. No doubt, when a person is out of control, terribly upset, and could conceivably be a danger to himself or to someone else, he may have to be separated from others for a short while in order to calm down. * * * If isolation is continued beyond a short time, the person isolated may begin to experience sensory deprivation, withdrawal, or perhaps psychotic or autistic behaviour."

Dr. George Lynn Hardman, Staff Psychiatrist, Roxbury Court Clinic, Boston; consultant to the Massachusetts Department of Youth Services:

> "It is my professional opinion that confining a child in isolation for punishment serves no treatment purpose whatsoever. On the contrary, because the child's problem or problems are in no way being dealt with during the period in which he is

confined in isolation, the child's behavior deteriorates rather than improves in the course of his isolation. The isolation of a child only inhibits that child's emotional development. * * *"

"It is my professional opinion that even a child who is acting out violently should not be isolated. * * * When a violent child is locked in a sparsely furnished room and left alone, he feels panic which may cause him to persist in his violent outbursts which may in turn cause staff to justify his continued isolation. * * *"

"It is my professional opinion that no human being, adult or child, should ever under any circumstances be confined in the barren, dark cell known as a 'bug-out' room which I observed in Annex B. Such cells are similar to those used to test experimentally the effects of sensory deprivation; well-adjusted adult volunteers have been found to hallucinate in such an environment within a matter of hours."

See also Lollis v. New York State Department of Social Services, 322 F.Supp. 473 (S.D.N.Y.1970). I hold that isolation of children under the circumstances as described in my findings of fact for the solitary confinement rooms of Annex B to be cruel and unusual punishment and enjoin any use of these confinement cells.

Further this Court holds that because the conditions of confinement in Annex B are anti-rehabilitative, use of Annex B is enjoined as a violation of equal protection and due process of law. If a boy were confined indoors by his parents, given no education or exercise and allowed no visitors, and his medical needs were ignored, it is likely that the state would intervene and remove the child for his own protection. See R.I.G.L. § 14–1–34. Certainly, then, the state acting in its *parens patriae* capacity cannot treat the boy in the same manner and justify having deprived him of his liberty. Children are not chattels.

Maximum Security—ACI

Plaintiffs attack confinement of juveniles at the ACI on two theories—that the administrative transfer procedures do not meet the requirements of due process and equal protection and that, regardless of the procedures used, confinement of juveniles with adults at a penal institution is constitutionally impermissible.

It appears that the original decision to transfer a boy to Maximum Security is made by defendant Devine and is subject to the approval of defendant Affleck. No rules have been promulgated defining the circumstances under which such a transfer would be deemed warranted, nor are there any other forms of institutionalized controls on defendants' discretion. The constitutionality of these transfer procedures was upheld by the Rhode Island Supreme Court in Long v. Langlois, 93 R.I. 23, 170 A.2d 618 (1961). *Long* appears to be decided on the theory that juveniles confined to the Training School have no claim to constitutional rights, 170 A.2d at 619, and so has been overruled by In re Gault, 387 U.S. 1, 87 S.Ct. 1428, 18 L.Ed. 2d 527 (1967).

In Shone v. State of Maine, 406 F.2d 844 (1st Cir.1969), the First Circuit Court of Appeals held that transfer of a juvenile from the Maine Boy's Training Center to the Men's Correctional Center, on an administrative finding of incorrigibility without benefit of those procedural safeguards that were afforded juveniles committed directly to the Men's Center, was a violation of due process and equal protection of the laws. The holding turned upon findings that the Correctional Center was functionally distinct from the Training Center and that the fact that controlled the juvenile's transfer was no part of the original adjudication as to whether he was a juvenile offender. *Shone* relied upon the reasoning of Baxstrom v. Herold, 383 U.S. 107, 86 S.Ct. 760, 15 L.Ed.2d 620 (1966) and of Specht v. Patterson, 386 U.S. 605, 87 S.Ct. 1209, 18 L.Ed.2d 326 (1967).

From the testimony of Bernard Humes and James Young it is evident that boys are transferred to Maximum Security for their behavior after they are committed to the Training School, behavior such as running away, and that the transfers are accomplished without notice or hearing.

The Boys' Training School and the ACI Maximum Security appear to be functionally distinct both in fact and in law.

The criminal courts of Rhode Island may commit a minor to the ACI upon conviction of a criminal offense. R.I.G.L. § 12–19–6.

Under *Shone*, it appears that the practices employed by defendants in transferring juveniles to the ACI pursuant to their authority under R.I.G.L. § 13–4–12 are violative of due process and equal protection.[13]

There is a substantial question whether a boy who has not been afforded the full protections of the criminal adjudicatory process may be confined to the ACI at all. Apparently this argument was not presented to the *Shone* court. As the court in State ex rel. Londerholm v. Owens, 197 Kan. 212, 416 P.2d 259, 269 (1966) so succinctly stated:

> "The validity of the whole juvenile system is dependent upon its adherence to its protective, rather than its penal, aspects. Dispensing with formal constitutional safeguards can be justified only so long as the proceedings are not, in any sense, criminal.
>
> "We hold confinement in a penal institution will convert the proceedings from juvenile to criminal and require the observance of constitutional safeguards. The non-criminal aspect is the legal backbone of the constitutionality of all American juvenile

---

[13] The plaintiff in *Shone* had been adjudicated a juvenile delinquent and had been transferred from the Training School to the Men's Correctional Center on a finding of "incorrigibility." The *Shone* court was not faced with the situation of a boy confined to a Training School for truancy, or some other non-criminal reason, who is then transferred to an adult institution for behaviour which is also not criminal. In such a situation I have considerable doubt whether a judicial hearing could cure the unconstitutionality of the transfer.

court legislation. If after a juvenile proceeding, the juvenile can be committed to a place of penal servitude, the entire claim of *parens patriae* becomes a hypocritical mockery."

For similar holdings, see also Baker v. Hamilton, 345 F.Supp. 345 (W.D.Ky.1972); United States ex rel. Stinnett v. Hegstrom, 178 F.Supp. 17 (D.Conn.1959); White v. Reid, 125 F.Supp. 647 (D.D.C. 1954); Boone v. Danforth, 463 S.W.2d 825 (Mo.1971); In re Rich, 125 Vt. 373, 216 A.2d 266 (1966); State ex rel. McGilton v. Adams, 143 W.Va. 325, 102 S.E.2d 145.

This Court is greatly disturbed by the testimony of two plaintiffs who have been confined to the ACI that they learned little there other than how to better commit crimes, that they were threatened with homosexual attacks, and that they had not participated in any rehabilitative programs. Such a situation surely cannot be in society's best interest. I note that a report by a committee appointed by the Governor of Rhode Island strongly recommended that the practice of incarcerating juveniles at the ACI be stopped.

The Court recognizes that some of these juveniles may be detrimental to the atmosphere of the Training School and are better confined elsewhere. Confinement with adult felons in a prison is not the only alternative open to defendants for dealing with these boys. I draw upon the wisdom of United States ex rel. Stinnett v. Hegstrom, 178 F.Supp. 17, 20:

> "The letter of the Attorney General quoted in the report points out the difficulty of controlling dangerous and hardened young criminals at the National Training School. The records in the cases of the petitioners now before this court indicate that they are serious disciplinary problems. It is probable that they need stricter custody and supervision than the general population of the Training School. This must be provided, however, outside the general penal population, or the purposes of the juvenile acts will be defeated and the cogent reasons which have led the courts to sanction custody of juveniles without full criminal proceedings will become hollow pretense."

Plaintiffs' motion for preliminary injunction is granted. Defendants are enjoined from transferring or confining any member of the plaintiff class in the Adult Correctional Institution.[a]

Annex C and Annex C Cellblock

It appears that Annex C is used primarily for two purposes; that is, to punish juveniles who have caused discipline problems and to detain juveniles who have run away in a somewhat more escape proof facility. According to defendants, the primary mission of Annex C is security from escape. Annex C cellblock serves the same purposes.

[a] The editors have "corrected" what appear to be simple transposing errors in the official report.

The class of inmates at the BTS consists of several subclasses according to the reasons for their confinement. There are boys there (1) who have been voluntarily committed by their parents; (2) who have been adjudicated dependent or neglected by their parents; (3) who have been convicted of delinquency; that is, who have committed an offense which, if committed by an adult, would be a felony, or otherwise more than once violated a law; (4) who have been adjudicated wayward, that is, deserted home without good cause, or habitually associated with dissolute, etc. persons, or leading an immoral or vicious life, or habitually disobedient, or truant, or violated a law; and (5) those awaiting trial. For all of these subclasses the legislature has decreed rehabilitative non-penal treatment.

The question is to what extent confinement in Annex C and in its cellblock can be justified as necessary to the ends of rehabilitation. The connection between this confinement and rehabilitation may be thought to exist through several links. First, as defendants have argued, they have to have the boys to treat them, that is, they cannot treat a boy who is run away. So they seek to justify this confinement as both actually necessary to stop yet another run away attempt and as a psychological deterrent to future attempts. They also argue their responsibility is to keep these boys out of the outside community until they have been reformed and are ready to return. Another link is the need to segregate boys, both to remove them as an obstacle to the rehabilitation of others, and to reform them. Presumably, segregated juveniles are themselves helped to reform by segregation by removing them from situations with which they cannot cope and by depriving them of "privileges" which they then presumably have incentive to earn back. There is also some evidence that on at least one occasion segregation has been necessary due to racial tensions. Defendants assert that Annex C and its cellblock are the only facilities they have in which they can segregate juveniles or keep them from running away.

Whatever the reasons, confinement in Annex C and its cellblock is punishment. The conditions of confinement are themselves detrimental to rehabilitation. It is conceivable perhaps, that this would not be so for security confinement in some other facility, but, as defendants assert, all they have is Annex C. Yet it is also clear that the conditions of confinement in Annex C and the cellblock are not the least restrictive means available to defendants for achieving their purposes of segregation and preventive detention, assuming arguendo these are permissible purposes.

Specifically, as to Annex C, I find no reason to deprive inmates of outdoors exercise. A well fenced exercise yard is available and is part of the institution. It should be used to provide a minimum of three hours of outdoors exercise daily, weather permitting. Defendants must provide daily outdoors exercise for all inmates of the BTS. I would note that this relief is in accord with testimony that the Assistant Director of the Department of Social and Rehabilitative Services wanted the inmates to have outdoors exercise.

As to education, there is a bitterly cruel irony in removing a boy from his parents because he is truant from school and then confining him to a small room, without exercise, where he gets no education because he already knows how to work the few math problems which constitute education at Annex C. Boys confined to Annex C are entitled to the same education received by inmates at the Training School proper. Whether equal educational opportunity is a fundamental right triggering strict judicial review, see Serrano v. Priest, 5 Cal.3d 584, 96 Cal.Rptr. 601, 487 P.2d 1241, 1255 (1971) or not, I find that denying education to inmates of Annex C which they would obtain in the BTS proper does not serve any permissible interest. Defendants are enjoined from confining any members of the plaintiff class at Annex C without providing them education which is the equivalent in duration, subject matters, materials, and otherwise, with that provided in the BTS proper (excluding Cottage B). Inmates confined to the B Cottages are also to be provided equivalent education. As to plaintiffs' prayer that all inmates at the BTS be provided with a full day of school which meets the Standards for Approval of Secondary Schools promulgated by the Rhode Island Department of Education, the motion for preliminary injunction is denied. The BTS may or may not offer adequate substitutes for a full day of schooling. The record is bare.

This Court sees no reason for feeding boys on a schedule which will insure their hunger. So long as defendants adhere to the present feeding schedule, and/or serve dinner to inmates before 6 p.m., they are enjoined from confining inmates in Annex C without allowing them daily canteen rights and the right to keep food in their rooms.

Even with these changes in conditions at Annex C, confinement there will be worse than confinement in the cottages. Plaintiffs accordingly ask that all boys who were transferred to Annex C without a judicial hearing be sent back to the cottages and further seek to enjoin defendants from transferring any juvenile to Annex C and confining any juvenile to the Annex C cellblock. These motions are denied. The Court finds itself in need of considerably more expert testimony before it attempts to rule on these questions. The Court invites both sides to present expert evidence at the hearing on the merits. Considerable harm might result to the community were this Court to summarily deny defendants' use of Annex C.

Although these motions for preliminary injunction are denied, the Court would like to make some seminal observations. As to the transfer procedures, the loss of liberty entailed by a boy in a transfer to Annex C or the cellblock may well require that such transfers be done in accordance with due process of law. Nolan v. Scafati, 430 F.2d 548 (1st Cir.1970); Cluchette v. Procunier, 328 F.Supp. 767 (N.D. Cal.1971).

It may also be that transfer to Annex C, if eventually found to be permissible at all, may well be limited to one or possibly two of the subclasses at the BTS, those adjudicated delinquent and those awaiting trial for delinquency. Assuming that no rehabilitative justification may be found for Annex C,[14] then Annex C may only be justified in terms of society's need to be protected. It would be foolish to ignore the reality that society may have been harmed by a delinquent's offenses and should be protected against them. The same may be true for a juvenile awaiting trial for delinquency. But I take it that the presumption of innocence attaches to juveniles awaiting trial. See In re Winship, 397 U.S. 358, 363, 90 S.Ct. 1068, 25 L.Ed.2d 368 (1970). It may be that the only permissible purpose for confining

[14] Affidavits from plaintiffs' two experts are vehement in their condemnation of use of Annex C and its cellblock. Dr. Jerome Miller stated:

"It is my firm belief that these two facilities, Annex C and the isolation cells above Annex C, should not be used under any imaginable circumstances to house juveniles. In light of the fact that there is not enough possibility for programs to be developed in either of these two cell blocks, and that the juveniles will remain in their rooms for most of each day, I believe that one who comes out of Annex C or Annex C lock-up will be less able to cope with the real world, than when he entered either of those two units. Most likely, the juvenile will unlearn whatever social skills he might have possessed or relearn others which involve survival in that kind of a circumstance i.e. survival of being alone, survival without sensory stimulation. In addition, children incarcerated in either of these two settings will fall behind educationally and vocationally. Most important, however, the juveniles will fall behind in their social inter-action skills. Everything that I saw in Annex C and in Annex C lock-up led me to believe that the programming in those two units will not help rehabilitate the youths incarcerated in them, but will most likely heighten their chances to return one day to a penal institution. I make this statement simply because incarcerating juveniles in that type of surrounding, can only have destructive results. The most likely resulting detrimental effect will be that the youth will further continue to develop his own self-image as 'the criminal.'

Specifically as to the upstairs lock-up in Annex C, I would never use them under any circumstances. The results of using such medieval facilities will be at best to produce little criminals or at worst to produce very sick youngsters."

Dr. Hardman's affidavit concurs:

"7. I have been told that boys confined in Annex C are locked in their rooms for as much as 20 hours a day, that they are never permitted outdoors for exercise, that the only indoor exercise they receive on a regular basis is calisthenics, that the only education available to them is one hour of math and history studies daily, that the only indoor recreation available to them is television, card games, or ping pong, and that they receive virtually no attention from any professionally trained personnel. Assuming that these facts are true, it is my professional opinion that confinement under these circumstances serves no treatment purpose whatsoever, severely inhibits any further emotional development of the boys, and predisposes these boys to regard themselves as prisoners, as 'cons.' When a boy leaves an institution with an image of himself as a 'con,' chances are great that he will become an adult 'con.'

8. Boys confined in Annex C under the circumstances enumerated in paragraph 7 above will in my professional opinion become progressively more emotionally stunted. Boys in their teens are at a developmental stage when they are in great flux. They are at a period in their life when their behavior can be changed with proper attention to their emotional needs. I am familiar with the principles of behavioral conditioning and with the principle of differential reinforcement, but I know of no sound psychiatric principle or theory which condones a system which deprives boys in need of help of those things which are indisputably beneficial to them such as fresh air, large muscle exercise, and a full day of academic or vocational training. If behavior is to be shaped by a system of increasing privileges, it is my professional opinion that proper psychiatric treatment dictates that only those pleasurable things which are not necessary to a boy's growth such as television, cigarettes, movies, card games and ping pong be treated as privileges to be earned.

9. It is my professional opinion that confinement of boys in the cellblock which I observed on the second floor above Annex C can serve no treatment purpose whatsoever and in addition will have a detrimental impact upon any boy confined there. It is my professional opinion that there is no justification for ever placing a child in this cellblock."

these awaiting trial juveniles is "to make certain that those detained are present when their cases are finally called for trial." Hamilton v. Love, 328 F.Supp. 1182, 1191 (E.D.Ark.1971). See also Constitutional Limitations on the Conditions of Pretrial Detention, 79 Yale L.J. 941, 955 (1970).

As to the other subclasses of inmates, society needs very little or no protection against them. "Wayward" children have not violated any criminal laws, except perhaps misdemeanor offenses, see R.I.G.L. § 14–1–3. I doubt whether the legislature could pass laws to imprison a boy for truancy; yet for exactly this reason boys have been confined to the BTS and eventually to Annex C. As the Supreme Court has said, "[D]ue process requires that the nature and duration of commitment bear some reasonable relationship to the purpose for which the individual is committed." McNeil v. Director, Patuxent Institution, 407 U.S. 245, 92 S.Ct. 2083, 32 L.Ed.2d 719 (1972). The same must be said for boys voluntarily committed by their parents.

Children who are committed to the BTS because they are dependent or have been neglected by their parents are confined on what must be a pure *parens patriae* theory. They are at the BTS because of their parents' actions, not their own. To cause them to suffer deprivations under law because of their status is constitutionally forbidden. Robinson v. California, 370 U.S. 660, 82 S.Ct. 1417, 8 L.Ed.2d 758 (1962); see also Weber v. Aetna Casualty & Surety Co., 406 U.S. 164, 92 S.Ct. 1400, 31 L.Ed.2d 768 (1972).

If boys from any subclass at the BTS commit offenses under the criminal laws while at the BTS, they may be charged with delinquency and given a judicial hearing.

These are merely preliminary observations, as is the following:

> "But traditional legal standards of precisely equal justice are not always compatible with the social welfare precept of aid according to need. Offender rehabilitation is purportedly the primary aim of the juvenile system; to accomplish this goal, each youth must be treated according to his particular needs. A purely legal solution—based on equal justice under law—would nullify the rehabilitative nature of the juvenile process by either imposing social sanctions upon one who does not require them, or withholding treatment from one who needs it. Thus, one must be wary, lest, *Kent, Gault,* and their progeny, which seek to impose upon the juvenile process the legal standards of criminal justice, be misdirected to deprive the juvenile system of its opportunity to devise social controls which do not merely 'fit the crime,' but which are responsive to individual needs."

Kittrie, Can the Right to Treatment Remedy the Ills of the Juvenile Process, 57 Geo.L.J. 848, 860 (1969).

The Court repeats that it invites both sides to present testimony from experts in this field.

Solitary Confinement

Plaintiffs ask for an injunction restraining the isolation of a juvenile in a room for more than two hours unless a psychiatrist certifies in writing to the Court and counsel for the plaintiffs that the juvenile, if released, would be either a danger to himself or a danger to the others in the institution, but in no case may a juvenile be isolated in a room for more than 24 hours within a seven day period.

Plaintiffs have introduced some expert testimony by affidavit, arguing that isolation is contrary to rehabilitation. They argue that the effects of isolation on a juvenile are far worse than on an adult. To quote from an expert affidavit submitted in Lollis v. New York State Department of Social Services, supra:

> "Isolation as a 'treatment' is punitive, destructive, defeats the purposes of any kind of rehabilitation efforts and harkens back to medieval times. There is no justification for such treatment unless one wants to dehumanize a young person in trouble and wants to create more trouble with such a person in the future."

Plaintiffs have demonstrated probability of success in showing that plaintiff juveniles have a claim to rehabilitative treatment. See Wyatt v. Stickney, 325 F.Supp. 781 (M.D.Ala.1971). This Court is convinced that solitary confinement may be psychologically damaging, anti-rehabilitative, and, at times inhumane.

However, the Court does not feel that there is sufficient expert testimony on the record of what constitutes solitary confinement as opposed to segregation and at what point it becomes destructive. In the absence of such evidence the Court finds it impossible to frame an equitable order and so denies the motion for preliminary injunction. From the record, however, it appears that solitary confinement is used as a solution to problems caused by juveniles at the BTS. The Court would urge defendants to find individualized methods of treatment for problem boys before final hearing on this matter.

Minimal Conditions of Confinement

Plaintiffs seek an injunction prohibiting confinement of juveniles in any facility without providing them the following:

a) A room equipped with lighting sufficient for an inmate to read by until 10:00 p.m.;

b) sufficient clothing to meet seasonal needs;

c) bedding, including blankets, sheets, pillows, pillow cases and mattresses; such bedding must be changed once a week;

d) personal hygiene supplies, including soap, toothpaste, towels, toilet paper, and a toothbrush;

e) a change of undergarments and socks every day;

f) minimum writing materials; pen, pencil, paper and envelopes;

g) prescription eyeglasses, if needed;

h) equal access to all books, periodicals and other reading materials located in the Training School;

i) daily showers;

j) daily access to medical facilities, including the provision of a 24-hour nursing service;

k) general correspondence privileges.

Although these minimal requirements may be provided in the cottages at the Training School, the record indicates that these have not been made available at all times in all facilities of the BTS. These are substantially the same as the regulations for minimal conditions of confinement of adult inmates at the ACI, which were promulgated by the State following this Court's order in Morris v. Travisono, 310 F.Supp. 857 (D.R.I.1970), final consent decree entered April 20, 1972.

The state has offered no reason to justify this discrimination against juveniles. The Court is hard pressed to think of any reason to justify this discrimination which would serve the purpose of rehabilitation. While defendants' carrot-and-stick program at the BTS which uses loss of privileges and gain of privileges to spur socially acceptable behaviour from the juveniles might be thought to justify this, there are floors on the power of defendant administrators to deprive inmates of "privileges." It is clear that the state does not consider these minimal conditions of confinement to be "privileges" for adults, nor does this Court consider them to be "privileges" for juveniles. Society has bargained with these juveniles and it should be an honest bargain. They have been confined through a process offering them fewer protections than adults have; they may not now be treated worse than the adult inmates are. Defendants are ordered to provide these minimum conditions of confinement.

Plan for Further Rehabilitative Treatment

Plaintiffs move that defendants be required to submit a plan to this Court within thirty days:

"(A) Whereby appropriate and adequate treatment will be provided to the inmates of the Youth Correctional Center and said plan shall include provision for removing all juveniles from the Minimum-Medium Security Building of the Adult Correctional Institution to an appropriate alternative facility. Implementation of this plan is to occur within 90 days of the Court's ruling on this motion;

"(B) Whereby appropriate and adequate vocational training will be made available to all inmates at the Training School;

"(C) Whereby an appropriate and adequate drug rehabilitation program will be made available to all inmates of the Training School;

"(D) Whereby an appropriate and adequate individual psychiatric counseling program will be made available to those inmates which from a medical standpoint shall benefit from such treatment as determined by a proper psychiatric examination of each inmate of the Training School."

The various aspects of the proposed plan will be discussed separately.

Closing Annex C (Part A)

Part (A) of plaintiffs' motion is denied as premature. As indicated, the Court feels itself in need of further expert testimony on the issue of Annex C.

Drug Rehabilitation Programs (Part C)

While there is some deposition evidence of drug problems at the BTS, the record is virtually barren of the extent of the problem and of defendants' efforts to meet the problem. Plaintiffs have not demonstrated irreparable injury and so this request for injunctive relief is denied. Cf. Addicts Rights Org. v. Hendrick, No. 2941, Pa. C.P., (Nov. 12, 1971).

Vocational Training Program (Part B)

There are no vocational training programs at any of the facilities of the BTS. By affidavit of Dr. John Finger, plaintiffs argue that vocational training is necessary to rehabilitate these boys. Defendants have submitted affidavits heatedly denying this and defending their present program.

This Court is not inclined to interfere with the running of the Training School on such a scanty record and in the absence of a clear showing of deprivation of a constitutional right. It may be that members of the plaintiff class have a claim to positive rehabilitative treatment in the form of vocational training, but there is insufficient showing that vocational training is a necessary part of a rehabilitation plan. The Court would welcome testimony from experts for both sides on this issue at hearing on permanent relief.

Psychiatric Counseling Program (Part D)

There is no regular psychiatric or psychological counseling program at the Training School, nor is there a psychiatrist or clinical psychologist on the BTS staff. A type of group therapy program has been instituted in the cottages of the BTS proper, but not in Annex C.

Defendants have argued to this Court that the measure of the BTS is not to be judged by its physical plant but by the number of adequately trained personnel available to the boys. On such a theory the lack of regular psychiatric care for the inmates is even less defensible. The Court does not wish to suggest that "delinquency" is a disease or medical condition. See Szasz, The Right to Health, 57 Geo.L.J. 734 (1969). Such a suggestion would open a Pandora's box. See Note, Conditioning and Other Technologies Used to "Treat?" "Rehabilitate?" "Demolish?" Prisoners and Mental Patients, 45 So. Cal.L.Rev. 616 (1972). But it is manifest that denial of psychiatric care to some of the inmates is to ignore their needs and may hasten a process of deterioration. Plaintiffs' motion is granted and defendants are ordered to submit an appropriate plan within thirty days.

Conclusion

In closing, the Court emphasizes that this judgment does not reflect on defendants' choice of theory of rehabilitative techniques being employed in cottages at the Training School proper. The Court realizes that defendants have been handicapped by lack of adequate facilities and trained personnel to deal with the plaintiff class, and that the remedy for this situation will involve the expenditure of state funds. See United States v. Alsbrook, D.C., 336 F.Supp. 973, 980 n. 15. The issue is not the good faith or bad faith of defendants, but rather the issue is of the protection of the constitutional rights of these boys. As the First Circuit Court of Appeals has said:

> "Nor can it be any excuse for continuous, as distinguished from temporary accidental, inhumane treatment * * * that the representatives of the state were doing the best they could."

Rozecki v. Gaughan, 459 F.2d 6 (1st Cir.1972).

Plaintiffs will prepare an order reflecting the rulings of this opinion.

NOTE

In In re Doe, 120 R.I. 885, 390 A.2d 390 (1978), a family court judge found the state director of mental health in contempt of court for failing to place a juvenile in a designated psychiatric facility at an approximate cost of $65,000 a year even though monies at the director's disposal for that purpose had been exhausted. In reversing the contempt decree, the Rhode Island Supreme Court considered Inmates etc. v. Affleck, concluding:

> Nevertheless, the rehabilitative goal does not mandate that antisocial behavior be treated without regard to expense or the availability of appropriated funds in a context, where as here, according to prior psychiatric evaluations, the prognosis is guarded and the outcome is doubtful.

Id. at 894, 390 A.2d at 395.

C. TRANSFERS

CRUZ v. COLLAZO

United States District Court, District of Puerto Rico, 1978.
450 F.Supp. 235.

OPINION AND ORDER

TOLEDO, DISTRICT JUDGE.

The complaint in this case was filed on June 1, 1977, and the jurisdiction of this Court was invoked under Title 28, United States Code, Sections 1343(3), 1651, 2201 and 2202. It is alleged that plaintiff Pedro A. Vega Cruz is a juvenile presently within the custody of the Secretary of the Department of Social Services of the

Commonwealth of Puerto Rico and residing at the Guaynabo State Home for Boys.   *   *   *

On November 10, 1977, defendants informed the Court that plaintiff had been transferred to the Industrial School for Boys in Mayaguez. Thereafter, on November 11, plaintiff filed a motion for a Temporary Restraining Order alleging therein that the Mayaguez Industrial School was a maximum security juvenile institution which housed hardened delinquents and that he had been transferred thereto without a hearing all of this in deprivation of his constitutional rights to due process and equal protection. On November 14, 1977, we issued a Temporary Restraining Order ordering defendants to return plaintiff to the Guaynabo Juvenile Institution. On November 30, 1977, we issued an order, ordering the parties to submit memoranda on the issue of whether the requirements established by the United States Supreme Court in *In re Gault,* 387 U.S. 1, 87 S.Ct. 1428, 18 L.Ed.2d 527 (1967), apply to plaintiff's transfer from one juvenile institution to another juvenile institution of maximum security, without a hearing. In that order it was further provided that the Temporary Restraining Order issued in the case was extended, in the nature of a preliminary injunction, until the final disposition of said matter. Said memoranda having been duly filed, the matter now stands submitted for our consideration.

ANALYSIS

It is plaintiff's contention that the transfer of a juvenile from a nonsecure juvenile facility to which he has been committed, to a maximum security institution for hardened juvenile delinquents pursuant to an administrative determination, without a judicial hearing, is violative of the due process and equal protection provisions contained in the Federal Constitution.

Defendants' contention is to the effect that the transfer here in question is not violative of plaintiff's due process and equal protection rights. Defendants are in effect stating that plaintiff herein has no liberty interest at stake. This is so, they contend, because the law "* * * is very clear in that minors who are placed under the custody of the Secretary of Social Services are not committed to a particular institution by the Juvenile Court but to the custody of the Secretary to be placed in an institution adequate for the minor's rehabilitation, the institution to be determined by the Secretary." (Defendants' Memorandum of Law filed December 8, 1977). They emphasize that plaintiff was transferred from a juvenile institution administered by the Secretary to another juvenile institution administered by the Secretary and that there was no change in his classification or designation as a delinquent. The discretion of the Secretary, under 34 L.P.R.A. Section 2010(4) is strongly relied upon by defendants and the argument is made to the effect that in plaintiff's case the Secretary could have originally committed plaintiff to the Mayaguez Industrial School without any ensuing due process claim. It is also claimed that plaintiff was accorded a full due process treatment according to the mandates of In Re Gault, 387 U.S. 1, 87 S.Ct. 1428, 18 L.Ed.2d 527 (1967) at the adjudicative stage when he was adjudged a juvenile delinquent by the Puerto Rico Juvenile Court.

We find that the precise issue here in question, the transfer from one juvenile institution to another, albeit a maximum security one, is of first impression. The cases cited by the parties in support of their respective contentions involve either the transfer of juveniles to adult penal institutions [15] or of mentally ill patients from minimum to maximum security confinements or for indeterminate periods.[16] Both lines of cases present the risk of losing perspective of the proper analysis to be made in view of the constitutional right involved. Thus, in the present case a proper definition of the right invoked is essential to trigger the correct analysis.

We begin by stating that once the issue has been clearly defined as above, In Re Gault has no direct application herein. In that case the Supreme Court held that juvenile *adjudicative* proceedings must be conducted in compliance with due process standards. By its own terms, the decision does not cover the post adjudicative stage in juvenile proceedings.

In this type of case we must first determine whether a life, liberty, or property interest within the meaning of the Due Process Clause is at stake. * * *

In Meachum v. Fano, 427 U.S. 215, 96 S.Ct. 2532, 49 L.Ed.2d 451 (1976) the United States Supreme Court held that an individual's grievous loss as a result of state action is not by itself enough to trigger the application of the Due Process Clause:

> "We reject * * * the notion that any grievous loss visited upon a person by the State is sufficient to invoke the procedural protections of the Due Process Clause. In Board of Regents v. Roth, 408 U.S. 564, 92 S.Ct. 2701, 33 L.Ed.2d 548 (1972), a university professor was deprived of his job, a loss which was surely a matter of great substance, but because the professor had no property interest in his position, due process procedures were not required in connection with his dismissal. We there held that the determining factor is the nature of the interest involved rather than its weight." (Emphasis supplied.)

The liberty analysis to be made was further described by the United States Court of Appeals for the Sixth Circuit in Walker v. Hughes, supra, at p. 1251:

> "However, under *Meachum,* the emphasis is on whether there is entitlement to be 'free from bodily restraint,' Morrissey v. Brewer, supra, 408 U.S. at 484, 92 S.Ct. 2593, or 'to enjoy those privileges recognized as essential to the orderly pursuit of happiness.' Board of Regents v. Roth, supra, 408 U.S. at 572, 92 S.Ct. at 2706; Meyer v. Nebraska, 262 U.S. 390, 399, 43 S.Ct. 625,

---

[15] E.g. Inmates of Boys Training School v. Affleck, 346 F.Supp. 1354 (1972); Shone v. State of Maine, 406 F.2d 844 (1 C.A., 1969).

[16] E.g. Eubanks v. Clarke, 434 F.Supp. 1022 (1977); Baxstrom v. Herold, 383 U.S. 107, 86 S.Ct. 760, 15 L.Ed.2d 620.

67 L.Ed. 1042 (1923). In effect, *Meachum* equated the threshold test for the finding of a liberty interest with that for determining whether a property interest exists. Board of Regents v. Roth, supra, 408 U.S. at 577, 92 S.Ct. at 2709, laid down this criterion in examining the nature of an alleged property interest:

"To have a property interest in a benefit, a person clearly must have more than an abstract need or desire for it. He must have more than a unilateral expectation of it. He must * * * have a legitimate claim of entitlement to it." (Emphasis supplied.)

* * *

"For at least two reasons the requirement of an entitlement for the existence of a due process liberty interest, instead of a finding of grievous loss, is the prescribed approach. First, a standard of grievous loss would measure the weight of the individual interest rather than determining its nature, contrary to the intention of *Roth*, supra, 408 U.S. at 570–71, 92 S.Ct. 2701, and Morrissey, supra, 408 U.S. at 481, 92 S.Ct. 2593. Second, the requirement of an entitlement provides an appropriate basis for compromise between the need for the protection of individual interests and the need for government action unhampered by procedural burdens. A standard of grievous loss would interfere more directly with government responsibilities. The Supreme Court in Meachum v. Fano, supra, 427 U.S. at 225, 96 S.Ct. at 2538, recognized that fact in the context of prison management.

"[T]o hold as we are urged to do that any substantial deprivation imposed by prison authorities triggers the procedural protections of the Due Process Clause would subject to judicial review a wide spectrum of discretionary actions that traditionally have been the business of prison administrators rather than of the federal courts."

Thus for the Due Process Clause to apply in the present case plaintiff must show some kind of liberty entitlement not to be transferred to a maximum security juvenile institution. It should be borne in mind that such transfer entails no change of plaintiff's classification as a juvenile delinquent and that the transfer is one within the system of *juveniles* institutions in Puerto Rico.

In Meachum v. Fano, supra, the Supreme Court specifically rejected the theory that "any change in the conditions of confinement having a substantial adverse impact on the prisoner involved is sufficient to invoke the protections of the Due Process Clause * * *" Id. 427 U.S. at 224, 96 S.Ct. at 2538. In In Re Gault, supra, the Supreme Court specified the requirements of the Due Process Clause to be accorded in the adjudicative stage of juveniles. Here it is not contested that at said stage, plaintiff was accorded a fully constitutional adjudication. Given a valid adjudication of juvenile delinquency, plaintiff has been constitutionally deprived of his liberty to the extent that the State may confine him and to subject him to its juvenile institution system so long as the conditions of confinement do not otherwise violate the Constitution.

In *Meachum,* the Court implied that the Constitution by its own force does not require that a person be confined in any particular prison:

"* * * Confinement in any of the State's institutions is within the normal limits or range of custody which the conviction has authorized the State to impose. That life in one prison is much more disagreeable than in another does not in itself signify that a Fourteenth Amendment liberty interest is implicated when a prisoner is transferred to the institution with the more severe rules." [Id. 96 S.Ct. at 2538].

We must, therefore, inquire whether under the law of Puerto Rico a liberty interest has been created so as to accord plaintiff a cause of action. In his supplemental brief filed on November 22, 1977, plaintiff states as follows:

"* * * From an analysis of the Statute, it can be concluded that while the Statute governing judicial proceedings concerning juveniles in the Commonwealth of Puerto Rico does not expressly establish the right to a judicial hearing prior to a transfer from one institution to another, it does not deny that right either * * *"

Much as we would like to rule otherwise, under Meachum v. Fano, the statute's omission in creating a liberty expectancy to remain in one given juvenile institution compels us to decide that there is no such liberty interest at stake. There is no creation by omission.

Under the statute here at hand[17] the minors placed by the Juvenile Courts under the custody of the Puerto Rico Secretary of Social Services are not committed to a particular institution by the Juvenile Court but to the custody of the Secretary to be placed, within his discretion, in an institution adequate for the minor's rehabilitation.

In Meachum v. Fano, supra, the Supreme Court held that the discretion granted to Massachusetts prison officials precluded finding under Massachusetts law a created liberty interest to being not transferred to another prison. Such is precisely the case here. In *Meachum* the Court said:

[17] This section reads:

"If the judge shall find that the condition or behavior of the child brings him under the provisions of Section 2002 of this title, he may enter an order:

* * *

4. Placing the child under the custody of the Secretary of Health for commitment to an institution suitable for the treatment of children, or for his place-ment in a foster home; or he may provide the manner of the treatment, without the need of committing the minor; provided, that the Secretary of Health may not terminate the period of custody or remove the minor from the jurisdiction of the court, without the previous express authorization of the latter; * * *"

"* * * Massachusetts prison officials have the discretion to transfer prisoners for any number of reasons. Their discretion is not limited to instances of serious misconduct. As we understand it no legal interest or right of these respondents under Massachusetts law would have been violated by their transfer whether or not their misconduct had been proved in accordance with procedures that might be required by the Due Process Clause in other circumstances. Whatever expectation the prisoner may have in remaining in a particular prison so long as he behaves himself, it is too ephemeral and insubstantial to trigger procedural due process protections as long as prison officials have discretion to transfer him for whatever reason or for no reason at all." 427 U.S. at 228, 96 S.Ct. at 2540.

See also: Montayne v. Haymes, 427 U.S. 236, 96 S.Ct. 2543, 49 L.Ed.2d 466 (1976), wherein it was held that New York law did *not* create a liberty interest precluding transfer to another prison.

Although we do not think that the matters raised by plaintiff herein are "ephemeral" or "insubstantial" we are compelled to follow the doctrine laid in *Meachum* and thus DENY plaintiff's request for a preliminary and permanent injunction. The constitutional law of the day has seen fit to regard that plaintiff's claim is not encompassed within the liberty concept of the Due Process Clause of the Fourteenth Amendment.

Wherefore, in view of all of the above, plaintiff's request for a preliminary and permanent injunction is hereby denied.

It is so ordered.

NOTES

1. STANDARDS FOR THE ADMINISTRATION OF JUVENILE JUSTICE, REPORT OF THE NATIONAL ADVISORY COMMITTEE FOR JUVENILE JUSTICE AND DELINQUENCY PREVENTION. (U. S. Department of Justice, 1980).

4.71 Transfers from Less Secure to More Secure Facilities

Each state should classify the public and private facilities providing residential care for juveniles subject to the jurisdiction of family court over delinquency or noncriminal misbehavior according to the level of security maintained. A list of the facilities in each category should be published each year.

Before a juvenile placed in a residential facility may be transferred to a cottage, wing, or structure within that facility which meets the definition of a high security unit set forth in Standards 4.219–4.2194, or which has security features equivalent to those found in any more secure category of facility, or to another facility in a more secure category, a hearing should be held. At that hearing the juvenile should be entitled to all rights specified for disciplinary hearings in Standard 4.54(a)–(g).

A juvenile should only be transferred to a more secure facility or unit if:

a. The juvenile poses a danger to him/herself or others;

b.   The juvenile's actions demonstrate that he/she cannot be controlled in the facility or unit or placement due to its lack of security; or

c.   The service benefits to the particular juvenile of the more secure facility or unit substantially outweigh any detrimental effect of the greater constraints on liberty.

A copy of a decision approving transfer to a more secure facility or unit should be provided to the placing family court for review, to the juvenile, the juvenile's representative, and to the juvenile's parent or guardian.

Transfers from nonresidential programs to residential programs and from foster care to other residential programs should only be authorized after a judicial hearing pursuant to Standards 3.1810 or 3.1811.

4.72   Transfers from More Secure to Less Secure Facilities

Transfer from more secure to less secure facilities may be made without a hearing. Written notice of the transfer and of the reasons therefore should be provided to the juvenile, the juvenile's parent or guardian, and to the placing family court.

2.   Suppose a juvenile court enters an adjudication of delinquency and commits the juvenile to the Division of Youth Services, who assigns the juvenile to a halfway house. Can the juvenile court then order the Division to transfer the juvenile to a state training school? See In the Interest of J.N., 279 So.2d 50 (Fla.App.1973), holding that the juvenile court had exceeded its authority in ordering the transfer.

IN RE RICH

Supreme Court of Vermont, 1966.
125 Vt. 373, 216 A.2d 266.

BARNEY, JUSTICE. Since March 5, 1965, this petitioner, now eighteen years old, has been confined in the House of Correction by executive order, without sentence or conviction for a crime. He seeks release through habeas corpus, not only from that and associated temporary confinement at Waterbury State Hospital, but from all restraint stemming from juvenile proceedings ordering him to Weeks School in June, 1962, when he was fourteen. He has both a guardian ad litem and an attorney representing his interests before this Court.

By stipulation, the issues raised here are

*   *   *

2.   Was the transfer from the Weeks School to the House of Correction, under Executive Order of 5 March 1965, valid?

*   *   *

The matter began with a petition to the juvenile court for Franklin county by the state's attorney alleging that the petitioner had contributed to the delinquency of a fourteen year old school friend by encouraging and causing the friend to commit petty larceny by stealing a sum of money from that friend's own parents. A hearing was held June 11, 1962, attended by the boy, his mother who was his custodian, (the parents are divorced), the state's attorney, and various court personnel. At that time the judge had in hand the report of the investigation by a representative of the Department of

Social Welfare, as authorized by 33 V.S.A. § 613. The summons for the hearing gave notice to all upon whom it was served that such a report had been filed with the court on May 29, 1962. This report recited the boy's personal history with respect to his family situation and environment, school relationships, and previous behavior. Commitment to Weeks School for the remainder of his minority followed.

His later transfer to the House of Correction at Windsor on March 5, 1965, derived from his behavior at Weeks School, and was done under the authority of 28 V.S.A. § 415, which provides:

> A person confined in such school in execution of a sentence who does not obey the regulations of such school and is not of good deportment, may be transferred from such school to the house of correction, upon the written order of the governor, for the remainder of his original term, or until such time as the governor may by written order return him to such school, as provided in section 416 of this title.

The contents of the executive order disclose that he ran away from Weeks School twice, stealing a car on each occasion, once reaching Canada and once going to New York State. As a consequence, the order declares that he is no longer a fit subject for further care in an open juvenile training school, and that his presence is detrimental to the welfare of Weeks School and its charges. Since he was committed to Weeks School for the duration of his minority, his commitment to the House of Correction was for the same term, unless he was sooner lawfully discharged.

* * *

The validity of the whole juvenile system is dependent upon its adherence to its protective, rather than its penal aspects. In re Gomez, supra, 113 Vt. 224, 225, 32 A.2d 138. The dispensing with formal constitutional safeguards can be justified only so long as the proceedings are not, in any sense, criminal. The statutory purposes must not be belied by its procedures.

The House of Correction is defined by 28 V.S.A. § 103 as follows:

> There is hereby established at the state prison at Windsor a department thereof to be known as the house of correction for men, for the punishment, employment and reformation of men who are convicted of misdemeanors.

Confinement in a penal institution will convert the proceedings from juvenile to criminal and require the observance of constitutional criminal safeguards. White v. Reid, D.C., 125 F.Supp. 647, 649–651, also 126 F.Supp. 867, 871. Judge Armon W. Ketcham, Associate Judge of the Washington, D. C. Juvenile Court, has said that the noncriminal aspect "is the legal backbone of the constitutionality of all American juvenile court legislation. If, after such a juvenile proceeding, the juvenile can, by the discretionary act of an executive officer, be transferred to a place of penal servitude, the entire claim of 'parens patriae' becomes a hypocritical mockery." The Judge, quoted in Coleman "The Constitutional Rights of a Juvenile Delinquent" 50 Women Lawyers Journal 84 (1964), goes on to point out that such action confines a person in a penal institution without having been found guilty of a crime.

It is therefore essential to the constitutional validity of our juvenile court procedures that the power to connect it to a punitive proceeding in the criminal sense be removed. The rehabilitative caretaking offered in exchange for constitutional protections must be substantive and real, not mere verbiage. Otherwise the exchange is, in the words of Professor Paulsen, counterfeit. Paulsen "Fairness to the Juvenile Offender" supra, 41 Minn.L.R. 547, 576 (1957).

To this end we hold that any transfer from Weeks School to a penal institution must be founded upon a criminal prosecution and conviction attended by the constitutional guarantees appropriate to such a proceeding. Transfers under the authority of 28 V.S.A. § 415 can constitutionally be made only under such circumstances. This did not occur in this case and must be corrected by a return of the petitioner to Weeks School.

We recognize that, although recalcitrant Weeks School inmates usually are not transferred to the House of Correction without engaging in behavior chargeable as criminal, nevertheless this ruling will impose administrative and disciplinary problems on the institutions involved. It is fundamental, however, that solutions to these problems must meet constitutional standards.

Petition dismissed. The petitioner is discharged from his present confinement and remanded to the custody of the Superintendent of the Weeks School, who is commanded to receive him on the authority of the mittimus issued by the juvenile court for the county of Franklin dated June 11, 1962.

NOTES

1. Both the IJA–ABA and the National Advisory Committee Standards expressly disapprove of transfers from youth agencies to adult correctional agencies. See IJA–ABA Juvenile Justice Standards, Corrections Administration § 2.2(B) (1980) and Note 2 infra for the Advisory Committee Standard.

2. STANDARDS FOR THE ADMINISTRATION OF JUVENILE JUSTICE, REPORT OF THE NATIONAL ADVISORY COMMITTEE FOR JUVENILE JUSTICE AND DELINQUENCY PREVENTION. (U.S. Department of Justice, 1980).

4.73 Transfers Among Agencies

Transfers from a juvenile facility in which a juvenile has been placed by the family court to a facility under the jurisdiction of a separate agency for the care of the mentally ill or for the care of narcotic addicts or drug abusers, should only be permitted following a hearing before a family court judge.

Transfers of juveniles from youth agencies to adult correctional agencies should be prohibited.

Commentary

This standard recommends that a hearing before a family court judge be held before any transfer is made from a juvenile facility to a facility operated by an agency for the care of the mentally ill or mentally retarded or of drug addicts or abusers. It also recommends that committed juveniles never be transferred to adult jails.

The IJA/ABA, Correction Administration, supra at Standards 2.2 and 2.3; and National Advisory Committee on Criminal Justice Standards and Goals, The Report of the Task Force on Juvenile Justice and Delinquency Prevention, Standard 19.6(1) (1976) also prohibit the transfer of juveniles to adult jails and require that a due process hearing be held before a family court judge before a juvenile is transferred to a mental institution. Both are silent regarding transfers to institutions housing drug abusers and narcotic addicts. The American Correctional Association, Commission on Accreditation for Corrections, Manual of Standards for Juvenile Detention Facilities and Services, Standards 8005, 8006, and 8400–8403 (1978) is in accord with all provisions in this standard.

The prohibition against transferring juveniles to adult facilities is based on the differing philosophies underlying the juvenile and adult systems. As the court in White v. Reid, 125 F.Supp. 647 (D.D.C.1954) pointed out, "* * * the basic function and purpose of a penal institution is punishment as a deterrent to crime and that unless the institution to which a juvenile is committed is intended for and adapted to guidance, care, education and training rather than punishment, and unless its supervision is that of a guardian and not that of a prison guard or jailer, commitment to such institution is by reason of conviction of crime and cannot withstand an assault for violation of fundamental Constitution safeguards." Id. at 650. Baker v. Hamilton, 345 F.Supp. 345 (W.D.Ky.1972).

In a class action brought on behalf of all juveniles placed in an adult jail in Louisville, Kentucky, the court found that such placement violated the Fourteenth Amendment as well as state statutes in that it treated juveniles as adults for punitive purposes, yet did not accord them the same procedural due process accorded adults. *Baker.* Additionally, the court found that confinement to the adult jail violated the Eighth Amendment's prohibition against cruel and unusual punishment in that no attempt at rehabilitation was being made and that terrible living conditions prevailed at the jail. Id. at 353.

United States ex rel. Murray v. Owens, 341 F.Supp. 722, rev'd on other grounds, 465 F.2d 289 (2d Cir.1972), cert. den., 409 U.S. 1117 (1973) does not absolutely prohibit the confinement of juveniles in adult prisons, but holds that a New York statute which permits a 15-year-old to be committed to an adult facility while denying him a jury trial was unconstitutional. The court stated that, "* * * it is fundamentally unfair to try the offender as a child, but then to imprison him as an adult." Id. at 724.

This standard would forbid any transfers of juveniles to adult facilities. As the IJA/ABA, Corrections Administration, supra points out, "* * * the underlying rationale for a separate juvenile justice process applies equally to the administration of juvenile corrections. The juvenile justice process serves to protect juveniles from full exposure to the criminal justice system." IJA/ABA, Corrections Administration, supra at Standard 2.2 and Commentary. The attempt to eliminate bad influences emanating from "hardened" adult criminals is clear: the absolute prohibition of the transfer of juveniles to adult facilities to prevent such exposure. See IJA/ABA, Corrections

Administration, supra at Standard 2.2 and Commentary. Further, considerable administrative "initiative and leadership" will be needed to ensure the implementation of programs designed to habilitate juveniles. If this responsibility is shared by the same agency which controls adult facilities, policy could become obscured by the dual function. IJA/ABA, Corrections Administration, supra at Standard 2.2 and Commentary.

This standard also prohibits the administrative transfer of a committed juvenile to a facility which cares for mentally-ill or retarded persons or to one which cares for drug addicts or abusers. It has been held that a transfer of an adult from a prison to a mental health institution involves more than a simple administrative decision. U.S. ex rel. Schuster v. Herold, 410 F.2d 1071 (2d Cir.), cert. den., 396 U.S. 847 (1969) found that such transfers involve rights of an important nature. Not only does the transfer "effectively eliminate the possibility of [plaintiff's] parole, but it significantly increases the restraints on him, exposes him to extraordinary hardships, and causes him to suffer indignities, frustrations and dangers, both physical and psychological, which he is not required to endure in a typical prison setting." Id. at 1078. In addition, there is the "terrifying possibility" that a transferred prisoner may not be mentally ill or retarded at all or that he may remain in the mental facility for a period longer than his original sentence. Id. at 1078-9.

Finding that there was substantial disparity between the procedural protections afforded to those who were facing involuntary civil commitment to a mental institution from the outside and the mere administrative decision to have a prisoner transferred to a mental institution, the court held that the prisoner was deprived of equal protection of the law.

The court relied heavily on Baxtrom v. Herold, 383 U.S. 107 (1966) which held that, "Where the state has provided for a judicial proceeding to determine the dangerous propensities of all others civilly committed to [a mental facility] it may not deny this right to a person [who has been criminally convicted] solely on the ground that he was nearing the expiration of a prison term." Id. at 114. The court in *Schuster* cited other authority, including a New York State Court decision which extended *Baxtrom* to a youth transferred from a correctional school to an institution for defective delinquents. *Schuster*, 410 F.2d at 1082, citing People ex rel. Goldfinger v. Johnton, 43 Misc.2d 949, 280 N.Y.S.2d 304 (Sup.Ct.1967). The court held that a full hearing with all the safeguards afforded to civilians was required for incarcerated persons.

In Matthews v. Hardy, 137 U.S.App.D.C. 39 (1969) the court found that a transfer to a mental hospital from a prison must be accomplished by the same procedure as a civil commitment for four reasons: (1) there is a stigma attached to the mentally ill which is different from that attached to the criminal class in general; (2) there are more restrictions on one's freedom and routines in a mental hospital than in a prison; (3) the length of time spent in the mental hospital could be longer than the original sentence; and (4) a person mistakenly placed in a mental hospital might suffer irreparable "severe emotional and psychic harm." Id. at 42, 43.

Two state supreme courts have recently held that a juvenile faced with commitment to a mental institution is entitled to the protection of due process safeguards. In In re Michael E., 123 Cal.Rptr. 103, 538 P.2d 231 (1975), the California Supreme Court held, on both constitutional and statutory grounds, that the commitment of a ward of the juvenile court to a mental institution can only occur in accordance with the civil commitment statute of

California. The North Carolina Court of Appeals has similarly held that juveniles are entitled to the same due process protections as adults in any proceeding where a loss of liberty is a possible result. In re Myers, 25 N.C. App. 555, 214 S.E.2d 268 (1975).

The standard recommends that the states require a hearing before a family court judge prior to transferring a juvenile to a mental health or retardation facility. In Parham v. J.R., 442 U.S. 584 (1979) the Supreme Court ruled that some kind of inquiry should be made by a neutral fact finder to determine whether the statutory requirements for admission of a ward of an agency to the hospital are satisfied * * * [and] that the child's continuing need for commitment be reviewed periodically by a similarly independent procedure. Id. at 597. The Court felt that in balancing the interests of children, parents, and the state, an evaluation by a staff physician to determine the child's need for hospitalization provided sufficient due process safeguards when an agency sought to commit one of its wards to a mental facility. However, the Court stated that states were free to require a formal procedure if it saw fit to do so.

Relying on the lower court decisions cited infra, the National Advisory Committee believes that the risk of erroneous commitments of state wards is too great to allow a commitment without a prior adversarial hearing before the family court judge. *Parham*, 442 U.S. at 608 (Justice Brennan concurring and dissenting). As the Supreme Court acknowledged, there is a risk that children without natural parents will be lost in the shuffle or that commitments may be extended because of state agency difficulties in locating alternative placements. Id. at 600. These standards contemplate the use of the least restrictive alternative necessary to provide appropriate treatment. See Standard 4.410 and Commentary. Without an independent evaluation of the restrictiveness in relation to the necessary treatment, agencies will often use facilities which provide more control than is necessary since they are usually more readily available. Further, adverse social effects can result from mental health commitments. The use of hearings before the family court judge combined with reviews of the process, See Standard 3.189, will avoid these problems.

The standard also requires a hearing before a transfer of a juvenile from a juvenile facility to one which cares for drug abusers and narcotic addicts. As in mental institutionalization, more restraints, more danger, more rigid programming, indignities, and so forth, may occur in a drug treatment center as opposed to a juvenile facility. See *Schuster*, 410 F.2d at 1078. The psyche of a youth could be severely damaged if incorrectly placed in a drug center with persons of all ages who are addicted, undergoing withdrawal, or knowledgeable about hard drugs.

The procedures at the hearing should comply with Standard 3.171. Adequate notice must be given in advance to afford the juvenile opportunity to prepare a defense. See also Bunday v. Cannon, 328 F.Supp. 165 (D.Md. 1971), modified, 453 F.Supp. 856 (D.Md.1978) (adult prisoner denied due process). The presence of the person is required, unless the right has been knowingly and intelligently waived. See also Lynch v. Baxley, 386 F.Supp. 378 (M.D.Ala.1974). Counsel is required to enable the person to effectively utilize any of the due process protections. Id. at 389. A juvenile should also be able to confront and cross-examine witnesses and offer evidence on his/her own behalf. Rennie v. Klein, 462 F.Supp. 1131, 1147 (D.N.J.1978). "Because the stigmatization and loss of liberty attendant upon forced confinement are of the most profound consequence to the individual affected

* * *," due process requires that a judge be persuaded by "clear, unequivocal, and convincing evidence * * *" that the transfer is necessary. *Lynch,* 386 F.Supp. at 393; Addington v. Texas, 441 U.S. 418 (1979). These protections go far beyond the minimum due process procedures set forth by the Supreme Court in *Parham,* supra. The Court required no more than an inquiry to be conducted by a psychiatrist which probes the child's background and includes interviews with relevant persons in the life. *Parham,* 442 U.S. at 597. Nevertheless, the Court indicated that the states were free to adopt the more stringent procedures. It is the committee's belief that additional safeguards are warranted to protect the child.

The National Advisory Committee recommends the adoption of this standard as an action each state can take immediately, without a major reallocation of funds, to improve the administration of juvenile justice.

Chapter 10

PAROLE

THE PRESIDENT'S COMMISSION ON LAW ENFORCEMENT
AND ADMINISTRATION OF JUSTICE, TASK FORCE
REPORT: CORRECTIONS 149–54 (1967)

4. JUVENILE AFTERCARE

Juvenile aftercare is defined as the release of a child from an institution at the time when he can best benefit from release and from life in the community under the supervision of a counselor. Use of the term "aftercare" rather than "parole," though not yet fully accepted even within the field of juvenile correction, has been encouraged by persons interested in social service in order to separate juvenile programs from the legalistic language and concepts of adult parole. The concept of aftercare has wider acceptance than the term, but the survey of aftercare programs in the United States today reveals wide variations in structure and program content.

* * *

A. THE RATIONALE OF AFTERCARE

When the behavior of a juvenile becomes sufficiently antisocial to warrant confining him in an institution, a complex array of correctional services is set in motion. Part of it deals with the planning and operation of a program that will help him when he leaves the institution.

In the United States, children and youth from 8 to 21 years of age are committed to juvenile training schools. On any one day, the total population of these schools is about 42,000. Because of the wide range of age and experience, differing placement plans are essential. Pre-adolescent children need programs different in content and philosophy from those needed by young adults, who may have been in the labor force before confinement. To meet such varied needs, aftercare programs must be flexible and creative, rather than routine and superficial as they are in parts of this country today.

The rationale for aftercare is simple. Each juvenile must have a carefully planned, expertly executed, and highly individualized program if he is to return to life outside the institution and play a constructive role there. Successful reentry into society is often made difficult both by the effects of institutional life on a juvenile and by the attitudes of the community to which he returns. The aftercare plan for him must take both these factors into account.

Institutionalization does different things to different children. Some become more antisocial and more sophisticated in delinquency than they were when they entered the training school. Others

959

become dependent on the institution and must learn how to break the ties gradually.

Community settings also differ widely. Some juveniles go back to the very conditions in which their previous delinquency was rooted. Most must face the possibility of the stigma attached to confinement in a correctional institution.

Aftercare is traditionally described as the last point on the juvenile correctional continuum. Yet, because it is in some respects the last opportunity to achieve the correctional objective, planning for aftercare must be an integral part of institutional programs. Indeed, it should begin immediately after commitment to an institution.

A good aftercare plan uses many resources inside and outside the institution. Since implementation of the plan takes place within the community, the aftercare counselor should use a variety of community resources to make the juvenile's reentry meaningful and productive. He should be working with all details of the case related to the ward's community even during the period of confinement in the State institution, forestry camp, or other setting attached to the training school.

It has taken this Nation a long time to recognize the importance of aftercare services for young people leaving correctional institutions, forestry camps, or halfway houses. Few well-developed aftercare programs were in existence 15 years ago. Some States have not yet initiated organizationally sound programs. On the other hand, a few have developed programs which stand out as models for those emerging elsewhere.

II. SURVEY FINDINGS

A. An Overview of Aftercare Today

The major items in this survey include data from the 40 State-operated special aftercare programs, but not from programs administered by city and county correctional systems, private institutions, and noncorrectional services of child and public welfare departments, since full information could not be obtained from them.

The 40 States reported a total of about 48,000 youth under aftercare supervision. Estimates for the other States, based on a projection of that figure, indicate that about 59,000 are under aftercare supervision in the United States. The number of juveniles in State programs ranges from 110 to 13,000.

* * *

State operating costs range from $7,000 to over $4 million a year. Together the States are spending about $18 million a year. Average per capita cost is $320 a year.

This expenditure is small in comparison with the cost of State-operated juvenile institutions, which spend over $144 million a year to care for an average daily population of slightly over 42,000 at an average per capita cost of about $3,400 a year.

* * *

E. JUVENILE PAROLING AUTHORITIES

According to the standard, the authority to approve placement should be vested in the parent State agency. The decision on the readiness of the youngster for placement should be based on the considered opinion of the appropriate training school staff committee.

According to the data gathered in the survey, the authority to release juveniles from State training schools rests with a wide variety of persons, groups, or agencies.

* * *

In most cases, these authorities are composed of members appointed by the Governor. Only seven States in the Nation have aftercare boards on which the members serve full time. Over half the States that have aftercare boards do not pay the members—State officials or lay citizens—for this service. In eight States aftercare board chairmen are paid, and in seven the board members receive salaries ranging from $6,000 to $18,000 a year, most frequently at the lower figure. Most board members are unpaid, are not trained for the board's special responsibilities, and are politically appointed.

Use of a central board, a relatively new event in juvenile correction, has been debated extensively. Those favoring it say the board can make sounder decisions than any other kind of releasing authority. Those questioning its usefulness say that board members are, in effect, assuming staff functions and cannot possibly know the details of the cases well enough from reading reports or hearing short presentations to make proper decisions. They believe further that competent staff in the training school or other facilities within the parent agency is better equipped than any outside group to make realistic decisions based on a thorough awareness of the details of a case.

The trend in the mid-1950's was toward the establishment of juvenile aftercare boards. This trend has ended. A large group of juvenile correctional administrators is now urging establishment of a pattern in which the training school (or other facility such as a forestry camp or halfway house) would make release recommendations to the parent agency, which in turn would authorize release.

F. LENGTH OF AFTERCARE PERIOD

The survey found that approximately 59,000 young people—about 47,000 boys and 12,000 girls—received aftercare services during the most recently reported annual period, 1964–65. The boy-girl ratio, slightly less than 4 to 1, is the same as other findings in most other statistical reports on delinquency comparisons by sex.

The average length of stay under aftercare supervision varies. Of the States reporting, 12 keep their juveniles in active aftercare supervision programs for an average of less than 1 year; 25 give aftercare supervision for an average of 1 year or more.

The State reports show a trend toward keeping girls under aftercare supervision longer than boys. The explanation may lie in our society's attitude that the young female requires protection for a longer period than the young male. Girls are kept longer in institutional settings than boys are, and staff working with the delinquent girl feel she needs more intense and prolonged services than the delinquent boy does. Of 14 States reporting on length of aftercare supervision, 10 show an average substantially longer for girls than for boys; 4 report an average period longer for boys.

G. PERSONNEL

* * *

The standard for minimum educational requirements states that the juvenile aftercare worker should have a bachelor's degree with a major in the social or behavioral sciences, plus 1 year of graduate study in social work or a related field, or 1 year of paid full-time casework experience in correction.

Of the 40 States, 34 report that they have such a requirement. The survey found, however, that not all juvenile aftercare directors actually enforce this requirement when they hire aftercare workers. The fact of the matter is that many aftercare workers have less than a college education. The minimum standard is approved in principle but not observed in practice.

J. DIVERSIFIED AFTERCARE SERVICES

The standards call for the previous (sic—provision?) of diversified aftercare services and facilities for children returning to the community from the institution or other correctional facility.

The survey found that services to released juveniles range from superficial supervision, consisting of nothing more than the juvenile's written monthly reports, to highly sophisticated aftercare innovations that meet the standards of good practice.

The survey asked the question: "Does the aftercare program also operate foster homes, group homes, and half-way houses?" Of the 40 States with statewide programs, 12 answered yes, including 2 that reported they did not pay for foster care but did use free home placements and 3 that qualified their positive reply by stating that local child welfare departments found and supervised foster homes for aftercare placements. Individual foster homes are used more frequently than group foster homes. Four State-operated programs reported the use of halfway houses for aftercare.

Three types of imaginative or unusual rehabilitation programs were reported more frequently than others. They are best described as efforts at the use of groups in treatment, family centered services, and youth employment programs specifically designed for the released ward. Some of these programs were described as experimental and new. They occur only where the State-operated program is well established and has an adequate budget.

H. Caseload and Work Assignments

The standard calls for the juvenile aftercare counselor to have a maximum workload of 50 active supervision cases, with one pre-release investigation being considered as equal to three cases under active supervision. (Although no standard has been formulated on the matter, good practice calls for assignment of every child in a training school, or in some other facility of the parent agency, to an aftercare counselor, who should work with the parents and others in the interest of planning for the child's release.)

TABLE 5

Aftercare Caseloads in States Having Special Aftercare Staff

Size of caseload [1]	Number of States	Number of children under supervision	Category's percentage of total number under supervision
Under 30 cases	3	536	1.12
30–40 cases	10	8,612	17.98
41–50 cases	5	4,339	9.06
51–60 cases	5	2,244	4.68
61–70 cases	6	23,382	48.81
71–90 cases	9	4,875	10.18
Over 91 cases	2	3,914	8.17
Total	40	47,902	100.00

[1] Number of children under aftercare supervision. Does not include children in institutions.

Table 5 presents the variation in caseload size, the number of children under supervision, and each caseload category's percentage of the total number of children under supervision throughout the 40 States where special aftercare staff are employed. Average caseloads range from 30 to 125 supervision cases, with the median in the 61–70 range. Since these caseloads are not weighted for the number of investigations made or for the number of children worked with by the aftercare counselors in the institutions, the actual caseload size is substantially larger than is indicated in the supervision caseload.

* * *

I. Staff Development

According to the standard, a staff development program should be provided, with staff assigned specifically to the training function.

The findings in this survey reveal a great lack of inservice training programs. Aside from the 11 States that have no statewide aftercare services at all, 8 of the 40 that do have such services have no inservice training program.

* * *

ELLIOTT, PAROLE READINESS: AN INSTITUTIONAL DILEMMA, FEDERAL PROBATION, MARCH, 1964, at 26, 27, 29–30

One of the most far-reaching decisions made by the staff of a training school is when it decides that a boy is ready to leave the training school and return to the community. * * * All too frequently, the paramount question of whether a boy has worked through his more socially crippling conflicts is obscured by other considerations. Limitations of the training school program, uneven quality of personnel, inadequate budgets, and need to make room for new arrivals can reduce the problem of determining the length of stay to a compromise solution which is based only in part upon the boy's emotional and social readiness to assume his responsibilities in the open society.

Mistakes in the assessment of a boy's readiness for parole is compounded when the boy's conformity to the training school program over a stipulated length of time is utilized as the "rule of thumb" for determining his eligibility for release. A past study [1] of 88 training schools found that the majority employed rather loose and inconsistent methods of determining parole readiness. The term, "satisfactory institutional adjustment" or another similar designation was the most frequent reason given for individual release. Releasing a boy prematurely from the training school may result in a boy's continuing his delinquent behavior with greater sophistication. The training school is then vulnerable to public criticism even though the boy may receive adequate postinstitutional supervision and the services of community social agencies.

On the other hand, a boy may be released much later than the time that he has demonstrated an optimal readiness for parole. To allow a boy to maintain a long period of static adjustment in the training school can inhibit psychological movement toward release as well as make the later adjustment in the community more difficult.

The Fallacy of Institutional Conformity

The deleterious ramifications of the shortsighted reliance on institutional conformity as a prerequisite for successful community adjustment should be mentioned. It tends to create an atmosphere in which the boy's behavioral adherence to the multiplicity of rules and regulations is viewed as the primary goal of his training school experience. This short circuits his efforts in pursuing other goals which might better prepare him for his return to the community.

[1] Elizabeth A. Betz, "Release from Training Schools," Advances in Understanding the Offender, ed. by Majorie Bell. New York: National Probation and Parole Association, 1950, pp. 75–88.

This can easily occur when vestigial remains of a custodial tradition tend to eclipse broader considerations of treatment and rehabilitation.

* * *

A determination of parole readiness emerges as the natural outgrowth of periodic evaluations made on each boy by individual staff members through participation in conferences, informal discussions, and written reports. Accurate guideposts for determining parole readiness are needed along with revisions in current attitudes regarding significant indications for retaining a boy in a training school program.

Relatively consistent demonstrations of the following attitudes and personality characteristics are indicative of those changes which are hopeful omens for parole success.

(1) *When the boy has come to grips at his own level of understanding and ability with the questions of "Who am I?" and "What do I want?"* This is the beginning of accurate self-assessment, ego autonomy, personal responsibility, introspection, and the emergence of internal controls. Until a boy has begun to somehow understand and accept his own internal realities, motivations ambiguities, needs and conflicts, he will continue to react blindly and impulsively when he encounters these similar but confusing phenomena in his daily environment. A sometimes agonizing but always liberating self-awareness can be encouraged, stimulated, and channeled in a training school which allows experimentation within supportive limits. The institutional focus in this instance is upon fostering growth, not reducing the boy to a psychic automaton.

(2) *When the boy is able to maintain stable and productive relationships with others.* This would entail not only understanding the quality of the boy's relationships with his peers, but also with selected members of the training school staff. An analysis of the ways in which a boy relates to a significant other offers valuable insights into the boy's use of relationships, feelings about authority, and comfort in meeting the expectations of others.

(3) *When the boy has shown improvement in social functioning and has made constructive use of the resources of the training school.* An assessment of this area will offer definitive information about the accuracy of the boy's reality-testing and problem-solving abilities. The manner in which each boy approaches and handles the demands of daily life situations is a broad index of how he will cope with whatever problems he will encounter following his release.

There are certain displayed attitudes and modes of behavior which operate as benchmarks of a boy's unreadiness for release. Some of these danger signals are:

(1) *Protracted, pervasive resistance to authority.* Continuous and irrational rebellion, expressed both overtly and covertly regardless of the differential stimuli of the training school, portrays clearly the high pitch of a boy's unresolved internal and external conflicts. When a boy fails to exercise options in behavior and rigidly retains

his original distorted perceptions of reality, it can be safely assumed that disturbed behavior will be continued in some form even if the environment of the training school is replaced by the environment of the community.

(2) *Continued expression of manipulative behavior.* This can manifest itself in all sorts of ways—exploitation of others, overconformity, protestations of complete and total reformation, and the projection of blame onto factors over which the boy cannot be expected to exercise any control such as peers, parents, or the dysfunctional aspects of society.

(3) *Identification with a delinquent subculture.* When the structure and program of a training school inhibits the development of cross-cultural, cross-racial, and otherwise fluid social groupings in its population, a boy's membership in an ethnic or culturally deviant clique is often strengthened. There is small possibility that a boy's values and attitudes can be substantially altered when this phenomenon occurs.

Additional factors such as the nature of the boy's planned placement, the length and seriousness of the boy's offense history, the boy's ability to make reality-based decisions, and the boy's tolerance of stress need to be carefully weighed prior to a boy's release.

NORTH CAROLINA GENERAL STATUTES (1983 Cum. Supp.), Art. 52

§ 7A–654. Prerelease planning.

The Director of the Division of Youth Services shall be responsible for evaluation of the progress of each juvenile at least once every six months as long as the juvenile remains in the care of the Division. If the director determines that a juvenile is ready for release, he shall initiate a prerelease planning process. The prerelease planning process shall be defined by rules and regulations of the Division of Youth Services, but shall include the following:

(1) Written notification to the judge who ordered commitment;

(2) A prerelease planning conference shall be held involving as many as possible of the following: the juvenile, his parent, court counselors who have supervised the juvenile on probation or will supervise him on aftercare, and staff of the facility that found the juvenile ready for release. The prerelease planning conference shall include personal contact and evaluation rather than telephonic notification. (1979, c. 815, s. 1.)

§ 7A–655. Conditional release and final discharge.

The Division of Youth Services shall release a juvenile either by conditional release or by final discharge. The decision as to which type of release is appropriate shall be made by the Director based on the needs of the juvenile and the best interests of the State under rules and regulations governing release which shall be promulgated by the Division of Youth Services, according to the following guidelines:

(1) Conditional release is appropriate for a juvenile needing supervision after leaving the institution. As part of the prerelease planning process, the terms of conditional release shall be set out in writing and a copy given to the juvenile, his parent, the committing court, and the court counselor who will provide aftercare supervision. The time that a juvenile spends on conditional release shall be credited toward his maximum period of commitment to the Division of Youth Services.

(2) Final discharge is appropriate when the juvenile does not require supervision, has completed a maximum commitment for his offense, or is 18 years of age. (1979, c. 815, s. 1; 1983, c. 133, s. 1; c. 276, s. 1.)

§ 7A–656. Revocation of conditional release.

If a juvenile does not conform to the terms of his conditional release, the court counselor providing aftercare supervision may make a motion for review in the court in the district where the juvenile has been residing during aftercare supervision. The judge shall hold a hearing to determine whether there has been a violation. With respect to any hearing pursuant to this section, the juvenile:

(1) Shall have reasonable notice in writing of the nature and content of the allegations in the petition, including notice that the purpose of the hearing is to determine whether the juvenile has violated the terms of his conditional release to the extent that his conditional release should be revoked;

(2) Shall be permitted to be represented by an attorney at the hearing;

(3) Shall have the right to confront and cross-examine any persons who have made allegations against him;

(4) May admit, deny, or explain the violation alleged and may present proof, including affidavits or other evidence, in support of his contentions. A record of the proceeding shall be made and preserved in the juvenile's record.

If the judge determines that the juvenile has violated the terms of his conditional release, the judge may revoke the conditional release or make any other disposition authorized by this Subchapter.

If the judge revokes the conditional release, the Chief Court Counselor shall have the responsibility for returning the juvenile to the facility specified by the Division of Youth Services. (1979, c. 815, s. 1.)

IN RE OWEN E.

Supreme Court of California, 1979.
23 Cal.3d 398, 154 Cal.Rptr. 204, 592 P.2d 720.

CLARK, JUSTICE.

Director of California Youth Authority (CYA) appeals from juvenile court order vacating order of commitment of Owen E. to CYA custody. Director contends the juvenile court erred in redetermining a ward's rehabilitative needs, CYA having properly determined the ward's application for parole be denied in his best interests. We agree with the director and reverse the order.

Understanding of the posture of the cause before us is essential to our resolution of the issues. Owen was properly committed to a CYA facility in August 1974.[1] For 18 months he participated in an educational program, making normal progress towards rehabilitation. In Fall 1976 CYA denied Owen's application for parole because in its view he had not yet accepted responsibility for his actions resulting in his commitment and did not fully appreciate his obligations to society. Shortly thereafter and without pursuing an administrative appeal from the denial, Owen's mother petitioned the juvenile court to vacate the 1974 commitment. (§ 778.)[2] The juvenile court, considering the same matters deemed by CYA to necessitate a continuation of Owen's participation in its program, concluded his rehabilitative needs would best be satisfied if he were released from custody. It set aside its original order of commitment and placed Owen on probation in the custody of his mother and ordered continuing therapy in an outpatient program.

This is not a case wherein Owen challenges the propriety of the order finding him a ward of the court or of the order of commitment in the first instance. Nor is any claim made that because of the availability of new facts or information the order of commitment should be reconsidered as having been improvidently made. Nor

---

[1] In August 1974 Owen, then 17 years of age, intentionally shot and killed his father after an argument at the family home. Owen first denied then several days later admitted the killing. Following hearing and stipulation to the facts he was declared a ward of the juvenile court. (Welf. & Inst.Code, § 602.) He was committed to CYA in March 1975.

Unless otherwise specified, all following statutory references are to sections of the Welfare and Institutions Code.

[2] Section 778 provides: "Any parent or other person having an interest in a child who is a ward or dependent child of the juvenile court or the child himself through a properly appointed guardian may, upon grounds of change of circumstances or new evidence, petition the court in the same action in which the child was found to be a ward or dependent child of the juvenile court for a hearing to change, modify, or set aside any order of court previously made or to terminate the jurisdiction of the court. The petition * * * shall set forth in concise language any change of circumstance or new evidence which are alleged to require such change or order or termination of jurisdiction.

"If it appears that the best interests of the child may be promoted by the proposed change of order or termination of jurisdiction, the court shall order that a hearing be held and shall give prior notice, or cause prior notice to be given, to such persons and by such means as prescribed by Sections 776 and 779, and, in such instances as the means of giving notice is not prescribed by such sections, then by such means as the court prescribes."

does Owen seek relief on any ground for which the writ of habeas corpus might lie. He does not complain that the length of his confinement is disproportionate to the gravity of his misconduct or to his rehabilitative needs. He does not complain that conditions of his confinement are so onerous as to deny him any protected right—in fact, both Owen and CYA agree Owen has adapted well to its program.

Owen's sole complaint is simply that CYA has abused its discretion in denying him immediate relief from commitment. He seeks in effect to establish the juvenile court's superior authority to reconsider and overrule a discretionary determination made by CYA pursuant to authority vested in CYA by the Legislature.[3]

FACTUAL BASIS FOR GRANTING PAROLE OR VACATING COMMITMENT

At the juvenile court hearing on the motion to vacate his commitment, Owen claimed CYA could no longer serve his rehabilitative needs.[4] Owen testified he was entered in a college program at a CYA facility and had completed 39 units,[5] but had been denied permission to attend offgrounds college courses. He further testified he wished to pursue a professional baseball career, but baseball (hardball) facilities were not available at the facility.[6]

A psychiatrist, a clinical psychologist intern, a social worker and parole agent, and a program administrator, all CYA staff members who had worked with Owen, testified he had continuing rehabilitative needs best served by the CYA program. They testified to CYA concern for Owen's lack of insight into the criminal nature of his conduct, his failure to acknowledge his role as a wrongdoer, and a tendency to excuse or justify his conduct. In their views Owen's continued confinement to an environment which required him to recognize and conform to standards approved by society would be beneficial to him and would foster further rehabilitation. On the other hand, an early release as on parole would tend to give support to his attitude of having committed an excusable or justifiable act.

There was also testimony that, after the possibility arose Owen would be transferred to another facility when found to have possession of marijuana during the pendency of the instant petition, he

[3] We note that during the pendency of these proceedings the juvenile court order appealed from has been stayed but CYA, in recognition of Owen's continuing progress toward rehabilitation, has released him on parole.

[4] Owen's petition was supported by the testimony of a private psychiatrist, who stated there was only a "remote" likelihood of a repetition of Owen's behavior and that Owen could be reached through therapy as an outpatient for his continuing therapeutic needs. The witness also

stated Owen had benefited by his commitment to CYA; however, he gave equivocal testimony concerning Owen's continuing benefit under CYA's program.

[5] Owen had achieved a 3.02 grade point average on a maximum 4.0 scale.

[6] It appears that the denial of offgrounds course participation and the unavailability of baseball facilities precipitated application for parole and, upon denial of such application, the filing of the instant petition.

stated the school program had been of benefit to him and he wished to remain there.

APPLICABLE LAW

Owen contends the juvenile court is vested with final authority to determine his rehabilitative needs. He asserts the juvenile court's authority to vacate his commitment to CYA derives from section 779.[7] That portion of section 779 limiting the court's authority to "change, modify, or set aside" an order of commitment by requiring that it give "due consideration to the effect" of such an order "on the discipline and parole system of the Youth Authority," is critical to our resolutions herein.

Director claims the juvenile court may preempt CYA only when the court can identify a clear abuse of discretion. Owen, on the other hand, maintains the juvenile court judge, before exercising authority conferred by section 779, need only take CYA determinations into account, and that it had a right to "second guess" CYA. When reminded that section 779 required it to consider the effect of its order on CYA parole and discipline, the court in this case commented "I assure you that I have considered that and I have given it some thought, because I don't think that I should close my mind to the possibilities of my action, I think at the beginning of this hearing I should be aware of what possibilities might occur, what the effect of a court's order might be. [¶] Now, certainly I would agree that a Court should not step in in case after case with the Youth Authority unless there is a serious reason for it."

It is manifest that when the juvenile court grants relief pursuant to sections 778 and 779, and places a ward on probation, it necessarily makes a judgment which CYA is charged with making, based on the same evidence. Such action by the court is tantamount to the granting of parole, again on the basis of the same matters considered by CYA. When as here such court action is taken in response to CYA's refusal to grant parole, it is inescapable the court has substituted its judgment for that of CYA.

The Legislature has not clearly defined the circumstances under which a juvenile court may intervene in a matter concerning the rehabilitative needs of a ward it has committed to CYA. The only

---

[7] Section 779 provides in pertinent part: "The court committing a ward to the Youth Authority may thereafter change, modify, or set aside the order of commitment. Ten days' notice of the hearing of the application therefor shall be served by United States mail upon the Director of the Youth Authority. In changing, modifying, or setting aside such order of commitment, the court shall give due consideration to the effect thereof upon the discipline and parole system of the Youth Authority or of the correctional school in which the ward may have been placed by the Youth Authority. Except as in this section provided, nothing in this chapter shall be deemed to interfere with the system of parole and discharge now or hereafter established by law, or by rule of the Youth Authority, for the parole and discharge of wards of the juvenile court committed to the Youth Authority, or with the management of any school, institution, or facility under the jurisdiction of the Youth Authority. Except as in this section provided, nothing in this chapter shall be deemed to interfere with the system of transfer between institutions and facilities under the jurisdiction of the Youth Authority."

express direction is contained in section 779 that the court "shall give due consideration to the effect [of setting aside an order of commitment] upon the discipline and parole system of" CYA, and that the authority to set aside an order of commitment "shall be deemed to interfere with the system of parole and discharge now or hereafter established by law, or by rule of" CYA. (See fn. 7, ante.) CYA thus argues section 779 authorizes a juvenile court to intervene only when to do does not interfere with CYA's proper administration of paroles and discharges.

Although dealing with revocation rather than granting of parole, support for CYA's position is found in In re Ronald E. (1977) 19 Cal. 3d 315, 137 Cal.Rptr. 781, 562 P.2d 684. In that case a juvenile, already a ward of the court committed to CYA, engaged in other criminal activity while on parole. After making initial findings on charges under supplemental petitions (§ 707), but without issuing a dispositional order, the juvenile court referred the matter to CYA "for final disposition." CYA then relied on juvenile court findings in considering the question of parole revocations. We held the juvenile court proceedings were inappropriate to initiate revocation of CYA parole. "Examination of the statutes governing Youth Authority parole and revocation procedure indicates that the juvenile court should play no part in the parole revocation process. The Youth Authority Act provides that the board has the power to grant and revoke parole. (§ 1711.3.) * * * [¶] No role is specified for the juvenile court with respect to revocation of parole. The reason is clear: the Youth Authority Act contemplates that the board or its representative is to conduct the parole revocation hearing, and then itself determine whether a parole violation in fact occurred and take appropriate action with respect to revocation or continuation of parole. The juvenile court is not authorized to act essentially in the role of a Youth Authority parole revocation hearing officer, as it did in this case." (Id., at p. 327, 137 Cal.Rptr. at p. 789, 562 P.2d at p. 692.) [8]

While *Ronald E.* deals only with parole revocation, our courts have also held the juvenile court is without jurisdiction to release a ward on parole from CYA. (Breed v. Superior Court (1976) 63 Cal. App.3d 773, 778, 134 Cal.Rptr. 228.) In so holding the court particularly relied on that provision of section 779 precluding a juvenile court from interfering with the CYA's "system of parole and discharge now or hereafter established by law, or by rule of" CYA. (Id., at pp. 787, 788, 134 Cal.Rptr., at p. 237.) The court also stated the "Legislature has properly delegated to the Youth Authority the discretion to determine whether its facilities will be or are of benefit to the ward." (Id., at pp. 784–785, 134 Cal.Rptr., at p. 236.) *Breed* is consistent with our expression in In re Authur N. (1976) 16 Cal.3d 226, 127 Cal.Rptr. 641, 545 P.2d 1345 that commitment to CYA "removes the ward from the direct supervision of the juvenile court"

---

[8] We further held in *Ronald E.* that CYA could not rely "for any purpose"— including purposes of parole revocation— on juvenile court determinations not resulting in appealable orders.

and that it was the function of CYA to determine the proper length of its jurisdiction over a ward. (Id., at pp. 237–238, 127 Cal.Rptr., at p. 649, 545 P.2d, at p. 1353.)

In the related field of jurisdiction to determine the rehabilitative needs of persons convicted of crimes, we have concluded the Adult Authority had the exclusive power to determine questions of rehabilitation. "If * * * the court were empowered * * * to recall the sentence and grant probation if the court found that the defendant had become rehabilitated after his incarceration, there manifestly would be two bodies (one judicial and one administrative) determining the matter of rehabilitation, and it is unreasonable to believe that the Legislature intended such a result." * * * While different statutes—even different codes—regulate the division of responsibility between the concerned administrative agency and court, it appears to be as unreasonable to assume the Legislature intended that both the juvenile court and CYA are to regulate juvenile rehabilitation as it is to assume that both the superior court and Adult Authority are to regulate criminal rehabilitation.

In view of the foregoing it appears section 779 does not constitute authority for a juvenile court to set aside an order committing a ward to CYA merely because the court's view of the rehabilitative progress and continuing needs of the ward differ from CYA determinations on such matters arrived at in accordance with law. The critical question is thus whether CYA acted within the discretion conferred upon it in rejecting Owen's application for parole. If so, there is no basis for judicial intervention by the juvenile court.

CONCLUSION

Owen's petition is supported by little more than a showing that after 18 months of confinement he had made good progress toward parole or outright release, that he had legitimate ambitions which he claimed could best be achieved if not confined, and a lone expert opinion that rehabilitation could best be accomplished in some other environment. But even that expert recognized Owen's need for continued psychiatric treatment and acknowledged release might have a detrimental effect upon the therapeutic benefit derived from working toward a regular grant of parole. He also gave conflicting testimony as to whether Owen would continue to benefit by treatment in CYA facilities.

Witnesses for CYA raised serious questions whether Owen had assumed a proper degree of responsibility for his grievous misconduct. They were unanimously of the opinion his early release would tend to be viewed by Owen as approval of such misconduct, thereby damaging rehabilitative efforts. They were also of the view that while Owen had made a good adjustment during his 18 months of commitment, he would continue to benefit by other adjustments, particularly through recognition of the anti-social nature of his offense.

It fairly appears the record in the instant case discloses a debatable question whether Owen's rehabilitative needs could best be served by his continued commitment to CYA. CYA acted well within law and discretion vested in it by the Legislature in denying Owen's application for parole in 1976.[9] In enacting section 779 in context with the Youth Authority Act the Legislature did not intend to authorize the juvenile court to substitute its judgment for that of CYA in such circumstances. The fact the question of release is debatable does not invoke judicial intervention—such circumstance tends instead to give conclusive effect to CYA's determination.

Giving meaning to the intendment of section 779 together with policies set forth in the balance of the Youth Authority Act, we hold a juvenile court may not act to vacate a proper commitment to CYA unless it appears CYA has failed to comply with law or has abused its discretion in dealing with a ward in its custody. Section 779 does not authorize judicial intervention into the routine parole function of CYA, as was done in this case.

The order appealed from is reversed.

MOSK, RICHARDSON and MANUEL, JJ., concur.

BIRD, CHIEF JUSTICE, dissenting.

I must respectfully dissent.

*   *   *

Clearly, the case law does not support the majority's conclusion that the Legislature did not mean what it plainly stated in sections 775, 778 and 779. These statutes give juvenile courts the authority to set aside Youth Authority commitments to promote a ward's best interests. Nothing in these statutes purports to limit this power to situations where the Youth Authority "has failed to comply with law or has abused its discretion." (Maj. opn., ante, p. 208 of 154 Cal. Rptr., p. 724 of 592 P.2d.) To the contrary, the court is accorded great discretion in determining whether the circumstances justify a change in disposition or total termination of the court's jurisdiction.[10] (See fn. 1, ante; In re W.R.W. (1971) 17 Cal.App.3d 1029, 1037, 95 Cal.Rptr. 354.) "[I]n the absence of a clear showing of abuse of discretion, an appellate court is not free to interfere with the trial court's order." (In re Corey (1964) 230 Cal.App.2d 813, 831–832, 41 Cal.Rptr. 379, 391.)

[9] Although testimony at the hearing focused on Owen's rehabilitative needs, a second factor which CYA must consider in its decision to release or retain a ward in custody is the safety of the public. (§§ 1700, 1765; see In re Martinez (1970) 1 Cal.3d 641, 650, 83 Cal.Rptr. 382, 463 P.2d 734.) Here Owen stipulated to having fired a rifle bullet from a bedroom window into his father's head at a distance of 35 feet. CYA's program was designed not only for Owen's needs, but also to insure the public's safety upon his release, and Owen's failure to accept responsibility for his criminal conduct was a factor which was a legitimate concern to CYA.

[10] Indeed, the court has a *duty* to terminate its jurisdiction when it becomes convinced on the evidence that the ward no longer requires the court's supervision. (See, e.g., In re Francecisco (1971) 16 Cal.App.3d 310, 314, 94 Cal.Rptr. 186.)

In the present case, a review of the evidence establishes that the juvenile court did not abuse its broad discretion in finding "a very great change of circumstances" and in setting aside Owen's Youth Authority commitment. The annual review made by Owen's immediate supervisors at the Youth Authority indicated that Owen had made "superior progress" in achieving the goals set in his rehabilitation program, and that his schoolwork was "outstanding." The report also stated that Owen "possessed leadership qualities," avoided negative influences, and was a "self-starter." The report concluded that "he should have no problem whatsoever maintaining any job he should happen to have." Owen's evaluators recommended his release.

In addition, a psychiatrist testifying on Owen's behalf stated that Owen had arrived at a philosophical understanding of his role in his father's death and that the chance of a recurrence of such violence was remote. The Youth Authority's experts agreed that the killing was an isolated incident and that Owen was not a hazard to the community.

Further, the evidence was uncontradicted that Owen had the potential ability to play professional baseball. However, the Youth Authority facilities where he was confined were inadequate to develop this talent.

On this record, it is clear that substantial evidence supported the trial judge's determination in this case. The evidence showed that Owen had made significant progress in the Youth Authority, that he was not a threat to the safety of the public, and that his educational and professional opportunities would be enhanced by his release. Experts for both Owen and the Youth Authority testified that denial of release could impede his progress. The trial court's decision to set aside the Youth Authority commitment and to order outpatient psychiatric care for Owen was well within its discretion.

The trial court's order should be affirmed.

TOBRINER and NEWMAN, JJ., concur.

Rehearing denied; BIRD, C.J., and TOBRINER, J., dissenting.

STATE v. MacQUEEN

Supreme Court of Appeals of West Virginia, 1979.
163 W.Va. 620, 259 S.E.2d 420.

CAPLAN, CHIEF JUSTICE:

In this original proceeding in Prohibition, J.R., a juvenile, seeks to prohibit the Circuit Court of Kanawha County from further proceeding in a hearing on parole revocation. The petitioner was charged with violation of conditions Nos. 1 and 3 of his parole order. Condition No. 1 provides "[t]hat the child shall not violate the laws of this State, nor any state of the United States, nor of any city within the boundaries thereof". Condition No. 3 requires the petitioner to "report as directed by the Court or his probation officer".

The petitioner was adjudicated a juvenile delinquent subsequent to being found guilty of truancy and breaking and entering. He was placed in the Industrial School for Boys on or about April 15, 1978. In December of the same year, the petitioner was placed on parole for a period of one year or until further order of the court.

In January 1979, a petition was executed charging the petitioner with the commission of robbery by violence. The petition was never filed with the circuit court, but, pursuant thereto, the petitioner was taken into custody and placed in the Kanawha Home for Children in Dunbar. Two days later the petitioner was given notice of a proposed hearing on the alleged parole violations. The notice set forth the conditions of parole allegedly violated, the specific facts upon which the alleged violations were predicated, the fact that a probable cause hearing would be held and, if necessary, that a revocation hearing would be scheduled.

At the preliminary hearing it was determined that there was probable cause to believe a parole violation occurred and a parole revocation hearing was scheduled for February 13, 1979 in the Circuit Court of Kanawha County. At that hearing the petitioner's counsel moved to dismiss the parole revocation proceeding contending that the court had no statutory authority to proceed against a juvenile on an alleged parole violation; that the State by using W.Va.Code, 1931, 49–5–14, as amended, in conjunction with the revocation procedure for adult parolees was depriving the petitioner of due process of law; and that the petitioner's parole could not be revoked before he was convicted of a violation of state law upon a formal charge. Furthermore, says the petitioner, the standard of proof of such violation must be that of "proof beyond a reasonable doubt". The circuit court denied the motion but stayed the proceeding to permit the petitioner to seek prohibition here. This proceeding followed.

The petitioner contends that W.Va.Code, 1931, 49–5–14, as amended, deals solely with the modification of dispositional orders and does not encompass procedures for revocation of parole. We disagree. The order of December 11, 1978 placing the petitioner on parole was a dispositional order. The above statute provides in part, "[i]f the motion or request for review of disposition is based upon an alleged violation of a court order [it was alleged that the petitioner violated the court's order not to violate the law], the court may modify the dispositional order to a more restrictive alternative if it finds clear and convincing proof of substantial violation."

This petitioner, having been adjudicated a delinquent child, was committed to a rehabilitation facility and, under the provisions of W.Va.Code, 1931, 49–5–13(b)(6), as amended, was returned to the court "for further disposition". This was done pursuant to the continuing jurisdiction of the court in juvenile matters. W.Va.Code, 1931, 49–5–2, as amended. As noted, the court entered an order placing the petitioner on parole, this being the "further disposition" referred to above. We find that the court properly proceeded under W.Va.Code, 1931, 49–5–14, as amended.

It is the further assertion of the petitioner that the application of adult parole revocation procedure, in conjunction with W.Va.Code, 1931, 49–5–14, as amended, to the revocation of parole of a juvenile is constitutionally impermissible. It is of no moment that there is no express statutory procedures for juvenile parole revocation. We have found that the court can act to modify a dispositional order and that such act may be the revocation of parole which was granted by such dispositional order. It is of great moment, however, that a juvenile being subjected to parole revocation be afforded all of the constitutional protections afforded an adult.

Neither the United States Supreme Court nor this Court has expressly spoken to the procedural requirements due a juvenile in parole revocation proceedings. In a series of cases, however, the Supreme Court has held that juveniles are entitled to procedural protections previously denied them under the doctrine of *parens patriae.* The command of these cases is that the constitutional rights of the juvenile can no longer be ignored but that he must be afforded constitutional due process and fair treatment.

* * *

In Morrissey v. Brewer, 408 U.S. 471, 92 S.Ct. 2593, 33 L.Ed.2d 484 (1972), the Court addressed the issue of the extent to which, if any, constitutional due process must be afforded in parole revocation proceedings. First, it was decided that a parolee's liberty, although indeterminate is valuable and is within the protection of the Fourteenth Amendment; its termination, therefore, calls for some orderly process, however informal. However, that Court further said "that the revocation of parole is not part of a criminal prosecution and thus the full panoply of rights due a defendant in such a proceeding does not apply to parole revocations."

The Court, in *Morrissey,* then listed the following minimum requirements of due process to be afforded in parole revocations: "(a) written notice of the claimed violations of parole; (b) disclosure to the parolee of evidence against him; (c) opportunity to be heard in person and to present witnesses and documentary evidence; (d) the right to confront and cross-examine adverse witnesses (unless the hearing officer specifically finds good cause for not allowing confrontation); (e) a 'neutral and detached' hearing body * * *; and (f) a written statement by the factfinders as to the evidence relied on and reasons for revoking parole."

Morrissey v. Brewer, supra, has been cited by this Court for the proposition that certain due process rights shall be afforded to adults in parole revocation proceedings. * * * We perceive no reason why the same due process rights should not apply to juvenile parole revocations.

Many jurisdictions have held that juveniles are entitled to at least a minimum of procedural due process rights in parole revocation proceedings. * * *

We agree with the thrust of the above cited cases. The nature of the interest of the juvenile parolee is no less valuable than that of an adult parolee. The termination of liberty afforded by parole must be accomplished through some orderly process. The circuit court in the instant case is proceeding by orderly process to revoke the petitioner's parole. It is employing the process used in adult parole revocations together with the procedure for the modification of dispositional orders in juvenile cases as provided in W.Va.Code, 1931, 49–5–14, as amended.

Let us look now to the procedures followed in the instant case to determine whether this petitioner is being afforded the due process required by Morrissey and other authorities cited. He received written notice of the claimed parole violations and a disclosure of the evidence against him. There is no indication that he will not be afforded an opportunity to be heard and present evidence; that he will not be afforded the right to confront his accusers before a neutral and detached hearing body; and, that he will not be informed of the reasons for revocation should his parole be revoked. Clearly, the procedure being followed by the court will afford the petitioner the due process protections contemplated by the state and federal constitutions.

The petitioner's basic contention, however, is that his parole cannot be revoked on the ground that he violated the law unless he is convicted on a formal charge in an adjudicatory proceeding upon proof beyond a reasonable doubt. This contention is without merit. As noted, we have approved the procedure employed by the court so long as minimal due process protections are afforded.

The legislature, in requiring "clear and convincing proof of substantial violation", under W.Va.Code, 1931, 49–5–14, as amended, explicitly set forth a higher standard of proof than that required in adult revocation proceedings. Violation of parole of an adult may be proved if "it shall appear *to the satisfaction of the board* that the parolee has violated any condition of his release on parole." (emphasis supplied) W.Va.Code, 1931, 62–12–19, as amended. The *Morrissey* court noted that parole revocation is not a part of a criminal prosecution and that the full panoply of rights due a defendant in such proceeding need not be afforded in revocation of parole.

In determining whether the petitioner violated its order, the Court contemplates employing the standard of "clear and convincing proof", as provided by W.Va.Code, 1931, 49–5–14, as amended. This standard of proof in juvenile parole revocation proceedings is not constitutionally deficient. * * *

Parole revocation is not a criminal prosecution. It is a proceeding stemming from an alleged violation of the conditions imposed as a condition of release from confinement. The violation may be proved as noted herein and the revocation may be effected so long as the minimum requirements of due process are afforded. A conviction on a formal charge is not a prerequisite.

For the reasons stated herein the Writ of Prohibition is denied. Writ denied.

NOTE

In a case decided prior to Morrissey v. Brewer, discussed in State v. MacQueen, the Minnesota Supreme Court ruled that a juvenile on parole was entitled to none of the following claimed rights before his parole could be revoked:

"(a) Notice of any alleged violation of law.

"(b) Court-appointed counsel.

"(c) A fact hearing on the allegations.

"(d) Confrontation and cross-examination of witnesses.

"(e) Presentation of evidence in his own behalf.

"(f) Minimal demands of due process, including presumption of innocence, burden of proof beyond a reasonable doubt, and bail."

Loyd v. Youth Conservation Commission, 287 Minn. 12, 13, 177 N.W.2d 555, 556 (1970).

The court said:

If we are to encourage early parole of youthful offenders, as the Youth Conservation Act is aimed to achieve, we should not at the same time create procedural obstacles to the revocation of parole thereunder, for the officials can hardly be expected to grant early parole if they must also provide the individual with all due process rights every time he is suspected of violating the conditions of parole. Absent a showing of abuse or arbitrariness on the part of the officials, we must grant them discretion in taking such steps as are necessary to the welfare of the youthful offender and to public safety.

The Minnesota youth correctional system is grounded in the philosophy of parens patriae, namely, that the state has the inherent power to take such steps as are necessary for the protection and welfare of the child. See, State ex rel. Knutson v. Jackson, 249 Minn. 246, 82 N.W.2d 234; Peterson v. McAuliffe, 151 Minn. 467, 187 N.W. 226. This philosophy, admittedly under attack in some quarters, has operated well as applied to our system of rehabilitation. We regard the Youth Conservation Commission as a progressive and highly satisfactory correctional entity and nothing in this record compels us to encumber or restrict it.

Id. at 17, 177 N.W.2d at 558. Is there a significant difference in the need for flexibility when dealing with adults on parole and when dealing with juveniles on parole?

STATE EX REL. R.R. v. SCHMIDT

Supreme Court of Wisconsin, 1974.
63 Wis.2d 82, 216 N.W.2d 18.

ORIGINAL ACTION. Mandamus to the Department of Health and Social Services and Wilbur J. Schmidt as Secretary of said Department.

Petitioner, R.R., a juvenile, filed a petition for leave to commence an original action for writ of mandamus which leave was granted November 28, 1973. The writ is sought to compel the secretary of the Department of Health and Social Services (hereinafter, "Department") to provide petitioner and his attorney with copies of the hearing examiner's synopsis of testimony and recommendations which were filed subsequent to an administrative aftercare revocation hearing held at the Wisconsin School for Boys on October 2, 1973.

Petitioner was found delinquent by the Rock County court on November 23, 1970 and committed to the Department of Health and Social Services. He was thereafter committed by the Department to the Wisconsin School for Boys at Wales.

On August 1, 1973, petitioner was released on aftercare supervision and was alleged to have stolen two radios from the Donald Dresselhaus group home in Beloit. For this reason the Department sought to revoke petitioner's aftercare supervision and a hearing was held before an administrative hearing examiner at the Wisconsin School for Boys on October 2, 1973, at which petitioner was represented by the state public defender.

Subsequent to this hearing the examiner apparently prepared a report which was forwarded to the secretary of the H & SS Department. Neither petitioner nor his counsel was provided with a copy of this report, and petitioner was informed that the secretary determined that petitioner's supervision should be revoked.

Petitioner's counsel alleges, though this is denied by the Department, that such reports have in the past been supplied to him as a matter of departmental policy. When informed of the decision to revoke supervision, petitioner's counsel objected to his being denied a copy of the report.

HANLEY, JUSTICE. Three issues are raised on this original action.

1. In an administrative hearing concerning revocation of a juvenile's aftercare supervision, does the juvenile have a constitutional right to inspect and reply to the hearing examiner's report?

2. Do the fair-play provisions of the Wisconsin Administrative Procedure Act apply to such revocation hearings?

3. What effect, if any, has Sec. 48.78, Stats. upon the juvenile's right to inspect the hearing examiner's report?

Constitutional Right

Both parties agree that petitioner has a constitutional right to inspect the hearing examiner's report under the mandate of Zizzo v. United States (7th Cir.1972), 470 F.2d 105, 108, certiorari denied, 409 U.S. 1012, 93 S.Ct. 443, 34 L.Ed.2d 306. That case involved revocation of the parole of an adult criminal defendant and the due process procedures which must be followed when parole is revoked. The court concluded that the hearing examiner's report must be made known to the parolee and that he must be given an opportunity to object by written submission before adoption of the report, citing Morrissey v. Brewer (1972), 408 U.S. 471, 92 S.Ct. 2593, 33 L.Ed.2d 484, but holding that *Morrissey* is to be applied prospectively only to June 29, 1972.

In *Morrissey* the court defined those procedures necessary to comport with the requirements of the due process clause of the Fourteenth Amendment in cases concerning revocation of the parole of an adult defendant. The court first distinguished the factual situation of *Morrissey* from Mempa v. Rhay (1967), 389 U.S. 128, 88 S.Ct. 254, 19 L.Ed.2d 336, which involved safeguards required when probation is revoked in a case where no sentence had been imposed prior to probation:

> "We begin with the proposition that the revocation of parole is not part of a criminal prosecution and thus the full panoply of rights due a defendant in such a proceeding does not apply to parole revocations. Cf. Mempa v. Rhay, 389 U.S. 128, 88 S.Ct. 254, 19 L.Ed.2d 336 (1967). Parole arises after the end of the criminal prosecution, including imposition of sentence. Supervision is not directly by the court but by an administrative agency, which is sometimes an arm of the court and sometimes of the executive. Revocation deprives an individual, not of the absolute liberty to which every citizen is entitled, but only of the conditional liberty properly dependent on observance of special parole restrictions." Id. 408 U.S. at p. 480, 92 S.Ct. at p. 2600.

In outlining the procedures required to comply with due process in the *Morrissey* fact situation, the court stated:

> "We cannot write a code of procedure; that is the responsibility of each State. Most States have done so by legislation, others by judicial decision usually on due process grounds. Our task is limited to deciding the minimum requirements of due process. They include (a) written notice of the claimed violations of parole; (b) disclosure to the parolee of evidence against him; (c) opportunity to be heard in person and to present witnesses and documentary evidence; (d) the right to confront and cross-examine adverse witnesses (unless the hearing officer specifically finds good cause for not allowing confrontation); (e) a 'neutral and detached' hearing body such as a traditional parole board, members of which need not be judicial officers or lawyers; and (f) a written statement by the factfinders as to the evidence relied on and reasons for revoking parole. We emphasize there is no thought to equate this second stage of parole revocation to a criminal prosecution in any sense. It is a narrow inquiry; the process should be flexible enough to consider evidence including letters, affidavits, and other material that would not be admissible in an adversary criminal trial." Id. at pages 488, 489, 92 S.Ct. at page 2604.

In *Zizzo*, supra, the court held that several of the requirements cited in *Morrissey*, supra, led to the conclusion that a defendant in a parole revocation proceeding must be afforded access to the hearing examiner's report:

> "(f) a written statement by the factfinders as to the evidence relied on and reasons for revoking parole;" "(b) disclosure to the parolee of evidence against him;" "(d) the right to confront and

cross-examine adverse witnesses (unless the hearing officer specifically finds good cause for not allowing confrontation)."

In State ex rel. Bernal v. Hershman (1972), 54 Wis.2d 626, 196 N.W.2d 721, this court extended the rights granted to the parolee in Johnson v. Cady (1971), 50 Wis.2d 540, 185 N.W.2d 306 to a juvenile under "aftercare" supervision by the Department, adding the right to counsel to such revocation proceedings. The court stated 54 Wis.2d at page 630, 196 N.W.2d at page 724:

> "Since we see no essential constitutional difference between a parole of an adult and 'liberty under supervision' of a juvenile, we believe the procedure should be uniform as far as practical * * *"

Bernal preceded Morrissey v. Brewer, supra, by about two months in laying out some of the same requisites for revocation proceedings, e.g., advising of rights prior to hearing, timely written statement and notice of reasons revocation was recommended; administrative hearing with opportunity to present and cross-examine witnesses and present oral arguments; transcript if requested; prompt advisement of the board's decision and of its reasons and the evidence relied upon and impartial hearing officer.

Both the court's conclusion that for constitutional due process purposes there is no difference between parole revocation and revocation of a juvenile's "aftercare" supervision, and the language emphasized above, point to the conclusion that due process requires that the juvenile should be afforded a copy of the hearing examiner's report and the opportunity to object thereto by written submission prior to the decision of the department secretary.

Do the APA Fair Play Provisions (Secs. 227.07–227.13) Apply to "Aftercare"?

The petitioner then contends that, in addition to his constitutionally protected due process right to be afforded a copy of the hearing examiner's report and the opportunity to object thereto by written submission prior to the decision of the department secretary, the Fair Play Provisions of the Wisconsin Administrative Procedure Act— Secs. 227.07–227.13, Stats.—are herein applicable and that there exists a right to an oral argument before the department secretary prior to his determination of the issue. Such is, however, not the case.

This court has on numerous occasions addressed itself to the constitutional and statutory rights embodied in the Wisconsin Children's Code and has determined that, within constitutional limits, it is for the legislature, not the courts, to prescribe the procedures to be followed in juvenile court proceedings. In re D.M.D. v. State (1972), 54 Wis.2d 313, 195 N.W.2d 594. Absent a constitutional requirement thereto, this court will not legislatively engraft a judicially conceived procedural right on the Wisconsin Children's Code. The petitioner's request that this court engraft the right to oral argument before the department secretary prior to his determination of the issue is without merit.

The procedural guarantees which are constitutionally required in revocation hearings consist of the following:

(a) a written statement and notice or reasons revocation was recommended;

(b) the right to present and cross-examine witnesses;

(c) the right to present arguments and evidence orally before the hearing examiner;

(d) the right to a transcript if requested;

(e) a prompt notification of the decision; and

(f) the right to inspect and a written reply to the hearing examiner's report.

See State ex rel. Bernal v. Hershman, supra; State ex rel. Johnson v. Cady, supra. See also Morrissey v. Brewer, supra; Zizzo v. United States, supra. Yet, in the words of the United States Supreme Court, "the full panoply of rights due a defendant in such a proceeding [criminal prosecution] does not apply to parole revocations." Morrissey v. Brewer, supra, 408 U.S. at p. 480, 92 S.Ct. at p. 2600. The procedural aspects of such a revocation hearing are, however, to remain flexible and are not equated with those of a criminal prosecution or similar hearings. Morrissey v. Brewer, supra. This court does not believe and the United States Supreme Court has never held that there exists a due process constitutional right to an oral argument before the department secretary prior to his determination of the issue.

Similarly, it is the opinion of this court that there exists no statutory right to present an oral argument as guaranteed in the Wisconsin Administrative Procedure Act before the department secretary. The Wisconsin Children's Code makes no provision as to the applicability of Ch. 227, Stats. thereto and this court will not so legislate its application. Neither has this court deemed Ch. 227, Stats. as being applicable to adult parole revocation hearings. State ex rel. Johnson v. Cady, supra. The rights guaranteed by such a hearing have been specifically delineated and do not rise to the level of a criminal prosecution or a Ch. 227 hearing. Such being the case, the right to an oral argument before the department secretary is without statutory or constitutional basis and must be denied.

Applicability of Sec 48.78, Stats.

Sec. 48.78, Stats. provides:

"Confidentiality of records. Records kept or information received by the department, county agencies specified in s. 48.56, licensed child welfare agencies, licensed day care centers and licensed maternity hospitals regarding individuals in their care or legal custody shall not be open to inspection or their contents disclosed except by order of the court. This section does not apply to the confidential exchange of information between these agencies or other social welfare or law enforcement agencies regarding individuals in the care or legal custody of one of the agencies."

Since a constitutional due process right to the hearing examiner's report exists under *Zizzo*, supra, we hold that Sec. 48.78 cannot prevent the juvenile from access to the report.

It must be noted that the statute does not absolutely prevent disclosure. Disclosure may be ordered by the juvenile court, and the reasons for disclosure here would certainly appear to constitute good and sufficient cause.

Counsel for both parties call the court's attention to the following language in Johnson v. Cady, supra, 50 Wis.2d at p. 550, 185 N.W. 2d at p. 311:

> "We, therefore, hold that petitioner's right of review of a revocation hearing is by certiorari directed to the court of conviction."

Counsel contends this language appears to confer jurisdiction on a court in circumstances where such jurisdiction has been expressly withheld by the legislature. Obviously it was not the intention of this court to confer certiorari jurisdiction on county courts. To clarify the court's intention we add the following sentence to the language referred to:

> "When such court has certiorari jurisdiction; otherwise, to a court having said jurisdiction in the county where petitioner was convicted."

We conclude that the petitioner and his attorney are entitled to receive copies of the hearing examiner's report and recommendations which were filed subsequent to an administrative aftercare revocation hearing held on October 2, 1973.

Writ of Mandamus granted vacating revocation order and requiring disclosure of examiner's report.

NOTE

In In re D.B., 594 S.W.2d 207 (Tex.Civ.App., 1980), the court held that parole revocation hearings are not judicial adjudicatory proceedings to which jeopardy would attach or res judicata principles would apply. Therefore, a subsequent criminal prosecution for the conduct that served as the basis for the determination that a condition of parole was (or—in this case—was not) violated was barred neither by the double jeopardy provision nor by principles of res judicata.

*

Chapter 11

CONFIDENTIALITY IN THE JUVENILE PROCESS

A. EXPUNGEMENT AND SEALING OF RECORDS

IJA–ABA JUVENILE JUSTICE STANDARDS, STANDARDS
RELATING TO JUVENILE RECORDS AND
INFORMATION SYSTEMS (1980).

PART XVII: DESTRUCTION OF JUVENILE RECORDS

17.1 General policy *

It should be the policy of juvenile courts to destroy all unnecessary information contained in records that identify the juvenile who is the subject of a juvenile record so that a juvenile is protected from the possible adverse consequences that may result from disclosure of his or her record to third persons.

17.2 Cases terminating prior to adjudication of delinquency *

In cases involving a delinquency complaint, all identifying records pertaining to the matter should be destroyed when:

   A. the application for the complaint is denied;

   B. the complaint or petition is dismissed; or

   C. the juvenile is adjudicated not delinquent.

17.3 Cases involving an adjudication of delinquency *

In cases in which a juvenile is adjudicated delinquent, all identifying records pertaining to the matter should be destroyed when:

   A. no subsequent proceeding is pending as a result of the filing of a delinquency or criminal complaint against the juvenile;

   B. the juvenile has been discharged from the supervision of the court or the state juvenile correctional agency;

   C. two years have elapsed from the date of such discharge; and

   D. the juvenile has not been adjudicated delinquent as a result of a charge that would constitute a felony for an adult.

* Reprinted with permission from Standards Relating to Juvenile Records and Information Systems, Copyright 1980, Ballinger Publishing Company.

* Reprinted with permission from Standards Relating to Juvenile Records and Information Systems, Copyright 1980, Ballinger Publishing Company.

* Reprinted with permission from Standards Relating to Dispositional Procedures, Copyright 1980, Ballinger Publishing Company.

17.7 Effect of destruction of a juvenile record *

A. Whenever a juvenile's record is destroyed by a juvenile court, the proceeding should be deemed to have never occurred and the juvenile who is the subject of the record and his or her parents may inform any person or organization, including employers, banks, credit companies, insurance companies, and schools that, with respect to the matter in which the record was destroyed, he or she was not arrested, he or she did not appear before a juvenile court, and he or she was not adjudicated delinquent or neglected.

B. Notwithstanding subsection A., in any criminal or delinquency case, if the juvenile is not the defendant and is called as a witness, the juvenile may be ordered to testify with respect to whether he or she was adjudicated delinquent and matters relating thereto.

PART XX: ACCESS TO POLICE RECORDS

20.1 Police records not to be public records*

Records and files maintained by a law enforcement agency pertaining to the arrest, detention, adjudication, or disposition of a juvenile's case should not be a public record.

20.2 Access by the juvenile and his or her representatives *

A juvenile, his or her parents, and the juvenile's attorney should, upon request, be given access to all records and files collected or retained by a law enforcement agency which pertain to the arrest, detention, adjudication, or disposition of a case involving the juvenile.

20.3 Disclosure to third persons *

A. Information contained in law enforcement records and files pertaining to juveniles may be disclosed to:

1. law enforcement officers of any jurisdiction for law enforcement purposes;

2. a probation officer, judge, or prosecutor for purposes of executing the responsibilities of his or her position in a matter relating to the juvenile who is the subject of the record;

3. the state juvenile correctional agency if the juvenile is currently committed to the agency;

4. a person to whom it is necessary to disclose information for the limited purposes of investigating a crime, apprehending a juvenile, or determining whether to detain a juvenile;

5. a person who meets the criteria of Standards 5.6 and 5.7.

B.   Information contained in law enforcement records and files pertaining to a juvenile should not be released to law enforcement officers of another jurisdiction unless the juvenile was adjudicated delinquent or convicted of a crime or unless there is an outstanding arrest warrant for the juvenile.

C.   Information that is released pertaining to a juvenile should include the disposition or current status of the case.

PART XXII: DESTRUCTION OF POLICE RECORDS

22.1   Procedure and timing of destruction of police records *

Upon receipt of notice from a juvenile court that a juvenile record has been destroyed or if a juvenile is arrested or detained and has not been referred to a court, a law enforcement agency should destroy all information pertaining to the matter in all records and files, except that if the chief law enforcement officer of the agency, or his or her designee, certifies in writing that certain information is needed for a pending investigation involving the commission of a felony, that information, and information identifying the juvenile, may be retained in an intelligence file until the investigation is terminated or for one additional year, whichever is sooner.

IN RE SMITH

Family Court, City of New York, New York County, 1970.
63 Misc.2d 198, 310 N.Y.S.2d 617.

NANETTE DEMBITZ, JUDGE.   This is a motion by respondent-juveniles at the close of a juvenile delinquency proceeding against them, for an order directing the expungement of all court and police records relating to it and to their arrests.

The police took the 14 and 15 year old respondents into custody during a demonstration in front of a public school.   Then, the proceeding in this court was initiated by juvenile delinquency petitions, attested by policemen, alleging acts by respondents which would constitute, if committed by adults, the crimes of unlawful assembly and riot, under Penal Law secs. 240.05 and 240.10.   At the opening of trial, counsel for the New York City Police Department, representing the petitioners, was granted permission to withdraw the petitions, on his motion on the ground that he did "not believe that we have enough evidence here to make out a prima facie case." Respondents' present motion to expunge the court and police records relating to the petitions and to their arrests, contends that these records will stand as obstacles to respondents' progress for years to come, particularly if they seek public employment after completing school.

While respondents' motion presents judicial questions of first impression, the handicap of a juvenile court record or a police record

* Reprinted with permission from Standards Relating to Juvenile Records and   Information Systems, Copyright 1980, Ballinger Publishing Company.

to a youth trying to gain a foothold in the job market, has concerned commentators on justice for juveniles and the underprivileged.[1]   The most frequent respondents in juvenile delinquency cases in New York City, as elsewhere, appear to be children of the minorities and of the poor, as indeed are the instant respondents.   The Court obviously cannot determine this case on the basis of the general social commentaries cited by respondents' diligent counsel.   However, having considered the instant circumstances, the legal grounds for relief, and the jurisdiction of this Court, it has concluded that the motion should, with some modifications in the requested remedy, be granted.

A.   Employers' Access to Court and Police Records

Despite the prohibition on inspection of Family Court files, employers secure knowledge of a juvenile delinquency petition in a job applicant's past, through a simple expedient—requiring him, as a condition of seeking employment, to obtain a court clerk's certificate of his record in this Court.[2]

As to arrest records, the New York City Police Department's regulations on confidentiality explicitly make exceptions for the release of information, in the discretion of the commanding officer, to the New York City Department of Personnel, the United States Civil Service Commission, the State Liquor Authority, and to any City agency as to any incumbent employee (Regulations of New York City Police Dept., c. 2 par. 6.0).   The regulation does not differentiate between juvenile and adult arrest records, which are maintained in separate files but on the same forms and in the same central office.

While a police spokesman stated that the discretion to release information to the specified agencies about job applicants is not presently exercised, it appears that the practice varies from time to time (See Matter of Adler v. Lang, 21 A.D.2d 107, 108, 248 N.Y.S.2d 549, 551, 1st Dept., 1964).   In any event, there is no question that arrest records are made available as to applicants for employment in the Housing, Transit or City Police or any other "uniformed service" (e.g., firemen, court officers), and also as to applicants to the Police Department's licensing division for hack owner's or driver's licenses.

With respect to private employers, there is reason to doubt that the prohibition on access to police arrest records is rigidly enforced.[3]

---

[1] E.g., Sparer, Employability and the Juvenile "Arrest" Record (Publ. by Center for Study of Unemployed Youth, N.Y.Univ.Grad.Sch. of Social Work, 1966); Note, Juvenile Delinquents: The Police, State Courts, and Individualized Justice, 79 Harv.Law Rev. (1966), 775, 801; Gough, Expungement of Adjudication Records of Juvenile and Adult Offenders, Washington Univ.Law Quart. (1966) 156, 171–172.   Compare Hambel v. Levine, 243 App.Div. 530, 275 N.Y.S. 702 (2nd Dept., 1934).

[2] And the Armed Forces secure the Family Court record of an applicant for enlistment by requiring him to sign a waiver of confidentiality.

[3] See Matter of Campbell v. Adams, 206 Misc. 673, 674, 133 N.Y.S.2d 876, 877 (Sup.Ct.Queens, 1954).   It is so well-known in New York City that private investigators can secure police arrest records (and this Court having seen records thus obtained), that this Court takes judicial notice of this circumstance.   As to the theoretical privacy of police records, see Sears Roebuck & Co. v. Hoyt, 202 Misc. 43, 48, 107 N.Y.S.2d 756, 761 (Sup.Ct.Jefferson, 1951);   Hale v. New York City, 251 App.Div. 826, 296

Additionally, arrest records unquestionably are disclosed to any employer who obtains a waiver of confidentiality from the job applicant.

B. *Handicap to Respondents From Their Court and Police Records*

While a Court Clerk's certificate would show that the juvenile delinquency petitions against respondents were "withdrawn" and this termination *might* also be inserted on the police arrest records, knowledge of this outcome would be unlikely to dissipate a potential employer's suspicions and doubts as to respondents' reliability. Employers, like the general public, tend to conclude from a charge and an arrest that "where there is smoke, there must be fire," and they may automatically disqualify applicants with arrest records when there are sufficient untarnished applicants.

Thus, even with the fair standards and procedures required of the New York City Civil Service Commission, it nevertheless disqualified an applicant for employment in part because of an arrest on a charge that was later dismissed—and there the arrest and the dismissal occurred ten years before the application for employment (*Lang*, above, 21 A.D.2d at p. 112, 248 N.Y.S.2d at p. 555). See also Cuccio v. Dept. of Personnel-Civil Service Commission of N.Y.C., 40 Misc.2d 345, 346–347, 243 N.Y.S.2d 220, 221–222 (Sup.Ct.N.Y., 1963).[4] Indeed, "about 75% of the employment agencies sampled * * * in the New York City area * * * do not refer any applicant with a record regardless of whether the arrest was followed by a conviction."[5] While less specific data is available as to the consequences of juvenile than of adult arrest records, it would seem that they are equally onerous, depending on the stage of life of the job-seeker.

C. *Grounds for Judicial Relief*

Thus, in the economic world that respondents must prepare to enter, there tends to be a presumption of guilt from an arrest record, rather than the presumption of innocence that in the world of legal theory prevails until conviction. On the instant motion, this Court—like respondents, their parents, and their community—must concern itself with the law in action, with the true impact, whether intended or unintended, of the system of justice upon their lives.

1. For an employer to draw any suspicion or inference of respondents' misconduct from their arrests and delinquency petitions would be especially unfair because the withdrawal of the petitions was due to a complete lack of evidence rather than a mere procedural

---

N.Y.S. 443 (2nd Dept., 1937); New York City Charter, sec. 1114.

[4] While a spokesman for the incumbent New York City Civil Service Commissioners stated that current policy is to ignore arrests, he noted that even when the present Commissioners are unable to prevent consideration of arrests by the employer-agencies, which have discretion to select one out of each three eligibles.

[5] The Challenge of Crime in a Free Society (Pres.Comm. on Law Enforc., 1967) 75.

And see Morrow v. District of Columbia, 417 F.2d 728, 731 (D.C.Cir.1969), summarizing extensive study of handicap of arrest records in securing employment; also Report of California Assembly Interim Committee on Criminal Procedure (1961) 68; Schwartz and Skolnick, Two Studies of Legal Stigma, 10 Social Problems 133, 136 (1962).

snag (this Court noticing that in practice petitioners attempt to establish a prima facie case if they have even a scintilla of evidence). Accordingly, respondents' motion is supported by analogy to the judicial power to grant protection against injury from a false, defamatory connotation.[6]

2.   Since there is no evidence of respondents' misconduct, there is no public interest from a law-enforcement standpoint in maintaining these records, except for statistical purposes (that is, without preserving respondents' names on them). See Wheeler v. Goodman, 306 F.Supp. 58, 65–66 (W.D.N.C.1969): "Criminal investigation is not subserved in the least by retention of the files" of persons who have "committed no crimes."

Any reliance by law-enforcement officers on respondents' arrest records not only would be unsound, but also might be seriously harmful. For respondents' arrest records would render them a likely focus of police suspicion in the event of any neighborhood illegality; the records would tend to pin on them the burdensome—and sometimes self-fulfilling—tag of "trouble-maker."

In sum, the Court and police records in their present form pose threats of injury to the respondents without justification in the public interest in law-enforcement—and indeed contrary to the public interest in helping deprived youths climb out of the poverty ghetto. Accordingly, a second and significant basis for relief for respondents is that the State's maintenance of the records constitutes an infringement of the Constitutional guarantees of due process and equal protection of the law.

3.   Besides the above general grounds for judicial relief, respondents, as juveniles, can voice a special plea. Mindful of the stresses, spontaneity, and plasticity of youth, the draftsmen of the Family Court Act sought to forestall future handicaps for young people even from adjudications of delinquency (see Sec. 783); *a fortiori* the juvenile should be protected against the effects of a withdrawn petition. Again, the Act attempts to safeguard juveniles from adverse use of their arrest records (Sec. 784), and indeed to prevent the very existence of a juvenile "arrest" record, by using the phrase "taken into custody" instead of "arrest" (Fam.Ct.Act, secs. 721–724). Certainly, these provisions were intended to be more than "an empty gesture" (see Lang, above, 21 A.D.2d at pp. 110–111, 248 N.Y.S.2d at pp. 553–554; also Anonymous v. N.Y.C. Transit Authority, 4 A.D.2d 953, 167 N.Y.S.2d 715 (2nd Dept., 1957); and the courts must effectuate the legislative intent when it is frustrated by unforeseen practices.

---

[6] See e.g., McGovern v. Van Riper, 137 N.J.Eq. 24, 43 A.2d 514, 519 (1955); State ex rel. Reed v. Harris, 348 Mo. 426, 153 S.W.2d 834 (1941); People ex rel. Gow v. Bingham, 57 Misc. 66, 75, 107 N.Y.S. 1011, 1017 (Sup.Ct.Kings, 1907) (approved in Hawkins v. Kuhne, 153 App. Div. 216, 219, 137 N.Y.S. 1090, 1091, 2nd Dept., 1912, aff'd 208 N.Y. 555, 101 N.E. 1104), granting injunctive relief against dissemination of fingerprints or photographs prior to conviction because of defamatory connotation; see also Application of American Society for Testing and Materials, 231 F.Supp. 686, 689 (E.D.Pa. 1964).

4. It might be argued that relief is inappropriate because there has been no proof of the imminence of injury to respondents from the instant records. But the appearance as well as the actuality of fairness is essential in the administration of justice. To maintain records of unproven charges against respondents appears unfair, because of the potential harm from these waste-products of the legal system, even if they are never in fact used adversely. Respondents should be freed from the fear of an unfair handicap in securing employment—particularly in the civil service, which offers a primary path for upward mobility to minority youths like respondents.

Furthermore, it is unfeasible to condition relief on an actual or imminent adverse use of the records because respondents may be unaware that their records are the cause of a rejection for employment. Compare Serrales v. Viader, 149 N.Y.S.2d 175 (Sup.Ct.N.Y., 1954) affirmed 285 App.Div. 947, 139 N.Y.S.2d 896. Thus, orders of expungement have been issued without such a showing, so that an arrestee would not be "haunted" indefinitely by his record (see United States v. Kalish, 271 F.Supp. 968, 970 (D.P.R.1967)).

* * *

While there is a division of authority as to the instant type of motion, this court holds that respondents are entitled to relief with respect to their records on the four grounds above-stated; further, that relief in the form of expungement should be granted, because an order merely prohibiting dissemination of their Court and arrest records would be inadequate.[7] Respectfully disagreeing with Weisberg v. Police Dept., 46 Misc.2d 846, 847, 260 N.Y.S.2d 554, 555 (Sup. Ct.Nassau, 1965), in this Court's opinion an expungement order based on an adversary proceeding does not conflict with the salutary statutes prohibiting public officers, on their own, from destroying public records.

D. *Propriety of Grant of Relief by this Court*

Clearly this Court, like all courts, has inherent power over its own records, including the power to expunge or obliterate them. And relief in the instant case is dictated by the principle that a court must exercise its power over its records when necessary to prevent injustice and unwarranted injury—that a court "will not allow itself to be made the instrument of wrong".

This Court's power to order a change in the Police Department's juvenile arrest records is implicit in the authority granted it in section 784 of the Family Court Act as to their inspection, which has received a broad construction. Such power should also be deemed ancillary to the Court's broad powers in juvenile delinquency cases. A major

---

[7] While such an order was viewed as the maximum proper relief in some police record cases (see Roesch v. Ferber, 48 N.J.Super. 231, 137 A.2d 61, 65, 1957, cited by petitioners) it appears insufficient for several reasons: (1) employers could nevertheless secure Court and arrest records through requiring a waiver of confidentiality; (2) use of the records by law-enforcement officers themselves is unjustifiable and potentially harmful; and (3) preservation of the records even with this prohibition would not erase the fear of their disclosure and the appearance of unfairness.

criterion as to ancillary jurisdiction is whether the court needs the additional authority in order to implement its decisions. Certainly this Court's governance of respondents' arrest records is necessary to secure to them the full benefit of its order approving withdrawal of the petitions. And this Court's control of the effects of a juvenile arrest is highly appropriate, considering that the arrest is merely preparatory and preliminary to a Court proceeding.

*   *   *

This Court, therefore, rejects the argument that only a court of general equitable jurisdiction has the power to direct a change in the police records, and it holds that it has concurrent authority over them as well as over its own records. The Family Court was intended to have wide powers and wide discretion "so that its action may fit the particular needs of those before it". With this function and with its expertise on the dilemmas facing underprivileged youth, it is incumbent upon *this* Court to undertake responsibility for fulfilling the hope and the promise that a youth will suffer no impediments in his future because of his juvenile record.

E. *Form of Order*

In order to preserve, with a minimum of administrative effort, a record of the petitions and arrests for use in statistical or other surveys, the requested destruction of the records herein will not be directed. Appropriate and adequate relief will be secured by the physical obliteration of the surnames of respondents and of their parents from the docket books, files, cards and all other records in the office of the Clerk of this Court and the offices of the Police Department (except for the Court petition itself), such obliterations to be made in the presence of respondents and/or their attorney at a time convenient to the parties within thirty days. The Clerk of this Court is to place the petitions in a sealed file separate from the regular petition files.

The reason for preservation of the petition is that employers frequently commence their investigation of an applicant by asking him if he has ever been arrested or taken into custody or appeared in court. Complete protection for respondents and other juveniles from unfair discrimination due to untenable arrests and dismissed charges can only be afforded by a statutory prohibition on employers' inquiries or a statutory procedure for nullifying abortive arrests.[8] Absent such legislation, job applicants who admit an arrest may be rejected out-of-hand; if the employer is willing to make further inquiry, however, it would be to respondents' interest to secure a certificate detailing from the endorsements on the petition the precise history of this proceeding.

[8] See statutes collected in Expungement of Adjudication Records, cited above note 1, Wash.Univ.Law Quart. at 172, 174–178; Note, Employment of Former Criminals, 55 Cornell Law.Journ. (1970) 306, 315–316, as to California statute providing that under specified circumstances an individual is permitted to deem an arrest a nullity, so that he may validly answer in the negative the question "Were you ever arrested?"

NOTES

1.   In Edward M. v. O'Neill, 291 Pa.Super. 531, 436 A.2d 628 (1981) the court detailed the circumstances under which a person has a due process right to expungement of juvenile records.

* * *

B

Next we address the propriety of Judge Dandridge's orders of August 21, 1979, granting the petitions to expunge the fingerprints and photographs of the individual juveniles.   The issue before us is whether expungement is the proper remedy regardless of the possible merit to the petitioners' claim.

The Commonwealth argues that the juvenile petitioners were not legally entitled to the remedy of expungement.   In support of this contention the Commonwealth cites Commonwealth v. Malone, 244 Pa.Super. 62, 366 A.2d 584 (1976).   In that case we held that in certain circumstances due process guarantees an individual the right to have his arrest record expunged.   In a subsequent case, Commonwealth v. Rose, 263 Pa.Super. 349, 351, 397 A.2d 1243, 1244 (1979), we relied on *Malone* in stating:

> The judicial remedy of expunction is an adjunct to the inherent rights of Due Process and is not dependent on express statutory authority. However, expunction is proper only in cases where acquittal is consistent with a finding of real innocence and is not a result of legal technicalities unrelated to questions of guilt or innocence.

Thus where an accused is indicted but never tried because the indictments were *nol prossed* upon the district attorney's confession that he would be unable to establish a prima facie case at trial, due process requires the Commonwealth to present compelling evidence justifying retention of the arrest record.   * * * However, where the record shows that the Commonwealth made out a prima facie case of guilt on the part of the accused, he will then have the burden to affirmatively demonstrate nonculpability, otherwise his petition to expunge will be denied.   Commonwealth v. Mueller, 258 Pa.Super. 219, 223, 392 A.2d 763, 765 (1978).   If nonculpability is established, the court must weigh the Commonwealth's interest in retaining the accused's arrest record against the accused's interest in being free from whatever disabilities the record may create.   Id.

In Commonwealth v. Briley, 278 Pa.Super. 363, 420 A.2d 582 (1980) the remedy of expungement was extended to the petitioners who had successfully completed the Accelerated Rehabilitative Disposition Program (hereafter ARD), see Pa.R.Crim.P. 175 et seq., 42 Pa.C.S.A.   There we held that the Commonwealth has the burden of justifying retention of the individual's arrest record.

As noted above, the judicial remedy of expungement is an adjunct to due process and proper where acquittal is consistent with a finding of real innocence.   Although ARD cannot be said to be equivalent to a finding of "real innocence", this court relied on the *Malone* and *Rose* line of cases in concluding that ARD program participants may be entitled to expungement. First, while acknowledging that placement in ARD is not a jury's acquittal, we stated that in practical effect the program is not that different in that once the candidate successfully completes the program, the Commonwealth was forever barred from convicting him on the charges lodged.   As a second reason for holding that expungement is an available remedy we stated:

Here, by moving the lower court for appellant's admission into the ARD program, the Commonwealth demonstrated its belief that the nature of appellant's offense and his background and character were such that the interests of society would be best served were he not prosecuted, but diverted out of the criminal justice system as quickly as possible.

278 Pa.Super. 363, 420 A.2d at 586.

In the instant case Judge Dandridge ordered the expungement of all photographs and fingerprint records of juvenile appellees, Ronald Forrest and Vander Clayborne. Both appellees had been adjudicated delinquent on the charges for which they had been photographed and fingerprinted prior to the orders of Judge Dandridge. Given this, appellants argue that the juveniles would not have been stigmatized by the retention of these records and are therefore not entitled to expungement. We agree.

As discussed at length above, the judicial remedy of expungement is rarely available. Initially we held that expungement is only proper where the defendant is innocent, not where acquittal is the result of legal technicalities. However, a principled extension of the remedy was found in *Briley* because of the singular nature of the ARD program: The similarity between the disposition and a jury's acquittal; the stringent qualifications the individual must possess before the Commonwealth will recommend entry into the program; and the Commonwealth's own admission in recommending ARD that diversion out of the criminal justice system will benefit society. In all cases, however, expungement is rooted in the accused's right to due process, as we stated in Commonwealth v. Malone:

Punishment of the innocent is the clearest denial of life, liberty and property without due process of law. To remedy such a situation, an individual must be afforded a hearing to present his claim that he is entitled to an expungement—that is because an innocent individual has a right to be free from unwarranted punishment, a court has the authority to remedy the denial of that right by ordering expungement of the arrest record.

244 Pa.Super. at 69, 366 A.2d at 588. Thus the remedy of expungement is not available to the appellees because they were adjudicated delinquent. Therefore, even if the photographing and fingerprinting of juveniles were found to be violative of the Juvenile Act, expungement would not be proper.

Id. at 540–43, 436 A.2d at 632–34.

2. In S. v. City of New York, 32 N.Y.2d 592, 347 N.Y.S.2d 54, 300 N.E.2d 426 (1973), the New York Court of Appeals affirmed, "without prejudice to a new application addressed to the discretion of the Family Court, to determine whether or not it should seal the records of this case * * *," an order of the Family Court denying relief to a juvenile whose PINS adjudication was reversed on appeal for failure of proof beyond a reasonable doubt. The juvenile had asked for "the expungement of all court and police records relating to his arrest, trial and adjudication."

3. Statutes authorizing the expungement or sealing of criminal and juvenile records have been supported as enlightened rehabilitative tools. The leading statement of this position appears in Gough, The Expungement of Adjudication Records of Juvenile and Adult Offenders: A Problem of Status, 1966 Wash.U.L.Q. 147. One of the rare statements in opposition to the practice of expungement appears in Kogon & Loughery, Sealing and

Expungement of Criminal Records—The Big Lie, 61 J. of Crim.L., C & PS 378 (1970) in which the authors conclude:

> [W]e reaffirm our conviction that sealing and expungement practices should be abandoned and not merely altered. They have no utility in the administration of criminal justice.

> Criminal and delinquency records can be neither sealed nor destroyed altogether, physically or practically. The record comes out inevitably, with the result that efforts to conceal it work invariably to the offender's detriment.

> Record manipulation does not address itself to the real problem. The pursuit of record manipulation practices results in our deluding ourselves, and, worse, in deluding offenders who have made a good adjustment.

> The only way to breach the barriers standing in the way of an offender's reintegration into the society is to assault them frontally. The remedy lies in a radically different approach—leaving the record alone while constantly striving to improve its quality, and mounting an educational program, with statutory supports, designed to liberalize public attitudes toward offenders.

> All of the above is predicated upon our belief that we must destroy the myth that if we can only find a way to wipe out a "sin" somehow, so that it was really never committed, then and only then can we relate to the offender as a fellow human being. Such a pathway, we are convinced, is illusory, doomed to failure, and only serves to perpetuate a cruel hoax on the offender.

Id. at 391.

IN RE FAKETTY

Michigan Court of Appeals, 1982.
121 Mich.App. 266, 328 N.W.2d 551.

Before R.B. Burns, P.J., and J.H. Gillis and V.J. Brennan, JJ.

Per Curiam.

Patrick Scott Faketty appeals, by leave granted, from a decision of the circuit court which affirmed the probate court's refusal to order the Michigan Department of Corrections to expunge the appellant's juvenile record from its files.

In 1962, appellant, then 11 years old, acquired a juvenile record for malicious destruction of property. On January 22, 1978, he attained the age of 27 years. In August, 1979, appellant was placed under the jurisdiction of the Michigan Department of Corrections. Appellant's juvenile record appeared in the department's files and was allegedly critical to the denial of his requests to participate in community placement programs.

On September 23, 1980, appellant petitioned the probate court, pursuant to JCR 1969, 13, for expunction of his juvenile record and for an order directing the Department of Corrections to expunge the juvenile record from its files. The probate judge granted the petition for expunction of the juvenile record maintained by the probate court. However, he denied the petition regarding expunction of the record from the Michigan Department of Corrections' files on the basis that the department was not a "law enforcement agency" within the meaning of JCR 1969, 13. The probate court's decision was affirmed on appeal to the circuit court. We granted leave to appeal.

JCR 1969, 13 provides:

"The court may retain a child's juvenile court delinquency records other than those involving motor vehicle violations until the child is 27, when they must be expunged. The court may retain a child's motor vehicle violation citations and summonses until the child is 19, when they must be expunged. The court shall expunge neglect records 25 years after its jurisdiction over the last child in the family ends. The court may at any time order the expunction of its own files and records and any law enforcement agency files and records pertaining to a juvenile, including fingerprints and photographs, on a showing of good cause."

This case presents a question of first impression, namely, whether the Department of Corrections is a "law enforcement agency" within the meaning of JCR 1969, 13.

The Michigan Law Enforcement Officers Training Council Act of 1965, section 2(c), M.C.L. § 28.602(c); M.S.A. § 4.450(2)(c), contains the following definition:

" 'Police officer' or 'law enforcement officer' means a member of a police force or other organization of a city, county, township, village or of the state, regularly employed as such and *who is responsible for the prevention and detection of crime and the enforcement of the general criminal laws of this state,* but shall not include any person serving as such solely by virtue of his occupying any other office or position." (Emphasis added.)

See also, OAG, 1977–1978, No. 5133, p. 83 (April 1, 1977).

We believe that, as used in JCR 1969, 13, the term "law enforcement agency" refers to those agencies charged with the prevention and detection of crime and enforcement of the general criminal laws of this state.

The jurisdiction of the Department of Corrections is set forth in M.C.L. § 791.204; M.S.A. § 28.2274:

"Subject to constitutional powers vested in the executive and judicial departments of the state, the department shall have exclusive jurisdiction over the following: (a) Probation officers of this state, and the administration of all orders of probation, (b) pardons, reprieves, commutations and paroles, and (c) penal institutions, correctional farms, probation recovery camps, prison labor and industry, wayward minor programs and youthful trainee institutions and programs for the care and supervision of youthful trainees."

The powers which the Legislature has extended to the department are related solely to the administration of penal institutions, probation, pardons, paroles and commutations and other aspects of the department's corrections functions. It is clear that the department is not charged with the enforcement of the general criminal laws of this state. The probate court and the circuit court correctly ruled that the department is not a "law enforcement agency" within JCR 1969, 13.

Appellant also contends that expunction of the juvenile record from the department's files is required because, had the court rule been complied with, the department would never have received the record. Appellant argues that upon attaining the age of 27 on January 22, 1978, the record should have been expunged. Appellate contends that since he did not come under the jurisdiction of the department until August, 1979, had the court rule been complied with, the department would never have received information pertaining to his juvenile record. We disagree.

The mandatory expunction provided in JCR 1969, 13, applies only to the probate court's own records. The expunction of law enforcement agency files is discretionary, to be granted upon a showing of good cause. In the present case, appellant did not petition the juvenile court to expunge his juvenile record from law enforcement agency files until September 23, 1980, long after he came under the jurisdiction of the Department of Corrections. Therefore, the juvenile record was properly available to the department through the files of the law enforcement agencies whose records were not expunged until October, 1980. Moreover, the juvenile record was available to the department through a presentence report prepared by federal court authorities pursuant to a 1970 federal conviction.

Affirmed.

V.J. BRENNAN, JUDGE (dissenting).

I respectfully dissent. I find that the Department of Corrections is a "law enforcement agency" for the purposes of JCR 1969, 13 because the courts and police agencies cannot enforce the law without the department. I cannot agree with the majority's finding that the department's powers are related solely to administration.

Moreover, a finding that the Department of Corrections is a "law enforcement agency" is a reasonable interpretation which supports what appears to me to be the purpose of the rule, to give an individual a fresh start. The majority's construction allows the Department of Corrections to have an individual's juvenile record before a review panel when it decides whether to grant or deny prisoner requests, perhaps becoming a factor in its decision making.[9] On the other hand, the courts and other agencies do not have access to those records per JCR 1969, 13. If a court or law enforcement agency is restricted from using a juvenile record because of the

---

[9] In this case, appellant acquired a juvenile record in Schoolcraft County for malicious destruction of property. Appellant was 11 years old at the time. Appellant's juvenile record was allegedly critical to the Department of Corrections' denial of his requests for an opportunity to participate in various work release programs.

expunction of the record, how does the Department of Corrections obtain any greater privilege or right to the juvenile record? Surely, priorities would dictate that the courts have all available information about a defendant at the sentencing stage. Since the rule prohibits the courts from having access to the juvenile record at that critical stage, I think it naturally follows that the rule was also intended to prohibit the Department of Corrections, as a law enforcement agency, from having access to the record. Therefore, I would order the expunction of the appellant's juvenile record from the file of the Department of Corrections.

B. COLLATERAL USES OF JUVENILE RECORDS

1. USE OF JUVENILE RECORDS IN SUBSEQUENT CRIMINAL CASES

Some statutes and court rules prohibit the use of any evidence given in any juvenile case in any other case, civil or criminal. Other statutes authorize the limited use of juvenile "law enforcement records" to aid in the investigation and prosecution of later juvenile or criminal cases. And the student will recall (See Chapter 3, section E, supra) that the circumstances under which physical evidence may be obtained from juveniles are circumscribed by constitutional limitations as well as by legislation and judicial decisions.

IJA–ABA JUVENILE JUSTICE STANDARDS, STANDARDS RELATING TO JUVENILE RECORDS AND INFORMATION SYSTEMS (1980).

19.6 Juveniles' fingerprints; photographs *

* * *

B. If latent fingerprints are found during the investigation of an offense and a law enforcement officer has reason to believe that they are those of the juvenile in custody, he or she may fingerprint the juvenile regardless of age or offense for purposes of immediate comparison with the latent fingerprints. If the comparison is negative, the fingerprint card and other copies of the fingerprints taken should be immediately destroyed. If the comparison is positive and the juvenile is referred to court, the fingerprint card and other copies of the fingerprints should be delivered to the court for disposition. If the juvenile is not referred to court, the prints should be immediately destroyed.

C. If the court finds that a juvenile has committed an offense that would be a felony for an adult, the prints may be retained by the local law enforcement agency or sent to the [state depository] provided that they be kept separate from those of adults under special security measures limited to inspection for comparison purposes by law enforcement officers or by staff of the [state depository] only in the investigation of a crime.

* Reprinted with permission from Standards Relating to Juvenile Records and   Information Systems, Copyright 1980, Ballinger Publishing Company.

* * *

E. Any photographs of juveniles, authorized under subsection D., that are retained by a law enforcement agency should be destroyed:

> 1. immediately, if it is concluded that the juvenile did not commit the offense which is the subject of investigation; or

> 2. upon a judicial determination that the juvenile is not delinquent; or

> 3. when the juvenile's police record is destroyed pursuant to Standard 22.1.

WEST VIRGINIA CODE ANNOTATED (1980)

§ 49–7–3. Proceedings under chapter not to be evidence against child, or be published; adjudication not deemed conviction and not bar to civil service eligibility.

Any evidence given in any cause or proceeding under this chapter, or any order, judgment or finding therein, or any adjudication upon the status of juvenile delinquent heretofore made or rendered, shall not in any civil, criminal or other cause or proceeding whatever in any court, be lawful or proper evidence against such child for any purpose whatsoever except in subsequent cases under this chapter involving the same child; nor shall the name of any child, in connection with any proceedings under this chapter, be published in any newspaper without a written order of the court; nor shall any such adjudication upon the status of any child by a juvenile court operate to impose any of the civil disabilities ordinarily imposed by conviction, nor shall any child be deemed a criminal by reason of such adjudication, nor shall such adjudication be deemed a conviction, nor shall any such adjudication operate to disqualify a child in any future civil service examination, appointment, or application.

ILLINOIS ANNOTATED STATUTES, Chapter 37
(1984–5 P.P.Supp.)

702–8. Confidentiality of law enforcement records

§ 2–8. Confidentiality of Law Enforcement Records. (A) Inspection and copying of law enforcement records maintained by law enforcement agencies which relate to a minor who has been arrested or taken into custody before his 17th birthday shall be restricted to the following:

(1) Any local, State or federal law enforcement officers of any jurisdiction or agency when necessary for the discharge of their official duties during the investigation or prosecution of a crime which would be a felony if committed by an adult.

(2) Prosecutors, probation officers, social workers, or other individuals assigned by the court to conduct a pre-adjudication or pre-disposition investigation, and individuals responsible for supervising or providing temporary or permanent care and custody for minors

pursuant to the order of the juvenile court, when essential to performing their responsibilities.

(3) Prosecutors and probation officers:

(a) In the course of a trial when institution of criminal proceedings has been permitted under Section 2–7 or required under Section 2–7; or

(b) When institution of criminal proceedings has been permitted under Section 2–7 or required under Section 2–7 and such minor is the subject of a proceeding to determine the amount of bail; or

(c) When criminal proceedings have been permitted under Section 2–7 or required under Section 2–7 and such minor is the subject of a pre-trial investigation, pre-sentence investigation, fitness hearing, or proceedings on an application for probation.

(4) Adult and Juvenile Prisoner Review Board.

(5) Authorized military personnel.

(6) Persons engaged in bona fide research, with the permission of the Presiding Judge of the Juvenile Court and the chief executive of the respective law enforcement agency; provided that publication of such research results in no disclosure of a minor's identity and protects the confidentiality of the minor's record.

(B) No law enforcement officer or other person or agency may knowingly transmit to the Department of Corrections, Adult Division or the Department of Law Enforcement or to the Federal Bureau of Investigation any fingerprint or photograph relating to a minor who has been arrested or taken into custody before his 17th birthday, unless the court in proceedings under this Act authorizes the transmission or enters an order under Section 2–7 permitting or requiring the institution of criminal proceedings.

(C) The records of law enforcement officers concerning all minors under 17 years of age must be maintained separate from the records of arrests and may not be open to public inspection or their contents disclosed to the public except by order of the court or when the institution of criminal proceedings has been permitted under Section 2–7 or required under Section 2–7 or such a person has been convicted of a crime and is the subject of pre-sentence investigation or proceedings on an application for probation.

(D) Law enforcement officers may not disclose the identity of any minor in releasing information to the general public as to the arrest, investigation or disposition of any case involving a minor.

STATE v. CONNER

Missouri Court of Appeals, Western District, 1980.
607 S.W.2d 784.

Before WASSERSTROM, C.J., Presiding, and SHANGLER and MANFORD, JJ.

WASSERSTROM, CHIEF JUDGE.

Defendant appeals from his conviction by jury of burglary second degree and stealing. His two Points Relied On are: (1) * * * (2) that the trial court should have suppressed certain fingerprint evidence.

* * *

II.

The crime in this case was committed in November 1978, when a residence was entered by means of breaking a glass pane. The police examined the broken glass and found fingerprints thereon which they sent to the fingerprint examiner employed by the Kansas City, Missouri police department for examination and report. The examiner compared the prints submitted with fingerprints on file, including both those in the adult and those in the juvenile files. In the course of that examination the examiner consulted fingerprint cards taken of defendant in 1973, under an order of the juvenile court, when defendant was 13 years old. The comparison of the latent prints submitted by the police with the 1973 prints on record showed the fingerprints from the scene of the crime to be those of defendant.

Upon receipt of that report the police arrested defendant and took new fingerprints. The new fingerprints were also found to match the latent fingerprints on the broken glass.

Prior to trial, defendant moved to suppress from use in evidence the 1973 fingerprint record and also the 1978 fingerprint record. With respect to the 1973 fingerprints, defendant argues that its use would violate (and he now argues that its use did violate) Rule 122.03, which substantially rescripts Section 211.321(2). That Rule provides:

> "All records of juveniles made and retained by law enforcement officers and agencies shall be kept separate from the records of other persons and shall not be open to inspection or their contents disclosed or distributed, except by order of the judge of the juvenile court. This Rule shall not apply to all such records of a juvenile in a case in which the court has dismissed the petition under Rule 118.04 to permit prosecution under the general law. The term 'records', as used in this Rule, shall include but is not limited to fingerprints and photographs of the juvenile." [10]

Defendant further argues that the use of the 1978 fingerprint cards was unlawful, because those prints were taken in connection with an unlawful arrest which was "the fruit of a poisoned tree."

To support his position that the use of the 1973 prints directly, and the 1978 prints indirectly, violated Rule 122.03, defendant argues

---

[10] Defendant makes no reliance on Section 211.271(3) which prohibits use as evidence of "all reports and records of the juvenile court." Defendant concedes that fingerprints taken under the circumstances such as here are admissible in evidence under State v. Jones, 571 S.W.2d 741 (Mo.App.1978). However, no argument was made or considered in *Jones* respecting Section 211.321(2) or Rule 122.03.

"that before the fingerprints of a person, taken when he was a juvenile by order of the juvenile court, can be used for a purpose other than that for which they were originally ordered to be taken, there must be a further order of the juvenile court permitting their further use." Defendant offers no citation of authority to support that broad statement as to the effect of Rule 122.03. We cannot accept the construction so suggested.

Rather the purpose of Rule 122.03 and the related statute appears to be to prevent a broad, unrestricted use of juvenile records by the general public. This was the general objective to which the prohibition was addressed, as indicated by the opinion in State ex rel. Arbeiter v. Reagan, 427 S.W.2d 371, l.c. 377 (Mo. banc 1968) where the court remarked upon concerns "that in practice juvenile records are widely circulated to law enforcement officers, social agencies, the FBI and even to prospective employers." So also in Nation Juvenile Law Center, Law and Tactics in Juvenile Cases (2d Ed.1974), at page 161, in speaking of abuse of juvenile records, it is stated that "it is common for law enforcement agencies to exchange fingerprint records, or to transmit them to the central depository maintained by the Federal Bureau of Investigation. Once taken, fingerprints will normally be retained in the permanent files of these agencies, where access to them may be open to virtually countless persons and agencies." Further demonstrating this worry about the potential for abuse is the inquiry which led to Op.Atty.Gen. No. 93 (Jan. 16, 1958), in which questions were put by the Missouri State Highway Patrol to the Missouri Attorney General as to whether juvenile records might be furnished to the National Automobile Theft Bureau and similar agencies, to insurance companies and attorneys interested in civil actions, and to other law enforcement agencies and authorities.

As still further evidence of this basic underlying concern to provide a curb on overbroad general public usage, see Comment to Rule 122.01 which states: "No apparent reason exists why the court cannot, in granting consent to fingerprint or photograph a juvenile, impose limiting conditions upon its consent, such as that neither the originals nor copies of the fingerprints or photographs be released to other municipal, state or federal agencies without express consent of the court." See also the Comment to Rule 122.02 which states that that rule and the cognate statute (which provides that juvenile records "shall be open to inspection only by order of the judge of the juvenile court") "represents a public policy decision by the General Assembly to ensure the confidential, *nonpublic* nature of juvenile court records." (emphasis added)

The use of the defendant's 1973 fingerprint records in this case was not of a nature within the concern outlined above. The use here was not a general public use, but instead was restricted to a narrow use for local investigations by the very agency which originally took the prints under order of the juvenile court and which has had custody of the fingerprint cards ever since. The use of the 1973 fingerprint records made in this case did not violate the policy or scope of Rule 122.03 or the related statute. The motion to suppress was therefore properly overruled. Defendant's point 2 is disallowed.

The judgments of conviction and sentence are affirmed.

All concur.

NOTES

1.

"When the appellant was originally fingerprinted by Wheeling police, one set of prints was sent to the latent fingerprint section of the FBI in Washington, D.C. These prints were the ones used for the comparisons. Consequently, the State urges us to hold that the expungement requirement of W.Va.Code, 49–5–17 [11] does not apply to any federal body, and that juvenile fingerprint cards in federal records may be used for identification purposes. This we refuse to do. The Legislature has clearly indicated its intent that juvenile records not be used for any purpose other than those specifically provided for by statute. If the Legislature had intended to do what the State urges us to do, it would have done so. As we said in *Van Isler*, supra: 'We will not expand upon the legislatively created exceptions to the legislatively imposed general rule of confidentiality of juvenile records.' Id. at 838.

It is undisputed that the fingerprints used for the comparisons were taken from the appellant when he was a juvenile, in connection with juvenile proceedings. The admission into evidence of the juvenile fingerprint card and the results of comparisons between that card and prints lifted from the scene of the break-in was error requiring reversal of the appellant's conviction. It is, therefore, not necessary to consider the appellant's argument based on W.Va.Code, 49–7–3, which deals with evidence given in a juvenile proceeding."

State v. Lucas, 299 S.E.2d 21, 22–3 (W.Va.1982).

2. The student should consider the efficacy of various sanctions for violating confidentiality requirements. Suppose the police fail to follow a court order requiring expungement, and the non-expunged material is later used in identifying the "once-juvenile-now-adult" as the perpetrator of another crime? Or, suppose, instead, that a statute commands automatic expungement under particular circumstances and the statute is violated? Consider these questions in light of Commonwealth v. Gordon, 621 S.W.2d 27 (Ky.1981):

The sole issue on this appeal is whether a photograph of a juvenile, retained in violation of KRS 208.196 and used as identification of a suspect (then an adult) in a criminal prosecution, is a violation of the fourth amendment.

Following the commission of an armed robbery in July of 1979, the victims viewed numerous photographs on the wall of Louisville police

---

[11] W.Va.Code, 49–5–17(a) [1978] provides:

"One year after the child's eighteenth birthday, or one year after personal or juvenile jurisdiction shall have terminated, whichever is later, the records of a juvenile proceeding conducted under this chapter, including law-enforcement files and records, fingerprints, physical evidence and all other records pertaining to said proceeding shall be expunged by operation of law. When records are expunged, they shall be returned to the court in which the case was pending and kept in a separate confidential file and not opened except upon order of the court."

headquarters. One of them was that of respondent, taken 16 days before his eighteenth birthday. It was there in relation to another totally unrelated criminal charge. One of the witnesses tentatively identified respondent. Following his subsequent arrest, respondent agreed to a line-up where he was positively identified.

Following a suppression hearing, the trial court admitted evidence of the photograph and evidence of the line-up. The Court of Appeals, in a split decision, reverse the trial court, based on the admitted violation of KRS 208.196. We disagree.

Essentially, the Court of Appeals ruled that since the photograph was illegally retained by the police, its use in identification was unconstitutional and any evidence flowing from said use was, in effect, the "fruit of the poisonous tree". KRS 208.196 is as follows:

"Physical evidence—How obtained and utilized—Disposition. (1) Physical evidence shall be obtained and utilized in the investigation of public offenses involving children in the same manner as it is obtained and utilized the investigation of public offenses involving adults. (2) All records and physical evidence so obtained shall be surrendered to the court upon elimination of a child as a suspect in the case. (3) Any person who violates the provisions of this section shall be guilty of a class B misdemeanor."

This statute is clearly for the benefit and for protection of juveniles. It does not actually or impliedly confer any constitutional rights on the protected parties. It provides a method of enforcement by providing misdemeanor sanctions. In the present case respondent was an adult when the photograph was viewed and is, therefore, not within the protective aegis of the statute. The statute is a deterrent to specific conduct of police authorities and is not constitutional in nature.

The decision of the Court of Appeals is reversed and the judgment of the trial court is reinstated.

2. USE OF JUVENILE RECORDS IN ADULT SENTENCING

YOUNG v. STATE

Oklahoma Court of Criminal Appeals, 1976.
553 P.2d 192.

OPINION

BLISS, JUDGE:

Petitioner, Terry Ray Young, was convicted upon his plea of guilty in the District Court, Tulsa County, Case No. CRF–75–2699, for the offense of Unauthorized Use of a Motor Vehicle, in violation of 47 O.S.1971, § 4–102. Pursuant thereto, the trial court sentenced the petitioner to a term of imprisonment of eighteen (18) months. Petitioner timely filed a motion to withdraw his plea of guilty, which upon hearing was overruled by the District Court, Tulsa County, and from this ruling the instant petition for writ of certiorari has been filed in this Court. We assume jurisdiction and proceed to dispose of the matter.

The instant appeal is predicated solely upon the contention that the trial court, at the sentencing hearing, erred in considering a presentence investigation and report [12] which contained specific references to the petitioner's prior juvenile record.   The petitioner contends that consideration of a prior juvenile record is an improper consideration in determining what sentence will be imposed against an adult offender and such a consideration violates the statutory proscription in 10 O.S.1971, § 1127, and this Court's prior holding in Lauen v. State, Okl.Cr., 515 P.2d 578 (1973).   Title 10 O.S.1971, § 1127, provides in pertinent part:

> "* * * A disposition of any child under this Act, or any evidence given in such cause, shall not in any civil, criminal or other cause or proceeding in any court be lawful or proper evidence against the child for any purpose whatever, except in subsequent cases against the same child under this Act * * *."

Petitioner alludes to this Court's language in Lauen v. State, supra, wherein the Court states:

> "* * * They [juvenile records] are not a proper consideration in the assessment of the punishment to be imposed upon defendant. Although the above section of the statute refers to 'evidence given in such cause,' it is this Court's opinion the language 'for any purpose whatever' prohibits the use of these records in an argument.   Consequently, the manifestation of a juvenile record influencing an imposed punishment will be grounds for modification."

Thus at issue is this Court's prior construction of 10 O.S.1971, § 1127, concluding that the statute prohibits use of an adult offender's prior juvenile record during an aggravation mitigation hearing as

---

[12] Title 22 O.S.Supp.1975, § 982, mandatorily provides for a presentence investigation and report as follows:

"Whenever a person is convicted of a felony except when the death sentence is imposed, the court shall, before imposing sentence to commit any felon to incarceration by the Department of Corrections, order a presentence investigation to be made by the Division of Probation and Parole of the Department. The Division shall thereupon inquire into the circumstances of the offense, and the criminal record, social history and present condition of the convicted person; and shall make a report of such investigation to the court, including a recommendation as to appropriate sentence, and specifically a recommendation for or against probation. Such reports must be presented to the judge so requesting, within a reasonable time, and upon the failure to so present the same, the judge may proceed with sentencing. Whenever, in the opinion of the court or the Division, it is desirable, the in-

vestigation shall include a physical and mental examination of the convicted person. The reports so received shall not be referred to, or be considered, in any appeal proceedings. Before imposing sentence, the court shall advise the defendant or his counsel and the district attorney of the factual contents and the conclusions of any presentence investigation or psychiatric examination and afford fair opportunity, if the defendant so requests, to controvert them. If either the defendant or the district attorney desires, such hearing shall be ordered by the court providing either party an opportunity to offer evidence proving or disproving any finding contained in such report, which shall be a hearing in mitigation or aggravation of punishment.

"If the district attorney and the defendant desire to waive such presentence investigation and report, both shall execute a suitable waiver subject to approval of the court, whereupon the judge shall proceed with the sentencing."

contemplated by 22 O.S.1971, § 973,[13] and the applicability of this construction to the use of a presentence investigation report containing the prior juvenile record of an adult offender before the court.

We are compelled to re-examine and ascertain the intent of the legislative enactment, 10 O.S.1971, § 1127, and the viability of our holding in Lauen v. State, supra.

Many states have statutory provisions comparably worded to 10 O.S.1971, § 1127, and its apparent restriction of the use of juvenile records. Particularly instructive is the lengthy discourse in People v. McFarlin, 389 Mich. 557, 208 N.W.2d 504, 64 A.L.R.3d 1274 (1973), wherein a statute comparably worded to 10 O.S.1971, § 1127, was construed not to prohibit a presentence investigation report from including information concerning the juvenile history of an adult offender. The court observed that decisions of other states although not controlling, revealed the clear weight of judicial authority is in favor of full disclosure of a defendant's past, including his juvenile court history, to the sentencing judge. People v. McFarlin, 208 N.W.2d 510. * * *

We note that the heretofore quoted portion of the language of 10 O.S.1971, § 1127, has been carried forward without substantial change since the legislative enactment in S.L.1909, Ch. 13, Art. I, § 594, which in pertinent part reads:

> "* * * A disposition of any child under this Act or any evidence given in such cause, shall not in any civil, criminal or other cause or proceedings whatever in any court be lawful or proper evidence against such child for any purpose whatever, except in subsequent cases against the same child under this Act. * * *"

The intent of this particular statutory language obviously was formulated several decades prior to the enactment of the presentence investigation report procedure. At the time of the drafting of this statutory language, the trial judge in determining the sentence, in a situation where discretion of sentence was conferred upon the court, would only have the alternative of hearing other evidence in mitigation or aggravation of punishment upon motion by either party. Greater emphasis is now placed upon a particularized sentence for a particular individual, and this is evidenced by the enacted presentence investigation procedure and the particular statutes regarding the sentencing powers of the court * * *.

In Williams v. New York, 337 U.S. 241, 69 S.Ct. 1079, 93 L.Ed. 1337 (1949), the Supreme Court of the United States stated:

---

[13] Title 22 O.S.1971, § 973, provides as follows:

"After a plea or verdict of guilty in a case where the extent of the punishment is left with the court, upon the suggestion of either party that there are circumstances which may be properly taken into view, either in aggravation or mitigation of the punishment, may in its discretion hear the same summarily at a specified time and upon such notice to the adverse party as it may direct."

"* * * Highly relevant—if not essential—to his selection of an appropriate sentence is the possession of the fullest information possible concerning the defendant's life and characteristics. And modern concepts individualizing punishment have made it all the more necessary that a sentencing judge not be denied an opportunity to obtain pertinent information by a requirement of rigid adherence to restrictive rules of evidence properly applicable to the trial.

*   *   *

"Under the practice of individualizing punishments, investigational techniques have been given an important role. Probation workers making reports of their investigations have not been trained to prosecute but to aid offenders. Their reports have been given a high value by conscientious judges who want to sentence persons on the best available information rather than on guesswork and inadequate information * * *." (Footnotes omitted)

In People v. McFarlin, supra, the court observed:

"The modern view of sentencing is that the sentence should be tailored to the particular circumstances of the case and the offender in an effort to balance both society's need for protection and its interest in maximizing the offender's rehabilitative potential. While the resources allocated for rehabilitation may be inadequate and some persons question whether rehabilitation can be achieved in the prison setting, this view of sentencing is the present policy of the state. A judge needs complete information to set a proper individualized sentence. A defendant's juvenile court history may reveal a pattern of law-breaking and his response to previous rehabilitative efforts. This, together with information concerning underlying social or family difficulties, and a host of other facts are essential to an informed sentencing decision, especially if the offender is a young adult.

"Some adult offenders may indeed serve longer prison sentences because of information developed from the official juvenile court record. But others, because the presentence report is a complete and reliable chronicle, may serve shorter sentences or not be imprisoned at all. Such differentiation in sentencing predicated on differences in the backgrounds of offenders is contemplated by the indeterminate sentencing and probation acts. The objectives of those acts and of the restriction on the use of a juvenile record are entirely reconcilable."

Thus, the court concluded that a presentence investigation and report may contain the juvenile history of the adult offender. Also, in Berfield v. State, 458 P.2d 1008 (Alaska 1969), the Alaska court stated:

"A judge, of all persons, should be most cognizant of the existence and meaning of AS 47.10.080(g), and of the fact that under that statute a juvenile offender may not be considered a criminal even though he has suffered a criminal conviction. But the judge cannot simply ignore that phase of appellant's life— before he reached 18 years of age—as though it did not exist— particularly when appellant was only 21 years old when sentenced. The judge is not required to operate in a vacuum. In sentencing a 21 year old person, the life, characteristics, and background behavior of that person prior to reaching the age of 18 years might be highly relevant. It should be noted that the judge cannot consider a juvenile offense as a criminal conviction for the purpose of prescribing a mandatory sentence. But that was not done in this case. The judge's consideration of factors relating to appellant's life, characteristics, background and behavior prior to reaching the age of 18 years does not mean that he considered appellant a criminal or that he was using the juvenile offenses as criminal convictions in determining the sentence to impose." (Footnotes omitted)

In Walker v. State, Tex.Cr.App., 493 S.W.2d 239 (1973), the Texas Court observed:

"It makes a great deal of sense that the judge should have before him a thorough report of the accused's past record and background, when considering his motion for probation. The very purpose of granting probation is to release a convicted defendant who shows himself capable of adhering to certain conditions. The present appellant was 18 years old at the time of trial. The principles just enunciated apply even more so in such a case. It would be ridiculous to conclude that an 18-year-old with a lengthy juvenile record should be granted the same consideration as someone of the same age with a spotless record."

We are of the opinion that the juvenile history of an adult offender is competent and relevant information of the social history of the adult offender and it is properly included in a presentence investigation and report to facilitate the trial court's determination of the appropriate sentence for the particular adult offender. We conclude that such information is not "evidence against the child" within the proscription of 10 O.S.1971, § 1127. In Mitchell v. Gladden, 229 Or. 192, 366 P.2d 907 (1961), that court noted:

"* * * There is no proscription against the use of such evidence against a person after he has reached his majority. The obvious purpose of the statute is to protect a child from the stigma of his wrongdoing in his effort to rehabilitate himself. When he is no longer a child and when it is demonstrated by his conviction that he has not rehabilitated himself, there is no longer any reason to preclude the use of the evidence in the juvenile proceedings for the purpose of fixing his sentence * * *."

Consistent with our conclusion is the fact that the Legislature has not enacted mandatory expungement statutes. Our current expungement statute, 10 O.S.1971, § 1506, reads as follows:

"Whenever any person who as a minor has been adjudged to be a delinquent child, or a child in need of supervision, by the District Court or the now defunct juvenile, children's or county court and is reformed and has been of good behavior since reaching majority, the court may upon expiration of five (5) years after said person attains majority upon its own motion or upon the petition of the probation officer or probation counselor, or said person, either with or without a formal hearing as the court determines, ascertain whether said delinquent, or a child in need of supervision, has been of good behavior since majority."

A child who having a juvenile record, upon reaching majority, leads a life of good behavior for five years is entitled to have his records expunged and obliterated. However, the court may continue the matter for a period of one year at its discretion. Certainly the retention of juvenile records must serve some purpose and we find one just and appropriate purpose is the use of a prior juvenile record in the sentencing of an adult offender who obviously has not been benefited from society's efforts to rehabilitate him.

In conclusion we are of the opinion that the trial court's consideration of an adult offender's juvenile record should be limited to the "hard-core" legal facts such as the pertinent facts of adjudication, disposition and the rehabilitative history surrounding the disposition.

For all the above and foregoing reasons, we find the trial court did not err in the consideration of the petitioner's juvenile record as reflected in the presentence investigation and report and thus the petition for certiorari is denied.

Brett, P.J., specially concurs.

Bussey, J., concurs.

Brett, Presiding Judge (specially concurring).

I concur in the decision reached in the majority's opinion. I feel it necessary to emphasize, however, that today's holding is limited to the use of defendant's juvenile court record in a pre-sentencing report authorized by 22 O.S.Supp., § 982, the purpose of which is to aid the trial judge in tailoring punishment to fit the individual offender. These confidential juvenile court records are not directly available, for example, to the office of the prosecutor.

I emphasize also that today's opinion limits the portions of the juvenile records available to the court to "hard-core legal facts such as the pertinent facts of adjudication, disposition and rehabilitative history surrounding the disposition." This limitation upon availability is, I believe, wise and necessary because records made of the social and family history of a juvenile offender often describe in some detail the characteristics, habits and life style of his family, friends and associates which information may not be germane to the decision to be made by the court and may constitute an unreasonable invasion of the privacy of those persons.

NOTES

1.   In In re Robert G., 296 Md. 175, 461 A.2d 1 (1983), the prosecutor sought juvenile records to aid him in determining whether to seek a death sentence.   A section of the Maryland Code authorized disclosure of a juvenile court record "by order of the court upon good cause shown."   The Court of Appeals of Maryland held that the judge who ordered disclosure of the defendant's juvenile record did not abuse his discretion in determining that good cause was shown.

2.   IJA–ABA JUVENILE JUSTICE STANDARDS, STANDARDS RELATING TO JUVENILE RECORDS AND INFORMATION SYSTEMS (1980).

18.4   Admissibility of juvenile records *

An adjudication of any juvenile as a delinquent, or the disposition ordered upon such an adjudication, or any information or record obtained in any case involving such a proceeding, should not be lawful or proper evidence against such juvenile for any purpose in any proceeding except:

A.   in subsequent proceedings against the same juvenile for purposes of disposition or sentencing, if the record of the prior proceeding has not been destroyed;

B.   in an appeal of the same case, information or records obtained for or utilized in the initial trial of the matter should be admissible upon appeal, if the information or record is otherwise lawful and proper evidence; and

C.   in a criminal trial involving the same matter after waiver of juvenile court jurisdiction.   Evidence not otherwise admissible in a criminal trial is not made admissible by its being introduced at the waiver hearing.

3.   USE OF JUVENILE RECORDS TO IMPEACH WITNESSES

STATE v. BROWN

Superior Court of New Jersey, 1975.
132 N.J.Super. 584, 334 A.2d 392.

ALTERMAN, J.D.C., Temporarily Assigned.

This is a motion for discovery in a criminal case.   Defendant stands indicted in two counts for assault with intent to rob while armed.   The victims of the alleged offenses are both juveniles.

Defendant seeks to compel the State to disclose the record of delinquency adjudications against each juvenile or, alternatively, to reveal whether the juveniles are presently on probation and whether juvenile delinquency complaints are now pending against either of them.   The prosecution contends that such information is nondiscoverable because of the State's established policy of maintaining the confidentiality of juvenile proceedings.

The Legislature has provided:

No disposition under this act shall operate to impose any of the civil disabilities ordinarily imposed by virtue of a criminal

---

* Reprinted with permission from Standards Relating to Juvenile Records and   Information Systems, Copyright 1980, Ballinger Publishing Company.

conviction, nor shall a juvenile be deemed a criminal by reason of such disposition.

The disposition of a case under this act shall not be admissible against the juvenile in any criminal or penal case or proceeding in any other court except for consideration in sentencing. [N.J.S.A. 2A:4–64] [14]

But, relying on Davis v. Alaska, 415 U.S. 308, 94 S.Ct. 1105, 39 L.Ed.2d 347 (1974), defendant asserts that his Sixth Amendment right to confrontation is impinged if he is deprived of any information which is useful in affecting a witness' credibility.

In Davis v. Alaska the court examined the conflict between the accused's constitutionally guaranteed right "to be confronted with the witnesses against him" and the state's interest in protecting the anonymity of juvenile offenders. There, the juvenile was a crucial witness in proving defendant's identification, but the trial court prevented the defense from making inquiry as to the witness' probation status under a juvenile court adjudication at the time that he originally identified defendant. The court held that in the attendant circumstances "the right of confrontation is paramount to the State's policy of protecting a juvenile offender." 415 U.S. at 319, 94 S.Ct. at 1113, 39 L.Ed.2d at 355.

Davis does not hold, however, that past adjudications of delinquency are always admissible to affect a witness' credibility. Rather, the language of the court clearly distinguishes between the use of juvenile adjudications for the purpose of impeaching the general credibility of a witness and the use of that evidence in cross-examination to reveal the bias, prejudice or ulterior motive of a witness.

There is no authority in this State for permitting prior adjudications of juvenile delinquency to be used for the purpose of impeaching the general credibility of a witness. On the contrary, use of juvenile adjudications for this purpose has been prohibited—either against a defendant in a criminal case, * * * or against a nonparty witness. * * * New Jersey's policy of maintaining the confidentiality of juvenile proceedings is sustained within present constitutional limits by continuing the distinction made by the court in *Davis.* Accordingly, the motion for disclosure of the witness' record of juvenile adjudications is denied.

The alternative motion for disclosure of juvenile records which would reveal whether the witnesses are presently on probation or whether any juvenile complaint is now pending against them, portends a particularized attack on credibility. In this case, as in the *Davis* case, the juveniles are crucial prosecution witnesses. The Defendant is entitled to have the jury assess their testimony carefully and diligently. Defense counsel bears the burden of exposing any bias, prejudice or ulterior motive that affects the reliability of that

[14] The statute continues the longstanding policy that juvenile convictions may not be used to affect the credibility of a witness. See L.1903, c. 219, as amended by L.1908, c. 236; 2 C.S. 1910.

testimony. This endeavor is severely hampered if the accused is deprived of information which may form the basis of such an attack.

We are committed to the imperative that a trial should serve as a vehicle for the disclosure of the truth. To that end, our rules provide for broad pretrial discovery in criminal cases, and require the prosecution to reveal any relevant record of prior conviction of persons who are known to have relevant evidence or information. R. 3:13–3(a). The necessity for that disclosure in advance of trial is not diminished because the State's witness is a juvenile.

The State's policy of confidentiality of juvenile records is not absolute. While procedural and social records in juvenile matters are required to be safeguarded from indiscriminate public inspection, the court is nevertheless authorized to permit specified persons or agencies to inspect juvenile records upon a showing of good cause. N.J. S.A. 2A:4–65; R. 5:10–7. The defendant's need to prepare an effective cross-examination of a juvenile prosecution witness is a valid reason to disclose otherwise confidential information. Accordingly, for the limited purpose of making a specific attack on the witness' credibility, the alternative motion is granted.

It is the sense of the statutory mandate and of the rule, however, that any disclosure of juvenile records should be strictly circumscribed so that only information required by the particular circumstances is revealed. Therefore, the court will inspect the records, if any, of the proposed juvenile witnesses, and will advise the State and defendant whether each of the juveniles is presently on probation for a juvenile offense and whether any complaints are now pending against each juvenile in the Juvenile and Domestic Relations Court of this county. See State in Interest of A.S., 130 N.J.Super. 388, 327 A.2d 260 (J.D.R.Ct.1974).

NOTES

1. In *Brown*, supra, the juvenile whose record was used to impeach his credibility was the victim of the alleged offenses, i.e. was a witness for the prosecution. In People v. Puente, 98 Ill.App.3d 936, 54 Ill.Dec. 25, 424 N.E.2d 775 (1981), the juvenile record of a witness for the defense was held to be usable to impeach him on the same basis as was used to permit the usage in *Brown*.

2. In Matter of Welfare of C.D.L., 306 N.W.2d 819 (Minn.1981), the Minnesota court permitted the use of juvenile records to impeach a "defense" witness in a juvenile delinquency adjudication hearing.

3. In Camitsch v. Risley, 705 F.2d 351 (9th Cir.1983), the court limited the availability of juvenile records for impeachment to adjudications of delinquency and probation status;

"In Davis v. Alaska, 415 U.S. 308, 94 S.Ct. 1105, 39 L.Ed.2d 347 (1974), the Supreme Court held that Alaska's interest in the confidentiality of a juvenile's record of delinquency must yield to a criminal defendant's right to effective cross-examination where 'serious damage to the State's case would have been a real possibility' had defense counsel been permitted to introduce the prior delinquency adjudication of the witness and his 'vulnerable' status as a probationer as evidence of his pro-prosecution bias. 415 U.S. at 319, 94 S.Ct. at 1111.   Camitsch attempts to expand the right of a criminal defendant under certain circumstances to introduce a juvenile offender's 'record' (i.e., the fact of a delinquency adjudication and probationary status) into a general right to rummage through the otherwise confidential case files of every juvenile witness. *Davis* will not stretch that far.

"In general, when we speak of a witness's or defendant's 'record,' we refer to a set of facts about that person, consisting of each previous arrest, whether the arrest led to conviction, and if so, the sentence imposed and served.   Those facts are usually transcribed onto a single document, which is also called the defendant's 'record' (or sometimes, 'rap sheet').   This is obviously something quite different from: (1) the case file assembled by the prosecutor in relation to each charge against the person; (2) the case file assembled by the prison authorities during his period of incarceration; or (3) the case file assembled by his probation officer during his probationary period.   Yet on occasion all three of these cases files may be referred to generally as 'records,' creating confusion.

"The right which *Davis* extended to encompass juvenile witnesses is the right to impeach a witness by showing that he has a 'record' in the precise, and not the loose, sense of that word—that is, the right to let the jury know that this witness is still facing pending criminal charges, has a prior conviction, or is still on probation.   Such matters tend to give the witness a motive to aid the prosecution, or at least not to give truthful information that might jeopardize his chances to make a favorable plea agreement, shorten his sentence, or finish his probation successfully.   *Davis* was necessary because many states sealed the records of juveniles, so that it was not possible for the jury to find out that the juvenile witness was, for example, on probation at the time he agreed to testify for the prosecution.

"*Davis* does not change the fact, however, that the sensitive, informal information found in a juvenile case file may be shielded from disclosure.   *Davis* makes a careful balancing of the interests of the juvenile and the state in protecting disclosure of the fact of delinquency against the interests of the criminal defendant in showing bias on the part of the juvenile witness.   That balance comes out very differently if the juvenile's interest is not in simply hiding the fact that he has been found delinquent and placed on probation, but in keeping private such information in case files as what his teachers think about him, who his friends are, whether his mother is affectionate or distant, etc., etc., etc.

"In short, *Davis* requires that the fact of adjudication as a delinquent be disclosed along with the fact of probationary status. But it does not require, nor should it be stretched to appear to require, disclosure of the private information found in a juvenile's case file.

"Camitsch also wished to use the information contained in J.E.'s file—informal reports by probation authorities, social workers and psychiatrists—in order to attack her competency as a witness. After an *in camera* inspection and *voir dire* of the witness, the trial judge found her to be competent, and the state supreme court upheld that determination as a matter of state law. 626 P.2d at 1256. Camitsch does not allege that this determination was erroneous, but rather that had he had access to the file he might have been able to persuade the trial court to make a different finding. We are unable to find a constitutional violation on these facts.

Id. at 353–4.

4. IJA–ABA JUVENILE JUSTICE STANDARDS, STANDARDS RELATING TO JUVENILE RECORDS AND INFORMATION SYSTEMS (1980).

5.7 Access to juvenile records for law enforcement or judicial purposes limited *

A. Access to juvenile records should not be provided to a law enforcement agency by a juvenile agency unless:

  1. the consent of the juvenile who is the subject of the record or his or her parents is obtained in accordance with Standard 5.4; or

  2. a judge determines, after *in camera* examination of the record of a designated juvenile, that such access is relevant and necessary.

B. Juvenile records should only be produced for a legal proceeding pursuant to a subpoena.

C. Juvenile records, other than records retained by or for a juvenile court, and the information contained therein, should not be admissible in any proceeding unless:

  1. the juvenile who is the subject of the record or his or her parents consent to the disclosure of the record or information in accordance with Standard 5.4 and the record or information is otherwise admissible; or

  2. a judge determines, after examining the record or information *in camera*, that the record or information is not all or a part of a social or psychological history (prepared by or for a juvenile agency other than a juvenile court), that it is relevant and necessary for the purpose of the proceeding, and that the admission of the record or information is warranted notwithstanding that its admission may be inconsistent with the juvenile's expectation of privacy.

D. In cases in which a juvenile's record is admitted pursuant to subsection C. 2., the reasons for its admission should be set forth in writing and made a part of the record.

4. USE OF JUVENILE RECORDS FOR RESEARCH

NOTE

IJA–ABA JUVENILE JUSTICE STANDARDS, STANDARDS RELATING TO JUVENILE RECORDS AND INFORMATION SYSTEMS (1980).

5.6 Access for research or evaluation *

A. Any person who seeks access to or information from juvenile records for purposes of research or evaluation should file a formal written application with the juvenile agency that has custody of the records. A copy of the application should also be sent to the juveniles' privacy committee.

B. The juvenile agency should approve the application if, after considering the views of the juveniles' privacy committee, and after examining the application, the applicant, and such other information that may be available, the juvenile agency is satisfied that:

  1. the applicant has adequate training and qualifications to undertake the proposed research or evaluation project;

  2. the proposed project is to be undertaken for valid educational, scientific, or other public purposes;

  3. the application includes an acceptable and detailed description of the proposed project including a specific statement of the information required and the purpose for which the project requires the information;

  4. the proposed project is designed to preserve the anonymity of the juveniles who are the subject of records or information to which access is sought;

  5. the applicant has agreed in a sworn statement not to reproduce any information from a juvenile record, except for internal purposes, and has agreed not to disclose any information from a juvenile record to an unauthorized person; and

  6. the applicant has agreed to provide a list of the names and addresses of each person who will be a member of the staff of the proposed project and to provide a sworn statement, signed by each of them, not to disclose any information from a juvenile record to an unauthorized person.

C. Before approving or disapproving an application for research or evaluation, the juvenile agency should make written findings with respect to the criteria set forth in subsection B.

D. Upon approving or disapproving an application, the written findings and conclusion with respect to the application should be filed with the juveniles' privacy committee.

E. Any final reports, findings, or conclusions of the research or evaluation project should be a public record and should be presented so that individual juveniles cannot be identified either directly or indirectly.

F. A juvenile agency that approves a research or evaluation project and the juveniles' privacy committee should have the right to inspect any approved project. If at any time the juvenile agency has reason to believe that the project is not being carried forward as agreed or is being conducted in a manner contrary to the research application, it should terminate the project's access to records or impose such other restrictions as may be necessary and proper.

G. If an application filed pursuant to this standard is disapproved, the applicant should be given the right to appeal the disapproval to a court of general jurisdiction.

———

Suppose the IJA–ABA Standard was in force. How would you rule on an application by a feature writer for a newspaper of general circulation to conduct research in juvenile court files? Suppose, instead, that the request came from Giraldo Rivera who proposed to use the results of the research in a future 20/20 program? See, Seattle Times Co. v. County of Benton, 99 Wash.2d 251, 661 P.2d 964 (1983).

INDEX

References are to pages